TAX PLANNING (Chapter 4; PFP Sheets 20–22)

How is a taxable income determined? (Exhibit 4-1, page 92)

How is a federal income tax return prepared? (pages 99–104)

What type of tax assistance is available? (pages 105–109)

What if my tax return is audited? (pages 109–110)

WEB SITES FOR TAX PLANNING

Internal Revenue Service
www.irs.ustreas.gov
Tax forms & tips
www.1040.com
www.taxweb.com

File your taxes online
www.taxsoft.com
Ernst & Young
www.ey.com/us/tax
H&R Block
www.hrblock.com

TurboTax
www.intuit.com/turbotax
State income tax information
www.taxadmin.org
www.best.com/~ftmexpat/html/taxsites.statelaw.html
www.homel.gte.net/brcpa/statelink.htm

BANKING SERVICES (Chapter 5; PFP Sheets 23–28)

How is electronic banking changing financial services? (pages 125–127)

How do changing interest rates affect financial service decisions? (Exhibit 5-3, page 128)

What are the main types of financial institutions? (pages 129–133)

How can I compare savings accounts and savings plans? (pages 134–141)

How do I reconcile my checking account? (page 147–148)

WEB SITES FOR BANKING SERVICES

Current rates for savings instruments
www.bankrate.com/bankrate/publ/tips.htm
www.banx.com
www.usatoday.com/money/savebox.htm
Federal Deposit Insurance Corporation
www.fdic.gov
U.S. Savings Bonds
www.publicdebt.treas.gov/sav/sav.htm

Federal Reserve System
www.bog.frb.fed.us
Purchasing government notes & bonds
www.frbsf.org
Current value of U.S. savings bonds
www.ny.frb.org
American Bankers Association
www.aba.com

American Savings Education Council
www.asec.com
Financial calculators for savings
www.centura.com/formulas/ca/c.html
Making payments on the Internet
www.checkfree.com
Online banking information
www.orcc.com/banking.htm/

CONSUMER CREDIT (Chapters 6, 7; PFP Sheets 29–31)

What are the main types of consumer credit? (pages 158–165)

How much credit can I afford to use? (pages 165–166)

Should I cosign a loan for a friend or relative? (pages 166–167)

What information is in a person's credit file? (pages 167–169)

How is a credit application evaluated by a lender? (page 172–175)

What federal laws exist to protect the rights of borrowers?
(Exhibit 6-11, page 180)

What is the best way to compare different credit plans?
(pages 189–194)

How is the cost of credit determined? (pages 194–196)

What are some of the signs of credit overuse?
(Exhibit 7-4, page 205)

Where can I seek assistance in case of credit problems?
(pages 205–206)

WEB SITES FOR USING CONSUMER CREDIT WISELY AND COMPARING CREDIT COSTS

RAM Research Group
www.ramresearch.com
Comparison of costs & features
www.cardtrak.com
Current loan & credit card rates
www.bankrate.com/bankrate/publ/tips.htm
www.banx.com
National Center for Financial Education
www.ncfe.org

Credit reports information
www.equifax.com
www.experian.com
www.tuc.com
Consumer Credit law information
www.ftc.gov
www.bog.frb.fed.us
www.pirg.org
FinanCenter
www.financenter.com

National Foundation for Consumer Credit
www.nfcc.org
National Credit Counseling Services
www.nccs.org
Debt Counselors of America
www.dca.org
Credit cost calculators
www.centura.com/formulas/ca/c.html

Irwin/McGraw-Hill

*A Division of The **McGraw·Hill** Companies*

This book is printed on acid-free paper.

3 4 5 6 7 8 9 0 VNH/VNH 9 3 2 1 0 9

ISBN 0-256-24608-4
ISBN 0-256-26234-9 (personal financial planner)
ISBN 0-256-26295-0 (set)
ISBN 0-07-290743-6 (*Business Week* edition)

Vice president and Editorial director: *Michael W. Junior*
Publisher: *Craig S. Beytien*
Developmental editor: *Martin D. Quinn*
Senior marketing manager: *Katie Rose-Matthews*
Project manager: *Paula M. Buschman*
Senior production supervisor: *Madelyn S. Underwood*
Designer: *Kiera Cunningham*
Supplement coordinator: *Linda Huenecke*
Compositor: *Electronic Publishing Services, Inc.*
Typeface: *10/12 Times Roman*
Printer: *Von Hoffmann Press, Inc*

Library of Congress Cataloging-in-Publication Data

Kapoor, Jack R.
     Personal finance / Jack R. Kapoor, Les R. Dlabay, Robert J.
  Hughes. — 5th ed.
        p.   cm. — (Irwin/McGraw-Hill series in finance, insurance,
  and real estate)
    Includes bibliographical references and index.
    ISBN 0-256-24608-4
    1. Finance, Personal.   I. Dlabay, Les R.   II. Hughes, Robert
  James, 1946-   .   III. Title.   IV. Series.
  HG179.K37 1999
  332.024—dc21   98-23632

http://www.mhhe.com

PERSONAL FINANCE

Fifth Edition

JACK R. KAPOOR
College of DuPage

Les R. Dlabay
Lake Forest College

Robert J. Hughes
Dallas County Community College

Irwin
McGraw-Hill

Boston   Burr Ridge, IL   Dubuque, IA   Madison, WI   New York   San Francisco   St. Louis
Bangkok   Bogotá   Caracas   Lisbon   London   Madrid   Mexico City   Milan   New Delhi   Seoul
Singapore   Sydney   Taipei   Toronto

PERSONAL FINANCE

THE IRWIN/McGraw-Hill Series in Finance, Insurance, and Real Estate

Stephen A. Ross
Sterling Professor of Economics and Finance
Yale University
Consulting Editor

FINANCIAL MANAGEMENT

Benninga and Sarig
Corporate Finance: A Valuation Approach

Block and Hirt
Foundations of Financial Management
Eighth Edition

Brealey and Myers
Principles of Corporate Finance
Fifth Edition

Brealey, Myers and Marcus
Fundamentals of Corporate Finance
Second Edition

Brooks
PC FinGame: The Financial Management Decision Game
Version 2.0 - DOS and Windows

Bruner
Case Studies in Finance: Managing for Corporate Value Creation
Third Edition

Chew
The New Corporate Finance: Where Theory Meets Practice
Second Edition

Grinblatt and Titman
Financial Markets and Corporate Strategy

Helfert
Techniques of Financial Analysis: A Modern Approach
Ninth Edition

Higgins
Analysis for Financial Management
Fifth Edition

Hite
A Programmed Learning Guide to Finance

Kester, Fruhan, Piper and Ruback
Case Problems in Finance
Eleventh Edition

Nunnally and Plath
Cases in Finance
Second Edition

Parker and Beaver
Risk Management: Challenges and Solutions

Ross, Westerfield and Jaffe
Corporate Finance
Fifth Edition

Ross, Westerfield and Jordan
Essentials of Corporate Finance
Second Edition

Ross, Westerfield and Jordan
Fundamentals of Corporate Finance
Fourth Edition

Schall and Haley
Introduction to Financial Management
Sixth Edition

Smith
The Modern Theory of Corporate Finance
Second Edition

White
Financial Analysis with an Electronic Calculator
Third Edition

INVESTMENTS

Ball and Kothari
Financial Statement Analysis

Bodie, Kane and Marcus
Essentials of Investments
Third Edition

Bodie, Kane and Marcus
Investments
Fourth Edition

Cohen, Zinbarg and Zeikel
Investment Analysis and Portfolio Management
Fifth Edition

Farrell
Portfolio Management: Theory and Applications
Second Edition

Hirt and Block
Fundamentals of Investment Management
Sixth Edition

Jarrow
Modeling Fixed Income Securities and Interest Rate Options

Morningstar, Inc. and Remaley
U.S. Equities OnFloppy Educational Version
Annual Edition

Shimko
The Innovative Investor
Excel Version

FINANCIAL INSTITUTIONS AND MARKETS

Flannery and Flood
Flannery and Flood's ProBanker: A Financial Services Simulation

Johnson
Financial Institutions and Markets: A Global Perspective

Rose
Commercial Bank Management
Third Edition

Rose
Money and Capital Markets: Financial Institutions and Instruments in a Global Marketplace
Sixth Edition

Rose and Kolari
Financial Institutions: Understanding and Managing Financial Services
Fifth Edition

Santomero and Babbel
Financial Markets, Instruments, and Institutions

Saunders
Financial Institutions Management: A Modern Perspective
Second Edition

INTERNATIONAL FINANCE

Eun and Resnick
International Financial Management

Kester and Luehrman
Case Problems in International Finance
Second Edition

Levi
International Finance
Third Edition

Levich
International Financial Markets: Prices and Policies

Stonehill and Eiteman
Finance: An International Perspective

REAL ESTATE

Berston
California Real Estate Principles
Seventh Edition

Brueggeman and Fisher
Real Estate Finance and Investments
Tenth Edition

Corgel, Smith and Ling
Real Estate Perspectives: An Introduction to Real Estate
Third Edition

Lusht
Real Estate Valuation: Principles and Applications

Sirmans
Real Estate Finance
Second Edition

FINANCIAL PLANNING AND INSURANCE

Allen, Melone, Rosenbloom and VanDerhei
Pension Planning: Pension, Profit-Sharing, and Other Deferred Compensation Plans
Eighth Edition

Crawford
Life and Health Insurance Law
Eighth Edition (LOMA)

Harrington and Niehaus
Risk Management and Insurance

Hirsch
Casualty Claim Practice
Sixth Edition

Kapoor, Dlabay and Hughes
Personal Finance
Fifth Edition

Kellison
Theory of Interest
Second Edition

Lang
Strategy for Personal Finance
Fifth Edition

Skipper
International Risk and Insurance: An Environmental-Managerial Approach

William, Smith and Young
Risk Management and Insurance
Eighth Edition

… To my parents, Ram and Sheila Kapoor; my wife, Theresa; and my children, Karen, Kathryn, and Dave

To my mother, Mary Dlabay, and the memory of my father, Les; my wife Linda; and my children, Carissa and Kyle

To my mother, Barbara Y. Hughes; and my wife, Peggy

PREFACE

"Double Your Money in Five Years"
"Eliminate Your Credit Card Payments"
"Obtain Your Dream Job"
"Travel to a Different Country Each Year"
"Cut Your Auto Insurance Rates by One-Third"

This book *cannot* promise you any of these. However, it *can* promise you the opportunity, along with your efforts, to achieve these and many other personal financial goals.

Legislative actions, technological developments, and an expanding global economy affect personal financial planning. This atmosphere of change makes it crucial that all spending, saving, borrowing, and investing decisions be wise, informed choices. *Personal Finance,* Fifth Edition, recognizes these dynamic circumstances and continues to provide the information and the decision-making tools needed to plan and implement successful personal financial planning activities.

DECISION MAKING AND OPPORTUNITY COSTS

Each day we are bombarded with choices for shopping, television watching, and other activities. Such choices can be difficult; however, *Personal Finance,* Fifth Edition, offers many tools to make these decisions easier. The steps in the financial planning decision-making process are introduced in Chapter 1. This step-by-step approach will help students identify and evaluate choices as well as understand the consequences of their decisions in terms of opportunity costs. Examples of personal financial decision trade-offs are highlighted with a graphic icon in the margin throughout the book.

QUANTITATIVE ANALYSIS FOR FINANCIAL PLANNING

"The numbers confuse me." If that sounds like you, you came to the right place! Commonly used financial planning calculations are explained in several formats: in text material, examples, and the Financial Planning Calculations boxes. The Key Formulas feature at the end of selected chapters summarizes the important quantitative concepts and provides an illustrative example for each formula. Finally, the Financial Planning Problems at the end of each chapter and the *Student Resource Manual* reinforce students' ability to use quantitative aspects of financial planning.

PERSONAL FINANCIAL PLANNING FOR VARIED LIFE SITUATIONS

Each of us may look, sound, and even act like others, but we are still different! The financial needs of single-person, single-parent, two-income, mixed-generation, special-needs, and other types of households are addressed throughout the text. Different financial situations and the effect they have on financial planning are illustrated in text examples, the Financial Planning for Life's Situations boxes, and the Life Situation Case at the end of each chapter. These examples and cases highlight the effects of marriage, divorce, childbirth, career changes, health difficulties, retirement, and death of household members on financial planning activities.

EMPHASIS ON REAL-WORLD APPLICATIONS

"That's nice, but what about the *real world?*" The Financial Planning in Action boxes illustrate actual uses of financial planning tools to help refine students' research and decision-making abilities. In addition, the Projects and Application Activities at the end of each chapter emphasize the use of decision-making, analytical, writing, and computer skills. The activities that involve technology are highlighted with a graphic icon in the margin. Each chapter also concludes with suggested financial planning activities and Web sites that help in the development of a personal financial plan.

TECHNOLOGY TO ENHANCE DECISION MAKING

The World Wide Web, financial planning software, and other technology are emphasized throughout the book with text content, examples, applications, problem-solving exercises, and financial decision situations. Also included at the end of each chapter is a new feature, "Using the Internet to Create a Personal Financial Plan."

NEW CONTENT AND FEATURES IN THIS EDITION

An expanded emphasis on technology, opportunity costs, and decision-making exercises is just one of several new features for this edition of *Personal Finance*. In addition, many content and instructional features have been added or revised to better serve both students and instructors.

Revised and Updated Chapter Content

Chapter 1 includes expanded discussion of the steps in the financial planning process. This process serves as a foundation for all other topics of study throughout the text. Chapter 2 has been reorganized with increased coverage of technology and how it can be used to conduct career searches. Expanded coverage of résumés, cover letters, and interviewing now appears in an appendix immediately following Chapter 2.

Chapter 3 has expanded coverage of evaluating one's financial situation using various ratios. Updated coverage of recent changes to tax laws related to capital gains, retirement accounts, and educational expenses appears in Chapter 4.

Chapter 5 has updated and expanded coverage of electronic banking services, including ATM fees, lost debit cards, point-of-sale transactions, stored-value cards, smart cards, and cybercash. The consumer credit unit (Chapters 6 and 7) provides updated information on credit reports, the Fair Credit Reporting Act, bankruptcy, and using the Internet to obtain credit and financial planning information.

The purchasing decision unit (Chapters 8 and 9) is condensed, with the transportation buying and leasing information now included as an appendix that follows Chapter 8. This chapter also includes expanded coverage of the Federal Trade Commission Telemarketing Sales Rule, new and common scams and frauds on the Internet, and the new federal auto leasing disclosure rule. Chapter 9 includes information on using the Internet to locate housing and mortgage information.

The insurance unit (Chapters 10 through 12) is streamlined, with the basics of insurance material condensed and placed at the beginning of the home and auto insurance chapter. Obtaining health information on the World Wide Web and the Health Insurance Portability and Accountability Act are discussed in Chapter 11. An updated discussion of types of life insurance policies and using the Internet to obtain life insurance information is included in Chapter 12.

In the investment unit (Chapters 13 through 17), the introductory chapter includes revised coverage of planning a long-term investment program. Chapter 14 provides more information on the techniques used to evaluate stock investments. Chapter 15 presents various bond analysis techniques and suggestions for investing in bonds for different life situations. Chapter 16 includes a new discussion on using the Internet to evaluate and select mutual funds. Chapter 17 presents new information on real estate investment trusts, along with Web sites for researching real estate investments.

The retirement and estate planning unit (Chapters 18 and 19) now includes a discussion of retirement housing traps, revised tax laws related to retirement accounts, and software for retirement planning, along with information on recent changes in estate taxes.

Modifications and Innovations in Pedagogy

The Opening Case for every chapter is new or updated to emphasize contemporary personal finance concerns and decision making in a changing economic and social environment.

The new "Did You Know?" feature provides interesting facts and financial planning tips about how personal finance affects students' lives.

Descriptive titles for each of the end-of-chapter Financial Planning Problems and Projects and Application Activities have been added to highlight different problems and exercises.

Another new end-of-chapter feature is "Using the Internet to Create a Personal Financial Plan." Students are directed to Web sites to complete financial planning activities. These exercises will train students not only to hone their financial planning skills but also to utilize the latest technology to do so. Students will also be better able to use the Personal Financial Planner to chart their course for making financial decisions.

Chapter summaries have been added to the *English/Spanish Glossary* to enhance the instructional value of that supplement. Now students will be able to get the overall picture of each chapter in their native language; the comfort level this will provide will enhance understanding. In addition, many new terms have been added for the Fifth Edition.

The *Business Week* edition of *Personal Finance* offers a subscription to this valuable information source that will keep students up to date on investments, taxes, credit, insurance, consumer buying, and other personal finance topics. Students who purchase the *Business Week* edition will receive a subscription to the magazine plus access to the *Business Week* Web site. Reading timely journals will benefit students' personal financial planning throughout their lives; this is a great way to get them started!

Financial Planning Awareness for Young Adults

In several chapters, we've introduced a new boxed essay feature, "Jonathan Hoenig Speaks," that offers insight into various financial planning topics from the perspective of a young adult. Mr. Hoenig is a radio personality and writer who encourages young people to be informed and take action on their personal finances. His radio show, "The Capitalist Pig," airs in 18 states. Mr. Hoenig has appeared on MTV, on CNN, and in several prestigious periodicals, including *Forbes*. His unique, insightful, and often brash brand of advice appeals directly to today's young people and calls on them to start their financial planning *now*.

TEXT FEATURES

Personal Finance continues to provide instructors and students with features and materials to create a learning environment that can be adapted to any educational setting.

Chapter Format

Each chapter starts with an opening case and related discussion questions to introduce the chapter content with a real-world situation.

The Learning Objectives, presented at the beginning of each chapter, are integrated throughout the chapter and instructional supplements. These objectives are highlighted at the start of each major section in the chapter and appear again in the end-of-chapter summary, which reviews key points for each objective. The learning objectives are also used to organize the end-of-chapter review questions, problems, and exercises, as well as materials in the *Instructor's Manual, Student Resource Manual,* and *Test Bank.*

Key terms appear in bold type and are highlighted in the margin. The end-of-chapter glossary repeats these key terms and includes a text page reference after the definition of each term. A variety of essays, activities, and financial analysis features enhance the chapter content.

In this edition, boxed essays and other features are used in each chapter to build student interest and highlight important topics. Four different types of boxed features are used in this edition; they include the following:

- "Financial Planning for Life's Situations" offers information that can assist students when faced with special situations and unique financial planning decisions.
- "Financial Planning in Action" provides opportunities for practical applications of text concepts. These features allow students to apply and interact with real-world decision-making situations.

■ "Financial Planning Calculations" presents numerous mathematical applications relevant to personal financial situations.

■ "Jonathan Hoenig Speaks" provides radio personality and writer Jonathan Hoenig's unique perspective on various personal finance topics.

Each chapter contains several "Did You Know?" features with facts, information, and financial planning assistance.

The integrated use of the Personal Financial Planner is highlighted with a PFP graphic in the margin. This visual, placed near the text material needed to complete each Personal Financial Planner worksheet, helps students to better integrate this instructional supplement into the teaching-learning process.

The Concept Check at the end of each major section provides questions to help students assess their knowledge of the main ideas covered in that section.

End-of-Chapter Features

The wide variety of end-of-chapter materials begins with a chapter summary and glossary followed by Review Questions to assess students' retention of major chapter concepts. Next, the Financial Planning Problems require the application of key chapter material and formulas in analytic situations.

The Projects and Application Activities section provides a variety of decision-making, critical thinking, analytical, writing, and computer activities. The technology activities are noted with an icon in the margin. Next, students can test their understanding and decision-making abilities with the Life Situation Case. Finally, the Using the Internet to Create a Personal Financial Plan feature encourages students to plan, research, and implement specific financial planning activities using the World Wide Web and the Personal Financial Planner.

Continuous Case

The six-part continuous case, which appears at the end of each text part (after Chapters 4, 7, 9, 12, 17, and 19), allows students to apply course concepts in an evolving life situation. This feature encourages students to evaluate the changes that affect a family and then respond to the resulting shift in needs, resources, and priorities.

Appendixes

The end-of-text appendixes provide additional information and ideas for successful financial planning.

■ Appendix A, "Using a Financial Planner and Other Financial Planning Information Sources," offers an overview of various financial planning information sources along with suggestions for finding and evaluating a financial planner.

■ Appendix B, "Technology for Personal Financial Planning: The Internet and Software," provides an introduction to using the World Wide Web for finding personal finance information. Also discussed are some computer programs commonly used for personal financial planning.

■ Appendix C, "The Time Value of Money: Future Value and Present Value Computations," presents a foundation for calculating financial computations. It provides both formulas and tables.

■ Appendix D, "Using Electronic Calculators for Financial Decisions," explains the basics for common personal calculations using an electronic calculator with special function keys for financial computations.

■ Appendix E, "Consumer Agencies and Organizations," lists the address, phone number, and Web site for various government and private organizations that may be contacted for information or assistance.

The information in these references will enhance students' ability to make informed personal financial decisions.

INSTRUCTIONAL SUPPLEMENTS

Few textbooks provide the innovative and practical instructional resources for both students and teachers that this text does. The comprehensive teaching-learning package for *Personal Finance* includes the following.

STUDENT SUPPLEMENTS

The Personal Financial Planner, free with every book purchased from Irwin/McGraw-Hill, consists of over 70 worksheets for creating and implementing a personal financial plan. The Personal Financial Planner worksheets are highlighted in the textbook near the related material using an icon and sheet number in the margin. The Personal Financial Planner is organized by topic area (and keyed to the main sections of the textbook) with visual tabs for ease of use when developing and implementing a personal financial plan. The Personal Financial Planner also includes suggested web sites for creating a personal financial plan. Teaching suggestions for using the Personal Financial Planner are in the *Instructor's Manual.*

The *Student Resource Manual with Supplementary Readings and Cases* allows students to review and apply text concepts. Each chapter contains a chapter overview, a pretest, self-guided study questions, a posttest, problems, applications, cases, and recent articles from *Business Week.* Together these exercises reinforce important text concepts and offer students additional opportunities to use their critical thinking and writing skills.

The Personal Finance Software consists of a Windows-based, computerized version of the Personal Financial Planner and other financial tools for performing personal finance calculations.

The *English-Spanish Glossary* that accompanies *Personal Finance* includes a Spanish translation of all key terms and definitions from the text. In addition, it provides a summary of each chapter in Spanish.

Ready Notes provide students with a printout of each PowerPoint slide for ease in notetaking. Each page has lines alongside each slide within which students can write.

Instructor Supplements

The *Instructor's Manual* includes a "Course Planning Guide" with instructional strategies, course projects, and supplementary resource lists. The "Chapter Teaching Materials" section of the *Instructor's Manual* provides a chapter overview, the chapter objectives with summaries, introductory activities, and detailed lecture outlines with teaching suggestions. This section also includes concluding activities, ready-to-duplicate quizzes, supplementary lecture materials and activities, and answers to concept checks, end-of-chapter questions, problems, and cases.

The *Instructor's Manual Disk* presents the teaching resources, chapter outlines, lecture outlines, supplementary lectures, chapter quizzes, and textbook answers in a format for use in designing a customized teaching plan with word processing software.

The *Transparency Acetates* package consists of 60 ready-to-use transparency acetates that highlight the major concepts of each chapter.

The *PowerPoint* software offers more than 300 visual presentations that may be used for lectures, handouts, or class exercises. The *Ready Notes* provide students with condensed copies of all Power-Point slides, providing a notetaking guide as well as a self-paced content outline.

The *Test Bank* consists of over 1,500 true-false, multiple-choice, and essay questions. These test items are organized by the learning objectives for each chapter. This manual also includes answers, text page references, and an indication of difficulty level.

Computest offers the test items for *Personal Finance* on computer disk. This program makes it possible to create tests based on chapter, type of questions, and difficulty level. Computest 4 allows instructors to combine their own questions with test items created by the authors of *Personal Finance.* This system can be used to edit existing questions and create numerous different versions of each test. The program accepts graphics, allows password protection of saved tests, and may be used on a computer network.

The *Personal Finance Videos,* produced by Coastline Community College, enhance the teaching-learning process. Each video program has a "Viewing Guide" with a synopsis of the content, discussion questions, and suggestions for follow-up activities.

THE *PERSONAL FINANCE* WEB SITE

In an effort to provide students and teachers with the most up-to-date information and instructional resources, The *Personal Finance* Web Site is available. This World Wide Web location includes study tips, updates of text material, links to useful *Personal Finance* Web sites, and e-mail links to the authors.

The *Personal Finance* Web Site is located at http://www.mhhe.com/business/finance/kdh.

McGRAW-HILL LEARNING ARCHITECTURE

The McGraw-Hill Learning Architecture, or MHLA, provides online course content delivery and class management. MHLA enables instructors to put their own materials online and to use McGraw-Hill content as the basis for their course. Instructors can send and receive messages to students. They can make class announcements and check on students' progress. Students can submit assignments and take tests online. Please see your local McGraw-Hill sales representative for more details.

ACKNOWLEDGEMENTS

We express our deepest appreciation for the efforts of the colleagues who provided extensive comments that contributed to the quality of the book you are using.

Peter K. Drysdale
Texas A&M University

Dennis R. Keefe
Michigan State University

Michael P. Griffin
University of Massachusetts at Dartmouth

Sherilyn Benson
Dixie College

Jim Evans
Johnson County Community College

Michael Jones
Delgado Community College

David Haeberle
Indiana University

Bill Tozer
Washington State University

Kenneth St. Clair
Cedarville College

Kenneth Mark
Kansas City, Kansas Community College

Carlene Creviston
Ball State University

Jimidean Murphy
South Plains College

Tom Chilcote
Messiah College

Many talented professionals at McGraw-Hill Higher Education have contributed to the development of *Personal Finance,* Fifth Edition. We are especially grateful to Marty Quinn, Craig Beytien, Paula Buschman, Linda Huenecke, Katie Rose-Mathews, and Mike Junior.

In addition, Jack Kapoor expresses special appreciation to Theresa and Dave Kapoor and Kathryn Thumme for their typing, proofreading, and research assistance. Finally, we thank our wives and families for their patience, understanding, encouragement, and love throughout the years since we started this project.

A NOTE OF APPRECIATION

Thousands of students at colleges and universities throughout the world have used the previous editions of *Personal Finance.* We are honored that instructors and students have chosen our text to learn about personal financial decision making. A text should always be evaluated by the people who use it. We welcome your comments, suggestions, and questions. Finally, we truly hope that as a result of studying personal finance, you will have a fulfilling life that brings economic prosperity along with satisfying personal relationships.

Jack R. Kapoor
Les R. Dlabay
Robert J. Hughes

Contents in Brief

CONTENTS

Part III

Making Your Purchasing Decisions

PART IV

INSURING YOUR RESOURCES

PART V

INVESTING YOUR FINANCIAL RESOURCES

PART VI

CONTROLLING YOUR FINANCIAL FUTURE

APPENDIXES

PERSONAL FINANCE

PART I

PLANNING YOUR PERSONAL FINANCES

"What should I do first when making financial decisions?" This question should come immediately to mind as you encounter situations requiring financial decisions. Part I of *Personal Finance* provides the foundation for studying and using personal financial planning techniques. Chapter 1 presents the steps in the financial planning process. This framework is the basis for all financial decisions, large and small.

Chapter 2 explores the personal, social, and economic factors that influence your career choices. For example, changing consumer demand affects the availability of employment opportunities. Careful career planning allows you to gain financial independence and personal fulfillment.

An important starting point of your financial activities is knowing your current financial status. In Chapter 3, you will learn how to determine your current financial situation using financial statements such as a personal balance sheet and cash flow statement. These documents provide a starting point for your financial planning activities.

Wise financial decisions also depend on valid information. Developing a habit of maintaining clear financial records will help you establish a spending and saving plan that meets your unique needs and goals.

Finally, Chapter 4 emphasizes the importance of taxes for personal financial planning and knowing the current tax laws and regulations that affect you. This chapter will assist you in selecting appropriate tax strategies for different financial and personal situations.

CHAPTER 1

PERSONAL FINANCIAL PLANNING
An Introduction

OPENING CASE

FINANCIAL DECISIONS FOR TWO SISTERS AND A CHILD

How does a person cope with daily living expenses while also trying to plan for long-term financial security? For Tamara Lopez, this has not been easy. Since the death of her husband seven months ago, Tamara and her daughter Kelly, age 3, have lived with Tamara's sister. This arrangement has helped them handle the stress caused by their loss.

Tamara's husband died with less than $3,000 in savings and only $20,000 in life insurance. Tamara had not worked in recent years. Instead, she stayed home to take care of Kelly. Tamara not only needs to return to work and obtain child care services, but she also wants to help her sister, Boni, who has provided emotional and financial support for her and Kelly.

Boni has a different set of financial problems. Three years ago, Boni had a skiing accident that left her partially paralyzed. She faces several financial concerns, such as annual maintenance costs for her electric wheelchair. Boni's disability insurance benefits have provided only 60 percent of her previous salary, and she now needs to obtain employment.

After eight months of physical therapy, Boni worked to expand her computer skills. The Americans with Disabilities Act (ADA) requires that employers make accommodations for applicants who have disabilities but are otherwise qualified for employment. ADA allows Boni more opportunities than were available in the past.

"I've been offered a job in the accounting department of that investment company over on Haverhill Street," Boni told Tamara.

"That's great!" responded Tamara. "What about their health, life, and disability insurance plans?"

"They are just about what I need," said Boni. "Now how about you? Have you been able to find a sitter for Kelly?"

"Well, not yet," said Tamara, "but I'm sure we'll work out something. Together we have gotten through all of our difficulties so far."

QUESTIONS

1. What financial goals and activities should be a priority for Tamara as a single parent?
2. What actions should Boni consider to manage her unique financial situation?
3. How might Tamara and Boni work together to manage their current and future financial situations?

After studying this chapter, you will be able to

L.O.1 Analyze the process for making personal financial decisions.

L.O.2 Develop personal financial goals.

L.O.3 Assess personal and economic factors that influence personal financial planning.

L.O.4 Determine personal and financial opportunity costs associated with personal financial decisions.

L.O.5 Identify strategies for achieving personal financial goals for different life situations.

THE FINANCIAL PLANNING PROCESS

L.O.1 Analyze the process for making personal financial decisions.

When it comes to handling money, are you an *explorer,* someone who is always searching through uncharted areas? Are you a *passenger,* just along for the ride on the money decision-making trip of life? Or are you a *researcher,* seeking answers to the inevitable money questions of life?

Most people want to handle their finances so that they get full satisfaction from each available dollar. Typical financial goals include such things as a new car, a luxury home, advanced career training, extended travel, and self-sufficiency during working and retirement years. To achieve these and other goals, however, people need to identify and set priorities. Financial and personal satisfaction are the result of an organized process that is commonly referred to as *personal money management* or *personal financial planning.*

personal financial planning

Personal financial planning is the process of managing your money to achieve personal economic satisfaction. This planning process allows you to control your financial situation. Every person, family, or household has a unique financial position, and any financial activity must therefore also be unique, that is, carefully planned to meet specific needs and goals.

A comprehensive financial plan can enhance the quality of your life and increase your satisfaction by reducing uncertainty about your future needs and resources. The specific advantages of personal financial planning include

- Increased effectiveness in obtaining, using, and protecting your financial resources throughout your lifetime.
- Increased control of your financial affairs by avoiding excessive debt, bankruptcy, and dependence on others for economic security.
- Improved personal relationships resulting from well-planned and effectively communicated financial decisions.
- A sense of freedom from financial worries obtained by looking to the future, anticipating expenses, and achieving your personal economic goals.

EXHIBIT 1–1   **The Financial Planning Process**

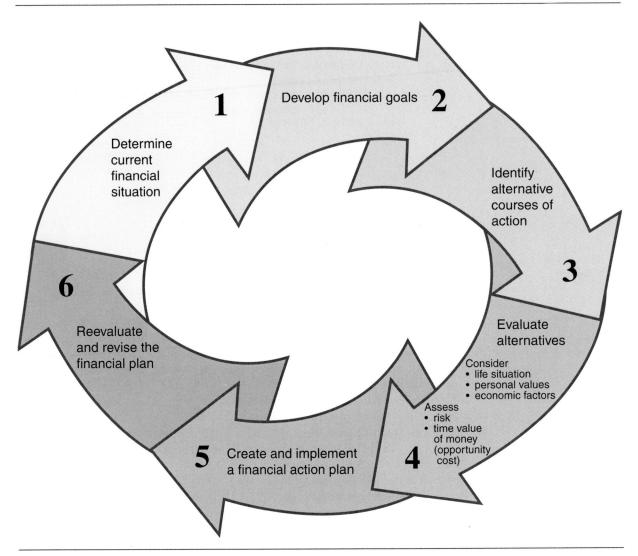

PFP

Sheet 1

We all make hundreds of decisions each day. Most of these decisions are quite simple and have few consequences. Others are complex and have long-term effects on our personal and financial situations. While everyone makes decisions, few people consider how to make better decisions. As Exhibit 1–1 shows, the financial planning process is a logical procedure that consists of six steps: (1) determining your current financial situation, (2) developing financial goals, (3) identifying alternative courses of action, (4) evaluating alternatives, (5) creating and implementing a financial action plan, and (6) reevaluating and revising the plan.

Step 1: Determine Your Current Financial Situation

In this first step of the financial planning process, you must determine your current financial situation with regard to income, savings, living expenses, and debts. Preparing a list of current balances and amounts spent for various items gives you a foundation for financial planning activities. The personal financial statements discussed in Chapter 3 will provide the information you need to match your goals with your current income and your potential earning power.

Step 2: Develop Financial Goals

In this step of the financial planning process, you should analyze your financial values and goals. This involves identifying how you feel about money and why you feel that way. Is the way you feel about money based on factual knowledge or on the influence of others? Are your financial priorities based on social pressures, household needs, or desires for luxury items? How will economic conditions affect your goals and priorities? The purpose of this analysis is to differentiate your needs from your wants.

Specific financial goals are vital to financial planning. Others can suggest financial goals for you; however, *you* must decide which goals to pursue. Your financial goals can range from spending all of your current income to developing an extensive savings and investment program for your future financial security. The goals you choose should be based on your household situation, your values, and your current financial situation.

Step 3: Identify Alternative Courses of Action

Developing alternatives is crucial for making good decisions. Although many factors will influence the available alternatives, your possible courses of action will usually fall into these categories:

- *Continue the same course of action*. For example, you may determine that the amount you have saved each month is still appropriate.
- *Expand the current situation*. You may choose to save a larger amount each month.
- *Change the current situation*. You may decide to use a money market account instead of a regular savings account.
- *Take a new course of action*. You may decide to use your monthly saving budget to pay off credit card debts.

Not all of these categories will apply to every decision situation; however, they do represent possible courses of action. For example, if you want to stop working full time to go to school, you must generate several alternatives under the category "Take a new course of action."

Creativity in decision making is vital to effective choices. Considering all of the possible alternatives will help you make more effective and satisfying decisions. For instance, most people believe they must own a car to get to work or school. However, they should consider other alternatives such as public transportation, carpooling, renting a car, shared ownership of a car, or a company car.

Remember, when you decide not to take action, you elect to "do nothing," which can be a dangerous alternative.

Step 4: Evaluate Alternatives

In this step, you need to evaluate possible courses of action, taking into consideration your life situation, personal values, and current economic conditions. How will the ages of dependents affect your saving goals? In what ways do you like to spend leisure time? How will changes in interest rates affect your financial situation? A later section in this chapter discusses these factors in greater detail.

EXHIBIT 1–2

Types of Risk

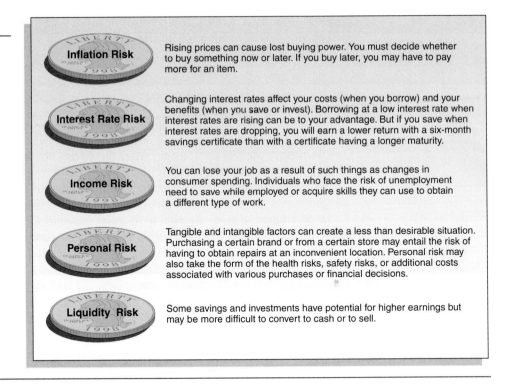

Inflation Risk — Rising prices can cause lost buying power. You must decide whether to buy something now or later. If you buy later, you may have to pay more for an item.

Interest Rate Risk — Changing interest rates affect your costs (when you borrow) and your benefits (when you save or invest). Borrowing at a low interest rate when interest rates are rising can be to your advantage. But if you save when interest rates are dropping, you will earn a lower return with a six-month savings certificate than with a certificate having a longer maturity.

Income Risk — You can lose your job as a result of such things as changes in consumer spending. Individuals who face the risk of unemployment need to save while employed or acquire skills they can use to obtain a different type of work.

Personal Risk — Tangible and intangible factors can create a less than desirable situation. Purchasing a certain brand or from a certain store may entail the risk of having to obtain repairs at an inconvenient location. Personal risk may also take the form of the health risks, safety risks, or additional costs associated with various purchases or financial decisions.

Liquidity Risk — Some savings and investments have potential for higher earnings but may be more difficult to convert to cash or to sell.

In the evaluation process, you should also look at the consequences and risks associated with each alternative. Every option in life can have positive or negative effects. Various information sources are available to help you assess these possible outcomes.

opportunity cost

Financial Decision
Trade-Off

Consequences of Choices   Every decision closes off alternatives. For example, a decision to invest in stock may mean you cannot take a vacation. A decision to go to school full time may mean you cannot work full time. **Opportunity cost** is what you give up by making a choice. This cost, commonly referred to as the *trade-off* of a decision, cannot always be measured in dollars. It may refer to the money you forgo by attending school rather than working, but it may also refer to the time you spend shopping around to compare brands for a major purchase. In either case, the resources you give up (money or time) have a value that is lost.

Decision making will be an ongoing part of your personal and financial situation. Thus, you will need to consider the lost opportunities that will result from your decisions. Since decisions vary based on each person's situation and values, opportunity costs will differ for each person. Some people value their time too highly to do extensive comparison shopping. Satisfying personal decisions are based on the various opportunity costs associated with financial activities.

Evaluating Risk   Uncertainty is a part of every decision. Selecting a college major and choosing a career field involve risk. What if you don't like working in this field or cannot obtain employment in it? Other types of decisions involve a very low degree of risk, such as putting money in a savings account or purchasing items that cost only a few dollars. Your chances of losing something of great value are low in these situations.

In many financial decisions, identifying and evaluating risk is difficult (see Exhibit 1–2). The best way to consider risk is to gather information based on your experience and the experiences of others, and to use financial planning information sources.

EXHIBIT 1–3

Financial Planning Information Sources

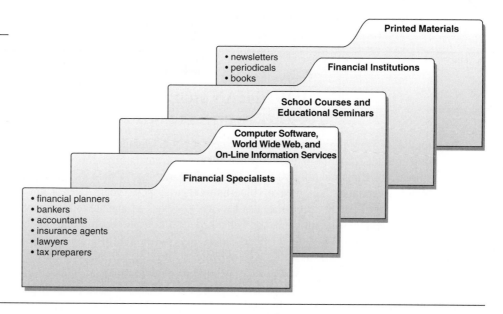

- newsletters
- periodicals
- books

Printed Materials

Financial Institutions

School Courses and Educational Seminars

Computer Software, World Wide Web, and On-Line Information Services

Financial Specialists

- financial planners
- bankers
- accountants
- insurance agents
- lawyers
- tax preparers

Sheet 2

Financial Planning Information Sources   When you travel, you often need a road map. Traveling the path of financial planning requires a different kind of map. Relevant information is required at each stage of the decision-making process. This book provides the foundation you need to make decisions in the area of personal financial planning. Changing personal, social, and economic conditions will require that you continually supplement and update your knowledge. Exhibit 1–3 offers an overview of the informational resources available when making personal financial decisions. Appendix A, "Using a Financial Planner and Other Financial Planning Information Sources," provides supplementary details.

Step 5: Create and Implement a Financial Action Plan

In this fifth step of the financial planning process, you develop an action plan. This requires choosing ways to achieve your goals. For example, you can increase your savings by reducing your spending or by increasing your income through extra time on the job. If you are concerned about year-end tax payments, you may increase the amount withheld from each paycheck, file quarterly tax payments, or shelter your current income in a tax-deferred pension program. As you achieve your immediate or short-term goals, the goals next in priority will come into focus.

To implement your financial action plan, you may need assistance from others. For example, you may use the services of an insurance agent to purchase property insurance or the services of an investment broker to purchase stocks, bonds, or mutual funds. All of your own efforts should be geared toward achieving your financial goals. Specific strategies for implementing various financial planning activities are the basis of this book.

Step 6: Reevaluate and Revise Your Plan

Financial planning is a dynamic process that does not end when you take a particular action. You need to regularly assess your financial decisions. You should do a complete review of your finances at least once a year. Changing personal, social, and economic factors may require more frequent assessments.

JONATHAN HOENIG SPEAKS
INTRODUCTION

The future was covered in coffee grounds.

I had just made a vanilla latte, the warm foam peaking over the flimsy cardboard cup. The café was packed—seemingly hundreds of blue-haired socialites barking about their frou-frou drinks. "My cappuccino is lacking," one shrieked, and I checked my watch to see how long it had been since I had tasted fresh air or seen the sun. My first job, slinging coffee for suburbia's self-professed hoy-poloy. In a word, it stank—$5.15 an hour doesn't exactly inspire dedication or dreams, and as a 15-year-old high school student I was beginning to realize that "making a buck" took a lot longer than I had previously believed. Minutes melted into months, and I spent hours contemplating why I subjected myself to the crabby nature of corporate coffee. A feeling of satisfaction or pride? Yeah, right! It was the money.

I was making dough, but not much. A few hours after school each week did not qualify me for the American Express Gold Card, but it was adding up. After stashing some savings, I started to become interested in the stock market—you know, those series of pages in the back part of the newspaper between the movie listings and sports scores. But which stock to buy? A soapy-eyed regular had suggested Starbucks (SBUX), not for refreshment but *investment*. I'm game and decided to go for it. Days later, my check was sent to a local brokerage firm and I became part owner in the burgeoning coffee kingdom. Now I wasn't just working for somebody else. As a shareholder, I was an owner in the company. I was working for myself!

Weeks later, while relishing my paltry 15-minute lunch break, I check the paper. My tiny stake in the equity market (12 shares of Starbucks stock) was still on the rise. Wow, I'm making money! Serious money. More in one day than I had made in a whole week of mopping floors, scooping up coffee grounds, and listening to people bark about the temperature of their grande hazelnut mochas.

Cleaning the coffee grounds from under my fingernails, my shirt soaked with sweat, I mutter the obvious: *I'm in the wrong business.*

Now, years later, I am the host of "Capitalist Pig," a financial radio show heard in Chicago and on Public Radio International's "Marketplace." I have put myself through college and already started saving for retirement with a pack of well-diversified mutual funds.

You can do the same thing! Taking control of your finances will be among the most empowering things you will ever do. Money, after all, is what makes the world go 'round. Being financially responsible will ensure that you can be a part of this world. Despite the rhetoric of teachers, clergy, and hundreds of "Sesame Street" reruns, being a nice person isn't tantamount to success. After evaluating reams of scholarly research and interviewing dozens of economic leaders, I reaffirm the tried and true: *Money talks.* Organize and effectively marshal your finances, and the future becomes yours to determine.

You are not your parents! What worked for them no longer works for us. For starters, there's no more job security and there may not be Social Security in the future. Nobody is there to take care of you except *you.* But the good news is, you *can* do it yourself, and live even better doing it. It's not "work, work, work," but "work smarter."

This is freedom we are talking about! The ability to choose the direction of one's life without worrying about money is the true crystallization of the American Dream.

OK, so money "can't buy me love," but it can snag me a better apartment, a cooler car, and a dinner that doesn't come out of a styrofoam carton. By getting control of your finances, you'll have the autonomy to live as you see fit. You've just got to get started—and it's not that difficult.

It's the future, and it's just a bit down the road. You should be part of it. Getting your finances together is taking that first, albeit vitally important step.

Let's get moving!

When life events affect your financial needs, this financial planning process will provide a vehicle for adapting to those changes. Regularly reviewing this decision-making process will help you make priority adjustments that will bring your financial goals and activities in line with your current life situation.

CONCEPT CHECK 1-1

1. What are the main elements of every decision we make?
2. What are some of the risks associated with financial decisions?
3. What are some common sources of financial planning information?
4. Why should you reevaluate your actions after making a personal financial decision?

DEVELOPING PERSONAL FINANCIAL GOALS

Since the United States is one of the richest countries in the world, it is difficult to understand why so many Americans have money problems. The answer seems to be the result of two main factors. The first is poor planning. The second is poor financial planning habits in areas such as spending and the use of credit. Another cause of money problems is extensive advertising, selling efforts, and product availability. Achieving personal financial satisfaction starts with clear financial goals.

Types of Financial Goals

Two factors commonly influence your financial aspirations for the future. The first is the time frame in which you would like to achieve your goals. The second is the type of financial need that drives your goals.

Timing of Goals   What would you like to do tomorrow? Believe it or not, that question involves goal setting. *Short-term goals* are goals to be achieved within the next year or so, such as saving for a vacation or paying off small debts. *Intermediate goals* have a time frame of two to five years. *Long-term goals* involve financial plans that are more than five years off, such as retirement savings, money for children's college educations, or the purchase of a vacation home.

Goal frequency is another ingredient in the financial planning process. Some goals, such as vacations or money for gifts, may be set annually. Other goals, such as a college education, a car, or a house, occur less frequently.

> **DID YOU KNOW?**
>
> A survey conducted by the Consumer Federation of America (CFA) and NationsBank estimates that 65 million American households will probably fail to realize one or more of their major life goals largely due to a lack of a comprehensive financial plan. In households with annual incomes of less than $100,000, savers who say they have financial plans also report about twice as much savings and investments as do savers without plans.

Goals for Different Financial Needs   A goal of obtaining increased career training is different than a goal of saving money to pay a semiannual auto insurance premium. Different personal and financial needs affect goal-setting activities.

Consumable goals usually occur on a periodic basis and involve items that are used up relatively quickly, such as food, clothing, and entertainment. Such purchases, if made unwisely, can have a negative effect on your financial situation.

FINANCIAL PLANNING IN ACTION

CREATING FINANCIAL GOALS

Based on your current situation or expectations for the future, create two financial goals, one short-term and one long-term, using the following guidelines:

1. Create realistic goals based on your life situation.

      a. Short-Term Goal

_____

_____

_____

_____

_____

      b. Long-Term Goal

_____

_____

_____

_____

_____

2. State your goals in specific, measurable terms.

    a. _____

       _____

    b. _____

       _____

3. Describe the time frame for accomplishing your goals.

    a. _____

       _____

    b. _____

       _____

4. Indicate an action to be taken to achieve your goals.

    a. _____

       _____

    b. _____

       _____

Durable goals usually involve infrequently purchased, expensive items such as appliances, cars, and sporting equipment. Most durable goals consist of tangible items. However, many people overlook *intangible goals*. These goals may relate to personal relationships, health, education, and leisure. Goal setting for these life circumstances is also necessary for your overall well-being.

Goal-Setting Guidelines

An old saying goes, "If you don't know where you're going, you might end up somewhere else and not even know it." Goal setting is central to financial decision making. Your financial goals are the basis for planning, implementing, and measuring the progress of your spending, saving, and investing activities. Exhibit 1–4 offers typical goals and financial activities for various life situations.

To guide financial decision making, your financial goals should be stated to take the following factors into account:

1. *Financial goals should be realistic.* Financial goals should be based on your income and life situation. For example, it is probably not realistic to buy a new car each year if you are a full-time student.
2. *Financial goals should be stated in specific, measurable terms.* Knowing exactly what your goals are will help you create a plan that is designed to achieve them.

EXHIBIT 1–4   **Financial Goals and Activities for Various Life Situations**

Common Financial Goals and Activities	Life Situation	Specialized Financial Activities
Obtain appropriate career training.	Young, single (18–35)	Establish financial independence. Obtain disability insurance to replace income during prolonged illness. Consider home purchase for tax benefit.
Create an effective financial recordkeeping system.	Young couple with children under 18	Carefully manage the increased need for the use of credit. Obtain an appropriate amount of life insurance for the care of dependents. Use a will to name guardian for children.
Develop a regular savings and investment program.	Single parent with children under 18	Obtain adequate amounts of health, life, and disability insurance. Contribute to savings and investment fund for college. Name a guardian for children and make other estate plans.
Accumulate an appropriate emergency fund.	Young dual-income couple, no children	Coordinate insurance coverage and other benefits. Develop savings and investment program for changes in life situation (larger house, children). Consider tax-deferred contributions to retirement fund.
Purchase appropriate types and amounts of insurance coverage.	Older couple, no dependent children at home	Consolidate financial assets and review estate plans. Obtain health insurance for postretirement period. Plan retirement housing, living expenses, recreational activities, and part-time work.
Create and implement a flexible budget.	Mixed-generation household (elderly individuals and children under 18)	Obtain long-term health care insurance and life/disability income for care of younger dependents. Use dependent care service if needed. Provide arrangements for handling finances of elderly if they become ill. Consider splitting of investment cost, with elderly getting income while alive and principal going to surviving relatives.
Evaluate and select appropriate investments.		
Establish and implement a plan for retirement goals.		
Make will and develop an estate plan.	Older, single	Make arrangement for long-term health care coverage. Review will and estate plan. Plan retirement living facilities, living expenses, and activities.

Sheet 3

For example, the goal of "accumulating $5,000 in an investment fund within three years" is a clearer guide to planning than the goal of "putting money into an investment fund."

3. *Financial goals should have a time frame.* In the preceding example, the goal is to be achieved in three years. A time frame helps you measure your progress toward your financial goals.

EXHIBIT 1–5

Life Situation Influences on Your Financial Decisions

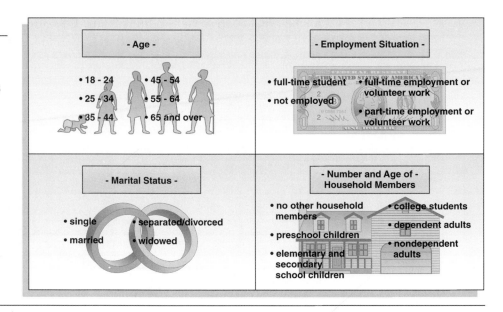

4. *Financial goals should indicate the type of action to be taken.* Your financial goals are the basis for the various financial activities you will undertake.

The Financial Planning in Action box on page 12 gives you an opportunity to set financial goals.

C O N C E P T   C H E C K   1–2

1. What are examples of long-term goals?
2. How can consumable goals affect a person's financial situation?
3. What are the four main characteristics of useful financial goals?

INFLUENCES ON PERSONAL FINANCIAL PLANNING

L.O.3 Assess personal and economic factors that influence personal financial planning.

Many factors influence daily financial decisions, ranging from age and household size to interest rates and inflation. Three main elements affect financial planning activities: life situation, personal values, and economic factors.

Life Situation and Personal Values

Why do people in their 50s spend money differently than those in their 20s? Personal factors such as age, income, household size, and personal beliefs influence your spending and saving patterns. Your life situation or lifestyle is created by a combination of factors.

As our society changes, different types of financial needs evolve. Today people tend to get married at a later age, and more households have two incomes. Many other households are headed by single parents. More than 2 million women provide care for both dependent children and parents. We are also living longer; over 80 percent of all Americans now living are expected to live past age 65.

adult life cycle

As Exhibit 1–5 shows, the **adult life cycle**—the stages in the family and financial needs of an adult—is an important influence on your financial activities and decisions. Your life situation is also affected by marital status, household size, and employment, as well as events such as

- Graduation (at various levels of education).
- Engagement and marriage.
- The birth or adoption of a child.
- A career change or a move to a new area.
- Changes in health.
- Divorce.
- Retirement.
- The death of a spouse, family member, or other dependent.

Your financial planning decisions must adapt to changes in your life situation and require ongoing communication among household members and others affected by those decisions.

values

In addition to being defined by your family situation, you are defined by your **values**—the ideas and principles that you consider correct, desirable, and important. Values have a direct influence on such decisions as spending now versus saving for the future or continuing school versus getting a job.

Financial Decision
Trade-Off

Different values and attitudes regarding financial planning can cause conflict. For example, research reveals that when selecting a financial institution, men tend to value rate of return while women value service. Many money problems result from misunderstandings among family members with different values. Thus, communication among household members is vital.

Economic Factors

economics

Daily economic activities are another important influence on financial planning. In our society, the forces of supply and demand play an important role in setting prices. **Economics** is the study of how wealth is created and distributed. The economic environment includes various institutions, principally business, labor, and government, that must work together to satisfy our needs and wants. Many principles and changing conditions of our economy can affect your personal financial decisions.

Market Forces   Prices of goods and services are generally determined by supply and demand. Just as a high demand for a consumer product forces its price up, a high demand for money pushes up interest rates. This price of money reflects the limited supply of money and the demand for it.

At times, the price of an item may seem to be unaffected by the forces of supply and demand, but in fact at such times other economic factors may also be influencing its price. Although factors such as production costs and competition influence prices, the market forces of supply and demand remain in operation.

Financial Institutions   Most people do business with a financial institution. Banks, savings and loan associations, credit unions, insurance companies, and investment companies are common financial institutions. Financial institutions provide services that facilitate financial activities in our economy. They accept savings, handle checking accounts, sell insurance, and make investments on behalf of others.

While various government agencies regulate financial activities, the Federal Reserve System, our nation's central bank, has significant responsibility in our economy. *The Fed,* as it is called, is concerned with maintaining an adequate money supply. It achieves this by influencing borrowing, interest rates, and the buying or selling of government securities. The Fed attempts to make adequate funds available for consumer spending and business expansion while keeping interest rates and consumer prices at an appropriate level.

Global Influences   The global marketplace is also an influence on financial activities. Our economy is affected by both the financial activities of foreign investors and competition from foreign companies. American business competes against foreign companies for the spending dollars of American consumers.

When the level of exports of U.S.-made goods is lower than the level of imported goods, more U.S. dollars leave the country than the dollar value of foreign currency coming into the United States. This reduces the funds available for domestic spending and investment. Also, if foreign companies decide not to invest their dollars in the United States, the domestic money supply is reduced. This reduced money supply can result in higher interest rates.

Economic Conditions   Newspapers and business periodicals regularly publish current economic statistics. Exhibit 1–6 provides an overview of some economic indicators that influence financial decisions. Your personal financial decisions are most heavily influenced by consumer prices, consumer spending, and interest rates.

inflation

1. Consumer Prices   **Inflation** is a rise in the general level of prices. In times of inflation, the buying power of the dollar decreases. For example, if prices increased 5 percent during the last year, items that cost $100 then would now cost $105. This means it now takes more money to buy the same amount of goods and services.

The main cause of inflation is an increase in demand without a comparable increase in supply. For example, if people have more money to spend because of pay increases or borrowing but the same amounts of goods and services are available, the increased demand can bid up prices for those goods and services.

Inflation is most harmful to people who live on fixed incomes. Due to inflation, retired people whose incomes may not change are able to afford smaller amounts of goods and services.

Inflation can also adversely affect lenders of money. Unless an adequate interest rate is charged, amounts repaid by borrowers in times of inflation have less buying power than the money they borrowed. If you pay 10 percent interest on a loan and the inflation rate is 12 percent, the dollars you pay the lender have lost buying power. For this reason, interest rates rise in periods of inflation.

> ### DID YOU KNOW?
>
> Not all consumer prices change by the same amount. In 1972, a one-pound box of sugar cost 18 cents. In 1997, that same box of sugar cost $1.15, a 538 percent increase. During the same time period, a five-pound bag of flour rose from 49 cents to $1.61, a 228 percent increase.

The rate of inflation varies. During the late 1950s and early 1960s, the annual inflation rate was in the 1 to 3 percent range. During the late 1970s and early 1980s, the cost of living increased 10 to 12 percent annually. At a 12 percent annual inflation rate, prices double (and the value of the dollar is cut in half) in about six years. To find out how fast prices (or your savings) will double, use the *rule of 72*: Just divide 72 by the annual inflation (or interest) rate. An annual inflation rate of 8 percent, for example, means prices will double in nine years ($72 \div 8 = 9$).

More recently, the annual price increase for most goods and services as measured by the consumer price index has been in the 3 to 5 percent range. The *consumer price index (CPI),* published by the Bureau of Labor Statistics, is a measure of the average change in the prices urban consumers pay for a fixed basket of goods and services.

EXHIBIT 1–6   **Changing Economic Conditions and Financial Decisions**

Economic Factor	What It Measures	How It Influences Financial Planning
Consumer prices	The value of the dollar; changes in inflation	If consumer prices increase faster than your income, you are unable to purchase the same amount of goods and services; higher consumer prices will also cause higher interest rates.
Consumer spending	The demand for goods and services by individuals and households	Increased consumer spending is likely to create more jobs and higher wages; high levels of consumer spending and borrowing can also push up consumer prices and interest rates.
Interest rates	The cost of money; the cost of credit when you borrow; the return on your money when you save or invest	Higher interest rates make buying on credit more expensive; higher interest rates make saving and investing more attractive and discourage borrowing.
Money supply	The dollars available for spending in our economy	Interest rates tend to decline as more people save and invest; but higher saving (and lower spending) may also reduce job opportunities.
Unemployment	The number of people without employment who are willing and able to work	People who are unemployed should reduce their debt level and have an emergency savings fund for living costs while out of work; high unemployment reduces consumer spending and job opportunities.
Housing starts	The number of new homes being built	Increased home building results in more job opportunities, higher wages, more consumer spending, and overall economic expansion.
Gross domestic product (GDP)	The total value of goods and services produced within a country's borders, including items produced with foreign resources	The GDP provides an indication of a nation's economic viability resulting in employment and opportunities for personal financial wealth.
Trade balance	The difference between a country's exports and its imports	If a country exports more than it imports, interest rates may rise and foreign goods and foreign travel will cost more.
Dow Jones Average, S&P 500, other stock market indexes	The relative value of stocks represented by the index	These indexes provide an indication of the general movement of stock prices.

Although different indexes are computed for various cities, the CPI may not be a reliable measure of your personal living costs. You do not buy goods and services in the same proportions that are used in calculating the CPI. However, the CPI will give you an indication of changes in prices and in the value of the dollar, and this information can assist you in your financial planning.

2. Consumer Spending   Total demand for goods and services in the economy influences employment opportunities and the potential for income. As consumer purchasing increases, the financial resources of current and prospective employees expand. This situation improves the financial condition of many households.

In contrast, reduced spending causes unemployment, since staff reduction commonly results from a company's reduced financial resources. The financial hardships of unemployment are a major concern of business, labor, and government. Retraining programs, income assistance, and job services can help people adjust.

3. Interest Rates   In simple terms, interest rates represent the cost of money. Like everything else, money has a price. The forces of supply and demand influence interest rates. As the amount consumers save and invest increases the supply of money, interest rates tend to decrease. However, as consumer, business, government, and foreign borrowing increase the demand for money, interest rates tend to rise.

Interest rates affect your financial planning. The earnings you receive as a saver or an investor reflect current interest rates as well as a *risk premium* based on such factors as the length of time your funds will be used by others, expected inflation, and the extent of uncertainty about getting your money back. Risk is also a factor in the interest rate you pay as a borrower. People with poor credit ratings pay a higher interest rate than people with good credit ratings. Interest rates influence many financial decisions.

Sheet 4

C O N C E P T   C H E C K   1–3

1. How do age, marital status, household size, employment situation, and other personal factors affect financial planning?
2. How can the Federal Reserve System and the trade balance affect the money supply and interest rates?
3. How might the uncertainty of inflation make personal financial planning difficult?

OPPORTUNITY COSTS AND THE TIME VALUE OF MONEY

L.O.4 Determine personal and financial opportunity costs associated with personal financial decisions.

Have you ever noticed that you always give up something when you make choices? In every financial decision, you sacrifice something to obtain something else that you consider more desirable. For example, you might forgo current consumption to invest funds for future purchases or long-term financial security. Or you might gain the use of an expensive item now by making credit payments from future earnings. In either case, you should carefully consider the trade-off between the alternatives. Opportunity costs may be viewed in terms of both personal and financial resources (see Exhibit 1–7).

Personal Opportunity Costs

An important personal opportunity cost involves time that when used for one activity cannot be used for other activities. Time used for studying, working, or shopping will not be available for other uses. The allocation of time should be viewed like any decision: Select your use of time to meet your needs, achieve your goals, and satisfy personal values.

Other personal opportunity costs relate to health. Poor eating habits, lack of sleep, or avoiding exercise can result in illness, time away from school or work, increased health care costs, and reduced financial security. Like financial resources, your personal resources (time, energy, health, abilities, knowledge) require management.

EXHIBIT 1-7

Opportunity Costs and Financial Decision Making

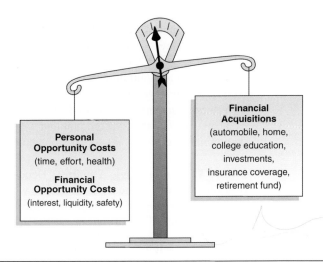

Financial Opportunity Costs

time value of money

Financial Decision Trade-Off

Like time, money used in one way cannot be used in other ways. Thus, you are constantly making choices among various financial decisions. In making those choices, you must consider the **time value of money**, the increases in an amount of money as a result of interest earned. Saving or investing a dollar instead of spending it today results in a future amount greater than a dollar. Every time you spend, save, invest, or borrow money, you should consider the time value of that money as an opportunity cost. Spending money from your savings account means lost interest earnings; however, what you buy with that money may have a higher priority than those earnings. Borrowing to make a purchase involves the opportunity cost of paying interest on the loan, but your current needs may make this trade-off worthwhile.

The opportunity cost of the time value of money is also present in these financial decisions:

- Setting aside funds in a savings plan with little or no risk has the opportunity cost of potentially higher returns from an investment with greater risk.
- Having extra money withheld from your paycheck in order to receive a tax refund has the opportunity cost of the lost interest the money could earn in a savings account.
- Making annual deposits in a retirement account can help you avoid the opportunity cost of having inadequate funds later in life.
- Purchasing a new automobile or home appliance has the potential benefit of saving you money on future maintenance and energy costs.

Interest Calculations   Three amounts are used to calculate the time value of money for savings in the form of interest earned:

- The amount of the savings (commonly called the *principal*).
- The annual interest rate.
- The length of time the money is on deposit.

These three items are multiplied to obtain the amount of interest. Simple interest is calculated as follows:

$$\boxed{\begin{array}{c}\text{Amount in}\\\text{savings}\end{array}} \times \boxed{\begin{array}{c}\text{Annual}\\\text{interest rate}\end{array}} \times \boxed{\begin{array}{c}\text{Time}\\\text{period}\end{array}} = \boxed{\text{Interest}}$$

For example, $500 on deposit at 6 percent for six months would earn $15 ($500 × 0.06 × $\frac{6}{12}$, or ½ year).

You can calculate the increased value of your money from interest earned in two ways. You can calculate the total amount that will be available later (future value), or you can determine the current value of an amount desired in the future (present value).

future value

Future Value of a Single Amount   Deposited money earns interest that will increase over time. **Future value** is the amount to which current savings will increase based on a certain interest rate and a certain time period. For example, $100 deposited in a 6 percent account for one year will grow to $106. This amount is computed as follows:

$$\text{Future value} = \$100 + (\$100 \times 0.06 \times 1 \text{ year}) = \$106$$

Original amount   Amount of
in savings   interest earned

The same process could be continued for a second, third, and fourth year, but the computations would be time consuming. Future value tables simplify the process (see Exhibit 1–8). To use a future value table, multiply the amount deposited by the factor for the desired interest rate and time period. For example, $650 at 8 percent for 10 years would have a future value of $1,403.35 ($650 × 2.159). The future value of an amount will always be greater than the original amount. As Exhibit 1–8A shows, all the future value factors are larger than 1.

Future value may be referred to as *compounding*, since interest is earned on previously earned interest. Compounding allows the future value of a deposit to grow faster than it would if interest were paid only on the original deposit.

The sooner you make deposits, the greater the future value will be. Depositing $1,000 in a 5 percent account at age 40 will give you $3,387 at age 65. However, making the $1,000 deposit at age 25 would result in an account balance of $7,040 at age 65.

Future Value of a Series of Deposits   Quite often, savers and investors make regular deposits. An *annuity* is a series of equal deposits or payments. To determine the future value of equal yearly savings deposits, use Exhibit 1–8B. For this table to be used, the deposits must earn a constant interest rate. If you deposit $50 a year at 7 percent for six years, starting at the end of the first year, you will have $357.65 at the end of that time ($50 × 7.153). The Financial Planning Calculations box on page 22 presents examples of using future value to achieve financial goals.

present value

Present Value of a Single Amount   Another aspect of the time value of money involves determining the current value of a desired amount for the future. **Present value** is the current value for a future amount based on a certain interest rate and a certain time period. Present value computations, also called *discounting,* allow you to determine how much to deposit now to obtain a desired total in the future. Present value tables (part C of Exhibit 1–8) can be used in making the computations. If you want $1,000 five years from now and you earn 5 percent on your savings, you need to deposit $784 ($1,000 × 0.784).

The present value of the amount you want in the future will always be less than the future value, since all of the factors in part C of Exhibit 1–8 are less than 1 and interest earned will increase the present value amount to the desired future amount.

EXHIBIT 1–8

Time Value of Money Tables (condensed)

A. Future Value of $1 (single amount)

Year	Percent				
	5%	6%	7%	8%	9%
5	1.276	1.338	1.403	1.469	1.539
6	1.340	1.419	1.501	1.587	1.677
7	1.407	1.504	1.606	1.714	1.828
8	1.477	1.594	1.718	1.851	1.993
9	1.551	1.689	1.838	1.999	2.172
10	1.629	1.791	1.967	2.159	2.367

B. Future Value of a Series of Deposits (annuity)

Year	Percent				
	5%	6%	7%	8%	9%
5	5.526	5.637	5.751	5.867	5.985
6	6.802	6.975	7.153	7.336	7.523
7	8.142	8.394	8.654	8.923	9.200
8	9.549	9.897	10.260	10.637	11.028
9	11.027	11.491	11.978	12.488	13.021
10	12.578	13.181	13.816	14.487	15.193

C. Present Value of $1 (single amount)

Year	Percent				
	5%	6%	7%	8%	9%
5	0.784	0.747	0.713	0.681	0.650
6	0.746	0.705	0.666	0.630	0.596
7	0.711	0.665	0.623	0.583	0.547
8	0.677	0.627	0.582	0.540	0.502
9	0.645	0.592	0.544	0.500	0.460
10	0.614	0.558	0.508	0.463	0.422

D. Present Value of a Series of Deposits (annuity)

Year	Percent				
	5%	6%	7%	8%	9%
5	4.329	4.212	4.100	3.993	3.890
6	5.076	4.917	4.767	4.623	4.486
7	5.786	5.582	5.389	5.206	5.033
8	6.463	6.210	5.971	5.747	5.535
9	7.108	6.802	6.515	6.247	5.995
10	7.722	7.360	7.024	6.710	6.418

See Appendix C at the end of the book for more complete future value and present value tables.

Present Value of a Series of Deposits   You can also use present value computations to determine how much you need to deposit so that you can take a certain amount out of the account for a desired number of years. For example, if you want to take $400 out of an investment account each year for nine years and your money is earning an annual rate of

FINANCIAL PLANNING CALCULATIONS

ANNUAL CONTRIBUTIONS TO ACHIEVE A FINANCIAL GOAL

Achieving specific financial goals often requires regular deposits to a savings or investment account. By using time value of money calculations, you can determine the amount you should save or invest to achieve a specific goal for the future.

Example 1

Jonie Emerson has two children who will start college in 10 years. She plans to set aside $1,500 a year for her children's college educations during that period and estimates she will earn an annual interest rate of 5 percent on her savings. What amount can Jonie expect to have available for her children's college educations when they start college?

Calculation:

$1,500 × Future value of a series of deposits,
5%, 10 years

$1,500 × 12.578 (Exhibit 1–8B) = $18,867

Example 2

Don Calder wants to accumulate $50,000 over the next 10 years as a reserve fund for his parents' retirement living expenses and health care. If he earns an average of 8 percent on his investments, what amount must he invest each year to achieve this goal?

Calculation:

$50,000 ÷ Future value of a series of deposits,
8%, 10 years

$50,000 ÷ 14.487 (Exhibit 1–8B) = $3,452.80

Don needs to invest approximately $3,450 a year for 10 years at 8 percent to achieve the desired financial goal.

PFP

Sheet 5

8 percent, you can see from Exhibit 1–8D that you would need to make a current deposit of $2,498.80 ($400 × 6.247).

The formulas for calculating future and present values, as well as tables covering a wider range of interest rates and time periods, are presented in Appendix C. Time value of money computations using a financial calculator are presented in Appendix D. Computer programs for calculating time value of money are also available.

CONCEPT CHECK 1–4

1. How can you use future value and present value computations to measure the opportunity cost of a financial decision?
2. Use the time value of money tables in Exhibit 1–8 to calculate the following:
   a. The future value of $100 at 7 percent in 10 years.
   b. The future value of $100 a year for six years earning 6 percent.
   c. The present value of $500 received in eight years with an interest rate of 8 percent.

EXHIBIT 1–9

Components of Personal Financial Planning

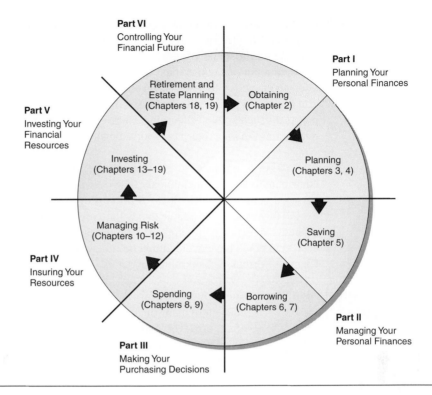

Part VI
Controlling Your Financial Future

Part I
Planning Your Personal Finances

Retirement and Estate Planning (Chapters 18, 19)

Obtaining (Chapter 2)

Part V
Investing Your Financial Resources

Investing (Chapters 13–19)

Planning (Chapters 3, 4)

Managing Risk (Chapters 10–12)

Saving (Chapter 5)

Part IV
Insuring Your Resources

Spending (Chapters 8, 9)

Borrowing (Chapters 6, 7)

Part II
Managing Your Personal Finances

Part III
Making Your Purchasing Decisions

ACHIEVING FINANCIAL GOALS

L.O.5 Identify strategies for achieving personal financial goals for different life situations.

Throughout life, we all have needs that can be satisfied with the intelligent use of financial resources. Financial planning involves deciding how to obtain, protect, and use those resources. By using the eight major areas of personal financial planning to organize your financial activities, you can avoid many common money mistakes.

Components of Personal Financial Planning

This book is designed to provide a framework for the study and planning of personal financial decisions. Exhibit 1–9 presents an overview of the eight major personal financial planning areas. To achieve a successful financial situation, you must coordinate these components through an organized plan and wise decision making.

Obtaining (Chapter 2)   You obtain financial resources from employment, investments, or ownership of a business. Obtaining financial resources is the foundation of financial planning, since these resources are used for all financial activities.

Planning (Chapters 3, 4)   Planned spending through budgeting is the key to achieving goals and future financial security. Efforts to anticipate expenses and financial decisions can also help reduce taxes. The ability to pay your fair share of taxes—no more, no less—is vital to increasing your financial resources.

Saving (Chapter 5)   Long-term financial security starts with a regular savings plan for emergencies, unexpected bills, replacement of major items, and the purchase of special

liquidity

goods and services, such as a college education, a boat, or a vacation home. Once you have established a basic savings plan, you may use additional money for investments that offer greater financial growth.

An amount of savings must be available to meet current household needs. **Liquidity** refers to the ability to readily convert financial resources into cash without a loss in value. The need for liquidity will vary based on a person's age, health, and family situation. Savings plans such as interest-earning checking accounts, money market accounts, and money market funds earn a return on your savings while providing a high degree of liquidity.

bankruptcy

Borrowing (Chapters 6, 7)   Maintaining control over your credit-buying habits will contribute to your financial goals. The overuse and misuse of credit is a major cause of personal economic difficulties. **Bankruptcy** is a situation in which a person's debts exceed the resources available to pay those debts. This may result in legal proceedings to arrange payments to creditors. The more than 1 million people who declare bankruptcy each year could have avoided this trauma with wise spending and borrowing decisions. Chapter 7 discusses bankruptcy in detail.

DID YOU KNOW?

In 1980, bankruptcies began to rise steadily. As of 1997, over 1.2 million personal bankruptcies were filed.

Spending (Chapters 8, 9)   Financial planning is designed not to prevent your enjoyment of life but to help you obtain the things you want. Too often, however, people make purchases without considering the financial consequences. Some people shop compulsively, creating financial difficulties. You should detail your living expenses and your other financial obligations in a spending plan. Spending less than you earn is the only way to achieve long-term financial security.

Managing Risk (Chapters 10–12)   Adequate insurance coverage is another component of personal financial planning. Certain types of insurance are commonly overlooked in financial plans. For example, the number of people who suffer disabling injuries or diseases at age 50 is greater than the number who die at that age, so people may need disability insurance more than they need life insurance. Yet surveys reveal that most people have adequate life insurance but few have disability insurance. The insurance industry is more aggressive in selling life insurance than in selling disability insurance, thus putting the burden of obtaining adequate disability insurance on you.

Many households have excessive or overlapping insurance coverage. Insuring property for more than it is worth may be a waste of money, as may both a husband and a wife having similar health insurance coverage.

Investing (Chapters 13–17)   While many types of investment vehicles are available, people invest for two primary reasons. Those interested in *current income* select investments that pay regular dividends or interest. In contrast, investors who desire *long-term growth* choose stocks, mutual funds, real estate, and other investments with potential for increased value in the future.

You can achieve investment diversification by including a variety of assets in your portfolio—for example, stocks, bond mutual funds, real estate, and collectibles such as rare coins. Obtaining investment advice is easy; however, it is more difficult to obtain investment advice to meet your individual needs and goals.

Retirement and Estate Planning (Chapters 18, 19)   Most people desire financial security upon completion of full-time employment. But retirement planning also involves thinking about your housing situation, your recreational activities, and possible part-time or volunteer work.

EXHIBIT 1–10   **Financial Planning in Action**

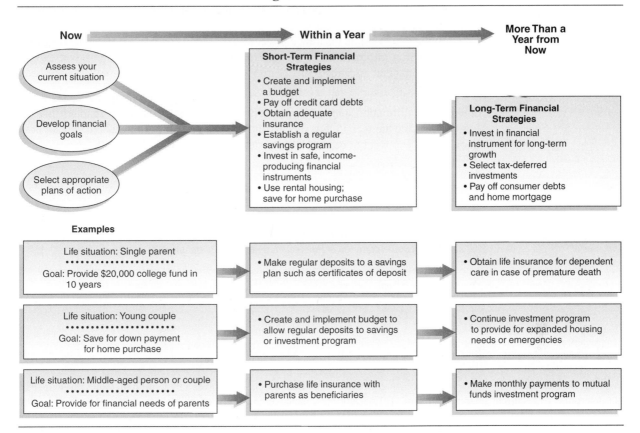

Transfers of money or property to others should be timed, if possible, to minimize the tax burden and maximize the benefits for those receiving the financial resources. A knowledge of property transfer methods can help you select the best course of action for funding current and future living costs, educational expenses, and retirement needs of dependents.

Developing a Flexible Financial Plan

financial plan

A **financial plan** is a formalized report that summarizes your current financial situation, analyzes your financial needs, and recommends future financial activities. You can create this document on your own, seek assistance from a financial planner, or use a money management software package (see Appendixes A and B). Exhibit 1–10 offers a framework for developing and implementing a financial plan, along with examples for several life situations.

Implementing Your Financial Plan

You must to have a plan before you can implement it. However, once you have clearly assessed your current situation and identified your financial goals, what do you do next?

The most important strategy for success is the development of financial habits that contribute to both short-term satisfaction and long-term financial security, including:

1. Using a well-conceived spending plan will help you stay within your income while you save and invest for the future. The main source of financial difficulties is overspending.
2. Having appropriate insurance protection will help you prevent financial disasters.
3. Becoming informed about tax and investment alternatives will help you expand your financial resources.

Achieving your financial objectives requires two things: a willingness to learn and appropriate information sources. *You* must provide the first element; the chapters that follow will provide the second. For successful financial planning, know where you are now, know where you want to be, and be persistent in your efforts.

CONCEPT CHECK 1–5

1. What are the main components of personal financial planning?
2. Identify some common actions taken to achieve financial goals.

SUMMARY

L.O.1   Analyze the process for making personal financial decisions.

Personal financial planning involves the following process: (1) determine your current financial situation; (2) develop financial goals; (3) identify alternative courses of action; (4) evaluate alternatives; (5) create and implement a financial action plan; and (6) reevaluate and revise the financial plan.

L.O.2   Develop personal financial goals.

Financial goals should (1) be realistic; (2) be stated in specific, measurable terms; (3) have a time frame; and (4) indicate the type of action to be taken.

L.O.3   Assess personal and economic factors that influence personal financial planning.

Financial decisions are affected by a person's life situation (income, age, household size, health), personal values, and economic factors (prices, interest rates, and employment opportunities).

L.O.4   Determine personal and financial opportunity costs associated with personal financial decisions.

Every decision involves a trade-off with things given up. Personal opportunity costs include time, effort, and health. Financial opportunity costs are based on the time value of money. Future value and present value calculations enable you to measure the increased value (or lost interest) that results from a saving, investing, borrowing, or purchasing decision.

L.O.5   Identify strategies for achieving personal financial goals for different life situations.

Successful financial planning requires specific goals combined with spending, saving, investing, and borrowing strategies based on your personal situation and various social and economic factors.

GLOSSARY

adult life cycle   The stages in the family situation and financial needs of an adult.   (p. 15)

bankruptcy   A situation in which a person's debts exceed the resources available to pay those debts.   (p. 24)

economics   The study of how wealth is created and distributed.   (p. 15)

financial plan   A formalized report that summarizes your current financial situation, analyzes your financial needs, and recommends future financial activities.   (p. 25)

future value   The amount to which current savings will increase based on a certain interest rate and a certain time period; also referred to as *compounding*.   (p. 20)

inflation   A rise in the general level of prices.   (p. 16)

liquidity   The ability to readily convert financial resources into cash without a loss in value.   (p. 24)

opportunity cost   What a person gives up by making a choice.   (p. 8)

personal financial planning   The process of managing your money to achieve personal economic satisfaction.   (p. 5)

present value   The current value for a future amount based on a certain interest rate and a certain time period; also referred to as *discounting*.   (p. 20)

time value of money   Increases in an amount of money as a result of interest earned.   (p. 19)

values   Ideas and principles that a person considers correct, desirable, and important.   (p. 15)

R E V I E W   Q U E S T I O N S

1. Explain how you can use the steps in the financial planning process to develop a plan for a specific area of your personal life situation.   (L.O.1)
2. Identify some financial goals and suggest specific financial activities that would be appropriate for the following life situations.   (L.O.2)
   a. An unemployed worker who is the single parent of two school-age children.
   b. A dual-income couple in their 40s with no children.
   c. A couple expecting their second child in four months.
   d. A woman supporting both her school-age daughter and her retired father.
3. What is the relationship between current interest rates and financial opportunity costs?   (L.O.3)
4. How does future value differ from present value?   (L.O.4)
5. What is the purpose of a financial plan?   (L.O.5)

F I N A N C I A L   P L A N N I N G   P R O B L E M S

(Note: Some of these problems require the use of the time value of money tables in Appendix C.)

1. *Calculating Future Value of Property.* Ben Collins plans to buy a house for $65,000. If that real estate is expected to increase in value by 5 percent each year, what will its approximate value be seven years from now?   (L.O.3)
2. *Using the Rule of 72.* Using the rule of 72, approximate the following amounts.   (L.O.3)
   a. If land in an area is increasing 6 percent a year, how long will it take for property values to double?
   b. If you earn 10 percent on your investments, how long will it take for your money to double?
   c. At an annual interest rate of 5 percent, how long will it take for your savings to double?
3. *Determining the Inflation Rate.* In the late 1980s, selected automobiles had an average cost of $12,000. The average cost of those same automobiles is now $15,000. What was the "rate of inflation" for these automobiles between the two time periods?   (L.O.3)
4. *Computing Future Living Expenses.* A family spends $28,000 a year for living expenses. If prices increase by 4 percent a year for the next three years, what amount will the family need for their living expenses?   (L.O.3)

5. *Calculating Earnings on Savings.* What would be the yearly earnings for a person with $6,000 in savings at an annual interest rate of 5.5 percent?   (L.O.4)
6. *Computing Time Value of Money.* Using time value of money tables, calculate the following.   (L.O.4)
   a. The future value of $450 six years from now at 7 percent.
   b. The future value of $800 saved each year for 10 years at 8 percent.
   c. The amount a person would have to deposit today (present value) at a 6 percent interest rate to have $1,000 five years from now.
   d. The amount a person would have to deposit today to be able to take out $500 a year for 10 years from an account earning 8 percent.
7. *Calculating Future Value of a Series of Amounts.* Elaine Romberg prepares her own income tax return each year. A tax preparer would charge her $60 for this service. Over a period of 10 years, how much does Elaine gain from preparing her own tax return? Assume she can earn 6 percent with a savings certificate.   (L.O.4)

P R O J E C T S   A N D   A P P L I C A T I O N   A C T I V I T I E S

1. *Researching Personal Finance on the Internet.* Using Web sites such as www.quicken.com or www. kiplinger.com and search engines, obtain information about commonly suggested actions related to various personal financial planning decisions. What are some of the best sources of information on the Internet to assist you with financial planning?   (L.O.1)

2. *Comparing Financial Planning Actions.* Survey friends, relatives, and others to determine the process they use when making financial decisions. How do these people measure risk when making financial decisions?   (L.O.1)

3. *Using Financial Planning Experts.* Prepare a list of financial planning specialists (investment advisers, credit counselors, insurance agents, real estate brokers, tax preparers) in your community that can assist people with personal financial planning. Prepare a list of questions that might be asked of these financial planning professionals by *(a)* a young person just starting out on his or her own, *(b)* a young couple planning for their children's education and for their own retirement, and *(c)* a person nearing retirement.   (L.O.1, 3)

4. *Setting Financial Goals.* Using Sheet 3 in the *Personal Financial Planner,* create one short-term and one long-term goal for people in these life situations: *(a)* a young single person, *(b)* a single parent, *(c)* a married person with no children, and *(d)* a retired person.   (L.O.2)

5. *Analyzing Changing Life Situations.* Ask friends, relatives, and others how their spending, saving, and borrowing activities changed when they decided to continue their education, change careers, or have children.   (L.O.3)

6. *Researching Economic Conditions.* Use library resources, such as *The Wall Street Journal,* or the World Wide Web to determine recent trends in interest rates, inflation, and other economic indicators. Information about the consumer price index (measuring changes in the cost of living) may be obtained at www.bls.gov. Report how this economic information might affect your financial planning decisions.   (L.O.3)

7. *Comparing Alternative Financial Actions.* What actions would be necessary to compare a financial planner that advertises "One Low Fee Is Charged to Develop Your Personal Financial Plan" and one that advertises "You Are Not Charged a Fee, My Services Are Covered by the Investment Company for Which I Work."   (L.O.4, 5)

8. *Determining Opportunity Costs.* What is the relationship between current interest rates and financial opportunity costs? Using time value of money calculations, state one or more goals in terms of an annual savings amount and the future value of this savings fund.   (L.O. 2, 4)

9. *Researching Financial Planning Software.* Visit software retailers to obtain information about the features and cost of various personal financial planning activities. Informa- tion about programs such as Managing Your Money, Microsoft Money, and Quicken may be obtained on the Internet.   (L.O.5)

LIFE SITUATION CASE 1

TRIPLE TROUBLE FOR THE "SANDWICH GENERATION"

Until recently, Fran and Ed Blake's personal finances ran smoothly. Both have maintained well-paying jobs while raising two children. The Blakes have a daughter who is completing her freshman year of college and a son three years younger. They have been able to save for the education of their children. Currently they have $22,000 in various savings and investment funds set aside for education. With education costs increasing faster than inflation, they are uncertain as to the adequacy of this amount.

In recent months, Fran's mother has required extensive medical attention and personal care assistance. Unable to live alone, she is now a resident of a long-term care facility. The cost of this service is $2,050 a month, with annual increases of about 7 percent. While a major portion of the cost is covered by her Social Security and pension, Fran's mother is unable to cover the entire cost. Their desire to help adds to the financial burden of the Blakes.

The Blakes are like millions of other Americans who have financial responsibilities for both dependent children and aging parents. Commonly referred to as the "sandwich generation," this group is squeezed on one side by the cost of raising and educating children and on the other side by the financial demands of caring for aging parents.

Finally, the Blakes, ages 47 and 43, are also concerned about saving for their own retirement. While they have consistently made annual deposits to a retirement fund, various current financial demands may force them to tap into this money.

QUESTIONS

1. What actions have the Blakes taken that would be considered wise financial planning choices?

2. What areas of financial concern do the Blakes face? What actions might be appropriate to address these concerns?

3. Using time value of money calculations (tables in Appendix C), compute the following:

   a. At 12 percent, what would be the value of the $22,000 education funds in three years?

   b. If the cost of long-term care is increasing at 7 percent a year, what will be the approximate monthly cost for Fran's mother eight years from now?

   c. Fran and Ed plan to deposit $1,500 a year to their retirement fund for 35 years. If they earn an average annual return of 9 percent, what will be the value of their retirement fund after 35 years?

USING THE INTERNET TO CREATE A PERSONAL FINANCIAL PLAN 1

STARTING YOUR FINANCIAL PLAN

Planning is the foundation of success in every aspect of life. Assessing your current financial situation along with setting goals sets the start of successful financial planning.

Web Sites for Financial Planning

- Goal setting information and investment planning at **www.personalwealth.com**
- The FinanCenter provides answers to questions and calculations related to budgeting, automobiles, savings, investments, credit, and housing at **www.financenter.com/**
- "The Motley Fool" offers a wide range of personal finance information at **www.fool.com/** as does **www.quicken.com (www.qfn.com),** the Cable News Network financial news service at **cnnfn.com/index.hmtl**, and the Center for Financial Well Being at **www.healthycash.com/ center**
- Selected articles from *Money* magazine at **www.money.com**, from *Kiplinger's Personal Finance* magazine at **www.kiplinger.com,** and *Business Week* at **www.businessweek.com**
- Information on Federal Reserve activities, publications, and access to the Web sites of the 12 Federal Reserve Banks at **www.bog.frb.fed.us**; each Federal Reserve Bank has a Web site with publications, links to other Web sites, and current economic data; these include the Boston Federal Reserve Bank at **www.bos.frb.org** and the New York Federal Reserve Bank at **www.ny.frb.org**
- Current consumer price index and inflation information at **www.bls.gov**, **www.stls.frb.org/fred/data/cupdate.html**, and **www.westegg .com/inflation**

- Current economic data at **www.stats.bls.gov/eag.table.htm**
- Financial planning calculators for computing the time value of money at **www-sci.lib.uci.edu/HSG/RefCalculator.html** and **www.centura.com/formulas/ca/c.html** and **www.moneyadvisor.com/calc**

(Note: Addresses and content of Web sites change, and new sites are created daily. Use the search engines discussed in Appendix B to update and locate Web sites for your current financial planning needs.)

PFP SHEETS: 1–5

Short-Term Financial Planning Activities

1. Prepare a list of personal and financial information for you and family members. Also create a list of financial service organizations you use (see PFP Sheets 1, 2)
2. Set financial goals related to various current and future needs (see PFP Sheet 3).
3. Monitor current economic conditions (inflation, interest rates) to determine possible actions to take related to your personal finances (see PFP Sheet 4).

Long-Term Financial Planning Activities

1. Based on various financial goals, calculate the necessary savings deposits needed to achieve those goals.
2. Identify various financial planning actions for you and other household members for the next 2–5 years.

CHAPTER 2

FINANCIAL ASPECTS OF CAREER PLANNING

OPENING CASE

IF YOU STAY READY, YOU DON'T HAVE TO GET READY

He knew it was going to happen. He just didn't know when. However, Kevin Larkin was ready.

When Kevin's company, Sun Electronics, announced it would lay off 600 workers, most people in the organization panicked. In contrast, Kevin volunteered to leave!

Kevin didn't have another job offer, nor was he offered a generous severance package. But Kevin did have a knowledge of his career skills and an ability to find another employment position. In other words, Kevin was prepared for the uncertainty that occurs in a volatile economy with increased foreign competition and technology. Through ongoing training, he continually upgraded his technical skills while also improving his ability to work on project teams.

Since Kevin knew things were changing in the electronics industry, he was not surprised when the downsizing announcement came. However, unlike other Sun employees, Kevin had prepared for that moment. In addition to ongoing training, he maintained a strong dedication to Sun. His on-the-job performance, creativity, and initiative were admired by both supervisors and co-workers. When investigating other employment opportunities, Kevin used vacation time and made sure his work was made up or covered by others.

Overall, Kevin Larkin is an ideal example of a person who managed his career. He did not let changes in the economy and employment marketplace surprise him. He continuously readied himself for those inevitable events.

QUESTIONS
1. What actions did Kevin take to ensure his future employment potential?
2. What factors commonly affect future employment opportunities?
3. Are the actions Kevin took valid for most career situations?

LEARNING
OBJECTIVES

After studying this chapter, you will be able to

L.O.1 Describe the activities associated with career planning and advancement.

L.O.2 Evaluate the factors that influence employment opportunities.

L.O.3 Implement employment search strategies.

L.O.4 Assess the financial and legal concerns related to obtaining employment.

L.O.5 Analyze the techniques available for career growth and advancement.

FINANCIAL AND PERSONAL ASPECTS OF CAREER CHOICE

L.O.1 Describe the activities associated with career planning and advancement.

job

career

Have you ever wondered why some people find great satisfaction in their work while others want only to put in their time? As with other personal financial decisions, career selection and professional growth require planning. The average person changes jobs about seven times during a lifetime. Most likely, therefore, you will reevaluate your choice of a job on a regular basis.

The lifework you select is a key to your financial well-being and personal satisfaction. You may select a **job,** an employment position obtained mainly to earn money. Many people work in one or more jobs during their lives without considering their interests or opportunities for advancement. Or you may select a **career,** a commitment to a profession that requires continued training and offers a clear path for occupational growth.

In many career areas, opportunities for advancement provide strong financial potential. However, entry-level salaries may be low. In contrast, strong earnings potential may not be available in jobs where the position and duties are more fixed. Workers may have to change jobs to improve their long-term financial capacity.

Trade-Offs of Career Decisions

While many factors affect daily living habits and financial choices, your employment situation probably affects them the most. Your income level, business associates, and available leisure time are a direct result of the work you do. Some people work so they can pursue their hobbies and recreational activities, while others have a chosen career field that reflects their interests, values, and goals.

Like other decisions, career choice and professional development alternatives have risks and opportunity costs. In recent years, many people in our society have placed family values and personal fulfillment above monetary reward and professional recognition. Career choices require a continual evaluation of trade-offs related to personal, social, and economic factors. For example:

EXHIBIT 2–1
_____

**Education and
Income**

As of the late-1990s, estimated lifetime earnings for
workers, based on the completed level of education, was:

Non–high school graduate

$608,810

High school graduate

$820,870

Some college

$992,890

College graduate
(bachelor's degree)

$1,420,850

Professional degree

$3,012,530

SOURCE: U.S. Bureau of the Census.

Financial Decision
Trade-Off

- Some people select employment that is challenging and offers strong personal satisfaction rather than employment in which they can make the most money.
- Some people refuse a transfer or a promotion that would require moving their families to a new area or reducing leisure time.
- Many parents opt for part-time employment or flexible hours to allow more time for their children.
- Many people give up secure job situations because they prefer to operate their own businesses.

Your ability to assess your personal values, needs, and goals will be an important basis for evaluating the personal and financial opportunity costs of your career choice.

Career Training and Skill Development

Your level of formal training affects your financial success. Exhibit 2–1 shows the influence of education on income. The statistics in this exhibit do not mean you will automatically earn a certain amount because you have a college degree. They imply that more education increases your *potential* earning power. However, other factors, such as field of study, also influence future income.

In addition to formal career training, successful managers, employers, and career counselors stress the importance of traits adaptable to most work situations. While some of these traits can be acquired in school, others require experiences in other situations. The traits that successful people usually possess include

- An ability to work well with others in a variety of settings.
- A desire to do tasks better than they have to be done.
- An interest in reading a wide variety of materials.
- A willingness to cope with conflict and adapt to change.
- An awareness of accounting, finance, and marketing fundamentals.
- A knowledge of technology and computer software such as word processing, spreadsheet, database, Web search, and graphics programs.
- An ability to solve problems creatively in team settings.
- A knowledge of research techniques and library resources.
- Well-developed written and oral communication skills.
- An understanding of both their own motivations and the motivations of others.

These competencies give people flexibility, making it easy to move from one organization to another and to successfully change career fields.

Personal Factors

You might be able to identify a satisfying career using guidance tests that measure your abilities, interests, and personal qualities. Aptitude tests, interest inventories, and other types of career assessment tests are available at school career counseling offices. You can use a book that allows you to take these tests at home. For a fee, testing services will mail you the results of your completed test.

> **DID YOU KNOW?**
>
> Prospective workers who are most desirable to employers possess technical skills (such as computer use and financial analysis), have the ability to communicate, and are team players.

What Do You Do Best?   *Aptitudes* are natural abilities that people possess. The ability to work well with numbers, problem-solving skills, and physical dexterity are examples of aptitudes.

What Do You Enjoy?   *Interest inventories* determine the activities that give you satisfaction. These instruments measure qualities related to various types of work. People with strong social tendencies may be best suited for careers that involve dealing with people, while people with investigative interests may be best suited for careers in research areas.

Does a Dream Job Exist?   Test results will not tell you which career to pursue. They will only give you an indication of your aptitudes and interests. Another important dimension of career selection is your personality. Do you perform best in structured or high-pressure situations, or do you prefer unstructured or creative work environments? The financial aspects of the career are also likely to be a concern.

Some experts say the best job is the one you look forward to on Monday morning. You want a job in which financial rewards, location, and work satisfaction are balanced. Some people adapt to any work situation, while others constantly think the next job will be the best. A vital ingredient in career choice is flexibility, since change will be a constant part of your work life and the job market.

Many people are able to obtain employment based on various interests and experiences. A person with volunteer experience might be hired as executive director of a community organization. Or a person who enjoys planning parties and other events may work as a meeting planner. The Financial Planning in Action box on page 35 can help you plan actions for obtaining a job or changing careers.

Career Decision Making

Changing personal and social factors will require you to continually assess your work situation. Exhibit 2–2 on page 34 provides an approach to career planning and advancement.

EXHIBIT 2–2   **Stages of Career Planning and Advancement**

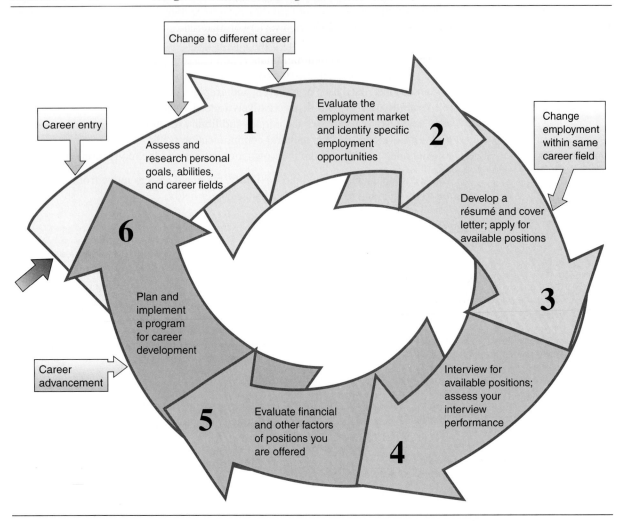

Change to different career

Career entry

Change employment within same career field

1. Assess and research personal goals, abilities, and career fields

2. Evaluate the employment market and identify specific employment opportunities

3. Develop a résumé and cover letter; apply for available positions

4. Interview for available positions; assess your interview performance

5. Evaluate financial and other factors of positions you are offered

6. Plan and implement a program for career development

Career advancement

As you can see, the different entry points depend on your personal situation. Your career goals will also affect how you use this process. If you desire more responsibility on the job, for example, you may obtain advanced training or change career fields.

This process is a suggested framework for planning, changing, or advancing in a career. Your specific strategies will depend on opportunity costs, the alternatives you identify, and your career area. Methods for obtaining employment are quite different for a college professor, an accountant, a computer sales representative, and a government social worker. Talking to people in your field of interest can be very valuable to career planning.

CONCEPT CHECK   2–1

1. How does a *job* differ from a *career?*
2. What opportunity costs are associated with career decisions?
3. What skills would be of value in most employment situations?

FINANCIAL PLANNING IN ACTION

DEVELOPING A CAREER ACTION PLAN

For each of the following elements of career planning,

   a. Describe your current situation in this area.

   b. State a specific goal you have in this area.

   c. Describe the time frame for accomplishing this goal.

   d. Indicate actions to take to achieve the goal.

1. *Personal and Career Interests:* What do you enjoy doing? How would you like to improve or expand your interests?

   a. _____

   b. _____

   c. _____

   d. _____

2. *Career Skills:* What type of work situation do you enjoy? How would you like to improve or expand your career skills? What new career skills do you desire?

   a. _____

   b. _____

   c. _____

   d. _____

3. *Education:* What education and career training do you desire?

   a. _____

   b. _____

   c. _____

   d. _____

4. *Employment Position:* Have you selected career fields of interest to you? What type of employment situation do you desire?

   a. _____

   b. _____

   c. _____

   d. _____

CAREER OPPORTUNITIES: NOW AND IN THE FUTURE

L.O.2 Evaluate the factors that influence employment opportunities.

Your job search should start with an assessment of the career choice factors shown in Exhibit 2–3 on page 36.

Social Influences

Various demographic and geographic trends influence employment opportunities. Demographic trends affecting the job market include the following:

- An increase in the number of working parents expands the demand for food service and child care.
- An increase in leisure time among some segments of the population results in an increased interest in personal health, physical fitness, and recreational products and services.
- An increase in the number of older people raises the demand for travel services, health care, and retirement facilities.
- An increased demand for additional employment training increases career opportunities for teachers and trainers within business organizations.

EXHIBIT 2–3

Factors Influencing Your Career Opportunities

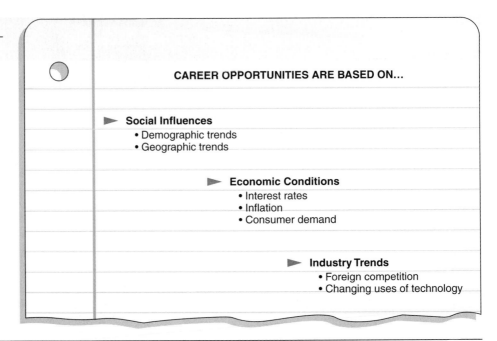

CAREER OPPORTUNITIES ARE BASED ON...

► **Social Influences**
  • Demographic trends
  • Geographic trends

► **Economic Conditions**
  • Interest rates
  • Inflation
  • Consumer demand

► **Industry Trends**
  • Foreign competition
  • Changing uses of technology

Changes in the locations of jobs influence employment opportunities. In recent years, some of the fastest-growing job markets include major cities in Florida, North Carolina, and Arizona; Atlanta, Georgia; Boulder, Colorado; Boise, Idaho; San Jose, California; Austin, Texas; Salt Lake City, Utah; and Albuquerque, New Mexico. Geographic location also influences income level. The Bureau of Labor Statistics reports that the mid-Atlantic and north-central areas of the United States have the highest average earnings.

In considering geographic areas, be sure to assess salary levels. Average incomes are high in such metropolitan areas as Boston, New York, and Chicago; however, the prices of food, housing, and other living expenses are also high. What appears to be a big salary may actually mean a lower standard of living than in a geographic area with lower salaries and lower living costs.

Economic Conditions

High interest rates, price increases, or decreased demand for goods and services can reduce career opportunities. While you cannot eliminate the effects of economic factors on employment trends, these factors affect some businesses more than others. For example, high interest rates reduce employment in housing-related industries, since people are less likely to buy homes when interest rates are high. Uncertainty about the stock market results in fewer investment transactions, reducing employment opportunities with financial institutions.

Trends in Industry and Technology

Two factors have reduced manufacturing employment in our economy. First, increased competition from companies in Asia, Europe, and other regions has reduced demand for American-made products. Second, automated production methods have decreased the need for manual workers and other entry-level employees in factories.

FINANCIAL PLANNING FOR LIFE'S SITUATIONS

COMMUTING TO THE NEXT ROOM

To meet the needs of family situations, many organizations allow some employees to do all or some work at home. *Telecommuting* involves using a computer and other technology (fax machine, modem, networking, e-mail) to work at home instead of at a company office or factory. Workers can care for children or dependent parents while saving time and energy by not traveling to a different location. Companies save money by requiring less office space.

Telecommuting is best suited to jobs that do not require regular in-person contact with others. The work must be of a type that can be done through computer networks and other telecommunications equipment. This employment arrangement is most common among staff writers, researchers, economists, accounting clerks, word processing clerks, database supervisors, and computer programmers. Companies find that telecommuting helps them to keep talented employees who do not want to work in a structured environment.

Another flexible employment arrangement is operating a business out of your home. Over 5 million people in the United States operate home businesses. The most common home-based businesses are sales, information

processing, construction and contracting, personal care services, arts and crafts, consulting, and clerical support.

Would running your own business be an appropriate career for you? That depends on your personality and abilities. Are you a highly motivated, confident individual? Do you have the ability to manage different phases of a business? Are you someone who enjoys challenges and is willing to take risks?

If you are planning to start your own business, consider three main issues. First, become knowledgeable about your product or service. Next, identify your potential customers, select an appropriate location, and study competitors. Finally, consider your financial sources. Most entrepreneurs use a combination of personal funds and loans.

You can obtain assistance with starting a home-based business from a lawyer, local banker, accountant, or insurance agent. For additional information about running your own business, contact the Small Business Administration, Attn.: Public Information Office, 1441 L St. NW, Washington, DC 20416; Web site: www.sba.gov. Also useful is the Web site of the National Association for the Self-Employed at selfemployed.nase.org/NASE.

Employment stability has a strong influence on a person's financial situation for both the short and long term. For example, workers in various technology fields, where scientific advances can quickly make products (and jobs) obsolete, must be ready to cope with personal financial uncertainty. (See the Financial Planning for Life's Situations box.)

While career opportunities have dwindled in some sectors of our economy, opportunities in other sectors have grown. Service industries that are expected to have the greatest employment potential into the 21st century are

DID YOU KNOW?

Between 1991 and 1995, most job growth in the U.S. economy, 6 million of 7.7 million new jobs, occurred in companies with fewer than 100 employees.

- *Computer technology*—systems analysts, computer operators, Web site developers, Internet operations managers, and repair personnel and service technicians for data processing equipment.
- *Health care*—medical assistants, physical therapists, physical therapy assistants, home health workers, laboratory technicians, registered nurses, and health care administrators.
- *Business services*—Web consultants, trainers, employee benefit managers, and operations consultants.
- *Social services*—Child care workers, elder care coordinators, family counselors, and social service agency administrators.
- *Sales and retailing*—retail salespeople, marketing representatives, and sales managers with technical knowledge in the areas of electronics, medical products, and financial services.

- *Hospitality and food services*—travel agents, resort and hotel administrators, food service managers, and meeting planners.
- *Management and human resources*—clerical supervisors, recruiters, interviewers, employee benefit administrators, and employment service workers.
- *Education*—corporate trainers, special education teachers, adult education instructors, and teachers for elementary, secondary, and postsecondary schools.
- *Financial services*—insurance agents, actuaries, investment brokers, and others with a knowledge of accounting and taxes.

Sheet 6

Business demands in the 21st century will include expanded reading and communication skills. More and more employees are being called on to read scientific and technical journals and financial reports and to write speeches and journal articles. Your career success and potential for advancement are likely to be dependent on these communication skills. In addition, computer skills and the ability to communicate in a second language will enhance your career potential.

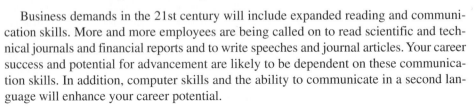

CONCEPT CHECK 2–2

1. What are some examples of demographic and economic factors that affect career opportunities?
2. How does technology affect available employment positions?

EMPLOYMENT SEARCH STRATEGIES

L.O.3 Implement employment search strategies.

We have all heard about job applicants who send out hundreds of résumés with very little success, while others get several offers. What are the differences between these two groups? The answer usually relates to an ability to expand one's experiences and use job search techniques effectively.

Obtaining Employment Experience

A common concern among people seeking employment is a lack of work experience. Many opportunities are available to obtain work-related training.

Part-Time Employment   Summer and part-time work can provide experience along with the chance to see if you enjoy a particular career field. The increased use of temporary employees has opened up opportunities to obtain experience in many career areas. Part-time work may also be of value for people who are changing careers and need experience in a different career field.

More and more workers are taking advantage of temporary job assignments as a channel to a full-time position. Many organizations do not have the resources to develop or attract employees with the right skills. As a result, the number of temporary employment services and "interim" workers continues to increase. Working as a "temp" can give you valuable experience as well as contacts in various fields of employment. Further information may be obtained at the Web site of the National Association of Temporary and Staffing Services (NATSS) at www.natss.org.

Volunteer Work   Involvement in community organizations and government agencies can provide excellent opportunities to acquire skills, establish good work habits, and

EXHIBIT 2–4

Career Information Sources

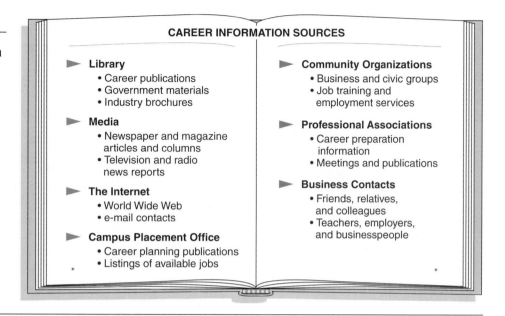

CAREER INFORMATION SOURCES

► **Library**
- Career publications
- Government materials
- Industry brochures

► **Media**
- Newspaper and magazine articles and columns
- Television and radio news reports

► **The Internet**
- World Wide Web
- e-mail contacts

► **Campus Placement Office**
- Career planning publications
- Listings of available jobs

► **Community Organizations**
- Business and civic groups
- Job training and employment services

► **Professional Associations**
- Career preparation information
- Meetings and publications

► **Business Contacts**
- Friends, relatives, and colleagues
- Teachers, employers, and businesspeople

make contacts. Volunteering to work at the gift shop of a museum, for example, gives you experience in retailing. You may participate in a recycling project, assist at a senior citizens' center, or help supervise youth activities at a park district. These types of activities will help you develop skills that could be applicable to other types of work situations.

Internships   In very competitive fields, an internship will give you the experience you need to obtain employment. During an internship, you can make contacts about available jobs. Applying for an internship is similar to applying for a job. Nine out of 10 four-year colleges and universities offer cooperative education and internships as part of their academic programs.

Campus Projects   Class assignments and campus activities are frequently overlooked as work-related experience. You can obtain valuable career skills on campus from experience in

- Managing, organizing, and coordinating people and activities as an officer or committee chairperson of a campus organization.
- Public speaking in class, campus, and community presentations.
- Goal setting, planning, supervising, and delegating responsibility in community service and class projects.
- Financial planning and budgeting gained from organizing fund-raising projects, managing personal finances, and handling funds for campus organizations.
- Conducting research for class projects, community organizations, and campus activities.

Using Career Information Sources

Career planning and advancement, like other financial decisions, are enhanced by the use of current and relevant information. Exhibit 2–4 provides an overview of the main sources of career information.

JONATHAN HOENIG SPEAKS
PERSONAL CAREER STRATEGIES

In the 1950s, large corporations regularly recruited staff with the understanding that "work" was a commitment in the truest sense. You were "in" for life, a gold watch waiting patiently in the storage closet.

Times have changed: The "company man" is dead. Then again, so is the company. In its stead lies an unfortunate assemblage of temp jobs, free-lance gigs, and internships. All without benefits. All without perks. All featuring wages not seen since the abolishment of indentured servitude.

Enter the entrepreneur! Entrepreneurship is not merely working for yourself, but *thinking* for yourself. The eradication of corporate loyalty mandates a fiercely independent, almost Machiavellian approach to kicking butt in the business world. Despite the legions of human resources directors espousing the virtues of "team players," the new business mentality is decidedly individualistic.

Regardless of who signs your paychecks, don't be misled: *You work for yourself.* An entrepreneurial attitude is a realistic response to corporate America's increasingly frigid indifference. Don't concern yourself with the "company;" your interest should always be *you.* Exemplary performance record? Boss's favorite? Irrelevant. When profits slip, that same 'ole chum who served you bratwurst at the company picnic will issue pink slips like parking tickets. The ax falls, and no one's head is spared.

But you've got nothing to worry about. Never before has there been a better time to ditch the suit for 501s and work for yourself. Technology is cheaper, faster, and more accessible than at any time in history. With a modem and fax machine, you can sell to Indonesia just as easily as to Indiana. No excuses: Get a laptop and get crankin'!

Armed with sufficient technology and a tangy dollop of moxie, you can compete with any Fortune 500, no questions asked. One of the inherent advantages of being an entrepreneur is the ability to work faster, cheaper, and more effectively than the big shots. No permission, approval, or signatures needed. You can easily fill the lucrative "cracks" big corporations leave behind. Chances are they will hire you to do so. The nimble entrepreneur will find an abundance of opportunity. When being free-lanced by a former employer, remember to *make 'em pay.*

A disclaimer: The mythology is a bit misleading. Poser entrepreneurs boast of being able to "miss work for a ballgame," but the real ones find they don't have an abundance of time. You'll work hard—arguably harder than you did while working for big business—*but you'll enjoy the pain!* Enjoyment is key: You could be miserable in corporate America, so at least enjoy what you're doing.

Library Materials   Most school and community libraries have extensive career information sources, ranging from job search guides to in-depth materials on specific careers, employment levels, salaries, and career forecasts. The *Occupational Outlook Handbook* covers all aspects of career planning and job search and provides detailed information on jobs in various career clusters. Other helpful government resources related to careers are the *Dictionary of Occupational Titles* and the *Occupational Outlook Quarterly.*

Mass Media Career Information   Most newspapers offer articles and columns with job search and career trend information. Newspapers, television reports, and radio reports also provide useful information about economic and social influences on careers. Changes in interest rates, consumer demand, and foreign trade are good indicators of job availability in certain occupational categories.

World Wide Web   The Internet offers a variety of information sources related to job opportunities, preparing a résumé, interviewing, and other career planning topics. See Appendix B for additional information.

Campus Placement Office   Your school probably has a career planning and placement service to assist you. This office is likely to have materials on various career planning topics and can assist you in creating a résumé and preparing for an interview.

Community Organizations   Every community has business and civic groups you can use in your career search. Public meetings featuring industry leaders and business owners provide opportunities to become acquainted with local businesspeople.

Professional Associations   Various professions have organizations to promote their career areas. These organizations include the American Marketing Association, the Independent Insurance Agents of America, the American Society of Women Accountants, and the National Association of Real Estate Brokers. The *Encyclopedia of Associations* can help you identify organizations representing careers that interest you.

networking

Business Contacts   Professional contacts can advise you about career preparation and job opportunities. Friends, relatives, people you meet through community and professional organizations, and people you meet through school, work, church, or other activities are all potential business contacts. **Networking** is the process of making and using contacts to obtain and update career information. Campus programs such as organizations, sports, and lectures can provide valuable contacts. Every person you talk to is a potential career contact who may provide career information or assistance.

informational interview

Although the contacts you make may not be able to hire you, if jobs are available they can refer you to the right person. They can also help you get an **informational interview,** a meeting at which you gather information about a career or an organization. Informational interviews are valuable sources of career planning information because they allow you to interact with people involved in a work setting.

Identifying Job Opportunities

Sheet 7

Before you apply for employment, you need to identify job openings that match your interests and abilities.

Job Advertisements   Advertisements in newspapers and professional periodicals can be valuable sources of available positions. Newspapers such as *The Wall Street Journal,* the *New York Times,* the *Chicago Tribune,* and the *Los Angeles Times* have job listings covering a wide geographic area. You should also check local and regional newspapers. For opportunities in a specific career field, refer to specialized publications such as *Advertising Age, Marketing News,* the *Journal of Accountancy,* and *American Banker.* Since 80 to 90 percent of available jobs are not advertised to the general public, other job search techniques are critical.

DID YOU KNOW?

Campus recruiters estimate that only 20 to 30 percent of job candidates prepare for the interview.

Career Fairs   Career fairs, commonly held on campuses and at convention centers, offer an opportunity to make contact with several firms in a short time span. Be prepared to quickly communicate your potential contributions to an organization. By making yourself memorable to the recruiter, you are likely to be called for an in-depth interview at a later date.

Employment Agencies   Another source of job leads is employment agencies. These for-profit organizations match job hunters with prospective employers. Often the hiring company pays the fee charged by the employment agency; however, be careful when you are asked to pay a fee and have no guarantee of a job. The Federal Trade Commission cautions job seekers about employment service firms that require large fees in advance or use 900 numbers. Also, be sure you understand any contracts before signing them.

Government-supported employment services are also available. Contact your state employment service or your state department of labor for further information.

job creation

Job Creation   After researching a particular company or industry, design a presentation that communicates how your abilities could contribute to that organization. **Job creation** involves developing an employment position that matches your skills with the needs of an organization.

As you develop skills in areas you enjoy, you may be able to create a demand for your services. For example, a person who enjoyed researching business and economic trends was hired by a major corporation to make presentations for its managers at various company offices. Other people with an ability to design promotions and advertising might be hired by a nonprofit organization that needs to expand awareness of its services.

Other Job Search Methods   Your ability to locate existing and potential employment positions is limited only by your imagination and initiative. Commonly overlooked sources of jobs include the following:

- Visit companies where you would like to work, and make face-to-face contacts. Create an impression that you are someone who can contribute to that organization.
- Successful organizations continually look for quality employees. Telephone and business directories can provide names of organizations that employ people with your qualifications.
- Search the World Wide Web for information about potential jobs and organizations that may be in search of someone with your abilities and skills.
- Talk with alumni who work in your field. Graduates who are familiar with your school and major can help you focus your career search.

To improve your job search efforts, work as many hours a week *getting* a job as you expect to work each week *on* the job. Maintaining an ongoing relationship with contacts can be a valuable source of information about future career opportunities.

résumé

cover letter

Applying for Employment

Many qualified people never get the job they deserve without a presentation of skills and experiences. This process usually involves three elements.

DID YOU KNOW?

The first 30 seconds of a job interview are crucial. In that brief time, a judgment is usually made to determine your potential for the specific job position and within the organization.

1. The **résumé,** a summary of education, training, experience, and qualifications, provides prospective employers with an overview of your potential contributions to an organization.
2. A **cover letter** is the correspondence that you send with a résumé to communicate your interest in a job and to obtain an interview.
3. The *interview* is the formal meeting used to discuss your qualifications in detail.

Additional information on résumés, cover letters, and interviews is presented in the appendix to this chapter.

CONCEPT   CHECK   2–3

1. How can a person obtain employment-related experiences without working in a job situation?
2. What types of career information sources can be helpful in identifying job opportunities?
3. How does the information in a cover letter differ from the information in a résumé?

FINANCIAL AND LEGAL ASPECTS OF EMPLOYMENT

L.O.4 Assess the financial and legal concerns related to obtaining employment

"We would like you to work for us." This is the result you wanted from your job search. When offered an employment position, you should examine a range of factors. Carefully assess the organization, the specific job, and the salary and other financial benefits. Also, become aware of your legal rights as an employee.

Accepting an Employment Position

Before accepting a position, do further research about the job and the company. Request information about your specific duties and job expectations. If someone currently has a similar position, ask to talk to that person. If you are replacing a person who is no longer with the company, obtain information about the circumstances of that person's departure.

The Work Environment   Investigate the work environment. The term *corporate culture* refers to management styles, work intensity, dress codes, and social interactions within an organization. For example, some companies have rigid lines of communication, while others have an open-door atmosphere. Are the values, goals, and lifestyles of current employees similar to yours? If not, you may find yourself in an uncomfortable situation that doesn't allow you to perform according to your capabilities.

Also consider company policies and procedures. For example, how does the company handle salary increases, evaluations of employees, and promotions? Talking with current workers can help you answer such questions.

Factors Affecting Salary   Your initial salary will be influenced by your education and training, company size, and salaries for comparable positions. To ensure a fair starting salary, talk to people in similar positions at other companies and check business journals for information about salary levels. In addition, make sure you clearly understand company procedures and policies for raises. In recent years, increased emphasis has been placed on team results for salary increases and on rewards for expanded learning.

Performance quality and work responsibilities are the main influences on salary advances. Meet regularly with your supervisor to obtain performance evaluations and suggestions for professional growth. Communicate your desire for increased work responsibilities and greater financial rewards. Meeting and exceeding organizational expectations should enhance your monetary position. If not, you may wish to consider other employment opportunities.

Evaluating Employee Benefits

Escalating health care costs, changing family situations, and concerns about retirement have increased the attention given to supplementary compensation benefits.

FINANCIAL PLANNING FOR LIFE'S SITUATIONS

EMPLOYEE BENEFITS TO MEET VARIED NEEDS

At Wilton Conner Packaging Company (Charlotte, NC), employees get their laundry done on premises for $1 a load. Long-term employees at John Nuveen Company (Chicago, IL) qualify for college tuition payments for their children. At some locations of MBNA America Bank (Wilmington, DE), workers may use services such as an espresso bar, a barber shop, shoe repair, film processing, and a travel agency.

These are just a few of the attempts companies are making to meet the varied needs of employees. Organizations are realizing that a strong effort to maintain a loyal, committed work force benefits their long-term financial success. One survey reports that about 30 percent of companies offer on-site gift stores, while 22 percent have on-site medical care.

To allow parents more time with their families, some companies are using a compressed workweek know as the *9/80.* Employees on this schedule put in 80 hours of work over 9 days instead of the usual 10. This gives employees a three-day weekend every other week. Other methods

used to meet the needs of workers with children or dependent parents include flextime, job sharing, on-site child care, and telecommuting.

Electronic technology is also contributing to meeting employee needs. Many companies use interactive computer technology to allow workers to access benefits information, make changes in their benefits package, and conduct related business using personal computers. Once connected to this type of system, employees can obtain real-time information on the market value of pension plan investments. In addition, they can choose a health plan, research HMOs, and select a doctor.

SOURCES: Stephanie Armour, "Perking Up Employees: Fringe Benefits on the Rise," *USA Today,* October 8, 1997, pp. 1B, 2B; Carol Kleiman, "Companies That Still Make People—Not Profit—Top Priority," *Chicago Tribune,* June 16, 1996, sec. 6, p. 1; Lynn Asinof, "Click & Shift: Workers Control Their Benefits On-Line," *The Wall Street Journal,* November 21, 1997, pp. C1, C17; Kathy Bergen, "Timely Exercise: Compact Schedules Help Workers Stretch," *Chicago Tribune,* March 2, 1997, sec. 5, pp. 1, 6.

Meeting Employee Needs   In recent years, nonsalary employee benefits have expanded to meet the needs of different life situations. The increasing number of two-income and single-parent households has resulted in a greater need for child care benefits and leaves of absence to care for newborn children, newly adopted children, and other dependents. The need for elder care benefits for employees with dependent parents or grandparents continues to increase. Child care benefits are offered in a variety of forms, ranging from direct payments for child care to facilities on company premises.

Other employee benefits designed to meet employees' needs include flexible work schedules; work-at-home arrangements; legal assistance; counseling for health, emotional, and financial needs; and exercise and fitness programs. Such benefits not only enhance the quality of employees' lives but are profitable for organizations because happier, healthier employees miss fewer workdays and have a higher level of productivity. (See the Financial Planning for Life's Situations box on page 45.)

cafeteria-style employee benefits

Financial Decision Trade-Off

Cafeteria-style employee benefits are programs that allow workers to base their job benefits on a credit system and personal needs. Flexible selection of employee benefits has become common. A married employee with children may opt for increased life and health insurance, while a single parent may use benefit credits for child care services. The Financial Planning in Action box on page 45 suggests benefits for different life situations. Like any financial decision, employee benefits involve a trade-off, or opportunity cost, that you must assess.

Many organizations offer *flexible spending plans*, also called *expense reimbursement accounts.* This arrangement allows you to set aside part of your salary for paying medical

FINANCIAL PLANNING IN ACTION

SELECTING EMPLOYEE BENEFITS

Commonly recommended employee benefits for various life situations are listed below. Based on your current life situation or expectations for the future, list the employee benefits that would be most important to you.

Single, no children

- Disability income insurance to maintain earning power
- Health insurance
- Contributions to a retirement program
- Educational assistance, such as tuition reimbursement

Young family

- Comprehensive health insurance
- Life insurance
- Child care services

Single parent

- Health insurance
- Life insurance
- Disability income insurance
- Dependent care benefits

Married, no children

- Health and disability insurance
- Retirement program contributions
- Maternity coverage and parental leave (young couple)
- Long-term health care needs (older couple)

Mixed-generation household

- Health and disability insurance
- Child care services
- Elder care benefits

Life situation _____

_____

Desired employee benefits _____

_____

_____

_____

_____

_____

or dependent care expenses. These funds are not subject to income or Social Security taxes. However, money not used for the specified purpose is forfeited. Therefore, you must carefully plan the amount to be designated for a flexible spending plan.

In a similar manner, a *medical-spending account (MSA)* allows people who are self-employed or work for a company with 50 or fewer employees the opportunity to pay health care costs with pretax dollars. The MSA has two components: (1) health insurance coverage with a high deductible and (2) a tax-deferred savings account for paying medical expenses. Money in this account may be taken out for other uses; however, the funds are then taxed, along with an additional 15 percent tax penalty. While MSAs have tax-saving implications, the high deductible may not be affordable for many households.

When matching dependent health care needs and medical insurance plans, consider the following:

- Types of services available and location of health care providers.
- Direct costs (insurance premiums) to you.
- Anticipated out-of-pocket costs (deductibles and coinsurance amounts).

Chapter 11 discusses medical and disability insurance in detail.

As people live longer, profit-sharing plans and retirement programs are increasing in importance. In addition to Social Security benefits, some employers contribute to a pension

FINANCIAL PLANNING CALCULATIONS

TAX-EQUIVALENT EMPLOYEE BENEFITS

Employee benefits that are nontaxable have a higher financial value than you may realize. A $100 employee benefit on which you are taxed is not worth as much as a nontaxable $100 benefit. This formula is used to calculate the *tax-equivalent value* of a nontaxable benefit:

$$\frac{\text{Value of the benefit}}{(1 - \text{Tax rate})}$$

For example, receiving a life insurance policy with a non-taxable annual premium of $350 is comparable to receiving a taxable employee benefit worth $486 if you are in the 28 percent tax bracket. This tax-equivalent amount is calculated as follows:

$$\frac{\$350}{(1 - 0.28)} = \frac{\$350}{0.72} = \$486$$

A variation of this formula, which would give the *after-tax* value of an employee benefit, is

$$\text{Taxable value of the benefit} (1 - \text{Tax rate})$$

For the above example, the calculation would be

$$\$486(1 - 0.28) = \$486(0.72) = \$350$$

In other words, a taxable benefit with a value of $486 would have an after-tax value of $350 since you would have to pay $136 ($486 × 0.28) in tax on the benefit.

These simple calculations can help you assess and compare different employee benefits within a company or in considering different jobs. Remember to also consider the value of employee benefits in terms of your personal and family needs and goals.

plan. *Vesting* is the point at which retirement payments made by the organization on your behalf belong to you even if you no longer work for the organization. Vesting schedules vary, but all qualified plans (those for which an employer may deduct contributions to the plan for tax purposes) must (1) be 100 percent vested on completion of five years of service or (2) have 20 percent vesting after three years and full vesting, in stages, after seven years. Vesting refers only to the employer's pension contributions; employee contributions belong to the employees regardless of the length of their service with the organization.

Workers are commonly allowed to make personal contributions to company-sponsored retirement programs. These plans usually involve several premixed portfolios, making it easy for employees to choose investments for their retirement funds. Retirement plans are discussed in Chapters 4 and 18.

Comparing Benefits　Two methods used to assess the monetary value of employee benefits are market value calculations and future value calculations.

Market value calculations determine the specific monetary value of employee benefits—the cost of the benefits if you had to pay for them. For example, you may view the value of one week's vacation as $\frac{1}{52}$ of your annual salary, or you may view the value of a life insurance benefit as what it would cost you to obtain the same coverage. You can use this method to determine the difference between two job offers with different salaries and employee benefits.

Future value calculations, as discussed in Chapter 1, enable you to assess the long-term worth of employee benefits such as pension programs and retirement plans. For example, you can compare the future value of payments contributed to a company retirement fund to that of other saving and investment options.

You should also take tax considerations into account when you assess employment benefits. A *tax-exempt* benefit is one on which you won't have to pay income tax, but a *tax-deferred* benefit requires the payment of income tax at some future time, such as at retirement. In recent years, the federal government has required that taxes be paid on certain types of nonfinancial benefits. For example, the value of a company car used for personal travel is considered taxable income.

Sheet 12

To be exempt from federal income tax, a benefit plan must be "nondiscriminatory"; that is, lower-paid workers must receive benefits comparable to those given to highly paid executives. If executives are given life insurance coverage in which the premium constitutes a higher proportion of their salaries, the excess value of the insurance premium is taxable. When assessing employment compensation and benefits, consider their taxability, since an untaxed benefit of lower value may be worth more than a benefit of higher value that is subject to taxation (see the accompanying Financial Planning Calculations box).

Your Employment Rights

Employees have legal rights both during the hiring process and on the job. For example, an employer cannot refuse to hire a woman or terminate her employment because of pregnancy, nor can it force her to go on leave at an arbitrary point during her pregnancy. In addition, a woman who stops working due to pregnancy must get full credit for previous service, accrued retirement benefits, and accumulated seniority. Other employment rights include the following:

> ### DID YOU KNOW?
>
> More and more employers are using credit reports as hiring tools. As of 1997, federal law requires that job applicants be told if credit histories are being used in the hiring process.

- A person may not be discriminated against in the employment selection process on the basis of age, race, color, religion, sex, marital status, national origin, or mental or physical disabilities.
- Minimum-wage and overtime pay legislation apply to individuals in certain work settings.
- Workers' compensation (for work-related injury or illness), Social Security, and unemployment insurance are required benefits.

CONCEPT CHECK 2–4

1. How does a person's life situation determine the importance of certain employee benefits?
2. What methods can be used to measure the monetary value of employee benefits?

LONG-TERM CAREER DEVELOPMENT

L.O.5 Analyze the techniques for career growth and advancement.

A job is for today, but a career can be for a lifetime. Will you always enjoy the work you do today? Will you be successful in the career you select? These questions cannot be answered right away; however, certain skills and attitudes can lead to a fulfilling work life.

Every day you can perform duties that contribute to your career success. Communicating and working well with others will enhance your chances for financial advancement and promotion. Flexibility and openness to new ideas will expand your abilities, knowledge, and career potential.

Develop efficient work habits. Use lists, goal setting, note cards, and other time management techniques. Combine increased productivity with quality. All of your work activities should reflect your best performance. This extra effort will be recognized and rewarded.

Finally, learn to anticipate problems and areas for action. Creativity and a willingness to assist others can help the entire organization and contribute to your work enjoyment and career growth.

Training Opportunities

Many technology-work situations did not exist a few years ago. Many of the job skills you will need in the future have yet to be created. Your desire for increased education is a primary determinant of your career success and financial advancement. Continue to learn about new technology and the global economy.

Various methods for updating and expanding your knowledge are available. Formal methods include company programs, seminars offered by professional organizations, and graduate and advanced college courses. Many companies encourage and pay for continuing education.

Informal methods for updating and expanding your knowledge include reading and discussion with colleagues. Newspapers, news magazines, business periodicals, and professional journals offer a wealth of information on business, economic, and social trends. Informal meetings with co-workers and associates from other companies are a valuable source of current career information.

Career Paths and Advancement

mentor

As with other financial decisions, career choices must be reevaluated in light of changing values, goals, economic conditions, and social trends. As Exhibit 2–5 shows, you will evolve through a series of career stages, each with specific tasks and challenges. A successful technique for coping with the anxieties associated with career development is to gain the support of an established person in your field. A **mentor** is an experienced employee who serves as a teacher and counselor for a less experienced person in a career field. A relationship with a mentor can provide such benefits as personalized training, access to influential people, and emotional support during difficult times.

Your efforts to attract a mentor start with excellent performance. Show initiative, be creative, and be alert to meeting the needs of others. Maintain visibility and display a desire to learn and grow by asking questions and volunteering for new assignments.

Sheet 13

A prospective mentor should be receptive to assisting others and to helping them grow in both the technical and social areas of a career. Many organizations have formal mentor programs with an experienced employee assigned to oversee the career development of a new employee. Some mentor relationships involve retired individuals who desire to share their knowledge and experience.

Changing Careers

At some time in their lives, most workers change jobs. About 10 million career moves occur each year. People change jobs to obtain a better or different position within the same career field or to move into a new career field. Changing jobs may be more difficult than selecting the first job. Unless their present situation is causing mental stress or physical illness, most people are unwilling to exchange the security of an existing position for the uncertainty of an unfamiliar one.

The following may be indications that it is time to move on:

- Low motivation toward your current work.
- Physical or emotional distress caused by your job.
- Consistently poor performance evaluations.

EXHIBIT 2–5

Stages of Career Development: Characteristics and Concerns

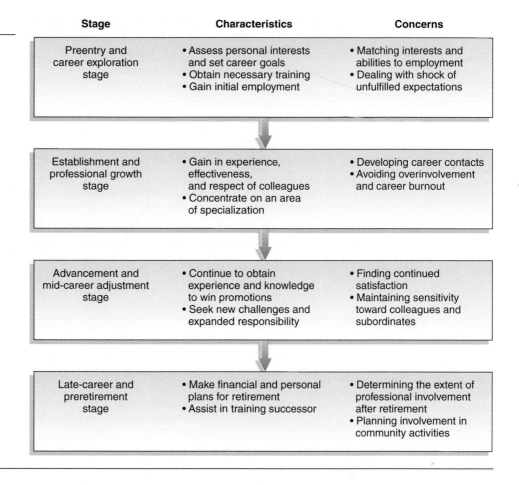

Stage	Characteristics	Concerns
Preentry and career exploration stage	• Assess personal interests and set career goals • Obtain necessary training • Gain initial employment	• Matching interests and abilities to employment • Dealing with shock of unfulfilled expectations
Establishment and professional growth stage	• Gain in experience, effectiveness, and respect of colleagues • Concentrate on an area of specialization	• Developing career contacts • Avoiding overinvolvement and career burnout
Advancement and mid-career adjustment stage	• Continue to obtain experience and knowledge to win promotions • Seek new challenges and expanded responsibility	• Finding continued satisfaction • Maintaining sensitivity toward colleagues and subordinates
Late-career and preretirement stage	• Make financial and personal plans for retirement • Assist in training successor	• Determining the extent of professional involvement after retirement • Planning involvement in community activities

- A lack of social interactions with co-workers.
- Limited opportunity for salary or position advancement.
- A poor relationship with your superior.

A decision to change careers may require minor alterations in your life (such as going from retail sales to industrial sales), or it may mean extensive retraining and starting at an entry level in a new field. As with every other financial decision, no exact formula exists for deciding whether you should make a career change. However, follow these guidelines. First, carefully assess the financial and personal costs and benefits of changing careers in relation to your needs and goals and those of your household. Giving up benefits such as health insurance may be costly to a family, but the expanded career opportunities in a new field may be worth the trade-off. Then determine whether a career change will serve your needs and goals and those of other household members.

In many industries, job security is a thing of the past. Company mergers, downsizing, and economic conditions may result in forced career changes. Layoffs cause emotional and financial stress for individuals and families. To cope with job termination while seeking new employment, counselors recommend that you

- Maintain appropriate eating, sleep, and exercise habits.
- Get involved in family and community activities; new career contacts are possible anywhere.

- Improve your career skills through personal study, formal classes, or volunteer work.
- Target your job search to high-growth industries or small businesses.
- Consider opportunities with nonprofit organizations, government agencies, temporary employment, or consultant work.
- Target your skills and experience to the needs of an organization.

CONCEPT   CHECK   2–5

1. What types of activities would you recommend for people who desire career advancement and professional growth?
2. What factors should a person consider before changing jobs or career fields?

SUMMARY

L.O.1   Describe the activities associated with career planning and advancement.

Career planning and advancement involve the following stages and activities: (1) assess and research personal goals, abilities, and career fields; (2) evaluate the employment market and identify specific employment opportunities; (3) develop a résumé and cover letter for use in applying for available positions; (4) interview for available positions; (5) evaluate financial and other elements of the positions you are offered; and (6) plan and implement a program for career development.

L.O.2   Evaluate the factors that influence employment opportunities.

Consider the selection of a career in relation to personal abilities, interests, experience, training, and goals; social influences affecting employment, such as demographic trends; changing economic conditions; and industrial and technological trends.

L.O.3   Implement employment search strategies.

For successful career planning and development, consider doing the following. Obtain employment or related experiences by working part-time or by participating in campus and community activities. Use career information sources to learn about employment fields and identify job opportunities. Prepare a résumé and cover letter that effectively present your qualifications for a specific employment position. Practice interview skills that project enthusiasm and competence.

L.O.4   Assess the financial and legal concerns related to obtaining employment.

Evaluate the work environment and compensation package of prospective employers. Assess employee benefits on the basis of their market value, future value, and taxability and your personal needs and goals. Prospective and current employees have legal rights with regard to fair hiring practices and equal opportunity on the job.

L.O.5   Analyze the techniques available for career growth and advancement.

Informal and formal education and training opportunities are available to foster professional development and facilitate career changes.

GLOSSARY

cafeteria-style employee benefits   Programs that allow workers to base their job benefits on a credit system and personal needs.   (p. 44)

career   A commitment to a profession that requires continued training and offers a clear path for occupational growth. (p. 31)

cover letter   A letter that accompanies a résumé and is designed to express interest in a job and obtain an interview. (p. 42)

informational interview   A company visit or meeting at which one gathers information about a career or an organization.   (p. 41)

job   An employment position obtained mainly to earn money, without regard for interests or opportunities for advancement.   (p. 31)

job creation   The development of an employment position that matches your skills with the needs of an organization. (p. 42)

mentor   An experienced employee who serves as a teacher and counselor for a less experienced person in a career field. (p. 48)

networking   The process of making and using contacts for obtaining and updating career information.   (p. 41)

résumé   A summary of a person's education, training, experience, and other job qualifications.   (p. 42)

R E V I E W   Q U E S T I O N S

1. Explain the potential benefits of advanced training for both short-term and long-term career success.   (L.O.1)
2. Describe a situation in which economic or social trends could affect jobs.   (L.O.2)
3. What actions could a person take to improve the chances of obtaining and maintaining employment?   (L.O.3)
4. Describe a situation in which a person's selection of a job might be based on the benefits the company offers.   (L.O.4)
5. What actions could a person take to maintain employability despite changes in social and economic trends?   (L.O.5)

F I N A N C I A L   P L A N N I N G   P R O B L E M S

1. *Determining the Future Value of Education.* Jenny Franklin estimates that as a result of completing her master's degree, she will earn $6,000 a year more for the next 40 years.   (L.O.1)
   a. What would be the total amount of these additional earnings?
   b. What would be the *present value* of these additional earnings based on an annual interest rate of 6 percent? (Use Table C–4 in Appendix C.)
2. *Comparing Living Costs.* Brad Edwards is earning $42,000 a year in a city located in the Midwest. He is interviewing for a position in a city with a cost of living 12 percent higher than where he currently lives. What would be the minimum salary he would need at his new job to maintain the same standard of living?   (L.O.2)
3. *Calculating Future Value of Salary.* During a job interview, Pam Thompson is offered a salary of $23,000. The company gives annual raises of 6 percent. What would be Pam's salary during her fifth year on the job?   (L.O.3)
4. *Computing Future Value.* Calculate the future value of a retirement account in which you deposit $2,000 a year for 30 years with an annual interest rate of 8 percent. (Use the tables in Appendix C.)   (L.O.4)
5. *Comparing Taxes for Employee Benefits.* Which of the following employee benefits has the greater value? Use the formula given in the Financial Planning Calculations box on page 46 to compare these benefits. (Assume a 28 percent tax rate.)   (L.O.4)
   a. A nontaxable pension contribution of $4,300 or the use of a company car with a taxable value of $6,325.
   b. A life insurance policy with a taxable value of $450 or a nontaxable increase in health insurance coverage valued at $340.
6. *Comparing Employment Offers.* Bill Mason is considering two job offers. Job 1 pays a salary of $36,500 with $4,500 of nontaxable employee benefits. Job 2 pays a salary of $34,700 and $6,120 of nontaxable benefits. Which position would have the higher monetary value? Use a 28 percent tax rate.   (L.O.4)

P R O J E C T S   A N D   A P P L I C A T I O N   A C T I V I T I E S

1. *Researching Career Views.* Interview several people about influences on their current employment situation. How did various personal, economic, and social factors affect their career choices and professional development?   (L.O.1)
2. *Researching Career Planning Activities.* Interview a person who recently made a major career change. What personal and economic factors influenced this decision? What specific career planning activities did the person use?   (L.O.1)
3. *Comparing Career Alternatives.* Using Sheet 6 in the *Personal Financial Planner,* research two careers you might consider. Compare employment requirements, duties on the job, and future potential.   (L.O.2)
4. *Projecting Future Career Opportunities.* Based on a Web search or library resources, obtain articles, employment data projections, and other information about the careers with the most future potential. Prepare a report or visual presentation (slides, poster, or video) communicating the types of careers that are likely be most in demand in the future.   (L.O.2)
5. *Searching Employment Opportunities on the Internet.* Using Web sites such at www.ajb.dni.us or www. careermosiac.com (or Web search engines), obtain information about positions available in your areas of interest.   (L.O.3)

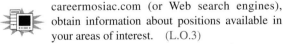

6. *Participating in an Informational Interview.* Arrange an informational interview at a local company or with a business contact you have made. Prepare questions to ask related to needed skills in this employment field, current

trends for the industry, and future prospects for this
career area.   (L.O.3)

7. *Searching the Web for Benefit Information.* Using a Web
search or library information, obtain information about
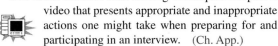
various employee benefits such as health insur-
ance, retirement plans, child care, life insurance,
and tuition reimbursement.   (L.O.4)

8. *Analyzing Employee Benefits.* Using Sheet 12 in the
Personal Financial Planner, obtain information about
various employee benefits from current or prospective
employers.   (L.O.4)

9. *Obtaining Career Advancement Information.* Talk with
several people employed in various types of careers
(large company, international business, individual entre-

preneur, nonprofit, or government). Prepare an outline or
other visual presentation describing the training and professional development activities they have found most
valuable.   (L.O.5)

10. *Creating a Personal Data Sheet.* Using Sheet 8 in the
Personal Financial Planner, plan the content and format
for a résumé that you might use in the near future.
(Ch. App.)

11. *Preparing for an Interview.* Based on library research, a
Web search, and experiences of others, obtain information about effective interviewing techniques. Prepare a
video that presents appropriate and inappropriate
actions one might take when preparing for and
participating in an interview.   (Ch. App.)

LIFE SITUATION CASE 2

BEING YOUR OWN BOSS

"I can't stand it anymore. It was another one of those days!"
Stan Vernon proclaimed as he walked in the door.

"Well, stop complaining and change jobs," his wife Calley
retorted.

"But it's been the same everywhere," complained Stan. "I
think it's time to take a different approach."

Later that week, while looking through the classified
section of the newspaper, Stan spotted an opportunity to buy
a company that provided computerized accounting, payroll,
and financial analysis services to small businesses. This
investment would allow Stan to use his career skills while
giving him experience in running his own company.

"This seems to be an opportunity for you to do what you
enjoy and not have to answer to others," advised Calley.
"Let's go over and talk to the current owner."

"That's a good idea," commented Stan. "But how much
should we pay for the company?"

Calley responded, "Start by asking how much they want
for it!"

QUESTIONS

1. What might affect a person's decision to own a business
rather than work for someone else?

2. What factors should Stan analyze when placing a value on
the business he is considering for purchase?

3. If Stan can invest his funds at 6 percent and expects to
have an annual profit from the business of $60,000 for 10
years, what would be the present value of that series of
cash inflows? (See Appendix C.)

4. In addition to running his own business, what other
employment alternatives could give Stan more flexibility
in his career?

USING THE INTERNET TO CREATE A PERSONAL FINANCIAL PLAN 2

CAREER PLANNING AND EMPLOYMENT SEARCHES

Your selection of a career and professional development activities will influence many aspects of your life, including financial resource availability, leisure time, living location, and acquaintances.

Web Sites for Career Planning

■ Career planning tips at **www.jobtrak.com/jobguide, www.careermag.com,** and **www.mapping-your-future .org**
■ Listings of available jobs at **www.careermosiac.com** and **www.careerpath.com**
■ Résumé preparation information and other career planning assistance at **www.occ.com** and **www.jobweb.com**
■ Career information from U.S. Department of Labor and state agencies at **www.ajb.dni.us**
■ Current career planning articles from *Money* magazine at **www.money.com**, from *Kiplinger's Personal Finance* magazine at **www.kiplinger.com,** *Business Week* at **www.businessweek.com**, *Worth* magazine at **www.worth .com**, and *Smart Money* at **www.smartmoney.com**

(NOTE: Addresses and content of Web sites change, and new sites are created daily. Use the search engines discussed in Appendix B to update and locate Web sites for your current financial planning needs.)

PFP SHEETS: 6–13

Short-Term Financial Planning Activities

1. Explore various career areas in relation to your interests, abilities, and goals   (see PFP Sheet 6).
2. Develop a résumé and sample cover letter for use in a job search   (see PFP Sheets 8, 9).
3. Research prospective employers and develop a strategy for effective interviewing   (see PFP Sheets 10, 11)

Long-Term Financial Planning Activities

1. Analyze employee benefits based on your current and possible future financial needs   (see PFP Sheet 12).
2. Develop a plan of action for professional development and career advancement   (see PFP Sheet 13).

Résumés, Cover Letters, and Interviews

DEVELOPING A RÉSUMÉ

Every business must present its product or service to potential customers in an effective manner. In the same way, you must market yourself to prospective employers by developing a résumé, creating a letter to obtain an interview, and interviewing for available positions.

Résumé Elements

A *résumé* is a summary of your education, training, experience, and other job qualifications. This personal-information sheet is vital in your employment search. The main components of a résumé are as follows.

1. The Personal Data Section   Start with your name, address, and telephone number. Both a school and home address and telephone number may be appropriate. Do not include your birth date, sex, height, and weight in a résumé unless they apply to specific job qualifications.

2. The Career Objective Section   You may omit this section from your résumé. A vague career objective will be meaningless to a prospective employer, and one that is too specific might prevent you from being considered for another position within the organization. Your career objective is probably best communicated in your cover letter. As an alternative, consider a "Summary" section with a synopsis of your capabilities.

3. The Education Section   This section should include dates, schools attended, fields of study, and degrees earned. Courses directly related to your career field may be highlighted. If your grade point average is exceptionally high, include it to demonstrate your ability to excel.

4. The Experience Section   In this section, list organizations, dates of involvement, and responsibilities for all previous employment, work-related school activities, and community service. Highlight computer skills, technical abilities, and other specific competencies that are in demand by organizations. Use action verbs to communicate how your experience and talents will benefit the organization (see Exhibit 2–A).

EXHIBIT 2–A

**Sample Action
Verbs to
Communicate
Career-Related
Experiences**

- Achieved...
- Administered...
- Coordinated...
- Created...
- Designed...
- Developed...
- Directed...
- Edited...
- Initiated...
- Implemented...
- Managed...
- Monitored...
- Organized...
- Planned...
- Produced...
- Researched...
- Summarized...
- Supervised...
- Trained...
- Updated...

5. The Related Information Section   List honors or awards to communicate your ability to produce quality work. List other interests and activities if they relate to your career. However, avoid a long list of hobbies and other interests, which can give the impression that work is not your top priority.

6. The References Section   In this section, list people who can verify your skills and competencies. These individuals may be teachers, previous employers, supervisors, or business colleagues. Be sure to obtain permission from the people you plan to use as references. References are usually not included in a résumé; however, you will need to have this information available if a prospective employer requests it.

Types of Résumés

Three commonly used types of résumés are the chronological résumé, the functional résumé, and the targeted résumé. The *chronological résumé* (see Exhibit 2–B) presents your education, work experience, and other information in a reverse-time sequence (the most recent item first). This type of résumé is most appropriate for people with a continuous school and work record. Many people find it to be the best vehicle for presenting their career qualifications.

The *functional résumé* (see Exhibit 2–C) is suggested for people with diverse skills and time gaps in their experience. This résumé emphasizes your abilities and skills in categories such as communication, supervision, project planning, human relations, and research. Each section provides information about experiences and qualifications rather than dates, places, and job titles. This type of résumé is especially appropriate if you are changing careers or your most recent experiences are not directly related to the available position.

You may want to develop a *targeted résumé,* that is, a résumé for a specific job. Such a résumé highlights the capabilities and experiences most appropriate to the available

EXHIBIT 2–B

A Chronological Résumé

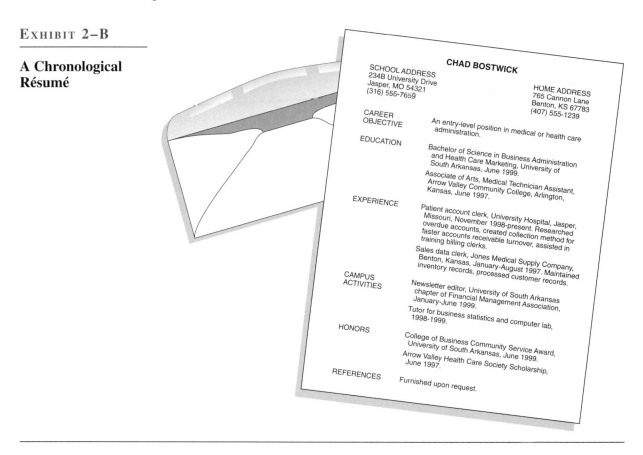

CHAD BOSTWICK

SCHOOL ADDRESS
234B University Drive
Jasper, MO 54321
(316) 555-7659

HOME ADDRESS
765 Cannon Lane
Benton, KS 67783
(407) 555-1239

CAREER OBJECTIVE
An entry-level position in medical or health care administration.

EDUCATION
Bachelor of Science in Business Administration and Health Care Marketing, University of South Arkansas, June 1999.

Associate of Arts, Medical Technician Assistant, Arrow Valley Community College, Arlington, Kansas, June 1997.

EXPERIENCE
Patient account clerk, University Hospital, Jasper, Missouri, November 1998-present. Researched overdue accounts, created collection method for faster accounts receivable turnover, assisted in training billing clerks.

Sales data clerk, Jones Medical Supply Company, Benton, Kansas, January-August 1997. Maintained inventory records, processed customer records.

CAMPUS ACTIVITIES
Newsletter editor, University of South Arkansas chapter of Financial Management Association, January-June 1999.

Tutor for business statistics and computer lab, 1998-1999.

HONORS
College of Business Community Service Award, University of South Arkansas, June 1999.

Arrow Valley Health Care Society Scholarship, June 1997.

REFERENCES
Furnished upon request.

---

position. The format may be similar to the chronological or functional résumé except it includes a very specific career objective. The targeted résumé takes extra time and research to prepare; however, this effort increases your opportunity for obtaining an interview.

Résumé Preparation

No formula exists for the preparation of an effective résumé; however, a résumé must be presented in a professional manner. Many candidates are disqualified due to poor résumés. Personal computers and laser printers make the résumé design process easier. Many quick-print businesses specialize in the preparation and reproduction of résumés.

Limit your résumé to one page. Send a two-page résumé only if you have enough material to fill three pages; then use the most valid information to prepare an impressive two-page presentation.

Use a format that highlights how your experiences will contribute to the company's needs. Underline or italicize items if appropriate. Remember, résumés are usually skimmed very quickly; in fact, some companies use scanning software to check for key words related to education and technical expertise.

Words and phrases that commonly impress prospective employers include: "foreign language skills," "computer experience," "achievement," "research experience," "flexible," "team projects," and "overseas study or experience."

For best results, seek guidance in preparing and evaluating your résumé. Counselors, the campus placement office, and friends may find errors and suggest improvements.

PFP

Sheet 8

Exhibit 2–C

A Functional Résumé

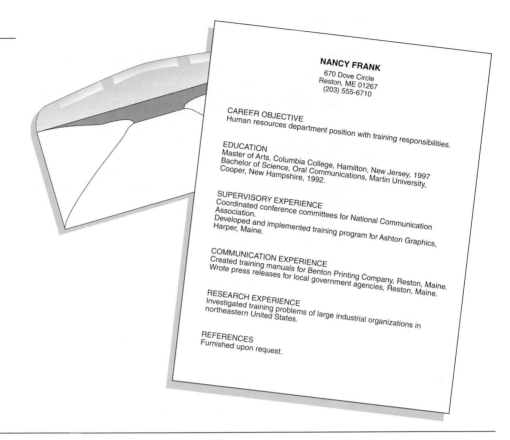

NANCY FRANK
670 Dove Circle
Reston, ME 01267
(203) 555-6710

CAREER OBJECTIVE
Human resources department position with training responsibilities.

EDUCATION
Master of Arts, Columbia College, Hamilton, New Jersey, 1997
Bachelor of Science, Oral Communications, Martin University,
Cooper, New Hampshire, 1992.

SUPERVISORY EXPERIENCE
Coordinated conference committees for National Communication
Association.
Developed and implemented training program for Ashton Graphics,
Harper, Maine.

COMMUNICATION EXPERIENCE
Created training manuals for Benton Printing Company, Reston, Maine.
Wrote press releases for local government agencies, Reston, Maine.

RESEARCH EXPERIENCE
Investigated training problems of large industrial organizations in
northeastern United States.

REFERENCES
Furnished upon request.

Résumé Delivery Methods

Traditionally, résumés have been mailed or hand delivered. When presenting a résumé in person, you have an opportunity to observe the company environment and make a positive impression about your career potential. Electronic résumé delivery may be done by fax, by e-mail, and posting on Web sites.

Résumé Alternatives

Thousands of résumés are sent each day. To stand out, applicants have tried various creative approaches. Employers report receiving résumés in the form of comic strips, "wanted" posters, advertisements, and menus; résumés attached to balloons, pizzas, and plants; and résumés on video and computer disks. Some of these efforts were effective; however, most employers view them as frivolous. A creative approach is probably most appropriate in fields such as advertising, journalism, photography, and public relations.

Instead of a résumé, some career counselors recommend a *targeted application letter* describing your background, experience, and accomplishments. After researching a position and company, you can communicate how your specific skills will benefit the organization.

Finally, you might create a *performance portfolio* containing tangible evidence of your experience. This printed or computerized presentation could include product designs, advertisements, marketing plans, published articles, photos, tables of sales results, financial charts, or other data.

CREATING A COVER LETTER

cover letter

Your résumé must be targeted to a specific organization and job. A **cover letter** is designed to express your interest in a job and help you obtain an interview. This letter accompanies your résumé and usually consists of an introductory paragraph, one or two development paragraphs, and a concluding paragraph.

Introduction

The introductory paragraph should get the reader's attention. Indicate your reason for writing by referring to the job or type of employment in which you are interested. Communicate what you have to offer the company based on your experience and qualifications.

Development

The development section should highlight the aspects of your background that specifically qualify you for the job. Refer the employer to your résumé for more details. At this point, elaborate on experiences and training that will contribute to the organization's needs in the future.

Conclusion

The concluding paragraph should request action from the employer. Ask for the opportunity to discuss your qualifications and potential with the employer in more detail; in other words, get an interview! Include information to make contacting you convenient, such as telephone numbers and the times when you are available. Close your letter by summarizing how you can benefit the organization.

You should create a separate cover letter for each position for which you apply. A poorly prepared cover letter usually guarantees rejection. Be sure to address your correspondence to the appropriate person in the organization.

A résumé and cover letter are your ticket to the interview. You may possess outstanding qualifications and career potential, but you need an interview to communicate this information. The time, effort, and care you take to present yourself on paper will help you achieve your career goal.

Sheet 9

THE JOB INTERVIEW

"Why should we hire you?" This may be an unexpected question; however, you may need to answer it. The interview phase of job hunting is limited to candidates who possess the specific qualifications the employer wants. Being invited for an interview puts you closer to receiving a job offer.

Preparing for the Interview

Prepare for your interview by obtaining additional information about your prospective employer. The best sources of company information include

- Library resources such as annual reports or recent articles.
- Internet searches of company and industry information.
- Observations during company visits.

- Observations of company products in stores or other places.
- Informal interviews with current and past employees.
- Discussions with people knowledgeable about the company or industry.

Sheet 10

During your research, try to obtain information about the company's past and current activities. Facts about its operations, competitors, recent successes, planned expansion, and personnel policies will be helpful when you discuss your potential contributions to the company.

Another preinterview activity is preparation of questions such as

- What training opportunities are available to employees who desire advancement?
- What qualities do your most successful employees possess?
- What do your employees like best about working here?
- What actions of competitors are likely to affect the company in the near future?

Also, prepare questions about your specific interests and about the particular organization with which you are interviewing. Request information about company policies and employee benefits.

Sheet 11

Successful interviewing requires practice. By using a video recorder or working with friends, you can develop the confidence needed for effective interviewing. Work to organize ideas, speak clearly and calmly, and communicate enthusiasm. Prepare specific answers regarding your strengths. Many campus organizations and career placement offices offer opportunities for practice by conducting mock interviews. Prepare concise answers for specific questions (see Exhibit 2–D) explaining how your experience will contribute to the future of the company. If appropriate, plan to bring photos or other evidence of your past efforts.

As you get ready for the interview, keep in mind that proper dress and grooming are important. Current employees are the best source of information about how to dress. In general, dress more conservatively than employees do. A business suit is usually appropriate for both men and women. Avoid trendy and casual styles, and don't wear too much jewelry. Confirm the time and location of the interview. Take copies of your résumé, your reference list, and a small notebook for writing down ideas during the interview. Plan to arrive about 10 minutes earlier than your appointed time.

The Interview Process

A *screening interview* is an initial, usually brief meeting with applicants that reduces the pool of job candidates. In the screening interview, interviewees are processed on the basis of overall impression and a few general questions. Screening interviews may be conducted on college campuses by corporate recruiters. Success in such an interview qualifies you for closer consideration by the employer.

Once you are judged to be a strong candidate for a job, your next interview can last from one hour to several days. The *selection interview,* which is reserved for the finalists in the job search, may involve a series of activities, including responses to questions, meetings with several people on the staff, and a seminar presentation.

The first part of the selection interview usually occurs in an informal setting. This arrangement is designed to help you relax and to establish rapport. Next, a brief discussion of the available position may take place. The main part of the interview involves questions to assess your abilities, potential, and personality. Interviews may include situations or questions to determine how you react under pressure. Remain calm. Answer clearly in a controlled manner. In the last portion of the interview, you are usually given an opportunity to ask questions.

EXHIBIT 2–D
_____

**Common Interview
Questions**

Education and Training Questions

What education and training qualify you for this job?
Why are you interested in working for this company?
In addition to going to school, what activities have helped you to expand your interests and knowledge?
What did you like best about school?
What did you like least?

Work and Other Experience Questions

In what types of situations have you done your best work?
Describe the supervisors who motivated you most.
Which of your past accomplishments are you most proud of?
Have you ever had to coordinate the activities of several people?
Describe some people whom you have found difficult to work with.
Describe a situation in which your determination helped you achieve a specific goal.
What situations frustrate you?
Other than past jobs, what experiences have helped prepare you for this job?
What methods do you consider best for motivating employees?

Personal Qualities Questions

What are your major strengths?
What are your major weaknesses? What have you done to overcome your weaknesses?
What do you plan to be doing 5 or 10 years from now?
Which individuals have had the greatest influence on you?
What traits make a person successful?
How well do you communicate your ideas orally and in writing?
How would your teachers and your past employers describe you?
What do you do in your leisure time?
How persuasive are you in presenting ideas to others?

Computers are also being used for interviews. Applicants respond to on-screen questions instead of to an interviewer. In addition, computers test an applicant's abilities in job-related situations, such as those that a bank teller or retail clerk might encounter.

Most interviewers conclude the selection interview by telling you when you can expect to hear from the company. While waiting, consider doing two things. First, send a follow-up letter within a day or two expressing your appreciation for the opportunity to interview. If you don't get the job, this thank-you letter can make a positive impression that improves your chances for future consideration. Second, do a self-evaluation of your interview performance. Write down the areas that you could improve. Try to remember the questions you were asked that were different than what you expected.

CHAPTER 3

MONEY MANAGEMENT STRATEGY
Financial Statements and Budgeting

Opening Case

"WE SPENT HOW MUCH ON WHAT?"

"Here we go again," complained Ben. "Every time we try to use a budget, we end up arguing and still don't have enough money."

Yolanda replied, "Maybe if we kept track of everything we spend, we would have some idea of where our money goes."

"No, not that!" Ben exclaimed. "I have a friend who keeps a notebook and lists everything he spends. That would drive me crazy."

"Well, we can't keep going like we have," responded Yolanda. "A year ago, we owed $4,500 on the credit cards. Now it's up to $7,000. And we don't have anything in savings. How will we ever be able to have a down payment for a house?"

Ben and Yolanda decided to sort all their check stubs, receipts, and credit card statements to see where their money was going. Last year, they spent over $2,000 in restaurants and charged over $800 on their vacation.

"I didn't realize we spent that much on those things," commented Ben. "We also had auto main-tenance costs of $1,650 and donated $1,800 to the homeless shelter and the church. Those are things we had to do and wanted to do."

Yolanda replied, "But now that we know how we spend our money, what do we do next?"

Ben conceded, "Maybe it's time we spent a few dollars on a notebook and file folders to record and sort our spending receipts in the future."

QUESTIONS

1. What would Ben and Yolanda learn by sorting their expenses into various categories? What categories should they use?
2. How can knowing where their money goes help Ben and Yolanda plan their spending?
3. What are various attitudes people have about budgeting?
4. What financial goals might Ben and Yolanda consider to address some of their money management concerns?

After studying this chapter, you will be able to

L.O.1	Recognize relationships among financial documents and money management activities.	**L.O.3**	Develop a personal balance sheet and cash flow statement.
L.O.2	Create a system for maintaining personal financial records.	**L.O.4**	Create and implement a budget.
		L.O.5	Calculate savings needed for achieving financial goals.

PLANNING FOR SUCCESSFUL MONEY MANAGEMENT

L.O.1 Recognize relationships among financial documents and money management activities.

"Each month I have too much month and not enough money. If the month were only 20 days long, budgeting would be easy." Most of us have heard a comment like this when it comes to budgeting and money management.

Your daily spending and saving decisions are the center of financial planning. You must coordinate these decisions with your needs, goals, and personal situation and with financial information. When people watch a baseball or football game, they usually know the score. In financial planning, knowing the score is also important. Maintaining financial records and planning your spending are essential to successful personal financial management. The time and effort you devote to these recordkeeping activities will yield benefits in the form of clear information and informed financial decisions. **Money management** refers to the day-to-day financial activities necessary to manage current personal economic resources while working toward long-term financial security.

money management

Opportunity Cost and Money Management

Consumers can choose from more than 25,000 items in a supermarket, from more than 11,000 periodicals, and from as many as 500 cable television stations. Daily decision making is a fact of life, and trade-offs are associated with each choice made. Selecting an alternative means you give up something else. In terms of money management decisions, examples of trade-off situations, or *opportunity costs,* include the following:

Financial Decision
Trade-Off

- Spending money on current living expenses reduces the amount you can use for saving and investing for long-term financial security.
- Saving and investing for the future reduce the amount you can spend now.
- Buying on credit results in payments later and a reduction in the amount of future income available for spending.
- Using savings for purchases results in lost interest earnings and an inability to use savings for other purposes.
- Comparison shopping can save you money and improve the quality of your purchases but uses up something of value you cannot replace: your time.

EXHIBIT 3–1   **Money Management Activities**

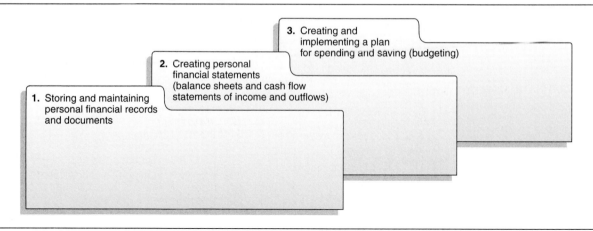

1. Storing and maintaining personal financial records and documents

2. Creating personal financial statements (balance sheets and cash flow statements of income and outflows)

3. Creating and implementing a plan for spending and saving (budgeting)

As you develop and implement various money management activities, you need to assess continually the financial and personal costs and benefits associated with these financial decisions.

Components of Money Management

As Exhibit 3–1 shows, three major money management activities are interrelated. Personal financial records and documents are the foundation of systematic resource use. They provide written evidence of business transactions, ownership of property, and legal matters. Personal financial statements enable you to measure and assess your financial position and progress. Your spending plan, or budget, is the basis for effective money management.

CONCEPT CHECK 3–1

1. What opportunity costs are associated with money management activities?
2. What are the three major money management activities?

A SYSTEM FOR PERSONAL FINANCIAL RECORDS

L.O.2 Create a system for maintaining personal financial records.

People have said that computers would result in fewer paper documents. How wrong they were! Today computers are generating more paperwork than ever. Much of that paperwork relates to financial matters. Invoices, credit card statements, insurance policies, and tax records are the basis of financial recordkeeping and personal economic choices.

An organized system of financial records provides a basis for

- Handling daily business affairs, including payment of bills on time.
- Planning and measuring financial progress.
- Completing required tax reports.
- Making effective investment decisions.
- Determining available resources for current and future buying.

EXHIBIT 3–2   **Where to Keep Your Financial Records**

Home File

1. Personal and Employment Records (Chapter 2)
- Current résumé
- Employee benefit information
- Social Security numbers
- Birth certificates

2. Money Management Records (Chapter 3)
- Current budget
- Recent personal financial statements (balance sheet, income statement)
- List of financial goals
- List of safe deposit box contents

3. Tax Records (Chapter 4)
- Paycheck stubs, W-2 forms, 1099 forms
- Receipts for tax-deductible items
- Records of taxable income
- Past income tax returns and documentation

4. Financial Services Records (Chapter 5)
- Checkbook, unused checks
- Bank statements, canceled checks
- Savings statements
- Location information and number of safe deposit box

5. Credit Records (Chapters 6, 7)
- Unused credit cards
- Payment books
- Receipts, monthly statements
- List of credit account numbers and telephone numbers of issuers

6. Consumer Purchase & Automobile Records (Chapter 8)
- Warranties
- Receipts for major purchases
- Owner's manuals for major appliances
- Automobile service and repair records
- Automobile registration
- Automobile owner's manual

7. Housing Records (Chapter 9)
- Lease (if renting)
- Property tax records
- Home repair, home improvement receipts

8. Insurance Records (Chapters 10–12)
- Original insurance policies
- List of insurance premium amounts and due dates
- Medical information (health history, prescription drug information)
- Claim reports

9. Investment Records (Chapters 13–17)
- Records of stock, bond, and mutual fund purchases and sales
- List of investment certificate numbers
- Brokerage statements
- Dividend records
- Company annual reports

10. Estate Planning and Retirement Records (Chapters 18–19)
- Will
- Pension plan information
- IRA statements
- Social Security information
- Trust agreements

Safe Deposit Box

- Birth, marriage, and death certificates
- Citizenship papers
- Adoption, custody papers
- Military papers
- Serial numbers of expensive items
- Photographs or video of valuable belongings

- Certificates of deposit
- List of checking and savings account numbers and financial institutions
- Credit contacts
- List of credit card numbers and telephone numbers of issuers

- Mortgage papers, title deed
- Automobile title
- List of insurance policy numbers and company names
- Stock and bond certificates
- Rare coins, stamps, gems, and other collectibles
- Copy of will

Personal Computer System

- Current and past budgets
- Summary of checks written and other banking transactions
- Past income tax returns prepared with tax preparation software
- Account summaries and performance results of investments
- Computerized version of wills, estate plans, and other documents

As Exhibit 3–2 shows, most financial records are kept in one of three places: a home file, a safe deposit box, or a home computer. A home file should be used to keep records for current needs and documents with limited value. Your home file may be a series of folders, a cabinet with several drawers, or even a cardboard box. Whatever method you use, it is most important that your home file be simply organized to allow quick access to required documents and information.

safe deposit box

Important financial records and valuable articles should be kept in a location that provides better security than a home file. A **safe deposit box** is a private storage area at a financial institution with maximum security for valuables and difficult-to-replace documents. Access to the contents of a safe deposit box requires two keys. One key is issued to you; the other is kept by the financial institution where the safe deposit box is located. Items commonly kept in a safe deposit box include stock certificates, contracts, a list of insurance policies, and valuables such as rare coins and stamps.

DID YOU KNOW?

In the United States, people keep various documents and valuables in 30 million safe deposit boxes in banks, savings and loans, and credit unions. While these boxes are usually very safe, each year a few people lose the contents of their safe deposit boxes through theft, fire, or natural disasters. Such losses are usually covered by the financial institution's insurance.

The number of financial records and documents may seem overwhelming; however, they can easily be organized into 10 categories (see Exhibit 3–2). These groups correspond to the major topics covered in this book. You may not need to use all of these records and documents at present. As your financial situation changes, you can add others.

How long should you keep personal finance records? The answer to this question differs for various documents. Records such as birth certificates, wills, and Social Security data should be kept permanently. Records on property and investments should be kept as long as you own these items. Federal tax laws dictate the length of time you should keep tax-related information. Copies of tax returns and supporting data should be saved for six years. Normally, an audit will go back only three years; however, under certain circumstances the Internal Revenue Service may request information from six years back. Financial experts recommend keeping documents related to the purchase and sale of real estate indefinitely.

Sheet 14

CONCEPT CHECK 3–2

1. What are the benefits of an organized system of financial records and documents?
2. What suggestions would you give for creating a system for organizing and storing financial records and documents?
3. What influences the length of time you should keep financial records and documents?

PERSONAL FINANCIAL STATEMENTS FOR MEASURING FINANCIAL PROGRESS

L.O.3 Develop a personal balance sheet and cash flow statement.

Every journey starts somewhere. You need to know where you are before you can go somewhere else. Personal financial statements tell you the starting point of your financial journey.

Most of the financial documents we have discussed come from financial institutions, other business organizations, or the government. Two documents that you create yourself, the personal balance sheet and the cash flow statement, are called *personal financial statements*. These reports provide information about your current financial position and present a summary of your income and spending. The main purposes of personal financial statements are to

- Report your current financial position in relation to the value of the items you own and the amounts you owe.
- Measure your progress toward your financial goals.

- Maintain information about your financial activities.
- Provide data you can use when preparing tax forms or applying for credit.

The Personal Balance Sheet: Where Are You Now?

balance sheet

The current financial position of an individual or a family is a common starting point for financial planning. A **balance sheet,** also called a *net worth statement,* or *statement of financial position,* reports what you own and what you owe. You prepare a personal balance sheet to determine your current financial position using the following process:

$$\boxed{\text{Items of value} \atop \text{(what you own)}} - \boxed{\text{Amounts owed} \atop \text{(what you owe)}} = \boxed{\text{Net worth} \atop \text{(your wealth)}}$$

For example, if your possessions are worth $4,500 and you owe $800 to others, your net worth is $3,700.

Step 1. Listing Items of Value   Available cash and money in bank accounts combined with other items of value are the foundation of your current financial position. **Assets** are cash and other tangible property with a monetary value. The balance sheet for Rose and Edgar Gomez (Exhibit 3–3) lists their assets under four categories:

assets

liquid assets

1. **Liquid assets** are cash and items of value that can easily be converted to cash. Money in checking and savings accounts is liquid and available to the Gomez family for current spending. The cash value of their life insurance may be borrowed if needed. While assets other than liquid assets can also be converted into cash, the process is not quite as easy.
2. *Real estate* includes a home, condominium, vacation property, or other land that a person or family owns.
3. *Personal possessions* are a major portion of assets for most people. Included in this category are automobiles and other personal belongings. While these items have value, they may be difficult to convert to cash quickly. You may list your possessions on the balance sheet at their original cost. However, these values probably need to be revised over time, since a five-year-old television set, for example, is worth less now than when it was new. Thus, you may wish to list your possessions at their current value (also referred to as *market value*). This method takes into account the fact that such things as a home or jewelry increase in value over time. You can estimate current value by looking at ads for the selling price of comparable automobiles, homes, or other possessions. Or you may use the services of an appraiser.
4. *Investment assets* are funds set aside for long-term financial needs. The Gomez family will use their investments for such things as financing their children's education, purchasing a vacation home, and planning for retirement. Since investment assets usually fluctuate in value, the amounts listed should reflect their value at the time the balance sheet is prepared.

DID YOU KNOW?

According to the Bureau of the Census, U.S. Department of Commerce, the most common assets held by households are motor vehicles, homes, savings accounts, U.S. savings bonds, certificates of deposit, mutual funds, stocks, corporate bonds, and retirement accounts.

Step 2. Determining Amounts Owed   Looking at the total assets of the Gomez family, you might conclude that they have a strong financial position. However, their debts must also be considered. **Liabilities** are amounts owed to others but do not include items not yet due, such as next month's rent. A liability is a debt you owe now, not something you may owe in the future. Liabilities fall into two categories:

liabilities

EXHIBIT 3–3   **Creating a Personal Balance Sheet**

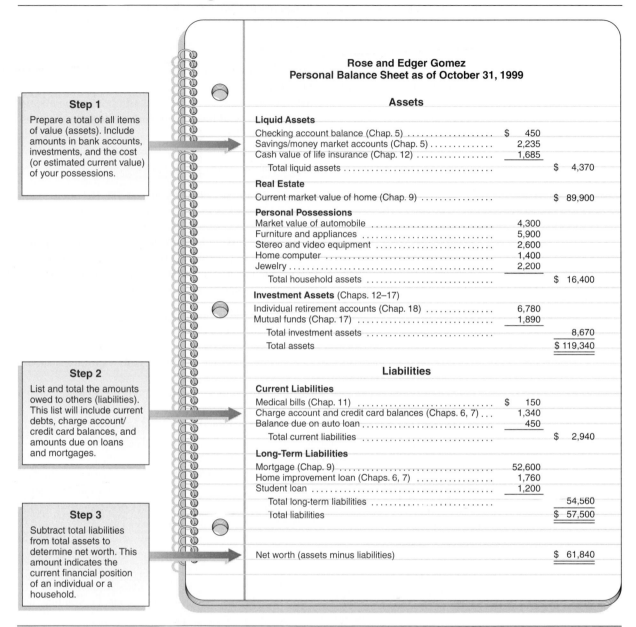

Step 1

Prepare a total of all items of value (assets). Include amounts in bank accounts, investments, and the cost (or estimated current value) of your possessions.

Step 2

List and total the amounts owed to others (liabilities). This list will include current debts, charge account/ credit card balances, and amounts due on loans and mortgages.

Step 3

Subtract total liabilities from total assets to determine net worth. This amount indicates the current financial position of an individual or a household.

Rose and Edger Gomez
Personal Balance Sheet as of October 31, 1999

Assets

Liquid Assets

Checking account balance (Chap. 5)	$ 450	
Savings/money market accounts (Chap. 5)	2,235	
Cash value of life insurance (Chap. 12)	1,685	
Total liquid assets		$ 4,370

Real Estate

Current market value of home (Chap. 9)	$ 89,900

Personal Possessions

Market value of automobile	4,300	
Furniture and appliances	5,900	
Stereo and video equipment	2,600	
Home computer	1,400	
Jewelry	2,200	
Total household assets		$ 16,400

Investment Assets (Chaps. 12–17)

Individual retirement accounts (Chap. 18)	6,780	
Mutual funds (Chap. 17)	1,890	
Total investment assets		8,670
Total assets		$ 119,340

Liabilities

Current Liabilities

Medical bills (Chap. 11)	$ 150	
Charge account and credit card balances (Chaps. 6, 7)	1,340	
Balance due on auto loan	450	
Total current liabilities		$ 2,940

Long-Term Liabilities

Mortgage (Chap. 9)	52,600	
Home improvement loan (Chaps. 6, 7)	1,760	
Student loan	1,200	
Total long-term liabilities		54,560
Total liabilities		$ 57,500

Net worth (assets minus liabilities)	$ 61,840

NOTE: Various asset and liability items are discussed in the chapters listed next to them.

current liabilities

1. **Current liabilities** are debts you must pay within a short time, usually less than a year. These liabilities include such things as medical bills, tax payments, insurance premiums, cash loans, and charge accounts.

long-term liabilities

2. **Long-term liabilities** are debts you do not have to pay in full until more than a year from now. Common long-term liabilities include auto loans, educational loans, and mortgages. A *mortgage* is an amount borrowed to buy a house or other real estate that will be repaid over a period of 15, 20, or 30 years. Similarly, a home improvement loan may be repaid to the lender over the next 5 to 10 years.

The debts listed in the liability section of a balance sheet represent the amount owed at the moment; they do not include future interest payments. However, each debt payment is likely to include a portion of interest. Chapters 6 and 7 discuss the cost of borrowing further.

net worth

Step 3. Computing Net Worth   Your **net worth** is the difference between your total assets and your total liabilities. This relationship can be stated as

$$\text{Assets} - \text{Liabilities} = \text{Net worth}$$

Net worth is the amount you would have if all assets were sold for the listed values and all debts were paid in full. Also, total assets equal total liabilities plus net worth. The balance sheet of a business is commonly expressed as

$$\text{Assets} = \text{Liabilities} + \text{Net worth}$$

As Exhibit 3–3 shows, Rose and Edgar Gomez have a net worth of $61,840. Since very few, if any, people liquidate all assets, the amount of net worth has a more practical purpose: It provides a measurement of your current financial position.

A person may have a high net worth but still have financial difficulties. Having many assets with low liquidity means not having the cash available to pay current expenses. **Insolvency** is the inability to pay debts when they are due; it occurs when a person's liabilities far exceed available assets. Bankruptcy, discussed in Chapter 7, may be an alternative for a person in this position.

insolvency

You can increase your net worth in various ways, including

- Increasing your savings.
- Reducing spending.
- Increasing the value of investments and other possessions.
- Reducing the amounts you owe.

Sheet 15

Remember, your net worth is *not* money available for use but an indication of your financial position on a given date.

Evaluating Your Financial Position

A personal balance sheet helps you measure progress toward financial goals. Your financial situation improves if your net worth increases each time you prepare a balance sheet. It will improve more rapidly if you are able to set aside money each month for savings and investments.

As with net worth, the relationship among various balance sheet items can give an indication of your financial position. In general, a lower *debt ratio*—liabilities divided by net worth—indicates a more favorable financial position. For example, if you have $50,000 in debts and a net worth of $25,000, your debt ratio is 2 ($50,000/$25,000); but if you have $25,000 in debts and a net worth of $50,000, your debt ratio is 0.5 ($25,000/$50,000).

Another balance sheet relationship is the *current ratio,* liquid assets divided by current liabilities. This relationship indicates the likelihood that you will be able to pay your upcoming debts. For instance, if you have $4,000 in liquid assets and $2,000 in current liabilities, your current ratio is 2 ($4,000/$2,000). This means you have $2 in liquid assets for every $1 in current liabilities.

In addition to the debt ratio and current ratio, other commonly used financial ratios to assess a person's financial situation include

- *Liquidity ratio* (liquid assets divided by monthly expenses). This ratio indicates the number of months in which expenses can be paid if an emergency arises.

FINANCIAL PLANNING IN ACTION

MONITORING YOUR CASH FLOW

A cash flow statement can help you plan your spending and attain your financial goals. Over the next month, list all sources of cash and the payments you make using a format similar to this:

Step 1: Cash inflows. List the dates, sources, and amounts of cash inflows from employment and other income sources.

Date	Source	Amount
_____	_____	_____
_____	_____	_____

Step 2: Cash outflows. List the dates, items, and amounts for all payments.

Date	Item	Amount
_____	_____	_____
_____	_____	_____

Date	Item	Amount
_____	_____	_____
_____	_____	_____
_____	_____	_____

Step 3: Net cash flow. Deduct the total cash outflows from the total cash inflows to determine your net cash surplus or deficit.

Total cash inflows	$_____
Less: Total cash outflows	$_____
Equals: Net cash surplus (deficit)	$_____

Were you surprised at any of your spending patterns? Were you able to make all payments on time? Were you able to put some money into savings? What actions could you take to increase your income or decrease your expenses?

- *Debt-payments ratio* (monthly credit payments divided by take-home pay). This measurement provides an indication of how much of a person's earning goes for debt payments (excluding a home mortgage). Most financial planners recommend that the debt-payments ratio be less than 20 percent.
- *Savings ratio* (amount saved each month divided by gross income). Financial experts recommend a savings rate of about 10 percent.

The Cash Flow Statement: Where Did Your Money Go?

cash flow

Each day, financial events can affect your net worth. When you receive a paycheck or pay living expenses, your total assets and liabilities change. **Cash flow** is the actual inflow and outflow of cash during a given time period. Income from employment will probably represent your most important *cash inflow;* however, other income, such as interest earned on a savings account, should also be considered. In contrast, payments for items such as rent, food, and loans are *cash outflows.*

cash flow statement

A **cash flow statement** (Exhibit 3–4) is a summary of cash receipts and payments for a given period, such as a month or a year. This report provides data on your income and spending patterns, which will be helpful when preparing a budget. (See the Financial Planning in Action feature on this page.) A checking account can provide information for your cash flow statement. Deposits to the account are your *inflows;* checks written are

EXHIBIT 3–4   **Creating a Cash Flow Statement of Income and Outflows**

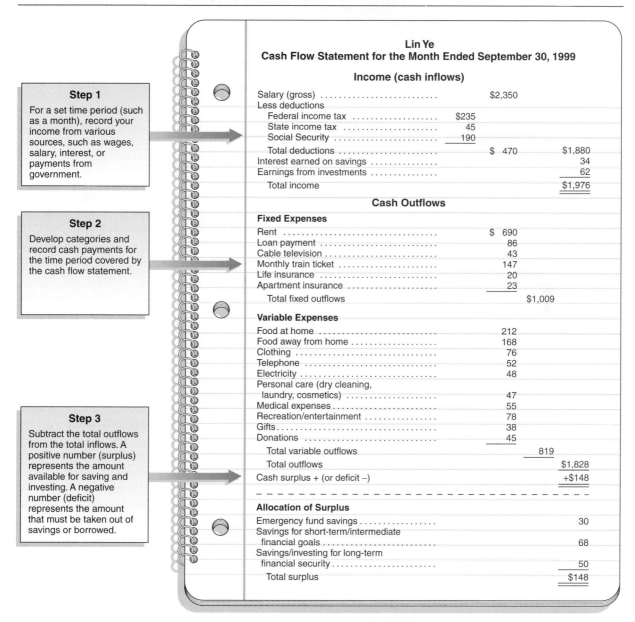

Step 1

For a set time period (such as a month), record your income from various sources, such as wages, salary, interest, or payments from government.

Step 2

Develop categories and record cash payments for the time period covered by the cash flow statement.

Step 3

Subtract the total outflows from the total inflows. A positive number (surplus) represents the amount available for saving and investing. A negative number (deficit) represents the amount that must be taken out of savings or borrowed.

Lin Ye
Cash Flow Statement for the Month Ended September 30, 1999

Income (cash inflows)

Salary (gross)		$2,350	
Less deductions			
Federal income tax	$235		
State income tax	45		
Social Security	190		
Total deductions		$ 470	$1,880
Interest earned on savings			34
Earnings from investments			62
Total income			$1,976

Cash Outflows

Fixed Expenses

Rent	$ 690	
Loan payment	86	
Cable television	43	
Monthly train ticket	147	
Life insurance	20	
Apartment insurance	23	
Total fixed outflows		$1,009

Variable Expenses

Food at home	212	
Food away from home	168	
Clothing	76	
Telephone	52	
Electricity	48	
Personal care (dry cleaning, laundry, cosmetics)	47	
Medical expenses	55	
Recreation/entertainment	78	
Gifts	38	
Donations	45	
Total variable outflows	819	
Total outflows		$1,828
Cash surplus + (or deficit –)		+$148

– –

Allocation of Surplus

Emergency fund savings	30
Savings for short-term/intermediate financial goals	68
Savings/investing for long-term financial security	50
Total surplus	$148

your *outflows.* Of course, in using this system, when you do not deposit the entire amounts received, you must also note the spending of undeposited amounts in your cash flow statement.

The process for preparing a cash flow statement is

Total cash received during the time period	−	Cash outflows during the time period	=	Cash surplus or deficit

income

Step 1. Record Income   Creating a cash flow statement starts with identifying the cash received during the time period involved. **Income** is the inflows of cash for an individual or a household. For most people, the main source of income is money received from a job. Other common income sources include

- Wages, salaries, and commissions.
- Self-employment business income.
- Saving and investment income (interest, dividends, rent).
- Gifts, grants, scholarships, and educational loans.
- Government payments, such as Social Security, public assistance, and unemployment benefits.
- Amounts received from pension and retirement programs.
- Alimony and child support payments.

take-home pay

In Exhibit 3–4, notice that Lin Ye's monthly salary (or *gross income*) of $2,350 is her main source of income. However, she does not have use of the entire amount. **Take-home pay,** also called *net* pay, is a person's earnings after deductions for taxes and other items. Lin's deductions for federal, state, and Social Security taxes are $470. Her take-home pay is $1,880. This amount, plus earnings from savings and investments, is the income she has available for use during the current month.

discretionary income

Take-home pay is also called *disposable income,* the amount a person or household has available to spend. **Discretionary income** is money left over after paying for housing, food, and other necessities. Studies report that discretionary income ranges from less than 5 percent for people under age 25 to more than 40 percent for older people.

Step 2. Record Cash Outflows   Cash payments for living expenses and other items make up the second component of a cash flow statement. Lin Ye divides her cash outflows into two major categories: fixed expenses and variable expenses. While every individual and household has different cash outflows, these main categories, along with the subgroupings Lin uses, can be adapted to most situations.

1. *Fixed expenses* are payments that do not vary from month to month. Rent or mortgage payments, installment loan payments, cable television service fees, and a monthly train ticket for commuting to work are examples of constant or fixed cash outflows.

For Lin, another type of fixed expense is the amount she sets aside each month for payments due once or twice a year. For example, Lin pays $240 every March for life insurance. Each month, she records a fixed outflow of $20 for deposit in a special savings account so that the money will be available when her insurance payment is due.

2. *Variable expenses* are flexible payments that change from month to month. Common examples of variable cash outflows are food, clothing, utilities (such as electricity and telephone), recreation, medical expenses, gifts, and donations. The use of a checkbook or some other recordkeeping system is necessary for an accurate total of cash outflows.

Step 3. Determine Net Cash Flow   The difference between income and outflows can be either a positive (*surplus*) or a negative (*deficit*) cash flow. A deficit exists if more cash goes out than comes in during a given month. This amount must be made up by withdrawals from savings or by borrowing. The effect of a net cash flow on net worth is shown in the Financial Planning for Life's Situations feature on page 73.

When you have a cash surplus, as Lin did (Exhibit 3–4), this amount is available for saving, investing, or paying off debts. Each month, Lin sets aside money for her *emergency fund* in a savings account that she would use for unexpected expenses or to pay living costs if she did not receive her salary. She deposits the rest of the surplus in savings

Sheet 16

FINANCIAL PLANNING FOR LIFE'S SITUATIONS

MEASURING YOUR FINANCIAL PROGRESS

People commonly prepare a balance sheet on a periodic basis, such as every three or six months. Between those points in time, use your budget and cash flow statement to plan and measure spending and saving activities. For example, during a certain calendar year, you might prepare a balance sheet on January 1, June 30, and December 31. Your budget would serve to plan your spending and saving between these points in time, and your cash flow statement of income and outflows would document your actual spending and saving. This relationship may be illustrated as shown below.

Changes in your net worth are the result of the relationship between cash inflows and outflows. In periods when your outflows exceed your inflows, you must draw on savings or borrow (buy on credit). When this happens, lower assets (savings) or higher liabilities (due to the use of

credit) result in a lower net worth. When inflows exceed outflows, putting money into savings or paying off debts will result in a higher net worth. In general, the relationship between the cash flow statement and the balance sheet may be expressed as follows:

Cash Flow Statement	Balance Sheet
If cash inflows (income) are greater than cash outflows	Net worth increases
If cash outflows (payments) are greater than cash inflows (income)	Net worth decreases

Using a budget, creating a cash flow statement, and developing a balance sheet on a periodic basis can help you improve your financial situation.

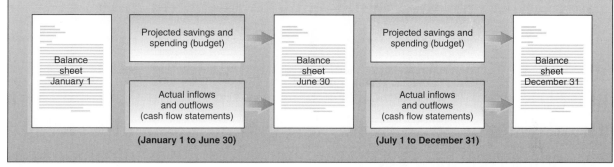

and investment plans that have two purposes. The first is the achievement of short-term and intermediate financial goals, such as a new car, a vacation, or reenrollment in school; the second is long-term financial security—her retirement.

A cash flow statement provides the foundation for preparing and implementing a spending, saving, and investment plan, discussed in the next section.

DID YOU KNOW?

The most common advice from financial planners: "Save more." "Save all you can." "Cut your spending so you can save more."

CONCEPT CHECK 3–3

1. What are the main purposes of personal financial statements?
2. What does a personal balance sheet tell about your financial situation?
3. How can you use a balance sheet for personal financial planning?
4. What information does a cash flow statement present?

EXHIBIT 3–5   **Creating and Implementing a Budget**

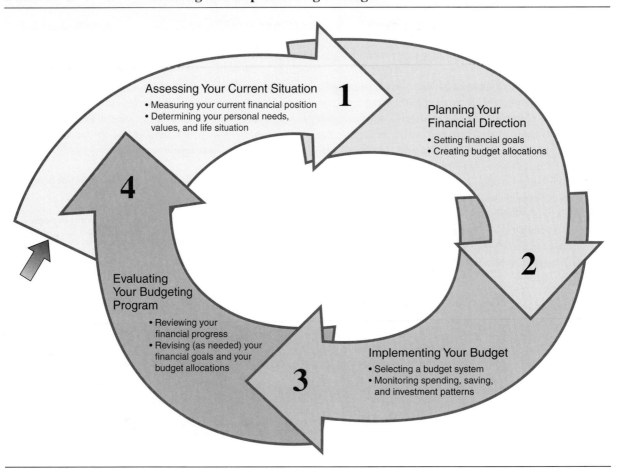

Assessing Your Current Situation
- Measuring your current financial position
- Determining your personal needs, values, and life situation

1

Planning Your Financial Direction
- Setting financial goals
- Creating budget allocations

2

4

Evaluating Your Budgeting Program
- Reviewing your financial progress
- Revising (as needed) your financial goals and your budget allocations

3

Implementing Your Budget
- Selecting a budget system
- Monitoring spending, saving, and investment patterns

THE BUDGETING PROCESS

L.O.4 Create and implement a budget.

budget

A **budget,** or *spending plan,* is necessary for successful financial planning. The common financial problems of overusing credit, lacking a regular savings program, and failing to ensure future financial security can be minimized through budgeting. The main purposes of a budget are to help you

- Live within your income.
- Spend your money wisely.
- Reach your financial goals.
- Prepare for financial emergencies.
- Develop wise financial management habits.

Budgeting may be viewed as a four-phase process (see Exhibit 3–5).

Assessing Your Current Situation

The financial statements and documents discussed in the first sections of this chapter provide a starting point for your daily money management activities. In addition, this first phase of the budgeting process involves making choices based on your personal situation.

EXHIBIT 3–6   **Common Financial Goals**

Personal Situation	Short-Term Goals (less than 2 years)	Intermediate Goals (2–5 years)	Long-Term Goals (over 5 years)
Single person	Complete college Pay off auto loan	Take a vacation Pay off education loan Return to school for graduate degree	Buy a vacation home Provide for retirement income
Married couple (no children)	Take an annual vacation Buy a new car	Remodel home Build a stock portfolio	Buy a retirement home Provide for retirement income
Parent (young children)	Increase life insurance Increase savings	Increase investments Buy a new car	Accumulate a college fund Move to a larger home

Measuring Your Current Financial Position   A personal balance sheet is an effective scorecard for measuring financial progress. Increases in net worth as a result of increased assets or decreased debt are evidence of an improved financial position. A regular assessment of your financial standing using a personal balance sheet can provide a point of reference for money management decisions.

Determining Your Personal Needs, Values, and Life Situation   Each day, you make many decisions that communicate your *lifestyle* by indicating how you spend your time and money. The clothes you wear, the food you eat, and the interests you pursue contribute to your lifestyle. Some people spend time and money on automobiles or stereo equipment; other people travel, plant gardens, or engage in church or community activities. These actions reflect a lifestyle influenced by three factors:

- *Career.* Your job situation will influence the amount of income, the way you spend your leisure time, and even the people with whom you associate.
- *Family.* The size of your household and the ages of its members will also affect your lifestyle. The spending priorities of a couple without children will differ from those of a couple with several youngsters.
- *Values.* Ideas and beliefs you regard as important will influence your interests, activities, and purchasing habits. For example, a desire to assist needy families may result in donations or volunteer time at a homeless shelter.

These factors combine to create planned spending patterns that your financial goals reflect.

Planning Your Financial Direction

This phase of your budgeting activities involves setting financial goals and deciding on budget allocations for various spending and saving categories.

Setting Financial Goals   Future plans are an important dimension of your financial direction. Financial goals are plans for future activities that require you to plan your spending, saving, and investing. Exhibit 3–6 gives examples of common financial goals based on life situation and time.

As discussed in Chapter 1, financial goals should be realistic, be stated in specific, measurable terms, have a definite time frame, and indicate the type of action to be taken. Your personal financial statements and budgeting allow you to achieve your financial goals with

Exhibit 3–7   **Typical After-Tax Budget Allocations for Different Life Situations**

Budget Category	Student	Working Single (no dependents)	Couple (children under 18)	Single Parent (young children)	Parents (children over 18 in college)	Couple (over 55, no dependent children)
Housing (rent or mortgage payment; utilities; furnishings and appliances)	0–25%	30–35%	25–35%	20–30%	25–30%	25–35%
Transportation	5–10	15–20	15–20	10–18	12–18	10–18
Food (at home and away from home)	15–20	15–25	15–25	13–20	15–20	18–25
Clothing	5–12	5–15	5–10	5–10	4–8	4–8
Personal and health care (including child care)	3–5	3–5	4–10	8–12	4–6	6–12
Entertainment and recreation	5–10	5–10	4–8	4–8	6–10	5–8
Reading and education	10–30	2–4	3–5	3–5	6–12	2–4
Personal insurance and pension payments	0–5	4–8	5–9	5–9	4–7	6–8
Gifts, donations, and contributions	4–6	5–8	3–5	3–5	4–8	3–5
Savings	0–10	4–15	5–10	5–8	2–4	3–5

sources: Bureau of Labor Statistics; *American Demographics; Money; The Wall Street Journal.*

1. Your cash flow statement—telling you what you received and spent over the past month.
2. Your balance sheet—reporting your current financial position (where you are now).
3. Your budget—planning spending and saving to achieve financial goals.

Creating Budget Allocations   Next, you should assign amounts to spending categories. How much you budget for various items will depend on your current needs and plans for the future. The following sources can help you plan your spending:

- Your cash flow statement.
- Sample budgets from government reports.
- Articles in magazines such as *Kiplinger's Personal Finance Magazine* and *Money.*
- Estimates of future income and expenses and anticipated changes in inflation rates.

Exhibit 3–7 suggests budget allocations for different life situations. Although this information can be of value when creating budget categories, maintaining a detailed record of your spending for several months is a better source for your personal situation. Don't become discouraged about keeping track of your spending. Use a simple system, such as a notebook or your checkbook. Remember, a budget is an *estimate* for spending and saving intended to help you make better use of your money, not to reduce your enjoyment of life.

A format similar to the one used for the cash flow statement can be the basis for your budget. A very common budgeting mistake is to save the amount you have left at the end of the month. When you do that, you often have *nothing* left for savings. Since savings are vital to long-term financial security, advisers suggest that they be budgeted as a fixed expense. The following sections outline a suggested budget format.

Step 1. Income   As Exhibit 3–8 shows, you should first estimate available money for a given period of time. A common budgeting period is a month, since many payments, such as rent or mortgage, utilities, and credit cards, are due each month. In determining available income, include only money that you are sure you'll receive. Bonuses, gifts, or unexpected income should not be considered until the money is actually received.

If you get paid once a month, planning is easy since you will work with a single amount. But if you get paid weekly or twice a month, you will need to plan how much of each paycheck will go for various expenses. If you get paid every two weeks, plan your spending based on the two paychecks you will receive each month. Then, during the two months each year that have three paydays, you can put additional amounts into savings, pay off some debts, or make a special purchase.

Budgeting income may be difficult if your earnings vary by season or your income is irregular, as with sales commissions. In these situations, attempt to estimate your income based on the past year and on your expectations for the current year. Estimating your income on the low side will help avoid overspending and resulting financial difficulties.

Step 2. Emergency Fund and Savings   To set aside money for unexpected expenses as well as future financial security, the Fraziers (see Exhibit 3–8) have budgeted several amounts for savings and investments. Financial advisers suggest that an emergency fund representing three to six months of living expenses be established for use in periods of unexpected financial difficulty. This amount will vary based on a person's life situation and employment stability. A three-month emergency fund is probably adequate for a person with a stable income or secure employment, while a person with erratic or seasonal income may need to set aside an emergency fund sufficient for six months or more of living expenses.

The Fraziers also set aside an amount each month for their automobile insurance payment, which is due every six months. Both this amount and the emergency fund are put into a savings account that will earn interest. The *time value of money,* discussed in Chapter 1, refers to increases in an amount of money as a result of interest earned. Savings methods for achieving financial goals are discussed later in this chapter.

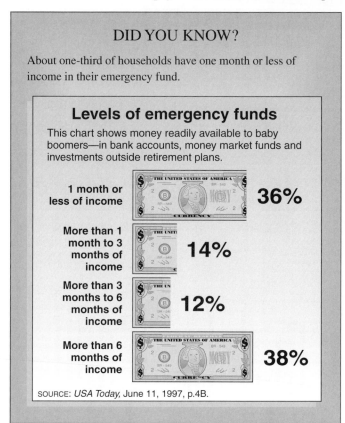

DID YOU KNOW?

About one-third of households have one month or less of income in their emergency fund.

Levels of emergency funds

This chart shows money readily available to baby boomers—in bank accounts, money market funds and investments outside retirement plans.

1 month or less of income   **36%**

More than 1 month to 3 months of income   **14%**

More than 3 months to 6 months of income   **12%**

More than 6 months of income   **38%**

SOURCE: *USA Today,* June 11, 1997, p.4B.

Step 3. Fixed Expenses   Definite obligations are the basis for this portion of a budget. As Exhibit 3–8 shows, the Fraziers have fixed expenses for housing, taxes, and loan payments. They make a monthly payment of $29 for life insurance. The budgeted total for the Fraziers' fixed expenses is $806, or 28 percent of estimated available income.

Step 4. Variable Expenses   Planning for variable expenses is not as easy as budgeting savings or fixed expenses. Variable expenses will fluctuate due to household situation, time of year, health, economic conditions, and a wide variety of other factors. A major portion of the Fraziers' planned spending—over 60 percent of their budgeted income— is for variable living costs.

EXHIBIT 3–8   The Fraziers Develop and Implement a Monthly Budget

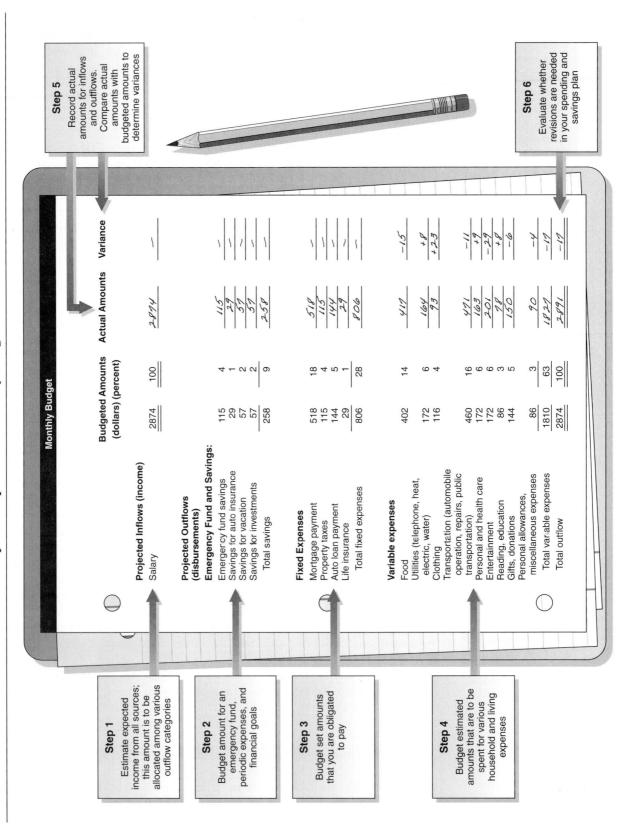

Monthly Budget

	Budgeted Amounts (dollars) (percent)		Actual Amounts	Variance
Projected Inflows (income)				
Salary	2874	100	2874	—
Projected Outflows (disbursements)				
Emergency Fund and Savings:				
Emergency fund savings	115	4	115	—
Savings for auto insurance	29	1	29	—
Savings for vacation	57	2	57	—
Savings for investments	57	2	57	—
Total savings	258	9	258	—
Fixed Expenses				
Mortgage payment	518	18	518	—
Property taxes	115	4	115	—
Auto loan payment	144	5	144	—
Life insurance	29	1	29	—
Total fixed expenses	806	28	806	—
Variable expenses				
Food	402	14	417	−15
Utilities (telephone, heat, electric, water)	172	6	164	+8
Clothing	116	4	93	+23
Transportation (automobile operation, repairs, public transportation)	460	16	471	−11
Personal and health care	172	6	163	+9
Entertainment	172	6	201	−29
Reading, education	86	3	78	+8
Gifts, donations	144	5	150	−6
Personal allowances, miscellaneous expenses	86	3	90	−4
Total variable expenses	1810	63	1827	−17
Total outflow	2874	100	2891	−17

Step 1
Estimate expected income from all sources; this amount is to be allocated among various outflow categories

Step 2
Budget amount for an emergency fund, periodic expenses, and financial goals

Step 3
Budget set amounts that you are obligated to pay

Step 4
Budget estimated amounts that are to be spent for various household and living expenses

Step 5
Record actual amounts for inflows and outflows. Compare actual amounts with budgeted amounts to determine variances

Step 6
Evaluate whether revisions are needed in your spending and savings plan

The Fraziers base their estimates on their needs and desires for the items listed and on expected changes in the cost of living. The *consumer price index (CPI)* is a measure of changes in the general price level of consumer goods and services in the United States. This government statistic indicates changes in the buying power of a dollar. As consumer prices increase due to inflation, people must spend more to buy the same amount. Changes in the cost of living will vary depending on where you live and what you buy.

As mentioned in Chapter 1, the *rule of 72* can help you budget for price rises. At a 6 percent inflation rate, prices will double in 12 years (72 ÷ 6); at an 8 percent inflation rate, prices will double in only 9 years (72 ÷ 8).

Implementing Your Budget

Step 5. Recording Amounts in a Budgeting System   Although your checkbook will give you a fairly complete record of your expenses, it does not serve the purpose of planning for spending. A budget requires that you outline how you will spend available income. Various types of budgeting systems exist, from informal procedures to computerized spending plans.

A *mental budget* exists only in a person's mind. This simple system may be appropriate for a person with limited resources and minimal financial responsibilities. The major drawback of a mental budget is the danger of forgetting what amounts you plan to spend on various items.

A *physical budget* involves the use of envelopes, folders, or containers to hold the money or slips of paper that represent amounts allocated for spending categories. This system allows you to actually see where your money goes. Envelopes would contain the amount of cash or a note listing the amount to be used for "Food," "Rent," "Clothing," "Auto Payment," "Entertainment," or some other expense.

Financial advisers and experienced money managers recommend a *written budget.* The exact system and the amount of detail will depend on the time, effort, and information that you put into the budgeting process. A written budget can be kept on notebook paper or in a specialized budgeting book available in office supply stores or bookstores. A common budget format is a spreadsheet that has several monthly columns for comparing budgeted and actual amounts for various expense items.

As the use of personal computers has increased, so too has the use of *computerized budgeting systems.* In addition to creating a spreadsheet budget presentation, a home computer is capable of doing other financial recordkeeping tasks such as writing checks and projecting the future value of savings accounts. Information about the use of a personal computer for financial recordkeeping and planning is available through computer stores, books, and articles in magazines such as *PC Computing* (also refer to Appendix B). It takes time and effort to learn the system and enter data; however, a computerized budgeting and recordkeeping procedure can yield fast and accurate financial planning data.

Having a spending plan will not eliminate financial worries. A budget will work only if you follow it. Changes in income, expenses, and goals will require changes in your spending plan. Money management experts advise that a successful budget should be

- *Well planned.* A good budget takes time and effort to prepare. Planning a budget should involve everyone affected by it. Children can learn important money management lessons by helping to develop and use the family budget.
- *Realistic.* If you have a moderate income, don't expect to save immediately enough money for an expensive car or a lavish vacation. A budget is designed not to prevent you from enjoying life but to help you achieve what you want most.

- *Flexible.* Unexpected expenses and changes in your cost of living will require a budget that you can easily revise. Also, varied life situations, such as two-income families or the arrival of a baby, may require an increase in certain types of expenses.
- *Clearly communicated.* Unless you and others affected by a budget are aware of the spending plan, the budget will not work. It should be written and available to all household members. Many variations of written budgets are possible, including a notebook or a computerized system.

Monitoring Spending and Saving Patterns   After you have established your spending plan, you will need to keep records of your actual income and expenses similar to those you keep in preparing an income statement. In Exhibit 3–8, notice that the Fraziers estimated specific amounts for income and expenses. These are presented under "Budgeted Amounts." The family's spending was not always the same as planned. A **budget variance** is the difference between the amount budgeted and the actual amount received or spent. The total variance for the Fraziers was a $17 **deficit,** since their actual spending exceeded their planned spending by this amount. The Fraziers would have had a **surplus** if their actual spending had been less than they had planned.

budget variance

deficit

surplus

Variances for income should be viewed as the opposite of variances for expenses. Less income than expected would be a deficit, while more income than expected would be a surplus.

Spending more than planned for an item may be justified by reducing spending for another item or by putting less into savings. However, it may be necessary to revise your budget and financial goals.

Sheet 17

Evaluating Your Budgeting Program

Like most decision-making activities, budgeting is a circular, ongoing process. You will need to review and perhaps revise your spending plan on a regular basis.

Step 6. Reviewing Your Financial Progress   The results of your budget may be obvious—having extra cash in checking, falling behind in your bill payments, and so on. However, such obvious results may not always be present. Occasionally, you will have to sit down (with other household members, if appropriate) and review areas where spending has been more or less than expected.

Sheet 18

As Exhibit 3–9 shows, you can prepare an annual summary to compare actual spending with budgeted amounts. This type of summary may also be prepared every three or six months. A spreadsheet computer program can be useful for this purpose. The summary will help you see areas where changes in your budget may be necessary. This review process is vital to both successful short-term money management and long-term financial security.

Revising Your Goals and Budget Allocations   What should you cut first when a budget shortage occurs? This question doesn't have easy answers, and the answers will vary for different household situations. The most common overspending areas are entertainment and food, especially away-from-home meals. Purchasing brand name and generic items, buying quality used products, avoiding credit card purchases, and renting rather than buying are common budget adjustment techniques.

At this point in the budgeting process, you may also revise your financial goals. Are you making progress toward achieving your objectives? Have changes in personal or economic conditions affected the desirability of certain goals? Have new goals surfaced

Exhibit 3–9   **An Annual Budget Summary**

Item	Monthly Budget	Jan.	Feb.	Mar.	Apr.	May	June	July	Aug.	Sept.	Oct.	Nov.	Dec.	Actual	Budgeted*
							Actual Spending (cash outflows)							Annual Totals	
Income	2,730	2,730	2,730	2,730	2,940	2,730	2,730	2,730	2,730	2,850	2,850	2,850	2,850	33,450	32,760
Savings	150	150	150	200	150	90	50	30	100	250	250	150	40	1,610	1,800
Mortgage/rent	826	826	826	826	826	826	826	826	826	826	826	826	826	9,912	9,912
Housing costs (insurance, utilities)	190	244	238	189	176	185	188	146	178	198	177	201	195	2,283	2,280
Telephone	50	43	45	61	56	54	52	65	45	43	52	49	47	618	600
Food (at home)	280	289	277	245	234	278	261	298	320	301	298	278	324	3,401	3,360
Food (away from home)	80	61	78	84	81	123	109	89	83	69	76	83	143	1,089	960
Clothing	100	98	78	123	156	86	76	111	124	89	95	123	111	1,268	1,200
Transportation (auto operation, public transportation)	340	302	312	333	345	291	281	390	313	299	301	269	301	3,809	4,080
Credit payments	249	249	249	249	249	249	249	249	249	249	249	249	249	2,988	2,988
Insurance (life, health, other)	45	—	—	135	—	—	135	—	—	135	—	—	135	540	540
Health care	140	176	145	189	122	111	156	186	166	134	189	193	149	1,912	1,680
Recreation	80	61	98	123	98	61	45	89	98	65	89	89	111	1,033	960
Reading, education	40	32	54	44	34	39	54	12	38	54	34	76	45	516	480
Gifts, donations	100	102	110	94	89	123	89	95	94	113	89	99	134	1,229	1,200
Personal miscellaneous expense	60	89	45	61	54	98	59	54	49	71	65	90	56	799	720
Total	2,730	2,702	2,705	2,964	2,674	2,626	2,642	2,638	2,743	2,892	2,786	2,771	2,864	33,001	32,760

*Monthly amount times 12.

that should be given a higher priority than those that have been your major concern? Addressing these issues while creating an effective saving method will help ensure accomplishment of your financial goals.

C O N C E P T   C H E C K   3–4

1. What are the main purposes of a budget?
2. How does a person's life situation affect goal setting and amounts allocated for various budget categories?
3. What are the main steps in creating a budget?
4. What are commonly recommended qualities of a successful budget?
5. What actions might you take when evaluating your budgeting program?

SAVING TECHNIQUES TO ACHIEVE FINANCIAL GOALS

L.O.5 Calculate savings needed for achieving financial goals.

Saving of current income (as well as investing, which is discussed in Part V) is the basis for an improved financial position and long-term financial security. Common reasons for saving include the following:

- To set aside money for irregular and unexpected expenses.
- To pay for the replacement of expensive items, such as appliances or an automobile, or to have money for a down payment on a house.
- To buy special items such as home video or recreational equipment or to pay for a vacation.
- To provide for long-term expenses such as the education of children or retirement.
- To earn income from the interest on savings for use in paying living expenses.

Selecting a Saving Technique

Traditionally, the United States ranks fairly low among industrial nations in savings rate. A low savings rate tends to slow economic growth with fewer funds available for business borrowing and for creation of new jobs. Low savings also affect the personal financial situations of people. Studies reveal that the majority of Americans do not have an adequate amount set aside for emergencies. A study conducted by the Consumer Federation of America revealed that one in five American households are "nonsavers" with nothing saved for their major goals.

Since most people find saving difficult, financial advisers suggest several methods to make it easier. One method is to write a check each payday and deposit it in a special savings account at a distant financial institution. This savings deposit can be a percentage of income, such as 5 or 10 percent, or a specific dollar amount. Always "pay yourself first." To guarantee setting something aside for savings, view savings as a fixed expense in your spending plan.

Another method is *payroll deduction,* which is available at many places of employment. Under a *direct deposit* system, an amount is automatically deducted from your salary and deposited in a savings or investment account.

EXHIBIT 3–10

Using Savings to Achieve Financial Goals

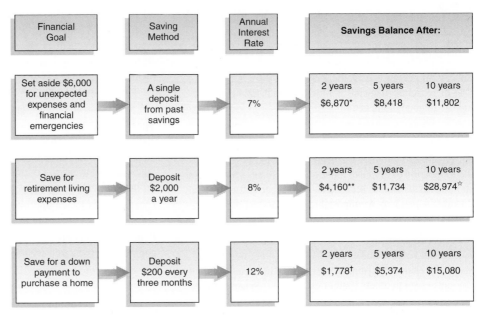

Financial Goal	Saving Method	Annual Interest Rate	Savings Balance After:		
			2 years	5 years	10 years
Set aside $6,000 for unexpected expenses and financial emergencies	A single deposit from past savings	7%	$6,870*	$8,418	$11,802
Save for retirement living expenses	Deposit $2,000 a year	8%	$4,160**	$11,734	$28,974☆
Save for a down payment to purchase a home	Deposit $200 every three months	12%	$1,778†	$5,374	$15,080

* Based on the future value of $1 tables in Chapter 1 and Appendix C.
** Based on the future value of a series of deposits tables in Chapter 1 and Appendix C.
☆ With annual $2,000 deposits, this same retirement account would grow to over $500,000 in 40 years.
† Based on quarterly compounding, explained in Chapter 5.

Finally, saving coins or spending less on certain items can help you save. Each day, put your change in a container. In a short time, you will have enough money to make a substantial deposit in a savings account. You can also increase your savings by taking a sandwich to work instead of buying your lunch or by refraining from buying snacks or magazines.

How you save, however, is less important than making regular periodic savings deposits that will help you achieve financial goals. Small amounts of savings can grow faster than most people realize. For example, at 5 percent interest, compounded daily, just $1 a day for 10 years will give you $4,700.

Calculating Savings Amounts

Sheet 19

To achieve your financial objectives, you should convert your savings goals into specific amounts. While certain saving methods involve keeping money at home, those funds should be deposited in an interest-earning savings plan on a regular basis. To earn interest, you must learn to "hide" money, not in your home but in an account at a financial institution or with an investment company.

Your use of a savings or investment plan is vital to the growth of your money. As Exhibit 3–10 shows, using the time value of money calculations, introduced in Chapter 1, can help you achieve your financial goals.

CONCEPT CHECK 3–5

1. What are some suggested methods to make saving easy?
2. What methods are available to calculate amounts needed to reach savings goals?

SUMMARY

L.O.1   Recognize relationships among financial documents and money management activities.

Successful money management requires effective coordination of personal financial records, personal financial statements, and budgeting activities.

L.O.2   Create a system for maintaining personal financial records.

An organized system of financial records and documents is the foundation of effective money management. This system should provide ease of access as well as security for financial documents that may be impossible to replace.

L.O.3   Develop a personal balance sheet and cash flow statement.

A personal balance sheet, also known as a *net worth statement,* is prepared by listing all items of value (assets) and all amounts owed to others (liabilities). The difference between your total assets and your total liabilities is your net worth. A cash flow statement is a summary of cash receipts and payments for a given period, such as a month or a year. This report provides data on your income and spending patterns.

L.O.4   Create and implement a budget.

The budgeting process involves four phases: (1) assessing your current personal and financial situation, (2) planning your financial direction by setting financial goals and creating budget allowances, (3) implementing your budget, and (4) evaluating your budgeting program.

L.O.5   Calculate savings needed for achieving financial goals.

Future value and present value calculations may be used to compute the increased value of savings for achieving financial goals.

GLOSSARY

assets   Cash and other property with a monetary value.   (p. 67)

balance sheet   A financial statement that reports what an individual or a family owns and owes; also called a *net worth statement.*   (p. 67)

budget   A specific plan for spending income.   (p. 74)

budget variance   The difference between the amount budgeted and the actual amount received or spent.   (p. 80)

cash flow   The actual inflow and outflow of cash during a given time period.   (p. 70)

cash flow statement   A financial statement that summarizes cash receipts and payments for a given period.   (p. 70)

current liabilities   Debts that must be paid within a short time, usually less than a year.   (p. 68)

deficit   The amount by which actual spending exceeds planned spending.   (p. 80)

discretionary income   Money left over after paying for housing, food, and other necessities.   (p. 72)

income   Inflows of cash to an individual or a household.   (p. 72)

insolvency   The inability to pay debts when they are due because liabilities far exceed the value of assets.   (p. 69)

liabilities   Amounts owed to others.   (p. 67)

liquid assets   Cash and items of value that can easily be converted to cash.   (p. 67)

long-term liabilities   Debts that are not required to be paid in full until more than a year from now.   (p. 68)

money management   Day-to-day financial activities necessary to manage current personal economic resources while working toward long-term financial security.   (p. 63)

net worth   The difference between total assets and total liabilities.   (p. 69)

safe deposit box   A private storage area at a financial institution with maximum security for valuables.   (p. 66)

surplus   The amount by which actual spending is less than planned spending.   (p. 80)

take-home pay   Earnings after deductions for taxes and other items; also called *disposable income.*   (p. 72)

REVIEW QUESTIONS

1. Why are money management activities vital for financial planning success?   (L.O.1)
2. What guidelines could a person use when deciding whether to store records and documents in a home file, a safe deposit box, or a home computer system?   (L.O.2)
3. How should a person respond to a cash flow deficit?   (L.O.3)
4. To what extent does a budget affect a person's overall financial situation?   (L.O.4)
5. How do a person's savings habits reflect her or his ability to achieve long-term financial security?   (L.O.5)

FINANCIAL PLANNING PROBLEMS

1. *Creating Personal Financial Statements.* Based on the procedures presented in the chapter, prepare your current personal balance sheet and a cash flow statement for the next month.   (L.O.3)

2. *Calculating Balance Sheet Amounts.* Based on the following data, compute the total assets, total liabilities, and net worth.   (L.O.3)

   Liquid assets, $3,670
   Investment assets, $8,340
   Current liabilities, $2,670
   Household assets, $89,890
   Long-term liabilities, $76,230

3. *Preparing a Personal Balance Sheet.* Use the following items to prepare a balance sheet and a cash flow statement. Determine the total assets, total liabilities, net worth, total cash inflows, and total cash outflows.   (L.O.3)

   Rent for the month, $650
   Monthly take-home salary, $1,950
   Cash in checking account, $450
   Savings account balance, $1,890
   Spending for food, $345
   Balance of educational loan, $2,160
   Current value of automobile, $7,800
   Telephone bill paid for month, $65
   Credit card balance, $235
   Loan payment, $80
   Auto insurance, $230
   Household possessions, $3,400
   Stereo equipment, $2,350
   Payment for electricity, $90
   Lunches/parking at work, $180
   Donations, $70
   Home computer, $1,500
   Value of stock investment, $860
   Clothing purchase, $110
   Restaurant spending, $130

4. *Computing Balance Sheet Amounts.* For each of the following situations, compute the missing amount.   (L.O.3)

   a. Assets $45,000; liabilities $16,000; net worth $_____

   b. Assets $76,500; liabilities $_____; net worth $18,700.

   c. Assets $34,280; liabilities $12,965; net worth $_____

   d. Assets $_____; liabilities $38,345; net worth $52,654

5. *Determining Budget Variances.* Fran Bowen created the following budget:

   Food, $350
   Transportation, $320
   Housing, $950
   Clothing, $100
   Personal expenses and recreation, $275

   She actually spent $298 for food, $337 for transportation, $982 for housing, $134 for clothing, and $231 for personal expenses and recreation. Calculate the variance for each of these categories, and indicate whether it was a *deficit* or a *surplus.*   (L.O.4)

6. *Calculating the Effect of Inflation.* Bill and Sally Kaplan have an annual spending plan that amounts to $36,000. If inflation is 5 percent a year for the next three years, what amount will the Kaplans need for their living expenses? (L.O.4)

7. *Computing Time Value of Money for Savings.* Use future value and present value calculations (see tables in Appendix C) to determine the following.   (L.O.5)

   a. The future value of a $500 savings deposit after eight years at an annual interest rate of 7 percent.

   b. The future value of saving $1,500 a year for five years at an annual interest rate of 8 percent.

   c. The present value of a $2,000 savings account that will earn 6 percent interest for four years.

8. *Calculating Present Value of a Savings Fund.* Hal Thomas wants to establish a savings fund from which a community organization could draw $800 a year for 20 years. If the account earns 6 percent, what amount would he have to deposit now to achieve this goal?   (L.O.5)

PROJECTS AND APPLICATION ACTIVITIES

1. *Researching Money Management Information.* Using the World Wide Web, library sources, friends, relatives, and others, obtain information on common suggestions for successful money management.   (L.O.1)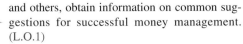

2. *Developing a Financial Document System.* Working with two or three others in your class, use Sheet 14 in the *Personal Financial Planner* to develop a system for filing and maintaining personal financial records.   (L.O.2)

3. *Comparing Financial Record Systems.* Conduct a survey of people of various ages to determine the system they use to keep track of various financial documents and records. (L.O.2)

4. *Creating Personal Financial Statements.* Using Sheets 15 and 16 in the *Personal Financial Planner,* or some other format, prepare a personal balance sheet and cash flow statement.   (L.O.3)

5. *Researching Household Asset Information on the Internet.* Using the World Wide Web or library research, find information about the assets commonly held by households in the United States. How have the values of assets, liabilities, and net worth of U.S. consumers changed in recent years?   (L.O.3)

6. *Researching Money Management Software.* Use the World Wide Web, store visits, or advertisements to determine the software a person might use to prepare personal financial statements, create a budget, and monitor spending, saving, and investing.   (L.O.3, 4)

7. *Analyzing Budgeting Situations.* Discuss with several people how the budget in Exhibit 3–8 (p. 78) might be changed based on various budget variances. If the household faced a decline in income, what spending areas might be reduced first?   (L.O.4)

8. *Comparing Budgeting Systems.* Ask two or three friends or relatives about their budgeting systems. Obtain information on how they maintain their spending records. Create a visual presentation (video or slide presentation) that communicates wise budgeting techniques.   (L.O.4)

9. *Analyzing Saving Habits.* Interview a young single person, a young couple, and a middle-aged person about their financial goals and savings habits. What actions do they take to determine and achieve various financial goals?   (L.O.5)

LIFE SITUATION CASE 3

OUT OF WORK BUT NOT OUT OF BILLS

Due to lower sales, the company for which Ed Weston works was cutting back on its work force. Even though Ed had been with the company for seven years, most of his duties were being performed by new, automated equipment.

After getting the word about losing his job, Ed talked with his wife, Alice, and their two children (ages 12 and 9) about ways they could reduce spending. The Westons started by making up a list of three things: (1) bills they had to pay each month, (2) areas where they could reduce spending, and (3) sources of funds to help them pay current expenses. Each family member had several ideas to help them cope with the difficult financial burden that was likely to occur over the next few weeks and months.

Before Ed was unemployed, the Westons had a monthly take-home income of $3,165. Each month, the money went for the following items: $880 for rent, $180 for utilities, $560 for food, $480 for automobile expenses, $300 for clothing, $280 for insurance, $250 for savings, and $235 for personal and other items. After the loss of Ed's job, the household's monthly income is $1,550, from his wife's wages and his unemployment benefits. The Westons also have savings accounts, investments, and retirement funds of $28,000.

QUESTIONS

1. What budget items might Ed and his family consider reducing to cope with their financial difficulties?

2. How should they use their savings and retirement funds during this financial crisis? What additional sources of funds might be available to the Westons during this period of unemployment?

3. What other current and future financial actions would you recommend to the Westons?

USING THE INTERNET TO CREATE A PERSONAL FINANCIAL PLAN 3

DEVELOPING PERSONAL FINANCIAL STATEMENTS AND A SPENDING PLAN

Money management activities are the basis for most financial planning activities. Creation of a financial document filing system, a personal balance sheet, a cash flow statement, and a budget provide you with tools for setting, implementing, and achieving financial goals.

Web Sites for Money Management

- Goal setting and money management information at **www.personalwealth.com**
- The FinanCenter provides answers to questions and calculations related to budgeting, automobiles, savings, investments, credit, and housing at **www.financenter. com/**
- Current data from the Consumer Expenditure Survey of the Bureau of Labor Statistics, U.S. Dept. of Labor available at **www.stats.bls.gov**
- Goal setting information and money management assistance at **www.personalwealth.com** and **www.networth. quicken.com**
- Budgeting information at **www.lifeadvice.com** and **www.americanexpress.com/student**
- Money management information from the National Center for Financial Education at **www.ncfe.org**
- Savings information at **www.savingsnet.com**

(Note: Addresses and content of Web sites change, and new sites are created daily. Use the search engines discussed in Appendix B to update and locate Web sites for your current financial planning needs.)

PFP SHEETS: 14–19

Short-Term Financial Planning Activities

1. Develop a filing system to organize your financial records and documents. (see PFP Sheet 14).
2. Create a personal balance sheet (see PFP Sheet 15) and a personal cash flow statement (see PFP Sheet 16).
3. Based on your current financial situation, set short-term financial goals and develop a budget (see PFP Sheet 17). Monitor your spending for various categories (see PFP Sheet 18).
4. Accumulate an appropriate amount for an emergency fund.

Long-Term Financial Planning Activities

1. Set long-term financial goals related to education, housing, or retirement (see PFP Sheet 3).
2. Develop a savings plan, such as automatic withdrawals, to achieve long-term financial goals.

CHAPTER 4

Planning Your Tax Strategy

OPENING CASE

We Owe *How* Much in Taxes?

Now that his daughter, Mandy, is two, Melvin Eckert has decided to restart his full-time business. Since Mandy's birth, Melvin has stayed home to care for her while his wife, Nina, continued her career as a human resources supervisor for a health care products company. Her salary and employee benefits provide the family with adequate financial resources. However, Melvin misses his career activities.

Before Mandy's birth, Melvin worked as an independent distributor and technical consultant for companies that made computer software used by small businesses. He represented several software companies and earned a commission based on sales. He also earned fees for helping companies set up computer systems.

When Melvin resumes his full-time career activities, he will need a car, business clothes, equipment, and supplies. The family will have child care expenses for Mandy. In addition, with two working parents, the Eckerts will likely eat meals away from home more often.

While certain business-related expenses are deductible from Melvin's income, the net earnings from his business will be subject to two types of federal taxes. First, the profit will be added to the family's tax return as ordinary income at a tax rate of 28 percent. Second, Melvin will have to pay a self-employment tax on his net earnings of about 15 percent as contributions for future Social Security benefits. In all, after deducting his business expenses, Melvin will pay about 43 cents of federal income tax for every dollar earned. And he still has to pay the state income tax.

"By the time we pay our extra household expenses, business expenses, and taxes, we'll have less than 20 cents per dollar I earn," Melvin commented to Nina. "Is it worth it?"

"That depends," replied Nina. "If you enjoy your work, that has to count for something."

"Well," responded Melvin, "I'm sure the government will enjoy my work, since they'll get a big chunk of the money."

Questions

1. What financial and personal factors can affect a person's decision to work?
2. What are the tax benefits and drawbacks associated with owning your own business?
3. How might the Eckerts evaluate the financial and personal benefits of Melvin's working?

After studying this chapter, you will be able to

L.O.1   Describe the importance of taxes for personal financial planning.

L.O.2   Calculate taxable income and the amount owed for federal income tax.

L.O.3   Prepare a federal income tax return.

L.O.4   Identify tax assistance sources.

L.O.5   Select appropriate tax strategies for different financial and personal situations.

TAXES AND FINANCIAL PLANNING

L.O.1 Describe the importance of taxes for personal financial planning.

Taxes are an everyday financial fact of life. You pay some taxes every time you get a paycheck or make a purchase. However, most people concern themselves with taxes only around April. With about one-third of each dollar you earn going for taxes, an effective tax strategy is vital for successful financial planning. If you know and understand the tax rules and regulations, you may be able to reduce your tax liability. Your purchases, investments, and other financial decisions can affect the amount you pay in taxes.

The U.S. Bureau of the Census reports that about two out of three American households have no money left after paying for taxes and normal living expenses. For most of us, taxes are a significant factor in financial planning. Each year, the Tax Foundation determines how long the average person works to pay taxes. In recent years, "Tax Freedom Day" came in early May. This means that the time people worked from January 1 until early May represents the portion of the year worked to pay their taxes.

In more specific terms, the tax burden for many households is 25 to 30 percent. This financial obligation includes the many types of taxes discussed later in this section. To help you cope with these taxes, common goals related to tax planning include

- Knowing the current tax laws and regulations that affect you.
- Maintaining complete and appropriate tax records.
- Making purchase and investment decisions that can reduce your tax liability.

You should gear tax planning efforts toward paying your fair share of taxes while taking advantage of tax benefits appropriate to your personal and financial situation.

The principal purpose of taxes is to finance government activities. As citizens, we expect government to provide services such as police and fire protection, schools, road maintenance, parks and libraries, and safety inspection of food, drugs, and other products. Most people pay taxes in four major categories: taxes on purchases, taxes on property, taxes on wealth, and taxes on earnings.

Taxes on Purchases

excise tax

You probably pay sales tax on many of your purchases. This state and local tax is added to the purchase price of products. Many states exempt food and drugs from sales tax to reduce the economic burden of this tax on the poor. In recent years, all but five states (Alaska, Delaware, Montana, New Hampshire, and Oregon) have had a general sales tax. An **excise tax** is imposed by the federal and state governments on specific goods and services, such as gasoline, cigarettes, alcoholic beverages, tires, air travel, and telephone service.

Taxes on Property

Real estate property tax is a major source of revenue for local governments. This tax is based on the value of land and buildings. The increasing amount of real estate property taxes is a major concern of homeowners. Retired people with limited pension incomes may encounter financial difficulties if local property taxes increase rapidly.

Some areas also impose personal property taxes. State and local governments may assess taxes on the value of automobiles, boats, furniture, and farm equipment.

Taxes on Wealth

estate tax

An **estate tax** is imposed on the value of a person's property at the time of his or her death. This tax is based on the fair market value of the deceased individual's investments, property, and bank accounts less allowable deductions and other taxes. Estate taxes are discussed in greater detail in Chapter 19.

inheritance tax

Money and property passed on to heirs may also be subject to a tax. An **inheritance tax** is levied on the value of property bequeathed by a deceased person. This tax is paid for the right to acquire the inherited property.

Individuals are allowed to give money or items valued at $10,000 or less in a year to a person without being subject to taxes. Gift amounts greater than $10,000 are subject to federal tax. Amounts given for the payment of tuition or medical expenses are not subject to federal gift taxes. Some states impose a gift tax on amounts that a person, before his or her death, transfers to another person since the action may have been intended to avoid estate and inheritance taxes.

Taxes on Earnings

The two main taxes on wages and salaries are Social Security and income taxes. Social Security taxes are used to finance the retirement, disability, and life insurance benefits of the federal government's Social Security program. Chapters 11 and 18 discuss various aspects of Social Security. Income tax is a major financial planning factor for most people. Some workers are subject to federal, state, and local income taxes. Currently, only seven states do not have a state income tax.

Throughout the year, your employer will withhold income tax payments from your paycheck, or you may be required to make estimated tax payments if you own your own business. Both types of payments are only estimates of your income taxes. You may need to pay an additional amount, or you may get a tax refund. The following sections will assist you in preparing your federal income tax return and planning your future tax strategies.

DID YOU KNOW?

In 1996, total taxes as a percentage of income for a two-earner family were estimated to be at 38.4 percent, up from 38.1 percent in 1995. For a single-earner family, total taxes as a percentage of income were estimated to increase to 36.4 percent from 36.1 percent in 1995. (SOURCE: Arthur P. Hall, "Family Tax Burden Up Three Years in a Row," *Consumers' Research,* January 1997, pp. 20–21.)

CONCEPT   CHECK   4–1

1. How should you consider taxes in your financial planning?
2. What types of taxes do people frequently overlook when making financial decisions?

INCOME TAX FUNDAMENTALS

L.O.2 Calculate taxable income and the amount owed for federal income tax.

Each year, millions of Americans are required to pay their share of income taxes to the federal government. The process involves computing taxable income, determining the amount of income tax owed, and comparing this amount with the income tax payments withheld or made during the year. Being aware of the income tax deadlines and the potential penalties for tax code violations is another basic aspect of the income tax process.

Step 1: Determining Adjusted Gross Income

taxable income

Taxable income is the net amount of income, after allowable deductions, on which income tax is computed. Exhibit 4–1 presents the components of taxable income and the process used to compute it.

Types of Income   Most, but not all, income is subject to taxation. Your gross, or total, income can consist of three main components:

earned income

1. **Earned income** is money received for personal effort. Earned income is usually in the form of wages, salary, commission, fees, tips, or bonuses.

investment income

2. **Investment income** (sometimes referred to as *portfolio income*) is money received in the form of dividends, interest, or rent from investments.

passive income

3. **Passive income** results from business activities in which you do not actively participate, such as a limited partnership.

Other types of income subject to federal income tax include alimony, awards, lottery winnings, and prizes. Cameron Clark won $30,533 in prizes on the television game show "Wheel of Fortune." In addition to paying California sales tax of $1,154, Cameron had to sell the car stereo, ping-pong table, camping gear, water ski equipment, bass guitar, and art drawing table and chair he won to pay the federal income tax. He did get to keep the Toyota Tercel, Honda Scooter, Gucci watches, and Australian vacation.

exclusion

Total income is also affected by exclusions. An **exclusion** is an amount not included in gross income. For example, the foreign income exclusion allows U.S. citizens working and living in another country to exclude a certain portion ($70,000) of their incomes from federal income taxes.

Exclusions are also referred to as **tax-exempt income,** or income that is not subject to tax. For example, interest earned on most state and city bonds is exempt from federal income tax. **Tax-deferred income** is income that will be taxed at a later date. The earnings on an individual retirement account (IRA) are an example of tax-deferred income. While these earnings are credited to the account now, you do not pay taxes on them until you withdraw them from the account.

> **DID YOU KNOW?**
>
> While earnings on money market funds may be reported to savers as "interest," the IRS considers this income as dividends. In contrast, credit union earnings are called "dividends," although these funds are actually interest.

tax-exempt income

tax-deferred income

Exhibit 4–1   **Computing Taxable Income and Your Tax Liability**

Step 1: Determining Adjusted Gross Income . . . .

Step 2: Computing Taxable Income . . . .

Step 3: Calculating Taxes Owed . . . .

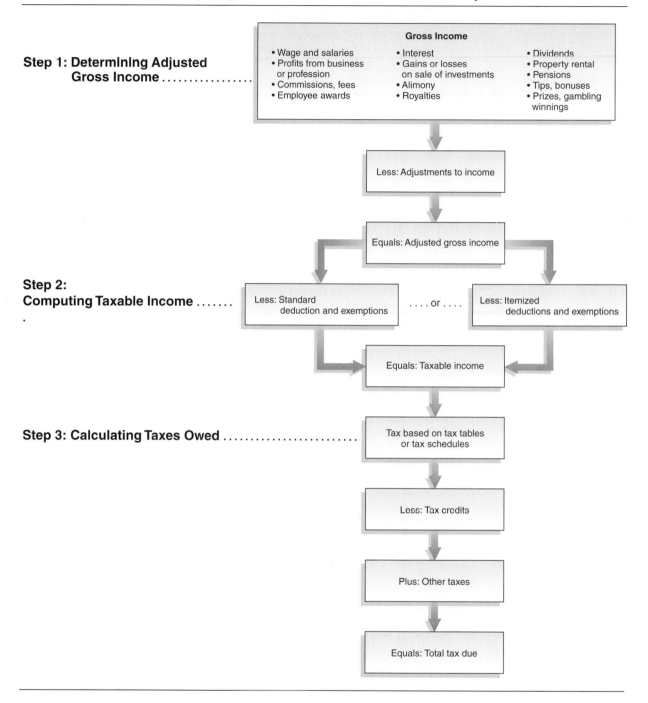

adjusted gross income (AGI)

Adjustments to Income   **Adjusted gross income (AGI)** is gross income after certain reductions have been made. These reductions, called *adjustments to income,* include contributions to an individual retirement account (IRA) or a Keogh retirement plan, penalties for early withdrawal of savings, and alimony payments. Adjusted gross income is used as the basis for computing various income tax deductions, such as medical expenses.

tax shelter

Certain adjustments to income, such as tax-deferred retirement plans, are a type of tax shelter. **Tax shelters** are investments that provide immediate tax benefits and a reasonable expectation of a future financial return. In recent years, tax court rulings and changes in the tax code have disallowed various types of tax shelters that were considered excessive.

Step 2: Computing Taxable Income

tax deduction

standard deduction

Deductions A **tax deduction** is an amount subtracted from adjusted gross income to arrive at taxable income. Every taxpayer receives at least the **standard deduction,** a set amount on which no taxes are paid. As of 1997, single people received a standard deduction of $4,150 (married couples filing jointly, $6,900). Blind and people 65 and over receive higher standard deductions.

itemized deductions

Many people qualify for more than the standard deduction. **Itemized deductions** are expenses a taxpayer is allowed to deduct from adjusted gross income. Common itemized deductions include the following:

- *Medical and dental expenses,* including doctors' fees, prescription medications, hospital expenses, medical insurance premiums, hearing aids, eyeglasses, and medical travel that has not been reimbursed or paid by others. The amount of this deduction is the medical and dental expenses that exceed 7.5 percent (as of 1997) of adjusted gross income. If your AGI is $20,000, for example, you must have more than $1,500 in unreimbursed medical and dental expenses before you can claim this deduction. If your medical and dental bills amount to $1,600, you qualify for a $100 deduction.
- *Taxes*—state and local income tax, real estate property tax, and state or local personal property tax.
- *Interest*—mortgage interest, home equity loan interest, and investment interest expense up to an amount equal to investment income.
- *Contributions* of cash or property to qualified charitable organizations. Contribution totals greater than 20 percent of adjusted gross income are subject to limitations.
- *Casualty and theft losses*—financial losses resulting from natural disasters, accidents, or unlawful acts. Deductions are for the amount exceeding 10 percent of AGI, less $100, for losses *not* reimbursed by an insurance company or other source. California residents commonly report casualty losses due to earthquake damage.
- *Moving expenses* when a change in residence is associated with a new job that is at least 50 miles farther from your former home than your old main job location. Deductible moving expenses include only the cost of transporting taxpayer and household members and the cost of moving household goods and personal property.
- *Job-related and other miscellaneous expenses* such as unreimbursed job travel, union dues, required continuing education, work clothes or uniforms, investment expenses, tax preparation fees, and safe deposit box rental (for storing investment documents). The total of these expenses must exceed 2 percent of adjusted gross income to qualify as a deduction. Such miscellaneous expenses as gambling losses to the extent of gambling winnings and physical or mental disability expenses that limit employability are not subject to the 2 percent limit.

The standard deduction *or* total itemized deductions, along with the value of your exemptions (see the next section), is subtracted from adjusted gross income to obtain your taxable income. The accompanying Financial Planning in Action box can help you determine which items to include in your taxable income when you calculate your federal income tax.

FINANCIAL PLANNING IN ACTION

IS IT TAXABLE INCOME? IS IT DEDUCTIBLE?

Certain financial benefits individuals receive are not subject to federal income tax. Indicate whether each of the following items would or would not be included in taxable income when you compute your federal income tax.

Indicate whether each of the following items would or would not be deductible when you compute your federal income tax.

Is it taxable income . . . ?	Yes	No
1. Lottery winnings	___	___
2. Child support received	___	___
3. Worker's compensation benefits	___	___
4. Life insurance death benefits	___	___
5. Municipal bond interest earnings	___	___
6. Bartering income	___	___

Is it deductible . . . ?	Yes	No
7. Life insurance premiums	___	___
8. Cosmetic surgery for improved looks	___	___
9. Fees for traffic violations	___	___
10. Mileage for driving to volunteer work	___	___
11. An attorney's fee for preparing a will	___	___
12. Income tax preparation fee	___	___

NOTE: These taxable income items and deductions are based on the 1997 tax year and may change due to changes in the tax code.

ANSWERS: 1, 6, 10, 12—yes; 2, 3, 4, 5, 7, 8, 9, 11—no.

You are required to maintain records to document your tax deductions. Financial advisers recommend a home filing system (see Exhibit 4–2) for storing receipts and other tax documents. Canceled checks can serve as proof of payment for such deductions as charitable contributions, medical expenses, and business-related expenses. Travel expenses can be documented in a daily log with records of mileage, tolls, parking fees, and away-from-home costs.

Generally, you should keep tax records for three years from the date you file your return. However, you may be held responsible for providing back documentation up to six years. Records such as past tax returns and housing documents should be kept indefinitely.

exemption

Exemptions An **exemption** is a deduction from adjusted gross income for yourself, your spouse, and qualified dependents. A dependent must not earn more than a set amount unless he or she is under age 19 or is a full-time student under age 24; you must provide more than half of the dependent's support; and the dependent must reside in your home or be a specified relative and must meet certain citizenship requirements. The Social Security number of each dependent must be reported on the tax return, regardless of age.

For 1997, taxable income was reduced by $2,650 for each exemption claimed. This amount is revised annually based on inflation. Increased exemptions and standard deductions eliminate or reduce the taxes many low-income Americans pay. For 1997, a family of four did not have to pay federal income tax on the first $17,500 of gross income ($6,900 for the standard deduction and $10,600 for four exemptions). After deducting the amounts for exemptions, you obtain your taxable income, which is the amount used to determine taxes owed.

EXHIBIT 4–2

**A Tax
Recordkeeping
System**

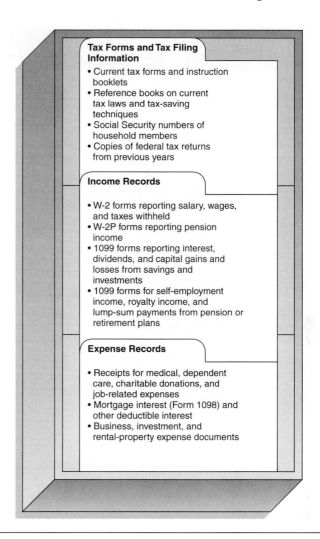

**Tax Forms and Tax Filing
Information**
- Current tax forms and instruction booklets
- Reference books on current tax laws and tax-saving techniques
- Social Security numbers of household members
- Copies of federal tax returns from previous years

Income Records
- W-2 forms reporting salary, wages, and taxes withheld
- W-2P forms reporting pension income
- 1099 forms reporting interest, dividends, and capital gains and losses from savings and investments
- 1099 forms for self-employment income, royalty income, and lump-sum payments from pension or retirement plans

Expense Records
- Receipts for medical, dependent care, charitable donations, and job-related expenses
- Mortgage interest (Form 1098) and other deductible interest
- Business, investment, and rental-property expense documents

Step 3: Calculating Taxes Owed

Your taxable income is the basis for computing the amount of your income tax. The use of tax rates and the benefits of tax credits are the final phase of the tax computation process.

Tax Rates   Use your taxable income in conjunction with the appropriate tax table or tax schedule. Before 1987, there were 14 tax rates, ranging from 11 to 50 percent. For 1997, the five-rate system for federal income tax was as shown here:

Rate on Taxable Income	Single Taxpayers	Married Taxpayers	Heads of Households
15%	Up to $24,650	Up to $41,200	Up to $33,050
28	$24,650–$59,750	$41,200–$99,600	$30,050–$85,350
31	$59,750–$124,650	$99,600–$151,750	$85,350–$138,200
36	$124,650–$271,050	$151,750–$271,050	$138,200–$271,050
39.6	Over $272,050	Over $271,050	Over $271,050

FINANCIAL PLANNING CALCULATIONS

TAX CREDITS VERSUS TAX DEDUCTIONS

Many people confuse *tax credits* with *tax deductions.* Is one better than the other? A tax *credit,* such as eligible child care or dependent care expenses, results in a dollar-for-dollar reduction in the amount of taxes owed. A *tax deduction,* such as an itemized deduction in the form of medical expenses, mortgage interest, or charitable contributions, reduces the taxable income on which your taxes are based.

Here is how a $100 tax credit compares with a $100 tax deduction:

As you might expect, tax credits are less readily available than tax deductions. To qualify for a $100 child care tax credit, you may have to spend $500 in child care expenses. In some situations, spending on deductible items may be more beneficial than qualifying for a tax credit. A knowledge of tax law and careful financial planning will help you use both tax credits and tax deductions to maximum advantage.

> **$100 Tax Credit**
>
> ↓
>
> Reduces your taxes by $100.

> **$100 Tax Deduction**
>
> ↓
>
> Reduces your taxable income by $100. The amount of your tax reduction depends on your tax bracket. Your taxes will be reduced by $15 if you are in the 15 percent tax bracket and by $28 if you are in the 28 percent tax bracket.

A separate tax rate schedule exists for married persons who file separate income tax returns.

marginal tax rate

The 15, 28, 31, 36, and 39.6 percent rates are referred to as **marginal tax rates.** These rates are used to calculate tax on the last (and next) dollar of taxable income. After deductions and exemptions, a person in the 28 percent tax bracket pays 28 cents in taxes for every dollar of taxable income in that bracket.

average tax rate

In contrast, the **average tax rate** is based on the total tax due divided by taxable income. Due to deductions and tax credits, this rate is less than a person's marginal tax rate. For example, a person with taxable income of $40,000 and a total tax bill of $4,200 would have an *average tax rate* of 10.5 percent ($4,200 ÷ $40,000). Self-employed people are likely to have a higher average tax rate due to self-employment taxes, which include payments toward future Social Security benefits.

Taxpayers who benefit from the special treatment given to certain income and receive special deductions may be subject to an additional tax. The *alternative minimum tax (AMT)* is designed to ensure that those who receive tax breaks also pay their fair share of taxes. Further discussion of the AMT is beyond the scope of this book; you may obtain information from the Internal Revenue Service (IRS).

tax credit

Tax Credits   The tax owed may be reduced by a **tax credit,** an amount subtracted directly from the amount of taxes owed. One example of a tax credit is the credit given for child care and dependent care expenses. This amount lowers the tax owed by an individual or a couple. A tax credit differs from a deduction in that a tax credit has a full dollar effect in lowering taxes, whereas a deduction reduces the taxable income on which the tax liability is computed. (See the accompanying Financial Planning Calculations box.)

EXHIBIT 4–3

W-2 Form

a Control number		OMB No. 1545-0008

b Employer's identification number 37 – 19876541	**1** Wages, tips, other compensation 23,972.09	**2** Federal income tax withheld 2,678.93

c Employer's name, address, and ZIP code	**3** Social security wages 23,972.09	**4** Social security tax withheld 1,725.99
Information Data, Inc. 9834 Collins Blvd. Benton, NJ 08734	**5** Medicare wages and tips	**6** Medicare tax withheld
	7 Social security tips	**8** Allocated tips

d Employee's social security number 123-45-6789	**9** Advance EIC payment	**10** Dependent care benefits

e Employee's name, address, and ZIP code	**11** Nonqualified plans	**12** Benefits included in box 1
Barbara Victor 124 Harper Lane Parmont, NJ 07819	**13** See Instrs. for box 13	**14** Other

15 Statutory employee ☐	Deceased ☐	Pension plan ☐	Legal rep. ☐	Hshld. emp. ☐	Subtotal ☐	Deferred compensation ☐

16 State Employer's state I.D. No. 37 – 19876541	**17** State wages, tips, etc.	**18** State income tax	**19** Locality name	**20** local wages, tips, etc.	**21** Local income tax

(1)   Department of the Treasury—Internal Revenue Service

Form **W-2** **Wage and Tax Statement**

Copy B To Be Filed With Employee's FEDERAL Tax Return

This information is being furnished to the Internal Revenue Service.

Low-income workers can benefit from the *earned-income credit (EIC).* This federal tax regulation, for working parents with taxable income under a certain amount ($29,290 with more than one child in 1997), can result in a tax credit of more than $2,500. Families that do not earn enough to owe federal income taxes are also eligible for the EIC. When these families file a tax return and attach Schedule EIC, they receive a check from the IRS for the amount of their credit.

Making Tax Payments

Your payment of income taxes to the federal government will be made in one of two ways: through payroll withholding or through estimated tax payments.

Withholding   The pay-as-you-go system requires an employer to deduct federal income tax from your pay and send it to the government. The withheld amount is based on the number of exemptions and the expected deductions claimed on the W-4 form. For example, a married person with children would have less withheld than a single person with the same salary, since the married person will owe less tax at year-end.

After the end of the year, you will receive a W-2 form (see Exhibit 4–3), which reports your annual earnings and the amounts that have been deducted for federal income tax, Social Security, and, if applicable, state income tax. A copy of the W-2 form is filed with your tax return to document your earnings and the amount you have paid in taxes. The difference between the amount withheld and the tax owed is either the additional amount you must pay or the refund you will receive.

Many taxpayers view an annual tax refund as a "windfall," extra money they can count on each year. However, these taxpayers are forgetting the opportunity cost of withholding excessive amounts. In 1996, about 56 million American households received an average

Financial Decision
Trade-Off

refund of $1,300, for a total of more than $72.8 billion. Invested at 5 percent for a year, these refunds represented over $3.64 billion in lost interest. Some people view their extra tax withholding as "forced savings." However, a payroll deduction plan for savings could serve the same purpose and would enable them to earn the interest instead of giving the government an interest-free loan.

Students and low-income individuals may file for exemption from withholding if they paid no federal income tax last year and do not expect to pay any in the current year. Dependents may not be exempt from withholding if they have any unearned income and if their total gross income will exceed $500. Being exempt from withholding results in not having to file for a refund and allows you to make more use of your money during the year. However, even if federal income tax is not withheld, Social Security taxes will still be deducted.

Estimated Payments   People with income from savings, investments, independent contracting, royalties, and lump-sum payments from pensions or retirement plans have their earnings reported on Form 1099. People in these situations and others who do not have taxes withheld may be required to make tax payments during the year (April 15, June 15, September 15, and January 15 as the last payment for the previous tax year). These payments are based on the person's estimate of taxes due at year-end. Underpayment or failure to make these estimated payments can result in penalties and interest charges. These penalties are usually avoided if withholding and estimated payments total more than your tax liability for the previous year or at least 90 percent of the current year's tax.

Deadlines and Penalties

Most people are required to file their federal income tax return each April 15. If you are not able to file on time, you can use Form 4868 to obtain an automatic four-month extension. This extension is for the 1040 form and other documents, but it does not delay your payment liability. You must submit the estimated amount owed along with Form 4868 by April 15. Failure to file on time can result in a penalty of 5 percent for just one day.

People who make quarterly deposits for estimated taxes must submit their payments by April 15, June 15, and September 15 of the current tax year, with the final payment due by January 15 of the following year.

The IRS can impose penalties and interest for violations of the tax code. Failure to file a tax return can result in a 25 percent penalty in addition to the taxes owed.

Underpayment of quarterly estimated taxes requires paying interest on the amount you should have paid. Underpayment due to negligence or fraud can result in penalties of 50 to 75 percent. The good news is that if you claim a refund several months or years late, the IRS will pay you interest. Refunds must be claimed within three years of filing the return or within two years of paying the tax.

Sheet 20

C O N C E P T   C H E C K   4–2

1. How does tax-exempt income differ from tax-deferred income?
2. What information is needed to compute taxable income?
3. When would you use the standard deduction instead of itemized deductions?
4. What is the difference between your marginal tax rate and your average tax rate?
5. How does a tax credit affect the amount owed for federal income tax?

FILING YOUR FEDERAL INCOME TAX RETURN

L.O.3 Prepare a federal income tax return.

As you stare at those piles of papers, you know it's time to do your taxes! Submitting your federal income tax return requires several decisions and activities. First, you must determine whether you are required to file a return. Next, you need to decide which basic form best serves your needs and whether you are required to submit additional schedules or supplementary forms. Finally, you must prepare your return.

Who Must File?

Every citizen or resident of the United States and every U.S. citizen who is a resident of Puerto Rico is required to file a federal income tax return if his or her income is above a certain amount. The amount is based on the person's *filing status* and other factors such as age. For example, single persons under 65 had to file a return on April 15, 1998 (for tax year 1997), if their gross income exceeded $6,800; single persons over 65 had to file if their gross income exceeded $7,800. The amount at which you are required to file will change each year based on changes in the standard deduction and in the allowed personal exemptions. If your gross income is less than this amount but taxes were withheld from your earnings, you will need to file a return to obtain a refund.

Your filing status is affected by such factors as marital status and dependents. The five filing status categories are

- *Single*—never-married, divorced, or legally separated individuals with no dependents.
- *Married, filing joint return*—combines the income of a husband and a wife.
- *Married, filing separate returns*—each spouse is responsible for his or her own tax. Under certain conditions, a married couple can benefit from this filing status.
- *Head of household*—an unmarried individual or a surviving spouse who maintains a household (paying for more than half of the costs) for a child or a dependent relative.
- *Qualifying widow or widower*—an individual whose spouse died within the past two years and who has a dependent; this status is limited to two years after the death of a spouse.

In some situations, you may have a choice of filing status. In such cases, compute your taxes under the available alternatives to determine the most advantageous filing status.

Which Tax Form Should You Use?

Although about 400 federal tax forms and schedules exist (see Exhibit 4–4), you have a choice of three basic forms when filing your income tax. Recently, about 20 percent of taxpayers used Form 1040EZ or Form 1040A; about 60 percent used the regular Form 1040. Your decision in this matter will depend on your type of income, the amount of your income, the number of your deductions, and the complexity of your tax situation.

Form 1040EZ   You may use Form 1040EZ if

- You are single or married filing a joint return, under age 65, and claim no dependents.
- Your income consisted only of wages, salaries, and tips and not more than $400 of taxable interest.
- Your taxable income is less than $50,000.
- You do not itemize deductions or claim any adjustments to income or any tax credits.

EXHIBIT 4–4   **The Most Commonly Used Federal Income Tax Forms**

Form	Title	Purpose
1040EZ	Income Tax Return	For single taxpayers or married taxpayers filing jointly with no dependents, taxable income of less than $50,000, no deductions
1040A	Income Tax Return	For taxpayers with taxable income of less than $50,000 and no itemized deductions who may take an IRA deduction and have certain tax credits
1040	Income Tax Return	For taxpayers with more complex tax situations who do not qualify for use of 1040EZ or 1040A
1040PC	Income Tax Return for Computerized Returns	For filing a tax return prepared on a personal computer
1040X	Amended Income Tax Retrun	To correct income or deductions reported in a previous year
Schedule A	Itemized Deductions	To claim deductions for medical expenses, certain state and local taxes, interest, donations, casualty losses, moving expenses, and other deductible expenses
Schedule B	Interest and Dividend Income	To report interest and/or dividend income of over $400
Schedule C	Profit or Loss from Business or Profession	To report income and expenses from self-employment
Schedule C-EZ	Net Profit from Business	To report net profit of a sole proprietorship with gross receipts of less than $25,000 and expenses of less than $2,000
Schedule D	Capital Gains and Losses	To report gains and losses on the sale of investments
Schedule E	Supplemental Income Schedule	To report income and expenses from rental property, royalties, partnerships, estates, and trusts
Schedule EIC	Earned-Income Credit	To calculate tax credit for low-income working families
Schedule R	Credit for the Elderly or Disabled	To claim a tax credit for elderly or disabled persons in low-income categories
Schedule SE	Social Security Self-Employment Tax	To calculate self-employment Social Security tax based on profit from a business or profession
2106	Employee Business Expenses	To report employee-related travel expenses and reimbursements for these expenses
2119	Sale of Your Home	To report the sale and/or exchange of your primary place of residence
2441	Credit for Child and Dependent Care Expenses	To calculate the tax credit for child care or dependent care costs for individuals in certain income groups
3903	Moving Expenses	To calculate the deductible expenses related to a change of residence based on job-distance restrictions
4562	Depreciation and Amortization	To calculate business depreciation expenses for various types of assets
4684	Casualties and Thefts	To report nonbusiness casualty and theft losses less any reimbursement from insurance or other sources
4868	Application for Automatic Extension	To request a four-month delay in filing your federal tax return; does not delay time for payment of taxes
5329	Return for IRA and Qualified Retirement Plans Taxes	To report excess contributions, premature distributions, or excess distributions related to a retirement plan
8283	Noncash Charitable Contributions	To report a charitable deduction of property or services
8606	Nondeductible IRA Contributions	To report contributions to an individual retirement arrangement that are not deductible for tax purposes
8615	Computation of Tax for Children under Age 14 Who Have Investment Income of More than $1,300	To report income and capital gains from investments
8829	Expenses for Business Use of Your Home	To report expenses related to the use of your home for business purposes
8839	Qualified Adoption Expenses	To report expenses associated with adoption of a child

Form 1040EZ allows people with less complicated situations to file with a minimum of effort. For example, Margie Collins, a college freshman, had a part-time job at a health center. Since she was single, earned less than the amount needed to file, and had $43 in interest income, Margie was able to use Form 1040EZ to obtain a refund of income tax withheld during the past year.

Form 1040A This form would be used by people who have less than $50,000 in taxable income from wages, salaries, tips, unemployment compensation, interest, or dividends and use the standard deduction. With Form 1040A, you can also take deductions for individual retirement account (IRA) contributions and a tax credit for child care and dependent care expenses.

If you qualify for either Form 1040EZ or Form 1040A, you may wish to use one of them to simplify filing your tax return. You may not necessarily use either form if the regular Form 1040 lets you pay less tax.

Form 1040 Form 1040 is an expanded version of Form 1040A that includes sections for all types of income. You are required to use this form if your income is over $50,000 or if you can be claimed as a dependent on your parents' return *and* you had interest or dividends over a set limit.

Form 1040 allows you to itemize your deductions. You can list various allowable expenses (medical costs, home mortgage interest, real estate property taxes) that will reduce taxable income and the amount you owe the government. You should learn about all the possible adjustments to income, deductions, and tax credits for which you may qualify.

> **DID YOU KNOW?**
>
> The Internal Revenue Service oversees more than 17,000 pages of laws and regulations with 480 different tax forms.

Form 1040PC This condensed version of Form 1040 must be created by using tax preparation software. This coded information uses numbers and letters that are read by a scanner at the IRS. The use of this form increases the speed of processing your federal tax return.

Form 1040X This form is used to amend a previously filed tax return. If you discovered income that was not reported, or if you found additional deductions, you should file Form 1040X to pay the additional tax or to obtain a refund.

Completing the Federal Income Tax Return

The major sections of Form 1040 (see Exhibit 4–5) correspond to tax topics discussed in the previous sections of this chapter:

1. *Filing status and exemptions.* Your tax rate is determined by your filing status and allowances for yourself, your spouse, and each person you claim as a dependent.
2. *Income.* Earnings from your employment (as reported by your W-2 form) and other income, such as savings and investment income, are reported in this section of Form 1040.
3. *Adjustments to income.* As discussed later in the chapter, if you qualify, you may deduct contributions (up to a certain amount) to an individual retirement account (IRA) or other qualified retirement program.
4. *Tax computation.* In this section, your adjusted gross income is reduced by your itemized deductions (see Exhibit 4–6) or by the standard deduction for your tax situation. In addition, an amount is deducted for each exemption to arrive at your taxable income. That income is the basis for determining the amount of your tax (see Exhibit 4–7).

EXHIBIT 4–5 **Federal Income Tax Return—Form 1040**

1. Your marriage and household situation will affect your taxable income and tax rate

2. Your earnings and other sources of income will be reported in this section

3. Adjusted gross income results from certain deductions and will be used as a basis for computing other deductions

Form **1040** Department of the Treasury—Internal Revenue Service (P) 19
U.S. Individual Income Tax Return
For the year Jan. 1—Dec. 31, 1997, or other tax year beginning , 19 , 1997, ending , 19 OMB No. 1545-0074
IRS Use Only—Do not write or staple in this space.

Label
(See instructions on page 10.)
Use the IRS label. Otherwise please print or type.

Your first name and initial: EDWARD L. Last name: RAMERIZ
Your social security number: 123 45 6789

If a joint return, spouse's first name and initial: MARGE S. Last name: RAMERIZ
Spouse's social security number: 123 54 9876

Home address (number and street). If you have a P.O. box, see page 10.: 8734 CONNER LANE Apt. no.

For help in finding line instructions, see pages 2 and 3 in the booklet.

City, town, or post office, state, and ZIP code. If you have a foreign address, see page 10.: COLLINS, IA 51733

Presidential Election Campaign (See page 10.)
Do you want $3 to go to this fund? ... Yes No
If a joint return, does your spouse want $3 to go to this fund? ...
Note: Checking "Yes" will not change your tax or reduce your refund.

Filing Status
Check only one box.

1 Single
2 ☒ Married filing joint return (even if only one had income)
3 Married filing separate return. Enter spouse's social security no. and full name here. ▶
4 Head of household (with qualifying person). (See page 10.) If the qualifying person is a child but not your dependent, enter this child's name here. ▶
5 Qualifying widow(er) with dependent child (year spouse died ▶ 19). (See page 10.)

Exemptions

6a ☒ Yourself. If your parents (or someone else) can claim you as a dependent on his or her tax return, do not check box 6a.
b ☒ Spouse
No. of boxes checked on 6a and 6b: 2
No. of your children on 6c who: 2

c Dependents:
(1) First name Last name	(3) Dependent's social security number	(4) Dependent's relationship to you	(5) No. of months lived in your home in 1997
JOHN RAMERIZ	987 65 4321	SON	12
SANDY RAMERIZ	789 56 1234	DAUGHTER	12

• lived with you
• did not live with you due to divorce or separation (see page 11)

If more than six dependents, see page 10.

Dependents on 6c not entered above

d Total number of exemptions claimed ...
Add numbers entered on lines above: 4

Income

Attach Copy B of your Forms W-2, W-2G, and 1099-R here.

If you did not get a W-2, see page 12.

Enclose, but do not attach, any payment. Also, please use Form 1040-V.

7 Wages, salaries, tips, etc. Attach Form(s) W-2	7	52,862 —
8a Taxable interest. Attach Schedule B if required	8a	280 —
b Tax exempt interest. DON'T include on line 8a. 8b		
9 Dividends. Attach Schedule B if required	9	
10 Taxable refunds, credits, or offsets of state and local income taxes (see page 12)	10	
11 Alimony received	11	
12 Business income or (loss). Attach Schedule C or C-EZ	12	
13 Capital gain or (loss). Attach Schedule D	13	360 —
14 Other gains or (losses). Attach Form 4797	14	
15a Total IRA distributions 15a b Taxable amount (see page 13)	15b	
16a Total Pensions and annuities 16a b Taxable amount (see page 13)	16b	
17 Rental real estate, royalties, partnerships, S corporations, trusts, etc. Attach Schedule E	17	
18 Farm income or (loss). Attach Schedule F	18	
19 Unemployment compensation	19	
20a Social security benefits 20a b Taxable amount (see page 14)	20b	
21 Other income. List type and amount—see page 15	21	
22 Add the amounts in the far right column for lines 7 through 21. This is your total income ▶	22	53,502 —

Adjusted Gross Income

If line 32 is under $29,290 (under $9,770 if a child did not live with you), see EIC inst. on page 21.

23 Your IRA deduction (see page 16)	23	2000 —	
24 Medical savings account deduction. Attach Form 8853	24		
25 Moving expenses. Attach 3903 or 3903-F	25		
26 One-half of self-employment tax. Attach Schedule SE.	26		
27 Self-employed health insurance deduction (see page 17)	27		
28 Keogh and self-employed SEP and SIMPLE plans	28		
29 Penalty on early withdrawal of savings	29		
30a Alimony paid. b Recipient's SSN ▶	30a		
31 Add lines 23 through 30a		30	2000 —
32 Subtract line 31 from line 22. These are your adjusted gross income ▶		31	51,502 —

For Privacy Act and Paperwork Reduction Act Notice, see page 38. Cat. No. 12599G Form **1040**

5. *Tax credits.* Any tax credits for which you qualify are subtracted at this point.

6. *Other taxes.* Any special taxes, such as self-employment tax, are included at this point.

7. *Payments.* Your total withholding and other payments are indicated in this section.

8. *Refund or amount you owe.* If your payments exceed the amount of income tax you owe, you are entitled to a refund. If the opposite is true, you must make an additional payment. Taxpayers who want their refunds sent directly to a bank will no longer need to complete a separate form. Instead, the necessary account information will be recorded directly on the Form 1040, 1040A, or 1040EZ.

9. *Your signature.* Forgetting to sign a tax return is one of the most common filing errors.

EXHIBIT 4–5   *(continued)*

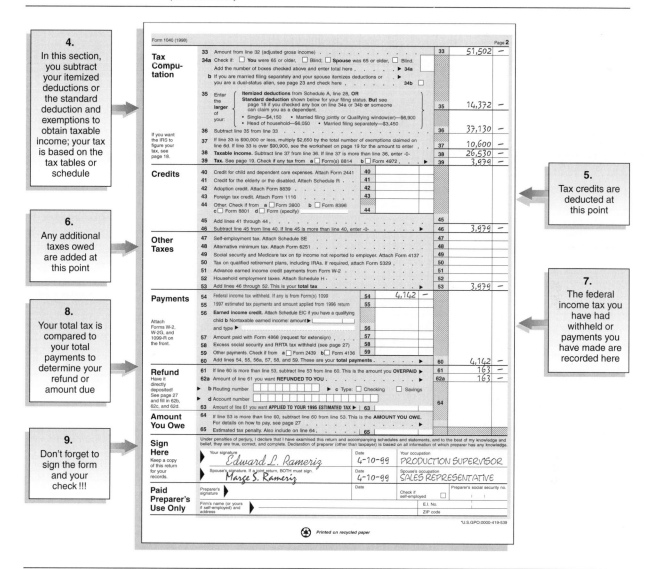

4.
In this section, you subtract your itemized deductions or the standard deduction and exemptions to obtain taxable income; your tax is based on the tax tables or schedule

5.
Tax credits are deducted at this point

6.
Any additional taxes owed are added at this point

7.
The federal income tax you have had withheld or payments you have made are recorded here

8.
Your total tax is compared to your total payments to determine your refund or amount due

9.
Don't forget to sign the form and your check !!!

NOTE: These forms are used in a recent year; the current forms may not be exactly the same. Obtain current income tax forms and current tax information from your local IRS office, post office, public library, or at www.irs.ustreas.gov.

Filing State Income Tax Returns

All but seven states (Alaska, Florida, Nevada, South Dakota, Texas, Washington, and Wyoming) have a state income tax. In most states, the tax rate ranges from 1 to 10 percent and is based on some aspect of your federal income tax return, such as adjusted gross income or taxable income. For further information about the income tax in your state, contact the state department of revenue. States usually require income tax returns to be filed when the federal income tax return is due. For help in planning your tax activities, see Exhibit 4–8.

EXHIBIT 4-6   **Schedule A for Itemized Deductions—Form 1040**

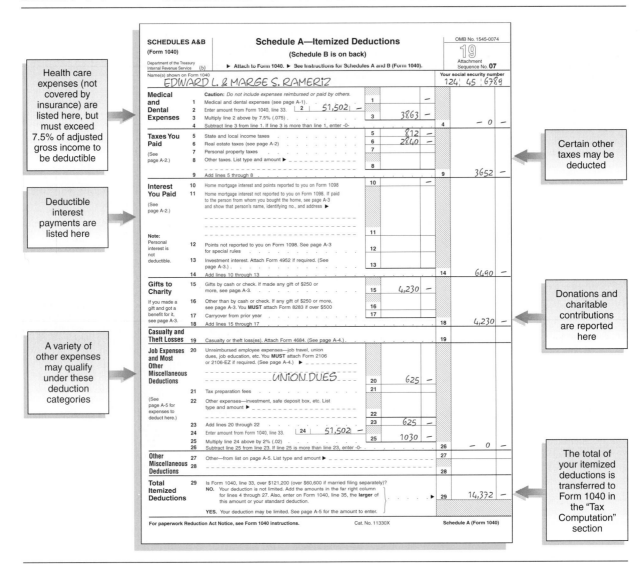

Health care expenses (not covered by insurance) are listed here, but must exceed 7.5% of adjusted gross income to be deductible

Deductible interest payments are listed here

A variety of other expenses may qualify under these deduction categories

Certain other taxes may be deducted

Donations and charitable contributions are reported here

The total of your itemized deductions is transferred to Form 1040 in the "Tax Computation" section

CONCEPT CHECK 4-3

1. In what ways does your filing status affect preparation of your federal income tax return?
2. What factors affect your choice of a 1040 form?

TAX ASSISTANCE AND THE AUDIT PROCESS

L.O.4 Identify tax assistance sources.

In the process of completing your federal income tax return, you may seek additional information or assistance. After filing your return, you may be identified for a tax audit. If this happens, several policies and procedures protect your rights.

EXHIBIT 4–7   **Tax Tables and Tax Rate Schedules**

Tax Table

If line 38 (taxable income) is–		And you are–			
At least	But less than	Single	Married filing jointly *	Married filing separately	Head of a household
		Your tax is–			
26,000					
26,000	26,050	4,083	3,904	4,609	3,904
26,050	26,100	4,097	3,911	4,623	3,911
26,100	26,150	4,111	3,919	4,637	3,919
26,150	26,200	4,125	3,926	4,651	3,926
26,200	26,250	4,139	3,934	4,665	3,934
26,250	26,300	4,153	3,941	4,679	3,941
26,300	26,350	4,167	3,949	4,693	3,949
26,350	26,400	4,181	3,956	4,707	3,956
26,400	26,450	4,195	3,964	4,721	3,934
26,450	26,500	4,209	3,971	4,735	3,971
26,500	26,550	4,223	3,979	4,749	3,979
26,550	26,600	4,237	3,986	4,763	3,986
26,600	26,650	4,251	3,994	4,777	3,994
26,650	26,700	4,265	4,001	4,791	4,001
26,700	26,750	4,279	4,009	4,805	4,009
26,750	26,800	4,293	4,016	4,819	4,016
26,800	26,850	4,307	4,024	4,833	4,024
26,850	26,900	4,321	4,031	4,847	4,031
26,900	26,950	4,335	4,039	4,861	4,039
26,950	27,000	4,349	4,046	4,875	4,046

* This column must also be used by a qualifying widow(er).

Tax Rate Schedules

Schedule Y-1—Use if your filing status is **Married filing jointly or Qualifying widow(er)**

If the amount on Form 1040, line 38, is: Over–	But not over–	Enter on Form 1040, line 39		of the amount over–
$0	$22,750	-----------	15%	$0
41,200	55,100	$6,180.00 +	28%	41,200
99,600	115,000	22,532.00 +	31%	99,600
151,750	250,000	36,698.50 +	36%	151,750
271,050	----------	81,646.50 +	39.6%	271,050

Caution: *Use **only** if you taxable income (Form 1040, line 38) is $100,000 or more. If less, use the* **Tax Table**. *Even though you cannot use the tax rate schedules below if your taxable income is less than $100,000, all levels of taxable income are shown so taxpayers can see the tax rate that applies to each level.*

NOTE: These were the federal income tax rates for a recent year. Current rates may vary due to changes in the tax code and adjustments for inflation. Obtain current income tax booklets from your local IRS office, post office, bank, or public library.

Tax Information Sources

As with other aspects of personal financial planning, many resources are available to assist you with your taxes. The IRS offers a wide variety of services to taxpayers. Libraries and bookstores offer books and other publications that are updated annually.

IRS Services   If you wish to do your own tax return or just to expand your knowledge of tax regulations, the IRS has four main methods of assistance:

1. *Publications.* The IRS offers hundreds of free booklets and pamphlets. You can obtain these publications at a local IRS office, by mail request, or by a telephone call to the office listed in your tax packet or your local telephone directory. Especially helpful is *Your Federal Income Tax* (IRS Publication 17). You may obtain IRS publications and tax forms by calling 1–800–TAX–FORM or online at http://www.irs.ustreas.gov.
2. *Recorded messages.* The IRS Tele-Tax system allows you access to about 150 telephone tax tips covering everything from filing requirements to reporting gambling income. Your push-button phone gives you 24-hour-a-day access to this recorded information. Telephone numbers can be found in your tax packet or your telephone directory, or call 1–800–829–4477.

EXHIBIT 4–8

Tax-Planner Calendar

January	February	March
• Establish a recordkeeping system for your tax information • If you expect a refund, file your tax return for the previous year • Make your final estimated quarterly payment for the previous year for income not covered by withholding	• Check to make sure you received W-2 and 1099 forms from all organizations from which you had income during the previous year; these should have been received by January 31; if not, contact the organization	• Organize your records and tax information in preparation for filing your tax return; if you expect a refund, file as soon as possible

April	May	June
• April 15 is the deadline for filing your federal tax return; if it falls on a weekend, you have until the next business day (usually Monday) • If necessary file for an automatic extension for filing your tax forms	• Review your tax return to determine whether any changes in withholding, exemptions, or marital status have not been reported to your employer	• The second installment for estimated tax is due June 15 for income not covered by withholding

July	August	September
• With the year half over, consider or implement plans for a personal retirement program such as an IRA or a Keogh	• Tax returns are due August 15 for those who received the automatic four-month extension	• The third installment for estimated tax is due September 15 for income not covered by withholding

October	November	December
• Determine the tax benefits of selling certain investments by year-end • Prepare a preliminary tax form to determine the most advantageous filing status	• Make any last-minute changes in withholding by your employer to avoid penalties for too little withholding • Determine if you qualify for an IRA; if so, consider opening one	• Determine if it would be to your advantage to make payments for next year before December 31 of the current year • Decide if you can defer income for the current year until the following year

NOTE: Children born before the end of the year give you a full-year exemption, so plan accordingly!

3. *Phone hot line.* You can obtain information about specific problems through an IRS-staffed phone line. The appropriate telephone number is listed in your local telephone directory, or call 1–800–829–1040. You are not asked to give your name when you use this service, so your questions are anonymous.

4. *Walk-in service.* You can visit your local or district IRS office to obtain assistance with your taxes. More than 500 of these facilities are available to taxpayers. Be aware, however, that information IRS employees provide is not always reliable.

Various studies in recent years have reported incorrect answers over 30 percent of the time. You can be held liable for taxes owed even if you based your calculations on information provided by IRS employees.

5. *CD-ROM.* The Internal Revenue Service also sells a CD-ROM with over 2,000 tax forms and publications.

In addition, the IRS has videos, free speakers for community groups, and teaching materials for schools to assist taxpayers.

Other Publications   Each year, several tax guides are published and offered for sale. These publications include *J. K. Lasser's Your Income Tax* and *Consumer Reports Books Guide to Income Tax Preparation.* You can purchase them at bookstores, drugstores, or supermarkets or use them at your library.

The Internet   As with other personal finance topics, extensive information may be found on the Internet, especially the World Wide Web. The Internal Revenue Service (www.irs.ustreas.gov) is a good starting point. Personal finance magazines, such as *Kiplinger's Personal Finance Magazine* and *Money,* as well as other financial planning information services, offer a variety of tax information, such as Life Net (www.lifenet. com) and The Tax Prophet (www.taxprophet.com/indexshtml). In addition, the Web sites of companies that sell tax software and tax-related organizations can be useful. Conducting a Web search can help you locate current information on a specific tax topic.

Computerized Tax Preparation and Electronic Filing

More and more taxpayers are using personal computers for tax recordkeeping and tax form preparation. A spreadsheet program can be very helpful in maintaining and updating tax data on various income and expense categories. Software packages such as *TaxCut, Personal Tax Edge,* and *TurboTax* allow you to complete and print finished versions of needed tax forms and schedules. See Appendix B for additional information.

> **DID YOU KNOW?**
>
> In 1996, the average cost (including postage, copies, books, software, and phone) for filing a federal tax return was $79.40. In addition, Americans spend 5.4 billion hours each year preparing federal tax forms. Between 1984 and 1994, the number of federal tax forms increased by 100.

The IRS has been expanding its acceptance of computer-readable tax forms. Electronic filing of federal tax returns now exceeds 15 million returns annually. With electronic filing, taxpayers have received their refunds within three weeks. The additional cost tax preparers charge for this service is usually between $15 and $70. The IRS also allows filing of tax returns through online computer services. Filing electronically doesn't eliminate all paperwork. You still have to mail in your W-2 forms and a check if you owe taxes.

Telefile is a file-by-phone system that has been tested in various geographic areas. It allows taxpayers to call a toll-free number, using a touch-tone phone, to file their tax returns. A follow-up written or voice "signature" confirmation is required.

The IRS is also planning to use computerized *expert systems* to answer tax inquiries. Through a series of on-screen questions, the IRS clerk can first help taxpayers identify their problems and then provide the solutions. This method is intended to reduce the proportion of incorrectly answered inquiries.

Tax Preparation Services

Over 40 million U.S. taxpayers pay someone to do their income taxes. The fee for this service can range from $40 at a tax preparation service for a simple return to more than $2,000 to a certified public accountant for a complicated return.

JONATHAN HOENIG SPEAKS
The Tax Man (or Woman) Cometh

Any attempt to calculate your investment return must include the least exciting, most annoying financial subject. Taxes. Even the word makes me cringe!

The government *will* get their share of your money—no exceptions. Smart tax planning helps pay less tax legally. The federal government isn't fooling around: Those who avoid paying taxes get socked with high-priced penalties or jail time. Pay your taxes on time. Horizontal stripes just aren't "in" these days.

Toward the first of the year, you will begin to receive a series of statements from the jobs at which you have worked or financial institutions where you hold accounts. This includes brokerage firms, banks, mutual funds, and other intermediaries. Scrounge up the receipts from any charitable donations you've made (canceled checks are OK) and proof of any work-related expenses you plan on writing off. Keep these materials together: Lost forms waste time and money!

Form 1040 has several sections to be aware of. "Filing Status" determines the filing category in which you belong. Married? Single? Each category has a particular schedule of taxes. Generally, your income should be added up, including any losses. Figure your taxable income, factor in additional credits or taxes, and write a check. *You've just paid your taxes!*

For those with a home business, complicated returns, or sketchy paperwork, some professional tax guidance is highly recommended—*and worth it!* Spending some bucks on a registered CPA might seem daunting, but will ensure that your return is filed accurately and rapidly.

Many people like doing their own taxes. This experience can help you improve your understanding of your financial situation. The IRS claims that anyone with an eighth-grade education can fill out a 1040 form. The average person takes a little more than two hours to complete Form 1040, compared with 57 minutes for Form 1040A and 22 minutes for the one-page 1040EZ. Doing your own taxes, however, can be complicated, particularly if you have sources of income other than salary. The sources available for professional tax assistance include the following:

- Tax services range from local, one-person operations to national firms with thousands of offices, such as H&R Block.
- Enrolled agents—government-approved tax experts—prepare returns and provide tax advice. You may contact the National Association of Enrolled Agents at 1–800–424–4339 for information about enrolled agents in your area.
- Many accountants offer tax assistance along with their other business services. A certified public accountant (CPA) with special training in taxes can help you with tax planning and the preparation of your annual return.
- Attorneys usually do not complete tax returns; however, you can use an attorney's services when you are involved in a tax-related transaction or when you have a difference of opinion with the IRS.

Even if you hire a professional tax preparer, you are responsible for supplying accurate and complete information. Hiring a tax preparer will not guarantee that you pay the *correct* amount. A study by *Money* magazine of 41 tax preparers reported fees ranging from $375 to $3,600, with taxes due ranging from $31,846 to $74,450 for the same fictional family. If

EXHIBIT 4–9

How to Avoid Common Filing Errors

- Organize all tax-related information for easy access.
- Follow instructions carefully. Many people deduct total medical and dental expenses rather than the amount of these expenses that exceeds 7.5 percent of adjusted gross income.
- Use the proper tax rate schedule or tax table column.
- Be sure to claim the correct number of exemptions and the correct amounts of standard deductions.
- Consider the alternative minimum tax that may apply to your situation. Be sure to pay self-employment tax and tax on early IRA withdrawals.
- Check your arithmetic several times.
- Sign your return (both spouses must sign a joint return), or the IRS won't process it.
- Be sure to include the correct Social Security number(s) and to record amounts on the correct lines.
- Attach necessary documentation such as your W-2 forms and required supporting schedules.
- Put your Social Security number, the tax year, and a daytime telephone number on your check—and be sure to sign the check!
- Make the check payable to *Internal Revenue Service*, not *IRS* (which could be altered to *MRS* and someone's name).
- Keep a photocopy of your return.
- Put the proper postage on your mailing envelope.
- Finally, check everything again—and file on time! Care taken when you file your income tax can result in "many happy returns."

Sheet 21

you owe more tax because your return contains errors or you have made entries that are not allowed, it is your responsibility to pay that additional tax, plus any interest and penalties.

Beware of tax preparers and other businesses that offer your refund in advance. These "refund anticipation loans" frequently charge very high interest rates for this type of consumer credit. A study by the Consumer Protection Board in New York State revealed interest rates as high as 520 percent (on an annualized basis).

What If Your Return Is Audited?

tax audit

The Internal Revenue Service reviews all returns to make sure they have been completed properly. Computers check the arithmetic. If you have made an error, your tax is automatically refigured and you will receive either a bill or a refund. If you have made an entry that is not allowed, you will be notified by mail. In contrast, a **tax audit** is a detailed examination of your tax return by the IRS. In most audits, the IRS requests more information to support the entries on your tax return. You therefore must keep accurate records to support your return. Keep receipts, canceled checks, and other evidence to prove amounts that you claim. Avoiding common filing mistakes (see Exhibit 4–9) helps minimize your chances of an audit.

Who Gets Audited?   A little over 1 percent of all tax filers—about 1.1 million people—are audited each year. While the IRS does not reveal its basis for selecting the returns that it audits, several indicators are evident. People who claim large or unusual deductions increase their chances of an audit.

Tax advisers suggest including a brief explanation or a copy of receipts for deductions that may be questioned. Individuals with high incomes who have had large losses due to tax shelters or partnerships, or who have had their tax returns questioned in the past, may also be targeted for an audit.

Types of Audits   The simplest and most common type of audit is the *correspondence audit*. This mail inquiry requires you to clarify or document minor questions about your tax return. You usually have 30 days to provide the requested information, and you respond by mail.

The *office audit* requires that you visit an IRS office to clarify some aspect of your tax return. This type of audit usually takes an hour or two.

The *field audit* is more complex. An IRS agent visits you at your home, your place of business, or the office of your accountant so that you will have access to records. A field audit may be done to verify whether an individual has an office in the home as claimed.

Your Audit Rights   When you receive an audit notice, you have the right to request more time to prepare. Also, you can ask the IRS for clarification of items being questioned. When you are audited, the following suggestions can be helpful:

- Decide whether you will bring your tax preparer, accountant, or lawyer.
- Be on time for your appointment; bring only relevant documents.
- Present substantiating records and receipts in a logical, calm, and confident manner; maintain a positive attitude that avoids hostility.
- Make sure the information you present is consistent with the tax law.
- Keep your answers aimed at the auditor's questions. Answer questions clearly and completely. Be as brief as possible; you can never tell an auditor too little.

People under stress tend to talk too much. IRS auditors are trained to create silence and listen in case the taxpayer blurts out damaging information. The five best responses to questions during the audit are: "Yes," "No," "I don't recall," "I'll have to check on that," and "What specific items do you want to see?"

If you disagree with the results of the audit, you may request a conference at the Regional Appeals Office. Although most differences of opinion are settled at this stage, some taxpayers take their cases further. A person may go to the U.S. tax court, the U.S. claims court, or the U.S. district court. Some tax disputes have gone to the U.S. Supreme Court.

C O N C E P T   C H E C K   4–4

1. What are the main sources available to help people prepare their taxes?
2. What appeal process do taxpayers have if they disagree with an audit decision of the IRS?

TAX-PLANNING STRATEGIES

L.O.5 Select appropriate tax strategies for different financial and personal situations.

tax avoidance

tax evasion

Most people want to pay their fair share of taxes—no more, no less. They do this by practicing **tax avoidance,** the use of legitimate methods to reduce one's taxes. In contrast, **tax evasion** is the use of illegal actions to reduce one's taxes. To minimize taxes owed, the following guidelines can be helpful:

- If you expect to have the *same* or a *lower* tax rate next year, *accelerate deductions* into the current year. Pay real estate property taxes or make your January mortgage payment in December. Make charitable donations by December 31.

EXHIBIT 4–10	**Special Tax Situations**
Business in your home	You may deduct any ordinary and necessary expenses related to starting and maintaining your business, including a portion of your rent or mortgage if that portion of your home is used exclusively for business. It must be your principal place of business. (Individuals who are employed elsewhere and claim an office at home are likely to be challenged by the IRS on this deduction.)
Divorced persons	Child support payments have no tax consequences. They are neither deductible by the payer nor included in the recipient's income. Alimony is tax deductible by the payer and must be included as income by the recipient. Exemptions for children are generally claimed by the parent who has custody for a longer period during the tax year.
Single parents	A single parent may claim "head of household" filing status, which has greater advantages than "single" status. Working parents may qualify for a child care tax credit. Low-income families may qualify for the earned-income credit (EIC).
Retired persons	Individuals over age 59½ may withdraw tax-deferred funds from a retirement plan without penalty. Of course, these funds must be reported as ordinary income. As of 1997, retirees with total incomes, including Social Security, exceeding $44,000 (couples) and $34,000 (others) pay income tax on up to 85 percent of their Social Security benefits. Those with incomes between $25,000 and $34,000 (singles) or $32,000 and $44,000 (couples) continue to be taxed on up to 50 percent of their benefits.

NOTE: Individual circumstances and changes in the tax laws can affect these examples.

- If you expect to have a *lower* or the *same* tax rate next year, *delay the receipt of income* until next year. This means income will be taxed at a lower rate or at a later date.
- If you expect to have a *higher* tax rate next year, consider *delaying deductions,* since they will have a greater benefit. A $1,000 deduction at 28 percent lowers your taxes $280; at 31 percent, your taxes are lowered $310.
- If you expect to have a *higher* tax rate next year, *accelerate the receipt of income* to have it taxed at the current lower rate.

As Exhibit 4–10 shows, people in different life situations can take advantage of various tax rules. When considering financial decisions in relation to your taxes, remember that purchasing, investing, and retirement planning are the areas most heavily affected by tax laws.

Consumer Purchasing

The buying decisions most directly affected by taxes are the purchase of a residence, the use of credit, and job-related expenses.

Place of Residence   Owning a home is one of the best tax shelters available to most people. Both real estate property taxes and interest on the mortgage are deductible (as itemized deductions) and thus reduce your taxable income. While renting may seem less expensive than owning, the after-tax cost of owning a home often makes owning financially advantageous. Chapter 9 presents specific calculations for comparing renting and buying.

Consumer Debt   Until 1990, some or all of the interest paid on credit cards, charge accounts, and personal loans was deductible for federal income tax purposes. This is no longer true. Current tax laws, however, still leave homeowners borrowing power for

> ### DID YOU KNOW?
>
> Each year, over 90,000 taxpayers do not receive their refunds. The undeliverable checks total over $60 million, an average of more than $600 per check. These refund checks were returned by the post office because they were unable to deliver them. Taxpayers due a refund may contact the IRS at 1–800–829–1040.

consumer purchases. You can deduct interest on loans (of up to $100,000) secured by your primary or secondary home up to the actual dollar amount you have invested in it—the difference between the market value of the home and the amount you owe on it. These *home equity loans,* which are *second mortgages,* are discussed in greater detail in Chapters 6 and 9. Current tax laws allow you to use that line of credit to buy a car, consolidate credit card or other debts, or finance other personal expenses. Some states place restrictions on home equity loans.

As of 1998, a person may claim a deduction for interest expense on qualified education loans. This deduction is allowed only for interest paid during the first 60 months in which interest payments are required.

Job-Related Expenses   As previously mentioned, certain work expenses, such as union dues, some travel and education costs, and business tools, may be included as itemized deductions. Job search expenses are also deductible if you incur them when seeking employment in your current occupational category. Such expenses may include transportation to interviews, résumé preparation and duplication, and employment agency or career counseling fees. Remember, only the portion of these expenses that exceeds 2 percent of adjusted gross income is deductible. Expenses related to finding your first job or obtaining work in a different field are not deductible.

Investment Decisions

A major area of tax planning involves the wide variety of decisions that relate to investing.

Tax-Exempt Investments   Interest income from municipal bonds, which are issued by state and local governments, and other tax-exempt investments is not subject to federal income taxes. While municipal bonds have lower interest rates than other investments, the *after-tax* income may be higher. For example, if you are in the 28 percent tax bracket, earning $100 of tax-exempt income would be worth more to you than earning $125 in taxable investment income. The $125 would have an after-tax value of $90: $125 less $35 (28 percent of $125) for taxes.

Tax-Deferred Investments   Although, from a tax standpoint, tax-deferred investments, whose income will be taxed at a later date, are less beneficial than tax-exempt investments, they also have financial advantages. According to the basic opportunity cost concept, paying a dollar in the future instead of today gives you the opportunity to invest (or spend) it now. Examples of tax-deferred investments include

- *Tax-deferred annuities,* usually issued by insurance companies. These investments are discussed in Chapter 20.
- *Series EE U.S. Treasury bonds.* Interest on these bonds is exempt from federal income tax if it is used to pay tuition at a college, university, or qualified technical school. Chapter 5 gives further details.
- *Retirement plans* such as IRA, Keogh, or 401(k) plans. The next section discusses the tax implications of these plans.

capital gains

Capital gains, profits from the sale of a capital asset such as stocks, bonds, or real estate, are also tax deferred; you do not have to pay the tax on these profits until the asset is sold. As of 1997, *long-term* capital gains (on investments held more than 18 months) are taxed at 20 percent. Certain assets, however, such as art, antiques, stamps, and other

FINANCIAL PLANNING CALCULATIONS

SHORT-TERM AND LONG-TERM CAPITAL GAINS

You will pay a lower tax rate on the profits from stocks and other investments if you hold the asset for more than 18 months. As of 1997, a taxpayer in the 28 percent tax bracket would pay $280 in taxes on a $1,000 short-term capital gain (assets held for less than 18 months). However, that same taxpayer would only pay $200 on the $1,000 (a 20 percent capital gains tax) if the investment was held for more than 18 months.

	Short-Term Capital Gain (assets held less than 18 months)	Long-Term Capital Gain (assets held 18 months or more)
Capital gain	$1,000	$1,000
Capital gains tax rate	28%	20%
Capital gains tax	$280	$200
Tax savings		$80

collectibles, are still taxed at the pre-1997 capital gains rate—28 percent. Starting in 2001, the capital gains tax rate on assets held for more than five years will be 18 percent.

Short-term capital gains (on investments held for less than 18 months) are taxed as ordinary income (see the Financial Planning Calculations box). Taxpayers in the 15 percent tax bracket have lower capital gains tax rates for both short-term and long-term investments.

The sale of an investment for less than its purchase price is, of course, a *capital loss.* Capital losses can be used to offset capital gains and up to $3,000 of ordinary income. Unused capital losses may be carried forward into future years to offset capital gains or ordinary income up to $3,000 per year.

Capital gains of $500,000 on the sale of a home may be excluded by a couple filing a joint return ($250,000 for singles). This exclusion is allowed each time a taxpayer sells or exchanges a principal residence—however, only once every two years.

Self-Employment   Owning your own business has certain tax advantages. Self-employed persons may deduct expenses such as health and life insurance as business costs. However, business owners have to pay self-employment tax (Social Security) in addition to the regular tax rate.

Children's Investments   In past years, parents made investments on their children's behalf and listed the children as owners. This process, known as *income shifting,* attempted to reduce the taxable income of parents by shifting the ownership of investments to children in lower tax brackets. A child under 14 with investment income of more than $1,300 is taxed at the parent's top rate. For investment income under $1,200, the child receives a deduction of $650 and the next $650 is taxed at his or her own rate, which is probably lower than the parent's rate. This income-shifting restriction does not apply to children 14 and older, so it is possible to take advantage of income shifting with them.

Retirement Plans

A major tax strategy of benefit to working people is the use of tax-deferred retirement plans such as individual retirement accounts (IRAs), Keogh plans, and 401(k) plans.

Deductible IRA   When IRAs were first established, every working person was allowed to deduct up to $2,000 per year for IRA contributions. The contributions to and earnings from these accounts are not taxed until they are withdrawn. Today a regular IRA deduction is available only to people who do not participate in employer-sponsored retirement plans and have an adjusted gross income under a certain amount. In 1998, this amount was $40,000 for single taxpayers and $60,000 for jointly filing taxpayers. These amounts are scheduled to increase over the next 10 years.

In general, amounts withdrawn from deductible IRAs are included in gross income. An additional 10 percent penalty is usually imposed on withdrawals made before age 59½ unless the withdrawn funds are on account of death or disability, for medical expenses, or for qualified higher education expenses.

Roth IRA   In 1997, Congress created the Roth IRA (also called the IRA Plus). While the $2,000 annual contribution to this plan is not tax deductible, the earnings on the account are tax free after five years. The funds from the Roth IRA may be withdrawn before age 59½ if the account owner is disabled, for educational expenses, or for the purchase of a first home. Like the regular IRA, the Roth IRA is limited to people with an adjusted gross income under a certain amount.

Deductible IRAs provide tax relief up front as contributions reduce current taxes. However, taxes must be paid when the withdrawals are made from the deductible IRA. In contrast, the Roth IRA does not have immediate benefits, but the investment grows in value on a tax-free basis. Withdrawals from the Roth IRA are exempt from federal and state taxes.

Education IRA   Also created in 1997, the Education IRA is designed to assist parents in saving for the college education of their children. Once again, the annual contribution (limited to $500) is not tax deductible and is limited to taxpayers with an adjusted gross income under a certain amount. However, as with the Roth IRA, the earnings accumulate tax free.

Keogh Plan   If you are self-employed and own your own business, you can establish a Keogh plan. This retirement plan, also called an HR10 plan, may combine a profit-sharing plan and a pension plan of other investments purchased by the employee. In general, with a Keogh, people may contribute 25 percent of their annual income, up to a maximum of $30,000, to this tax-deferred retirement plan.

401(k) Plan   The part of the tax code called 401(k) authorizes a tax-deferred retirement plan sponsored by an employer. This plan allows you to contribute a greater tax-deferred amount (a maximum of $10,000 for 1998) than you can contribute to an IRA. However, most companies set a limit on your contribution, such as 15 percent of your salary. Many employers provide a matching contribution in their 401(k) plans. For example, a company may contribute 50 cents for each $1 contributed by an employee. This results in an immediate 50 percent return on your investment.

Tax planners advise people to contribute as much as possible to a Keogh or 401(k) plan since (1) the increased value of the investment accumulates on a tax-free basis until the funds are withdrawn and (2) contributions reduce your adjusted gross income for computing your current tax liability. Chapter 18 discusses these retirement plans in greater detail.

Changing Tax Strategies

Someone once said that "death and taxes are the only certainties of life." Changing tax laws seem to be another certainty. Each year, the IRS modifies the tax form and filing procedures. In addition, Congress frequently passes legislation that changes the tax code.

Sheet 22

These changes require that you regularly determine how to take best advantage of the tax laws for personal financial planning. Finally, carefully consider changes in your personal situation and your income level. You should carefully monitor your personal tax strategies to best serve both your daily living needs and your long-term financial goals.

CONCEPT CHECK 4–5

1. How does tax avoidance differ from tax evasion?
2. What common tax-saving methods are available to most individuals and households?

SUMMARY

L.O.1   Describe the importance of taxes for personal financial planning.

Tax planning can influence spending, saving, borrowing, and investing decisions. A knowledge of tax laws and maintenance of accurate tax records allow you to take advantage of appropriate tax benefits. An awareness of income taxes, sales taxes, excise taxes, property taxes, estate taxes, inheritance taxes, gift taxes, and Social Security taxes is vital for successful financial planning.

L.O.2   Calculate taxable income and the amount owed for federal income tax.

Taxable income is determined by subtracting adjustments to income, deductions, and allowances for exemptions from gross income. Your total tax liability is based on the published tax tables or tax schedules, less any tax credits.

L.O.3   Prepare a federal income tax return.

The major sections of Form 1040 require you to calculate (1) your filing status, (2) exemptions, (3) income from all sources, (4) adjustments to your income, (5) standard deduction or itemized deductions, (6) tax credits for which you qualify, (7) other taxes you owe, (8) amounts you have withheld or paid in advance, and (9) your refund or the additional amount you owe.

L.O.4   Identify tax assistance sources.

The main sources of tax assistance are IRS services and publications, other publications, the Internet, computer software, and professional tax preparers such as commercial tax services, enrolled agents, accountants, and attorneys.

L.O.5   Select appropriate tax strategies for different financial and personal situations.

You may reduce your tax burden through careful planning and making financial decisions related to consumer purchasing, the use of debt, investments, and retirement planning.

GLOSSARY

adjusted gross income (AGI)   Gross income reduced by certain adjustments, such as contributions to an individual retirement account (IRA) and alimony payments.   (p. 92)

average tax rate   Total tax due divided by taxable income.   (p. 96)

capital gains   Profits from the sale of a capital asset such as stocks, bonds, or real estate.   (p. 112)

earned income   Money received for personal effort, such as wages, salary, commission, fees, tips, or bonuses.   (p. 91)

estate tax   A tax imposed on the value of a person's property at the time of his or her death.   (p. 90)

excise tax   A tax imposed on specific goods and services, such as gasoline, cigarettes, alcoholic beverages, tires, and air travel.   (p. 90)

exclusion   An amount not included in gross income. (p. 91)

exemption   A deduction from adjusted gross income for yourself, your spouse, and qualified dependents.   (p. 94)

inheritance tax   A tax levied on the value of property bequeathed by a deceased person.   (p. 90)

investment income   Money received in the form of dividends interest, or rent from investments. Also called *portfolio income.*   (p. 91)

itemized deductions   Expenses that can be deducted from adjusted gross income, such as medical expenses, real estate property taxes, home mortgage interest, charitable contributions, casualty losses, and certain work-related expenses. (p. 93)

marginal tax rate   The rate used to calculate tax on the last (and next) dollar of taxable income.   (p. 96)

passive income   Income resulting from business activities in which you do not actively participate.   (p. 91)

standard deduction   A set amount on which no taxes are paid.   (p. 93)

taxable income   The net amount of income, after allowable deductions, on which income tax is computed.   (p. 91)

tax audit   A detailed examination of your tax return by the Internal Revenue Service.   (p. 109)

tax avoidance   The use of legitimate methods to reduce one's taxes.   (p. 110)

tax credit   An amount subtracted directly from the amount of taxes owed.   (p. 96)

tax deduction   An amount subtracted from adjusted gross income to arrive at taxable income.   (p. 93)

tax-deferred income   Income that will be taxed at a later date.   (p. 91)

tax evasion   The use of illegal actions to reduce one's taxes.   (p. 110)

tax-exempt income   Income that is not subject to tax. (p. 91)

tax shelter   An investment that provides immediate tax benefits and a reasonable expectation of a future financial return.   (p. 93)

R E V I E W   Q U E S T I O N S

1. How might careful tax planning help lower a person's tax burden?   (L.O.1)
2. What types of income could help reduce a person's taxable income?   (L.O.2)
3. Why should a person reconsider his or her filing status each year?   (L.O.3)
4. What actions can help a person reduce the chances of an IRS audit?   (L.O.4)
5. How can taxes affect a person's investment decisions?   (L.O.5)

F I N A N C I A L   P L A N N I N G   P R O B L E M S

1. *Computing Taxable Income.* Thomas Franklin arrived at the following tax information:

   Gross salary, $41,780
   Interest earnings, $225
   Dividend income, $80
   One personal exemption, $2,650
   Itemized deductions, $3,890
   Adjustments to income, $1,150

   What amount would Thomas report as taxable income? (L.O.1)

2. *Determining Tax Deductions.* If Lola Harper had the following itemized deductions, should she use Schedule A or the standard deduction? The standard deduction for her tax situation is $6,050.   (L.O.2)

   Donations to church and other charities, $1,980
   Medical and dental expenses exceeding 7.5 percent of adjusted gross income, $430
   State income tax, $690
   Job-related expenses exceeding 2 percent of adjusted gross income, $1,610

3. *Calculating Average Tax Rate.* What would be the average tax rate for a person who paid taxes of $4,864.14 on a taxable income of $39,870?   (L.O.2)

4. *Determining a Refund or Taxes Owed.* Based on the following data, would Ann and Carl Wilton receive a refund or owe additional taxes?   (L.O.2)

   Adjusted gross income, $43,190
   Itemized deductions, $11,420

   Child care tax credit, $80
   Federal income tax withheld, $6,784
   Amount for personal exemptions, $7,950
   Tax rate on taxable income, 15 percent

5. *Selecting Federal Tax Forms.* Which 1040 form should each of the following individuals use?   (L.O.3)
   a. A high school student with an after-school job and interest earnings of $480 from savings accounts.
   b. A college student who, due to ownership of property, is able to itemize deductions rather than take the standard deduction.
   c. A young, entry-level worker with no dependents and income only from salary.

6. *Using Federal Tax Tables.* Using the tax table in Exhibit 4–7, determine the amount of taxes for the following situations:
   a. A head of household with taxable income of $26,210
   b. A single person with taxable income of $26,888
   c. A married person filing a separate return with taxable income of $26,272

7. *Comparing Taxes on Investments.* Would you prefer a fully taxable investment earning 10.7 percent or a tax-exempt investment earning 8.1 percent? Why?   (L.O.5)

8. *Future Value of a Tax Savings.* On December 30, you decide to make a $1,000 charitable donation. If you are in the 28 percent tax bracket, how much will you save in taxes for the current year? If you deposit that tax savings in a savings account for the next five years at 8 percent, what will be the future value of that account?   (L.O.5)

PROJECTS AND APPLICATION EXERCISES

1. *Searching the Internet for Tax Information.* Using the World Wide Web (such as *Kiplinger's Personal Finance* magazine at www.kiplinger.com or *Money* magazine at www.money.com) or library resources, obtain information about the tax implications of various financial planning decisions. (L.O.1)

2. *Researching Tax-Exempt Income.* Using library resources or the World Wide Web, determine the types of income that are exempt from federal income tax. (L.O.2)

3. *Planning Your Tax Payment.* Survey several people about whether they get a federal tax refund or owe taxes each year. Obtain information about the following: *(a)* Do they usually get a refund or have to pay when they file their federal tax return? *(b)* Is their situation (refund or payment) planned? *(c)* What are the reasons they want to get a refund each year? *(d)* Are there situations where getting a refund may not be a wise financial decision? (L.O.2)

4. *Researching Current Tax Forms.* Obtain samples of current tax forms you would use to file your federal income tax return. These may be ordered by mail, obtained at a local IRS office or post office, or obtained on the Internet at www.irs.ustreas.gov. (L.O.4)

5. *Researching Tax Questions.* Use IRS publications and other reference materials to answer a specific tax question. Contact an IRS office to obtain an answer for the same question. What differences, if any, exist between the information sources? (L.O.4)

6. *Analyzing Tax Preparation Software.* Visit a retailer that sells tax preparation software, or visit the Web sites of software companies to determine the costs and features of programs you may use to prepare and file your federal income tax return. (L.O.4)

7. *Reducing Tax Errors.* Create a visual presentation (video or slide presentation) that demonstrates actions a person might take to reduce errors when filing a federal tax return. (L.O.4)

8. *Comparing Tax Services.* Using Sheet 21 in the *Personal Financial Planner,* obtain information from two different tax preparation companies about the services they offer and the costs of their services. (L.O.4)

9. *Determining Tax-Planning Activities.* Survey friends and relatives about their tax-planning strategies. You may use Sheet 22 from the *Personal Financial Planner* to obtain questions for your survey. (L.O.5)

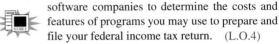

LIFE SITUATION CASE 4

A SINGLE FATHER'S TAX SITUATION

Ever since his wife's death, Eric Stanford has faced difficult personal and financial circumstances. His job provides him with a fairly good income but keeps him away from his daughters, ages 8 and 10, nearly 20 days a month. This requires him to use in-home child care services that consume a large portion of his income. Since the Stanfords live in a small apartment, this arrangement has been very inconvenient.

Due to the costs of caring for his children, Eric has only a minimal amount withheld from his salary for federal income taxes. This makes more money available during the year, but for the last few years he has had to make large payments in April—another financial burden.

Although Eric has created an investment fund for his daughters' college education and for his retirement, he has not sought to select investments that offer tax benefits. Overall, he needs to look at several aspects of his tax-planning activities to find strategies that will best serve his current and future financial needs.

Eric has assembled the following information for the current tax year:

Earnings from wages, $42,590
Interest earned on savings, $125

IRA deduction, $2,000
Checking account interest, $65
Three exemptions at $2,650 each
Current standard deduction for filing status, $6,050
Amount withheld for federal income tax, $3,178
Tax credit for child care, $400
Filing status: head of household

QUESTIONS

1. What are Eric's major financial concerns in his current situation?

2. In what ways might Eric improve his tax-planning efforts?

3. Is Eric typical of many people in our society with regard to tax planning? Why or why not?

4. What additional actions might Eric investigate with regard to taxes and personal financial planning?

5. Calculate the following
   a. What is Eric's taxable income? (Refer to Exhibit 4–1, page 92.)
   b. What is his total tax liability? (Use Exhibit 4–7, page 105.) What is his average tax rate?
   c. Based on his withholding, will Eric receive a refund or owe additional tax? What is the amount?

USING THE INTERNET TO CREATE A PERSONAL FINANCIAL PLAN 4

TAX PLANNING ACTIVITIES

Taxes are a fact of financial planning. However, various actions can be taken to reduce the time and money that goes toward taxes.

Web Sites for Tax Planning

- Access to federal tax forms, IRS regulations, and other tax information at **www.irs.ustreas.gov**
- Tax planning suggestions from Ernst & Young at **www.ey.com/us/tax** and H&R Block at **www.hrblock.com**
- Federal forms and tax tips at **www.1040.com** and **www.taxweb.com**
- Prepare your tax form and file online at **www.taxsoft.com**
- Software information for TurboTax at **www.intuit.com/turbotax**
- State income tax information and forms at **www.tax-admin.org, www.best.com/~ftmexpat/html/taxsites.statelaw.html,** and **homel.gte.net/brcpa/statelink.htm**

(Note: Addresses and content of Web sites change, and new sites are created daily. Use the search engines discussed in Appendix B to update and locate Web sites for your current financial planning needs.)

PFP SHEETS: 20–22

Short-Term Financial Planning Activities

1. Develop a system for filing and storing various tax records related to income, deductible expenses, and current tax forms (see Exhibit 4–2).
2. Using the IRS and other Web sites, identify recent changes in tax laws that may affect your financial planning decisions.
3. Using current IRS tax forms and tax tables, estimate your tax liability for the current year   (see PFP Sheet 20).
4. Compare the cost of tax preparation services   (see PFP Sheet 21).

Long-Term Financial Planning Activities

1. Identify saving and investing decisions that would minimize future income taxes.
2. Develop a plan for actions to be taken related to your current and future tax situation   (see PFP Sheet 22).

CONTINUOUS CASE FOR PART I

GETTING STARTED: PLANNING FOR THE FUTURE

Life Situation
Single, age 22; starting a career; no dependents

Financial Goals
- Evaluate current financial situation
- Establish a personal financial plan
- Develop a budgeting system for
  spending and savings

Financial Data	
Monthly income	$2,400
Living expenses	1,980
Assets	6,200
Liabilities	1,270

While in college, Pam Jenkins worked part time and was never concerned about long-term financial planning. Rather than creating a budget, she used her checkbook and savings account (which usually had a very low balance) to handle her financial needs.

After completing college, Pam began her career as a sales representative for a clothing manufacturer located in California. After one year, her assets consist of a 1992 Chevrolet, a television set, a stereo, and some clothing and other personal belongs, with a total value of $6,200.

Since a portion of her income is based on commissions, her monthly income varies from one month to the next. This situation has made it difficult for Pam to establish a realistic budget. During lean months, she has had to resort to using her credit card to make ends meet. In fact, her credit card debt, $1,270, is her only liability at this time. Her only

other source of income is a large tax refund. In the past, she has always used tax refunds to finance major purchases (a vacation or furniture) or pay off credit card debt.

QUESTIONS
1. What financial decisions should Pam be thinking about at this point in her life?
2. What are some financial goals that Pam might want to accomplish within the next few years?
3. How should Pam budget for fluctuations in her income caused by commission earnings?
4. Assume Pam's federal tax refund is $1,100. Given her current situation, what should she do with the refund?
5. Based on her life situation, what type of tax planning should Pam consider?

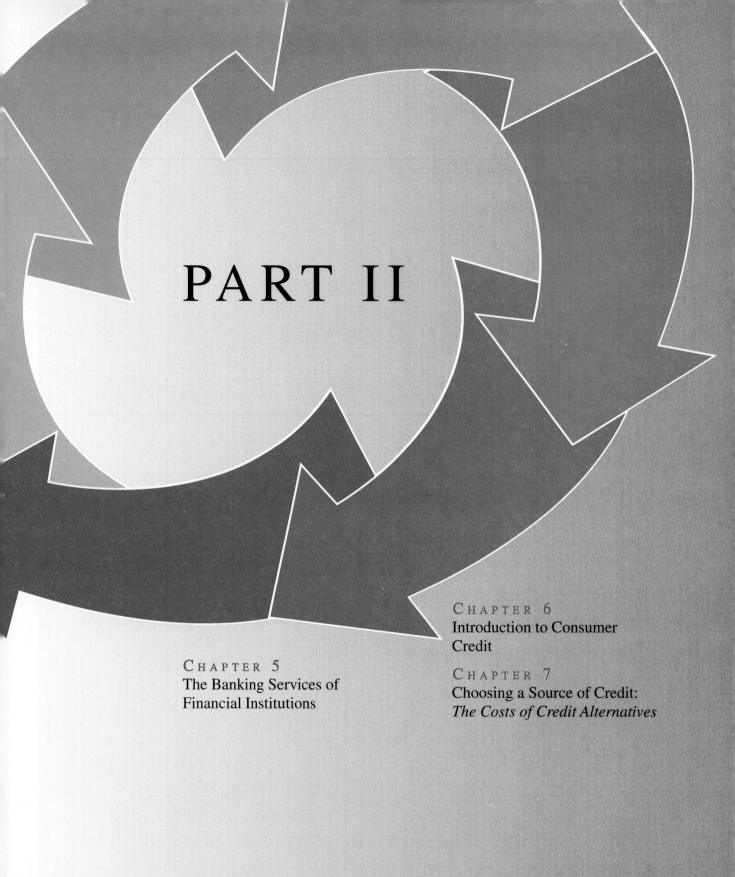

PART II

MANAGING YOUR PERSONAL FINANCES

"What I would really like to have is . . ." Each of us would probably complete that sentence in a slightly different way, as our personal values and goals reflect our beliefs and priorities. Whatever our choices may be, we achieve our financial goals by saving for future events. In Part II of *Personal Finance*, you will learn about a wide range of financial services that can help you plan, manage, and save appropriately.

Throughout your life, you will use the services of various financial institutions such as banks, credit unions, mortgage companies, and investment brokers. These organizations can assist you with your financial planning activities. However, you must be ready to evaluate their services in relation to costs and other factors. Chapter 5 will assist you in identifying factors that affect selection and use of financial services.

As you work toward achieving your personal financial goals, you are likely to use credit. Chapter 6 describes advantages and disadvantages of credit and helps you differentiate among various types of credit. Finally, Chapter 7 analyzes the major sources and costs of credit.

Knowledge about the types of credit, how to establish credit, how to avoid credit problems, and the costs associated with different credit sources can serve you in both the short-term and long-term financial planning processes.

CHAPTER 5

THE BANKING SERVICES
OF FINANCIAL INSTITUTIONS

OPENING CASE

PRESS ONE TO WITHDRAW CASH ...
PRESS TWO TO DEPOSIT CASH ...
PRESS THREE FOR HIGH BANKING FEES!

Carter Yuma was visiting the cash machine near his place of work for the third time that week. "Wow! Another cash withdrawal," commented his friend Edwin. "You must have tons of money in that checking account."

"Well, not really," Carter confessed. "I can use this ATM card to access either my checking or savings account."

"You mean after you've used up everything in your checking account, you start taking money out of your savings?" asked Edwin. "Doesn't this machine make it too easy for you to overspend?"

"It's just that I've been so busy at work the last few weeks, so I've been eating at restaurants a lot, and my cash is used up quickly," replied Carter.

A couple of weeks later, Carter received his bank statement, which included a couple of surprises.

"Oh no!" he exclaimed. "Withdrawing cash from my checking account made me fall below the minimum balance for the account, so they charged me $7.50. My 11 cash withdrawals resulted in more fees. And what's this? Another charge for an overdraft! All those cash withdrawals and fees really hit me hard! And my savings account is down to $78!"

QUESTIONS

1. What benefits and costs are associated with automatic teller machines?
2. How does the use of financial services like ATMs affect a person's overall financial plan?
3. What could Carter do to reduce his banking fees and manage his money more wisely?

LEARNING
OBJECTIVES

After studying this chapter, you will be able to

L.O.1 Analyze factors that affect selection and use of financial services.

L.O.2 Compare the types of financial institutions.

L.O.3 Compare the costs and benefits of various savings plans.

L.O.4 Identify the factors used to evaluate different savings plans.

L.O.5 Compare the costs and benefits of different types of checking accounts.

L.O.6 Describe the activities involved in using a checking account.

A STRATEGY FOR MANAGING CASH

L.O.1 Analyze factors that affect selection and use of financial services.

With over 11,000 banks, 2,000 savings and loan associations, and 12,000 credit unions, an extensive financial services market exists. These organizations provide a variety of services for your daily payment and savings needs. Today a trip to "the bank" may mean a visit to a credit union, an automatic teller machine in a shopping mall, or checking an account balance on the World Wide Web. In recent years, financial services have expanded. A bank is no longer the only source of checking accounts. Mortgages are available from a range of financial institutions.

While some financial decisions relate directly to goals, your daily activities require the use of financial services for various business transactions. Exhibit 5–1 provides an overview of financial services for managing cash flows and moving toward financial goals. In simplest terms, the growth of current savings can be achieved only by spending less than is taken in. As discussed in Chapter 3, you implement the savings principle "pay yourself first" by using various financial services.

Meeting Daily Money Needs

Buying groceries, paying the rent, and other routine spending activities require a cash management plan.

Financial Decision Trade-Off

Managing Cash on Hand   Cash, check, credit card, or automatic teller machine (ATM) card are the common payment choices for most people. While most people desire ease of payment, they must also consider fees and the potential for impulse buying and overspending. For example, in recent years ATM fees have risen from nothing to $1 or $2 per cash withdrawal and even higher charges for balance inquiries. If you make two $1 transaction fees a week and could invest your money at 5 percent, this convenience will cost you more than $570 over a five-year period.

EXHIBIT 5–1

Financial Services for Managing Cash Flow

Financial Services for Short-Term Needs
- Daily purchases
- Living expense payments
- Emergency fund

Cash Availability
- Check cashing
- Automatic teller machines
- Traveler's checks
- Foreign currency exchange

Savings
- Regular savings account
- Money market account

Checking
- Regular checking
- NOW accounts
- Electronic funds transfer
- Cashier's checks
- Money orders

Credit Cards
- All-purpose cards
- Cash advances

Financial Services for Long-Term Goals
- Major purchases
- Long-term financial security

Savings
- Certificates of deposit
- U.S. savings bonds

Credit Services
- Cash loans for autos, education, and other purposes
- Mortgages
- Home equity loans

Investment Services
- Individual retirement accounts (IRAs)
- Brokerage service
- Investment advice
- Mutual funds

Other Services
- Insurance (auto, home, life, health)
- Trust service
- Tax preparation
- Safe deposit boxes
- Budget counseling
- Estate planning

Whenever possible, cash not needed for current expenses should be deposited in various interest-earning accounts and investment plans. As you will see later in this chapter and in Chapters 13 through 17, savings bonds, money market accounts, mutual funds, and other investments may be used to achieve long-term financial goals.

Sources of Quick Cash　No matter how carefully you manage your money, there may be times when you will need more cash than you currently have available. To cope with that situation, you have two basic choices: liquidate savings or borrow. A savings account, certificate of deposit, mutual fund, or other investment may be raided when you need funds. Alternatively, a credit card cash advance or a personal loan may be appropriate. Remember, however, that both using savings and increasing borrowing reduce your net worth and your potential to achieve long-term financial security.

Types of Financial Services

Banks and other financial institutions offer services to meet a variety of needs. These services fall into four main categories.

time deposits

1. Savings　Safe storage of funds for future use is a basic need for everyone. These services, commonly referred to as **time deposits,** include money in savings accounts and certificates of deposit. Selection of a savings plan is commonly based on the interest rate earned, liquidity, safety, and convenience. These factors are discussed later in the chapter.

demand deposits

2. Payment Services　The ability to transfer money to other parties is a necessary part of daily business activities. Checking accounts and other payment methods, commonly called **demand deposits,** are also covered later in the chapter.

3. Borrowing   Most people use credit at some time during their lives. Credit alternatives range from short-term accounts, such as credit cards and cash loans, to long-term borrowing, such as a home mortgage. Chapters 6 and 7 discuss the types and costs of credit.

4. Other Financial Services   Insurance protection, investment for the future, real estate purchases, tax assistance, and financial planning are additional services you may need for successful financial management. With some financial plans, someone else manages your funds. A **trust** is a legal agreement that provides for the management and control of assets by one party for the benefit of another. This type of arrangement is most commonly created through a commercial bank or a lawyer. Parents who want to set aside certain funds for their children's education may use a trust. The investments and money in the trust are managed by a bank, and the necessary amounts go to the children for their educational expenses. Trusts are covered in more detail in Chapter 19.

trust

To simplify the maze of financial services and to attract customers, many financial institutions offer all-in-one accounts. An **asset management account,** also called a *cash management account,* provides a complete financial services program for a single fee. Investment brokers and other financial institutions offer this all-purpose account, which usually includes

asset management account

- A minimum balance of $5,000, $10,000, or as much as $25,000.
- A checking account and an ATM card.
- One or more all-purpose credit cards.
- A line of credit to obtain quick cash loans.
- Access to various types of investments such as stocks, bonds, mutual funds, commodities, and government securities; one account allows customers access to over 1,600 mutual funds.
- Use of online services for banking transactions and for buying and selling investments.
- A *sweep,* a feature in which cash that is not needed in the checking account or invested earns a money market interest rate.
- A single monthly statement that summarizes all transactions and types of accounts.

Sheet 23

Asset management accounts are offered by companies such as American Express, Charles Schwab, Merrill Lynch, and Prudential.

Electronic Banking Services

Years ago, people had to conduct banking activities only during set business hours, usually nine in the morning to three in the afternoon. Today things are different. Several million Americans bank or pay bills online, and 24-hour access is possible. Computerized financial services (see Exhibit 5–2) provide fast, convenient, and efficient systems for recording inflows and outflows of funds.

Direct Deposit   Each year, more and more workers are receiving only a pay stub on payday. Their earnings are being automatically deposited into their checking or savings accounts. This process can save time, effort, and money for all parties. Government agencies are also increasing use of direct deposits to reduce costs. State and federal government checks going to contractors, Social Security retirees, and welfare recipients are deposited electronically into their bank accounts.

Automatic Payments   Many utility companies, lenders, and other businesses allow customers to use an automatic payment system with bills paid through direct withdrawal

EXHIBIT 5–2

Electronic Banking Transactions

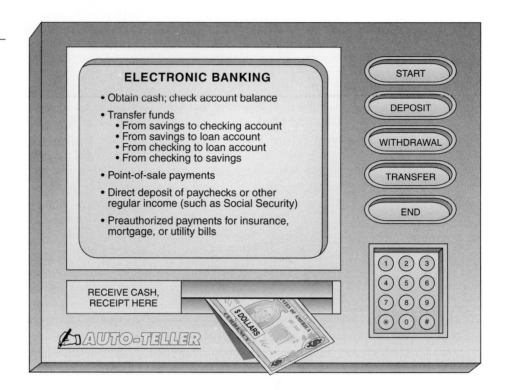

ELECTRONIC BANKING

- Obtain cash; check account balance
- Transfer funds
  - From savings to checking account
  - From savings to loan account
  - From checking to loan account
  - From checking to savings
- Point-of-sale payments
- Direct deposit of paychecks or other regular income (such as Social Security)
- Preauthorized payments for insurance, mortgage, or utility bills

START
DEPOSIT
WITHDRAWAL
TRANSFER
END

RECEIVE CASH, RECEIPT HERE

AUTO-TELLER

from a bank account. Experts recommend that you stagger your payments based on when paychecks are received. This allows you to pay bills in an orderly fashion while stabilizing your cash flow. Also, check bank statements regularly to make sure the correct amounts have been deducted from your account. A minor error can result in an overdrawn account and expensive fees.

automatic teller machine (ATM)

Automatic Teller Machines   An **automatic teller machine (ATM),** or simply *cash machine,* is a computer terminal that allows customers to conduct banking transactions. In addition, some ATMs sell bus passes, postage stamps, gift certificates, and mutual funds.

With more than 120,000 cash machines, most people are aware of ATM convenience. In addition to cash machines at banks, malls, and movie theaters, temporary ATMs are placed at sporting events, fairs, and community events.

debit card

A **debit card** or *cash card,* activates ATM transactions and is linked to a bank account. A debit card is in contrast to a *credit card,* since you are spending existing funds rather than borrowing additional money. Using a debit card, along with your personal identification number (PIN), is similar to writing a check with the amount of the transaction (cash withdrawal or purchase) deducted from your bank account.

ATM Fees   ATM convenience can be expensive. As the opening case points out, a person who uses an ATM several times a week, like Carter Yuma, can incur service charges of several hundred dollars a year. Surveys reveal that in casinos, the surcharges often add up to $3 to $5 per transaction. An ATM transaction on a cruise ship can cost $9 or more.

Several states, along with Congress, have enacted or are considering legislation to limit ATM fees or to require financial institutions to warn consumers if they will be assessed a surcharge for using an ATM, and give them a chance to cancel the transaction. To reduce ATM fees, experts suggest that you

- Compare ATM fees at different financial institutions before opening an account. Get the fee schedule in writing.
- Use your own bank's ATM whenever possible to avoid surcharges imposed when using the ATM of another financial institution.
- Withdraw larger cash amounts, as needed, to avoid fees on several small transactions.
- Consider using personal checks, traveler's checks, and credit cards when away from home.

Lost Debit Cards   A lost or stolen debit card can be expensive. If you notify the financial institution within two days of losing the card, your liability for unauthorized use is $50. If you wait any longer, you can be liable for up to $500 of unauthorized use for up to 60 days; beyond that time, your liability is unlimited. However, some card issuers use the same rules for lost or stolen debit cards as used for credit cards—a $50 maximum.

You are not liable for unauthorized use if, for example, a con artist uses your account number to make a purchase. Reporting the fraud within 60 days of receiving your bank statement protects your right not to be charged for this transaction.

Plastic Payments   While cash and checks are still the most popular method of paying, various access cards are gaining in acceptance and use.

<table>
<tr><td>

DID YOU KNOW?

The average cash machine customer withdraws money 72 times a year with an average amount of $87 and pays fees of $155. (SOURCE: David J. Morrow, "Is Your A.T.M. Ripping You Off?" *The New York Times*, May 4, 1997, sec. 3, p. 1.)

</td><td>

1. Point-of-Sale Transactions   ATM cards are accepted by many retail stores and restaurants. Your financial institution may issue two types of debit cards for these transactions. An *online card* operates like an ATM card, with an instant transfer of funds from your account. Online transactions require that you enter your secret personal identification number (PIN) to authorize the transaction.

Offline card transactions are processed like credit card charges; your PIN is not required. However, these transactions do not increase the amount owed. Instead, the funds are deducted from your bank account after a day or two.

</td></tr>
</table>

2. Stored-Value Cards   Prepaid cards for buying telephone service, transit fares, highway tolls, laundry service, library fees, and school lunches are becoming very common. While some of these access cards, such as phone cards, are disposable (or become collector's items), others are reloadable "stored-value" cards.

At the 1996 Summer Olympics in Atlanta, cards in denominations of $10, $20, $50, and $100 were issued by Visa USA. The price of a purchase is subtracted by an electronic card reader in the store. The remaining value is stored in a microchip implanted in the card.

3. Smart Cards   "Smart Cards," sometimes called "electronic wallets," look like ATM cards; however, they also include a microchip. This minicomputer stores prepaid amounts for buying goods and services. In addition, the card stores data about a person's account balances, transaction records, insurance information, and medical history. Smart cards are expected to see expanded use in the future as the services they offer increase.

4. Electronic Cash   CyberCash Inc. (Web site: www.cybercash.com) is one of the main contenders in the market that is developing electronic money. The company plans to create electronic replicas of all existing payment systems—cash, checks, credit cards, and coins.

EXHIBIT 5–3

Changing Interest Rates and Decisions Related to Financial Services

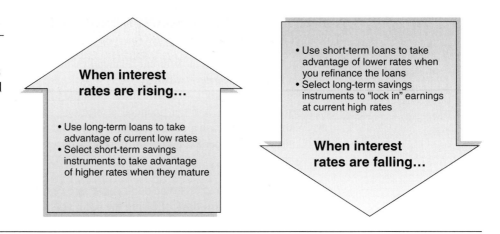

When interest rates are rising...

- Use long-term loans to take advantage of current low rates
- Select short-term savings instruments to take advantage of higher rates when they mature

- Use short-term loans to take advantage of lower rates when you refinance the loans
- Select long-term savings instruments to "lock in" earnings at current high rates

When interest rates are falling...

Opportunity Costs of Financial Services

When making budget decisions about spending and saving, consider the trade-off between current satisfaction and long-term financial security. In a similar manner, you consider opportunity cost—what you give up—when you evaluate, select, and use financial services. The money you save by shopping around for a low-cost checking account must be balanced against the value of the time you spend gathering information. Other common trade-offs related to financial services include the following:

Financial Decision Trade-Off

- Higher returns of long-term savings and investment plans may be achieved at the cost of *low liquidity,* the inability to obtain your money quickly.
- The convenience of a 24-hour automatic teller machine or a bank branch office near your home or place of work must be weighed against service fees.
- The "no fee" checking account that requires a non-interest-bearing $500 minimum balance means lost interest of nearly $400 at 6 percent compounded over 10 years.

You should evaluate costs and benefits in both monetary and personal terms to choose the financial services that best serve your needs.

Financial Services and Economic Conditions

Changing interest rates, rising consumer prices, and other economic factors also influence financial services. For successful financial planning, be aware of the current trends and future prospects for interest rates (see Exhibit 5–3 and the Financial Planning in Action box on page 129). You can learn about these trends and prospects by reading *The Wall Street Journal,* the business section of daily newspapers, and business periodicals such as *Business Week, Forbes,* and *Fortune.*

CONCEPT CHECK 5–1

1. What is the relationship between financial services and overall financial planning?
2. What are the major categories of financial services?
3. What financial services are available through electronic banking systems?
4. Why shouldn't you select financial services only on the basis of monetary factors?
5. How do changing economic conditions affect the use of financial services?

FINANCIAL PLANNING IN ACTION

UNDERSTANDING INTEREST RATES

When people discuss higher or lower interest rates, they could be talking about one of many types of interest rates. Some interest rates refer to the cost of borrowing by a business; others refer to the cost of buying a home. Your awareness of various types of interest rates can help you plan your spending, saving, borrowing, and investing. The accompanying table describes the most commonly reported interest rates and gives their *annual average* for selected years.

Using the business section of a newspaper, *The Wall Street Journal,* the World Wide Web or other business information sources, obtain current numbers for some or all of these interest rates. How might the current trend in interest rates affect your financial decisions?

	1970	1975	1980	1985	1990	1994	1997	Current
Prime rate—an indication of the rate banks charge large corporations	7.91%	7.85%	15.26%	9.93%	10.01%	7.15%	8.50%	____%
Discount rate—the rate financial institutions are charged to borrow funds from Federal Reserve banks	5.95	6.25	11.77	7.69	6.98	3.60	5.00	____
T-bill rate—the yield on short-term (13-week) U.S. government debt obligations	6.39	5.78	11.43	7.48	7.51	4.29	5.29	____
Treasury bond rate—the yield on long-term (30-year) U.S. government debt obligations	6.86	8.19	11.39	10.97	8.61	7.37	5.93	____
Mortgage rate—the amount individuals are paying to borrow for the purchase of a new home	8.45	9.00	12.66	11.55	10.13	8.35	7.00	____
Corporate bond rate—the cost of borrowing for large U.S. corporations	8.04	8.83	11.94	11.37	9.32	7.97	6.71	____
Certificate of deposit rate—the rate for six-month time deposits at savings institutions	7.65	6.89	12.99	8.25	8.17	4.96	5.74	____

SOURCE: Federal Reserve Statistical Release: *Selected Interest Rates* (G-13).

TYPES OF FINANCIAL INSTITUTIONS

L.O.2 Compare the types of financial institutions.

Many types of businesses, such as insurance companies, investment brokers, and credit card companies, have become involved in financial services previously limited to banks. Companies such as General Motors, Sears, and AT&T now issue or sponsor credit cards. Banks have also expanded their competitive efforts by opening offices that specialize in financial services such as investments, insurance, or real estate. Increased competition has brought about the opening of many limited-service offices, sometimes called *non-banks.* These limited-service offices specialize in a particular banking activity, such as savings or personal loans.

EXHIBIT 5–4

Types of Financial Institutions

Deposit-Type Institutions	Nondeposit Institutions
• Commercial banks • Savings and loan associations • Mutual savings banks • Credit unions	• Life insurance companies • Investment companies • Finance companies • Mortgage companies • Pawnshops • Check-cashing outlets

In contrast, *financial supermarkets* offer a range of financial services. One advantage of financial supermarkets is the convenience of one-stop shopping. The trade-off for this convenience is often higher costs and less personalized service. Also, many of these financial institutions are not covered by federal deposit insurance.

Despite changes in the banking environment, many familiar financial institutions still serve your needs. Most of these institutions have expanded their services. As Exhibit 5–4 shows, financial institutions fall into two major categories: deposit-type institutions and nondeposit institutions.

Deposit-Type Institutions

The financial institutions that most people use on a daily basis serve as intermediaries between suppliers (savers) and users (borrowers) of funds. These deposit-type institutions include commercial banks, savings and loan associations, mutual savings banks, and credit unions.

commercial bank

Commercial Banks   A **commercial bank** offers a full range of financial services to individuals, businesses, and government agencies. In addition to checking, savings, and lending, commercial banks offer many other services. Commercial banks are organized as corporations, with individual investors (stockholders) contributing the capital the banks need to operate. National banks are chartered by the federal government and state banks by state governments. State-chartered banks are usually subject to fewer restrictions than federally chartered banks.

In recent years, banks have opened full-service branch offices in grocery stores. These are truly "financial supermarkets," offering everything from automatic teller machines and loans to safe deposit boxes. As of mid-1998, over 3,000 such branches were in operation.

DID YOU KNOW?

While the number of commercial banks in the United States dropped from 14,199 in 1986 to 9,586 in 1996, the total number of branches grew to 57,188 from 45,303 during that same period. (SOURCE: "Trend Spotter," *Worth,* May 1997, p. 28.)

Savings and Loan Associations   While the commercial bank traditionally served mainly businesses and other customers with large amounts of money, the **savings and loan association (S&L)** specialized in savings accounts and loans for mortgages. In recent years, savings and loan associations have expanded their services to include interest-bearing checking accounts, specialized savings plans, loans to businesses, and other investment and financial planning services. Like banks, savings and loan associations have either federal or state charters.

savings and loan association (S&L)

The high interest rates of the late 1970s and early 1980s resulted in financial difficulties for many savings and loan associations. Many S&Ls issued mortgages at low rates, while savers demanded higher earnings on deposits. In addition, some large savings and loan associations made many loans in high-growth, high-cost areas. When an economic downturn occurred in these areas, loans were not paid back, resulting in big losses for the lenders. These difficulties caused failures, mergers, and increased regulation of S&Ls.

mutual savings bank

Mutual Savings Banks   Another financial institution that concentrates on serving individuals is the **mutual savings bank,** which is owned by depositors and, like the traditional savings and loan association, specializes in savings accounts and mortgage loans. Mutual savings banks are located mainly in the northeastern United States. Unlike the profits of other types of financial institutions, the profits of a mutual savings bank go to the depositors, paying higher rates on savings.

credit union

Credit Unions   A **credit union** is a user-owned, nonprofit, cooperative financial institution. Traditionally, credit union members had to have a common bond such as work, church, or community affiliation. As the common bond restriction was loosened, the membership of credit unions increased. Today more than 10 million people belong to over 12,000 credit unions in the United States.

Each year surveys conducted by consumer organizations and others report lower fees for checking accounts, lower loan rates, and higher levels of user satisfaction for credit unions compared to other financial institutions. Most credit unions continue to expand their services; many now offer credit cards, mortgages, home equity loans, direct deposit, cash machines, safe deposit boxes, and investment services.

DID YOU KNOW?

For 14 consecutive years, credit unions have topped the annual consumer satisfaction survey conducted by *American Banker.* Over 70 percent of credit union members said they were "very satisfied" with the service they receive compared to 53 percent of bank customers. (SOURCE: "News about Credit Unions," January 5, 1998, p. 1, Credit Union National Association, Box 431, Madison, WI 53701.)

Nondeposit Institutions

Financial services are also available from institutions such as life insurance companies, investment companies, finance companies, mortgage companies, pawnshops, and check-cashing outlets.

Life Insurance Companies   While the main purpose of life insurance is to provide financial security for dependents, many life insurance policies contain savings and investment features. Chapter 12 discusses these policies. In recent years, life insurance companies have expanded the financial services they offer include investment and retirement planning.

money market fund

Investment Companies   Investment companies, also referred to as *mutual funds,* offer banking-type services. A common service of these organizations is the **money market fund,** a combination savings-investment plan in which the investment company uses your money to purchase a variety of short-term financial instruments. Your earnings are based on the interest the investment company receives. Unlike most banks, savings and loan associations, and credit unions, investment company accounts are not covered by federal deposit insurance.

Investors in money market funds are usually allowed to write a limited number of checks on their accounts. This service gives the convenience of liquidity.

Finance Companies   Making loans to consumers and small businesses is the main function of finance companies. These loans have short and intermediate terms with higher rates than most other lenders charge. Some finance companies have expanded their activities to offer other financial planning services.

FINANCIAL PLANNING FOR LIFE'S SITUATIONS

HIGH-COST FINANCIAL SERVICES: THE ALTERNATIVE FINANCIAL SECTOR

Would you pay $8 to cash a $100 check? Or pay $2.25 to send a $40 payment to someone? Many consumers without ready access to financial services (such as people with low incomes) may use what is called the *alternative financial sector (AFS)*. These services include pawn shops, rent-to-own programs, check-cashing outlets, money orders, and rapid-refund tax services as alternatives to traditional financial services.

Compared to the traditional financial sector, AFS services are very expensive. Offers of "quick cash" and "low payments" attract consumers who do not have a regular banking account or credit card. Some observers believe the growth of these services is related to deregulation of banking and uneven income growth in our society. However, most loans through the AFS are small, and traditional financial institutions typically would not choose to be involved with such transactions.

Another example of the AFS is a "check-deferral transaction" that allows consumers to get a cash advance against their next paycheck. In Cleveland, Tennessee, at a local Check Into Cash outlet, a $200 two-week advance costs $38 (resulting in a possible annual cost of $988). When a check-cashing company receives $120 in exchange for a $100 advance, the $20 fee for a two-week advance amounts to a 500 percent annual interest rate. Cash advance customers find the service helps them avoid the high fees associated with bounced checks.

SOURCES: Roger Swagler, John Burton, and Joan Koonce Lewis, "The Alternative Financial Sector: An Overview," *Advancing the Consumer Interest,* Fall 1995, pp. 7–12; Roger Swagler, John Burton, and Joan Koonce Lewis, "The Operations, Appeals and Costs of the Alternative Financial Sector: Implications for Financial Counselors," *Financial Counseling and Planning* 6 (1995), pp. 93–98; Rodney Ho, "Fees of Quick-Cash Chains Draw Scrutiny," *The Wall Street Journal,* June 10, 1997, pp. B1, B2.

Mortgage Companies   Mortgage companies are organized primarily to provide loans to purchase homes. Chapter 9 discusses further the activities of mortgage companies.

Pawnshops   Pawnshops make loans based on the value of tangible possessions such as jewelry or other valuable items. Many low- and moderate-income families use these organizations to obtain cash loans quickly. Pawnshops charge higher fees than other financial institutions. Today there are more pawnshops than ever in U.S. history, and they may be found in large cities, small towns, and suburbs throughout the nation.

Check-Cashing Outlets   About 17 percent of U.S. households do not have bank accounts, and most financial institutions will not cash a check unless the person has an account. The more than 6,000 check-cashing outlets (CCOs) can charge anywhere from 1 to 20 percent of the face value of a check; the average cost is between 2 and 3 percent. However, for a low-income family, that can be a significant portion of the total household budget (see the "Financial Planning for Life's Situation" box).

CCOs offer a wide variety of services, including electronic tax filing, money orders, private postal boxes, utility bill payment, and the sale of bus and subway tokens. Once again, you can usually obtain most of these services for less at other locations.

Cyberbanking

Banking through the telephone, personal computer, and online services continues to expand. Hundreds of banks now have "cyber" branches where customers can check balances, pay bills, transfer funds, compare savings plans, and apply for loans on the Internet. Wells

EXHIBIT 5–5

**Which Financial
Institution Should
You Choose?**

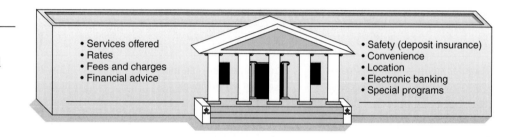

- Services offered
- Rates
- Fees and charges
- Financial advice

- Safety (deposit insurance)
- Convenience
- Location
- Electronic banking
- Special programs

Fargo (www.wellsfargo.com) and Bank of America (www.bankamerica.com) were two of the first banks to do business on the Web.

The Security First Network Bank (www.sfnb.com) was one of the first financial institutions to operate exclusively on the Internet. Access to all accounts and transactions is available 24 hours a day, seven days a week.

Despite expanded use of online banking activities, privacy and security of transactions give a cause of anxiety. High fees are also a concern; online services can reduce a bank's operating costs, but these lower costs are not always passed on to customers.

Comparing Financial Institutions

The basic concerns of a financial services customer are simple: Where can I get the best return on my savings? How can I minimize the cost of checking? Will I be able to borrow money when I need it?

As you use financial services, decide what you want from the organization that will serve your needs. With the financial marketplace constantly changing, you must assess the various services and other factors before selecting an organization (see Exhibit 5–5).

The services the financial institution offers are likely to be a major factor. Personal service is important to many customers. Convenience may be provided by business hours, close-by branch offices and automatic teller machines, and banking-by-mail service. Convenience and service have a cost, so be sure to compare fees and other charges at several financial institutions.

Finally, you should consider safety factors and interest rates. Obtain information about earnings you will receive on savings and checking accounts and the rate you will pay for borrowed funds. Most financial institutions have deposit insurance to protect customers against losses; however, not all of them are insured by federal government programs. Investigate the type of protection your money will have.

Your selection of a financial institution should be based on valid information. Never assume that one will provide a better interest rate or service than another. You need to compare banks, savings and loan associations, and credit unions with other providers of financial services.

CONCEPT   CHECK   5–2

1. What are examples of deposit-type financial institutions?
2. What factors do consumers usually consider when selecting a financial institution to meet their saving and checking needs?

EXHIBIT 5–6   **Savings Alternatives**

Type of Account	Benefits	Drawbacks
Regular savings accounts/pass-book accounts/share accounts	Low minimum balance Ease of withdrawal Insured	Low rate of return
Certificates of deposit (CDs)	Guaranteed rate of return for time of CD Insured	Possible penalty for early with-drawal Minimum deposit
Interest-earning checking accounts	Checking privileges Interest earned Insured	Service charge for going below minimum balance Cost for printing checks; other fees may apply
Money market accounts	Favorable rate of return (based on current interest rates) Allows some check writing Insured	Higher minimum balance than regular savings accounts No interest or service charge if below a certain balance
Money market funds	Favorable rate of return (based on current interest rates) Some check writing	Minimum balance Not insured
U.S. savings bonds	Fairly good rate of return (varies with current interest rates) Low minimum deposit Government guaranteed Exempt from state and local income taxes	Long maturity Lower rate when redeemed before five years

TYPES OF SAVINGS PLANS

L.O.3 Compare the costs and benefits of various savings plans.

As Chapter 3 emphasized, you need a savings program to attain your financial goals. The evaluation of various savings plans is the starting point of this process.

Changes in financial services have created a wide choice of savings alternatives (see Exhibit 5–6). While the number of savings plans may seem overwhelming, they can be grouped into these main categories: regular savings accounts, club accounts, certificates of deposit, interest-earning checking accounts, money market accounts and funds, and savings bonds. Investment vehicles, such as U.S. Treasury bills, are discussed in later chapters.

Regular Savings Accounts

Traditionally called *passbook accounts, regular savings accounts* usually involve a low or no minimum balance. Today, instead of a passbook showing deposits and withdrawals, some savers receive a monthly or quarterly statement with a summary of transactions.

A regular savings account usually allows you to withdraw money as needed. However, these *time deposits* may require a waiting period of up to 30 days to obtain your funds.

share account

Banks, savings and loan associations, and other financial institutions offer regular savings accounts. At a credit union, these savings plans are called **share accounts**.

DID YOU KNOW?

The Consumer Federation of America and the Credit Union National Association estimate that savers could earn up to $16 billion more in annual interest on deposits if they shifted funds from a savings or money market deposit account to a six-month certificate of deposit.

Club Accounts

Club accounts, offered mainly at smaller financial institutions, are designed to meet a specific goal. Examples are vacation and Christmas club accounts in which you make a weekly deposit. Usually you cannot withdraw money until a certain time (such as November 1 for Christmas clubs) without incurring a penalty. While a club account is a forced-savings method, it usually pays very low interest.

Certificates of Deposit

certificate of deposit (CD)

Higher earnings are commonly available to savers when they leave money on deposit for a set time period. A **certificate of deposit (CD)** is a savings plan that requires that a certain amount be left on deposit for a stated time period (ranging from 30 days to five or more years) to earn a specific rate of return. These time deposits can be an attractive and safe savings alternative. However, most financial institutions impose a penalty for early withdrawal of CD funds.

Types of CDs   Financial institutions offer certificates of deposit with a variety of features:

1. *Rising-rate* or *bump-up* CDs may give you higher rates at various intervals, such as every six months. However, beware of ads that highlight a higher rate in the future. This rate may be in effect only for the last couple of months for an 18- or 24-month CD. Also, some bump-ups may require a rather large minimum investment.
2. *Stock-indexed* CDs have earnings based on the stock market. In times of strong stock performance, your CD earnings can be higher than those on other CDs. At other times, however, you may earn no interest and may even lose part of your savings.
3. *Callable CDs* start with higher rates and usually have long-term maturities, as high as 10 to 15 years. These savings plans also have the benefit of federal deposit insurance. However, the bank may "call" the account after a stipulated period, such as one or two years, if interest rates drop. When the call option is exercised, the saver receives the original investment principal and any interest that has been earned. Remember, don't be drawn in by the high initial rate on a callable CD; it could change in a few years. Also, if it is not called, you may not have the flexibility to withdraw without a substantial penalty.
4. *Global CDs* combine higher interest with a hedge on future changes in the dollar compared to other currencies. As exchange rates change, your earnings can fluctuate. A weaker U.S. dollar (compared to a given foreign currency) can result in a higher return on your savings. In contrast, a stronger dollar will result in a lower rate of return. Some global CDs offered by U.S. banks have federal deposit insurance; others do not.
5. *Promotional CDs* attempt to attract savers with gifts or special rates. A Boulder, Colorado, bank offered Rolex watches, archery equipment, and Zodiac inflatable boats in lieu of interest. Be sure to balance the value of the item against the lost interest.

Managing CDs   When saving with a CD or *rolling over* a CD (buying a new one at maturity), carefully assess all earnings and costs. Do not allow your financial institution to automatically roll over your money into another CD for the same term. If interest rates have dropped, you might consider a shorter maturity. Or if you believe rates are at a peak and you won't need the money for some time, obtain a CD with a longer term.

Consider creating a CD *portfolio* with CDs maturing at different times, for example, $2,000 in a three-month CD, $2,000 in a six-month CD, $2,000 in a one-year CD, and $2,000 in a two-year CD. This will give you some degree of liquidity and flexibility when you reinvest your funds.

Don't hesitate to buy CDs by mail from a financial institution in another state. You might earn as much as a full percentage point higher than your local bank offers. Also, when interest rates stay low, consider other savings alternatives such as savings bonds, mutual funds, and government securities. Current information about CD rates at various financial institutions may be obtained at http://www.bankrate/com.

Interest-Earning Checking Accounts

Checking accounts can also be savings vehicles. These interest-earning accounts, which usually pay a low interest rate, are discussed in the next section of this chapter.

Money Market Accounts and Funds

money market account

To meet consumer demand for higher savings rates, a savings plan with a floating interest rate was created. A **money market account** is a savings account that requires a minimum balance and has earnings based on market interest rates. Money market accounts allow you to write a limited number of checks to make large payments or to transfer money to other accounts. Since money market accounts may impose a fee when you go below the required minimum balance, usually $1,000, consider a regular savings account or a payroll deduction savings plan.

Both money market *accounts* and money market *funds* offer earnings based on current interest rates, and both have minimum-balance restrictions and allow check writing. The major difference is in safety. Money market accounts at banks and savings and loan associations are covered by federal deposit insurance. This is not true of money market funds, which are a product of investment and insurance companies. Since money market funds invest mainly in short-term (less than a year) government and corporate securities, however, they are usually quite safe.

U.S. Savings Bonds

Years ago, the low return on savings bonds made their purchase a patriotic act rather than a wise savings choice. In recent years, however, the Treasury Department has used a floating interest rate on savings bonds. Earnings rise and fall based on changes in the level of interest rates in the economy.

Series EE bonds may be purchased for amounts ranging from $25 to $15,000 (face values of $50 to $30,000, respectively). Interest accrues on these bonds until they reach their maturity value (double the purchase price).

You must hold bonds at least five years to earn the stated rate. If redeemed within five years of purchase, you earn a lower rate. Between the time the bond is six months and five years old, your money earns a slightly higher rate every six months. Series EE bonds continue to earn interest for 30 years, well beyond the maturity date.

The main tax advantages of Series EE bonds are that (1) the interest earned is exempt from state and local taxes and (2) you do not have to pay federal income tax on earnings until the bonds are redeemed.

EE bonds that have reached maturity value may be exchanged for Series HH bonds to defer the taxes. The taxes owed for interest earned on the EE bonds will not be due until the HH bonds are cashed in or reach maturity. Series HH bonds pay interest in cash twice a year. This interest is taxed as current income. The semiannual interest payments of HH bonds make them a popular source of retirement income.

Investors may purchase up to $15,000 ($30,000 maturity face) of U.S. savings bonds a year. This amount applies to any person, so parents may buy an additional $15,000 in each child's name.

Redeemed Series EE bonds may be exempt from federal income tax if the funds are used to pay tuition and fees at a college, university, or qualified technical school for yourself or a dependent. The bonds must be purchased by an individual who is at least 24 years old, and they must be issued in the names of one or both parents. These provisions have been designed to assist low- and middle-income households; people whose incomes exceed a certain amount do not qualify for the exemption.

Banks and other financial institutions that sell U.S. savings bonds no longer issue the actual bond. Instead you receive a receipt or, if desired, a "gift certificate." The bonds are then sent from the Federal Reserve bank within 15 business days. For an update on U.S. savings bond rates and other information, call 1–800–US BONDS. The Web site for savings bonds is at www.publicdebt.treas.gov/sav/sav.htm.

Lost, stolen, or destroyed savings bonds will be replaced by the government free of charge.

A table of savings bond redemption values (Form PD 3600) is available from the Savings Bond Marketing Office, 800 K St., NW, Washington, DC 20226.

PFP

Sheet 24

CONCEPT CHECK 5–3

1. What are the main types of savings plans offered by financial institutions?
2. How does a money market *account* differ from a money market *fund?*
3. What are the benefits of U.S. savings bonds?

EVALUATING SAVINGS PLANS

L.O.4 Identify the factors used to evaluate different savings plans.

Your selection of a savings plan will be influenced by the rate of return, inflation, tax considerations, liquidity, safety, restrictions, and fees.

Rate of Return

rate of return

Earnings on savings can be measured by the **rate of return,** or *yield,* the percentage of increase in the value of your savings from earned interest. For example, a $100 savings account that earned $5 after a year would have a rate of return, or yield, of 5 percent. This rate of return was determined by dividing the interest earned ($5) by the amount in the savings account ($100).

Compounding   The yield on your savings will usually be greater than the stated interest rate. **Compounding** refers to interest that is earned on previously earned interest.

compounding

EXHIBIT 5–7
_____

**Compounding
Frequency
Increases the
Savings Yield**

Shorter compounding periods result in higher yields. This chart shows the growth of $10,000, five-year CDs paying the same rate of 8 percent, but with different compounding methods.

End of Year	Compounding Method			
	Daily	Monthly	Quarterly	Annually
1	$10,832.78	$10,830.00	$10,824.32	$10,800.00
2	11,743.91	11,728.88	11,716.59	11,664.00
3	12,712.17	12,702.37	12,682.41	12,597.12
4	13,770.82	13,756.66	13,727.85	13,604.89
5	14,917.62	14,898.46	14,859.46	14,693.28
Annual yield	8.33%	8.30%	8.24%	8.00%

SOURCE: United States League of Savings Institutions.

Each time interest is added to your savings, the next interest amount is computed on the new balance in the account. Future value and present value calculations, introduced in Chapter 1, take compounding into account.

The more frequent the compounding, the higher your rate of return will be. For example, $100 in a savings account that earns 6 percent compounded annually will increase $6 after a year. But the same $100 in a 6 percent account compounded daily will earn $6.19 for the year. Although this difference may seem slight, large amounts held in savings for long periods of time will result in far higher differences (see Exhibit 5–7).

Truth in Savings   The *Truth in Savings* law (Federal Reserve Regulation DD) requires financial institutions to disclose the following information on savings account plans they offer:

- Fees on deposit accounts.
- The interest rate.
- The annual percentage yield (APY).
- Other terms and conditions of the savings plan.

*annual percentage
yield (APY)*

Truth in Savings (TIS) defines **annual percentage yield (APY)** as the percentage rate expressing the total amount of interest that would be received on a $100 deposit based on the annual rate and frequency of compounding for a 365-day period. This law defines a year as 365 days rather than 360, 366, or some other number. TIS eliminates the confusion caused by the more than 8 million variations of interest calculation methods previously used by financial institutions. APY reflects the amount of interest a saver should expect to earn. (See the accompanying Financial Planning Calculations box for additional information on APY.)

In addition to setting the formula for computing the annual percentage yield, Truth in Savings (1) requires disclosure of fees and APY earned on any statements provided to customers, (2) establishes rules for advertising deposit accounts, and (3) restricts the method of calculating the balance on which interest is paid. Financial institutions are also required to calculate interest on the full principal balance in the account each day.

Inflation

The rate of return you earn on your savings should be compared with the inflation rate. When the inflation rate was over 10 percent, people with money in savings accounts earning 5 or 6 percent were experiencing a loss in the buying power of that money. In general,

FINANCIAL PLANNING CALCULATIONS

ANNUAL PERCENTAGE YIELD

The Truth in Savings law, which took effect in 1993, requires that financial institutions report in advertisements, if a rate is quoted, and to savings plan customers the annual percentage yield (APY). The formula for APY is

$$APY = 100\,[(1 + \text{Interest/Principal})^{365/\text{days in term}} - 1]$$

The *principal* is the amount of funds on deposit. *Interest* is the total dollar amount earned during the term on the principal. *Days in term* is the actual number of days over which interest is earned.

When the number of days in the term is 365 (that is, where the stated maturity is 365 days) or where the account does not have a stated maturity, the APY formula is simply

$$APY = 100\,(\text{Interest/Principal})$$

APY provides a consistent comparison for savings plans with different interest rates, different compounding frequencies, and different time periods. APY may be easily viewed in terms of a $100 deposit for a 365-day year. For example, an APY of 6.5 percent would mean $6.50 interest for a year.

as the inflation rate increases, the interest rates offered to savers also increase. This gives you an opportunity to select a savings option that will minimize the erosion of your dollars on deposit.

Tax Considerations

Like inflation, taxes reduce earnings on savings. For example, a 10 percent return for a saver in a 28 percent tax bracket means a real return of 7.2 percent (the accompanying Financial Planning Calculations feature shows how to compute the after-tax savings rate of return). As discussed in Chapter 4 and discussed further in Part V, several tax-exempt and tax-deferred savings plans and investments can increase your real rate of return.

Also, remember that taxes are usually not withheld from savings and investment income. Consequently, you may owe additional taxes at year-end due to earnings on savings.

Liquidity

Financial Decision
Trade-Off

Liquidity allows you to withdraw your money on short notice without a loss of principal or fees. Some savings plans impose penalties for early withdrawal or have other restrictions. With certain types of savings certificates and accounts, early withdrawal may be penalized by a loss of interest or a lower earnings rate.

You should consider the degree of liquidity you desire in relation to your savings goals. To achieve long-term financial goals, many people trade off liquidity for a higher return.

Safety

Most savings plans at banks, savings and loan associations, and credit unions are insured by agencies affiliated with the federal government. This protection prevents a loss of money due to the failure of the insured institution.

While a few financial institutions have failed in recent years, savers with deposits covered by federal insurance have not lost any money. Depositors of failed organizations

FINANCIAL PLANNING CALCULATIONS

AFTER-TAX SAVINGS RATE OF RETURN

The taxability of interest on your savings reduces your real rate of return. In other words, you lose some portion of your interest to taxes. This calculation consists of the following steps:

1. Determine your top tax bracket for federal income taxes.
2. Subtract this rate, expressed as a decimal, from 1.0.
3. Multiply the result by the yield on your savings account.
4. The product, expressed as a percentage, is your after-tax rate of return.

For example,

1. You are in the 28 percent tax bracket.
2. $1.0 - 0.28 = 0.72$.
3. If the yield on your savings account is 6.25 percent, $0.0625 \times 0.72 = 0.045$.
4. Your after-tax rate of return is 4.5 percent.

You may use the same procedure to determine the *real rate of return* on your savings based on inflation. For example, if you are earning 6 percent on savings and inflation is 5 percent, your *real rate of return* (after inflation) is 5.7 percent: $.06 \times (1 - 0.05) = 0.057$.

have either been paid the amounts in their accounts or have had the accounts taken over by a financially stable institution.

As a result of financial troubles in the savings and loan industry, the coverage of the Federal Deposit Insurance Corporation (FDIC), which provides deposit insurance for banks, was extended to savings and loan associations. The FDIC administers separate insurance funds, the Bank Insurance Fund and the Savings Association Insurance Fund. Credit unions may obtain deposit insurance through the National Credit Union Association (NCUA). Some state-chartered credit unions have opted for a private insurance program.

The FDIC insures deposits of up to $100,000 per person per financial institution; a joint account is considered to belong proportionally to each name on the account. For example, if you have a $70,000 individual account and an $80,000 joint account with a relative in the same financial institution, $10,000 of your savings will not be covered by federal deposit insurance ($70,000 plus one-half of $80,000 exceeds the $100,000 limit). However, by using combinations of individual, joint, and trust accounts in different financial institutions, it may be possible to have federal deposit insurance cover amounts that exceed $100,000. Remember, the maximum coverage of federal deposit insurance is based on each depositor, not on each account. The best advice is to never keep more than $100,000 in one financial institution. Be careful, however, since different branch offices count as the same institution. (Further information on deposit insurance is available at www.fdic.gov.)

Since not all financial institutions have federal deposit insurance, investigate this matter when you are selecting a savings plan. Additional information on the regulation and consumer protection aspects of financial institutions is included in Appendix E.

Restrictions and Fees

Other limitations can affect your choice of a savings program. For example, there may be a delay between the time interest is earned and the time it is added to your account. This means it will not be available for your immediate use. Also, some institutions charge a transaction fee for each deposit or withdrawal. Such fees can mount when you make several transactions each month.

Sheet 25

In the past, some financial institutions had promotions offering a "free" gift when a certain savings amount was deposited. To receive this gift, you had to leave your money on deposit for a certain time period, or you may have received less interest, since some of the earnings were used to cover the cost of the "free" items. Economists tell us that "there is no such thing as a free lunch"; the same holds true for toasters and television sets.

CONCEPT CHECK 5–4

1. When would you prefer a savings plan with high liquidity over one with a high rate of return?
2. What is the relationship between compounding and the future value of an amount?
3. How do inflation and taxes affect earnings on savings?

SELECTING PAYMENT METHODS

L.O.5 Compare the costs and benefits of different types of checking accounts.

With about 90 percent of business transactions conducted by check, a checking account is a necessity for most people.

Types of Checking Accounts

Checking accounts fall into three major categories: regular checking accounts, activity accounts, and interest-earning checking accounts.

> **DID YOU KNOW?**
>
> A survey of 243 banks in 25 major U.S. cities found that a free checking account with no minimum-balance requirement was offered in 17 cities. The study also revealed penalties ranging from $10 to $27 for a bounced check. (SOURCE: Ellen Stark, "How to Get the Best Deal in a Checking Account," *Money,* May 1997, pp. 126–127.)

Regular Checking Accounts   *Regular checking accounts* usually have a monthly service charge that you may avoid by keeping a minimum balance in the account. Some financial institutions will waive the monthly fee if you keep a certain amount in savings. Avoiding the monthly service charge can be beneficial. For example, a monthly fee of $7.50 results in $90 a year. However, you lose interest on the minimum-balance amount in a non-interest-earning account.

Activity Accounts   *Activity accounts* charge a fee for each check written and sometimes a fee for each deposit in addition to a monthly service charge. However, you do not have to maintain a minimum balance. An activity account is most appropriate for people who write only a few checks each month and are unable to maintain the required minimum balance.

Interest-Earning Checking Accounts   *Interest-earning checking accounts,* sometimes called **NOW accounts** (NOW stands for *negotiable order of withdrawal*), usually require a minimum balance. If the account balance goes below this amount, you may not earn interest and will likely incur a service charge.

NOW account

share draft account

The **share draft account** is an interest-earning checking account at a credit union. Credit union members write checks, called *share drafts,* against their account balances.

EXHIBIT 5–8

Checking Account Selection Factors

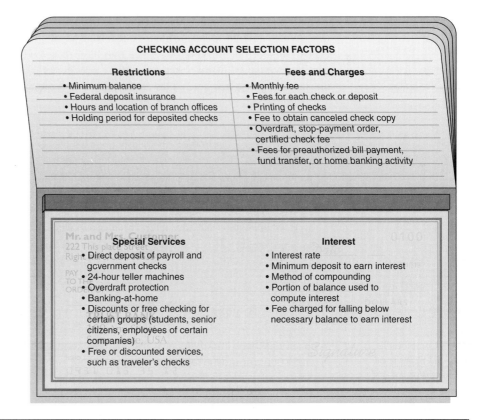

CHECKING ACCOUNT SELECTION FACTORS

Restrictions	Fees and Charges
• Minimum balance	• Monthly fee
• Federal deposit insurance	• Fees for each check or deposit
• Hours and location of branch offices	• Printing of checks
• Holding period for deposited checks	• Fee to obtain canceled check copy
	• Overdraft, stop-payment order, certified check fee
	• Fees for preauthorized bill payment, fund transfer, or home banking activity

Special Services	Interest
• Direct deposit of payroll and government checks	• Interest rate
• 24-hour teller machines	• Minimum deposit to earn interest
• Overdraft protection	• Method of compounding
• Banking-at-home	• Portion of balance used to compute interest
• Discounts or free checking for certain groups (students, senior citizens, employees of certain companies)	• Fee charged for falling below necessary balance to earn interest
• Free or discounted services, such as traveler's checks	

Evaluating Checking Accounts

Would you rather have a checking account that pays interest and requires a $1,000 minimum balance or an account that doesn't pay interest and requires a $300 minimum balance? This decision requires evaluating factors such as restrictions, fees and charges, interest, and special services (see Exhibit 5–8).

Restrictions   The most common limitation on checking accounts is the amount you must keep on deposit to earn interest or avoid a service charge. Until recently, financial institutions also placed various restrictions on the holding period for deposited checks; that is, they required a period of time for checks to clear before you were allowed to use the funds. The Expedited Funds Availability Act requires that funds from local checks be available within two business days and funds from out-of-town checks be withheld for no more than five business days.

Financial Decision Trade-Off

PFP

Sheet 26

Fees and Charges   Nearly all financial institutions require a minimum balance or impose service charges for checking accounts. When using an interest-bearing checking account, compare your earnings with any service charge or fee. Also, consider the cost of lost or reduced interest due to the need to maintain the minimum balance.

Checking account fees have increased in recent years. Items such as check printing, overdraft fees, and stop-payment orders have doubled or tripled in price at some financial institutions. Some institutions will "bait" you with fancy checks at a low price and then charge a much higher price when you reorder. You may be able to purchase checks at a lower cost from a mail-order company that advertises in magazines or the Sunday newspaper.

JONATHAN HOENIG SPEAKS
BANK ON IT

In mid-1995, a major Chicago-based bank started offering its customers a revolutionary "service": the live-teller surcharge. Three dollars extra to speak to a live teller.

Customers went ballistic, consumer groups freaked out, and social pundits lamented the seemingly inhumane vibe. The bank eventually loosened the rules in a feeble attempt to quell the commotion.

In the increasingly competitive banking industry, it is an unprecedented buyer's market. Pressure from brokerage firms, mutual funds companies, and financial service providers has caused traditional banks to reinvent; bidding has become the gilded "one-stop shop" for your hard-earned cash. *Pass the passbook,* because today's banks offer a smattering of services that would make even a Rockefeller reel.

No matter what the size of your account, remember this: *The customer is always right.* Most banks are so desperate to retain market share that they regularly negotiate terms to keep you around. Your list of demands should include (but not be limited to) free checking, reduced ATM surcharges, improved CD interest rates, and minimal overdraft protection. While you're at it, make sure they throw in one heck of a shiny new toaster.

If you savor the solitude, banking via PC is always an option. But even as human interaction becomes a "premium" service, remember that it's *your* money. Banks that leave the "customer" out of "customer service" will get what they deserve: bankruptcy.

Interest   As discussed earlier, the interest rate, the frequency of compounding, and the interest computation method will affect the earnings on your checking account.

Special Services   Financial institutions commonly offer checking account customers services such as 24-hour teller machines and home banking services. To attract new accounts, some banks offer "buyer protection insurance" to checking account customers. This insurance protects products bought by check against damage or loss and also extends manufacturers' warranties.

Financial institutions are attempting to reduce the paper and postage costs associated with checking accounts. One solution is to not return canceled checks to customers. The financial institution then uses microfilm to store checks and provides customers with detailed statements summarizing the checks written. If a customer requests a copy of a canceled check, the institution reproduces the copy from its microfilm file for a fee.

overdraft protection

Overdraft protection is an automatic loan made to checking account customers for checks written in excess of the available balance. This service is convenient but costly. Most overdraft plans make loans based on $50 or $100 increments. An overdraft of just a dollar might trigger a $50 loan and corresponding finance charges of perhaps 18 percent. But overdraft protection can be less costly than the fee charged for a check you write when you do not have enough money on deposit to cover it. That fee may be $15 or more. Many financial institutions will allow you to cover checking account overdrafts with an automatic transfer from a savings account for a nominal fee.

Beware of checking accounts that offer several services (safe deposit box, traveler's checks, low-rate loans, and travel insurance) for a single monthly fee. This may sound

Sheet 27

FINANCIAL PLANNING IN ACTION

COMPARING CHECKING ACCOUNT COSTS

Comparisons of interest earned and service charges and fees for checking accounts can be confusing. To assist you with this analysis, use the following calculation. Remember: Not all items listed here will apply to every type of checking account.

Inflows	*Outflows*
Step 1.	**Step 2.**
Multiply average monthly balance $ _____ by average rate of return _____ percent to determine annual earnings	Monthly service charge $ _____ × 12 = $ _____
	Average number of checks written per month _____ × charge per check × 12 $ _____
	Average number of deposits per month _____ × charge per deposit × 12 $ _____
	Fee for dropping below minimum balance $ _____ × number of times below minimum $ _____
	Lost interest: Opportunity cost _____ percent × required minimum balance $ _____ $ _____
Total estimated annual inflow $ _____	Total estimated annual outflow $ _____

Step 3.

Estimated annual inflows less annual outflows =

+ Net earnings for account (Step 1)
− Net cost for account (Step 2)

+/− $ _____

NOTE: This calculation does not take into account charges and fees for services such as overdrafts, stop payments, ATM use, and check printing. Be sure to also consider these costs when selecting a checking account.

like a good value; however, financial experts observe that such accounts benefit only a small group of people who make constant use of the services offered.

The accompanying Financial Planning in Action box offers a method for comparing the costs of various types of checking accounts.

Other Payment Methods

While personal checks are the most common payment form, other methods are available. A *certified check* is a personal check with guaranteed payment. The amount of the check is deducted from your balance when the financial institution certifies the check. A *cashier's check* is a check of a financial institution. You may purchase one by paying the amount of the check plus a fee. You may purchase a *money order* in a similar manner from financial institutions, post offices, and stores. Certified checks, cashier's checks, and money orders allow you to make a payment that the recipient knows is valid.

Traveler's checks allow you to make payments when you are away from home. This payment form requires you to sign each check twice. First, you sign the traveler's checks when you purchase them. Then, to identify you as the authorized person, you sign them again as you cash them.

Electronic traveler's checks, in the form of a prepaid travel card, are starting to be used. The card will allow travelers visiting other nations to get local currency from an ATM.

CONCEPT CHECK 5–5

1. What factors are commonly considered when selecting a checking account?
2. Are checking accounts that earn interest preferable to regular checking accounts? Why or why not?

USING A CHECKING ACCOUNT

L.O.6 Describe the activities involved in using a checking account.

After you select a checking account, you will follow several procedures in using the account.

Opening a Checking Account

Deciding who the owner of the account will be is your starting point for opening a checking account. Only one person is allowed to write checks on an *individual account*. A *joint account* has two or more owners, with any authorized person allowed to write checks if it is specified as an "or" account. In contrast, an "and" account with two owners requires the signatures of both owners on checks. This arrangement is commonly used by businesses and other organizations.

Both an individual account and a joint account require a signature card. This document is a record of the official signatures of the person or persons authorized to write checks on the account.

Making Deposits

A *deposit ticket* is the form you use for adding money to your checking account (see Exhibit 5–9 on page 146). On this document, you list the amounts of the cash and checks being deposited. Each check you deposit requires an *endorsement*—your signature on the back of the check—to authorize the transfer of the funds into your account. The following are three common endorsement forms:

EXHIBIT 5–9

Deposit Ticket

DEPOSIT TICKET

Barbara Carter
7640 Moontree Lane
Elton, NE 67844

DATE _____ April 10 _____ 19 99

First National Bank
of Elton

⑆000000000⑆ ⑆5 5 303 79⑈ 3323

CHECKS AND OTHER ITEMS ARE RECEIVED FOR DEPOSIT SUBJECT TO THE PROVISIONS OF THE UNIFORM COMMERCIAL CODE OR ANY APPLICABLE COLLECTION AGREEMENT.

CASH	CURRENCY	17	—	
	COIN	2	50	
LIST CHECKS SINGLY		16	25	
		11	37	00-0000/0000
TOTAL FROM OTHER SIDE				
TOTAL		47	12	USE OTHER SIDE FOR ADDITIONAL LISTING
LESS CASH RECEIVED		10	—	
NET DEPOSIT		37	12	BE SURE EACH ITEM IS PROPERLY ENDORSED

- A *blank endorsement* is your signature. Use this endorsement form only when you are actually depositing or cashing a check, since a check may be cashed by anyone once its back has been signed.
- A *restrictive endorsement* consists of the words *for deposit only,* followed by your signature. This endorsement form is especially useful when you are depositing checks by mail.
- A *special endorsement* allows you to transfer a check to an organization or another person. On this endorsement form, the words *pay to the order of* are followed by the name of the organization or person and then by your signature.

Federal regulations require that endorsements be on the reverse of the left side of the check, using no more than 1½ inches of space from the top. They may be handwritten, typed, rubber-stamped, or printed.

Writing Checks

Before writing a check, record the information in your check register and deduct the amount of the check from your balance. Otherwise, you will think you have more money available than you really do. Many checking account customers use duplicate checks to maintain a record of their current balance.

The procedure for proper check writing, displayed in Exhibit 5–10, consists of the following steps:

1. Record the current date.
2. Write the name of the person or organization receiving the payment.
3. Record the amount of the check in figures.
4. Write the amount of the check in words; checks for less than a dollar should be written as "only 79 cents," for example, with the word *dollars* on the check crossed out.
5. Sign the check in the same way you signed the signature card when you opened your account.
6. Make a note of the reason for payment, to assist with budget and tax preparation.

Check-writing software is available as a separate program or as part of a financial planning package such as Microsoft Office or Quicken. These programs can easily prepare

EXHIBIT 5–10

A Personal Check

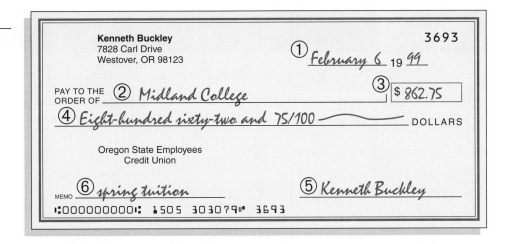

Kenneth Buckley
7828 Carl Drive
Westover, OR 98123

3693

① February 6 19 99

PAY TO THE ② Midland College
ORDER OF

③ $ 862.75

④ Eight-hundred sixty-two and 75/100 ———— DOLLARS

Oregon State Employees
Credit Union

MEMO ⑥ spring tuition

⑤ Kenneth Buckley

⑆000000000⑆ 1505 303079⑆ 3693

checks while also maintaining your financial records such as the check register, personal financial statements, and a budget.

A *stop-payment order* may be necessary if a check is lost or stolen or if a business transaction was not completed in a satisfactory manner. A verbal stop-payment order is valid for 14 days; a written order stays in effect for six months. After that time, it may be necessary to renew the order and fill out a new stop-payment form. Most banks, however, do not honor checks with "stale" dates. The fee for a stop payment commonly ranges from $10 to $20. If several checks are missing or you lose your checkbook, the bank may suggest closing that account and opening a new one. This action is likely to be less costly than paying several stop-payment fees.

Maintaining a Checking Account

Each month, you will receive a *bank statement,* a summary of the transactions for a checking account. This document reports deposits made, checks paid, interest earned, and fees for items such as service charges and printing of checks. The balance reported on the bank statement will probably differ from the balance in your checkbook. Reasons for a difference are checks that you have written but have not yet cleared, deposits you have made since the bank statement was prepared, interest added to your account, and deductions for fees and charges.

To determine your true balance, you should prepare a *bank reconciliation.* This report accounts for differences between the bank statement and your checkbook balance. The steps you take in this process, shown in the Financial Planning Calculations box on page 148, are as follows:

1. Compare the checks you have written over the past month with those reported as paid on your bank statement. Use the canceled checks from the financial institution, or compare your check register with the check numbers reported on the bank statement (many financial institutions no longer return canceled checks to customers). *Subtract* from the *bank statement balance* the total of the checks written but not yet cleared.
2. Determine whether any recent deposits are not on the bank statement. If so, *add* the amount of the deposits to the *bank statement balance.*
3. *Subtract* any fees or charges on the bank statement from your *checkbook balance.*
4. *Add* any interest earned to your *checkbook balance.*

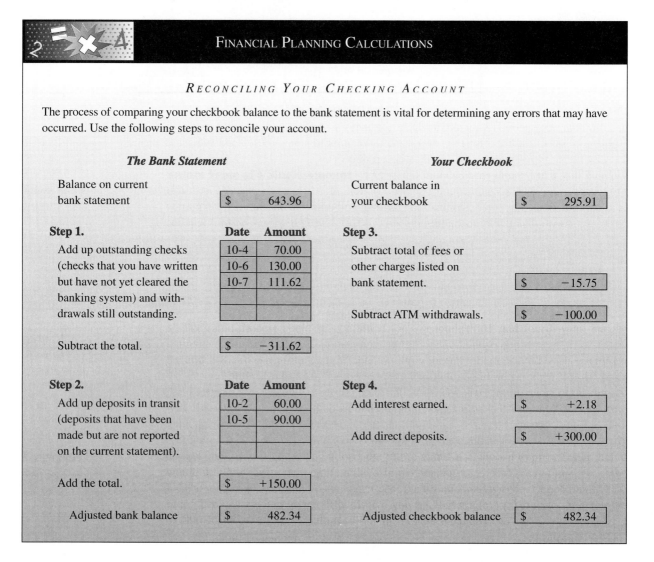

FINANCIAL PLANNING CALCULATIONS

RECONCILING YOUR CHECKING ACCOUNT

The process of comparing your checkbook balance to the bank statement is vital for determining any errors that may have occurred. Use the following steps to reconcile your account.

The Bank Statement			*Your Checkbook*	
Balance on current bank statement	$ 643.96		Current balance in your checkbook	$ 295.91

Step 1. | **Date** | **Amount** | **Step 3.** |
Add up outstanding checks (checks that you have written but have not yet cleared the banking system) and withdrawals still outstanding.	10-4	70.00	Subtract total of fees or other charges listed on bank statement.	$ −15.75
	10-6	130.00		
	10-7	111.62	Subtract ATM withdrawals.	$ −100.00
Subtract the total.	$ −311.62			

Step 2. | **Date** | **Amount** | **Step 4.** |
Add up deposits in transit (deposits that have been made but are not reported on the current statement).	10-2	60.00	Add interest earned.	$ +2.18
	10-5	90.00	Add direct deposits.	$ +300.00
Add the total.	$ +150.00			
Adjusted bank balance	$ 482.34		Adjusted checkbook balance	$ 482.34

PFP

Sheet 28

At this point, the revised balances for both your checkbook and the bank statement should be the same. If the two do not match, check your math, making sure every check and deposit was recorded correctly in your checkbook and on the bank statement.

Many people do not take the time to reconcile their accounts; however, failure to do this could cost you money. If the bank subtracts more for a check than the amount for which you wrote it and you don't complain within a year, the bank may not be liable to correct the error. Regulations covering this situation vary from state to state.

CONCEPT CHECK 5–6

1. How does a blank endorsement differ from a special endorsement?
2. What common difficulties do people encounter when reconciling their checking accounts?

KEY FORMULAS

Page	Topic	Formula
139	Annual percentage yield (APY)	$APY = 100 [(1 + Interest/Principal)^{365/days\ in\ term} - 1]$
		Principal = The amount of funds on deposit
		Interest = The total dollar amount earned on the principal
		Days in term = The actual number of days in the term of the account
	When the number of days in the term is 365 or where the account does not have a stated maturity, the APY formula is simply	$APY = 100 (Interest/Principal)$
		Example:
		$100 \left[\left(1 + \frac{\$56.20}{\$1,000} \right)^{\frac{365}{365}} - 1 \right] = 0.0562 = 5.62\%$
140	After-tax rate of return	Interest rate $\times$ (1 − Tax rate)
		Example:
		$.05 \times (1 - 0.28) = 0.036 = 3.6\%$

SUMMARY

L.O.1   Analyze factors that affect selection and use of financial services.

Financial products such as savings plans, checking accounts, loans, and trust services are used for managing daily financial activities. Technology, opportunity costs, and economic conditions affect the selection and use of financial services.

L.O.2   Compare the types of financial institutions.

Commercial banks, savings and loan associations, mutual savings banks, credit unions, life insurance companies, investment companies, finance companies, mortgage companies, pawnshops, and check-cashing outlets may be compared on the basis of services offered, rates and fees, safety, convenience, and special programs available to customers.

L.O.3   Compare the costs and benefits of various savings plans.

Commonly used savings plans include regular savings accounts, club accounts, certificates of deposit, interest-earning checking accounts, money market accounts, money market funds, and U.S. savings bonds.

L.O.4   Identify the factors used to evaluate different savings plans.

Savings plans may be evaluated on the basis of rate of return, inflation, tax considerations, liquidity, safety, restrictions, and fees.

L.O.5   Compare the costs and benefits of different types of checking accounts.

Regular checking accounts, activity accounts, and interest-earning checking accounts can be compared with regard to restrictions (such as a minimum balance), fees and charges, interest, and special services.

L.O.6   Describe the activities involved in using a checking account.

Checking account activities include opening an account, making deposits, writing checks, and reconciling the account.

GLOSSARY

annual percentage yield (APY)   The percentage rate expressing the total amount of interest that would be received on a $100 deposit based on the annual rate and frequency of compounding for a 365-day period.   (p. 138)

asset management account   An all-in-one account that includes savings, checking, borrowing, investing, and other financial services for a single fee; also called a *cash management account.*   (p. 125)

automatic teller machine (ATM)   A computer terminal used to conduct banking transactions.   (p. 126)

certificate of deposit (CD)   A savings plan requiring that a certain amount be left on deposit for a stated time period to earn a specified interest rate.   (p. 135)

commercial bank   A financial institution that offers a full range of financial services to individuals, businesses, and government agencies.   (p. 130)

compounding   A process that calculates interest based on previously earned interest.   (p. 137)

credit union   A user-owned, nonprofit cooperative financial institution that is organized for the benefit of its members. (p. 131)

debit card   A plastic access card used in computerized banking transactions; also called a *cash card* or *ATM card.* (p. 126)

demand deposits   Funds in checking accounts.   (p. 124)

money market account   A savings account offered by banks, savings and loan associations, and credit unions that requires a minimum balance and has earnings based on market interest rates.   (p. 136)

money market fund   A savings-investment plan offered by investment companies, with earnings based on investments in various short-term financial instruments.   (p. 131)

mutual savings bank   A financial institution that is owned by depositors and specializes in savings accounts and mortgage loans.   (p. 131)

NOW account   An interest-bearing checking account; NOW is an abbreviation for *negotiable order of withdrawal.* (p. 141)

overdraft protection   An automatic loan made to checking account customers to cover the amount of checks written in excess of the available balance in the checking account. (p. 143)

rate of return   The percentage of increase in the value of savings as a result of interest earned; also called *yield.* (p. 137)

savings and loan association (S&L)   A financial institution that traditionally specialized in savings accounts and mortgage loans.   (p. 130)

share account   A regular savings account at a credit union.   (p. 135)

share draft account   An interest-bearing checking account at a credit union.   (p. 141)

time deposits   Money in savings accounts and certificates. (p. 124)

trust   A legal agreement that provides for the management and control of assets by one party for the benefit of another.   (p. 125)

Review Questions

1. Why is a knowledge of interest rates important for successful financial planning?   (L.O.1)
2. How can users of financial services get the most for their money?   (L.O.2)
3. Why would a two-year certificate of deposit pay a higher rate than a six-month CD?   (L.O.3)
4. What relationship exists between risk and rate of return for savings plans?   (L.O.4)
5. What opportunity costs are associated with selecting and using a checking account?   (L.O.5)
6. How does careful management of a checking account help a person avoid becoming a victim of check fraud?   (L.O.6)

Financial Planning Problems

1. *Determining Savings Goals.* What would be common savings goals for a person who buys a five-year CD paying 8.75 percent instead of an 18-month savings certificate paying 7.5 percent?   (L.O.4)
2. *Computing Future Value.* What would be the value of a savings account started with $500, earning 6 percent (compounded annually) after 10 years?   (L.O.5)
3. *Calculating Present Value.* Brenda Young desires to have $10,000 eight years from now for her daughter's college fund. If she will earn 7 percent (compounded annually) on her money, what amount should she deposit now? Use the present value of a single amount calculation.   (L.O.5)
4. *Computing Future Value of Annual Deposits.* What amount would you have if you deposited $1,500 a year for 30 years at 8 percent (compounded annually)? (Use Appendix C.)   (L.O.5)
5. *Comparing Taxable and Tax-Free Yields.* With a 28 percent marginal tax rate, would a tax-free yield of 7 percent or a taxable yield of 9.5 percent give you a better return on your savings? Why?   (L.O.5)
6. *Computing APY.* What would be the annual percentage yield for a savings account that earned $56 in interest on $800 over the past 365 days?   (L.O.5)
7. *Calculating Opportunity Cost.* What is the annual opportunity cost of a checking account that requires a $350 minimum balance to avoid service charges? Assume an interest rate of 6.5 percent.   (L.O.5)
8. *Comparing Costs of Checking Accounts.* What would be the net *annual* cost of the following checking accounts? (L.O.5)
   a. Monthly fee, $3.75; processing fee, 25 cents per check; checks written, an average of 22 a month.

b. Interest earnings of 6 percent with a $500 minimum balance; average monthly balance, $600; monthly service charge of $15 for falling below the minimum balance, which occurs three times a year (no interest earned in these months).

9. *Computing Checking Account Costs.* Based on the following information, determine the true balance in your checking account. (L.O.6)

Balance in your checkbook, $356
Balance on bank statement, $472
Service charge and other fees, $15
Interest earned on the account, $4
Total of outstanding checks, $187
Deposits in transit, $60

PROJECTS AND APPLICATION ACTIVITIES

1. *Researching Financial Services.* Using the World Wide Web or library resources, obtain information about new developments in financial services. How have technology, changing economic conditions, and new legislation affected the types and availability of various saving and checking financial services? (L.O.1)

2. *Monitoring Economic Conditions.* Research current economic conditions (interest rates, inflation) using *The Wall Street Journal,* other library resources, or the World Wide 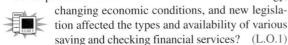 Web. Based on current economic conditions, what actions would you recommend to people who are saving and borrowing money? (L.O.1)

3. *Comparing Financial Institutions.* Collect advertisements and promotional information from several financial institutions, or locate the Web sites of financial institutions such as Wells Fargo Bank (www.wellsfargo.com) and Bank of America (www.bankamerica.com). Create a list of factors 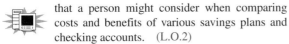 that a person might consider when comparing costs and benefits of various savings plans and checking accounts. (L.O.2)

4. *Obtaining Opinions about Financial Services.* Survey several people to determine awareness and use of various financial services such as online banking, "smart cards," and check-writing software. (L.O.2)

5. *Researching Credit Unions.* Using the Web site for the Credit Union National Association (www.cuna.org) or other sources, obtain information about joining a credit union and the services this type of financial institution offers. (L.O.2)

6. *Comparing Savings Plans.* Collect advertisements from several financial institutions with information about the savings plans they offer. (You may do this using the Web sites of various financial institutions.) Using Sheet 25 in the *Personal Financial Planner,* compare the features and potential earnings of two or three savings plans. (L.O.3,4)

7. *Researching Current Savings Rates.* Using library sources (such as *The Wall Street Journal* and other current business periodicals) or Web sites (such as 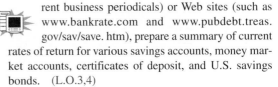 www.bankrate.com and www.pubdebt.treas. gov/sav/save. htm), prepare a summary of current rates of return for various savings accounts, money market accounts, certificates of deposit, and U.S. savings bonds. (L.O.3,4)

8. *Comparing Checking Accounts.* Using Sheets 26 and 27 in the Personal Financial Planner, compare the features and costs of checking accounts at two different financial institutions. Online searches of bank Web sites may be useful. (L.O.5,6)

9. *Analyzing Check-Writing Software.* Visit software retailers to obtain information about the features in various personal computer programs used for maintaining a checking 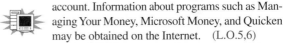 account. Information about programs such as Managing Your Money, Microsoft Money, and Quicken may be obtained on the Internet. (L.O.5,6)

10. *Researching Checking Accounts.* Several states require that banks offer basic checking accounts. For example, in Illinois, New York, New Jersey, and Minnesota, check services with minimal fees must be made available for consumers making a limited number of transactions. Obtain information about the availability of these types of *life-line* accounts in your area. (L.O.5,6)

LIFE SITUATION CASE 5

CHECKING OUT FINANCIAL SERVICES

Carla and Ed Johnson have separate checking accounts. Each pays part of the household and living expenses. Carla pays the mortgage and telephone bill, while Ed pays for food and utilities and makes the insurance and car payments. This arrangement allows them the freedom to spend whatever extra money they have each month without needing to explain their actions to each other. Carla and Ed believe their separate accounts have minimized disagreements about money. Since both spend most of their money each month, they have low balances in their checking accounts, resulting in a monthly charge totaling $15.

In the same financial institution where Carla has her checking account, the Johnsons have $600 in a passbook savings account that earns 1.8 percent interest. If the savings account balance exceeded $1,000, they would earn 2.65 percent. If the balance stayed above $1,000, they would not have to pay the monthly service charge on Carla's checking account. The financial institution has a program that moves money from checking to savings. This program would allow the Johnsons to increase their savings and work toward a secure financial future.

Ed has his checking account at a bank that offers an electronic banking system allowing a customer to obtain cash at many locations 24 hours a day. Ed believes this feature is valuable when cash is needed to cover business expenses and personal spending. For an additional monthly fee, the bank would also provide Ed with a credit card, a safe deposit box, and a single monthly statement summarizing all transactions.

While most people plan their spending for living expenses, few plan their use of financial services. Therefore, many people are charged high fees for checking accounts and earn low interest on their savings. Despite a wide choice of financial institutions and services, you can learn to compare their costs and benefits. Your awareness of financial services and your ability to evaluate them are vital skills for a healthy personal economic future.

QUESTIONS

1. Which financial services are most important to Carla and Ed Johnson?
2. What efforts are the Johnsons currently making to assess their use of financial services in relation to their other financial activities?
3. How should the Johnsons assess their needs for financial services? On what bases should they compare financial services?
4. What should the Johnsons do to improve their use of financial services?

USING THE INTERNET TO CREATE A PERSONAL FINANCIAL PLAN 5

SELECTING SAVINGS AND CHECKING ACCOUNT SERVICES

The use of payment services and savings programs influences other aspects of financial planning. Attempts to minimize banking fees while maximizing earnings on funds are common objectives.

Web Sites for Selecting Banking Services

- Current rates for various savings instruments at **usatoday.com/money/savebox.htm, www.bankrate.com/bankrate/publ/tips.htm,** and **www.banx.com**
- The Federal Deposit Insurance Corporation provides access to consumer information, press releases, and banking statistics at **www.fdic.gov**
- Current information on U.S. savings bonds at **www.publicdebt.treas.gov/sav/sav.htm**
- Information on Federal Reserve activities, publications, and access to the Web sites of other Federal Reserve Banks is available at **www.bog.frb.fed.us;** the Federal Reserve Bank of San Francisco offers details for buying U.S. savings bonds and Treasury notes and bonds at www.frbsf.org; the Federal Reserve Bank Web site has a redemption calculator for determining the current value of U.S. savings bonds at **www.ny.frb.org**
- Information about banking services from the American Bankers Association at **www.aba.com**
- Savings information from the American Savings Education Council at **www.asec.org**
- Financial calculators for savings at **www.centura.com/formulas/ca/c.html**

- Information on making payments on the Internet at **www.checkfree.com**
- Online banking information at **www.orcc.com/banking.htm/**

(Note: Addresses and content of Web sites change, and new sites are created daily. Use the search engines discussed in Appendix B to update and locate Web sites for your current financial planning needs.)

PFP SHEETS: 23–28

Short-Term Financial Planning Activities

1. Identify various financial services needed for savings, payment, and money management activities. Identify financial institutions that might be used to obtain these financial services (see PFP sheet 23).
2. Compare the rates of return, fees, and other factors for different savings plans that might be used to meet your financial goals (see PFP Sheets 24, 25).
3. Compare the features and costs of checking services at various financial institutions (see PFP Sheet 26, 27).

Long-Term Financial Planning Activities

1. Identify saving decisions that would best help you achieve long-term financial goals.
2. List the economic conditions (inflation, current interest rates) and personal factors to monitor, related to the costs and benefits of financial services, as your personal life situation changes over time.

CHAPTER 6

INTRODUCTION TO CONSUMER CREDIT

OPENING CASE

FEE IF YOU DO, FEE IF YOU DON'T

What if you had to pay a fee for *not* using your credit card? Or what if your credit card company charged $25 if you decided to close your account? Advanta Corporation, the nation's 10th largest credit card issuer, is telling its cardholders it may do exactly that in a notice being mailed with its current billing. If Advanta, based in Spring House, Pennsylvania, succeeds, other banks may soon follow.

Banks are increasingly turning to fee income to prop their balance sheets because the income they earn from interest on loans is becoming a smaller piece of their income pie. For example, First Chicago NBD Corporation counts on its credit card operation to provide more than 20 percent of its total income. Since 1992, the money First Chicago earned by charging customers and clients a fee for its services has grown 25 percent, from $2 billion to 2.5 billion.

Consumer advocates don't like this trend. Stephen Brobeck, executive director of the Consumer Federation of America (CFA), said, "We need incentives for consumers to cut up their credit card accounts, not keep them."

Brobeck said the CFA is opposed only to the account termination fee proposed by Advanta, not the fee for nonusage. Brobeck believes that charging a fee for termination of an account discourages consumers from shopping for the best deal in the marketplace. A credit card industry spokesperson noted, however, that consumers carrying a balance frequently roll their balance to a new card if they receive an offer of a lower interest rate, even if it's only for an introductory period.

Advanta says it doesn't know when, or if, it will impose the new fees. "By mailing the notices, we're just reserving the right to impose fees," said Darcy Rudney, a spokesperson for the credit card company.

QUESTIONS:

1. For what two activities may Advanta cardholders have to pay a fee in the future?
2. Why are banks turning to fees to increase their income?
3. Why is the Consumer Federation of America opposed to account termination fees?

SOURCE: Adapted from John Schmeltzer, "Fee If You Do, Fee If You Don't: Credit Card Firm May Levy Non-Use Charge," *Chicago Tribune*, June 12, 1997.

After studying this chapter, you will be able to

L.O.1 Define consumer credit and analyze its advantages and disadvantages.

L.O.2 Differentiate among various types of credit.

L.O.3 Assess your credit capacity and build your credit rating.

L.O.4 Describe the information creditors look for when you apply for credit.

L.O.5 Identify the steps you can take to avoid and correct credit mistakes.

L.O.6 Describe the laws that protect you if you have a complaint about consumer credit.

WHAT IS CONSUMER CREDIT?

L.O.1 Define consumer credit and analyze its advantages and disadvantages.

credit

consumer credit

Financial Decision Trade-Off

"Charge it!" "Cash or credit?" "Put it on my account." As these phrases indicate, the use of credit is a fact of life in personal and family financial planning. When you use credit, you satisfy needs today and pay for this satisfaction in the future. While the use of credit is often necessary and even advantageous, responsibilities and disadvantages are associated with its use.

Credit is an arrangement to receive cash, goods, or services now and pay for them in the future. **Consumer credit** refers to the use of credit for personal needs (except a home mortgage) by individuals and families in contrast to credit used for business purposes.

Although Polonius cautioned, "Neither a borrower nor a lender be," using and providing credit have become a way of life for many people and businesses in today's economy. In January, you pay a bill for electricity that you used in December. A statement arrives in the mail for medical services that you received last month. You write a check for $40, a minimum payment on a $300 department store bill. With a bank loan, you purchase a new car. These are all examples of using credit: paying later for goods and services obtained now.

Most consumers have three alternatives in financing current purchases: They can draw on their savings, use their present earnings, or borrow against their expected future income. Each of these alternatives has trade-offs. If you continually deplete your savings, little will be left for emergencies or retirement income. If you spend your current income on luxuries instead of necessities, your well-being will eventually suffer. And if you pledge your future income to make current credit purchases, you will have little or no spendable income in the future.

Consumer credit is based on trust in people's ability and willingness to pay bills when due. It works because people by and large are honest and responsible. But how does consumer credit affect our economy, and how is it affected by our economy?

The Importance of Consumer Credit in Our Economy

Consumer credit dates back to colonial times. While credit was originally a privilege of the affluent, farmers came to use it extensively. No direct finance charges were imposed; instead, the cost of credit was added to the prices of goods. With the advent of the automobile in the early 1900s, installment credit, in which the debt is repaid in equal installments over a specified period of time, exploded on the American scene.

All economists now recognize consumer credit as a major force in the American economy. Any forecast or evaluation of the economy includes consumer spending trends and consumer credit as a sustaining force. To paraphrase an old political expression, as the consumer goes, so goes the U.S. economy.

The aging of the baby boom generation has added to the growth of consumer credit. The 25–44 age group currently represents about 30 percent of the population but holds nearly 60 percent of the outstanding debt. The people in this age group have always been disproportionate users of credit, since consumption is highest as families are formed and homes are purchased and furnished. Thus, while the extensive use of debt by this age group is nothing new, the fact that it has grown rapidly has added to overall debt use.

Uses and Misuses of Credit

Using credit to purchase goods and services may allow consumers to be more efficient or more productive or to lead more satisfying lives. There are many valid reasons for using credit. A medical emergency may leave a person strapped for funds. A homemaker returning to the work force may need a car. It may be possible to buy an item now for less money than it will cost later. Borrowing for a college education is another valid reason. But it is probably not reasonable to borrow for everyday living expenses or finance a Corvette on credit when a Ford Escort is all your budget allows.

"Shopaholics" and young adults are most vulnerable to misusing credit. College students are a prime target for credit card issuers, and issuers make it very easy for students to get credit cards. Wendy Leright, a 25-year-old teacher in Detroit, knows this all too well. As a college freshman, she applied for and got seven credit cards, all bearing at least an 18.9 percent interest rate and a $20 annual fee. Although unemployed, she used the cards freely, buying expensive clothes for herself, extravagant Christmas presents for friends and family, and even a one-week vacation in the Bahamas. "It got to a point where I didn't even look at the price tag," she said. By her senior year, Wendy had amassed $9,000 in credit card debt and couldn't make the monthly payments of nearly $200. She eventually turned to her parents to bail her out. "Until my mother sat me down and showed me how much interest I had to pay, I hadn't even given it a thought. I was shocked," Wendy said. "I would have had to pay it off for years."[1]

Using credit increases the amount of money a person can spend to purchase goods and services now. But the trade-off is that it decreases the amount of money that will be available to spend in the future. However, many people expect their incomes to increase and therefore expect to be able to make payments on past credit purchases and still make new purchases.

Here are some questions you should consider before you decide how and when to make a major purchase, for example, a car:

Financial Decision
Trade-Off

- Do I have the cash I need for the down payment?
- Do I want to use my savings for this purchase?
- Does the purchase fit my budget?
- Could I use the credit I need for this purchase in some better way?

- Could I postpone the purchase?
- What are the opportunity costs of postponing the purchase? (Alternative transportation costs, a possible increase in the price of the car)
- What are the dollar costs and the psychological costs of using credit? (Interest, other finance charges, being in debt and responsible for making a monthly payment)

If you decide to use credit, make sure the benefits of making the purchase now (increased efficiency or productivity, a more satisfying life, etc.) outweigh the costs (financial and psychological) of using credit. Thus, credit, when effectively used, can help you have more and enjoy more. When misused, credit can result in default, bankruptcy, and loss of creditworthiness.

Advantages of Credit

Consumer credit enables people to enjoy goods and services now—a car, a home, an education, help in emergencies—and pay for them through payment plans based on future income.

Credit cards permit the purchase of goods even when funds are low. Customers with previously approved credit may receive other extras, such as advance notice of sales and the right to order by phone or to buy on approval. In addition, many shoppers believe it is easier to return merchandise they have purchased on account. Credit cards also provide shopping convenience and the efficiency of paying for several purchases with one monthly payment.

Credit is more than a substitute for cash. Many of the services it provides are taken for granted. Every time you turn on the water tap, flick the light switch, or telephone a friend, you are using credit.

It is safer to use credit, since charge accounts and credit cards let you shop and travel without carrying a large amount of cash. You need a credit card to make a hotel reservation, rent a car, and shop by phone. You also use credit cards for identification when cashing checks, and the use of credit provides you with a record of expenses.

The use of credit cards can provide up to a 50-day "float," the time lag between when you make the purchase and when the lender deducts the balance from your checking account. This float, offered by many credit card issuers, includes a grace period of 20 to 25 days. During the grace period, no finance charges are assessed on current purchases if the balance is paid in full each month within 25 days after billing.

Some large corporations, such as General Electric Company and General Motors Corporation, issue their own Visa and MasterCard and offer rebates on purchases. For example, every time you make a purchase with the GM MasterCard, 5 percent of the purchase price is set aside for you in a special GM Card Rebate account. When you are ready to buy or lease a GM car or truck, you just cash in your rebate at the GM dealership. Similarly, with a Discover card, you can earn a cash bonus of up to 1 percent based on your total purchases during the year. In the late 1990s, however, some corporations began to eliminate these cards.

Finally, credit indicates stability. The fact that lenders consider you a good risk usually means you are a responsible individual. However, if you do not repay your debts in a timely manner, you will find that credit has many disadvantages.

Disadvantages of Credit

When considering the use of credit, remember that credit costs money and may lead you to overspend, resulting in loss of merchandise or income, and tie up your future income.

Perhaps the greatest disadvantage of using credit is the temptation to overspend, especially during periods of inflation. It seems easy to buy today and pay tomorrow using cheaper dollars. But continual overspending leads to serious trouble.

Whether or not credit involves security (something of value to back the loan), failure to repay a loan may result in loss of income, valuable property, and your good reputation. It can even lead to court action and bankruptcy. Misuse of credit can create serious long-term financial problems, damage to family relationships, and a slowing of progress toward financial goals. Therefore, you should approach credit with caution and avoid using it more extensively than your budget permits.

Although credit allows more immediate satisfaction of needs and desires, it does not increase total purchasing power. Credit purchases must be paid for out of future income; therefore, credit ties up the use of future income. Furthermore, if your income does not increase to cover rising costs, your ability to repay credit commitments will diminish. Before buying goods and services on credit, consider whether they will have lasting value, whether they will increase your personal satisfaction during present and future income periods, and whether your current income will continue or increase.

Finally, credit costs money. It is a service for which you must pay. Paying for purchases over a period of time is more costly than paying for them with cash. Purchasing with credit rather than cash involves one very obvious trade-off: the fact that it will cost more due to monthly finance charges and the compounding effect of interest on interest.

In summary, the use of credit provides immediate access to goods and services, flexibility in money management, safety and convenience, a cushion in emergencies, a means of increasing resources, and a good credit rating if you pay your debts back in a timely manner. But remember, the use of credit is a two-sided coin. An intelligent decision as to its use demands careful evaluation of your current debt, your future income, the added cost, and the consequences of overspending.

CONCEPT CHECK 6–1

1. What is consumer credit?
2. Why is consumer credit important to our economy?
3. What are the uses and misuses of credit?
4. What are the advantages and disadvantages of credit?

TYPES OF CREDIT

L.O.2 Differentiate among various types of credit.

closed-end credit

open-end credit

Two basic types of consumer credit exist: closed-end credit and open-end credit. With **closed-end credit,** you pay back one-time loans in a specified period of time and in payments of equal amounts. With **open-end credit,** loans are made on a continuous basis and you are billed periodically for at least partial payment. Exhibit 6–1 shows examples of closed-end and open-end credit.

Closed-End Credit

Closed-end credit is used for a specific purpose and involves a specified amount. Mortgage loans, automobile loans, and installment loans for purchasing furniture or appliances are examples of closed-end credit. An agreement, or contract, lists the repayment

EXHIBIT 6–1
_____

Types of Credit

Closed-End Credit
• Mortgage loans
• Automobile loans
• Installment loans (Installment sales contract, installment cash credit, single lump-sum credit)

Open-End Credit
• Cards issued by: Department stores, Bank cards (Visa, MasterCard, American Express)
• Travel & Entertainment (T&E)
• Overdraft protection

terms—the number of payments, the payment amount, and how much the credit will cost. Closed-end payment plans usually involve a written agreement for each credit purchase. A down payment or trade-in may be required, with the balance to be repaid in equal weekly or monthly payments over a period of time. Generally, the seller holds title to the merchandise until the payments have been completed.

The three most common types of closed-end credit are installment sales credit, installment cash credit, and single lump-sum credit. *Installment sales credit* is a loan that allows you to receive merchandise, usually high-priced items such as large appliances or furniture. You make a down payment and usually sign a contract to repay the balance, plus interest and service charges, in equal installments over a specified period.

Installment cash credit is a direct loan of money for personal purposes, home improvements, or vacation expenses. You make no down payment and make payments in specified amounts over a set period.

Single lump-sum credit is a loan that must be repaid in total on a specified day, usually within 30 to 90 days. Lump-sum credit is generally, but not always, used to purchase a single item. As Exhibit 6–2 shows, consumer installment credit reached over $1 trillion in 1995.

Open-End Credit

Using a credit card issued by a department store, using a bank credit card (Visa, MasterCard) to make purchases at different stores, charging a meal at a restaurant, and using overdraft protection are examples of open-end credit. As you will soon see, you do not apply for open-end credit to make a single purchase, as you do with closed-end credit. Rather, you can use open-end credit to make any purchases you wish if you do not exceed *line of credit* your **line of credit,** the maximum dollar amount of credit the lender has made available to you. You may have to pay **interest,** a periodic charge for the use of credit, or other *interest* finance charges. Some creditors allow you a grace period of 20 to 25 days to pay a bill in full before you incur any interest charges.

You may have had an appointment with a doctor or a dentist that you did not pay for until later. Professionals and small businesses often do not demand immediate payment but will charge interest if you do not pay the bill in full within 30 days. *Incidental credit* is a credit arrangement that has no extra costs and no specific repayment plan.

Many retailers use open-end credit. Customers can purchase goods or services up to a fixed dollar limit at any time. Usually you have the option to pay the bill in full within 30 days without interest charges or to make set monthly installments based on the account balance plus interest.

revolving check credit Many banks extend **revolving check credit**. Also called a *bank line of credit*, this is a prearranged loan for a specified amount that you can use by writing a special check. Repayment is made in installments over a set period. The finance charges are based on the amount of credit used during the month and on the outstanding balance.

EXHIBIT 6–2

**Consumer
Installment Credit**

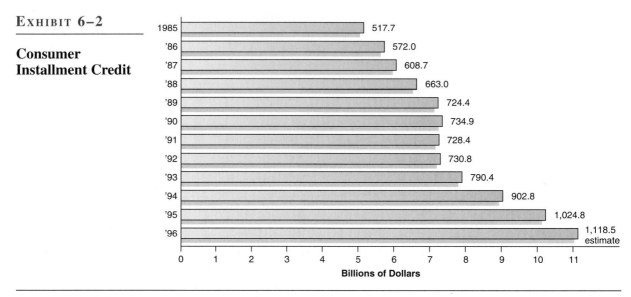

1985	517.7
'86	572.0
'87	608.7
'88	663.0
'89	724.4
'90	734.9
'91	728.4
'92	730.8
'93	790.4
'94	902.8
'95	1,024.8
'96	1,118.5 estimate

Billions of Dollars

SOURCE: *Statistical Abstract of the United States.*

Credit Cards   Credit cards are extremely popular. According to a recent *American Banker* survey, 8 out of 10 U.S. households carry one or more credit cards. Two out of three households have at least one retail credit card, 56 percent have one or more Visa cards, and 47 percent have at least one MasterCard.[2]

One-third of all credit card users generally pay off their balances in full each month. These cardholders are often known as *convenience users.* Others are borrowers; they carry balances beyond the grace period and pay finance charges. As Exhibit 6–3 illustrates, consumers use more than 1 billion credit cards to buy clothing, meals, vacations, gasoline, groceries, doctor visits, and other goods and services on credit.[3]

About 25,000 financial institutions participate in the credit card business, and the vast majority of them are affiliated with Visa International or the Interbank Card Association, which issues MasterCard. The Financial Planning for Life's Situations box on page 163 provides a few helpful hints for choosing a credit card.

Cobranding is the linking of a credit card with a business trade name offering "points" or premiums toward the purchase of a product or service. Cobranding has become increasingly popular since the success of General Motors Corporation's credit card, launched in 1992. Cobranded credit cards offer rebates on products and services such as health clubs, tax preparation services from H&R Block, and gasoline purchases. Banks are realizing that cobranded credit cards help build customer loyalty. *Smart cards,* the ultimate plastic embedded with a computer chip that can store 500 times the data of a credit card, are on their way.

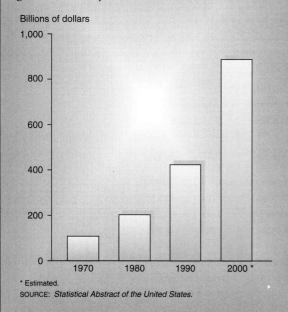

DID YOU KNOW?

Americans will charge more than $830 billion on their credit cards in the year 2000. The average cardholder has more than nine credit cards, including bank, retail, gasoline, and telephone cards.

Billions of dollars

* Estimated.
SOURCE: *Statistical Abstract of the United States.*

EXHIBIT 6–3

**Credit Card
Holders and
Credit Cards Held**

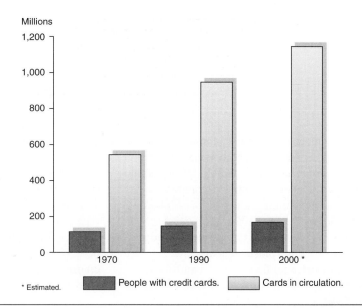

Millions

* Estimated.   People with credit cards.   Cards in circulation.

SOURCE: *Statistical Abstract of the United States.*

Smart cards combine credit cards, a driver's license, a health care ID with your medical history and insurance information, frequent-flier miles, and telephone cards. A single smart card, for example, can be used to buy an airline ticket, store it digitally, and track frequent-flier miles. In the near future, smart cards will provide a crucial link between the World Wide Web and the physical world. Smart cards could make up half of the $7.3 billion in online sales expected by 2000. "The Internet combined with the development of electronic cash will finally start the smart-card revolution in the U.S.," according to Keith S. Kendrick, senior vice president at AT&T Universal Card. Citibank, Chase Manhattan Corporation, and Wells Fargo & Company have begun testing the smart credit/debit cards.[4]

debit card
Don't confuse credit cards with debit cards. Although they may look alike, the **debit card**, as the name implies, electronically subtracts from your account at the moment you buy goods or services, while the credit card extends credit and delays your payment. Debit cards are most commonly used at automatic teller machines, but they are increasingly being used to purchase goods at point-of-sale terminals in stores and service stations.

Debit cards are often called *bank cards*, *ATM cards*, *cash cards*, and *check cards*. While cash advances on credit cards can look attractive, remember that interest usually accrues from the moment you accept the cash, and you must also pay a transaction fee. One cash advance could cost you the money you were saving for a birthday gift for that special someone.

You are never responsible for charges on a debit card you haven't accepted. If you report a lost or stolen debit card within two days, federal regulations limit your liability to $50. After two days, your liability is limited to $50 plus any amount resulting from your failure to notify the issuer. If your debit card is lost or stolen, you must work directly with the issuer.

Protecting Yourself against Debit/Credit Card Fraud   In a country where consumers owe more than $½ trillion on their credit cards, estimates of $2 billion to $3 billion in credit fraud losses—just two to three one-thousandths of 1 percent—may not seem all that terrible. But it *is* terrible to victims of fraud. Though they may be protected financially,

JONATHAN HOENIG SPEAKS
CREDIT CHAOS

The bubonic plague of personal finance comes in the form of a 17 percent or higher interest rate on your credit card. You'll have to do a lot of bargain shopping and coupon clipping to compensate for your constantly compounding finance charges. Bummer? *Yes.* Your fault? Yes. Just because you have access to credit doesn't mean you should necessarily partake of the plastic. Credit cards can be a useful part of personal finance or a painful experience best likened to televisions "Cop Rock." Rule of thumb: *Don't buy things you can't afford.*

Thankfully, most young people seem to be following the rules these days. According to *Scholars and Cents,* an independent study sponsored by Visa USA, more than half of young people surveyed pay their credit card balance in full each month. Compared to the majority of cardholders, 60 percent of whom carry a balance, young people are demonstrating their financial savvy in record numbers.

Paying cash? You'll still deal with debt. Certain types, like school loans, car payments, and mortgages, are designed to be paid over longer periods of time. This is reflected in a lower interest rate. A credit card bill, and other types of "unsecured" debt, however, should be paid as soon as possible.

The Visa survey suggests young people are headed in the right direction. Ninety-four percent of college students recognize the importance of establishing and maintaining a good credit history.

they are forced to endure major inconvenience. Many fraud victims are devastated emotionally. The negative effects can linger for years. Moreover, all of us pay the costs of credit card fraud through higher prices, higher interest rates, and increased inconvenience.

How can you protect yourself against credit card fraud? You can take several measures:

- Sign your new cards as soon as they arrive.
- Treat your cards like money. Store them in a secure place.
- Shred anything with your account number before throwing it away.
- Don't give your card number over the phone or online unless you initiate the call.
- Don't write your card number on a postcard or the outside of an envelope.
- Remember to get your card and receipt after a transaction, and double-check to be sure it's yours.
- If your billing statement is incorrect or your credit cards are lost or stolen, notify your card issuers immediately.
- If you don't receive your billing statement, notify the company immediately.
- If you are a victim of credit card fraud, call the Experian Consumer Education Department at 1–800–301–7195.

DID YOU KNOW?

By 2000, credit card debt will reach $660.9 billion.

Card type	Billions of Dollars
Bank cards	486.0
Retail store cards	98.9
Travel and Entertainment cards	35.3
Other cards	33.7
Oil company cards	4.1
Phone cards	3.0

SOURCE: *Statistical Abstract of the United States 1996,* Table 793, p. 517

FINANCIAL PLANNING FOR LIFE'S SITUATIONS

CHOOSING A CREDIT CARD?

When choosing a credit card, it pays to shop around. Follow these suggestions to select the card that best meets your needs.

1. Department stores and gasoline companies are good places to obtain your first credit card. Pay your bills in full and on time, and you will begin to establish a good credit history.

2. Bank cards are offered through banks and savings and loan associations. Fees and finance charges vary considerably (from 8 to 21.6 percent), so shop around.

3. If you usually pay your bill in full, try to deal with a financial institution with an interest-free grace period, which is the time after a purchase has been made and before a finance charge is imposed, typically 25 to 30 days.

4. If you're used to paying monthly installments, look for a card with a low monthly finance charge. Be sure you understand how that finance charge is calculated.

5. Consider obtaining a card from an out-of-state financial institution if it offers better terms than those offered locally.

6. Be aware of some credit cards that offer "no fee" or low interest but start charging interest from the day you purchase an item.

7. Watch out for some credit cards that do not charge annual fees but instead charge a "transaction fee" each time you use the card.

8. If you're paying only the minimum amounts on your monthly statement, you need to plan your budget more carefully. The longer it takes for you to pay off a bill, the more interest you pay. The finance charges you pay on an item could end up being more than the item is worth.

9. With a grace period of 25 days, you actually get a free loan when you pay bills in full each month.

10. To avoid delays that may result in finance charges, follow the card issuer's instructions as to where, how, and when to make bill payments.

11. If you have a bad credit history and problems getting a credit card, look for a savings institution that will give you a secured credit card if you open a savings account. Your line of credit will be determined by the amount you have on deposit.

12. Beware of offers of easy credit. No one can guarantee to get you credit.

13. Think twice before making a 900 number telephone call for a credit card. You will pay from $2 to $50 for the 900 call and may never receive a credit card.

14. Be aware of credit cards offered by "credit repair" companies or "credit clinics." These firms may also offer to clean up your credit history for a fee. But remember, only time and good credit habits will repair your credit report if you have a poor credit history.

15. If you are a victim of credit card fraud, immediately report it to the National Consumers League Fraud hot line at 1–800–846–7661 on weekdays.

16. If you don't have a list of your credit issuers' telephone numbers, you may be able to obtain them by calling the 800 number directory assistance at 1–800–555–1212.

17. Travel and entertainment (T&E) cards often charge higher annual fees than most credit cards. Usually you must make payment in full within 30 days of receiving your bill or typically no further purchases will be approved on the account.

18. Often additional credit cards on your account for a spouse or child (over 18) are available with a minimum additional fee or no fee at all.

19. Be aware that debit cards are not credit cards but simply a substitute for a check or cash. The amount of the sale is subtracted from your checking account.

SOURCES: American Institute of Certified Public Accountants, U.S. Office of Consumer Affairs, and Federal Trade Commission.

■ Request a copy of your credit report every few years. Reviewing your report will tell you if anyone has applied for credit in your name and whether any accounts are being used without your knowledge, with the billing statement being sent to a different address.[5]

Travel and Entertainment (T&E) Cards   T&E cards are really not credit cards, because the monthly balance is due in full. However, most people think of Diners Club

FINANCIAL PLANNING CALCULATIONS

HOW MUCH CAN YOU BORROW WITH A HOME EQUITY LOAN?

Depending on your income and the equity in your home, you can apply for a line of credit for anywhere from $10,000 to $250,000 or more.

Some lenders let you borrow only up to 75 percent of the value of your home, less the amount of your first mortgage. At some banks you may qualify to borrow up to 85 percent! This higher lending limit may make the difference in your ability to get the money you need for home improvements, education, or other expenses.

Use the following chart to calculate your home loan value, which is the approximate amount of your home equity line of credit.

	Example	Your Home
Approximate market value of your home	$100,000	$ _____
Multiply by .85	× .85	× .85
Approximate loan value	85,000	_____
Subtract balance due on mortgage(s)	50,000	_____
Approximate credit limit available	$35,000	$ _____

In the above example, your home loan value (the amount for which you could establish your account) is $35,000.

Once your account is established, you can write a check for any amount you need up to $35,000.

In choosing a home equity loan,

1. Find out if your lending institution protects you against rising interest rates.
2. Compare the size of your lender's fee with those of other institutions.
3. Find out if your lender charges an inactivity fee.
4. Make sure high annual fees and other costs do not outweigh the tax advantage of a home equity loan, especially if you are borrowing only a small amount.
5. Be careful of interest-only payments on home equity loans.
6. Find out whether your lender has the right to change the terms and conditions of your plan or to terminate your plan.
7. Make sure that all of the interest you hope to finally deduct on your home equity loan is in fact deductible.
8. Carefully evaluate your reasons for using the equity in your home for loans.
9. Know the full costs and risks of home equity loans before you make a commitment to a lending institution.

SOURCES: Adapted from *Home Equity Loan Guide,* Household Bank, F.S.B., August 1991, p. 3, and *Home Equity Loans: A Consumer's Guide,* American Institute of CPAs, n.d.

or American Express cards as credit cards because they don't pay the moment they purchase goods or services.

home equity loan

Home Equity Loans   A **home equity loan** is based on the difference between the current market value of your home and the amount you still owe on your mortgage. With such a loan, you can borrow up to $100,000 or more on your home. Depending on the value of the home, you can borrow up to 85 percent of its appraised value, less the amount you still owe on your mortgage. The interest you pay on a home equity loan is tax deductible, unlike interest on other types of loans.

A home equity loan is usually set up as a revolving line of credit, typically with a variable interest rate. A *revolving line of credit* is an arrangement whereby borrowings are permitted up to a specified limit and for a stated period, usually 5 to 10 years. Once the line of credit has been established, you draw from it only the amount you need at any one time (see the Financial Planning Calculations box above). Today many lenders offer home equity lines of credit. But your home is your largest asset. You should use the home equity loan only for major items such as education, home improvements, or medical bills and not for daily expenses. Remember, if you miss payments on a home equity loan, you can lose your home. Furthermore, when you sell your home, you probably will be required to pay off your equity line in full. If you plan to sell your house in the near future, consider whether annual fees to maintain the account and other costs of setting up an equity credit line make sense.

How much credit do you need? There is no single, universal formula to guide consumers on whether they need credit or on how much credit they can safely handle. People have different wants and needs. In addition, social and economic background and status play a part in what people want and need.

CONCEPT CHECK 6–2

1. What are the two main types of consumer credit?
2. What is a debit card?
3. What is a home equity loan?

MEASURING YOUR CREDIT CAPACITY

L.O.3 Assess your credit capacity and build your credit rating.

The only way to determine how much credit you can assume is to first learn how to make an accurate and sensible personal or family budget. Budgets, as you learned in Chapter 3, are simple, carefully considered spending plans. With budgets, you first provide for basic necessities such as rent or mortgage, food, and clothing. Then you provide for items such as home furnishings and other heavy, more durable goods.

Can You Afford a Loan?

Financial Decision
Trade-Off

Before you take out a loan, ask yourself whether you can meet all of your essential expenses and still afford the monthly loan payments. You can make this calculation in two ways. One is to add up all of your basic monthly expenses and then subtract this total from your take-home pay. If the difference will not cover the monthly payment and still leave funds for other expenses, you cannot afford the loan.

A second and more reliable method is to ask yourself what you plan to give up to make the monthly loan payment. If you currently save a portion of your income that is greater than the monthly payment, you can use these savings to pay off the loan. But if you do not, you will have to forgo spending on entertainment, new appliances, or perhaps even necessities. Are you prepared to make this trade-off? Although it is difficult to precisely measure your credit capacity, you can follow certain rules of thumb.

General Rules of Credit Capacity

Debt Payments-to-Income Ratio   The debt payments-to-income ratio is calculated by dividing your monthly debt payments (not including house payment, which is a long-term liability) by your net monthly income. Experts suggest that you spend no more than 20 percent of your net (after-tax) income on credit payments. Thus, as Exhibit 6–4 shows, a person making $1,068 per month after taxes should spend no more than $213 on credit payments per month.

The 20 percent estimate is the maximum; however, 15 percent is much better. The 20 percent estimate is based on the average family, with average expenses; it does not take

EXHIBIT 6–4

How to Calculate Debt Payments-to-Income Ratio

Monthly gross income	$1,500
Less:	
All taxes	270
Social Security	112
Monthly IRA contribution	50
Monthly net income	$ 1,068
Monthly installment credit payments:	
Visa	25
MasterCard	20
Discover card	15
Education loan	—
Personal bank loan	—
Auto loan	153
Total monthly payments	$ 213
Debt payments-to-income ratio ($213/$1,068)	19.94%

Sheet 29

major emergencies into account. If you are just beginning to use credit, you should not consider yourself safe if you are spending 20 percent of your net income on credit payments.

Debt-to-Equity Ratio   The debt-to-equity ratio is calculated by dividing your total liabilities by your net worth. In calculating this ratio, do not include the value of your home and the amount of its mortgage. If your debt-to-equity ratio is about 1, that is, if your consumer installment debt roughly equals your net worth (not including your home or the mortgage), you have probably reached the upper limit of debt obligations.

The debt-to-equity ratio for business firms in general ranges between 0.33 and 0.50. The larger this ratio, the riskier the situation for lenders and borrowers. Of course, you can lower the debt-to-equity ratio by paying off debts.

None of the above methods is perfect for everyone; the limits given are only guidelines. Only you, based on the money you earn, your current obligations, and your financial plans for the future, can determine the exact amount of credit you need and can afford. You must be your own credit manager.

Keep in mind that you adversely affect your credit capacity if you cosign a loan for a friend or a relative.

Cosigning a Loan

What would you do if a friend or a relative asked you to cosign a loan? Before you give your answer, make sure you understand what cosigning involves. Under a recent Federal Trade Commission rule, creditors are required to give you a notice to help explain your obligations. The cosigner's notice says,

> You are being asked to guarantee this debt. Think carefully before you do. If the borrower doesn't pay the debt, you will have to. Be sure you can afford to pay if you have to, and that you want to accept this responsibility.
>
> You may have to pay up to the full amount of the debt if the borrower does not pay. You may also have to pay late fees or collection costs, which increase this amount.
>
> The creditor can collect this debt from you without first trying to collect from the borrower. The creditor can use the same collection methods against you that can be used against the borrower, such as suing you, garnishing your wages, etc. If this debt is ever in default, that fact may become a part of *your* credit record.[6]

Cosigners Often Pay   Some studies of certain types of lenders show that as many as three of four cosigners are asked to wholly or partially repay the loan. That statistic should not surprise you. When you are asked to cosign, you are being asked to take a risk that a professional lender will not take. The lender would not require a cosigner if the borrower met the lender's criteria for making a loan.

In most states, if you do cosign and your friend or relative misses a payment, the lender can collect the entire debt from you immediately without pursuing the borrower first. Also, the amount you owe may increase if the lender decides to sue to collect. If the lender wins the case, they may be able to take your wages and property.

If You Do Cosign   Despite the risks, at times you may decide to cosign. Perhaps your child needs a first loan or a close friend needs help. Here are a few things to consider before you cosign:

1. Be sure you can afford to pay the loan. If you are asked to pay and cannot, you could be sued or your credit rating could be damaged.
2. Consider that even if you are not asked to repay the debt, your liability for this loan may keep you from getting other credit you want.
3. Before you pledge property such as your automobile or furniture to secure the loan, make sure you understand the consequences. If the borrower defaults, you could lose the property you pledge.
4. Check your state law. Some states have laws giving you additional rights as a cosigner.
5. Request that a copy of overdue-payment notices be sent to you so that you can take action to protect your credit history.

Building and Maintaining Your Credit Rating

If you apply for a charge account, credit card, car loan, personal loan, or mortgage, your credit experience, or lack of it, will be a major consideration for the creditor. Your credit experience may even affect your ability to get a job or buy life insurance. A good credit rating is a valuable asset that should be nurtured and protected. If you want a good rating, you must use credit with discretion: Limit your borrowing to your capacity to repay, and live up to the terms of your contracts. The quality of your credit rating is entirely up to you.

In reviewing your creditworthiness, a creditor seeks information from a credit bureau. Most creditors rely heavily on credit reports in considering loan applications.

Credit Bureaus

credit bureaus

Credit bureaus collect credit and other information about consumers. There are three major credit bureaus: Experian Information Solutions (formerly TRW, Inc.), Trans Union Credit Information Company, and Equifax Services, Inc. Each bureau maintains over 190 million credit files on individuals based on 2 billion items of information received each month from lenders.[7] In addition, several thousand regional credit bureaus collect credit information about consumers. These firms sell the data to creditors that evaluate credit applications.

The Federal Trade Commission receives more consumer complaints about credit bureaus than about any other industry, on average 9,000 a year.[8] A common complaint involves mixups between people with identical surnames (see Life Situation Case 6 on page 184). However, the accuracy of credit reports has improved recently, due primarily to public outcry and the threat of stricter federal laws.

Who Provides Data to Credit Bureaus?

Credit bureaus obtain their data from banks, finance companies, merchants, credit card companies, and other creditors. These sources regularly send reports to credit bureaus containing information about the kinds of credit they extend to customers, the amounts and terms of that credit, and customers' paying habits. Credit bureaus also collect some information from other sources, such as court records.

What Is in Your Credit Files?

As the sample credit report in Exhibit 6–5 shows, the credit bureau file contains your name, address, Social Security number, and birth date. It may also include the following information:

> Your employer, position, and income.
> Your former address.
> Your former employer.
> Your spouse's name, Social Security number, employer, and income.
> Whether you own your home, rent, or board.
> Checks returned for insufficient funds.

Your credit file may also contain detailed credit information. Each time you buy from a reporting store on credit or take out a loan at a bank, a finance company, or some other reporting creditor, a credit bureau is informed of your account number and the date, amount, terms, and type of credit. As you make payments, your file is updated to show the outstanding balance, the number and amounts of payments past due, and the frequency of 30-, 60-, or 90-day delinquencies. Any suits, judgments, or tax liens against you may appear as well. However, a federal law protects your rights if the information in your credit file is erroneous.

Fair Credit Reporting

Fair Credit Reporting Act

You can see that fair and accurate credit reporting is vital to both creditors and consumers. In 1971, Congress enacted the **Fair Credit Reporting Act**, which regulates the use of credit reports, requires the deletion of obsolete information, and gives consumers access to their files and the right to have erroneous data corrected. Furthermore, the act allows only authorized persons to obtain credit reports.

In the early 1990s, TRW, Inc. (now Experian Information Solutions, Inc.), settled lawsuits alleging that the credit-reporting giant used sloppy procedures that created errors in consumer credit files, inadequately investigated consumer complaints about inaccuracies, allowed errors to recur in credit files, and illegally sold consumer data to firms for their mailing lists.

Credit bureaus provide lists of creditworthy consumers for companies to offer credit. These are called prescreened lists. You can remove your name from all Experian-generated mail and telephone lists by sending your full name and addresses for the past five years to Experian, Consumer Opt Out, P.O. Box 919, Allen, TX 75013, or call 1–800–353–0809. Your name will be shared with Equifax and Trans Union, the other two national credit-reporting systems.

Who May Obtain a Credit Report?

Your credit report may be issued only to properly identified persons for approved purposes. It may be furnished in response to a court order or in accordance with your own

EXHIBIT 6–5

Sample Credit Report

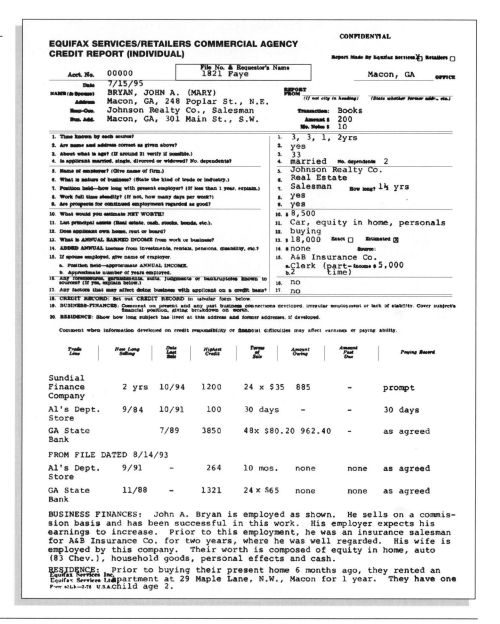

written request. A credit report may also be provided to someone who will use it in connection with a credit transaction, underwriting of insurance, or some other legitimate business need or in determining eligibility for a license or other benefit granted by a government agency. Your friends and neighbors may not obtain credit information about you. If they request such information, they may be subject to fine and imprisonment.

The credit bureaus contend that current laws protect consumers' privacy, but many consumer organizations believe that anyone with a personal computer and a modem can easily access credit bureau files.

FINANCIAL PLANNING IN ACTION

GET YOUR CREDIT REPORT FROM THE BIG THREE

To obtain a copy of your credit report, call or write the following organizations:

- *Equifax*. (www.equifax.com) You may order a copy of your credit report by calling 1–800–685–1111. Or write to Equifax, P.O. Box 105873, Atlanta, GA 30348. Be sure to include your full name, address, Social Security number, date of birth, and daytime telephone number. To fax your request, simply dial 1–404–612–2668. The maximum cost is $8.
- *Trans Union*. (www.tuc.com) Call Trans Union at 1–800–916–8800. Or write to Trans Union Corporation at P.O. Box 390, Philadelphia, PA 19064-0390. You'll need

to provide the following information: your full name (spouse's name if applicable), current address, previous address if you've moved in the past two years, your Social Security number, your spouse's Social Security number (if applicable), your date of birth, current employment, signature, and telephone number. The cost is $8.
- *Experian*. (www.experian.com) To obtain a copy, call 1–800–643–3334 or 1–888–EXPERIAN.

You can order a consolidated report of the information collected by the major bureaus by contacting Confidential Credit File, Credco, 9444 Balboa Avenue, #500, San Diego, CA 92123; or call 1–800–443–9342. The cost is $30.95.

Time Limits on Adverse Data

Most of the information in your credit file may be reported for only seven years. If you have declared personal bankruptcy, however, that fact may be reported for 10 years. After 7 or 10 years, a credit reporting agency can't disclose the information in your credit file unless you are being investigated for a credit application of $50,000 or more or for an application to purchase life insurance of $50,000 or more.

Incorrect Information in Your Credit File

Credit bureaus are required to follow reasonable procedures to ensure that subscribing creditors report information accurately. However, mistakes may occur. Your file may contain erroneous data or records of someone with a name similar to yours. When you notify the credit bureau that you dispute the accuracy of its information, it must reinvestigate and modify or remove inaccurate data. You should give the credit bureau any pertinent data you have concerning an error. If you contest an item on your credit report, the reporting agency must remove the item unless the creditor verifies that the information is accurate.

If you are denied credit, insurance, employment, or rental housing based on the information in the report, you can get a copy of your credit report free within 60 days of your request. You should review your credit files every few years even if you are not planning to apply for a big loan. Married women and young adults should make sure that all accounts for which they are individually and jointly liable are listed in their credit files. The Financial Planning in Action box above shows how to get your credit reports.

What Are the Legal Remedies?

Any consumer reporting agency or user of reported information that willfully or through negligence fails to comply with the provisions of the Fair Credit Reporting Act may be sued by the affected consumer. If the agency or the user is found guilty, the consumer may be awarded actual damages, court costs, and attorneys' fees and, in the case of willful

EXHIBIT 6–6   **What If You Are Denied Credit?**

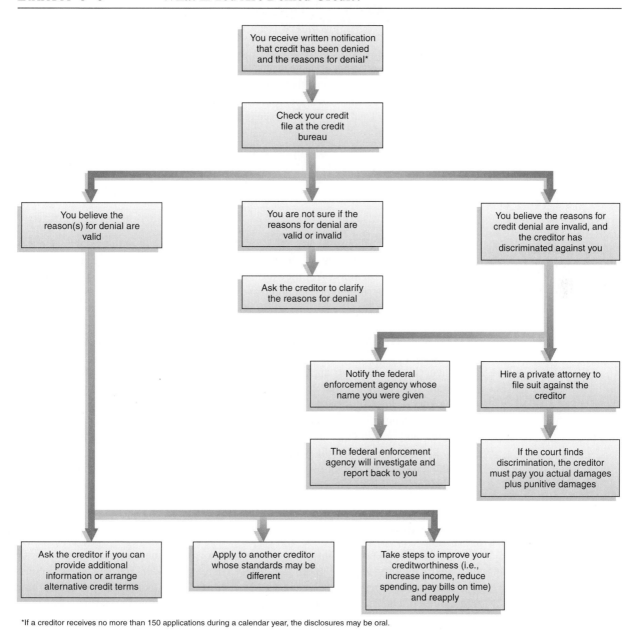

*If a creditor receives no more than 150 applications during a calendar year, the disclosures may be oral.

SOURCE: Reprinted courtesy of Office of Public Information, Federal Reserve Bank Minneapolis, Minneapolis, MN 55480.

noncompliance, punitive damages as allowed by the court. The action must be brought within two years of the occurrence or within two years after the discovery of material and willful misrepresentation of information. An unauthorized person who obtains a credit report under false pretenses may be fined up to $5,000, imprisoned for one year, or both. The same penalties apply to anyone who willfully provides credit information to someone not authorized to receive it.

Exhibit 6–6 outlines the steps you can take if you are denied credit.

CONCEPT CHECK 6–3

1. What are the general rules for measuring credit capacity?
2. What can happen if you cosign a loan?
3. What can you do to build and maintain your credit rating?
4. What is the Fair Credit Reporting Act?
5. How do you correct erroneous information in your credit file?
6. What are your legal remedies if a credit reporting agency engages in unfair reporting practices?

APPLYING FOR CREDIT

L.O.4 Describe the information creditors look for when you apply for credit.

A Scenario from the Past

Mary and John Jones have joint income that is more than enough for them to make payments on their dream house. Yet they are turned down for a mortgage loan. The lender says Mary might become pregnant and leave her job.

In fact, however, it is illegal for a creditor to ask or assume anything about a woman's childbearing plans. It is even illegal to discourage the Joneses from applying for a loan because Mary is of childbearing age. Also, Mary's income must be acknowledged fully by the lender.

Equal Credit Opportunity Act (ECOA)

When you are ready to apply for credit, you should know what creditors think is important in deciding whether you are creditworthy. You should also know what they cannot legally consider in their decisions. The **Equal Credit Opportunity Act (ECOA)** starts all credit applicants off on the same footing. It states that race, color, age, sex, marital status, and certain other factors may not be used to discriminate against you in any part of a credit dealing. Credit rights of women are protected under the ECOA. Women should build and protect their own credit histories, using the checklist shown in the Financial Planning for Life's Situations box on page 174.

What Creditors Look For

When a lender extends credit to its customers, it recognizes that some customers will be unable or unwilling to pay for their purchases. Therefore, lenders must establish policies for determining who will receive credit. Most lenders build their credit policies around the *five Cs of credit*: **character, capacity, capital, collateral,** and **conditions** (see the Financial Planning in Action box on page 175).

character

capacity

capital

collateral

conditions

Creditors use different combinations of the five Cs to reach their decisions. Some creditors set unusually high standards, and others simply do not make certain kinds of loans. Creditors also use different kinds of rating systems. Some rely strictly on their own instinct and experience. Others use a credit-scoring or statistical system to predict whether an applicant is a good credit risk. They assign a certain number of points to each characteristic that has proven to be a reliable sign that a borrower will repay. Then they rate the applicant on this scale.

Typical questions in a credit application appear in Exhibit 6–7, and Exhibit 6–8 shows how your credit application might be scored. In addition, during the loan application process, lenders may evaluate many of the following criteria to determine whether you are a good credit risk.

EXHIBIT 6–7

Sample Credit Application Questions

- Amount of loan requested
- Proposed use of the loan
- Your name and birth date
- Social Security and driver's license numbers
- Present and previous street addresses
- Present and previous employers and their addresses
- Present salary
- Number and ages of dependents
- Other income and sources of other income
- Have you ever received credit from us?

- If so, when and at which office?
- Checking account number, institution, and branch
- Savings account number, institution, and branch
- Name of nearest relative not living with you
- Relative's address and telephone number
- Your marital status
-

EXHIBIT 6–8

How a Consumer's Application Is Scored

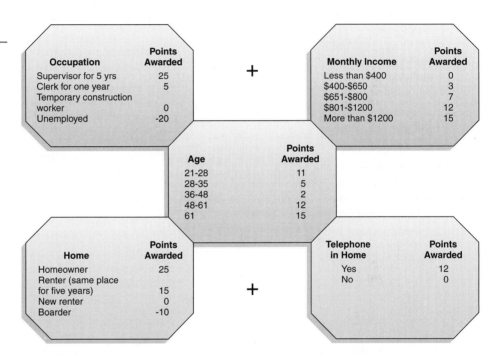

Age   Eugene and Ethel Esposito, a retired couple, and many older people have complained that they were denied credit because they were over a certain age or that when they retired, their credit was suddenly cut off or reduced.

The ECOA is very specific about how a person's age may be used in credit decisions. A creditor may ask about your age, but if you're old enough to sign a binding contract (usually 18 or 21 years old, depending on state law), a creditor may not

Turn you down or decrease your credit because of your age.
Ignore your retirement income in rating your application.
Close your credit account or require you to reapply for it because you have reached a certain age or retired.
Deny you credit or close your account because credit life insurance or other credit-related insurance is not available to people of your age.

WOMEN'S CHECKLIST FOR BUILDING AND PROTECTING THEIR CREDIT HISTORIES

It is simple and sensible to build and protect your own credit history. Here are some steps to get you started.

If you are single:

- Open a checking or savings account, or both.
- Apply for a local department store card.
- Take out a small loan from your bank. Make timely payments.

If you are already married:

- Establish credit in your maiden name or your first name.
- Open your own accounts.
- Try to have separate credit card accounts in your own name.
- Review your joint accounts.
- Make sure that creditors report your credit history to credit bureaus in both names.

If you are getting married:

- Write to your creditors and ask them to continue maintaining your credit file separately.
- You can choose to use your first name and your maiden name (Sue Smith), your first name and your husband's last name (Sue Jones), or your first name and a combined last name (Sue Smith-Jones).
- Once you have picked a name, use it consistently.

If you have recently been separated or divorced:

- Close all of your joint accounts. Your credit record could suffer if your ex-partner is delinquent.
- Meet your creditors and clear your credit record if your ex-partner has hurt your credit rating.

If you are widowed:

- Notify all creditors and tell them whether you or the executor of the estate will handle payment.

- Transfer all existing joint loans to your name alone. You may also want to renegotiate repayment terms.
- Transfer joint credit card accounts to your name alone or reapply for new accounts.
- Seek professional advice, if needed.

And remember that a creditor *cannot:*

1. Refuse you individual credit in your own name if you are creditworthy.
2. Require a spouse to cosign a loan. Any creditworthy person can be your cosigner if one is required.
3. Ask about your birth control practices or family plans or assume that your income will be interrupted to have children.
4. Consider whether you have a telephone listing in your own name.

A creditor *must:*

5. Evaluate you on the same basis as applicants who are male or who have a different marital status.
6. Consider income from part-time employment.
7. Consider reliable alimony, child support, or separate-maintenance payments.
8. Consider the payment history of all joint accounts that accurately reflects your credit history.
9. Report the payment history on an account if you use the account jointly with your spouse.
10. Disregard information on accounts if you can prove that it does not reflect your ability or willingness to repay.

SOURCE: Reprinted courtesy of Office of Public Information, Federal Reserve Bank of Minneapolis, Minneapolis, MN 55480.

Public Assistance   You may not be denied credit because you receive Social Security or public assistance. But, as with age, certain information related to this source of income could have a bearing on your creditworthiness.

Housing Loans   The ECOA covers your application for a mortgage or a home improvement loan. It bans discrimination due to characteristics such as your race, color, or sex or to the race or national origin of the people in the neighborhood where you live or want to buy your home. Creditors may not use any appraisal of the value of your property that considers the race of the people in your neighborhood.

FINANCIAL PLANNING IN ACTION

THE FIVE CS OF CREDIT

Here is what lenders look for in determining your creditworthiness.

Credit History

1. Character: Will you repay the loan?

	Yes	No
Do you have a good attitude toward credit obligations?	___	___
Have you used credit before?	___	___
Do you pay your bills on time?	___	___
Have you ever filed for bankruptcy?	___	___
Do you live within your means?	___	___

Stability

How long have you lived at your present address? ___ yrs.

Do you own your home? ___ ___

How long have you been employed by your present employer? ___ yrs.

Income

2. Capacity: Can you repay the loan?

Your salary and occupation? $___ ; ___

Place of occupation? _____

How reliable is your income?   Reliable ___ ; Not reliable ___

Any other sources of income? $_____

Expenses

Number of dependents? _____

Do you pay any alimony or child support?   Yes ___ ; No ___

Current debts? $_____

Net Worth

3. Capital: What are your assets and net worth?

What are your assets? $_____

What are your liabilities? $_____

What is your net worth? $_____

Loan Security

4. Collateral: What if you don't repay the loan?

What assets do you have to secure the loan? (Car, home, furniture?)   _____

What sources do you have besides income? (Savings, stocks, bonds, insurance?)   _____

Job Security

5. Conditions: What general economic conditions can affect your repayment of the loan?

How secure is your job?   Secure ___ ; Not secure ___

How secure is the firm you work for?   Secure ___ ; Not secure ___

SOURCE: Adapted from William M. Pride, Robert J. Hughes, and Jack R. Kapoor, *Business,*

What If Your Application Is Denied?

Ask Questions If Your Application Is Denied   If you receive a notice that your application has been denied, the ECOA gives you the right to know the specific reasons for denial. If the denial is based on a credit report, you are entitled to know the specific information in the credit report that led to it. After you receive this information from the creditor, you should visit or telephone the local credit bureau to find out what information it reported. The bureau cannot charge you a disclosure fee if you ask to see your file within 60 days of being notified of a denial based on a credit report. You may ask the bureau to investigate any inaccurate or incomplete information and correct its records.

CONCEPT   CHECK   6–4

1. What is the Equal Credit Opportunity Act?
2. What are the five Cs of credit?
3. What can you do if your credit application is denied?

AVOIDING AND CORRECTING CREDIT MISTAKES

L.O.5 Identify the steps you can take to avoid and correct credit mistakes.

Has a department store's computer ever billed you for merchandise that you returned to the store or never received? Has a credit company ever charged you for the same item twice or failed to properly credit a payment on your account?

The best way to maintain your credit standing is to repay your debts on time. But complications may still occur. To protect your credit and save your time, your money, and your future credit rating, you should learn how to correct any mistakes and misunderstandings that crop up in your credit accounts. If a snag occurs, first try to deal directly with the creditor. The credit laws can help you settle your complaints.

The **Fair Credit Billing Act (FCBA),** passed in 1975, sets procedures for promptly correcting billing mistakes, refusing to make credit card or revolving credit payments on defective goods, and promptly crediting your payments.

Fair Credit Billing Act (FCBA)

The act defines a billing error as any charge for something you did not buy or for something bought by a person not authorized to use your account. Also included among billing errors is any charge that is not properly identified on your bill (that is, for an amount different from the actual purchase price) or that was entered on a date other than the purchase date. A billing error may also be a charge for something you did not accept on delivery or was not delivered according to agreement.

Finally, billing errors include errors in arithmetic; failure to reflect a payment or other credit to your account; failure to mail the statement to your current address, provided you notified the creditor of an address change at least 20 days before the end of the billing period; and questionable items or items about which you need additional information.

In Case of a Billing Error

If you think your bill is wrong or you want more information about it, follow these steps. First, notify the creditor *in writing* within 60 days after the bill was mailed. A telephone call will not protect your rights. Be sure to write to the address the creditor lists for billing inquiries, to give the creditor your name and account number, and to say that you believe the bill contains an error and what you believe the error to be. State the suspected amount of the error or the item you want explained. Then pay all the parts of the bill that are not in dispute. While waiting for an answer, you do not have to pay the disputed amount or any minimum payments or finance charges that apply to it.

The creditor must acknowledge your letter within 30 days, unless it can correct your bill sooner. Within two billing periods, but in no case longer than 90 days, either your account must be corrected or you must be told why the creditor believes the bill is correct. If the creditor made a mistake, you need not pay any finance charges on the disputed amount. Your account must be corrected, and you must be sent an explanation of any amount you still owe.

If no error is found, the creditor must promptly send you an explanation of the reasons for that determination and a statement of what you owe, which may include any finance

EXHIBIT 6–9   **Steps Involved in the Process of Resolving a Billing Dispute**

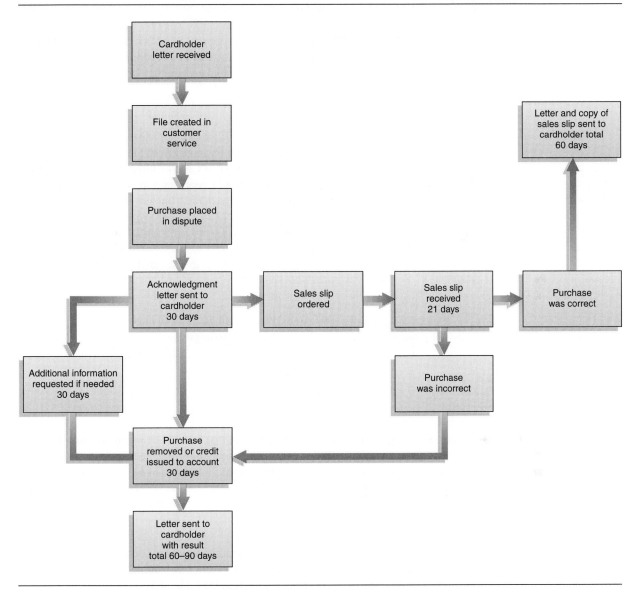

SOURCE: Courtesy of Charge-It-System®, Billing Errors Section, *Cardholder Tips*, March 1992, n.p.

charges that have accumulated and any minimum payments you missed while you were questioning the bill. Exhibit 6–9 summarizes the steps in resolving a billing dispute.

Your Credit Rating during the Dispute

A creditor may not threaten your credit rating while you are resolving a billing dispute. Once you have written about a possible error, a creditor is prohibited from giving out information that would damage your credit reputation to other creditors or credit bureaus. And until your complaint has been answered, the creditor may not take any action to collect the disputed amount.

After explaining the bill, the creditor may report you as delinquent on the amount in dispute and take action to collect if you do not pay in the time allowed. Even so, you can still disagree in writing. Then the creditor and the credit bureau must report that you have challenged your bill and give you the name and address of each recipient of information about your account. When the matter has been settled, the creditor must report the outcome to each recipient of the information. Remember, you may also place your version of the dispute in your credit record.

Defective Goods or Services

Your new sofa arrives with only three legs. You try to return it, but no luck. You ask the merchant to repair or replace it; still no luck. The Fair Credit Billing Act provides that you may withhold payment on any damaged or shoddy goods or poor services that you have purchased with a credit card as long as you have made a sincere attempt to resolve the problem with the merchant.

CONCEPT CHECK 6–5

1. What is the Fair Credit Billing Act?
2. What must you do to protect your rights if a billing error occurs?
3. What happens to your credit rating during the billing dispute?

COMPLAINING ABOUT CONSUMER CREDIT

L.O.6 Describe the laws that protect you if you have a complaint about consumer credit.

If you have a complaint about credit, first try to solve your problem directly with the creditor. Only if that fails should you use more formal complaint procedures. This section describes how to file a complaint with the federal agencies responsible for administering consumer credit protection laws.

Complaints about Banks

If you have a complaint about a bank in connection with any of the federal credit laws, or if you think any part of your business with a bank has been handled in an unfair or deceptive way, you may get advice and help from the Federal Reserve System. You don't need to have an account at the bank to file a complaint. (See Exhibit 6–10.)

Protection under Consumer Credit Laws

You may also take legal action against a creditor. If you decide to file a lawsuit, there are important consumer credit laws you should know about.

Truth in Lending and Consumer Leasing Acts   If a creditor fails to disclose information required under the Truth in Lending Act or the Consumer Leasing Act, gives inaccurate information, or does not comply with the rules regarding credit cards or the right to cancel them, you may sue for actual damages, that is, any money loss you suffer. Class action suits are also permitted. A class action suit is a suit filed on behalf of a group of people with similar claims.

Exhibit 6–10

Complaint Form to Report Violations of Federal Credit Laws

COMPLAINT FORM   **Federal Reserve System**

Name _____   Name of Bank _____

Address _____   Address _____
                    Street   City   State   Zip

_____
City   State   Zip

Daytime telephone _____   Account number (if applicable) _____
              (include area code)

The complaint involves the following service: Checking Account ☐   Savings Account ☐   Loan ☐

Other: Please specify _____

I have attempted to resolve this complaint directly with the bank: No ☐   Yes ☐

      If "No", an attempt should be made to contact the bank and resolve the complaint.

      If "Yes", name of person or department contacted is _____
                                                                                          Date

MY COMPLAINT IS AS FOLLOWS (Briefly describe the events in the order in which they happened, including specific dates and the bank's actions to which you object. Enclose copies of any pertinent information or correspondence that may be helpful. Do not send us your only copy of any document):

_____
_____
_____
_____
_____
_____
_____
_____
_____
_____
_____
_____

This information is solicited under the Federal Trade Commission Improvement Act. Providing the information is voluntary, complete information is necessary to expedite investigation of your complaint. Routine use of the information may include disclosing it to bank(s) or others involved or to other governmental agencies as deemed appropriate.

Date _____   Signatures _____

                                                                      _____

SOURCE: Board of Governors of the Federal Reserve System.

Equal Credit Opportunity Act   If you think you can prove that a creditor has discriminated against you for any reason prohibited by the ECOA, you may sue for actual damages plus punitive damages (that is, damages for the fact that the law has been violated) of up to $10,000.

Fair Credit Billing Act   A creditor that fails to comply with the rules applying to the correction of billing errors automatically forfeits the amount owed on the item in question and any finance charges on it, up to a combined total of $50, even if the bill was correct. You may also sue for actual damages plus twice the amount of any finance charges.

Fair Credit Reporting Act   You may sue any credit-reporting agency or creditor for violating the rules regarding access to your credit records and correction of errors in your credit file. Again, you are entitled to actual damages plus any punitive damages the court allows if the violation is proven to have been intentional.

Consumer Credit Reporting Reform Act   An unfavorable credit report can force you to pay a higher interest rate on a loan or cost you a loan, an insurance policy, an apartment rental, or even a job offer. The Consumer Credit Reporting Reform Act of 1997 places the burden of proof for accurate credit information on the credit-reporting agency rather than on you. Under this law, the creditor must certify that disputed data are accurate. If a creditor or the credit bureau verifies incorrect data, you can sue for damages. The federal government and state attorneys general can also sue creditors for civil damages.

Exhibit 6–11   **Summary of Federal Consumer Credit Laws**

Act (date effective)	Major Provisions
Truth in Lending Act (July 1, 1969)	Provides specific cost disclosure requirements for the annual percentage rate and the finance charges as a dollar amount
	Requires disclosure of other loan terms and conditions
	Regulates the advertising of credit terms
	Provides the right to cancel a contract when certain real estate is used as security
(January 25, 1971)	Prohibits credit card issuers from sending unrequested cards; limits a cardholder's liability for unauthorized use of a card to $50
(October 1, 1982)	Requires that disclosures for closed-end credit (installment credit) be written in plain English and appear apart from all other information
	Allows a credit customer to request an itemization of the amount financed if the creditor does not automatically provide it
Fair Credit Reporting Act (April 24, 1971)	Requires disclosure to consumers of the name and address of any consumer reporting agency that supplied reports used to deny credit, insurance, or employment
	Gives consumers the right to know what is in their files, have incorrect information reinvestigated and removed, and include their versions of a disputed item in the file
	Requires credit-reporting agencies to send the consumer's version of a disputed item to certain businesses or creditors
	Sets forth identification requirements for consumers wishing to inspect their files
	Requires that consumers be notified when an investigative report is being made
	Limits the amount of time certain information can be kept in a credit file
Fair Credit Billing Act (October 28, 1975)	Establishes procedures for consumers and creditors to follow when billing errors occur on periodic statements for revolving credit accounts
	Requires creditors to send a statement setting forth these procedures to consumers periodically
	Allows consumers to withhold payment for faulty or defective goods or services (within certain limitations) when purchased with a credit card
	Requires creditors to promptly credit customers' accounts and to return overpayments if requested
Equal Credit Opportunity Act (October 28, 1975)	Prohibits credit discrimination based on sex and marital status
	Prohibits creditors from requiring women to reapply for credit upon a change in marital status
	Requires creditors to inform applicants of acceptance or rejection of their credit application within 30 days of receiving a completed application
	Requires creditors to provide a written statement of the reasons for adverse action
(March 23, 1977)	Prohibits credit discrimination based on race, national origin, religion, age, or the receipt of public assistance
(June 1, 1977)	Requires creditors to report information on an account to credit bureaus in the names of both husband and wife if both use the account and both are liable for it
Fair Debt Collection Practices Act (March 20, 1978)	Prohibits abusive, deceptive, and unfair practices by debt collectors
	Establishes procedures for debt collectors contacting a credit user
	Restricts debt collector contacts with a third party
	Specifies that payment for several debts be applied as the consumer wishes and that no money be applied to a debt in dispute
Consumer Credit Reporting Reform Act (September 30, 1997)	Places the burden of proof for accurate credit information on credit issuers rather than on consumers
	Requires creditors to certify that disputed credit information is accurate
	Requires "credit repair" companies to give consumers a written contract that can be canceled within three business days
	Requires the big three credit bureaus (Experian, Equifax, and Trans Union) to establish a joint toll-free system that allows consumers to call and remove their names permanently from all prescreened lists
	Places the maximum cost of a credit report at $8; however, indigent persons, welfare recipients, unemployed persons, and jobhunters can get one free report annually

SOURCES: *Managing Your Credit,* rev. ed. (Prospect Heights, IL: Money Management Institute, Household Financial Services, 1988), p. 36; © Household Financial Services, Prospect Heights, Illinois; *Banking Legislation & Policy,* Federal Reserve Bank of Philadelphia, April–June, 1997, pp. 3–4.

EXHIBIT 6–12   **Federal Government Agencies that Enforce the Consumer Credit Laws**

If you think you've been discriminated against by:	You may file a complaint with the following agency:
A retailer, nonbank credit card issuer, consumer finance company, state-chartered credit union or bank, noninsured savings and loan institution	Federal Trade Commission (FTC) Equal Credit Opportunity Washington, DC 20580
A national bank	Comptroller of the Currency Consumer Affairs Division Washington, DC 20219
A Federal Reserve member bank	Board of Governors of the Federal Reserve System Director, Division of Consumer Affairs Washington, DC 20551
Other insured banks	Federal Deposit Insurance Corporation Office of Bank Customer Affairs Washington, DC 20429
Insured savings and loan institutions	Federal Home Loan Bank Board Equal Credit Opportunity Washington, DC 20552
The FHA mortgage program	Housing and Urban Development (HUD) Department of Health, Education and Welfare Washington, DC 20410
A federal credit union	National Credit Union Administration 2025 M Street, N.W. Washington, DC 20455

The Credit Card Consumer Protection Act was introduced in June 1997. If passed, this bill limits the fees credit card companies can charge and will require more disclosures to consumers. This bill prohibits fees to consumers when the balance is paid in full and on time each month.[9]

Exhibit 6–11 on page 180 summarizes the major federal consumer credit laws. The Federal Reserve System has set up a separate office in Washington, the Division of Consumer and Community Affairs, to handle consumer complaints. This division also writes regulations to carry out the consumer credit laws, enforces these laws for state-chartered banks that are members of the Federal Reserve System, and helps banks comply with these laws.

Your Rights under Consumer Credit Laws

If you believe you have been refused credit due to discrimination, you can do one or more of the following:

1. Complain to the creditor. Let the creditor know you are aware of the law.
2. File a complaint with the government. You can report any violations to the appropriate government enforcement agency (see Exhibit 6–12). Although the agencies use complaints to decide which companies to investigate, they cannot handle private cases. When you are denied credit, the creditor must give you the name and address of the appropriate agency to contact.

3. If all else fails, sue the creditor. You have the right to bring a case in a federal district court. If you win, you can recover your actual damages and punitive damages of up to $10,000. You can also recover reasonable attorneys' fees and court costs. A private attorney can advise you on how to proceed.

CONCEPT CHECK 6-6

1. What federal laws protect you if you have a complaint regarding consumer credit?
2. What are your rights under the consumer credit laws?

SUMMARY

L.O.1 Define consumer credit and analyze its advantages and disadvantages.

Consumer credit is the use of credit by individuals and families for personal needs. Among the advantages of using credit are the ability to purchase goods when they are needed and pay for them gradually, the ability to meet financial emergencies, convenience in shopping, and establishment of a credit rating. Disadvantages are that credit costs money, encourages overspending, and ties up future income.

L.O.2 Differentiate among various types of credit.

Closed-end and open-end credit are two types of consumer credit. With closed-end credit, the borrower pays back a one-time loan in a stated period of time and with a specified number of payments. With open-end credit, the borrower is permitted to take loans on a continuous basis and is billed for partial payments periodically.

L.O.3 Assess your credit capacity and build your credit rating.

Two general rules for measuring credit capacity are the debt payments-to-income ratio and the debt-to-equity ratio. In reviewing your creditworthiness, a creditor seeks information from one of the three national credit bureaus or a regional credit bureau.

L.O.4 Describe the information creditors look for when you apply for credit.

Creditors determine creditworthiness on the basis of the five Cs: character, capacity, capital, collateral, and conditions.

L.O.5 Identify the steps you can take to avoid and correct credit mistakes.

If a billing error occurs on your account, notify the creditor in writing within 60 days. If the dispute is not settled in your favor, you can place your version of it in your credit file. You may also withhold payment on any defective goods or services you have purchased with a credit card as long as you have attempted to resolve the problem with the merchant.

L.O.6 Describe the laws that protect you if you have a complaint about consumer credit.

If you have a complain about credit, first try to deal directly with the creditor. If that fails, you can turn to the appropriate consumer credit law. These laws include the Truth in Lending Act, the Consumer Leasing Act, the Equal Credit Opportunity Act, the Fair Credit Billing Act, the Fair Credit Reporting Act, and the Consumer Credit Reporting Reform Act.

GLOSSARY

capacity The borrower's financial ability to meet credit obligations. (p. 172)

capital The borrower's assets or net worth. (p. 172)

character The borrower's attitude toward his or her credit obligations. (p. 172)

closed-end credit One-time loans that the borrower pays back in a specified period of time and in payments of equal amounts. (p. 158)

collateral A valuable asset that is pledged to ensure loan payments. (p. 172)

conditions The general economic conditions that can affect a borrower's ability to repay a loan. (p. 172)

consumer credit The use of credit for personal needs (except a home mortgage). (p. 155)

Consumer Credit Reporting Reform Act Places the burden of proof for accurate credit information on the credit reporting agency. (p. 179)

credit An arrangement to receive cash, goods, or services now and pay for them in the future. (p. 155)

credit bureau   A reporting agency that assembles credit and other information about consumers.   (p. 167)

debit card   Electronically subtracts the amount of a purchase from the buyer's account at the moment the purchase is made.   (p. 161)

Equal Credit Opportunity Act (ECOA)   Bans discrimination in the extension of credit on the basis of race, color, age, sex, marital status, and other factors.   (p. 172)

Fair Credit Billing Act (FCBA)   Sets procedures for promptly correcting billing mistakes, refusing to make credit card payments on defective goods, and promptly crediting payments.   (p. 176)

Fair Credit Reporting Act   Regulates the use of credit reports, requires the deletion of obsolete information, and

gives consumers access to their files and the right to have erroneous data corrected.   (p. 168)

home equity loan   A loan based on the current market value of a home less the amount still owed on the mortgage. (p. 164)

interest   A periodic charge for the use of credit.   (p. 159)

line of credit   The dollar amount, which may or may not be borrowed, that a lender makes available to a borrower. (p. 159)

open-end credit   A line of credit in which loans are made on a continuous basis and the borrower is billed periodically for at least partial payment.   (p. 158)

revolving check credit   A prearranged loan from a bank for a specified amount; also called a *bank line of credit*.   (p. 159)

REVIEW QUESTIONS

1. Why is consumer credit important in our economy? (L.O.1)
2. What are some valid reasons for using consumer credit? (L.O.1)
3. Discuss advantages and disadvantages of using consumer credit.   (L.O.1)
4. What are the differences between closed-end and open-end credit?   (L.O.2)
5. Distinguish between credit cards and debit cards. Why might you use a debit card?   (L.O.2)
6. What are the two general rules for measuring credit capacity?   (L.O.3)
7. Why might you cosign a loan for a friend?   (L.O.3)

8. How does the Fair Credit Reporting Act protect consumers?   (L.O.3)
9. What can you do if your credit file contains incorrect information? What are your legal remedies?   (L.O.3)
10. What do creditors look for to determine your creditworthiness?   (L.O.4)
11. What steps can you take if your credit application is denied?   (L.O.4)
12. What can you do if your statement contains a billing error?   (L.O.5)
13. Is your credit rating affected if a dispute arises between you and the creditor? Explain.   (L.O.5)
14. What federal laws protect you if you have a complaint about consumer credit?   (L.O.6)

FINANCIAL PLANNING PROBLEMS

1. *Calculating the Amount for a Home Equity Loan.* A few years ago, Michael Tucker purchased a home for $100,000. Today the home is worth $150,000. His remaining mortgage balance is $50,000. Assuming Michael can borrow up to 80 percent of the market value of his home, what is the maximum amount he can borrow?   (L.O.2)
2. *Determining the Debt Payments-to-Income Ratio.* Louise McIntyre's monthly gross income is $2,000. Her employer withholds $400 in federal, state, and local income taxes and $160 in Social Security taxes per month. Louise contributes $80 per month for her IRA. Her monthly credit payments for Visa, MasterCard, and Discover cards are $35, $30, and $20, respectively. Her monthly payment on an automobile loan is $285. What is Louise's debt payments-to-income ratio? Is Louise living within her means? Explain.   (L.O.3)
3. *Calculating the Debt-to-Equity Ratio.* Robert Thumme owns a $140,000 townhouse and still has an unpaid mortgage of $110,000. In addition to his mortgage, he has the following liabilities:

Visa	$565
MasterCard	480
Discover card	395
Education loan	920
Personal bank loan	800
Auto loan	4,250
Total	$7,410

Robert's net worth (not including his home) is about $21,000. This equity is in mutual funds, an automobile, a coin collection, furniture, and other personal property. What is Robert's debt-to-equity ratio? Has he reached the upper limit of debt obligations? Explain.   (L.O.3)

4. *Calculating Net Worth and Determining Safe Credit Limit.*
   a. Calculate your net worth based on your present assets and liabilities.
   b. Refer to your net worth statement and determine your safe credit limit. Use the debt payments-to-income and debt-to-equity formulas.   (L.O.3)
5. *Using Credit Cards as an Identification.* Dinesh D'Souza flew to New York to attend his brother's wedding. Know-

ing that his family would be busy, he did not ask anyone to meet him at the airport. Instead, he planned to rent a car to use while in New York. He has no nationally known credit cards but is prepared to pay cash for the rental car. The car rental agency refuses to rent him a car, even though it has several cars available. Why do you think Dinesh is unable to rent a car?   (L.O.4)

6. *Determining What Creditors Look for in Approving Loans.* Jim Moniz, a recent college graduate, has accepted a teaching position at Hubbleville High School. Jim moved to Hubbleville and applied for a car loan at First National Bank. He had never used credit or obtained a loan. The bank notified him that it will not approve the loan unless he has a cosigner. On what basis has the bank denied Jim credit?   (L.O.4)

7. *Analyzing Feasibility of a Loan.* Fred Reinero has had a student loan, two auto loans, and three credit cards. He has always made timely payments on all obligations. He has a savings account of $2,400 and an annual income of $25,000. His current payments for rent, insurance, and utilities are about $1,100 per month. Fred has accumulated $12,800 in an individual retirement account. Fred's loan application asks for $10,000 to start up a small restaurant with some friends. Fred will not be an active manager; his partner will run the restaurant. Will he get the loan? Explain your answer.   (L.O.4)

PROJECTS AND APPLICATION ACTIVITIES

1. *Determining Whether to Use or Not Use Credit.* Survey friends and relatives to determine the process they used in deciding whether or not to use credit to purchase an automobile or a major appliance. What risks and opportunity costs did they consider?   (L.O.1)

2. *Analyzing Opportunity Costs Using Credit.* Think about the last three major purchases you made.   (L.O.1)
   a. Did you pay cash? If so, why?
   b. If you paid cash, what opportunity costs were associated with the purchase?
   c. Did you use credit? If so, why?
   d. What were the financial and psychological opportunity costs of using credit?

3. *Comparing Reasons for Using Credit.* Prepare a list of similarities and differences in the reasons the following individuals might have for using credit.   (L.O.2)
   a. A teenager.
   b. A young adult.
   c. A growing family of four.
   d. A retired couple.

4. *Using the Internet to Obtain Information about Credit Cards.* Choose one of the following organizations and visit its home page on the World Wide Web. Then prepare a report that summarizes the information the organization provides. How could this information help you in choosing your credit card?
   a. BankCard Holders of America—provides consumer information on your credit card rights.
   b. Credit Card Network—provides information on credit card rates.
   c. Federal Trade Commission—provides information on how to regain financial health, uses and misuses of credit cards, and many other related topics.   (L.O.2)

5. *Using your Home Equity to Obtain a Loan.* Visit your local financial institutions, such as commercial banks, federal savings banks, and credit unions, to obtain information about getting a home equity loan. Compare their requirements for the loan.   (L.O.2)

6. *Determining Whether to Cosign a Loan.* Talk to a person who has cosigned a loan. What experiences did this person have as a cosigner?   (L.O.3)

7. *Determining Net Worth and Credit Capacity.* What changes might take place in your personal net worth during different stages of your life? How might these changes affect your credit capacity?   (L.O.4)

8. *Assessing How Lenders Determine Creditworthiness.* Survey credit representatives such as bankers, managers of credit departments in retail stores, managers of finance companies, credit union officers, managers of credit bureaus, and savings and loan officers. Ask what procedures they follow in granting or refusing a loan. Write a report of your survey.   (L.O.4)

9. *Analyzing Credit-Related Problems.* Bring to class examples of credit-related problems of individuals or families. Suggest ways in which these problems might be solved.   (L.O.5)

10. *Evaluating Creditors and Seeking Help with Credit-Related Problems.* Compile a list of places a person can call to report dishonest credit practices, get advice and help with credit problems, and check out a creditor's reputation before signing a contract.   (L.O.6)

LIFE SITUATION CASE 6

ONLINE ACCESS TO CREDIT INFORMATION

Ann Smith applied for a credit card with a lower interest rate than she had seen advertised elsewhere. She considered herself a good credit risk because she had no late payments on her current credit cards and had a stable income. To her surprise, she was turned down!

Ann decided to order a credit report to find out why. Rather than send her request through the mail and wait for a few weeks for a hard copy to come in the mail, Ann signed up for a new online credit information service that she had seen advertised on the Web. The service takes orders on the Internet and sends information to customers through the mail or, even more quickly, through the Internet. Ann opted for the latter and received her report within two hours.

The report showed late payments on cards that she had never owned and charges in states she had never even visited. Ann was puzzled. She knew her name was a fairly common one and decided to investigate. She e-mailed the credit bureau explaining her problem. She requested that the credit bureau verify the charges in question and double-check the Social Security number of the person who made them.

The credit bureau investigated and found that her hunch was right. It removed the incorrect information from her report and, at Ann's request, sent the updated report to the credit card issuer that had recently turned her down. Ann was then able to obtain the lower-interest-rate card for which she had applied.

QUESTIONS

1. Why do you think Ann was denied credit?
2. What was the advantage of using the Internet to order the credit report?
3. What are some privacy issues involved in accessing credit information via the Internet?
4. What advice would you offer Ann to prevent a similar problem in the future?
5. What federal law protects Ann's rights in this situation?

Sources: "Consumers: Know Your Credit Rights," *Financial Responsibility,* American Express Company, Spring 1994; John O'Dell, "Online Credit Reports," *Los Angeles Times,* June 2, 1997.

USING THE INTERNET TO CREATE A PERSONAL FINANCIAL PLAN 6

ESTABLISHING AND MAINTAINING A CREDIT RECORD

The wise use of credit requires a knowledge of the process for establishing credit. In addition, you should develop an awareness of credit reports and the legal rights associated with using consumer credit.

Web Sites for Wise Use of Credit

- Credit card information from RAM Research Group at **www.ramresearch.com** and comparison of credit card costs and features at **www.cardtrak.com**
- Current rates for mortgages, home equity loans, credit cards, and consumer loans are at **www.bankrate.com/ bankrate/publ/tips.htm** and **www.banx.com**
- Wise use of credit information from the National Center for Financial Education at **www.ncfe.org**
- Information on credit reports at **www.equifax.com**, **experian.com**, and **www.tuc.com**
- Credit law information at **www.ftc.gov, www.bog.frb.fed. us,** and **www.pirg.org**

(Note: Addresses and content of Web sites change, and new sites are created daily. Use the search engines discussed in Appendix B to update and locate Web sites for your current financial planning needs.)

PFP SHEET: 29

Short-Term Financial Planning Activities

1. Prepare an inventory of current credit balances and monthly payments (see PFP Sheet 29).
2. Review your credit file for current accuracy of information.
3. Become familiar with consumer credit laws that may relate to various aspects of your use of credit.

Long-Term Financial Planning Activities

1. Describe actions that may be taken to reduce your credit balances (if applicable).
2. Create a plan for spending that provides for using credit at an appropriate level.

CHAPTER 7

CHOOSING A SOURCE OF CREDIT
The Costs of Credit Alternatives

OPENING CASE

THE PERKS AND PERILS OF CREDIT CARD "BONUSES"

Recently Brian has been barraged with promotions for credit cards that offer special "perks"—from cards that earn frequent-flier miles or give special rebates, to department store cards that offer discounts for first purchases. Many sound like good deals, but he wonders if there is a catch.

For people who habitually carry high levels of revolving debt, the interest rates these cards carry frequently obliterate the perks. By the time Brian gets the free tickets or product discounts, he may have paid the price and more in interest charges, advisers say.

Because consumer credit is so much a part of almost everyone's life, the International Credit Association (ICA) reminds consumers that although credit can be used for many valid reasons, it should never be viewed as extra money or a bonus. According to Diane Lambert, education director for the ICA, "Using credit wisely means knowing which type of credit is best for you in various buying situations."

Brian should evaluate special discounts on purchases and frequent-flier miles. He should weigh the additional perks against the amount he would save annually with a lower-interest-rate card. If he pays in full each month, interest rates won't really concern him, and extra bonuses might be the answer. But if he carries a monthly balance, a card with a low interest rate will be his best choice.

In addition, many credit educators encourage consumers not to use more than one-third of their extra monthly net incomes on credit payments. Extra money is money that is left after paying your basic living expenses: rent or mortgage, utilities, food, clothing, transportation, and medical expenses.

QUESTIONS

1. Why should people who habitually carry large monthly balances on their credit cards avoid card promotions for rebate programs?
2. How should Brain evaluate special discounts on purchases and frequent-flier miles?
3. What is the highest percentage of extra monthly income that credit educators recommend consumers carry in credit card payments?

SOURCES: Deborah Lohse, "Start Slashing Your Credit-Card Costs to Avoid Sting of Rising Interest Rates," *The Wall Street Journal*, April 27, 1994, pp. C1, C21; Terry Ruffolo, "How to Avoid Overextending Yourself and How to Build a Good Credit History," *Chicago Tribune*, April 25, 1997, p. C5.

LEARNING
OBJECTIVES

After studying this chapter, you will be able to

L.O.1   Analyze the major sources of consumer credit.

L.O.2   Determine the cost of credit by calculating interest using various interest formulas.

L.O.3   Develop a plan to manage your debts.

L.O.4   Evaluate various private and governmental sources that assist consumers with debt problems.

L.O.5   Assess the choices in declaring personal bankruptcy.

SOURCES OF CONSUMER CREDIT

L.O.1 Analyze the major sources of consumer credit.

Financial Decision
Trade-Off

Credit costs got you down? Well, you are not alone. Credit costs money; therefore, always weigh the benefits of buying an item on credit now versus waiting until you have saved enough money to pay cash. We can all get into credit difficulties if we do not understand how and when to use credit.

Financial and other institutions, the sources of credit, come in all shapes and sizes. They play an important role in our economy, and they offer a broad range of financial services. By evaluating your credit options, you can reduce your finance charges. You can reconsider your decision to borrow money, discover a less expensive type of loan, or find a lender that charges a lower interest rate.

Before deciding whether to borrow money, ask yourself these three questions: Do I need a loan? Can I afford a loan? Can I qualify for a loan? We discussed the affordability of loans and the qualifications required to obtain loans in the last chapter. Here we wrestle with the first question.

You should avoid credit in two situations. The first situation is one in which you do not need or really want a product that will require financing. Easy access to installment loans or possession of credit cards sometimes encourages consumers to make expensive purchases that they later regret. The solution to this problem is simple: After you have selected a product, resist any sales pressure to buy immediately and take a day to think it over.

The second situation is one in which you can afford to pay cash. Consider the trade-offs and opportunity costs involved. Paying cash is almost always cheaper than using credit. In fact, some stores even offer a discount for payment in cash.

What Kind of Loan Should You Seek?

As discussed in the last chapter, two types of credit exist: closed-end and open-end credit. Because installment loans carry a lower interest rate, they are the less expensive credit option for loans that are repaid over a period of many months or years. However, because credit cards usually provide a float period—a certain number of days during which no interest is charged—they represent the cheaper way to make credit purchases that are paid off in a month or two. Also, once you have a credit card, using it is always easier than taking out an installment loan. An alternative to a credit card is a travel and entertainment (T&E) card, such as an American Express or Diners Club card. A T&E card requires full payment of the balance due each month but does not impose a finance charge. Annual fees, however, can be high.

In seeking an installment loan, you may think first of borrowing from a bank or a credit union. However, less expensive credit sources are available.

Financial Decision
Trade-Off

Inexpensive Loans   Parents or family members are often the source of the least expensive loans. They may charge you only the interest they would have earned had they not made the loan—as little as the 3 percent they would have earned on a passbook account. Such loans, however, can complicate family relationships.

Also relatively inexpensive is money borrowed on financial assets held by a lending institution, for example, a bank certificate of deposit or the cash value of a whole life insurance policy. The interest rate on such loans typically ranges from 7 to 10 percent. But the trade-off is that your assets are tied up until you have repaid the loan.

Medium-Priced Loans   Often you can obtain medium-priced loans from commercial banks and credit unions. New-car loans, for example, may cost 8 to 12 percent; used-car loans and home improvement loans may cost slightly more.

Borrowing from credit unions has several advantages. These institutions provide free credit life insurance, are generally sympathetic to borrowers with legitimate payment problems, and provide personalized service. Credit unions can now offer the same range of consumer loans that banks and other financial institutions do. Over 70 million Americans belong to credit unions, and the number of credit union members has been growing steadily. About 12,000 credit unions exist in the United States today.

Expensive Loans   Though convenient to obtain, the most expensive loans available are from finance companies, retailers, and banks through credit cards. Finance companies often lend to people who cannot obtain credit from banks or credit unions. Typically, the interest ranges from 12 to 25 percent. If you are denied credit by a bank or a credit union, you should question your ability to afford the higher rate a loan company charges.

Borrowing from car dealers, appliance stores, department stores, and other retailers is also relatively expensive. The interest rates retailers charge are usually similar to those charged by finance companies, frequently 20 percent or more.

Banks lend funds not only through installment loans but also through cash advances on MasterCard or Visa cards. According to *Nilson Report,* an industry newsletter, the average American owes $2,733 in credit card debt and pays more than $465 in interest each year.[1] Credit card cobranding has become increasingly popular with banks and industries. Cobranded credit cards, such as Yahoo! Visa card will make shopping over the Internet easier and faster. Yahoo! will designate Visa as its "preferred card" and will promote Visa throughout its Web sites and to online merchants worldwide. Then there is Sinatra MasterCard® with "talent, style, class. Sinatra Has It All!" You receive a five-minute phone card with Sinatra's image and logo, and even receive free Sinatra compact disks.

One type of loan from finance companies is currently less expensive than most other credit. Loans of this kind, which often can be obtained at a rate of under 8 percent, are available from the finance companies of major automakers—General Motors Acceptance Corporation, Ford Motor Credit Corporation, and others. But a car dealer that offers you such a rate may be less willing to discount the price of the car or throw in free options.

Exhibit 7–1 on pages 190 and 191 summarizes the major sources of consumer credit: commercial banks, consumer finance companies, credit unions, life insurance companies, and savings and loan associations. This exhibit attempts to generalize the information and give an average picture of each source regarding the type of credit available, lending policies, and customer services. Due to the dramatic fluctuations in interest rates during the 1990s, it is no longer possible to provide a common range of annual percentage rates for each source of credit. Check with your local lender for current interest rates. Study and compare the differences to determine which source can best meet your needs and requirements.

Today borrowing and credit are more complex than ever. As more and more types of financial institutions offer financial services, your choices of what and where to borrow will widen. Online computer services such as America Online, CompuServe, and Prodigy may be used to compare interest rates for different loan sources and credit cards. Smart cards, or chip cards, will allow you to access accounts from your banks, transfer funds, and obtain account balances. These cards will facilitate electronic banking and bill payment. You will be able to access these smart card services from point-of-sale terminals, ATMs, the Internet, touch-tone phones, interactive TVs, screen phones, personal digital assistants, and cellular phones. For further information, see Appendix B. Shopping for credit is just as important as shopping for an automobile, furniture, or major appliances.

CONCEPT CHECK 7–1

1. What are the major sources of consumer credit?
2. What are some advantages and disadvantages of securing a loan from a credit union? From a finance company?

THE COST OF CREDIT

L.O.2 Determine the cost of credit by calculating interest using various interest formulas.

Truth in Lending law

The **Truth in Lending law** of 1969 was a landmark piece of legislation. For the first time, creditors were required to state the cost of borrowing as a dollar amount so that consumers would know exactly what the credit charges were and thus could compare credit costs and shop for credit.

If you are thinking of borrowing money or opening a credit account, your first step should be to figure out how much it will cost you and whether you can afford it. Then you should shop for the best terms. Two key concepts that you should remember are the finance charge and the annual percentage rate.

The Finance Charge and the Annual Percentage Rate (APR)

Credit costs vary. If you know the finance charge and the annual percentage rate (APR), you can compare credit prices from different sources. Under the Truth in Lending law, the creditor must inform you, in writing and before you sign any agreement, of the finance charge and the APR.

finance charge

The **finance charge** is the total dollar amount you pay to use credit. It includes interest costs and sometimes other costs such as service charges, credit-related insurance premiums, or appraisal fees.

Exhibit 7–1   Sources of Consumer Credit and Their Major Features

Credit Source	Commercial Banks	Consumer Finance Companies
Type of loan	Single-payment loans Personal installment loans Passbook loans Check-credit plans Credit card loans Second mortgages	Personal installment loans Second mortgages
Lending policies	Seek customers with established credit history Often require collateral or security Prefer to deal in large loans, such as auto, home improvement, and home modernization, with the exception of credit card and check-credit plans Determine repayment schedules according to the purpose of the loan Vary credit rates according to the type of credit, time period, customer's credit history, and the security offered May require several days to process a new credit application	Often lend to consumers without established credit history Often make unsecured loans Often vary rates according to the size of the loan balance Offer a variety of repayment schedules Make a higher percentage of small loans than other lenders Maximum loan size limited by law Process applications quickly, frequently on the same day the application is made
Cost	Lower than some lenders because they: Take fewer credit risks Lend depositors' money, which is a relatively inexpensive source of funds Deal primarily in large loans, which yield a larger dollar income without an increase in administrative costs	Higher than some lenders because they: Take greater credit risks Must borrow and pay interest on money to lend Deal frequently in small loans, which are costly to make and yield a small amount of income
Services	Offer several types of consumer credit plans May offer financial counseling Handle credit transactions confidentially	Provide credit promptly Make loans to pay off accumulated debts willingly Design repayment schedules to fit the borrower's income Usually offer financial counseling Handle credit transactions confidentially

Credit Unions	Life Insurance Companies	Federal Savings Banks (Savings and Loan Associations)
Personal installment loans Share draft–credit plans Credit-card loans Second mortgages	Single-payment or partial-payment loans	Personal installment loans (generally permitted by state-chartered savings associations) Home improvement loans Education loans Savings account loans Second mortgages
Lend to members only Make unsecured loans May require collateral or cosigner for loans over a specified amount May require payroll deductions to pay off loan May submit large loan applications to a committee of members for approval Offer a variety of repayment schedules	Lend on cash value of life insurance policy No date or penalty on repayment Deduct amount owed from the value of policy benefit if death or other maturity occurs before repayment	Will lend to all creditworthy individuals Often require collateral Loan rates vary depending on size of loan, length of payment, and security involved
Lower than some lenders because they: Take fewer credit risks Lend money deposited by members, which is less expensive than borrowed money Often receive free office space and supplies from the sponsoring organization Are managed by members whose services are usually donated Enjoy federal income tax exemptions	Lower than some lenders because they: Take no risk Pay no collection costs Secure loans by cash value of policy	Lower than some lenders because they: Lend depositors' money, which is a relatively inexpensive source of funds Secure most loans by savings accounts or real estate
Design repayment schedules to fit the borrower's income Generally provide credit life insurance without extra charge May offer financial counseling Handle credit transactions confidentially	Permit repayment at any time Handle credit transactions confidentially	Often offer financial counseling Specialize in mortgages and other housing-related loans Handle credit transactions confidentially

SOURCE: *Managing Your Credit* (Household International, 1988), pp. 18–19. © Household Financial Services, Prospect Heights, Illinois.

annual percentage rate (APR)

For example, borrowing $100 for a year might cost you $10 in interest. If there is also a service charge of $1, the finance charge will be $11. The **annual percentage rate (APR)** is the percentage cost (or relative cost) of credit on a yearly basis. The APR is your key to comparing costs, regardless of the amount of credit or how much time you have to repay it.

Suppose you borrow $100 for one year and pay a finance charge of $10. If you can keep the entire $100 for the whole year and then pay it all back at once, you are paying an APR of 10 percent:

Amount Borrowed	Month Number	Payment Made	Loan Balance
$100	1	0	$100
	2	0	100
	3	0	100
	.	.	.
	.	.	.
	.	.	.
	12	100 (plus $10 interest)	0

On the average, you had full use of $100 throughout the year. To calculate the average use, add the loan balance during the first and last month, then divide by 2:

$$\text{Average balance} = \frac{\$100 + \$100}{2} = \$100$$

But if you repay the $100 and the finance charge (a total of $110) in 12 equal monthly payments, you don't get the use of the $100 for the whole year. In fact, as shown next, you get the use of less and less of that $100 each month. In this case, the $10 charge for credit amounts to an APR of 18.5 percent.

Amount Borrowed	Month Number	Payment Made	Loan Balance
$100	1	0	$100.00
	2	8.33	91.67
	3	8.33	83.34
	4	8.33	75.01
	5	8.33	66.68
	6	8.33	58.35
	7	8.33	50.02
	8	8.33	41.69
	9	8.33	33.36
	10	8.33	25.03
	11	8.33	16.70
	12	8.33	8.37

Note that you are paying 10 percent interest even though you had the use of only $91.67 during the second month, not $100. During the last month, you owed only $8.37 (and had the use of $8.37), but the $10 interest is for the entire $100. As calculated in the previous example, the average use of the money during the year is $100 + $8.37 ÷ 2, or $54.18.

The accompanying Financial Planning Calculations feature shows how to calculate the APR.

FINANCIAL PLANNING CALCULATIONS

THE ARITHMETIC OF THE ANNUAL PERCENTAGE RATE (APR)

There are two ways to calculate the APR: using an APR formula and using the APR tables. The APR tables are more precise than the formula. The formula, given below, only approximates the APR:

$$r = \frac{2 \times n \times I}{P(N + 1)}$$

where

r = Approximate APR
n = Number of payment periods in one year
     (12, if payments are monthly; 52, if weekly)
I = Total dollar cost of credit
P = Principal, or net amount of loan
N = Total number of payments scheduled to pay off the loan

Let us compare the APR when the $100 loan is paid off in one lump sum at the end of the year and when the same loan is paid off in 12 equal monthly payments. The stated annual interest rate is 10 percent for both loans.

Using the formula, the APR for the lump-sum loan is

$$r = \frac{2 \times 1 \times \$10}{\$100(1 + 1)} = \frac{\$20}{\$100(2)} = \frac{\$20}{\$200} = 0.10,$$

or 10 percent

Using the formula, the APR for the monthly payment loan is

$$r = \frac{2 \times 12 \times \$10}{\$100(12 + 1)} = \frac{\$240}{\$100(13)} = \frac{\$240}{\$1,300}$$

$$= 0.1846, \text{ or } 18.46 \text{ percent (rounded to 18.5 percent)}$$

All creditors—banks, stores, car dealers, credit card companies, finance companies—must state the cost of their credit in terms of the finance charge and the APR. The law does not set interest rates or other credit charges, but it does require their disclosure so that you can compare credit costs and tackle the trade-offs.

Tackling the Trade-Offs

Financial Decision
Trade-Off

When you choose your financing, there are trade-offs between the features you prefer (term, size of payments, fixed or variable interest, or payment plan) and the cost of your loan. Here are some of the major trade-offs you should consider.

Term versus Interest Costs   Many people choose longer-term financing because they want smaller monthly payments. But the longer the term for a loan at a given interest rate, the greater the amount you must pay in interest charges. Consider the following analysis of the relationship between the term and interest costs.

A Comparison   Even when you understand the terms a creditor is offering, it's easy to underestimate the difference in dollars that different terms can make. Suppose you're buying a $7,500 used car. You put $1,500 down, and you need to borrow $6,000. Compare the following three credit arrangements:

	APR	Length of Loan	Monthly Payment	Total Finance Charge	Total Cost
Creditor A	14%	3 years	$205.07	$1,382.52	$7,382.52
Creditor B	14	4 years	163.96	1,870.08	7,870.08
Creditor C	15	4 years	166.98	2,015.04	8,015.04

How do these choices compare? The answer depends partly on what you need. The lowest-cost loan is available from creditor A. If you are looking for lower monthly payments, you could repay the loan over a longer period of time. However, you would have to pay more in total costs. A loan from creditor B—also at a 14 percent APR, but for four years—would add about $488 to your finance charge.

If that four-year loan were available only from creditor C, the APR of 15 percent would add another $145 to your finance charges. Other terms, such as the size of the down payment, will also make a difference. Be sure to look at all the terms before you make your choice.

Lender Risk versus Interest Rate   You may prefer financing that requires fixed payments or only a minimum of up-front cash. But both of these requirements can increase your cost of borrowing because they create more risk for your lender.

If you want to minimize your borrowing costs, you may need to accept conditions that reduce your lender's risk. Here are a few possibilities.

Variable Interest Rate   A variable interest rate is based on fluctuating rates in the banking system, such as the prime rate. With this type of loan, you share the interest rate risks with the lender. Therefore, the lender may offer you a lower initial interest rate than it would with a fixed-rate loan.

A Secured Loan   If you pledge property or other assets as collateral, you'll probably receive a lower interest rate on your loan.

Up-Front Cash   Many lenders believe you have a higher stake in repaying a loan if you pay cash for a large portion of what you are financing. Doing so may give you a better chance of getting the other terms you want. Of course, by making a large down payment, you forgo interest that you might earn in a savings account.

A Shorter Term   As you have learned, the shorter the period of time for which you borrow, the smaller the chance that something will prevent you from repaying and the lower the risk to the lender. Therefore, you may be able to borrow at a lower interest rate if you accept a shorter-term loan, but your payments will be high.

In the next section, you will see how the above-mentioned trade-offs can affect the cost of closed-end and open-end credit.

Calculating the Cost of Credit

The two most common methods of calculating interest are compound and simple interest formulas. Perhaps the most basic method is the simple interest calculation. Simple interest on the declining balance, add-on interest, bank discount, and compound interest are variations of simple interest.

simple interest

Simple Interest   **Simple interest** is the interest computed on principal only and without compounding; it is the dollar cost of borrowing money. This cost is based on three elements: the amount borrowed, which is called the *principal;* the rate of interest; and the amount of time for which the principal is borrowed.

You can use the following formula to find simple interest:

$$\text{Interest} = \text{Principal} \times \text{Rate of interest} \times \text{Time}$$

or

$$I = P \times r \times T$$

Example 1   Suppose you have persuaded a relative to lend you $1,000 to purchase a laptop computer. Your relative agreed to charge only 5 percent interest, and you agreed to repay the loan at the end of one year. Using the simple interest formula, the interest will be 5 percent of $1,000 for one year, or $50, since you have the use of $1,000 for the entire year:

$$I = \$1,000 \times 0.05 \times 1$$

$$= \$50$$

Using the APR formula discussed earlier,

$$APR = \frac{2 \times n \times I}{P(N + 1)} = \frac{2 \times 1 \times \$50}{\$1,000(1 + 1)} = \frac{\$100}{\$2,000} = 0.05, \text{ or 5 percent}$$

Note that the stated rate, 5 percent, is also the annual percentage rate.

declining balance method

Simple Interest on the Declining Balance   When more than one payment is made on a simple interest loan, the method of computing interest is known as the **declining balance method.** Since you pay interest only on the amount of the original principal that you have not yet repaid, the more frequent the payments, the lower the interest you will pay. Of course, the amount of credit you have at your disposal will also be lower.

Example 2   Using simple interest on the declining balance to compute interest charges, the interest on a 5 percent, $1,000 loan repaid in two payments, one at the end of the first half-year and another at the end of the second half-year, would be $37.50, as follows:
First payment:

$$I = P \times r \times T$$

$$= \$1,000 \times 0.05 \times \frac{1}{2}$$

$$= \$25 \text{ interest plus } \$500, \text{ or } \$525$$

Second payment:

$$I = P \times r \times T$$

$$= \$500 \times 0.05 \times \frac{1}{2}$$

$$= \$12.50 \text{ interest plus the remaining balance of } \$500, \text{ or } \$512.50$$

Total payment on the loan:

$$\$525 + \$512.50 = \$1,037.50$$

Using the APR formula,

$$APR = \frac{2 \times n \times I}{P(N + 1)} = \frac{2 \times 2 \times \$37.50}{\$1,000(2 + 1)} = \frac{\$150}{\$3,000} = 0.05, \text{ or 5 percent}$$

Note that using simple interest under the declining balance method, the stated rate, 5 percent, is also the annual percentage rate. The add-on interest, bank discount, and compound interest calculation methods differ from the simple interest method as to when, how, and on what balance interest is paid. For these methods, the real annual rate, or the annual percentage rate, differs from the stated rate.

add-on interest method

Add-On Interest   With the **add-on interest method,** interest is calculated on the full amount of the original principal. The interest amount is immediately added to the original principal, and payments are determined by dividing principal plus interest by the number of payments to be made. When only one payment is required, this method produces the same APR as the simple interest method. However, when two or more payments are to be made, the add-on method results in an effective rate of interest that is higher than the stated rate.

Example 3   Consider again the two-payment loan in Example 2. Using the add-on method, interest of $50 (5 percent of $1,000 for one year) is added to the $1,000 borrowed, giving $1,050 to be repaid—half (or $525) at the end of the first half-year and the other half at the end of the second half-year.

Even though your relative's stated interest rate is 5 percent, the real interest rate is

$$\text{APR} = \frac{2 \times n \times I}{P(N + 1)} = \frac{2 \times 2 \times \$50}{\$1,000(2 + 1)} = \frac{\$200}{\$3,000} = 0.066, \text{ or } 6.6 \text{ percent}$$

Note that using the add-on interest method means that no matter how many payments you are to make, the interest will always be $50. As the number of payments increases, you have use of less and less credit over the year. For example, if you make four quarterly payments of $262.50, you have use of $1,000 during the first quarter, about $750 during the second quarter, about $500 during the third quarter, and about $250 during the fourth and final quarter. Therefore, as the number of payments increases, the true interest rate, or APR, also increases.

Various other methods of determining the cost of credit, such as the bank discount method, the compound interest formula, amortization, and the use of tables, are presented in the appendix to this chapter.

Cost of Open-End Credit   As discussed earlier, open-end credit includes credit cards, department store charge cards, and check overdraft accounts that allow you to write checks for more than your actual balance. You can use open-end credit again and again until you reach a prearranged borrowing limit. The Truth in Lending law requires that open-end creditors let you know how the finance charge and the APR will affect your costs.

First, creditors must tell you how they calculate the finance charge. Creditors use various systems to calculate the balance on which they assess finance charges. Some creditors add finance charges after subtracting payments made during the billing period; this is called the **adjusted balance method.** Other creditors give you no credit for payments made during the billing period; this is called the **previous balance method.** Under the third—and the fairest—method, the **average daily balance method,** creditors add your balances for each day in the billing period and then divide by the number of days in the period.

adjusted balance method

previous balance method

average daily balance method

Here is a sample of the three billing methods:

	Adjusted Balance	**Previous Balance**	**Average Daily Balance**
Monthly interest rate	1½%	1½%	1½%
Previous balance	$400	$400	$400
Payments	$300	$300	$300 (payment on 15th day)
Interest charge	$1.50	$6.00	$3.75
	($100 × 1.5%)	($400 × 1.5%)	(average balance of $250 × 1.5%)

As the example shows, the finance charge varies for the same pattern of purchases and payments.

Second, creditors must tell you when finance charges on your credit account begin so that you know how much time you have to pay your bills before a finance charge is added. Some creditors, for example, give you a 20- to 25-day grace period to pay your balance in full before imposing a finance charge. But in most cases, the grace period applies only if you have no outstanding balance on your card. Therefore, if you want to take advantage of the interest-free period on your card, you must pay your bill in full every month.

The Truth in Lending law does not set rates or tell the creditor how to make interest calculations. It requires only that the creditor tell you the method that will be used. You should ask for an explanation of any terms you don't understand.

Cost of Credit and Expected Inflation   As you have seen, interest rates dictate when you must pay future dollars to receive current dollars. Borrowers and lenders, however, are less concerned about dollars, present or future, than about the goods and services those dollars can buy—that is, their purchasing power.

Inflation erodes the purchasing power of money. Each percentage point increase in inflation means a decrease of approximately 1 percent in the quantity of goods and services you can purchase with a given quantity of dollars. As a result, lenders, seeking to protect their purchasing power, add the expected rate of inflation to the interest rate they charge. You are willing to pay this higher rate because you expect inflation to enable you to repay the loan with cheaper dollars.

For example, if a lender expects a 4 percent inflation rate for the coming year and desires an 8 percent return on its loan, it will probably charge you a 12 percent nominal or stated rate (a 4 percent inflation premium plus an 8 percent "real" rate).

Return to Example 1, in which you borrowed $1,000 from your relative at the bargain rate of 5 percent for one year. If the inflation rate was 4 percent during that year, your relative's real rate of return was only 1 percent (5 percent stated interest minus 4 percent inflation rate) and your "real" cost was not $50 but only $10 ($50 minus $40 inflation premium).

Cost of Credit and Tax Considerations   Before the Tax Reform Act of 1986, the interest you paid on consumer credit reduced your taxable income. The new law did not affect the deductibility of home mortgage interest, but beginning in 1991 you can no longer deduct interest paid on consumer loans.

When you borrow from a bank or another lender, you usually arrange to repay the loan with interest by a specific date in a specified number of installments. But after several payments, you may decide to repay the entire loan at an earlier date than the one originally scheduled. How is interest calculated if you repay the loan early? See the Financial Planning Calculations feature on page 201.

Avoid the Minimum Monthly Payment Trap   The "minimum monthly payment" is the smallest amount you can pay and still be a cardholder in good standing. Banks often encourage you to make the minimum payment, such as 2 percent of your outstanding balance or $20, whichever is greater. Some statements refer to the minimum as the "cardholder amount due." But that is not the total amount you owe.

Consider the following examples. In each example, the minimum payment is based on 1/36 of the outstanding balance or $20, whichever is greater.

Example 1   You are buying new books for college. If you spend $500 on textbooks using a credit card charging 19.8 percent interest and make only the minimum payment,

Sheet 30

Financial Decision Trade-Off

FINANCIAL PLANNING FOR LIFE'S SITUATIONS

To Choose It, First Decide How You Plan to Use It

As you learned in the Opening Case, many bank cards offer added value through enhancements such as discounts on merchandise, rebates on purchases, travel and accident insurance, frequent-flier mileage, emergency card replacement, donations to nonprofit groups, and 24-hour customer service. The trick to finding the bank card that's right for you is to balance the benefits with the right price. You should consider interest rates and fees based on how you plan to use the card.

- *Annual fee.* If you plan to pay your balance in full each month, shop for a card that has a grace period and carries no annual fee, or a low annual fee, even if the trade-off is a higher interest rate. You plan to pay little or no interest anyway.
- *Low rates.* If you prefer to stretch out repayment, aim for a card with a lower interest rate. In general, lower-interest-rate cards tend to have tougher credit approval requirements, may not offer a grace period, and often have slightly higher annual fees. But if you qualify, the money you save on interest is likely to offset a higher fee.
- *Variable rates.* Some credit cards promote variable interest rates tied to an index like *The Wall Street Journal* "prime rate." You may benefit from lower interest rates when the index is low, but remember that when the index rises, you'll pay the higher rate even on purchases you've already made.
- *Grace period.* Not all credit cards offer a grace period. When you use such a card, the bank begins charging you interest on the day you make the purchase or the day the purchase is recorded on your account. Try to pay off your balance in

full each month to maintain the grace period and avoid paying interest.

- *Other fees.* Most automated teller machine (ATM) cards charge a special fee when you take a cash advance. Usually the fee is about 2 or 3 percent of the amount borrowed.

Many banks impose late fees even when payment arrives a day after the due date. Some banks charge a set fee, such as $10 or $15, while others charge a percentage, such as 5 percent, of the minimum payment due.

Most cards assess an over-credit-limit fee. For instance, if you charge $400 over your limit and the penalty is 5 percent, you will pay a $20 fee in addition to interest charges. A few companies charge lost-card replacement fees—usually $5 or $10.

Some credit card issuers allow you to skip a payment without a penalty. While this sounds like the bank is giving you a break, you will be charged interest during this period and will owe more in interest than you did before.

Once you decide on the right combination of features and price, you can begin shopping. Federal law requires that every mail solicitation, "take one" application, and application brochure carry a special box listing the interest rate, annual fee, length of grace period, and other fees. This will allow you to easily compare the costs of different card plans.

SOURCES: American Bankers Association; *Understanding Credit Card Costs* (San Francisco: Consumer Action, March 1994).

---

it will take you more than 2½ years to pay off the loan, adding $150 in interest charges to the cost of your purchase. The same purchase on a credit card charging 12 percent interest will cost only $78 extra.

Example 2 You purchase a $2,000 stereo system using a credit card with 19 percent interest and a 2 percent minimum payment. If you pay just the minimum every month, it will take you 265 months—over 22 years—to pay off the debt and will cost you nearly $4,800 in interest payments. Doubling the amount paid each month to 4 percent of the balance owed would allow you to shorten the payment time to 88 months from 265 months—or 7 years as opposed to 22 years—and save you about $3,680.

Example 3   You charge $2,000 in tuition and fees on a credit card charging 18.5 percent interest. If you pay off the balance by making the minimum payment each month, it will take you more than 11 years to repay the debt. By the time you have paid off the loan, you will have spent an extra $1,934 in interest alone—almost the actual cost of your tuition and fccs. Again, to be prudent, pay off the balance as quickly as possible.

See the Financial Planning for Life's Situations feature on page 198 for guidance in choosing the card that is right for you.

When the Repayment Is Early: The Rule of 78s

rule of 78s

Creditors sometimes use tables based on a mathematical formula called the **rule of 78s,** also called "the sum of the digits," to determine how much interest you have paid at any point in a loan. This formula dictates that you pay more interest at the beginning of a loan, when you have the use of more of the money, and pay less and less interest as the debt is reduced. Because all of the payments are the same in size, the part going to pay back the amount borrowed increases as the part representing interest decreases.

The laws of several states authorize the use of the rule of 78s as a means of calculating finance charge rebates when you pay off a loan early. The Truth in Lending law requires that your creditor disclose whether or not you are entitled to a rebate of the finance charge if you pay off the loan early. Loans for a year or less, however, usually do not allow for a finance charge rebate.

Read the Financial Planning Calculations feature to learn how to use the rule of 78s.

Credit Insurance

credit insurance

Credit insurance ensures the repayment of your loan in the event of death, disability, or loss of property. The lender is named the beneficiary and directly receives any payments made on submitted claims.

There are three types of credit insurance: credit life, credit accident and health, and credit property. The most commonly purchased type of credit insurance is credit life insurance, which provides for the repayment of the loan if the borrower dies. According to the Consumer Federation of America and the National Insurance Consumer Organization, most borrowers don't need credit life insurance. Those who don't have life insurance can buy term life insurance for less. Term life insurance is discussed in Chapter 12.

Credit accident and health insurance, also called *credit disability insurance,* repays your loan in the event of a loss of income due to illness or injury. Credit property insurance provides coverage for personal property purchased with a loan. It may also insure collateral property, such as a car or furniture. However, premiums for such coverages are quite high.

Sheet 31

C O N C E P T   C H E C K   7–2

1. Distinguish between the finance charge and the annual percentage rate.
2. What are the three variations of the simple interest formula?
3. Distinguish among the adjusted balance, previous balance, and average daily balance methods of calculating the cost of open-end credit.
4. What is the rule of 78s?

FINANCIAL PLANNING CALCULATIONS

THE RULE OF 78s

How to Use the Rule of 78s

The first step is to add up all the digits for the number of payments scheduled. For a 12-installment loan, add the numbers 1 through 12:

$$1 + 2 + 3 + 4 + 5 + 6 + 7 + 8 + 9 + 10 + 11 + 12 = 78$$

The answer—"the sum of the digits"—explains how the rule was named. One might say that the total interest is divided into 78 parts for payment over the term of the loan.

In the first month, before making any payments, you have the use of the whole amount borrowed, and therefore you pay 12/78 of the total interest in the first payment; in the second month, you still have the use of 11 parts of the loan and pay 11/78 of the interest; in the third, 10/78; and so on down to the final installment, 1/78.

Adding all the numbers in a series of payments is rather tedious. We can arrive at the answer quickly by using this formula:

$$\frac{N}{2} \times (N + 1)$$

N is the number of payments. For a 12-month loan, it looks like this:

$$\frac{12}{2} \times (12 + 1) = 6 \times 13 = 78$$

A Loan for Karen and Mike

Let us suppose that Karen and Mike borrow $3,000 from the National Bank to redecorate their home. Interest comes to $225, and the total of $3,225 is to be paid in 15 equal installments of $215.

Using the rule of 78s, we can determine how much of each installment represents interest. We add all the numbers from 1 through 15:

$$\frac{15}{2} \times (15 + 1) = 7.5 \times 16 = 120$$

Total interest is divided into 120 parts. The first payment will include 15 parts of the total interest, or 15/120

$$\left(\frac{\$225}{120} \times 15 = \$28.13\right)$$

the second, 14/120

$$\left(\frac{\$225}{120} \times 14 = \$26.25\right)$$

and so on.

Notice in the following table that the interest decreases with each payment and the repayment of the amount borrowed increases with each payment:

Payment Number	Interest	Reduction of Debt	Total Payment
1	$ 28.13	$ 186.87	$ 215.00
2	26.25	188.75	215.00
3	24.37	190.63	215.00
4	22.50	192.50	215.00
5	20.63	194.37	215.00
6	18.75	196.25	215.00
7	16.87	198.13	215.00
8	15.00	200.00	215.00
9	13.13	201.87	215.00
10	11.25	203.75	215.00
11	9.37	205.63	215.00
12	7.50	207.50	215.00
13	5.63	209.37	215.00
14	3.75	211.25	215.00
15	1.87	213.13	215.00
	$225.00	$3,000.00	$3,225.00

How Much Is the Rebate?

Now let's assume Karen and Mike want to pay off the loan with the fifth payment. We know the total interest is divided into 120 parts. To find out how many parts will be rebated, we add up the numbers for the remaining 10 installments, which will be prepaid:

$$\frac{10}{2} \times (10 + 1) = 5 \times 11 = 55$$

Now we know that 55/120 of the interest will be deducted as a rebate; it amounts to $103.12:

$$\frac{55}{120} \times \$225 = \frac{\$12,375}{120} = \$103.12$$

We see that Karen and Mike do not save two-thirds of the interest (which would be $150) by paying off the loan in one-third of the scheduled time. But the earlier they repay the loan, the higher the portion of interest they do save. The rule of 78s favors lenders.

SOURCE: *The Rule of 78s* (Philadelphia: Federal Reserve Bank of Philadelphia, May 1989).

MANAGING YOUR DEBTS

L.O.3 Develop a plan to manage your debts.

A sudden illness or the loss of your job may make it impossible for you to pay your bills on time. If you find you cannot make your payments, contact your creditors at once and try to work out a modified payment plan with them. If you have paid your bills promptly in the past, they may be willing to work with you. Do not wait until your account is turned over to a debt collector. At that point, the creditor has given up on you.

Automobile loans present special problems. Most automobile financing agreements permit your creditor to repossess your car anytime you are in default on your payments. No advance notice is required. If your car is repossessed, you may have to pay the full balance due on the loan, as well as towing and storage costs, to get it back. If you cannot do this, the creditor may sell the car. Try to solve the problem with your creditor when you realize you will not be able to meet your payments. It may be better to sell the car yourself and pay off your debt than to incur the added costs of repossession.

> **DID YOU KNOW?**
>
> Citibank offers a 16-page booklet on personal money management for young people, *Max Moore Detective in Money Town.* Call 1–800–833–9666 for your free copy.

If you are having trouble paying your bills, you may be tempted to turn to a company that claims to offer assistance in solving debt problems. Such companies may offer debt consolidation loans, debt counseling, or debt reorganization plans that are "guaranteed" to stop creditors' collection efforts. Before signing with such a company, investigate it. Be sure you understand what services the company provides and what they will cost you. Do not rely on verbal promises that do not appear in your contract. Also, check with the Better Business Bureau and your state or local consumer protection office. It may be able to tell you whether other consumers have registered complaints about the company.

A constant worry for a debtor who is behind in payments is the fear of debt collection agencies. However, as you will see in the next section, a federal agency protects certain legal rights that you possess in your dealings with such agencies.

Debt Collection Practices

Fair Debt Collection Practices Act (FDCPA)

The Federal Trade Commission enforces the **Fair Debt Collection Practices Act (FDCPA),** which prohibits certain practices by agencies that collect debts for creditors. The act does not apply to creditors that collect debts themselves. While the act does not erase the legitimate debts consumers owe, it does regulate the ways debt collection agencies do business.

Exhibit 7–2 summarizes the steps you may take if a debt collector calls.

Warning Signs of Debt Problems

Bill Kenney is in his early 30s. He has a steady job with an annual income of $40,000 a year. Bill, his wife, and their two children enjoy a comfortable life. A new car is parked in the driveway of their home, a home furnished with such modern conveniences as a new microwave oven, a new freezer, an electric washer and dryer, a videocassette recorder, and a large-screen color television set.

> **DID YOU KNOW?**
>
> Visa International offers *Credit Cards: An Owner's Manual,* with a budget worksheet and financial fitness quiz. Call 1–800–847–2511 for your free copy.

However, Bill Kenney is in debt. He is drowning in a sea of bills; most of his income is tied up in repaying debts. Foreclosure proceedings on his home have been instituted, while several stores have court orders to repossess practically every major appliance in it. His current car payment is overdue, and three charge accounts at local stores are several months delinquent.

This case is neither exaggerated nor isolated. Unfortunately, a large number of people are in the same floundering state. These people's problem is

EXHIBIT 7–2   **What to Do If a Debt Collector Calls**

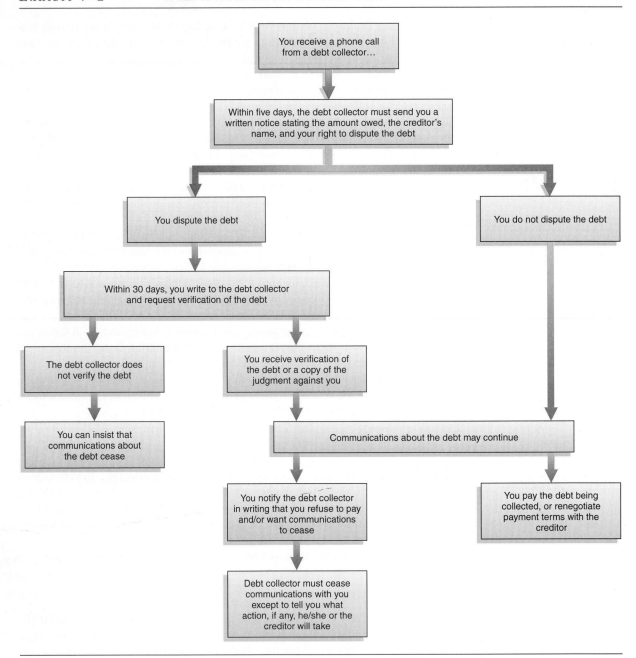

SOURCE: Reprinted courtesy of Office of Public Information, Federal Reserve Bank of Minneapolis, Minneapolis, MN 55480.

immaturity. Mature consumers have certain information; they demonstrate self-discipline, control their impulses, and use sound judgment; they accept responsibility for money management; and they are able to postpone and govern expenditures when overextension of credit appears likely. As Exhibit 7–3 on page 203 shows, overextension of credit is the second most common reason consumers are unable to pay their bills on time.

EXHIBIT 7–3	Reason for Default		Primary or Contributing Cause of Default (percent of cases)
Why Consumers Don't Pay	Loss of income		48
	Unemployment	24	
	Illness	16	
	Other	8	
	Overextension		25
	Defective goods or services or other perceived consumer fraud		20
	Fraudulent use of credit		4
	Other		3

SOURCE: Reprinted courtesy of Office of Public Information, Federal Reserve Bank of Minneapolis, Minneapolis, MN 55480.

Referring to overindebtedness as the nation's number two family financial problem, a nationally noted columnist on consumer affairs lists the following as frequent reasons for indebtedness:[2]

1. *Emotional problems,* such as the need for instant gratification, as in the case of a man who can't resist buying a costly suit or a woman who impulsively purchases an expensive dress in a trendy department store.
2. *The use of money to punish,* such as a husband who buys a new car without consulting his wife, who in turn buys a diamond watch to get even.
3. *The expectation of instant comfort* among young couples who assume that by use of the installment plan, they can have immediately the possessions their parents acquired after years of work.
4. *Keeping up with the Joneses,* which is more apparent than ever, not only among prosperous families but among limited-income families too.
5. *Overindulgence of children,* often because of the parents' own emotional needs, competition with each other, or inadequate communication regarding expenditures for the children.
6. *Misunderstanding or lack of communication among family members.* For example, a salesperson visited a Memphis family to sell them an expensive freezer. Although the freezer was beyond the means of this already overindebted family and too large for their needs anyway, the husband thought his wife wanted it. Not until later, in an interview with a debt counselor, did the wife relate her concern when she signed the contract; she had wanted her husband to say no.
7. *The amount of the finance charges,* which can push a family over the edge of their ability to pay, especially when they borrow from one company to pay another and these charges pyramid.

Exhibit 7–4 on page 205 lists the danger signals of potential debt problems.

The Serious Consequences of Debt

If the causes of indebtedness vary, so too does a mixture of other personal and family problems that frequently occur with overextension of credit.

Loss of a job because of garnishment proceedings may occur in a family that has a disproportionate amount of income tied up in debts. Another possibility is that such a family is forced to neglect vital areas. In the frantic effort to rob Peter to pay Paul, skimping

FINANCIAL PLANNING FOR LIFE'S SITUATIONS

MONEY MANAGEMENT IN CYBERSPACE

Whether you're developing a plan for reaching your financial goals or searching for a low-interest credit card, you can look to the Internet for a world of free information. Many web sites provide interactive worksheets that allow you to plug in personal information and obtain customized reports. Here are some suggestions.

FinanCenter This provides nifty payment calculators that help you figure out the actual dollars paid in interest over the period of a credit card debt or the maximum amount you should borrow at your current income. If your payments have been piling up, take a deep breath before traveling here. (www.financenter.com)

Bank Rate Monitor Looking for the best credit card rates available or up-to-the-minute news on the credit industry? Then log on here. The site posts a survey of card rates and even lets you apply on-line for some cards. You can also scroll through a list of suggestions for cutting your credit card debt. (www.bankrate.com)

RAM Research Created by this independent bank research organization, the site contains everything you ever wanted to know about credit cards. It includes a database of 10,000 financial institutions, and news and statistics on the credit industry. If you've had credit problems and want to reestablish your credit rating, see the section on secured cards. (www.ramresearch.com)

American Consumer Credit Counseling, Inc. This is where to turn if you have a credit problem. You can take a test to determine if you are heading into financial difficulties. Read up on the legal ins and outs of indebtedness,

whether to consider bankruptcy, and how the Fair Credit Reporting Act works. (www.consumercredit.com)

American Association of Individual Investors (AAII) The AAII web site covers the fundamentals of investing, with an array of subjects that will interest both the novice and the advanced investor. You can dive into portfolio management or brush up on investment terminology. There's also a special section on using computers to manage your finances. (www.aaii.org)

National Association of Personal Financial Advisors (NAPFA) NAPFA offers consumer information on what to expect from a financial planner, as well as how and why to choose one. A handy search tool lets you pinpoint an advisor close to home. (www.napfa.org)

International Association for Financial Planning Check in here to learn how to assess your financial situation and ways to set budget goals. The site also features a section on determining whether or not you need a financial planner. (www.iafp.org)

Securities and Exchange Commission (SEC) Here you'll find a wealth of information about this U.S. government regulatory agency, including a straightforward discussion on the essentials of investing. You can tap into the EDGAR database to view the information that the SEC requires companies to file. (www.sec.gov)

Source: *Teacher$ Talk,* TIAA-CREF (New York: Spring 1997), p. 5.

may seriously affect the family's health and neglect the educational needs of children. Excessive indebtedness may also result in heavy drinking, neglect of children, marital difficulties, and drug abuse. But help is available to those debtors who seek it. See the accompanying Financial Planning for Life's Situations feature.

CONCEPT CHECK 7–3

1. What is the Fair Debt Collection Practices Act?
2. What are the most frequent reasons for indebtedness?
3. What are common danger signals of potential debt problems?

EXHIBIT 7–4

Danger Signals of Potential Debt Problems

1. Paying only the minimum balance on credit card bills each month
2. Increasing the total balance due on credit accounts each month
3. Missing payments, paying late, or paying some bills this month and others next month
4. Intentionally using the overdraft or automatic loan features on checking accounts or taking frequent cash advances on credit cards
5. Using savings to pay routine bills such as groceries or utilities
6. Receiving second or third payment notices from creditors
7. Not talking to your spouse about money or talking *only* about money
8. Depending on overtime, moonlighting, or bonuses to meet everyday expenses
9. Using up your savings
10. Borrowing money to pay old debts
11. Not knowing how much you owe until the bills arrive
12. Going over your credit limit on credit cards
13. Having little or nothing in savings to handle unexpected expenses
14. Being denied credit because of a negative credit bureau report
15. Getting a credit card revoked by the issuer
16. Putting off medical or dental visits because you can't afford them right now

If your household is experiencing more than two of these warning signals, it's time to examine your budget for ways to reduce expenses.

SOURCES: *Advice for Consumers Who Use Credit* (Silver Springs, MD: Consumer Credit Counseling Service of Maryland, Inc.); *How to Be Credit Smart* (Washington, DC: Consumer Credit Education Foundation).

CONSUMER CREDIT COUNSELING SERVICES

L.O.4 Evaluate various private and governmental sources that assist consumers with debt problems.

Consumer Credit Counseling Service (CCCS)

If you are having problems paying your bills and need help, you have several options. You can contact your creditors and try to work out an adjusted repayment plan yourself, or you can check your telephone directory for a nonprofit financial counseling program to get help.

The **Consumer Credit Counseling Service (CCCS)** is a local, nonprofit organization affiliated with the National Foundation for Consumer Credit (NFCC). Branches of the CCCS provide debt counseling services for families and individuals with serious financial problems. It is not a charity, a lending institution, or a governmental or legal agency. The Consumer Credit Counseling Service is supported by contributions from banks, consumer finance companies, credit unions, merchants, and other community-minded organizations and individuals.

According to the NFCC, in 1996 more than 1.5 million consumers contacted CCCS offices for help with their personal financial problems. More than 225 CCCS offices opened in 1996, bringing the total number of locations to about 1,300. Now more than 90 percent of the U.S. population has convenient access to CCCS services.

To find an office near you, check the white pages of your local telephone directory under Consumer Credit Counseling Service, or call 1-800-388-CCCS. All information is kept strictly confidential. Exhibit 7–5 on page 206 reveals the characteristics of the typical CCCS client.

What the CCCS Does

Credit counselors are aware that most people who are in debt over their heads are basically honest people who want to clear up their indebtedness. Too often, the problems of such people arise from a lack of planning or a miscalculation of what they earn. Therefore, the

EXHIBIT 7–5	Following are the characteristics of the typical client of the Consumer Credit Counseling Service:	
Profile of a CCCS Client	**Age:**	35
	Sex:	Male 51%, female 49%
	Marital status:	Single 25%, married 52%
		Separated, divorced, or widowed 23%
	Number in family:	3.3
	Buying or own home:	38%
	Average monthly gross income:	$2,056
	Average total debt:	$18,312
	Average number of creditors:	11

SOURCES: National Foundation for Consumer Credit, Inc. (Silver Springs, MD); Consumer Credit Insurance Association (Chicago); Consumer Credit Counseling Service (Chicago); TransUnion Corporation; *Chicago Tribune,* August 9, 1992, Sec. 6, p. 10.

CCCS is as concerned with preventing the problems as with solving them. As a result, its activities are divided into two parts:

1. Aiding families with serious debt problems by helping them manage their money better and setting up a realistic budget and plan for expenditures.
2. Helping people prevent debt problems by teaching them the necessity of family budget planning, providing education to people of all ages regarding the pitfalls of unwise credit buying, suggesting techniques for family budgeting, and encouraging credit institutions to provide full information about the costs and terms of credit and to withhold credit from those who cannot afford to repay it.

Anyone who is overburdened by credit obligations can phone, write, or visit a CCCS office. The CCCS requires that an applicant complete an application for credit counseling and then arranges an appointment for a personal interview with the applicant.

CCCS counseling is usually free. However, when the CCCS administers a debt repayment plan, it sometimes charges a nominal fee to help defray administrative costs.

Alternative Counseling Services

In addition to the CCCS, universities, military bases, credit unions, local county extension agents, and state and federal housing authorities sometimes provide nonprofit counseling services. These organizations usually charge little or nothing for such assistance. You can also check with your local bank or consumer protection office to see whether it has a listing of reputable, low-cost financial counseling services.

> **DID YOU KNOW?**
>
> MasterCard offers a brochure, *In the Red,* which has advice and resources for managing debt. Call 1–800–633–1185 for your free copy.

To get individualized recommendations on the quickest and most inexpensive way to pay off credit card balances, request a Debt Zapper report from the Bankcard Holders of America, 524 Branch Drive, Salem, Virginia 24153, or call (703) 481–1110 to request a form on which you state the balance, interest rate, and minimum amount due each month for all of your credit cards and any extra money you can spare each month to help whittle down the debt. For $15, you will receive a schedule that tells you exactly how much money to pay on each card every month until the debts are gone. You may visit this organization at this Web site: www.epn.com/bha.

Another organization that offers financial counseling is Debtors Anonymous, General Service Board, P.O. Box 20322, New York, New York 10025.

But what if a debtor suffers from an extreme case of financial woes? Is there any relief? The answer is yes: bankruptcy proceedings.

1. What is the Consumer Credit Counseling Service?
2. What are the two major activities of the Consumer Credit Counseling Service?
3. What options other than the CCCS do consumers have for financial counseling?

DECLARING PERSONAL BANKRUPTCY

L.O.5 Assess the choices in declaring personal bankruptcy.

Jan Watson typifies the new face of bankruptcy. A 43-year-old freelance commercial photographer from Point Reyes, California, she was never in serious financial trouble until she began incurring big medical costs last year and reached for her credit cards to pay the bills. Since Jan didn't have health insurance, her debt quickly mounted and soon reached $17,000. It was too much for her to pay off with her $25,000-a-year freelance income. Her solution: Declare personal bankruptcy and the immediate freedom it would bring from creditors' demands.

Ms. Watson's move put her in familiar company, demographically speaking. An increasing number of bankruptcy filers are well-educated, middle-class baby boomers with an overwhelming level of credit card debt. These baby boomers make up 44 percent of the adult population, but they account for 59 percent of personal bankruptcies. In that group, the people most likely to be in bankruptcy are between 40 and 44 years old, an age group that is usually assumed to be economically established. Increasingly, too, the bankruptcy debtor is likely to be female. Women now account for 28.6 percent of bankruptcy filers, up from 17 percent only a decade ago.

In 1994, the U.S. Senate unanimously passed a bill that will reduce the time and cost of bankruptcy proceedings. The bill strengthens creditor rights and enables more individuals to weather bankruptcy proceedings without selling their assets.

Unfortunately for some debtors, bankruptcy has become an acceptable tool of credit management. During the last nine years, the personal bankruptcy rate has increased 20 percent annually. According to the American Bankruptcy Institute, a record 1.2 million people declared bankruptcy in 1996, the highest rate since the U.S. bankruptcy code took effect in 1979 (see Exhibit 7–6 on page 208).[3] Bankruptcy courts have turned to regular Saturday sessions to handle the overflow.

The U.S. Bankruptcy Act of 1978: The Last Resort

Nationwide, the overwhelming majority of bankruptcies like Jan Watson's are filed under Chapter 7 of the U.S. bankruptcy code. If your situation is hopeless, you have two choices in declaring personal bankruptcy: Chapter 7 (a straight bankruptcy) and Chapter 13 (a wage earner plan) bankruptcy. Both choices are undesirable, and neither should be considered an easy way out.

Chapter 7 bankruptcy

Chapter 7 Bankruptcy   In a **Chapter 7 bankruptcy,** a debtor is required to draw up a petition listing his or her assets and liabilities. The debtor submits the petition to a U.S. district court and pays a filing fee. A person filing for relief under the bankruptcy code is called a *debtor;* the term *bankrupt* is not used.

Chapter 7 is a straight bankruptcy in which many, but not all, debts are forgiven. Most of the debtor's assets are sold to pay off creditors. However, certain assets of the debtor are protected. These assets are $7,500 equity in a home; $1,200 equity in a car or truck; $200 per item in household goods; up to $400 worth of any other property; $750 worth

EXHIBIT 7-6

U.S. Bankruptces, 1961-95

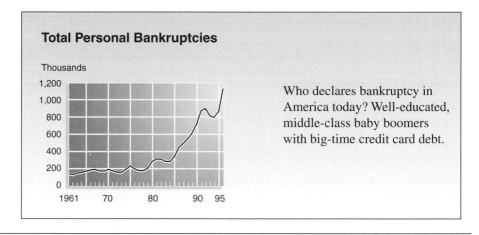

Total Personal Bankruptcies

Thousands

Who declares bankruptcy in America today? Well-educated, middle-class baby boomers with big-time credit card debt.

SOURCES: Administrative Office of the United States Courts; *Economic Policy Review,* Federal Reserve Bank of New York, July 1997, p. 84.

of trade tools, books, and so on; $500 worth of personal jewelry; Social Security Payments; and unemployment compensation.

However, some creditors still try to collect. In 1997, for example, the Federal Trade Commission negotiated a settlement agreement with Sears, Roebuck and Company ensuring that Sears makes full refunds totaling more than $100 million to consumers. More than 200,000 consumers whose debts were discharged in bankruptcy proceedings had been forced by Sears to continue payments or face illegal collection efforts.

The discharge of debts in Chapter 7 does not affect alimony, child support, certain taxes, fines, certain debts arising from educational loans, or debts that you fail to properly disclose to the bankruptcy court. At the request of a creditor, the bankruptcy judge may also exclude from the discharge debts resulting from loans you received by giving the lender a false financial statement. Furthermore, debts arising from fraud, embezzlement, driving while intoxicated, larceny, or certain other willful or malicious acts may also be excluded.

According to recent research by Purdue's Credit Research Center, Chapter 7 bankrupts average $19,800 in annual after-tax income and credit card debts of $17,544. Increasingly, credit card issuers have been targeting less affluent consumers. From 1993 to 1996, the proportion of households with incomes under $20,000 that received credit card offers rose from 40 to 58 percent. In addition, issuers are increasingly marketing to recent bankrupts and teenagers.[4]

Chapter 13 bankruptcy   **Chapter 13 Bankruptcy**   In a **Chapter 13 bankruptcy,** a debtor with a regular income proposes to a bankruptcy court a plan for extinguishing his or her debts from future earnings or other property over a period of time. In such a bankruptcy, the debtor normally keeps all or most of his or her property.

During the period the plan is in effect, which can be as long as five years, the debtor makes regular payments to a Chapter 13 trustee. The trustee, in turn, distributes the money to the creditors. Under certain circumstances, the bankruptcy court may approve a plan permitting the debtor to keep all property even though the debtor repays less than the full amount of the debts. Certain debts not dischargeable in Chapter 7, such as those based on fraud, may be discharged in Chapter 13 if the debtor successfully completes the plan. To file a Chapter 13 bankruptcy, a person must have regular income and not more than $100,000 in unsecured debts or $350,000 in secured debts.

Effect of Bankruptcy on Your Job and Your Future Credit

Financial Decision
Trade-Off

Different people have different experiences in obtaining credit after they file bankruptcy. Some find obtaining credit more difficult. Others find obtaining credit easier because they have relieved themselves of their prior debts or because creditors know they cannot file another bankruptcy case for a period of time. Obtaining credit may be easier for people who file a Chapter 13 bankruptcy and repay some of their debts than for people who file a Chapter 7 bankruptcy and make no effort to repay their debts. The bankruptcy law prohibits your employer from discharging you simply because you have filed a bankruptcy case.

One caution: Don't confuse a personal bankruptcy with a business (or Chapter 11) bankruptcy. The Chapter 11 bankruptcy is a reorganization ordered by the court because a business is unable to pay its debts.

Should a Lawyer Represent You in a Bankruptcy Case?

When 29-year-old Lynn Jensen of San Garbriel, California, lost her $35,000-a-year job, she ended up filing for bankruptcy using a "how to file for bankruptcy" book because she could not afford a lawyer. Like Lynn, you have the right to file your own bankruptcy case and to represent yourself at all court hearings. In any bankruptcy case, however, you must complete and file with a bankruptcy court several detailed forms concerning your property, debts, and financial condition. Many people find it easier to complete these forms with the assistance of experienced bankruptcy counsel. In addition, you may discover that your case will develop complications, especially if you own a substantial amount of property or your creditors object to the discharge of your debts. Then you will require the advice and assistance of a lawyer.

Choosing a bankruptcy lawyer may be difficult. Some of the least reputable lawyers make easy money by handling hundreds of bankruptcy cases without adequately considering individual needs. Recommendations from those you know and trust, and from employee assistance programs, are most useful.

What Are the Costs?   The monetary costs to the debtor under Chapter 13 include the following:

1. *Court costs.* The debtor must pay a filing fee to the clerk of the court at the time of filing his or her petition. The filing fee may be paid in up to four installments if the court grants authorization.
2. *Attorneys' fees.* These fees are usually the largest single item of cost. Often the attorney does not require them to be paid in advance at the time of filing but agrees to be paid in installments after receipt of a down payment.
3. *Trustees' fees and costs.* The trustees' fees are established by the bankruptcy judge in most districts and by a U.S. trustee in certain other districts.

Although it is possible to reduce these costs by purchasing the legal forms in a local stationery store and completing them yourself, an attorney is strongly recommended.

There are also intangible costs to bankruptcy. For example, obtaining credit in the future may be difficult, since bankruptcy reports are retained in credit bureaus for 10 years. Therefore, you should take the extreme step of declaring personal bankruptcy only when no other options for solving your financial problems exist.

Since you now know everything you ever wanted to know about consumer credit, read the Financial Planning in Action feature on page 210 to test your credit IQ.

FINANCIAL PLANNING FOR LIFE'S SITUATIONS

WHAT'S YOUR CREDIT IQ?

Credit-Ability Scorecard

Test your credit IQ. For each question, circle the letter that best describes your credit habits.

1. **I pay my bills when they are due.**
   (A) Always   (B) Almost Always   (C) Sometimes

2. **After paying my regular bills each month, I have money left from my income.**
   (A) Yes   (B) Sometimes   (C) Never

3. **I know how much I owe on my credit cards each month before I receive my bills.**
   (A) Yes   (B) Sometimes   (C) No

4. **When I get behind in my payments, I ignore the past-due notices.**
   (A) Never or Not Applicable   (B) Sometimes
   (C) Always

5. **When I need more money for my regular living expenses, I take out a loan or use my line of credit on my credit card or checking account.**
   (A) Never   (B) Sometimes   (C) Often

6. **If I want to see a copy of my credit report, I would contact . . .**
   (A) A credit reporting agency   (B) My lenders
   (C) My lawyer

7. **My credit record shows that I am current on all my loans and charge accounts.**
   (A) Yes   (B) Don't know   (C) No

8. **I pay more than the minimum balance due on my credit card accounts.**
   (A) Always   (B) Sometimes   (C) Never

9. **To pay off my current credit and charge card accounts, it would take me . . .**
   (A) 4 months or less   (B) 5 to 8 months
   (C) Over 8 months

10. **My consumer loans (including auto loans, but not mortgage payment) and credit card bills each month average more than 20% of my take-home pay.**
    (A) No   (B) Sometimes   (C) Always

11. **If I had serious credit problems, I would contact my creditors to explain the problem.**
    (A) Yes   (B) Probably   (C) No

12. **If I default (don't repay) on a loan, that fact can stay on my credit report for . . .**
    (A) 7 years   (B) 3 years   (C) 1 year

Assign a score of 3 for each "A" answer, 2 for each "B" answer, and 1 for each "C" response. Total the score.

If you scored:

31–36   You have an excellent knowledge of credit and its responsible use.

24–30   You should take steps toward a better understanding of your personal finances and of the credit process.

18–23   You probably need to take a serious look at your personal finances; consider controlling your spending and keeping on a tight budget.

12–17   You may be heading for serious trouble; consider seeking help, such as nonprofit consumer credit counseling services.

SOURCE: *How to Be Credit Smart* (Washington, DC: Consumer Credit Education Foundation, 1994).

CONCEPT CHECK 7–5

1. What is the purpose of Chapter 7 bankruptcy?
2. What is the difference between Chapter 7 and Chapter 13 bankruptcy?
3. How does bankruptcy affect your job and future credit?
4. What are the costs of declaring bankruptcy?

KEY FORMULAS

Page	Topic	Formula

193 — **Calculating annual percentage rate (APR)**

$$\text{APR} = \frac{2 \times \text{Number of payment periods in one year} \times \text{Dollar cost of credit}}{\text{Loan amount (Total number of payments to pay off the loan} + 1)}$$

$$= \frac{2 \times n \times I}{P(N + 1)}$$

Example:

P = Principal borrowed, $100; n = number of payments in one year, 1;
I = Dollar cost of credit, $8

$$\text{APR} = \frac{2 \times 1 \times \$8}{\$100(1 + 1)} = \frac{\$16}{\$200} = 0.08, \text{ or 8 percent}$$

For 12 equal monthly payments,

$$\text{APR} = \frac{2 \times 12 \times \$8}{\$100(12 + 1)} = \frac{\$192}{\$1,300} = 0.1476, \text{ or 14.76 percent}$$

194 — **Calculating simple interest**

$$\frac{\text{Interest}}{\text{(in dollars)}} = \text{Principal borrowed} \times \text{Interest rate} \times \text{Length of loan in years}$$

$$I = P \times r \times T$$

Example:

From above: P = $100; r = 0.08; T = 1

$$I = \$100 \times 0.08 \times 1 = \$8$$

217 — **Calculating compound interest**

$$\text{Total future value of a loan} = \text{Principal} (1 + \text{Rate of interest})^{\text{Time in years}}$$
$$F = P(1 + r)^T$$

Example:

From above: P = $100; r = 0.08; T = 1

$$F = \$100(1 + 0.08)^1 = \$100 (1.08) = \$108$$

218 — **Calculating total monthly payment (principal + interest) on a conventional loan**

$$\frac{\text{Monthly}}{\text{payment}} = \frac{\text{Loan} \times \text{Monthly interest rate} \times (1 + \text{Monthly interest rate})^{\text{Time in months}}}{(1 + \text{Monthly interest rate})^{\text{Time in months}} - 1}$$

$$MP = P \times \frac{i \times (1 + i)^T}{(1 + i)^T - 1}$$

Example:

From above: P = $100; i = 0.08

In a 12-month loan,

$$MP = \frac{\$100 \times 0.08(1 + 0.08)^{12}}{(1 + 0.08)^{12} - 1} = \frac{\$100 \times 0.08/12 \times (1 + 0.0066)^{12}}{(1 + 0.0066)^{12} - 1} = \$8.70$$

200 — **Rule of 78s**

$$\frac{\text{Number of payments}}{2} \times (\text{Number of payments} + 1)$$

$$\frac{N}{2} \times (N + 1)$$

Example:

In a 12-month loan,

$$\frac{12}{2} \times (12 + 1) = 6(13) = 78$$

SUMMARY

L.O.1   Analyze the major sources of consumer credit.

The major sources of consumer credit are commercial banks, savings and loan associations, credit unions, finance companies, life insurance companies, and family and friends. Each of these sources has unique advantages and disadvantages.

L.O.2   Determine the cost of credit by calculating interest using various interest formulas.

Compare the finance charge and the annual percentage rate (APR) as you shop for credit. Under the Truth in Lending law, creditors are required to state the cost of borrowing so that you can compare credit costs and shop for credit.

L.O.3   Develop a plan to manage your debts.

The Fair Debt Collection Practices Act prohibits certain practices by debt collection agencies. Debt has serious consequences if a proper plan for managing it is not implemented.

L.O.4   Evaluate various private and governmental sources that assist consumers with debt problems.

If you cannot meet your obligations, contact your creditors immediately. Before signing up with a debt consolidation company, investigate it thoroughly. Better yet, contact your local Consumer Credit Counseling Service or other debt counseling organizations.

L.O.5   Assess the choices in declaring personal bankruptcy.

A debtor's last resort is to declare bankruptcy, permitted by the U.S. Bankruptcy Act of 1978. Consider the financial and other costs of bankruptcy before taking this extreme step. A debtor can declare Chapter 7 (straight) bankruptcy or Chapter 13 (wage earner plan) bankruptcy.

GLOSSARY

add-on interest method   A method of computing interest in which interest is calculated on the full amount of the original principal.   (p. 196)

adjusted balance method   The assessment of finance charges after payments made during the billing period have been subtracted.   (p. 196)

annual percentage rate (APR)   The percentage cost (or relative cost) of credit on a yearly basis. The APR yields a true rate of interest for comparisons with other sources of credit.   (p. 192)

average daily balance method   A method of computing finance charges that uses a weighted average of the account balance throughout the current billing period.   (p. 196)

Chapter 7 bankruptcy   One type of personal (or straight) bankruptcy in which many debts are forgiven.   (p. 207)

Chapter 13 bankruptcy   A voluntary plan that a debtor with regular income develops and proposes to a bankruptcy court.   (p. 208)

Consumer Credit Counseling Service (CCCS)   A local, nonprofit organization that provides debt counseling services for families and individuals with serious financial problems.   (p. 205)

credit insurance   Any type of insurance that ensures repayment of a loan in the event the borrower is unable to repay it.   (p. 199)

declining balance method   A method of computing interest when more than one payment is made on a simple interest loan.   (p. 195)

Fair Debt Collection Practices Act (FDCPA)   A federal law, enacted in 1978, that regulates debt collection activities.   (p. 201)

finance charge   The total dollar amount paid to use credit.   (p. 189)

previous balance method   A method of computing finance charges that gives no credit for payments made during the billing period.   (p. 196)

rule of 78s   A mathematical formula to determine how much interest has been paid at any point in a loan term.   (p. 199)

simple interest   Interest computed on the principal only and without compounding.   (p. 194)

Truth in Lending law   A federal law that requires creditors to disclose the annual percentage rate (APR) and the finance charge as a dollar amount.   (p. 189)

REVIEW QUESTIONS

1. What might be the best source of consumer credit for you? What are some potential advantages and disadvantages of this source?   (L.O.1)
2. Which method of calculating the cost of open-end credit is most favorable to a borrower? Why?   (L.O.2)
3. Does the rule of 78s favor lenders or borrowers? Explain.   (L.O.2)
4. Discuss the validity of the most frequent reasons given for indebtedness.   (L.O.3)

5. Why might people with debt problems seek assistance from the Consumer Credit Counseling Service or other debt counseling organizations?   (L.O.4)

6. What might be some consequences of declaring a straight (Chapter 7) bankruptcy or a wage earner plan (Chapter 13) bankruptcy?   (L.O.5)

FINANCIAL PLANNING PROBLEMS

1. *Calculating the Finance Charge on a Loan.* Dave borrowed $500 for one year and paid $50 in interest. The bank charged him a $5 service charge. What is the finance charge on this loan?   (L.O.2)

2. *Calculating the Annual Percentage Rate.* In problem 1, Dave borrowed $500 on January 1, 1998, and paid it all back at once on December 31, 1998. What was the APR? (L.O.2)

3. *Calculating the Annual Percentage Rate.* If Dave paid the $500 in 12 equal monthly payments, what was the APR? (L.O.2)

4. *Comparing the Costs of Credit Cards.* Bobby is trying to decide between two credit cards. One has no annual fee and an 18 percent interest rate, and the other has a $40 annual fee and an 8.9 percent interest rate. Should he take the card that's free or the one that costs $40?   (L.O.2)

5. *Calculating Cash Advance Fee and the Dollar Amount of Interest.* Sidney took a $200 cash advance by using checks linked to her credit card account. The bank charges a 2 percent cash advance fee on the amount borrowed and offers no grace period on cash advances. Sidney paid the balance in full when the bill arrived. What was the cash advance fee? What was the interest for one month at an 18 percent APR? What was the total amount she paid? What if she had made the purchase with her credit card (assuming no over-credit limit) and paid off the bill in full promptly?   (L.O.2)

6. *Comparing the Cost of Credit during Inflationary Periods.* Dorothy lacks cash to pay for a $600 dishwasher. She could buy it from the store on credit by making 12 monthly payments of $52.74. The total cost would then be $632.88. Instead, Dorothy decides to deposit $50 a month in the bank until she has saved enough money to pay cash for the dishwasher. One year later, she has saved $642— $600 in deposits plus interest. When she goes back to the store, she finds the dishwasher now costs $660. Its price has gone up 10 percent, the current rate of inflation. Was postponing her purchase a good trade-off for Dorothy? (L.O.2)

7. *Comparing Costs of Credit Using Three Calculation Methods.* You have been pricing a compact disk player in several stores. Three stores have the identical price of $300. Each store charges 18 percent APR, has a 30-day grace period, and sends out bills on the first of the month. On further investigation, you find that store A calculates the finance charge by using the average daily balance method, store B uses the adjusted balance method, and store C uses the previous balance method. Assume you purchased the disk player on May 5 and made a $100 payment on June 15. What will the finance charge be if you made your purchase from store A? From store B? From store C?   (L.O.2)

8. *Determining Interest Cost Using Simple Interest Formula.* What are the interest cost and the total amount due on a six-month loan of $1,500 at 13.2 percent simple annual interest?   (L.O.2)

9. *Calculating Interest Paid Using the Rule of 78s.* Return to the example of Karen and Mike in "Financial Planning Calculations: The Rule of 78s." Assume Karen and Mike pay off their loan with the 11th payment. How much interest will they save? Remember that the interest over 15 months is divided into 120 parts and you need to know how many payments will be prepaid. Fill in the blanks:

$$\frac{N}{2} \times (N11) = 2 \times (\underline{\quad}11) \times = \underline{\quad} \times \underline{\quad} = \underline{\quad}.$$

Now multiply the rebate fraction by the total amount of interest on the loan: $\underline{\quad} \times \underline{\quad} = \$\underline{\quad}$ rebate.   (L.O.2)

10. *Calculating the Total Cost of a Purchase, the Monthly Payment, and an APR.* After visiting several automobile dealerships, Richard selects the used car he wants. He likes its $10,000 price, but financing through the dealer is no bargain. He has $2,000 cash for a down payment, so he needs an $8,000 loan. In shopping at several banks for an installment loan, he learns that interest on most automobile loans is quoted at add-on rates. That is, during the life of the loan, interest is paid on the full amount borrowed even though a portion of the principal has been paid back. Richard borrows $8,000 for a period of four years at an add-on interest rate of 11 percent. What is the total interest on Richard's loan? What is the total cost of the car? What is the monthly payment? What is the annual percentage rate (APR)?   (L.O.2)

PROJECTS AND APPLICATION ACTIVITIES

1. *Determining Criteria If a Loan Is Needed.* Survey friends and relatives to find out what criteria they used to determine the need for credit.   (L.O.1)

2. *Comparing Costs of Loans from Various Lenders.* Prepare a list of sources of inexpensive loans, medium-priced loans, and expensive loans in your area. What are the trade-offs in obtaining a loan from an "easy" lender?   (L.O.1)

3. *Using Current Information on Obtaining the Best Credit Terms.* Choose a current issue of *Worth, Money, Kiplinger's Personal Finance Magazine,* or *Business Week*

and summarize an article that provides suggestions on how you can choose the best yet least expensive source of credit.   (L.O.2)

4. *Using the Internet to Obtain Information about the Costs of Credit.* As pointed out in the beginning of this chapter, credit costs money; therefore, you must conduct the 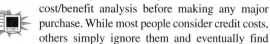 cost/benefit analysis before making any major purchase. While most people consider credit costs, others simply ignore them and eventually find themselves in financial difficulties. To help consumers avoid this problem, each of the following organizations has a home page on the Internet:

Finance Center, Inc., helps consumers save money when purchasing, financing, or refinancing a new home, car, or making a credit card transaction.

Bankcard Holders of America provides individualized recommendations on the quickest and most inexpensive way to pay off credit card balances.

Debtors Anonymous offers financial counseling to debt-ridden consumers.

Bank Rate Monitor™ is America's consumer rate source for mortgages, credit cards, auto loans, home equity loans, and personal loans.

Choose one of the above organizations and visit its home page. Then prepare a report that summarizes the information the organization provides. Finally, decide how this information could help you better manage your credit and its costs.

5. *Choosing between the Features and Costs of a Loan.* When you choose financing, what are the trade-offs between the features you prefer (term, size of payments, fixed or variable interest, or payment plan) and the cost of your loan?   (L.O.2)

6. *Calculating the Cost of Credit Using Three APR Formulas.* How are the simple interest, simple interest on the declining balance, and add-on interest formulas used in determining the cost of credit?   (L.O.2)

7. *Handling Harassment from Debt Collection Agencies.* Your friend is drowning in a sea of overdue bills and is being harassed by a debt collection agency. Prepare a list of the steps your friend should take if the harassment continues.   (L.O.3)

8. *Seeking Assistance from the Consumer Credit Counseling Services.* Visit a local office of the Consumer Credit Counseling Service. What assistance can debtors obtain from this office? What is the cost of this assistance, if any?   (L.O.4)

9. *Assessing the Choices in Declaring Personal Bankruptcy.* What factors would you consider in assessing the choices in declaring personal bankruptcy? Why should personal bankruptcy be the choice of last resort?   (L.O.4)

L I F E   S I T U A T I O N   C A S E   7

FINANCING SUE'S GEO METRO

After shopping around, Sue Wallace decided on the car of her choice, a used Geo Metro. The dealer quoted her a total price of $8,000. Sue decided to use $2,000 of her savings as a down payment and borrow $6,000. The salesperson wrote this information on a sales contract that Sue took with her when she set out to find financing.

When Sue applied for a loan, she discussed loan terms with the bank lending officer. The officer told her that the bank's policy was to lend only 80 percent of the total price of a used car. Sue showed the officer her copy of the sales contract, indicating that she had agreed to make a $2,000, or 25 percent, down payment on the $8,000 car, so this requirement caused her no problem. Although the bank was willing to make 48-month loans at an annual percentage rate of 15 percent on used cars, Sue chose a 36-month repayment schedule. She believed she could afford the higher payments, and she knew she would not have to pay as much interest if she paid off the loan at a faster rate. The bank lending officer provided Sue with a copy of the Truth-in-Lending Disclosure Statement shown here.

Truth-in-Lending Disclosure Statement (Loans)

Annual Percentage Rate	Finance Charge	Amount Financed	Total of Payments 36
The cost of your credit as a yearly rate.	The dollar amount the credit will cost you.	The amount of credit provided to you or on your behalf.	The amount you will have paid after you have made all payments as scheduled.
15%	$1,487.64	$6,000.00	$7,487.64

You have the right to receive at this time an itemization of the Amount Financed.

☒ I want an itemization.   ☐ I do not want an itemization.

Your payment schedule will be:

Number of Payments	Amount of Payments	When Payments Are Due
36	$207.99	1st of each month

Sue decided to compare the APR she had been offered with the APR offered by another bank, but the 20 percent APR of the second bank (bank B) was more expensive than the 15 percent APR of the first bank (bank A). Here is her comparison of the two loans:

	Bank A 15% APR	Bank B 20% APR
Amount financed	$6,000.00	$6,000.00
Finance charge	1,487.64	2,027.28
Total of payments	7,487.64	8,027.28
Monthly payments	207.99	222.98

The 5 percent difference in the APRs of the two banks meant Sue would have to pay $15 extra every month if she got her loan from the second bank. Of course, she got the loan from the first bank.

QUESTIONS

1. What is perhaps the most important item shown on the disclosure statement? Why?
2. What is included in the finance charge?
3. What amount will Sue receive from the bank?
4. Should Sue borrow from bank A or bank B? Why?

USING THE INTERNET TO CREATE A PERSONAL FINANCIAL PLAN 7

COMPARING CREDIT SOURCES AND COSTS

Credit is available from many, many sources. Your awareness of the differences among financial institutions related to borrowing costs and other factors, while wisely managing your debt, will help you avoid financial difficulties.

Web Sites for Comparing Credit Costs

- RAM Research provides an opportunity to compare credit card costs and features at **www.cardtrak.com** and a library of credit information at **www.ramresearch.com**
- Current rates for mortgages, home equity loans, credit cards, and consumer loans at **www.bankrate.com/ bankrate/publ/tips.htm** and **www.banx.com**
- Credit card information from the FinanCenter at **www.financenter.com/**
- The National Foundation for Consumer Credit provides information on financial problems and credit reports at **www.nfcc.org;**
- National Credit Counseling Services assistance may be obtained at **www.nccs.org** and the Debt Counselors of America at **www.dca.org**
- Information for the Bankcard Holders of America at **www.epn.com/bha**

- Financial calculators for cost of credit at **www.centura. com/formulas/ca/c.html**

(Note: Addresses and content of Web sites change, and new sites are created daily. Use the search engines discussed in Appendix B to update and locate Web sites for your current financial planning needs.)

PFP SHEETS: 30–31

Short-Term Financial Planning Activities

1. Evaluate your current use of credit cards. Compare various credit card offers related to APR, annual fee, grace period, and other fees (see PFP Sheet 30).
2. Compare various credit sources for loans related to various financial needs (see PFP Sheet 31).

Long-Term Financial Planning Activities

1. Investigate various actions commonly taken to avoid debt problems.
2. Prepare a spending plan to minimize the use of credit.

APPENDIX

OTHER METHODS OF DETERMINING THE COST OF CREDIT

BANK DISCOUNT METHOD

When the *bank discount rate* method is used, interest is calculated on the amount to be paid back and you receive the difference between the amount to be paid back and the interest amount. That is, if your relative lends you $1,000 less $50 (interest at 5 percent), you receive $950.

Example 1 Using the APR formula, you find the true interest rate, or the annual percentage rate, is 5.263 percent, not the stated 5 percent:

$$\text{APR} = \frac{2 \times n \times I}{P(N + 1)} = \frac{2 \times 1 \times \$50}{\$950(1 + 1)} = \frac{\$100}{\$1,900} = 0.05263, \text{ or } 5.263 \text{ percent}$$

COMPOUND INTEREST

Unlike simple interest, *compound interest* is the interest paid on the original principal *plus* the accumulated interest. With interest compounding, the greater the number of periods for which interest is calculated, the more rapidly the amount of interest on interest and interest on principal builds.

Annual compounding means there is only *one* period annually for the calculation of interest. With such compounding, interest charges on a *one-year* loan are identical whether they are figured on a simple interest basis or on an annual compound basis. However, a new interest formula, based on the simple interest formula, must be used if there is annual compounding for two or more years or compounding with more than one compound period per year.

COMPOUND FORMULA

A compact formula that describes compound interest calculations is

$$F = P(1 + r)^T$$

where

F = Total future repayment value of a loan
       (principal *plus* total accumulated or compound interest)
P = Principal
r = Rate of interest per year, or annual interest rate
T = Time in years

Before the compound interest formula can be used for *multiple*-period compounding, two important adjustments must be made.

First, adjust the *annual* interest rate (r) to reflect the number of compounding periods per year. For example, a 5 percent annual rate of interest, compounded half-yearly, works out to 2.5 percent (5 percent divided by 2) per half-year.

Second, adjust the time factor (T), which is measured in years, to reflect the *total* number of compounding periods. For example, your loan for one year compounded half-yearly works out to two compound periods (1 year multiplied by 2 compounding periods per year) over the length of the loan.

Example 2   Suppose your relative compounds interest semiannually and you make two payments, six months apart. Using the compound interest formula, here is the annual percentage rate:

$$F = P(1 + r)^T$$
$$F = \$1{,}000(1 + 0.05)^{1 \times 2}$$
$$= \$1{,}000(1 + 0.025)^2$$
$$= \$1{,}000(1.050625)$$
$$= \$1{,}050.625$$

That is, you are paying $50.63 in interest for a one-year, $1,000 loan. Now, using the APR formula, you find the APR is 6.75 percent:

$$\text{APR} = \frac{2 \times n \times I}{P(N + 1)}$$
$$= \frac{2 \times 2 \times \$50.63}{\$1{,}000(2 + 1)}$$
$$= \frac{\$202.52}{\$3{,}000}$$
$$= 0.0675, \text{ or } 6.75 \text{ percent}$$

If your relative chose to compound interest daily (365 compounding periods per year), the solution to this problem would be quite complicated. A calculator or a compound interest table can make interest calculations more manageable. See Appendix B for compound interest tables.

The following table summarizes the effects on the APR when the interest on a one-year, $1,000 loan is calculated using the simple interest, declining balance, add-on interest, bank discount, and compound interest methods:

Method	Amount Borrowed	Stated Interest	Total Interest	Number of Payments	APR
Simple interest*	$1,000	5%	$50.00	1	5.00%
Declining balance*	1,000	5	37.50	2	5.00
Add-on*	1,000	5	50.00	2	6.60
Bank discount	1,000(–50)	5	50.00	1	5.26
Compound interest	1,000	5	50.63	2	6.75

*Discussed in the chapter.

The methods of calculating interest described here are just some of the more common methods in use. As you have seen, the method of interest calculation can substantially affect the amount of interest paid, and you should be aware not only of the stated or nominal interest rates but also of how the stated rates are used in calculating total interest charges. Furthermore, the simple interest and bank discount methods assume you have the full use of the principal over the length of the loan. Rather than making periodic payments, you are obligated to repay the loan in one or two lump sums. Most borrowers, however, are unable to repay loans, especially home loans (mortgages) and auto loans, in one or two lump-sum payments. They must make equal periodic payments to pay off a loan and interest over the length of the loan. This concept is known as *amortization*.

AMORTIZATION

Amortization is the process of gradually reducing a debt through scheduled periodic payments. For example, if a five-year auto loan is repaid in 60 equal monthly payments, each of these payments is applied to reduce the principal and pay interest on the total amount borrowed. Over the initial years of the loan, most of the monthly payment is used to pay interest; the rest reduces the principal. As the loan approaches maturity, more of the monthly payment is used to pay off the principal than to pay interest.

The following formula can be used to calculate the monthly payment (principal and interest) on an installment loan or a conventional mortgage loan:

$$\frac{\text{Monthly}}{\text{payment}} = \text{Loan} \times \frac{\text{Monthly interest rate} \times (1 + \text{Monthly interest rate})^{T \times 12}}{(1 + \text{Monthly interest rate})^{T \times 12} - 1}$$

Because a monthly mortgage payment is required, both the annual interest rate and the total length of the loan must be adjusted by 12 (months).

Example 3   On a 30-year mortgage loan for $60,000 at a 12 percent annual interest rate, what is the monthly payment (MP)? Substitute the numbers into the formula:

$$MP = \$60,000 \times \frac{\dfrac{0.12}{12} \times \left(1 + \dfrac{0.12}{12}\right)^{30 \times 12}}{\left(1 + \dfrac{0.12}{12}\right)^{30 \times 12} - 1}$$

$$= \$60,000 \times \frac{0.01 \times (1 + 0.01)^{360}}{(1 + 0.01)^{360} - 1}$$

$$= \$60,000 \times \frac{0.01 \times 35.9496}{35.9496 - 1}$$

$$= \$60,000 \times \frac{0.359496}{34.9496}$$

$$= \$60,000 \times 0.010286$$

$$= \$617.17$$

USE OF TABLES

Finding the monthly payment on a mortgage or consumer installment loan may become rather complicated when the problem must be solved manually. Fortunately, the use of tables can simplify the task. Notice how easily the problem in Example 3 is solved by using the table at the end of this appendix.

Just find the P&I constant for 12 percent and a 30-year term, which is 10.29 for a $1,000 loan. Since the loan in Example 3 is for $60,000, multiply 10.29 by 60. The result, $617.40, is fairly close to the $617.17 found by using the formula.

Example 4   What is the total finance charge on a 30-year, $60,000 loan at a 10.5 percent annual interest rate?

Using the table on the next page, you find the constant for a 10.5 percent, $1,000 loan with a 30-year term is 9.15. Since the loan is for $60,000, multiply the constant by 60. The result is a $549 monthly payment, which includes principal and interest.

For a 30-year loan, you must make 360 monthly payments of $549, totaling $197,640. Since you borrowed $60,000 but repaid $197,640, the difference must be the finance charge, which amounts to $137,640! Surprised?

You will come to a similar conclusion if you use the monthly payment formula presented in Example 3.

P&I Constants per $1,000 of Loan Amount

Interest Rate	15 Years	20 Years	25 Years	30 Years	Interest Rate	15 Years	20 Years	25 Years	30 Years
6.00%	8.44	7.16	6.44	6.00	10.62%	11.13	10.07	9.53	9.24
6.12	8.51	7.24	6.52	6.08	10.75	11.21	10.15	9.62	9.33
6.25	8.57	7.31	6.60	6.16	10.87	11.29	10.24	9.71	9.43
6.37	8.64	7.38	6.67	6.24	11.00	11.37	10.32	9.80	9.52
6.50	8.71	7.46	6.75	6.32	11.12	11.44	10.41	9.89	9.62
6.62	8.78	7.53	6.83	6.40	11.25	11.52	10.49	9.98	9.71
6.75	8.85	7.60	6.91	6.49	11.37	11.60	10.58	10.07	9.81
6.87	8.92	7.68	6.99	6.57	11.50	11.68	10.66	10.16	9.90
7.00	8.99	7.75	7.07	6.65	11.62	11.76	10.75	10.26	10.00
7.12	9.06	7.83	7.15	6.74	11.75	11.84	10.84	10.35	10.09
7.25	9.13	7.90	7.23	6.82	11.87	11.92	10.92	10.44	10.19
7.37	9.20	7.98	7.31	6.91	12.00	12.00	11.01	10.53	10.29
7.50	9.27	8.06	7.39	6.99	12.12	12.08	11.10	10.62	10.38
7.62	9.34	8.13	7.47	7.08	12.25	12.16	11.19	10.72	10.48
7.75	9.41	8.21	7.55	7.16	12.37	12.24	11.27	10.81	10.58
7.87	9.48	8.29	7.64	7.25	12.50	12.33	11.36	10.90	10.67
8.00	9.56	8.36	7.72	7.34	12.62	12.41	11.45	11.00	10.77
8.12	9.63	8.44	7.80	7.42	12.75	12.49	11.54	11.09	10.87
8.25	9.70	8.52	7.88	7.51	12.87	12.57	11.63	11.18	10.96
8.37	9.77	8.60	7.97	7.60	13.00	12.65	11.72	11.28	11.06
8.50	9.85	8.68	8.05	7.69	13.12	12.73	11.80	11.37	11.16
8.62	9.92	8.76	8.14	7.78	13.25	12.82	11.89	11.47	11.26
8.75	9.99	8.84	8.22	7.87	13.37	12.90	11.98	11.56	11.36
8.87	10.07	8.92	8.31	7.96	13.50	12.98	12.07	11.66	11.45
9.00	10.14	9.00	8.39	8.05	13.62	13.07	12.16	11.75	11.55
9.12	10.22	9.08	8.48	8.14	13.75	13.15	12.25	11.85	11.65
9.25	10.29	9.16	8.56	8.23	13.87	13.23	12.34	11.94	11.75
9.37	10.37	9.24	8.65	8.32	14.00	13.32	12.44	12.04	11.85
9.50	10.44	9.32	8.74	8.41	14.12	13.40	12.53	12.13	11.95
9.62	10.52	9.40	8.82	8.50	14.25	13.49	12.62	12.23	12.05
9.75	10.59	9.49	8.91	8.59	14.37	13.57	12.71	12.33	12.15
9.87	10.67	9.57	9.00	8.68	14.50	13.66	12.80	12.42	12.25
10.00	10.75	9.65	9.09	8.78	14.62	13.74	12.89	12.52	12.35
10.12	10.82	9.73	9.18	8.87	14.75	13.83	12.98	12.61	12.44
10.25	10.90	9.82	9.26	8.96	14.87	13.91	13.08	12.71	12.54
10.37	10.98	9.90	9.35	9.05	15.00	14.00	13.17	12.81	12.64
10.50	11.05	9.98	9.44	9.15					

CONTINUOUS CASE FOR PART II

USING FINANCIAL SERVICES: SAVINGS, CHECKING, AND CREDIT

Life Situation
Newly married couple: Pam, 26; Josh, 28; renting an apartment

Financial Goals
- Establish a joint checking account
- Develop a savings fund for emergencies and long-term financial security
- Reduce monthly debt payments

Financial Data

Monthly income	$ 5,840
Living expenses	3,900
Assets	13,500
Liabilities	7,800

Pam Jenkins recently married Josh Brock. Pam continues to work as a sales representative for a clothing manufacturer, and her monthly income has averaged $2,840 a month over the past year. Josh is employed as a computer programmer and earns $3,000 a month.

The Brocks' combined monthly income, $5,840, allows them to enjoy a comfortable lifestyle. Yet they have been unable to save any money for emergencies. According to Josh, "It's hard to believe, but we don't even have a savings account because we spend everything we make each month." Every month, they deposit each of their paychecks in separate checking accounts. Josh pays the rent and makes the car payment. Pam buys the groceries and pays the monthly utilities. They use the money left over to purchase new clothes and the other "necessities" of life that they both want. To make matters worse, they often resort to using their credit cards for everyday purchases when they both run out of money at the end of the month. As a result, they have credit card debts totaling $2,800.

QUESTIONS

1. What should the Brocks do to increase the amount of money they set aside for emergencies?
2. Pam and Josh Brock have separate checking accounts. Do you think they should give up their separate checking accounts and open a joint checking account?
3. If you were Pam or Josh Brock, how would you go about paying off your credit card debts and other liabilities?
4. What would you recommend to the Brocks regarding their future use of credit?

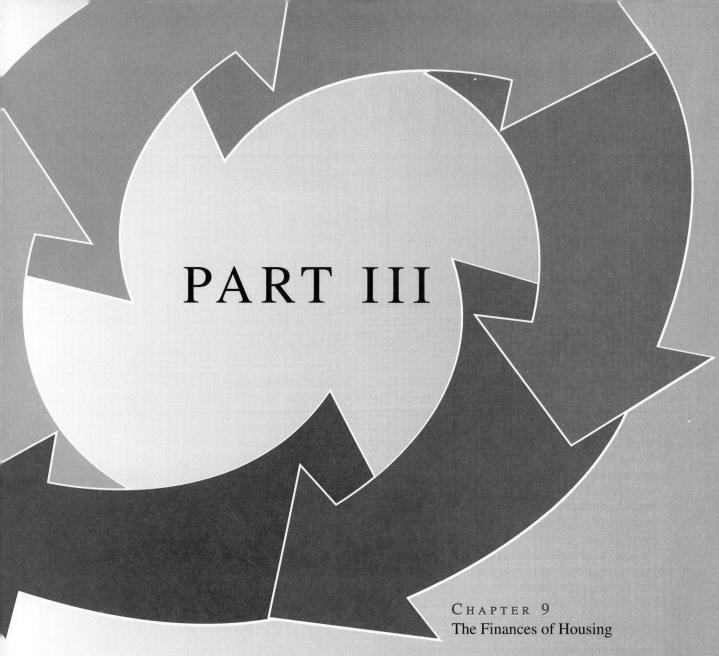

PART III

MAKING YOUR PURCHASING DECISIONS

Each day you face tens of thousands of product choices. These alternatives offer many courses of action for satisfying needs and wants. Part III of *Personal Finance* emphasizes the importance of wise buying in the spending phase of financial planning. As you will see in Chapter 8, effective buying includes gathering information, identifying alternatives, obtaining financing, and continually evaluating costs and benefits associated with buying decisions.

A competent consumer also assesses postpurchase satisfaction. Your ability to resolve consumer complaints through various governmental and legal means is a skill that will serve you well throughout your life.

In Chapter 9, you will assess housing alternatives and identify the factors that influence your choice. Your needs, lifestyle, and financial resources will determine whether you decide to rent, buy, or have a home built.

CHAPTER 8

CONSUMER PURCHASING STRATEGIES AND LEGAL PROTECTION

Opening Case

"IT'S IN THE MAIL"

As Marge Upton got home from another long day at the office, she realized that she needed to get her mother a birthday gift. The stores were long closed. However, Marge had just received one of the 14 billion catalogs sent to U.S. consumers each year.

Looking through the catalog, Marge saw a sweater her mother would probably like. "This looks very nice," she thought. "And it's quite reasonably priced."

Since the company accepted orders on its Web site 24 hours a day, Marge placed an order for the sweater using a credit card. Within a week, she received it. However, when she opened the package, she noticed the style of the sweater was different than it looked in the catalog. "Oh no, this isn't what I wanted," she thought.

Marge called the catalog company to find out how to return the item. The company told her to send the sweater back for a refund. However, Marge had to pay the return postage and was not refunded the initial shipping and handling charges.

Later that day, Marge saw a table lamp in a catalog. "This is a nice gift for Mom," she thought. She sent a in check for the lamp and within a week received a notice that the item would not be available for four to six weeks.

Frustrated by her online mail-order shopping experiences, Marge was not sure what to do next. She thought maybe it was time to forget about buying by mail or the Internet and consider the Home Shopping Network!

QUESTIONS

1. What benefits and drawbacks are associated with mail-order shopping?
2. What actions might a consumer take before making a mail-order purchase?
3. What options are available to consumers who are dissatisfied with a mail-order or other consumer purchase?

After studying this chapter, you will be able to

L.O.1 Assess the financial implications of consumer purchasing decisions.

L.O.2 Evaluate the alternatives in consumer purchasing decisions.

L.O.3 Implement strategies for effective purchasing.

L.O.4 Identify steps to take to resolve consumer problems.

L.O.5 Evaluate the legal alternatives available to consumers.

FINANCIAL IMPLICATIONS OF CONSUMER DECISIONS

L.O.1 Assess the financial implications of consumer purchasing decisions.

Every person who makes personal financial decisions is a consumer. Regardless of age, income, or household situation, we all use goods and services every day. Daily buying decisions require a trade-off between current spending and saving for the future. While some people shop for recreation and others only when necessary, both groups use techniques to help them get the most for their money. Wise buying decisions contribute to both your current personal satisfaction and your long-term financial security.

Economic, social, and personal factors all affect daily buying habits (see Exhibit 8–1 on page 227). These factors are the basis for spending, saving, investing, and achieving personal financial goals. In very simple terms, the only way you can have long-term financial security is to refrain from spending all of your current income. In addition, as Exhibit 8–1 shows, overspending leads to misuse of credit and to financial difficulties.

Addictive shopping may characterize as many as 15 million Americans. Overspenders may shop to obtain an emotional boost, or use credit cards to purchase items they cannot afford because friends have these items, or try to impress others by having every credit card on the market. Overspending patterns frequently result from the absence of a systematic decision process for making purchases.

Throughout your life, you make buying decisions that reflect many influences. As discussed throughout this book, you should consider opportunity costs to maximize the satisfaction you obtain from available financial resources. Commonly overlooked trade-offs in buying decisions include

Financial Decision
Trade-Off

- Paying a higher price over time when buying on credit items that you need now.
- Buying unknown, possibly poor-quality brands because they are less expensive.
- Selecting less expensive brands that may be difficult to service or repair.
- Ordering by mail or online, which saves time and money but may make it harder to return, replace, or repair purchases.
- Taking time and effort to comparison-shop to save money and obtain better after-sale service.

Your buying decisions reflect many aspects of your personality, life situation, values, and goals. Combine this fact with the complexity of the marketplace, and you can see that most purchase decisions require analysis.

CONCEPT CHECK 8–1

1. What factors commonly influence a person's daily buying choices?
2. How are daily buying decisions related to overall financial planning?

CONSUMER PURCHASING: A RESEARCH-BASED APPROACH

L.O.2 Evaluate the alternatives in consumer purchasing decisions.

Shopping decisions are based on a specific decision-making process. Exhibit 8–2 on page 228 presents steps for effective purchasing. This consumer buying process will be most valuable with large purchases such as appliances, sports equipment, home improvements, and vacations. When buying such items, most people want to take time and effort to get the most for their money. However, you probably make many routine purchases of low-cost items, such as food and clothing, without thinking about them, and often this is exactly what you should do. Following all of the steps in the consumer buying process for low-cost items may not be the best use of your time. Taking time to evaluate all your purchases, however, can increase the satisfaction you receive from each dollar you spend.

Phase 1: Preshopping Activities

In the first phase of the consumer purchasing process, define your needs and obtain relevant information. These activities are the foundation for buying decisions that will help you achieve your personal goals.

Problem Identification   Objective decision making should start with an open mind. Some people always buy the same brand when another brand at a lower price could also serve their needs or when another brand at the same price may provide better quality. A narrow view of the problem is a weakness in problem identification. You may think the problem is "the need to get a car" when the real problem is "the need for transportation."

Information Gathering   Information is power. The better informed you are, the better buying decisions you are likely to make. Knowing the least expensive place to buy an appliance or being aware of the ingredients in a food product can enhance your financial and physical well-being. Information for buying decisions commonly falls into three areas:

1. *Costs*—what is the price at various locations?
2. *Options*—who offers which items, brands, and services?
3. *Consequences*—how might a purchase affect my time, health, and financial situation?

EXHIBIT 8–1

Consumer Buying Influences and Financial Implications

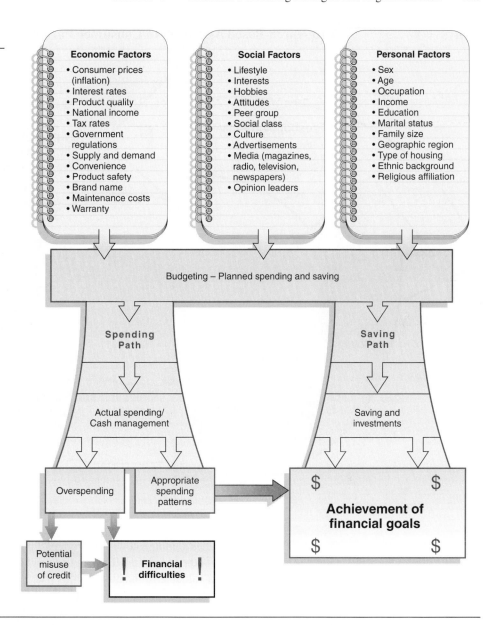

Some people spend very little time gathering and evaluating buying information. At the other extreme are people who spend much time and effort obtaining consumer information. While information is necessary for wise purchasing, too much information can create confusion and frustration. The best course of action lies somewhere between these two extremes. Many simple, routine purchases may require no information other than experience, while expensive items merit some information gathering.

The main sources of consumer information are personal contacts, business organizations, media reports, independent testing organizations, government agencies, and online sources. You should evaluate the information received from any source for reliability, completeness, relevance, and objectivity.

Exhibit 8–2   **A Research-Based Approach to Consumer Purchases**

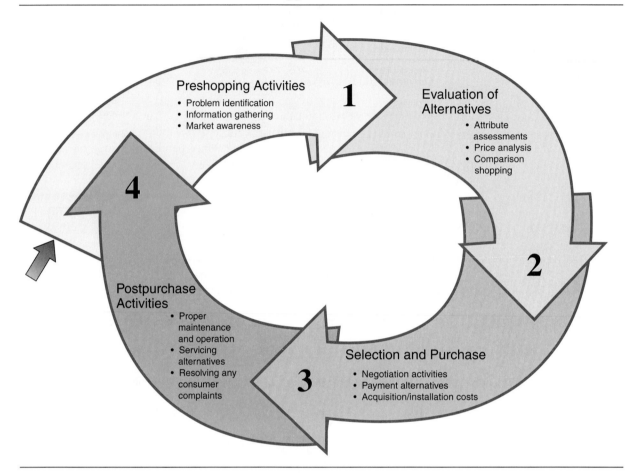

Preshopping Activities

- Problem identification
- Information gathering
- Market awareness

1

Evaluation of Alternatives

- Attribute assessments
- Price analysis
- Comparison shopping

2

4

Postpurchase Activities

- Proper maintenance and operation
- Servicing alternatives
- Resolving any consumer complaints

3

Selection and Purchase

- Negotiation activities
- Payment alternatives
- Acquisition/installation costs

Personal Contacts   Besides gaining knowledge from past purchases, you can learn from the buying experiences of others. Information about product performance, brand quality, and prices can give you a valuable foundation for this phase of the buying process.

Business Organizations   Advertising is the most common source of consumer information. Each day you are exposed to several hundred ads on billboards, in publications, at stores, and on television and radio. Advertising that provides information about product price, quality, and availability can be helpful. Many ads, however, appeal to emotions and provide little assistance for making purchasing choices.

Other business information sources are the product label and the package. Like advertising, a product label contains helpful information such as ingredients, weight, and price, as well as attempts to stimulate sales.

Despite state and federal laws prohibiting false advertising, deceptive or misleading ads may be present. You may wish to make use of more objective information from sources such as the following.

Media Information   Television, radio, newspapers, and magazines are among the most valuable, easily available, and least expensive consumer information sources. Besides advertisements, these media sources provide purchasing advice and consumer information.

Many magazines and newspapers have columns and special articles on topics such as wise spending, budgeting, and insurance. Special-topic magazines are helpful when buying automobiles, boats, cameras, computers, stereos, video recorders, or sports equipment.

Independent Testing Organizations   Since 1936, Consumers Union has been providing information about the quality of products and services. Each month *Consumer Reports* presents test results on items ranging from automobiles, vacuum cleaners, and personal computers to hand soap, orange juice, and hot dogs. As our economy has become more service oriented, Consumers Union has increased its coverage of subjects such as apartment renting, health care, insurance, investments, legal services, tax preparers, and banking services. *Consumer Reports* and other consumer publications may be accessed through online computer services and the World Wide Web. For further information, see Appendix B.

Underwriters Laboratories (UL) is a business-sponsored organization that tests products for electrical and fire safety. Items that pass the tests display the UL symbol. This emblem assures consumers that the product has met safety standards.

Government Agencies   Local, state, and federal government funds are used to provide publications and other information services for consumers (for example, see Exhibit 8–3 on page 230). Beyond printed information, government agencies inform consumers through toll-free telephone numbers, Web sites, and community displays at shopping centers, county fairs, and libraries. Appendix E details government sources of information on various consumer topics.

Online Sources   The Internet now provides one of the most extensive sources of consumer information. Most companies, magazines, newspapers, consumer organizations, and government agencies have Web sites with product information and shopping suggestions. For additional information on using the Internet and World Wide Web for consumer information, see Appendix B.

Marketplace Awareness   Preshopping research results in expanded awareness of the buying environment. This includes an awareness of

- Store, mail-order, and online sources of an item.
- Available brands and features.
- Pricing techniques for the item.
- The most reliable sources of information.

Based on marketplace factors, you can create and evaluate a list of product attributes for the second phase of the research-based consumer purchasing approach.

Phase 2: Evaluation of Alternatives

Every purchasing situation usually has several acceptable alternatives. Alternatives are based on questions such as: Is it possible to delay the purchase or to do without the item? Will you pay for the item with cash or buy it on credit? Which brands should you consider? How do the price, quality, and service compare at different stores? Is it possible to rent the item instead of buying it? Considering such alternatives will result in more effective purchasing decisions.

Attribute Assessments   Each alternative should be evaluated on the basis of factors such as personal values and goals; available time and money; costs and benefits; and specific needs with regard to product size, quality, quantity, and features. Exhibit 8–4 presents a

Exhibit 8–3

Telemarketing Sales Rule

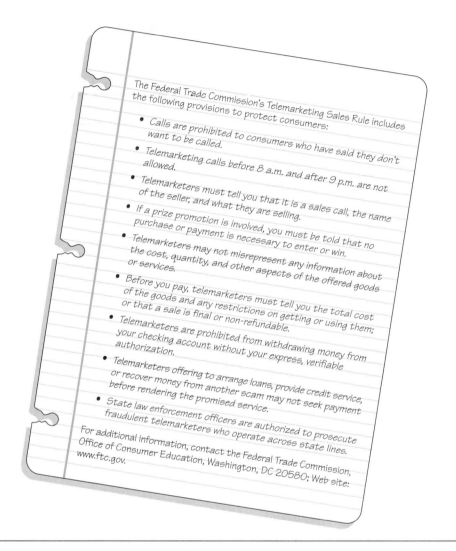

The Federal Trade Commission's Telemarketing Sales Rule includes the following provisions to protect consumers:

- Calls are prohibited to consumers who have said they don't want to be called.
- Telemarketing calls before 8 a.m. and after 9 p.m. are not allowed.
- Telemarketers must tell you that it is a sales call, the name of the seller, and what they are selling.
- If a prize promotion is involved, you must be told that no purchase or payment is necessary to enter or win.
- Telemarketers may not misrepresent any information about the cost, quantity, and other aspects of the offered goods or services.
- Before you pay, telemarketers must tell you the total cost of the goods and any restrictions on getting or using them; or that a sale is final or non-refundable.
- Telemarketers are prohibited from withdrawing money from your checking account without your express, verifiable authorization.
- Telemarketers offering to arrange loans, provide credit service, or recover money from another scam may not seek payment before rendering the promised service.
- State law enforcement officers are authorized to prosecute fraudulent telemarketers who operate across state lines.

For additional information, contact the Federal Trade Commission, Office of Consumer Education, Washington, DC 20580; Web site: www.ftc.gov.

consumer buying matrix that you may use to evaluate alternatives. In this exhibit, a consumer is considering the purchase of one of three brands of notebook computers using the following steps:

1. Identify attributes such as features, performance, design, and warranty, and assign a weight based on the importance of each attribute.
2. Select the brands to be evaluated.
3. Rate (from 1 to 10) each brand based on the attributes identified in step 1. Multiply the rating number by the weight. For example, in Exhibit 8–4, brand A received a rating of 6 for "features," giving a weighted score of 1.8 ($6 \times .3$).
4. Total and assess the results. Besides this numeric evaluation, consider other factors such as price, store reputation, and your personal situation.

As you research consumer purchases, you will identify the attributes that are important to you. Helpful sources for this task are friends who own the product, salespeople, and periodicals such as *Consumer Reports*. The specific attributes will vary depending on the product or service. When buying a cordless telephone, for example, you might consider

EXHIBIT 8–4

Consumer Buying Matrix

Item _NOTEBOOK COMPUTER_

Information Sources/Comments _CONSUMER MAGAZINE/BRAND C SLOW COMPARED TO_

OTHERS TESTED; FRIEND/BRAND B PERFORMS WELL

Attribute	Weight	Alternatives					
		Brand _A_ Price _$2,150_		Brand _B_ Price _$2,029_		Brand _C_ Price _$1,899_	
		Rating (1-10)	Weighted Score	Rating (1-10)	Weighted Score	Rating (1-10)	Weighted Score
FEATURES	.3	6	1.8	8	2.4	10	3
PERFORMANCE	.4	9	3.6	7	2.8	5	2
DESIGN	.1	8	.8	8	.8	7	.7
WARRANTY	.2	9	1.8	6	1.2	4	.8
■ Totals	1.0		8.0		7.2		6.5

sound quality, ring loudness, number memory, and the range of use; you might assess a microwave oven on the basis of size, ease of operation, power settings, and exterior finish; and you are likely to select a provider of services based on training, experience, and reputation. As previously mentioned, independent testing organizations can assist you in evaluating desirable attributes.

Price Analysis   Research shows that prices can vary for all types of products. For a camera, prices may range from under $200 to well over $500. The price of aspirin may range from less than 50 cents to over $3 for 100 five-grain tablets. While differences in quality and attributes may exist among the cameras, the aspirin are the same in quantity and quality. Differences in quality (based on information from others and on your personal evaluation of product attributes) need to be assessed in relation to price. When the quality and quantity are the same (as with aspirin), the lowest price is likely to be the wisest choice, except, perhaps, if the place of purchase is not convenient.

When prices and quality differ (as in the buying matrix in Exhibit 8–4), you have two alternatives. If all the choices are within your available resources, you may purchase the item with the highest number of weighted "quality points," or you may divide the price of each item by its quality points to determine which item gives you the best value per dollar spent.

Always be cautious of the common belief that "you get what you pay for." Many studies have revealed low relationships between price and quality, especially for expensive, highly technical products. To obtain the best value for your dollar, you should use other comparison shopping activities. The lowest price for one item at a store does not mean all prices are the lowest at that store. Consumers need to continue comparing different stores and brands and not assume one will always be the best.

Comparison Shopping   Many people view comparison shopping as a waste of time. While this may be true in certain situations, you can benefit from comparison shopping when

- Buying expensive or complex items.
- Buying items that you purchase often.
- Comparison shopping can be done easily (as with advertisements or several mail-order catalogs).
- Different sellers offer different prices and services, creating a competitive environment.
- Product quality or prices vary greatly.

The next major section of this chapter provides additional details on comparison shopping techniques. (The "Financial Planning for Life's Situations" box provides information on shopping for services.)

Phase 3: Selection and Purchase

Once you've done your research and evaluations, you are ready for a few last-minute activities and decisions. Certain products, such as real estate or automobiles, may be purchased using price negotiation. Negotiation may also be used in other buying situations to obtain a lower price or additional features. Two vital factors in negotiation are (1) having all the necessary information about the product and buying situation and (2) dealing with a person who has the authority to give you a lower price or additional features, such as the owner or store manager.

Using cash or credit should be considered in terms of the costs and benefits. Paying cash gives you the benefit of not paying finance charges; however, you also have the opportunity costs of not earning interest on the amount paid and not having the amount in savings for emergencies. Before using credit, evaluate the various financial and opportunity costs based on

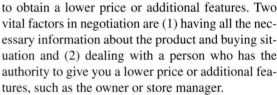

DID YOU KNOW?

Most auto manufacturers offer nearly identical models under different names. Certain Mercury models are also available as Fords. General Motors offers the nearly identical Buick LeSabre, Oldsmobile 88, and Pontiac Bonneville. The Dodge Caravan and Plymouth Voyager are twin minivans.

Sheet 32

Financial Decision
Trade-Off

- Different places to borrow.
- Different types of credit accounts.
- Different down payment amounts.
- Different lengths of time to complete payments.

You can make more intelligent decisions about using credit by reviewing the material in Chapters 6 and 7.

The final aspect of the purchase phase is getting all acquisition and installation costs in writing. Many bargains have disappeared due to the "add-on" costs of hookup charges, delivery fees, and the like. Know exactly what the purchase price includes.

Phase 4: Postpurchase Activities

Some buying situations involve postpurchase tasks. Maintenance and ownership costs may be associated with the item. Correct use can result in improved performance and fewer long-term repairs. When you need repairs not covered by a warranty, you should follow a pattern similar to that followed in making the original purchase to obtain the repair service. Investigate, evaluate, and negotiate a variety of servicing options.

FINANCIAL PLANNING FOR LIFE'S SITUATIONS

BUYING SERVICES IS DIFFERENT

You can see a microwave oven in action, and you can view recordings from a video camera. But how do you compare and evaluate education, child care, home improvements, automobile repairs, and other services? Our society is increasing its spending on services. Many experts estimate that in the future, over 80 percent of our purchases will be for services. Renting furniture, leasing a car, traveling to a vacation resort, and buying computer time are becoming increasingly common.

Buying services presents special problems. First, services are intangible, so it is difficult to assess their quality. Second, services must be performed before you can judge their quality. This limits comparison shopping. Finally, variations among sources of services can be great. For example, two home improvement firms may charge the same price but provide very different results.

Your primary decision in selecting a service concerns the type of business you choose. National firms usually provide fast service at a low cost. In contrast, local businesses may be more concerned with quality and customer satisfaction. Certain types of services, such as automobile repair shops and hairstylists, require certification in some states. Investigate this aspect of the companies you plan to patronize.

When obtaining price information for expensive services, get written estimates of costs, work to be performed, time it will take, and terms of payment. Such estimates will help ensure that you get what you pay for. Also, get information about the guarantee the company offers for customer satisfaction.

For services, the main indicator is the reputation of the business. The experiences of previous customers can help you choose service organizations.

Sheet 33

In some situations, you may not be satisfied with a purchase. Know how to cope with complaint situations. The final two sections of this chapter discuss how to handle consumer complaints and the legal alternatives available to consumers.

One final point about the purchasing process: Remember that it is an ongoing activity that requires continual reevaluation. You have to consider not only what you have learned from gathering information about products and services and from buying experiences but also changes in your values, goals, personal resources, and life situation. These changes will make every purchasing decision a new experience with different alternatives and different opportunity costs.

CONCEPT CHECK 8–2

1. What are the major sources of consumer information?
2. What are the benefits and drawbacks of using advertising to gather information for a consumer purchase?
3. What relationship exists between a person's life situation and the attributes the person desires in a consumer purchase?
4. Why is buying services more difficult than buying products?

EXHIBIT 8–5

**Practical
Purchasing
Strategies**

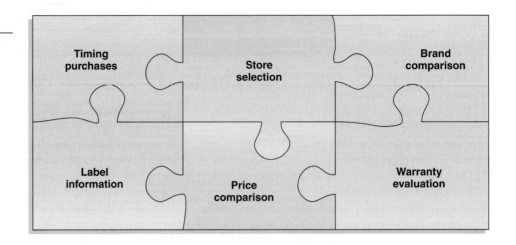

PRACTICAL PURCHASING STRATEGIES

L.O.3 Implement strategies for effective purchasing.

Several buying styles are common among people. Some shoppers look for ways to save on the brands they regularly buy, while others buy the lowest-priced brands or look for the best bargains and are not brand loyal. To achieve your buying goals, use the techniques listed in Exhibit 8–5.

Timing Purchases

In the past, certain items would go on sale at the same time each year. People could obtain bargains by buying winter clothing in midwinter or late winter or summer clothing in midsummer or late summer. Many people save by buying holiday items and other products at reduced prices in late December and early January. In recent years, as retail competition has become more intense, sales and discounts occur throughout the year. Also, "back-to-school" sales have broadened to include anything a college student might need.

Weather reports and other news can also help you plan your purchasing strategies. A crop failure can quickly result in higher prices for certain food products. Changing economic conditions and political difficulties in foreign countries may result in higher prices and reduced supplies of certain products. An awareness of such situations can help you buy when prices are relatively low.

DID YOU KNOW?

Between 1987 and 1995, sales at secondhand stores grew 92 percent. The National Association of Resale and Thrift Shops has a membership of more than 1,000 retailers.

Store Selection

Your decision to shop at a particular store is probably influenced by the quality and variety of merchandise. Also important are the store's policies on matters such as check cashing, exchanges, and frequency of sales. Most stores offer customers various services, including free parking and delivery, telephone and mail orders, and product advice. Finally, your selection of a store is affected by store hours, location, reputation, and the accessibility of shopping alternatives. Exhibit 8–6 provides an overview of the major types of retailers.

Social, economic, and technological influences have resulted in several alternatives to store shopping. One alternative is the **cooperative,** a nonprofit organization whose member-owners may save money on certain products or services. As discussed in Chapter 5,

cooperative

EXHIBIT 8–6 **Types of Retailers**

	Benefits	Limitations
Traditional Stores		
Department stores	Wide variety of products grouped by department	Possible inexperience or limited knowledge of sales staff
Specialty stores	Wide selection of a specific product line; knowledgeable sales staff	Prices generally higher; location and shopping hours may not be convenient
Discount stores	Convenient parking; low prices	Self-service format; minimal assistance from sales staff
Contemporary Retailers		
Convenience stores	Convenient location; long hours; fast service	Prices generally higher than those of other types
Catalog showroom	Brand-name items; discount prices	Limited services from sales staff; no delivery or installation
Factory outlet	Brand-name items; low prices	May offer only "seconds" or "irregulars"; few services; returns may not be allowed
Hypermarket	Full supermarket combined with general merchandise discount store	Clerks not likely to offer specialized service or product information
Warehouse, Superstore	Large quantities of items at discount prices	May require membership fee; limited services; inventory items may vary
Nonstore Shopping		
Cooperative	Nonprofit, member owned and operated, resulting in lower prices	Limited product line; few customer services; may sell only to members
Direct selling (mail order, telephone sales, home demonstrations, television home shopping, online shopping)	Convenience; saves time and perhaps money	Possible delays in delivery; companies may not give what they promise; sometimes difficult to return purchases and get refunds

a credit union is an example of a financial services cooperative. Food cooperatives, usually based in a community group or church, buy grocery items in large quantities. The money these bulk purchases save is passed on to the co-op's members in the form of lower food prices. Although most food co-ops have a limited scope, some have thousands of members and have expanded their services to provide low-cost groceries to nonmembers. Cooperatives have also been organized to provide less expensive child care, recreational equipment, health care, cable television, and burial services.

Brand Comparison

impulse buying

Comparison shopping is the process of considering alternative stores, brands, and prices. In contrast, **impulse buying** is unplanned purchasing. While some impulse buying may be acceptable, too much can cause financial problems.

Since food and other products come in different brands, customers have a choice. *Brand-name* products are highly advertised items available in many stores. You are probably familiar with brands such as Green Giant, Nabisco, Del Monte, Kellogg's, Kraft, Levi-Strauss, Sony, Kodak, and Tylenol. Brand-name products are usually more expensive than nonbrand products, but they offer a consistency of quality for which people are willing to pay.

Financial Decision Trade-Off

generic item

Store-brand products, sold by one chain of stores, are low-cost alternatives to famous-name products. These products have labels that identify them with a specific retail chain, such as Safeway, Kroger, A&P, Osco, Walgreen's, and Kmart. Since store-brand products are commonly manufactured by the same companies that produce brand-name counterparts, they allow consumers to save money. Private and store-brand items can result in extensive savings over time. For example, a weekly savings of $6 on groceries results in more than $1,500 over five years.

For many products, a third brand alternative is the plain-package, nonbrand **generic item.** Generic alternatives for certain products provide you with a low-cost choice. While for some items the generic equivalent may be lower in quality than the national and store brands, other items, such as plain aspirin, bleach, granulated sugar, and salt, are equal in quality to national and store brands.

Label Information

Certain label information is helpful; however, other information is nothing more than advertising. Federal law requires that food labels contain information about the common name of the product, the name and address of the manufacturer or distributor, the net weight of the product, and a list of the ingredients in decreasing order of weight. Food labels (1) must have nutrition information on all processed foods; (2) must define terms such as *low fat, light, low sodium,* and *high fiber;* and (3) allow scientifically established health claims that have been shown to help reduce the risk of disease. Product labeling for appliances includes information about operating costs that can assist you in selecting the most energy-efficient models of refrigerators, washing machines, and air conditioners.

open dating

Open dating, information that describes the freshness or shelf life of a perishable product, also appears on labels. Open dating was originally used for bakery and dairy products; now it is also used for most other foods. Phrases such as "Use before May 1999" or "Not to be sold after October 8" appear on most grocery items.

Price Comparison

unit pricing

Unit pricing uses a standard unit of measurement to compare the prices of packages of different sizes. The process for calculating and using the unit price is as follows:

1. Determine the common unit of measurement, such as ounces, pounds, gallons, or number of sheets (for items such as paper towels and facial tissues).
2. Divide the price by the number of common units; for example, an 8-ounce package of breakfast cereal selling for $1.52 has a unit price of 19 cents per ounce, while an 11-ounce package costing $1.98 has a unit price of 18 cents per ounce.
3. Compare the unit prices for various sizes, brands, and stores to determine the best buy for your situation.

Remember, the package with the lowest unit price may not be the best buy for you since it may contain more food than you would use before spoilage occurs.

Two common techniques that offer customers reduced prices are coupons and rebates. Each year, billions of coupons are distributed on packages and through newspapers, magazines, and the mail. These coupons are especially valuable if you already plan to buy the products. One family saved about $8 a week on their groceries by using

Sheet 34

FINANCIAL PLANNING CALCULATIONS

NET PRESENT VALUE OF A CONSUMER PURCHASE

The time value of money (see Chapter 1 and Reference C) may be used to evaluate the financial benefits of buying home appliances and other items. For example, when you purchase a washing machine and a clothes dryer, the money you save by not driving to and using a laundromat could be considered a cash *inflow* (since money not going out is like money coming in). The cost of the appliances

would be the current cash *outflow*. If the appliances have an expected life of 10 years, the *net present value* calculations might be as shown below.

You can use this calculation format to assess the financial benefits of a consumer purchase by comparing the cost savings achieved by the purchase over time with the current price of the item purchased.

Step 1. Estimated amount saved on weekly washing and drying at laundromat:

$4.75 times 52 weeks	$ 247.00
Savings from not driving to laundromat: six miles a week at 15 cents a mile times 52 weeks	46.80
Less: Estimated cost of hot water and electricity to operate appliances at home	−13.80
Total annual savings	$ 280.00

Step 2. Multiply annual savings by the present value of a series (Exhibit 1–8D in Chapter 1 or Exhibit C–4 in Appendix C) for 6 percent over 10 years (6 percent is the average expected return from a savings account).

	7.360
	2,060.80

Step 3. Subtract the cost of the washing machine and the clothes dryer.
The result is the net present value of the savings obtained by buying the appliances.*

	−875.00
	$1,185.80

*A negative net present value would indicate that the financial aspects of the purchase are not desirable.

coupons. This resulted in $416 over a year and $2,080 over five years (not counting interest earned had that amount been put in a savings account).

rebate
A **rebate** is a partial refund of the price of a product. This technique was originally used to promote sales of automobiles, but it is now used for selling almost every type of product.

The following guidelines are helpful in comparing prices:

- More convenience (location, hours, sales staff) usually means higher prices.
- Ready-to-use products (convenience foods, preassembled toys, furniture) usually have higher prices.
- Large packages are usually the best buy; however, be sure to use unit pricing to compare different sizes, brands, and stores.
- "Sale" may not always mean saving money; the sale price at one store may be higher than the regular price at another store.

Warranty Evaluation

warranty
Most products come with some guarantee of quality. A **warranty** is a written guarantee from the manufacturer or distributor that specifies the conditions under which the product can be returned, replaced, or repaired. Federal law requires that sellers of products

EXHIBIT 8–7

Wise Buying Techniques: A Summary

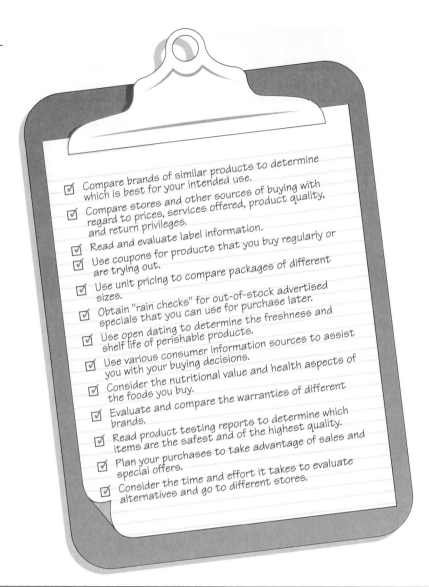

☑ Compare brands of similar products to determine which is best for your intended use.

☑ Compare stores and other sources of buying with regard to prices, services offered, product quality, and return privileges.

☑ Read and evaluate label information.

☑ Use coupons for products that you buy regularly or are trying out.

☑ Use unit pricing to compare packages of different sizes.

☑ Obtain "rain checks" for out-of-stock advertised specials that you can use for purchase later.

☑ Use open dating to determine the freshness and shelf life of perishable products.

☑ Use various consumer information sources to assist you with your buying decisions.

☑ Consider the nutritional value and health aspects of the foods you buy.

☑ Evaluate and compare the warranties of different brands.

☑ Read product testing reports to determine which items are the safest and of the highest quality.

☑ Plan your purchases to take advantage of sales and special offers.

☑ Consider the time and effort it takes to evaluate alternatives and go to different stores.

that cost more than $15 and have a warranty make this document available to customers before purchase. Frequently this disclosure is printed in the catalog or on the package.

An *express warranty,* usually in written form, is created by the seller or manufacturer and has two forms: the *full* warranty and the *limited* warranty. A full warranty states that a defective product can be fixed or replaced in a reasonable amount of time. A limited warranty covers only certain aspects of the product, such as parts, or requires the buyer to incur part of the costs for shipping or repairs.

An *implied warranty* covers a product's intended use or other basic understandings that are not in writing. For example, an implied *warranty of title* indicates that the seller has the right to sell the product. An implied *warranty of merchantability* guarantees that the product is fit for the ordinary uses for which it is intended: A toaster must toast bread, and a stereo must play CDs or tapes. Since implied warranties vary from state to state, contact your state consumer protection office for additional information.

EXHIBIT 8–8

**Sources of
Common
Consumer
Complaints**

Motor vehicle purchases, repairs
Mail-order purchases
Magazine subscriptions
Work-at-home, business opportunities
Landlord–tenant relations
Investment scams
Telemarketing
Computers, home electronics
Health clubs, diet programs
Online services, product sales

Home remodeling, home repairs
Credit card promotions, practices
Financial service companies
Insurance companies
Contests and sweepstakes
Dry cleaning, laundry companies
Travel services, travel packages
Health care service
Rent-to-own companies
Telecommunications, electronic devices

SOURCES: Council of Better Business Bureaus, National Association of Attorneys General, National Fraud Information Center.

service contract

A **service contract** is an agreement between a business and a consumer to cover the repair costs of a product. Even though service contracts are frequently called *extended warranties,* they are not warranties. For a fee, they insure the buyer of a product against losses due to the cost of certain repairs. Owners of automobiles, home appliances, and other equipment buy these contracts to protect themselves against large repair expenses. Service contracts are very profitable for businesses, since many more people buy them than need repair service. Buying a service contract may not be the best use of your money. Most companies that sell service contracts pay out less than 10 cents in costs for every dollar received from consumers. A wiser action may be to set aside money for needed repairs.

Exhibit 8–7 summarizes techniques that can assist you in your buying decisions.

CONCEPT CHECK 8–3

1. What types of brands are commonly available to consumers?
2. What information on food labels can be helpful to consumers?
3. In what situations can comparing prices help in purchasing decisions?
4. How does a service contract differ from a warranty? What rights do purchasers of products have even if no written warranty exists?

RESOLVING CONSUMER COMPLAINTS

L.O.4 Identify steps to take to resolve consumer problems.

Every business transaction is a potential problem. Most customer difficulties result from defective products, low quality, short product lives, unexpected costs, deceptive pricing, and poor repairs. These problems are most commonly associated with the products and services listed in Exhibit 8–8. Federal consumer agencies estimate annual consumer losses from fraudulent business activities at $10 billion to $40 billion for telemarketing and mail order, $3 billion for credit card fraud and credit "repair" scams, and $10 billion for investment swindles.

Most people do not anticipate problems with a purchase. However, problems do arise, and it's best to be prepared for them. The process for resolving differences between buyers and sellers includes the steps presented in Exhibit 8–9 on page 241. To help ensure success when you make a complaint, keep a file of receipts, names of people you talked to, dates of attempted repairs, copies of letters you wrote, and costs incurred. Having

FINANCIAL PLANNING FOR LIFE'S SITUATIONS

BEWARE OF THESE COMMON (AND NOT SO COMMON) FRAUDS

Foreign Scams.   About 800 people received a letter from a Nigerian bank promising all or part of $30 million. The letter requested the recipient's bank account number so the money could be transferred. There was another catch: To receive the fortune, the recipient would have to pay between $100,000 to $1 million in taxes—in advance! Fourteen people, none of them U.S. residents, sent checks totaling about $20 million.

Telemarketing Scams.   Telemarketing fraud and common telephone scams include sweepstakes and prize offers, travel packages, investments, charities, recovery swindles, work-at-home schemes, magazine or publication sales, advanced loan fees and credit arrangers, lotteries and lottery tickets, and business opportunities.

Advance-Fee Loans.   Fraudulent loan brokers misrepresenting the availability of credit use the "advance-fee" loan scam. They guarantee to get you a loan or other type of credit—but you must pay *before* you apply. After getting the money in advance, the con artists commonly disappear.

Credit Repair.   Companies offer to clean up the credit reports of consumers with poor credit histories. After paying hundreds or thousands of dollars, bilked consumers find out these companies can do nothing to improve their credit reports.

Automatic Debit Scams.   Automatic debiting of your checking account can be a legitimate payment method for monthly bills such as a mortgage or utilities. However, many fraudulent telemarketers use this technique to improperly take money from a person's checking account. *Do not* give out checking account information over the phone unless you are familiar with the company and agree to pay for something.

Fraudulent Diet Products.   Americans spend an estimated $6 billion a year on fraudulent diet products such as "The Amazing Skin Patch Melts Away Body Fat," "Lose Weight While You Sleep," and "Lose All the Weight You Can for Just $99." A sensible meal plan combined with regular exercise will help you take off the pounds without taking dollars out of your wallet.

Fraudulent Health Claims.   Spotting false health claims may be as easy as being cautious of phrases such as "scientific breakthrough," "miraculous cure," "exclusive product," "secret ingredient," or "ancient remedy."

Common health fraud schemes occur in the areas of cancer, AIDS-HIV, and arthritis.

Magazine Subscription Scams.   Beware of telephone sales pitches for "free," "prepaid," or "special" magazine subscription offers. One consumer received a call stating that as a "preferred customer" the company had prepaid seven magazine subscriptions for 60 months. All that would be required would be a "small" weekly service fee of $3.43. The magazines would cost nearly $900 over the five-year period.

Toll-Free Scams.   Calls to 800 and 888 numbers are almost always free. However, there are some exceptions. Companies that provide audio entertainment or information services may charge for calls to 800, 888, and other toll-free numbers, but only if they follow the Federal Trade Commission's 900-number rule.

International Phone Scams.   Be cautious when calling an unfamiliar telephone number—it could be a costly international telephone call. Scam artists confuse callers by promoting calls to "809" numbers in the Dominican Republic. While these telephone numbers may look like domestic calls, international rates apply.

Prepaid Phone Card Scams.   Selling prepaid calling cards for a living can result in telecommunications fraud. Most phone card scams reported have involved multilevel marketing. Also common is requesting investors to pay a fairly large up-front fee to become a distributor. Another fraud warning is a company that is selling phone cards with a very low per-minute charge.

Online and High-Tech Scams.   According to the National Consumers League, the five most common Internet scams are pyramid schemes, Internet-related services, equipment sales, business opportunities, and work-at-home offers. Be leery of overstated claims and promises, especially if they require money or a credit card number. Deceptive use of online discussion groups can lead potential investors to believe a company is an outstanding investment opportunity. Paging licenses and 900 numbers are the most often reported high-tech information superhighway scams.

Further information about various frauds and deceptive business practices is available at www.fraud.org and www.ftc.gov.

EXHIBIT 8–9

Suggested Steps for Resolving Consumer Complaints

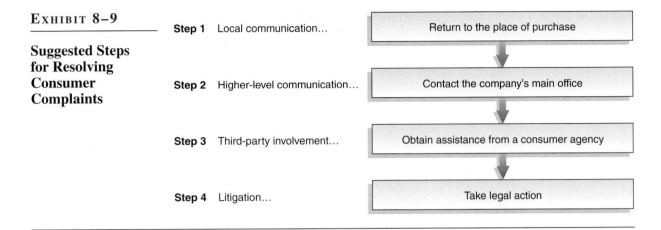

Step 1   Local communication…   Return to the place of purchase

Step 2   Higher-level communication…   Contact the company's main office

Step 3   Third-party involvement…   Obtain assistance from a consumer agency

Step 4   Litigation…   Take legal action

written documents can help resolve a problem in your favor. An automobile owner kept detailed records and receipts for all gasoline purchases, oil changes, and repairs. When a warranty dispute occurred, the person was able to prove proper maintenance and received a refund for the defective vehicle.

Step 1: Return to Place of Purchase

Most consumer complaints are resolved at the original sales location. Since most business firms are concerned about their reputations for honesty and fairness, they usually honor legitimate complaints. As you talk with the salesperson, customer service person, or store manager, avoid yelling, threatening a lawsuit, or demanding unreasonable action. In general, a calm, rational, yet persistent approach is recommended.

Federal law allows three business days to cancel a contract for $25 or more if the agreement was signed away from the seller's regular place of business. This "cooling-off" law does not apply to purchases made at a retail business in a fixed location or for transactions made by mail or phone. This law was originally designed to protect consumers from questionable door-to-door salespeople. The cancellation right also applies to home equity loans, health club memberships, and discount buying clubs, no matter where the contract is signed. Most states allow a cooling-off period when buying timeshare vacation property; others also cover campground memberships.

> **DID YOU KNOW?**
>
> The American Association of Retired Persons estimates that more than 14,000 fraudulent telemarketing businesses are operating in the United States, costing consumers an annual loss of about $40 billion.

Step 2: Contact Company Headquarters

Consumer advisers suggest you express dissatisfaction at the corporate level if your problem is not resolved at the local store. A letter like the one in Exhibit 8–10 may be appropriate. You can obtain addresses of companies you may wish to contact from the *Consumer's Resource Handbook,* published by the U.S. Office of Consumer Affairs; Standard & Poor's *Register of Corporations, Directors, and Executives;* Dun & Bradstreet's *Million Dollar Directory;* or other reference books available at your library. The Web sites of major companies also offer a method to communicate with these organizations.

EXHIBIT 8–10   **Sample Complaint Letter**

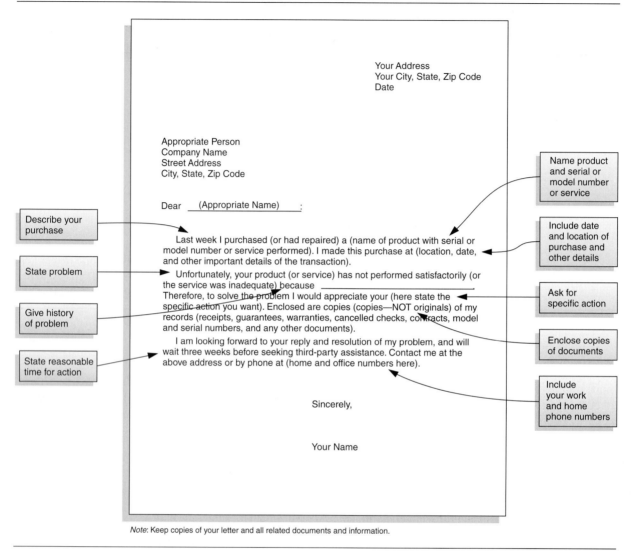

Note: Keep copies of your letter and all related documents and information.

source: *Consumer's Resource Handbook.*

You can obtain a company's hot line number by using a directory of toll-free numbers in the library or calling 1–800–555–1212, the toll-free information number. Some companies print the toll-free hot-line number on product packages. The Society of Consumer Affairs Professionals in Business estimates that 70 percent of consumer complaints made to company toll-free numbers are resolved on the first contact.

Step 3: Obtain Consumer Agency Assistance

If you do not receive satisfaction from the company, several consumer, business, and government organizations are available. These include national organizations specializing in issues such as automobile safety, nuclear energy, and nutrition, and local organizations that handle complaints, conduct surveys, and provide legal assistance.

The Better Business Bureaus are a network of offices throughout the country that resolve complaints against local merchants. Better Business Bureaus are sponsored by local business organizations, and companies are not obligated to respond to the complaints they handle. The Better Business Bureau in your area can be of most value to you before you make a purchase. Its files will tell you about the experiences of others who dealt with a firm with which you are planning to do business.

mediation

Mediation involves the use of a third party to settle grievances. In mediation, an impartial person—the *mediator*—tries to resolve a conflict between a customer and a business through discussion and negotiation. Mediation is a nonbinding process. It can save you more time and money than other dispute settlement methods.

arbitration

Arbitration is the settlement of a difference by a third party—the *arbitrator*—whose decision is legally binding. After both sides agree to abide by the arbitrator's decision, each side presents its case to the arbitrator. Arbitrators are selected from a pool of volunteers. Most major automobile manufacturers and many industry organizations have arbitration programs to resolve consumer complaints.

A vast network of government agencies is also available to consumers. Problems with local restaurants or food stores may be handled by a city or county health department. Every state has a variety of agencies to handle problems involving deceptive advertising, fraudulent business practices, banking, insurance companies, and utility rates.

Federal agencies available to help resolve consumer difficulties and provide information are listed in Appendix E. When you are uncertain about which agency to use, contact your U.S. representative in Washington, DC. This office can help channel your concern to the most appropriate consumer protection agency.

Step 4: Take Legal Action

The next section discusses the various alternatives available to consumers to resolve consumer problems.

CONCEPT CHECK 8–4

1. What are common causes of consumer problems and complaints?
2. How can most consumer complaints be resolved?
3. How does arbitration differ from mediation?

LEGAL OPTIONS FOR CONSUMERS

L.O.5 Evaluate the legal alternatives available to consumers.

What should you do if all of the previously mentioned avenues of action failed to bring about a resolution of a consumer complaint? One of the following legal actions might be appropriate.

Small Claims Court

small claims court

Every state has a court system to settle minor disagreements. In **small claims court,** a person may file a claim involving amounts below a set dollar limit. The maximum varies from state to state, ranging from $500 to $10,000; most states have a limit of between $1,500 and $3,000. The process usually takes place without the involvement of a lawyer, although in many states attorneys are allowed in small claims court.

To make best use of small claims court, experts suggest the following tips:

- Become familiar with the court's location, procedures, and filing fees (usually ranging from $5 to $50).
- Observe other cases to learn more about the process.
- Present your case in a polite, calm, and concise manner.
- Submit evidence such as photographs, contracts, receipts, and other documents.
- Use witnesses who can testify on your behalf.

While obtaining a favorable judgment in small claims court may be easy, the collection process is frequently difficult. Since the defendant may not appear, you may have to pay a sheriff to serve a court order or use a collection agency to get your money.

Class-Action Suits

class-action suit

Occasionally, a number of people have the same complaint, for example, people who have been injured by a defective product, customers who have been overcharged by a utility company, or travelers who have been cheated by a charter tour business. Such people may qualify for a class-action suit. A **class-action suit** is a legal action taken by a few individuals on behalf of all the people who have suffered the same alleged injustice. These people, called a *class,* are represented by one lawyer or by a group of lawyers working together.

> **DID YOU KNOW?**
>
> A class-action suit can be expensive. After winning $2.19 in back interest, Dexter J. Kamilewicz also noted a $91.33 "miscellaneous deduction" on his mortgage escrow account. This charge was his portion for lawyers he never knew he hired to win a class-action suit.
> Source: Barry Meier, "Math of a Class-Action Suit: 'Winning' $2.19 Costs $91.33," *The New York Times,* November 21, 1995, pp. A1, C4.

Once a situation qualifies as a class-action suit, all of the affected parties must be notified of the suit. At this point, a person may decide not to participate in the class-action suit and instead file an individual lawsuit. If the court ruling is favorable to the class, the funds awarded may be divided among all of the people involved, used to reduce rates in the future, or assigned to public funds for government use. Recent class-action suits included auto owners who were sold unneeded replacement parts for their vehicles and a group of investors who sued a brokerage company for unauthorized buy-and-sell transactions that resulted in high commission charges.

Using a Lawyer

When small claims court or a class-action suit is not appropriate, you may seek the services of an attorney. The most common sources of available lawyers are referrals from people you know, the local branch of the American Bar Association, and telephone directory listings. Lawyers advertise in newspapers, on television, and in other media. However, you must be aware that impressive advertising does not mean competent legal counsel.

Deciding when to use a lawyer is difficult. In general, straightforward legal situations such as appearing in small claims court, renting an apartment, or defending yourself on a minor traffic violation usually do not require legal counsel. But for more complicated matters such as writing a will, settling a real estate purchase, or suing for injury damages caused by a product, it is probably wise to obtain the assistance of an attorney.

When selecting a lawyer, you should consider several questions. Is the lawyer experienced in your type of case? Will you be charged on a flat fee basis, at an hourly rate, or on a contingency basis? Is there a fee for the initial consultation? How and when will you be required to make payment for services?

Sheet 35

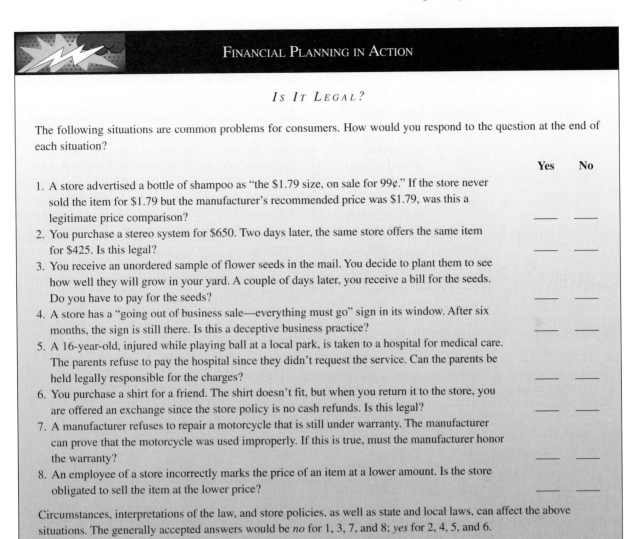

FINANCIAL PLANNING IN ACTION

IS IT LEGAL?

The following situations are common problems for consumers. How would you respond to the question at the end of each situation?

	Yes	No
1. A store advertised a bottle of shampoo as "the $1.79 size, on sale for 99¢." If the store never sold the item for $1.79 but the manufacturer's recommended price was $1.79, was this a legitimate price comparison?	___	___
2. You purchase a stereo system for $650. Two days later, the same store offers the same item for $425. Is this legal?	___	___
3. You receive an unordered sample of flower seeds in the mail. You decide to plant them to see how well they will grow in your yard. A couple of days later, you receive a bill for the seeds. Do you have to pay for the seeds?	___	___
4. A store has a "going out of business sale—everything must go" sign in its window. After six months, the sign is still there. Is this a deceptive business practice?	___	___
5. A 16-year-old, injured while playing ball at a local park, is taken to a hospital for medical care. The parents refuse to pay the hospital since they didn't request the service. Can the parents be held legally responsible for the charges?	___	___
6. You purchase a shirt for a friend. The shirt doesn't fit, but when you return it to the store, you are offered an exchange since the store policy is no cash refunds. Is this legal?	___	___
7. A manufacturer refuses to repair a motorcycle that is still under warranty. The manufacturer can prove that the motorcycle was used improperly. If this is true, must the manufacturer honor the warranty?	___	___
8. An employee of a store incorrectly marks the price of an item at a lower amount. Is the store obligated to sell the item at the lower price?	___	___

Circumstances, interpretations of the law, and store policies, as well as state and local laws, can affect the above situations. The generally accepted answers would be *no* for 1, 3, 7, and 8; *yes* for 2, 4, 5, and 6.

Other Legal Alternatives

legal aid society

The cost of legal services can be a problem, especially for low-income consumers. A **legal aid society** is one of a network of publicly supported community law offices that provide legal assistance to people who cannot afford their own attorney. These community agencies provide this assistance at a minimal cost or without charge.

Prepaid legal services provide unlimited or reduced-fee legal assistance for a set fee. Some of these programs provide certain basic services, such as telephone consultation and preparation of a simple will, for an annual fee ranging from $50 to $150 or more. More complicated legal assistance would require an additional fee, usually at a reduced rate. Other programs do not charge an advance fee but allow members to obtain legal services at discount rates. There are also comprehensive plans in which a high prepaid fee covers the legal needs of most families. In general, prepaid legal programs are designed to prevent minor troubles from becoming complicated legal problems.

Personal Consumer Protection

While many laws, agencies, and legal tools are available to protect your rights, none will be of value to you unless you use them. Consumer protection experts suggest that to prevent being taken in by deceptive business practices, you should

1. Do business with reputable companies that have a proven record of satisfying customers.
2. Avoid signing contracts and other documents that you do not understand.
3. Be cautious about offerings that seem too good to be true—they probably are!
4. Compare the cost of buying on credit with the cost of paying cash; also, compare the interest rates the seller offers with those offered by a bank or a credit union.
5. Avoid rushing to get a good deal; successful con artists depend on impulse buying.

To achieve financial well-being, be aware of and use the various information sources available to consumers to make effective purchasing decisions.

CONCEPT CHECK 8–5

1. In what types of situations would small claims court and class-action suits be helpful?
2. Describe some situations in which you might use the services of a lawyer.

SUMMARY

L.O.1 Assess the financial implications of consumer purchasing decisions.

A variety of economic, social, and personal factors influence daily buying decisions. Overspending and poor money management are frequent causes of overuse of credit and other financial difficulties.

L.O.2 Evaluate the alternatives in consumer purchasing decisions.

A research-based approach to consumer buying involves problem identification, information gathering, and increased marketplace awareness. In this approach, purchase alternatives are assessed on the basis of quality, price, performance, style, company reputation, and service.

L.O.3 Implement strategies for effective purchasing.

Timing purchases, comparing stores and brands, using label information, computing unit prices, and evaluating warranties are common strategies for effective purchasing.

L.O.4 Identify steps to take to resolve consumer problems.

Most consumer problems can be resolved by following these steps: (1) Return to the place of purchase; (2) contact the company's main office; (3) obtain assistance from a consumer agency; and (4) take legal action.

L.O.5 Evaluate the legal alternatives available to consumers.

Small claims court, class-action suits, the services of a lawyer, legal aid societies, and prepaid legal services are legal means for handling consumer problems that cannot be resolved through communication with the business involved or through the help of a consumer protection agency.

GLOSSARY

arbitration   The settlement of a difference by a third party whose decision is legally binding.   (p. 243)

class-action suit   A legal action taken by a few individuals on behalf of all the people who have suffered the same alleged injustice.   (p. 244)

cooperative   A nonprofit organization whose member-owners may save money on certain products or services.   (p. 234)

generic item   A plain-package, nonbrand version of a product, offered at a lower price than that of the brand-name version(s).   (p. 236)

impulse buying   Unplanned purchasing.   (p. 235)

legal aid society   One of a network of publicly supported community law offices that provide legal assistance to consumers who cannot afford their own attorney.   (p. 245)

mediation   The attempt by an impartial third party to resolve a difference between two parties through discussion and negotiation.   (p. 243)

open dating   Information about freshness or shelf life found on the package of a perishable product.   (p. 236)

rebate   A partial refund of the price of a product.   (p. 237)

service contract   An agreement between a business and a consumer to cover the repair costs of a product.   (p. 239)

small claims court   A court that settles legal differences involving amounts below a set limit and employs a process in which the litigants usually do not use a lawyer.   (p. 243)

unit pricing   The use of a standard unit of measurement to compare the prices of packages of different sizes.   (p. 236)

warranty   A written guarantee from the manufacturer or distributor of a product that specifies the conditions under which the product can be returned, replaced, or repaired.   (p. 237)

R E V I E W   Q U E S T I O N S

1. Why might the effects of daily shopping decisions be overlooked when viewing one's financial planning activities?   (L.O.1)
2. How can a person use a research process to make wise purchasing decisions?   (L.O.2)
3. What effect can small changes in buying habits have on a person's financial well-being?   (L.O.3)

4. What relationship exists between wise shopping decisions and avoiding consumer problems?   (L.O.4)
5. What would be an indication that a consumer problem might require legal action?   (L.O.5)

F I N A N C I A L   P L A N N I N G   P R O B L E M S

1. *Analyzing Influences on Consumer Buying.* Use advertisements, recent news articles, and personal observations to point out the economic, social, and personal factors that influence the purchases of people in the following life situations.   (L.O.1)
   a. A retired person.
   b. A single parent with children ages five and nine.
   c. A dual-income couple with no children.
   d. A person with a dependent child and a dependent parent.
2. *Comparing Buying Alternatives.* Tammy Monahan is considering the purchase of a home entertainment center. The product attributes she plans to consider and the weights she gives to them are

Portability	.1
Sound projection	.6
Warranty	.3

   Tammy related the brands as follows:

	Portability	Sound Projection	Warranty
Brand A	6	8	7
Brand B	9	6	8
Brand C	5	9	6

   Using the consumer buying matrix (Exhibit 8–4), conduct a quantitative product evaluation rating for each brand. What other factors is Tammy likely to consider when making her purchase?
3. *Researching Consumer Purchases.* Using the consumer buying matrix (Exhibit 8–4), analyze a consumer purchase you plan to make sometime in the future. What factors affected the selection of the attributes and weights you chose for this purchase analysis?   (L.O.2)
4. *Calculating the Cost of Credit.* John Walters is comparing the cost of credit to the cash price of an item. If John makes a $60 down payment and pays $32 a month for 24 months, how much more will that amount be than the cash price of $685?   (L.O.2)
5. *Computing Unit Prices.* Calculate the unit price of each of the following items: (L.O.3)

Item	Price	Size	Unit Price
Motor oil	$1.95	2.5 quarts	____ cents/quart
Cereal	2.17	15 ounces	____ cents/ounces
Canned fruit	0.89	13 ounces	____ cents/ounces
Facial tissue	2.25	300 tissues	____ cents/100 tissues
Shampoo	3.96	17 ounces	____ cents/ounces

6. *Calculating the Present Value of a Consumer Purchase.* What would be the net present value of a microwave oven that costs $159 and will save you $68 a year in time and food away from home? Assume an average return on your savings of 7 percent.   (L.O.3)
7. *Computing Net Present Value.* Use the feature "Financial Planning Calculations: Net Present Value of a Consumer Purchase" (p. 237) to analyze a past or a future purchase.   (L.O.3)
8. *Calculating Future Value.* You can purchase a service contract for all of your major appliances for $160 a year. If the appliances are expected to last for 10 years and you earn 5 percent on your savings, what would be the future value of the amount you will pay for the service contract?   (L.O.3)

9. *Comparing Automobile Purchases.* Based on financial and opportunity costs, which of the following do you believe would be the wiser purchase? (Chapter Appendix)

   Vehicle 1: A three-year-old car with 45,000 miles, costing $6,700 and requiring $385 of immediate repairs.

   Vehicle 2: A five-year-old car with 62,000 miles, costing $4,500 and requiring $760 of immediate repairs.

10. *Calculating Motor Vehicle Operating Costs.* Calculate the approximate yearly operating cost of the following vehicle. (Chapter Appendix)

Annual depreciation, $2,500
Annual mileage, 13,200
Current year's loan interest, $650
Miles per gallon, 24
Insurance, $680
License and registration fees, $65
Average gasoline price, $1.18 per gallon
Oil changes/repairs, $370
Parking/tolls, $420

PROJECTS AND APPLICATION ACTIVITIES

1. *Obtaining Consumer Information.* Using the World Wide Web, library resources, or a survey of acquaintances, determine the major factors people consider when *(a)* buying food, *(b)* selecting a store at which to shop, and *(c)* using information from advertisements. (L.O.1)

2. *Comparing Consumer Information Sources.* Obtain a recent issue of *Consumer Reports* (or go to http://www.ConsumerReports.org) to evaluate and compare different 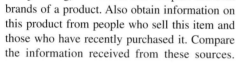 brands of a product. Also obtain information on this product from people who sell this item and those who have recently purchased it. Compare the information received from these sources. (L.O.2)

3. *Evaluating Consumer Information Sources.* Develop guidelines that consumers could use to evaluate different sources of consumer information (advertising, salespeople, friends, government publications, Internet sites). Consider the *(a)* objectivity, *(b)* accuracy, *(c)* clarity, and *(d)* usefulness of these sources. Prepare a video or other visual presentation to communicate your guidelines. (L.O.2)

4. *Researching Consumer Information on the Internet.* Locate Web sites that would provide you and others with useful information when buying various consumer products. (L.O.3)

5. *Determining Brand Loyalty.* Conduct a survey of several people regarding brand loyalty. For what products do these people usually buy a certain brand? What factors (price, location, information) may influence their selection of another brand? (L.O.3)

6. *Solving Consumer Problems.* Interview one or two people who have had a complaint about a product or company.

What difficulties did they encounter? What actions did they take? Was the complaint resolved in a satisfactory manner? (L.O.4)

7. *Identifying and Solving Consumer Problems.* Collect magazine or newspaper advertisements that appear to be 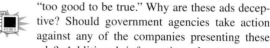 "too good to be true." Why are these ads deceptive? Should government agencies take action against any of the companies presenting these ads? Additional information about common frauds may be obtained at www.fraud.org. (L.O.4)

8. *Comparing Legal Services.* Prepare a survey of legal services available to students and others in your community. Use Sheet 33 in the *Personal Financial Planner* to compare the fees and services provided by lawyers and other sources of legal assistance. (L.O.5)

9. *Comparing Used Cars.* Use Sheet 37 in the *Personal Financial Planner* to compare different sources of used motor vehicles. (Chapter Appendix)

10. *Searching the Internet for Transportation Information.* Using various search engines, identify World Wide Web sites that could assist consumers with evaluating and comparing automobile prices. (Chapter Appendix)

11. *Evaluating Motor Vehicle Leases.* Use Sheet 38 in the *Personal Financial Planner* to compare the costs of buying and leasing a motor vehicle. (Chapter Appendix)

12. *Comparing Auto Service.* Compare the prices different types of automotive service businesses (specialty shops, dealers, service stations) charge for the purchase and installation of a battery, muffler, and tires. (Chapter Appendix)

LIFE SITUATION CASE 8

MAKING MARKETPLACE DECISIONS

Anthony Carlton just completed his college degree and has taken a job in a nearby city. As he prepares to move into his new apartment, Anthony realizes he must make a purchasing

decision regarding furniture. He starts the buying process by talking to his parents and friends.

His dad suggests that Anthony lease some furniture until he is sure how long he will live in this area. "No sense buying things that you might have to sell or move a long distance," he advises.

"I can get you a great deal on some furniture," offered Anthony's friend Steve. Anthony responded, "I don't have that much cash available." Steve replied, "No problem, we have an easy payment plan at our store."

While continuing to think about the situation, Anthony comes across an advertisement by a "rent-to-buy" store. He calls the company and finds out that the very low payments make it possible to get the furniture available almost immediately. In addition, the salesperson on the phone commented that "within just a few years, these items can be yours to keep."

Anthony continues to read articles about buying furniture and talks to others about the purchase. As he obtains more buying information, Anthony becomes increasingly uncertain about what action to take. Finally, he exclaims, "Maybe I can just sit on the floor!"

QUESTIONS

1. What information sources are likely to be most helpful to Anthony?
2. How should Anthony evaluate the costs and benefits of the alternatives available for resolving his buying problem?
3. What other alternatives may be available to Anthony?

USING THE INTERNET TO CREATE A PERSONAL FINANCIAL PLAN 8

COMPARISON SHOPPING AND BUYING MOTOR VEHICLES

Daily buying actions such as comparing prices, evaluating brands, and avoiding fraud allow you to wisely use resources for both current living expenses and long-term financial security.

Web Sites for Comparison Shopping

- Current *Consumer Reports* articles at **www.Consumer-Reports.org;** extensive information on various consumer topics are links to other sites at **www.consumerworld.org**
- A comparison of brands, prices, and features for various products may be accessed at **www.compare.net** and **www.pricescan.com**
- Consumer information related to food, health, money, product safety, and transportation at **www.consumer.gov;** access to publications from the Consumer Information Center at **www.pueblo.gsa.gov;** Federal Trade Commission consumer information at **www.ftc.gov**
- The National Fraud Information Center Web site offers fraud warnings and links to federal, state, and local consumer agencies at **www.fraud.org;** the Better Business Bureau offers a directory of BBB offices, information on marketplace scams, and links to other BBB Web sites at **www.bbb.org**
- Legal information related to various consumer and personal finance topics at **www.nolo.com** and **www.consumerlawpage.com**
- CARveat Emptor has links to various aspects of researching, selecting, negotiating, and leasing motor vehicles at **www.well.com/user/kr2;** new and used car prices at

www.edmunds.com and **www.kbb.com;** auto leasing information at **www.leasesource.com**
- Driving safety information at **www.hwysafety.org** and crash data and insurance injury, collision, and theft loss information at **www.carsafety.org**

(Note: Addresses and content of Web sites change, and new sites are created daily. Use the search engines discussed in Appendix B to update and locate additional Web sites.)

PFP SHEETS: 32–39

Short-Term Financial Planning Activities

1. Compare the cash and credit, and various brands, for the purchase of a major consumer item you may need in the near future. (see PFP Sheets 32, 33).
2. Conduct a unit pricing comparison at several stores (see PFP Sheet 34).
3. Determine current transportation needs related to new and used motor vehicles along with comparing buying and leasing options (see PFP Sheets 36–38).

Long-Term Financial Planning Activities

1. Determine buying guidelines for major purchases (appliances, furniture, home entertainment equipment). Identify brands, store locations, and savings plans to avoid buying on credit.
2. Identify and compare various legal services available for use (see PFP Sheet 35).
3. Identify motor vehicles that would provide the lowest operating and insurance costs. (see PFP Sheet 39).

APPENDIX

BUYING AND OPERATING MOTOR VEHICLES

BUYING A USED VEHICLE

Sheet 36

The average used car costs $9,000 less than the average new car. The cost of a new car exceeded $20,000 in the mid-1990s. New cars cost an average of about 50 cents a mile to own and operate; used cars cost an average of about 35 cents a mile. While many people prefer a previously owned vehicle, higher new-car prices have created increased demand and higher costs for used cars. Americans spend over $100 billion a year to purchase more than 20 million used cars.

Sources of Used Vehicles

New-Car Dealers   New-car dealers usually have a good supply of used vehicles. These automobiles are late-model vehicles received as trade-ins for new-car purchases. New-car dealers generally give you a better warranty on a used car than other sellers and have a service department to recondition the cars they sell. These services mean higher used-car prices at new-car dealers than at other used-car sources.

Used-Car Dealers   Used-car dealers specialize in previously owned vehicles. They usually offer vehicles that are older than those offered by new-car dealers. If they give warranties, the coverage is likely to be limited. In exchange for these shortcomings, however, you will probably be able to obtain a lower price from a used-car dealer than from a new-car dealer. Be aware, though, that some used-car dealers obtain vehicles that have been poorly maintained by their previous users.

Private Parties   Individuals selling their own cars are another common source of used cars. A private-party sale can be a bargain if the vehicle was well maintained; it can also be a nightmare. Since few consumer protection regulations apply to private-party sales, caution is suggested when using this used-car source. Ask past owners if they have a record of regular maintenance and repairs for vehicles you are considering.

Other Sources   Other used-car sources include auctions and dealers that sell automobiles previously owned by businesses, auto rental companies, and government agencies. Government automobiles and the automobiles of auto rental companies are usually serviced regularly. However, most of these vehicles have had many different drivers or, like police vehicles, have undergone extreme use. Attempt to avoid a vehicle that seems to be in good shape but has experienced heavy use.

Consumer Protection for Used-Car Buyers

The Federal Trade Commission (FTC) requires businesses that sell used cars to place a buyer's guide sticker in the windows of cars available for sale. This disclosure must state whether the car comes with a warranty and, if so, what protection the dealer will provide. If no warranty is offered, the car is sold "as is" and the dealer assumes no responsibility for any repairs, regardless of any oral claims. About one-half of all the used cars sold by dealers come without a warranty, and if you buy such a car, you must pay for any repairs needed to correct problems. Be sure to get in writing any promises made by the salesperson.

While a used car may not have an *express warranty,* most states have *implied warranties* that protect basic rights of the used-car buyer. An implied warranty of merchantability means the product is guaranteed to do what it is supposed to do. Thus, the used car is guaranteed to run—at least for awhile!

The buyer's guide required by the FTC encourages you to have the used car inspected by a mechanic and to get all promises in writing. You also receive a list of the 14 major systems of an automobile and some of the major problems that may occur in these systems. This list can be helpful in comparing the vehicles and warranties offered by different dealers. FTC used-car regulations do not apply to vehicles purchased from private owners. Limited information may be available; however, ask the seller whether you can see the receipts for maintenance and repairs.

You should follow two general rules when you buy a used vehicle. First, buy your vehicle from a source that gives some assurance of the vehicle's reliability. Second, make a detailed investigation of the vehicle's condition and performance potential.

The Inspection Process

The appearance of a used car can be deceptive. A well-maintained engine may be inside a body with unsightly rust; a clean, shiny exterior may conceal major operational problems. Therefore, you should conduct a used-car inspection as outlined in Exhibit 8–A.

Have a trained and trusted mechanic of *your* choice check the car to estimate the costs of potential repairs. This service will help you avoid surprises when the vehicle becomes yours. Some businesses use computers to check the engine and other mechanisms. A van carrying the computer will go right to the location where the vehicle is for sale.

Although federal law makes odometer tampering illegal, the problem still exists. Mileage may be turned back to give a vehicle a newer appearance. Signs of possible odometer fraud are the failure of digits to line up straight or the presence of broken plastic in the speedometer case. If the brake pedal, tires, or upholstery look very old or very new for the number of miles on the odometer, odometer tampering may have occurred.

Before making your final decision, find out whether there have been safety recalls on the car. If so, have the necessary adjustments been made? Information about recalls may be obtained from the National Highway Traffic Safety Administration, a division of the U.S. Department of Transportation. This agency has an auto safety hot line (1–800–424–9393) for consumers to check on auto recalls.

Used-Car Price Negotiation

The final phase of used-car buying is price. Begin to determine a fair price by checking newspaper ads for the prices of comparable vehicles. Other sources of current used-car

EXHIBIT 8–A   **Checking Out a Used Car**

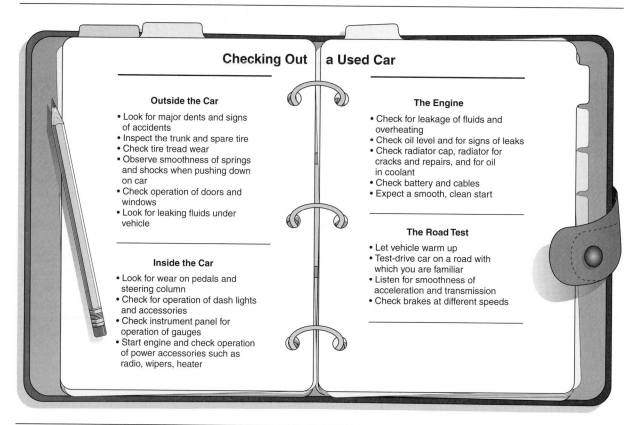

Checking Out a Used Car

Outside the Car

- Look for major dents and signs of accidents
- Inspect the trunk and spare tire
- Check tire tread wear
- Observe smoothness of springs and shocks when pushing down on car
- Check operation of doors and windows
- Look for leaking fluids under vehicle

Inside the Car

- Look for wear on pedals and steering column
- Check for operation of dash lights and accessories
- Check instrument panel for operation of gauges
- Start engine and check operation of power accessories such as radio, wipers, heater

The Engine

- Check for leakage of fluids and overheating
- Check oil level and for signs of leaks
- Check radiator cap, radiator for cracks and repairs, and for oil in coolant
- Check battery and cables
- Expect a smooth, clean start

The Road Test

- Let vehicle warm up
- Test-drive car on a road with which you are familiar
- Listen for smoothness of acceleration and transmission
- Check brakes at different speeds

---

prices are *Edmund's Used Car Prices* and the National Automobile Dealers Association's *Official Used Car Guide,* commonly called the *blue book.* These publications are available at banks, credit unions, libraries, and bookstores. Since the blue book is updated monthly, some automobile sellers and buyers use the *black book,* a weekly report of automobile auction sales published by National Auto Research of Gainesville, Georgia.

A number of factors influence the basic price of a used car. The number of miles the car has been driven and the car's features and options affect price. A low-mileage car will have a higher price than a comparable car with high mileage. The overall condition of the car and the demand for the model also affect price.

Used-car prices follow the trend in new-car sales. If more people buy new cars and trade in or sell their present cars, the increased supply of used cars keeps their prices down. However, when the demand for new cars is low and people keep their cars longer, the prices of used cars increase. Information about the market value and safety of used motor vehicles may be obtained from online computer services (see Appendix B).

PFP

Sheet 37

PURCHASING A NEW VEHICLE

You may be interested in a vehicle with "AC, pwr mrrs, ABS, and P/S." When you decode these abbreviations, you will know the vehicle has air conditioning, power mirrors, antilock brakes, and power steering. Gathering information, selecting options for your new car, and determining price are the primary steps in buying a new car.

Gathering Information

An important source of new-car price information is the *sticker price.* This is displayed in printed form on the vehicle with the suggested retail price of the new car and its optional equipment. This information label presents the base price of the car as well as details about the costs of accessories and other items. The dealer's cost, or *invoice price,* is an amount less than the sticker price.

The difference between the sticker price and the dealer's cost is the range available for negotiation. This range is larger for full-size, luxury cars; subcompacts usually do not have a wide negotiation range. Dealer's cost for a vehicle (in relation to the sticker price) varies based on the size of the car. For example, on subcompact and compact cars, the dealer's cost is usually between 87 and 94 percent of the sticker price. On full-size cars and vans, the cost is between 80 and 84 percent of the list price.

Information about dealer's cost is available from several sources. *Edmund's New Car Prices,* available in libraries and bookstores, is helpful. More sophisticated car cost data can be obtained from computerized services such as Consumers Union, publisher of *Consumer Reports.*

Obtaining a favorable deal may depend on the time of day, the month, and the year. Usually you will get the most attention during the morning or early afternoon. Salespeople may give you a better price near the end of the month to make their quota. Finally, some experts recommend that you buy your new car at the end of the model year (in late summer), in winter, or in early spring, when auto sales tend to be slow.

Selecting Options

Optional equipment falls into three categories:

1. Mechanical devices that improve performance and operation, such as a larger engine, special transmission, power steering, power brakes, and cruise control.
2. Comfort and convenience options, including reclining seats, air conditioning, stereo systems, power locks, rear window defoggers, and tinted glass.
3. Aesthetic features that add to the vehicle's visual appeal, such as metallic paint, special trim, and plush upholstery.

Color is an option that may make your car safer. Tests that involved viewing vehicles on backgrounds of concrete, meadows, and snow determined that the most visible colors were luminous orange, white (although white was difficult to see in snow and bright sunshine), and light shades of orange, gray, and blue. The colors most difficult to see were browns, greens, dark gray, dark blue, and black. Cars whose colors are the same as the cars in company ads will probably have the highest resale value, since these ads use the colors that research has shown to be most appealing.

Several options may be available for a single price. For example, a *convenience package* may include power door locks, power windows, power mirror adjustment, and a push-button trunk opener. The package price may save you money. However, do you want all of these items? Remember too that these power items may increase the operating cost of the vehicle by reducing fuel efficiency.

You may save money on optional equipment by selecting the deluxe edition of a model. Items that cost extra with the basic, low-price edition may be included as standard equipment with the higher-priced limited edition. Again, be sure you want all of the options, and compare the prices of the two editions to make sure the additional accessories justify the cost difference. Your willingness to accept different editions or comparable models of a different make will improve your negotiating position.

A *service contract* can cover the cost of repairs not included in the warranty provided by the manufacturer. Service contracts range from $400 to over $1,000; however, they do not always include everything you might expect. Most of these contracts contain a list of parts not covered, along with other provisions. All service contracts cover failure of the engine cooling system; however, some contracts exclude coverage of such failures if caused by overheating.

Because of costs and exclusions, service contracts may not be a wise financial decision. You can minimize your concern about expensive repairs by setting aside a fund of money to pay for them. Then, if you need repairs, the money to pay for them will be available. If the automobile performs as expected, you will be able to use the money in other ways. Most people spend less on repair costs than they would be charged for a service contract.

Determining a Purchase Price

Traditionally, car buyers negotiated prices. However, more and more auto dealers are experimenting with various forms of one-price selling.

Price Bargaining   Start price bargaining by comparing the prices of similar automobiles at several dealers. This information provides background on selling prices in relation to the sticker price. Be prepared to be flexible about the car you choose. Your determination to buy a specific make, model, and style weakens your negotiating position.

Use dealer's cost information to get a vehicle price that is only a couple of hundred dollars over the dealer's cost. The closer your price is to the dealer's cost, the better the deal you are getting. Don't be fooled by a price far below the sticker price; the dealer's cost is the number that should be of concern.

Will you receive a better deal by purchasing a car off the lot or by ordering one from the factory? The answer is not clear. Selling a car in stock helps a dealer clear inventory; however, you may not get a good price deal on the car if it is in high demand among potential buyers. Moreover, the car on the lot may have options you don't want. Ordering a car means waiting several weeks or months, but it eliminates the dealer's inventory carrying cost.

To prevent confusion in determining the true price of the new car, do not mention a trade-in vehicle until the cost of the new car has been settled. Then ask how much the dealer is willing to pay for your old car. If the offer price is not acceptable, sell the old car on your own.

A typical negotiating conversation might go like this:

Customer: "I'm willing to give you $15,600 for the car. That's my top offer."
Auto salesperson: "Let me check with my manager." After returning, "My manager says $16,200 is the best we can do."
Customer (who should be willing to walk out at this point): "I can go to $15,650."
Auto salesperson: "We have the car you want, ready to go. How about $15,700?"

If the customer agrees, the dealer has gotten $100 more than the customer's "top offer!"

Set-Price Dealers   An increasing number of auto dealers and manufacturers now use no-haggling car selling. The prices are presented for customers to accept or reject as stated. Instead of spending time negotiating price, emphasis shifts to the features and benefits of the vehicle. Some believe this method of selling cars may result in realistic sticker prices. However, resistance to this approach comes from customers who like to negotiate and competitors who undercut one-price dealers.

FINANCIAL PLANNING FOR LIFE'S SITUATIONS

MOTOR VEHICLE SALES TECHNIQUES

Be cautious. To avoid buying a vehicle you do not want or cannot afford, be on guard for situations like these:

- "My manager won't approve this deal. But if you are willing to pay for shipping, we have a deal." *Lowballing* occurs when a new-car buyer is quoted a very low price that increases when add-on costs are included at the last moment.

- "We can easily give you $8,000 on your trade-in. That's more than $1,200 above its market value." *Highballing* occurs when a new-car buyer is offered a very high amount for a trade-in vehicle, with the extra amount made up by increasing the new-car price.

- "How much can you afford per month?" Be sure to also ask how many months. Also, compare the total finance charge and annual percentage rate (APR) among different lenders.

- "What will it take to put you in this car today?" "I have this car ready for you today." "Take it overnight and see how you like it." Each of these types of subtle pressure is designed to lower your guard and give the seller an edge in negotiating a deal.

- "A small deposit will hold this vehicle for you." Never leave a deposit unless you are ready to buy a vehicle or are willing to lose that amount. Very few dealers will refund a deposit.

- "Your price is only $100 above our cost." However, many hidden costs may have been added in to get the dealer's cost.

- "You can have this $8,000 car for $7,000 with our 12 percent financing over five years." The total cost of the vehicle will be over $9,300. Once again, compare financing terms among different lenders.

Beware of sales agreements with preprinted amounts. Cross out numbers you believe are not appropriate for your purchase. One story has it that a car salesperson had $500 stored in the memory of his calculator. That amount was automatically added to the total vehicle price, unless the customer noticed.

Set prices may also mean a "value pricing" approach in which a manufacturer offers a vehicle equipped with popular options and priced close to the dealer's cost. However, this set selling price may not give the best deal. Therefore, some dealers will negotiate the supposedly nonnegotiable price.

Car Buying Services   You may also consider a *car buying service,* a business that helps you obtain a specific new car at a reasonable price with minimal effort. Also referred to as an *auto broker,* such a business offers desired models with options for prices ranging between $50 and $200 over the dealer's cost. First, the auto broker charges a small fee for price information on desired models. Then, if you decide to buy a car, the auto broker arranges the purchase with a dealer near your home. Car buying services are frequently available through credit unions, churches, community organizations, and motor clubs. In recent years, about 15 to 20 percent of all motor vehicles were purchased using a buying service or broker.

Online Car Buying   At first, the World Wide Web was a dynamic source of auto buying information. As this marketplace of ideas has expanded to a marketplace of products, consumers can now buy a car online. Several car buying services have set up shop on the Internet. In addition, some traditional dealers have set up Web sites to attract customers from outside their usual geographic areas.

The Sales Agreement   Before the sale is completed, you must sign a *sales agreement,* a legal document that contains the specific details of an automobile purchase. As with any contract, make sure you understand the sales agreement before signing. Also, be sure everything you expect from the deal is presented in the sales agreement. If an item isn't in writing, you have no assurance it will be included.

The sales agreement or another receipt will serve as proof of any deposit you pay. Obtain in writing the conditions that would allow you to get back your deposit. Make your deposit as small as possible to cut your losses in case you cancel the deal and are unable to get a refund.

Consumer Protection for New-Car Buyers

New-car warranties provide buyers with some assurance of quality. These warranties vary in the time and mileage of the protection they offer and in the parts they cover. The main conditions of a warranty are (1) coverage of basic parts against manufacturer's defects; (2) power train coverage for the engine, transmission, and drive train; and (3) the corrosion warranty, which usually applies only to holes due to rust, not to surface rust. Other important conditions of a warranty are a statement regarding whether the warranty is transferable to other owners of the car and details about the charges, if any, that will be made for major repairs in the form of a *deductible.*

In the past, when major problems occurred with a new car and the warranty didn't solve the difficulty, many consumers lacked a course of action. As a result, all 50 states and the District of Columbia enacted *lemon laws* that require a refund for the vehicle after the owner has made repeated attempts to obtain servicing. In general, these laws apply to situations in which a person has made four attempts to get the same problem corrected and situations in which the vehicle has been out of service for more than 30 days within 12 months of purchase or the first 12,000 miles. The terms of the state laws vary; contact your state consumer protection office for details (see Appendix E). The lemon laws resulted in various arbitration programs of automobile manufacturers, which were discussed in the chapter.

Financing an Automobile Purchase

You may pay cash for your car. However, as motor vehicles increase in cost, many people buy them on credit.

Financing Sources   As discussed in Chapter 7, car loans are available from banks, credit unions, consumer finance companies, and other financial institutions. Many lenders will *preapprove* you for a certain loan amount. This lets you know how much you can afford to spend. Preapproval also separates financing from negotiating the price of the car. Until the new-car price is set, you should not indicate that you intend to use the dealer's credit plan. Studies have revealed that low-cost loans are frequently offset by increased vehicle prices.

Dealer financing is another option. In an effort to make automobile buying more attractive, General Motors Acceptance Corporation, Ford Motor Credit Company, and Chrysler Financial Corporation have created credit plans such as balloon payment loans, variable-rate loans, and special loans for recent college graduates. With a *balloon payment loan,* which is illegal in some states, you make payments smaller than the payments on a regular loan for 48 months. After 48 months, you have the option to (*a*) continue to make payments until the balance has been paid; (*b*) return the car to the dealer for a fee; or (*c*) sell the car, pay off the loan, and keep any leftover funds.

Obtaining the Best Financing   The lowest interest rate or the lowest payment does not necessarily mean the best credit plan. Select the length of your auto loan carefully. Otherwise, after two or three years the value of your car may be less than the amount you

EXHIBIT 8–B

Comparing Rebates and Special Financing: An Example

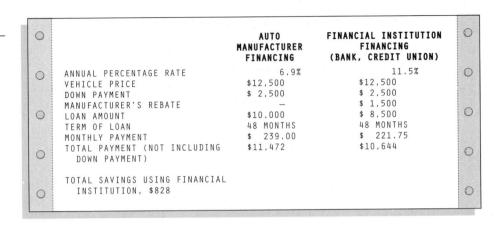

	AUTO MANUFACTURER FINANCING	FINANCIAL INSTITUTION FINANCING (BANK, CREDIT UNION)
ANNUAL PERCENTAGE RATE	6.9%	11.5%
VEHICLE PRICE	$12,500	$12,500
DOWN PAYMENT	$ 2,500	$ 2,500
MANUFACTURER'S REBATE	—	$ 1,500
LOAN AMOUNT	$10,000	$ 8,500
TERM OF LOAN	48 MONTHS	48 MONTHS
MONTHLY PAYMENT	$ 239.00	$ 221.75
TOTAL PAYMENT (NOT INCLUDING DOWN PAYMENT)	$11,472	$10,644

TOTAL SAVINGS USING FINANCIAL INSTITUTION, $828

still owe; this situation is referred to as *upside-down* or *negative equity*. If you default on your loan or sell the car at this time, you will have to pay the difference—a very unpleasant situation!

The annual percentage rate (APR) is the best indicator of the true cost of credit. The federal truth in lending law requires that the APR be clearly stated in advertising and other communications. Low payments may seem to be a good deal, but they mean you will be paying longer and your total finance charges will be higher. Consider both the APR and the finance charge when comparing credit terms of different lenders.

Automobile manufacturers frequently offer opportunities for low-interest financing. They may offer rebates at the same time, giving buyers a choice between a rebate and a low-interest loan. Carefully compare low-interest financing and the rebate (see Exhibit 8–B). Special rebates are sometimes offered to students, teachers, credit union members, real estate agents, and other groups.

LEASING A MOTOR VEHICLE

In the past, doctors, lawyers, and small-business owners were about the only people who leased. In recent years, more than one-fourth of all cars and small trucks went out the door under lease. When federal tax laws eliminated deductions for consumer loan interest and sales tax, buying an automobile had fewer financial benefits and leasing became more attractive in some situations. *Leasing* is a contractual agreement with monthly payments for the use of an automobile over a set time period, typically three, four, or five years. At the end of the lease term, the vehicle is usually returned to the leasing company.

Advantages of Leasing

The main advantages of leasing a vehicle include the following:

- Leasing requires only a small cash outflow for the security deposit, usually amounting to two monthly payments, whereas buying can require a large cash outflow for the purchase price or a down payment.
- The monthly lease payments are usually lower than monthly financing payments for a purchased automobile.
- The lease agreement provides detailed records for people who use their automobiles for business purposes.

Disadvantages of Leasing

Common drawbacks of automobile leasing include the following:

- You have no ownership interest in the vehicle.
- You must meet requirements similar to those for qualifying for credit.
- You may have additional costs for extra mileage, certain repairs, turning the car in early, or even a move to another state.

Types of Leases

With a *closed-end,* or "walk-away," lease, the most common type, you return the vehicle at the end of the lease after paying any additional costs for damage or extra mileage. This type of lease commits you for the full term; getting out early will probably require a large fee. Since you have no risk with regard to the residual value of the car, your payments are higher with a closed-end lease than with an open-end lease.

An *open-end,* or "finance," lease, which is easier to terminate than a closed-end lease, may require you to pay the difference between the expected value of the leased automobile and the amount for which the leasing company sells it. The current market value will probably be determined by an independent appraiser. If the appraised value is equal to or greater than the estimated ending value specified in the lease, you will not owe an additional amount. However, if the appraised value is less than that value, you will be required to make an *end-of-lease* payment.

The *single-payment* lease allows customers to obtain a discount on the motor vehicle rental agreement. The manufacturer or finance company reduces its default risk and administrative costs. The customer must decide whether the discount available with this prepaid lease is worth the lost earnings (opportunity costs) from savings.

Financial Decision
Trade-Off

Financial Aspects of Leasing

When leasing, you arrange for the dealer to sell the vehicle through a financing company. As a result, be sure you know the true cost, including

1. The *capitalized cost,* which is the price of the vehicle. The average car buyer pays about 92 percent of the list price for a vehicle; the average leasing arrangement has a capitalized cost of 96 percent of the list price.
2. The *money factor,* which is the interest rate being paid on the capitalized cost.
3. The monthly payment and number of payments.
4. The *residual value,* or the expected value of the vehicle at the end of the lease. After the final payment, you may need to decide whether to return, keep, or sell the vehicle. If the current market value is greater than the residual value, you may be able to sell it for a profit. If the residual value is less than the market value (which is the typical case), returning the vehicle to the leasing company is usually the best decision. However, you may want to buy the vehicle for continued use.

A recommended guideline for evaluating leases is the "2 percent rule." A two-year, no-money-down lease may be a good deal if the monthly payment is 2 percent or less of the car's suggested retail price. After this guideline is met, you should investigate other terms of the lease.

Individuals who lease automobiles are protected by the Consumer Leasing Act, administered by the Federal Trade Commission, which requires disclosure of various terms and conditions of the leasing agreement (see Exhibit 8–C).

EXHIBIT 8–C

Terms and Conditions of an Automobile Lease

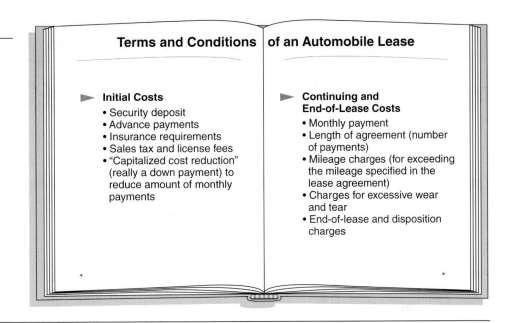

Terms and Conditions of an Automobile Lease

▶ **Initial Costs**
- Security deposit
- Advance payments
- Insurance requirements
- Sales tax and license fees
- "Capitalized cost reduction" (really a down payment) to reduce amount of monthly payments

▶ **Continuing and End-of-Lease Costs**
- Monthly payment
- Length of agreement (number of payments)
- Mileage charges (for exceeding the mileage specified in the lease agreement)
- Charges for excessive wear and tear
- End-of-lease and disposition charges

Avoiding Lease Traps

When considering a lease agreement for a motor vehicle, beware of the following common pitfalls:

- Not knowing the total cost of the agreement, including the cost of the vehicle, not just the monthly payment.
- Making a larger up-front payment than is required or paying unnecessary add-on costs.
- Negotiating the monthly payment rather than the capitalized cost of the vehicle.
- Not having the value of any trade-in vehicle reflected in the lease.
- Signing a contract you don't understand.

PFP

Sheet 38

Compare monthly payments and other terms among several leasing companies. People have been known to pay over $24,000 to lease a vehicle that was worth only $20,000 at the start of the lease agreement. Comparison of leasing terms is available with online computer services. For further information, see Appendix B. The Financial Planning in Action feature on page 260 provides a guideline for comparing buying and leasing.

FINANCIAL ASPECTS OF AUTOMOBILE OWNERSHIP

Most people spend more of their income on transportation than on any other item except housing and food. For many households, when insurance, license plates, and road taxes are included, the amount spent on an automobile also exceeds the amount spent on food. Over a period of 50 years, you can expect to spend over $200,000 on automobile costs, more than seven times the amount an average person spends on education.

FINANCIAL PLANNING IN ACTION

BUYING VERSUS LEASING AN AUTOMOBILE

To compare the costs of purchasing and leasing a vehicle, use the following framework.

Purchase Costs	Example	Your Figures	Leasing Costs	Example	Your Figures
Total vehicle cost, including sales tax ($15,000)			Security deposit ($300)		
Down payment (or full amount if paying cash)	$ 2,000	$_____	Monthly lease payments: $300 × 48-month length of lease	$14,400	$_____
Monthly loan payment: $336 × 48-month length of financing (this item is zero if vehicle is not financed)	16,128	_____	Opportunity cost of security deposit: $300 security deposit × 4 years × 6 percent	72	_____
Opportunity cost of down payment (or total cost of the vehicle if it is bought for cash): $2,000 × 4 years of financing/ownership × 6 percent	480	_____	End-of-lease charges (if applicable)*	1,500	_____
Less: Estimated value of vehicle at end of loan term/ownership period	−3,000	_____	Total cost to lease	$15,972	_____
Total cost to buy	$15,608	_____			

*With a closed-end lease, charges for extra mileage or excessive wear and tear; with an open-end lease, end-of-lease payment if appraised value is less than estimated ending value.

Automobile Operating Costs

Your driving costs will vary based on two main factors: the size of your automobile and the number of miles you drive. The American Automobile Association recently estimated that, given an annual mileage of 10,000, a subcompact would cost 39.8 cents a mile, a midsize car 46.6 cents, and a full-size car 58.4 cents. These cost estimates are obtained by considering two categories of expenses:

Fixed Ownership Costs	Variable Operating Costs
Depreciation	Gasoline and oil
Interest on auto loan	Tires
Insurance	Maintenance and repairs
License, registration, taxes, and fees	Parking and tolls

Fixed Ownership Costs   The largest fixed expense associated with a new automobile is *depreciation,* the loss in the vehicle's value due to time and use. For example, federal tax guidelines assume a motor vehicle depreciates 52 percent during the first two years of its expected five-year life. For a $15,000 car, that means someone who can deduct the cost of the vehicle for tax purposes would have $7,800 in business expenses over the first two years.

Since money is not paid out for depreciation, many people do not consider it an expense. However, this decreased value of an automobile is a cost that owners incur as time goes by.

While depreciation is considered a fixed cost of automobile ownership, the actual amount of the decreased value depends on two factors: the extent to which the automobile is used and the care taken to maintain it. Low-mileage, well-maintained automobiles retain a larger portion of their original value than do other automobiles. Also, certain high-quality, expensive models, such as BMWs and Cadillacs, depreciate at a slower rate than other models. Not all automobiles depreciate. Very old vehicles in excellent condition may even *appreciate,* or increase in value.

Another fixed ownership cost is the interest charged when financing an automobile purchase. This charge is based on the loan amount, the interest rate, and the length of the loan.

Other fixed costs associated with automobile ownership are insurance, license and registration fees, and taxes. Fixed costs are easier to anticipate than variable costs.

Sheet 39

Variable Operating Costs   Some automobile expenses vary in relation to the extent of use. Costs such as gasoline, oil, and tires increase with the number of miles an automobile is driven. Planning for these expenses is easier if the number of miles you drive during a given period of time is fairly constant. Unexpected trips will increase such costs.

As a car gets older, maintenance and repair costs usually increase. Expect to replace relatively low-priced components such as fan belts, hoses, the battery, or the muffler. Budgeting an amount for more costly repairs, such as repair of brakes, can minimize the financial burden.

Automobile Expense Records   An awareness of the total cost of owning and operating an automobile can help your overall financial planning. An automobile expense record should include the dates of odometer readings. Recording your mileage each time you buy gas will allow you to compute fuel efficiency. For tax-deductible travel, the Internal Revenue Service requires specific information about the mileage, locations, dates, and purposes of trips. Use a notebook to keep records of regular operating expenses such as gas, oil, parking, and tolls. Also, consider keeping files on maintenance, repair, and replacement part costs. Finally, keep a record of infrequent expenditures such as insurance payments and license and registration fees (see Exhibit 8–D).

Proper Maintenance

People who sell, repair, or drive automobiles for a living stress the importance of regular vehicle care. While owner's manuals and articles suggest mileage or time intervals for certain servicing, more frequent oil changes or tune-ups can minimize major repairs and maximize the life of your car.

Automotive systems that should be monitored and maintained on a regular basis are the engine, cooling system, transmission, brakes, steering mechanism, exhaust components, and suspension. Exhibit 8–E presents additional details on automobile maintenance. This figure is not intended to be a complete guide; however, it should serve as a reminder of areas that could result in expensive problems.

Automobile Servicing Sources

A variety of businesses offer automobile maintenance and repair service.

Car Dealers   The service department of a car dealer offers a wide range of car care services. Since car dealers are required to perform routine maintenance, major repairs, and

EXHIBIT 8–D

Estimating Annual Automobile Ownership and Operating Costs

Model year _____ *1999* _____   Make, Size, Model _____ FORD TAURUS _____

Fixed Ownership Costs	Variable Operating Costs

Fixed Ownership Costs

1. Depreciation
$ *18,000* purchase price divided by *6* years estimated life of vehicle* $ *3,000*

2. Interest on Auto Loan
Cost of financing the vehicle if buying on credit $ *100*

3. Insurance
Cost of liability and property insurance on the vehicle for the year $ *600*

4. License, Registration Fee, and Taxes
Cost of registering vehicle for state and city license fees $ *50*

Variable Operating Costs

5. Gasoline
12,000 estimated miles per year divided by *24* miles per gallon times the $ *1.44* average price of gasoline per gallon $ *720*

6. Oil Changes
Cost of regular oil changes during the year $ *54*

7. Tires
Cost of tires purchased during the year $ *110*

8. Maintenance/Repairs
Cost of planned or other expected maintenance $ *156*

9. Parking and Tolls
Regular fees for parking and highway toll charges $ *310*

Total Fixed Costs	$ *4,350*	
Divided by miles driven equals fixed cost per mile	*36.25* ¢	

Total Variable Costs	$ *1,350*	
Divided by miles driven equals variable cost per mile	*11.25* ¢	

Total Costs	$ *5,700*	
Divided by miles driven equals total cost per mile	*47.5* ¢	

*This estimate of vehicle depreciation is based on a *straight-line* approach—equal depreciation each year. A more realistic approach would be larger amounts in the early years of ownership, such as 25 to 30 percent the first year and 30 to 35 percent the second year. Most cars lose 90 percent of their value by the time they are seven years old.

body work, they have a complete inventory of parts for most vehicles. The charges by car dealers for servicing may be higher than those of other repair businesses.

Service Stations   Gas stations may provide convenience and reasonable prices for routine maintenance and repairs. However, the number of full-service stations has declined due to lower profits and competition from other automobile servicing businesses. Today most people buy gas at a combination gas station and convenience store. For automobile servicing, drivers must consider other alternatives.

EXHIBIT 8–E   **Extended Vehicle Life through Proper Maintenance**

- Regular oil changes
- Check fluids (brake, power steering, transmission)
- Inspect hoses and belts for wear
- Tune-up (new spark plugs, fuel filter, air filter) every 12,000–15,000 miles
- Check and clean battery cables and terminals
- Check spark plug wires after 50,000 miles

- Flush radiator and service transmission every 25,000 miles
- Keep lights, turn signals, horn in working condition
- Check muffler and exhaust pipes
- Check tires for wear; rotate tires every 7,500 miles
- Check condition of brakes

Automobile Repair Shops   Independent repair shops serve a wide variety of automobile servicing needs at fairly competitive prices. As with any service, the quality of these repair shops varies. Talk with previous customers before selecting an automobile repair shop.

Department and Discount Stores   Mass merchandise retailers such as Sears and Kmart offer convenient automobile service. These retailers usually emphasize the sale of tires, batteries, mufflers, and other replacement parts. They also replace brakes and do oil changes and tune-ups.

Specialty Shops   These limited-service businesses offer a single product or service at a reasonable price with fast results. Mufflers, tires, automatic transmissions, and oil changes are among the items specialty businesses provide.

Since automobile maintenance and repairs can be expensive, be sure to seek out competent service for your money. To avoid unnecessary expense, be aware of the common repair frauds presented in Exhibit 8–F. Remember to deal with reputable auto service businesses. Be sure to get a written, detailed estimate in advance as well as a detailed, paid receipt for the service completed. Studies of consumer problems consistently rank auto repairs as one of the top consumer ripoffs.

Many people avoid problems and minimize costs by working on their own vehicles. This can save money for routine maintenance and minor repairs such as oil changes, tune-ups, and replacement of belts, hoses, and batteries. Many books on automobile servicing are available at libraries and bookstores. Also, some high schools and community colleges offer basic automobile maintenance courses.

Selling Your Automobile

At some time, you may be on the selling side of an automobile transaction. The decision to sell a car on your own may result from a low trade-in offer from a dealer. The selling process starts with awareness of documents you must file with your state vehicle registration department. Contact this agency to obtain the necessary forms as well as information about the regulations that affect the sale of an automobile.

Use current advertisements in local newspapers, along with the used-car price guides discussed earlier, to assist you in setting a sales price. Maintenance and minor repairs will help improve your car's appearance and increase its value and customer appeal.

Next, make others aware of the car. Put a "for sale" sign, with a telephone number on it, in a location that will allow many people to see it. Information about the car can be distributed through store, church, or community bulletin boards. Advertisements in local newspapers will increase the number of people who are aware that the car is for sale.

Exhibit 8–F

**Common
Automobile
Repair Frauds**

The majority of automobile servicing sources are fair and honest. Sometimes, however, consumers waste dollars when they fall prey to the following tricks:

- When checking the oil, the attendant puts the dipstick only partway down and then shows you that you need oil.
- An attendant cuts a fan belt or punctures a hose. Watch carefully when someone checks under your hood.
- A garage employee puts some liquid on your battery and then tries to convince you that it is leaking and you need a new battery.
- Removing air from a tire instead of adding air to it can make an unwary driver open to buying a new tire or paying for an unneeded patch on a tire that is in perfect condition.
- The attendant puts grease near a shock absorber or on the ground and then tells you your present shocks are dangerous and you need new ones.
- You are charged for two gallons of antifreeze with a radiator flush when only one gallon was put in.

Dealing with reputable businesses and having a basic knowledge of your automobile are the best methods of avoiding deceptive repair practices.

Ask people who express interest in buying your car to provide you with their addresses and telephone numbers, and have them make appointments to see and test-drive the car. As a precaution, be sure to accompany prospective buyers on the road test. If you have kept a file of maintenance and repair receipts, use this information to document the condition of the car. In negotiating price, consider the condition, mileage, and potential demand for the vehicle.

When completing the transaction, be sure to meet the associated legal requirements, such as the payment of title, vehicle registration, and other fees. To avoid getting a bad check or handling large amounts of cash, insist that the car be paid for with a cashier's check or a money order. Provide the buyer with a receipt containing the details of the transaction.

CHAPTER 9

THE FINANCES OF HOUSING

Opening Case

TWO CAN BUY MORE CHEAPLY THAN ONE

During a time when mortgage rates were very high, Nina Cortez and her sister, Cathy, were unable to buy the home they desired. Their parents had given them $3,000 for a down payment, but that amount was not enough for the type of house they wanted.

After finishing college, Nina rented an apartment for seven years. During that time, she was able to save $8,000 for a down payment on a home. Also, she now earns enough money from her job to be able to afford the monthly costs of a home.

Cathy, recently divorced, has less than $3,000 in savings. Despite her weak financial situation, Cathy wants a home for herself and her son.

During the past eight months, mortgage rates in their region of the country fell 1.5 percentage points. Nina and Cathy have decided to combine their resources to purchase a home. The *co-ownership* arrangement allows them to buy a home valued at $12,000 more than the home they could have afforded a year ago.

However, Nina and Cathy had better ask themselves a few questions before buying a home. What happens to the house if one of them marries or accepts a job transfer to another city? What if one of them can no longer meet the financial requirements of the home? How will they share maintenance responsibilities and costs? Nina and Cathy need to answer these questions before entering a co-ownership housing arrangement.

QUESTIONS

1. What factors affect a person's ability to buy a house?
2. What are common sources for a down payment?
3. Why should home buyers not use all of their savings to make the down payment on a home?
4. What problems could arise in a co-ownership housing arrangement?

After studying this chapter, you will be able to

L.O.1	Evaluate available housing alternatives.		*L.O.4*	Calculate the costs associated with purchasing a home.
L.O.2	Analyze the costs and benefits associated with renting.		*L.O.5*	Develop a strategy for selling a home.
L.O.3	Implement the home-buying process.			

EVALUATING HOUSING ALTERNATIVES

L.O.1 Evaluate available housing alternatives.

As you walk in various neighborhoods, you are likely to see a variety of housing types. As you assess housing alternatives, you need to identify the factors that will influence your choice. Your needs, lifestyle, and financial resources will determine whether you decide to rent, buy, or have a home built.

Your Lifestyle and Your Choice of Housing

While the concept of lifestyle—how you spend your time and money—may seem intangible, it materializes in your consumer purchases. Every buying decision is a statement about your lifestyle. Your lifestyle, needs, desires, and attitudes are reflected in your choice of a place to live. For example, some people want a kitchen large enough for family gatherings. Career-oriented people may want a lavish bathroom or a home spa where they can escape the pressures of work. Among the lifestyle factors that influence housing choices are status, fashion, individualism, and ecological concerns. As you select housing, you might consider the alternatives in Exhibit 9–1 on page 268.

While personal preferences are the foundation of a housing decision, financial factors may modify the final choice. Traditional financial guidelines suggest that "you should spend no more than 25 or 30 percent of your take-home pay on housing" or "your home should cost about 2½ times your annual income." While changes in our economy and our society no longer make these guidelines completely valid, you need some sort of financial guideline to determine the amount to spend on housing. A budget and other financial records discussed in Chapter 3 can help you evaluate your income, living costs, and other financial obligations to determine an appropriate amount for your housing expenses.

Sheet 40

Opportunity Costs of Housing Choices

While the selection of housing is usually based on life situation and financial factors, also consider what you might have to give up. The opportunity costs of your housing decision will vary; however, some common trade-offs include

267

EXHIBIT 9–1

Different Housing for Different Life Situations

Life Situation	Possible Housing Types
Young single	Rental housing requires limited maintenance activities and offers mobility in the event of a job transfer
	Purchase a home or a condominium for financial and tax benefits
Single parent	Rental housing provides a suitable environment for children and some degree of home security
	Purchase low-maintenance housing that meets the financial and social needs of family members
Young couple, no children	Rental housing offers convenience and flexibility of lifestyle
	Purchase housing for financial benefits and to build long-term financial security
Couple, young children	Rental housing can provide appropriate facilities for children in a family-oriented area
	Purchase a home to meet financial and other family needs
Couple, children no longer at home	Rental housing offers convenience and flexibility for changing needs and financial situations
	Purchase housing that requires minimal maintenance and meets lifestyle needs
Retired person	Rental housing can meet financial, social, and physical needs
	Purchase housing that requires minimal maintenance, offers convenience, and provides needed services

Financial Decision
Trade-Off

- The interest earnings lost on the money used for a down payment on a home.
- The interest lost on the security deposit for an apartment.
- The time and cost of commuting to work when you live in an area that offers less expensive housing or more living space.
- The loss of tax advantages and equity growth when you rent a city apartment to be close to your work.
- The time and money you spend when you repair and improve a lower-priced home.
- The time and effort involved when you have a home built to your personal specifications.

Like every other financial choice, a housing decision requires consideration of what you give up in time, effort, and money.

Renting versus Buying Housing

PFP

Sheet 41

The choice between renting and buying your residence is fundamental. You may resolve this dilemma by evaluating various lifestyle and financial factors. Exhibit 9–2 can help you assess renting and buying alternatives. Mobility is a primary motivator of renters, while buyers usually want permanence.

As you can see in the Financial Planning in Action feature on page 270, the choice between renting and buying is usually not clear-cut. In general, renting is less costly in the short run, but homeownership also has financial advantages.

Housing Information Sources

As with other consumer purchases, housing information is available. Start your data search with basic resources such as this book and books available in libraries. Consult the real estate section of your newspaper for articles about renting, buying, financing, remodeling,

EXHIBIT 9–2

Evaluating Housing Alternatives

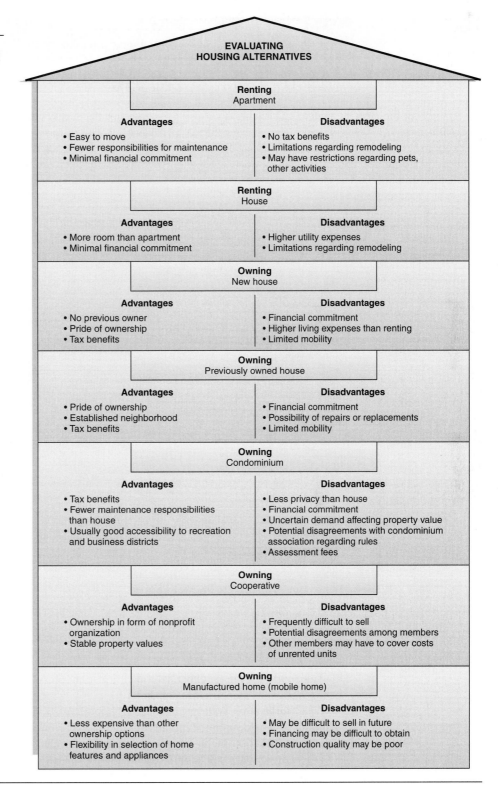

EVALUATING
HOUSING ALTERNATIVES

Renting
Apartment

Advantages	Disadvantages
• Easy to move • Fewer responsibilities for maintenance • Minimal financial commitment	• No tax benefits • Limitations regarding remodeling • May have restrictions regarding pets, other activities

Renting
House

Advantages	Disadvantages
• More room than apartment • Minimal financial commitment	• Higher utility expenses • Limitations regarding remodeling

Owning
New house

Advantages	Disadvantages
• No previous owner • Pride of ownership • Tax benefits	• Financial commitment • Higher living expenses than renting • Limited mobility

Owning
Previously owned house

Advantages	Disadvantages
• Pride of ownership • Established neighborhood • Tax benefits	• Financial commitment • Possibility of repairs or replacements • Limited mobility

Owning
Condominium

Advantages	Disadvantages
• Tax benefits • Fewer maintenance responsibilities than house • Usually good accessibility to recreation and business districts	• Less privacy than house • Financial commitment • Uncertain demand affecting property value • Potential disagreements with condominium association regarding rules • Assessment fees

Owning
Cooperative

Advantages	Disadvantages
• Ownership in form of nonprofit organization • Stable property values	• Frequently difficult to sell • Potential disagreements among members • Other members may have to cover costs of unrented units

Owning
Manufactured home (mobile home)

Advantages	Disadvantages
• Less expensive than other ownership options • Flexibility in selection of home features and appliances	• May be difficult to sell in future • Financing may be difficult to obtain • Construction quality may be poor

FINANCIAL PLANNING IN ACTION

RENTING VERSUS BUYING YOUR PLACE OF RESIDENCE

Comparing the costs of renting and buying involves consideration of a variety of factors. The following framework and example provide a basis for assessing these two housing alternatives. The apartment in the example has a monthly rent of $700, and the home costs $85,000. A 29 percent tax rate is assumed.

Although the numbers in this example favor buying, remember that in any financial decision, calculations provide only part of the answer. You should also consider your needs and values and assess the opportunity costs associated with renting and buying.

	Example	Your Figures
Rental Costs		
Annual rent payments	$ 8,400	$ _____
Renter's insurance	170	_____
Interest lost on security deposit (amount of security deposit		
times after-tax savings account interest rate)	80	_____
Total annual cost of renting	$ 8,650	_____
Buying Costs		
Annual mortgage payments	$10,500	_____
Property taxes (annual costs)	2,000	_____
Homeowner's insurance (annual premium)	400	_____
Estimated maintenance and repairs (1%)	850	_____
After-tax interest lost on down payment and closing costs	1,030	_____
Less (financial benefits of home ownership):		
Growth in equity	−264	_____
Tax savings for mortgage interest (annual mortgage interest times tax rate)	−2,866	_____
Tax savings for property taxes (annual property taxes times tax rate)	−560	_____
Estimated annual appreciation (3%)*	−2,550	_____
Total annual cost of buying	$ 8,540	_____

*This is a nationwide average; actual appreciation of property will vary by geographic area and economic conditions.

and other housing topics. Other helpful information sources are friends, real estate agents, and government agencies (see Appendix E).

The World Wide Web has become an important source of housing information. In addition to providing home-buying tips and mortgage rates, online sites can be used to access available housing in an area. For example, the *Chicago Tribune* real estate section is available at www.chicago.tribune.com/homes. Many real estate Web sites include video presentations of both rental units and homes for sale. A home buyer can easily view properties and judge them based on factors such as location, price range, desired number of rooms, and other features. As banks and other financial institutions expand online services, the mortgage application process is also being handled through Web sites.

Concept Check 9–1

1. How does a person's employment and household situation influence the selection of housing?
2. What are some common opportunity costs associated with the selection of housing?

RENTING YOUR RESIDENCE

L.O.2 Analyze the costs and benefits associated with renting.

Are you interested in a "2-bd. garden apt, a/c, crptg, mod bath, lndry, sec $850"? Not sure? Translated, this means a two-bedroom garden apartment (at or below ground level) with air conditioning, carpeting, a modern bath, and laundry facilities. An $850 security deposit is required.

At some point in your life, you are likely to rent your place of residence. You may rent when you are first on your own and cannot afford to buy a home or later in life when you want to avoid the activities required to maintain your own home. About 35 percent of U.S. households live in rental units.

As a tenant, you pay for the right to live in a residence owned by someone else. Exhibit 9–3 on page 272 presents the activities involved in finding and living in a rental unit.

Selecting a Rental Unit

An apartment is the most common type of rental housing. Apartments range from modern, luxury units with extensive recreational facilities to simple one- and two-bedroom units in quiet neighborhoods.

If you need more room, you should consider renting a house. The increased space will cost more, and you will probably have more responsibility for maintaining the property. If you need less space, you may rent a room in a house, over a garage, or in a basement.

The main sources of information on available rental units are newspaper ads, real estate and rental offices, and people you know. When comparing rental units, consider the factors presented in Exhibit 9–4 on page 273.

Advantages of Renting

The three main advantages of renting are mobility, fewer responsibilities, and lower initial costs.

Mobility   Renting offers mobility when a location change is necessary or desirable. A new job, a rent increase, the need for a larger apartment, or the desire to live in a different community can make relocation necessary. It is easier to move when you are renting than when you own a home. After you have completed school and started your career, renting makes it easier for you to move to meet job transfer demands.

Financial Decision Trade-Off

Fewer Responsibilities   Renters have fewer responsibilities than homeowners because they usually do not have to be concerned with maintenance and repairs. However, they are expected to do regular household cleaning. Renters also have fewer financial concerns. Their main housing costs are rent and utilities, while homeowners incur expenses related to property taxes and upkeep.

EXHIBIT 9–3   **Housing Rental Activities**

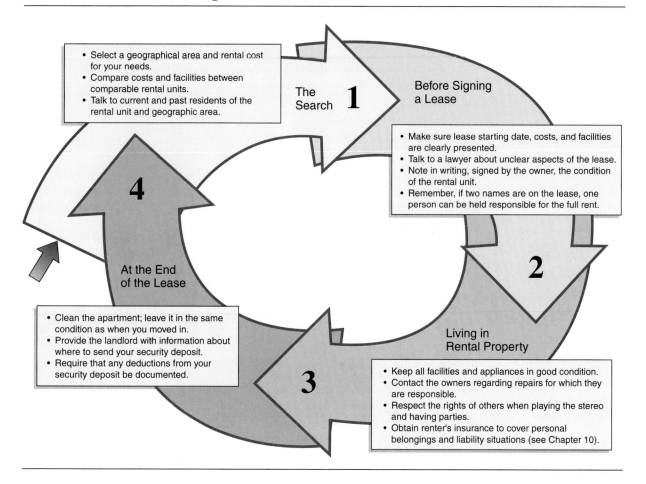

- Select a geographical area and rental cost for your needs.
- Compare costs and facilities between comparable rental units.
- Talk to current and past residents of the rental unit and geographic area.

The Search **1**

Before Signing a Lease

- Make sure lease starting date, costs, and facilities are clearly presented.
- Talk to a lawyer about unclear aspects of the lease.
- Note in writing, signed by the owner, the condition of the rental unit.
- Remember, if two names are on the lease, one person can be held responsible for the full rent.

4

At the End of the Lease

- Clean the apartment; leave it in the same condition as when you moved in.
- Provide the landlord with information about where to send your security deposit.
- Require that any deductions from your security deposit be documented.

2

Living in Rental Property

3

- Keep all facilities and appliances in good condition.
- Contact the owners regarding repairs for which they are responsible.
- Respect the rights of others when playing the stereo and having parties.
- Obtain renter's insurance to cover personal belongings and liability situations (see Chapter 10).

Lower Initial Costs   It is less expensive to take possession of a rental unit than to buy a home. While new tenants usually pay a security deposit, a new home buyer is likely to have initial costs of several thousand dollars.

Disadvantages of Renting

Renting offers few financial benefits, imposes a restricted lifestyle, and entails legal concerns.

Few Financial Benefits   Renters do not enjoy the financial advantages homeowners do. They neither receive tax deductions for mortgage interest and property taxes nor benefit from the increased value of real estate. They are subject to rent increases over which they have little control.

Restricted Lifestyle   Renters are generally limited in the types of activities they can pursue in their place of residence. Noise from a stereo system or parties may be monitored closely. Tenants are often subject to restrictions regarding pets and decoration.

EXHIBIT 9–4

Selecting an Apartment

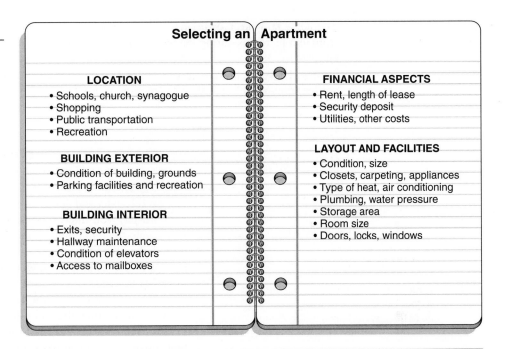

Selecting an Apartment

LOCATION
- Schools, church, synagogue
- Shopping
- Public transportation
- Recreation

BUILDING EXTERIOR
- Condition of building, grounds
- Parking facilities and recreation

BUILDING INTERIOR
- Exits, security
- Hallway maintenance
- Condition of elevators
- Access to mailboxes

FINANCIAL ASPECTS
- Rent, length of lease
- Security deposit
- Utilities, other costs

LAYOUT AND FACILITIES
- Condition, size
- Closets, carpeting, appliances
- Type of heat, air conditioning
- Plumbing, water pressure
- Storage area
- Room size
- Doors, locks, windows

lease

Legal Concerns   Most tenants sign a **lease,** a legal document that defines the conditions of a rental agreement. This document provides the following information:

- A description of the property, including the address.
- The name and address of the owner/landlord (the *lessor*).
- The name of the tenant (the *lessee*).
- The effective date of the lease.
- The length of the lease.
- The amount of the security deposit.
- The amount and due date of the monthly rent.
- The location at which the rent must be paid.
- The date and amount due of charges for late rent payments.
- A list of the utilities, appliances, furniture, or other facilities that are included in the rental amount.
- The restrictions regarding certain activities (pets, remodeling).
- The tenant's right to sublet the rental unit.
- The charges for damages or for moving out of the rental unit later (or earlier) than the lease expiration date.
- The conditions under which the landlord may enter the apartment.

Standard lease forms include conditions you may not want to accept. The fact that a lease is printed does not mean you must accept it as is. Negotiate with the landlord about lease terms you consider unacceptable.

Some leases give you the right to *sublet* the rental unit. Subletting may be necessary if you must vacate the premises before the lease expires. Subletting allows you to have another person take over rent payments and live in the rental unit.

Most leases are written, but oral leases are also valid. With an oral lease, one party must give a 30-day notice to the other party before terminating the lease or imposing a rent increase.

A lease provides protection to both the landlord and the tenant. The tenant is protected from rent increases during the lease term unless the lease contains a provision allowing an increase. In most states, the tenant cannot be locked out or evicted without a court hearing. However, the lease gives the landlord the right to take legal action against a tenant for nonpayment of rent or destruction of property.

Costs of Renting

A *security deposit* is usually required when you sign a lease. This is an amount of money the landlord holds to cover the cost of damages done to the rental unit during the lease period. The security deposit is usually one month's rent.

Several state and local governments require that the landlord pay you interest on your security deposit. After you vacate the rental unit, your security deposit should be refunded within a reasonable time. Many states require that it be returned within 30 days of the end of the lease. If money is deducted from your security deposit, you have the right to an itemized list of the cost of repairs.

As a renter, you will incur other living expenses besides monthly rent. For many apartments, water is covered by the rent; however, other utilities are not. If you rent a house, you will probably pay for heat, electricity, water, and telephone. When you rent, you should obtain insurance coverage for your personal property. Renter's insurance is discussed in Chapter 10.

> ### DID YOU KNOW?
>
> Renter's insurance is one of the most overlooked expenses of people who live in apartments. Damage or theft of personal property (clothing, furniture, stereo equipment, jewelry) is usually not covered by the landlord's insurance policy.

Sheet 42

CONCEPT CHECK 9–2

1. What are the main benefits and drawbacks of renting a place of residence?
2. Which components of a lease are likely to be most negotiable?

THE HOME-BUYING PROCESS

L.O.3 Implement the home-buying process.

Many people dream of having a place of residence they can call their own. Homeownership is a common financial goal. Exhibit 9–5 presents the process for achieving this goal. This section covers the first three steps of the home-buying process; the next section discusses the final two steps.

Step 1: Determine Homeownership Needs

In the first phase of the home-buying process, you should consider the benefits and drawbacks of this major financial commitment. In addition, you should evaluate different types of housing units and determine the amount you can afford.

Evaluate Owning Your Place of Residence

What Are the Benefits of Homeownership?   Whether you purchase a house, a condominium, or a manufactured home, you can enjoy the pride of ownership, financial benefits, and lifestyle flexibility of homeownership.

EXHIBIT 9–5   **The Home Buying Process**

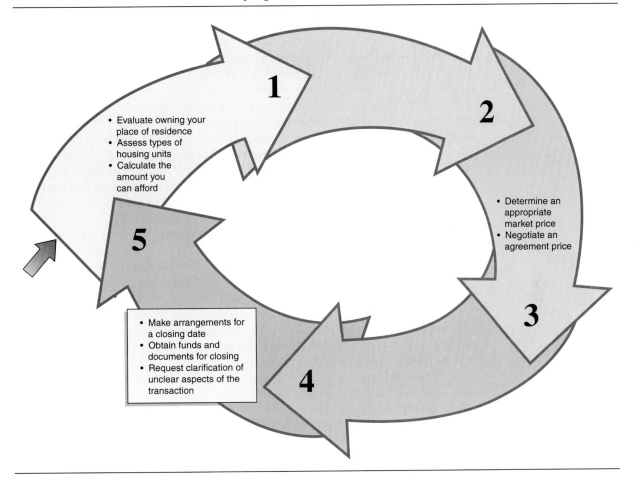

1. *Pride of ownership*. Having a place to call their own is a primary motive of many home buyers. Stability of residence and a personalized living location can be important. Pride of ownership may be reflected in community activities.

2. *Financial benefits*. Homeownership has financial benefits. One benefit is the deductibility of mortgage interest and real estate tax payments for federal income tax purposes. A potential benefit is increases in the value of the property. Finally, homeowners in most states may be able to borrow against the equity in their homes. *Equity* is the home value less the amount owed on the mortgage.

3. *Lifestyle flexibility*. While renting gives you mobility, homeownership gives you more opportunity to express individuality. Homeowners have greater freedom than renters in decorating their dwellings and entertaining guests.

What Are the Drawbacks of Homeownership?   The American dream of buying one's own home does not guarantee a glamorous existence. This investment imposes financial risks, limited mobility, and higher living costs.

1. *Financial risks.* Among the financial risks associated with buying a home is obtaining money for a down payment. Obtaining mortgage financing may also be a problem due to your situation or current economic conditions. Finally, changing property values in an area can affect your financial investment.

2. *Limited mobility.* Homeownership does not provide the ease of changing living location that renting does. If changes in your situation make it necessary for you to sell your home, doing so may be difficult. High interest rates can result in a weak demand for housing.

3. *Higher living costs.* As most homeowners will verify, owning your place of residence can be expensive. The homeowner is responsible for maintenance and costs of repainting, repairs, and home improvements.

Real estate taxes are a major expense of homeowners. When the federal government cuts services in an attempt to reduce its budget, state and local governments have to accept the responsibility for many of these services. The result will be higher property taxes. Even for homeowners who no longer have mortgage payments, higher property values and higher tax rates mean higher real estate taxes. Higher taxes affect homeowners more directly than renters, who pay them in the form of higher rent. It is harder for homeowners to counter the effects of high taxes by moving to less expensive housing.

Assess Types of Housing That Can Be Purchased   Seven common options are available to home buyers:

1. *Single-family dwellings* are the most popular form of housing. These residences include previously owned houses, new houses, and custom-built houses. Older houses may be preferred by people who want a certain style and quality of housing.

2. *Multiunit dwellings,* dwellings with more than one living unit, include duplexes and townhouses. A *duplex* is a building that contains two separate homes. A *townhouse* contains two, four, or six single-family living units. While multifamily housing appeals to some people, others want more privacy.

condominium

3. **Condominiums** are individually owned housing units in a building with several such units. Individual ownership does not include the common areas, such as hallways, outside grounds, and recreational facilities. These areas are owned by the condominium association, which is run by the people who own the housing units. The condominium association oversees the management and operation of the housing complex. Condominium owners are charged a monthly fee to cover the maintenance, repairs, improvements, and insurance for the building and the common areas. A condominium is not a type of building structure; it is a legal form of homeownership. Many housing units previously rented as apartments have been converted to condominiums, with some individuals purchasing their living units. These conversions created difficulties for people who could not or did not want to buy the units they previously rented.

cooperative housing

4. **Cooperative housing** is a form of housing in which a building containing a number of units is owned by a nonprofit organization whose members rent the units. The living units of a co-op, unlike condominiums, are owned not by the residents but by the co-op. Rents in a co-op can increase quickly if living units become vacant, since the remaining residents must cover the maintenance costs of the building.

manufactured home

5. **Manufactured homes** are housing units that are fully or partially assembled in a factory and then moved to the living site. There are two basic types of manufactured homes. One type is the *prefabricated* home, with components built in a factory and then assembled at the housing site. This type of housing may be popular, since mass production can help keep building costs lower.

6. *Mobile homes* are a second type of manufactured home. However, since very few mobile homes are moved from their original sites, the term is not completely accurate. These housing units are typically less than 1,000 square feet in size; however, they usually offer the same features a conventional house does, for example, fully equipped kitchens, fireplaces, cathedral ceilings, and whirlpool baths. The site for a mobile home may be

either purchased or leased in a development specifically designed for such housing units. As of the early 1990s, over 8 million mobile homes were in use in the United States.

The safety of mobile homes is continually debated. Fires occur no more frequently in these housing units than in other types of homes. But due to the size and construction of mobile homes, a fire spreads faster in them than in conventional houses. Manufacturers' standards for the fire safety of mobile homes are higher now than in the past. Still, when a fire occurs in a mobile home, the unit is often completely destroyed.

Another common concern about mobile homes is their tendency to depreciate in value. When this occurs, an important benefit of homeownership is eliminated. Depreciation may make it difficult to obtain financing to purchase a mobile home.

7. *Building a home* is also an option. Some people want a home built to their specifications. Before you begin such a project, be sure you possess the knowledge, money, and perseverance needed to complete it. When choosing a contractor to coordinate the project, consider the following:

- Does the contractor have the experience needed to handle the type of building project you require?
- Does the contractor have a good working relationship with the architect, materials suppliers, electricians, plumbers, carpenters, and other personnel needed to complete the project?
- What assurance do you have about the quality of materials?
- What arrangements must be made for payments during construction?
- What delays in the construction process will be considered legitimate?
- Is the contractor licensed and insured?
- Is the contractor willing to provide names, addresses, and phone numbers of satisfied customers?
- Have local consumer agencies received any complaints about this contractor?

Your written contract should include a time schedule, cost estimates, a description of the work, and a payment schedule.

Financial Decision Trade-Off

You can save as much as 25 percent of the cost of a new house by supervising its construction. Home-building suppliers and owners of homes under construction can suggest quality tradespeople. Inexpensive blueprints are available from the U.S. Department of Housing and Urban Development; these building plans can save you thousands of dollars in architect fees.

Determine How Much You Can Afford   As you determine how much of your budget you will spend on a home, consider the price of the house along with its size and quality.

Price   The amount you can afford to spend is affected by funds available for a down payment, your income, and your current living expenses. Other factors you should consider are current mortgage rates, the potential future value of the property, and your ability to make monthly mortgage, tax, and insurance payments. To determine how much you can afford to spend on a home, have a loan officer at a mortgage company or other financial institution prequalify you. This service is usually provided without charge.

Size and Quality   You may not get all the features you want in your first home, but financial advisers suggest you get into the housing market by purchasing what you can afford. As you move up in the housing market, your second or third home can include more of the features you want.

Ideally, the home you buy will be in good condition. In certain circumstances, however, you may be willing to buy a *handyman's special*, a home that needs work and that you are able to get at a lower price because of its condition. You will then need to put more money into the house for repairs and improvements or to invest *sweat equity* by doing some of the work yourself. Home improvement information and assistance are available from hardware stores and other home product retailers.

Step 2: Find and Evaluate a Property to Purchase

Next, you should select a location, consider using the services of a real estate agent, and conduct a home inspection.

Selecting a Location   An old adage among real estate people is that the three most important factors to consider when buying a home are *location*, *location*, and *location!* Perhaps you prefer an urban, a suburban, or a rural setting. Or perhaps you want to live in a small town or in a resort area near a lake or skiing facilities. In selecting a neighborhood, compare your values and lifestyle with those of current residents.

zoning laws

Be aware of **zoning laws**, restrictions on how the property in an area can be used. The location of businesses and the anticipated construction of industrial buildings or a highway may influence your buying decision.

If you have or plan to have a family, you should assess the school system. Educators recommend that schools be evaluated on program variety, achievement level of students, percentage of students who go on to college, dedication of faculty members, facilities, school funding, and involvement of parents. Homeowners without children also benefit from strong schools, since the educational advantages of a community help to maintain property values.

Using a Real Estate Agent   A real estate agent can help you assess your housing needs and determine the amount you can afford to spend. Real estate agents have information about areas of interest to you. The Multiple Listing Service, usually in a computerized format, provides information about the homes available for sale in a geographic area that meet your needs.

Video programs and online computer services with homes for sale are becoming increasingly available. A home buyer can view potential properties on-screen based on location, price range, desired number of rooms, and other features. In addition, various software is available for planning and financing a home purchase (see Appendix B).

The main services a real estate agent provides include (1) presenting your offer to the seller, (2) negotiating a settlement price, (3) assisting you in obtaining financing, and (4) representing you at the closing. A real estate agent will also recommend lawyers, insurance agents, home inspectors, and mortgage companies to serve your needs.

Since the seller of the home usually pays the real estate agent's commission, the buyer may not incur a direct cost. However, this expense may be reflected in the price paid for the home. In some states, the agent could be working for the seller. In others, the agent may be working for the buyer and may be a *dual agent*, working for both the buyer and the seller. When this dual agency exists, some states require that the buyers sign a disclosure acknowledging that they are aware that the agent is working for both buyer and seller.

Many states now have *buyer agents* who represent the buyer's interests. In these situations, the buyer agent may be paid by either the seller or the buyer.

EXHIBIT 9–6   **Conducting a Home Inspection**

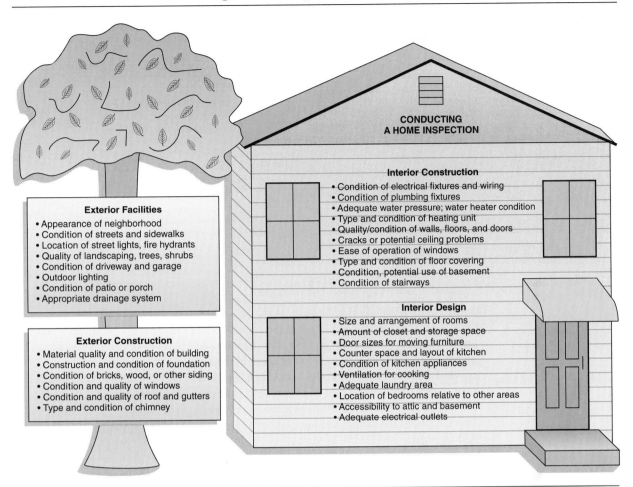

**CONDUCTING
A HOME INSPECTION**

Interior Construction
- Condition of electrical fixtures and wiring
- Condition of plumbing fixtures
- Adequate water pressure; water heater condition
- Type and condition of heating unit
- Quality/condition of walls, floors, and doors
- Cracks or potential ceiling problems
- Ease of operation of windows
- Type and condition of floor covering
- Condition, potential use of basement
- Condition of stairways

Interior Design
- Size and arrangement of rooms
- Amount of closet and storage space
- Door sizes for moving furniture
- Counter space and layout of kitchen
- Condition of kitchen appliances
- Ventilation for cooking
- Adequate laundry area
- Location of bedrooms relative to other areas
- Accessibility to attic and basement
- Adequate electrical outlets

Exterior Facilities
- Appearance of neighborhood
- Condition of streets and sidewalks
- Location of street lights, fire hydrants
- Quality of landscaping, trees, shrubs
- Condition of driveway and garage
- Outdoor lighting
- Condition of patio or porch
- Appropriate drainage system

Exterior Construction
- Material quality and condition of building
- Construction and condition of foundation
- Condition of bricks, wood, or other siding
- Condition and quality of windows
- Condition and quality of roof and gutters
- Type and condition of chimney

Conducting a Home Inspection   Before reaching your decision about a specific home, conduct a complete evaluation of the property. An evaluation by a trained home inspector can minimize future problems. Do not assume everything is in proper working condition because someone lives there now. Being cautious and determined will save you headaches and unplanned expenses. The mortgage company will usually conduct an *appraisal* to determine the fair market value of the property; although the appraisal is not a detailed inspection, it does help to assess the condition of the home. Exhibit 9–6 presents a detailed format for inspecting a home. A home purchase agreement may include the right to have a contractor or several professionals (roofer, plumber, electrician) inspect the property.

Step 3: Price the Property

After you have selected a home, determine an offer price and negotiate a final buying price.

Determining the Home Price   What price should you offer for the home? The main factors you should consider are recent selling prices in the area, current demand for housing, the length of time the home has been on the market, the owner's need to sell, financing

Exhibit 9–7

The Components
of a Home
Purchase
Agreement

Components of a Home Purchase Agreement

In a real estate transaction, the contract between buyer and seller contains the following information:

❑ The names and addresses of the buyer and seller

❑ A description of the property

❑ The price of the property

❑ The amount of the mortgage that will be needed

❑ The amount of the earnest money deposit

❑ The date and time of the closing

❑ Where the closing will take place

❑ A provision for extension of the closing date

❑ A provision for disposition of the deposit money if something goes wrong

❑ Adjustments to be made at the closing

❑ Details of what is included in the sale—home appliances, drapes, carpeting, and other items

❑ Special conditions of the sale

❑ Inspections the buyer can make before the closing

❑ Property easements, such as the use of an area of the property for utility lines or poles

SOURCE: *Homeownership: Guidelines for Buying and Owning a Home* (Richmond, VA: Federal Reserve Bank of Richmond).

options, and features and condition of the home. Each of these factors can affect your offer price. For example, you will have to offer a higher price in times of low interest rates and high demand for homes. On the other hand, a home that has been on the market for over a year could mean an opportunity to offer a lower price. The services of a real estate agent or an appraiser can assist you in assessing the current value of the home.

Your offer will be in the form of a *purchase agreement*, or contract (see Exhibit 9–7). This document constitutes your legal offer to purchase the home. Usually, however, your first offer price will not be accepted.

Negotiating the Purchase Price   If your initial offer is accepted, you have a valid contract to buy the home. If your offer is rejected, you have several options, depending on the seller. A counteroffer from the owner indicates a willingness to negotiate a price settlement. If the counteroffer is only slightly lower than the asking price, you are expected to move closer to that price with your next offer. If the counteroffer is quite a bit off the asking price, you are closer to the point where you might split the difference to arrive at the purchase price. If no counteroffer is forthcoming, you may wish to make another offer to see whether the seller is willing to do any negotiating. Be cautious in your negotiations if you are not using a *buyer-agent*. Remember, in that situation, the agent represents the interests of the seller.

In times of high demand for housing, negotiating may be minimized; this situation is referred to as a *seller's market,* since the current homeowner is likely to have several offers for the property. In contrast, when home sales are slow, a *buyer's market* exists and a lower price is likely.

When you buy a previously owned home, your negotiating power is based on current market demand and the current owner's need to sell. When you buy a new home, a slow market may mean lower prices or an opportunity to obtain various amenities (fireplace, higher-quality carpeting) from the builder at a lower cost.

Once a price has been agreed on, the purchase contract becomes the basis for the real

earnest money

estate transaction. At this time, the buyer must present **earnest money**, a portion of the purchase price deposited as evidence of good faith to show that the purchase offer is serious.

At the closing of the home purchase, the earnest money is applied toward the down payment. This money is returned if the sale cannot be completed due to circumstances beyond the buyer's control.

Home purchase agreements often contain a *contingency clause*. This contract condition states that the agreement is binding only if a certain event occurs. For example, a real estate contract may stipulate that the contract will not be valid unless the buyer obtains financing for the purchase within a certain period of time, or it may make the purchase of a home contingent on the sale of the buyer's current home.

CONCEPT CHECK 9–3

1. What are the advantages and disadvantages of owning a home?
2. What guidelines can be used to determine the amount to spend for a home purchase?
3. How can the quality of a school system benefit even homeowners in a community who do not have school-age children?
4. What services are available to home buyers from real estate agents?
5. How does a *seller's* market differ from a *buyer's* market?

THE FINANCES OF HOME BUYING

L.O.4 Calculate the costs associated with purchasing a home.

After you have decided to purchase a specific home and have agreed on a price, you will probably need to obtain a loan. Financing a home purchase requires obtaining a mortgage, being aware of the types of mortgages, and settling the real estate transaction.

Step 4: Obtain Financing

Determine Amount of Down Payment   The amount of cash available for a down payment will affect the size of the mortgage loan you require. A large down payment, such as 20 percent or more, will make it easier for you to obtain a mortgage.

Personal savings, pension plan funds, sales of investments or other assets, and assistance from relatives are the most common sources of down payment money. Parents can help their children purchase a home by giving them a cash gift or a loan, depositing money with the lender to reduce the interest rate on the loan, cosigning the loan, or acting as comortgagors.

Private mortgage insurance (PMI) is usually required if the down payment is less than 20 percent. This coverage protects the lender from financial loss due to default. PMI charges, which the borrower pays, vary depending on the amount of the down payment. These costs may be paid in full at closing or are sometimes financed over the life of the mortgage, depending on the type of financing. After building up 20 or 25 percent equity in a home, a home buyer may contact the lender to cancel PMI.

Qualifying for a Mortgage   Do you have funds for a down payment? Do you earn enough to make mortgage payments while covering other living expenses? Do you have a good credit rating? Unless you pay cash for a home, a favorable response to these questions is necessary. A **mortgage** is a long-term loan on a specific piece of property such as a home or other real estate. Payments on a mortgage are usually made over 15, 20, or 30 years. Banks, savings and loan associations, credit unions, and mortgage companies are

mortgage

EXHIBIT 9–8   **Housing Affordability and Mortgage Qualification Amounts**

	Example A	Example B
Step 1: Determine your monthly gross income (annual income divided by 12).	$36,000 ÷ 12	
Step 2: With a down payment of at least 10 percent, lenders use 28 percent of monthly gross income as a guideline for PITI (principal, interest, taxes, and insurance) and 36 percent of monthly gross income as a guideline for PITI plus other debt payments.	$ 3,000 × .36 $ 1,080	$ 3,000 × .28 $ 840
Step 3: Subtract other debt payments (e.g., payments on an auto loan) and an estimate of the monthly costs of property taxes and homeowner's insurance.	− 180 − 200	— − 200
(a) Affordable monthly mortgage payment	$ 700	$ 640
Step 4: Divide this amount by the monthly mortgage payment per $1,000 based on current mortgage rates—a 10 percent, 30-year loan, for example (see Exhibit 9–9)—and multiply by $1,000.	÷ $ 8.78 × $ 1,000	÷ $ 8.78 × $ 1,000
(b) Affordable mortgage amount	$79,727	$72,893
Step 5: Divide your affordable mortgage amount by 1 minus the fractional portion of your down payment (e.g., 1 − .1 with a 10 percent down payment).	÷ .9	÷ .9
(c) Affordable home purchase price	$88,585	$80,992

NOTE: The two ratios lending institutions use (step 2) and other loan requirements are likely to vary based on a variety of factors, including the type of mortgage, the amount of the down payment, your income level, and current interest rates.

the most common home financing sources. *Mortgage brokers* can help home buyers obtain financing, since they are in contact with several financial institutions. However, a mortgage broker may charge higher fees than a lending institution with which you deal directly.

To qualify for a mortgage, you must meet criteria similar to those for other loans. The home you buy serves as security, or *collateral*, for the mortgage. The major factors that affect the affordability of your mortgage are your income, other debts, the amount available for a down payment, the length of the loan, and current mortgage rates. The results calculated in Exhibit 9–8 are (*a*) the monthly mortgage payment you can afford, (*b*) the mortgage amount you can afford, and (*c*) the home purchase price you can afford.

The procedures in Exhibit 9–8 include the following:

1. Indicate your monthly gross income.
2. Multiply your monthly gross income by 0.28 (or 0.36 if you have other debts, such as an auto loan). Lenders commonly use 28 and 36 percent as guidelines to determine the amount most people can comfortably afford for housing.
3. After subtracting the monthly debt payments and an estimate of the monthly cost for property taxes and homeowner's insurance, you arrive at your *affordable monthly mortgage payment* (*a*).
4. Divide (*a*) by the factor from Exhibit 9–9, based on your mortgage term (in years) and rate. Then multiply your answer by $1,000 to convert your figure to thousands of dollars. This gives you your *affordable mortgage amount* (*b*). Exhibit 9–9 provides the amount you need to pay back $1,000 over 15, 20, 25, or 30 years based on various interest rates.
5. To obtain your *affordable home purchasing price* (*c*), divide (*b*) by the amount you will be financing, such as 0.9 when you make a 10 percent down payment.

These sample calculations are typical of those most financial institutions use; however, the actual qualifications for a mortgage may vary by lender and by the type of mortgage.

PFP

Sheet 43

Exhibit 9–9	Term Rate	30 Years	25 Years	20 Years	15 Years
Mortgage Payment Factors (principal and interest factors per $1,000 of loan amount)	6.0%	$ 6.00	$ 6.44	$ 7.16	$ 8.43
	6.5	6.32	6.67	7.45	8.71
	7.0	6.65	7.06	7.75	8.98
	7.5	6.99	7.39	8.06	9.27
	8.0	7.34	7.72	8.36	9.56
	8.5	7.69	8.05	8.68	9.85
	9.0	8.05	8.39	9.00	10.14
	9.5	8.41	8.74	9.32	10.44
	10.0	8.78	9.09	9.65	10.75
	10.5	9.15	9.44	9.98	11.05
	11.0	9.52	9.80	10.32	11.37
	11.5	9.90	10.16	10.66	11.68
	12.0	10.29	10.53	11.01	12.00
	12.5	10.67	10.90	11.36	12.33
	13.0	11.06	11.28	11.72	12.65
	13.5	11.45	11.66	12.07	12.98
	14.0	11.85	12.04	12.44	13.32
	14.5	12.25	12.42	12.80	13.66
	15.0	12.64	12.81	13.17	14.00

In addition, current mortgage interest rates will affect the amount of the mortgage loan for which you qualify.

The mortgage loan for which you can qualify is larger when interest rates are low than when they are high. For example, a person who can afford a monthly mortgage payment of $700 will qualify for a 30-year loan of

$105,263 at 7 percent
$ 95,368 at 8 percent
$ 86,956 at 9 percent
$ 79,726 at 10 percent
$ 73,529 at 11 percent
$ 68,027 at 12 percent

> **DID YOU KNOW?**
>
> Among lenders, interest rates on a 30-year mortgage can vary as much as two percentage points within a single geographic region.

As interest rates rise, fewer people are able to afford the cost of an average-priced home.

Evaluating Points   When you compare costs at several mortgage companies, the interest rate you are quoted is not the only factor to consider. The required down payment and the points charged will affect the interest rate. **Points** are prepaid interest charged by the lender. Each *discount point* is equal to 1 percent of the loan amount and should be viewed as a premium you pay for obtaining a lower mortgage rate. In deciding whether to take a lower rate with more points or a higher rate with fewer points, do the following:

points

1. Determine the difference between the monthly payments you will make for two different situations.
2. Determine the difference between the points charged for the two different rates or at two different lenders.
3. Divide the result in step 2 by the result in step 1. This will tell you how many months it will take for the lower monthly payment to offset the higher cost of the points.

If you plan to live in your home longer than the time calculated in step 3, paying the points and taking the lower mortgage rate is probably the best action. This decision will, however, be affected by the amount of funds available to pay the points at the time of closing. If you sell your home sooner than the time calculated in step 3, the higher mortgage rate with fewer discount points may be better. Online computer services may be used to compare current mortgage rates and to apply for a mortgage. For further information, see Appendix B.

The Application Process   Applying for a mortgage involves three main phases:

1. After completing the mortgage application, a meeting between lender and borrower is scheduled. The borrower presents evidence of employment, income, ownership of assets, and amounts of existing debts. At this point, most lenders charge an application fee of between $100 and $300.
2. The lender obtains a credit report and verifies other aspects of the borrower's application and financial status.
3. The mortgage is either approved or denied. The decision is based on the potential borrower's credit and financial history and an evaluation of the home, including its location, condition, and value. Home buyers who are denied a mortgage may seek recourse under the Equal Credit Opportunity Act of the Fair Credit Reporting Act.

The loan commitment is the financial institution's decision to provide the funds needed to purchase a specific property. At this point, the purchase contract for the home becomes legally binding. The approved mortgage application usually *locks in* an interest rate for 30 to 60 days.

Fixed-Rate, Fixed-Payment Mortgages   As Exhibit 9–10 shows, fixed-rate, fixed-payment mortgages are one of the two major types of mortgages.

conventional mortgage

amortization

Conventional Mortgages   The **conventional mortgage** has equal payments over usually 15, 20, or 30 years based on a fixed interest rate. This mortgage offers home buyers certainty about future loan payments. The mortgage payments are set at a level that allows **amortization** of the loan; that is, the balance owed is reduced with each payment. Since the amount borrowed is large, the payments made during the early years of the mortgage are applied mainly to interest, with only small reductions in the principal of the loan. As the amount owed declines, the monthly payments have an increasing impact on the loan balance. Near the end of the mortgage term, nearly all of each payment is applied to the balance.

For example, a $75,000, 30-year, 10 percent mortgage would have monthly payments of $658.18. The payments would be divided as follows:

	Interest		Principal	Remaining Balance	
For the first month	$625.00	($75,000 × 0.10 × 1/12)	$ 33.18	$74,966.82	($75,000 − $33.18)
For the second month	624.72	($74,966.82 × 0.10 × 1/12)	33.46	74,933.36	($74,966.82 − $33.46)
For the 360th month	5.41		649.54	− 0 −	

In the past, many conventional mortgages were *assumable*. This feature allowed a home buyer to continue with the seller's original agreement. Assumable mortgages were especially attractive if the mortgage rate was lower than market interest rates at the time of the sale. Today, due to volatile interest rates, few assumable mortgages are offered.

EXHIBIT 9–10   **Types of Mortgage Loans**

Loan Type	Benefits	Drawbacks
Fixed-Rate, Fixed-Payment		
1. Conventional 30-year mortgage	■ Fixed monthly payments for 30 years provide certainty of principal and interest payments.	■ Higher initial rates than adjustables.
2. Conventional 15- or 20-year mortgage	■ Lower rate than 30-year fixed; faster equity buildup and quicker payoff of loan.	■ Higher monthly payments.
3. FHA/VA fixed-rate mortgage (30-year and 15-year)	■ Low down payment requirements and fully assumable with no prepayment penalties.	■ May require substantial points; may have application red tape and delays.
4. "Balloon" loan (3–10-year terms)	■ May carry discount rates and other favorable terms, particularly when the home seller provides the loan.	■ At the end of the 3–10-year term, the entire remaining balance is due in a lump-sum or "balloon" payment, forcing the borrower to find new financing.
Adjustable-Rate, Variable-Payment		
6. Adjustable rate mortgage (ARM)— payment changes on 1-year, 3-year, and 5-year schedules	■ Lower initial rates than fixed-rate loans, particularly on the one-year adjustable. Generally assumable by new buyers. Offers possibility of future rate and payment decreases. Loans with rate "caps" may protect borrowers against increases in rates. Some may be convertible to fixed-rate plans.	■ Shifts far greater interest rate risk onto borrowers than fixed-rate loans. May push up monthly payments in future years.
7. Graduated-payment mortgage (GPM)—payment increases by prearranged increments during first 5 to 7 years, then levels off	■ Allows buyers with marginal incomes to qualify. Higher incomes over next 5–7 years expected to cover gradual payment increases. May be combined with adjustable-rate mortgage to further lower initial rate and payment.	■ May have higher annual percentage rate (APR) than standard fixed-rate or adjustable-rate loans. May involve negative amortization— increasing debt owed by lender.
8. Growing-equity mortgage (GEM)— contributes rising portions of monthly payments to payoff of principal debt. Typically pays off in 15–18 years rather than 30	■ Lower up-front payments, quicker loan payoff than conventional fixed-rate or adjustable-rate loans.	■ May have higher effective rates and higher down payments than other loans in the marketplace.

SOURCE: *Real Estate Today,* National Association of Realtors®.

Government-Guaranteed Financing Programs   *Government-guaranteed financing programs* include loans insured by the Federal Housing Authority (FHA) and loans guaranteed by the Veterans Administration (VA). These government agencies do not provide the mortgage money; rather, they help home buyers obtain low-interest, low-down-payment loans.

EXHIBIT 9–11

Mortgage Rates through the Years

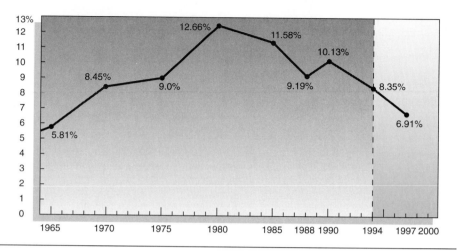

SOURCE: Board of Governors of the Federal Reserve System.

To qualify for an FHA-insured loan, a person must meet certain conditions related to the down payment and fees. Most low- and middle-income people can qualify for the FHA loan program. The minimum down payment ranges from 3 to 5 percent, depending on the loan size. This lower down payment makes it easier for a person to purchase a home. FHA-insured loans have interest rates lower than market interest rates, since the FHA's involvement reduces the risk for the lending institution. The borrower is required to pay a fee for insurance that protects the lender from financial loss due to default. Despite the protection given the lender, the lower-than-market interest rate can result in extra prepaid interest, *points*, as a condition of the loan.

The VA-guaranteed loan program assists eligible armed services veterans with home purchases. As with the FHA program, the funds for VA loans come from a financial institution or a mortgage company, with the risk reduced by government participation. A VA loan can be obtained without a down payment. The points charged by the lending institution must be paid by the home seller; however, the veteran is usually responsible for other charges, such as origination and funding fees.

Both FHA-insured loans and VA-guaranteed loans can be attractive financing alternatives and are assumable by future owners when the house is sold to qualifying individuals. Both impose limits on the amount one can borrow, however, and a backlog of processing applications and approving loans may occur during periods of high demand for housing.

balloon mortgage

Balloon Mortgages   The high mortgage rates of the early 1980s (Exhibit 9–11) led to innovative lending plans for home buyers. One such plan is the **balloon mortgage,** which has fixed monthly payments and a very large final payment, usually after three, five, or seven years. This financing plan is designed for people who wish to buy a home during periods of high interest rates but expect to be able to refinance the loan or sell the home before or when the balloon payment is due. Most balloon mortgages allow conversion to a conventional mortgage (for a fee) after a year if certain conditions are met. Some financial counselors advise against the use of a balloon mortgage, since you have to pay mortgage processing and closing costs when you refinance. Beware that being unable to refinance in time can result in a major financial loss.

Adjustable-Rate, Variable-Payment Mortgages   As noted in Exhibit 9–10, adjustable-rate, variable-payment mortgages are a major category of financing available to home buyers.

adjustable-rate mortgage (ARM)

Adjustable-Rate Mortgages   The **adjustable rate mortgage (ARM),** also referred to as a flexible-rate mortgage or a variable-rate mortgage, has an interest rate that increases or decreases during the life of the loan. When mortgage rates were at record highs, many people took out variable-rate home loans, expecting rates would eventually go down. ARMs usually have a lower initial interest rate than fixed-rate mortgages; however, the borrower, not the lender, bears the risk of future interest rate increases.

rate cap

A **rate cap** restricts the amount by which the interest rate can increase or decrease during the ARM term. This limit prevents the borrower from having to pay an interest rate significantly higher than the one in the original agreement. Most rate caps limit increases (or decreases) in the mortgage rate to one percentage point in a year and to no more than five points over the life of the loan.

payment cap

A **payment cap** keeps the payments on an adjustable-rate mortgage at a given level or limits the amount to which those payments can rise. When mortgage payments do not rise but interest rates do, the amount owed can increase in months in which the mortgage payment does not cover the interest owed. This increased loan balance, called *negative amortization,* means the amount of the home equity is decreasing instead of increasing. As a result of these increases in the amount owed, the borrower usually has to make payments for a period longer than planned. Beware: Some adjustable-rate mortgages may stretch out as long as 40 years.

Consider several factors when you evaluate adjustable-rate mortgages. First, determine the frequency of and restrictions on allowed changes in interest rates. Second, consider the frequency of and restrictions on changes in the monthly payment. Third, investigate the possibility that the loan will be extended due to negative amortization, and find out whether the mortgage agreement limits the amount of negative amortization. Finally, find out what index the lending institution will use to set the mortgage interest rate over the term of the loan. A lending institution will revise the rate for an adjustable-rate mortgage based on changes in the rates on U.S. Treasury securities, the Federal Home Loan Bank Board's mortgage rate index, or its own cost-of-funds index. Studies reveal that an ARM can be less costly over the life of a mortgage as long as interest rates remain fairly stable.

Convertible ARMs allow the home buyer to change an adjustable-rate mortgage to a fixed-rate mortgage during a certain period, such as the time between the second and fifth year of the loan. A conversion fee, typically between $250 and $500, must be paid to obtain a fixed rate, usually 0.25 to 0.50 percent higher than the current rates for conventional 30-year mortgages.

Sheet 44

graduated-payment mortgage

Graduated-Payment Mortgages   A **graduated-payment mortgage** is a financing agreement in which payments rise to different levels every 5 or 10 years during the term of the loan. During the early years, the payments are relatively low. This type of mortgage is especially beneficial for people who anticipate increases in income in the future.

growing-equity mortgage

Growing-Equity Mortgages   A **growing-equity mortgage** provides for increases in payments that allow the amount owed to be paid off more quickly. With such a mortgage, a person would be able to pay off a 30-year home loan in 15 to 18 years. A growing-equity mortgage may be desired by individuals who want to build equity in their homes quickly.

Other Financing Methods   To assist first-time home buyers, builders and financial institutions offer financing plans to make the purchase easier.

FINANCIAL PLANNING FOR LIFE'S SITUATIONS

SHOULD YOU PAY OFF YOUR MORTGAGE EARLY?

People who have a mortgage might consider paying it off early. Make sure the mortgage does not include a *prepayment penalty,* a fee borrowers pay for the privilege of retiring a loan early. Most mortgages do not include this penalty. Before paying off your mortgage early, however, consider the tax deductions you may lose and your lost earnings on the money you use to retire this debt.

Instead of paying off your entire mortgage early, consider paying an additional amount each month—for example, $25. Since this amount will be applied to the loan principal, you will save interest and pay off the mortgage in a shorter time than the contracted period. Paying an additional $25 a month on a $75,000, 30-year, 10 percent mortgage will save you over $34,000 in interest and enable you to pay off the loan in less than 25 years.

Beware of organizations that promise to help you make additional payments on your mortgage. This is something you could do on your own, and they are likely to charge you a fee for doing it. In addition, these organizations frequently collect money from you every two weeks but make a payment only once a month, which gives them the use of thousands of *your* dollars to invest for *their* gain.

---

buy-down

Buy-Downs   A **buy-down** is an interest rate subsidy from a home builder or a real estate developer that reduces the mortgage payments during the first few years of the loan. This assistance is intended to stimulate sales among home buyers who cannot afford conventional financing. After the buy-down period, the mortgage payments increase to the level that would have existed without the financial assistance.

shared appreciation mortgage (SAM)

Shared Appreciation Mortgages   The **shared appreciation mortgage (SAM)** is an arrangement in which the borrower agrees to share the increased value of the home with the lender when the home is sold. This agreement provides the home buyer with a below-market interest rate and lower payments than a conventional loan. To obtain these conditions, the borrower typically must agree to give the lending institution 30 to 50 percent of the home's appreciation when the home is sold. Shared appreciation agreements are also common when parents provide financial assistance to their children for the purchase of a home.

As your personal and financial circumstances change, other mortgage plans may have benefits.

second mortgage

Second Mortgages   A **second mortgage**, more commonly called a *home equity loan,* allows a homeowner to borrow on the paid-up value of the property. Traditional second mortgages allow a homeowner to borrow a lump sum against the equity and repay it in monthly installments. Recently, lending institutions have offered a variety of home equity loans, including a line of credit program that allows the borrower to obtain additional funds. You need to be careful when using a home equity line of credit. This revolving credit plan can keep you continually in debt as you request new cash advances.

A home equity loan makes it possible to deduct the interest on consumer purchases on the federal income tax return. However, it creates the risk of losing the home if required payments on both the first and second mortgages are not made. To help prevent this financial disaster, some states restrict the use of home equity loans. In Texas, for example, a second mortgage may be used only for home improvement expenses.

reverse mortgage

Financial Decision
Trade-Off

Reverse Mortgages   Programs are available to assist people who have a high equity in their homes and need cash. **Reverse mortgages** provide elderly homeowners with tax-free income in the form of a loan that is paid back (with interest) when the home is sold or the homeowner dies. You must be 62 to qualify. These financing plans, also called *home equity conversion mortgages,* have two main formats. A *reverse mortgage annuity* guarantees the homeowner a monthly income for life. In contrast, a reverse mortgage may have a *set term,* at the end of which the loan would be due. This format is likely to offer a higher monthly income; however, an elderly person faces the prospect of having to sell the home before he or she desires to do so. Reverse mortgages are increasing in availability through both government agencies and private lending institutions.

refinance

Sheet 45

Refinancing   During the term of your mortgage, you may want to **refinance** your home, that is, obtain a new mortgage on your current home at a lower interest rate. Before taking this action, be sure the costs of refinancing do not offset the savings of a lower interest rate. Refinancing is most advantageous when you can get a rate 2 or 3 percent lower than your current rate and when you plan to own your present home for at least two more years. Divide the costs of refinancing by the amount saved each month to determine the time you need to cover your costs. Also, be sure to consider the tax deductibility of refinancing costs. Another financing decision involves making extra payments on your mortgage (see the Financial Planning for Life's Situations feature on page 288).

Step 5: Close the Purchase Transaction

Before finalizing the transaction, do a *walk-through* to inspect the conditions and facilities of the home you plan to buy. You can use a Polaroid or video camera to collect evidence for any last-minute items you may need to negotiate.

The *closing* involves a meeting among the buyer, seller, and lender of funds, or representatives of each party, to complete the transaction. Documents are signed, last-minute details are settled, and appropriate amounts are paid. A number of expenses are incurred at the closing. The **closing costs,** also referred to as *settlement costs,* are the fees and charges paid when a real estate transaction is completed (see Exhibit 9–12 on page 290).

> ### DID YOU KNOW?
>
> If you still owe $60,000 on a $100,000, 9.5 percent mortgage with 20 years left to pay, refinancing the $60,000 for 30 years at 7.5 percent will reduce your monthly payments from $834 to $417. This will result in savings of over $106,000 in interest. Refinancing with a 20-year mortgage would result in even a larger savings.

closing costs

title insurance

Title insurance is one closing cost. This coverage has two phases. First, the title company defines the boundaries of the property being purchased and conducts a search to determine whether the property is free of claims such as unpaid real estate taxes. Second, during the mortgage term, the title company protects the owner and the lender against financial loss resulting from future defects in the title and from other unforeseen property claims not excluded by the policy.

deed

Also due at closing time is the fee for recording the deed. The **deed** is the document that transfers ownership of property from one party to another. With a *warranty deed*, the seller guarantees the title is good. This document certifies that the seller is the true owner of the property, there are no claims against the title, and the seller has the right to sell the property.

Mortgage insurance is another possible closing cost. If required, mortgage insurance protects the lender from loss resulting from a mortgage default.

EXHIBIT 9–12   **Common Closing Costs**

At the transaction settlement of a real estate purchase and sale, the buyer and seller will encounter a variety of expenses that are commonly referred to as *closing costs.*

	Cost Range Encountered	
	By the Buyer	By the Seller
Title search fee	$50–$150	—
Title insurance	$100–$600	$100–$600
Attorney's fee	$50–$700	$50–$700
Property survey	—	$100–$400
Appraisal fee	$100–$300	—
Recording fees; transfer taxes	$15–$30	$15–$30
Credit report	$25–$75	—
Termite inspection	$50–$150	—
Lender's origination fee	1–3% of loan amount	—
Reserves for home insurance and property taxes	Varies	—
Interest paid in advance (from the closing date to the end of the month)	Varies	—
Real estate broker's commission	—	5–7% of purchase price

NOTE: The amounts paid by the buyer are in addition to the down payment.

The Real Estate Settlement Procedures Act (RESPA) helps home buyers understand the closing process and closing costs. This legislation requires that loan applicants be given certain information, including an estimate of the closing costs, before the actual closing. Obtaining this information as early as possible will allow you to plan for the closing costs. Information on RESPA is available online at www.hud.gov/fha/res/respa_hm.html.

escrow account

At the time of closing and when you make your monthly payments, you will probably deposit money to be used to pay home-related expenses. For example, the lender will require that you have property insurance on the home. An **escrow account** is money, usually deposited with the lending institution, for the payment of property taxes and homeowner's insurance. This account protects the lender from financial loss due to unpaid real estate taxes or damage from fire or other hazards.

As a new home buyer, you might also consider purchasing an agreement that gives you protection against defects in the home. Implied warranties created by state laws may cover some problem areas; however, other repair costs can occur. Home builders and real estate sales companies offer warranties to buyers. Coverage offered commonly provides protection against structural, wiring, plumbing, heating, and other mechanical defects. However, most home warranty programs have many limitations.

In addition, a new homeowner may purchase a service contract from a real estate company such as Century 21 or Remax. This agreement warrants appliances, plumbing, air conditioning and heating systems, and other select items for one year. As with any service contract, you must decide whether the coverage provided and the chances of repair expenses justify the cost.

Home Buying: A Final Word

For most people, buying a home is the most expensive and one of the most complex activities they will undertake. As a reminder, Exhibit 9–13 provides an overview of the major elements you need to consider when making this critical financial decision.

EXHIBIT 9–13

The Main Elements of Buying a Home

- **Location.** Consider the community and geographic region. A $100,000 home in one area may be an average-priced house, while in another part of the country it may be fairly expensive real estate. The demand for homes in an area is largely affected by the economy and the availability of jobs.

- **Down payment.** While making a large down payment reduces your mortgage payments, you may need the funds for closing costs, moving expenses, repairs, or furniture.

- **Mortgage application.** When applying for a home loan, you will likely be required to provide copies of recent tax returns, a residence and employment history, information about bank and investment accounts, a listing of debts, and evidence of auto and real estate ownership (if any).

- **Points.** You may need to select between a higher rate (no discount points) and a lower rate requiring points paid at closing.

- **Closing costs.** Settlement costs can range from 2 to 6 percent of the loan amount. This means you could need as much as $6,000 to finalize a $100,000 mortgage; this amount is in addition to your down payment.

- **PITI.** Your monthly payment for principal, interest, taxes, and insurance is an important budget item. Beware of buying "too much house" and not having enough for other living expenses.

- **Maintenance costs.** As any homeowner will tell you, owning a home can be expensive. Set aside funds for repair and remodeling expenses.

CONCEPT CHECK 9–4

1. What are the main sources of money for a down payment?
2. What factors affect a person's ability to qualify for a mortgage?
3. How do changing interest rates affect the amount of mortgage a person can afford?
4. How do discount points affect the cost of a mortgage?
5. Under what conditions might an adjustable-rate mortgage be appropriate?
6. When might refinancing a mortgage be advisable?
7. How do closing costs affect a person's ability to afford a home purchase?

SELLING YOUR HOME

L.O.5 Develop a strategy for selling a home.

Most people who buy a home will eventually be on the other side of a real estate transaction. Selling your home requires preparing it for selling, setting a price, and deciding whether to sell it yourself or use a real estate agent.

Preparing Your Home for Selling

The effective presentation of your home can result in a fast and financially favorable sale. Real estate salespeople recommend that you make needed repairs and paint worn exterior and interior areas. Clear the garage and exterior areas of toys, debris, and old vehicles, and keep the lawn cut and the leaves raked. Keep the kitchen and bathroom clean. Avoid offensive odors by removing garbage and keeping pets and their areas clean. Remove excess furniture and dispose of unneeded items to make the house, closets, and storage areas look larger. When showing your home, open drapes and turn on lights to give it a pleasant atmosphere. This effort will give your property a positive image and make it attractive to potential buyers.

Determining the Selling Price

appraisal

Putting a price on your home can be difficult. You risk not selling it immediately if the price is too high, and you may not get a fair amount if the price is too low. An **appraisal,** an estimate of the current value of the property, can provide a good indication of the price you should set. An asking price is influenced by recent selling prices of comparable homes in your area, demand in the housing market, and available financing based on current mortgage rates.

The home improvements you have made may or may not increase the selling price. A hot tub or an exercise room may have no value for potential buyers. Among the most desirable improvements are energy-efficient features, a remodeled kitchen, an additional or remodeled bathroom, added rooms and storage space, a converted basement, a fireplace, and an outdoor deck or patio.

The time to think about selling your home is when you buy it and every day you live in it. Daily maintenance, timely repairs, and home improvements will increase the future sales price.

> ### DID YOU KNOW?
>
> An appraisal is likely to cost between $200 and $300. However, this expense can help people selling a home on their own to get a realistic view of the property's value.

Sale by Owner

Financial Decision Trade-Off

Each year, about 10 percent of home sales are made by the home's owners. If you decide to sell your home without using a real estate professional, price the home and advertise it through local newspapers and with an information sheet describing it in detail. Obtain a listing sheet from a real estate office as an example of the information to include on your flier. Distribute the sheet at stores and in other public areas.

When selling your home on your own, obtain information about the availability of financing and financing requirements. This information will help you and potential buyers to determine whether a sale is possible. Use the services of a lawyer or title company to assist you with the contract, the closing, and other legal matters.

Require potential buyers to provide their names, addresses, telephone numbers, and background information, and show your home only by appointment. As a security measure, show it only when two or more adults are at home. Selling your own home can save you several thousand dollars in commission; however, it requires an investment of time and effort.

Listing with a Real Estate Agent

If you decide to sell your home with the assistance of a real estate agent, you can choose from among many real estate businesses in your area. These businesses range from firms owned by one person to nationally franchised and advertised companies. Primary selection factors should be the real estate agent's knowledge of your community and the agent's willingness to actively market your home.

Your real estate agent will provide you with various services. These services include suggesting a selling price, making potential buyers and other agents aware of your home, providing advice on features to highlight, conducting showings of your home, and handling the financial aspects of the sale. A real estate agent can also help screen potential buyers to determine whether they will qualify for a mortgage.

Discount real estate brokers are available to assist sellers who are willing to take on certain duties and want to reduce selling costs. Companies such as Save More Real Estate and Help-U-Sell Real Estate charge a flat fee or 1 to 2 percent of the selling price instead of the customary 6 percent.

CONCEPT CHECK 9–5

1. What actions are recommended when planning to sell your home?
2. What factors affect the selling price of a home?
3. What should you consider when deciding whether to sell your home on your own or to use the services of a real estate agent?

SUMMARY

L.O.1   Evaluate available housing alternatives.

Your needs, life situation, and financial resources are the major factors that influence your selection of housing. Assess renting and buying alternatives in terms of their financial and opportunity costs.

L.O.2   Analyze the costs and benefits associated with renting.

The main advantages of renting are mobility, fewer responsibilities, and lower initial costs. The main disadvantages of renting are few financial benefits, a restricted lifestyle, and legal concerns.

L.O.3   Implement the home-buying process.

Home buying involves five major stages: (1) determining homeownership needs, (2) finding and evaluating a property

to purchase, (3) pricing the property, (4) financing the purchase, and (5) closing the real estate transaction.

L.O.4   Calculate the costs associated with purchasing a home.

The costs associated with purchasing a home include the down payment; mortgage origination costs; closing costs such as a deed fee, prepaid interest, attorneys' fees, payment for title insurance, and a property survey; and an escrow account for homeowner's insurance and property taxes.

L.O.5   Develop a strategy for selling a home.

When selling a home, you must decide whether to make certain repairs and improvements, determine a selling price, and choose between selling the home yourself and using the services of a real estate agent.

GLOSSARY

adjustable-rate mortgage (ARM)   A home loan with an interest rate that can change during the mortgage term due to changes in market interest rates; also called a *flexible-rate mortgage* or a *variable-rate mortgage*.   (p. 287)

amortization   The reduction of a loan balance through payments made over a period of time. (p. 284)

appraisal   An estimate of the current value of a property. (p. 292)

balloon mortgage   A home loan with fixed monthly payments and a large final payment, usually after three, five, or seven years.   (p. 286)

buy-down   An interest rate subsidy from a home builder or a real estate developer that reduces a home buyer's mortgage payments during the first few years of the loan.   (p. 288)

closing costs   Fees and charges paid when a real estate transaction is completed; also called *settlement costs*. (p. 289)

condominium   An individually owned housing unit in a building with several such units.   (p. 276)

conventional mortgage   A fixed rate, fixed-payment home loan with equal payments over 15, 20, or 30 years.   (p. 284)

cooperative housing   A form of housing in which a building containing a number of housing units is owned by a nonprofit organization whose members rent the units.   (p. 276)

deed   A document that transfers ownership of property from one party to another.   (p. 289)

earnest money   A portion of the price of a home that the buyer deposits as evidence of good faith to indicate a serious purchase offer.   (p. 280)

escrow account   Money, usually deposited with the lending financial institution, for the payment of property taxes and homeowner's insurance.   (p. 290)

graduated-payment mortgage   A home financing agreement in which payments rise to different levels every 5 or 10 years during the loan term.   (p. 287)

growing-equity mortgage   A home loan agreement that provides for payment increases to allow the amount owed to be paid off more quickly.   (p. 287)

lease   A legal document that defines the conditions of a rental agreement.   (p. 273)

manufactured home   A housing unit that is fully or partially assembled in a factory before being moved to the living site.   (p. 276)

mortgage   A long-term loan on a specific piece of property such as a home or other real estate.   (p. 281)

payment cap   A limit on the payment increases for an adjustable-rate mortgage.   (p. 287)

points   Prepaid interest charged by a lending institution for a mortgage; each discount point is equal to 1 percent of the loan amount.   (p. 283)

rate cap   A limit on the increases and decreases in the interest rate charged on an adjustable-rate mortgage.   (p. 287)

refinance   The process of obtaining a new mortgage on a home to get a lower interest rate.   (p. 289)

reverse mortgage   A loan, based on the equity in a home, that provides elderly homeowners with tax-free income and is paid back with interest when the home is sold or the homeowner dies.   (p. 289)

second mortgage   A cash advance based on the paid-up value of a home; also called a *home equity loan*.   (p. 288)

shared appreciation mortgage (SAM)   A home loan agreement in which the borrower agrees to share the increased value of the home with the lender when the home is sold.   (p. 288)

title insurance   Insurance that, during the mortgage term, protects the owner or the lender against financial loss resulting from future defects in the title and from other unforeseen property claims not excluded by the policy.   (p. 289)

zoning laws   Restrictions on how the property in an area can be used.   (p. 278)

R E V I E W   Q U E S T I O N S

1. What factors should a person consider when selecting a place of residence?   (L.O.1)
2. Why will most people rent a place of residence at some point in their lives?   (L.O.2)
3. Why is location commonly considered the most important influence on the value of a home?   (L.O.3)
4. What information and documents are typically required from a prospective borrower when applying for a mortgage?   (L.O.4)
5. When selling a home, what actions could enhance the value of the property?   (L.O.5)

F I N A N C I A L   P L A N N I N G   P R O B L E M S

1. *Determining Appropriate Housing.* What type of housing would you suggest for people in the following life situations?   (L.O.1)
   a. A single parent with two school-age children.
   b. A two-income couple without children.
   c. A person with both dependent children and a dependent parent.
   d. A couple near retirement with grown children.
2. *Comparing Renting and Buying.* Based on the following data, would you recommend buying or renting?

Rental Costs	Buying Costs
Annual rent, $7,380	Annual mortgage payments, $9,800
Insurance, $145	($9,575 is interest)
Security deposit, $650	Property taxes, $1,780
	Insurance/maintenance, $1,050
	Down payment/closing costs, $4,500
	Growth in equity, $225
	Estimated annual appreciation, $1,700

   Assume an after-tax savings interest rate of 6 percent and a tax rate of 28 percent.   (L.O.2)
3. *Analyzing the Buy-versus-Rent Decision.* Use the buy-versus-rent analysis on page 270 to compare two residences you might consider.   (L.O.2)

4. *Estimating a Monthly Mortgage Payment.* Estimate the affordable monthly mortgage payment, the affordable mortgage amount, and the affordable home purchase price for the following situation (see Exhibit 9–8).   (L.O.4)
   Monthly gross income, $2,950
   Down payment to be made—15 percent of purchase price
   Other debt (monthly payment), $160
   Monthly estimate for property taxes and insurance, $210
   30-year loan at 10.5 percent.
5. *Calculating Monthly Mortgage Payments.* Based on Exhibit 9–9, what would be the monthly mortgage payments for each of the following situations?
   a. A $40,000, 15-year loan at 11.5 percent.
   b. A $76,000, 30-year loan at 9 percent.
   c. A $65,000, 20-year loan at 10 percent.
   What relationship exists between the length of the loan and the monthly payment? How does the mortgage rate affect the monthly payment?   (L.O.4)
6. *Comparing Total Mortgage Payments.* Which mortgage would result in higher total payments?   (L.O.4)
   Mortgage A: $985 a month for 30 years
   Mortgage B: $780 a month for 5 years and $1,056 for 25 years

7. *Evaluating a Refinance Decision.* Kelly and Tim Jones plan to refinance their mortgage to obtain a lower interest rate. They will reduce their mortgage payments by $56 a month. Their closing costs for refinancing will be $1,670. How long will it take them to cover the cost of refinancing?   (L.O.4)

8. *Future Value of an Amount Saved.* You estimate that you can save $3,800 by selling your home yourself rather than using a real estate agent. What would be the future value of that amount if invested for five years at 7 percent? (L.O.5)

PROJECTS AND APPLICATION ACTIVITIES

1. *Comparing Housing Alternatives.* Interview several people about the factors that influenced their current residence.   (L.O.1)

2. *Comparing Rental Situations.* Using Sheet 42 in the *Personal Financial Planner,* compare the costs, facilities, and features of apartments and other rental housing in your area. You may obtain this information through newspaper advertisements, rental offices, or online searches of the World Wide Web.   (L.O.2)

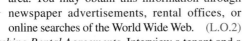

3. *Researching Rental Agreements.* Interview a tenant and a landlord to obtain their views about potential problems associated with renting. How do their views on tenant–landlord relations differ?   (L.O.2)

4. *Comparing Home-Buying Alternatives.* Visit the sales office for a condominium, a new home, and a mobile home. Based on the information obtained, prepare a written or an oral presentation comparing the benefits and potential concerns of these housing alternatives.   (L.O.3)

5. *Using a Real Estate Agent.* Interview a real estate agent about the process involved in selecting and buying a home. Ask about housing prices in your area and the services the agent provides. Also, obtain information about

the agent's opinion as to what will happen to housing prices and interest rates over the next six months?   (L.O.3)

6. *Comparing Types of Mortgages.* Talk with people who have different types of mortgages. What suggestions do they offer about obtaining home financing? What were their experiences with closing costs when they purchased their homes?   (L.O.4)

7. *Comparing Mortgage Companies.* Using Sheet 44 in the *Personal Financial Planner,* contact several mortgage companies and other financial institutions to obtain information about current mortgage rates, application fees, and the process for obtaining a mortgage.   (L.O.4)

8. *Searching the Web for Mortgage Rates.* Using Web sites such as www.financenter.com, www.interest.com, or www.bestrate.com, obtain information on current mortgage rates available in different parts of the country.   (L.O.4)

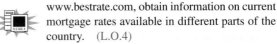

9. *Analyzing Homes for Sales.* Visit a couple of homes for sale. What features do you believe would appeal to potential buyers? What efforts were made to attract potential buyers to the open houses?   (L.O.5)

LIFE SITUATION CASE 9

HOUSING DECISIONS

When Mark and Valerie Bowman first saw the house, they didn't like it. However, it was a dark, rainy day. They viewed the house more favorably on their second visit, which they had expected to be a waste of time. Despite cracked ceilings, the need for a paint job, and a kitchen built in the 1950s, the Bowmans saw a potential to create a place they could call their own.

Beth Franklin purchased her condominium four years ago. She obtained a mortgage rate of 9.75 percent, which was very good then. Recently, when interest rates dropped, Beth was considering refinancing her mortgage at a lower rate.

Matt and Peggy Zoran had been married for five years and were still living in an apartment. Several of the Zorans' friends had purchased homes recently. However, Matt and Peggy were

not sure they wanted to follow this example. Although they liked their friends' homes and had viewed photographs of homes currently on the market, they also liked the freedom from maintenance responsibility they enjoyed as renters.

QUESTIONS

1. How could the Bowmans have benefited from buying a home that needed improvements?
2. How might Beth Franklin have found out when mortgage rates were at a level that would make refinancing her condominium more affordable?
3. Although the Zorans had good reasons for continuing to rent, what factors might make it desirable for an individual or a family to buy a home?

USING THE INTERNET TO CREATE A PERSONAL FINANCIAL PLAN 9

SELECTING AND FINANCING HOUSING

Housing represents a major budget expenditure. This area of financial planning requires careful analysis of needs along with a comparison of the costs and benefits of housing alternatives.

Web sites for Housing

- Comparing renting and buying at **www.financenter.com**
- A step-by-step guide to buying a home at **www.maxsol. com/homes/steps.htm**
- Assistance with various aspects of home buying (housing prices, mortgage rates) may be obtained at **www. homefair.com/home, www.homeshark.com,** and **www. ired.com**
- Mortgage rate information at **www.bankrate.com, www.loan-page.com, www.hsh.com,** and **www.micro-surf.com**
- Adjustable rate mortgage information at **www.maxsol. com/homes/comparm.htm**
- Fannie Mae's Web site at **www.homepath.com** includes information on home buying, mortgages, refinancing, and other home ownership topics.
- Housing and mortgage information from the Department of Housing and Urban Development at **www.hud.gov**
- Information of prepaying a mortgage at **alfredo.wustl. edu/mort/**
- Information about reverse mortgages may be obtained at **www.hud.gov/rvrsmort.html**

- Financial calculators for mortgage costs at **www.centura.com/formulas/ca/c.html**

(Note: Addresses and content of Web sites change, and new sites are created daily. Use the search engines discussed in Appendix B to update and locate Web sites for your current financial planning needs.)

PFP SHEETS: 40–45

Short-Term Financial Planning Activities

1. Compare your current housing situation with your housing needs and financial situation (see PFP Sheet 40).
2. Conduct an analysis to compare renting and buying of housing (see PFP Sheet 41).
3. Compare various rental alternatives, as needed (see PFP Sheet 42).
4. Determine your housing and mortgage affordability, and compare various sources of mortgages (see PFP Sheets 43).

Long-Term Financial Planning Activities

1. Monitor changing interest rates and assess refinancing alternatives (see PFP Sheet 45).
2. Develop a plan for assessing housing needs and costs in the future.

Continuous Case for Part III

Spending Patterns for Financial Security

Life Situation
Young married couple: Pam, 30; Josh, 32; two children, ages 1 and 3

Financial Goals	Financial Data	
• Improve daily spending habits	Monthly income	$ 3,600
• Purchase a new home	Living expenses	3,125
• Acquire a second motor vehicle	Assets	33,850
	Liabilities	1,520

The Brocks now have two preschool-age children. Their household income has declined because Pam has "retired" for awhile to care for the children. To compensate for their lower monthly income, Pam and Josh have cut back to the basics and purchase only the "necessities" each month. Still, their expenses total $3,125 a month. However, the Brocks have managed to pay down their liabilities over the past four years; now their liabilities total $1,520.

Housing needs are also changing for the Brocks as their family increases in size. At present, they pay $750 in rent for a two-bedroom apartment. To purchase a home for a comparable monthly payment, the Brocks would have to relocate farther from Josh's place of employment.

In addition to buying a home, the Brocks need to purchase a second automobile. Currently Pam must drive Josh to the train station (creating many inconveniences for her and the children) if she wants to use the car for various business and education activities. If they move to the suburbs, the situation will only get worse.

Questions
1. What major factors are affecting the Brocks' spending habits?
2. Based on a monthly income of $3,600, an estimated $240 per month for property taxes and homeowner's insurance, current mortgage interest rates of 9 percent, and a down payment of at least 10 percent, what would it cost the Brocks to purchase a home?
3. What tax advantages will the Brocks realize by purchasing a home rather than renting?
4. What transportation alternatives should the Brocks consider? If they decide that they need a second motor vehicle, how should they finance it?

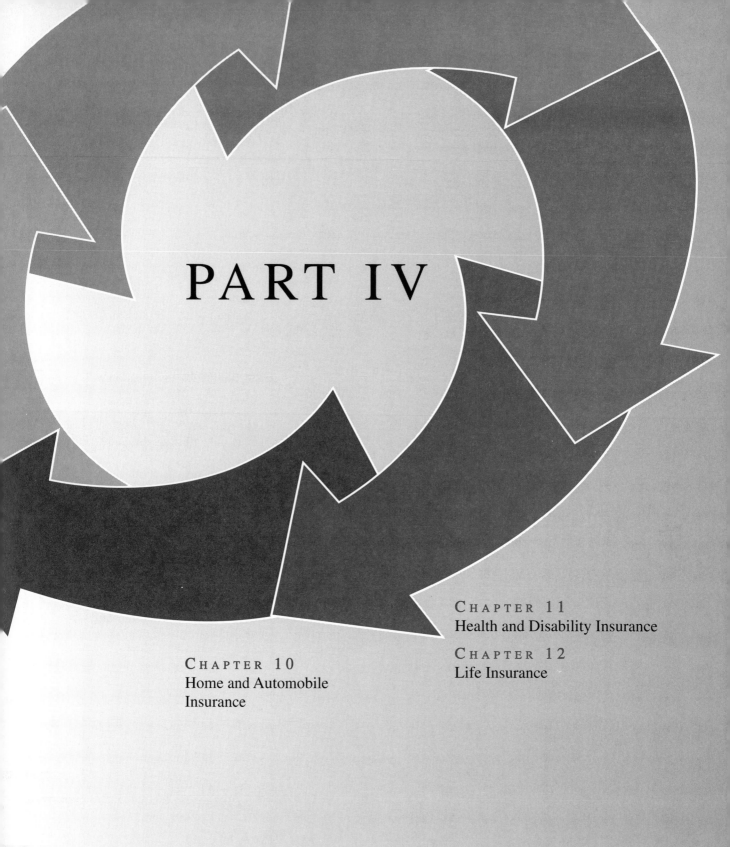

PART IV

INSURING YOUR RESOURCES

"Should I buy term or whole life?" "Does a $500 or a $1,000 deductible better serve my needs?" Your life situation, personal values, economic conditions, and various opportunity costs are central to every financial choice, including personal risk management.

Part IV of *Personal Finance* gives you a basic knowledge of ways to protect your financial resources. Personal risk management is something we must all practice. However, people often avoid this issue and, as a result, increase their risk of financial calamity.

Many people view insurance as a topic that is beyond their understanding. However, as with any area of personal finance, you can become knowledgeable about insurance through your efforts and the assistance of others.

Chapter 10 emphasizes the importance of property and liability insurance and explains the insurance coverages and policy types available to you. Chapter 11 explores health and disability income insurance and explains their importance in financial planning. Chapter 12 deals with determining life insurance needs and creating a plan to buy life insurance and annuities.

Home, auto, health, disability, and life insurance are the cornerstones of every financial plan. As your insurance needs evolve due to changing personal needs and priorities, you will be able to contact professionals and ask appropriate questions to help guide you to wise financial decisions.

CHAPTER 10

HOME AND AUTOMOBILE INSURANCE

Opening Case

ROAD TRIPS ARE FUN AS LONG AS YOU'RE INSURED

José and Marty are excited about their spring break trip to Florida. They have decided to rent a car because Marty drives a clunker and José doesn't want to put miles on the Honda his parents gave him as a graduation gift. When they go to pick up the car, the sales agent asks them if they want a loss-damage and collision-damage waiver, which would cost them $10 per day. They don't want to spend an extra $70 on this trip, but neither one knows if his personal insurance covers rental cars. What should they do?

Motorists usually decline trip insurance. They get the same or better protection from their personal auto insurance. However, sometimes there are gaps in personal coverage. If you don't know the rules and decline the rental agency's offer, you may be driving uninsured. For example, Marty may not have comprehensive and collision coverage on his "clunker" because he knows it isn't worth enough to need the additional coverage. This means he also won't be covered on the rental car.

If Marty's or José's auto policy doesn't cover collision or theft when driving a rental car, they have another option. Certain credit cards will protect them against damage or theft if the card is used when paying for the rental. But again, there may be limitations. Visa offers coverage only with its gold cards; MasterCard gives it with gold cards and some standard cards; American Express covers all its U.S. personal card members. Randy Petersen, editor of the newsletter *InsideFlyer,* always charges rental cars on his Diner's Club card. "It is the only charge card that offers a primary coverage of rental cars," he said. "The other cards only offer secondary coverage, meaning that they kick in after your primary insurance has been exhausted. Diner's Club stands head and shoulders above the rest in this area."

If José and Marty don't know their rental car insurance rules, they are better off checking with their auto insurer or credit card company. Otherwise, the safest thing would be to pay the additional $10 per day.

QUESTIONS

1. Why do most motorists decline additional coverage when they rent a car? What are the limitations of this strategy?
2. What other option do Marty and José have if their personal auto insurance does not cover rental cars?
3. What additional research could they do before they rent a car again?

SOURCES: Jane Bryant Quinn, "Driving Home a Point: Make Sure You're Covered When You Drive a Rental Car," *Chicago Tribune,* December 12, 1996, p. C7; Echo and Kevin Garrett, "Insuring Rental Cars Is Trickier Than Ever," *Investor's Business Daily,* September 18, 1996, p. A1.

After studying this chapter, you will be able to

L.O.1 Develop a risk management plan using insurance.

L.O.2 Discuss the importance of property and liability insurance.

L.O.3 Explain the insurance coverages and policy types available to homeowners and renters.

L.O.4 Analyze factors that influence the amount of coverage and cost of home insurance.

L.O.5 Identify the important types of automobile insurance coverages.

L.O.6 Evaluate factors that affect the cost of automobile insurance.

INSURANCE AND RISK MANAGEMENT: AN INTRODUCTION

L.O.1 Develop a risk management plan using insurance.

Insurance deals with property and people. By providing protection against the many risks of financial uncertainty and unexpected losses, insurance makes it possible for people to plan confidently for the future.

What Is Insurance?

insurance

Insurance is protection against possible financial loss. Although many types of insurance exist, they all have one thing in common: They give you the peace of mind that comes from knowing that money will be available to meet the needs of your survivors, pay medical expenses, protect your home and belongings, and cover personal or property damage caused by your car.

Life insurance replaces income that would be lost if the policyholder died. Health insurance helps meet medical expenses when the policyholder gets sick or helps replace income lost when illness makes it impossible for the policyholder to work. Automobile insurance helps cover property and personal damage caused by the policyholder's car. Home insurance covers the policyholder's place of residence and its associated financial risks, such as damage to personal property and injuries to others.

insurance company

insurer

policy

premium

insured

policyholder

An **insurance company,** or **insurer,** is a risk-sharing firm that agrees to assume financial responsibility for losses that may result from an insured risk. A person joins the risk-sharing group (the insurance company) by purchasing a contract (a **policy**). Under the policy, the insurance company agrees to assume the risk for a fee (the **premium**) that the person (the **insured,** or the **policyholder**) pays periodically.

Insurance provides protection against many risks of financial uncertainty and unexpected losses. The financial consequences of failing to obtain the right amount and type of insurance can be disastrous. Consider the following trade-offs of being without insurance:

301

1. What will happen to your family if the main wage earner dies prematurely without an adequate amount of life insurance? Weigh the yearly cost of insurance premiums against the cost your family will face if regular income stops coming in.
2. What if the main wage earner becomes permanently disabled and is unable to support the family? Again, consider the psychological and financial costs versus the benefits of disability income.
3. What if you have unexpected medical or automobile accident expenses and lack major medical or automobile insurance? Most people will agree that the cost of such insurance protection is a better trade-off than not having the coverage.
4. What might happen if your property is stolen, destroyed, or damaged and you are not insured against such losses?
5. What if a repairperson sues you for an injury suffered from falling down the stairs in your house and you don't carry liability insurance?

Since these trade-offs are usually unacceptable alternatives, most Americans choose to be covered by various types of insurance.

Financial Decision Trade-Off

Types of Risks

You face risks every day. You can't cross the street without some danger that you'll be hit by a car. You can't own property without taking the chance that it will be lost, stolen, damaged, or destroyed. Insurance companies offer financial protection against such dangers and losses by promising to compensate the insured for a relatively large loss in return for the payment of a much smaller but certain expense called the *premium.*

Risk, peril, and *hazard* are important terms in insurance. While in popular use these terms tend to be interchangeable, each has a distinct, technical meaning in insurance terminology.

risk

Basically, **risk** is uncertainty or lack of predictability. In this instance, it refers to the uncertainty as to loss that a person or a property covered by insurance faces. Insurance companies frequently refer to the insured person or property as the *risk.*

peril

Peril is the cause of a possible loss. It is the contingency that causes someone to take out insurance. People buy policies for financial protection against perils such as fire, windstorms, explosions, robbery, accidents, and premature death.

hazard

Hazard increases the likelihood of loss through some peril. For example, defective house wiring is a hazard that increases the likelihood of the peril of fire.

The most common risks are classified as personal risks, property risks, and liability risks. *Personal risks* are the uncertainties surrounding loss of income or life due to premature death, illness, disability, old age, or unemployment. *Property risks* are the uncertainties of direct or indirect losses to personal or real property due to fire, windstorms, accidents, theft, and other hazards. *Liability risks* are possible losses due to negligence resulting in bodily harm or property damage to others. Such harm or damage could be caused by an automobile, professional misconduct, injury suffered on one's property, and so on.

pure risk

Personal risks, property risks, and liability risks are types of **pure risk,** or *insurable risk,* since there would be a chance of loss only if the specified events occurred. Pure risks are accidental and unintentional risks for which the nature and financial cost of the loss can be predicted.

speculative risk

A **speculative risk** is a risk that carries a chance of either loss or gain. Starting a small business that may or may not succeed is an example of speculative risk. So is gambling. Speculative risks are legally defined as uninsurable.

Risk Management Methods

Risk management is an organized strategy for protecting and conserving assets and people. It helps reduce financial losses caused by destructive events. Risk management is a long-range planning process. People's risk management needs change at various points in their lives. If you understand risks and how to manage them, you can provide better protection for yourself and your family against the effects of personal risks, property risks, and liability risks. In this way, you can reduce your financial losses and thereby improve your chances for economic, social, physical, and emotional well-being throughout your life. Since you will probably be unable to afford to cover all risks, you need to understand how to obtain the best protection you can afford. A combination of strategic alternatives to cover major risks is usually advisable.

Most people think of risk management as buying insurance. However, insurance is not the only method of dealing with risk, and in certain situations, other methods may be less costly. In this section, we discuss the four general risk management techniques.

1. Risk Avoidance   You can avoid the risk of an automobile accident by not driving to work. General Motors can avoid the risk of product failure by not introducing new cars. Risk avoidance would be practiced in both instances, but at a very high cost. You might have to give up your job, and General Motors might lose out to competitors that introduce new models.

In some situations, however, risk avoidance is a practical approach. At the personal level, people avoid risks by not smoking or by not walking through high-crime neighborhoods. At the business level, jewelry stores avoid losses through robbery by locking their merchandise in vaults before closing. Obviously, no person or business can avoid all risks. By the same token, no one should assume all risks are unavoidable.

2. Risk Reduction   You may reduce risks; however, you cannot avoid them. You can reduce the risk of injury in an auto accident by wearing a seat belt. You can install smoke alarms and fire extinguishers in your home to protect life and reduce potential damage in case of fire. You can reduce the risk of becoming ill by eating a balanced diet and exercising.

3. Risk Assumption   Risk assumption means taking on responsibility for the loss or injury that may result from a risk. Generally, it makes sense to assume a risk when the potential loss is too small to worry about, when effective risk management has reduced the risk, when insurance coverage is too expensive, and when there is no other way to obtain protection against a loss. For instance, you might decide not to purchase collision insurance on an older car. Then, if an accident occurs, you will bear the costs of fixing the car.

self-insurance

Self-insurance is the process of establishing a monetary fund to cover the cost of a loss. Self-insurance does not eliminate risks; it only provides means for covering losses. Many people self-insure by default, not by choice.

4. Risk Shifting   The most common method of dealing with risk is to shift, or transfer, it to an insurance company or some other organization. Insurance is thus the protection against loss afforded by the purchase of an insurance policy from an insurance company.

Exhibit 10–1 summarizes various risks and appropriate strategies for managing them.

Planning an Insurance Program

Because all people have their own needs and goals, many of which change over the years, a personal insurance program should be tailored to those needs and goals and to the

EXHIBIT 10-1   **Examples of Risks and Risk Management Strategies**

	Risks		Strategies for Reducing Financial Impact	
Personal Events	**Financial Impact**	**Personal Resources**	**Private Sector**	**Public Sector**
Disability	Loss of one income Loss of services Increased expenses Other losses	Savings, investments Family observing safety precautions Other resources	Disability insurance Other strategies	Disability insurance
Illness	Loss of one income Catastrophic hospital expenses Other losses	Health-enhancing behavior	Health insurance Health maintenance organizations Other strategies	Military health care Medicare, Medicaid
Death	Loss of one income Loss of services Final expenses Other expenses	Estate planning Risk reduction Other resources	Life insurance Other strategies	Veteran's life insurance Social Security survivor's benefits
Retirement	Decreased income Other expenses	Savings Investments Hobbies, skills Other resources	Retirement and/or pensions Other strategies	Social Security Pension plan for government employees
Property loss	Catastrophic storm damage to property Repair or replacement cost of theft	Property repair and upkeep Security plans Other resources	Automobile insurance Homeowner's insurance Flood insurance (joint program with government)	Flood insurance (joint program with business)
Liability	Claims and settlement costs Lawsuits and legal expenses Loss of personal assets and income Other expenses	Observing safety precautions Maintaining property Other resources	Homeowner's insurance Automobile insurance Malpractice insurance Other strategies	

changes they undergo. In the early years of marriage, when children are young and the family is growing, most families need certain kinds of insurance protection. This protection may include property insurance on an apartment or a house, life and disability insurance for the major wage earner, and adequate health insurance (with maternity benefits for the wife) for the whole family.

Later, when the family has a higher income and different financial requirements, protection needs will change. There might be a long-range provision for the children's education, more life insurance to match higher income and living standards, and revised health insurance protection. Still later, when the children have grown and are on their own, retirement benefits will be a consideration, further changing the family's personal insurance program.

The accompanying Financial Planning in Action feature on page 306 suggests several guidelines to follow in planning your insurance program. Exhibit 10–2 outlines the steps in developing a personal insurance program.

EXHIBIT 10–2   **Creating a Personal Insurance Program**

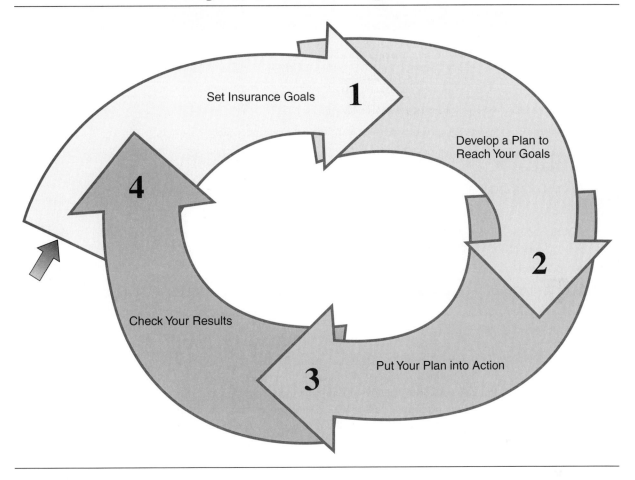

1. Set Insurance Goals   In managing risks, your goals are to minimize personal, property, and liability risks. Your insurance goals should define what you expect to do to cover the basic risks present in your life situation. Covering the basic risks means providing a financial resource to cover costs resulting from a loss.

Suppose your goal is to buy a new car. You must plan to make the purchase and to protect yourself against accidents. Auto insurance on the car lets you enjoy the car without worrying that an auto accident might leave you worse off, financially and physically, than before.

Each individual has unique goals. Income, age, family size, lifestyle, experience, and responsibilities enter into the goals you set, and the insurance you buy must reflect those goals. In general, financial advisers say that a basic risk management plan must set goals to reduce

- Potential loss of income due to the premature death, illness, accident, or unemployment of a wage earner.
- Potential loss of income and extra expense resulting from the illness, disability, or death of a spouse.
- Additional expenses due to the injury, illness, or death of other family members.
- Potential loss of real or personal property due to fire, theft, or other hazards.
- Potential loss of income, savings, and property due to personal liability.

Financial Planning in Action

How Can You Plan an Insurance Program?

Did You: Yes   No

- Seek advice from a competent and reliable insurance adviser?   ☐   ☐
- Determine what insurance you need to provide your family with sufficient protection if you die? ☐   ☐
- Consider what portion of the family protection you need is met by Social Security and by group insurance, if any?   ☐   ☐
- Decide what other needs must be met by insurance (funeral expenses, savings, retirement annuities, etc.)?   ☐   ☐
- Decide what types of insurance best meet your needs?   ☐   ☐
- Plan on an insurance program and stick to it except for periodic reviews of changing needs and changing conditions?   ☐   ☐
- Buy more insurance than you need or can afford?   ☐   ☐
- Drop one policy for another (unless the new policy provides the same coverage for less money)?   ☐   ☐

2. Develop a Plan to Reach Your Goals   Planning is a sign of maturity, a way of taking control of life instead of letting life happen to you. What risks do you face? Which risks can you afford to take without having to back away from your goals? What resources—public programs, personal assets, or private risk-sharing plans—are available to you?

To understand and use the resources at your command, you need good information. In terms of insurance, this means a clear picture of the available insurance, the soundness and reliability of different insurers, and the comparative costs of the coverage you need.

3. Put Your Plan into Action   As you carry out your plan, you obtain financial and personal resources, budget them, and use them to reach your risk management goals. If, for example, you find the insurance protection you have is not enough to cover your basic risks, you may purchase additional coverage, change the kind of insurance coverage you have, restructure your personal or family budget to cover additional insurance costs, and strengthen your savings or investment programs to reduce the long-term risk of economic hardship.

The best risk management plans have an element of flexibility. Savings accounts or other cash, for example, are available as emergency funds for any number of unexpected financial problems. The best plans are also flexible enough to allow you to respond to changing life situations. Your goal should be an insurance program that expands (or contracts) with the changing scope of your protection needs.

4. Check Your Results   Evaluate your insurance plan periodically, at least every two or three years or whenever your family circumstances change. Among the questions you should ask yourself are: Does it work? Does it adequately protect my plans and goals? An effective risk manager consistently checks the outcomes of decisions and is alert to changes that may reduce the effectiveness of the current risk management plan.

A young working couple may be entirely happy with their life and health insurance coverage. But when they add an infant to the family, it's time to review the protection

JONATHAN HOENIG SPEAKS
INSURE? SURE!

Ever been to Vegas? Ever made a bet?

Buying insurance is essentially making a bet that you *don't* want to win. While you can't *plan* on experiencing many of life's calamities, you *should* plan for them. Without the appropriate insurance, a single event—often an unexpected accident—can completely trash your hard-earned assets.

Never smoked? Healthy as a horse? It doesn't matter! Insurance is specifically designed for those situations you hope will never occur. When those situations do occur, however, you'll find that savvy spending on appropriate insurance was money well spent.

Life insurance takes care of your dependents if you die. If you have a spouse, children, or other loved ones who are directly dependent on your income, life insurance is a *must*. Young people generally find they don't need life insurance.

Health insurance "foots" the medical bills if you get sick. If you've ever paid full price for a medical prescription, you are probably aware that health care costs have skyrocketed. Even a seemingly simple procedure can often cost thousands of dollars. So everyone needs health insurance, and thankfully many employers offer group plans at reasonable rates. Be sure to inquire about health insurance when applying for a job; the level of insurance offered might affect your interest in working for a particular company. Working solo? Bummer. Individuals who purchase private policies will pay more for equivalent coverage.

Keep in mind that there are insurance products available for any number of scenarios, so do your homework and evaluate your needs. As always, read everything and ask a ton of questions.

Statistics show that each year 1 out of 106 people die, 1 out of 70 have an automobile accident, and 1 out of 88 households catch on fire. That "1" could easily be you.

---

plans. Suddenly the risk of financial catastrophe to the family (should one or both parents die or become disabled) is much greater. Yesterday's decisions about insurance coverage need revision.

The needs of a single person differ from those of a family, a single parent, a couple, or a group of unrelated adults living in the same household. All of these people face similar risks, but their financial responsibility to others differs greatly. In each case, the vital question is: Have I provided the financial resources and risk management strategy needed to take care of my basic responsibilities for my own well-being and the well-being of others?

To put your risk management plan to work, you must answer four basic questions: (1) What should be insured, (2) for how much, (3) what kind of insurance should I buy, and (4) from whom?

Sheet 46

CONCEPT CHECK 10–1

1. What is the purpose of insurance?
2. How are the most common risks classified?
3. What is the difference between pure risk and speculative risk?
4. What are the methods of managing risk?
5. What are the steps in planning your personal insurance coverage?

THE ROLE OF PROPERTY AND LIABILITY INSURANCE IN YOUR FINANCIAL PLAN

L.O.2 Discuss the importance of property and liability insurance.

In recent years, major disasters have caused catastrophic amounts of property loss in the United States. Hurricane Hugo cost $4.2 billion in damages. Fires in Oakland, California, caused insured losses of $1.2 billion. Hurricane Andrew resulted in $7.3 billion of insurance claims. The Midwest floods of 1993 resulted in over $12 billion of damage.

Since most people invest large amounts of money in their homes and motor vehicles, protecting these assets from loss is a great concern. Each year, homeowners and renters lose billions of dollars from more than 3 million burglaries, 500,000 fires, and 200,000 instances of damage from other hazards. The cost of injuries and property damage caused by automobiles is also very great. Most people use insurance to reduce their chances of economic loss from these risks.

Every aspect of personal financial decision making involves a trade-off among alternatives. Many events that might affect your home or your automobile—for example, a robbery in your home or an automobile accident—can result in great financial losses. The price you pay for home and automobile insurance may be viewed as an investment in financial protection against these losses. Although the costs of home and automobile insurance may seem high, the financial losses from which insurance protects you are much higher. Property and liability insurance offer protection from financial losses that may arise from a wide variety of situations.

An automobile insurance company once paid $3,600 for damages to a car in an accident caused by a mouse. The critter apparently got into the car while it was parked and then crawled up the driver's pants leg while the car was on an interstate highway. The driver lost control of the vehicle and crashed into a roadside barrier. Another claim resulted when a barbecued steak fell off a 17th-floor balcony and dented a car.

While these incidents have a humorous side, most accidents—and the property losses and legal actions connected with them—do not. The main types of risks related to a home and an automobile are (1) property damage or loss and (2) your responsibility for injuries to others or damage to the property of others.

Potential Property Losses

Houses, automobiles, furniture, clothing, and other personal belongings are a substantial financial commitment for most people. Property owners face two basic types of risks. The first is *physical damage* caused by hazards such as fire, wind, water, and smoke. These hazards can cause destruction of your property or temporary loss of its use. For example, if a windstorm causes a large tree branch to break your automobile windshield, you lose the use of the vehicle while it is being repaired. The second type of risk property owners face is *loss of use* due to robbery, burglary, vandalism, or arson.

Liability Protection

In a wide variety of circumstances, a person may be judged legally responsible for injuries or damages. For example, if a child walks across your property, falls, and sustains severe injuries, the child's family may be able to recover substantial damages from you as a result of the injuries. If you accidentally damage a rare painting while assisting a friend with home repairs, the friend may take legal action against you to recover the cost of the painting.

liability

negligence

Liability is legal responsibility for the financial cost of another person's losses or injuries. In many situations, your legal responsibility can be caused by **negligence,** failure to take ordinary or reasonable care. Doing something in a careless manner, such as

EXHIBIT 10–3   **Home Insurance Coverage**

Building and other structures

Personal property

Loss of use/necessary living expenses while home is uninhabitable

Personal liability and related coverages

improperly supervising children at a swimming pool or failure to remove items from a frequently used staircase, may be ruled as negligence in a liability lawsuit.

strict liability

vicarious liability

Despite taking great care, a person may still be held liable in a situation. **Strict liability** is present when a person is held responsible for intentional or unintentional actions. **Vicarious liability** occurs when a person is held responsible for the actions of another person. If the behavior of a child causes financial or physical harm to others, the parent may be held responsible; if the activities of an employee cause damage, the employer may be held responsible.

Liability lawsuits affect society as well as individuals. The settlements for such cases result in higher insurance premiums and higher prices for goods and services. In an effort to keep liability insurance costs down, most states have taken action to limit damage awards. The purpose of these legislative measures is to keep insurance premiums reasonable for businesses and consumers. Florida's liability award limit, for example, was imposed on the condition that premiums be reduced for insurance customers.

CONCEPT   CHECK   10–2

1. What property and liability risks might some people overlook?
2. How could a person's life situation influence the need for certain types of property and liability insurance?

PRINCIPLES OF HOME AND PROPERTY INSURANCE

L.O.3 Explain the insurance coverages and policy types available to homeowners and renters.

homeowner's insurance

Your home and personal belongings are probably a major portion of your assets. Whether you rent your dwelling or own a house, condominium, or mobile home, property insurance is vital. **Homeowner's insurance** is coverage for your place of residence and its associated financial risks, such as damage to personal property and injuries to others (see Exhibit 10–3).

Homeowner's Insurance Coverages

A homeowner's policy provides coverages for the building and other structures, additional living expenses, personal property, personal liability and related coverages, and specialized coverages.

Building and Other Structures   The main component of homeowner's insurance is protection against financial loss due to damage or destruction to a house or other structures. Your dwelling and attached structures are covered for fire and other damages. Detached structures on the property, such as a garage, toolshed, or bathhouse, are also protected. Finally, the coverage includes trees, shrubs, and plants.

Additional Living Expenses   If damage from a fire or other event prevents the use of your home, *additional living expense coverage* pays for the cost of living elsewhere. While your home is being repaired, this coverage reimburses you for the cost of living in a temporary location. Some policies limit additional living expense coverage to 10 to 20 percent of the home's coverage and limit payments to a maximum of six to nine months; other policies pay the full cost incurred for up to a year.

Personal Property   Your household belongings, such as furniture, appliances, and clothing, are covered for damage or loss up to a portion of the insured value of the home, usually 55, 70, or 75 percent. For example, a home insured for $80,000 might have $56,000 (70 percent) of coverage for household belongings.

personal property floater

Personal property coverage commonly has limits for the theft of certain items, such as $1,000 for jewelry, $2,000 for firearms, and $2,500 for silverware. Items with a value exceeding these limits can be protected with a **personal property floater,** which covers the damage or loss of a specific item of high value. A floater requires a detailed description of the item and periodic appraisals to verify its current value. This coverage protects the item regardless of its location; thus, the item is insured while you are traveling or transporting it.

Floaters to protect home computers and related equipment are recommended. This additional coverage can prevent financial loss due to damage or loss of your computer. Contact your insurance agent to determine whether the equipment is covered against damage from mischievous pets, spilled drinks, dropping, or power surges.

Personal property coverage usually provides protection against the loss or damage of articles taken with you when away from home. For example, possessions taken on vacation or used while at school are usually covered up to a policy limit. Property that you rent, such as some power tools or a rug shampoo machine, is insured while it is in your possession.

household inventory

In the event of damage or loss of property, you must be able to prove both ownership and value. A **household inventory** is a list or other documentation of personal belongings, with purchase dates and cost information. You can get a form for such an inventory from an insurance agent. Exhibit 10–4 provides a reminder of the items you should include in the inventory. For items of special value, you should have receipts, serial numbers, brand names, model names, and written appraisals of value.

Your household inventory can include photographs or a video recording of your home and its contents. Make sure the closet and storage area doors are photographed open. On the backs of the photographs, indicate the date and the value of the objects. Regularly update your inventory, photos, and appraisal documents. Keep a copy of each document in a secure location such as a safe deposit box.

Sheet 47

Personal Liability and Related Coverages   Each day, we face the risk of financial loss due to injuries to others or damage to property for which we are responsible. The following are examples of this risk:

- A neighbor or guest falls on your property, resulting in permanent disability.
- A spark from burning leaves on your property starts a fire that damages a neighbor's roof.
- A member of your family accidentally breaks an expensive glass statue while at another person's house.

EXHIBIT 10–4   **Household Inventory Contents**

In each of these situations, you could be held responsible for the costs incurred. The personal liability component of a homeowner's policy protects you from financial losses resulting from legal action or claims against you or family members due to damages to the property of others. This coverage includes the cost of legal defense.

Not all of the individuals who come to your property are covered by your liability insurance. While a baby-sitter or others who assist you occasionally are probably covered, regular employees, such as a housekeeper or a gardener, may require worker's compensation coverage.

EXHIBIT 10–5

Types of Home Insurance Policies

The policies below cover perils provided for in the basic and broad forms, including

Basic Form (HO–1)	<table><tr><td>■ Fire, lightning</td><td>■ Smoke</td></tr><tr><td>■ Windstorm, hail</td><td>■ Vandalism or malicious mischief</td></tr><tr><td>■ Explosion</td><td>■ Theft</td></tr><tr><td>■ Riot or civil commotion</td><td>■ Glass breakage</td></tr><tr><td>■ Aircraft</td><td>■ Volcanic eruption</td></tr><tr><td>■ Vehicles</td><td></td></tr></table>
Broad Form (HO–2)	Covers all basic-form risks, plus <table><tr><td>■ Falling objects</td><td>■ Tearing apart of heating system or appliance</td></tr><tr><td>■ Weight of ice, snow, or sleet</td><td>■ Freezing</td></tr><tr><td>■ Discharge of water or steam</td><td>■ Accidental damage from electrical current</td></tr></table>
Special Form (All risk) (HO–3)	Covers all basic and broad-form risks, plus any other risks except those specifically excluded from the policy, such as <table><tr><td>■ Flood</td><td>■ War</td></tr><tr><td>■ Earthquake</td><td>■ Nuclear accidents</td></tr></table>
Tenants Form (HO–4)	Covers personal belongings against the risks covered by the basic and broad forms of the homeowner's policies
Comprehensive Form (HO–5)	Expands coverage of HO–3 to include endorsements for items such as replacement cost coverage on contents and guaranteed replacement cost coverage on buildings
Condominium Form (HO–6)	Covers personal belongings and additions to the living unit
Country Home Form (HO–7)	For nonfarm business rural residents with coverage on agricultural buildings and equipment
Modified Coverage Form (HO–8)	This older-home policy covers residences with high replacement cost relative to current market value. For example, decorative woodwork in a Victorian home would be very costly to duplicate; coverage pays for the restoration of property, but not necessarily with the same materials as used in the original. The other major coverages of each policy are ■ Personal liability ■ Medical payments for guests on the property ■ Additional living expenses

umbrella policy

Most homeowner's policies provide a basic personal liability coverage of $100,000, but additional amounts are frequently recommended. An **umbrella policy,** also called a *personal catastrophe policy,* supplements your basic personal liability coverage. This added protection covers you for personal injury claims such as libel, slander, defamation of character, and invasion of property. Extended liability policies are sold in amounts of $1 million or more and are useful for individuals with substantial net worth. If you are a business owner, you may need other types of liability coverage.

medical payments coverage

Medical payments coverage pays the costs of minor accidental injuries on your property and minor injuries caused by you, family members, or pets away from home. Settlements under medical payments coverage are made without determining fault. This protection allows fast processing of small claims, generally up to $5,000. Suits for more severe personal injuries are covered by the personal liability portion of the homeowner's policy. Medical payments coverage does not cover the people who live in the home being insured.

Should you or a family member accidentally damage another person's property, the *supplementary coverage* of homeowner's insurance will pay for these minor mishaps. This protection is usually limited to $500 or $1,000. Again, payments are made regardless of fault. Any property damage claims for greater amounts would require action under the personal liability coverage.

Specialized Coverages   Homeowner's insurance usually does not cover losses from floods and earthquakes. People living in areas with these two risks need to obtain special coverage. In various communities, the National Flood Insurance Program makes flood insurance available. This protection is a coverage separate from the homeowner's policy. An insurance agent or the Federal Emergency Management Agency of the Federal Insurance Administration (see Appendix E) can give you additional information about this coverage. Ninety percent of the people who lost their homes in the 1993 Midwest floods had no flood insurance.

endorsement

Earthquake insurance can be obtained as an **endorsement,** or addition of coverage, to the homeowner's policy. Since the most severe earthquakes occur in the Pacific Coast region, most insurance against this risk is bought by people in that region. Remember, however, that every state is vulnerable to earthquakes and this insurance coverage is available in all areas for an additional charge. Lenders frequently require insurance against both floods and earthquakes for a mortgage to buy a home in areas with these risks.

Renter's Insurance

For people who rent, home insurance coverages include personal property protection, additional living expenses coverage, and personal liability and related coverages. Protection against financial loss due to damage or loss of personal property is the main component of renter's insurance. While more than 9 out of 10 homeowners have insurance, only about 4 out of 10 renters are covered. Often renters believe they are covered under the insurance policy of the building owner. In fact, the building owner's property insurance does not cover tenants' personal property unless the building owner can be proven negligent. If faulty wiring causes a fire and damages a tenant's property, the renter may be able to collect for damages from the building owner. Renter's insurance is relatively inexpensive and provides protection from financial loss due to many of the same risks covered in homeowner's policies.

Home Insurance Policy Forms

Until the mid-1950s, a homeowner had to buy separate coverage for fire, theft, and other risks. Then the insurance industry developed a series of package policies. The *basic form (HO–1)* and the *broad form (HO–2)* were the first such policies; they provided the primary coverages shown in Exhibit 10–5. Today very few companies still sell these two forms of homeowner's insurance.

The *special form (HO–3)* of a homeowner's policy covers the building for all causes of loss or damage except those specifically excluded by the policy. Common exclusions are flood, earthquake, war, and nuclear accidents (see also Exhibit 10–6). Personal property is covered for the risks listed in the policy.

EXHIBIT 10–6

Not Everything Is Covered

Certain personal property is specifically excluded from the coverage provided by homeowner's insurance:

- Articles separately described and specifically insured, such as jewelry, furs, boats, or expensive electronic equipment.
- Animals, birds, or fish.
- Motorized land vehicles, except those used to service an insured's residence, that are not licensed for road use.
- Any device or instrument for the transmission and recording of sound, including any accessories or antennas, while in or on motor vehicles. This includes stereo tape players, stereo tapes, and citizens' band radios.
- Aircraft and parts.
- Property of roomers, boarders, and other tenants who are not related to any insured.
- Property contained in an apartment regularly rented or held for rental to others by any insured.
- Property rented or held for rental to others away from the residence premises.
- Business property in storage, or held as a sample, or for sale, or for delivery after sale.
- Business property pertaining to business actually conducted on the residence premises.
- Business property away from the residence premises.

The *tenants form (HO–4)* protects the personal property of renters against the specific risks listed in the policy. As mentioned, renter's insurance does not include coverage on the building or other structures.

Condominium owner's insurance (HO–6) protects personal property of condominium owners and any additions or improvements made to the living unit, such as bookshelves, electrical fixtures, and wall or floor coverings. Insurance on the building and other structures is purchased by the condominium association.

The *modified coverage form (HO–8)*, or older-home policy, provides the same coverages as the basic form at a more reasonable cost because the homes are older and more difficult to replace.

Manufactured housing units and mobile homes usually qualify for insurance coverage with conventional policies. However, certain mobile homes may require a special arrangement and higher rates since their construction makes them more prone to fire and wind damage. The cost of mobile home insurance coverage is most heavily affected by location and by the method used to attach the housing unit to the ground. This type of property insurance is quite expensive; a $20,000 mobile home can cost as much to insure as a $60,000 house.

In addition to the property and liability risks previously discussed, home insurance policies include coverage for

- Credit card fraud, check forgery, and counterfeit money.
- The cost of removing damaged property.
- Emergency removal of property to protect it from damage.
- Temporary repairs after a loss to prevent further damage.
- Fire department charges in areas with such fees.

CONCEPT CHECK 10–3

1. What main coverages are included in home insurance policies?
2. What is the purpose of personal liability coverage?
3. How does renter's insurance differ from other home insurance policies?

EXHIBIT 10–7

Determining the Amount of Home Insurance You Need

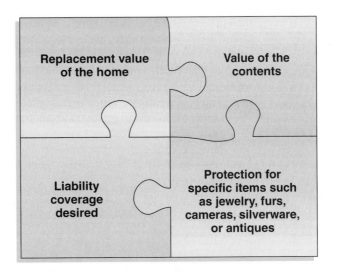

HOME INSURANCE COST FACTORS

L.O.4 Analyze factors that influence the amount of coverage and cost of home insurance.

Some studies estimate that as many as two-thirds of homes in the United States are not insured or are underinsured. Financial losses caused by fire, theft, wind, and other risks amount to billions of dollars each year. Since most homeowners have a mortgage on their property, their lending institutions usually require that they have insurance. When purchasing insurance, you can get the best value for each premium dollar by selecting the appropriate amount of coverage and being aware of the factors that affect insurance costs.

How Much Coverage Do You Need?

Several factors affect how much insurance coverage you need for your home and property (see Exhibit 10–7). Your insurance protection should be based on the amount of money you need to rebuild or repair your house, not the amount you paid for it. As construction costs rise, you should increase the amount of coverage. In recent years, most insurance policies have had a built-in inflation clause that increases coverage as property values increase. This increased coverage is based on an index of property values and the cost of living in your area.

coinsurance clause

In the past, most homeowner's policies contained a provision requiring that the building be insured for at least 80 percent of the replacement value. Under this **coinsurance clause,** the homeowner would have to pay for part of the losses if the property was not insured for the specified percentage of the replacement value. While a few companies still use a coinsurance clause, most companies today suggest full coverage.

If you are financing a home, the lending institution will require you to have property insurance in an amount that covers its financial investment. Remember, too, that the amount of insurance on your home will determine the coverage on the contents. Personal belongings are generally covered up to an amount ranging from 55 to 75 percent of the insurance on the dwelling.

actual cash value (ACV)

Insurance companies base claim settlements on one of two methods. Under the **actual cash value (ACV)** method, the payment you receive is based on the current replacement cost of a damaged or lost item less depreciation. This means you would get $180 for a five-year-old television set that cost you $400 and had an estimated life of eight years if the same set now costs $480. Your settlement amount is determined by taking the current cost of $480 and subtracting five years of depreciation from it—$300 for five years at $60 a year.

replacement value

Under the **replacement value** method for settling claims, you receive the full cost of repairing or replacing a damaged or lost item; depreciation is not considered. However, many companies limit the replacement cost to 400 percent of the item's actual cash value. Replacement value coverage costs about 10 to 20 percent more than ACV coverage.

Factors That Affect Home Insurance Costs

Sheet 48

The main influences on the premium paid for home and property insurance are the location of the home, the type of structure, the coverage amount and policy type, discounts, and differences among insurance companies.

Location of Home   The location of the residence affects insurance rates. So do the efficiency of the fire department, the available water supply, and the frequency of thefts in the area. If more claims have been filed in an area, home insurance rates for people living there will be higher.

Type of Structure   The type of home and the construction materials influence the costs of insurance coverage. A brick house, for example, would cost less to insure than a similar house made of wood. However, earthquake coverage is more expensive for a brick home than for a wood dwelling. Also, the age and style of the house can create more potential risks and increase insurance costs.

Coverage Amount and Policy Type   The policy you select and the financial limits of coverage affect the premium you pay. It costs more to insure a $150,000 home than a $100,000 home. The comprehensive form of homeowner's policy costs more than a tenant's policy.

The *deductible* amount in your policy also affects the cost of your insurance. If you increase the amount of your deductible, your premium will be lower since the company will pay out less in claims. The most common deductible amount is $250. Increasing the deductible from $250 to $500 or $1,000 can reduce the premium 15 percent or more.

Home Insurance Discounts   Most companies offer incentives that reduce home insurance costs. Your premium may be lower if you have smoke detectors or a fire extinguisher. Deterrents to burglars, such as dead bolt locks or an alarm system, can also save you money. Some companies offer home insurance discounts to policyholders who are nonsmokers or may give a discount for being "claim free" for a certain number of years.

Sheet 49

Company Differences   Studies show that you can save up to 25 percent on homeowner's insurance by comparing companies. Contact both insurance agents who work for one company and independent agents who represent several. The information you obtain will enable you to compare rates. Home insurance rates may be compared using information from the World Wide Web. For further information, see Appendix B.

Don't select a company on the basis of price alone. Also consider service and coverage. Not all companies settle claims in the same way. For example, a number of homeowners had two sides of their houses dented by hail. Since the type of siding used in these houses was no longer available, all of the siding had to be replaced. Some insurance companies paid for the complete replacement of the siding, while others paid only for the replacement of the damaged areas. State insurance commissions, other government agencies, and consumer organizations can provide information about the reputations of insurance companies. *Consumer Reports* regularly publishes a satisfaction index of property insurance companies based on speed of settling claims, claim settlement amounts, and ease of reaching a claim representative.

CONCEPT CHECK 10–4

1. What major factors influence the cost of home insurance?
2. What actions can a person take to reduce the cost of home insurance?

AUTOMOBILE INSURANCE COVERAGES

L.O.5 Identify the important types of automobile insurance coverages.

Each year, motor vehicle crashes cost over $140 billion in lost wages and medical costs. The National Traffic Safety Administration estimates that alcohol use is a factor in over 60 percent of automobile accidents. Such accidents result in thousands of highway deaths and injuries and over $30 billion in costs. These automobile accidents create a risk that affects many people financially and emotionally. Automobile insurance cannot eliminate the costs of automobile accidents; however, it does reduce the financial impact.

financial responsibility law

A **financial responsibility law** is state legislation that requires drivers to prove their ability to cover the cost of damage or injury caused by an automobile accident. All states have such laws to protect the public from physical harm and property damage losses caused by drivers. When injuries or significant property damage occur in an accident, the drivers involved are required to file a report with the state and to show financial responsibility. As of 1997, over 40 states had compulsory automobile insurance laws. In other states, most people meet the financial responsibility requirement by buying insurance, since very few have the financial resources needed to meet this legal requirement on their own. Exhibit 10–8 presents each state's minimum limits for financial responsibility. These amounts represent the minimum state requirement; higher coverage is recommended to protect the financial assets of individuals.

The main coverages provided by automobile insurance fall into two categories: bodily injury coverages and property damage coverages (see Exhibit 10–9). Other coverages include wage loss insurance, towing service, accidental death, and car rental when a vehicle is undergoing repairs due to an accident.

Bodily Injury Coverages

Most of the money automobile insurance companies pay in claims goes for legal expenses of injury lawsuits, medical expenses, and related costs. The main bodily injury coverages are bodily injury liability, medical payments coverage, and uninsured motorist's protection. No-fault systems in a number of states have influenced the process of settling bodily injury claims.

bodily injury liability

Bodily Injury Liability   **Bodily injury liability** covers the risk of financial loss due to legal expenses, medical expenses, lost wages, and other expenses associated with injuries caused by an automobile accident for which you were responsible. This insurance protects you from extensive financial losses.

Bodily injury liability is usually expressed as a split limit, such as 50/100 or 100/300. These amounts represent thousands of dollars of coverage. The first number (see Exhibit

EXHIBIT 10–8

Automobile Financial Responsibility/ Compulsory Insurance Minimum Limits (As of 1998)

State	Liability Limits	State	Liability Limits
Alabama*	20/40/10	Montana*	25/50/10
Alaska*	50/100/25	Nebraska*	25/50/25
Arizona*	15/30/10	Nevada*	15/30/10
Arkansas*	25/50/15	New Hampshire	25/50/25
California*	15/30/5	New Jersey*	15/30/5
Colorado*	25/50/15	New Mexico*	25/50/10
Connecticut*	20/40/10	New York*	25/50/10
Delaware*	15/30/10	North Carolina*	25/50/15
District of Columbia*	25/50/10	North Dakota*	25/50/25
Florida*	10/20/10	Ohio*	12.5/25/7.5
Georgia*	15/30/10	Oklahoma*	10/20/10
Hawaii*	20/40/10	Oregon*	25/50/10
Idaho*	25/50/15	Pennsylvania*	15/30/5
Illinois*	20/40/15	Rhode Island*	25/50/25
Indiana*	25/50/10	South Carolina*	15/30/5
Iowa*	20/40/15	South Dakota*	25/50/25
Kansas*	25/50/10	Tennessee*	20/50/10
Kentucky*	25/50/10	Texas*	20/40/15
Louisiana*	10/20/10	Utah*	25/50/15
Maine*	20/40/10	Vermont*	20/40/10
Maryland*	20/40/10	Virginia	25/50/20
Massachusetts*	20/40/5	Washington*	25/50/10
Michigan*	20/40/10	West Virginia*	20/40/10
Minnesota*	30/60/10	Wisconsin	25/50/10
Mississippi*	10/20/5	Wyoming*	25/50/20
Missouri*	25/50/10		

*State with compulsory automobile liability insurance.
†50/100 in cases where injury results in death.
SOURCE: Insurance Information Institute.

EXHIBIT 10–9

Automobile Insurance Coverage

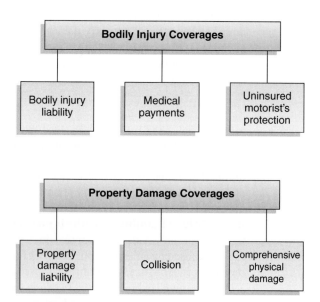

EXHIBIT 10–10

Automobile Liability Insurance Coverage

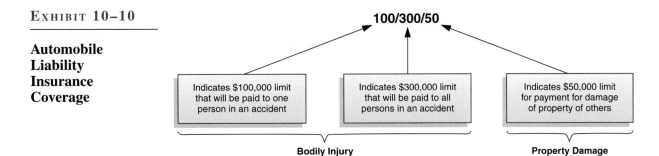

100/300/50

Indicates $100,000 limit that will be paid to one person in an accident

Indicates $300,000 limit that will be paid to all persons in an accident

Indicates $50,000 limit for payment for damage of property of others

Bodily Injury Liability

Property Damage Liability

10–10) is the limit for claims that can be paid to one person; the second number is the limit for each accident; the third number is discussed in the section on property damage coverages. With 100/300 bodily injury coverage, for example, a driver would have a limit of $100,000 that could be paid to one person in an accident for claims. In addition, there would be a $300,000 limit for all bodily injury claims from a single accident.

Medical Payments Coverage   While bodily injury liability pays for the costs of injuries to persons who were not in your automobile, **medical payments coverage** covers the costs of health care for people who were injured in your automobile, including yourself. This protection covers friends, car pool members, and others who ride in your vehicle. Medical payments insurance also provides medical benefits if you or a member of your family is struck by an automobile or injured while riding in another person's automobile.

medical payments coverage

Uninsured Motorist's Protection   If you are in an accident caused by a person without insurance, **uninsured motorist's protection** covers the cost of injuries to you and your family; in most states, however, it does not cover property damage. This insurance also provides protection against financial losses due to injuries caused by a hit-and-run driver or by a driver who has insufficient coverage to cover the cost of your injuries. *Under-insured motorist's coverage* provides financial protection when another driver has insurance but less coverage than needed to cover the financial damages brought upon you.

uninsured motorist's protection

No-Fault Insurance   Difficulties and high costs of settling claims for medical expenses and personal injuries resulted in the creation of the **no-fault system,** in which drivers involved in accidents collect medical expenses, lost wages, and related injury costs from their own insurance companies. The system is intended to provide fast and smooth methods of paying for damages without taking the legal action frequently necessary to determine fault.

no-fault system

In 1971, Massachusetts was the first state to implement no-fault insurance. As of 1993, nearly 30 states had some variation of the system. While no-fault automobile insurance was intended to reduce the time and cost associated with the settlement of automobile injury cases, this has not always been the result. One reason for continued difficulties is that no-fault systems vary from state to state. Some no-fault states set limits on medical expenses, lost wages, and other claim settlements, while other states allow lawsuits under certain conditions, such as permanent paralysis or death. Some states include property damage in no-fault insurance. Many consider Michigan's system, in which policies provide unlimited compensation for medical and rehabilitation costs and up to a set amount for lost income, an ideal no-fault system. Drivers should investigate the coverages and implications of no-fault insurance in their states.

FINANCIAL PLANNING IN ACTION

ARE YOU COVERED?

Often people believe their insurance will cover various financial losses. For each of the following situations, name the type of home or automobile insurance that would protect you.

1. While you are on vacation, clothing and other personal belongings are stolen. _____

2. Your home is damaged by fire, and you have to live in a hotel for several weeks. _____

3. You and members of your family suffer injuries in an automobile accident caused by a hit-and-run driver. _____

4. A deliveryperson is injured on your property and takes legal action against you. _____

5. Your automobile is accidentally damaged by some people playing baseball. _____

6. A person takes legal action against you for injuries you caused in an automobile accident. _____

7. Water from a local lake rises and damages your furniture and carpeting. _____

8. Your automobile needs repairs because you hit a tree. _____

9. You damaged a valuable tree when your automobile hit it, and you want to pay for the damage. _____

10. While riding with you in your automobile, your nephew is injured in an accident and incurs various medical expenses. _____

ANSWERS: (1) Personal property coverage of home insurance; (2) additional living expenses of home insurance; (3) uninsured motorist's protection; (4) personal liability coverage of home insurance; (5) comprehensive physical damage; (6) bodily injury liability; (7) flood insurance—requires coverage separate from home insurance; (8) collision; (9) property damage liability of automobile insurance; (10) medical payments.

Property Damage Coverages

Three coverages protect you from financial loss due to damage of property of others and damage to your vehicle: (1) property damage liability, (2) collision, and (3) comprehensive physical damage. (See the Financial Planning in Action feature.)

property damage liability

Property Damage Liability   When you damage the property of others, **property damage liability** protects you against financial loss. This coverage applies mainly to other vehicles; however, it also includes damage to street signs, lampposts, buildings, and other property. Property damage liability protects you and others covered by your policy when driving another person's automobile with permission. The policy limit for property damage liability is frequently given with your bodily injury coverages. The last number in 50/100/25 and 100/300/50, for example, is for property damage liability ($25,000 and $50,000, respectively).

collision

Collision   When your automobile is involved in an accident, **collision** insurance pays for the damage to the automobile regardless of fault. However, if another driver caused the accident, your insurance company may try to recover the repair costs for your vehicle through the other driver's property damage liability. The insurance company's right to recover the amount it pays for the loss from the person responsible for the loss is called *subrogation.*

The amount you can collect with collision insurance is limited to the retail value of the automobile at the time of the accident. This amount is usually based on the figures

FINANCIAL PLANNING CALCULATIONS

CLAIM SETTLEMENTS AND DEDUCTIBLES

Both collision and comprehensive coverage are commonly sold with a *deductible* to help reduce insurance costs. If a broken windshield costs $250 to replace and you have a $100 deductible on your comprehensive coverage, the insurance company will pay $150 of the damages.

Deductibles keep insurance premiums lower by reducing the number of small claims companies pay. Going from full-coverage comprehensive insurance to a $100 deductible may reduce the cost of that coverage by as much as 40 percent.

provided by some appraisal service such as the *Official Used Car Guide* of the National Association of Automobile Dealers. If you have an automobile with many add-on features or one that is several years old and has been restored, you should obtain a documented statement of its condition and value before an accident occurs.

comprehensive physical damage

Comprehensive Physical Damage   Another protection for your automobile involves financial losses from damage caused by a risk other than a collision. **Comprehensive physical damage** covers you for risks such as fire, theft, glass breakage, falling objects, vandalism, wind, hail, flood, tornado, lightning, earthquake, avalanche, or damage caused by hitting an animal. Certain articles in your vehicle, such as some radios and stereo equipment, may be excluded from this insurance. These articles may be protected by the personal property coverage of your home insurance. Like collision insurance, comprehensive coverage applies only to your car, and claims are paid without considering fault. (See the Financial Planning Calculations feature.)

Other Automobile Coverages

In addition to basic bodily injury and property damage coverages, other protection is available. Wage loss insurance will reimburse you for any salary or income lost due to injury in an automobile accident. Wage loss insurance is usually required in states with a no-fault insurance system; in other states, it is available on an optional basis.

Towing and emergency road service coverage pays for the cost of breakdowns and mechanical assistance. This coverage can be especially beneficial on long trips or during inclement weather. Towing and road service coverage pays for the cost of getting the vehicle to a service station or starting it when it breaks down on the highway, but not for the cost of repairs. If you belong to an automobile club, your membership may include towing coverage. Purchasing duplicate coverage as part of your automobile insurance could be a waste of money.

CONCEPT CHECK 10–5

1. What is the purpose of financial responsibility laws?
2. What are the main coverages included in most automobile insurance policies?
3. What is no-fault insurance?
4. How does collision coverage differ from comprehensive physical damage coverage?

AUTOMOBILE INSURANCE COSTS

L.O.6 Evaluate factors that affect the cost of insurance.

The average household spends about $1,000 for auto insurance each year. Automobile insurance premiums reflect the amounts insurance companies pay for injury and property damage claims. Your automobile insurance is directly related to coverage amounts and factors such as the vehicle, your place of residence, and your driving record.

Amount of Coverage

"How much coverage do I need?" This question affects the amount you pay for insurance. Our legal environment and increasing property values influence coverage amounts.

Legal Concerns   As discussed earlier, every state has laws that require or encourage automobile liability insurance coverage. Since very few people can afford to pay an expensive court settlement with their personal assets, most drivers buy automobile liability insurance.

Until the mid-1970s, bodily injury liability coverage of 10/20 was considered adequate. In fact, some states still use these amounts as their minimum limits for financial responsibility. However, in recent injury cases, some people have been awarded millions of dollars; thus legal and insurance advisers now recommend 100/300. As discussed earlier in this chapter, an umbrella policy can provide additional liability coverage of $1 million or more.

Property Values   Just as medical expenses and legal settlements have increased, so has the cost of automobiles. Therefore, a policy limit of more than $5,000 or $10,000 for property damage liability is appropriate; $50,000 or $100,000 is usually suggested.

The higher cost of automobile replacement parts also contributes to the need for increased property damage coverage. The list price for a 1993 Ford Taurus was $19,095. The Alliance of American Insurers determined that purchasing its parts individually would cost $62,701!

Automobile Insurance Premium Factors

Several factors influence the premium you pay for automobile insurance. The main factors are vehicle type, rating territory, and driver classification.

Automobile Type   The year, make, and model of your motor vehicle strongly influence your automobile insurance costs. Expensive replacement parts and complicated repairs due to body style contribute to higher rates. Also, certain makes and models are stolen more often than others. According to the Highway Loss Data Institute, the Nissan 300ZX, Ford Mustang convertible, BMW, and Corvette have high theft records. Occupant injury data for various types of vehicles also affect the rates paid.

rating territory

Rating Territory   In most states, your **rating territory** is the place of residence used to determine your automobile insurance premium. Various geographic locations have different costs due to differences in the number of claims made. For example, fewer accidents and less vandalism occur in rural areas than in large cities. New York City, Los Angeles, and Chicago have the highest incidence of automobile theft—more than 40,000 stolen vehicles each year.

driver classification

Driver Classification   You are compared with other drivers to set your automobile insurance premium. **Driver classification** is a category based on the driver's age, sex, marital status, driving record, and driving habits; drivers' categories are used to determine

WHAT TO DO IF YOU HAVE AN AUTO ACCIDENT

No one plans to have an auto accident; nevertheless, more than 18 million auto accidents occur each year. If you are involved in an auto accident, you should take the following actions:

■ Stop your vehicle, turn off your ignition, and remain at the scene of the accident.

■ Seek medical assistance for anyone who is injured. Do not move an injured person; that should be done by medical personnel.

■ Obtain the names and addresses of other drivers, passengers, and witnesses; make notes regarding the circumstances of the accident.

■ Assist in the preparation of a police report, if required, by providing your name, address, license number, and vehicle and insurance information. Do not admit fault.

■ Obtain a copy of the police accident report, if any; file the necessary accident documents with your insurance company and state or local government agencies.

automobile insurance rates. In general, young drivers have more frequent and severe accidents. As a result, they can expect to pay higher premiums. In recent years, some states have banned the use of sex as a factor in setting insurance premiums. As a result, young female drivers have had premium increases of from $200 to over $1,000. Insurance companies argue that young male drivers should pay more than young female drivers since they have more moving violations, license suspensions, and revocations.

Accidents and traffic violations also influence your driver classification. A poor driving record increases your insurance costs. Finally, you pay less for insurance if you do not drive to work than if you use your automobile for business. Belonging to a car pool instead of driving to work alone can reduce your insurance costs.

The number of claims you file with your insurance company also affects your premiums. Expensive liability settlements or extensive property damage will increase your rates. If you have many expensive claims or a poor driving record, your company may cancel your policy, making it difficult for you to obtain coverage from another company. To deal with this problem, every state has an **assigned risk pool** consisting of people who are unable to obtain automobile insurance. Some of these people are assigned to each insurance company operating in the state. They pay several times the normal rates, but they do get coverage. Once they establish a good driving record, they can reapply for insurance at regular rates. Critics of the assigned risk system contend that under this system good drivers help cover the costs of poor drivers. However, if assigned risk drivers were in accidents without insurance, the potential financial burden on society might be even greater.

assigned risk pool

Reducing Automobile Insurance Premiums

Methods for lowering automobile insurance costs include comparing companies and taking advantage of commonly offered discounts.

Comparing Companies   Rates and service vary among automobile insurance companies. Among companies in the same area, premiums can vary as much as 100 percent. If you relocate, don't assume your present company will offer the best rates in your new living area.

Also consider the service the local insurance agent provides. Will this company representative be available to answer questions, change coverages, and handle claims as needed? You can check a company's reputation for handling automobile insurance claims and other matters with sources such as *Consumer Reports* or your state insurance department. Ratings, recommendations, and strategies for choosing an auto insurance company may be obtained with an online computer service. Most states publish information with sample auto insurance rates for different companies to help consumers save money. See Appendix E for the address of your state insurance regulator.

Premium Discounts   The best way to keep your rates down is to establish and maintain a safe driving record. Taking steps to avoid accidents and traffic violations will mean lower automobile insurance premiums. In addition, most insurance companies offer various discounts. Drivers under 25 can qualify for reduced rates by completing a driver training program and maintaining good grades in school. When young drivers are away at school without a car, families are likely to get reduced premiums, since the student will not be using the vehicle on a regular basis.

Installing security devices such as a fuel shutoff switch, a second ignition switch, or an alarm system will decrease your chances of theft and lower your comprehensive insurance costs. Vehicles with antilock brakes may qualify for a discount. Being a nonsmoker can qualify you for lower automobile insurance premiums. Discounts are also offered for participating in a car pool and insuring two or more vehicles with the same company. Ask your insurance agent about other methods for lowering your automobile insurance rates.

Increasing the amount of deductibles will result in a lower premium. Also, some people believe an old car is not worth the amount paid for the collision and comprehensive coverages and therefore dispense with them. However, before doing this, be sure to compare the value of your car for getting you to school or work with the cost of these coverages.

If you change your driving habits, get married, or alter your driving status in other ways, be sure to notify the insurance company. Premium savings can result. Also, some employers make group automobile insurance available to workers. As with other types of group insurance plans, the cost of such insurance is usually lower than the cost of an individual policy.

Before you buy a motor vehicle, find out which makes and models have the lowest insurance costs. This information can result in a purchasing decision with many financial benefits.

Sheet 50

CONCEPT   CHECK   10–6

1. What factors influence how much a person pays for automobile insurance?
2. What actions can a person take to reduce the cost of automobile insurance?

SUMMARY

L.O.1   Develop a risk management plan using insurance.

The four general risk management techniques are risk avoidance, risk reduction, risk assumption, and risk shifting. In planning a personal insurance program, set your goals, make a plan to reach your goals, put your plan into action, and check your results.

L.O.2   Discuss the importance of property and liability insurance.

Owners of homes and automobiles face the risks of (1) property damage or loss and (2) legal actions by others for the costs of injuries or property damage. Property and liability insurance offer protection from financial losses that may arise from a wide variety of situations faced by owners of homes and users of automobiles.

L.O.3   Explain the insurance coverages and policy types available to homeowners and renters.

Homeowner's insurance includes protection for the building and other structures, additional living expenses, personal property, and personal liability. Renter's insurance includes the same coverages excluding protection for the building and other structures, which is the concern of the building owner. The main types of home insurance policies are the basic, broad, special, tenants, comprehensive, condominium, country home, and modified coverage forms. These policies differ in the risks and property they cover.

L.O.4   Analyze factors that influence the amount of coverage and cost of home insurance.

The amount of home insurance coverage is determined by the replacement cost of your dwelling and personal belongings. The cost of home insurance is influenced by the location of the home, the type of structure, the coverage amount, the policy type, discounts, and company differences.

L.O.5   Identify the important types of automobile insurance coverages.

Automobile insurance is used to meet states' financial responsibility laws and to protect drivers against financial losses associated with bodily injury and property damage. The major types of automobile insurance coverages are bodily injury liability, medical payments, uninsured motorist's, property damage liability, collision, and comprehensive physical damage.

L.O.6   Evaluate factors that affect the cost of automobile insurance.

The cost of automobile insurance is affected by the amount of coverage, automobile type, rating territory, driver classification, differences among insurance companies, and premium discounts.

G L O S S A R Y

actual cash value (ACV)   A claim settlement method in which the insured receives payment based on the current replacement cost of a damaged or lost item, less depreciation. (p. 315)

assigned risk pool   Consists of people who are unable to obtain automobile insurance due to poor driving or accident records and obtain coverage at high rates through a state program that requires insurance companies to accept some of them.   (p. 323)

bodily injury liability   Coverage for the risk of financial loss due to legal expenses, medical costs, lost wages, and other expenses associated with injuries caused by an automobile accident for which the insured was responsible.   (p. 317)

coinsurance clause   A policy provision that requires a homeowner to pay for part of the losses if the property is not insured for the specified percentage of the replacement value. (p. 315)

collision   Automobile insurance that pays for damage to the insured's car when it is involved in an accident.   (p. 320)

comprehensive physical damage   Automobile insurance that covers financial loss from damage to a vehicle caused by a risk other than a collision, such as fire, theft, glass breakage, hail, or vandalism.   (p. 321)

driver classification   A category based on the driver's age, sex, marital status, driving record, and driving habits; used to determine automobile insurance rates.   (p. 322)

endorsement   An addition of coverage to a standard insurance policy.   (p. 313)

financial responsibility law   State legislation that requires drivers to prove their ability to cover the cost of damage or injury caused by an automobile accident.   (p. 317)

hazard   A factor that increases the likelihood of loss through some peril.   (p. 302)

homeowner's insurance   Coverage for a place of residence and its associated financial risks.   (p. 309)

household inventory   A list or other documentation of personal belongings, with purchase dates and cost information. (p. 310)

insurance   Protection against possible financial loss. (p. 301)

insurance company   A risk-sharing firm that assumes financial responsibility for losses that may result from an insured risk.   (p. 301)

insured   A person covered by an insurance policy.   (p. 301)

insurer   An insurance company.   (p. 301)

liability   Legal responsibility for the financial cost of another person's losses or injuries.   (p. 308)

medical payments coverage   Home insurance that pays the cost of minor accidental injuries on one's property; also, automobile insurance that covers medical expenses for people injured in one's car.   (pp. 312, 319)

negligence   Failure to take ordinary or reasonable care in a situation.   (p. 308)

no-fault system   An automobile insurance program in which drivers involved in accidents collect medical expenses, lost wages, and related injury costs from their own insurance companies.   (p. 319)

peril   The cause of a possible loss.   (p. 302)

personal property floater   Additional property insurance to cover the damage or loss of a specific item of high value. (p. 310)

policy   A written contract for insurance.   (p. 301)

policyholder   A person who owns an insurance policy. (p. 301)

premium   The amount of money a policyholder is charged for an insurance policy.   (p. 301)

property damage liability   Automobile insurance coverage that protects a person against financial loss when that person damages the property of others.   (p. 320)

pure risk   A risk in which there is only a chance of loss; also called *insurable risk.*   (p. 302)

rating territory   The place of residence used to determine a person's automobile insurance premium.   (p. 322)

replacement value   A claim settlement method in which the insured receives the full cost of repairing or replacing a damaged or lost item.   (p. 316)

risk   Chance or uncertainty of loss; also used to mean "the insured."   (p. 302)

self-insurance   The process of establishing a monetary fund to cover the cost of a loss.   (p. 303)

speculative risk   A risk in which there is a chance of either loss or gain.   (p. 302)

strict liability   A situation in which a person is held responsible for intentional or unintentional actions.   (p. 309)

umbrella policy   Supplementary personal liability coverage; also called a *personal catastrophe policy.*   (p. 312)

uninsured motorist's protection   Automobile insurance coverage for the cost of injuries to a person and members of his or her family caused by a driver with inadequate insurance or by a hit-and-run driver.   (p. 319)

vicarious liability   A situation in which a person is held legally responsible for the actions of another person. (p. 309)

Review Questions

1. What is the role of risk management in financial planning?
2. What are the financial implications of having inadequate liability insurance?   (L.O.2)
3. How would a person determine which home insurance policy would be appropriate for his or her situation? (L.O.3)
4. How can a person reduce the cost of property insurance when buying a home or having one built?   (L.O.4)
5. Why does a deductible reduce the cost of collision and comprehensive insurance?   (L.O.5)
6. What factors might a person investigate when selecting an automobile insurance company?   (L.O.6)

Financial Planning Problems

1. *Calculating Property Loss Claim Coverage.* Most home insurance policies cover jewelry for $1,000 and silverware for $2,500 unless items are covered with additional insurance. If $3,500 worth of jewelry and $3,800 worth of silverware were stolen from a family, what amount of the claim would not be covered by insurance?   (L.O.2)
2. *Computing Actual Cash Value Coverage.* What amount would a person with actual cash value (ACV) coverage receive for two-year-old furniture destroyed by a fire? The furniture would cost $1,000 to replace today and had an estimated life of five years.   (L.O.3)
3. *Determining Replacement Cost.* What amount would it cost an insurance company to replace a family's personal property that originally cost $18,000? The replacement costs for the items have increased 15 percent.   (L.O.3)
4. *Calculating a Coinsurance Claim.* If Carissa Dalton has a $130,000 home insured for $100,000, based on the 80 percent coinsurance provision, how much would the insurance company pay on a $5,000 claim?   (L.O.3)
5. *Determining the Claim Amount (with Deductibles).* For each of the following situations, what amount would the insurance company pay?   (L.O.3)
    a. Wind damage of $785; the insured has a $500 deductible.
    b. Theft of a stereo system worth $1,300; the insured has a $250 deductible.
    c. Vandalism that does $375 of damage to a home; the insured has a $500 deductible.
6. *Calculating Auto Liability Claim Coverage.* Becky Fenton has 25/50/10 automobile insurance coverage. If two other people are awarded $35,000 each for injuries in an auto accident in which Becky was judged at fault, how much of this judgment would the insurance cover?   (L.O.4)
7. *Determining a Property Damage Liability Claim.* Kurt Simmons has 50/100/15 auto insurance coverage. One evening he lost control of his vehicle, hitting a parked car and damaging a storefront along the street. Damage to the parked car was $5,400, and damage to the store was $12,650. What amount will the insurance company pay for the damages? What amount will Kurt have to pay? (L.O.4)
8. *Calculating Future Value of Insurance Savings.* Beverly and Kyle Nelson currently insure their cars with separate companies, paying $450 and $375 a year. If they insured both cars with the same company, they would save 10 percent on the annual premiums. What would be the future value of the annual savings over 10 years based on an annual interest rate of 6 percent?   (L.O.5)

PROJECTS AND APPLICATIONS ACTIVITIES

1. *Determining Insurance Coverages.* Survey friends and relatives to determine the types of insurance coverages they have. Also, obtain information about the process used to select these coverages. (L.O.1)
2. *Researching Insurance on the Internet.* Locate Web sites that can provide you with useful information when selecting and comparing various insurance coverages. (L.O.1)
3. *Developing a Personal Insurance Plan.* Outline a personal insurance plan with the following phases: (*a*) identify personal, financial, and property risks; (*b*) set goals you might achieve when obtaining needed insurance coverages; and (*c*) describe actions you might take to achieve these insurance goals. (L.O.1)
4. *Analyzing Insurance Coverages.* Talk to a financial planner or an insurance agent about the financial difficulties faced by people who lack adequate home and auto insurance. What common coverages do many people overlook? (L.O.2)
5. *Maintaining a Household Inventory.* Survey several people about their household inventory records. In the event of damage or loss, would they be able to prove the value of their personal property and other belongings? (L.O.3)
6. *Comparing Home Insurance Costs.* Contact two or three insurance agents to obtain information about home or renter's insurance. Use Sheet 49 in the *Personal Financial Planner* to compare the coverages and costs. (L.O.3)
7. *Analyzing Home Insurance Policies.* Examine a homeowner's or renter's insurance policy. What coverages does the policy include? Does the policy contain unclear conditions or wording? (L.O.3)
8. *Reducing Home Insurance Costs.* Talk to several homeowners about the actions they take to reduce the cost of their home insurance. Conduct a search of the Internet to obtain Web sites that offer information about reducing home insurance costs. Prepare a video or other visual presentation to communicate your findings. (L.O.4)
9. *Determining Auto Insurance Coverages.* Survey several people to determine the types and amounts of automobile insurance coverage they have. Do most of them have adequate coverage? (L.O.5)
10. *Comparing Auto Insurance Costs.* Contact two or three insurance agents to obtain information about automobile insurance. Use Sheet 50 in the *Personal Financial Planner* to compare costs and coverages for various insurance companies. (L.O.6)
11. *Reducing Auto Insurance Costs.* Search the World Wide Web or talk to an insurance agent to obtain suggestions for reducing automobile insurance costs. (L.O.6)

LIFE SITUATION CASE 10

WE RENT, SO WHY DO WE NEED INSURANCE?

"Have you been down in the basement?" Nathan asked his wife, Erin, as he entered their apartment.

"No, What's up?" responded Erin.

"It's flooded because of all that rain we got last weekend!" he exclaimed.

"Oh no! We have the extra furniture my mom gave us stored down there. Is everything ruined?" Erin asked.

"The couch and coffee table are in a foot of water; the loveseat was the only thing that looked OK. Boy, I didn't realize the basement of this building wasn't waterproof. I'm going to call our landlady to complain."

As Erin thought about the situation, she remembered that when they moved in last fall, Kathy, their landlady, had informed them that her insurance policy covered the building but not the property belonging to each tenant. Because of this, they had purchased renter's insurance. "Nathan, I think our renter's insurance will cover the damage. Let me give our agent a call."

When Erin and Nathan purchased their insurance, they had to decide whether they wanted be insured for cash value or for replacement costs. Replacement was more expensive, but it meant they would collect enough to go out and buy new household items at today's prices. If they had opted for cash value, the couch Erin's mother had paid $1,000 for five years ago would be worth less than $500 today.

Erin made the call and found out their insurance did cover the furniture in the basement, and at replacement value after they paid the deductible. The $300 they had invested in renter's insurance last year was well worth it!

Not every renter has as much foresight as Erin and Nathan. According to figures from Cambridge Reports Inc., fewer than 3 in 10 renters have renter's insurance. Some aren't even aware they need it. They may assume they are covered by the landlord's insurance—but they aren't. This mistake can be costly.

Think about how much you have invested in your possessions and how much it would cost to replace them. Start with your stereo equipment or the color television and VCR that you bought last year. Experts suggest that people who rent start thinking about these things as soon as they move into their first apartment. Your policy should cover your personal belongings and provide funds for living expenses if you are dispossessed by a fire or other disaster.

SOURCES: Laura Castaneda "How to Shop for Insurance/Don't Go Overboard," *San Francisco Chronicle,* September 3, 1996, p. B1; Betty Lonngren, "Safe, Not Sorry: A Rental Policy Can Save the Day," *Chicago Tribune,* July 19, 1996, p. 26.

QUESTIONS

1. Why is it important for people who rent to have insurance?
2. Does the building owner's property insurance ever cover the tenant's personal property?
3. What is the difference between cash value and replacement value?
4. When shopping for renter's insurance, what coverage features should you look for?

USING THE INTERNET TO CREATE A PERSONAL FINANCIAL PLAN 10

OBTAINING HOME AND AUTO INSURANCE

Creation of an insurance plan including appropriate coverage for your home, personal property, and motor vehicles helps to avoid financial difficulties.

Web Sites for Home and Auto Insurance

- The Web site of the Insurance Research Council offers current information on various insurance research studies, policy issues, and IRC publications along with links to related Web sites at **www.ircweb.org**
- Answers to questions about basic information and current developments about auto and home insurance may be obtained at **www.insure.com**
- Home and auto insurance information at **www.iiaa. iix.com** and **www.iii.org**
- Insurance rate information at **www.insuremarket.com**
- Information about trends and current issues in the home-auto-property insurance industry at **www.ircweb.org**

(Note: Addresses and content of Web sites change, and new sites are created daily. Use the search engines discussed in Appendix B to update and locate Web sites for your current financial planning needs.)

PFP SHEETS: 46–50

Short-Term Financial Planning Activities

1. List current and needed insurance coverages (see PFP Sheet 46).
2. (a) Prepare an inventory of personal belongings (see PFP Sheet 47). (b) Compare the cost of home/renters insurance from two or more companies (see PFP Sheet 49).
3. Compare the cost of auto insurance from two or more companies (see PFP Sheet 50).

Long-Term Financial Planning Activities

1. Identify buying decisions that could reduce your future home and auto insurance costs.
2. Develop a plan to monitor changes in your life situation that would affect the need to change home or auto insurance coverages.

CHAPTER 11

HEALTH AND DISABILITY INSURANCE

HEALTH INSURANCE: YOU *CAN* TAKE IT WITH YOU

Hadiya had been experiencing chronic back pain for the past year-and-a-half at her job as an assembly line worker in a microchip plant. She was receiving treatment that was covered by her health insurance and had decided to look for a new career. A friend told her about a new employer in her area that offered retraining for office positions; this seemed ideal because the work would be less physical.

Unfortunately, Hadiya heard that if she changed jobs, her new insurance would not cover her pre-existing medical condition. A pre-existing condition is an illness or injury you had before you switched jobs, that you are receiving treatment for at the time you switch, or that you have been treated for in the past but that might recur. This meant she would not be able to continue her current treatment or get the back surgery her doctor recommended. She felt helpless and forced to stay with a job that was actually exacerbating her back problem.

Hadiya is not alone, but thanks to a new law that took effect July 1, 1997, her health insurance is now "portable." In other words, when she moves from one company to another, Hadiya will continue to receive coverage or will eventually be able to get coverage for her back problem even though it is a pre-existing medical condition.

The Health Insurance Portability and Accountability Act (HIPAA) works like this: If you or your family were covered under a former employer's health plan for at least 12 months, without an interruption of 63 or more days, a new plan will have to provide coverage with no limitation on pre-existing conditions. Hadiya just needs to request a certificate of insurance coverage from her former employer to prove her eligibility under a new plan.

Under HIPAA, Hadiya's new plan can refuse to cover her condition if it was diagnosed within six months before the date she enrolled. However, since her back problems began 18 months before she decided to change jobs, she cannot be refused coverage. Even people who fall within the six-month date will be able to get coverage for a pre-existing condition if they stay with the new plan for 12 months.

QUESTIONS:

1. What is portability?
2. How does the HIPAA work?
3. What does Hadiya need to do to prove she had insurance coverage?

SOURCES: Grace W. Weinstein, "Health Insurance: You Can Take It With You," *Investor's Business Daily,* June 17, 1997, p. A1; "Answering Your Questions on Health Insurance Reform," *Gannett News Service,* June 11, 1997.

LEARNING
OBJECTIVES

After studying this chapter, you will be able to

L.O.1 Explain why the costs of health insurance and health care have been increasing.

L.O.2 Define *health insurance* and *disability income insurance* and explain their importance in financial planning.

L.O.3 Recognize the need for disability income insurance.

L.O.4 Analyze the benefits and limitations of the various types of health care coverage.

L.O.5 Evaluate private sources of health insurance and health care.

L.O.6 Appraise the sources of government health care programs.

HEALTH CARE COSTS

L.O.1 Explain why the costs of health insurance and health care have been increasing.

Health insurance is one way people protect themselves against economic losses due to illness, accident, or disability. Health coverage is available through private insurance companies, service plans, health maintenance organizations, and government programs.

Employers often offer health insurance as part of an employee benefit package, called *group health insurance,* and health care providers sell it to individuals.

Affordable health care has become one of the most important social issues of our time. News broadcasts abound with special reports on "America's health care crisis" or politicians demanding "universal health insurance."

High Medical Costs

The United States has the highest per capita medical expenditures of any industrialized country in the world. In 1996, average per capita spending on health care totaled $3,759 a year, up from $1,000 in 1980. The United States spends twice as much on health care as the average for the 24 industrialized countries in Europe and North America.[1]

Health care costs rose by less than inflation during 1994–96, but increased 5 percent in 1997 and are expected to rise up to 10 percent in 1998. As Exhibit 11–1 shows, health care prices have risen much faster than the general price level as measured by the consumer price index.

Rapid Increase in Medical Expenditures Since federally sponsored health care began in 1965, U.S. health care expenditures rose from $41.6 billion, or about 6 percent of the gross domestic product (GDP), to over $1 trillion in 1997, or 13.6 percent of GDP.[2]

High Administrative Costs In the United States, administrative costs consume nearly 26 percent of health care dollars compared to 1 percent under Canada's socialized system. These costs include activities such as enrolling beneficiaries in a health plan, paying health

EXHIBIT 11–1

**Health Care Prices,
1961–96**

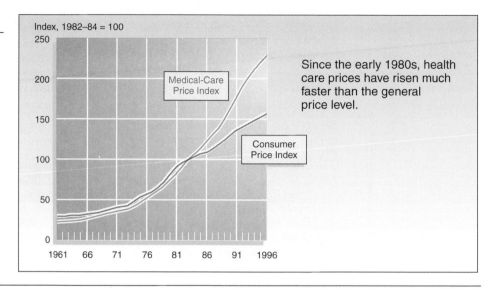

Index, 1982–84 = 100

Medical-Care Price Index

Consumer Price Index

Since the early 1980s, health care prices have risen much faster than the general price level.

SOURCES: *Economic Report of President,* 1997; *Economic Trends,* Federal Reserve Bank of Cleveland, May 1997, p. 15.

insurance premiums, checking eligibility, obtaining authorizations for specialist referrals, and filing reimbursement claims. More than 1,100 different insurance forms are now in use in the United States.

Americans without Insurance Coverage   At any given time, over 13 percent of Americans have incomes that are too high to qualify them for Medicare or Medicaid but too low to pay for medical insurance themselves. Currently 37 million Americans are uninsured or underinsured.

Why Does Health Care Cost So Much?

The high and rising costs of health care are attributable to many factors, including

- The use of sophisticated, expensive technologies.
- Duplication of tests and sometimes duplication of technologies that yield similar results.
- Increases in the variety and frequency of treatments, including allegedly unnecessary tests.
- The increasing number and longevity of elderly people.
- Regulations that result in cost shifting rather than cost reduction.
- The increasing number of accidents and crimes that require emergency medical services.
- Limited competition and restrictive work rules in the health care delivery system.
- Labor intensiveness and rapid average earnings growth for health care professionals and executives.
- Built-in inflation in the health care delivery system.
- Other major factors that cost billions of dollars each year, including fraud, administrative waste, malpractice insurance, excessive surgical procedures, a wide range of prices for similar services, and double health coverage such as medigap.[3]

According to the General Accounting Office, fraud and abuse account for nearly 10 percent of all dollars spent on health care. In 1995, that was a loss of about $17.7 billion to Medicare. "Rather than look for people who are nickel-and-diming the program, we've ratcheted up," says Donna Shalala, secretary of health and human services. "We have to demonstrate that we have the guts to go after the big players in health care."[4]

Because third parties—private health insurers and government—pay such a large part of the nation's health care bill, hospitals, doctors, and patients often lack the incentive to make the most economical use of health care services.

What Is Being Done about the High Costs of Health Care?

In the private sector, concerned groups such as employers, labor unions, health insurers, health care professionals, and consumers have undertaken a wide range of innovative activities to contain the costs of health care. These activities include

- Programs to carefully review health care fees and charges and the use of health care services.
- The establishment of incentives to encourage preventive care and provide more services out of hospitals where this is medically acceptable.
- Involvement in community health planning to help achieve a better balance between health needs and health care resources.
- The encouragement of prepaid group practices and other alternatives to fee-for-service arrangements.
- Community health education programs that motivate people to take better care of themselves.

What Can You Do to Reduce Personal Health Care Costs?

The best way to avoid the high cost of illness is to stay well. The prescription is the same as it has always been:

1. Eat a balanced diet, and keep your weight under control.
2. Avoid smoking, and don't drink to excess.
3. Get sufficient rest, relaxation, and exercise.
4. Drive carefully, and watch out for accident and fire hazards in the home.

CONCEPT CHECK 11–1

1. What are the reasons for rising health care expenditures?
2. What are various groups doing to curb the high costs of health care?
3. What can you do to reduce health care costs?

HEALTH INSURANCE AND FINANCIAL PLANNING

L.O.2 Define *health insurance* and *disability income insurance* and explain their importance in financial planning.

Although the United States spent about $1 trillion on health care in 1996 (see Exhibit 11–2 on page 334), the number of Americans without basic health insurance has been growing. In this wealthy country of 264 million people, 37 million citizens have no health insurance. Two-thirds of uninsured persons are either full-time workers or family members of full-time employees.

According to recent government reports, two-thirds of uninsured pregnant women fail to receive adequate prenatal care. Among children, 40 percent fail to receive basic

EXHIBIT 11–2   **U.S. National Health Expenditures, 1960-1997**

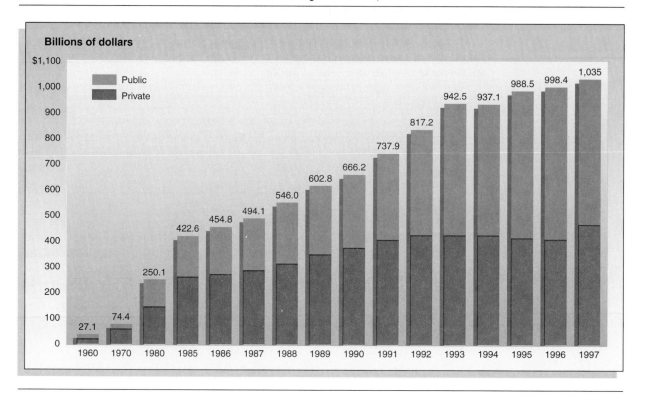

SOURCES: U.S. Department of Health and Human Services; Health Care Financing Administration; *U.S. Industrial Outlook, 1994* (Washington, DC: U.S. Department of Commerce, 1994), p. 42-7; HCFA press release, January 27, 1997; *Chicago Tribune,* January 13, 1998, p. 5.

childhood vaccinations, 25 percent don't see a doctor even once a year, and 31 percent in low-income families lack health coverage.[5]

A growing number of college students have been uninsured due to the growth of an older student population not covered by family policies. Today 40 percent of college students are older than 25.

What Is Health Insurance?

Health insurance is a form of protection whose primary purpose is to alleviate the financial burdens individuals suffer from illness or injury. Health insurance includes both medical expense insurance and disability income insurance.[6]

Health Insurance   Health insurance, like other forms of insurance, reduces the financial burden of risk by dividing losses among many individuals. It works in the same way as life insurance, homeowner's insurance, and automobile insurance. You pay the insurance company a specified premium, and the company guarantees you some degree of financial protection. Like the premiums and benefits of other types of insurance, the premiums and benefits of health insurance are figured on the basis of average experience. To establish rates and benefits, insurance company actuaries rely on general statistics that tell them how many people in a certain population group will become ill and how much their illnesses will cost.

Disability Income Insurance   Because you feel young and healthy now, you may over-look the very real need for disability income insurance. Disability income insurance, dis-cussed in detail in the next section, protects your most valuable asset: your ability to earn income. Most people are more likely to lose their incomes due to disability than to death. The fact is that for all age groups, disability is more likely than death.

Medical expense insurance and disability income insurance are an important part of your financial planning. To safeguard your family's economic security, both protections should be a part of your overall insurance program.

There are many ways individuals or groups of individuals can obtain health insurance protection. Planning a health insurance program takes careful study because the protec-tion should be shaped to the needs of the individual or family. For many families, how-ever, the task is simplified because the group health insurance they obtain at work already provides a foundation for their coverage.

Group Health Insurance

Group plans comprise more than 85 percent of all the health insurance issued by health and life insurance companies. Most of these plans are employer sponsored, and the employer often pays part or most of their cost. Group insurance will cover you and your immediate family. Group insurance seldom requires evidence that you are insurable if you enroll when you first become eligible for coverage.

The Health Insurance Portability and Accountability Act of 1996 (HIPPA) legislates new federal standards for health insurance portability, nondiscrimination in health insurance, and guaranteed renewability. The law provides tax breaks for long-term care insurance, authorizes various government agencies to investigate Medicare/Medicaid fraud and abuses, and permits establishing experimental *medical savings accounts* (MSAs). The MSA allowed small businesses and self-employed people to open medical savings accounts for the first time in 1997. The law permitted 750,000 people to open tax-free MSAs for routine health care costs and to buy high-deductible health insurance for major medical expenses. MSAs are allowed only until January 1, 2001.

This landmark legislation gives millions of workers the comfort of knowing that if they change jobs, they need not lose their health insurance. For example, a parent with a sick child can move from one group plan to another without lapses in health insurance and without paying more than other employees for coverage. In addition to providing health care portability, this law created a stable source of funding for fraud control activities.

The protection group insurance provides varies from plan to plan. The plan may not cover all of your health insurance needs; therefore, you will have to start thinking about supplementing it with individual health insurance.

Individual Health Insurance

Individual health insurance covers either one person or a family. If the kind of health insurance you need is not available through a group or if you need coverage in addition to the coverage a group provides, you should obtain an individual policy—a policy tai-lored to your particular needs—from the company of your choice. This requires careful shopping, because coverage and cost vary from company to company.

So find out what your group insurance will pay for and what it won't. Make sure you have enough insurance, but don't waste money by overinsuring.

Supplementing Your Group Insurance

A sign that your group coverage needs supplementing would be its failure to provide ben-efits for the major portion of your medical care bills, mainly hospital, doctor, and surgical charges. If, for example, your group policy will pay only $500 per day toward a hospital room and the cost in your area is $1,000, you should look for an individual policy that covers most of the remaining amount. Similarly, if your group policy will pay only about half the going rate for surgical procedures in your area, you need individual coverage for the other half.

coordination of benefits (COB)

In supplementing your group health insurance, consider the health insurance benefits your employer-sponsored plan provides for family members. Most group policy contracts have a **coordination of benefits (COB)** provision. The COB is a method of integrating the benefits payable under more than one health insurance plan so that the benefits received from all sources are limited to 100 percent of allowable medical expenses.

If you have any questions about your group plan, you should be able to get answers from your employer, union, or association. If you have questions about an individual policy, talk with your insurance company representative.

Medical Coverage and Divorce

Medical coverage of nonworking spouses is a concern when couples divorce. Under federal law, coverage under a former spouse's medical plan can be continued for 36 months if the former spouse works for a company with 20 or more employees.

Premiums, however, can run as high as $4,000 annually. If there are children and the parent who gets custody doesn't work, the working parent can usually still cover the children under an employer's group plan.

The federal *Consolidated Omnibus Budget Reconciliation Act of 1986 (COBRA)* requires many employers to offer employees and dependents who would otherwise lose group health insurance the option to continue their group coverage for a set period of time. Employees of private companies and state and local governments are covered by this law; employees of the federal government and religious institutions are not.

CONCEPT CHECK 11–2

1. What is health insurance, and what is its purpose?
2. What are group health and individual health insurance?
3. What is a coordination of benefits provision?

DISABILITY INCOME INSURANCE

L.O.3 Recognize the need for disability income insurance.

disability income insurance

Disability income insurance provides regular cash income lost by employees as the result of an accident, illness, or pregnancy. Disability income insurance is probably the most neglected form of available insurance protection. Many people who insure their houses, cars, and other property fail to insure their most valuable resource: their earning power. Disability can cause even greater financial problems than death. In fact, disability is often called "the living death." Disabled persons lose their earning power while continuing to incur normal family expenses. In addition, they often face huge expenses for the medical treatment and special care their disabilities require.

If you are between ages 35 and 65, your chances of being unable to work for 90 days or more due to a disabling illness or injury are about equal to your chances of dying. To be more specific, at age 40 you face a 12 percent chance of dying before reaching age 65 and a 19 percent chance of having at least one disability lasting 90 days or longer.[7] If you

EXHIBIT 11–3

Probability of Disability between Age 20 and Attained Age for Workers Eligible for Social Security Income

	Probability of Insured Disability from Age 20	
From Age 20 to Age	Males	Females
21	0.1%	0.0%
25	0.5	0.3
30	1.3	0.7
35	2.3	1.5
40	3.5	2.6
45	5.2	4.1
50	7.8	6.4
55	12.0	9.9
60	19.1	15.3
65	29.2	22.1
66	30.8	23.1
67	32.2	24.0

SOURCES: U.S. Department of Health and Human Services; Social Security Administration; *Source Book of Health Insurance Data* (Washington, DC: Health Insurance Association of America, 1991), p. 99.

have no disability income protection, you are betting that you will not be disabled, and that could be a very costly bet.

The probability of a male becoming temporarily or permanently disabled between ages 20 and 30 is 1.3 percent, but between ages 20 and 60 it increases to 19.1 percent (see Exhibit 11–3). Females are less prone to disability during their lifetimes and have only a 15.3 percent chance of becoming disabled between 20 and 60 years of age.[8]

Definition of Disability

Disability has several definitions. Some policies define it simply as the inability to do your regular work. Others have stricter definitions. For example, a dentist who is unable to do his or her regular work because of a hand injury but can earn income through related duties such as teaching dentistry would not be considered permanently disabled under certain policies.

Good disability plans pay when you are unable to work at your regular job; poor disability plans pay only when you are unable to work at any job. A good disability plan will also make partial disability payments when you return to work on a part-time basis.

Disability Insurance Trade-Offs

Following are some important trade-offs you should consider in purchasing disability income insurance.

Financial Decision Trade-Off

Waiting or Elimination Period   Benefits don't begin on the first day you become disabled. Usually there is a waiting or elimination period of between 30 and 90 days. Some waiting periods may be as long as 180 days. Generally, disability income policies with longer waiting periods have lower premiums. If you have substantial savings to cover three to six months of expenses, the reduced premiums of a policy with a long waiting period may be attractive. But if you need every paycheck to cover your bills, you are probably better off paying the higher premium for a short waiting period. Short waiting periods, however, are very expensive.

Duration of Benefits   The maximum time a disability income policy will pay benefits may be a few years, to age 65, or for life. You should seek a policy that pays benefits for life. If you became permanently disabled, it would be financially disastrous if your benefits ended at age 55 or 65.

Amount of Benefits   You should aim for a benefit amount that, when added to your other income, will equal 60 to 70 percent of your gross pay. Of course, the greater the benefits, the greater the cost.

Accident and Sickness Coverage   Consider both accident and sickness coverage. Some disability income policies will pay only for accidents, but you want to be insured for illness too.

Guaranteed Renewability   Ask for noncancelable and guaranteed renewable coverage. Either coverage will protect you against your insurance company dropping you if your health becomes poor. The premium for these coverages is higher, but the coverages are well worth the extra cost. Furthermore, look for a disability income policy that waives premium payments while you are disabled.

See whether you qualify for a lower premium if you agree to forgo part of your monthly benefit when Social Security or worker's compensation benefits begin. Most disability income policies coordinate their benefits with these programs.

Sources of Disability Income

Before you buy disability income insurance, remember that you may already have some form of such insurance. This coverage may come to you through your employer, Social Security, or worker's compensation.

Employer   Many, but not all, employers provide disability income protection for their employees through group insurance plans. Your employer may have some form of wage continuation policy that lasts a few months or an employee group disability plan that provides long-term protection. In most cases, your employer will pay part or all of the cost of this plan.

Social Security   Most salaried workers in the United States participate in the Social Security program. In this program, your benefits are determined by your salary and by the number of years you have been covered under Social Security. Your dependents also qualify for certain benefits, as Exhibits 11–4 and 11–5 show. However, Social Security has very strict rules. You must be totally disabled for 12 months or more, and you must be unable to do any work.

Worker's Compensation   If your accident or illness occurred at your place of work or resulted from your type of employment, you could be entitled to worker's compensation benefits in your state. Like Social Security benefits, these benefits are determined by your earnings and work history.

Other possible sources of disability income include Veterans Administration pension disability benefits, civil service disability benefits for government workers, state vocational rehabilitation benefits, state welfare benefits for low-income people, Aid to Families with Dependent Children, group union disability benefits, automobile insurance that provides benefits for disability from an auto accident, and private insurance programs such as credit disability insurance, which covers loan payments when you are

EXHIBIT 11-4 **Approximate Monthly Social Security Disability Benefits If You Became Disabled in 1997 and Had Steady Earnings**

Your Age	Your Family	Your Earnings in 1996				
		$20,000	$30,000	$40,000	$50,000	$62,700 or More[*]
25	You	$ 797	$1,063	$1,229	$1,354	$1,508
	You, your spouse, and your child[†]	1,195	1,595	1,844	2,032	2,262
35	You	797	1,063	1,229	1,354	1,485
	You, your spouse, and your child[†]	1,195	1,595	1,844	2,032	2,227
45	You	797	1,063	1,229	1,348	1,445
	You, your spouse, and your child[†]	1,195	1,595	1,844	2,023	2,168
55	You	797	1,063	1,214	1,297	1,363
	You, your spouse, and your child[†]	1,195	1,595	1,822	1,945	2,044
64	You	790	1,054	1,182	1,248	1,301
	You, your spouse, and your child[†]	1,185	1,581	1,773	1,872	1,951

[*]Earnings equal to or greater than the OASDI wage base from age 22 through 1996.
[†]Equals the maximum family benefit.
NOTE: The accuracy of these estimates depends on the pattern of your earnings in prior years.
SOURCE: *Social Security: Understanding the Benefits* (Washington, DC: Social Security Administration, January 1997), p. 36.

EXHIBIT 11-5 **Approximate Monthly Social Security Survivor's Benefits for a Worker Who Died in 1996 and Had Steady Earnings**

Worker's Age	Worker's Family	Your Earnings in 1996				
		$20,000	$30,000	$40,000	$50,000	$62,700 or More[*]
35	Spouse and one child[†]	$1,194	$1,594	$1,844	$2,032	$2,240
	Spouse and two children[††]	1,459	1,874	2,152	2,371	2,614
	One child only	597	797	922	1,016	1,120
	Spouse at age 60[§]	569	760	879	968	1,067
45	Spouse and one child[†]	1,194	1,594	1,844	2,030	2,184
	Spouse and two children[††]	1,459	1,874	2,152	2,370	2,549
	One child only	597	797	922	1,015	1,092
	Spouse at age 60[§]	569	760	879	968	1,041
55	Spouse and one child[†]	1,194	1,594	1,822	1,944	2,044
	Spouse and two children[††]	1,459	1,874	2,126	2,270	2,385
	One child only	597	797	911	972	1,022
	Spouse at age 60[§]	567	760	868	927	974

[*] Earnings equal to or greater than the OASDI wage base from age 22 through 1996.
[†] Amounts shown also equal the benefits paid to two children if no parent survives or surviving parent has substantial earnings.
[††] Equals the maximum family benefit.
[§] Amounts payable in 1996. Spouses turning 60 in the future would receive higher benefits.
NOTE: The accuracy of these estimates depends on the pattern of earnings in prior years.
SOURCE: *Social Security: Understanding the Benefits* (Washington, DC: Social Security Administration, January 1997), p. 37.

EXHIBIT 11–6

Disability Income Worksheet

How much income will you have available if you become disabled?

	Monthly Amount	After Waiting:	For a Period of:
Sick leave or short-term disability	_____	_____	_____
Group long-term disability	_____	_____	_____
Social Security	_____	_____	_____
Other government programs	_____	_____	_____
Individual disability insurance	_____	_____	_____
Credit disability insurance	_____	_____	_____
Other income:	_____	_____	_____
Savings	_____	_____	_____
Spouse's income	_____	_____	_____

Total monthly income while disabled: $_____

disabled. Use Exhibit 11–6 to determine how much income you will have available if you become disabled.

The availability and extent of these and other disability income sources vary widely in different parts of the country. Be sure to look into such sources carefully before calculating your need for additional disability income insurance.

Determining Your Disability Income Insurance Requirements

Sheet 51

Once you have found out what your benefits from the numerous public and private disability income sources would be, you should determine whether those benefits are sufficient to meet your disability income needs. If the sum of your disability benefits approaches your after-tax income, you can safely assume that should disability strike, you'll be in good shape to pay your day-to-day bills while recuperating.

You should know how long you would have to wait before the benefits begin (the waiting or elimination period) and how long they would be paid (the benefit period).

What if, as is often the case, Social Security and other disability benefits are not sufficient to support your family? In that case, you may want to consider buying disability income insurance to make up the difference.

Don't expect to insure yourself for your full salary. Most insurers limit benefits from all sources to no more than 70 to 80 percent of your take-home pay. For example, if you earn $400 a week, you could be eligible for disability insurance of about $280 to $320 a week. You will not need $400, because while you are disabled, your work-related expenses will be eliminated and your taxes will be far lower.

The Financial Planning in Action box on page 341 shows you how to compare different features among disability income policies.

CONCEPT CHECK 11–3

1. What is disability income insurance?
2. What are the three main sources of disability income?
3. How can you determine the amount of disability income insurance you need?

FINANCIAL PLANNING IN ACTION

DISABILITY INCOME POLICY CHECKLIST

Every disability income policy may have different features. The following checklist will help you compare policies you may be considering.

	Policy A	Policy B
1. How is disability defined?		
Inability to perform your own job?	____	____
Inability to perform any job?	____	____
2. Does the policy cover		
Accident?	____	____
Illness?	____	____
3. Are benefits available		
For total disability?	____	____
For partial disability?	____	____
Only after total disability?	____	____
Without a prior period of total disability?	____	____
4. Are full benefits paid, whether or not you are able to work, for loss of		
Sight?	____	____
Speech?	____	____
Hearing?	____	____
Use of limbs?	____	____

	Policy A	Policy B
5. What percentage of your income will the maximum benefit replace?	____	____
6. Is the policy noncancelable, guaranteed renewable, or conditionally renewable?	____	____
7. How long must you be disabled before premiums are waived?	____	____
8. Is there an option to buy additional coverage, without evidence of insurability, at a later date?	____	____
9. Does the policy offer an inflation adjustment feature?	____	____
If so, what is the rate of increase?	____	____
How often is it applied?	____	____
For how long?	____	____

	Policy A		Policy B	
10. What does the policy cost?	With Inflation Feature	Without Inflation Feature	With Inflation Feature	Without Inflation Feature
For a waiting period of ____ days and (30–180)	_____	_____	_____	_____
For a benefit period of ____? (1 yr.–lifetime)	_____	_____	_____	_____
Total	_____	_____	_____	_____

SOURCE: Health Insurance Association of America, Washington DC.

TYPES OF HEALTH INSURANCE COVERAGES

L.O.4 Analyze the benefits and limitations of the various types of health care coverage.

With today's high cost of health care, it makes sense to be as fully insured as you can afford. Combining the group plan available where you work with the individual policies insurance companies offer will enable you to put together enough coverage to give you peace of mind. A good health insurance plan should

- Offer basic coverage for hospital and doctor bills.
- Provide at least 120 days' hospital room and board in full.
- Provide at least a $1 million lifetime maximum for each family member.
- Pay at least 80 percent for out-of-hospital expenses after a yearly deductible of $500 per person or $1,000 per family.
- Impose no unreasonable exclusions.
- Limit your out-of-pocket expenses to no more than $3,000 to $5,000 a year, excluding dental, optical, and prescription costs.

Several types of health insurance coverage are available under group and individual policies.

Hospital Expense Insurance

hospital expense insurance

Hospital expense insurance pays part or the full amount of hospital bills for room, board, and other charges. Frequently a maximum amount is allowed for each day in the hospital, up to a maximum number of days. More people have hospital insurance than any other kind of health insurance.

Surgical Expense Insurance

surgical expense insurance

Surgical expense insurance pays part or the full amount of the surgeon's fees for an operation. A policy of this kind usually lists a number of specific operations and the maximum fee allowed for each. The higher the maximum fee allowed in the policy, the higher the premium charged. People often buy surgical expense insurance in combination with hospital expense insurance.

Physician Expense Insurance

physician expense insurance

Physician expense insurance helps pay for physician's care that does not involve surgery. Like surgical expense insurance, it lists maximum benefits for specific services. Its coverage may include visits to the doctor's office, X rays, and lab tests. This type of insurance is usually bought in combination with hospital and surgical insurance. The three types of insurance combined are called **basic health insurance coverage.**

basic health insurance coverage

Major Medical Expense Insurance

major medical expense insurance

Major medical expense insurance protects against the large expenses of a serious injury or a long illness. It adds to the protection offered by basic health insurance coverage. The costs of a serious illness can easily exceed the benefits under hospital, surgical, and physician expense policies. Major medical pays the bulk of the additional costs. The maximum benefits payable under major medical insurance are high—up to $1 million. Because major medical insurance offers such a wide range of benefits and provides high maximums, it contains two features to help keep the premium within the policyholder's means.

Financial Decision
Trade-Off

deductible

One of these features is a **deductible** provision that requires the policyholder to pay a basic amount before the policy benefits begin—for example, the first $500 per year under an individual plan and a lesser amount under a group plan. (Sometimes part or all of the deductible amount is covered by the benefits of a basic hospital and surgical plan.) The other feature is a **coinsurance** provision that requires the policyholder to share expenses beyond the deductible amount. Many policies pay 75 or 80 percent of expenses above the deductible amount; the policyholder pays the rest.

coinsurance

stop-loss

Some major medical policies contain a **stop-loss** provision. This requires the policy-holder to pay up to a certain amount, after which the insurance company pays 100 percent of all remaining covered expenses. Typically, the out-of-pocket payment is between $3,000 and $5,000.

Comprehensive Major Medical Insurance

comprehensive major medical insurance

Comprehensive major medical insurance is a type of major medical insurance that has a very low deductible amount, often $200 or $300, and is offered without a separate basic plan. This all-inclusive health insurance helps pay hospital, surgical, medical, and other bills. Many major medical policies have specific maximum benefits for certain expenses, such as hospital room and board and the cost of surgery.

Hospital Indemnity Policies

hospital indemnity policy

A **hospital indemnity policy** pays benefits only when you are hospitalized, but these benefits, stipulated in the policy, are paid to you in cash and you can use the money for medical, nonmedical, or supplementary expenses. While such policies have limited coverage, their benefits can have wide use. The hospital indemnity policy is not a substitute for basic or major medical protection but a supplement to it. Many people buy hospital indemnity policies in the hope that they will make money if they get sick, but the average benefit return does not justify the premium cost.

Dental Expense Insurance

Dental expense insurance provides reimbursement for the expenses of dental services and supplies and encourages preventive dental care. The coverage normally provides for oral examinations (including X rays and cleanings), fillings, extractions, inlays, bridgework, and dentures, as well as oral surgery, root canal therapy, and orthodontics.

Vision Care Insurance

A recent development in health insurance coverage is *vision care insurance*. An increasing number of insurance companies and prepayment plans are offering this insurance, usually to groups.

Vision and eye health problems are the second most prevalent chronic health care concerns, affecting 120 million Americans. A recent study by the Georgetown University Medical Center indicates that about 250,000 of the new cases of blindness each year are preventable through timely detection and treatment.[9] Good vision care insurance should cover diagnosing and treating eye diseases such as glaucoma, periodic eye examinations, eyeglasses, contact lenses, and eye surgery.

In considering vision and dental coverages, you should analyze their costs and benefits. Sometimes these coverages cost more than they are worth.

Dread Disease and Cancer Insurance Policies

Dread disease and cancer policies, which are usually sold through the mail, in newspapers and magazines, or by door-to-door salespeople working on commission, are notoriously poor values. Their appeal is based on unrealistic fears, and a number of states have prohibited their sale. Such policies provide coverage only for very specific conditions and are no substitute for comprehensive insurance.

Long-Term Care Insurance

long-term care insurance (LTC)

Long-term care insurance (LTC), virtually unknown 15 years ago, is growing faster than any other form of insurance in the country. *Long-term care* is day-in, day-out assistance that you might need if you ever have an illness or a disability that lasts a long time and leaves you unable to care for yourself. You may or may not need lengthy care in a nursing home, but you may need help at home with daily activities such as dressing, bathing, and doing household chores.

In the late-1990s, about 8 million men and women over age 65 are estimated to need long-term care. The number is expected to increase to 9 million by the year 2000 and to 12 million by the year 2020. Most of these older Americans will be cared for at home; family members and friends are the sole caregivers for 70 percent of the elderly population. However, a study by the U.S. Department of Health and Human Services indicates that 65-year-olds face at least a 40 percent lifetime chance of entering a nursing home, and about 10 percent will stay there five years or longer. The study estimates that 13.3 million Americans have an elderly parent or spouse who needs long-term care.[10] Because women generally outlive men by several years, they face a 50 percent greater likelihood than men of entering a nursing home after age 65.

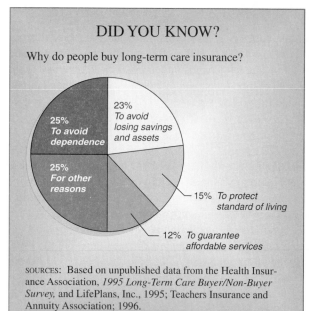

DID YOU KNOW?

Why do people buy long-term care insurance?

23% To avoid losing savings and assets

25% To avoid dependence

25% For other reasons

15% To protect standard of living

12% To guarantee affordable services

SOURCES: Based on unpublished data from the Health Insurance Association, *1995 Long-Term Care Buyer/Non-Buyer Survey,* and LifePlans, Inc., 1995; Teachers Insurance and Annuity Association; 1996.

Long-term care can be very expensive. As a national average, a year in a nursing home can cost $38,000. In some regions, it can cost as much as $60,000. The average cost for one year of nursing home care is projected to be $48,200 by 2001. Bringing an aide into your home just three times a week to help with dressing, bathing, preparing meals, and similar household chores can easily cost $1,000 a month.

The annual premium for LTC policies can range from under $900 up to $15,000, depending on your age and the choices you make. The older you are when you enroll, the higher your annual premium. Typically, individual insurance plans are sold to the 50-to-80 age group, pay benefits for a maximum of two to six years, and carry a dollar limit on the total benefits they will pay.

The number of policies in effect has more than doubled since 1990, to about 4 million. About 120 insurance companies cover 12 percent of people age 65 and over. But long-term care insurance is not for everyone; it is rarely recommended for people under 60. If you are over 60, you may consider it if you wish to protect your assets, but if you have substantial wealth ($1 million or more), or very little (less than $100,000), the premium can be a waste of money.[11] However, if your employer pays the premium, the Health Insurance Portability and Accountability Act of 1996 treats a long-term care premium as a tax-deductible expense for the employer.[12]

Explore services available in your community to help meet long-term care needs. Care given by family members can be supplemented by visiting nurses, home health aides, friendly visitor programs, home-delivered meals, chore services, adult day care centers, and respite services for caregivers who need a break from daily responsibilities.

These services are becoming more widely available. Some or all of them may be found in your community. Your local Area Agency on Aging or Office on Aging can help you locate the services you need. Call the Eldercare Locator at 1–800–677–1116 to locate your local office.

The Financial Planning in Action box on page 346 can help you compare the features of long-term care policies.

An insurance company usually allows you a minimum of 10 days to review your health insurance policy, so be sure to check the major provisions that affect your coverage. Deductible, coinsurance, and stop-loss provisions were discussed under major medical expense insurance. Other major provisions are described in the following sections.

Major Provisions in a Health Insurance Policy

All health insurance policies have certain provisions in common. Be sure you understand what your policy covers. Even the most comprehensive policy may be of little value if a provision in small print limits or denies benefits.

Eligibility   The eligibility provision defines who is entitled to benefits under the policy. Age, marital status, and dependency requirements are usually specified in this provision. For example, foster children usually are not automatically covered under the family contract, but stepchildren may be. Check with your insurance company to be sure.

Assigned Benefits   When you assign benefits, you sign a paper allowing your insurance company to make payments to your hospital or doctor. Otherwise, the payments will be made to you when you turn in your bills and claim forms to the company.

Internal Limits   A policy with internal limits will pay only a fixed amount for your hospital room no matter what the actual rate is, or it will cover your surgical expenses only to a fixed limit no matter what the actual charges are. For example, if your policy has an internal limit of $200 per hospital day and you are in a $300-a-day hospital room, you will have to pay the difference.

DID YOU KNOW?

Who pays for long-term care? Today most long-term care costs in the U.S. are paid out of private, personal resources.

35% Medicaid

42% Private Out-of-Pocket

19% Medicare

<1% Private Insurance and Other

4% Other Government Programs

SOURCES: Office of the Assistant Secretary for Planning and Evaluation, DHHS; *Congressional Research Service Issue Brief,* March 22, 1995.

copayment

Copayment   **Copayment** is a type of cost sharing. You pay a flat dollar amount each time you receive a covered medical service. Copayments of $3 to $10 for prescriptions and $5 to $15 for doctors' office visits are common. The amount of copayment does not vary with the cost of service.

Service Benefits   In a service benefits provision, insurance benefits are expressed in terms of entitlement to receive specified hospital or medical care rather than entitlement to receive a fixed dollar amount for each procedure. Service benefits are always preferable to a coverage stated in dollar amounts.

Benefit Limits   The benefit limits provision defines the maximum benefits possible, in terms of either a dollar amount or a number of days in the hospital. Many policies today have benefit limits ranging from $250,000 to unlimited payments.

Exclusions and Limitations   The exclusions and limitations provision specifies the conditions or circumstances for which the policy does not provide benefits. For example, the policy may exclude coverage for pre-existing conditions, cosmetic surgery, or routine checkups.

FINANCIAL PLANNING IN ACTION

LONG-TERM CARE POLICY CHECKLIST

The following checklist will help you compare LTC policies you may be considering:

	Policy A	Policy B
1. What services are covered?		
Skilled care	____	____
Intermediate care	____	____
Custodial care	____	____
Home health care	____	____
Adult day care	____	____
Other	____	____
2. How much does the policy pay per day?		
For skilled care	____	____
For intermediate care	____	____
For custodial care	____	____
For home health care	____	____
For adult day care	____	____
3. How long will benefits last?		
In a nursing home for:		
Skilled nursing care	____	____
Intermediate nursing care	____	____
Custodial care	____	____
At home:	____	____
4. Does the policy have a maximum lifetime benefit? If so, what is it?		
For nursing home care	____	____
For home health care	____	____
5. Does the policy have a maximum length of coverage for each period of confinement? If so, what is it?		
For nursing home care	____	____
For home health care	____	____
6. How long must I wait before pre-existing conditions are covered?	____	____
7. How many days must I wait before benefits begin?		
For nursing home care	____	____
For home health care	____	____
8. Are Alzheimer's disease and other organic mental and nervous disorders covered?	____	____

	Policy A	Policy B
9. Does this policy require:		
Physician certification of need?	____	____
An assessment of activities of daily living?	____	____
A prior hospital stay for:		
Nursing home care?	____	____
Home health care?	____	____
A prior nursing home stay for home health care coverage?	____	____
Other?	____	____
10. Is the policy guaranteed renewable?	____	____
11. What is the age range for enrollment?	____	____
12. Is there a waiver-of-premium provision:		
For nursing home care?	____	____
For home health care?	____	____
13. How long must I be confined before premiums are waived?	____	____
14. Does the policy offer an inflation adjustment feature? If so:	____	____
What is the rate of increase?	____	____
How often is it applied?	____	____
For how long?	____	____
Is there an additional cost?	____	____
15. What does the policy cost:		
Per year?		
With inflation feature	____	____
Without inflation feature	____	____
Per month?		
With inflation feature	____	____
Without inflation feature	____	____
16. Is there a 30-day free look?	____	____

SOURCE: *Guide to Long-Term Care Insurance* (Washington, DC: Health Insurance Association of America, 1994), pp. 11–12.

Coordination of Benefits   As discussed earlier, the coordination of benefits provision prevents you from collecting benefits from two or more group policies that would in total exceed the actual charges. Under this provision, the benefits from your own and your spouse's policies are coordinated to allow you up to 100 percent payment of your covered charges.

Guaranteed Renewable   With this policy provision, the insurance company cannot cancel a policy unless you fail to pay premiums when they are due. Also, it cannot raise premiums unless a rate increase occurs for all policyholders in that group.

Cancellation and Termination   This provision explains the circumstances under which the insurance company can terminate your health insurance policy. It also explains your right to convert a group contract into an individual contract.

Which Coverage Should You Choose?

Now that you are familiar with the types of health insurance available and some of their major provisions, how do you choose one? The most important thing to understand is that the more money you can pay for health insurance, the more coverage you can get.

For medical insurance, you have three choices. You can buy (1) basic, (2) major medical, or (3) both basic and major medical.

If your budget is very limited, it is a toss-up between choosing a basic plan or a major medical plan. In many cases, either plan will handle a major share of your hospital and doctor bills. In the event of an illness involving catastrophic costs, however, you will need the protection a major medical policy offers. Ideally, you should get a basic plan and a major medical supplementary plan or a comprehensive major medical policy that combines the values of both these plans in a single policy.

Health Insurance Trade-Offs

The benefits of health insurance policies differ, and the differences can have a significant impact on your premiums. Consider the following trade-offs.

Financial Decision
Trade-Off

Reimbursement versus Indemnity   A reimbursement policy provides benefits based on the actual expenses you incur. An indemnity policy provides specified benefits, regardless of whether the actual expenses are greater or less than the benefits.

Internal Limits versus Aggregate Limits   A policy with internal limits stipulates maximum benefits for specific expenses, such as the maximum reimbursement for daily hospital room and board. Other policies may limit only the total amount of coverage, such as $1 million major expense benefits, or may have no limits.

Deductibles and Coinsurance   The cost of a health insurance policy can be greatly affected by the size of the deductible (the amount you must pay toward medical expenses before the insurance company pays), the degree of coinsurance, and the share of medical expenses you must pay (for example, 20 percent).

Out-of-Pocket Limit   A policy that limits the total of the coinsurance and deductibles you must pay (for example, $2,000) will limit or eliminate your financial risk, but it will also increase the premium.

FINANCIAL PLANNING IN ACTION

HEALTH CARE WEB SITES ON THE INTERNET

http://www.HouseCall.com is an online encyclopedia of more than 30,000 pages of health information that incorporates data from news sources, including television, radio, newspapers, magazine and medical journals.

http://www.centerwatch.com provides information on ongoing international clinical research trials, new drug therapies, and a confidential patient notification service.

http://healthnet.ivi.com explains medical headlines, current issues, and newly approved drugs and answers other questions with advice from physicians.

http://pharminfo.com has health news from the publishers of *The New England Journal of Medicine* and is a pharmaceutical information network.

http://wwwicic.nci.nin.gov is a National Cancer Institute database that includes information about cancer and its treatment. All information on it is reviewed by oncology experts.

http://www.cdc.gov provides information from the Centers for Disease Control and Prevention on chronic diseases, injuries and disabilities, health risks, and prevention guidelines.

http://medicus.marhall.edu/medicus.htm is an online interactive patient service that simulates an actual patient encounter.

http://www.cpmc.columbia.edu/list.html has information on cholesterol in clinical vocabulary terms and is a site provided by Columbia University and Presbyterian Hospital in New York.

http://www.nih.gov provides online health care information from the National Institutes of Health, a federal agency, and a biomedical research center, with materials on AIDS research, women's health, and bone marrow transplantation.

http://www.nlm.nih.gov is the National Library of Medicine's Web page offering resources and information from more than 5 million medical books, journals, pamphlets, rare manuscripts, and films.

http://nhic-nt.health.org is the National Health Information Center's Web page, an online directory of more than 1,100 health-related organizations that provide health information.

http://chmis.org lists materials available from Community Health Management Information Systems. Communities across the country collaborate to address the need for comprehensive health information systems.

http://www.fda.gov is the Food and Drug Administration's site. It has documents from the Center for Drug Evaluation and Research, the National Center for Toxicological Research, and the Center for Food Safety and Applied Nutrition. The site includes the latest information from the FDA, including press statements, testimony, federal register notices, and enforcement reports.

SOURCE: *NCL Bulletin,* November–December 1996, p. 2.

Benefits Based on Reasonable and Customary Charges   A policy that covers "reasonable and customary" medical expenses limits reimbursement to the usual charges of medical providers in an area and helps prevent overcharging.

Sheet 52

Health Information Online

Recent studies indicate that consumers are seeking information on health and health care online to supplement traditional medical counsel. By far, the most consumer-friendly part of the Internet is the World Wide Web. While the rest of the Internet displays text only, the Web has the ability to display graphics and multimedia. Many legitimate providers of reliable health and medical information, including the federal Food and Drug Administration, are taking advantage of the Web's popularity by offering brochures and in-depth information on specific topics at their Web sites. The Financial Planning in Action feature on page 348 lists some good sources of health care Web sites on the Internet.

CONCEPT   CHECK   11-4

1. What are several types of health insurance coverage available under group and individual policies?
2. What are the major provisions of a health insurance policy?
3. How do you decide which coverage to choose?
4. How can you analyze the costs and benefits of your health insurance policy?

PRIVATE SOURCES OF HEALTH INSURANCE AND HEALTH CARE

L.O.5 Evaluate private sources of health insurance and health care.

Health insurance is available from more than 800 private insurance companies. Moreover, service plans such as Blue Cross/Blue Shield, health maintenance organizations, preferred provider organizations, government programs such as Medicare, fraternal organizations, and trade unions provide health insurance.

Private Insurance Companies

Insurance companies sell health insurance through either group or individual policies. Of these two types, group health insurance represents about 90 percent of all medical expense insurance and 80 percent of all disability income insurance.

The policies insurance companies issue provide for payment either directly to the insured for reimbursement of expenses incurred or, if assigned by the insured, to the provider of services.

Most private insurance companies sell health insurance policies to employers, who in turn offer them as fringe benefits to employees and employees' dependents. The premiums may be partially paid by employers. The Health Insurance Portability and Accountability Act, as discussed earlier, requires employers to keep detailed records of all employees and dependents covered by the company's health plan. Employers must be able to provide certificates of coverage for any employee covered since July 1, 1996.

Hospital and Medical Service Plans

Blue Cross and Blue Shield are statewide organizations similar to commercial health insurance companies. Each state has its own Blue Cross and Blue Shield. The nation's 69 Blues plans play an important role in providing private health insurance to about 67 million Americans.[13]

Blue Cross   **Blue Cross** plans provide *hospital care benefits* on essentially a "service type" basis. Through a separate contract with each member hospital, Blue Cross reimburses the hospital for covered services provided to the insured.

Blue Shield   **Blue Shield** plans provide benefits for *surgical and medical services* performed by physicians. The typical Blue Shield plan provides benefits similar to those provided under the benefit provisions of hospital-surgical policies issued by insurance companies.

managed care   During the 1970s and 1980s, increasing health care costs spurred the growth of managed care. **Managed care** refers to prepaid health plans that provide comprehensive health care to members. Managed care is offered by health maintenance organizations, preferred provider organizations, exclusive provider organizations, point-of-service plans, and traditional indemnity insurance companies.

Health Maintenance Organizations (HMOs)

health maintenance organization (HMO)

Prepaid managed care is designed to make the provision of health care services cost effective by controlling their use. Health maintenance organizations are an alternative to basic and major medical insurance plans. A **health maintenance organization (HMO)** is a health insurance plan that directly employs or contracts with selected physicians, surgeons, dentists, and optometrists to provide health care services in exchange for a fixed, prepaid monthly premium. HMOs operate on the premise that maintaining health through preventive care will minimize future medical problems.

The preventive care HMOs provide includes periodic checkups, screening programs, diagnostic testing, and immunizations. HMOs also provide a comprehensive range of other health care services. These services are divided into two categories: basic and supplemental. *Basic health services* include inpatient, outpatient, maternity, mental health, substance abuse, and emergency care. *Supplemental services* include vision, hearing, and pharmaceutical care, which are usually available for an additional fee.

Your membership in a typical HMO should cover office visits, routine checkups, hospital and surgical care, eye exams, laboratory and X-ray services, hemodialysis for kidney failure, and mental health services. See the Financial Planning for Life's Situations feature on page 351 for tips on how to use and choose an HMO.

In the late 1990s, HMOs are coming under fire from patients, doctors, unions, and federal and state governments. In 1997, President Clinton appointed a 34-member advisory committee to draft a patients' bill of rights and study what kind of legislation may be needed to enforce it. "Many Americans worry that lower costs mean lower quality and less attention to their rights," said the president. Senator Edward Kennedy charged that "too many managed-care firms and other insurance companies have decided that the shortest route to highest profits and a competitive edge is by denying patients the care they need and deserve." Furthermore, Health Access, a coalition of 215 consumer organizations, is drafting a very comprehensive state bill of rights for HMO members. It would set legal standards for everything from when HMOs can deny care to how long they can keep patients waiting on the telephone. In 1996, 35 states passed 56 laws to "regulate or weaken HMOs," according to Thomas Bodenheimer of the University of San Francisco School of Medicine.[14]

Preferred Provider Organizations (PPOs)

preferred provider organization (PPO)

A **preferred provider organization (PPO)** is a group of doctors and hospitals that agree to provide health care at rates approved by the insurer. In return, PPOs expect prompt payment and the opportunity to serve an increased volume of patients. The premiums for PPOs are slightly higher than those for HMOs. An insurance company or your employer contracts with a PPO to provide specified services at predetermined fees to PPO members.

Preferred provider organizations combine the best elements of the fee-for-service and HMO systems. PPOs offer the services of doctors and hospitals at discount rates or give breaks in copayments and deductibles.

PPOs provide their members with essentially the same benefits HMOs offer. However, while HMOs require members to seek care from HMO providers only (except for emergency treatment), PPOs allow members to use a preferred provider—or another provider—

FINANCIAL PLANNING FOR LIFE'S SITUATIONS

TIPS ON USING AND CHOOSING AN HMO

How to Use an HMO

When you first enroll in an HMO, you must choose a plan physician (family practitioner, internist, pediatrician, or obstetrician-gynecologist) who provides or arranges for all of your health care services. It is extremely important that you receive your care through the plan physician. If you don't, you are responsible for the cost of the service rendered.

The only exceptions to the requirement that care be received through the plan physician are medical emergencies. A medical emergency is a sudden onset of illness or a sudden injury that would jeopardize your life or health if not treated immediately. In such instances, you may use the facilities of the nearest hospital emergency room. All other care must be provided by hospitals and doctors under contract with the HMO.

How to Choose an HMO

If you decide to enroll in an HMO, you should consider these additional factors:

1. *Accessibility.* Since you must use plan providers, it is extremely important that they be easily accessible from your home or office.
2. *Convenient office hours.* Your plan physician should have convenient office hours.
3. *Alternative physicians.* Should you become dissatisfied with your first choice of a physician, the HMO should allow you the option to change physicians.

4. *Second opinions.* You should be able to obtain second opinions.
5. *Type of coverage.* You should compare the health care services offered by various HMOs, paying particular attention to whether you will incur out-of-pocket expenses or copayments.
6. *Appeal procedures.* The HMO should have a convenient and prompt system for resolving problems and disputes.
7. *Price.* You should compare the prices various HMOs charge to ensure that you are getting the most services for your health care dollar.

What to Do When an HMO Denies Treatment or Coverage

- *Get it in writing.* Ask for a letter detailing the clinical reasons your claim was denied and the name and medical expertise of the HMO staff member responsible, to better defend your case.
- *Know your rights.* The plan document or your HMO's member services department will tell you how experimental treatments are defined and covered and how the appeals process works.
- *Keep records.* Make copies of any correspondence, including payments and any reimbursements. Also, keep a written log of all conversations relevant to your claim.
- *Find advocates.* Enlist the help of your doctor, employer, and state insurance department to lobby your case before the HMO.

SOURCE: *Business Week*, May 19, 1997, p. 141.

---

exclusive provider organization (EPO)

point-of-service plan (POS)

each time a medical need arises. This combination of allowing free choice of physicians and low-cost care makes PPOs popular.

The **exclusive provider organization (EPO)** is the extreme form of the PPO. Services rendered by nonaffiliated providers are not reimbursed. Therefore, if you belong to an EPO, you must receive your care from affiliated providers or pay the entire cost yourself. Providers typically are reimbursed on a fee-for-service basis according to a negotiated discount or fee schedule.

Point-of-service plans (POSs), sometimes called *HMO-PPO hybrids* or *open-ended HMOs,* combine characteristics of both HMOs and PPOs. POSs use a network of selected contracted, participating providers. Employees select a primary care physician who controls referrals for medical specialists. If you receive care from a plan provider, you pay little or nothing, as in an HMO, and do not file claims. Medical care provided by out-of-plan providers will be reimbursed, but you must pay significantly higher copayments and deductibles. Hybrid plans are useful if you want to try managed care but don't want to be locked into a network of doctors. A drawback is that they cost more than HMOs.

The distinction among HMOs, PPOs, EPOs, and POSs is becoming blurred. As cost reduction pressures mount and these alternative delivery systems try to increase their market share, each tries to make its system more attractive. The evolution of health care plans will likely continue so that it will become increasingly difficult to characterize a particular managed care delivery system as adhering to any particular model.

Home Health Care Agencies

Home health care providers furnish and are responsible for the supervision and management of preventive medical care in a home setting in accordance with a medical order. Rising hospital care costs, new medical technology, and the increasing number of elderly and infirm people have helped make home care one of the fastest-growing areas of the health care industry.

Spending on home health care has been growing at an annual rate of about 20 percent over the past few years. This rapid growth reflects (1) the increasing proportion of older people in the U.S. population, (2) the lower costs of home health care compared to the costs of institutional health care, (3) insurers' active support of home health care, and (4) Medicare's promotion of home health care as an alternative to institutionalization.

Employer Self-Funded Health Plans

Certain types of health insurance coverage are made available by plans that employers, labor unions, fraternal societies, or communities administer. Usually these groups provide the amount of protection a specific group of people desires and can afford.

It is important to note that self-funded groups must assume the financial burden if medical bills are greater than the amount covered by premium income. While private insurance companies have the assets needed in such situations, self-funded plans often do not. The results can be disastrous.

In addition to the private sources of health insurance and health care discussed in this section, government health care programs cover over 35 million people. The next section discusses these programs.

DID YOU KNOW?

How do Americans choose a health plan? Here are the important criteria:

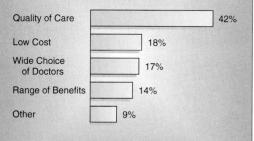

Quality of Care	42%
Low Cost	18%
Wide Choice of Doctors	17%
Range of Benefits	14%
Other	9%

SOURCES: Kaiser Family Foundation; Agency for Health Care Policy and Research; Princeton Survey Research Associates, September 1996.

CONCEPT CHECK 11-5

1. What are the major sources of health insurance and health care?
2. What are Blue Cross and Blue Shield plans? What benefits does each plan provide?
3. What are the differences among HMOs, PPOs, EPOs, and POSs?
4. What are home health care agencies?
5. What are employer self-funded health plans?

GOVERNMENT HEALTH CARE PROGRAMS

L.O.6 Appraise the sources of government health care programs.

Public opinion polls consistently show that Americans are unhappy, if not disgusted, with the nation's health care system. Increasingly, businesses and citizens have been calling for some kind of national health program.

Federal and state governments offer health coverage in accordance with laws that define the premiums and benefits they can offer. Specific requirements as to age, occupation, length of service, and family income may be used to determine eligibility for coverage. Two sources of government health insurance are Medicare and Medicaid.

Medicare

Medicare, established in 1965, is a federal health insurance program for people 65 or older, people of any age with permanent kidney failure, and people with certain disabilities. The program is administered by the Health Care Financing Administration. Local Social Security Administration offices take applications for Medicare, assist beneficiaries in filing claims, and provide information about the program.

Medicare has two parts: hospital insurance (Part A) and medical insurance (Part B). Medicare *hospital insurance* helps pay for inpatient hospital care, inpatient care in a skilled nursing facility, home health care, and hospice care. Hospital insurance is financed from a portion of the Social Security tax. Part A pays for all covered services for inpatient hospital care after you pay a single annual deductible ($760 in 1997). Once you meet this deductible, Medicare pays for all medically necessary inpatient hospital care for the remainder of the calendar year, regardless of the costs, the length of your stay, or the number of times you are hospitalized during the year.

Medicare *medical insurance* helps pay for doctors' services and a variety of other medical services and supplies not covered by hospital insurance. Each year, as soon as you meet the annual medical insurance deductible, medical insurance will pay 80 percent of the approved charges for the covered services that you receive during the rest of the year. In 1997, the annual deductible was $100. Voluntary medical insurance is financed from the monthly premiums paid by people who have enrolled in it and from general federal revenues.

And now the bad news. According to Medicare's own financial projections, under current tax and spending rules, the program will be insolvent by 2001. The recent budget agreement would slash Medicare growth by $115 billion over the next five years, extending the program's solvency until 2007.[15]

Use Exhibit 11–7 to compare Medicare HMO plans.

What Is Not Covered by Medicare?   Although Medicare is very helpful for meeting medical costs, it does not cover everything. In addition to the deductibles and coinsurance mentioned earlier, Medicare does not cover some medical expenses at all, including

- Care in a skilled nursing facility (SNF) beyond 100 days per benefit period.
- Skilled nursing care in facilities not approved by Medicare.
- Intermediate and custodial nursing care (the kind many nursing home residents need).
- Out-of-hospital prescription drugs.
- Private-duty nursing.
- Routine checkups, dental care, most immunizations, cosmetic surgery, routine foot care, eyeglasses, and hearing aids.
- Care received outside the United States except in Canada and Mexico, and then only in limited circumstances.

EXHIBIT 11–7

Medicare HMO Comparison Chart

	Plan 1	Plan 2	Plan 3
Hospital Services:			
Hospitalization			
Outpatient services			
Hospital emergency room			
Psychiatric inpatient care			
Other			
Professional Services:			
Physician office visits			
Laboratory and X-ray			
Chiropractic care			
Outpatient mental illness treatment			
Other			
Other Services:			
Skilled nursing facility care			
Home health care			
Durable medical equipment			
Ambulance services			
Out-of-area urgent/emergency care			
Prescription drugs			
Other			
Routine Care:			
Routine physical exam			
Routine eye exam			
Prescription eyeglasses/lenses			
Prescription eyeglasses/frames			
Routine hearing exam			
Hearing aid			
Mammograms/pap smears			
Other			
Statistics:			
Plan membership			
Number of primary care doctors available			
Counties serviced			
Out-of-pocket maximum			
Other			
Miscellaneous:			
Contract type			
Monthly premium			

SOURCE: *1997 Medicare Supplement Premium Comparison Guide,* Illinois Department of Insurance.

- Services Medicare does not consider medically necessary.
- Physician charges above Medicare's approved amount. The government has a fee schedule for physician charges and places limits on charges in excess of the Medicare approved amount when the physician does not accept Medicare's approved amount as payment in full.[16]

For a more complete description of Medicare coverage and costs, ask your local Social Security Administration office for a copy of *The Medicare Handbook*. For more information, call the Medicare Hotline at 1–800–772–1213.

EXHIBIT 11–8   **Medicare Supplement Policies: Plans A–J**

This chart indicates the benefits included in each of the 10 standardized Medicare Supplement plans. All companies selling Medicare Supplement policies must offer Plan A (Core Plan). The Core Plan includes:

- All Part A coinsurance expenses for:
  $190 per day for 61st through 90th day
  $380 per day for 91st through 150th day
- Upon exhaustion of Part A hospitalization benefits, full coverage of an additional 365 days per lifetime
- Part B coinsurance (20% of Medicare-approved expenses)
- First three pints of blood each calendar year

					Core Benefits				
A	B	C	D	E	F	G	H	I	J
		Skilled nursing coinsurance	Skilled nursing coinsurance	Skilled nursing coinsurance	Skilled nursing coinsurance	Skilled nursing coinsurance	Skilled nursing coinsurance	Skilled nursing coinsurance	Skilled nursing coinsurance
	Part A deductible	Part A deductible	Part A deductible	Part A deductible	Part A deductible	Part A deductible	Part A deductible	Part A deductible	Part A deductible
		Part B deductible			Part B deductible				Part B deductible
				Part B excess (100%)		Part B excess (80%)		Part B excess (100%)	Part B excess (100%)
		Foreign travel emergency	Foreign travel emergency	Foreign travel emergency	Foreign travel emergency	Foreign travel emergency	Foreign travel emergency	Foreign travel emergency	Foreign travel emergency
			At-home recovery			At-home recovery		At-home recovery	At-home recovery
							Basic drugs ($1,250)	Basic drugs ($1,250)	Extended drugs ($3,000)
				Preventive care					Preventive care

SOURCE: *1997 Medicare Supplement Premium Comparison Guide,* Illinois Department of Insurance, March 1997, p. 6.

medigap (MedSup) insurance

Medigap   Medicare was never intended to pay all medical costs. To fill the gap between Medicare payments and medical costs not covered by Medicare, many companies sell medigap insurance policies. **Medigap** or **MedSup insurance** is not sold or serviced by the federal government or state governments. Contrary to the claims made by advertising and insurance agents, Medicare supplement insurance is not a government-sponsored program.

Most states now have 10 standardized Medicare supplement policies designated by the letters A through J (see Exhibit 11–8). These newly standardized policies make it much easier to compare the costs of policies issued by different insurers. All Medicare policies must cover certain gaps in Medicare coverage, such as the daily coinsurance amount for hospitalization.

In addition to the basic benefits that must now be included in all newly issued Medicare supplement policies in most states, you should consider other policy features.

Medicaid

Title XIX of the Social Security Act provides for a program of medical assistance to certain low-income individuals and families. In 1965 the program, known as *Medicaid,* became federal law.

Medicaid is administered by each state within certain broad federal requirements and guidelines. Financed by both state and federal funds, it is designed to provide medical assistance to groups or categories of persons who are eligible to receive payments under one of the cash assistance programs such as Aid to Families with Dependent Children and Supplemental Security Income. The states may also provide Medicaid to medically needy individuals, that is, to persons who fit into one of the categories eligible for public assistance.

Many members of the Medicaid population are also covered by Medicare. Where such dual coverage exists, most state Medicaid programs pay for the Medicare premiums, deductibles, and copayments and for services not covered by Medicare. Medicaid differs from Medicare because eligibility for Medicaid depends on having very low income and assets. Once a person is eligible, Medicaid provides more benefits than does Medicare. Because Medicaid coverage is so comprehensive, people using it do not need to purchase supplemental insurance.

To qualify for federal matching funds, state programs must include inpatient hospital services; outpatient hospital services; laboratory and X-ray services; skilled nursing and home health services for individuals age 21 and older; family planning services; early and periodic screening, diagnosis, and treatment for individuals under 21; and physicians' services in the home, office, hospital, nursing home, or elsewhere.

Fight against Medicare/Medicaid Fraud and Abuse

> ### DID YOU KNOW?
>
> You can call 1–800–HHS–TIPS to report fraud and abuse in Medicare and Medicaid programs.

Nearly 70 percent of consumers believe the Medicare program would not go broke if fraud and abuse were eliminated. Moreover, nearly 80 percent are not aware of any efforts to reduce health care fraud and abuse. In 1997, President Clinton introduced the Medicare/Medicaid Anti-Waste, Fraud and Abuse Act, which established tough new requirements for health care providers that wish to participate in the Medicare/Medicaid program.

The Financial Planning for Life's Situations feature on page 357 provides some consumer tips on health and disability insurance.

Government Consumer Health Information Web Sites

With more than 60 central World Wide Web sites on eight separate Web domains, the Department of Health and Human Services (HHS) maintains one of the richest and most reliable sources of information on the Internet. HHS documents on the Web include information on health issues, research-related data, and access to HHS services, including interactive sites. Major HHS health information Web sites include the following.

Healthfinder   Healthfinder includes links to more than 1,250 Web sites, including over 250 federal sites and 1,000 state, local, not-for-profit, university, and other consumer health resources. Topics are organized in a subject index. With more than 7 million hits in its first two months of operation, Healthfinder is currently rated fifth among consumers' favorite Web sites on the "Web 100" list.

Medline   Medline, the world's most extensive collection of published medical information, is coordinated by the National Library of Medicine. Originally designed for

FINANCIAL PLANNING FOR LIFE'S SITUATIONS

CONSUMER TIPS ON HEALTH AND DISABILITY INSURANCE

1. If you pay your own premiums directly, try to arrange to pay them on an annual or quarterly basis rather than a monthly basis. It is cheaper.

2. Policies should be delivered to you within 30 days. If not, contact your insurer and find out, in writing, why. If a policy is not delivered in 60 days, contact the state department of insurance.

3. When you receive a policy, take advantage of the free-look provision. You have 10 days to look it over and obtain a refund if you decide it is not for you.

4. Unless you have a policy with no internal limits, read over your contract every year to see whether its benefits are still in line with medical costs.

5. Don't replace a policy because you think it is out of date. Switching may subject you to new waiting periods and new exclusions. Rather, add to what you have if necessary.

6. On the other hand, don't keep a policy because you've had it a long time. You don't get any special credit from the company for being an old customer.

7. Don't try to make a profit on your insurance by carrying overlapping coverages. Duplicate coverage is expensive. Besides, most group policies now contain a coordination of benefits clause limiting benefits to 100 percent.

8. Use your health emergency fund to cover small expenses.

9. If you're considering the purchase of a dread disease policy such as cancer insurance, understand that it is supplementary and will pay for only one disease. You should have full coverage before you consider it. Otherwise, it's a gamble.

10. Don't lie on your insurance application. If you fail to mention a pre-existing condition, you may not get paid. You can usually get paid even for that condition after one or two years have elapsed if you have had no treatment for the condition during that period.

11. Keep your insurance up to date. Some policies adjust to inflation better than others. Some insurers check that benefits have not been outdistanced by inflation. Review your policies annually.

12. Never sign a health insurance application (such applications are lengthy and detailed for individually written policies) until you have recorded full and complete answers to every question.

SOURCE: Health Insurance Association of America.

---

health professionals and researchers, MEDLINE is also valuable for students and for those seeking more specific information about health care. Free access to MEDLINE was initiated on June 26, 1997. "PubMed," a free online service, will provide direct Web links between MEDLINE abstracts and the publishers of full-text articles.

NIH Health Information Page   This Web site provides a single access point to the consumer health information resources of the National Institutes of Health, including the NIH Health Information Index, NIH publications and clearinghouses, and the Combined Health Information Database.

CONCEPT CHECK 11–6

1. What are the two sources of government health insurance?
2. What benefits do Part A and Part B of Medicare provide?
3. What is medigap, or MedSup, insurance?

SUMMARY

L.O.1   Explain why the costs of health insurance and health care have been increasing.

Health care costs, except during 1994–96, have gone up faster than the rate of inflation. Among the reasons for high and rising health care costs are the use of expensive technologies, duplication of tests and sometimes technologies, increases in the variety and frequency of treatments, unnecessary tests, the increasing number and longevity of elderly people, regulations that shift rather than reduce costs, the increasing number of accidents and crimes requiring emergency services, limited competition and restrictive work rules in the health care delivery system, rapid earnings growth among health care professionals, built-in inflation in the health care delivery system, and other factors.

L.O.2   Define *health insurance* and *disability income insurance* and explain their importance in financial planning.

Health insurance is protection that provides payment of benefits for a covered sickness or injury. Disability income insurance protects a person's most valuable asset: the ability to earn income.

Health insurance and disability income insurance are two protections against economic losses due to illness, accident, or disability. Both protections should be a part of your overall insurance program to safeguard your family's economic security.

L.O.3   Recognize the need for disability income insurance.

Disability income insurance provides regular cash income lost by employees as the result of an accident, illness, or pregnancy. Sources of disability income insurance include the employer, Social Security, worker's compensation, the Veterans Administration, the federal and state governments, unions, and private insurance.

L.O.4   Analyze the benefits and limitations of the various types of health care coverage.

Five basic types of health insurance are available under group and individual policies: hospital expense insurance, surgical expense insurance, physician's expense insurance, major medical expense insurance, and comprehensive major medical insurance. The benefits and limitations of each policy differ. Ideally, you should get a basic plan and a major medical supplementary plan, or a comprehensive major medical policy that combines the values of both of these plans in a single policy.

L.O.5   Evaluate private sources of health insurance and health care.

Health insurance and health care are available from private insurance companies, hospital and medical service plans such as Blue Cross/Blue Shield, health maintenance organizations (HMOs), preferred provider organizations (PPOs), exclusive provider organizations (EPOs), point-of-service plans (POSs), home health care agencies, and employer self-funded health plans.

L.O.6   Appraise the sources of government health care programs.

The federal and state governments offer health coverage in accordance with laws that define the premiums and benefits. Two well-known government health programs are Medicare and Medicaid.

GLOSSARY

basic health insurance coverage   Hospital expense insurance, surgical expense insurance, and physician expense insurance.   (p. 342)

Blue Cross   An independent, nonprofit membership corporation that provides protection against the cost of hospital care.   (p. 349)

Blue Shield   An independent, nonprofit membership corporation that provides protection against the cost of surgical and medical care.   (p. 349)

coinsurance   A provision under which both the insured and the insurer share the covered losses.   (p. 342)

comprehensive major medical insurance   A type of major medical insurance that has a very low deductible and is offered without a separate basic plan.   (p. 343)

coordination of benefits (COB)   A method of integrating the benefits payable under more than one health insurance plan.   (p. 336)

copayment   A provision under which the insured pays a flat dollar amount each time a covered medical service is received.   (p. 345)

deductible   An amount the insured must pay before benefits become payable by the insurance company.   (pp. 342, 347)

disability income insurance   Provides payments to replace income when an insured person is unable to work.   (p. 336)

exclusive provider organization (EPO)   Renders medical care from affiliated health care providers.   (p. 351)

health maintenance organization (HMO)   A health insurance plan that provides a wide range of health care services for a fixed, prepaid monthly premium.   (p. 350)

hospital expense insurance   Pays part or all of hospital bills for room, board, and other charges.   (p. 342)

hospital indemnity policy   Pays stipulated daily, weekly, or monthly cash benefits during hospital confinement. (p. 343)

long-term care insurance (LTC)   Provides day-in, day-out care for long-term illness or disability.   (p. 344)

major medical expense insurance   Pays most of the costs exceeding those covered by the hospital, surgical, and physician's expense policies.   (p. 342)

managed care   Prepaid health plans that provide comprehensive health care to members.   (p. 349)

medigap (MedSup) insurance   Supplements Medicare by filling the gap between Medicare payments and medical costs not covered by Medicare.   (p. 355)

physician expense insurance   Provides benefits for doctors' fees for nonsurgical care, X rays, and lab tests.   (p. 342)

point-of-service plan (POS)   A network of selected contracted, participating providers; also called an *HMO-PPO hybrid* or *open-ended HMO*.   (p. 351)

preferred provider organization (PPO)   A group of doctors and hospitals that agree to provide health care at rates approved by the insurer.   (p. 350)

stop-loss   A provision under which an insured pays a certain amount, after which the insurance company pays 100 percent of the remaining covered expenses.   (p. 343)

surgical expense insurance   Pays part or all of the surgeon's fees for an operation.   (p. 342)

R E V I E W   Q U E S T I O N S

1. Why does health care cost so much? What is being done about the high cost of health care? What can you do about it?   (L.O.1)
2. Define *health insurance* and *disability income insurance*. What is their importance in financial planning?   (L.O.2)
3. What are the sources of disability income?   (L.O.3)
4. What major types of health insurance coverage are available under group and individual policies?   (L.O.4)
5. What are the major provisions of a health insurance policy?   (L.O.4)

6. What are the benefits and limitations of the various types of health care coverage?   (L.O.4)
7. What are the private sources of health insurance and health care?   (L.O.5)
8. What are the government sources of health care programs?   (L.O.6)
9. What type of health care information can you obtain by using the Internet or an online computer service? (L.O.6)

F I N A N C I A L   P L A N N I N G   P R O B L E M S

1. *Calculating the Effect of Inflation on Health Care Costs.*   As of 1995, per capita spending on health care in the United States was about $3,600. If this amount increased by 5 percent a year, what would be the amount of per capita spending for health care in 10 years?   (L.O.1)
2. *Calculating the Amount of Disability Benefits.*   Georgia Braxton, a widow, has take-home pay of $600 a week. Her disability insurance coverage replaces 70 percent of her earnings after a four-week waiting period. What amount would she receive in disability benefits if an illness kept Georgia off work for 16 weeks?   (L.O.3)
3. *Calculating the Amount of Reimbursement from an Insurance Company.*   The Kelleher family has health insurance

coverage that pays 80 percent of out-of-hospital expenses after a $500 deductible per person. If one family member has doctor and prescription medication expenses of $1,100, what amount would the insurance company pay?   (L.O.4)
4. *Comparing the Costs of a Regular Health Insurance Policy and an HMO.*   A health insurance policy pay 65 percent of physical therapy costs after a $200 deductible. In contrast, an HMO charges $15 per visit for physical therapy. How much would a person save with the HMO if they had 10 physical therapy sessions costing $50 each? (L.O.5)

P R O J E C T S   A N D   A P P L I C A T I O N   A C T I V I T I E S

1. *Identifying Financial Resources Needed to Pay for Health Care Services.* List health care services that you and other members of your family have used during the past year. Assign an approximate dollar cost to each of these services, and identify the financial resources (savings, health insurance, government sources, etc.) you used to pay for them.   (L.O.1)

2. *Using Current Information to Obtain Costs of Health Care.* Choose a current issue of *Consumer Reports, Money, Business Week,* or *Kiplinger's Personal Finance* and summarize an article that updates the costs of health care. How may you use this information to reduce your health care costs?   (L.O.1)

3. *Reviewing an Employer's Health Benefit Package.* List the benefits included in your employee benefit package, such as health insurance, disability income insurance, and life insurance. Discuss the importance of such a benefit package to the consumer.   (L.O.2)

4. *Determining Social Security Disability Benefits.* Visit the Social Security Administration's Web page to determine approximate monthly Social Security disability benefits if you became disabled in the current year. Or call your Social Security office to request the latest edition of *Social Security: Understanding the Benefits.*   (L.O.3)

5. *Comparing Major Provisions in a Health Care Insurance Policy.* Obtain sample health insurance policies from insurance agents or brokers, and analyze the policies for definitions, coverages, exclusions, limitations on coverage, and amounts of coverage. In what ways are the policies similar? In what ways do they differ?   (L.O.4)

6. *Using the Internet to Obtain Information about Various Types of Health Insurance Coverages.* Visit the 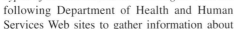 following Department of Health and Human Services Web sites to gather information about various types of health insurance coverages. Prepare a summary report on how this information may be useful to you.   (L.O.4)

   a. Healthfinder (http://www.healthfinder.gov)

   b. MEDLINE (http://www.medline.gov)

7. *Choosing a Source of Health Insurance and Health Care.* Visit the National Health Information Center's Web page (http://nhic-nt.health.org). The NHIC is an online directory of more than 1,100 health-related organizations that 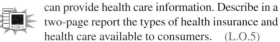 can provide health care information. Describe in a two-page report the types of health insurance and health care available to consumers.   (L.O.5)

8. *Using Current Information for People with Medicare.* Write to the U.S. Department of Health and Human Services (Health Care Financing Administration, Baltimore, MD 21207), and ask for the latest edition of *Guide to Health Insurance for People with Medicare.* On the basis of the information contained in this source, describe the changes that have been made in the hospital insurance and medical insurance provided by Medicare.   (L.O.6)

LIFE SITUATION CASE 11

MATERNITY HEALTH COVERAGE FOR PARENTS-TO-BE

Most expectant parents want their only surprise to be the boy-or-girl kind, not unexpected gaps in their maternity health coverage. While it is still important to know the ins and outs of your company's health plans, many parents-to-be find themselves stuck with charges the insurer refuses to pay. However, two recently passed pieces of legislation make maternity health coverage more "user friendly."

For example, new mothers were being forced to leave the hospital too quickly after delivery because health maintenance organizations were refusing to pay for additional nights in the hospital in an effort to reduce costs. However, in 1996 Congress passed the Newborns and Mothers Health Protection Act, which requires insurers to cover a minimum 48-hour maternity stay.

In another instance, workers who decided to leave one job for another after they or their spouses became pregnant were at greater risk of being excluded from receiving benefits for a pre-existing pregnancy. But under the Health Insurance Portability and Accountability Act, a worker is now entitled to immediate coverage in a new job if he or she had insurance immediately prior to taking the job. The guarantee of continuous coverage will not apply if a worker is without health insurance for more than 63 days between jobs.

Maternity care is often the biggest health care expense for many companies, ranging from around $4,500 for the normal birth of a healthly baby to tens of thousands of dollars for a birth complicated by problems for the mother or infant. For this reason, it can be the first place companies look to for savings. So despite these improvements in health insurance laws, benefits and health care experts recommend combing through every line of a company's maternity health plan description—before pregnancy occurs, if possible. That way, people who work for companies that offer different types of plans or different levels of coverage have time to switch.

Parents-to-be should ask their benefits department or insurer the following questions:

- Does the plan cover pregnancy and prenatal care?
- What deductibles or copayments will the parents owe, and will they be reimbursed for expenses before or after delivery?
- When does the insurance plan begin covering the baby as a dependent?
- Will the plan cover the services of birthing centers and/or midwives if the parents want them?
- Is the mother required to join a prenatal education program or maternity case management program to get full coverage?
- To what extent does the plan cover prenatal diagnostic tests?
- Does the insurer have to be notified within a certain amount of time after the mother is admitted to the hospital for delivery?
- How long can the mother and baby stay in the hospital after delivery, and how is one day measured for this purpose?

■ To what extent does the policy cover normal newborn nursery care? What about neonatal intensive care if needed?

QUESTIONS

1. Why do two new laws make it easier for expectant parents to count on adequate health care coverage?
2. What does the Newborns and Mothers Health Protection Act of 1996 require of insurers?
3. Are there any exceptions to the continuous coverage guarantee of the Health Insurance Portability and Accountability Act?

4. Why is it important to closely examine your company's maternity health plan description before you or your spouse becomes pregnant?

SOURCES: Deborah Lohse, "Prospective Parents Should Look Out for Gaps in Maternity Health Coverage," *The Wall Street Journal,* May 3, 1994, p. C1; Robert A. Rosenblatt, "Clinton Signs Major Package of Health Insurance Reforms Legislation," *Los Angeles Times,* August 22, 1996, p. A16; Sheryl Gay Stolberg, "Many Women Wary of Congress's Newfound Interest in Female Health Issues," *The New York Times,* May 26, 1997, p. 9.

USING THE INTERNET TO CREATE A PERSONAL FINANCIAL PLAN 11

COMPARING HEALTH INSURANCE PLANS

Changing programs and regulations influence your ability to be properly covered for health care and disability insurance coverage. Awareness of policy types, coverages, and limitations will help you plan this phase of your financial plan.

Web Sites for Health Insurance

■ Links to various health Web sites may be accessed at **www.healthseek.com**
■ Information from the Life and Health Information Foundation for Education at **www.life-line.org**
■ Information about health insurance options at **www.northcoast.com/unlimited/services_listing/greg_connors/gci.html**
■ Answers to common questions about long-term care at **www.service.com/answers/health_insurance.html**
■ Medicare from Social Security Administration at **www.ssa.gov**
■ Supplemental Medicare information from the National Association of Insurance Commissioners at **www.naic.org**
■ Current health insurance articles from *Money* magazine at **www.money.com,** from *Kiplinger's Personal Finance* magazine at **www.kiplinger.com,** *Business Week* at **www.businessweek.com,** *Worth* magazine at **www.worth.com,** and *Smart Money* at **www.dowjones.com/smartmoney**

(Note: Addresses and content of Web sites change, and new sites are created daily. Use the search engines discussed in Appendix B to update and locate Web sites for your current financial planning needs.)

PFP SHEETS: 50–51

Short-Term Financial Planning Activities

1. Assess your current habits that could improve your health and reduce medical costs.
2. Evaluate your need for expanded disability income insurance (see PFP Sheet 50).
3. Analyze current health insurance coverage in relation to family and household needs (see PFP Sheet 51).
4. Compare the cost of health insurance programs available from various sources.

Long-Term Financial Planning Activities

1. Identify possible future needs for supplemental Medicare and long-term care insurance coverages.
2. Develop a plan for reducing health care and medical insurance costs.

CHAPTER 12

LIFE INSURANCE

OPENING CASE

HOW MUCH IS ENOUGH?

Joanne and Glenn Kitsos recently had their second child and decided to make a change to their life insurance. "We've got two kids now, and we have to start thinking about the future," Joanne said.

The Kitsos and other new parents are among the people experts say ought to have life insurance. Anyone who has someone financially dependent on them or anyone whose death would cause someone to lose money should be insured.

"Term life insurance is 'extraordinarily cheap' when people are in their 20s and 30s, so people with children should purchase a sufficient amount," says Elliot S. Lipson, an Atlanta financial planner. "All too often, people buy expensive policies that offer savings or investment components but lack a basic benefit that is large enough to provide for their needs."

The amount you need isn't easy to determine because the total can be as little as five times and as much as 10 times your annual salary.

Jim Hunt, consultant to the Consumer Federation of America's insurance group, says the total need for an average couple with two young children is close to six to eight times their salary. For example, the Kitsos' combined income is $100,000, so they probably need a minimum of $600,000 in insurance and maybe a little more if they have no group life insurance at work.

Here are a few questions to ask when figuring how much life insurance you need:

- How much income will your dependents need every year if you die?
- How much income will your dependents have from other sources, such as investments, pensions, or savings, if you die?
- How much income will your dependents have access to from sources such as your spouse's salary or Social Security?

Once you've come up with a total, you have to decide whether you want term, whole life, or some hybrid variation.

Your goal, Hunt says, is to buy as much insurance as you need. But because of the costs of whole life insurance, that often means term. While whole life costs more in the early years, it guarantees that you will pay the same premium 10, 15, or even 20 years down the road.

The Kitsos started out with whole life insurance, but they have decided to switch to term insurance that will last until their kids graduate from college. They want to have enough insurance to cover their funeral costs and the cost of their children's college educations. But rather than using their insurance as an investment, they plan to invest more in mutual funds.

QUESTIONS

1. What is the advantage of buying life insurance when you are younger, and what is a good reason for having it?
2. What would be the total coverage needed for an average couple with two children and a combined income of $45,000?
3. What is one advantage of whole life insurance?
4. Is term insurance the right choice for the Kitsos? Why or why not?

SOURCES: Earl C. Gottschalk, Jr., "Avoiding the Big Mistakes along Life's Path," *The Wall Street Journal,* May 27, 1997, p. C1; Candy McCampbell, "How Much Insurance to Carry Is a Question Not Easily Answered," *Gannett News Service,* July 9, 1997, p. S12..

L E A R N I N G
O B J E C T I V E S

After studying this chapter, you will be able to

L.O.1 Define *life insurance* and describe its purpose and principle.

L.O.2 Determine your life insurance needs.

L.O.3 Distinguish between the two types of life insurance companies and analyze various types of life insurance policies these companies issue.

L.O.4 Select important provisions in life insurance contracts.

L.O.5 Create a plan to buy life insurance.

L.O.6 Recognize how annuities provide financial security.

LIFE INSURANCE: AN INTRODUCTION

Even though it may be impossible to put a price on your life, you probably own some life insurance—through a group plan where you work, as a veteran, or through a policy you bought yourself. Perhaps you are considering the purchase of additional life insurance to keep pace with inflation or cover your growing family. If so, you should prepare for that purchase by learning as much as possible about life insurance and how it can help you meet your needs.

This chapter will help you make decisions about life insurance. It describes what life insurance is and how it works, the major types of life insurance coverages, and how you can use life insurance to protect your family.

Consumer awareness of life insurance has changed very little over the years. Life insurance is still more often sold than bought. In other words, while most people actively seek to buy insurance for their property and health, they avoid a life insurance purchase until an agent approaches them. Still, at the beginning of 1997, life insurance in force reached a new high of $13.8 trillion. About 154 million Americans (78 percent of all households) now have life insurance.[1]

What Is Life Insurance?

L.O.1 Define life insurance and describe its purpose and principle.

Life insurance is neither mysterious nor difficult to understand. It works in the following manner. A person joins a risk-sharing group (an insurance company) by purchasing a contract (a policy). Under the policy, the insurance company promises to pay a sum of money at the time of the policyholder's death to the person or persons selected by him or her (the beneficiaries). In the case of an endowment policy, the money is paid to the policyholder (the insured) if he or she is alive on the future date (the maturity date) named in the policy. The insurance company makes this promise in return for the insured's agreement to pay it a sum of money (the premium) periodically.

The Purpose of Life Insurance

Most people buy life insurance to protect someone who depends on them from financial losses caused by their death. That someone could be the nonworking spouse and children of a single-income family. It could be the wife or husband of a two-income family. It could be an aging parent. It could be a business partner or a corporation.

Here are typical examples of how life insurance proceeds are used:

- Paying off a home mortgage or other debts at the time of death by way of a decreasing term policy.
- Providing lump-sum payments through an endowment to children when they reach a specified age.
- Providing an education or income for children.
- Making charitable bequests after death.
- Providing a retirement income.
- Accumulating savings.
- Establishing a regular income for survivors.
- Setting up an estate plan.
- Making estate and death tax payments.

Life insurance is one of the few ways to provide liquidity at the time of death.

The Principle of Life Insurance

The principle of home insurance discussed in Chapter 10 can be applied to the lives of persons. From records covering many years and including millions of lives, mortality tables have been prepared to show the number of deaths among various age groups during any year. In the 1950s, the life insurance industry developed and the National Association of Insurance Commissioners (NAIC) approved a mortality table known as the Commissioners 1958 Standard Ordinary (CSO) Mortality Table. In 1980, the NAIC approved a new Standard Ordinary Mortality Table based on experience during 1970–75 (Exhibit 12–1). Unlike the 1958 CSO table, which combined the mortality experience of males and females, the 1980 CSO table separates the experience by sex.

An Example   The data in the 1980 CSO table can be used to illustrate the insurance principle for human lives. Let us assume a group of 100,000 males, age 29, wish to contribute a sufficient amount to a common fund each year that $1,000 can be paid to the dependents of each group member who dies during the year. A glance at Exhibit 12–1 shows that the death rate for males at age 29 is 1.71 per thousand; therefore, 171 members of the group can be expected to die during the year.

Thus, each of the 100,000 members must contribute $1.71 at the beginning of the year to provide $1,000 for the dependents of each of the 171 who will die before the end of the year. If the survivors desire to continue the arrangements the following year, each of the remaining 99,829 members alive at the beginning of the next year, when they will be 30 years old, must contribute $1.73 to protect the dependents of the 173 individuals in the group who will die during that year.

If the group of 100,000 were females age 29, the per-member cost for providing $1,000 of benefits to those who died during the year would be $1.30, since the female mortality rate per 1,000 is 1.30 at 29 years of age. This example may help you see why life insurance premiums usually cost less for females than for males.

EXHIBIT 12–1   **1980 Commissioners Standard Ordinary Mortality Table**

Age	Male Mortality Rate per 1,000	Male Expectancy, Years	Female Mortality Rate per 1,000	Female Expectancy, Years	Age	Male Mortality Rate per 1,000	Male Expectancy, Years	Female Mortality Rate per 1,000	Female Expectancy, Years
0	4.18	70.83	2.89	75.83	50	6.71	25.36	4.96	29.53
1	1.07	70.13	0.87	75.04	51	7.30	24.52	5.31	28.67
2	0.99	69.20	0.81	74.11	52	7.96	23.70	5.70	27.82
3	0.98	68.27	0.79	73.17	53	8.71	22.89	6.15	26.98
4	0.95	67.34	0.77	72.23	54	9.56	22.08	6.61	26.14
5	0.90	66.40	0.76	71.28	55	10.47	21.29	7.09	25.31
6	0.85	65.46	0.73	70.34	56	11.46	20.51	7.57	24.49
7	0.80	64.52	0.72	69.39	57	12.49	19.74	8.03	23.67
8	0.76	63.57	0.70	68.44	58	13.59	18.99	8.47	22.86
9	0.74	62.62	0.69	67.48	59	14.77	18.24	8.94	22.05
10	0.73	61.66	0.68	66.53	60	16.08	17.51	9.47	21.25
11	0.77	60.71	0.69	65.58	61	17.54	16.79	10.13	20.44
12	0.85	59.75	0.72	64.62	62	19.19	16.08	10.96	19.65
13	0.99	58.80	0.75	63.67	63	21.06	15.38	12.02	18.86
14	1.15	57.86	0.80	62.71	64	23.14	14.70	13.25	18.08
15	1.33	56.93	0.85	61.76	65	25.42	14.04	14.59	17.32
16	1.51	56.00	0.90	60.82	66	27.85	13.39	16.00	16.57
17	1.67	55.09	0.95	59.87	67	30.44	12.76	17.43	15.83
18	1.78	54.18	0.98	58.93	68	33.19	12.14	18.84	15.10
19	1.86	53.27	1.02	57.98	69	36.17	11.54	20.36	14.38
20	1.90	52.37	1.05	57.04	70	39.51	10.96	22.11	13.67
21	1.91	51.47	1.07	56.10	71	43.30	10.39	24.23	12.97
22	1.89	50.57	1.09	55.16	72	47.65	9.84	26.87	12.28
23	1.86	49.66	1.11	54.22	73	52.64	9.30	30.11	11.60
24	1.82	48.75	1.14	53.28	74	58.19	8.79	33.93	10.95
25	1.77	47.84	1.16	52.34	75	64.19	8.31	38.24	10.32
26	1.73	46.93	1.19	51.40	76	70.53	7.84	42.96	9.71
27	1.71	46.01	1.22	50.46	77	77.12	7.40	48.04	9.12
28	1.70	45.09	1.26	49.52	78	83.90	6.97	53.45	8.55
29	1.71	44.16	1.30	48.59	79	91.05	6.57	59.35	8.01
30	1.73	43.24	1.35	47.65	80	98.84	6.18	65.99	7.48
31	1.78	42.31	1.40	46.71	81	107.48	5.80	73.60	6.98
32	1.83	41.38	1.45	45.78	82	117.25	5.44	82.40	6.49
33	1.91	40.46	1.50	44.84	83	128.26	5.09	92.53	6.03
34	2.00	39.54	1.58	43.91	84	140.25	4.77	103.81	5.59
35	2.11	38.61	1.65	42.98	85	152.95	4.46	116.10	5.18
36	2.24	37.69	1.76	42.05	86	166.09	4.18	129.29	4.80
37	2.40	36.78	1.89	41.12	87	179.55	3.91	143.32	4.43
38	2.58	35.87	2.04	40.20	88	193.27	3.66	158.18	4.09
39	2.79	34.96	2.22	39.28	89	207.29	3.41	173.94	3.77
40	3.02	34.05	2.42	38.36	90	221.77	3.18	190.75	3.45
41	3.29	33.16	2.64	37.46	91	236.98	2.94	208.87	3.15
42	3.56	32.26	2.87	36.55	92	253.45	2.70	228.81	2.85
43	3.87	31.38	3.09	35.66	93	272.11	2.44	251.51	2.55
44	4.19	30.50	3.32	34.77	94	295.90	2.17	279.31	2.24
45	4.55	29.62	3.56	33.88	95	329.96	1.87	317.32	1.91
46	4.92	28.76	3.80	33.00	96	384.55	1.54	375.74	1.56
47	5.32	27.90	4.05	32.12	97	480.20	1.20	474.97	1.21
48	5.74	27.04	4.33	31.25	98	657.98	0.84	655.85	0.84
49	6.21	26.20	4.63	30.39	99	1,000.00	0.50	1,000.00	0.50

SOURCE: *1997 Life Insurance Fact Book,* American Council of Life Insurance, pp. 107–08.

EXHIBIT 12–2

Expectation of Life at Birth in the United States (years)

Year	White			All Other			Total		
	Male	Female	Total	Male	Female	Total	Male	Female	Total
1900	46.6	48.7	47.6	32.5	33.5	33.0	46.3	48.3	47.3
1910	48.6	52.0	50.3	33.8	37.5	35.6	48.4	51.8	50.0
1920	54.4	55.6	54.9	45.5	45.2	45.3	53.6	54.6	54.1
1930	59.7	63.5	61.4	47.3	49.2	48.1	58.1	61.6	59.7
1940	62.1	66.6	64.2	51.5	54.9	53.1	60.8	65.2	62.9
1950	66.5	72.2	69.1	59.1	62.9	60.8	65.6	71.1	68.2
1960	67.4	74.1	70.6	61.1	66.3	63.6	66.6	73.1	69.7
1965	67.6	74.7	71.0	61.1	67.4	64.1	66.8	73.7	70.2
1970	68.0	75.6	71.7	61.3	69.4	65.3	67.1	74.7	70.8
1971	68.3	75.8	72.0	61.6	69.8	65.6	67.4	75.0	71.1
1972	68.3	75.9	72.0	61.5	70.1	65.7	67.4	75.1	71.2
1973	68.5	76.1	72.2	62.0	70.3	66.1	67.6	75.3	71.4
1974	69.0	76.7	72.8	62.9	71.3	67.1	68.2	75.9	72.0
1975	69.5	77.3	73.4	63.7	72.4	68.0	68.8	76.6	72.6
1976	69.9	77.5	73.6	64.2	72.7	68.4	69.1	76.8	72.9
1977	70.2	77.9	74.0	64.7	73.2	68.9	69.5	77.2	73.3
1978	70.4	78.0	74.1	65.0	73.5	69.3	69.6	77.3	73.5
1979	70.8	78.4	74.6	65.4	74.1	69.8	70.0	77.8	73.9
1980	70.7	78.1	74.4	65.3	73.6	69.5	70.0	77.4	73.7
1981	71.1	78.4	74.8	66.2	74.4	70.3	70.4	77.8	74.1
1982	71.5	78.7	75.1	66.8	74.9	70.9	70.8	78.1	74.5
1983	71.6	78.7	75.2	67.0	74.7	70.9	71.0	78.1	74.6
1984	71.8	78.7	75.3	67.2	74.9	71.1	71.1	78.2	74.7
1985	71.8	78.7	75.3	67.0	74.8	71.0	71.1	78.2	74.7
1986	71.9	78.8	75.4	66.8	74.9	70.9	71.2	78.2	74.7
1987	72.1	78.9	75.6	66.9	75.0	71.0	71.4	78.3	74.9
1988	72.2	78.9	75.6	66.7	74.8	70.8	71.4	78.3	74.9
1989	72.5	79.2	75.9	66.7	74.9	70.9	71.7	78.5	75.1
1990	72.7	79.4	76.1	67.0	75.2	71.2	71.8	78.8	75.4
1991	72.9	79.6	76.3	67.3	75.5	71.6	72.0	79.0	75.5
1992	73.2	79.7	76.5	67.8	75.6	71.8	72.3	79.0	75.7
1993	73.1	79.5	76.3	67.3	75.5	71.5	72.2	78.8	75.5
1994	73.2	79.6	76.4	67.5	75.8	71.7	72.3	79.0	75.7
1995	73.4	79.6	76.5	67.9	75.7	71.9	72.5	78.9	75.8

NOTE: Some data are revised.

SOURCES: National Center for Health Statistics; U.S. Department of Health and Human Services; Metropolitan Life Insurance Company; *1997 Life Insurance Fact Book,* p. 109.

How Long Will You Live?

Life expectancy, shown in Exhibit 12–1, does not indicate the age at which a person has the highest probability of dying. For example, the exhibit shows that the life expectancy of a male at age 30 is 43.24 years. This does not mean males 30 years old will probably die at age 73.24 years. It means 43.24 is the average number of years all males alive at age 30 will still live. Exhibit 12–2 shows that life expectancy in the United States has been steadily increasing since 1900.

Covering the financial need arising from the risk of untimely death is the function of life insurance. Modern life insurance policies are designed to meet almost every circumstance in which loss of earning power occurs.

1. What is the meaning of life insurance?
2. What is the purpose of life insurance?
3. What is the principle of life insurance?
4. What do life expectancy tables indicate?

DETERMINING YOUR LIFE INSURANCE NEEDS

L.O.2 Determine your life insurance needs.

You should consider a number of factors before you buy insurance. These factors include your present and future sources of income, other savings and income protection, group life insurance, group annuities (or other pension benefits), and Social Security. First, however, you should determine whether you need life insurance.

Do You Need Life Insurance?

If your death would cause financial stress for your spouse, children, parents, or anyone else you want to protect, you should consider purchasing life insurance. Your stage in the life cycle and the type of household you live in will influence this decision. Single persons living alone or with their parents usually have little or no need for life insurance. Consider Brian Brickman, 28, a bachelor who does not smoke, is in excellent health, and has no dependents. Brian owns a $100,000 condominium with a $90,000 mortgage. Since his employer provides a $100,000 group term life policy, he needs no additional life insurance. Larry Lucas, 32, and his wife, Liz, 30, are professionals, each earning $45,000 a year. The Lucases have no dependents. This two-earner couple may have a moderate need for life insurance, especially if they have a mortgage or other large debts. Households with small children usually have the greatest need for life insurance.

Determining Your Life Insurance Objectives

Before you consider types of life insurance policies, you must decide what you want your life insurance to do for you and your dependents.

First, how much money do you want to leave to your dependents should you die today? Will you require more or less insurance protection to meet their needs as time goes on?

Second, when would you like to be able to retire? What amount of income do you believe you and your spouse would need then?

Third, how much will you be able to pay for your insurance program? When you are older, are you most likely to earn more than, the same as, or less than you do now? Are the demands on your family budget for other living expenses likely to be greater or lower as time goes on?

When you have considered these questions and developed some approximate answers, you are ready to select the types and amounts of life insurance policies that will help you accomplish your objectives.

Once you have decided what you want your life insurance to accomplish, the next important decision is how much to buy.

Financial Decision
Trade-Off

Estimating Your Life Insurance Requirements

How much life insurance should you carry? This question is important for every person who owns or intends to buy life insurance. Because of the various factors involved, the question cannot be answered by mathematics alone. Nevertheless, an insurance policy puts a price on the life of the person insured, and therefore methods are needed to estimate what that price should be.

There are four general methods for determining the amount of insurance you may need: the easy method, the DINK method, the "nonworking" spouse method, and the "family need" method.

The Easy Method   Simple as this method is, it is remarkably useful. It is based on the insurance agent's rule of thumb that a "typical family" will need approximately 70 percent of your salary for seven years before they adjust to the financial consequences of your death. In other words, for a simple estimate of your life insurance needs, just multiply your current gross income by 7 (7 years) and 0.70 (70 percent).

Example:

$30,000 current income × 7 = $210,000; $210,000 × 0.70 = $147,000

Your figures:

$_____ current income × 7 = $_____ × 0.70 = $_____

This method assumes your family is "typical." You may need more insurance if you have four or more children, if you have above-average family debt, if any member of your family suffers from poor health, or if your spouse has poor employment potential.

The DINK (Dual Income, No Kids) Method   If you have no dependents and your spouse earns as much as or more than you do, you have very simple insurance needs. Basically, all you need to do is ensure that your spouse will not be unduly burdened by debts should you die. Here is an example of the DINK method:

	Example	Your Figures
Funeral expenses	$ 5,000	$_____
One-half of mortgage	60,000	_____
One-half of auto loan	7,000	_____
One-half of credit card balance	1,500	_____
One-half of personal debt	1,500	_____
Other debts	1,000	_____
Total insurance needs	$76,000	$_____

This method assumes your spouse will continue to work after your death. If your spouse suffers poor health or is employed in an occupation with an uncertain future, you should consider adding an insurance cushion to see him or her through hard times.

The "Nonworking" Spouse Method   Insurance experts have estimated that extra costs of up to $9,000 a year may be required to replace the services of a homemaker in a family with small children. These extra costs may include the cost of a housekeeper, child care, more meals out, additional carfare, laundry services, and so on. They do not include the lost potential earnings of the surviving spouse, who often must take time away from the job to care for the family.

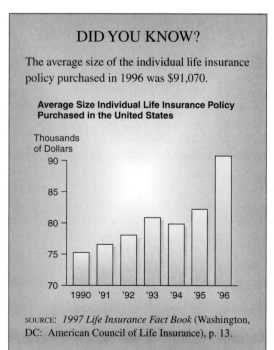

DID YOU KNOW?

The average size of the individual life insurance policy purchased in 1996 was $91,070.

Average Size Individual Life Insurance Policy Purchased in the United States

SOURCE: *1997 Life Insurance Fact Book* (Washington, DC: American Council of Life Insurance), p. 13.

EXHIBIT 12–3

A Worksheet to Calculate Your Life Insurance Needs

1. Five times your personal yearly income = _____ (1)

2. Total approximate expenses above and beyond your daily living costs for you and your dependents (e.g., tuition, care for a disabled child or parent) amount to = _____ (2)

3. Your emergency fund (3 to 6 months of living expenses) amounts to = _____ (3)

4. Estimated amount for your funeral expenses = (U.S. average is $5,000 to $10,000) +_____ (4)

5. Total estimate of your family's financial needs = (add lines 1 through 4) =_____ (5)

6. Your total liquid assets (e.g., savings accounts, CDs, money market funds, existing life insurance both individual and group, pension plan death benefits, and Social Security benefits −_____ (6)

7. Subtract line 6 from line 5 and enter the difference here. =_____ (7)

The net result (line 7) is an estimate of the shortfall your family would face upon your death. Remember, these are just rules of thumb. For a complete analysis of your needs, consult a professional.

SOURCE: *About Life Insurance,* Metropolitan Life Insurance Company, February 1997, p. 3; *The TIAA Guide to Life Insurance Planning for People in Education* (New York: Teachers Insurance and Annuity Association, January 1997), p. 3.

To estimate how much life insurance a homemaker should carry, multiply the number of years before the youngest child reaches age 18 by $9,000:

Example:

$$10 \text{ years} \times \$9,000 = \$90,000$$

Your figures:

$$\_\_\_\_\_ \text{ years} \times \$9,000 = \$_____$$

If the wage-earning spouse's job is not demanding or if there are teenage children, the $9,000 figure can be reduced. If the wage earner's job is especially demanding, there are more than two children under age 13, or anyone in the family suffers poor health or has special needs, the $9,000 figure should be adjusted upward.

Sheet 53

The "Family Need" Method   The first three methods assume you and your family are "typical" and ignore important factors such as Social Security and your liquid assets. Exhibit 12–3 provides a detailed worksheet for making a thorough estimation of your life insurance needs.

Although this method is quite thorough, you may believe it does not address all of your special needs. If so, you should obtain further advice from an insurance expert or a financial planner.

As you determine your life insurance needs, don't forget to consider the life insurance you may already have. You may have ample coverage through your employer and through mortgage and credit life insurance you may have purchased.

CONCEPT CHECK   12–2

1. How do you determine the need for life insurance?
2. What determines your life insurance objectives?
3. What are the four methods of estimating your life insurance requirements?

TYPES OF LIFE INSURANCE COMPANIES AND POLICIES

Types of Life Insurance Companies

L.O.3 Distinguish between the two types of life insurance companies and analyze various types of life insurance policies these companies issue.

nonparticipating policy

participating policy

You can purchase the new or extra life insurance you need from two types of life insurance companies: stock life insurance companies, owned by shareholders, and mutual life insurance companies, owned by their policyholders. About 95 percent of U.S. life insurance companies are stock companies, and about 5 percent are mutuals.

Stock companies generally sell **nonparticipating** (or *nonpar*) policies, while mutual companies specialize in the sale of **participating** (or *par*) policies. A participating policy has a somewhat higher premium than a nonparticipating policy, but a part of the premium is refunded to the policyholder annually. This refund is called the *policy dividend.*

There has been long and inconclusive debate about whether stock companies or mutual companies offer less expensive life insurance. You should check with both stock and mutual companies to determine which type offers the best policy for your particular needs at the lowest price.

If you wish to pay exactly the same premium each year, you should choose a nonparticipating policy with its guaranteed premiums. However, you may prefer life insurance whose annual price reflects the company's experience with its investments, the health of its policyholders, and its general operating costs, that is, a participating policy.

Nevertheless, as with other forms of insurance, price should not be your only consideration in choosing a life insurance policy. You should consider the financial stability, reliability, and service the insurance company provides. Currently about 1,700 life insurance companies in the United States sell life insurance.

Types of Life Insurance Policies

Both mutual insurance companies and stock insurance companies sell two basic types of life insurance: temporary and permanent insurance. Temporary insurance can be term, renewable term, convertible term, or decreasing term insurance. Permanent insurance is known by different names, including *whole life, straight life, ordinary life,* and *cash value life insurance.* As you will learn in the next section, permanent insurance can be limited payment, variable, adjustable, or universal life insurance. Other types of insurance policies—group life and credit life insurance—are generally temporary forms of insurance. Exhibit 12–4 shows the types of policies issued in 1994, and Exhibit 12–5 shows major types and subtypes of life insurance.

Term Life Insurance

term insurance

Term insurance is protection for a specified period of time, usually 1, 5, 10, or 20 years or up to age 65. A term insurance policy pays a benefit only if you die during the period it covers. If you stop paying the premiums, the insurance stops. Term insurance is therefore sometimes called *temporary life insurance.*

Renewability Option   The coverage of term insurance ends at the conclusion of the term, but you can continue it for another term if you have a renewable option. For example, the term insurance of The Teachers Insurance and Annuity Association is renewable at your option for successive five-year periods to age 70 without medical re-examination. Level premiums are paid during each five-year period. The premiums increase every five years.

EXHIBIT 12–4

Types of Life Insurance Policies Issued in 1994

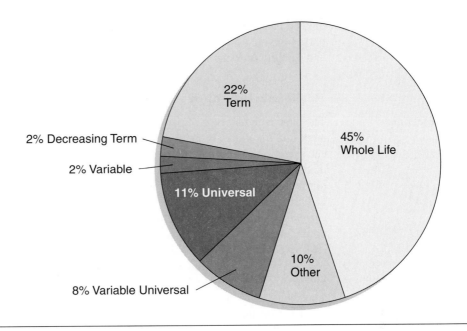

SOURCES: LIMRA International; *1997 Life Insurance Fact Book* (Washington, DC: American Council of Life Insurance), p. 18.

EXHIBIT 12–5

Major Types and Subtypes of Life Insurance

Term (temporary)	Whole, Straight, or Ordinary Life	Other Types
■ Term	■ Limited payment	■ Group life
■ Renewable term	■ Single premium	■ Credit life
■ Convertible term	■ Modified life	
■ Decreasing term	■ Variable life	
	■ Adjustable life	
	■ Universal life	
	■ Variable universal life	

Conversion Option   If you have convertible term insurance, you can exchange it for a whole life policy without a medical examination and at a higher premium. The premium for the whole life policy stays the same for the rest of your life.

Decreasing Term Insurance   Term insurance is also available in a form that pays less to the beneficiary as time passes. The insurance period you select might depend on your age or on how long you decide the coverage will be needed. For example, a decreasing term contract for 25 years might be appropriate as coverage of a mortgage loan balance on a house because the coverage will decrease as the balance on the mortgage decreases. You could get the same result by purchasing annual renewable term policies of diminishing amounts during the period of the mortgage loan. An annual renewable policy would offer more flexibility to change coverage if you were to sell the house or remortgage it. Mortgage insurance therefore is a form of decreasing term insurance, decreasing to keep pace with the principal balance on your mortgage loan. In 1997, a 35-year-old person buying a $100,000, 20-year decreasing term policy from the Teachers Insurance and Annuity Association would pay a first-year premium of $141.

Whole Life Insurance

whole life policy

The most common type of permanent life insurance is the **whole life policy** (also called a *straight life policy* or an *ordinary life policy*), in which you pay a specified premium each year for as long as you live. In return, the insurance company promises to pay a stipulated sum to the beneficiary when you die. The amount of your premium depends primarily on the age at which you purchase the insurance.

cash value

One important feature of the whole life policy is its cash value. **Cash value** (or *cash surrender value*) is an amount that increases over the years that you receive it if you give up the insurance. A table in the whole life policy enables you to tell exactly how much cash value the policy has at any given time (see Exhibit 12–6 on page 373).

Cash value policies may make sense for people who intend to keep the policies for the long term or for people who must be forced to save. But you should not have too low a death benefit just because you would like the savings component of a cash value life policy. The Consumer Federation of America Insurance Group (formerly known as NICO) suggests that you explore other savings and investment strategies before investing your money in a permanent life insurance policy.

nonforfeiture clause

Nonforfeiture Clause   Another important feature of the whole life policy is the **non-forfeiture clause.** This provision allows you not to forfeit all accrued benefits. For example, if you decide not to continue paying premiums, you can exercise certain options with your cash value.

To see the workings of the whole life policy and its cash value, let us suppose a 30-year-old woman wants to buy $30,000 worth of coverage. She might pay an annual premium of $435 for a whole life policy with no policy dividends. Here's how the cash would grow:

Age 35	$1,830
Age 40	4,260
Age 45	6,990
Age 50	9,960

The insurance company accumulates a substantial reserve during the early years of the whole life policy to pay the benefits in the later years when your chances of dying are greater. At first, the basic premium for whole life insurance is higher than that for term insurance. However, the premium for a whole life policy remains constant throughout your lifetime, whereas the premium for a term policy increases with each renewal.

Several types of whole life insurance have been developed to meet different objectives. A few of the more popular types are discussed next.

Limited Payment Policy   One type of whole life policy is called the *limited payment policy.* With this plan, you pay premiums for a stipulated period, usually 20 or 30 years, or until you reach a specified age, such as 60 or 65 (unless your death occurs earlier). However, you remain insured for life and the company will pay the face amount of the policy at your death. Because the premium payment period for a limited payment policy is shorter than that for a whole life policy, the annual premium is higher. For example, in 1997, a 35-year-old person buying a $25,000, 20-payment life policy at a preferred risk

EXHIBIT 12–6	Plan and Additional Benefits	Amount	Premium	Years Payable
An Example of Guaranteed Cash Values	Whole life (premiums payable to age 90)	$10,000	$229.50	55
	Waiver of premium (to age 65)		4.30	30
	Accidental death (to age 70)	10,000	7.80	35

A premium is payable on the policy date and every 12 policy months thereafter. The first premium is $241.60.

Explanation: To cancel the policy in the 10th year, the insured would get $1,719 in savings (cash value). He or she could use the $1,719 to purchase a $3,690 paid-up life policy or purchase an extended term policy that would be in effect for 19 years and 78 days.

Table of Guaranteed Values

End of Policy Year	Cash or Loan Value	Paid-up Insurance	Extended Term Insurance	
			Years	Days
1	$ 14	$ 30	0	152
2	174	450	4	182
3	338	860	8	65
4	506	1,250	10	344
5	676	1,640	12	360
6	879	2,070	14	335
7	1,084	2,500	16	147
8	1,293	2,910	17	207
9	1,504	3,300	18	177
10	1,719	3,690	19	78
11	1,908	4,000	19	209
12	2,099	4,300	19	306
13	2,294	4,590	20	8
14	2,490	4,870	20	47
15	2,690	5,140	20	65
16	2,891	5,410	20	66
17	3,095	5,660	20	52
18	3,301	5,910	20	27
19	3,508	6,150	19	358
20	3,718	6,390	19	317
Age 60	4,620	7,200	18	111
Age 65	5,504	7,860	16	147

Paid-up additions and dividend accumulations increase the cash values; indebtedness decreases them.

Direct Beneficiary: Helen M. Benson, wife of the insured
Owner: Thomas A. Benson, the insured
Insured: Thomas A. Benson   **Age and Sex:**   37 Male
Policy Date: November 1, 1998   **Policy Number:**   000/00
Date of Issue: November 1, 1998

SOURCE: *Sample Life Insurance Policy* (Washington, DC: American Council of Life Insurance, n.d.), p. 2.

FINANCIAL PLANNING FOR LIFE'S SITUATIONS

Do you qualify for preferred rates? These guidelines are used to determine preferred rates; standard rates are higher.

- **Blood profile:** All favorable values for cholesterol, triglycerides, and lipides.
- **Blood pressure:** May not exceed 140/90.
- **Urinalysis:** No abnormal findings. Presence of nicotine will disqualify the applicant for no-tobacco rates.
- **Personal history:** No history of or current treatment for high blood pressure, cancer, diabetes, mental or nervous disorders, or disorders of the heart, lungs, liver, or kidneys.

- **Build:** Weight may not exceed 115 percent of average for height.
- **Driving:** No convictions for reckless driving or driving under the influence of alcohol or drugs in the past five years; no more than three moving violations in the past three years; no more than one moving violation in the past six months.
- **Family history:** No family history (natural parents and siblings) of death from heart disease, cardiovascular impairments, cancer, or diabetes prior to age 60.

SOURCE: Ameritas Life Insurance Corporation, May 1997.

rate from the Teachers Insurance and Annuity Association (TIAA) would pay a $236.25 premium during the first year. In contrast, the premium for an ordinary life policy would be $183.50 for the same coverage. How do you qualify for preferred risk rates? See the Financial Planning for Life's Situations feature.

A special form of the limited payment plan is the single-premium policy. In this type of contract, you make only one very large premium payment.

Variable Life Insurance Policy   The cash values of a *variable life* insurance policy fluctuate according to the yields earned by a separate fund, which can be a stock fund, a money market fund, or a long-term bond fund. A minimum death benefit is guaranteed, but the death benefit can rise above that minimum to a level that depends on the earnings of the dollars invested in the separate fund. The premium payments for a variable life policy are fixed.

When you purchase a variable life policy, you assume the risk of poor investment performance. Therefore, the cash value of a variable life policy is not guaranteed. Life insurance agents selling variable life policies must be registered representatives of a broker-dealer licensed by the National Association of Securities Dealers and registered with the Securities and Exchange Commission. If you are interested in a variable life policy, be sure your agent gives you a prospectus that includes an extensive disclosure about the policy.

Adjustable Life Insurance Policy   The *adjustable life* insurance policy is another relatively recent type of whole life insurance. You can change such a policy as your needs change. For example, if you want to increase or decrease your coverage, you can change either the premium payments or the period of coverage.

universal life

Universal Life   Subject to certain minimums, **universal life** insurance, first introduced in 1979, is designed to let you pay premiums at any time in virtually any amount. The amount of insurance can be changed more easily in a universal life policy than in a traditional policy. The increase in the cash value of a universal life policy reflects the interest earned on short-term investments. Thus, the universal life policy clearly combines

EXHIBIT 12–7   **Comparison of Term, Whole Life, and Universal Life Insurance**

	Type of Policy	Period Covered	Cash Value	Insurance Protection	Premium	Coverage	Comments
Temporary	Term						
	Level	For a stated number of years, such as 1, 5, 20	None	High	Stays the same until renewal	Stays the same	Pure insurance coverage
	Decreasing	For a stated number of years, such as 1, 5, 20	None	High	Stays the same	Decreases	Least expensive type of insurance
Permanent	Whole life						Part insurance, part savings
	Straight	Whole life	Low	Moderate	Stays the same	Stays the same	
	Limited payment	Whole life	Low	Moderate	Stays the same	Stays the same	Paid up after a certain number of years
	Universal life	Varies	Low to high	Low to high	Varies	Varies	Combines renewable term insurance with a savings account paying market interest rates

Financial Decision
Trade-Off

term insurance and investment elements. About $2.2 trillion of universal life insurance was in force at the beginning of 1996.

Like the details of other types of policies, the details of universal life policies vary from company to company. The key distinguishing features of universal life policies are explicit, separate accounting reports to policyholders of (1) the charges for the insurance element, (2) the charges for company expenses (commissions, policy fees, etc.), and (3) the rate of return on the investment (cash value) of the policy. The rate of return is flexible; it is guaranteed to be not less than a certain amount (usually 4 percent), but it may be more, depending on the insurance company's decision.

What are the differences between universal life and whole life insurance? While both policy types have cash value, universal life gives you more direct control. With universal life, you control your outlay and can change your premium without changing your coverage. Whole life, in contrast, requires you to pay a specific premium every year, or the policy will lapse. Universal life allows you access to your cash value by a policy loan or withdrawal. Whole life allows only for policy loans.

Since your primary reason for buying a life insurance policy is the insurance component, the cost of that component should be your main consideration. Thus, universal life policies, which offer a high rate of return on the cash value but charge a high price for the insurance element, should generally be avoided.

Exhibit 12–7 compares some important features of term, whole life, and universal life policies.

Over the years, variations on term and whole life insurance have been developed. The details of these policies may differ among companies. Therefore, check with individual companies to determine the best policy for your needs.

Other Types of Life Insurance Policies

Group Life Insurance   In recent decades, *group life insurance* has become quite popular. A group insurance plan insures a large number of persons under the terms of a single policy without requiring medical examinations. In general, the principles that apply to other forms of insurance also apply to group insurance.

Fundamentally, group insurance is term insurance, which was described earlier. Usually the cost of group insurance is split between the employer and the employees such that the cost of insurance per $1,000 is the same for each employee, regardless of age. For older employees, the employer pays a larger portion of the costs of the group policy. Group life insurance provided $5 trillion of protection in 1996.

However, group life insurance is not always a good deal. Indeed, insurance advisers offer countless stories about employer-sponsored plans, or group plans offered through professional associations, offering coverage that costs 20, 50, or even 100 percent more than policies their clients could buy on the open market.[2]

If you want to compare rates and avoid a high-pressure pitch for permanent insurance, contact a low-load, no-commission insurer. One life insurance adviser recommends either USAA Life & Health Insurance Company (1–800–531–8000) or Ameritas Life Insurance Corporation (1–800–552–3553); both give quotes over the phone.

Credit Life Insurance   *Credit life insurance* is used to repay a personal debt should the borrower die before doing so. It is based on the belief that "no person's debts should live after him or her." It was introduced in the United States in 1917, when installment financing and purchasing became popular.

Credit life insurance policies for auto loans and home mortgages are not the best buy for the protection they offer. Instead, buy less expensive decreasing term insurance, discussed earlier.

In fact, some experts claim that credit life insurance policies are the nation's biggest ripoff. The Consumer Federation of America Insurance Group reports that only 42 percent of more than $2 billion in credit premiums charged in 1990 was paid out in claims.[3] Yet consumers had purchased $231.3 billion of credit insurance in 1995. Exhibit 12–8 shows the growth of individual, group, and credit life insurance in the United States.

Modern life insurance policies contain numerous provisions whose terminology can be confusing. Therefore, an understanding of these provisions is very important for the insurance buyer.

In our dynamic economy, inflation and interest rates change often. Therefore, experts recommend that you reevaluate your insurance coverage every two years. Be sure, of course, to update your insurance whenever your situation changes substantially. For example, the birth of another child or an increase in your home mortgage can boost your insurance needs.

DID YOU KNOW?

Americans purchased $1,850 billion of new life insurance in 1996. Of the 31.5 million new life insurance policies and certificates issued during the year, 13.4 million were individual policies and 18.1 million were group certificates.

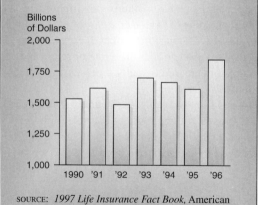

Life Insurance Purchases in the United States

SOURCE: *1997 Life Insurance Fact Book,* American Council of Life Insurance, p. 11.

CONCEPT   CHECK   12–3

1. What are the two types of life insurance companies?
2. What are the major types and subtypes of life insurance?

EXHIBIT 12–8   **Growth of Individual, Group, and Credit Life Insurance in Force in the United States**

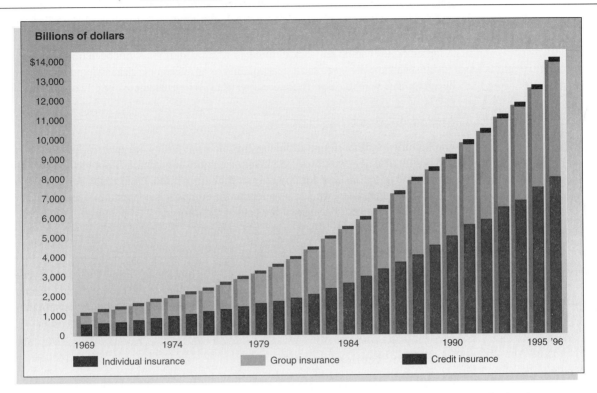

Most group life insurance contracts are issued to employers, though many are issued to unions, professional associations, and other groups.

SOURCE: *1997 Life Insurance Fact Book* (Washington, DC: American Council of Life Insurance), p. 11.

IMPORTANT PROVISIONS IN A LIFE INSURANCE CONTRACT

L.O.4 Select important provisions in life insurance contracts.

Your life insurance policy is valuable only if it meets your objectives. When your objectives change, however, it may not be necessary to give up the policy. Instead, study the policy carefully and discuss its provisions with your agent. Following are some of the most common provisions.

Naming Your Beneficiary

beneficiary

An important provision in every life insurance policy is the right to name your beneficiary. A **beneficiary** is a person who is designated to receive something, such as life insurance proceeds, from the insured. In your policy, you can name one or more persons as contingent beneficiaries who will receive your policy proceeds if the primary beneficiary dies before you do.

The Grace Period

When you buy a life insurance policy, the insurance company agrees to pay a certain sum of money under specified circumstances and you agree to pay a certain premium regularly.

The grace period allows 28 to 31 days to elapse, during which time you may pay the premium without penalty. After that time, the policy lapses if you have not paid the premium.

Policy Reinstatement

A lapsed policy can be put back in force, or reinstated, if it has not been turned in for cash. To reinstate the policy, you must again qualify as an acceptable risk, and you must pay overdue premiums with interest. There is a time limit on reinstatement, usually one or two years.

Incontestability Clause

incontestability clause

The **incontestability clause** stipulates that after the policy has been in force for a specified period (usually two years), the insurance company cannot dispute its validity during the lifetime of the insured for any reason, including fraud. One reason for this provision is that the beneficiaries, who cannot defend the company's contesting of the claim, should not be forced to suffer because of the acts of the insured.

Suicide Clause

suicide clause

The **suicide clause** provides that if the insured dies by suicide during the first two years the policy is in force, the death benefit will equal the amount of the premium paid. Generally, after two years, the suicide becomes a risk covered by the policy and the beneficiaries of a suicide receive the same benefit that is payable for death from any other cause.

Automatic Premium Loans

With an automatic premium loan option, if you do not pay the premium within the grace period, the insurance company automatically pays it out of the policy's cash value if that cash value is sufficient in your whole life policy. This prevents you from inadvertently allowing the policy to lapse.

Misstatement of Age Provision

The misstatement of age provision says that if the company finds out that your age was incorrectly stated, it will pay the benefits your premiums would have bought if your age had been correctly stated. The provision sets forth a simple procedure to resolve what could otherwise be a complicated legal matter.

Policy Loan Provision

A loan from the insurance company is available on a whole life policy after the policy has been in force for one, two, or three years, as stated in the policy. This feature, known as the *policy loan provision,* permits you to borrow any amount up to the cash value of the policy. However, a policy loan reduces the death benefit by the amount of the loan plus interest if the loan is not repaid.

Riders to Life Insurance Policies

rider

An insurance company can change the provisions of a policy by attaching a rider to it. A **rider** is any document attached to the policy that modifies its coverage by adding or excluding specified conditions or altering its benefits. A whole life insurance policy may include a waiver of premium disability benefit, an accidental death benefit, or both.

EXHIBIT 12–9

Effects of Inflation on a $100,000 Life Insurance Policy

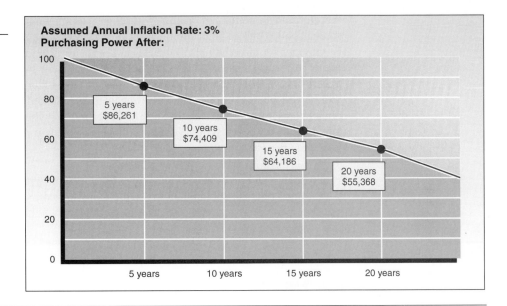

SOURCE: *The TIAA Guide to Life Insurance Planning for People in Education* (New York: Teachers Insurance and Annuity Association, January 1997), p. 8.

Waiver of Premium Disability Benefit   Under this provision, the company waives any premiums that are due after the onset of total and permanent disability. In effect, the company pays the premiums. The disability must occur before you reach a certain age, usually 60.

The waiver of premium rider is sometimes desirable. Don't buy it, however, if the added cost will prevent you from carrying needed basic life insurance. Some insurance companies include this rider automatically in all policies issued through age 55.

Accidental Death Benefit   Under this provision, the insurance company pays twice the face amount of the policy if the insured's death results from an accident. The accidental death benefit is often called **double indemnity.** Accidental death must occur within a certain time period after the injury, usually 90 days, and before the insured reaches a certain age, usually 60 or 65.

double indemnity

The accidental death benefit is expensive. Moreover, your chances of dying in the exact manner stated in the policy are very small, as are the chances that your beneficiary will collect the double payment.

Guaranteed Insurability Option   This option allows you to buy specified additional amounts of life insurance at stated intervals without proof of insurability. Thus, even if you do not remain in good health, you can increase the amount of your insurance as your income rises. This option is desirable if you anticipate the need for additional life insurance in the future.

Cost of Living Protection   This special rider is designed to help prevent inflation from eroding the purchasing power of the protection your policy provides. A *loss, reduction,* or *erosion of purchasing power* refers to the impact inflation has on a fixed amount of money. As inflation increases the costs of goods and services, that fixed amount will not buy as much in the future as it does today. Exhibit 12–9 shows the effects of inflation on a $100,000 life insurance policy.

Accelerated Benefits   *Accelerated benefits*, also known as *living benefits,* are life insurance policy proceeds paid to the policyholder *before* he or she dies. The benefits may be provided for directly in the policies, but more often they are added by riders or attachments to new or existing policies. A representative list of insurers that offer accelerated benefits is available from the National Insurance Consumer Helpline (NICH) at 1–800–942–4242. Although more than 150 companies offer some form of accelerated benefits, not all plans are approved in all states. NICH cannot tell you whether a particular plan is approved in any given state. For more information, check with your insurance agent or your state department of insurance.

Now that you know the various types of life insurance policies and the major provisions of and riders to such policies, you are ready to make your buying decisions.

CONCEPT CHECK 12–4

1. What are the most common provisions in life insurance contracts?
2. What is a beneficiary?
3. What is a rider?
4. What is the concept of double indemnity?

BUYING LIFE INSURANCE

L.O.5 Create a plan to buy life insurance.

You should consider a number of factors before buying life insurance. As discussed earlier in this chapter, these factors include your present and future sources of income, other savings and income protection, group life insurance, group annuities (or other pension benefits), Social Security, and, of course, the financial strength of the company.

From Whom to Buy?

Look for insurance coverage from financially strong companies with professionally qualified representatives. It is not unusual for a relationship with an insurance company to extend over a period of 20, 30, or even 50 years. For that reason alone, you should choose carefully when deciding on an insurance company or an insurance agent. Fortunately, you have a choice of sources.

Sources   Protection is available from a wide range of private and public sources, including insurance companies and their representatives; private groups such as employers, labor unions, and professional or fraternal organizations; government programs such as Medicare and Social Security; and financial institutions and manufacturers offering credit insurance.

Rating Insurance Companies   Some of the strongest, most reputable insurance companies in the nation provide excellent insurance coverage at reasonable costs. In fact, the financial strength of an insurance company may be a major factor in holding down premium costs for consumers.

Locate an insurance company by checking the reputations of local agencies. Ask members of your family, friends, or colleagues about the insurers they prefer.

EXHIBIT 12–10

Rating Systems of Major Rating Agencies

	A. M. Best	Standard & Poor's Duff & Phelps	Moody's	Weiss Research
Superior	A++ A+	AAA	Aaa	A+
Excellent	A A−	AA+ AA AA−	Aa1 Aa2 Aa3	A A− B+
Good	B++ B+	A+ A A−	A1 A2 A3	B B− C+
Adequate	B B−	BBB+ BBB BBB−	Baa1 Baa2 Baa3	C C− D+
Below average	C++ C+	BB+ BB BB−	Ba1 Ba2 Ba3	D D− E+
Weak	C C− D	B+ B B−	B1 B2 B3	E E−
Nonviable	E F	CCC CC C, D	Caa Ca C	F

For a more official review, consult *Best's Agents Guide* or *Best's Insurance Reports* at your public library. Exhibit 12–10 describes the rating systems used by A. M. Best and the other big four rating agencies. As a rule, you should deal with companies rated A++, A+, or A. In addition, *Consumer Reports, Kiplinger's Personal Finance,* and *Money* periodically provide satisfaction ratings on various types of insurance and insurance companies.

Choosing Your Insurance Agent   An insurance agent handles the technical side of insurance. However, that's only the beginning. The really important part of the agent's job is to apply his or her knowledge of insurance to help you select the proper kind of protection within your financial boundaries.

Choosing a good agent is among the most important steps in building your insurance program. How do you find an agent? One of the best ways to begin is by asking your parents, friends, neighbors, and others for their recommendations. However, note that you will seldom have the same agent all your life. The accompanying Financial Planning in Action feature offers guidelines for choosing an insurance agent.

You may also want to investigate an agent's membership in professional groups. Agents who belong to a local Life Underwriters Association are often among the more experienced agents in their communities. A **chartered life underwriter (CLU)** is a life insurance agent who has passed a series of college-level examinations on insurance and related subjects. Such agents are entitled to use the designation CLU after their names. Agents who have passed a series of examinations on property and casualty insurance are designated as *chartered property and casualty underwriters (CPCUs).*

Once you have found an agent, you must decide which policy is right for you. The best way to do this is to talk to your agent. Remember, doing so does not obligate you to buy insurance.

chartered life underwriter (CLU)

FINANCIAL PLANNING IN ACTION

GUIDELINES FOR CHOOSING AN INSURANCE AGENT

	Yes	No
1. Is your agent available when needed? Clients sometimes have problems that need immediate answers.	☐	☐
2. Does your agent advise you to have a financial plan? Each part of the plan should be necessary to your overall financial protection.	☐	☐
3. Does your agent pressure you? You should be free to make your own decisions about insurance coverage.	☐	☐
4. Does your agent keep up with changes in the insurance field? Agents often attend special classes or study on their own so that they can serve their clients better.	☐	☐
5. Is your agent happy to answer questions? Does he or she want you to know exactly what you are paying for with an insurance policy?	☐	☐

Comparing Policy Costs

Each life insurance company designs the policies it sells to make them attractive and useful to many policyholders. One policy may have features another policy doesn't; one company may be more selective than another company; one company may get a better return on its investments than another company. These and other factors affect the prices of life insurance policies.

In brief, five factors affect the price a company charges for a life insurance policy: the company's cost of doing business, the return on its investments, the mortality rate it expects among its policyholders, the features the policy contains, and competition among companies with comparable policies.

The prices of life insurance policies therefore vary considerably among life insurance companies. Moreover, a particular company will not be equally competitive for all policies. Thus, one company might have a competitively priced policy for 24-year-olds but not for 35-year-olds.

interest-adjusted index   Ask your agent to give you interest-adjusted indexes. An **interest-adjusted index** is a method of evaluating the cost of life insurance by taking into account the time value of money. Highly complex mathematical calculations and formulas combine premium payments, dividends, cash value buildup, and present value analysis into an index number that makes possible a fairly accurate cost comparison among insurance companies. The lower the index number, the lower the cost of the policy. The Consumer Federation of America Insurance Group offers a computerized service for comparing policy costs. Contact them at 1424 16th St. NW, Suite 604, Washington, DC, 20036, or at 202–387–6121. Insurance Information, Inc., in South Dennis, Massachusetts, provides price quotes for term insurance. For $50 it will run your age, health status, and occupation through computer data banks covering about 650 different policies and send you the names of the five policies suitable for you and sold in your state. Contact this company at 1–800–472–5800.

Price quote services offer convenient and free, no-obligation premium comparisons. TermQuote in Dayton, Ohio (1–800–444–TERM), represents about 75 insurance companies, and SelectQuote in San Francisco (1–800–343–1985) represents about 20 insurance companies. Shopping for life insurance may be done using online computer services (see Appendix B).

FINANCIAL PLANNING CALCULATIONS

DETERMINING THE COST OF INSURANCE

In determining the cost of insurance, don't overlook the time value of money. You must include as part of that cost the interest (opportunity cost) you would earn on money if you did not use it to pay insurance premiums. For many years, insurers did not assign a time value to money in making their sales presentations. Only recently has the insurance industry widely adopted interest-adjusted cost estimates.

If you fail to consider the time value of money, you may get the false impression that the insurance company is giving you something for nothing. Here is an example. Suppose you are 35 and have a $10,000 face amount, 20-year, limited-payment, participating policy. Your annual premium is $210, or $4,200 over the 20-year period. Your dividends over the 20-year payment period total $1,700, so your total net premium is $2,500 ($4,200 − $1,700). Yet the cash value of your policy at the end of 20 years is $4,600. If you disregard the interest your premiums could otherwise have earned, you might get the impression that the insurance company is giving you $2,100 more than you paid ($4,600 − $2,500). But if you consider the time

value of money (or its opportunity cost), the insurance company is not giving you $2,100. What if you had invested the annual premiums in a conservative stock mutual fund? At an 8 percent annual yield, your account would have accumulated to $6,180 in 20 years. Therefore, instead of having received $2,100 from the insurance company, you have paid the company $1,580 for 20 years of insurance protection:

Premiums you paid over 20 years	$4,200
Time value of money	1,980 ($6,180 − $4,200)
Total cost	6,180
Cash value	4,600
Net cost of insurance	1,580 ($6,180 − $4,600)

Be sure to request interest-adjusted indexes from your agent; if he or she doesn't give them to you, look for another agent. As you have seen in the example, you can compare the costs among insurance companies by combining premium payments, dividends, cash value buildup, and present value analysis into an index number.

The accompanying Financial Planning Calculations feature shows how to use an interest-adjusted index to compare the costs of insurance.

Obtaining a Policy

A life insurance policy is issued after you submit an application for insurance and the insurance company accepts the application. The application usually has two parts. In the first part, you state your name, age, and sex, what type of policy you desire, how much insurance you want, your occupation, and so forth. In the second part, you give your medical history. While a medical examination is frequently required for ordinary policies, usually no examination is required for group insurance.

The company determines your insurability by means of the information in your application, the results of the medical examination, and the inspection report. Of all applicants, 98 percent are found to be insurable, though some may have to pay higher premiums because of an existing medical condition.

Examining a Policy

Before the Purchase When you buy a life insurance policy, read every word of the contract and, if necessary, ask your agent for a point-by-point explanation of the language. Many insurance companies have rewritten their contracts to make them more understandable. Remember that these are legal documents and you should be familiar with what they promise, even though technical terms are used.

After the Purchase   After you buy new life insurance, you have a 10-day "free-look" period during which you can change your mind. If you do so, the company will return your premium without penalty.

It's a good idea to give your beneficiaries and your lawyer a photocopy of your policy. Your beneficiaries should know where the policy is kept, because to obtain the insurance proceeds, they will have to send it to the company upon your death, along with a copy of the death certificate.

Choosing Settlement Options

A well-planned life insurance program should cover the immediate expenses resulting from the death of the insured. However, that is only one of its purposes. In most instances, the primary purpose of life insurance is to protect dependents against a loss of income resulting from the premature death of the primary wage earner. Thus, selecting the appropriate settlement option is an important part of designing a life insurance program. Perhaps the most common settlement options are lump-sum payment, limited installment payment, life income option, and proceeds left with the company.

Financial Decision Trade-Off

Lump-Sum Payment   In the lump-sum payment option, the company pays the face amount of the policy in one installment to the beneficiary or to the estate of the insured. This form of settlement is the most widely used option.

Limited Installment Payment   This option provides for payment of the life insurance proceeds in equal periodic installments for a specified number of years after your death.

Life Income Option   Under the life income option, payments are made to the beneficiary for as long as she or he lives. The amount of each payment is based primarily on the sex and attained age of the beneficiary at the time of the insured's death.

Proceeds Left with the Company   Under this option, the life insurance proceeds are left with the insurance company at a specified rate of interest. The company acts as trustee and pays the interest to the beneficiary. The guaranteed minimum interest rate paid on the proceeds varies among companies.

Switching Policies

Sheet 54

Think twice if your agent suggests that you replace the whole life or universal life insurance you already own. According to a recent study by the Consumer Federation of America, consumers lose billions of dollars each year because they don't hold onto their cash life insurance policies long enough or because they purchase the wrong policies. The author of the study, James Hunt, Vermont's former insurance commissioner, notes that half of those who buy whole or universal life policies drop them within 10 years.

Before you give up this protection, make sure you are still insurable (check medical and any other qualification requirements). Also, remember that you are now older than you were when you purchased your policy and a new policy will therefore cost more. Moreover, the older policy may have provisions that are not duplicated in some of the new policies. This does not mean you should reject the idea of replacing your present policy; rather, you should proceed with caution. We recommend that you ask your agent or company for an opinion about the new proposal to get both sides of the argument.

FINANCIAL PLANNING IN ACTION

TEN GOLDEN RULES OF BUYING LIFE INSURANCE

Remember that your need for life insurance coverage will change over time. Your income may go up or down, or your family size might change. Therefore, it is wise to review your coverage periodically to ensure that it keeps up with your changing needs.

Follow these rules when buying life insurance:

	Yes	No
1. Understand and know what your life insurance needs are before you make any purchase, and make sure the company you choose can meet those needs.	☐	☐
2. Buy your life insurance from a company that is licensed in your state.	☐	☐
3. Select an agent who is competent, knowledgeable, and trustworthy.	☐	☐
4. Shop around and compare costs.	☐	☐
5. Buy only the amount of life insurance you need and can afford.	☐	☐
6. Ask about lower premium rates for nonsmokers.	☐	☐
7. Read your policy and make sure you understand it.	☐	☐
8. Inform your beneficiaries about the kinds and amount of life insurance you own.	☐	☐
9. Keep your policy in a safe place at home, and keep your insurance company's name and your policy number in a safe deposit box.	☐	☐
10. Check your coverage periodically, or whenever your situation changes, to ensure that it meets your current needs.	☐	☐

SOURCE: American Council of Life Insurance, 1001 Pennsylvania Avenue, NW, Washington, DC 20004-2599.

The accompanying Financial Planning in Action feature presents important guidelines to use in purchasing life insurance.

CONCEPT CHECK 12–5

1. How do insurance companies price their products?
2. How do insurance companies determine your insurability?
3. What should you do in examining a policy before and after the purchase?
4. What are the four most common settlement options?
5. Should you switch life insurance policies?

FINANCIAL PLANNING WITH ANNUITIES

L.O.6 Recognize how annuities provide financial security.

annuity

As you have seen so far, life insurance provides a set sum of money at your death. However, if you want to enjoy benefits while you are still alive, you might consider annuities. An annuity protects you against the risk of outliving your assets.

An **annuity** is a financial contract written by an insurance company that provides you with a regular income. Generally, you receive the income monthly, often with payments

EXHIBIT 12–11

Individual Annuity Mortality Table

Age of Male	U.S. Population Deaths per 1,000	U.S. Population Life Expectancy (years)	Age of Male	U.S. Population Deaths per 1,000	U.S. Population Life Expectancy (years)
50	5.89	27.94	71	33.15	12.72
51	6.42	27.10	72	35.93	12.14
52	6.99	26.28	73	38.82	11.58
53	7.61	25.46	74	41.84	11.02
54	8.30	24.65	75	45.07	10.48
55	9.02	23.85	76	48.67	9.95
56	9.78	23.06	77	52.74	9.44
57	10.59	22.29	78	57.42	8.93
58	11.51	21.52	79	62.77	8.45
59	12.54	20.76	80	68.82	7.98
60	13.68	20.02	81	75.52	7.53
61	14.93	19.29	82	82.78	7.11
62	16.28	18.58	83	90.41	6.70
63	17.67	17.88	84	98.42	6.32
64	19.11	17.19	85	107.25	5.96
65	20.59	16.51	86	117.12	5.61
66	22.16	15.85	87	127.17	5.29
67	23.89	15.20	88	137.08	4.99
68	25.85	14.56	89	147.28	4.70
69	28.06	13.93	90	158.68	4.43
70	30.52	13.32			

SOURCE: *1997 Life Insurance Fact Book* (Washington, DC: American Council of Life Insurance), pp. 107–08.

arranged to continue for as long as you live. The payments may begin at once (*immediate annuity*) or at some future date (*deferred annuity*). According to a recent Gallup Organization survey, the average owner of an annuity is a 66-year-old, retired person with an annual household income of less than $75,000. Life insurance companies issued 2.9 million individual annuities during 1995. About 95 percent of them were deferred annuities. The remainder were immediate annuities used to provide retirement income.[4] The annuity is often described as the opposite of life insurance: It pays while you live, while life insurance pays when you die.

As with the life insurance principle, discussed earlier, the predictable mortality experience of a large group of individuals is fundamental to the annuity principle. By determining the average number of years a large number of persons in a given age group will live, the insurance company can calculate the annual amount to pay to each person in the group over his or her entire life.

For example, for annuity purposes, the life expectancy of males age 76 is about 10 years (see Exhibit 12–11). Thus, if 1,000 males age 76 each pay a $10,000 premium (a total of $10 million), each is guaranteed a payment of $1,000 per year for life. Those who live beyond the 10-year average have their "excess" payments funded by those who die before 10 years have elapsed.

Because the annual payouts per premium amount are determined by average mortality experience, annuity contracts are more attractive for people whose present health, living habits, and family mortality experience suggest that they are likely to live longer than average. As a general rule, annuities are not advisable for people in poor health, although exceptions to this rule exist.

EXHIBIT 12–12

Tax-Deferred Annuity versus Taxable CD (a 30-year projection of performance; single deposit of $30,000)

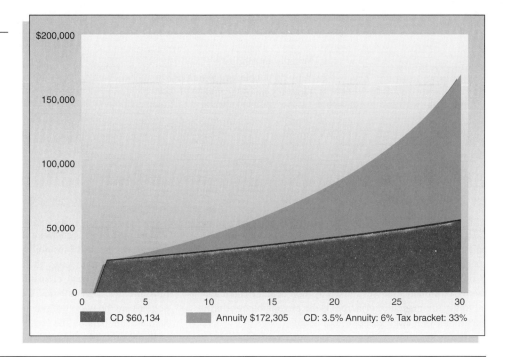

CD $60,134   Annuity $172,305   CD: 3.5% Annuity: 6% Tax bracket: 33%

Why Buy Annuities?

A primary reason for buying an annuity is to give you retirement income for the rest of your life. We discuss retirement income in Chapter 18, "Retirement Planning."

Although people have been buying annuities for many years, the appeal of variable annuities has increased recently due to a rising stock market. A *fixed annuity* states that the annuitant (the person who is to receive the annuity) will receive a fixed amount of income over a certain period or for life. With a *variable annuity,* the monthly payments vary because they are based on the income received from stocks or other investments.

Some of the growth in the use of annuities can be attributed to the passage of the Employee Retirement Income Security Act (ERISA) of 1974. Annuities are often purchased for individual retirement accounts (IRAs), which ERISA made possible. They may also be used in Keogh-type plans for self-employed people. As you will see in Chapter 18, contributions to both IRA and Keogh plans are tax deductible up to specified limits.

Tax Considerations

When you buy an annuity, the interest on the principal, as well as the interest compounded on that interest, builds up free of current income tax. The Tax Reform Act of 1986 preserves the tax advantages of annuities (and insurance) but curtails deductions for IRAs. With an annuity, there is no maximum annual contribution. Also, if you die during the accumulation period, your beneficiary is guaranteed no less than the amount invested.

Exhibit 12–12 shows the difference between an investment in an annuity and an investment in a certificate of deposit (CD). Remember, federal income tax on an annuity is deferred, whereas the tax on interest earned on a CD must be paid currently.

As with any other financial product, the advantages of annuities are tempered by drawbacks. In the case of variable annuities, these drawbacks include reduced flexibility and fees that lower investment return.

CONCEPT CHECK 12–6

1. What is an annuity?
2. Why do people buy annuities?
3. How are annuities taxed?

SUMMARY

L.O.1   Define *life insurance* and describe its purpose and principle.

Life insurance is a contract between an insurance company and a policyholder under which the company agrees to pay a specified sum to a beneficiary upon the insured's death. Most people buy life insurance to protect someone who depends on them from financial losses caused by their death. Fundamental to the life insurance principle is the predictable mortality experience of a large group of individuals.

L.O.2   Determine your life insurance needs.

In determining your life insurance needs, you must first determine your insurance objectives and then use the easy method, the DINK method, the "nonworking" spouse method, or the "family need" method. The "family need" method is recommended.

L.O.3   Distinguish between the two types of life insurance companies and analyze various types of life insurance policies these companies issue.

The two types of life insurance companies are stock companies, owned by stockholders, and mutual companies, owned by policyholders. In general, stock companies sell nonparticipating policies and mutual companies sell participating policies. The three basic types of life insurance are term, whole life, and endowment policies. Many variations and combinations of these types are available.

L.O.4   Select important provisions in life insurance contracts.

The naming of the beneficiary, the grace period, policy reinstatement, the incontestability clause, the suicide clause, automatic premium loans, the misstatement of age provision, and the policy loan provision are important provisions in most life insurance policies. Common riders in life insurance policies are the waiver of premium disability benefit, the accidental death benefit, the guaranteed insurability option, cost of living protection, and accelerated benefits.

L.O.5   Create a plan to buy life insurance.

Before buying life insurance, consider your present and future sources of income, group life insurance, group annuities (or other pension benefits), and Social Security. Then compare the costs of several life insurance policies. Examine your policy before and after the purchase, and choose appropriate settlement options.

L.O.6   Recognize how annuities provide financial security.

An annuity is the opposite of life insurance: It pays while you live, whereas life insurance pays when you die. An annuity provides you with a regular income during your retirement years. The Tax Reform Act of 1986 gives annuities favorable income tax treatment.

GLOSSARY

annuity   A contract that provides an income for as long as the person lives.   (p. 385)

beneficiary   A person designated to receive something, such as life insurance proceeds, from the insured.   (p. 377)

cash value   The amount received after giving up a life insurance policy.   (p. 372)

chartered life underwriter (CLU)   A life insurance agent who has passed a series of college-level examinations on insurance and related subjects.   (p. 381)

double indemnity   A benefit under which the company pays twice the face value of the policy if the insured's death results from an accident.   (p. 379)

incontestability clause   A provision stating that the insurer cannot dispute the validity of a policy after a specified period.   (p. 378)

interest-adjusted index   A method of evaluating the cost of life insurance by taking into account the time value of money.   (p. 382)

nonforfeiture clause   A provision that allows the insured not to forfeit all accrued benefits.   (p. 372)

nonparticipating policy   Life insurance that does not provide policy dividends; also called a *nonpar policy.*   (p. 370)

participating policy   Life insurance that provides policy dividends; also called a *par policy.*   (p. 370)

rider   A document attached to a policy that modifies its coverage.   (p. 378)

suicide clause   A provision stating that if the insured dies by suicide during the first two years the policy is in force, the death benefit will equal the amount of the premium paid. (p. 378)

term insurance   Life insurance protection for a specified period of time; sometimes called *temporary life insurance*. (p. 370)

universal life   A whole life policy that combines term insurance and investment elements.   (p. 374)

whole life policy   An insurance plan in which the policyholder pays a specified premium each year for as long as he or she lives; also called a *straight life policy* or an *ordinary life policy*.   (p. 372)

R E V I E W   Q U E S T I O N S

1. How can the principle of home insurance be applied to the lives of persons?   (L.O.1)
2. What does a life insurance mortality table indicate? (L.O.1)
3. What factors should you consider in determining whether or not you need life insurance?   (L.O.2)
4. Which type of insurance company, stock or mutual, would you prefer when purchasing life insurance? Why?   (L.O.3)

5. Which provisions in a life insurance policy would be important to you?   (L.O.4)
6. Discuss four settlement options available to most policyholders. Which one would you choose, and why?   (L.O.5)
7. What type of life insurance information can you obtain by using online computer services?   (L.O.5)
8. What are the roles of variable and fixed annuities in a life insurance program?   (L.O.6)

F I N A N C I A L   P L A N N I N G   P R O B L E M S

1. *Illustrating the Principle of Life Insurance.* A group of 100,000, males, age 35, wish to contribute each year an amount to a common fund sufficient to pay $1,000 to the dependents of each group member who dies during the year. Use the mortality table in Exhibit 12–1 to determine the following.   (L.O.1)
    a. How many members of the group can be expected to die during the year.
    b. What amount each of the 100,000 members must contribute at the beginning of the year to provide $1,000 for the dependents of those who die before the end of the year.
2. *Calculating the Amount of Life Insurance Needed Using the Easy Method.* You are the wage earner in a "typical family," with $30,000 gross annual income. Use the easy method to determine how much life insurance you should carry.   (L.O.2)
3. *Estimating Life Insurance Needs Using the DINK Method.* You and your spouse are in good health and have reasonably secure careers. Each of you makes about $28,000 annually. You own a home with an $80,000 mortgage, and you owe $10,000 on car loans, $5,000 in personal debts, and $3,000 on credit card loans. You have no other debts. You have no plans to increase the size of your family in the near future. Estimate your total insurance needs using the DINK method.   (L.O.2)

4. *Using the "Nonworking Spouse" Method to Determine Life Insurance Needs.* Tim and Allison are married and have two children, ages 4 and 7. Allison is a "nonworking" spouse who devotes all of her time to household activities. Estimate how much life insurance Tim and Allison should carry.   (L.O.2)
5. *Comparing the Costs of Life Insurance and Various Provisions in a Life Insurance Policy.* Obtain premium rates for $25,000 whole life, universal life, and term life policies from local insurance agents. Compare the costs and provisions of these policies.   (L.O.3)
6. *Calculating Your Life Insurance Needs.* Use Exhibit 12–3 to calculate your life insurance needs.   (L.O.3)
7. *Choosing the Settlement Options.* Review the settlement options on your family's life insurance policies, and discuss with your family which option would be the best choice for them at this time.   (L.O.5)
8. *Calculating Accumulated Account Values.* Assume you have $10,000 to invest for 10 years. You can invest in a certificate of deposit at 8.5 percent or a 10-year, tax-deferred annuity at 8.5 percent. Assume a 33 percent federal tax bracket. Use Exhibit 12–9 to find your accumulated account values. Which investment is better, and by how much?   (L.O.6)

P R O J E C T S   A N D   A P P L I C A T I O N   A C T I V I T I E S

1. *Planning for Life Insurance.* Choose a current issue of *Money, Kiplinger's Personal Finance, Consumer Reports,* or *Worth* magazine and summarize an article that provides

information on human life expectancy and how life insurance may provide financial security.   (L.O.1)

2. *Assessing the Need for Life Insurance.* Interview relatives and friends to determine why they purchased life insurance. Prepare an essay summarizing your findings.   (L.O.1)

3. *Comparing the Methods of Determining Life Insurance Requirements.* Analyze the four methods of determining life insurance requirements. Which method is best, and why?   (L.O.2)

4. *Comparing Premiums for Life Insurance Policies.* Choose one stock and one mutual life insurance company. Obtain and compare premiums for
   a. Term life insurance for $50,000.
   b. Whole life insurance for $50,000.
   c. Universal life insurance for $50,000.
   Prepare a summary table indicating which policy you would consider and why.   (L.O.3)

5. *Using the Internet to Obtain Information about Various Types of Life Insurance.* All major life insurance companies now maintain a Web page on the Internet. Visit a few

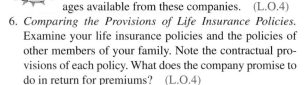

Web sites of companies such as Metropolitan Life, New York Life, Transamerica Life, Lincoln Benefit Life, or others of your choice. Then prepare a report that summarizes the various types of insurance coverages available from these companies.   (L.O.4)

6. *Comparing the Provisions of Life Insurance Policies.* Examine your life insurance policies and the policies of other members of your family. Note the contractual provisions of each policy. What does the company promise to do in return for premiums?   (L.O.4)

7. *Using the Services Provided by State Insurance Departments.* Contact your state insurance department to get information about whether your state requires interest-adjusted cost disclosure. Prepare a summary report of your finding.   (L.O.5)

8. *Assessing the Use and Need for Annuities.* Interview friends, relatives, and others who have bought annuities. Which type of annuity did they purchase, and why?   (L.O.6)

LIFE SITUATION CASE 12

MANY GLOOMY RETURNS

Like many consumers, Ram Reddy, a Houston pharmacist, based his decision to buy a life insurance policy on an elaborate chart showing what he thought the policy would earn over time. However, the policy has earned significantly less, and now, because the company cut the dividend it pays policyholders, Reddy has to pay an extra year of premiums for a policy that should have been paid for.

Unfortunately, Reddy didn't know what the insurance industry knows: These complicated computer-generated charts, called "illustrations," are based on optimistic assumptions that might not occur. The three of four policyholders who own whole life or other forms of cash value insurance, which offer an investment feature as well as a death benefit, may very well not earn as much as illustrated.

Although the charts generally carry disclaimers, too often the buyer, either through ignorance or on the advice of his or her agent, simply ignores it. That has made illustrations one of the most potent and misleading weapons in the insurance industry's sales arsenal.

Reddy says he read the fine print on his illustration that said the rates weren't guaranteed, but his agent told him that the company had never cut rates and that he shouldn't expect it to. "I absolutely did not think this could happen," Reddy says. "They promise one thing, but in reality something else happens."

QUESTIONS

1. Why must Ram Reddy pay an extra year of premiums to keep his life insurance policy?

2. Why do most life insurance buyers ignore disclaimers on illustrations?

SOURCE: Excerpted from Greg Steinmetz, "Sunny Charts Can Belie Gloomy Returns from Insurance," *The Wall Street Journal,* February 23, 1994, pp. B1–B11.

USING THE INTERNET TO CREATE A PERSONAL FINANCIAL PLAN 12

DETERMINING LIFE INSURANCE NEEDS

Providing for the financial needs of dependents is the primary goal of a life insurance program. Comparing policy types, coverage amounts, and other provisions will help to meet this financial purpose.

Web Sites for Life Insurance

■ Life insurance needs may be assessed at **www.rightquote. com**

■ Consumers can compare types of life insurance policies and costs for various insurers at **www.quickquote.com/, www.quotesmith.com, www.quickquote.com,** and **www. accuquote.com**

- Answers to questions about basic information and current developments about auto, home, and life insurance may be obtained at **www.insure.com**
- Life insurance rates and insurance planning assistance at **insuremarket.com** and **www.lifenet.com**
- Information on state insurance regulatory agencies from the National Association of Insurance Commissioners at **www.naic.org**

(Note: Addresses and content of Web sites change, and new sites are created daily. Use the search engines discussed in Appendix B to update and locate Web sites for your current financial planning needs.)

PFP SHEETS: 53–54

Short-Term Financial Planning Activities

1. Determine life insurance needs for your current life situation (see PFP Sheet 53).
2. Compare rates and coverages for different life insurance policies and companies (see PFP Sheet 54).
3. Evaluate the use of annuities in your financial plan.

Long-Term Financial Planning Activities

1. Identify information sources to monitor changes in life insurance coverages and costs offered by life insurance companies.
2. Develop a plan for reassessing life insurance needs as family and household situations change.

CONTINUOUS CASE FOR PART IV

MANAGING RISKS FOR EFFECTIVE FINANCIAL PLANNING

Life Situation
Pam, 36; Josh, 38; three children, ages 9, 7, and 4

Financial Goals
- Evaluate property and liability insurance needs
- Assess the need for disability insurance
- Determine additional life insurance needs

Financial Data

Monthly income	$4,300
Living expenses	4,075
Assets	150,850
Liabilities	99,520

Both Pam and Josh Brock are comfortable. They now have three children, are happy with their home, and are more financially secure than they were six years ago. In fact, everything seems to be right on track. Yet the Brocks still have financial needs they must address. Several changes have affected their financial planning:

- The value of their home has increased due to inflation and home improvements.
- They have purchased a used car to meet additional transportation needs.
- Josh's current place of employment offers him only 30 days of sick leave.
- Pam's life insurance policy is only for $2,000. Josh has life insurance coverage equal to approximately eight times his annual salary.

QUESTIONS

1. How should the Brocks determine whether they have enough insurance coverage for their home?
2. What factors should the Brocks consider in deciding whether to purchase collision insurance coverage for their used car?
3. When considering disability income insurance, what length of waiting period and duration of benefits should the Brocks consider?
4. Do you think Pam and Josh Brock have enough life insurance? If not, what changes would you recommend? Explain your answer.

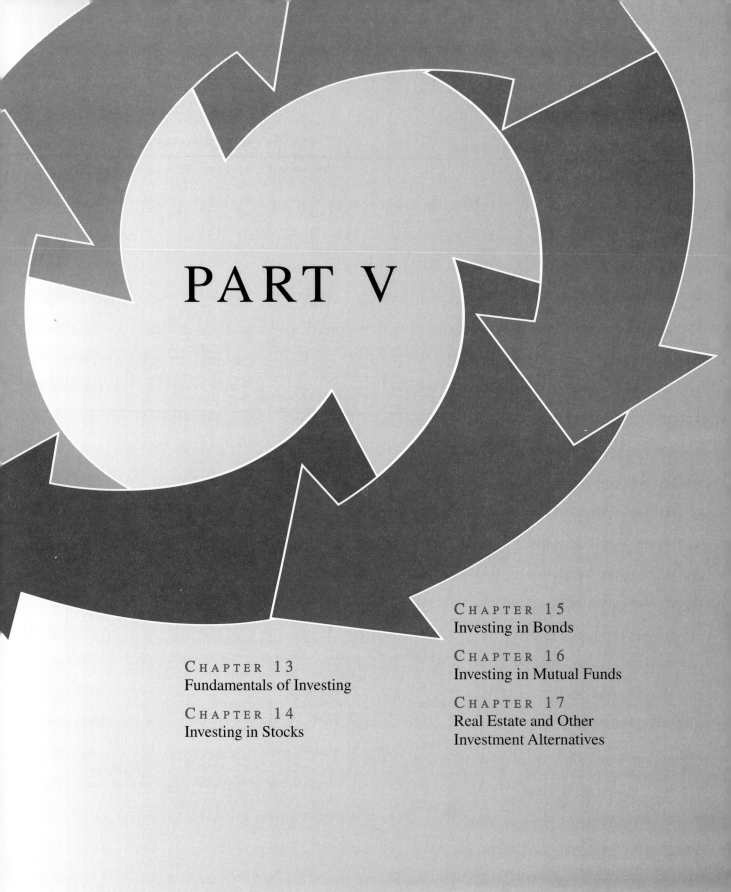

PART V

INVESTING YOUR FINANCIAL RESOURCES

How do most people achieve long-term financial security? Basically it is a simple, two-step process. First, spend less than you receive. Without a savings plan, no funds will be available for future use. Second, make appropriate investment choices based on your changing goals and life situation.

Part V of *Personal Finance* helps you put your financial plans into action through investing. Increasing your monetary resources to achieve personal financial goals is a central theme of your financial planning activities.

Knowing and using the fundamentals of investing is considered one of the most vital and exciting elements of financial planning. Investing in stocks, bonds, mutual funds, real estate, and other investment vehicles provides a basis for creating a diversified investment portfolio to help you meet your personal financial goals.

Chapter 13 explains why you should prepare for and establish an investment program. It describes how safety, risk, income, growth, and liquidity affect your investments. Chapter 14 identifies the most important features of common stock and discusses why people invest in stocks. Chapter 15 explores investing in corporate and government bonds. Chapter 16 describes the unique characteristics of investments in mutual funds. Chapter 17 discusses investing in real estate, precious metals, gems, and collectibles.

CHAPTER 13

FUNDAMENTALS OF INVESTING

OPENING CASE

REALITY 101: RETIREMENT PLANNING FOR THE YEAR 2000 AND BEYOND

Should college students worry about planning for retirement? You bet! Although it seems ironic, in reality there is no better time to begin an investment program than when you are young and have your entire career in front of you. The reason is quite simple: If you start an investment program when you are young, make sound investments, and let your investment earnings accumulate, you won't have to worry about finances when you reach retirement age. With this fact in mind, it's even possible for a person with an average salary to retire early. It just takes planning and discipline.

Take Mary and Peter Miller. Mary, 32, is a high school history teacher. Peter, 35, runs his own computer consulting business. Together they earn about $80,000 a year and enjoy their careers. Yet both want to make sure they have enough money to retire on when Peter reaches age 65.

When the Millers married just over 10 years ago, they established a long-term goal to accumulate a retirement nest egg of $1.5 million. While they can't remember why they chose this amount, they do remember their first conversation with Gina Reynolds, a financial planner whom a friend recommended. Ms. Reynolds explained that if they chose quality investments that earned a 12 percent average annual return and invested just $2,000 each year, their investment portfolio would be worth $1,534,180 at the end of 40 years when Peter reached age 65. She encouraged the Millers to begin investing right away. To drive this point home, she calculated that if they waited 10 years before starting their investment program and made the same investments for a 30-year period, their investment portfolio would be worth only $482,660. They would lose over $1 million.

Needless to say, the Millers realized it was time to start their investment program. To accomplish their investment goals, they developed a two-step plan. First, they began to put their financial affairs in order. Over a two-year period, they paid off their credit card debts and began paying cash for all purchases. They also managed to save $9,000, which became their emergency fund. Now it was time to get serious about their investment program and take the second step. They began investing in quality, long-term mutual funds, stocks, bonds, and real estate.

Today, after 10 years of disciplined investing, the Millers estimate that their investment portfolio is worth approximately $45,000. And while the current value of their investment portfolio is a long way from $1.5 million, Ms. Reynolds promises that if they keep investing in the same types of investments, they will accumulate more than $1.5 million by the time Peter reaches age 65.

QUESTIONS

1. With planning and discipline, even a person with an average salary can retire early. Would early retirement appeal to you? Why or why not?
2. Mary and Peter Miller want to retire by the time Peter reaches age 65. What specific steps have they taken to achieve their goal?

SOURCES: Sue Goldstein, "How to Save 15% of Your Income," *New Choices,* November 1996, p. 34; Valerie Lynn Gray, "How to Turn $100 into a Six-Figure Nest Egg," *Black Enterprise,* October 1996, pp. 123–24+; Peter Keating, "The Lifestyle You Want," *Money,* October 1996, pp. 95–98; Virginia Munger Kahn, "Learning to Love Risk," *Working Woman,* September 1996, p. 24+.

After studying this chapter, you will be able to

L.O.1 Explain why you should prepare for and establish an investment program.

L.O.2 Describe how safety, risk, income, growth, and liquidity affect your investment decisions.

L.O.3 Identify the major types of investment alternatives.

L.O.4 Recognize the role of the professional financial planner and your role in a personal investment program.

L.O.5 Use various sources of financial information that can reduce investment risks.

PREPARING FOR AN INVESTMENT PROGRAM

L.O.1 Explain why you should prepare for and establish an investment program.

Financial Decision
Trade-Off

The old saying goes "I've been rich and I've been poor, but believe me, rich is better." While being rich doesn't guarantee happiness, the accumulation of money does provide financial security and is a goal worthy of pursuit. Regardless of how much money you want or what you want to use the money for, the time value of money—a concept we have discussed throughout this text—can help you attain your financial goals. Mary and Peter Miller, the couple in the opening case for this chapter, are using the time value of money concept to accumulate an investment portfolio that eventually will be worth more than $1.5 million—and they started building their nest egg by investing just $2,000 a year! Their success is the result of planning, discipline, and choosing investments that have returned over 12 percent a year. By following the basic investment principles presented in this chapter along with the material on stocks, bonds, mutual funds, real estate, and other investments in the remaining chapters in Part V, you can build your own investment portfolio.

The decision to start an investment program is an important first step to accomplishing your long-term financial goals. Like other decisions, the decision to start an investment program is one you must make for yourself. No one is going to make you establish a financial plan. No one is going to make you save the money you need to fund an investment program. These things won't be done unless you want to do them. In fact, the *specific* goals you want to accomplish must be the driving force behind your investment program.

Establishing Investment Goals

To be useful, investment goals must be specific and measurable. They must be tailored to your particular financial needs. Some financial planners suggest that investment goals be stated in terms of money: By December 31, 2008, I will have total assets of $120,000. Other financial planners believe investors are more motivated to work toward

Sheet 55

goals that are stated in terms of the particular things they desire: By January 1, 2008, I will have accumulated enough money to purchase a second home in the mountains. The following questions will help you establish valid investment goals:

1. What will you use the money for?
2. How much money do you need to satisfy your investment goals?
3. How will you obtain the money?
4. How long will it take you to obtain the money?
5. How much risk are you willing to assume in an investment program?
6. What possible economic or personal conditions could alter your investment goals?
7. Considering your economic circumstances, are your investment goals reasonable?
8. Are you willing to make the sacrifices necessary to ensure that you meet your investment goals?
9. What will the consequences be if you don't reach your investment goals?

Investment objectives must always be oriented toward the future. In Chapter 1, we classified objectives as short term (less than two years), intermediate (two to five years), or long term (over five years). These same classifications are also useful in planning an investment program. For example, an investor may establish a short-term objective of accumulating $3,000 in a savings account over the next 18 months. The investor may then use the $3,000 to finance intermediate or long-term investment objectives.

Performing a Financial Checkup

Before beginning an investment program, your personal financial affairs should be in good shape. In this section, we examine several factors you should consider before making your first investment.

Financial Decision
Trade-Off

Learn to Live within Your Means   Often people must learn to live within their means before they begin investing. Many individuals regularly spend more than they make. They purchase items on credit and then must make monthly installment payments and pay finance charges ranging between 12 and 18 percent or higher. With this situation, it makes no sense to start an investment program until credit card and installment purchases, along with the accompanying finance charges, are reduced or eliminated. Therefore, you should limit credit purchases to only the necessities or to purchases required to meet emergencies. A good rule of thumb is to limit installment payments to 10 percent of your monthly pay after taxes. Eventually, the amount of cash remaining after the bills are paid will increase and can be used to start a savings program or finance other investments. A word of caution: Corrective measures take time, and it is impossible to improve a bad situation overnight.

Provide Adequate Insurance Protection   We discussed insurance in detail in Part IV, and will not cover that topic again here. However, it is essential that you consider insurance needs before beginning an investment program. The types of insurance and the amount of coverage will vary from one person to the next. Before you start investing, examine the amount of your insurance coverage for life insurance, hospitalization, your home and other real estate holdings, automobiles, and any other assets that may need coverage.

emergency fund

Start an Emergency Fund   Most financial planners suggest that an investment program should begin with the accumulation of an emergency fund. An **emergency fund** is a certain amount of money you can obtain quickly in case of immediate need. This money should be deposited in a savings account paying the highest available interest rate or in a liquid money market mutual fund.

The amount of money that should be put away in the emergency fund varies from person to person. However, most financial planners agree that an amount equal to three to nine months' living expenses is reasonable.[1] For example, Debbie Martin earns $30,000 a year. Her monthly expenses total $1,600. Before Debbie can begin investing, she must save at least $4,800 ($1,600 × 3 months) in a savings account or other near-cash investment to meet emergencies.

Have Access to Other Sources of Cash for Emergency Needs   Financial planners also recommend establishing a line of credit at a commercial bank, savings and loan association, credit union, or credit card company. A **line of credit** is a short-term loan that is approved before the money is actually needed. Because the necessary paperwork has already been completed and the loan has been preapproved, you can later obtain the money as soon as you need it. The cash advance provision offered by major credit card companies can also be used in an emergency.

However, both lines of credit and credit cards have a ceiling, or maximum dollar amount, that limits the amount of available credit. If you have already exhausted both of these sources of credit on everyday expenses, they will not be available in an emergency.

DID YOU KNOW?

The more you make, the more challenging your investment goals can be. Here are household income levels for U.S. families.

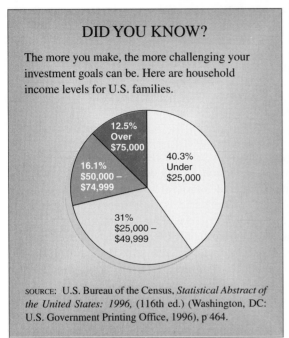

12.5% Over $75,000

16.1% $50,000 – $74,999

40.3% Under $25,000

31% $25,000 – $49,999

SOURCE: U.S. Bureau of the Census, *Statistical Abstract of the United States: 1996,* (116th ed.) (Washington, DC: U.S. Government Printing Office, 1996), p 464.

line of credit

Financial Decision Trade-Off

Getting the Money Needed to Start an Investment Program

Once you have established your investment goals and completed your personal financial checkup, it's time to start investing—assuming you have enough money to finance your investments. Unfortunately, that is a wrong assumption in many cases because the money doesn't automatically appear. In today's world, you must work to accumulate the money you need to start any type of investment program.

Priority of Investment Goals   How badly do you want to achieve your investment goals? Are you willing to sacrifice some purchases to provide financing for your investments? The answers to both questions are extremely important. Take Rita Johnson, a 32-year-old nurse in a large St. Louis hospital. As part of a divorce settlement in 1994, she received a cash payment of almost $55,000. At first, she was tempted to spend this money on a trip to Europe, a new BMW, and new furniture. But after some careful planning, she decided to invest $35,000 in a long-term certificate of deposit and the remainder in a conservative mutual fund. On May 31, 1998, these investments were valued at $79,000.

As pointed out earlier in this chapter, no one can make you save money to finance your investment program. You have to *want* to do it. Here are some suggestions to help you obtain the money you need.

1. *Pay yourself first.* Too often, people save or invest what is left over after they have paid everything else. As you might guess, nothing is left over in many cases, and the investment program is put on hold for another month. A second and much better approach is to (1) pay your monthly bills, (2) save a reasonable amount of money, and (3) use whatever money is left over for personal expenses such as clothes or entertainment.

Exhibit 13–1

Growth Rate for $2,000 Invested at the End of Each Year at Various Rates of Return for Different Time Periods

Rate of Return	Balance at End of Year					
	1	5	10	20	30	40
6%	$2,000	$11,274	$26,362	$73,572	$158,116	$309,520
7	2,000	11,502	27,632	81,990	188,922	399,280
8	2,000	11,734	28,974	91,524	226,560	518,120
9	2,000	11,970	30,386	102,320	272,620	675,780
10	2,000	12,210	31,874	114,550	328,980	885,180
11	2,000	12,456	33,444	128,406	398,040	1,163,660
12	2,000	12,706	35,098	144,104	482,660	1,534,180

2. *Participate in an elective savings program.* You can elect to have money withheld from your paycheck each payday and automatically deposited in an account at a bank, savings and loan association, or credit union. When you choose this option, it is much easier to put money into the account than it is to get money out of it. You can also make investing easier by arranging with a mutual fund or brokerage firm to take a fixed sum from your bank account automatically every month and invest it.

3. *Make a special savings effort one or two months each year.* Some financial planners recommend that you really cut back to the basics for one or two months each year to obtain additional money for investment purposes.

4. *Take advantage of gifts, inheritances, and windfalls.* During your lifetime, you will likely receive gifts, inheritances, salary increases, year-end bonuses, or federal income tax refunds. Often people opt to spend this extra money on something they could not afford under normal circumstances. A better approach is to use the money to fund your investment program.

The Value of Long-Term Investment Programs

Many people never start an investment program because they have only small sums of money. But even small sums grow over a long period of time. The Millers, the couple in the opening case for this chapter, began their investment program by investing $2,000 *each year* when they were in their 20s; yet they expect their investment portfolio to be worth more than $1.5 million by the time Peter reaches age 65. How did they do it? Simple: They took advantage of the time value of money. You can achieve the same type of result. For instance, if you invest $2,000 each year for 40 years at a 6 percent annual rate of return, your investment will grow to $309,520. The rate of return and the length of time your money is invested *do* make a difference. Exhibit 13–1 shows how much your investment portfolio will be worth at the end of selected time periods and with different rates of return.

Notice that the value of your investments increases each year because of two factors. First, it is assumed you will invest another $2,000 each year. For example, at the end of 10 years, you have invested a total of $20,000 ($2,000 × 10 years). Second, all investment earnings are allowed to accumulate and are added to your yearly deposits. Thus, the totals illustrated in Exhibit 13–1 are a result of continuous yearly deposits plus earnings on your investments.

Also, notice that if investments earn a higher rate of return, total portfolio values increase dramatically. For example, a $2,000 annual investment that earns 6 percent a year is worth $26,362 at the end of 10 years. But if the same $2,000 annual investment earns 12 percent each year, your investment portfolio value increases to $35,098 at the end of the same 10-year period. The search for higher returns is one reason many

Exhibit 13–2

A Personal Plan of Action for Investing

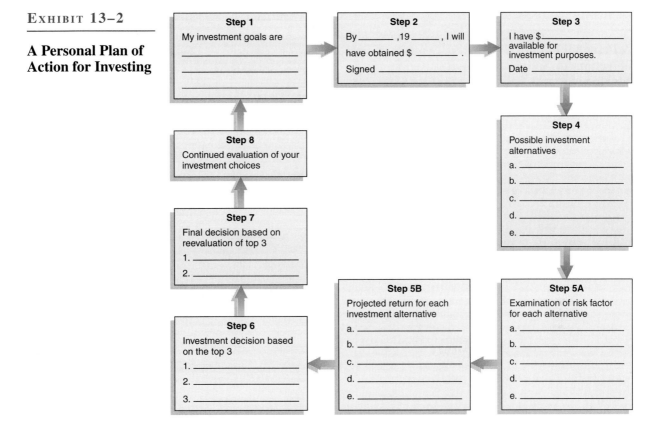

investors choose stocks and mutual funds that offer higher potential returns compared to certificates of deposit or savings accounts. You should know that to earn higher returns, you must take more chances. In fact, the material in the remainder of Part V will help you determine if you should invest in these more speculative investments.

The investment earnings illustrated in Exhibit 13–1 are taxable as ordinary income under current Internal Revenue Service guidelines. To avoid immediate taxation, you may want to invest your money in an individual retirement account (IRA), a 401(k) or 403(b) retirement account offered through your employer, or one of the tax-free investments described later in Part V. Although taxes are always a consideration, this complication does not reduce the importance of the time value of money. In fact, the time value of money is so important for a successful investment program that you may want to review this concept (see Chapter 1) before you begin to invest.

A Personal Plan of Action for Investing

To be a successful investor, you must develop a plan and then implement it. You begin investment planning by establishing realistic goals. The next step is to perform a personal financial checkup to make sure you are ready to invest. Then you must evaluate each investment opportunity, including the potential risk and return. At the very least, this requires some expert advice and careful study. Generally through a process of comparison and elimination, you can choose particular alternatives and combine them into an investment plan.

The steps required for an effective personal plan of action are presented in Exhibit 13–2. The first step is to summarize your investment goals. The second step is to determine

Exhibit 13–3

A Personal Plan of Action for Sally Morton

Step 1	Step 2	Step 3
My investment goals are *to begin a retirement program*	By *Jan. 1* ,20 *04* , I will have obtained $ *20,000* . Signed *Sally Morton*	I have *$14,000* available for investment purposes. Date *Jan. 1, 1999*

Step 8
Continued evaluation of your investment choices

Step 4
Possible investment alternatives
a. *Certificate of deposit*
b. *Stocks*
c. *Corporate Bonds*
d. *Mutual fund*
e. *Gold stocks*

Step 7
Final decision based on reevaluation of top 3
1. *Certificate of deposit*
2. *Mutual fund*

Step 5B
Projected return for each investment alternative
a. *4% - 6%*
b. *6% - 12%*
c. *6% - 8%*
d. *4% -10%*
e. *? ? ?*

Step 5A
Examination of risk factor for each alternative
a. *Low risk*
b. *More risk*
c. *Moderate risk*
d. *Moderate risk*
e. *Very high risk*

Step 6
Investment decision based on the top 3
1. *Certificate of deposit*
2. *Mutual fund*
3. *Corporate Bonds*

the amount of money you will obtain by a specific date. The total amount of money specified in step 2 should be based on the goals you have summarized in step 1. The amount of money you now have available for investment purposes is specified in step 3. For most investors, the money currently available for investment purposes has accumulated over a period of time. For example, Shannon and Fred Rogers began saving $200 a month to finance a future investment program over three years ago. They deposited the money in an interest-bearing savings account. Now, after three years, they have accumulated over $8,000 that they can use to purchase different investments. In step 4, specific investment alternatives are listed.

Because of the relationship between projected risks and returns for each investment alternative, step 5 is divided into two components. Step 5A examines the risk factor for each investment alternative. Step 5B examines the potential return associated with each alternative. The information needed to complete steps 5A and 5B should be based on your research of the investments listed in step 4. In step 6, you reduce the choice of investments to the top three. In step 7, you make a final decision to choose the top two alternatives. By choosing at least two alternatives, you build a certain amount of diversification into your investment program and avoid the pitfalls of putting all your eggs in one basket. As the total dollar value of your investments grows, you will probably want to continue to consider additional investments. After all, spreading potential risks among different investments is a key factor in a successful investment program.

Step 8 provides for continued evaluation of your investments. Investors' circumstances often change as they go through life. As a result, investors are often forced to adapt their planning to new situations. For example, if you accept a new job at a substantially higher salary, changes in investment goals may make your present personal plan of action obsolete. Also, different investments may become more or less attractive because of changes in economic and financial conditions. During the early 1980s, for example, many investors sold their common stocks and invested the money in certificates of deposit that paid high guaranteed interest. During the 1990s, many of the same investors cashed in their certificates of deposit, which were now paying lower interest rates, and purchased common stocks and mutual funds that offered more potential.

To illustrate the above planning process, let's fill in the blanks in Exhibit 13–2, using the case of Sally Morton, who accepted a position in advertising after college. After four years, Sally is earning $30,000 a year. Her take-home pay after deductions is $2,000 a month. Her living expenses are about $1,600 a month, which leaves a surplus of $400. After graduating from college, she immediately began saving a portion of each month's surplus. First, she established an emergency fund. Now she has $14,000 available for investment purposes. After much thought, Sally developed the personal plan of action illustrated in Exhibit 13–3.

Your own plan may be quite different from Sally's, but the principle is the same. Each person has different ideas and goals. Establish your investment goals first, and then follow through.

Financial Decision Trade-Off

C O N C E P T   C H E C K   13–1

1. Why should an investor develop specific investment goals?
2. Why should you perform a financial checkup?
3. How can an investor accumulate the money needed to fund an investment program?
4. What are the steps required for a personal plan of action?

FACTORS AFFECTING THE CHOICE OF INVESTMENTS

L.O.2 Describe how safety, risk, income, growth, and liquidity affect your investment decisions.

Millions of Americans have a savings account, buy stocks, bonds, or mutual funds, purchase gold and silver, or make similar investments. And they all have reasons for investing their money. Some people want to supplement their retirement income when they reach age 65, while others want to become millionaires before age 50. Although each investor may have specific, individual goals for investing, all investors must consider a number of different factors before choosing an investment alternative.

Safety and Risk

Sheet 56

The safety and risk factors are two sides of the same coin. You cannot evaluate any investment without assessing how safety relates to risk. Safety in an investment means minimal risk of loss. On the other hand, risk in an investment means a measure of uncertainty about the outcome. Investments range from very safe to very risky. At one end of the investment spectrum are very safe investments that attract conservative investors. Investments in this category include government bonds, savings accounts, certificates of deposit, and certain stocks and bonds. Mutual funds and real estate may also be very safe investments. Investors pick such investments because they know there is very little chance that investments of this kind will become worthless. Although anyone can choose investments like those just listed, there is usually a reason someone chooses conservative

JONATHAN HOENIG SPEAKS
Invest-Quest

Here's a question you don't hear every day: What's your asset allocation? Precious metals. Real estate. Even baseball cards! What the Wall Street hotshots call "asset allocation" is basically deciding *where* you are going to invest your money. Stocks aren't the only game in town, although for most investors, stocks should form the bulk of their overall investment portfolio.

Why? Common stocks have historically outperformed most investments over longer periods of time. Putting your money in the stock market is not a sure-fire way to get rich but a savvy move to protect your savings against inflation. Remember: Even if you don't spend a cent of Grandma's birthday check, every year inflation eats away your purchasing power. That's why many "safe" investments like CDs, savings accounts, or checking accounts can actually put you in the hole: Those type of investments are not designed to outpace inflation.

In a sense, every time you spend money, you are *investing*. Even a purchase as seemingly innocent as lunch qualifies. Is the "return on investment" (your nutritional and gastronomic enjoyment) worth the $3.50 they want for that bagel sandwich? Always keep an eye out for value. Often we lose money not on poor stock investments but on the daily "disposable" income that always seems to disappear. Just because everyone is talking about a particular book doesn't mean you have to buy it. Get it out of the library and save yourself the $20. Boom! A 100 percent return on investment.

Your money should work harder than you do, so unless you've got a mint-condition Michael Jordan rookie basketball card (street price approximately $1,500US) sitting around the attic, stick to a diversified portfolio of financial investments.

And save. It might seem "old school," but a penny saved truly *is* a penny earned.

---

investments. Many investors choose conservative investments because of the individual life situations in which they find themselves. For example, people in their 40s, 50s, or 60s usually make conservative investments because they are approaching retirement age and don't want to lose the nest egg they have built up over the years. Some people choose to invest one-time windfalls or inheritances in a conservative investment because they know it may be impossible to replace the money if it is lost. Finally, some investors simply dislike taking chances.

At the other end of the investment spectrum are very high-risk investments. Such investments offer the possibility of a larger dollar return, but if they are unsuccessful, you may lose most or all of your initial investment. Speculative stocks, certain bonds, mutual funds, real estate, derivatives, commodities, options, precious metals, precious stones, and collectibles are risk-oriented investments. Although many of these investments are discussed in detail in later chapters, they are often considered too risky for beginning investors.

By now, you probably realize the safety and risk factors are more complex than the simple definitions just presented. From an investor's standpoint, one basic rule sums up the relationship between the factors of safety and risk: *The potential return on any investment should be directly related to the risk the investor assumes.* For example, Ana Luna was injured in a work-related accident three years ago. After a lengthy lawsuit, she received a legal settlement totaling $420,000. As a result of the injury, she was no longer qualified to perform her old job as an assembler for an electronics manufacturer. When

Opportunity Cost

she thought about the future, she knew she needed to get a job, but realized she would be forced to acquire new employment skills. She also realized she had received a great deal of money that could be invested to provide a steady source of income not only for the next two years while she obtained job training but also for the remainder of her life. Having never invested before, she quickly realized her tolerance for risk was minimal. She had to conserve her $420,000 settlement. Eventually, after much discussion with professionals and her own research, she chose to invest about half of her money in certificates of deposit. For the remaining half, she chose three stocks that offered a 4 percent average dividend, a potential for growth, and a high degree of safety because of the financial stability of the corporations that issued the stocks.

A more risk-oriented investor might have criticized Ana's decisions as too conservative. In fact, this second type of investor (sometimes referred to as a *speculator*) might have chosen to invest in more speculative stocks that offer a greater potential for growth and increase in market value even though the corporations issuing the stocks are not paying dividends at the present time. The bottom line is: What is right for one investor may not be right for another!

The problem of assessing safety and risk is further complicated by the large number of potential investments from which to choose. You must determine how much risk you are willing to assume. Once you have determined the amount of risk you are comfortable with, you can choose different investments that hopefully will provide the expected return. To help you determine how much risk you are willing to assume, take the test for risk tolerance presented in the accompanying Financial Planning in Action box.

Components of the Risk Factor

The risk factor associated with a specific investment does change from time to time. For example, the stock of Computer-Tabulating-Recording Company was once considered a high-risk investment. Then this company changed its name to IBM and eventually became a leader in the computer industry. By the early 1980s, many conservative investors were purchasing IBM stock because of its safety and earnings potential. But in the early 1990s, many of these same investors sold their IBM stock because changes in the computer industry had brought financial problems for IBM. IBM was once again considered too risky for many investors. Now, as a result of solving many of its financial problems, IBM is once again considered a conservative choice for conservative investors.

When choosing an investment, you must carefully evaluate changes in the risk factor. In fact, the overall risk factor can be broken down into four components.

Inflation Risk   During periods of high inflation, there is a risk that the financial return on an investment will not keep pace with the inflation rate. To see how inflation reduces your buying power, let's assume you have deposited $10,000 in the bank at 4 percent interest. At the end of one year, your money will have earned $400 in interest ($10,000 × 4% = $400). Assuming an inflation rate of 6 percent, it will cost you an additional $600 ($10,000 × 6% = $600) or $10,600 to purchase the same amount of goods you could have purchased for $10,000 a year earlier. Thus, even though you earned $400, you lost $200 in purchasing power. And after paying taxes on the $400 interest, your loss of purchasing power is even greater.

Interest Rate Risk   The interest rate risk associated with a fixed-return investment in preferred stocks or government or corporate bonds is the result of changes in the interest rates in the economy. The value of preferred stocks, government bonds, or corporate bonds decreases when overall interest rates increase and rises when overall interest rates

A QUICK TEST TO MEASURE INVESTMENT RISK

The following quiz, adapted from one prepared by the T. Rowe Price group of mutual funds, can help you discover how comfortable you are with varying degrees of risk. Other things being equal, your risk tolerance score is a useful guide in deciding how heavily you should weight your portfolio toward safe investments versus more risk-oriented, speculative investments.

1. You're the winner on a TV game show. Which prize would you choose?
   - ☐ $2,000 in cash (1 point).
   - ☐ A 50 percent chance to win $4,000 (3 points).
   - ☐ A 20 percent chance to win $10,000 (5 points).
   - ☐ A 2 percent chance to win $100,000 (9 points).

2. You're down $500 in a poker game. How much more would you be willing to put up to win the $500 back?
   - ☐ More than $500 (8 points).
   - ☐ $500 (6 points).
   - ☐ $250 (4 points).
   - ☐ $100 (2 points).
   - ☐ Nothing—you'll cut your losses now (1 point).

3. A month after you invest in a stock, it suddenly goes up 15 percent. With no further information, what would you do?
   - ☐ Hold it, hoping for further gains (3 points).
   - ☐ Sell it and take your gains (1 point).
   - ☐ Buy more—it will probably go higher (4 points).

4. Your investment suddenly goes down 15 percent one month after you invest. Its fundamentals still look good. What would you do?
   - ☐ Buy more. If it looked good at the original price, it looks even better now (4 points).
   - ☐ Hold on and wait for it to come back (3 points).
   - ☐ Sell it to avoid losing even more (1 point).

5. You're a key employee in a start-up company. You can choose one of two ways to take your year-end bonus. Which would you pick?
   - ☐ $1,500 in cash (1 point).
   - ☐ Company stock options that could bring you $15,000 next year if the company succeeds, but will be worthless if it fails (5 points).

Your total score: _____

Scoring

5–18 points You are a more conservative investor. You prefer to minimize financial risks. The lower your score, the more cautious you are. When you choose investments, look for high credit ratings, well-established records, and an orientation toward stability. In stocks, bonds, and real estate, look for a focus on income.

19–30 points You are a less conservative investor. You are willing to take more chances in pursuit of greater rewards. The higher your score, the bolder you are. When you invest, look for high overall returns. You may want to consider bonds with higher yields and lower credit ratings, the stocks of newer companies, and real estate investments that use mortgage debt.

A primer on the ABCs of investing is available from T. Rowe Price, 100 E. Pratt St., Baltimore, MD 21202 (1–800–638–5660).

decrease. For example, suppose you purchase a $1,000 corporate bond issued by AMR, the parent company of American Airlines, that matures in 2012 and pays 9 percent interest until maturity. This means AMR will pay $90 ($1,000 × 9% = $90) each year until the maturity date in 2012. If bond interest rates for comparable bonds increase to 11 percent, the market value of your 9 percent bond will decrease. No one will be willing to purchase your bond at the price you paid for it since a comparable bond that pays 11 percent can be purchased for $1,000. As a result, you will have to sell your bond for less than $1,000 or hold it until maturity. If you decide to sell the bond, the approximate dollar price you could sell it for would be $818 ($90 ÷ 11% = $818). This price would provide the purchaser with an 11 percent return, and you would lose $182 ($1,000 − $818 = $182) because you owned a bond with a fixed interest rate of 9 percent during a period when overall interest rates in the economy increased. Of course, if overall interest rates declined, your bond would increase in value.

Business Failure Risk   The risk of business failure is associated with investments in common stock, preferred stock, and corporate bonds. With each of these investments, you face the possibility that bad management, unsuccessful products, or a host of other factors will cause the business to be less profitable than originally anticipated. Lower profits usually mean lower dividends or no dividends at all. If the business continues to operate at a loss, even interest payments and repayment of bonds may be questionable. The business may even fail and be forced to file for bankruptcy, in which case your investment may become totally worthless. Of course, the best way to protect yourself against such losses is to carefully evaluate the investments you make.

Market Risk   The prices of stocks, bonds, mutual funds, and other investments may fluctuate because of the behavior of investors in the marketplace. As a result, economic growth is not as systematic and predictable as most investors would like to believe. Generally, a period of rapid expansion is followed by a period of recession. During periods of recession, it may be quite difficult to sell investments such as real estate. Fluctuations in the market price for stocks and bonds may have nothing to do with the fundamental changes in the financial health of corporations. Such fluctuations may be caused by political or social conditions. For example, the price of petroleum stocks may increase or decrease as a result of political activity in the Middle East. In late 1997, the stock markets in Asia experienced substantial losses. As a result, investors who had purchased stocks listed on these exchanges lost money.

Investment Income

Investors sometimes purchase certain investments because they want a predictable source of income. The safest investments—passbook savings accounts, CDs, U.S. savings bonds, and U.S. Treasury bills—are also the most predictable sources of income for an investor. With these investments, the investor knows exactly what the interest rate is and how much income will be paid on a specific date.

If investment income is a primary objective, investors can also choose municipal bonds, corporate bonds, preferred stocks, utility stocks, or conservative common stock issues. When purchasing stocks or bonds for potential income, most investors are concerned about the issuing corporation's overall profits, future earnings picture, and dividend policies. For example, some corporations are very proud of their long record of consecutive dividend payments and will maintain that policy if at all possible (see Exhibit 13–4).

Other investments that provide income potential are mutual funds and real estate rental property. Although the income from mutual funds is not guaranteed, investors can choose funds whose primary objective is income. Income from real estate rental property is not guaranteed because the possibility of either vacancies or unexpected repair bills always exists. The more speculative investments, such as commodities, options, precious metals, gemstones, and collectibles, offer little, if any, potential for regular income.

Investment Growth

To investors, *growth* means their investments will increase in value. Often the greatest opportunity for growth is an investment in common stock. During the 1980s, investors found that stocks issued by corporations in the electronics, technology, energy, and health

EXHIBIT 13–4

Corporations with Consecutive Dividend Payments for at Least 95 Years

Corporation	Dividends Since	Type of Business
AT&T Corporation	1881	Telephone utility
DuPont (E. I.) de Nemours & Co.	1904	Chemicals
Exxon Corporation	1882	Chemical and petroleum products
General Electric Company	1899	Electrical equipment
Procter & Gamble Company	1891	Soap products
Texaco	1894	Chemical and petroleum products
Union Pacific Corporation	1900	Railroad

care industries provided the greatest growth potential. In fact, goods and services provided by companies in these industries have been in even greater demand in the 1990s.

When purchasing growth stocks, investors often sacrifice immediate cash dividends in return for greater dollar value in the future. For most growth companies, profits that would normally be paid to stockholders in the form of dividends are reinvested in the companies in the form of *retained earnings*. The money the companies keep can provide at least part of the financing they need for future growth and expansion and control the cost of borrowing money. As a result, they grow at an even faster pace. Growth financed by retained earnings normally increases the dollar value of a share of stock for the investor.

Certificates of deposit (assuming the interest is allowed to accumulate), government bonds, corporate bonds, mutual funds, and real estate may also offer growth possibilities. Precious metals, gemstones, and collectibles are more speculative investments that offer less predictable growth potential. Investments in commodities and options are more speculative investments that usually stress immediate returns as opposed to continued long-term growth.

Investment Liquidity

liquidity

Liquidity is the ease and speed with which an asset can be converted to cash without a substantial loss in dollar value. Investments range from near-cash investments to frozen investments from which it is impossible to get your money. Checking and savings accounts are very liquid investments because they can be quickly converted to cash. Certificates of deposit impose penalties for withdrawing money before the maturity date.

With other investments, you may be able to sell quickly, but market conditions, economic conditions, or many other factors may prevent you from regaining the amount of money you originally invested. For example, the owner of real estate may have to lower the asking price to find a buyer. And it may be difficult to find a buyer for investments in collectibles such as antiques and paintings.

CONCEPT CHECK 13–2

1. Why are safety and risk two sides of the same coin?
2. What are the four components of the risk factor?
3. How do income, growth, and liquidity affect the choice of an investment?

AN OVERVIEW OF INVESTMENT ALTERNATIVES

L.O.3. Identify the major types of investment alternatives.

When establishing an investment program, you should begin by gathering as much information as possible about investment alternatives. Then you will be able to decide whether purchasing stocks, bonds, mutual funds, real estate, or other investment alternatives is a better use of your money than putting it in the bank. Before examining these investment alternatives, let's review the typical financial services available at a bank, savings and loan association, or credit union. As discussed in Chapter 5, regular savings accounts provide a safe place to store money, especially your emergency fund. A second option is a certificate of deposit (CD). A CD's chief advantage over a passbook savings account is that the CD usually pays a higher rate of interest.

Once you have established your emergency fund and have some money accumulated for investment purposes, it's time to consider the investment alternatives most people choose. The remainder of this section provides a brief overview of different investment alternatives. The remaining chapters of Part V provide more detailed information on stocks, bonds, mutual funds, real estate, and other investment alternatives.

Stock or Equity Financing

equity capital

Equity capital is money that a business obtains from its owners. If a business is a sole proprietorship or a partnership, it acquires equity capital when the owners invest their own money in the business. In the case of a corporation, equity capital is provided by stockholders, who buy shares of its stock. Since all stockholders are owners, they share in the success of the corporation. This can make buying stock an attractive investment opportunity.

However, you should consider at least two factors before investing in stock. First, a corporation is not required to repay the money obtained from the sale of stock or to repurchase the stock at a later date. Assume you purchased 100 shares of Southwest Airlines stock. Later you decide to sell your Southwest stock. Your stock is sold to another investor, not back to the company. In many cases, a stockholder sells a stock because he or she thinks its price is going to decrease in value. The purchaser, on the other hand, buys that stock because he or she thinks its price is going to increase. This creates a situation in which either the seller or the buyer may lose money.

Second, a corporation is under no legal obligation to pay dividends to stockholders. Dividends are paid out of earnings, but if a corporation that usually pays dividends has a bad year, its board of directors can vote to omit dividend payments to help pay necessary business expenses. Corporations may also retain earnings to make additional financing available for expansion, research and product development, or other business activities.

There are two types of stock: *common stock* and *preferred stock.* Both types have advantages and disadvantages that you should consider before deciding which to use for an investment program. A share of common stock represents the most basic form of corporate ownership. Most large corporations sell common stock to satisfy a large part of their financing needs.

A corporation can issue many types of preferred stocks with different features and different dividends. The most important priority an investor in preferred stock enjoys is receiving cash dividends before common stockholders are paid any cash dividends. This factor is especially important when a corporation is experiencing financial problems and cannot pay cash dividends to both preferred and common stockholders. Other factors you should consider before purchasing both common or preferred stock are discussed in Chapter 14.

Corporate and Government Bonds

corporate bond

government bond

There are two types of bonds an investor should consider. A **corporate bond** is a corporation's written pledge to repay a specified amount of money, along with interest. A **government bond** is the written pledge of a government or a municipality to repay a specified sum of money, along with interest. Thus, when you buy a bond, you are loaning a corporation or government entity money for a period of time. Regardless of who issues the bond, you need to consider two major questions before investing in bonds. First, will the bond be repaid at maturity? The maturity dates for most bonds range between 1 and 30 years. An investor who purchases a bond has two options: keep the bond until maturity and then redeem it, or sell the bond to another investor. In either case, the value of the bond is closely tied to the ability of the corporation or government agency to repay the bond at maturity. Second, will the corporation or government agency be able to maintain interest payments to bondholders? Bondholders normally receive interest payments every six months. Again, if a corporation or government agency cannot pay the interest on its bonds, the value of those bonds will decrease.

Holding bonds until maturity is one method of making money on this type of investment. Investors also use two other methods that can provide more liberal returns on bond investments. Chapter 15 discusses each of these methods.

Mutual Funds

mutual fund

A **mutual fund** is an investment alternative chosen by people who pool their money to buy stocks, bonds, and other securities selected by professional managers employed by an investment company. Professional management is an especially important factor for investors with little or no previous experience in financial matters. Another reason investors choose mutual funds is *diversification*. Since mutual funds invest in a number of different securities, an occasional loss in one security is often offset by gains in other securities. As a result, the diversification provided by a mutual fund reduces risk.

The goals of one investor often differ from those of another. The managers of mutual funds realize this and tailor programs to meet individual needs and objectives. Some invest in U.S. companies, while others invest in stocks and bonds issued by companies in foreign countries. As a result of all the different investment alternatives, mutual funds range from very conservative to extremely speculative investments. For more information on global investments, read the accompanying Financial Planning for Life's Situation box.

Although investing money in a mutual fund provides professional management, even the best managers can make errors in judgment. The responsibility for choosing the right mutual fund is still the individual investor's decision. Chapter 16 presents more information on the different types of mutual funds, the costs involved, and techniques for evaluating these investments.

Real Estate

As a rule, real estate increases in value and eventually sells at a profit, but there are no guarantees. Success in real estate investments depends on how well you evaluate alternatives. Experts often tell would-be investors that the three most important factors when evaluating a potential real estate investment are *location, location,* and *location.* While location may be the most important factor, other factors may determine whether or not a piece of real estate is a good investment. For example, you should answer the following questions before making a decision to purchase any property:

1. Is the property priced competitively with similar properties?
2. What type of financing is available, if any?

FINANCIAL PLANNING FOR LIFE'S SITUATIONS

GLOBAL INVESTMENTS: SHOULD YOU TAKE THE PLUNGE?

In 1984, only 1 billion people were affected by free enterprise. But with the fall of communism and the enormous economic growth of many underdeveloped nations, free enterprise is expected to expand dramatically. In the future, almost 5 billion people will live in countries with some form of free enterprise or free market economy. As a result, the potential for economic growth of overseas investments is enticing many U.S. investors to rush into the foreign securities markets with the expectation of making a financial killing. Even now, overseas investments account for one out of every eight dollars invested by American mutual funds and pension funds. And the experts expect the amount of money and the number of people investing overseas will only increase in the future.

In some ways, investing in foreign securities is just like investing at home: Both offer opportunities and both incur risks. An investor can purchase shares of stock in individual foreign firms or, as most financial analysts recommend, purchase shares in a mutual fund. For the investor who has less than $200,000 to invest and is unaccustomed to the risks in overseas investments, global and international mutual funds offer more safety. While many investors think global and international funds invest in the same financial securities, there is a difference. Global funds buy stocks anywhere in the world, including the United States. International funds buy stocks only in foreign countries. Today more than 600 stock funds and more than 50 bond funds invest partly or entirely abroad.

When building an investment portfolio, most experts advise committing at least 10 percent of your foreign investments to rapidly developing countries in Africa, Eastern Europe, the Far East, or Latin America. These markets have the greatest potential for extraordinary growth in both production and consumption. The remaining 90 percent of your foreign investments should be placed in countries with more stable economies such as Britain, Canada, Germany, and Japan.

A Final Word of Caution

With rising interest rates and a possible economic slowdown in the United States over the next few years, the media are hyping foreign investments, leading many investors to believe they can reduce the risks on their domestic portfolios by running to their brokers and plunging into foreign investments. Yet many investors lost a lot of money in late 1997 when investments in Latin America, Asia, and the Pacific Rim nations declined in value. *Be warned:* Regardless of all the hype, there are no guarantees. You must evaluate foreign investments just as you would U.S. investments.

SOURCES: Ted C. Fishman, "The Joys of Global Investment," *Harper's,* February 1997, pp. 35–41; Joseph Nocera, "It's a Whole New World of Investing," *Fortune,* December 23, 1996, pp. 104–6; Lawrence A. Armour, "A Superstar's Global View," *Fortune,* December 23, 1996, pp. 147–48.

---

3. How much are the taxes?
4. What is the condition of the buildings and houses in the immediate area?
5. Why are the present owners selling the property?
6. Is there a chance that the property will decrease in value?

Any investment has disadvantages, and real estate is no exception. Many people were "taken" by unscrupulous promoters who sold inaccessible land in the Florida Everglades. Poor location can cause a piece of property to decrease in value. Also, to sell your property, you must find an interested buyer who is able to obtain enough money or financing to complete the transaction. Finding a buyer can be difficult if loan money is scarce, the real estate market is in a decline, or you overpaid for the property. If you are forced to hold your investment longer than you originally planned, you must also consider taxes and installment payments. Chapter 17 presents additional information on how to evaluate a real estate investment.

Exhibit 13–5

The Risks Involved in Typical Investment Alternatives

	Factors to Be Evaluated				
Type of Investment	Safety	Risk	Income	Growth	Liquidity
Savings accounts and CDs	High	Low	Low	Low	High
Common stock	Average	Average	Average	High	Average
Preferred stock	Average	Average	High	Average	Average
Corporate bonds	Average	Average	High	Low	Average
Government bonds	High	Low	Low	Low	High
Mutual funds	Average	Average	Average	Average	Average
Real estate	Average	Average	Average	Average	Low
Options	Low	High	N/A	Low	Average
Derivatives	Low	High	N/A	Low	Average
Commodities	Low	High	N/A	Low	Average
Precious metals, gemstones, and collectibles	Low	High	N/A	Low	Low

N/A = Not applicable.

Other Investment Alternatives

speculative investment

A **speculative investment** is a high-risk investment made in the hope of earning a relatively large profit in a short time. By its very nature, any investment may be speculative; that is, it may be quite risky. However, a *true* speculative investment is speculative because of the methods investors use to earn a quick profit. Typical speculative investments include

- Call options
- Put options
- Derivatives
- Commodities
- Precious metals
- Gemstones
- Coins
- Stamps
- Antiques and collectibles

Without exception, investments of this kind are normally referred to as speculative for one reason or another. For example, the gold market has many unscrupulous dealers who sell worthless gold-plated lead coins to unsuspecting, uninformed investors. With any speculative investment, it is extremely important to deal with reputable dealers and recognized investment firms. It pays to be careful. While investments in this category can lead to large dollar gains, they should not be used by anyone who does not fully understand the risks involved. Chapter 14 presents information on options. Chapter 17 provides information on precious metals, gemstones, and collectibles.

Summary of Factors That Affect Investment Choices

Earlier in this chapter, we examined how safety, risk, income, growth, and liquidity affect your investment choices. In the preceding section, we looked at available investment alternatives. Now let's compare the factors that affect the choice of investments with each alternative. Exhibit 13–5 ranks the alternatives in terms of safety, risk, income, growth, and liquidity.

EXHIBIT 13–6

Possible Investments for Financial Security, Safety and Income, Growth, and Speculation

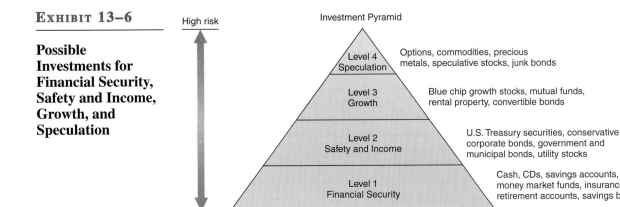

It is now appropriate to introduce the topic of diversification. **Diversification** is the process of spreading your assets among several types of investments to lessen risk. As already pointed out in this chapter, putting all your eggs in one basket is a common mistake among investors. Many financial planners suggest that to avoid this mistake, you should think of your investment program as a pyramid consisting of four levels, as illustrated in Exhibit 13–6. This approach to investing can provide financial growth and protection regardless of your age, marital status, income, or level of financial sophistication.

In Exhibit 13–6, the investments in level 1 provide the foundation for an investment program. After the foundation is established in level 1, most investors choose from the investment alternatives in level 2 and level 3. Be warned: Many investors may decide the investments in level 4 are too speculative for their investment programs. While investments at this level may provide spectacular dollar gains, they pose the risk that they will lose value or even become totally worthless.

diversification

CONCEPT   CHECK   13–3

1. Of all the investment alternatives presented in this chapter, which one is the most conservative?
2. What are two chief advantages of investing in mutual funds?
3. What factors should you consider before purchasing real estate for investment purposes?
4. How can the investment pyramid presented in Exhibit 13–6 help you build an investment program to reach your financial goals?

FACTORS THAT REDUCE INVESTMENT RISK

In this section, we examine the factors that can spell the difference between success and failure for an investor. We begin by examining the role of a financial planner. Then we consider your role in the investment process.

L.O.4 Recognize the role
of the professional
financial planner and your
role in a personal
investment program.

The Role of a Financial Planner

To achieve their financial goals, many people seek professional help. In many cases, they turn to stockbrokers, lawyers, accountants, bankers, or insurance agents. However, these professionals are specialists in one specific field and may not be qualified to provide the type of advice required to develop a thorough financial plan.

A *true* financial planner has had at least two years of training in securities, insurance, taxes, real estate, and estate planning and has passed a rigorous examination. As evidence of training and successful completion of a 10-hour qualifying examination, the Institute of Certified Financial Planners in Denver allows individuals to use the designation Certified Financial Planner (CFP). Similarly, the American College in Bryn Mawr, Pennsylvania, allows individuals to use the designation Chartered Financial Consultant (ChFC) if they complete the necessary requirements, have a minimum of three years' experience, and pass 10 two-hour exams.

Financial planners fall into two categories. The first category consists of financial planners who charge a fee but have no financial interest in the investment or insurance products they recommend. Most financial planners in this category charge consultant's fees that range between $100 and $250 an hour.

The second category consists of financial planners who earn a commission on any insurance, stocks, mutual funds, or other investments the client buys. These individuals are often employed by brokerage firms or financial services companies. Critics contend that the financial planning assistance such planners provide is just a marketing ploy to sell their investment or insurance products.

Many investors assume a financial planner is a professional and really doesn't want the investor's input. Nothing could be further from the truth. To provide better service, a financial planner must know what type of investment program you want to establish. Therefore, you should answer the following questions before choosing a financial planner:

1. What are your financial goals?
2. What is your financial worth today?
3. How much return do you expect from your investments?
4. How much risk are you willing to assume to achieve your investment goals?
5. Should your investments provide income for immediate needs or growth for the future?
6. What type of help do you want from a financial planner?

You should also ask some questions to determine whether you and the financial planner are on the same wavelength with regard to investment goals and objectives. Typical questions include the following:

1. How much training and experience does the financial planner have?
2. Can you talk to clients who have used the financial planner's services?
3. What do local bankers, lawyers, and accountants say about the financial planner?
4. How much will consultation with the financial planner cost?
5. How often will you receive financial reports that describe the investments in your portfolio and the value of those investments?
6. After the initial consultation, do you feel you will be able to achieve your investment objectives with the help of the financial planner?

The financial planner you select should prepare a personal financial plan that will help you achieve your long-term goals. As part of this plan, the financial planner should outline potential risks and benefits. Finally, the financial planner should suggest specific investments that are appropriate for you. Again, the key to developing the "right" plan

FINANCIAL PLANNING CALCULATIONS

CHARTING THE VALUE OF YOUR INVESTMENT

To monitor the value of their investments, many investors use a simple chart like the one illustrated here. To construct a chart like this one, place the original purchase price of your investment in the middle on the side of the chart. Then use price increments of a logical amount to show increases and decreases in dollar value.

Place individual dates along the bottom of the chart. For stocks, bonds, mutual funds, and similar investments, you may want to graph every two weeks and chart current values on, say, a Friday. For longer-term investments like real estate, you can chart current values every six months.

A Word of Caution

If an investment is beginning to increase or decrease in value, you should watch that investment more closely. You can still continue to chart at regular intervals, but you may want to check dollar values more frequently—in some cases, daily.

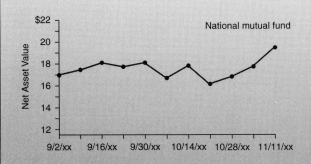

with the help of a financial planner is to ask questions about the plan. Actually, most reliable financial planners encourage questions, because this is one way to find out whether their clients understand their suggestions.

If, after a reasonable period of time, you become dissatisfied with your investment program, do not hesitate to discuss this with the financial planner. You may even find it necessary to choose another financial planner if your dissatisfaction continues. This step is not at all uncommon. But when all is said and done, it is *your* money and you must make the final decisions that will help you meet your investment goals.

Your Role in the Investment Process

Successful investors continually monitor the value of their investments. They never sit back and let their investments manage themselves. Obviously, different types of investments will require different methods of evaluation. Some basic elements of evaluation are described next.

Monitor the Value of Your Investment If you invest your money in a savings account or a certificate of deposit, most financial institutions will provide you with a detailed statement of all activity in the account. If you choose to invest in stocks, bonds, mutual funds, commodities, or options, you can determine the value of your holdings by looking at the price quotations reported daily in the financial section of your local newspaper. Your real estate holdings may be compared with similar properties currently for sale in the surrounding area. Finally, you can determine the value of your precious metals, gemstones, and collectibles by checking with reputable dealers and investment firms. Regardless of which type of investment you choose, close surveillance will keep you informed of whether your investment increases or decreases in value. The accompanying Financial Planning Calculations box presents further information on monitoring the value of your investments.

current yield

Keep Accurate and Current Records   Accurate recordkeeping is necessary for tax purposes. However, it can also help you spot opportunities to maximize profits or reduce dollar losses when you sell your investments. Accurate recordkeeping can also help you decide whether you want to invest additional funds in a particular investment. It will also enable you to do at least three simple calculations to help you monitor the success of an investment: current yield, total return, and annualized holding period yield.

Calculation of Current Yield   One of the most common calculations investors use to monitor the value of their investments is the current yield. The **current yield** is the yearly dollar amount of income generated by an investment divided by the investment's current market value. For example, assume you purchase stock in Ford Motor Company. Also assume Ford pays an annual dividend of $1.68 and is currently selling for $37 a share. The current dividend yield is 4.5 percent, as calculated below:

$$\text{Current yield} = \frac{\text{Annual income amount}}{\text{Market value}}$$

$$= \frac{\$1.68}{\$37}$$

$$= 0.045, \text{ or } 4.5 \text{ percent.}$$

This example involves common stock; however, the same procedure will work for bonds, mutual funds, and other investments that provide annual income. As a general rule, an increase in current yield is a healthy sign for any investment. A current yield of 6 percent is better than a 4.5 percent current yield.

total return

Calculation of Total Return   Although the current yield calculation is useful, you should also consider whether the investment is increasing or decreasing in dollar value. **Total return** is a calculation that includes not only the yearly dollar amount of income but also any increase or decrease in the original purchase price of the investment. The following formula is used to calculate total return:

$$\text{Total return} = \text{Current return} + \text{Future return}$$

While this concept may be used for any investment, let's illustrate it by using the assumptions for Ford stock presented in the preceding example. Assume, in addition, that you own 100 shares of the stock that you purchased for $32.50 a share and hold your stock for two years before deciding to sell it at the current market price of $45 a share. Your total return for this investment would be $1,586, as calculated below:

$$\text{Total return} = \text{Current return} + \text{Future return}$$

$$\$1,586 = \$336 \quad\quad + \$1,250$$

In this example, the current return of $336 results from the payment of dividends for two years ($1.68 per-share dividend $\times$ 100 shares $\times$ 2 years). The future return of $1,250 results from the increase in the stock price from $32.50 a share to $45 a share ($12.50 per-share increase $\times$ 100 shares = $1,250). (Of course, commissions to buy and sell your stock, a topic covered in the next chapter, would reduce your total return.)

In this example, the investment increased in value and the total return was greater than the current return. For an investment that decreases in value, the total return will be less than the current return. And while it may be obvious, we should point out that the larger the dollar amount of total return, the better.

annualized holding
period yield

Annualized Holding Period Yield   The **annualized holding period yield** calculation takes into account the total return, the original investment, and the time the investment is held. The following formula is used to calculate the annualized holding period yield:

$$\text{Annualized holding period yield} = \frac{\text{Total return}}{\text{Original investment}} \times \frac{1}{N}$$

where

$$N = \text{Number of years investment is held}$$

To illustrate this concept, let's return to your Ford investment, for which the total return was $1,586, the original investment was $3,250, and the holding period was two years. As shown below, the annualized holding period yield for this investment is 24.1 percent for each of the two years you held the investment:

$$\text{Annualized holding period yield} = \frac{\$1,586}{\$3,250} \times \frac{1}{2}$$

$$= 0.244$$

$$= 24.4 \text{ percent}$$

There is no meaningful average for annualized holding period yield because individual investments vary. But an increase in annualized holding period yield is a healthy sign. For instance, an annualized holding period yield of 9.2 percent is better than a 7 percent annualized holding period yield.

Tax Considerations

Generally, investment income falls into three categories: tax-exempt income, tax-deferred income, and taxable income. *Tax-exempt income* is income that is *not* subject to tax. For example, the interest paid on most state and city bonds is exempt from federal income tax. Also, the income earned on the new Roth individual retirement account is tax free. *Tax-deferred income* is income that will be taxed at a later date. The most common type of tax-deferred income is the income earned on a traditional individual retirement account (IRA). Both contributions and earnings on traditional IRAs accumulate tax free until you withdraw them at a later date; then you must pay federal income tax. The 401(k) and 403(b) retirement accounts provided by employers also provide tax-deferred income. Chapter 18 discusses these retirement plans in greater detail. The income from all other investments is *taxable income.*

With all three types of investment income, it is your responsibility to determine how taxes and current tax rulings affect your investments. Areas of concern include dividend, interest, and rental income, and capital gains and capital losses.

dividend

Dividends, Interest Income, and Rental Income   A **dividend** is a distribution of money, stock, or other property that a corporation pays to stockholders. Like wages or salaries, dividend income is reported on your federal tax return as ordinary income. Generally, a corporation will send you a Form 1099-DIV that states how much dividend income has been reported to the Internal Revenue Service in your name.

Interest from banks, credit unions, and savings and loan associations is subject to federal taxation. Usually, the payer will send you a Form 1099-INT that states how much interest income has been reported to the Internal Revenue Service in your name. Interest that you receive from promissory notes, loans, bonds, and U.S. securities must also be reported as income. With the exception of tax-free bonds, there is no exclusion for interest income. You must report the total of such income as ordinary income on your tax return.

Net income from rental property is also subject to federal taxation and is treated as ordinary income like wages or salaries. Generally, you must report all income and expenses on rental property on IRS Schedule E.

Capital Gains and Capital Losses   Under current tax laws, profits resulting from the sale of investments held for less than 18 months are taxed as ordinary income. For example, assume Joe Coit sold 100 shares of General Electric stock for a profit of $1,000. If this investment was held for less than 18 months and Joe is in the 28 percent tax bracket, Joe's tax on the $1,000 profit is $280 ($1,000 × 28% = $280). Investments held for longer than 18 months are treated as capital gains and are taxed at reduced tax rates. Under the current tax law, the maximum tax rate on capital gains is 20 percent for most taxpayers and 10 percent for people in the 15 percent tax bracket. If Joe Coit had held his General Electric stock for 18 months or longer, his profit would be treated as a capital gain. His tax on the $1,000 capital gain would be $200 ($1,000 × 20% = $200). Capital gains on assets purchased after year 2000 and held for more than five years will be taxed at even lower rates. For these assets, the 20 percent rate will drop to 18 percent and the 10 percent rate will drop to 8 percent.

Under current tax laws, capital losses are first used to offset capital gains. Up to $3,000 in capital losses may then be used each year to offset ordinary income. Any capital losses in excess of the $3,000 used to offset ordinary income may be used in future tax years.

DID YOU KNOW?

There are many different investment opportunities for people who start an individual retirement account (IRA).

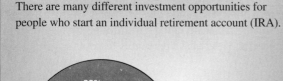
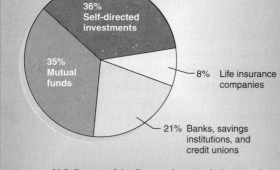

SOURCE: U.S. Bureau of the Census, *Statistical Abstract of the United States: 1996,* 116th ed. (Washington, DC: U.S. Government Printing Office), p. 527.

CONCEPT   CHECK   13–4

1. How can a financial planner help you achieve your investment goals?
2. How can calculations for current yield, total return, and annualized holding period yield help you monitor the value of your investments?
3. How do dividends, interest, and rental income differ from capital gains and losses?

SOURCES OF INVESTMENT INFORMATION

L.O.5. Use various sources of financial information that can reduce investment risks.

With most investments, more information is available than an investor can read and comprehend. Therefore, you must be selective in the type of information you use for evaluation purposes. With some investments, however, only a limited amount of information is available. For example, a wealth of information is available on stocks and mutual funds, whereas the amount of information on a metal such as cobalt or manganese may be limited to one source. Regardless of the number or availability of sources, always determine how reliable and accurate the information is. Following are sources of information you can use to evaluate present and future investments. Also, see Exhibit 13–7 for publications used by successful investors.

EXHIBIT 13–7

A Personal Reading List for Successful Investing

While individual investors have their favorite sources for investment information, it is quite likely that most successful investors use some of the following newspapers and periodicals on a regular basis.

Newspapers

- Local newspapers—published daily
- *The Wall Street Journal*—published daily
- *USA Today*—published daily
- *The New York Times*—published daily

Business Periodicals

- *Barron's*—published weekly
- *Business Week*—published weekly
- *Fortune*—published twice a month
- *Forbes*—published twice a month
- *Newsweek*—published weekly
- *U.S News & World Report*—published weekly

Personal Financial Publications

- *Consumer Reports*—published monthly
- *Kiplinger's Personal Finance*—published monthly
- *Money*—published monthly

Newspapers

The most readily available source of information for the average investor is the financial page of a daily metropolitan newspaper or *The Wall Street Journal.* There you will find a summary of the day's trading on the two most widely quoted stock exchanges in the United States, the New York Stock Exchange and the American Stock Exchange. In addition to stock coverage, most newspapers provide information on stocks traded in the over-the-counter markets, mutual funds, corporate and government bonds, commodities, options, and some metals. Detailed information on how to read price quotations for stocks, bonds, mutual funds, and other investments is presented in the remaining chapters of Part V.

Business Periodicals and Government Publications

Most business periodicals are published weekly, twice a month, or monthly. *Barron's, Business Week, Fortune, Forbes, Harvard Business Review,* and similar business periodicals provide not only general news about the overall economy but also detailed financial information about individual corporations. Some business periodicals—for example, *Advertising Age* and *Business Insurance*—focus on information about the firms in a specific industry. In addition to business periodicals, more general magazines such as *U.S. News & World Report, Time,* and *Newsweek* provide investment information as a regular feature. Finally, *Money, Consumer Reports, Smart Money, Kiplinger's Personal Finance,* and similar periodicals provide information and advice designed to improve your investment skills.

The U.S. government is the world's largest provider of information. Much of this information is of value to investors and is either free or available at minimal cost. U.S. government publications that investors may find useful include the *Federal Reserve Bulletin,* published by the Federal Reserve System, and the *Survey of Current Business,* published by the Department of Commerce. In addition, the Bureau of the Census provides statistical information that may be useful to investors.

Exhibit 13–8	Statistical Average	Type of Investment
Statistical Averages Used to Evaluate Investments	Dow Jones Industrial Average	Stocks
	Standard & Poor's 500 Stock Index	Stocks
	Value Line Stock Index	Stocks
	New York Stock Exchange Index	Stocks on New York Stock Exchange
	American Stock Exchange Index	Stocks on American Stock Exchange
	NASDAQ Composite Stock Index	Over-the-counter stocks
	Lipper Mutual Funds Index	Mutual funds
	Dow Jones Bond Average	Corporate bonds
	Barron's Money Rates	Interest rates
	New One-Family House Price Index	Real estate
	Dow Jones Spot Market Index	Commodities
	Sotheby's Fine Art Index	Art/paintings
	Linn's Trends of Stamp Values	Stamps

The Internet and Online Computer Services

While no one knows the exact number, experts estimate that there are more than 100 million Internet users worldwide.[2] In the United States alone, over 9.5 million Americans use the Internet.[3] Today more people have access to information provided by computers located in their homes or at libraries, universities, or businesses than ever before. More important, there is a wealth of information available on most personal finance topics and different investment alternatives. For example, you can obtain interest rates for certificates of deposit; current price information for stocks, bonds, and mutual funds; and brokers' recommendations to buy, hold, or sell a corporation's stock. You can even trade securities online just by asking the right questions or pushing the right button on your computer keyboard. You can also use computers and financial planning software to develop a personal financial plan.

To use your computer to generate information you really need, you must be selective. One of the best ways to access needed information is to use a gopher. A *gopher* is a research tool that helps you move through a menu system until you find the information you want. You can also do a word search for either the personal finance topic or investment alternative that you want to explore. Finally, federal, state, and local governments and most corporations have a home page where you can obtain valuable information.

Today thousands of Internet access providers allow users to connect to the Internet and use gophers, newsgroups, mailing lists, and e-mail. If you're a beginner, you may find it easier to use one of the commercial online companies like America Online, CompuServe, Prodigy, and Microsoft Network. These online companies usually provide subscribers with access to a broad range of information on a variety of topics as well as a connection to the Internet. As an added bonus, online services are often easier to use than a straight Internet connection arranged through an Internet service provider.

Corporate Reports

The federal government requires corporations selling new issues of securities to disclose information about corporate earnings, assets and liabilities, products or services, and the qualifications of top management in a *prospectus* that they must give to investors. In addition to the prospectus, all publicly owned corporations send their stockholders an annual report and quarterly reports that contain detailed financial data. Included in annual and quarterly corporate reports is a statement of financial position, which describes changes in assets, liabilities, and owners' equity. Also included in these reports is an income statement, which provides dollar amounts for sales, expenses, and profits or losses.

Statistical Averages

Investors often gauge the value of their investments by following one or more widely recognized statistical averages. Such an average is a statistical measure that indicates whether a broad investment category (stocks, bonds, mutual funds, etc.) is increasing or decreasing in value.

How much importance should you attach to statistical averages? These averages show trends and direction, but they do not pinpoint the actual value of a specific investment. Some of the more widely used statistical averages are listed in Exhibit 13–8 on page 418. The remaining chapters of Part V describe many of these averages.

Investor Services and Newsletters

Many stockbrokers and financial planners mail a free monthly or quarterly newsletter to their clients. In addition, investors can subscribe to services that provide investment information. The fees for investor services generally range from $30 to $750 a year.

Three widely used services are available for investors who specialize in stocks and bonds:

1. *Standard & Poor's Stock Reports.* These up-to-date reports on corporations cover such topics as recommendations, sales and earnings, prospects, recent developments, income statements, and statements of financial position.
2. *Value Line.* These reports supply detailed information about major corporations—earnings, dividends, sales, liabilities, and other financial data.
3. *Moody's Investors Service.* Moody's reports help investors evaluate potential investments in corporate securities and provide information similar to that contained in Standard & Poor's and Value Line reports.
4. *Morningstar Investment Reports.* Morningstar tracks thousands of mutual funds and issues monthly reports on safety, financial performance, and other important information that investors can use to evaluate a mutual fund.
5. *Wiesenberger Investment Reports.* The mutual fund information provided by Wiesenberger is similar to the detailed reports provided by Morningstar.

Other investment publications that may help you evaluate potential investments include Dun & Bradstreet's *Key Business Ratios;* the *Business One Investment Almanac,* published by Richard D. Irwin; the *Information Please Business Almanac,* published by Houghton Mifflin; *Hoover's Handbook of American Business,* published by the Referance Press; the *Commodity Yearbook;* and publications by the International Monetary Fund.

In addition to the preceding publications, each of the following securities exchanges provides information through printed materials and the Internet:

- American Stock Exchange.
- Chicago Mercantile Exchange.
- New York Stock Exchange (NYSE).
- Stock exchange markets (foreign exchanges).

PFP

Sheet 57

While each Internet home page may differ, each provides basic information about the exchange, offers educational material and a glossary of important terms, and describes how investors can profit from transactions through the exchange.

The preceding discussion of investor services and newsletters is not exhaustive, but it does give you some idea of the amount and scope of the information available to serious investors. Although most small investors find many of the services and newsletters described here too expensive for personal subscriptions, this information may be available from stockbrokers or financial planners. This type of information is also available at most public libraries.

CONCEPT CHECK 13–5

1. The most readily available source of information for the average investor is the daily newspaper. What types of information could you find in a newspaper?
2. Briefly describe the additional sources of information you can use to evaluate a potential investment.

KEY FORMULAS

Page	Topic	Formula
414	Current yield	$\text{Current yield} = \dfrac{\text{Annual income amount}}{\text{Market value}}$
	Example:	$\text{Current yield} = \dfrac{\$3.00}{\$50.00}$
		$\text{Current yield} = 0.06 = 6 \text{ percent}$
414	Total return	$\text{Total return} = \text{Current return} + \text{Future return}$
	Example:	$\text{Total return} = \$120 + \$710$
		$\text{Total return} = \$830$
415	Annualized holding period yield	$\text{Annualized holding period yield} = \dfrac{\text{Total return}}{\text{Original investment}} \times \dfrac{1}{N}$
		$N = \text{Number of years investment is held}$
	Example:	$\text{Annualized holding period yield} = \dfrac{\$830}{\$2,600} \times \dfrac{1}{4}$
		$\text{Annualized holding period yield} = 0.08 = 8 \text{ percent}$

SUMMARY

L.O.1 Explain why you should prepare for and establish an investment program.

Investment goals must be specific and measurable and should be classified as short term, intermediate, and long term. Before beginning an investment program, you must make sure your personal financial affairs are in order. This process begins with learning to live within your means and obtaining adequate insurance protection. The next step is the accumulation of an emergency fund equal to three to nine months' living expenses.

L.O.2   Describe how safety, risk, income, growth, and liquidity affect your investment decisions.

Although each investor may have specific, individual reasons for investing, all investors must consider the factors of safety, risk, income, growth, and liquidity. Especially important is the relationship between safety and risk. Basically, this concept can be summarized as follows: The potential return for any investment should be directly related to the risk the investor assumes.

L.O.3   Identify the major types of investment alternatives.

Investment alternatives include savings accounts, certificates of deposit, stocks, bonds, mutual funds, and real estate. More speculative investment alternatives include options, derivatives, commodities, precious metals, gemstones, and collectibles.

L.O.4   Recognize the role of the professional financial planner and your role in a personal investment program.

A qualified financial planner has had at least two years of training in securities, insurance, taxes, real estate, and estate planning and has passed a rigorous examination. Financial planners can help people achieve their investment goals. It is your responsibility to monitor the value of your investments and to keep accurate and current records.

L.O.5   Use various sources of financial information that can reduce investment risks.

Because more information on investments is available than most investors can read and comprehend, you must be selective in the type of information you use for evaluation purposes. Sources of information include newspapers, business periodicals, government publications, the Internet, corporate reports, and investor services.

G L O S S A R Y

annualized holding period yield   A yield calculation that takes into account the total return, the original investment, and the time the investment is held.   (p. 415)

corporate bond   A corporation's written pledge to repay a specified amount of money, along with interest.   (p. 408)

current yield   The yearly dollar amount of income generated by an investment divided by the investment's current market value.   (p. 414)

diversification   The process of spreading your assets among several types of investments to lessen risk.   (p. 411)

dividend   A distribution of money, stock, or other property that a corporation pays to stockholders.   (p. 415)

emergency fund   A certain amount of money you can obtain quickly in case of immediate need.   (p. 396)

equity capital   Money that a business obtains from its owners.   (p. 407)

government bond   The written pledge of a government or a municipality to repay a specified amount of money, along with interest.   (p. 408)

line of credit   A short-term loan that is approved before the money is actually needed.   (p. 397)

liquidity   The ease and speed with which an asset can be converted to cash without a substantial loss in dollar value. (p. 406)

mutual fund   An investment alternative chosen by people who pool their money to buy stocks, bonds, and other securities selected by professional managers employed by an investment company.   (p. 408)

speculative investment   A high-risk investment made in the hope of earning a relatively large profit in a short time. (p. 410)

total return   A calculation that includes the yearly dollar amount of income as well as any increase or decrease in the original purchase price of the investment.   (p. 414)

R E V I E W   Q U E S T I O N S

1. What four factors should you consider when performing a financial checkup?   (L.O.1)
2. Why should you establish an emergency fund before investing money in stocks, bonds, mutual funds, or other investments?   (L.O.1)
3. What suggestions did this chapter offer to help you get the money you need to start an investment program?   (L.O.1)
4. In your own words, describe the steps you would use to establish a personal plan of action like the one illustrated in Exhibit 13–2.   (L.O.1)
5. When choosing an investment, how are the safety and risk factors related?   (L.O.2)
6. The risk factor is broken into four individual components. Why is each component important?   (L.O.2)
7. What types of investors would concentrate on investment income? Investment growth? Investment liquidity? (L.O.2)
8. How do corporate and government bonds differ from common and preferred stock?   (L.O.3)

9. You may invest in stocks either directly or through a mutual fund. How do the two investment methods differ? (L.O.3)

10. What questions should you ask before investing in real estate? (L.O.3)

11. What factors account for the increased risk involved in the purchase of derivatives, commodities, options, precious metals, gemstones, and collectibles? (L.O.3)

12. Financial planners fall into two categories. What is the difference between the two? Which type of planner would you choose to help you attain your investment goals? (L.O.4)

13. What is your role in the investment process? (L.O.4)

14. Describe the types of investment information you can use to reduce investment risk. (L.O.5)

15. What type of investment information can you obtain by using the Internet or an online computer service? (L.O.5)

FINANCIAL PLANNING PROBLEMS

1. *Calculating the Amount for an Emergency Fund.* Beth and Bob Hernandez have total take-home pay of $3,200 a month. Their monthly expenses total $2,800. Calculate the amount this couple needs to establish an emergency fund. How did you calculate this amount? (L.O.1)

2. *Developing a Financial Plan.* Assume you are single and have graduated from college. Your monthly take-home pay is $2,100, and your monthly expenses total $1,800, leaving you with a monthly surplus of $300. Develop a personal plan of action for investing like the one illustrated in Exhibit 13–2. (L.O.1)

3. *Analyzing Income and Growth Investments.* List three personal factors that might lead some investors to emphasize income rather than growth in their investment planning. List three personal factors that might lead some investors to emphasize growth rather than income. (L.O.2)

4. *Comparing Investment Alternatives.* Choose three of the investment alternatives presented in this chapter, then rank them from high to low on safety, risk, and liquidity. Assume that 3 is the highest score and 1 is the lowest score for each factor. Based on your ranking, which one of the three alternatives would you choose for your own investment program? Why? (L.O.3)

5. *Calculating Return on Investment.* Assume you purchased 100 shares of IBM common stock for $54 a share, received an annual dividend of $1 per share, and sold your IBM stock for $76 a share at the end of three years. (L.O.4)

   a. Calculate the current yield for your IBM stock at the time you purchased it.

   b. Calculate the total return for your IBM investment at the end of three years.

   c. Calculate the annualized holding period yield for your IBM investment at the end of the three-year period.

6. *Calculating Return on an Investment.* Two years ago, you purchased 100 shares of Coca-Cola Company. Your purchase price for each share was $42. During the last two years, you have received the following dividend amounts: $.56 per share the first year and $.68 per share the second year. Also, assume that at the end of two years, you sold your Coca-Cola stock for $55.50 a share. (L.O.4)

   a. Calculate the current yield for your Coca-Cola stock at the time you purchased it.

   b. Calculate the current yield for your Coca-Cola stock at the time you sold it.

   c. Calculate the total return for your Coca-Cola investment when you sold the stock at the end of two years.

   d. Calculate the annualized holding period yield for your Coca-Cola investment at the end of the two-year period.

7. *Monitoring an Investment's Financial Performance.* Based on the following information, construct a graph that illustrates price movement for a share of the New York Venture Mutual Fund. Note: You may want to review the material presented in the Financial Planning Calculations feature on page 413. (L.O.4)

January	$18.70	July	$16.10
February	18.00	August	15.50
March	20.30	September	16.40
April	21.35	October	16.90
May	19.50	November	18.40
June	17.80	December	17.20

8. *Using Financial Information.* Suppose you just inherited 500 shares of General Motors stock. List five sources of information you could use to evaluate your inheritance. Beside each source, briefly state how the information it contains could help in your evaluation. (L.O.5)

PROJECTS AND APPLICATION ACTIVITIES

1. *Using Investment Information.* Choose a current issue of *Kiplinger's Personal Finance, Money,* or *Consumer Reports* and summarize an article that provides suggestions on how you could use your money more effectively. (L.O.1)

2. *Planning for an Investment Program.* Assume you are 28 years old, your take-home pay totals $2,200 a month, you have monthly living expenses that total $1,200, your monthly car payment is $300, and your credit card debts total $4,900. Using the information presented in this

chapter, develop a three-part plan to (1) reduce your monthly expense, (2) establish an emergency fund, and (3) save $4,000 to establish an investment program. (L.O.1)

3. *Using the Internet to Obtain Information about Money Management.* As pointed out at the beginning of this chapter, it doesn't make a lot of sense to establish an investment program until credit card and installment purchases are reduced or eliminated. While most people are responsible and make payments when they're supposed to, some

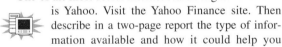 people get in trouble. To help avoid this problem, each of the following organizations has a home page on the Internet:

Debt Counselors of America provides individuals with information about how to manage consumer debt.

Equifax provides information about how you can obtain your credit report.

Finance Center, Inc. helps consumers save money when purchasing, financing, or refinancing a new home, car, or credit card transactions.

Choose one of the above organizations and visit its home page. Then prepare a report that summarizes the information provided by the organization. Finally, indicate if this information could help you manage your consumer debt. (L.O.1)

4. *Choosing Investment Alternatives.* From the investment alternatives described in this chapter, choose two specific investments you believe would help an individual who is 35 years old, is divorced, and earns $20,000 a year begin an investment program. Assume this individual has $30,000 to invest at this time. As part of your recommendation, compare each of your investment suggestions on safety, risk, income, growth, and liquidity. (L.O.2)

5. *Choosing Investment Alternatives.* Choose one of the investment alternatives presented in this chapter (stocks, bonds, mutual funds, real estate, or speculative investments) and prepare a two-page report describing why this investment would be appropriate for a woman who is 68 years old and has just lost her husband. Assume she is debt free and has inherited $175,000. (L.O.3)

6. *Explaining the Principle of Diversification.* Prepare a two-minute presentation describing why the principle of diversification is important when establishing an investment program. (L.O.3)

7. *Choosing a Financial Planner.* More than 200,000 people call themselves financial planners. Prepare a list of at least 10 questions you could use to determine whether any one of them could really help you achieve your financial goals. (L.O.4)

8. *Reporting Investment Income for Tax Purposes.* Choose three of the following sources of investment income. Then describe how each type is taxed by the federal government. (L.O.4)

   a. Dividend income
   b. Interest income
   c. Rental income
   d. Capital gains
   e. Capital losses

9. *Using Investment Information.* Assume you have established an emergency fund and have saved an additional $12,000 to fund an investment in common stock issued by AT&T Corporation. Using the sources of information discussed in this chapter, go to the library and obtain information about this company. Summarize your findings in a three-page report describing AT&T's current operations and the firm's past and present financial performance. Finally, indicate if you would purchase AT&T common stock based on the information in your report. (L.O.5)

10. *Using Investment Information.* Each year the publishers of *Fortune* magazine provide a special edition called the *Fortune Investor's Guide.* This guide is devoted to helping people learn about different investment alternatives. At the time of publication of this text, the latest guide was published on August 18, 1997. Obtain a copy of either this guide or one published on a later date, and summarize one of the articles highlighting an investment that could help you reach your investment goals. (L.O.5)

11. *Using the Internet to Obtain Investment Information.* One of the most useful Internet search engines available

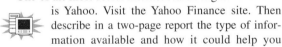 is Yahoo. Visit the Yahoo Finance site. Then describe in a two-page report the type of information available and how it could help you become a better investor. (L.O.5)

LIFE SITUATION CASE 13

FIRST BUDGET, THEN INVEST FOR SUCCESS!

Joe and Mary Garner, married 12 years, have an eight-year-old child. Six years ago, they purchased a home on which they owe about $110,000. They also owe $6,000 on their two-year-old automobile. All of their furniture is paid for, but they owe a total of $3,170 on two credit cards. Joe is employed as an engineer and makes $48,000 a year. Mary works as a part-time computer analyst and earns about $18,000 a year. Their combined monthly income after deductions is $3,950.

About six months ago, the Garners had what they now describe as a "financial meltdown." It all started one Monday afternoon when their air conditioner stopped cooling. Since their home was only six years old, they thought the repair ought to be a simple one—at least until the repair technician diagnosed their problem as a defective compressor. Unfortunately, the warranty on the compressor had run out about three months before the compressor broke down. According to the technician, it would cost over $1,200 to replace the compressor. At the time, they had about $2,000 in their savings account, which they had been saving for their summer vacation, and now they had to use their vacation money to fix the air conditioner.

For the Garners, the fact that they didn't have enough money to take a vacation was like a wake-up call. They realized they were now in their mid-30s and had serious cash problems. According to Joe, "We don't waste money, but there just never seems to be enough money to do the things we want to do." But according to Mary, "The big problem is that we never have enough money to start an investment program that could pay for our daughter's college education or fund our retirement."

Fortunately, they decided to take a "big" first step in an attempt to solve their financial problems. They began by examining their monthly expenses for the past month. Here's what they found:

Income (cash inflow)

Joe's take-home salary	$2,800	
Mary's take-home salary	1,150	
Total income		$3,950

Cash outflows

Monthly fixed expenses:

Home mortgage payment, including taxes and insurance	$1,190	
Automobile loan	315	
Automobile insurance	130	
Life insurance premium	50	
Total fixed expenses		$1,685

Monthly variable expenses:

Food and household necessities	$480	
Electricity	115	
Natural gas	50	
Water	35	
Telephone	55	
Family clothing allowance	130	
Gasoline and automobile repairs	120	
Personal and health care	100	
Recreation and entertainment	600	
Gifts and donations	300	
Minimum payment on credit cards	80	
Total variable expenses		$2,065
Total monthly expenses		$3,750
Surplus for savings or investments		$200

Once they realized they had a $200 surplus each month, they began to replace the $1,200 they had taken from their savings account to pay for repairing the air conditioner. Now it was time to take the next step.

QUESTIONS

1. How would you rate the financial status of the Garners before the air conditioner broke down?
2. The Garners have a $200 surplus at the end of each month. Based on their current financial condition, what do you think they should do with this money?
3. The Garners' take-home pay is almost $4,000 a month. Yet, after all expenses are paid, there is only a $200 surplus each month. Based on the information presented in this case, what expenses, if any, seem out of line and could be reduced to increase the surplus at the end of each month?
4. Given that both Joe and Mary Garner are in their mid-30s and want to retire when they reach age 65, what type of investment goals would be most appropriate for them?
5. How does the time value of money concept affect the types of long-term goals and the investments that a couple like the Garners might use to build their financial nest egg?
6. Based on the different investments described in this chapter, what specific types of investments (certificates of deposit, stocks, mutual funds, real estate, etc.) would you recommend for the Garners? Why?

USING THE INTERNET TO CREATE A PERSONAL FINANCIAL PLAN 13

DEVELOPING AN INVESTMENT PLAN

An investment program should consider safety, current income, growth potential, liquidity, and taxes. Your ability to set financial goals and select investment vehicles is crucial to long-term financial prosperity.

Web Sites for Investment Planning

- Investment planning information at **www.personal-wealth.com, www.quicken.com,** the FinanCenter at **www.financenter.com/,** "The Motley Fool" at **www.fool.com/,** the Cable News Network at **cnnfn.com/index.hmtl,** Bloomberg Personal at **www.bloomberg.com,** Money

Line at **www.moneyline.com,** the Daily Rocket at **www.dailyrocket.com,** and **www.investorama.com**

- Current investment articles from *Money* magazine at **www.money.com,** from *Kiplinger's Personal Finance* magazine at **www.kiplinger.com,** *Business Week* at **www.businessweek.com,** *Worth* magazine at **www.worth.com,** and *Smart Money* at **www.smartmoney.com**
- Basic information about investing is available at **www.invest-faq.com**
- At **www.investor.nasd.com,** investment newsletters, glossary, market data, and financial calculators from the National Association of Securities dealers.
- Information from the American Association of Individual Investors at **www.aaii.org**
- Investment club information at **www.better-investing.org**
- Information from the Securities and Exchange Commission about online financial swindles may be obtained at **www.sec/gov/consumer/cyberfr.htm**

(NOTE: Addresses and content of Web sites change, and new sites are created daily. Use the search engines discussed in Appendix B to update and locate Web sites for your current financial planning needs.)

PFP SHEETS: 55, 56, 57

Short-Term Financial Planning Activities

1. Set investment goals for various financial needs (see PFP Sheet 55).
2. Assess various types of investments for market risk, inflation, interest rate risk, and liquidity (see PFP Sheet 56).
3. Identify and evaluate investment information sources. (See PFP Sheet 57.)

Long-Term Financial Planning Activities

1. Identify saving and investing decisions that would serve your changing life situations.
2. Develop a plan for revising investments as family and household situations change.

CHAPTER 14

INVESTING IN STOCKS

OPENING CASE

BUY HOME DEPOT STOCK AND START BUILDING A FINANCIAL FUTURE

Back in 1991, Martha and Michael Kahn didn't have a lot of money. Their combined annual income was just over $45,000. Nevertheless, Martha talked Michael into saving about $1,000 with an eye toward beginning an investment program. On January 21, 1991, they purchased 100 shares of Home Depot common stock for $8.25 per share for a total outlay of $890, including the broker's commission.

Now, after eight years, the Kahns admit their first investment was based on a short conversation between Martha and her boss, Bart Thompson. Thompson had just made a sales call on Atlanta-based Home Depot and was "very impressed" with their operation. Their method of selling home improvement merchandise—hardware, lumber, paint, electrical products, plumbing products, and just about anything else the professional contractor or the do-it-yourselfer could need, all at one location at discounted prices—was working. Thompson went on to say that since Home Depot had less than 8 percent of the national market for this type of merchandise, there was still "a lot of room for expansion."

During the first 11 months they owned their Home Depot stock, the Kahns' stock increased to over $14 a share. Michael was tempted to sell. After all, they had almost doubled their original investment. However, Martha persuaded him that they should hold onto their investment a little longer.

Today the Kahns admit their decision to hold their Home Depot stock "a little longer" was one of the best they ever made. During the next seven years, Home Depot opened more stores and at the end of 1996 (the last year for which complete financial data are available) had 515 warehouse-style home centers in 40 states and 28 stores in three Canadian provinces. Gross sales increased to $19.5 billion. And for four consecutive years, Home Depot has been ranked by *Fortune* as America's most admired retailer. For the Kahns, the most important fact about their Home Depot investment was that their original $890 investment was now worth a staggering $18,000.

QUESTIONS

1. In 1996, *Fortune* named Home Depot America's most admired retailer. If you live in the United States, there is a good chance you have shopped in a Home Depot store. Based on your experience or the material in the opening case, what factors do your think have led to Home Depot's success?
2. Back in 1991, Martha and Michael Kahn purchased 100 shares of Home Depot stock for $8.25 a share; their total investment, including commission, was $890. At the beginning of 1998, their investment was worth over $18,000. If you were the Kahns, would you sell your Home Depot stock and take your profits? Explain your answer.

SOURCES: The Home Depot, Inc., *1996 Annual Report;* George Sutton and James R. Talbot, eds., *Hoover's 500 Profile of America's Largest Business Enterprises* (Austin, TX: The Business Press, 1996), p. 251; *Moody's Handbook of Common Stocks* (New York: Moody's Investors Service, 1997); Susan E. Kuhn, "Blue-Chip Stocks Offer Value in a Volatile Market," *Fortune,* July 25, 1994, pp. 29–30; Graham Button, "The Man Who Almost Walked Out on Ross Perot, *Forbes,* November 22, 1993, pp. 68–69+.

After studying this chapter, you will be able to

L.O.1 Identify the most important features of common stock.

L.O.4 Describe how stocks are bought and sold.

L.O.2 Discuss the most important features of preferred stock.

L.O.5 Explain the trading techniques used by long-term and short-term investors.

L.O.3 Explain how investors can evaluate stock investments.

COMMON STOCK

L.O.1 Identify the most important features of common stock.

Financial Decision Trade-Off

securities

Opportunity costs! The Kahns, the couple in the opening case, took a chance when they purchased 100 shares of Home Depot common stock. Their investment, which cost almost $900, could have gone down in value. But because the company has been successful, investors like the Kahns who purchased Home Depot stock have made a lot of money. That's the way it's supposed to work. Investors provide the money; the corporation uses the money to generate sales and earn profits; and the stockholders earn a return on their investment. Today a lot of people buy and sell stocks. Why? The most obvious answer is simple: They want larger returns than those more conservative investments offer. Between 1982 and 1997, the Standard & Poor's 500 Stock Index averaged a 19.18 percent annual return.[1] And during the last two years of that period, the same index averaged an annual return of over 30 percent.[2] Not bad when compared to returns offered by certificates of deposit and more conservative investments. However, before you decide to invest in stocks, you should realize that this type of investment involves more risk.

The term **securities** encompasses a broad range of investments, including stocks and bonds, mutual funds, options, and commodities that are traded on security exchanges or the over-the-counter markets. In this chapter, we examine stocks. There are two types of stocks, common and preferred stock. We discuss common stock in this section and preferred stock in the next. Exhibit 14–1 on page 428 shows a common stock certificate. Since common stockholders are the actual owners of the corporation, they share in its success. But before investing your money, it helps to understand why corporations issue common stock.

Why Corporations Issue Common Stock

Corporations issue common stock to finance their business start-up costs and help pay for their ongoing business activities. Today corporations are classified as either private corporations or public corporations. A *private corporation* is a corporation whose stock is owned by relatively few people and is not traded openly in stock markets. A *public corporation* is a corporation whose stock is traded openly in stock markets and may be

EXHIBIT 14–1

A Common Stock Certificate

purchased by individuals. Public corporations may have thousands or even millions of stockholders. American Telephone & Telegraph, for example, has over 2 million stockholders, while General Motors has almost 1 million. Corporate managers prefer selling common stock as a method of financing for several reasons.

A Form of Equity   Corporations don't have to repay the money a stockholder pays for stock. Generally, a stockholder in a public corporation may sell his or her stock to another individual. The selling price is determined by how much a buyer is willing to pay for the stock. Simply put, if the demand for a particular stock increases, the market value of the stock will increase. If the demand for a particular stock decreases, the market value of the stock will decrease. Demand for a stock changes when information about the firm or its future prospects is released to the general public. For example, information about expected sales revenues, earnings, expansions or mergers, or other important developments within the firm can increase or decrease the demand for, and ultimately the market value of, the firm's stock.

Dividends Not Mandatory   Dividends are paid out of profits, and dividend payments must be approved by the corporation's board of directors. Dividend policies vary among corporations, but most firms distribute between 30 and 70 percent of their earnings to stockholders. However, some corporations follow a policy of smaller dividend distributions to stockholders. In general, these are rapidly growing firms that retain a large share of their earnings for research and development, expansion, or major projects. On the other hand, utility companies and other financially secure enterprises may distribute 80 to 90 percent of their earnings. Always remember that if a corporation has had a bad year, board members may vote to omit dividend payments to stockholders.

Voting Rights and Control of the Company   In return for the financing provided by selling common stock, management must make concessions to stockholders that may restrict corporate policies. For example, corporations are required by law to have an annual meeting at which stockholders have a right to vote, usually casting one vote per share of stock. Stockholders may vote in person or by proxy. A **proxy** is a legal form that

proxy

lists the issues to be decided at a stockholders' meeting and requests that stockholders transfer their voting rights to some individual or individuals. The common stockholders elect the board of directors and must approve major changes in corporate policies. Typical changes in corporate policy include (1) an amendment of the corporate charter, (2) the sale of certain assets, (3) possible mergers, (4) the issuance of preferred stock or corporate bonds, and (5) changes in the amount of common stock.

preemptive right

Many states require that a provision for preemptive rights be included in the charter of every corporation. A **preemptive right** is the right of current stockholders to purchase any new stock the corporation issues before it is offered to the general public. By exercising their preemptive rights, stockholders are able to maintain their current proportion of corporate ownership. This may be important when the corporation is small and management control is a matter of concern to stockholders.

Finally, corporations are required by law to distribute annual and quarterly reports to stockholders. These reports contain details about sales, earnings, and other vital information.

Why Investors Purchase Common Stock

How do you make money by buying common stock? Basically, common stock investments can increase in three ways: income from dividends, dollar appreciation of stock value, and the possibility of increased value from stock splits.

Income from Dividends   While the corporation's board members are under no legal obligation to pay dividends, most board members like to keep stockholders happy (and prosperous). Few things will unite stockholders into a powerful opposition force more rapidly than omitted or lowered dividends. Therefore, board members usually declare dividends if the corporation's after-tax profits are sufficient for them to do so. Since dividends are a distribution of profits, investors must be concerned about future after-tax profits. In short, how secure is the dividend?

Corporate dividends for common stock may take the form of cash, additional stock, or company products. However, the last type of dividend is extremely unusual. If the board of directors declares a cash dividend, each common stockholder receives an equal amount per share. Although dividend policies vary, most corporations pay dividends on a quarterly basis. Some corporations, particularly those experiencing large swings in earnings, declare special year-end or extra dividends in addition to their regular quarterly dividends.

record date

Notice in Exhibit 14–2 that Coca-Cola Company has declared a quarterly dividend of $.14 per share to stockholders who own the stock on the record date of September 15. The **record date** is the date on which a stockholder must be registered on the corporation's books in order to receive dividend payments. When a stock is traded around the record date, the company must determine whether the buyer or the seller is entitled to the dividend. To solve this problem, this rule is followed: *Dividends remain with the stock until four business days before the record date.* On the fourth day before the record date, the stock begins selling ex-dividend. Investors who purchase an ex-dividend stock are not entitled to receive dividends for that quarter, and the dividend is paid to the previous owner of the stock.

For example, Coca-Cola declared a quarterly dividend of $.14 per share to stockholders who owned its stock on Monday, September 15, 1997. The stock went ex-dividend on Tuesday, September 9, 1997, four *business* days before the September 15 date. A stockholder who purchased the stock on September 9 or after was not entitled to this quarterly dividend payment. Coca-Cola made the actual dividend payment on October 1 to stockholders who owned the stock on the record date. Investors are generally very conscious of the date on which a stock goes ex-dividend, and the dollar value of the stock may go down by the value of the quarterly dividend.

EXHIBIT 14–2   **Typical Information on Corporate Dividends as Presented in** *The Wall Street Journal*

THE WALL STREET JOURNAL TUESDAY, JULY 22, 1997 **C17**

CORPORATE DIVIDEND NEWS

Dividends Reported July 21

Company	Period	Amt.	Payable date	Record date
REGULAR				
AK Steel Hldg pf	Q	.538⅛	10–15–97	9–15
AmSouth Bancorp	Q	.28	c10– 1–97	9–12
c-Corrected.				
ArchDanielsMidland	Q	.05	9– 2–97	8– 8
Arco Chemical Co	Q	.70	9– 5–97	8– 8
Bank of Montreal	Q	b.40	8–28–97	8– 7
Bryn Mawr Bank	Q	.18	9– 1 97	8– 1
Cavalier Homes	Q	.03	8–15–97	7–31
Chiquita Brands	Q	.05	9– 7–97	8–21
Citicorp ser16 dep	Q	.50	8–15–97	7–31
Citicorp ser17 dep	Q	.469	8–15–97	7–31
Citicorp ser20 dep	Q	.51⅞	8–15–97	7–31
Citicorp ser21 dep	Q	.53⅛	8–15–97	7–31
Citicorp ser22 dep	Q	.484⅜	8–15–97	7–31
Coca-Cola Co	Q	.14	10– 1–97	9–15
Computer Data Sys	S	.06	8–20–97	8– 8
Comsat Corp	Q	.05	9– 8–97	8– 8
Damen Finl Corp	Q	.06	8–15–97	7–31
Deb Shops Inc	Q	.05	8–22–97	7–31
Dime Financial	Q	.10	8–15–97	7–31
Dominion Resources	Q	.64½	9–20–97	8–29

Company	Period	Amount	Payable date	Record date
Student Loan Mktg	Q	.44	9–19–97	9– 5
StudentLnMk adjpfA	Q	.62½	9–30–97	9–16
Sunstone Hotel Inv	Q	.25	8–15–97	7–31
TCF Finl Corp	Q	.25	8–29–97	8– 8
TSI Inc	Q	.02½	8–18–97	8– 4
TejasGas 5.25%dep	Q	.65⅝	11– 3–97	10–17
TejasGas 9.96%dep	Q	.62¼	11– 3–97	10–17
Unitd Dominion Ind	Q	.07	9–30–97	9– 5
Value Line Inc	Q	.25	8–13–97	7–28
Versa Technologies	Q	.10	8–11–97	7–31
Webster City Fedl	Q	.20	8–20–97	8– 4
IRREGULAR				
CFB Capital I Inc	Q	.5547	7–15–97	r7–14
r-Revised.				
G&L Realty 10.25%pfA	M	.2135	8–15–97	8– 1
Orange Natl Bncp	Q	.10	9– 2–97	8–14
Peoples Finl Corp	Q	.12½	8–20–97	8– 5
FUNDS · REITS · INVESTMENT COS · LPS				
Colonial HiIncoMuni	M	.0455	8–15–97	7–31
Colonial IntermHi	M	.057	8–15–97	7–31
Colonial MuniInco	M	.04¼	8–15–97	7–31
CrossTimbers Rylty	M	.1108	8–14–97	7–31

Company	Period	Amount		Payable date	Record date
Weyco Group		s		10– 1–97	9– 2
s-3-for-1 stock split.					
INCREASED					
		–Amounts–			
		New	Old		
Dana Corp	Q	.27	.25	9–15–97	8–29
IBS Finl Corp	Q	.10	.08	9–16–97	8–27
Martin Industries	Q	.04	.038	8–15–97	8– 4
Michigan Finl Corp	Q	.20	n.19	8–20–97	8– 5
n-After adjustment of 5% stk div.					
Rohm & Haas Co	Q	.50	.45	9– 1–97	8– 8
FOREIGN					
Thorn Plc ADR		–	s	7–28–97	7–18
s-Revised dates for 6-for-7 reverse stock split.					
VitroSocAnon ADR		–	f0.1145	– –	7–25
INITIAL					
Educationl Develop	A	.01		8–14–97	8– 1
Fort Wayne Natl new	Q	.20		10– 1–97	9–10
Merrill Lynch & Co	Q	.20		8–27–97	8– 8
Ohio Valley Bank Corp new	Q	.20		8–10–97	7–28
Wells Financial Corp	Q	.12		8–21–97	7–31
Weyco Group new	Q	p.08		10– 1–97	9– 2
p-On post-split shares.					

Dollar Appreciation of Stock Value   In most cases, a stockholder purchases a stock and then holds onto that stock for a period of time. If the market value of the stock increases, the stockholder must decide whether to sell the stock at the higher price or continue to hold it. If the stockholder decides to sell the stock, the dollar amount of difference between the purchase price and the selling price represents his or her profit.

Let's assume that on July 23, 1995, you purchased 100 shares of Eastman Kodak stock at a cost of $56 a share. Your cost for the stock was $5,600 plus $80 in commission charges, for a total investment of $5,680. (Note: Commissions—a topic covered later in this chapter—are charged when you purchase stock *and* when you sell stock.) Let's also assume you held your 100 shares until July 23, 1997, and then sold them for $67 a share. During the two-year period you owned Eastman Kodak, the company paid dividends totaling $3.36 a share. Exhibit 14–3 shows your return on the investment. In this case, you made money because of quarterly dividend distributions and through an increase in stock value from $56 to $67 per share. As Exhibit 14–3 shows, your total return is $1,256. Of course, if the stock's value should decrease, or if the firm's board of directors reduces or votes to omit dividends, your return may be less than the original investment. With this information, it is also possible to calculate a current yield and an annualized holding period yield (see the Financial Planning Calculations feature on page 431).

Possibility Increased Value from Stock Splits   Investors can also increase potential

stock split

profits through a stock split. A **stock split** is a procedure in which the shares of stock owned by existing stockholders are divided into a larger number of shares. In 1996, for example, Nike's board of directors approved a 2-for-1 stock split. After the stock split, a stockholder who had previously owned 100 shares now owned 200 shares. The most common stock splits are 2-for-1, 3-for-1, and 4-for-1.

Why do corporations split their stock? In many cases, a firm's management has a theoretical ideal price range for the firm's stock. If the market value of the stock rises above the ideal range, a stock split brings the market value back in line. In the case of Nike, the

FINANCIAL PLANNING CALCULATIONS

CURRENT YIELD AND ANNUALIZED HOLDING PERIOD YIELD

Two calculations presented in Chapter 13 can be used to determine the current yield and the annualized holding period yield for the Eastman Kodak stock transaction illustrated in Exhibit 14–3.

The *current yield* is calculated by dividing the annual dividend per share by the market value per share. During year two, Eastman Kodak paid dividends totaling $1.76. At the end of year two, the market value for a share of stock was $67.

$$\text{Current yield} = \frac{\$1.76 \text{ annual dividend}}{\$67 \text{ market value}}$$

$$= 0.026, \text{ or } 2.6 \text{ percent}$$

The *annualized holding period yield* equals the total return divided by the original investment times $\frac{1}{N}$. N

equals the number of years the investment is held. (In Exhibit 14–3, the total return is $1,256.)

$$\text{Annualized holding period yield} = \frac{\$1,256 \text{ total return}}{\$5,680 \text{ original investment}} \times \frac{1}{2}$$

$$= 0.111, \text{ or } 11.1 \text{ percent}$$

The 2.6 percent current yield for the Eastman Kodak investment illustrated in Exhibit 14–3 is a little lower than the return on a passbook savings account. However, the annualized holding period yield of 11.1 percent is much higher.

EXHIBIT 14–3

Sample Stock Transaction for Eastman Kodak

Assumptions

100 shares of common stock purchased July 23, 1995, sold July 23, 1997; dividends of $3.36 per share for the two-year period.

Costs when purchased		Return when sold	
100 shares @ $56 =	$5,600	100 shares @ $67 =	$6,700
Plus commission	+ 80	Minus commission	−100
Total investment	$5,680	Total return	$6,600

Transaction summary	
Total return	$6,600
Minus total investment	−5,680
Profit from stock sale	$ 920
Plus dividends	+336
Total return for the transaction	$1,256

2-for-1 stock split reduced the market value to about one-half of the stock's previous market value. The lower market value for each share of stock was the result of dividing the dollar value of the company by a larger number of shares of common stock. Also, a decision to split a company's stock and the resulting lower market value makes the stock more attractive to the investing public. *Although there are no guarantees that a stock's market value will go up after a split, the investing public believes a potential for an increase in market value exists because the stock is offered at a lower price.*

A less common type of stock split occurs when the number of outstanding shares of common stock is reduced. This usually occurs when the market value of a corporation's stock has dropped to a point at which the directors consider it too low. In a *reverse split,* stockholders exchange their shares for a proportionately smaller number of shares. As a result, the market value is adjusted upward by a proportionate amount.

CONCEPT CHECK 14–1

1. Why do corporations issue common stock?
2. What are the typical issues on which stockholders vote?
3. Describe three reasons stockholders purchase common stock.
4. Why do corporations split their stock? Is a stock split good or bad for investors?

PREFERRED STOCK

L.O.2 Discuss the most important features of preferred stock.

In addition to purchasing common stock, you may purchase preferred stock. The most important priority an investor in preferred stock enjoys is receiving cash dividends before common stockholders are paid any cash dividends. This factor is especially important when a corporation is experiencing financial problems and cannot pay cash dividends to both preferred and common stockholders. Unlike the amount of the dividend on common stock, the dollar amount of the dividend on preferred stock is known before the stock is purchased. The dividend amount is either a stated amount of money for each share of pre-

par value

ferred stock or a certain percentage of the par value of the stock. The **par value** is an assigned (and often arbitrary) dollar value that is printed on a stock certificate. For example, if the par value for a preferred stock issue is $50 and the dividend rate is 6 percent, the dollar amount of the dividend is $3 ($50 × 6% = $3).

While preferred stock does not represent a legal debt that must be repaid, if the firm is dissolved or declares bankruptcy, preferred stockholders do have first claim to the corporation's assets after creditors (including bondholders).

callable preferred stock

Generally, preferred stock is callable. **Callable preferred stock** is stock that a corporation may exchange, at its option, for a specified amount of money. To understand why a corporation would call in a preferred stock issue, you must first realize that dividend rates paid by similar investments increase and decrease. If dividends are decreasing and similar investments provide a smaller return than the corporation's preferred stock issue, management may decide to call in the issue and substitute a new preferred stock that pays a lower dividend. Management may also decide to call in the preferred stock and issue common stock with no specified dividend. The dividend amount paid on a preferred issue can also affect the market value of the stock. For example, the preferred stock issue in the last example paid a 6 percent dividend. When the corporation issued that preferred stock, the 6 percent dividend was competitive with the dividends paid by corporations issuing preferred stocks at that time. If dividend rates on similar investments decrease, the market value of the 6 percent preferred stock issue will go up due to its higher dividend. On the other hand, if dividends paid on similar investments increase, the market value of the 6 percent preferred stock issue will fall due to its lower dividend rate.

Corporations issue preferred stock because it is an alternative method of financing that may attract investors who do not wish to buy common stock. Potential investors often regard preferred stock as a safer investment than common stock because the claim of preferred stock to both dividends and assets is prior to that of common stock. Yet preferred stock, like common stock, is equity financing that does not have to be repaid. And dividends on preferred stock, as on common stock, may be omitted by action of the board of directors.

Many small investors consider preferred stock to be as safe as corporate bonds. Generally, however, it is less safe, because corporate bonds represent borrowed money that must be repaid. Bondholders are more likely to receive interest payments until maturity and eventual repayment of their initial investment than preferred stockholders are to continue receiving dividends or recover their initial investment in the stock. To make preferred stock issues more attractive, some corporations may offer three additional features.

The Cumulative Feature of Preferred Stock

cumulative preferred stock

If the corporation's board of directors believes that omitting dividends is justified, it can vote to omit not only the dividends paid to common stockholders but also the dividends paid to preferred stockholders. One way preferred stockholders can protect themselves against omitted dividends is to purchase cumulative preferred stock. **Cumulative preferred stock** is stock whose unpaid dividends accumulate and must be paid before any cash dividend is paid to the common stockholders. If a corporation does not pay dividends to the cumulative preferred stockholders during one dividend period, the amount of the missed dividends is added to the following period's preferred dividends. If you own noncumulative preferred stock, an omitted dividend will not be made up later.

The Participation Feature of Preferred Stock

To make a preferred stock issue more attractive, corporations sometimes add a *participation feature*. This feature allows preferred stockholders to share with the common stockholders in the corporation's earnings. Participating preferred stock is a rare form of investment; this feature is used only when special measures are necessary to attract investors.[3]

The participation feature of preferred stock works like this: (1) The required dividend is paid to preferred stockholders; (2) a stated dividend, usually equal to the dividend amount paid to preferred stockholders, is paid to common stockholders; and (3) the remainder of the earnings available for distribution is shared by both preferred and common stockholders.

The Conversion Feature of Preferred Stock

Convertible preferred stock is preferred stock that can be exchanged, at the stockholder's option, for a specified number of shares of common stock. The conversion feature provides the investor with the safety of preferred stock and the possibility of greater speculative gain through conversion to common stock.

All of the information relating to the number of shares of common stock that may be obtained through conversion of preferred stock is stated in the corporate records and is usually printed on the preferred stock certificate. For example, assume Martin & Martin Manufacturing Corporation has issued a convertible preferred stock. Each share of preferred stock in this issue is convertible into two shares of common stock. Assume the market price of Martin & Martin's convertible preferred stock is $24 and the stock pays an annual dividend of $1.60 a share. Also assume the market price of the company's common stock is $9 and the common stock currently pays an annual dividend of $.54 a share. Under these circumstances, you would keep the preferred stock. If the market price of the common stock increased to above $12 a share, however, you would have an incentive to exercise the conversion option.

The decision to convert preferred stock to common stock is complicated by three factors. First, the dividends paid on preferred stock are more secure than the dividends paid on common stock. Second, the dividend yield for preferred stock is generally higher than the dividend yield for common stock. The dividend yield for Martin & Martin's preferred stock is $1.60 ÷ $24 = 0.07 = 7 percent, and the dividend yield for its common stock is $.54 ÷ $9 = 0.06 = 6 percent. Third, because of the conversion option, the market value of convertible preferred stock usually increases as the market value of common stock increases.

The next section discusses additional factors an investor should evaluate before purchasing either preferred stock or common stock.

CONCEPT CHECK 14–2

1. What is the most important priority a preferred stockholder has compared to common stockholders?
2. Why would a corporation call in preferred stock?
3. Describe three features corporations can offer to make preferred stock more attractive.

EVALUATION OF A STOCK ISSUE

L.O.3 Explain how investors can evaluate stock investments.

Financial Decision Trade-Off

How long would it take you to earn $2,500? One month? Two months? Three months? While everyone's answer is different, the fact is that $2,500 is a significant amount of money. Many investors expect to earn this much or more on their investments, and yet they are unwilling to spend the time required to become a good investor. In fact, many people purchase investments without doing *any* research. They wouldn't buy a car without a test drive or purchase a residence without comparing different houses, but for some unknown reason they invest without doing their homework. The truth is that there is no substitute for a few hours of detective work when choosing an investment. This section explains how to evaluate a potential stock investment.

Sources of Stock Information

A wealth of information is available to stock investors. Sources of this information include newspapers and business periodicals, corporate reports, the Internet, and investor services. Most local newspapers carry several pages of business news. *The Wall Street Journal* (published on weekdays) and *Barron's* (published once a week) are devoted almost entirely to financial and economic news. Obviously, different types of investments require different methods of evaluation, but a logical place to start the evaluation process for stock is with the most readily available source of information: the daily newspaper.

How to Read the Financial Section of the Newspaper

Most daily newspapers contain information about stocks listed on the New York Stock Exchange, the American Stock Exchange, and other major stock exchanges and stocks of local interest. Although not all newspapers print exactly the same information, they usually provide the basic information. Stocks are listed alphabetically, so your first task is to move down the table to find the stock you're interested in. Then, to read the stock quotation, you simply read across the table. The fifth row in Exhibit 14–4 gives detailed information about Exxon. (Each numbered entry in the list below the enlarged stock table refers to a numbered column of the stock table.)

If a corporation has more than one stock issue, the common stock is always listed first. Then the preferred stock issues are listed and are indicated by the letters *pf* behind the firm's name.

EXHIBIT 14–4

Financial Information about Common Stock Given in *The Wall Street Journal*

	1	2	3	4	5	6	7	8	9	10	11	12
	52 Weeks					**Yld**		**Vol**				**Net**
	Hi	**Lo**	**Stock**	**Sym**	**Div**	**%**	**PE**	**100s**	**Hi**	**Lo**	**Close**	**Chg**
	72¾	35⅝ ♣	ExecRisk	ER	.08	.1	21	690	69⅞	69¾	69⅞	+ ⅛
	65³⁄₁₆	36⅞ ♣	Exel	XL	1.60f	2.6	8	2086	63	61⁹⁄₁₆	62	−¹⁵⁄₁₆
	31¼	14⅝ ♣	Exide	EX	.08	.3	28	602	26	25⁷⁄₁₆	25⁷⁄₁₆	−⁹⁄₁₆
	20¾	10⅝	ExtndStayAm	ESA	...		cc	986	11¹³⁄₁₆	11½	11⅝	− ¼
s	67¼	49⅜	Exxon	XON	1.64	2.7	18	58318	60¹⁵⁄₁₆	58⅞	60⅞	+ 1⅞

-F-F-F-

8½	5⅛	FAC RltyTr	FAC		...	dd	186	7⅞	7⅝	7⅞	...
36⁷⁄₁₆	19⅝	F&M Ntl	FMN	.74	2.2	22	342	34	33½	33½	− ⁷⁄₁₆
91⁷⁄₁₆	59⅜	FMC Cp	FMC		...	12	732	67¾	66⅛	66⅜	−1⅛

1. Highest price paid for one share of Exxon during the past 52 weeks: $67¼, or $67.25
2. Lowest price paid for one share of Exxon in the past 52 weeks: $49⅜, or $49.375
3. Name of the company: Exxon
4. Ticker symbol or letters that identify a stock for trading: Xon
5. Total dividends paid per share during the last 12 months: $1.64
6. Yield percentage, or the percentage of return based on the dividend and current price of the stock: $1.64 ÷ $60.875 = 0.027 = 2.7%
7. Price-earnings (PE) ratio—the price of a share of stock divided by the corporation's earnings per share of stock outstanding over the last 12 months: 18
8. Number of shares of Exxon traded during the day, expressed in hundreds of shares: 5,831,800
9. Highest price paid for one share of Exxon during the day: $60¹⁵⁄₁₆, or $60.938
10. Lowest price paid for one share of Exxon during the day: $58⅞, or $58.875
11. Price paid in the close transaction of the day: $60⅞, or $60.875
12. Difference between the price paid for the last share today and the price paid for the last share on the previous day: + 1⅞, or plus $1.875 (in Wall Street terms, Exxon "closed up 1⅞" on this day)

SOURCE: Reprinted by permission of *The Wall Street Journal,* © 1998 by Dow Jones & Company. All rights reserved worldwide.

Classification of Stock Investments

When evaluating a stock investment, stockbrokers, financial planners, and investors often classify stocks into different categories. We will describe six commonly used classifications.

blue-chip stock

A **blue-chip stock** is a safe investment that generally attracts conservative investors. Stocks of this kind are issued by the strongest and most respected companies, such as AT&T, General Electric, and Kellogg. Characteristics to watch for when evaluating this type of stock include leadership in an industrial group, a history of stable earnings, and consistency in paying dividends.

income stock

An **income stock** is a stock that pays higher than average dividends. To be able to pay above-average dividends, a corporation must have a steady, predictable source of income. Stocks issued by Bristol-Myers Squibb, Dow Chemical, and Royal Dutch/Shell are often purchased for their higher-than-average dividends. Also, stocks issued by electric, gas, telephone, and other utility companies are generally classified as income stocks. Many investors seeking income may also include quality preferred stock issues in their portfolios.

growth stock

A **growth stock** is a stock issued by a corporation earning profits above the average profits of all the firms in the economy. Key factors to evaluate when choosing a growth stock include an expanding product line of quality merchandise and an effective research and development department. Retail expansion, state-of-the-art manufacturing facilities, and expansion into international markets are also characteristic of growth stocks. In fact, most growth companies retain a large part of their earnings to pay for their research and development efforts. As a result, such companies generally pay out less than 30 percent of their earnings in dividends to their stockholders. In the late-1990s, typical growth stocks include Adobe Systems; Southwest Airlines; Just For Feet, Inc.; and Home Depot.

cyclical stock

A **cyclical stock** is a stock that follows the business cycle of advances and declines in the economy. When the economy expands, the market value of a cyclical stock increases. When the economy declines, the market value of a cyclical stock decreases. Most cyclical stocks are in basic industries such as automobiles, steel, paper, and heavy manufacturing. Investors try to buy cyclical stocks just before the economy expands and sell them just before it declines. Assuming the economy continues to expand, most financial experts are predicting that Ford (automotive), Phelps Dodge (metals), and Motorola (electronics) will increase in value because of increased demand for their products during the first part of the next century.

defensive stock

A **defensive stock** is a stock that remains stable during declines in the economy. Generally, companies that issue such stocks have a history of stable earnings and are able to maintain dividend payments to stockholders during periods of economic decline. Many stocks that are classified as income stocks are also classified as defensive stocks because of their stable earnings and consistent dividend policies. Stocks in this classification include Procter & Gamble, Kellogg, and stocks issued by utility companies.

penny stock

A **penny stock** is a stock that typically sells for $1 to $10.[4] These stocks are issued by new companies or companies with erratic sales and earnings. Therefore, penny stocks are more volatile than more conservative stocks. These stocks are classified as high-risk investments and are more difficult to research because information about them is hard to find. They are also more difficult to track, and dramatic increases and decreases in market value are common. Unfortunately, when the bubble bursts, these stocks can become worthless. As a result, penny stocks should by purchased only by investors who understand *all* the risks.

Financial Decision
Trade-Off

Stock Advisory Services

In addition to newspapers, sources of information investors can use to evaluate potential stock investments are stock advisory services and the Internet. In choosing among the hundreds of stock advisory services that charge fees for their information, the investor must consider both the quality and the quantity of the information they provide. The information stock advisory services provide ranges from simple alphabetical listings to detailed financial reports.

Standard & Poor's reports, Value Line, and Moody's Investors Service were briefly described in the last chapter. Here we will examine a detailed report for Reebok International Ltd., a worldwide manufacturer and distributor of athletic footwear and apparel, that is published in the *Moody's Handbook of Common Stock* (see Exhibit 14–5).

The basic report illustrated in Exhibit 14–5 consists of six main sections. The top section of the report provides information about stock prices and capitalization, earnings, and dividends for Reebok. The "Background" section describes the company's major operations in detail. It lists specific products, including footwear, apparel for men, women, and children, and other business lines that complement the firm's existing product line. The next section, "Recent Developments," provides current information about the company's net income and sales revenue. Reebok reported net income of $20.3 million during the second quarter of 1997. During the same period, sales climbed 2.9 percent to $841.1 million. The "Prospects" section describes the company's outlook. It states, "The company expects substantial margin pressure over the next year or so as a

EXHIBIT 14–5   **Moody's Report for Reebok International, Ltd.**

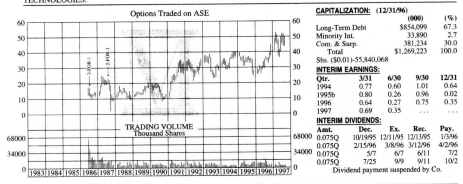

REEBOK INTERNATIONAL LTD.

LISTED	SYM.	LTPS♦	STPS♦	IND. DIV.	REC. PRICE	RANGE (52-WKS.)	YLD.	'96 YR.-END PR.
NYSE	RBK	90.3	97.2	- - -	51⅝	52⅞ - 32½	- - -	42

UPPER MEDIUM GRADE. GROSS MARGINS ARE EXPECTED TO SUFFER FROM CONTINUING INVESTMENT IN TECHNOLOGIES.

CAPITALIZATION: (12/31/96)

	(000)	(%)
Long-Term Debt	$854,099	67.3
Minority Int.	33,890	2.7
Com. & Surp.	381,234	30.0
Total	$1,269,223	100.0

Shs. ($0.01)-55,840,068

INTERIM EARNINGS:

Qtr.	3/31	6/30	9/30	12/31
1994	0.77	0.60	1.01	0.64
1995b	0.80	0.26	0.96	0.02
1996	0.64	0.27	0.75	0.35
1997	0.69	0.35	. . .	. . .

INTERIM DIVIDENDS:

Amt.	Dec.	Ex.	Rec.	Pay.
0.075Q	10/19/95	12/11/95	12/13/95	1/3/96
0.075Q	2/15/96	3/8/96	3/12/96	4/2/96
0.075Q	5/7	6/7	6/11	7/2
0.075Q	7/25	9/9	9/11	10/2

Dividend payment suspended by Co.

BACKGROUND:

Reebok International Ltd. designs, develops, and markets branded footwear and apparel worldwide. Categories in the Reebok footwear division include: aerobic, tennis, fitness, running, basketball, cycling, volleyball, walking and children's athletic footwear. The apparel division designs men's, women's and children's sportswear for aerobics, fitness and running in addition to offering casual clothes. The Rockport Co. is a market leader in casual and dress comfort shoes for men and women. Ellesse designs and markets high-end sports apparel, sportswear and athletic shoes. Avia Group International was sold in June 1996.

RECENT DEVELOPMENTS:

For the quarter ended 6/30/97, net income climbed 2.6% to $20.3 million from $19.8 million in the corresponding 1996 quarter. Net sales were $841.1 million, up 2.9% from $817.6 million in the year-earlier quarter. For the six months ended 6/30/97, net income declined 11.3% to $60.5 million from $68.2 million for the same period in 1996. Net sales rose 2.9% to $1.77 billion from $1.72 billion in the prior-year period. Net sales for the 1996 second quarter and six months included revenues of the Company's Avia subsidiary which was sold in June 1996. These revenues amounted to $22.6 million and $49.4 million in the second quarter and six months of 1996, respectively.

PROSPECTS:

The Company expects substantial margin pressure over the next year or so as a result of its continuing investment in new technologies. The favorable reception from both retailers and consumers concerning the new proprietary technologies has caused the Company to ramp up capacity faster than originally anticipated. While margins on these products should improve over the long term, they will return less than normal gross margins during the start-up phase. The Company will continue to expand its brand presence in better retail locations around the world.

STATISTICS:

YEAR	GROSS REVS. ($mill.)	OPER. PROFIT MARGIN %	RET. ON EQUITY %	NET INCOME ($mill.)	WORK CAP. ($mill.)	SENIOR CAPITAL ($mill.)	SHARES (000)	EARN. PER SH.$	DIV. PER SH.$	DIV. PAY. %	PRICE RANGE	P/E RATIO	AVG. YIELD %
87	1,389.2	22.4	28.3	165.2	267.7	12.6	112,561	1.49	0.15	10	25⅛ - 2⅛	9.1	1.1
88	1,785.9	13.7	19.8	137.0	457.8	112.7	112,951	1.20	0.275	23	18⅜ - 9½	11.6	2.0
89	1,822.1	15.5	20.7	175.0	581.3	110.3	113,856	1.53	0.30	20	19⅝ - 11⅛	10.0	2.0
90	2,159.2	13.8	17.7	176.6	735.9	105.8	114,428	1.54	0.30	19	20 - 8⅛	9.1	2.1
91	2,734.5	14.9	28.5	234.7	602.6	170.4	90,974	2.37	0.30	13	35⅛ - 10¾	9.7	1.3
92	3,022.6	7.8	13.7	a114.8	674.6	116.0	89,363	a1.24	0.30	24	35⅝ - 21⅜	23.0	1.1
93	2,893.9	13.3	26.4	223.4	730.8	134.2	83,691	2.53	0.30	12	38⅝ - 23	12.2	1.0
94	3,280.4	13.0	25.7	254.5	831.9	131.8	80,945	3.02	0.30	10	40¼ - 28⅜	11.4	0.9
95	3,481.5	8.3	18.4	b164.8	911.0	254.2	74,804	2.07	0.30	14	39⅝ - 24⅛	15.4	0.9
96	**3,478.6**	**8.0**	**36.4**	**139.0**	**946.1**	**854.1**	**55,840**	**2.00**	**0.30**	**15**	**45¼ - 25⅜**	**17.7**	**0.8**

♦Long-Term Price Score — Short-Term Price Score; See page 4a. STATISTICS ARE AS ORIGINALLY REPORTED. Adjusted for 2-for-1 stock split, 8/87; 3-for-1, 6/86. a-Incl. a net restructuring charge of $135.4 million and a net gain of $18 mill. from sale of stock. b-Incl. special after-tax charge of $44.9 mill.

INCORPORATED:
1979 — MA

PRINCIPAL OFFICE:
100 Technology Center Dr.
Stoughton, MA 02072
Tel.: (617) 341-5000

FAX: (617) 341-5087

ANNUAL MEETING:
In May

NUMBER OF STOCKHOLDERS:
7,179

TRANSFER AGENT(S):
First National Bank of Boston
Boston, MA

REGISTRAR(S):
First National Bank of Boston
Boston, MA

INSTITUTIONAL HOLDINGS:
No. of Institutions: 162
Shares Held: 37,511,793

OFFICERS:
Chmn., Pres. & C.E.O.
P. B. Fireman
Ex. V.P. & C.F.O.
K. Watchmaker
V.P. & Gen. Couns.
B. Nagler
Treasurer
L. S. Vannoni

SOURCE: *Moody's Handbook of Common Stock*, Fall 1997 (New York: Moody's Investors Service, Inc., 1997).

EXHIBIT 14–6   Value Line Report for Reebok International, Ltd.

REEBOK INT'L NYSE-RBK | RECENT PRICE **37** | P/E RATIO **14.2** (Trailing: 15.9 Median: 12.0) | RELATIVE P/E RATIO **0.82** | DIV'D YLD **Nil** | VALUE LINE **1676**

| TIMELINESS **3** Average (Relative Price Performance Next 12 Mos.) | High: | 17.6 | 25.2 | 18.4 | 19.6 | 20.0 | 35.1 | 35.6 | 38.6 | 40.1 | 39.6 | 45.3 | 52.9 | | Target Price Range 2000 2001 2002 |
| | Low: | 4.2 | 7.0 | 9.5 | 11.1 | 8.1 | 10.8 | 21.4 | 23.0 | 28.4 | 24.1 | 25.4 | 36.1 | | |

SAFETY **3** Average
(Scale: 1 Highest to 5 Lowest)
BETA 1.10   (1.00 = Market)

2000-02 PROJECTIONS

	Price	Gain	Ann'l Total Return
High	80	(+115%)	21%
Low	50	(+35%)	8%

Insider Decisions

	D	J	F	M	A	M	J	J	A
to Buy	0	0	0	0	0	0	0	0	0
Options	0	1	1	0	0	0	0	0	0
to Sell	0	0	3	0	0	0	0	1	0

Institutional Decisions

	4Q'96	1Q'97	2Q'97
to Buy	70	68	72
to Sell	83	82	74
Hld's(000)	37393	38765	38497

Percent shares traded: 18.0, 12.0, 6.0

Options: ASE
Shaded area indicates recession
Relative Price Strength

1981	1982	1983	1984	1985	1986	1987	1988	1989	1990	1991	1992	1993	1994	1995	1996	1997	1998	© VALUE LINE PUB., INC.	00-02	
.02	.05	.17	.84	3.20	8.70	12.34	15.81	16.00	18.87	30.06	33.82	34.58	40.53	46.54	62.30	64.60	70.80	Sales per sh	83.35	
--	--	.01	.08	.42	1.29	1.65	1.42	1.79	1.86	3.00	3.10	3.18	3.61	3.32	3.32	3.35	3.90	"Cash Flow" per sh	5.95	
--	--	.01	.08	.45	1.28	1.49	1.20	1.53	1.54	2.37	2.51	2.61	3.02	2.65	2.00	2.50	3.00	Earnings per sh A	5.00	
--	--	--	--	--	--	.20	.30	.30	.30	.30	.30	.30	.30	.30	.23	Nil	Nil	Div'ds Decl'd per sh E	.30	
--	--	--	.02	.02	.14	.41	.28	.16	.21	.41	.41	.24	.76	.35	.70	.70	.90	Cap'l Spending per sh	.90	
--	--	.01	.09	.93	2.82	5.20	6.12	7.42	8.71	9.05	9.38	10.12	12.24	11.97	6.83	9.30	12.40	Book Value per sh B	24.20	
75.34	75.34	75.34	78.33	95.90	105.67	112.56	112.95	113.86	114.43	90.97	89.36	83.69	80.94	74.80	55.84	56.50	56.50	Common Shs Outst'g C	57.00	
--	--	--	--	9.4	8.6	11.8	11.3	9.6	9.9	10.6	11.9	11.9	11.4	12.8	15.3	Bold figures are Value Line estimates		Avg Ann'l P/E Ratio	13.0	
--	--	--	--	.76	.58	.79	.94	.73	.74	.68	.72	.70	.75	.86	1.03			Relative P/E Ratio	.95	
--	--	--	--	--	--	1.1%	2.2%	2.1%	2.0%	1.2%	1.0%	1.0%	.9%	.9%	.7%			Avg Ann'l Div'd Yield	.5%	

CAPITAL STRUCTURE as of 9/30/97
Total Debt $873.6 mill. Due in 5 Yrs $774.8 mill.
LT Debt $683.0 mill.   LT Interest $47.8 mill.
(57% of Cap'l)

Leases, Uncapitalized Annual rentals $34.1 mill.

Pension Liability None

Pfd Stock None

Common Stock 56,305,774 shs.   (43% of Cap'l)
as of 11/7/97

	1389.2	1785.9	1822.1	2159.2	2734.5	3022.6	2893.9	3280.4	3481.5	3478.6	3650	4000	Sales ($mill)	4750
	23.1%	14.7%	17.0%	15.5%	16.3%	14.4%	14.9%	14.0%	11.6%	8.9%	8.8%	9.0%	Operating Margin	11.0%
	20.1	23.4	28.5	36.5	38.5	44.3	35.6	37.4	38.6	46.3	44.0	46.0	Depreciation ($mill)	55.0
	165.2	137.0	175.0	176.6	234.7	232.3	230.5	254.5	209.7	139.0	145	175	Net Profit ($mill)	285
	46.0%	40.6%	39.8%	40.1%	39.8%	39.4%	37.2%	36.9%	36.5%	35.4%	36.0%	34.0%	Income Tax Rate	35.0%
	11.9%	7.7%	9.6%	8.2%	8.6%	7.7%	8.0%	7.8%	6.0%	4.0%	4.0%	4.4%	Net Profit Margin	6.0%
	267.7	457.8	581.3	735.9	602.6	674.6	730.7	831.9	910.9	946.1	905	1030	Working Cap'l ($mill)	1365
	12.6	112.7	110.3	105.8	170.4	116.0	134.2	131.8	254.2	854.1	640	570	Long-Term Debt ($mill)	150
	584.8	690.7	844.3	996.7	823.5	838.7	846.6	990.5	895.3	381.2	525	700	Net Worth ($mill)	1380
	27.7%	17.3%	18.9%	16.6%	25.0%	25.3%	24.6%	23.2%	19.0%	12.8%	14.5%	15.5%	% Earned Total Cap'l	19.0%
	28.3%	19.8%	20.7%	17.7%	28.5%	27.7%	27.2%	25.7%	23.4%	36.4%	27.5%	25.0%	% Earned Net Worth	20.5%
	24.5%	16.2%	16.7%	14.3%	24.8%	24.4%	24.1%	23.2%	20.8%	31.0%	27.5%	25.0%	% Retained to Com Eq	19.5%
	13%	19%	19%	19%	13%	12%	11%	10%	11%	15%	Nil	Nil	% All Div'ds to Net Prof	6%

CURRENT POSITION (in mill)

	1995	1996	9/30/97
Cash Assets	80.4	232.4	139.9
Receivables	506.4	590.5	744.7
Inventory (FIFO)	635.0	544.5	562.8
Other	121.0	95.7	163.5
Current Assets	1342.8	1463.1	1610.9
Accts Payable	166.0	194.4	193.2
Debt Due	67.6	85.7	190.6
Other	198.3	234.9	294.0
Current Liab.	431.9	517.0	677.8

ANNUAL RATES

of change (per sh)	Past 10 Yrs.	Past 5 Yrs.	Est'd '94-'96 to '00-'02
Sales	28.0%	18.0%	9.0%
"Cash Flow"	19.0%	9.0%	9.5%
Earnings	15.5%	7.0%	12.0%
Dividends	--	-1.5%	1.5%
Book Value	23.5%	4.5%	15.0%

QUARTERLY SALES ($ mill.)

Calendar	Mar.31	Jun.30	Sep.30	Dec.31	Full Year
1994	857.4	776.8	937.1	709.1	3280.4
1995	935.5	788.7	1006	751.3	3481.5
1996	902.9	817.6	970.1	788.0	3478.6
1997	930.0	841.1	1009.1	869.8	3650
1998	1020	930	1100	950	4000

EARNINGS PER SHARE A

Calendar	Mar.31	Jun.30	Sep.30	Dec.31	Full Year
1994	.77	.60	1.01	.64	3.02
1995	.80	.40	.96	.46	D2.65
1996	.64	.27	.75	.35	D2.00
1997	.69	.35	.94	.52	2.50
1998	.80	.47	1.08	.65	3.00

QUARTERLY DIVIDENDS PAID E

Calendar	Mar.31	Jun.30	Sep.30	Dec.31	Full Year
1993	.075	.075	.075	.075	.30
1994	.075	.075	.075	.075	.30
1995	.075	.075	.075	.075	.30
1996	.075	.075	.075	--	.225
1997	--	--	--	--	--

BUSINESS: Reebok International, Ltd. designs, develops, and markets high-quality footwear and apparel products. 1996 sales breakdown: Reebok Footwear (domestic), 34%; Reebok Apparel (domestic), 9%; Reebok Int'l (footwear and apparel combined), 42%; Rockport, 13%; Avia, 2%. Sources prod. mostly from: China (34%), Indonesia (30%), Thailand (12%), and the Philippines (13%). For-eign sales: 44% of '96 total; advertising exp., 5.8%. Foot Locker, a division of Woolworth Corp., is the largest customer. 1996 depr. rate: 13.0%. Has 6,900 empl., 7,180 shrhldrs. Off./ Dir. own 15.0% of common stock (3/97 Proxy). Chrmn., Pres., and C.E.O.: P. Fireman. Inc.: MA. Addr.: 100 Technology Center Dr., Stoughton, MA 02072. Tel.: 617-341-5000. Internet: http://www.reebok.com.

We believe that a sales turnaround for Reebok is on the horizon, led by its new technology product lines. The company's domestic footwear sales have been sluggish through the first nine months of 1997, leading to a decline in net income of over 5% (excluding nonrecurring gains this year) compared to the prior-year period. However, Reebok has some exciting new product introductions planned for the December period, led by Allen Iverson's *DMX* basketball shoe (*The Answer*). This shoe, along with other *DMX* basketball shoes and *3D Ultralite* running shoes, will likely help U.S. footwear sales rebound beginning in the fourth quarter. All told, we expect the company's three new technology lines to represent about 25% of overall fourth-quarter sales versus only 12% in the September period.

We expect share earnings to increase by 20% in 1998. In addition to the sales growth that we anticipate from the innovative technology products, Reebok is also improving its distribution presence. It is rapidly increasing its sales to athletic-specialty stores, which generally enhance brand image and expose the shoes to the key trend setters, youth. This channel currently represents about 35% of overall domestic sales (versus 20% last year), and its backlog for the six months ending March 31, 1998, is up by 65%.

Margins, which will likely remain under pressure through the first half of next year, should help fuel earnings growth out to decade's end. Start-up costs associated with the introduction of the new lines have held margins down in the past few quarters. However, we expect revenues from these lines to begin to offset the expenses in the third quarter of 1998, resulting in wider margins. Furthermore, Reebok is consolidating its warehouses and implementing a global information system in Europe. We believe that these moves will significantly reduce operating expenses, commencing in 1999.

Reebok's stock price has declined by over 25% since our August report, due primarily, we think, to the overall weakness in the athletic footwear industry. But at its current quotation, the equity's 3- to 5-year appreciation potential is well above the market median.
Jonathan B. Chappell November 21, 1997

(A) Primary earnings. Excludes nonrecurring gains/(losses): '92, ($1.23); '93, (8¢); '95, (58¢); '97Q3, 32¢. Next earnings report due early February.
(B) Includes intangibles. In '96: $69.7 mill., $1.25 per share.
(C) In millions, adjusted for stock splits.
(D) Quarterly earnings do not sum to annual total due to changes in shares outstanding.
(E) Dividend suspended October 1996.

Company's Financial Strength	B++
Stock's Price Stability	35
Price Growth Persistence	65
Earnings Predictability	70

To subscribe call 1-800-833-0046.

result of its continuing investment in new technologies." The "Statistics" section provides important data on the company for the past 10 years. Among the topics included in this section are gross revenues, operating profit margin, return on equity, and net income. The final section of the report states, among other things, when and where the company was incorporated, where its principal office is located, who its transfer agent is, and who its main corporate officers are.

Exhibit 14–6 on page 438 presents a detailed research report for Reebok published by Value Line. While other stock advisory services provide basically the same types of information as that in Exhibits 14–5 and 14–6, it is the investor's job to interpret such information and decide whether the company's stock is a good investment. Online computer services such as America Online, CompuServe, Prodigy, and the Internet, may be used to research companies and to obtain current stock prices.

Corporate News

As mentioned in Chapter 13, the federal government requires corporations selling new issues of securities to disclose information about corporate earnings, assets and liabilities, products or services, and the qualifications of top management in a prospectus that they must give to investors. In addition to a prospectus, all publicly owned corporations send their stockholders an annual report and quarterly reports that contain detailed financial data. Even if you're not a stockholder, you can obtain an annual report from the corporation. For most corporations, all it takes is a call to an 800 telephone number. A written request to the corporation's headquarters can also help you obtain an annual report. To see how the information contained in an annual report can help you choose stock investments, read the accompanying Financial Planning for Life's Situation feature.

It is also possible to obtain much of the same information contained in a corporate annual report through the Internet. Today most corporations have a home page. Three factors make information obtained from the Internet especially useful. First, it is easily accessible. All you have to do is make an Internet connection and type in the name of the corporation. Most corporations provide not only financial information about the corporation but also the most recent news and press releases, information about new products, and even employment opportunities. Second, the information about a corporation obtained on the Internet is up to date. Finally, the Internet may provide more information about a corporation than is available in an annual report, quarterly reports, or other corporate publications.

Factors That Influence the Price of a Stock

bull market

bear market

A **bull market** occurs when investors are optimistic about a nation's economy and buy stocks. In a bull market, the fact that more investors are buying stock causes the value for both individual stocks and the stock market as a whole to increase. A **bear market** occurs when investors are pessimistic about the nation's economy and sell stocks. Because more investors are selling stock, the value of both individual stocks and the stock market as a whole declines.

But how do you determine whether it is the right time to buy or sell a particular stock? Many factors affect the market value of a stock. Therefore, you must also consider potential sales revenues, profits or losses, cash flow, and other important fundamentals when determining whether a stock will increase or decrease in value. In the remainder of this section, we examine numerical measures for a corporation and the fundamental, technical, and efficient market theories that investors use to determine whether a stock is priced right.

FINANCIAL PLANNING FOR LIFE'S SITUATIONS

GETTING TO THE BASICS OF ANNUAL REPORTS

One of the best resources you can use to determine the soundness of a stock investment is a corporation's annual report. These reports are an excellent tool for learning about a company, its management, its past performance, and its goals. But while thumbing through these glossy publications, you must always keep in mind that corporations use this medium to "toot their own horn." The letter from the chair of the board, the upbeat, smiling faces of the employees, and the artistic layout and beautiful photographs are nice to look at, but it's the accounting statements and footnotes that give the true picture of the financial health of a corporation. Understanding the items presented on these pages tucked away in the back of the report is the real key in determining if a company is making a profit. Once you know the basics of reading annual reports you will be in a better position to evaluate different investment opportunities.

Experts recommend that before investing you review and compare the annual reports a corporation has published over the last three years. Read the shareholders' letters to see if they met their goals each year. Are any areas of concern mentioned? Are the facts presented in a straightforward manner, or do you have to struggle to interpret their meaning? Learn to read between the lines to separate the hype from the truth. And watch for words like *except for,* *challenges,* and *contingencies.* Next, turn to the accounting statements section of the report. This is where you can compare the corporation's financial position by noting changes in its current assets, current liabilities, inventories, total liabilities, and owners' equity. Information on the income statement will enable you to determine if the corporation earned a profit. Be sure to look at the amounts reported for sales, expenses, and profit or loss figures. Finally, don't overlook the footnotes: they contain (and sometimes hide) important information.

book value

Numerical Measures for a Corporation   Although little correlation may exist between the market value of a stock and its book value, book value is widely reported in financial publications. Therefore, it deserves mention. The **book value** for a share of stock is determined by deducting all liabilities from the corporation's assets and dividing the remainder by the number of outstanding shares of common stock. For example, assume XYZ Corporation has assets of $6 million and liabilities of $3 million and has issued 100,000 shares of common stock. In this situation, the book value for a share of XYZ stock is $30 per share, as follows:

$$\frac{\overset{\textit{Assets}}{\$6,000,000} - \overset{\textit{Liabilities}}{\$3,000,000}}{100,000 \text{ shares of stock}} = \$30 \text{ per share}$$

Some investors believe they have found a bargain when a stock's market value is about the same as or lower than its book value. *Be warned:* Book value calculations may be misleading, because the dollar amount of assets used in the above formula may be understated or overstated on the firm's financial statements. For example, buildings are depreciated like the firm's other assets, yet buildings may increase, not decrease, in value. This dollar increase for buildings is not reported on a firm's financial statements. As a result, the book value may be incorrect. From a practical standpoint, most financial experts suggest that book value is just one piece of the puzzle and you must consider other factors along with book value when evaluating a possible stock investment.

earnings per share

Earnings per share are a corporation's after-tax earnings divided by the number of outstanding shares of common stock. For example, assume that in 1998 XYZ Corporation has after-tax earnings of $800,000. As mentioned previously, XYZ has 100,000 shares of common stock. This means XYZ's earnings per share are $8 ($800,000 ÷ 100,000 = $8). Most stockholders consider the amount of earnings per share important because it is a measure of the company's profitability. No meaningful average for this measure exists, mainly because the number of shares of a firm's stock is subject to change via stock splits and stock dividends. *As a general rule, however, an increase in earnings per share is a healthy sign for any corporation and its stockholders.*

The **price-earnings (PE) ratio** is the price of a share of stock divided by the corporation's earnings per share of stock outstanding over the last 12 months. For example, assume XYZ Corporation's common stock is selling for $96 a share. As determined earlier, XYZ's earnings per share are $8. XYZ's price-earnings ratio is therefore 12 ($96 ÷ $8 = 12). The price-earnings ratio is a key factor that serious investors use to evaluate stock investments. *A low price-earnings ratio indicates that a stock may be a good investment, and a high price-earnings ratio indicates that it may be a poor investment.* Generally, you should study the price-earnings ratio for a corporation over a period of time. For example, if XYZ's price-earnings ratio has ranged from 12 to 30 over the past three years, its current price-earnings ratio of 12 indicates that it is a potentially good investment. If XYZ's current price-earnings ratio were 27—toward the high end of the range—it may be a poor investment at this time. For most corporations, price-earnings ratios range between 5 and 25.

The **beta** is an index reported in many financial publications that compares the risk associated with a specific stock issue with the risk of the stock market in general. The beta for the stock market in general is 1.0. The majority of stocks have betas between 0.5 and 2.0. Generally, conservative stocks have low betas and speculative stocks have high betas. For example, assume XYZ Corporation's stock has a beta of 0.50. This means its stock is less responsive than the market. When the market in general increases by 10 percent, XYZ's stock will go up 5 percent. If, on the other hand, ABC Corporation has a beta of 2.0, this means ABC's stock is twice as responsive as the market. When the market in general decreases by 10 percent, ABC's stock will go down 20 percent. Take another look at the Value Line report in Exhibit 14–6. The beta for Reebok International is reported at the top on the left side and is 1.10. This means that if the stock market as a whole goes up 10 percent, the market value of Reebok's stock will increase 11 percent. If the value of the stock market as a whole decreases by 10 percent, the market value of Reebok's stock will decrease by 11 percent. Thus, the market value of Reebok's stock is slightly more volatile than the stock market as a whole.

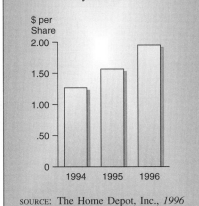

DID YOU KNOW?

One of the reasons Martha and Michael Kahns' (the couple in the opening case) investment in Home Depot has increased is the firm's increase in earnings per share over the last three years.

SOURCE: The Home Depot, Inc., *1996 Annual Report.*

price-earnings (PE) ratio

beta

Investment Theories   Three different investment theories are sometimes used by investors to determine a stock's value. The **fundamental theory** is based on the assumption that a stock's intrinsic or real value is determined by the company's future earnings. If a corporation's expected earnings are higher than its present earnings, the corporation's stock should increase in value. If its expected earnings are lower than its present earnings, the stock should decrease in value. In addition to expected earnings, fundamentalists consider (1) the financial strength of the company, (2) the type of industry the company is in, (3) new-product development, and (4) the economic growth of the overall economy.

fundamental theory

JONATHAN HOENIG SPEAKS
STOCK ME UP

Ever open a lemonade stand?

Hot summer afternoons are always punctuated by the legions of prepubescent tykes determined to corner the market in discount beverages. You might have been one of these young Trumps. I know I was. Running the lemonade stand, even for a few hours, was a harmless exposure to a burgeoning business. I learned about budgeting, inventory, and marketing. And slippage. It was the slippage that eventually leveled my lemony-sweet, tycoon fantasies. What can I say, *I got thirsty!*

Companies are run by management but *owned* by shareholders. When you invest in shares of a publicly traded company, you become part owner; literally *sharing* in the company's success. Successful companies make shareholders money, and that's important! Don't forget: The only reason you should be investing in common stock is to make money. Stick to fundamental research and bet on success.

Fundamental research is Wall Street talk for looking at the books. Is the company profitable? How competent is management? What are the profit margins? What are the earnings?

A bit of research and a lot of common sense are your best tools for making sound investment decisions. Luckily, many of the "professional" tools the hedge fund bigshots use are now available to us all. One great source is FreeEDGAR (www.freeedgar.com), a comprehensive database of Securities and Exchange Commission filings. Hidden in these harmless pages of hypertext are a company's deepest financial secrets. Even a casual sift can turn up a golden nugget. For example, the always-telling 13-D form, filed by any investor owning more than 5 percent of the shares, is a good sign of institutional interest. Savvy researchers can punch up the company's website, check out earnings estimates at Zacks (www.zacks.com.), and buy shares at rock-bottom commissions—all without leaving their chairs.

As for my lemonade stand, it was not a great investment. What I lost in capital I gained in other forms: primarily a really great sugar high.

technical theory

The **technical theory** is based on the assumption that a stock's market value is determined by the forces of supply and demand in the stock market as a whole. It is based *not* on the expected earnings or the intrinsic value of an individual corporation's stock but on factors found in the market as a whole. Typical technical factors are the total number of shares traded, the number of buy orders, and the number of sell orders over a period of time. Technical analysts, sometimes called *chartists,* construct charts that plot past price movements and other market averages. These charts allow them to observe trends and patterns for the market as a whole that enable them to predict whether a specific stock's market value will increase or decrease.

efficient market theory

The **efficient market theory,** sometimes called the *random walk theory,* is based on the assumption that stock price movements are purely random. Advocates of the efficient market theory assume the stock market is completely efficient and buyers and sellers have considered all of the available information about an individual stock. Any news on an individual corporation, an oil embargo, or a change in the tax laws that may affect the value of a stock is quickly absorbed by all investors seeking a profit. Thus, a stock's current market price reflects its true value. The efficient market theory rejects both the fundamental theory and the technical theory. According to this theory, it is impossible for an investor to outperform the average for the stock market as a whole over a long period of time.

Before completing this section, you may want to examine the Financial Planning in Action box on page 443.

Sheet 58

FINANCIAL PLANNING IN ACTION

EVALUATING CORPORATE STOCK

No checklist can serve as a foolproof guide for choosing a common or preferred stock. However, the following questions will help you evaluate a potential stock investment.

Category 1: The Basics

1. What is the corporation's name? _____

    _____

2. What are the corporation's address and telephone number? _____

    _____

3. Have you requested the latest annual report and quarterly report? ☐ Yes   ☐ No

4. What information about the corporation is available on the Internet?

    _____

    _____

5. Where is the stock traded?

    _____

6. What types of products or services does this firm provide? _____

    _____

7. Briefly describe the prospects for this company. (Include significant factors like product development, plans for expansion, plans for mergers, etc.)

    _____

    _____

    _____

    _____

Category 2: Dividend Income

8. Is the corporation currently paying dividends? If so, how much? _____

9. What is the current yield for this stock? _____

10. Has the dividend payout increased or decreased over the past seven years? _____

11. How does the yield for this investment compare with those for other potential investments? _____

    _____

Category 3: Financial Performance

12. Is the corporation profitable? What are the firm's earnings per share for the last 3 years?

    _____

13. Have profits increased over the last seven years?
    ☐ Yes   ☐ No

14. What is the firm's beta? _____

15. What is the firm's current PE ratio? _____

16. How does the firm's PE ratio compare with other firms in general? With other firms in the same industry? _____

    _____

17. Are this year's sales higher than last year's sales?
    ☐ Yes   ☐ No

18. Have sales increased over the last seven years?
    ☐ Yes   ☐ No

19. Briefly describe any other information that you obtained from *Moody's, Value Line, Standard & Poor's,* or other stock advisory services.

    _____

    _____

    _____

A Word of Caution

When you use a checklist, there is always a danger of overlooking important relevant information. The above checklist is not all-inclusive, but it does provide some very sound questions that you should answer before making a decision to invest in stock. Quite simply, it is a place to start. If you need other information, *you* are responsible for obtaining it and for determining how it affects your potential investment.

1. What sources of information would you use to evaluate a stock issue?
2. How would you define (1) a blue-chip stock, (2) an income stock, (3) a growth stock, (4) a cyclical stock, (5) a defensive stock, and (6) a penny stock?
3. What are the formulas for book value, earnings per share, and the price-earnings ratio?
4. Do you think the fundamental theory, the technical theory, or the efficient market theory best describes price movements for the stock market? Why?

BUYING AND SELLING STOCKS

L.O.4 Describe how stocks are bought and sold.

primary market

investment bank

initial public offering (IPO)

To purchase a pair of Levi Strauss jeans, you simply walk into a store that sells Levi's, choose a pair, and pay for your purchase. To purchase common or preferred stock, you generally have to work through a financial representative. In turn, your financial representative must buy the stock in either the primary or secondary market. In the **primary market,** you purchase financial securities, via an investment bank or other representative, from the issuer of those securities. An **investment bank** is a financial firm that assists corporations in raising funds, usually by helping to sell new security issues.

New security issues sold through an investment bank can be issued by corporations that have sold stocks and bonds before and need to sell new issues to raise additional financing. The new securities can also be initial public offerings. An **initial public offering (IPO)** occurs when a corporation sells stock to the general public for the first time. Since 1990, more than 3,400 different IPOs have raised over $210 billion that was used to start new businesses or finance new corporate growth and expansion.[5] *Be warned:* The promise of quick profits often lures investors to purchase IPOs. An IPO is generally classified as a high-risk investment—one made in the hope of earning a relatively large profit in a short time. Depending on the corporation selling the new security, IPOs are usually too risky for most people.

Examples of stocks sold through the primary market are the common stock issues sold by Home Depot, Microsoft, and Lucent Technologies. Investors bought these stocks through brokerage firms acting as agents for an investment banking firm, and the money they paid for common stock flowed to the corporations that issued the stock. In fact, the only time the corporation receives money from the sale of stock is when its stock is sold in the primary market.

secondary market

After a stock has been sold through the primary market, it is traded through the secondary market. The **secondary market** is a market for existing financial securities that are currently traded among investors. Once the above stocks are sold in the primary market, they can be sold time and again in the secondary market. The fact that stocks can be sold in the secondary market improves the liquidity of stock investments because the money you pay for stock goes to the seller of the stock.

Primary Markets for Stocks

How would you sell $100 million worth of common stocks or preferred stocks? For a large corporation, the decision to sell stocks is often complicated, time consuming, and expensive. There are basically two methods.

First, a large corporation may use an investment bank to sell and distribute the new stock issue. Most large corporations that need a lot of financing use this method. If this method is used, analysts for the investment bank examine the corporation's financial position to determine whether the new issue is financially sound and how difficult it will be to sell.

If the investment bank is satisfied that the new stock is a good risk, it will buy the stock and then resell the stock to its customers—commercial banks, insurance companies, pension funds, mutual funds, and the general public. The investment bank's commission, or spread, ranges from less than 1 percent for a utility firm to as much as 25 percent for a small company selling stock for the first time.[6] The size of the spread depends on the quality and financial health of the issuing corporation. The commission allows the investment bank to make a profit while guaranteeing that the corporation will receive the financing it needs.

If the investment bank's analysts believe the new issue will be difficult to sell, the investment bank may agree to take the stock on a best-efforts basis, without guaranteeing that the stock will be sold. Because the corporation must take back any unsold stocks after a reasonable time, most large corporations are unwilling to accept this arrangement. If the stock issue is too large for one investment bank, a group of investment bankers may form an *underwriting syndicate*. Then each member of the syndicate is responsible for selling only a part of the new issue.

The second method used by a corporation trying to obtain financing through the primary market is to sell directly to current stockholders. Usually, promotional materials describing the new stock issue are mailed to current stockholders. These stockholders may then purchase the stock directly from the corporation. As mentioned earlier in this chapter, most states require that a provision for preemptive rights be included in the charters of corporations chartered within their boundaries. This provision gives current stockholders the right to purchase any new stock the corporation issues before it is offered to the general public.

You may ask, "Why would a corporation try to sell its own stock?" The most obvious reason for doing so is to avoid the investment bank's commission. Of course, a corporation's ability to sell a new stock issue without the aid of an investment bank is tied directly to investors' perception of the corporation's financial health.

DID YOU KNOW?

To diversify their holdings, Americans are buying foreign stocks.

SOURCE: U.S. Bureau of the Census, *Statistical Abstract of the United States: 1996*, 116th ed. (Washington, DC: U.S. Government Printing Office, 1996).

Secondary Markets for Stocks

account executive

How do you buy or sell stock in the secondary market? To purchase common or preferred stock, you usually have to work through a financial representative—your account executive. An **account executive**, or *stockbroker,* is a licensed individual who buys or sells securities for his or her clients. (Actually, *account executive* is the more descriptive title because such individuals handle all types of securities, not just stocks.) Then your account executive must buy or sell for you in a securities marketplace, at a securities exchange or through the over-the-counter market.

securities exchange

Securities Exchanges   A **securities exchange** is a marketplace where member brokers who represent investors meet to buy and sell securities. The securities sold at a particular exchange must first be listed, or accepted for trading, at that exchange. Generally, the securities issued by nationwide corporations are traded at either the New York Stock Exchange or the American Stock Exchange. The securities of regional corporations are traded at smaller, regional exchanges. These exchanges are located in Chicago, San Francisco,

Philadelphia, Boston, and several other cities. The securities of very large corporations may be traded at more than one exchange. American firms that do business abroad may also be listed on foreign securities exchanges—in Tokyo, London, or Paris, for example.

The New York Stock Exchange (NYSE) is the largest securities exchange in the United States. This exchange lists stocks for over 2,500 corporations with a total market value of about $5 trillion.[7] The NYSE has 1,366 members, or *seats*. Most of these members represent brokerage firms that charge commissions on security trades made by their representatives for their customers. Other members are called *specialists* or *specialist firms*. A **specialist** is an individual on the floor of the exchange who buys *or* sells a particular stock in an effort to maintain an orderly market.

specialist

The cost of a seat is determined largely by sales volume and stock prices on the exchange. The lowest price for a seat on the NYSE in the 1900s was $17,000, paid in 1942. In the late 1990s, a seat sold for approximately $1 million.

Before a corporation's stock is approved for listing on the NYSE, the corporation must meet five criteria:

1. Its annual earnings before income taxes must be at least $2.5 million in the most recent year.
2. It must own net tangible assets valued at $40 million or more.
3. The market value of its publicly held stock must equal or exceed $40 million.
4. At least 1.1 million shares of its common stock must be publicly owned.
5. At least 2,000 stockholders must each own 100 or more shares of its stock.

The American Stock Exchange (AMEX) and various regional exchanges also have listing requirements, but typically these are less stringent than the NYSE requirements. The stock of corporations that cannot meet the NYSE requirements, find it too expensive to be listed on the NYSE, or choose not to be listed on the NYSE is often traded on the American Stock Exchange, on one of the regional exchanges, or through the over-the-counter market.

The Over-the-Counter Market   Not all securities are traded on organized exchanges. Stocks issued by several thousand companies are traded in the over-the-counter market. The **over-the-counter (OTC) market** is a network of dealers who buy and sell the stocks of corporations that are not listed on a securities exchange. Today these stocks are not really traded over the counter. The term was coined more than 100 years ago when securities were sold "over the counter" in stores and banks.

over-the-counter (OTC) market

Most over-the-counter securities are traded through NASDAQ (pronounced "nazz-dack"). **NASDAQ** is an electronic marketplace for almost 5,000 different stocks. In addition to providing price information, this computerized system allows investors to buy and sell shares of companies listed on NASDAQ. When you want to buy or sell shares of a company that trades on NASDAQ—say, Microsoft—your account executive sends your order into the NASDAQ computer system, where it shows up on the screen with all the other orders from people who want to buy or sell Microsoft. Then a NASDAQ specialist sitting at a computer terminal matches buy and sell orders for Microsoft. Once a match is found, your order is completed.

NASDAQ

Begun in 1971 and regulated by the National Association of Securities Dealers, NASDAQ is the third largest securities market in the world in terms of volume, trailing only the NYSE and Tokyo Stock Exchange. It is known for its innovative, forward-looking growth companies. Although many securities are issued by smaller companies, some large firms, including Intel, Microsoft, MCI, Apple Computer, and Lotus Development, also trade on NASDAQ.

Brokerage Firms and Account Executives

Sheet 61

While all account executives can buy or sell stock for you, most investors expect more from their account executives. Ideally, an account executive should provide information and advice to be used in evaluating potential investments. Many investors begin their search for an account executive by asking friends or business associates for recommendations. This is a logical starting point, but remember that some account executives are conservative while others are more risk oriented.

Before choosing an account executive, you should have already determined your short-term and long-term financial objectives. Then you must be careful to communicate those objectives to the account executive so that he or she can do a better job of advising you. Needless to say, account executives may err in their investment recommendations. To help avoid a situation in which your account executive's recommendations are automatically implemented, you should be *actively* involved in the decisions of your investment program and you should never allow your account executive to use his or her discretion without your approval. Watch your account for signs of churning.

churning

Churning is excessive buying and selling of securities to generate commissions. From a total dollar return standpoint, this practice usually leaves the client worse off or at least no better off. Churning is illegal under the rules established by the Securities and Exchange Commission; however, it may be difficult to prove. Finally, keep in mind that account executives generally are not liable for client losses that result from their recommendations. In fact, most brokerage firms require new clients to sign a statement in which they promise to submit any complaints to an arbitration board. This arbitration clause generally prevents a client from suing an account executive or a brokerage firm. Above all, remember you are investing *your* money and you should make the final decisions with the help of your account executive.

The Typical Transaction   Once you and your account executive have decided on a particular transaction, it is time to execute an order to buy or sell. Today most investors telephone their account executives and place a market, limit, stop, or discretionary order. A

market order

market order is a request to buy or sell a stock at the current market value. Since the stock exchange is an auction market, the account executive's representative will try to get the best price available and the transaction will be completed as soon as possible.

Exhibit 14–7 illustrates how a market order to sell stock is actually executed. You should note two things. First, every stock listed on the NYSE is traded at a specific computer-equipped trading post on the floor of the exchange. A computer monitor above the post indicates current price information for all stocks traded at each trading post. Second, each transaction is recorded, and the pertinent information (stock symbol, number of shares, and price) is transmitted to interested parties through a communications network called a *ticker tape*. Payment for stocks is generally required within three business days of the transaction. Then, in about four to six weeks, a stock certificate is sent to the purchaser of the stock, unless the securities are left with the brokerage firm for safekeeping. Today it is common practice for investors to leave stock certificates with a brokerage firm. Because the stock certificates are in the broker's care, transfers when the stock is sold are much easier. The phrase "left in the street name" is used to describe investor-owned securities held by a brokerage firm.

limit order

A **limit order** is a request to buy or sell a stock at a specified price. When you purchase stock, a limit order ensures that you will buy at the best possible price but not above a specified dollar amount. When you sell stock, a limit order ensures that you will sell at the best possible price but not below a specified dollar amount. For example, if you place

EXHIBIT 14–7

**The Steps Involved
in a Typical
Transaction for
Stock Traded
on the New York
Stock Exchange**

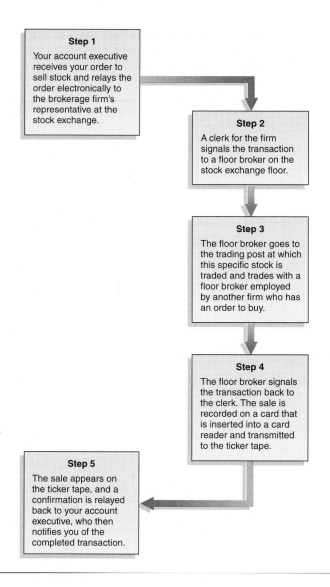

a limit order to buy Kellogg common stock for $86 a share, the stock will not be purchased until the price drops to $86 a share or lower. Likewise, if your limit order is to sell Kellogg for $86 a share, the stock will not be sold until the price rises to $86 a share or higher. *Be warned:* Limit orders are executed if and when the specified price or better is reached and *all* other previously received orders have been fulfilled. Let's assume you enter a limit order to purchase Microsoft stock at $135. If the stock drops to $135, all purchase orders will be filled in the sequence in which they were received. If the price of Microsoft begins to increase before your order can be filled, you may miss an investment opportunity because you were unable to buy the stock at the specified price.

Many stockholders are certain that they want to sell their stock if it reaches a specified price. A limit order does not guarantee that this will be done. With a limit order, as mentioned above, orders by other investors may be placed ahead of your order. If you want to guarantee that your order will be executed, you place a special type of limit order known as a stop order. A **stop order** (sometimes called a *stop-loss order*) is an order to sell a particular stock at the next available opportunity after its market price reaches a

stop order

specified amount. This type of order is used to protect an investor against a sharp drop in price and thus stop the dollar loss on a stock investment. For example, assume you purchased General Motors common stock at $56 a share. Two weeks after making your investment, General Motors is facing multiple product liability lawsuits. Fearing that the market value of your stock will decrease, you enter a stop order to sell your General Motors stock at $48. This means that if the price of the stock decreases to $48 or lower, the account executive will sell it. While a stop order does not guarantee that your stock will be sold at the price you specified, it does guarantee that it will be sold at the next available opportunity. Both limit and stop orders may be good for one day, one week, one month, or good until canceled (GTC).

discretionary order

You can also choose to place a discretionary order. A **discretionary order** is an order to buy or sell a security that lets the account executive decide when to execute the transaction and at what price. Financial planners advise against using a discretionary order for two reasons. First, a discretionary order gives the account executive a great deal of authority. If the account executive makes a mistake, it is the investor who suffers the dollar loss. Second, financial planners argue that only investors (with the help of their account executives) should make investment decisions.

Computerized Transaction   While most people still prefer to use telephone orders to buy and sell stocks, a growing number of investors are using computers to complete security transactions. A good investment software package can help you evaluate potential investments, monitor the value of your investments, *and* place buy and sell orders online. As a rule of thumb, the more active the investor is, the more sense it makes to use computers. Other reasons that justify using a computer include

1. The size of your investment portfolio.
2. The ability to manage your investments closely.
3. The capability of your computer and the software package.

While computers can make the investment process easier and faster, you should realize that *you* are still responsible for analyzing the information and making the final decision to buy or sell a security. All the computer does is provide more information and, in most cases, complete transactions more quickly and economically.

Commission Charges   Most brokerage firms have a minimum commission ranging from $25 to $40 for buying and selling stock. Additional commission charges are based on the number of shares and the value of stock bought and sold. On the trading floor of a stock exchange, stocks are traded in round lots or odd lots. A **round lot** is 100 shares or multiples of 100 shares of a particular stock. An **odd lot** is fewer than 100 shares of a particular stock. Exhibit 14–8 shows typical commission charges for stock transactions.

round lot

odd lot

Notice that the commission full-service brokers charge is higher than that charged by discount brokers or firms that let investors trade online. Full-service brokers usually spend more time with each client and provide research information. Discount brokers, on the other hand, generally just buy or sell securities on behalf of the client. When you choose a discount broker, you should understand that you will have to make your own decisions. In fact, many discount brokers charge for research information. Like discount brokers, firms that let investors buy or sell stocks online charge for research information if it is available. *Be warned:* A discount brokerage firm may charge higher commissions than a full-service brokerage firm. This generally occurs when the transaction is small, involving a total dollar amount of less than $1,000, and the investor is charged the discount brokerage firm's minimum commission charge.

Exhibit 14–8

Typical Commission Charges for Stock Transactions through a Full-Service Broker and a Discount Broker

Brokerage Firm	Commissions (100 shares at $30 per share)	Brokerage Firm	Commissions (100 shares at $30 per share)
Full Service		**Discount**	
Dean Witter	$84	Charles Schwab	$55
A. G. Edwards	83	Fidelity	54
Kemper	88	Olde Discount	40
Merrill Lynch	86	Quick & Reilly	49
Paine Webber	89	**Electronic Trading**	
Prudential	90	Ameritrade	$ 8
Smith Barney Shearson	91	E. Schwab	29
		E*Trade	15

SOURCES: Jeanhee Kim, "Hidden Costs of El Cheapo Brokers," *Money,* January 6, 1996, p. 53; Tricia Welsh, "Keep Your Broker Honest," *Fortune/1994 Investor's Guide*, Fall 1993, p. 170. © 1993 Time, Inc. All rights reserved.

Securities Regulation

Government regulation of securities trading began as a response to abusive and fraudulent practices in the sale of stocks. Individual states were the first to react early in this century. Later federal legislation was passed to regulate the interstate sale of securities.

State Regulation   In 1911, Kansas enacted the first state law regulating securities transactions. Within a few years, a number of other states passed similar laws. Most of the state laws provide for (1) registration of securities, (2) licensing of brokers and securities salespeople, and (3) prosecution of any individual who sells fraudulent stocks and bonds. These state laws are often called *blue-sky laws* because they were designed to stop the sale of securities that had nothing to back them up except the sky.

Federal Regulation   The Securities Act of 1933, sometimes referred to as the *Truth in Securities Act,* provides for full disclosure of important facts about corporations issuing new securities. Such corporations are required to file a registration statement containing specific information about their earnings, assets, and liabilities; their products or services; and the qualifications of their top management. This act also requires publication of a prospectus, a summary of information contained in the registration statement.

The Securities Exchange Act of 1934 created the Securities and Exchange Commission (SEC). The Securities and Exchange Commission is the agency that enforces federal securities regulations. The 1934 act gave the SEC the power to regulate trading on the New York Stock Exchange and the American Stock Exchange. It also empowered the SEC to make brokers and securities dealers pass an examination before being allowed to sell securities, and it required that registration statements be brought up to date periodically.

Eight other federal acts were passed primarily to protect investors:

- The Maloney Act of 1938 made the National Association of Securities Dealers (NASD) responsible for the self-regulation of the over-the-counter securities market.
- The Investment Company Act of 1940 placed investment companies that sell mutual funds under the jurisdiction of the SEC.
- The Investment Advisers Act of 1940 required financial advisers with more than 15 clients to register with the SEC.
- The Federal Securities Act of 1964 extended the SEC's jurisdiction to companies whose stock is sold over the counter if they have total assets of at least $1 million or more than 500 stockholders of any one class of stock.

- The Securities Investor Protection Act of 1970 created the Securities Investor Protection Corporation (SIPC). This organization provides insurance of up to $500,000 per customer, including $100,000 for any cash deposited with a brokerage firm that fails.
- The Securities Acts Amendments of 1975 eliminated fixed commissions and allowed more competition among brokerage firms.
- The Insider Trading Sanctions Act of 1984 strengthened the penalty provisions of the 1934 Securities Exchange Act. Under this act, people are guilty of insider trading if they use information that is available only to account executives or other employees of brokerage firms. The act also expanded the SEC's power to investigate such illegal behavior.
- The Insider Trading Act of 1988 made the top management of brokerage firms responsible for reporting transactions based on inside information to the SEC. This act also enabled the SEC to levy fines of up to $1 million for failure to report such violations of the law.

CONCEPT CHECK 14–4

1. What is the difference between the primary market and the secondary market?
2. Describe the steps required to buy or sell stock on a securities exchange.
3. Assume you want to purchase stock. Would you use a full-service broker or a discount broker? Would you ever trade stocks online?
4. What are the two main federal acts that regulate the securities industry? What do they regulate?

LONG-TERM AND SHORT-TERM INVESTMENT STRATEGIES

L.O.5 Explain the trading techniques used by long-term and short-term investors.

Once you purchase stock, the investment may be classified as either long term or short term. Generally, individuals who hold an investment for a long period of time are referred to as *investors*. Typically, long-term investors hold their investments for at least a year or longer. Individuals who routinely buy and then sell stocks within a short period of time are called *speculators* or *traders*.

Long-Term Techniques

In this section, we discuss the long-term techniques of buy and hold, dollar cost averaging, direct investment programs, and dividend reinvestment programs.

The Buy-and-Hold Technique   Many long-term investors purchase stock and hold onto it for a number of years. When they do this, their investment can increase in value in three ways. First, they are entitled to dividends if the board of directors approves dividend payments to stockholders. Second, the price of the stock may go up. Third, the stock may be split. Although there are no guarantees, stock splits usually increase the value of a stock investment over a long period of time. Remember Martha and Michael Kahn, the couple in the opening case for this chapter? Back when they didn't have a lot of money, they purchased 100 shares of Home Depot common stock. Although they were tempted to sell after just 11 months, they made the decision to use a buy-and-hold technique while their Home Depot stock continued to increase in value. As a result, their investment in Home Depot was worth $18,000 at the time of publication of this book.

EXHIBIT 14–9

**Dollar Cost
Averaging**

Year	Investment	Stock Price	Shares Purchased
1996	$2,000	$50	40.0
1997	2,000	65	30.8
1998	2,000	60	33.3
Total	$6,000		104.1

dollar cost averaging

Dollar Cost Averaging   **Dollar cost averaging** is a long-term technique used by investors who purchase an equal dollar amount of the same stock at equal intervals. Assume you invest $2,000 in Johnson & Johnson's common stock each year for a period of three years. The results of your investment program are illustrated in Exhibit 14–9. Notice that when the price of the stock increased in 1997, you purchased fewer shares of stock. When the price decreased in 1998, you purchased more shares of stock. The average cost for a share of stock, determined by dividing the total investment ($6,000) by the total number of shares (104.1), is $57.64. Another application of dollar cost averaging occurs when employees purchase shares of their company's stock through a payroll deduction plan over an extended period of time.

Investors use dollar cost averaging to avoid the common pitfall of buying high and selling low. In the situation shown in Exhibit 14–9, you would lose money only if you sold your stock at less than the average cost of $57.64. Thus, with dollar cost averaging, you can make money if the stock is sold at a price higher than the average purchase price.

direct investment plan

dividend reinvestment plan

Direct Investment and Dividend Reinvestment Plans   Today a large number of corporations offer direct investment plans. A **direct investment plan** allows stockholders to purchase stock directly from a corporation without having to use an account executive or a brokerage firm. Similarly, a **dividend reinvestment plan** allows current stockholders the option to reinvest or use their cash dividends to purchase stock of the corporation. For stockholders, the chief advantage of both types of plans is that these plans enable them to purchase stock without paying a commission charge to a brokerage firm. (Note: A few companies may charge for dividend reinvestment, but the charge is less than what most brokerage firms charge.) As an added incentive, some corporations even offer their stock at a small discount to encourage stockholders to use their direct investment and dividend reinvestment plans. Also, with the dividend reinvestment plan, investors can take advantage of dollar cost averaging, discussed in the last section. For corporations, the chief advantage of both types of plans is that they provide an additional source of capital. As an added bonus, they are providing a service to their stockholders.

Short-Term Techniques

In addition to the long-term techniques presented in the preceding section, investors sometimes use more speculative, short-term techniques. In this section, we discuss buying stock on margin, selling short, and trading in options. *Be warned:* The methods presented in this section are quite risky; do not use them unless you fully understand the underlying risks.

Buying Stock on Margin

margin

When buying stock on **margin,** an investor borrows part of the money needed to buy a particular stock. The margin requirement is set by the Federal Reserve Board and is subject to periodic change. The current margin requirement is 50 percent, which means an

EXHIBIT 14–10

A Typical Margin Transaction

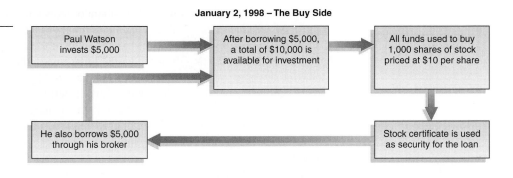

January 2, 1998 – The Buy Side

Paul Watson invests $5,000

After borrowing $5,000, a total of $10,000 is available for investment

All funds used to buy 1,000 shares of stock priced at $10 per share

He also borrows $5,000 through his broker

Stock certificate is used as security for the loan

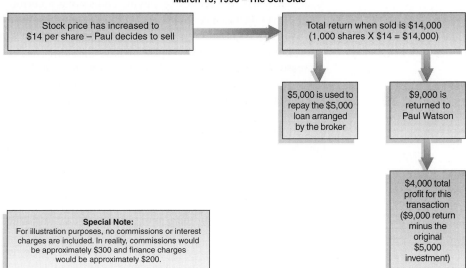

March 15, 1998 – The Sell Side

Stock price has increased to $14 per share – Paul decides to sell

Total return when sold is $14,000 (1,000 shares X $14 = $14,000)

$5,000 is used to repay the $5,000 loan arranged by the broker

$9,000 is returned to Paul Watson

$4,000 total profit for this transaction ($9,000 return minus the original $5,000 investment)

Special Note:
For illustration purposes, no commissions or interest charges are included. In reality, commissions would be approximately $300 and finance charges would be approximately $200.

investor may borrow up to half of the stock purchase price. Usually the brokerage firm either lends the money or arranges the loan with another financial institution. Investors buy on margin because doing so offers them the potential for greater profits. Exhibit 14–10 gives an example of buying stock on margin.

As Exhibit 14–10 shows, it is more profitable to use margin. In effect, the financial leverage (often defined as the use of borrowed funds to increase the return on an investment) allowed Paul Watson, who is single and 32 years old, to purchase a larger number of shares of stock. Since the dollar value of each share increased, Watson obtained a larger profit by buying the stock on margin.

In this example, Paul Watson's stock did exactly what it was supposed to do: It increased in market value. Had the value of the stock gone down, buying on margin would have increased his loss. For example, Watson would have lost $3,000 if the price of the stock had dropped from $10 a share (the original purchase price) to $7 a share.

If the market value of a margined stock decreases to approximately one-half of the original price, the investor will receive a *margin call* from the brokerage firm. After the margin call, the investor must pledge additional cash or securities to serve as collateral for the loan. If the investor doesn't have acceptable collateral or cash, the margined stock is sold and the proceeds are used to repay the loan. The exact price at which the brokerage firm issues the margin call is determined by the amount of money the investor borrowed when he or she purchased the stock. Generally, the more money the investor borrows, the sooner he or she will receive a margin call if the market value of the margined stock drops.

In addition to facing the possibility of larger dollar losses, the investor must pay interest on the money borrowed to purchase stock on margin. Most brokerage firms charge 1 to 3 percent above the prime rate. Normally, bankers define the prime rate as the interest rate they charge their best business customers. Interest charges can absorb the potential profits if the value of margined stock does not increase rapidly enough and the margined stocks must be held for long periods of time.

Selling Short

selling short

Your ability to make money by buying and selling securities is related to how well you can predict whether a certain stock will increase or decrease in market value. Normally, the investor buys stocks and assumes they will increase in value, a procedure referred to as *buying long*. But not all stocks increase in value. In fact, the value of a stock may decrease, for many reasons. Typical reasons include lower corporate sales revenues, lower profits, reduced dividends, product failures, and product liability lawsuits. With this fact in mind, investors often use a procedure called *selling short* to make money when the value of a stock is falling. **Selling short** is selling stock that has been borrowed from a brokerage firm and must be replaced at a later date. When you sell short, you sell today, knowing you must buy or *cover* your short transaction at a later date. To make money in a short transaction, you must take these steps:

1. Arrange to *borrow a stock certificate* for a certain number of shares of a particular stock from a brokerage firm.
2. *Sell the borrowed* stock, assuming it will drop in value in a reasonably short period of time.
3. *Buy the stock at a lower price* than the price it sold for in step 2.
4. Use the stock purchased in step 3 to *replace the stock that was borrowed from the brokerage firm* in step 1.

For example, Betty Malone, who is divorced and 28 years old, believes General Motors stock is overpriced because of lower demand for cars and numerous other factors. As a result, she decides to sell short 100 shares of General Motors (Exhibit 14–11).

As Exhibit 14–11 shows, Betty Malone's total return for this short transaction was $700 because the stock did what it was supposed to do in a short transaction: decrease in value. A price decrease is especially important when selling short because you must replace the stock borrowed from the brokerage firm with stock purchased (hopefully at a lower market value) at a later date. If the stock increases in value, you will lose money because you must replace the borrowed stock with stock purchased at a higher price. If the price of the General Motors stock in Exhibit 14–11 had increased from $56 to $63, Betty Malone would have lost $700.

There is usually no special or extra brokerage charge for selling short, since the brokerage firm receives its regular commission when the stock is bought and sold. Before selling short, consider two factors. First, since the stock you borrow from your broker is actually owned by another investor, you must pay any dividends the stock earns before you replace the stock. After all, you borrowed the stock and then sold the borrowed stock. Eventually, dividends can absorb the profits from your short transaction if the price of the stock does not decrease rapidly enough. Second, to make money selling short, you must be correct in predicting that a stock will decrease in value. If the value of the stock increases, you lose.

EXHIBIT 14–11

**An Example of
Selling Short**

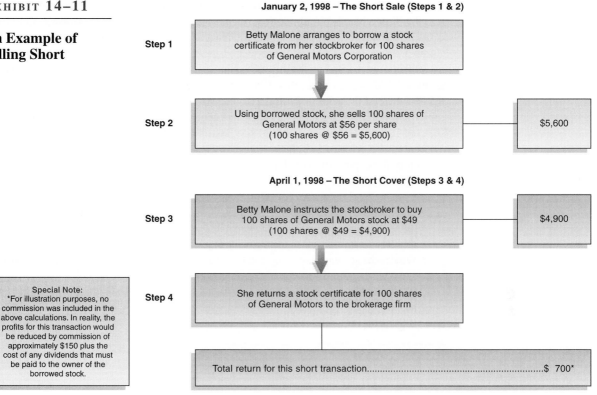

January 2, 1998 – The Short Sale (Steps 1 & 2)

Step 1 — Betty Malone arranges to borrow a stock certificate from her stockbroker for 100 shares of General Motors Corporation

Step 2 — Using borrowed stock, she sells 100 shares of General Motors at $56 per share (100 shares @ $56 = $5,600) — $5,600

April 1, 1998 – The Short Cover (Steps 3 & 4)

Step 3 — Betty Malone instructs the stockbroker to buy 100 shares of General Motors stock at $49 (100 shares @ $49 = $4,900) — $4,900

Step 4 — She returns a stock certificate for 100 shares of General Motors to the brokerage firm

Total return for this short transaction..$ 700*

Special Note:
*For illustration purposes, no commission was included in the above calculations. In reality, the profits for this transaction would be reduced by commission of approximately $150 plus the cost of any dividends that must be paid to the owner of the borrowed stock.

Trading in Options

option

An **option** gives an investor the right to buy or sell a stock at a predetermined price during a specified period of time. Options are usually available for three-, six-, or nine-month periods. An investor who thinks the market price of a stock will increase during a short period of time may decide to purchase a call option. A **call option** is sold by a stockholder and gives the purchaser the right to *buy* 100 shares of a stock at a guaranteed price before a specified expiration date. For instance, Bob Gray invests $300 to purchase a call option on Digital Equipment stock. His call option enables him to buy 100 shares of Digital Equipment before the expiration date at a guaranteed price of $35 per share. In this case, if the price of Digital Equipment stock does increase, Bob can make money in one of two ways:

call option

1. Before the expiration date, he can sell his call option to another investor. Since his option is more valuable as a result of the stock's higher price, he can sell the option to another investor at a price higher than what he paid for it.
2. He can exercise his option and purchase the stock at the price guaranteed by the option ($35). Since the stock price guaranteed by the option is lower than the market price, he can make a profit by selling the stock at a higher price. Because of the commissions involved in buying and selling stock when using this method, most investors would prefer the first method.

Be warned: For Bob Gray to use either of the preceding methods, the price for Digital Equipment stock must increase to $35 or above. If the market value of Digital Equipment's stock does not increase before the expiration date, Bob will lose the $300 he paid for the call option.

put option

Some stock owners who believe the price of their stock will go down during the option period will purchase a put option to safeguard their investment. A **put option** is the right to *sell* 100 shares of a stock at a guaranteed price before a specified expiration date. For example, Patsy Jones owns 100 shares of Eastman Kodak. She decides to safeguard her investment from a drop in value by purchasing a put option for $350. Her put option enables her to sell 100 shares of Eastman Kodak before the expiration date, at a guaranteed price of $70 a share. If the price of Eastman Kodak stock decreases to $70 or less, Patsy can make money if she sells the option to another investor at a higher price than what she paid for it. She could also exercise her option to sell Eastman Kodak stock before the expiration date at a guaranteed price of $70. If the value for Eastman Kodak does not decrease to $70 or less before the expiration date, Patsy will lose the $350 that she paid for the put option.

CONCEPT CHECK 14–5

1. How can an investor make money using the buy-and-hold technique?
2. What is the advantage of using dollar cost averaging? Of using direct investment plans and dividend reinvestment plans?
3. Why would an investor buy stock on margin? Why would an investor use the selling-short technique?
4. What is the difference between a call option and a put option?

KEY FORMULAS

Page	Topic	Formula
440	Book value	$$\text{Book value} = \frac{\text{Assets} - \text{Liabilities}}{\text{Number of outstanding shares of common stock}}$$ *Example:* $$\text{Book value} = \frac{\$135,000,000 - \$60,000,000}{3,750,000}$$ $$= \$20 \text{ per share}$$
441	Earnings per share	$$\text{Earnings per share} = \frac{\text{After-tax earnings}}{\text{Number of outstanding shares of common stock}}$$ *Example:* $$\text{Earnings per share} = \frac{\$11,250,000}{3,750,000}$$ $$= \$3.00 \text{ per share}$$
441	Price-earnings (PE) ratio	$$\text{PE ratio} = \frac{\text{Price per share}}{\text{Earnings per share of stock outstanding over the last 12 months}}$$ *Example:* $$\text{Price-earnings ratio} = \frac{\$54}{\$3.00}$$ $$= 18$$

SUMMARY

L.O.1 Identify the most important features of common stock.

Corporations sell common stock to finance their business start-up costs and help pay for their ongoing business activities. People invest in common stock because of dividend income, appreciation of value, and the possibility of gain through stock splits. Dividend payments to common stockholders must be approved by a corporation's board of directors. In return for providing the money needed to finance the corporation, stockholders have the right to elect the board of directors. They must also approve changes to corporate policies that include (1) an amendment to the corporate charter, (2) the sale of certain assets, (3) possible mergers, (4) the issuance of preferred stock or corporate bonds, and (5) changes in the amount of common stock.

L.O.2 Discuss the most important features of preferred stock.

The most important priority an investor in preferred stock enjoys is receiving cash dividends before any cash dividends are paid to common stockholders. Still, dividend distributions to both preferred and common stockholders must be approved by the board of directors. To make preferred stock issues more attractive, corporations may add a cumulative feature, a participating feature, and/or a conversion feature to these issues.

L.O.3 Explain how investors can evaluate stock investments.

A number of factors can make a share of stock increase or decrease in value. When evaluating a particular stock issue, most investors begin with the information contained in daily newspapers. Classification of stocks, stock advisory services, annual reports, quarterly reports, information contained on the Internet, numerical measures, and the funda-mental, technical, and efficient market investment theories can all be used to help evaluate a stock investment.

L.O.4 Describe how stocks are bought and sold.

A corporation may sell a new stock issue through an investment bank or directly to current stockholders. Once the stock has been sold in the primary market, it can be sold time and again in the secondary market. In the secondary market, investors purchase stock listed on a securities exchange or traded in the over-the-counter market. Most securities transactions are made through an account executive who works for a brokerage firm. A growing number of investors are using computers to complete security transactions. In fact, a good investment software package can help you evaluate potential investments, monitor the value of your investments, and place buy and sell orders online. Most brokerage firms charge a minimum commission for buying or selling stock. Additional commission charges are based on the number and value of the stock shares that are bought or sold. Individual states and the federal government have enacted a number of regulations to protect investors.

L.O.5 Explain the trading techniques used by long-term and short-term investors.

Purchased stock may be classified as either a long-term investment or a speculative investment. Long-term investors typically hold their investments for at least a year or longer; speculators (sometimes referred to as *traders*) usually sell their investments within a shorter time period. Traditional trading techniques long-term investors use include the buy-and-hold technique, dollar cost averaging, direct investment plans, and dividend reinvestment plans. More speculative techniques include buying on margin, selling short, and trading in options.

GLOSSARY

account executive A licensed individual who buys or sells securities for his or her clients; also called a *stockbroker.* (p. 445)

bear market Occurs when investors are pessimistic about a nation's economy and sell stocks. (p. 439)

beta An index that compares the risk associated with a specific stock issue with the risk of the stock market in general. (p. 441)

blue-chip stock A safe investment that generally attracts conservative investors. (p. 435)

book value Determined by deducting all liabilities from the corporation's assets and dividing the remainder by the number of outstanding shares of common stock. (p. 440)

bull market Occurs when investors are optimistic about a nation's economy and buy stocks. (p. 439)

callable preferred stock Stock that a corporation may exchange, at its option, for a specified amount of money. (p. 432)

call option The right to buy 100 shares of a stock at a guaranteed price before a specified expiration date.   (p. 455)

churning The excessive buying and selling of securities to generate commissions.   (p. 447)

cumulative preferred stock A stock whose unpaid dividends accumulate and must be paid before any cash dividend is paid to the common stockholders.   (p. 433)

cyclical stock A stock that follows the business cycle of advances and declines in the economy.   (p. 436)

defensive stock A stock that remains stable during declines in the economy. (p. 436)

direct investment plan   A plan that allows stockholders to purchase stock directly from a corporation without having to use an account executive or a brokerage firm.   (p. 452)

discretionary order   An order to buy or sell a security that lets the account executive decide when to execute the transaction and at what price.   (p. 449)

dividend reinvestment plan   A plan that allows current stockholders the option to reinvest or use their cash dividends to purchase the stock of the corporation.   (p. 452)

dollar cost averaging   A long-term technique used by investors who purchase an equal dollar amount of the same stock at equal intervals.   (p. 452)

earnings per share   A corporation's after-tax earnings divided by the number of outstanding shares of common stock.   (p. 441)

efficient market theory   An investment theory based on the assumption that stock price movements are purely random; also called the *random walk theory*.   (p. 442)

fundamental theory   An investment theory based on the assumption that a stock's intrinsic or real value is determined by the company's future earnings.   (p. 441)

growth stock   A stock issued by a corporation earning profits above the average profits of all the firms in the economy.   (p. 435)

income stock   A stock that pays higher than average dividends.   (p. 435)

initial public offering (IPO)   Occurs when a corporation sells stock to the general public for the first time.   (p. 444)

investment bank   A financial firm that assists corporations in raising funds, usually by helping to sell new security issues.   (p. 444)

limit order   A request to buy or sell a stock at a specified price.   (p. 447)

margin   A speculative technique whereby an investor borrows part of the money needed to buy a particular stock.   (p. 452)

market order   A request to buy or sell a stock at the current market value.   (p. 447)

NASDAQ (pronounced "nazzdack")   An electronic marketplace for almost 5,000 different stocks.   (p. 446)

odd lot   Fewer than 100 shares of a particular stock.   (p. 449)

option   The right to buy or sell a stock at a predetermined price during a specified period of time.   (p. 455)

over-the-counter (OTC) market   A network of dealers who buy and sell the stocks of corporations that are not listed on a securities exchange.   (p. 446)

par value   An assigned (and often arbitrary) dollar value that is printed on a stock certificate.   (p. 432)

preemptive right   The right of current stockholders to purchase any new stock the corporation issues before it is offered to the general public.   (p. 429)

penny stock   A stock issue that typically sells for $1 to $10.   (p. 436)

price-earnings (PE) ratio   The price of a share of stock divided by the corporation's earnings per share of stock outstanding over the last 12 months.   (p. 441)

primary market   A market in which an investor purchases financial securities, via an investment bank or other representative, from the issuer of those securities.   (p. 444)

proxy   A legal form that lists the issues to be decided at a stockholders' meeting and requests that stockholders transfer their voting rights to some individual or individuals.   (pp. 428, 429)

put option   The right to sell 100 shares of a stock at a guaranteed price before a specified expiration date.   (p. 456)

record date   The date on which a stockholder must be registered on the corporation's books in order to receive dividend payments.   (p. 429)

round lot   One hundred shares or multiples of 100 shares of a particular stock.   (p. 449)

secondary market   A market for existing financial securities that are currently traded among investors.   (p. 444)

securities   Investments, including stocks and bonds, mutual funds, options, and commodities, that are traded on securities exchanges or the over-the-counter market.   (p. 427)

securities exchange   A marketplace where member brokers who represent investors meet to buy and sell securities.   (p. 445)

selling short   Selling stock that has been borrowed from a brokerage firm and must be replaced at a later date.   (p. 454)

specialist   An individual on the floor of an exchange who buys or sells a particular stock in an effort to maintain an orderly market.   (p. 446)

stock split   A procedure in which the shares of common stock owned by existing stockholders are divided into a larger number of shares.   (p. 430)

stop order   An order to sell a particular stock at the next available opportunity after its market price reaches a specified amount.   (p. 448)

technical theory   An investment theory based on the assumption that a stock's market value is determined by the forces of supply and demand in the stock market as a whole.   (p. 442)

REVIEW QUESTIONS

1. From a manager's perspective, explain the advantages and disadvantages of using stock to finance a corporation's activities. (L.O.1)
2. Why would you choose common stock compared with other investment alternatives? (L.O.1)
3. Why do corporations issue preferred stock? (L.O.2)
4. Why do investors purchase preferred stock? (L.O.2)
5. What type of financial information do *The Wall Street Journal, Barron's,* and local newspapers contain? (L.O.3)
6. Describe the six classifications of stock discussed in this chapter. Which classification do you believe would be appropriate for your own investment program? (L.O.3)
7. What type of information can an investor obtain from stock advisory services? (L.O.3)
8. For most corporations, information is available in annual reports, in quarterly reports, and on the Internet. If you

needed information about a corporation, which source would you choose? Why? (L.O.3)
9. Why would an investor calculate book value, earnings per share, and price-earnings ratio for a particular corporation's stock? (L.O.3)
10. How important are the primary market and the investment bank when a corporation is selling stock for the first time? (L.O.4)
11. What steps are involved in the sale of stock in the secondary market? (L.O.4)
12. Describe the long-term investment techniques of buy and hold, dollar cost averaging, direct investment plan, and dividend reinvestment plan. (L.O.5)
13. What are the advantages and disadvantages of buying stock on margin? Of selling short? (L.O.5)
14. What are the dangers of trading in options? (L.O.5)

FINANCIAL PLANNING CALCULATIONS

1. *Calculating Dividend Amounts.* Betty and John Martinez own 220 shares of Exxon common stock. Exxon's quarterly dividend is $.41 per share. What is the amount of the dividend check the Martinez couple will receive for this quarter? (L.O.1)
2. *Determining the Number of Shares after a Stock Split.* In May, stockholders of Coca-Cola Company approved a 2-for-1 stock split. After the split, how many shares of Coca-Cola stock will an investor have if she or he owned 360 shares before the split? (L.O.1)
3. *Calculating Total Return.* Tammy Jackson purchased 100 shares of All-American Manufacturing Company stock at $29½ a share. One year later, she sold the stock for $38 a share. She paid her broker a $34 commission when she purchased the stock and a $42 commission when she sold it. During the 12 months she owned the stock, she received $184 in dividends. Calculate Tammy's total return on this investment. (L.O.1)
4. *Calculating Total Return.* Marie and Bob Houmas purchased 200 shares of General Electric stock for $95 a share. One year later, they sold the stock for $104 a share. They paid their broker a $350 commission when they purchased the stock and a $425 commission when they sold it. During the 12 months they owned the stock, they received $576 in dividends. Calculate the total return on this investment. (L.O.1)
5. *Determining a Preferred Dividend Amount.* James Hayes owns Ohio Utility preferred stock. If this preferred stock issue pays 6¼ percent based on a par value of $25, what is the dollar amount of the dividend for one share of Ohio Utility? (L.O.2)
6. *Calculating the Dividend for a Cumulative Preferred Stock Issue.* Wyoming Sports Equipment issued a $3 cumulative preferred stock issue. In 1997, the firm's board

of directors voted to omit dividends for both the company's common stock and its preferred stock issues. Also, the corporation's board of directors voted to pay dividends in 1998. (L.O.2)
   a. How much did the preferred stockholders receive in 1997?
   b. How much did the common stockholders receive in 1997?
   c. How much did the preferred stockholders receive in 1998?
7. *Calculating Book Value, Earnings per Share, and Price-Earnings Ratio.* As a stockholder of Bozo Oil Company, you receive its annual report. In the financial statements, the firm has reported assets of $9 million, liabilities of $5 million, after-tax earnings of $2 million, and 750,000 outstanding shares of common stock. (L.O.3)
   a. Calculate the book value of a share of Bozo Oil's common stock.
   b. Calculate the earnings per share of Bozo Oil's common stock.
   c. Assuming a share of Bozo Oil's common stock has a market value of $40, what is the firm's price-earnings ratio?
8. *Using Dollar Cost Averaging.* For four years, Mary Nations invested $3,000 each year in America Bank stock. The stock was selling for $34 in 1995, for $48 in 1996, $37 in 1997, and for $52 in 1998. (L.O.5)
   a. What is Mary's total investment in America Bank?
   b. After four years, how many shares does Mary own?
   c. What is the average cost per share of Mary's investment?
9. *Using Margin.* Bill Campbell invested $4,000 and borrowed $4,000 to purchase shares in Wal-Mart. At the time of his investment, Wal-Mart stock was selling for $25 a share. (L.O.5)

a. If Bill paid a $50 commission, how many shares could he buy if he used only his own money and did not use margin?

b. If Bill paid a $100 commission, how many shares could he buy if he used his $4,000 and borrowed $4,000 on margin to buy Wal-Mart stock?

c. Assuming Bill did use margin, paid a $250 commission to buy and sell his Wal-Mart stock, and sold his stock for $33 a share, how much profit did he make on his Wal-Mart investment?

10. *Selling Short.* After researching Toro common stock, Sally Jackson is convinced that the stock is overpriced. She contacts her account executive and arranges to sell short 200 shares of Toro. At the time of the sale, a share of common stock had a value of $35. Six months later, Toro was selling for $23 a share, and Sally instructs her broker to cover her short transaction. Total commissions to buy and sell the stock were $120. What is her profit for this short transaction?   (L.O.5)

PROJECTS   AND   APPLICATION   ACTIVITIES

1. *Surveying Investors.* Survey investors who own stock. Then explain, in a short paragraph, their reasons for owning stock.   (L.O.1)

2. *Determining the Effect of a Stock Split on a Stock's Market Value.* Use the *Reader's Guide to Periodical Literature,* the Internet, and/or issues of *The Wall Street Journal* to locate a stock that has experienced a 2-for-1 split.   (L.O.1)

   a. What is the name of the corporation that had the 2-for-1 stock split?

   b. When did the stock split?

   c. What was the price the day before the stock split?

   d. What was the price the day after the stock split?

   e. What was the price a month after the stock split?

   f. At the end of one month, do you think the stock split was good for an individual investor?

3. *Interviewing an Account Executive.* Interview an account executive about the cumulative feature, participation feature, and conversion feature of preferred stock. What do these features mean to preferred stockholders?   (L.O.2)

4. *Using Library Information.* Divide a sheet of paper into three columns. In the first column, list sources of information you can use to evaluate stock investments. In the second column, state where you would find each of these sources. In the third column, describe the types of information each source would provide.   (L.O.3)

5. *Using Stock Advisory Services.* Pick a stock of interest to you and research the company at the library by examining the information contained in reports published by Moody's, Standard & Poor's, Value Line, or Business periodicals like *Business Week, Money,* or *Kiplinger's*

Personal Finance. Then write a one- or two-page summary of your findings. Based on your research, would you still want to invest in this stock? Why or why not?   (L.O.3)

6.   *Using the Internet.* Choose a stock that you think would be a good investment. Then research the stock using the Internet.

   a. Based on the information contained on the corporation's home page, would you still want to invest in the stock? Explain your answer.

   b. What other investment information would you need to evaluate the stock? Where would you obtain this information?

7. *Conducting Library Research.* Conduct library research on the fundamental theory, the technical theory, and the efficient market theory described in this chapter. How do these theories explain the movements of a stock traded on the NYSE or over-the-counter market?   (L.O.3)

8. *Exploring Career Opportunities.* Prepare a list of questions you could use to interview an account executive about career opportunities in the field of finance.   (L.O.4)

9. *Using Long-Term Investment Techniques.* Interview people who have used the long-term investment techniques of buy and hold, dollar cost averaging, direct investment plan, and dividend reinvestment plan. Describe your findings.   (L.O.5)

10. *Analyzing Short-Term Investments.* Prepare a chart that describes the similarities and differences among buying stock on margin, selling short, and trading in options.   (L.O.5)

LIFE   SITUATION   CASE   14

RESEARCH INFORMATION AVAILABLE FROM MOODY'S AND VALUE LINE

This chapter stressed the importance of evaluating potential investments. Now it's your turn to try your skill at evaluating a potential investment in Reebok International, Ltd. Assume

you could invest $10,000 in the common stock of this company. To help you evaluate this potential investment, carefully examine Exhibits 14–5 and 14–6, which reproduce the research reports on Reebok International from Moody's and Value Line, respectively. Both reports were published in the fall of 1997.

QUESTIONS

1. Based on the research provided by Moody's and Value Line, would you buy Reebok International stock? Justify your answer.
2. What other investment information would you need to evaluate Reebok International common stock? Where would you obtain this information?
3. On Thursday, January 8, 1998, Reebok International common stock was selling for $29.50. Using a newspaper, determine the current price for a share of Reebok common stock. Based on this information, would your Reebok investment have been profitable if you had purchased the common stock for $29.50 a share? (Hint: Reebok stock is listed on the New York Stock Exchange.)
4. Assuming you purchased Reebok International stock on January 8, 1998, and based on your answer to question 3, would you want to hold or sell your Reebok stock? Explain your answer.

USING THE INTERNET TO CREATE A PERSONAL FINANCIAL PLAN 14

INVESTING IN STOCKS

For many investors, selection of stocks for their portfolio is an important element that helps achieve various investment goals.

Web Sites for Investing in Stocks

- Current stock market information and data at **www.personalwealth.com**
- Information about investing in stocks at **www.stockmaster.com** and **www.onr.com/stocks.html**
- Stock quotes and other financial data at **www.wsrn.com, quote.yahoo.com, www.quote.com,** and **my.excite.com/stocks**
- Information on activities and resources of various stock exchanges: American Stock Exchange at **www.amex.com;** New York Stock Exchange at **www.nyse.com;** and **www.nasdaq.com**
- Company annual report information at **www.zpub.com** and company information at **www.hoovers.com**
- News about investing in high-tech stocks at **www.tech-stocks.com** and **www.newshub.com**

(Note: Addresses and content of Web sites change, and new sites are created daily. Use the search engines discussed in Appendix B to update and locate Web sites for your current financial planning needs.)

PFP SHEETS: 58, 61

Short-Term Financial Planning Activities

1. Identify investments goals that might be appropriate for investing in stocks for your various financial goals and life situation.
2. Research potential stocks based on your various financial goals. Consider risk, potential growth, income, and recent market performance.
3. Monitor current economic conditions that may affect the value of individual stocks as well as the stock market as a whole.
4. Compare the cost of various investment broker services.

Long-Term Financial Planning Activities

1. Identify stock investing decisions that might be used for achieving long-term financial goals.
2. Develop a plan for investing in stocks as family and household situations change.

CHAPTER 15

INVESTING IN BONDS

OPENING CASE

COCA-COLA IS THE ONE FOR ME!

Back in 1987, Betty and Matthew Randall bought 12 corporate bonds issued by Coca-Cola Enterprises. The bonds paid 8½ percent interest and will mature in 2012. Each bond cost $994. With commission, the total investment was $12,048. Each year since 1987, the Randalls have collected $85 in interest payments, and as interest rates in the economy have fallen, their bonds' market value has increased.

Were the Randalls just lucky? No, not at all! Although it may seem overly simple, the Randalls began their search for an investment by thinking about the products they used daily. Since Coca-Cola was their favorite soft drink, and since they bought the product on a regular basis, they assumed Coca-Cola was rolling in profits. Betty researched Coca-Cola Corporation and found that the parent company, Coca-Cola, had many diverse subsidiaries. She also found that the company had issued stocks, bonds, and other financial securities to finance its operations.

After much discussion, the Randalls decided to purchase corporate bonds issued by Coca-Cola Enterprises, a major subsidiary of Coca-Cola. Moody's Investors Service rated these bonds A3.

According to Moody's, bonds in this category possess many favorable investment attributes and are considered upper-medium-grade obligations. In addition to paying 8½ percent interest, or $85, each year, the Coca-Cola bonds have increased in market value due to falling interest rates in the economy. Falling interest rates in the economy make bonds with a fixed interest rate, like those issued by Coca-Cola Enterprises, more valuable.

QUESTIONS

1. Based on what you have learned thus far, would you buy bonds issued by Coca-Cola Enterprises?
2. What might make a particular investment, such as Coca-Cola bonds, a good investment for one person and a poor investment for another person?

SOURCES: Gary Hoover, ed., Hoover's *500 Profiles of America's Largest Business Enterprises* (Austin, TX: The Reference Press, 1996), pp. 134–13; Moody's Investors Service, *Moody's Handbook of Common Stocks*, Fall 1997; Moody's Investors Service, *Moody's Industrial Manual*, Vol. 1, 1997, pp. 2997; Moody's Investors Service, *Moody's Bond Record*, December 1997, p. 56.

L E A R N I N G
O B J E C T I V E S

After studying this chapter, you will be able to

L.O.1 Describe the characteristics of corporate bonds.

L.O.2 Discuss why corporations issue bonds.

L.O.3 Explain why investors purchase corporate bonds.

L.O.4 Discuss why federal, state, and local governments issue bonds.

L.O.5 Evaluate bonds when making an investment.

Financial Decision
Trade-Off

Opportunity costs! The Randalls, the couple in the opening case, took a chance when they purchased 12 corporate bonds issued by Coca-Cola Enterprises. Their investment, which cost over $12,000, could have gone down in value. But because they took the time to evaluate the investment using reliable sources, they could be reasonably certain that their investment would increase in value. Since 1987, each Coca-Cola bond they purchased has earned 8½ percent interest annually. That's over $1,000 per bond! In addition, the market value of the bonds has increased.

Coca-Cola Enterprises, the company that issued the bonds, also took advantage of the concept of opportunity costs when it sold bonds. It agreed to pay bondholders 8½ percent interest until the bonds mature in 2012. It also agreed to repay the Randalls' original investment when the bonds mature. In return, Coca-Cola's managers obtained the money they needed to produce more products that could be sold to consumers, provide more jobs for employees, and ultimately earn larger profits.

We begin this chapter by describing the basic characteristics of corporate bonds that define the relationship between investors, like the Randalls, and corporations, like Coca-Cola Enterprises, that sell bonds to obtain financing.

CHARACTERISTICS OF CORPORATE BONDS

L.O.1 Describe the characteristics of corporate bonds.

corporate bond

face value

A **corporate bond** is a corporation's written pledge to repay a specified amount of money with interest. Exhibit 15–1 on page 464 illustrates a typical corporate bond. Note that it states the dollar amount of the bond, the interest rate, and the maturity date. The **face value** is the dollar amount the bondholder will receive at the bond's maturity. The usual face value of a corporate bond is $1,000, but the face value of some corporate bonds may be as high as $50,000. The total face value of all the bonds in an issue usually runs into millions of dollars (see Exhibit 15–2 on page 465). Between the time of purchase and the maturity date, the corporation pays interest to the bondholder, usually every six months, at the stated interest rate. For example, assume you purchase the $1,000 Mobil Corporation bond illustrated in Exhibit 15–1 and the interest rate for this bond is 8½ percent. In this situation, you receive interest of $85 ($1,000 × 8.5% = $85) a year from Mobil. The interest is paid semiannually, or every six months, in $42.50 installments until the bond matures.

EXHIBIT 15–1

**A Typical
Corporate Bond**

maturity date

The **maturity date** of a corporate bond is the date on which the corporation is to repay the borrowed money. At the maturity date, the bondholder returns the bond to the corporation and receives cash equal to the bond's face value. Maturity dates for bonds generally range from 1 to 30 years after the date of issue.

bond indenture

The actual legal conditions for a corporate bond are described in a bond indenture. A **bond indenture** is a legal document that details all of the conditions relating to a bond issue. Often containing over 100 pages of complicated legal wording, the bond indenture remains in effect until the bonds reach maturity or are redeemed by the corporation.

trustee

Since corporate bond indentures are very difficult for the average person to read and understand, a corporation issuing bonds appoints a trustee. The **trustee** is a financially independent firm that acts as the bondholders' representative. Usually the trustee is a commercial bank or some other financial institution. The corporation must report to the trustee periodically regarding its ability to make interest payments and eventually redeem the bonds. In turn, the trustee transmits this information to the bondholders along with its own evaluation of the corporation's ability to pay. If the corporation fails to live up to all the provisions in the indenture agreement, the trustee may bring legal action to protect the bondholders' interests.

CONCEPT CHECK 15–1

1. What is the usual face value for a corporate bond?
2. What is the annual interest amount for a $1,000 bond issued by Zenith Corporation that pays 6¼ percent interest?
3. How does a trustee evaluate the provisions contained in a bond indenture?

EXHIBIT 15–2

Advertisement for a 7½ Percent Convertible Debenture Bond Issued by Meditrust

This announcement is neither an offer to sell nor a solicitation of an offer to buy any of these securities. The offering is made only by the Prospectus Supplement and the related Prospectus. Copies of the prospectus Supplement and the related Prospectus may be obtained from the undersigned in any state in which this announcement is circulated and where such securities may lawfully be offered.   *March 1994*

Meditrust

$90,000,000

7½% Convertible Debentures Due 2001

Price 100%

NWM
NATWEST MARKETS
Corporate & Investment Banking

The abovesigned acted as agent in the placement of these securities.

WHY CORPORATIONS SELL CORPORATE BONDS

L.O.2 Discuss why corporations issue bonds.

Corporations like Meditrust (see Exhibit 15–2) sell corporate bonds to help finance their ongoing business activities. They often sell bonds when it is difficult or impossible to sell stock. The sale of bonds can also improve a corporation's financial leverage—the use of borrowed funds to increase the corporation's return on investment. Finally, the interest paid to bond owners is a tax-deductible expense and thus can be used to reduce the taxes the corporation must pay. While a corporation may use both bonds and stocks to finance its activities, there are important distinctions between the two. Corporate bonds are a form of *debt financing,* whereas stock is a form of *equity financing.* Bond owners must be repaid at a future date; stockholders do not have to be repaid. Interest payments on bonds are required; dividends are paid to stockholders at the discretion of the board of directors. Finally, in the event of bankruptcy, bondholders have a claim to the assets of the corporation prior to that of stockholders.

Financial Decision Trade-Off

Before issuing bonds, a corporation must decide what type of bond to issue and how the bond issue will be repaid.

Types of Bonds

debenture

Most corporate bonds are debentures. A **debenture** is a bond that is backed only by the reputation of the issuing corporation. If the corporation fails to make either interest payments or repayment at maturity, debenture bondholders become general creditors, much like the firm's suppliers. In the event of corporate bankruptcy, general creditors, including debenture bondholders, can claim any asset not specifically used as collateral for another financial obligation.

mortgage bond

To make a bond issue more appealing to conservative investors, a corporation may issue a mortgage bond. A **mortgage bond** (sometimes referred to as a *secured bond*) is a corporate bond that is secured by various assets of the issuing firm. A first mortgage bond may be backed by a lien on a specific asset, usually real estate. A general mortgage bond is secured by all the fixed assets of the firm that are not pledged as collateral for other financial obligations. A mortgage bond is considered more secure than a debenture because corporate assets or collateral may be sold to repay the bondholders if the corporation defaults on interest or repayment. Because of this added security, interest rates on mortgage bonds are usually lower than interest rates on debentures.

subordinated debenture

A third type of bond a corporation may issue is called a *subordinated* debenture. A **subordinated debenture** is an unsecured bond that gives bondholders a claim secondary to that of other designated bondholders with respect to both interest payments and assets. Investors who purchase subordinated debentures usually enjoy higher interest rates than other bondholders because of the increased risk associated with this type of bond.

Convertible Bonds

convertible bond

A special type of bond a corporation may issue is a convertible bond. A **convertible bond** can be exchanged, at the owner's option, for a specified number of shares of the corporation's common stock. This conversion feature allows investors to enjoy the lower risk of a corporate bond but also take advantage of the speculative nature of common stock. For example, Westinghouse Electric Corporation's $1,000 bond issue with a 2007 maturity date is convertible. Each bond can be converted to 64.5 shares of the company's common stock. This means you could convert the bond to common stock whenever the price of the company's common stock is $15.50 ($1,000 ÷ 64.5 5 $15.50) or higher.

Financial Decision
Trade-Off

In reality, there is no guarantee that Westinghouse bondholders will convert to common stock even if the market value of the common stock does increase to $15.50 or higher. The reason for choosing not to exercise the conversion feature in this example is quite simple. As the market value of the common stock increases, the market value of the convertible bond *also* increases. By not converting to common stock, bondholders enjoy the interest income from the bond in addition to the increased market value of the bond caused by the price movement of the common stock.

The corporation gains three advantages by issuing convertible bonds. First, the interest rate on a convertible bond is often 1 to 2 percent lower than that on traditional bonds. Second, the conversion feature attracts investors who are interested in the speculative gain that conversion to common stock may provide. Third, if the bondholder converts to common stock, the corporation no longer has to redeem the bond at maturity.

Convertible bonds, like all potential investments, must be carefully evaluated. Remember, not all convertible bonds are quality investments.

Provisions for Repayment

call feature

Today most corporate bonds are callable. A **call feature** allows the corporation to call in or buy outstanding bonds from current bondholders before the maturity date. In the 1990s, investors have seen a large number of bonds called because corporations can replace high-interest bond issues with new bond issues that have lower interest rates. The money needed to call a bond may come from the firm's profits, the sale of additional stock, or the sale of new bonds that have a lower interest rate.

In most cases, corporations issuing callable bonds agree not to call them for the first 5 to 10 years after the bonds have been issued. When a call feature is used, the corporation may have to pay the bondholders a *premium*, an additional amount above the face value of the bond. The amount of the premium is specified in the bond indenture; a $10 to $50 premium over the bond's face value is common.

sinking fund

A corporation may use one of two methods to ensure that it has sufficient funds available to redeem a bond issue. First, the corporation may establish a sinking fund. A **sinking fund** is a fund to which annual or semiannual deposits are made for the purpose of redeeming a bond issue. To retire a $100 million bond issue that matures in 2017, Outboard Marine Corporation (OMC) agreed to make annual sinking fund payments of $5 million on April 15 of each year between 1998 and 2016. A sinking fund provision in the bond indenture is generally advantageous to bondholders. Such a provision forces the corporation to make arrangements for bond repayment before the maturity date. If the terms of the provision are not met, the trustee or bondholders may take legal action against the company.

serial bonds

Second, a corporation may issue serial bonds. **Serial bonds** are bonds of a single issue that mature on different dates. For example, Seaside Productions used a 20-year, $100 million bond issue to finance its expansion. None of the bonds matures during the first 10 years. Thereafter, 10 percent of the bonds mature each year until all the bonds are retired at the end of the 20-year period.

Detailed information about provisions for repayment, along with other vital information (including maturity date, interest rate, bond rating, call provisions, trustee, and details about collateral), is available from Moody's Investors Service, Standard & Poor's Corporation, and other financial service companies. Take a look at the information provided by Moody's Investors Service for the Bell Atlantic of Pennsylvania bond illustrated in the Financial Planning in Action box on page 468.

CONCEPT CHECK 15–2

1. Why do corporations sell bonds?
2. What are the differences among a debenture, a mortgage bond, and a subordinated debenture?
3. Why would an investor purchase a Westinghouse Electric convertible bond?
4. Describe three reasons a corporation would sell convertible bonds.
5. Explain the methods corporations can use to repay a bond issue.

WHY INVESTORS PURCHASE CORPORATE BONDS

L.O.3 Explain why investors purchase corporate bonds.

Investors purchase corporate bonds for three reasons: (1) interest income, (2) possible increase in value, and (3) repayment at maturity.

Interest Income

As mentioned earlier, bondholders normally receive interest payments every six months. The dollar amount of interest is determined by multiplying the interest rate by the face value of the bond. For example, if IBM issues a 7½ percent bond with a face value of $1,000, the investor will receive $75 ($1,000 × 7.5% = $75) a year, paid in installments of $37.50 at the end of each six-month period.

FINANCIAL PLANNING IN ACTION

THE "HOW TO" OF RESEARCHING A BOND

How do you find out whether or not a corporate bond is callable? Where can you find out who the trustee for a specific bond issue is? These are only two of the multitude of questions that concern investors who are trying to evaluate bond investments. Fortunately, the answers are easy to obtain if you know where to look.

Today the most readily available source of detailed information about a corporation, including information about its bond issues, is Moody's *Industrial Manuals*. Individual subscriptions to this series of publications are too expensive for most investors, but the series is available

at both college and public libraries. It includes individual manuals on industrial companies, public utilities, banks and financial institutions, and transportation companies. Each manual contains detailed information on major companies in the United States, including the company's history, operations, products, and bond issues.

The following data on a corporate bond issued by Bell Atlantic Company of Pennsylvania will give you an idea of the contents of the "Long-Term Debt" section of a Moody's report.

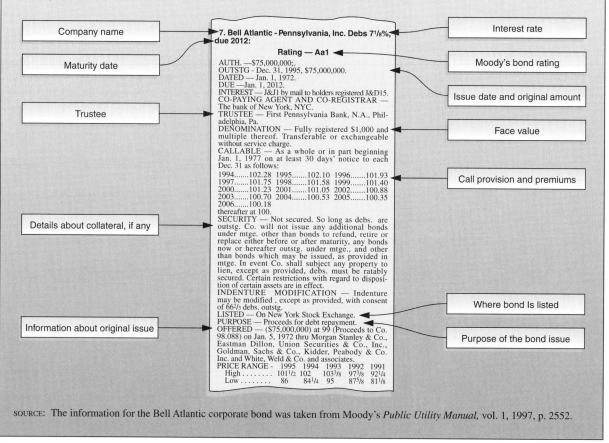

SOURCE: The information for the Bell Atlantic corporate bond was taken from Moody's *Public Utility Manual,* vol. 1, 1997, p. 2552.

---

registered bond

coupon bond

The method used to pay bondholders their interest depends on whether they own registered bonds, coupon bonds, or zero-coupon bonds. A **registered bond** is registered in the owner's name by the issuing company. Interest checks for registered bonds are mailed directly to the bondholder of record. A **coupon bond** is issued with detachable coupons that the bondholder must present to a paying agent *or* the issuer to receive interest payments. *Be* *warned:* Coupon bonds are bearer bonds, and the rightful owner of this type of bond can be out of luck if they are lost or stolen. Anyone—rightful owner or thief—can collect interest payments if he or she has physical possession of the bond's coupons. While some coupon bonds are still in circulation, they are no longer issued by corporations.

zero-coupon bond

A **zero-coupon bond** is sold at a price far below its face value, makes no annual or semiannual interest payments, and is redeemed for its face value at maturity. With a zero-coupon bond, the buyer receives a return based on the bond's increased market value as its maturity date approaches. For example, assume you purchased a Waste Management zero-coupon bond for $350 in 1995 and Waste Management will pay you $1,000 when the bond matures in 2012. For holding the bond 18 years, you will receive interest of $650 ($1,000 face value − $350 purchase price = $650 interest) at maturity.

Before investing in zero-coupon bonds, you should consider at least two factors. First, even though all of the interest on these bonds is paid at maturity, the IRS requires you to report interest each year—that is, as you earn it, not when you actually receive it. Second, zero-coupon bonds are more volatile than other types of bonds. When evaluating such bonds, as in evaluating any other type of bond, the most important criterion is the quality of the issuer. It pays to be careful.

Dollar Appreciation of Bond Value

Most beginning investors think that a $1,000 bond is always worth $1,000. In reality, the price of a corporate bond may fluctuate until the maturity date. Changes in overall interest rates in the economy are the primary cause of most bond price fluctuations. Changing bond prices that result from changes in overall interest rates in the economy are an example of interest rate risk, discussed in Chapter 13. In fact, there is an inverse relationship between a bond's market value and overall interest rates in the economy. When IBM issued the bond mentioned earlier, the $7\frac{1}{2}$ percent interest rate was competitive with the interest rates offered by other corporations issuing bonds at that time. If overall interest rates fall, the IBM bond will go up in market value due to its higher, $7\frac{1}{2}$ percent, interest rate. On the other hand, if overall interest rates rise, the market value of the IBM bond will fall due to its lower, $7\frac{1}{2}$ percent, interest rate.

When a bond is selling for less than its face value, it is said to be selling at a *discount*. When a bond is selling for more than its face value, it is said to be selling at a *premium*. Generally, investors consult *The Wall Street Journal, Barron's,* or a local newspaper to determine the price of a bond. Information on how to read bond quotations is provided later in this chapter.

It is also possible to approximate a bond's market value using the following formula:

$$\text{Approximate market value} = \frac{\text{Annual interest amount}}{\text{Current interest rate}}$$

For example, assume you purchase a New York Telephone bond that pays $4\frac{7}{8}$ percent interest based on a face value of $1,000. Also assume new corporate bond issues of comparable quality are currently paying 7 percent. The approximate market value is $696, as follows:

$$\text{Annual interest} = \$1,000 \times 4\frac{7}{8} \text{ percent}$$
$$= \$1,000 \times 4.875 \text{ percent}$$
$$= \$48.75$$

$$\text{Approximate market value} = \frac{\text{Annual interest amount}}{\text{Current interest rate}} = \frac{\$48.75}{7\%}$$
$$= \$696$$

EXHIBIT 15–3

Sample Corporate Bond Transaction for Borden, Inc.

Assumptions

Interest, 8⅜ percent; maturity date, 2016; purchased October 8, 1988; sold October 8, 1997

Costs when purchased		Return when sold	
1 bond @ $680	$680	1 bond @ $1,030	$1,030
Plus commission	+ 25	Minus commission	− 25
Total investment	$705	Dollar return	$1,005

Transaction summary

Dollar return	$1,005
Minus total investment	− 705
Profit from bond sale	$ 300
Plus interest ($83.75 for 9 years)	+ 754
Total profit and interest on the transaction	$1,054

The market value of a bond may also be affected by the financial condition of the company or government unit issuing the bond, the factors of supply and demand, and the proximity of the bond's maturity date.

Bond Repayment at Maturity

Corporate bonds are repaid at maturity. When you purchase a bond, you have two options: You may keep the bond until maturity and then redeem it, or you may sell the bond at any time to another investor. In either case, the value of your bond is closely tied to the corporation's ability to repay its bond indebtedness. For example, the retailer Color Tile and Carpet filed for reorganization under the provisions of the U.S. Bankruptcy Act. As a result, the bonds issued by Color Tile immediately dropped in value due to questions concerning the prospects for bond repayment at maturity.

A Typical Bond Transaction

Financial Decision Trade-Off

Assume that on October 8, 1988, you purchased an 8⅜ percent corporate bond issued by Borden, Inc. Your cost for the bond was $680 plus a $25 commission charge, for a total investment of $705. Also assume you held the bond until October 8, 1997, when you sold it at its current market value of $1,030. Exhibit 15–3 shows the return on your investment.

In this example, you made a total return of $1,054, which came from two sources. After paying commissions for buying and selling your Borden bond, you made $300 because the market value of the bond increased from $680 to $1,030. The increase in the value of the bond resulted because overall interest rates in the economy declined during the nine-year period in which you owned the bond. Also, Borden established a reputation for efficiency and productivity during this period. Increased efficiency and productivity help ensure that Borden will be able to repay bondholders when the bond reaches maturity in the year 2016.

You also made money on your Borden bond because of interest payments. For each of the nine years you owned the bond, Borden paid you $83.75 ($1,000 × 8.375% = $83.75) interest. Thus, you received interest payments totaling $754.

Of course, you should remember that the price of a corporate bond can decrease and that interest payments and eventual repayment may be a problem for a corporation that encounters financial difficulties or enters bankruptcy. In addition to purchasing individual bonds, some investors prefer to purchase bond funds. To help you decide whether you should purchase individual bonds or bond funds, read the accompanying Financial Planning for Life's Situations box.

FINANCIAL PLANNING FOR LIFE'S SITUATIONS

ARE BOND FUNDS RIGHT FOR YOU?

Simply put, bond funds are an indirect way of owning bonds, debt instruments, and IOUs issued by the U.S. Treasury, corporations, or state, city, and local school districts. Many financial experts recommend bond funds for small investors because these investments offer diversification and professional management. Diversification spells safety because an occasional loss incurred with one bond issue is usually offset by gains from other bond issues in the fund. Also, professional managers should be able to do a better job of picking bonds than individual investors. But before investing, consider two factors. First, even the best portfolio managers make mistakes. Second, it may cost more to purchase bond funds than individual bonds. As with most investments, the key to making money with funds is evaluation.

Evaluating Bond Funds

Martha Hernandez, a working mother with one child, received $44,000 following the death of her grandmother. After some careful planning, she decided to invest $34,000 in two high-quality corporate bond funds. She used the remaining $10,000 to pay off some credit card debts and establish an emergency fund. During the next two years, she earned over 11 percent on her bond investments—not bad during a period when CDs were paying between 5 and 6 percent.

Martha's 11 percent return wasn't just luck. She began by establishing an investment goal: Find a safe investment with minimal risk. After establishing her goal, she talked with an account executive at Merrill Lynch and asked for five suggestions that would enable her to attain her goal. Of the five original suggestions, three were conservative bond funds.

Next, Martha took a crucial step that many investors forget: She decided to do her own research and not just rely on the account executive's suggestions. She contacted the firms that managed each of the three bond funds and asked them to mail her both a prospectus and an annual report. After receiving the information, she was able to (1) determine each fund's investment objective, (2) identify the investments each fund contained, and (3) calculate the approximate fees and expenses charged by each fund.

Then she made a trip to the library, where she analyzed the performance of each of the three bond funds in the special mutual fund editions of *Business Week, Kiplinger's Personal Finance,* and *Money.* Each publication ranked the three bond funds according to the total return for the previous 12 months, three years, and five years. Although past performance is no guarantee of future performance, it may be one of the best predictors available. Based on the account executive's suggestions and her own research, she chose the "top" two bond funds.

Martha admits that she spent almost 30 hours researching her investments, but believes the time was well spent. When you consider the amount of money she made on her bond fund investments during the first two years—over $7,400—she made almost $250 an hour.

SOURCES: Jason Zweig, "This Summer's Blockbusters . . . Bond Funds," *Money,* June 1997, pp. 134–36+; Werner Renberg, "The Lowdown on Bond Funds," *Black Enterprise,* September 1996, p. 48; Steven T. Golberg, "Buy Bonds or Bond Funds?" *Kiplinger's Personal Finance,* July 1996. pp. 77–78+.

The Mechanics of a Bond Transaction

Bonds are purchased in much the same manner as stocks. Corporate bonds may be purchased in the primary market or the secondary market. (Remember, in the *primary* market, an investor purchases financial securities, via an investment bank or other representative, from the issuer of those securities. In the *secondary* market, existing financial securities are traded among investors.) In the secondary market, corporate bonds issued by larger, well-recognized companies are traded on either the New York Bond Exchange or the American Bond Exchange. The actual steps involved in purchasing a bond listed on an exchange are similar to the steps required to purchase stocks listed on a stock exchange (see Exhibit 14–7 in Chapter 14). You can also purchase corporate bonds directly from account executives who make a market or maintain an inventory for certain bonds. Generally, if you purchase a $1,000 bond through an account executive, you should expect to pay a minimum commission of between $25 and $50. If you purchase more bonds, the commission usually drops to $5 to $20 per bond. You should also expect to pay commissions when you sell bonds.

CONCEPT CHECK 15–3

1. Describe the three reasons investors purchase bonds.
2. What are the differences among a registered bond, a coupon bond, and a zero-coupon bond?
3. In what ways can interest rates in the economy affect the price of a corporate bond?
4. Why is the value of a bond closely tied to the issuing corporation's ability to repay its bond indebtedness?
5. How are corporate bonds bought and sold?

GOVERNMENT BONDS AND DEBT SECURITIES

L.O.4 Discuss why federal, state, and local governments issue bonds.

In addition to corporations, the U.S. government and state and local governments issue bonds to obtain financing. In this section, we discuss bonds issued by these three levels of government.

Treasury Bills, Notes, and Bonds

Financial Decision
Trade-Off

The federal government sells bonds and securities to finance both the national debt and the government's ongoing activities. The main reason investors choose U.S. government securities is that most investors consider them risk free. In fact, some financial planners refer to them as the ultimate safe investment because their quality is considered to be higher than that of any other investment. Because they are backed by the full faith and credit of the U.S. government and carry a decreased risk of default, they offer lower interest rates than corporate bonds. The U.S. Treasury Department issues four principal types of bonds and securities: Treasury bills, Treasury notes, Treasury bonds, and U.S. government savings bonds. Treasury bills, notes, and bonds can be purchased directly from the 12 Federal Reserve banks or one of their 25 branches. When investors purchase U.S. government securities through the Federal Reserve System, they pay no commission charge. The Federal Reserve System conducts auctions to sell Treasury bills, notes, and bonds. Buyers interested in purchasing these securities at such auctions may bid competitively or noncompetitively. If they bid competitively, they must specify the price or interest yield they are willing to accept. If they bid noncompetitively, they are willing to accept the average interest rate and to pay the average price at which the securities are sold. Treasury securities may also be purchased through banks or brokers, which charge a commission. U.S. government savings bonds can be purchased through the Federal Reserve banks and branches, commercial banks, savings and loan associations, or other financial institutions. U.S. government securities can be held until maturity or redeemed before maturity. Interest paid on U.S. government securities is taxable for federal income tax purposes but is exempt from state and local taxation. Current information on prices and interest rates appears in *The Wall Street Journal* and other financial publications.

Treasury Bills   A *Treasury bill,* sometimes called a *T-bill,* is sold in a minimum unit of $10,000 with additional increments of $1,000 above the minimum. The maturity for a T-bill ranges from three months to one year.

T-bills are discounted securities, and the actual purchase price you pay is less than the maturity value of the T-bill. Let's assume you purchase a one-year, $10,000 T-bill with a stated interest rate of 5 percent. To determine the discount amount ($500), multiply the maturity value by the interest rate ($10,000 × 5% = $500). To determine the purchase price ($9,500), subtract the discount amount from the maturity value ($10,000 − $500 = $9,500).

In reality, the actual yield on T-bills is slightly higher than the stated interest rate. In the above example, you received $500 interest on a $9,500 investment, which represents a 5.3 percent return, as follows:

$$\text{Current yield for a T-bill} = \frac{\text{Discount amount}}{\text{Purchase price}}$$

$$= \frac{\$500}{\$9,500}$$

$$= 0.053 = 5.3 \text{ percent}$$

Treasury Notes   A *Treasury note* is issued in $5,000 units with two- or three-year maturities. You can also purchase a $1,000 Treasury note with either a 5-year or a 10-year maturity. Interest rates for Treasury notes are slightly higher than those for Treasury bills, because investors must wait longer to get their money back and therefore demand more compensation in the form of higher interest. Interest for Treasury notes is paid every six months.

Treasury Bonds   A *Treasury bond* is issued in minimum units of $1,000 and has a 30-year maturity. Interest rates for Treasury bonds are generally higher than those for either Treasury bills or Treasury notes. Again, the primary reason for the higher interest rates is the length of time investors must hold Treasury bonds. Like interest on Treasury notes, interest on Treasury bonds is paid every six months.

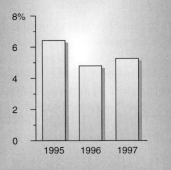

DID YOU KNOW?

Interest rates for U.S. government savings bonds purchased after May 1995 and held for more than 5 years

SOURCE: Federal Reserve Bank, January 12, 1998.

U.S. Government Savings Bonds   Generally, Series EE bonds are purchased and held until maturity. These bonds are issued with maturity values ranging from $50 to $10,000. The purchase price for Series EE bonds is one-half of their maturity value. Thus, a $100 bond costs $50 when purchased. At the time of publication, Series EE bonds purchased after May 1997 provide a guaranteed return that is based on the yield paid on five-year Treasury notes. The actual interest rate you receive on Series EE bonds is 90 percent of the average yields paid on five-year Treasury notes for the proceeding six months. This average yield is calculated on May 1 and November 1 of each year.

The interest on Series EE bonds, which some financial planners call *accrued interest,* is exempt from state and local taxes and accumulates free from federal taxation until the bonds are redeemed. Savings bonds may be redeemed anytime from six months to 30 years after purchase to receive the amount paid plus interest. Once these bonds are cashed in, the interest on them is subject to federal taxation. As discussed in Chapter 5, if the income derived from savings bonds is used to pay college tuition, it is exempt from federal taxation.

You can also postpone federal taxation of the interest paid on Series EE bonds if you convert them to Series HH bonds. Series HH bonds pay out interest semiannually if you hold them for more than six months.

JONATHAN HOENIG SPEAKS
RELEASED FROM BONDAGE

Riddle me this: If a 7-Eleven is open 24 hours a day, 7 days a week, 365 days a year, then *why* do the doors have locks? No answer?

Same question: If stocks have historically outperformed bonds, then why bother making bonds a part of your portfolio? Simple answers: *diversity.*

Buying bonds or other fixed-income investment diversifies a portfolio across asset classes, which "smoothes out" a portfolio's overall return. By venturing outside the stock market, bond investors are purchasing securities with incongruent correlations. Corporate bonds, bank certificates of deposit, and U.S. Treasury securities pay investors interest income. This yield can drastically boost your return, especially when the stock market sags. In addition

to the bond's yield, the price of bonds itself fluctuates with interest rates. When not held to "maturity," it is quite possible to lose money investing in individual bonds.

Generally, you need serious cash to purchase a diversified portfolio of individual bonds, so those looking for fixed-income exposure might want to use bond mutual funds. These funds, which are not federally insured, are offered in a variety of different risk profiles.

Thinking safety? In lieu of putting cash under your mattress, try a money market fund. Available through every major fund company, these investments function as really short-term bond funds and are perfect surrogates for the savings account.

Federal Agency Debt Issues

In addition to the bonds and securities issued by the Treasury Department, debt securities are issued by federal agencies, which include the Federal National Mortgage Association (sometimes referred to as Fannie Mae), the Federal Housing Administration (FHA), the Government National Mortgage Association (sometimes referred to as Ginnie Mae), and the Federal Home Loan Mortgage Corporation (which somehow became know as Freddie Mac).

Although agency debt issues are, for practical purposes, risk free, they offer a slightly higher interest rate than government securities issued by the Treasury Department. Generally, their minimum denomination is $25,000. Securities issued by federal agencies have maturities ranging from 1 year to 40 years, with an average life of about 15 years.

State and Local Government Securities

municipal bond

A **municipal bond,** sometimes called a *muni,* is a debt security issued by a state or local government. In the United States, there are 50 state governments. In addition, approximately 50,000 municipal entities—cities, counties, school districts, and special taxing districts—may sell municipal bonds.[1] Such securities are used to finance the ongoing activities of state and local governments and major projects such as airports, schools, toll roads, and toll bridges, and may be purchased directly from the government entity that issued them or through account executives.

general obligation bond

revenue bond

State and local securities are classified as either general obligation bonds or revenue bonds. A **general obligation bond** is backed by the full faith, credit, and unlimited taxing power of the government that issued it. A **revenue bond** is repaid from the income generated by the project it is designed to finance.

Although both general obligation and revenue bonds are relatively safe, defaults have occurred in recent years. In the 1990s, default rates have been high for tax-exempt bonds used to finance health care facilities. In Florida alone, $20 million in health care bonds went sour just one year after they were issued. Unfortunately, tax-exempt bonds used to fund other government projects have also cost investors millions of dollars. Pilot Point Development Authority issued tax-exempt bonds to construct a hotel and marina development in Charleston, South Carolina. Before the project was completed, Pilot Point Development Authority stopped making interest payments on its bonds. Losses to investors who purchased these bonds totaled an estimated $21 million.[2] The largest municipal bond default in recent history occurred when Washington Public Power Supply was unable to pay off its debt as scheduled on municipal bonds worth more than $2 billion, and thousands of investors lost money.

If the risk of default worries you, you can purchase insured municipal bonds. A number of states offer to guarantee payments on selected securities. Also, there are three large private insurers: the Municipal Bond Insurance Association, the American Municipal Bond Assurance Corporation, and the Financial Guaranty Insurance Corporation.

Financial Decision Trade-Off

Even if a municipal bond issue is insured, however, financial experts worry about the insurer's ability to pay off in the event of default on a large bond issue. Most advise investors to determine the underlying quality of a bond whether or not it is insured. Also, guaranteed municipal securities carry a slightly lower interest rate than uninsured bonds because of the reduced risk of default.

Like a corporate bond, a municipal bond may be callable by the government unit that issued it. Typically, some call protection exists. In most cases, the municipality that issues the bond agrees not to call it for the first 10 years. *Be warned:* Your municipal bond may be called if interest rates fall and the government entity that issued the bond can sell new bonds with lower rates. For example, in the past few years, thousands of municipal bondholders who purchased high-yielding municipal bonds in the 1980s have been shocked to have their bonds called. Many were counting on another 10 to 15 years of 12 percent or higher yields to finance their retirement. Although they were repaid the principal invested in the bond that was called, they faced the challenge of reinvesting their money when interest rates were at a 20-year low. If the bond is not called, the investor has two options. First, the bond may be held until maturity, in which case the investor will be repaid its face value. Second, the bond may be sold to another investor. However, it may be difficult to find a buyer for some municipal bond issues.

One of the most important features of municipal securities is that the interest on them may be exempt from federal taxes. Whether or not the interest on municipal bonds is tax exempt depends on how the funds obtained from their sale are used. *It is your responsibility, as an investor, to determine whether or not municipal bonds are taxable.* Municipal bonds exempt from federal taxation are generally exempt from state and local taxes only in the state where they are issued.

To some extent, the tax advantages associated with municipal bonds have diminished because recent tax law changes lowered the maximum federal income tax rate for individuals. (Before those changes were enacted, the maximum rate for individuals was 50 percent!) But even with the lower tax rates, municipal bonds are still very popular among wealthy investors. Because of their tax-exempt status, the interest rates on municipal bonds are lower than those on taxable bonds. By using the following formula, you can calculate the *taxable equivalent yield* for a municipal security:

$$\text{Taxable equivalent yield} = \frac{\text{Tax-exempt yield}}{1.0 - \text{Your tax rate}}$$

EXHIBIT 15–4

Yields for Tax-Exempt Investments

The following information can be used to compare the return on tax-exempt investments with the returns offered by taxable investments.

Tax-Exempt Yield	Equivalent Yields for Taxable Investments				
	15% Tax Rate	28% Tax Rate	31% Tax Rate	36% Tax Rate	39.6% Tax Rate
4%	4.71%	5.56%	5.80%	6.3%	6.6%
5	5.88	6.94	7.25	7.8	8.3
6	7.06	8.33	8.70	9.4	9.9
7	8.24	9.72	10.14	10.9	11.6
8	9.41	11.11	11.59	12.5	13.2
9	10.59	12.50	13.04	14.1	14.9
10	11.76	13.89	14.49	15.6	16.6

For example, the taxable equivalent yield on a 5 percent, tax-exempt municipal bond for a person in the 28 percent tax bracket is 6.9 percent, as follows:

$$\text{Taxable equivalent yield} = \frac{0.05}{1.0 - 0.28} = 0.069, \text{ or } 6.9 \text{ percent}$$

If this taxpayer had been in the 39.6 tax bracket, the taxable-equivalent yield for a 5 percent, tax-exempt investment would increase to 8.3 percent. Once you have calculated the taxable equivalent yield, you can compare the return on tax-exempt securities with the return on taxable securities. Exhibit 15–4 illustrates the yields for tax-exempt investments and their taxable equivalent yields.

CONCEPT CHECK   15–4

1. What are the denominations and maturities for a Treasury bill, a Treasury note, and a Treasury bond?
2. How is the interest rate for Series EE savings bonds calculated?
3. What is the difference between a general obligation bond and a revenue bond?
4. What risks are involved when investing in municipal bonds?
5. Assume a taxpayer in the 28 percent tax bracket invests in a 6 percent, tax-exempt municipal bond. Use the above formula to find the taxable equivalent yield.

THE INVESTOR'S DECISION TO BUY OR SELL BONDS

L.O.5 Evaluate bonds when making an investment.

Sheet 59

One basic principle we have stressed throughout this text is the need to evaluate any potential investment. Certainly corporate *and* government bonds are no exception. Only after you have completed your evaluation should you purchase bonds. Of course, a decision to sell bonds also requires evaluation. In this section, we examine methods you can use to evaluate bond investments.

How to Read the Bond Section of the Newspaper

Not all local newspapers contain bond quotations, but *The Wall Street Journal* and *Barron's* publish complete and thorough information on this subject. In bond quotations,

EXHIBIT 15–5

Financial Information about Corporate Bonds Available in *The Wall Street Journal*

NEW YORK EXCHANGE BONDS

CORPORATION BONDS
Volume, $21,225,000

Bonds	Cur Yld	Vol	Close	Net Chg
AMR 8.10s98	8.0	6	101 13/16	+ 11/16
AMR 9s16	7.6	30	118 1/4	− 5/8
ATT 4 3/4 98	4.8	3	99 5/8	+ 5/32
ATT 4 3/8 99	4.5	25	98 1/8	...
ATT 6s00	6.0	15	100 1/8	− 1/8
ATT 5 1/8 01	5.2	12	98 1/4	+ 1/8
ATT 7 1/8 02	6.8	69	104 3/4	− 1/8
ATT 6 3/4 04	6.4	30	104 3/4	+ 3/8
ATT 7s05	6.6	12	106	...
ATT 8.2s05	7.8	10	105 3/8	+ 1 5/8
ATT 7 3/4 07	7.0	7	111	+ 1
ATT 8 1/8 22	7.5	1142	108 1/4	...
ATT 8 1/8 24	7.6	47	107 5/8	− 1/4
ATT 8 5/8 31	7.8	45	111 1/4	− 1/4
AlaBn 6.2s99t	6.3	5	98 1/2	...
AlskAr 6 7/8 14	cv	41	121	+ 1
AlldC zr98	...	37	96 1/16	+ 1/16
AlldC zr2000	...	10	85 3/8	+ 3/8
AlldC zr09	...	100	47 7/8	+ 3/8
Allwst 7 1/4 14	cv	11	91	− 3
Alza 5s06	cv	27	105	...
Alza zr14	...	22	45 3/4	− 1/4
Amoco 8 5/8 16	8.1	1	106 5/8	− 1 1/4
Amresco 8 3/4 99	8.8	1	100	− 3/4
Amresco 10s03	9.9	27	101	...
Amresco 10s04	9.8	15	102	− 1/2
AnnTaylr 8 3/4 00	8.7	14	100 3/8	...

Quotations as of 4 p.m. Eastern Time
Monday, January 12, 1998

Volume $21,420,000

SALES SINCE JANUARY 1
(000 omitted)

1998	1997	1996
$128,120	$199,947	$183,283

	Domestic Mon.	Domestic Fri.	All Issues Mon.	All Issues Fri.
Issues traded	298	280	305	291
Advances	139	117	142	119
Declines	98	106	100	111
Unchanged	61	57	63	61
New highs	52	66	52	66
New lows	6	4	7	4

Dow Jones Bond Averages

−1997− High	−1997− Low	−1998− High	−1998− Low		−−−1998−−− Close	−−−1998−−− Chg.	−−−1998−−− %Yld	−−1997−− Close	−−1997−− Chg.
105.13	101.09	105.40	105.24	20 Bonds	105.40	+0.13	6.82	103.02	+ 0.02
102.89	97.64	103.02	102.69	10 Utilities	102.78	+0.09	6.89	100.01	− 0.13
107.49	104.54	108.01	107.59	10 Industrials	108.01	+0.17	6.75	106.03	+ 0.17

1. The name (often abbreviated) of the issuing firm is ATT. The bond pays annual interest at the rate of 6¾ percent of the face value, or $1,000 × 6¾% = $67.50 per year. It matures in the year 2004.
2. The current yield, or return, based on today's market price is $67.50 ÷ $1,047.50, or 6.4 percent.
3. On this day, 30 bonds were traded.
4. The last price for a ATT bond during the day was $1,000 × 104.75, or $1,047.50.
5. The last price paid on this day was .375% × $1,000, or $3.75, higher than the last price paid on the previous trading day. In Wall Street terms, the ATT bond "closed up ⅜" on this day.

SOURCE: Reprinted by permission of *The Wall Street Journal,* January 13, 1998, p. C20.

prices are given as a percentage of the face value, which is usually $1,000. Thus, to find the actual market price for a bond, you must multiply the face value ($1,000) by the newspaper quote. For example, a price quoted as 84 means a selling price of $1,000 × 84% = $840. Purchases and sales of bonds are reported in tables like that shown at the top of Exhibit 15–5. The eighth row of Exhibit 15–5 gives the detailed information for an ATT corporate bond. (The numbers in this list refer to the actual columns in the newspaper quotation.)

For government bonds, most financial publications include two price quotations. The first price quotation, or the *bid price,* is the highest price a dealer is willing to pay for a government security. The bid price represents the amount that a seller could receive for a government bond. The second price quotation, or the *asked price,* represents the lowest price at which a dealer is willing to sell a government security. The asked price represents the amount for which a buyer could purchase the security. In addition to price quotations, financial publications provide information about the interest rates, maturity dates, and yields of government securities.

Annual Reports and the Internet

As pointed out earlier in this chapter, bondholders must be concerned about the financial health of the corporation or government unit that issues bonds. To understand how important financial information is when evaluating a bond issue, consider the following two questions:

- Will the bond be repaid at maturity?
- Will you receive interest payments until maturity?

While it may be difficult to answer these questions with 100 percent accuracy, the information contained in a firm's annual report is the logical starting point. Today there are three ways to obtain a corporation's annual report. First, you can either write or telephone the corporation and request an annual report. (Hint: Many corporations have 800 telephone numbers for investor use.) Second, most corporations maintain an Internet Web site that contains detailed information about their financial performance. Often you can access this information by simply typing in a corporation's name, locating the topic "financial information" or "annual report," and clicking your mouse. Third, some financial publications provide a reader's service that allows investors to use a toll-free telephone number or a postcard to obtain an annual report.

Regardless of how you obtain an annual report, you should look for signs of financial strength or weakness. Is the firm profitable? Are sales revenues increasing? Are the firm's long-term liabilities increasing? In fact, there are many questions bondholders should ask before making a decision to buy a bond. To help you determine the right questions to ask when evaluating a bond issue, read the accompanying Financial Planning in Action feature. Also, you may want to examine the bond's rating and perform the calculations described on pages 480–81 before investing your money.

Bond Ratings

To determine the quality and risk associated with bond issues, investors rely on the bond ratings provided by Moody's Investors Service, Inc., and Standard & Poor's Corporation. Both companies rank thousands of corporate and municipal bonds.

As Exhibit 15–6 illustrates, bond ratings generally range from AAA (the highest) to D (the lowest). For both Moody's and Standard & Poor's, the first four individual categories represent investment-grade securities. Investment-grade securities are suitable for conservative investors who want a safe investment that provides a predictable source of income. Bonds in the next two categories are considered speculative in nature. Finally, the C and D categories are used to rank bonds that may be in default due to poor prospects of repayment or even continued payment of interest. Although bond ratings may be flawed or inaccurate, most investors regard the work of both Moody's and Standard & Poor's as highly reliable.

Generally, U.S. government securities issued by the Treasury Department and various federal agencies are not graded because they are risk free for practical purposes. The rating of long-term municipal bonds is similar to that of corporate bonds. In addition, Standard & Poor's rates shorter-term municipal bonds maturing in three years or less with the following designations:

SP–1 Very strong or strong capacity to pay principal and interest. Those issues determined to possess overwhelming safety characteristics receive a plus (+) designation.

SP–2 Satisfactory capacity to pay principal and interest.

SP–3 Speculative capacity to pay principal and interest.[3]

Bond Yield Calculations

yield

For a bond investment, the **yield** is the rate of return earned by an investor who holds a bond for a stated period of time. Two methods are used to measure the yield on a bond investment.

Financial Planning in Action

Evaluating Corporate Bonds

No checklist can serve as a foolproof guide for choosing a corporate or government bond. However, the following questions will help you evaluate a potential bond investment. (Usual sources of information include *Moody's Industrial Manuals* and *Standard & Poor's Stock and Bond Guide*.)

Category 1: Information about the Corporation

1. What is the corporation's name? _____

2. What are the corporation's address and telephone number?
   _____
   _____

3. What type of products or services does this firm provide?
   _____
   _____

4. Briefly describe the prospects for this company. (Include significant factors like product development, plans for expansion, plans for mergers, etc.) _____
   _____
   _____
   _____
   _____

Category 2: Bond Basics

5. What type of bond is this? _____

6. What is the face value for this bond? _____

7. What is the interest rate for this bond? _____

8. What is the annual interest amount for this bond? _____

9. When are interest payments made to bondholders? _____

10. Is the corporation currently paying interest as scheduled?
    ☐ Yes   ☐ No

11. What is the maturity date for this bond? _____

12. What is Moody's rating for this bond? _____

13. What is Standard & Poor's rating for this bond? _____

14. What do these ratings mean? _____
    _____
    _____

15. What was the original issue date? _____

16. Who is the trustee for this bond issue? _____
    _____

17. Is the bond callable? If so, when? _____
    _____

18. Is the bond secured with collateral? If so, what?
    ☐ Yes   ☐ No _____

19. How did the corporation use the money from this bond issue? _____
    _____

Category 3: Financial Performance

20. Has the firm's total debt increased over the last three years?
    ☐ Yes   ☐ No

21. Is the corporation profitable? If so, how profitable?
    ☐ Yes   ☐ No $ _____

22. Have profits increased over the last seven years?
    ☐ Yes   ☐ No

23. Are this year's sales higher than last year's sales?
    ☐ Yes   ☐ No

24. Have sales increased over the last seven years?
    ☐ Yes   ☐ No

25. Briefly describe any other information that you obtained from Moody's, Standard & Poor's, or other advisory services.
    _____
    _____
    _____
    _____

A Word of Caution

When you use a checklist, there is always a danger of overlooking important relevant information. The above checklist is not a cure-all, but it does provide some very sound questions that you should answer before making a decision to invest in bonds. Quite simply, it is a place to start. If you need other information, *you* are responsible for obtaining it and for determining how it affects your potential investment.

Exhibit 15–6   **Description of Bond Ratings Provided by Moody's Investors Service and Standard & Poor's Corporation**

Quality	Moody's	Standard & Poor's	Description
High-grade	Aaa	AAA	Bonds that are judged to be of the best quality. They carry the smallest degree of investment risk and are generally referred to as *gilt edge*. Interest payments are protected by a large or exceptionally stable margin, and principal is secure.
	Aa	AA	Bonds that are judged to be of high quality by all standards. Together with the first group, they comprise what are generally known as *high-grade* bonds. They are rated lower than the best bonds because their margins of protection may be smaller.
Medium-grade	A	A	Bonds that possess many favorable investment attributes and are to be considered upper medium-grade obligations. The factors giving security to principal and interest are considered adequate.
	Baa	BBB	Bonds that are considered medium-grade obligations; i.e., they are neither highly protected nor poorly secured.
Speculative	Ba	BB	Bonds that are judged to have speculative elements; their future cannot be considered well assured. Often their protection of interest and principal payment is very moderate.
	B	B	Bonds that generally lack characteristics of the desirable investment. Assurance of interest and principal payments or of maintenance of other terms of the contract over a long period of time may be low.
Default	Caa	CCC	Bonds that are of poor standing. Such issues may be in default, or elements of danger with respect to principal or interest, may be present .
	Ca	CC	Bonds that represent obligations that are highly speculative.
	C		The lowest-rated class in Moody's designation. These bonds are regarded as having extremely poor prospects of attaining any real investment standing.
		C	Rating given to bonds where a bankruptcy petition has been filed.
		D	Bond issues in default.

SOURCES: *Moody's Bond Survey,* December 1997, Moody's Investors Service, 99 Church St., New York, NY 10007; *Standard & Poor's Stock and Bond Guide,* 1997 edition, Standard & Poor's Corporation, 25 Broadway, New York, NY 10004.

current yield   The **current yield** is determined by dividing the annual income amount of any investment by its current market value. For bonds, the following formula may help you complete this calculation:

$$\text{Current yield on a corporate bond} = \frac{\text{Annual interest amount}}{\text{Current market value}}$$

For example, assume you own an AT&T corporate bond that pays 7.5 percent interest on an annual basis. This means that each year you will receive $75 ($1,000 $\times$ 7.5% = $75). Also assume the current market price of the AT&T bond is $960. The current yield is 7.8 percent, as follows:

$$\text{Current yield} = \frac{\$75}{\$960}$$

$$= 0.078, \text{ or } 7.8 \text{ percent}$$

The yield calculation allows you to compare a bond investment with the yields of other investment alternatives, which include certificates of deposit, common stock, preferred stock, and mutual funds. Naturally, the higher the current yield, the better! A current yield of 10 percent is better than a current yield of 7.8 percent.

yield to maturity

The **yield to maturity** is a yield calculation that takes into account the relationship among a bond's maturity value, the time to maturity, the current price, and the dollar amount of interest. The formula for calculating the yield to maturity is as follows:

$$\text{Yield to maturity} = \frac{\text{Annual interest amount} + \dfrac{\text{Face value} - \text{Market value}}{\text{Number of periods}}}{\dfrac{\text{Market value} + \text{Face value}}{2}}$$

For example, assume that on January 1, 1995, you purchased at the current market price of $830 a corporate bond with a $1,000 face value issued by Fruit of the Loom. The bond pays 7 percent annual interest, and its maturity date is 2011. The yield to maturity is 8.7 percent, as follows:

$$\text{Yield to maturity} = \frac{\$70 + \dfrac{\$1,000 - \$830}{17}}{\dfrac{\$830 + \$1,000}{2}}$$

$$= \frac{\$80}{\$915}$$

$$= 0.087, \text{ or } 8.7 \text{ percent}$$

In this situation, the yield to maturity takes into account two types of return on the bond. First, you will receive interest income from the purchase date until the maturity date. Second, at maturity you will receive a payment for the face value of the bond. If you purchased the bond at a price below the face value, the yield to maturity will be greater than the stated interest rate. If you purchased the bond at a price above the face value, the yield to maturity will be less than the stated interest rate. Like the current yield, the yield to maturity allows an investor to compare returns on a bond investment with other investments. Also, like the current yield, the higher the yield to maturity, the better. A yield to maturity of 9 percent is better than a yield to maturity of 7 percent. One additional calculation, times interest earned, is described in the accompanying Financial Planning Calculations box.

Other Sources of Information

Investors can use two additional sources of information to evaluate potential bond investments. First, both business periodicals and government publications can provide information about the economy and interest rates and detailed financial information about a corporation or government entity that issues bonds. You can locate many of these sources at your college or public library.

Second, most bonds are sold through brokerage firms and account executives. Ideally, an account executive should provide both information and advice about potential investments. Many experts urge you to remember one basic rule: It is always *your* money, and *you* should be the one who makes the final decision about which investment is best for you. Your account executive's role is to make suggestions and provide information that may enable you to make a more informed decision.

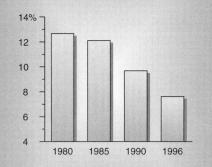

DO YOU KNOW

Average interest yields paid on corporate bonds in 1980, 1985, 1990, and 1996.

SOURCE: U.S. Bureau of the Census, *Statistical Abstract of the United States: 1997,* 117th ed. (Washington, DC: U.S. Government Printing Office, 1997), p. 524.

FINANCIAL PLANNING CALCULATIONS

THE TIMES INTEREST EARNED RATIO:
ONE TOOL TO HELP YOU EVALUATE BOND ISSUES

After evaluating Coca-Cola Enterprises, Betty and Matthew Randall (the couple in the opening case) wanted to purchase the firm's corporate debentures. But they were concerned about the corporation's ability to make future interest payments. Their account executive, Mike Foster, suggested that one way to measure a corporation's ability to pay interest is to calculate a ratio called the *times interest earned ratio,* illustrated below:

$$\text{Times interest earned} = \frac{\text{Operating income before interest and taxes}}{\text{Interest expense}}$$

For example, Coca-Cola Enterprises had interest expense of $351 million and operating income before interest and taxes of $545 million in 1996 (the latest year for which actual figures are available at the time of this publication). The times interest earned ratio for Coca-Cola Enterprises is 1.55 to 1, as follows:

$$\text{Times interest earned} = \frac{544 \text{ million}}{351 \text{ million}}$$

$$= 1.55 \text{ to } 1$$

Although the average for the times interest earned ratio varies from industry to industry, a higher number is better than a lower number. According to Mike Foster's calculations, Coca-Cola Enterprises is earning slightly over 1.5 times the amount required to pay the annual interest on its long-term notes, bonds, and other financial obligations. With a times interest earned ratio of 1.55 to 1, Coca-Cola Enterprises could experience a "significant" drop in earnings and still meet its financial obligations.

SOURCES: Based on information contained in Coca-Cola Enterprises, *The 1996 Annual Report.*

CONCEPT CHECK 15–5

1. What is the market value for a bond with a face value of $1,000 and a newspaper quotation of 77¼?
2. What type of information is contained in a corporation's annual report? On a corporation's Web page?
3. How important are bond ratings when evaluating a bond issue?
4. Why should you calculate the current yield and yield to maturity on a bond investment?
5. What type of assistance should you expect from your account executive when choosing a bond investment?

KEY FORMULAS

Page	Topic	Formula

469   Approximate market value

$$\text{Approximate market value} = \frac{\text{Annual interest amount}}{\text{Comparable interest rate}}$$

Example:

$$\text{Approximate market value} = \frac{\$80}{0.095}$$

$$= \$842.11$$

---

473   Current yield for a T-bill

$$\text{Current yield} = \frac{\text{Discount amount}}{\text{Purchase price}}$$

Example:

$$\text{Current yield} = \frac{\$550}{\$9,450}$$

$$= 0.058 = 5.8 \text{ percent}$$

---

475   Taxable equivalent yield

$$\text{Taxable equivalent yield} = \frac{\text{Tax-exempt yield}}{1.0 - \text{Your tax rate}}$$

Example:

$$\text{Taxable equivalent yield} = \frac{0.06}{1.0 - 0.28}$$

$$= 0.083 = 8.3 \text{ percent}$$

---

480   Current yield for a corporate bond

$$\text{Current yield} = \frac{\text{Annual interest amount}}{\text{Current market value}}$$

Example:

$$\text{Current yield} = \frac{\$75}{\$800}$$

$$= 0.094 = 9.4 \text{ percent}$$

---

481   Yield to maturity

$$\text{Yield to maturity} = \frac{\text{Annual interest amount} + \dfrac{\text{Face value} - \text{Market value}}{\text{Number of periods}}}{\dfrac{\text{Market value} + \text{Face value}}{2}}$$

Example:

$$\text{Yield to maturity} = \frac{\$60 + \dfrac{\$1,000 - \$900}{10}}{\dfrac{\$900 + \$1,000}{2}}$$

$$= 0.074 = 7.4 \text{ percent}$$

SUMMARY

L.O.1   Describe the characteristics of corporate bonds.

A corporate bond is a corporation's written pledge to repay a specified amount of money with interest. All of the details about a bond (face value, interest rate, maturity date, repayment, etc.) are contained in the bond indenture. The trustee is the bond holder's representative

L.O.2   Discuss why corporations issue bonds.

Corporations issue bonds and other securities to help finance their ongoing activities. Bonds may be debentures, mortgage bonds, subordinated debentures, or convertible bonds. Most bonds are callable. To ensure that the money will be available when needed to repay bonds, most corporations establish a sinking fund. Corporations can also issue serial bonds that mature on different dates.

L.O.3   Explain why investors purchase corporate bonds.

Investors purchase corporate bonds for three reasons: (1) interest income, (2) possible increase in value, and (3) repayment at maturity. The method used to pay bondholders their interest depends on whether they own registered bonds, coupon bonds, or zero-coupon bonds. Corporate bonds can be bought or sold through account executives who represent brokerage firms.

L.O.4   Discuss why federal, state, and local governments issue bonds.

Bonds issued by the U.S. Treasury and federal agencies are used to finance the national debt and the ongoing activities of the federal government. The U.S. Treasury issues four principal types of bonds: Treasury bills, Treasury notes, Treasury bonds, and Series EE savings bonds. State and local governments issue bonds to finance their ongoing activities and special projects such as airports, schools, toll roads, and toll bridges. U.S. government bonds can be purchased through Federal Reserve banks and branches, commercial banks, savings and loan associations, and other financial institutions. Municipal bonds are generally sold through the government entity that issued them or account executives.

L.O.5   Evaluate bonds when making an investment.

Some local newspapers, *The Wall Street Journal,* and *Barron's* provide bond investors with some of the information they need to evaluate a bond issue. Detailed financial information can be obtained by requesting a printed copy of the corporation's annual report or accessing its Internet Web site. To determine the quality of a bond issue, most investors study the ratings provided by Standard & Poor's and Moody's. Investors can also calculate a current yield and a yield to maturity to evaluate bond issues.

The current yield is determined by dividing the annual interest dollar amount of the bond by its current market value. The yield to maturity takes into account the relationship among a bond's maturity value, the time to maturity, the current price, and the dollar amount of interest.

GLOSSARY

bond indenture   A legal document that details all of the conditions relating to a bond issue.   (p. 464)

call feature   A feature that allows the corporation to call in or buy outstanding bonds from current bondholders before the maturity date.   (p. 466)

convertible bond   A bond that can be exchanged, at the owner's option, for a specified number of shares of the corporation's common stock.   (p. 466)

corporate bond   A corporation's written pledge to repay a specified amount of money with interest.   (p. 463)

coupon bond   A bond that is issued with detachable coupons that the bondholder presents to a paying agent or the issuing company to receive interest payments.   (p. 468)

current yield   Determined by dividing the annual income amount of any investment by its current market value. (p. 480)

debenture   A bond that is backed only by the reputation of the issuing corporation.   (p. 465)

face value   The dollar amount the bondholder will receive at the bond's maturity.   (p. 463)

general obligation bond   A bond backed by the full faith, credit, and unlimited taxing power of the government that issued it.   (p. 474)

maturity date   For a corporate bond, the date on which the corporation is to repay the borrowed money.   (p. 464)

mortgage bond   A corporate bond that is secured by various assets of the issuing firm.   (p. 466)

municipal bond   A debt security issued by a state or local government.   (p. 474)

registered bond   A bond that is registered in the owner's name by the issuing company.   (p. 468)

revenue bond   A bond that is repaid from the income generated by the project it is designed to finance.   (p. 474)

serial bonds   Bonds of a single issue that mature on different dates.   (p. 467)

sinking fund   A fund to which annual or semiannual deposits are made for the purpose of redeeming a bond issue.   (p. 467)

subordinated debenture   An unsecured bond that gives bondholders a claim secondary to that of other designated bondholders with respect to both interest payments and assets.   (p. 466)

trustee   A financially independent firm that acts as the bondholders' representative.   (p. 464)

yield   The rate of return earned by an investor who holds a bond for a stated period of time.   (p. 478)

yield to maturity   A yield calculation that takes into account the relationship among a bond's maturity value, the time to maturity, the current price, and the dollar amount of interest.   (p. 481)

zero-coupon bond   A bond that is sold at a price far below its face value, makes no annual or semiannual interest payments, and is redeemed for its face value at maturity.   (p. 469)

R E V I E W   Q U E S T I O N S

1. In your own words, define the following terms: (L.O.1)
   a. Corporate bond
   b. Maturity date
   c. Bond indenture
2. What does a trustee do? Whom does a trustee represent?   (L.O.1)
3. From an investor's view, how do the following bonds differ?   (L.O.2)
   a. Debenture bond
   b. Mortgage bond
   c. Subordinated bond
   d. Convertible bond
4. Describe two ways a corporation can pay off a bond issue at maturity.   (L.O.2)
5. Discuss three different reasons investors purchase bonds for investment purposes.   (L.O.3)
6. Describe how bonds are bought and sold.   (L.O.3)
7. What is the difference between a U.S. Treasury bill, a Treasury note, and a Treasury bond?   (L.O.4)

8. How is the purchase price for a U.S. government savings bond determined?   (L.O.4)
9. What is the difference between a general obligation bond and a revenue bond?   (L.O.4)
10. Describe the type of bond information provided in *The Wall Street Journal, Barron's,* or a local newspaper.   (L.O.5)
11. What type of information is contained in a corporation's annual report? How could it help you as a prospective bondholder?   (L.O.5)
12. How important are the bond ratings provided by Moody's and Standard & Poor's?   (L.O.5)
13. Describe how to calculate the current yield for a bond investment.   (L.O.5)
14. Describe how to calculate the yield to maturity for a bond investment.   (L.0.5)
15. How can business periodicals, government publications, and account executives help you evaluate a bond issue?   (L.O.5)

F I N A N C I A L   P L A N N I N G   P R O B L E M S

1. *Calculating Interest.* What is the annual interest amount for a $1,000 bond that pays 8¼ percent interest?   (L.O.1)
2. *Explaining Different Types of Corporate Bonds.* Dorothy Martin wants to invest $10,000 in corporate bonds. Her account executive suggested that she consider debentures, mortgage bonds, and convertible bonds. Since she has never invested in bonds, she is not sure how these types of bonds differ. How would you explain their differences to her?   (L.O.2)
3. *Evaluating Zero-Coupon Bonds.* List the reasons investors might want to buy zero-coupon bonds. Then list the reasons investors might want to avoid zero-coupon bonds. Based on these lists, do you consider zero-coupon bonds a good alternative for your investment program? Why or why not?   (L.O.2)
4. *Analyzing Why Investors Purchase Bonds.* In your own words, explain how each of the following factors is a reason to invest in bonds.   (L.O.3)
   a. Interest income.
   b. Possible increase in value.
   c. Repayment at maturity.

5. *Explaining Different Types of Treasury Securities.* Complete the following table: (L.O.4)

	Minimum Amount	Maturity Range	How Interest Is Paid
Treasury bill	_____	_____	_____
Treasury note	_____	_____	_____
Treasury bond	_____	_____	_____

6. *Calculating Tax-Equivalent Yield.* Assume you are in the 28 percent tax bracket and purchase a 7 percent, tax-exempt municipal bond. Use the formula presented in this chapter to calculate the taxable equivalent yield for this investment.   (L.O.4)
7. *Evaluating a Corporate Bond Issue.* Choose a corporate bond listed on the New York Bond Exchange, and use *Moody's Industrial Manuals* (available at your college or public library) to answer the following questions about this bond issue.   (L.O.5)
   a. What is Moody's rating for the issue?

b. What is the purpose of the issue?

c. Does the issue have a call provision?

d. Who is the trustee for the issue?

e. What collateral, if any, has been pledged as security for the issue?

f. Based on the information you have obtained, would the bond be a good investment for you? Why or why not?

8. *Calculating Yields.* Assume you purchased a corporate bond at its current market price of $850 on January 1, 1995. It pays 9 percent interest and will mature on December 31, 2004, at which time the corporation will pay you the face value of $1,000.   (L.O.5)

a. Determine the current yield on your bond investment at the time of purchase.

b. Determine the yield to maturity on your bond investment.

PROJECTS AND APPLICATION ACTIVITIES

1. *Explaining the Purpose of a Bond Indenture.* Prepare a one-minute oral presentation that describes the type of information contained in a bond indenture.   (L.O.1)

2. *Investigating a New Bond Issue.* Locate an advertisement for a new bond issue in *The Wall Street Journal, Barron's, The New York Times,* or a local newspaper. Then go to the

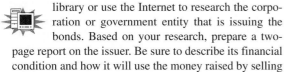

library or use the Internet to research the corporation or government entity that is issuing the bonds. Based on your research, prepare a two-page report on the issuer. Be sure to describe its financial condition and how it will use the money raised by selling the bonds.   (L.O.2)

3. *Interviewing an Account Executive.* Talk to an account executive or a banker about the differences among debentures, mortgage bonds, and subordinated debentures. Describe your findings.   (L.O.2)

4. *Making Investment Decisions.* Assume you just inherited 10 Westinghouse Electric Corporation bonds and each bond is convertible to 64.5 shares of the corporation's common stock.   (L.O.2)

a. What type of information would you need to help you decide whether to convert your bonds to common stock?

b. Where would you obtain this information?

c. Under what conditions would you convert your bonds to common stock?

d. Under what conditions would you keep the bonds?

5. *Analyzing Why Investors Purchase Bonds.* Survey at least two investors who own either corporate or government bonds. Then answer the following questions.   (L.O.3)

a. Why did these investors purchase the bonds?

b. How long have they invested in bonds?

c. Do they consider their bond issues to be conservative or speculative investments?

d. Why did they decide to purchase bonds instead of other investments like certificates of deposit, stocks, mutual funds, or real estate?

6. *Using the Internet to Obtain Investment Information.* Use one of the Internet search engines to locate the Web site for the Federal Reserve Bank of San Francisco. Then pre-

pare a report that summarizes the information provided on Treasury bills, Treasury notes, and Treasury bonds.   (L.O.4)

7. *Using the Internet to Obtain Investment Information.* Use one of the Internet search engines to locate the Web site for the Federal Reserve Bank of San Francisco. Then pre-

pare a report that summarizes the information provided on U.S. government savings bonds.   (L.O.4)

8. *Reading Financial Information in the Newspaper.* Using information from the local newspaper or *The Wall Street Journal,* answer the following questions on the bond issues listed below.   (L.O.5)

Newspaper _____   Date _____

	Current Yield	Volume	Close Price
IBM 7½ 13	_____	_____	_____
SouBell 7¼ 25	_____	_____	_____
TmeWar 7.48 08	_____	_____	_____
Unisys 8¼ 00	_____	_____	_____

9. *Analyzing Yields.* In your own words, describe what affects the current yield and the yield to maturity for a bond?   (L.O.5)

10. *Evaluating a Bond Transaction.* Choose a corporate bond that you would consider purchasing. Then, using

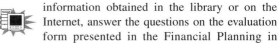

information obtained in the library or on the Internet, answer the questions on the evaluation form presented in the Financial Planning in Action feature on page 479. Based on your research, would you still purchase this bond? Explain your answer. (L.O.5)

A LESSON FROM THE PAST

Back in 1985, Mary Goldberg, a 34-year-old divorcee, got a telephone call from a Wall Street account executive who said that one of his other clients had given him her name. Then he told her his brokerage firm was selling a new corporate bond issue in New World Explorations, a company heavily engaged in oil exploration in the western United States. The bonds in this issue paid investors 13.2 percent a year. He then went on to say that the minimum investment was $10,000 and that if she wanted to take advantage of this "once in a life-time" opportunity, she had to move fast. To Mary, it was an opportunity that was too good to pass up, and she bit hook, line, and sinker. She sent the account executive a check—and never heard from him again. When she went to the library and tried to research her bond investment, she found there was no such company as New World Explorations. She lost her $10,000 and quickly vowed she would never invest in bonds again. From now on, she would put her money in the bank, where it was guaranteed.

Over the years, she continued to deposit money in the bank and accumulated more than $90,000. Things seemed to be pretty much on track until one of her certificates of deposit (CDs) matured. When she went to renew the CD, the bank officer told her interest rates had fallen and current CD interest rates ranged between $4\frac{1}{2}$ and $5\frac{1}{4}$ percent. To make matters worse, the banker told Mary that only the bank's 36-month CD offered the $5\frac{1}{4}$ percent interest rate. CDs with shorter maturities paid lower interest rates.

Faced with the prospects of lower interest rates, Mary decided to shop around for higher interest rates. She called several local banks and got pretty much the same answer. That's when one of her friends suggested that she talk to Peter Manning, an account executive for Smith Barney. Manning told her there were conservative corporate bonds and quality stock issues that offered higher returns. But, he warned her, these investments were *not* guaranteed. If she wanted higher returns, she would have to take some risks.

While Mary wanted higher returns, she also remembered how she had lost $10,000 investing in corporate bonds. When she told Peter Manning about her bond investment in the fictitious New World Exploration, he was quick to point out that she made some pretty serious mistakes. For starters, she bought the bonds over the phone from someone she didn't know, and she bought them without doing any research. He assured her that the bonds and stocks he would recommend would be issued by real companies, and she would be able to find "a lot of information" on each of his recommendations at the library. For starters, he suggested the following three investments:

1. ATT $8\frac{1}{8}$ 2022 (corporate bond issued by AT&T Corporation with a current market value of $1,030).
2. IBM $7\frac{1}{2}$ 2013 (corporate bond issued by International Business Machines Corporation with a current market value of $1,040).
3. General Electric common stock (listed on the New York Stock Exchange and selling for $65 a share with annual dividends of $1.04 per share).

QUESTIONS

1. According to Mary Goldberg, the chance to invest in New World Explorations was "too good to pass up." Unfortunately, it was too good to be true, and she lost $10,000. Why do you think so many people are taken in by get-rich-quick schemes?
2. During the last part of the 1990s, investors were forced to look for ways to squeeze additional income from their investment portfolios. Do you think investing in corporate bonds or quality stocks is the best way to increase income? Why or why not?
3. Using information obtained in the library or on the Internet, answer the following questions about Peter Manning's investment suggestions. (Hint: For the bond issues, you may want to examine *Moody's Industrial Manuals.* For the stock issue, you may want to use *Moody's Handbook of Common Stock.*)
   a. What is Moody's rating for the AT&T bond?
   b. What is Moody's rating for the IBM bond?
   c. What do these ratings mean?
   d. How would you describe the common stock issued by General Electric?
4. Based on your research, which investment would you recommend to Mary Goldberg? Why?
5. Assuming you recommend one of the above investments, how much of Mary's $90,000 would you invest? What would you do with the remainder of her money?
6. Using a current newspaper, *The Wall Street Journal,* or *Standard & Poor's Stock and Bond Guide,* determine the current market value for each of the three investments suggested in this case. Based on this information, would these investments have been profitable if Mary had purchased them on October 1, 1997?

USING THE INTERNET TO CREATE A PERSONAL FINANCIAL PLAN 15

INVESTING IN BONDS

Inclusion of bonds in an investment portfolio can be useful when attempting to achieve various financial goals when certain life situations, business conditions, and economic trends arise.

Web Sites for Investing in Bonds

• Bonds Online Internet provides information about investing in bonds at **www.bonds-online.com**
• Current bond investment articles from *Money* magazine at **www.money.com,** *Kiplinger's Personal Finance* magazine at **www.kiplinger.com,** *Business Week* at **www.businessweek.com,** *Worth* magazine at **www. worth.com,** and *Smart Money* at **www.smartmoney.com**
• T-Bill Direct provides information on how to buy and sell Treasury bills, notes, and bonds) at **www.netfactory.com/mondenet/tbdira1.html**
• The Federal Reserve Bank of San Francisco offers details for buying U.S. savings bonds and Treasury notes and bonds at **www.frbsf.org**
• Information on the bond market in emerging international markets at **www.bradynet.org**

(Note: Addresses and content of Web sites change, and new sites are created daily. Use the search engines discussed in Appendix B to update and locate Web sites for your current financial planning needs.)

PFP SHEET: 59

Short-Term Financial Planning Activities

1. Assess various type of bond investments that might be appropriate for your various financial goals and life situation.
2. Compare the recent performance of various corporate bonds that could be appropriate investments for you.
3. Research the recent performance of federal government and municipal bonds. Determine how these might be used in your investment portfolio.

Long-Term Financial Planning Activities

1. Identify bond investing situations that could help minimize risk.
2. Develop a plan for selecting bond investments in the future.

CHAPTER 16

INVESTING IN MUTUAL FUNDS

OPENING CASE

JANUS WORLDWIDE: A DREAM COME TRUE FOR THE GLOVERS

What a year! Mike and Kathy Glover, both in their 30s, invested $24,500 in the Janus Worldwide mutual fund. When they made their investment, just about everyone was talking about global investments. The Janus fund seemed to be one of the best and was definitely a high flyer during the first nine months of 1997. Then the economies in Hong Kong, Indonesia, and other Pacific Rim countries began to experience financial troubles, and investors got scared. Their Janus global fund, like many other investments in stocks and mutual funds, took a real hit during October 1997. Fortunately, by the end of the year, their fund had recovered and was worth almost $29,000. For the 12-month period, they had earned over 15 percent on their investment. Was it luck? No, not at all, according to Kathy. They had done their homework.

They began their research with a trip to the library. Both admitted they were overwhelmed with the amount of information they found on investments. Some of the more interesting articles stressed the need to diversify and place 10 to 30 percent of one's assets in global investments. According to another article, global investors enjoyed two major advantages. First, global investments provide investors with diversification. Second, economies in Denmark, Ireland, Norway, Spain, Indonesia, Malaysia, and Taiwan are expanding faster than the U.S. economy's 2.7 percent annual growth rate.

Based on their research, the Glovers decided to go global, but they had to decide if they wanted to invest in individual stocks or global mutual funds. The articles they read pointed out that purchasing individual, global stocks was a road full of potholes. For starters, evaluating foreign firms may be more difficult than evaluating U.S.

firms because reliable accounting information is often scarce. It was easier to get reliable information about global mutual funds. Just by calling an 800 phone number, they could obtain a prospectus, an annual report, and information about the fund manager. *Business Week, Forbes, Money, Barron's, The Wall Street Journal,* and other financial publications provided information about global mutual fund investments. For these reasons, most financial planners recommended global mutual funds for investors with less than $200,000 to invest.

After spending more than 10 hours researching Janus Worldwide, a $6 billion global fund that invests in over 200 different stocks, they decided to invest $24,500. Was their decision a good one? Twelve months later, their $24,500 investment had earned almost $4,500.

QUESTIONS

1. Today many financial planners recommend that you invest 10 to 30 percent of your assets in global investments. Given the recent economic upheavals in the Pacific Rim and other parts of the world, does this seem like a reasonable recommendation? Why or why not?
2. An investor who wants to go global can purchase individual stocks in foreign firms or shares in global mutual funds. If you wanted to invest in global investments, which method would you prefer? Explain your answer.

SOURCE: Lawrence A. Armour, "A Globetrotter from Denver," *Fortune,* June 23, 1997, pp. 181–82+; Lisa Reilly Cullen, "These First-Class Funds Go Round the World for Profits." *Money,* May 1997, pp. 50–52; Michael Sivy, "How to Cash in on the Asia Boom," *Money,* May 1997, pp. 108+.

After studying this chapter, you will be able to

L.O.1 Describe the characteristics of investments in mutual funds.

L.O.2 Classify mutual funds by investment objective.

L.O.3 Evaluate mutual funds for investment purposes.

L.O.4 Describe how and why mutual funds are bought and sold.

mutual fund

If you ever thought about buying stocks or bonds but decided not to, your reasons were probably like most other people's: You didn't know enough to make a good decision, and you lacked enough money to diversify your investments among several choices. These same two reasons explain why people invest in mutual funds. By pooling your money with money from other investors, a mutual fund can do for you what you can't do on your own. Specifically, a **mutual fund** is an investment alternative chosen by people who pool their money to buy stocks, bonds, and other financial securities selected by professional managers who work for investment companies. Mutual funds are an excellent choice for many individuals. In many cases, they can also be used for retirement accounts, including 401(k), 403(b), and individual retirement accounts.

Financial Decision
Trade-Off

The Glovers, the couple in the opening case, did their homework and made a decision to purchase Janus Worldwide. That's the way it's supposed to work: You research different investment alternatives and then make an informed decision. Does it work? Well, the Glovers' investment earned almost $4,500 during a 12-month period. You can earn the same type of financial returns on your investments.

Let's begin with a basic concept: *Mutual funds, like all potential investments, must be evaluated.* An investment in mutual funds is based on the concept of opportunity costs, which we have discussed throughout this text. Simply put, you have to be willing to take some chances if you want to get larger returns on your investments. Before deciding whether mutual funds are the right investment for you, read the material presented in the next section.

WHY INVESTORS PURCHASE MUTUAL FUNDS

L.O.1 Describe the characteristics of investments in mutual funds.

The major reasons investors purchase mutual funds are *professional management* and *diversification*. Most investment companies do everything possible to convince you that they can do a better job of picking securities than you can. Sometimes these claims are true, and sometimes they are just so much hot air. Still, investment companies do have professional fund managers with years of experience who devote large amounts of time to picking just the "right" securities for their funds' portfolios. *Be warned:* Even the best portfolio managers make mistakes. So you, the investor, must be careful!

The diversification mutual funds offer spells safety, because an occasional loss incurred with one investment contained in a mutual fund is usually offset by gains from

EXHIBIT 16–1

Types of Securities Included in the Portfolio of Fundamental Investors Mutual Fund

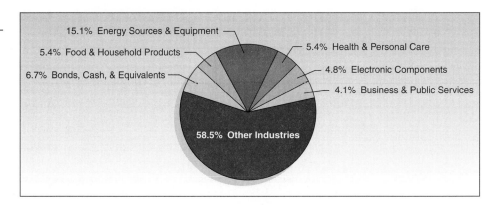

10 Largest Holdings

Company	Market Value (in millions)	Percent of net assets
Atlantic Richfield	$198.8	2.8%
Texas Instruments	160.0	2.2
Royal Dutch Petroleum	109.8	1.5
Exxon	104.9	1.5
Pfizer	103.6	1.4
Time Warner	99.9	1.4
Seagram	94.9	1.3
AT&T	91.9	1.3
Intel	91.7	1.3
Disney	89.8	1.3

SOURCE: *1997 Fund Facts and Prospectus for the Fundamental Investors Mutual Fund,* The American Funds Group, One Market Steuart Tower, Suite 1800, San Francisco, CA 94105.

other investments in the fund. For example, consider the diversification provided in the portfolio of the Fundamental Investors fund, shown in Exhibit 16–1. With $10 billion in assets, this fund is one of the larger mutual funds in the United States. According to information contained in the latest Fundamental Investors Web page, common stocks represent approximately 92 percent of the fund's investments. The fund invests in seven different industrial areas, a particularly attractive feature for investors who seek diversification. Also, notice the 10 largest holdings listed in Exhibit 16–1. Cash, preferred stock, and bonds make up the remaining 8 percent of the fund.[1]

Characteristics of Mutual Funds

investment company

Barron's *Dictionary of Finance and Investment Terms* defines an **investment company** as a firm that, for a management fee, invests the pooled funds of small investors in securities appropriate to its stated investment objectives.[2] Although the investment company concept originated in Europe and then spread to the United States in the late 1800s, investment companies didn't gain real popularity until the last 25 years. In 1970, there were 361 mutual funds. In 1997, there were over 6,000 mutual funds, and 70 percent are owned by households.[3] Today mutual funds may be classified as either closed-end funds or open-end funds.

closed-end fund

Closed-End or Open-End Mutual Funds   Approximately 10 percent of all mutual funds are closed-end funds offered by investment companies. A **closed-end fund** is a mutual fund whose shares are issued by an investment company only when the fund is organized. As a result, only a certain number of shares are available to investors. After all the shares originally issued have been sold, an investor can purchase shares only from another investor who is willing to sell them. Shares of closed-end funds are traded on the floors of stock exchanges. Like the prices of stocks, the prices of shares for closed-end funds are determined by the factors of supply and demand, by the value of stocks and other investments contained in the fund's portfolio, and by investor expectations. A special section of *The Wall Street Journal* provides information about closed-end funds.

open-end fund

net asset value (NAV)

Approximately 90 percent of all mutual funds are classified as open-end funds. An **open-end fund** is a mutual fund whose shares are issued and redeemed by the investment company at the request of investors. Investors are free to buy and sell shares at the net asset value. The **net asset value (NAV)** per share is equal to the current market value of securities contained in the mutual fund's portfolio minus the mutual fund's liabilities divided by the number of shares outstanding:

$$\text{Net asset value} = \frac{\text{Value of the fund's portfolio} - \text{Liabilities}}{\text{Number of shares outstanding}}$$

For example, assume the portfolio of all investments contained in the New American Frontiers Mutual Fund has a current market value of $124 million. The fund also has liabilities totaling $4 million. If this mutual fund has 6 million shares outstanding, the net asset value per share is $20:

$$\text{Net asset value} = \frac{\text{Value of the fund's portfolio} - \text{Liabilities}}{\text{Number of shares outstanding}}$$

$$= \frac{\$124 \text{ million} - \$4 \text{ million}}{6 \text{ million shares}}$$

$$= \$20 \text{ per share}$$

For most mutual funds, the net asset value is calculated at least once a day. In addition to buying and selling shares on request, most open-end funds provide their investors with a wide variety of services, including payroll deduction programs, automatic reinvestment programs, automatic withdrawal programs, and the option to change shares in one fund to another fund within the same fund family—all topics discussed later in this chapter.

load fund

Load Funds and No-Load Funds   Before investing in mutual funds, you should compare the cost of this type of investment with the cost of other investment alternatives, such as purchasing stocks or bonds. With regard to cost, mutual funds are classified as load funds, low-load funds, or no-load funds. A **load fund** (sometimes referred to as an *"A" fund*) is a mutual fund in which investors pay a commission every time they purchase shares. The commission charge, sometimes referred to as the *sales fee,* may be as high as 8½ percent of the purchase price for investments under $10,000. (Typically, this fee declines for investments over $10,000.) The "stated" advantage of a load fund is that the fund's sales force (account executives, financial planners, or brokerage divisions of banks and other financial institutions) will explain the mutual fund to investors and offer advice as to when shares of the fund should be bought or sold. A **low-load fund,** as the name implies, charges a lower commission than a load fund. This commission usually ranges between 1 and 3 percent of the purchase price for investments under $10,000. While exceptions exist, the average charge for load funds ranges between 3 and 5 percent today.

low-load fund

EXHIBIT 16–2

Summary of Expenses Paid to Invest in the Vista Growth and Income Mutual Fund

Expense Summary

	Class A Shares
Shareholder Transaction Expenses	
Maximum Sales Charge Imposed on Purchases (as a percentage of offering price)	4.75%
Maximum Deferred Sales Charge (as a percentage of the lower of original purchase price or redemption proceeds)*	None
Annual Fund Operating Expenses (as a percentage of average net assets)	
Investment Advisory Fee	0.40%
12b-1 Fee**	0.25%
Shareholder Servicing Fee	0.25%
Other Expenses	0.40%
Total Fund Operating Expenses	1.30%

Examples

Your investment of $1,000 would incur the following expenses, assuming 5% annual return:	1 Year	3 Years	5 Years	10 Years
Class A Shares†	$60	$87	$115	$197
Class B Shares:				
Assuming complete redemption at the end of the period†† †††	$70	$90	$121	$198
Assuming no redemptions†††	$18	$57	$ 97	$198

* The maximum deferred sales charge on Class B shares applies to redemptions during the first year after purchase; the charge generally declines by 1% annually thereafter (except in the fourth year), reaching zero after six years. See "How to Buy, Sell and Exchange Shares."

** Long-term shareholders in mutual funds with 12b-1 fees, such as Class A and Class B shareholders of the Fund, may pay more than the economic equivalent of the maximum front-end sales charge permitted by rules of the National Association of Securities Dealers, Inc.

†Assumes deduction at the time of purchase of the maximum sales charge

††Assumes deduction at the time of redemption of the maximum applicable deferred sales charge.

†††Ten-year figures assume conversion of Class B shares to Class A shares at the beginning of the ninth year after purchase. See "How to Buy, Sell and Exchange Shares."

SOURCE: Excerpted from the *Vista Growth and Income Fund Prospectus,* January 10, 1998.

no-load fund

Financial Decision Trade-Off

A **no-load fund** is a mutual fund in which the individual investor pays no sales charge. No-load funds don't charge commissions when you buy shares because they have no sales-people. If you want to buy shares of a no-load fund, you must deal directly with the investment company. The usual means of contact is by telephone or mail. As an investor, you must decide whether to invest in a load fund, a low-load fund, or a no-load fund. Some investment salespeople have claimed that load funds outperform no-load funds. But many financial analysts suggest there is no significant difference between mutual funds that charge commissions and those that do not.[4] *Since no-load funds offer the same investment opportunities load funds offer, you should investigate them further before deciding which type of mutual fund is best for you.* Although the sales commission should not be the decisive factor, the possibility of saving an 8½ percent load charge is a factor to consider. For example, suppose Barbara Harrington invests $10,000 in a mutual fund that charges an 8½ percent sales fee. Since this fee is deducted in advance, her initial $10,000 investment is reduced by $850. Simply put, she now has $9,150 that she can use to buy shares in this load fund. By comparison, Mary Hernandez decides to invest $10,000 in a no-load mutual fund. Since there is no sales fee, she can use the entire $10,000 to purchase shares in this

EXHIBIT 16–3	Type of Fee or Charge	Customary Amount
	Load fund	Up to 8½ percent of the purchase
Typical Fees Associated with Mutual Fund Investments	Low-load fund	Between 1 and 3 percent of the purchase
	No-load fund	No sales charge
	Management fee	0.25 to 1 percent per year of the fund's total assets
	Contingent deferred sales load	1 to 6 percent of withdrawals the first year and then declines
	12b-1 fee	Approximately 1 percent of the fund's assets

no-load fund. Depending on the load fund's performance, it may take Barbara a year or more to "catch up" and cover the cost of the sales fee.

Management Fees and Other Charges   In evaluating a specific mutual fund, you should consider management fees and other charges. The companies that sponsor mutual funds charge management fees. This fee, which is disclosed in the fund's prospectus, is a fixed percentage of the fund's asset value. Today annual management fees range between 0.25 and 1 percent of the fund's asset value.

contingent deferred sales load

Instead of charging investors a fee when they purchase shares in a mutual fund, some mutual funds charge a **contingent deferred sales load** (sometimes referred to as a *back-end load* or a *"B" fund*). These fees range from 1 to 6 percent on withdrawals during the first year you own the fund. *Generally,* the deferred charge declines until there is no withdrawal charge if you own the shares in the fund for more than five to seven years. Obviously, this deferred sales fee is designed to discourage early withdrawals. If all other factors are equal, a fund that doesn't charge a contingent deferral sales load is superior to a fund that does.

12b-1 fee

The investment company may also levy a **12b-1 fee** to defray the costs of advertising and marketing a mutual fund. Approved by the Securities and Exchange Commission in 1980, annual 12b-1 fees are calculated on the value of a fund's assets and may exceed 1 percent of a fund's assets per year. Note: A true no-load fund has neither a sales fee nor a 12b-1 fee.)

The investment company's prospectus must provide all details relating to management fees, contingent deferred sales fees, 12b-1 fees, and other expenses. Exhibit 16–2 on page 494 reproduces the summary of expenses (sometimes called a *fee table*) taken from the Vista Growth and Income Fund. Notice that this fee table has three separate parts. The first part describes shareholder transaction expenses. For this fund, the maximum sales charge is 4.75 percent. The second part describes the fund's annual operating expenses. For this fund, management fees, 12b-1 fees, and other expenses are reported. (For the Vista Growth and Income Fund, annual operating expenses total 1.30 percent of the fund's net assets.) The third part illustrates the total fees and expenses you would pay on a $1,000 investment assuming a 5 percent annual return and redemption at the end of 1, 3, 5, and 10 years.

Exhibit 16–3 on this page summarizes load, low-load, and no-load charges. In addition, it reports management fees, contingent deferred sales loads, and 12b-1 charges.

CONCEPT CHECK   16–1

1. What are two major reasons investors purchase mutual funds?
2. How do a closed-end fund and an open-end fund differ?
3. What are the typical fees charged for a load, low-load, and no-load mutual fund?
4. What are the typical management fees, contingent deferred sales loads, and 12b-1 fees?

JONATHAN HOENIG SPEAKS
MUTUAL MADNESS

The maligned. The marvelous. The misunderstood. The *mutual fund!*

How deceptively simple: Your hard-earned, minimum-wage dollars are dumped into a pool of cash and given to a professional money manager to worry about. "Pool" of course, being relative: At $63 billion, Fidelity Magellan (the nation's largest mutual fund) probably qualifies as a lake—or a small ocean, for that matter.

You pick the fund. The fund manager picks the stocks.

In the oceans of mutual funds available, where should your investment dollars drop? Choices abound. Interested in small-cap-growth-and-value-biotechnology firms in unincorporated areas of lower Jakarta? There are mutual funds to satiate even the most arcane investment taste. More realistically, there is a growing number of investment opportunities for the socially conscious. Many funds avoid investing in companies that manufacture tobacco, sell firearms, or treat employees unfairly. Many times, these "socially responsible" mutual funds outperform their less restrictive brethren.

The ultra-rich, megabucks high-rollers are advised to sell this book and head for Vegas. Those, however, who *don't* want to lose money are politely asked to heed the following suggestion: *Read the prospectus.* A "prospectus" is merely Wall Street talk for a booklet explaining the risks and rules of a particular mutual fund. It summarizes the fund's objective, outlines the fees (no "free" lunch on Wall Street!) and profiles past performance. You'll also be introduced to the fund's portfolio manager. This individual makes the decisions about where to invest your money. Check out her education. Hmm, I wonder how *she* did in second-year macro!

When it comes to picking a fund, be leery of a few years of supercharged returns. Often one year's Puff Daddy is another year's Vanilla Ice. Serious consideration should be given to expenses, which over time can have a major effect on overall returns.

Ask questions. Lots of them. Because when it comes to your money, more is never enough.

CLASSIFICATIONS OF MUTUAL FUNDS

L.O.2 Classify mutual funds by investment objective.

The managers of mutual funds tailor their investment portfolios to the investment objectives of their customers. Usually a fund's objectives are plainly disclosed in its prospectus. For example, the objectives of the American Mutual Fund are described as follows:

> The fund strives for the balanced accomplishment of three investment objectives—current income, capital growth, and conservation of principal. The fund seeks to fulfill each of its objectives as follows:
>
> *Current income* primarily by the selection of investments whose dividends appear well protected.
>
> *Capital growth* primarily by the purchase of equity-type securities of companies that Capital Research and Management Company, the investment adviser, expects are likely to participate in the growth of the American economy.
>
> *Conservation of principal* by careful selection, broad diversification, and constant supervision of investments that should serve to reduce risk and thereby preserve principal.[5]

While it may be helpful to categorize the 6,000-plus mutual funds into different categories, note that different sources of investment information may use different categories for the same mutual fund. In most cases, the name of the category gives a pretty good clue to the types of investments included within the category. The *major* fund categories according to *The Wall Street Journal* are described in alphabetical order as follows.[6]

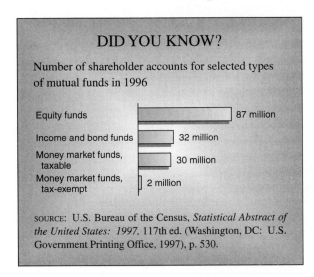

DID YOU KNOW?

Number of shareholder accounts for selected types of mutual funds in 1996

Equity funds	87 million
Income and bond funds	32 million
Money market funds, taxable	30 million
Money market funds, tax-exempt	2 million

SOURCE: U.S. Bureau of the Census, *Statistical Abstract of the United States: 1997*, 117th ed. (Washington, DC: U.S. Government Printing Office, 1997), p. 530.

Stock Funds

- *Capital appreciation funds* seek rapid growth, often by buying and changing investments within the fund's portfolio.
- *Global stock funds* invest in stocks of companies throughout the globe, including the United States.
- *Growth funds* invest in companies expecting higher-than-average revenue and earnings growth.
- *Growth and income funds* invest for increases in dollar values and dividend growth.
- *Small cap funds* invest in smaller, lesser known companies that offer higher growth potential.
- *Sector funds* invest in companies within the same industry.
- *Utility funds* invest in companies that provide utility services to their customers.

Bond Funds

- *High-yield (junk) bond funds* invest in high-yield, high-risk corporate bonds.
- *Intermediate bond funds* invest in investment-grade corporate debt of up to 10-year maturities.
- *Long-term bond funds* invest in corporate bond issues with maturities in excess of 10 years.
- *Long-term (U.S) bond funds* invest in U.S. Treasury and U.S. zero-coupon bonds.
- *Municipal bond funds* invest in municipal bonds that provide investors with tax-free interest income.
- *Short-term (U.S.) government bond funds* invest in U.S. Treasury issues.

Stock and Bond Funds

- *Balanced funds* invest in both stocks and bonds with the primary objective of conserving principal.
- *Stock/bond blend funds* invest in both stocks and bonds to achieve multipurpose objectives that may include flexible income, flexible portfolios, global securities, and convertible securities.

family of funds

A **family of funds** exists when one investment company manages a group of mutual funds. Each fund within the family has a different financial objective. For instance, one fund may be a money market fund and another a growth fund. Most investment companies offer exchange privileges that enable shareholders to switch among the mutual funds in a fund family. For example, if you own shares in the Franklin growth fund, you may, at your discretion, switch to the Franklin income fund. Generally, investors may give instructions to switch from one fund to another within the same family either in writing or over the telephone. The family-of-funds concept makes it convenient for shareholders to switch their investments among funds as different funds offer more potential, financial reward, or security. Charges for exchanges, if any, are generally small for each transaction. For funds that do charge, the fee may be as low as $5 per transaction.

market timer

**Financial Decision
Trade-Off**

Many financial analysts suggest that the true mark of a quality mutual fund investment is the fund's ability to increase the investor's return during good times and maintain that return during bad times. To help accomplish this task, a large number of investors have turned to market timers. A **market timer** is an individual who helps investors decide when to switch their investment from one fund to another fund, usually within the same family of funds. Market timers usually charge an annual fee of 1½ to 3 percent of the dollar value of the funds they manage. When evaluating market timers, keep in mind that the services they offer are a relatively recent innovation. Thus, it may be hard to judge their long-term track record accurately. Early research indicates that market timers must be evaluated on their individual investment philosophy and their past performance, and it is impossible to pass judgment on *all* market timers as a group.

CONCEPT CHECK 16–2

1. How important is the investment objective as stated in a fund's prospectus?
2. What is a family of funds? How is it related to shareholder exchanges?
3. How does a market timer help people manage their mutual fund investments?

EVALUATION OF MUTUAL FUNDS

L.O.3 Evaluate mutual funds for investment purposes.

If you suspect there are mutual funds designed to meet just about any conceivable investment objective, you are probably right. Hundreds of mutual funds trade daily under the headings "capital appreciation," "small-cap," and "growth-income." It is your job to determine which fund is right for you. This section will help you decide which fund can help you achieve your investment objectives.

Often the decision to buy or sell shares in mutual funds is "too easy" because investors assume they do not need to evaluate these investments. Why question what the professional portfolio managers decide to do? Yet the professionals do make mistakes. The responsibility for choosing the right mutual fund rests with you, the individual investor. After all, you are the only one who knows how a particular mutual fund can help you achieve your financial objectives. Some of the basic means for evaluating mutual funds are described next, but first read the Financial Planning for Life's Situations feature to see how one investor obtained the information he needed to evaluate mutual funds.

How to Read the Mutual Funds Section of the Newspaper

Most local newspapers, *The Wall Street Journal,* and *Barron's* provide information about mutual funds. For most investors, the Friday *Wall Street Journal* provides the most complete financial coverage (see Exhibit 16–4). Information about net asset value, change in net asset value, the fund family and fund name, fund objective, fund performance, ranking among similar funds, sales commission, and annual expenses is provided. On other days, coverage in *The Wall Street Journal,* local newspapers, or other financial publications generally provides less information. Much of this same information is also available on the Internet.

The letters beside the name of a specific fund can be very informative. You can find out what they mean by looking at the footnotes that accompany the newspaper's mutual fund quotations. Generally, "NL" means no load, "p" means a 12b-1 distribution fee is charged, "r" means a redemption charge may be made, and "t" means both the p and r footnotes apply.

FINANCIAL PLANNING FOR LIFE'S SITUATIONS

HOW CHARLES GOODWIN USES THE INTERNET TO OBTAIN INVESTMENT INFORMATION

Five years ago, Charles Goodwin felt the world was passing him by. He had just moved to a small town in East Texas. While he enjoyed the more relaxed lifestyle, he missed a lot of the conveniences he took for granted when he lived in the metropolitan Dallas/Fort Worth area. One convenience he missed the most was his trips to the public library. Ironically, he had never considered himself a bookworm, but he did enjoy researching his investments. Unfortunately, the local library in the nearest small town just didn't have the "stuff" Charles used to make his investment decisions. In fact, the most recent publication the library had was a two-year-old copy of *Morningstar Mutual Funds*. The libraries in nearby towns were equally out of date.

The Internet to the Rescue

Charles quickly realized he would have to find another source of investment information if he was to continue evaluating his investments. One of his friends suggested that he consider going online, but Charles was reluctant. The thought of using a computer was a little frightening, but if he wanted current and valid information he had to do something. He purchased a computer and selected an online service. Then he began "surfing" the Net in search of useful investment information. Now he admits that using the computer was really easy. By accessing the Internet and typing the name of a professional advisory service or the name of the investment company sponsoring a mutual fund, he could get all kinds of information. And he could get current market values for the mutual funds and individual stocks in his portfolio. As an added bonus, he could get information at any time of the day or night, seven days a week.

Useful Web Sites for Investors

If you are interested in using the Internet to obtain research information, you may want to begin with the Web sites listed below:

1. Business Week Online (www.businessweek.com) provides the current issue of the magazine, archives, and an assortment of investment information.
2. Morningstar Net (www.morningstar.net) provides detailed information about mutual fund investments.
3. NASD Regulation (www.nasdr.com) provides information you can use to check out stockbrokers and account executives.
4. S&P Investor Service (www.stockinfo.standardpoor.com) provides financial news along with individual stock recommendations.
5. Securities and Exchange Commission (www.sec.gov) providers a wealth of information about companies issuing stock, bonds, and mutual funds.
6. USA Today Money (www.usatoday.com/money/mfront/htm) provides a variety of information about investments and personal finance topics.
7. Yahoo Fiance (www.quote.yahoo.com) provides current market prices for stocks, bonds, and mutual funds and other useful investment information.

SOURCES: David C. Churbuck, "Data for Cheapskates," *Forbes,* June 17, 1997, p. 173; Gary Weiss, "Web of Hype and Glory," *Business Week,* June 16, 1997, pp. 108+; Derek Gordon, "Grab the Best Fund Info at Morningstar's Site," *Money,* March 1997, p. 28; Manuel Schiffres and Steven T. Goldberg, "The World According to Morningstar," *Kiplinger's Personal Finance,* February 1997, pp. 89–91.

In many cases, the search for a no-load fund starts with a newspaper quotation. Therefore, the NL footnote is especially important. As pointed out earlier, no-load mutual funds do not charge sales fees. Since no-load funds offer the same investment opportunities load funds do, financial experts often recommend these funds.

Other Factors and Sources to Consider

The newspaper coverage described in the last section is a good means of monitoring the value of your mutual fund investments. However, other sources of information provide a more complete basis for evaluating mutual fund investments.

EXHIBIT 16–4   **Financial Information about Mutual Funds Available in**
The Wall Street Journal

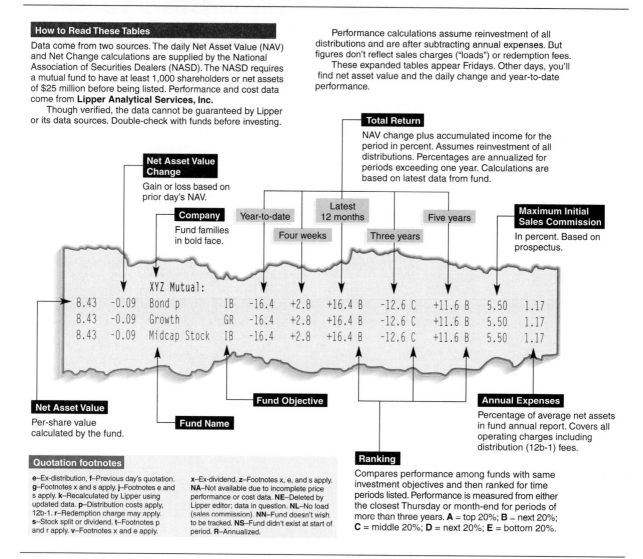

How to Read These Tables

Data come from two sources. The daily Net Asset Value (NAV) and Net Change calculations are supplied by the National Association of Securities Dealers (NASD). The NASD requires a mutual fund to have at least 1,000 shareholders or net assets of $25 million before being listed. Performance and cost data come from **Lipper Analytical Services, Inc.**

Though verified, the data cannot be guaranteed by Lipper or its data sources. Double-check with funds before investing.

Performance calculations assume reinvestment of all distributions and are after subtracting annual expenses. But figures don't reflect sales charges ("loads") or redemption fees.

These expanded tables appear Fridays. Other days, you'll find net asset value and the daily change and year-to-date performance.

Net Asset Value Change

Gain or loss based on prior day's NAV.

Company

Fund families in bold face.

Total Return

NAV change plus accumulated income for the period in percent. Assumes reinvestment of all distributions. Percentages are annualized for periods exceeding one year. Calculations are based on latest data from fund.

Year-to-date   Latest 12 months   Five years

Four weeks   Three years

Maximum Initial Sales Commission

In percent. Based on prospectus.

XYZ Mutual:

8.43	-0.09	Bond p	IB	-16.4	+2.8	+16.4 B	-12.6 C	+11.6 B	5.50	1.17
8.43	-0.09	Growth	GR	-16.4	+2.8	+16.4 B	-12.6 C	+11.6 B	5.50	1.17
8.43	-0.09	Midcap Stock	IB	-16.4	+2.8	+16.4 B	-12.6 C	+11.6 B	5.50	1.17

Net Asset Value

Per-share value calculated by the fund.

Fund Name

Fund Objective

Ranking

Compares performance among funds with same investment objectives and then ranked for time periods listed. Performance is measured from either the closest Thursday or month-end for periods of more than three years. **A** = top 20%; **B** – next 20%; **C** = middle 20%; **D** = next 20%; **E** = bottom 20%.

Annual Expenses

Percentage of average net assets in fund annual report. Covers all operating charges including distribution (12b-1) fees.

Quotation footnotes

e–Ex-distribution. **f**–Previous day's quotation. **g**–Footnotes x and s apply. **j**–Footnotes e and s apply. **k**–Recalculated by Lipper using updated data. **p**–Distribution costs apply, 12b-1. **r**–Redemption charge may apply. **s**–Stock split or dividend. **t**–Footnotes p and r apply. **v**–Footnotes x and e apply.

x–Ex-dividend. **z**–Footnotes x, e, and s apply. **NA**–Not available due to incomplete price performance or cost data. **NE**–Deleted by Lipper editor; data in question. **NL**–No load (sales commission). **NN**–Fund doesn't wish to be tracked. **NS**–Fund didn't exist at start of period. **R**–Annualized.

SOURCE: *The Wall Street Journal,* January 16, 1998, p. C24.

Financial Objectives—Again   In Chapter 13, we talked about establishing investment goals and objectives. In this chapter, we have looked at the investment objectives of mutual funds. Here our aim is to point out the relationship between the two. In establishing your own investment goals and objectives, you must evaluate the personal factors of age, family situation, income, and future earning power. Only then can you establish short-term, intermediate, and long-term objectives. Now you must find a mutual fund whose investment objectives match your own. As mentioned earlier in this chapter, a mutual fund's prospectus provides a detailed description of a fund's investment objective. Once you have found a match, you need to gather as much information as possible about the fund and the investment company that sponsors it.

Mutual Fund Prospectus An investment company sponsoring a mutual fund must give potential investors a prospectus. According to financial experts, the prospectus is usually the first piece of information investors receive, and they should read it completely before investing. Although it may look foreboding, a commonsense approach to reading a fund's prospectus can provide valuable insights. In fact, most investors find that a fund's prospectus can provide a wealth of information. As pointed out earlier, the prospectus summarizes the fund's objective. Also, the fee table provides a summary of the fees charged by a fund. In addition to information about objectives and fees, the prospectus should provide the following:

- A statement describing the risk factor associated with the fund.
- A description of the fund's past performance.
- A statement describing the type of investments contained in the fund's portfolio.
- Information about dividends, distributions, and taxes.
- Information about the fund's management.

Finally, the prospectus provides information about how to purchase shares, exchange privileges (if any), and how to redeem shares.

Mutual Fund Annual Report Once you are a shareholder, the investment company will send you an annual report. A fund's annual report contains a letter from the president of the investment company, from the fund manager, or both. *Caution: Don't forget the role of the fund manager in determining a fund's success.* One important question is how long the present fund manager has been managing the fund. If a fund has performed well under its present manager over a 5- or 10-year period, there is a strong likelihood that it will continue to perform well under that manager in the future.

The annual report also contains detailed financial information about the fund's assets and liabilities, statement of operations, and statement of changes in net assets. Next, the annual report includes a schedule of investments. (Take a second look at the partial schedule of investments for the Fundamental Investors Mutual Fund in Exhibit 16–1.) Finally, the fund's annual report should include a letter from the fund's independent auditors that provides an opinion as to the accuracy of the fund's financial statements.

Financial Publications Investment-oriented magazines like *Business Week, Forbes, Kiplinger's Personal Finance,* and *Money* are another source of information about mutual funds. Each of these publications provides an annual survey of mutual funds and ranks them on a number of important investment criteria. Exhibit 16–5 on page 502 illustrates a portion of *Business Week*'s mutual fund survey for 1997.

A fund's past long-term performance is no guarantee of future success, but it is a valid predictor. To gauge this variable, most annual surveys include information about a fund's total return. In Exhibit 16–5, total returns for 1 year, 3 years, 5 years, and 10 years are reported for each fund included in the survey. Also included in the *Business Week* survey is information about

- The fund's overall rating when compared with *all* other funds.
- The fund's rating when compared with funds in the same category.
- The size of the fund.
- The sales charge and expense ratio for each fund.
- Trends over selected 30-month periods for the last 10 years.
- Portfolio data, including turnover, PE ratio, and largest holdings.
- Risk of loss factor for each fund.
- A toll-free telephone number for each fund.

EXHIBIT 16–5   **A Portion of the 1996 Mutual Fund Survey by *Business Week* Magazine**

Equity Funds

MUTUAL FUND SCOREBOARD

How to Use the Tables

BUSINESS WEEK RATINGS
Overall ratings are based on five-year risk-adjusted returns. They are calculated by subtracting a fund's risk-of-loss factor (see RISK) from historical pretax total return. To get a positive rating, the fund must beat the S&P 500 on a risk-adjusted basis. Category ratings are based on risk-adjusted returns of the funds in that category. The ratings are as follows:

♠ ♠ ♠ SUPERIOR
♠ ♠   VERY GOOD
♠   GOOD
AVG   AVERAGE
♦   BELOW AVERAGE
♦ ♦   POOR
♦ ♦ ♦ VERY POOR

MANAGEMENT CHANGES
♟ indicates the fund's manager has held the job at least 10 years; ♙ indicates a new manager since Dec. 31, 1995.

S&P 500 COMPARISON
The pretax total returns for the S&P 500 are as follows: 1996, 22.9%; three-year average (1994-1996), 19.7%; five-year average (1992-96), 15.2%; 10-year average (1987-96), 15.3%.

CATEGORY
Each U.S. diversified fund is classified by market capitalization of the stocks in the portfolio and by the nature of those stocks. If the median market cap is greater than $5 billion, the fund is large-cap; from $1 billion to $5 billion,

mid-cap; and less than $1 billion, small-cap. "Value" funds are those whose stocks have price-to-earnings and price-to-book ratios lower than that of the S&P 500. "Growth" funds have higher than average p-e's and p-b's. "Blend" funds are those in which the ratios are about average. Hybrids mix stocks and bonds, and possibly other assets. World funds generally include U.S. stocks, foreign funds do not. Sector and regional foreign funds are as indicated.

FUND	OVERALL RATING (COMPARES RISK-ADJUSTED PERFORMANCE OF EACH FUND AGAINST ALL FUNDS)	CATEGORY (COMPARES RISK-ADJUSTED PERFORMANCE OF FUND WITHIN CATEGORY)	RATING	SIZE ASSETS $MIL.	% CHG. 1995-6	FEES SALES CHARGE (%)	EXPENSE RATIO (%)	1996 RETURNS (%) PRE-TAX	AFTER-TAX	YIELD
AARP BALANCED STOCK & BOND		Domestic Hybrid		445.9	61	No load	0.88	13.2	11.9	2.8
AARP CAPITAL GROWTH	♦	Large-cap Blend	♦ ♦ ♦	877.2	24	No load	0.90	20.6	17.4	0.9
AARP GROWTH & INCOME ♟	♠ ♠ ♠	Large-cap Blend	♠ ♠ ♠	4606.5	41	No load	0.69	21.6	19.4	2.5
ACORN ♟	♠	Small-cap Growth	♠ ♠ ♠	2853.7	19	No load	0.57	22.6	19.2	0.7
ACORN INTERNATIONAL		Foreign		1771.7	39	No load	1.20	20.7	20.0	0.6
AIM AGGRESSIVE GROWTH	♦	Small-cap Growth	♠ ♠	2724.0	18	5.50‡	1.08†	14.3	12.7	0.0
AIM BALANCED A	AVG	Domestic Hybrid	♦	333.7	263	4.75	1.43†	19.3	17.6	2.5
AIM BLUE CHIP A (a) ♙	AVG	Large-cap Growth	♠ ♠	158.0	115	5.50	1.26†	23.8	18.6	0.4
AIM CHARTER A	AVG	Large-cap Blend	♦ ♦	2804.2	35	5.50	1.17†	19.6	17.3	1.4
AIM CONSTELLATION A	♦	Mid-cap Growth	AVG	11915.2	62	5.50	1.20†	16.3	15.2	0.0

SOURCE: *Business Week,* February 3, 1997, pp. 82+.

A number of mutual fund guidebooks are available at your local bookstore or public library. You can also order these publications by phone. Some of the more popular publications are

1. Gerald Perritt, *The Mutual Fund Almanac* (1–800–326–6941)
2. Gordon Williamson, *The 100 Best Mutual Funds You Can Buy* (1–800– 748–5552)
3. *Money Letters Mutual Funds Almanac* (1–800–433–1528)
4. *Individual Investor's Guide to Low-Load Mutual Funds,* American Association of Individual Investors (312–280–0170)
5. *Investment Company Institute Directory of Mutual Funds* (202–326–5800)
6. *The Investor's Guide to Low-Cost Mutual Funds,* Mutual Fund Education Alliance (816–454–9422)
7. *Mutual Fund Fact Book,* Investment Company Institute (202–326–5800)
8. Sheldon Jacobs, *The Handbook for No-Load Fund Investors* (1–800–252–2042).

Professional Advisory Services   A number of subscription services provide detailed information on mutual funds. Standard and Poor's Corporation, Lipper Analytical Services, Morningstar, Inc., Value Line, and Wiesenberger Investment Companies are five widely used sources of such information. Exhibit 16–6 illustrates the type of information provided by Morningstar, Inc., for the Davis NY Venture fund. Although the Morningstar

EXHIBIT 16–5   *(concluded)*

SALES CHARGE
The cost of buying a fund. Many funds take this "load" out of the initial investment, and for ratings purposes, returns are reduced by these charges. Loads may be levied on withdrawals.

EXPENSE RATIO
Expenses for 1996 as a percentage of average net assets, a measure of how much shareholders pay for management. Footnotes indicate if the ratio includes a 12(b)-1 plan, which spends shareholder money on marketing. The average is 1.29%.

PRETAX TOTAL RETURN
A fund's net gain to investors, including reinvestment of dividends and capital gains at month-end prices.

AFTERTAX TOTAL RETURN
Pretax return adjusted for federal taxes. Assumes ordinary income

and capital gains taxed at highest rate applicable in each year; uses 31% tax rate on income since 1991. Capital gains are assumed to be long-term.

YIELD
Income distributions as a percent of net asset value, adjusted for capital gains distributions.

TREND
A fund's relative performance during the four 30-month periods from Jan. 1, 1987 to Dec. 31, 1996. Boxes read from left to right, and the level of green indicates performance relative to all other funds in that period: ■ for the top quartile; ▣ for the second quartile; ▢ for the third quartile; ☐ for the bottom quartile. An empty box indicates no data for that period.

TURNOVER
Trading activity, the lesser of pur-

chases or sales divided by average monthly assets.

% CASH
Portion of fund assets not invested in stocks or bonds. A negative number means the fund has borrowed to buy securities.

% FOREIGN
Portion of funds assets invested in non-U.S. securities.

PRICE-EARNINGS RATIO
The average, weighted price-earnings ratio of stocks in a fund's portfolio, based on last 12 months' earnings.

UNTAXED GAINS
Percentage of assets in portfolio that are unrealized and undistributed capital gains. A negative figure indicates losses that may offset future gains.

LARGEST HOLDING
Comes from the latest available fund reports.

RISK
Potential for losing money in a fund, or risk-of-loss factor. For each fund, the three-month Treasury bill return is subtracted from the monthly total return for each of the 60 months in the ratings period. When a fund has not performed as well as Treasury bills, the monthly result is negative. The sum of these negative numbers is divided by the number of months. The result is a negative number, and the greater its magnitude, the higher the risk of loss. This number is the basis for BW ratings, category ratings, and the RISK column.

BEST & WORST QUARTERS
The fund's highest and lowest quarterly returns of the past five years.

AVERAGE ANNUAL TOTAL RETURNS (%)						TREND	PORTFOLIO DATA						RISK	BEST		WORST		TELEPHONE
3 YEARS		5 YEARS		10 YEARS		BW 10-YEAR	TURNOVER	CASH	FOREIGN	P-E	UNTAXED	LARGEST HOLDING	LEVEL					
PRETAX	AFTERTAX	PRETAX	AFTERTAX	PRETAX	AFTERTAX	ANALYSIS		%	%	RATIO	GAINS (%)	COMPANY (% ASSETS)		QTR	%RET	QTR	%RET	
Less than three years of data available							Low	3	11	22	17	Xerox(1)						800-322-2282
12.3	10.8	11.5	9.8	13.3	11.4		Average	2	12	21	38	Hewlett-Packard(3)	High	II 95	10.8	I 94	−8.1	800-322-2282
18.2	16.2	15.9	14.2	13.9	12.0		Low	2	15	22	34	Xerox(3)	Low	II 95	8.8	I 94	−3.3	800-322-2282
11.1	8.7	17.6	15.5	16.1	13.5		Low	2	20	26	43	Newell(2)	Average	IV 92	16.0	I 94	−5.5	800-922-6769
8.1	7.9						Low	8	98	25	23	WM-Data CI B(3)						800-922-6769
23.8	22.9	24.9	24.0	18.8	17.4		Average	6	2	38	28	Cascade Communs.(1)	High	IV 92	26.4	II 92	−12.5	800-347-4246
15.0	13.8	14.0	13.0	11.4	9.7		Average	9	13	27	10	Gucci Group(1)	Average	II 95	11.0	II 92	−4.1	800-347-4246
19.6	17.0	12.9	11.0	13.8	12.6		Average	5	7	25	18	General Electric(4)	Average	I 95	9.1	I 92	−4.1	800-347-4246
15.8	13.3	11.4	9.6	15.1	12.4		High	2	9	26	17	FNMA(2)	Average	II 95	11.1	I 92	−4.1	800-347-4246
16.9	15.8	16.6	16.0	19.2	16.5		Average	7	5	33	24	Cisco Systems(1)	High	IV 92	19.6	II 92	−9.3	800-347-4246

report is just one page long, it provides a wealth of information designed to help you decide if this is the right fund for you. Notice that the information is divided into various sections. At the top, a small box entitled "Historical Profile" contains information about financial return, risk, and rating. Notice that Davis NY Venture is rated 5 stars, Morningstar's highest rating. The report also provides statistical information over the past 12 years. The middle section of the report provides information about the fund manager(s), performance, risk analysis, and portfolio analysis. The last section at the very bottom describes the investment philosophy of the fund. Generally, the analysis section summarizes Morningstar's research. Here it says,

> The fund's appeal is obvious. Its top decile 1997 ranking makes the third year in a row it has been tops in its category.

As you can see, the research information for the Davis NY Venture fund is pretty upbeat. However, other research firms like Lipper Analytical Services, Value Line, and Wiesenberger Investment Companies, as well as Morningstar, Inc., will also tell you if a fund is a poor performer that offers poor investment potential.

In addition, various mutual fund newsletters provide financial information to subscribers for a fee. All of these sources are rather expensive, but their reports may be available from brokerage firms or libraries.

EXHIBIT 16-6   **Mutual Fund Research Information Provided by Morningstar, Inc.**

Volume 32, Issue 1, January 23, 1998. Reprinted with permission.

Davis NY Venture A

	Ticker	Load	NAV	Yield	SEC Yield	Total Assets	Mstar Category
	NYVTX	4.75%	$22.33	1.0%	—	$7,223.8 mil	Large Value

Prospectus Objective: Growth

Davis New York Venture Fund - Class A seeks growth of capital.

The fund invests primarily in equities issued by companies with market capitalizations of at least $250 million, though it may also hold securities of smaller companies. It may invest in securities of foreign issuers.

Class A shares have front loads; B shares have deferred loads, higher 12b-1 fees, and conversion features; C shares have level loads. Prior to Oct. 1, 1995, the fund was named New York Venture Fund.

Class	Exp%	Sales Fees	Rec. Hold (Years)
A	0.89	4.75%L	6.5+
B	1.78	4.00%D,0.75%B	6.0–6.5
C	1.73	1.00%D,0.75%B	0.0–6.5

Portfolio Manager(s)

Christopher C. Davis. Since 10-95. MA'87 U. of St. Andrews. Davis is a vice chairman with Davis Selected Advisers. He also serves as chairman of Shelby Cullom Davis Financial Consultants, Inc., and as a director at Rosenwald, Roditi & Co., an offshore investment management company. Previously, Davis served as an associate with Tanaka Capital Management for two years and a portfolio accountant with State Street Bank and Trust Co. for one year. Other funds currently managed: Selected American, Davis Financial.

Performance 12-31-97

	1st Qtr	2nd Qtr	3rd Qtr	4th Qtr	Total
1993	8.89	-0.17	10.40	-3.27	16.09
1994	-3.43	1.30	1.88	-1.60	-1.93
1995	10.57	12.32	11.11	1.86	40.56
1996	5.23	2.62	4.91	11.69	26.54
1997	1.94	16.70	11.91	0.40	33.68

Trailing	Total Return%	+/- S&P 500	+/-Wil Large Value	%Rank All	%Rank Cat	Growth of $10,000
3 Mo	0.40	-2.47	-3.41	60	62	10,040
6 Mo	12.36	1.79	-3.35	11	19	11,236
1 Yr	33.68	0.33	2.30	4	7	13,368
3 Yr Avg	33.47	2.34	2.54	1	2	23,775
5 Yr Avg	22.04	1.79	2.55	2	4	27,069
10 Yr Avg	21.07	3.03	3.68	3	3	67,691
15 Yr Avg	19.47	1.96	0.57	1	2	144,198

Tax Analysis	Tax-Adj Ret%	%Rank Cat	%Pretax Ret	%Rank Cat
3 Yr Avg	31.34	2	93.6	9
5 Yr Avg	19.94	3	90.5	13
10 Yr Avg	18.35	3	87.0	17

Potential Capital Gain Exposure: 34% of assets

Analysis by Laura Lallos 01-09-98

Davis New York Venture Fund hasn't been spoiled by success.

Investors flooded the fund last year, and cash was as high as 15% at times. The fund thus lagged its fully invested counterpart, Selected American, by a few points. But it still edged past the S&P 500 and was one of the best-performing large-cap value funds.

Nonetheless, manager Chris Davis is contemplating closing the fund. While the volume of assets isn't a problem, given the fund's large-cap focus and low turnover, the velocity of asset flows is overwhelming. He says his first loyalty is to current shareholders—which includes the board of directors, who are paid in shares of the fund in what is unfortunately a rare arrangement.

The fund's appeal is obvious. Its top-decile 1997 ranking makes the third year in a row it has been tops in its category. Its slight struggle with rising rates in 1994 hasn't marred its stellar long-term record. Davis is proving his worth as day-to-day manager, and Shelby Davis remains involved in shaping the fund.

The fund has its dangers, though: Davis is keeping a concentrated stake in the financials that have driven returns. While some value managers are selling, he added to the sector's prospects, given demographics. He calls these firms "growth in disguise"; under the same rubric, he added to oil services names as prices have fallen.

Davis sees growth in all of his value purchases. For example, he considers Nike to be "growth under a cloud". He was even able to add to some "true growth" tech holdings such as Hewlett-Packard during their late-year weakness. This growth focus has kept the fund out of cyclicals, which has been a plus lately.

Davis has modest expectations going forward, noting that historical stock returns are around 7%. But less-exciting markets will only highlight this fund's relative worth.

Address:	124 E. Marcy Street
	Santa Fe, NM 87501
	800–279–0279 / 505–983–4335
Inception:	02-17-69
Advisor:	Davis Selected Advisers
Subadvisor:	Davis Selected Advisers
Distributor:	Davis Distributors
NTF Plans:	Schwab Inst.

Minimum Purchase:	$1000	Add: $25	IRA: $250
Min Auto Inv Plan:	$1000	Systematic Inv: $25	
Sales Fees:	4.75%L, 0.25%S		
Management Fee:	0.75% max./0.50% min.		
Actual Fees:	Mgt: 0.57%	Dist: 0.18%	
Expense Projections:	3Yr: $75	5Yr: $95	10Yr: $153
Annual Brokerage Cost:	0.06%	Income Distrib: Annually	

Total Cost (relative to category):   Average

Historical Profile

Return	High
Risk	Average
Rating	★★★★★ Highest

Investment Style
Equity
Average Stock %

▼ Manager Change
▽ Partial Manager Change
► Mgr Unknown After
◄ Mgr Unknown Before

Fund Performance vs. Category Average
▨ Quarterly Fund Return
  +/– Category Average
— Category Baseline

Performance Quartile (within Category)

	1986	1987	1988	1989	1990	1991	1992	1993	1994	1995	1996	12-97	History
	9.20	6.98	7.64	9.15	8.16	10.51	11.06	11.97	11.16	14.52	17.50	22.33	NAV
	22.00	-1.49	21.38	34.75	-2.90	40.55	12.04	16.09	-1.93	40.56	26.54	33.68	Total Return %
	3.32	-6.75	4.77	3.06	0.22	10.07	4.42	6.03	-3.24	3.03	3.59	0.33	+/- S&P 500
	-0.23	-5.08	-1.42	9.61	4.69	14.91	-2.35	2.64	2.42	-2.91	7.46	2.30	+/- Wilshire LV
	1.01	2.63	3.15	5.01	2.02	2.22	1.55	2.32	1.08	1.08	1.06	1.10	Income Return %
	20.99	-4.12	18.22	29.74	-4.93	38.33	10.49	13.77	-3.00	39.48	25.47	32.58	Capital Return %
	.17	.74	.32	.6	.22	.13	.30	.31	.73	.4	.9	.7	Total Rtn % Rank Cat
	0.10	0.22	0.22	0.40	0.17	0.19	0.17	0.26	0.12	0.15	0.18	0.23	Income $
	1.68	2.14	0.56	0.70	0.54	0.65	0.53	0.58	0.45	1.01	0.70	0.83	Capital Gains $
	0.99	0.93	1.01	0.97	0.97	0.97	0.91	0.89	0.87	0.90	0.87	0.89	Expense Ratio %
	1.56	1.48	2.42	2.45	3.78	1.84	1.36	0.85	1.19	1.11	1.30	0.98	Income Ratio %
	98	55	38	58	47	52	26	24	13	15	19	24	Turnover Rate %
	146.8	159.2	239.3	308.2	341.9	459.0	547.9	937.7	1,090.5	1,798.2	2,658.6	4,655.5	Net Assets $mil

Risk Analysis

Time Period	Load-Adj Return %	Risk %Rank All	Cat	Morningstar Return Risk		Morningstar Risk-Adj Rating
1 Yr	27.33					
3 Yr	31.32	64	62	1.60	0.73	★★★★★
5 Yr	20.86	78	92	1.60	1.01	★★★★
10 Yr	20.49	70	68	1.85	0.92	★★★★★

Average Historical Rating (146 months):   4.7★s

¹1=low, 100=high

Category Rating (3 Yr)
Worst ① ② ③ ④ ⑤ Best
Return High
Risk Average

Other Measures	Standard Index S&P 500	Best Fit Index S&P 500
Alpha	2.7	2.7
Beta	0.96	0.96
R-Squared	87	87
Standard Deviation	15.12	
Mean	29.87	
Sharpe Ratio	2.09	

Portfolio Analysis 11-30-97

Share change since 10-97 Total Stocks: 119

		Sector	PE	YTD Ret%	% Assets
⊖	IBM	Technology	17.5	39.33	3.89
⊖	Wells Fargo	Financials	33.4	28.19	3.47
⊖	Hewlett-Packard	Technology	21.1	25.25	3.39
⊖	American Express	Financials	20.6	59.89	3.01
⊖	McDonald's	Retail	20.4	5.94	2.80
⊖	General Re	Financials	17.8	35.95	2.71
⊕	Travelers Group	Financials	19.4	79.87	2.57
⊖	BankAmerica	Financials	17.5	49.15	2.50
⊖	Morgan Stanley/Dean Witter	Financials	18.2	80.77	2.38
⊖	Halliburton	Energy	32.2	74.29	2.35
⊕	Burlington Northern Santa Fe	Services	16.0	9.06	2.20
⊖	Masco	Cyclicals	22.8	43.45	2.19
⊖	Philip Morris	Staples	17.0	24.65	2.13
⊕	Texas Instruments	Technology	8.7	42.20	2.05
⊖	Citicorp	Financials	17.8	24.94	2.00
⊖	Nestle (Reg) (ADR)	Staples	—	—	1.96
⊖	SmithKline Beecham (ADR)	Health	34.6	54.42	1.93
⊖	Crescent Real Estate Eq	Financials	35.6	64.69	1.51
⊖	AirTouch Communications	Services	67.0	64.61	1.40
⊖	SunAmerica	Financials	23.8	44.91	1.40
⊖	Allstate	Financials	14.1	58.44	1.35
⊖	Burlington Resources	Energy	15.7	-9.96	1.34
⊖	Union Pacific	Services	19.7	7.00	1.33
⊖	Motorola	Technology	31.8	-5.91	1.28
⊖	Nike	Durables	14.7	-34.30	1.25

Current Investment Style

Style: Value Blnd Growth / Large Med Small

	Stock Port Avg	Relative S&P 500 Current	Hist	Rel Cat
Price/Earnings Ratio	23.8	0.88	0.9	1.07
Price/Book Ratio	4.3	0.70	0.7	1.04
Price/Cash Flow	17.6	0.99	0.9	1.33
3 Yr Earnings Growth	16.6	0.77	1.3	0.82
1 Yr Earnings Est%	19.3	1.48	—	1.74
Debt % Total Cap	40.7	0.91	1.0	0.84
Med Mkt Cap $mil	29,125	0.9	1.4	2.02

Special Securities

	% of assets 11-30-97
● Restricted/Illiquid Secs	Trace
● Emerging-Markets Secs	Trace
● Options/Futures/Warrants	Yes

Composition	% of assets 11-30-97	Market Cap	
Cash	11.1	Giant	51.4
Stocks*	88.4	Large	30.8
Bonds	0.0	Medium	17.6
Other	0.5	Small	0.2
		Micro	0.1
*Foreign (% of stocks)	6.7		

Sector Weightings	% of Stocks	Rel S&P	5-Year High	Low
Utilities	0.0	0.0	8	0
Energy	11.6	1.3	13	5
Financials	41.7	2.6	62	37
Cyclicals	5.1	0.4	8	1
Durables	1.6	0.5	4	0
Staples	6.8	0.6	16	6
Services	10.0	0.7	14	5
Retail	3.2	0.6	7	0
Health	5.9	0.5	15	3
Technology	14.0	1.1	16	6

MORNINGSTAR   Mutual Funds

SOURCE: *Morningstar Mutual Funds*, January 23, 1998, p. 70. (Morningstar, Inc., 25 W. Wacker Drive, Chicago, IL 60606).

EXHIBIT 16–7   **Opening Page for the Web Site for the Vangaurd Family of Mutual Funds**

| THE**Vanguard**GROUP. | Our Funds | Investor Education | Planning Center | Account Services |

welcome to Vanguard Online.

Using Our Site

Fund Prices

Accessing Your Account

Obtaining Materials

Opening An Account

About Vanguard

Contacting Vanguard

Career Opportunities

Our site is best viewed by browsers that support the capabilities of Netscape Navigator® version 3.0 or higher, and Microsoft® Internet Explorer version 3.0 or higher.

top stories

Ian MacKinnon on Bonds Why invest in bond funds when the stock market is booming? Managing Director Ian A. MacKinnon explains why in this interview, an excerpt from the new edition of "In the Vanguard."

Check Out Investor's Quarterly Adding mutual funds to your Vanguard Brokerage Services account through FundAccess? Information about Vanguard and non-Vanguard funds is now available online.

Economic Week in Review: April 27–May 1, 1998 A look at economic indicators for the week.

did you know?

The Vanguard Guide to Investing During Retirement can help you determine whether you're financially ready to retire and how to invest your money after you retire.

features

▸ **Retirement Resource Center**

▸ **Roth IRA Guide**

▸ **Tax Center**

▸ **Proxy Voting**

▸ **Institutional Investors: Vanguard Bridge**

▸ **Financial Planning, Investment Advice, And Trust Services**

▸ **Brokerage Services**

▸ **Services For Advisers**

▸ **Mutual Fund Quiz**

SOURCE: The above information was taken from the Internet on May 2, 1998. (The Vanguard Internet address is http://www.vanguard.com.)

The Internet   Many investors have found a wealth of information about mutual fund investments on the Internet. Basically, there are three ways to access information. First, you can obtain current market values for mutual funds by using one of the Internet search engines, such as Yahoo. All you have to do is type in the symbol for the mutual fund and depress the Enter key. Don't know the fund symbol? No problem. Just type in the name of the fund, and the computer will respond with the correct symbol. In addition to current market values, you can obtain a price history and a profile for the fund.

Second, most investment companies that sponsor mutual funds have a Web page. To obtain information, all you have to do is access one of the Internet search engines and type in the name of the fund. Before reading on, take a look at Exhibit 16–7, the opening page for the Vanguard Investment Company. Generally, statistical information about individual funds, procedures for opening an account, available literature (including a prospectus and an annual report), and different investor services are provided. *Be warned:* Investment companies want you to become a shareholder. As a result, the Web sites for *some* investment companies read like a sales pitch. Read between the glowing descriptions and look at the facts before investing your money.

Finally, professional advisory services, covered in the previous section, offer online research reports for mutual funds. Many investors have found that the research reports provided by companies like Morningstar, Inc., and Lipper Analytical Services are well

FINANCIAL PLANNING IN ACTION

EVALUATION OF A MUTUAL FUND

No checklist can serve as a foolproof guide for choosing a mutual fund. However, the following questions will help you evaluate a potential investment in such a fund.

Category 1: Fund Characteristics

1. What is the value of the assets of this fund?_____

_____

2. What is this fund's Morningstar rating? _____
3. What is the minimum investment? _____
4. Does the fund allow telephone exchanges?
   ☐ Yes   ☐ No
5. Is there a fee for telephone exchanges?
   ☐ Yes   ☐ No

Category 2: Costs

6. Is there a front-end load charge? If so, how much is it?

_____

7. Is there a redemption fee? If so, how much is it? _____

_____

8. How much is the annual management fee? _____

_____

9. Is there a 12b-1 fee? If so, how much is it? _____
10. What is the fund's expense ratio? _____

Category 3: Diversification

11. What is the fund's objective? _____

_____

12. What types of securities does the fund's portfolio include?

_____

13. How many securities does the fund's portfolio include?

_____

14. How many types of industries does the fund's portfolio

   include? _____

_____

Category 4: Fund Performance

15. How long has the fund manager been with the fund?

_____

16. How would you describe the fund's performance over the

   past 12 months? _____

_____

17. How would you describe the fund's performance over the

   past five years? _____

_____

18. How would you describe the fund's performance over the

   past 10 years? _____

_____

Category 5: Conclusion

19. Based on the above information, do you think an investment in this fund will help you achieve your investment goals?
   ☐ Yes   ☐ No

20. Explain your answer to question 19. _____

_____

_____

_____

_____

_____

A Word of Caution

When you use a checklist, there is always a danger of overlooking important relevant information. The above checklist is not a cure-all, but it does provide some very sound questions that you should answer before making a mutual fund investment decision. Quite simply, it is a place to start. If you need other information, *you* are responsible for obtaining it and for determining how it affects your potential investment.

worth the $5 to $10 fee charged for online services. While the information is basically the same as that in the reports described in the previous section, the ability to obtain the information quickly without having to wait for research materials to be mailed or to make a trip to the library is a real selling point.

For more information on the evaluation process, study the checklist provided in the Financial Planning in Action feature on page 506.

CONCEPT CHECK 16–3

1. How can the following help you evaluate a mutual fund?
   a. Newspapers
   b. The fund's objective
   c. The prospectus
   d. The annual report
   e. Financial publications
   f. Professional advisory services
   g. The Internet

THE MECHANICS OF A MUTUAL FUND TRANSACTION

L.O.4 Describe how and why mutual funds are bought and sold.

In this section, we discuss three important topics. First, we examine how shareholders can make money by investing in closed-end funds or open-end funds. Next, we look at the options used to purchase shares in a mutual fund. Finally, we examine the options used to withdraw shares from a mutual fund.

Return on Investment

income dividends

capital gain distributions

As with other investments, the purpose of investing in a closed-end fund or an open-end fund is to earn a financial return. Shareholders in such funds can receive a return in one of three ways. First, both types of funds pay income dividends. **Income dividends** are the earnings a fund pays to shareholders after it has deducted expenses from its dividend and interest income. Second, investors can earn capital gain distributions. **Capital gain distributions** are the payments made to a fund's shareholders that result from the sale of securities in the fund's portfolio. These amounts generally are paid once a year. Third, as with stock and bond investments, you can buy shares in both types of funds at a low price and then sell them after the price has increased. For example, assume you purchased shares in the American Capital Enterprise Mutual Fund at $13.50 per share and sold your shares two years later at $16 per share. In this case, you made $2.50 ($16 selling price − $13.50 purchase price) per share. With this financial information and dollar amounts for income dividends and capital gain distributions, you can calculate a total return for your mutual fund investment. Before completing this section, you may want to examine the actual procedure used to calculate the dollar amount of total return and percentage of total return in the accompanying Financial Planning Calculations box.

The profit that results from an increase in value is referred to as a *capital gain*. Note the difference between a capital gain distribution and a capital gain. A capital gain distribution occurs when *the fund* distributes profits that result from *the fund* selling securities in the portfolio at a profit. On the other hand, a capital gain is the profit that results when

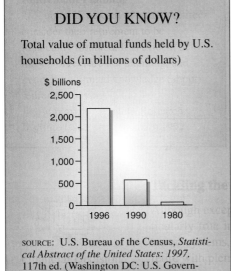

DID YOU KNOW?

Total value of mutual funds held by U.S. households (in billions of dollars)

$ billions

1996	~2,200
1990	~550
1980	~100

SOURCE: U.S. Bureau of the Census, *Statistical Abstract of the United States: 1997,* 117th ed. (Washington DC: U.S. Government Printing Office, 1997), p. 510.

FINANCIAL PLANNING CALCULATIONS

CALCULATING TOTAL RETURN FOR MUTUAL FUNDS

In Chapter 13, we defined total return as a calculation that includes not only the yearly dollar amount of income but also any increase or decrease in market value from the original purchase price of an investment. For mutual funds, you can use the following calculation to determine the dollar amount of total return:

$$
\begin{array}{l}
\text{Income dividends} \\
+ \ \text{Capital gain distributions} \\
+ \ \text{Change in share market value} \\
\hline
\text{Dollar amount of total return}
\end{array}
$$

For example, assume you purchased 100 shares of Majestic Growth Fund for $12.20 per share for a total investment of $1,220. During the next 12 months, you received income dividends of $.36 a share and capital gain distributions of $.42. Also, assume you sold your investment at the end of 12 months for $13.30 a share. As illustrated below, the dollar amount for total return is $188:

Income dividends = 100 × $0.36 =		$ 36
Capital gain distributions = 100 × $0.42 =		+ 42
Change in share value = $13.30 − $12.20		
= $1.10 × 100 =		+ 110
Dollar amount of total return		$ 188

To calculate the percent of total return, divide the dollar amount of total return by the original cost of your mutual fund investment. The percent of total return for the above example is 15.4 percent, as follows:

$$
\begin{aligned}
\text{Percent of total return} &= \frac{\text{Dollar amount of total return}}{\text{Original cost of your investment}} \\[2mm]
&= \frac{\$188}{\$1,220} \\[2mm]
&= 0.154, \text{ or } 15.4\%
\end{aligned}
$$

you sell your shares in the mutual fund for more than you paid for them. Of course, if the price of a fund's shares goes down between the time of your purchase and the time of sale, you incur a loss.

Income dividends, capital gain distributions, and financial gains and losses from the sale of closed-end or open-end funds are subject to taxation. At the end of each year, investment companies are required to send each shareholder a statement specifying how much he or she received in dividends and capital gain distributions. Although investment companies may provide this information as part of their year-end statement, most funds use IRS Form 1099 DIV. Capital gains or losses that result from your decision to sell shares in one of your mutual funds must also be reported as taxable income.

To ensure having all of the documentation you need for tax reporting purposes, it is essential that *you* keep accurate records. The same records will help you monitor the value of your mutual fund investments and make more intelligent decisions with regard to buying and selling these investments.

Purchase Options

You can buy shares of a closed-end fund through the New York Stock Exchange and various other stock exchanges. You can purchase shares of an open-end, no-load fund by contacting the investment company that sponsors the fund. You can purchase shares of an open-end, load fund through a salesperson who is authorized to sell them, through an account executive of a brokerage firm, or directly from the investment company that sponsors the fund. Because of the unique nature of open-end fund transactions, we will examine how investors buy and sell shares in this type of mutual fund.

**Financial Decision
Trade-Off**

To purchase shares in an open-end mutual fund, you may use four options: regular account transactions, voluntary savings plans, contractual savings plans, and reinvestment plans. The most popular and least complicated method of purchasing shares in an open-end fund is through a regular account transaction. When you use a regular account transaction, you decide how much money you want to invest and simply buy as many shares as possible. Commissions, if any, are deducted from the amount of the investment, and the remainder is used to purchase shares.

Voluntary savings plans allow you to open an account with an investment company for as little as $25. For most investment companies, the minimum amount for opening this type of account ranges between $250 and $2,500. At the time of the initial purchase, you declare an intent to make regular minimum purchases of the fund's shares. The chief advantage of the voluntary savings plan is that it allows you to make smaller purchases than the minimum purchases required by the regular account method described above. For most voluntary savings plans, the minimum purchase ranges from $25 to $100 for each purchase after the initial investment. Although there is no penalty for not making regular purchases, most investors feel an "obligation" to make purchases on a regular basis, and, as pointed out throughout this text, small monthly investments are a great way to save for long-term objectives. Funds try to make investing as easy as possible. Most offer payroll deduction plans, and many will deduct, upon proper shareholder authorization, a specified amount from a shareholder's bank account. Also, many investors can choose mutual funds as a vehicle to invest money that is contributed to a 401(k), 403(b), or individual retirement account. Chapter 18 provides more information on the tax advantages of different types of retirement accounts.

Contractual savings plans require you to make regular purchases over a specified period of time, usually 10 to 15 years. These plans are sometimes referred to as *front-end load funds* because almost all of the commissions are paid in the first few years of the contract period. You will incur penalties if you do not fulfill the purchase requirements. For example, if you drop out of a contractual savings plan before completing the purchase requirements, you sacrifice the prepaid commissions. Many financial experts and government regulatory agencies are critical of contractual savings plans. As a result, the Securities and Exchange Commission and many states have imposed new rules on investment companies offering contractual savings plans.

reinvestment plan

You may also purchase shares in an open-end fund by using the fund's reinvestment plan. A **reinvestment plan** is a service provided by an investment company in which income dividends and capital gain distributions are automatically reinvested to purchase additional shares of the fund. Most reinvestment plans allow shareholders to use reinvested money to purchase shares without having to pay additional sales charges or commissions. *Be warned:* When your dividends or capital gain distributions are reinvested, you must still report these transactions as taxable income.

All four purchase options allow you to buy shares over a long period of time. As a result, you can use the principle of *dollar cost averaging,* which was explained in Chapter 14. Dollar cost averaging allows you to average many individual purchase prices over a long period of time. This method helps you avoid the problem of buying high and selling low. With dollar cost averaging, you can make money if you sell your mutual fund shares at a price higher than their *average* purchase price.

Withdrawal Options

Because closed-end funds are listed on securities exchanges, it is possible to sell shares in such a fund to another investor. Shares in an open-end fund can be sold on any business day to the investment company that sponsors the fund. In this case, the shares are

Financial Decision Trade-Off

redeemed at their net asset value. All you have to do is give proper notification and the fund will send you a check. With some funds, you can even write checks to withdraw money from the fund.

In addition, most funds have provisions that allow investors with shares that have a minimum net asset value of at least $5,000 to use four options to systematically withdraw money. First, you may withdraw a specified, fixed dollar amount each investment period until your fund has been exhausted. Normally, an investment period is three months, and most funds require investors to withdraw a minimum amount, ranging from $25 to $50, each investment period.

A second option allows you to liquidate or "sell off" a certain number of shares each investment period. Since the net asset value of shares in a fund varies from one period to the next, the amount of money you receive will also vary. Once the specified number of shares has been sold, a check is mailed directly to you.

Sheet 60

A third option allows you to withdraw a fixed percentage of asset growth. For example, assume you arrange to receive 60 percent of the asset growth of your investment, and the asset growth of your investment amounts to $800 in a particular investment period. For that period, you will receive a check for $480 ($800 × 60% = $480). If no asset growth occurs, no payment is made to you. Under this option, your principal remains untouched.

A final option allows you to withdraw all income that results from income dividends and capital gains earned by the fund during an investment period. Under this option, your principal remains untouched.

CONCEPT CHECK 16–4

1. How can you make money when investing in mutual funds?
2. What options can you use to purchase shares in a mutual fund?
3. What options can you use to withdraw money from a mutual fund?

KEY FORMULAS

Page	Topic	Formula

493   Net asset value

$$\text{Net asset value} = \frac{\text{Value of a funds portfolio} - \text{Liabilities}}{\text{Number of shares outstanding}}$$

Example:

$$\text{Net asset value} = \frac{\$24,500,000 - \$2,500,000}{1,800,000}$$

$$= \$12.22 \text{ per share}$$

---

508   Total return

Income dividends
+ Capital gain distributions
+ Change in market value
———————————————————
Dollar amount of total return

Example:

Dollar amount of $ 120
                     + 80
                     +320
                     $520

---

508   Percent of total return

$$\text{Percent of total return} = \frac{\text{Dollar amount of total return}}{\text{Original cost of investment}}$$

Example:

$$\text{Percent of total return} = \frac{\$\ 520}{\$4{,}500}$$

$$= 0.116, \text{ or } 11.6\%$$

SUMMARY

L.O.1   Describe the characteristics of investments in mutual funds.

The major reasons investors choose mutual funds are professional management and diversification. Mutual funds are also a convenient way to invest money. There are two types of mutual funds. A closed-end fund is a mutual fund whose shares are issued only when the fund is organized. An open-end fund is a mutual fund whose shares are sold and redeemed by the investment company at the net asset value (NAV) at the request of investors. Mutual funds are also classified as load, low-load, or no-load funds. Both load and low-load funds charge a commission every time an investor purchases shares. No commission is charged to purchase shares in a no-load fund. Other possible fees include management fees, contingent deferred sales loads, and 12b-1 fees.

L.O.2   Classify mutual funds by investment objective.

The major categories of mutual funds, in terms of the types of securities in which they invest, are capital appreciation, global stock, growth, growth-income, small-cap, sector, utility, high-yield (junk) bond, intermediate bond, long-term bond, long-term (U.S.) bond, municipal bond, short-term (U.S.) bond, balanced, and stock/bond blend funds. Today

many investment companies use a family-of-funds concept, which allows shareholders to switch their investments among funds as different funds offer more potential, financial reward, or security.

L.O.3   Evaluate mutual funds for investment purposes.

The responsibility for choosing the "right" mutual fund rests with you, the investor. The information in newspapers, the financial objectives of the fund, the information in the prospectus and annual reports, financial publications, professional advisory services, and the Internet can all help you evaluate a mutual fund.

L.O.4   Describe how and why mutual funds are bought and sold.

The shares of a closed-end fund are bought and sold on organized stock exchanges. The shares of an open-end fund may be purchased through a salesperson who is authorized to sell them, through an account executive of a brokerage firm, or from the investment company that sponsors the fund. The shares in an open-end fund can be sold to the investment company that sponsors the fund. A number of purchase and withdrawal options are available.

GLOSSARY

capital gain distributions   The payments made to a fund's shareholders that result from the sale of securities in the fund's portfolio.   (p. 507)

closed-end fund   A mutual fund whose shares are issued by an investment company only when the fund is organized.   (p. 493)

contingent deferred sales load   A 1 to 6 percent charge that shareholders pay when they withdraw their investment from a mutual fund.   (p. 495)

family of funds   A group of mutual funds managed by one investment company.   (p. 497)

income dividends   The earnings a fund pays to shareholders after it has deducted expenses from its dividend and interest income.   (p. 507)

investment company   A firm that, for a management fee, invests the pooled funds of small investors in securities appropriate to its stated investment objectives.   (p. 492)

load fund A mutual fund in which investors pay a commission (as high as 8½ percent) every time they purchase shares. (p. 493)

low-load fund A mutual fund that charges a lower commission (usually between 1 and 3 percent) than a load fund. (p. 493)

market timer An individual who helps investors decide when to switch their investments from one fund to another fund, usually within the same family of funds. (p. 498)

mutual fund An investment alternative chosen by people who pool their money to buy stocks, bonds, and other financial securities selected by professional managers who work for an investment company. (p. 491)

net asset value (NAV) The current market value of the securities contained in the mutual fund's portfolio minus the

mutual fund's liabilities divided by the number of shares outstanding. (p. 493)

no-load fund A mutual fund in which the individual investor pays no sales charge. (p. 494)

open-end fund A mutual fund whose shares are issued and redeemed by the investment company at the request of investors. (p. 493)

reinvestment plan A service provided by an investment company in which shareholder income dividends and capital gain distributions are automatically reinvested to purchase additional shares of the fund. (p. 509)

12b-1 fee A fee that an investment company levies to defray the costs of advertising and marketing a mutual fund. (p. 495)

REVIEW QUESTIONS

1. Why would an investor prefer to invest in mutual funds instead of purchasing individual stocks or bonds? (L.O.1)
2. Describe the difference between a closed-end fund and an open-end fund. (L.O.1)
3. How do you calculate net asset value? Why is this calculation important? (L.O.1)
4. What are the typical sales fees for a load fund, a low-load fund, and a no-load fund? (L.O.1)
5. In your own words, explain how the following affect a mutual fund investment. (L.O.1)
   a. Management fees.
   b. Contingent deferred sales loads.
   c. 12b-1 fees.
6. How important is the investment objective(s) for a mutual fund? (L.O.2)
7. Why do you think fund managers offer so many different kinds of mutual funds? (L.O.2)
8. What is a family of funds? How does it affect mutual fund investments? (L.O.2)

9. Many financial experts say that purchasing a mutual fund is "too easy." Do you think this statement is true or false? Why? (L.O.3)
10. A common footnote in mutual fund quotations is NL. What does NL mean? (L.O.3)
11. What types of information appear in a fund's prospectus? In an annual report? (L.O.3)
12. List four magazines that publish annual surveys for mutual funds. (L.O.3)
13. What type of information is available from professional advisory services? From the Internet? (L.O.3)
14. What is the difference between income dividends, capital gain distributions, and capital gains? (L.O.4)
15. Whom would you contact to purchase a closed-end fund? An open-end fund? (L.O.4)
16. Explain the four options an investor can use to purchase shares in an open-end mutual fund. (L.O.4)
17. Explain the four options an investor can use to redeem shares in an open-end mutual fund. (L.O.4)

FINANCIAL PLANNING PROBLEMS

1. *Calculating Net Asset Value.* Given the information below, calculate the net asset value for the Boston Equity mutual fund. (L.O.1)

Total assets	$225,000,000
Total liabilities	$5,000,000
Total number of shares	4,400,000

2. *Calculating Net Asset Value.* Given the following information, calculate the net asset value for the New Empire small-cap mutual fund. (L.O.1)

Total assets	$350,000,000
Total liabilities	$10,000,000
Total number of shares	17,000,000

3. *Calculating Sales Fees.* Jan Throng invested $15,000 in the Aim Charter Mutual Fund. The fund charges a 5.50 percent commission when shares are purchased. Calculate the amount of commission Jan must pay. (L.O.1)

4. *Calculating Sales Fees.* Bill Matthews invested $9,800 in the John Hancock growth and income fund. The fund charges a 5.3 percent commission when shares are purchased. Calculate the amount of commission Bill must pay. (L.O.1)

5. *Determining Management Fees.* Mike Jackson invested a total of $8,500 in the ABC Mutual Fund. The management fee for this particular fund is 0.70 percent of the total

investment amount. Calculate the management fee Mike must pay this year.   (L.O.1)

6. *Calculating Contingent Deferred Sales Loads.* Mary Canfield purchased the New Dimensions bond fund. While this fund doesn't charge a front-end load, it does charge a contingent deferred sales load of 4 percent for any withdrawals in the first five years. If Mary withdraws $6,000 during the second year, how much is the contingent deferred sales load?   (L.O.1)

7. *Matching Mutual Funds with Investor Needs.* This chapter classified mutual funds into different categories based on the nature of their investments. Using the following information, pick a mutual fund category that you consider suitable for each investor described and justify your choice.   (L.O.2)

   a. A 25-year-old single investor with a new job that pays $30,000 a year.

   Mutual fund category _____

   Why? _____

   b. A single parent with two children who has just received a $100,000 divorce settlement, has no job, and has not worked outside the home for the past five years.

   Mutual fund category _____

   Why? _____

   c. A husband and wife who are both in their early 60s and retired.

   Mutual fund category _____

   Why? _____

8. *Finding Total Return.* Assume that one year ago, you bought 100 shares of a mutual fund for $15 per share, you received a $.75-per-share distribution during the past 12 months, and the market value of the fund is now $18. Calculate the total return for this investment if you were to sell it now.   (L.O.3)

9. *Finding Percent of Total Return.* Given the information in question 8, calculate the percent of total return for your $1,500 investment.   (L.O.3)

10. *Using Dollar Cost Averaging.* Over a four-year period, Matt Ewing purchased shares in the Stein Roe Venture Fund. Using the following information, answer the questions that follow. You may want to review the concept of dollar cost averaging in Chapter 14 before completing this problem.   (L.O.4)

Year	Investment Amount	Price per Share
1998	$3,000	$40 per share
1999	$3,000	$50 per share
2000	$3,000	$60 per share
2001	$3,000	$45 per share

   a. At the end of four years, what is the total amount invested?

   b. At the end of four years, what is the total number of mutual fund shares purchased?

   c. At the end of four years, what is the average cost for each mutual fund share?

PROJECTS AND APPLICATION ACTIVITIES

1. *Deciding If Mutual Funds Are Right for You.* Assume you are 35, are divorced, and have just received a $120,000 legal settlement. Prepare a two-page report on the major advantages and disadvantages of investing in mutual funds.   (L.O.1)

2. *Applying Terms to Mutual Fund Investments.* Using recent newspapers, magazines, mutual fund reports, or the Internet, find examples of the following concepts.   (L.O.1)

   a. The net asset value for a mutual fund.
   b. An example of a load fund.
   c. An example of a no-load fund.
   d. The management fee for a specific mutual fund.
   e. A fund that charges a contingent deferred sales load.
   f. A fund that charges a 12b-1 fee.

3. *Understanding Fees Associated with Mutual Fund Investments.* Assume you are single, are 28 years old, and have decided to invest $8,000 in mutual funds.   (L.O1)

   a. Prepare a chart that shows the typical charges for load funds, low-load funds, no-load funds, management fees, contingent deferred sales loads, and 12b-1 fees.

   b. Calculate the following fees for your $8,000 mutual fund investment: (1) a 5 percent load charge, (2) an annual 0.50 percent management fee, and (3) an annual 1 percent 12b-1 fee.

4. *Matching Mutual Funds with Investor Needs.* This chapter explored a number of different classifications of mutual funds.   (L.O.2)

   a. Based on your age and current financial situation, which type of mutual fund seems appropriate for your investment needs? Explain your answer.

   b. As people get closer to retirement, their investment goals often change. Assume you are now 45 and have accumulated $80,000 in a retirement account. In this situation, what type of mutual fund would you choose? Why?

   c. Assume you are now 60 years of age and have accumulated $300,000 in a retirement account. Also, assume you would like to retire when you are 65. What type of mutual funds would you choose to help you reach your investment goals? Why?

5. *Using Information to Evaluate Mutual Funds.* Obtain specific information on either the Aim Charter mutual fund or the Aim Value mutual fund. Then describe how each source of information could help you evaluate a mutual fund.   (L.O.3)

   a. Newspapers.
   b. The fund's investment objective.

c. The fund's prospectus.

d. The fund's annual report.

e. Financial publications.

f. Professional advisory services.

g. The Internet.

After researching one of the Aim funds, would you invest in the fund? Why or why not?

6. *Evaluating Mutual Funds.* Choose one of the following mutual funds and use information from newspapers, magazines, mutual fund reports, or the Internet to complete the mutual fund evaluation form presented in the Financial Planning in Action feature on page 506. Then answer the following questions.   (L.O.3)

Name of Fund	Type of Fund
Ameristar Capital Growth Fund	Growth fund
Arrow Equity Fund	Growth fund
Highmark Balanced Fund	Balanced fund
Janus Mercury Fund	Capital appreciation
USAA Group S&P Index Fund	Growth and income

a. Which fund did you choose?

b. Why did you choose this fund?

c. Do you think this fund could help you achieve your investment objectives? Explain your answer.

7. *Applying the Concept of Dollar Cost Averaging.* In a one-page report, explain how the concept of dollar cost averaging applies to the options used to purchase mutual funds. (L.O.4)

8. *Reading a Prospectus.* Obtain a mutual fund prospectus to determine the options you can use to purchase and redeem shares. Then prepare a chart that illustrates which options can be used to purchase and redeem shares in the fund, and answer the following questions.   (L.O.4)

a. Which purchase option would appeal to you?

b. Assuming you are now of retirement age, which withdrawal option would appeal to you?

LIFE SITUATION CASE 16

THE WRONG MUTUAL FUND?

According to Mike and Della Hanson, a Salt Lake City couple in their middle 30s, mutual funds were one of the biggest disappointments in their lives. In September 1994, they invested $11,500 in the Fidelity Select American Gold mutual fund. Three years later, their original investment had gained *only* 3.3 percent, or less than $400, during a period when most mutual funds were posting huge profits. What went wrong?

Three years after their investment, the Hansons admitted they had invested money without researching the Fidelity Select American Gold fund. They made their investment choice because Mike had heard a "high-powered" financial planner on a radio talk show raving about gold as the "ultimate" safe investment. Over the next two days, Mike convinced Della that gold was an investment that could be trusted. The Hansons would have purchased the gold coins the talk show host was selling, but Mike lost the 800 phone number. For lack of some other way to invest in gold, they decided to purchase shares in the Fidelity Select American Gold mutual fund. Besides, they reasoned, shares in a mutual fund would be a better investment compared to purchasing individual coins because mutual funds provided diversification and professional management. Both thought they were choosing the right investment. What could be better than a mutual fund that "specialized" in gold? Their investment would be a safe choice even if other investments went down in value.

The Hanson also thought that since everybody was investing in mutual funds, they had to be the perfect investment. After all, there were over 6,000 different funds to choose

from. Indeed, it seemed almost fashionable to invest in mutual funds. Because of professional management and diversification, there was no need to evaluate a mutual fund. Certainly the fund manager knew more about picking the investments contained in the fund's portfolio than they did. It seemed mutual funds were almost guaranteed to increase in value. But after earning about 1 percent a year, they realized that "almost guaranteed" was not the same thing as "guaranteed."

At the time of their investment, both had heard good things about Fidelity mutual funds. A number of their friends had opened accounts with Fidelity and had done well. And Fidelity made it so easy! Just fill out an application, send the money, and let the professional managers make all the decisions. In fact, the Hansons didn't realize that Fidelity, the nation's largest mutual fund family, offered approximately 150 mutual funds ranging all the way from very conservative to very speculative investments. Simply put, they chose the wrong Fidelity mutual fund. Had the Hansons chosen the Fidelity Select Electronics fund, their original investment would have increased almost 45 percent and been worth nearly $17,000.

QUESTIONS

1. Often investors indicate that diversification and professional management are the two main reasons they choose mutual fund investments. How important do you consider these two factors? Why?

2. At the time of this publication, Fidelity offered approximately 150 mutual funds ranging from very conservative to very speculative investments. Why do you think a fund family would offer so many investment alternatives?

3. According to the Hansons, everybody was investing in mutual funds—indeed, it almost seemed fashionable to invest in mutual funds. In your own words, what did Mike and Della Hanson do wrong?

4. Obtain information about the Fidelity Select American Gold fund and the Fidelity Select Electronics fund at the library or by using the Internet. Then complete a mutual fund evaluation form (see the Financial Planning in Action on page 506) for each fund and answer the following questions.

   a. What sources of information did you use to evaluate each fund?

   b. What fees must investors pay to invest in each fund?
   c. What is the investment objective for each fund?
   d. How would you describe the fund's financial performance over the past 12 months? The past three years? The past five years?
   e. How would you rate the risk associated with each fund?
   f. Would you invest your money in either of these funds? Justify you answer.

   SOURCE: Values for the Fidelity Select American Gold fund and the Fidelity Select Electronics fund based on information from *Kiplinger's Personal Finance,* August 1997, p. 66.

USING THE INTERNET TO CREATE A PERSONAL FINANCIAL PLAN 16

INVESTING IN MUTUAL FUNDS

Diversification through the use of mutual funds provides investors with convenience and professional management. The variety of mutual funds contributes to the investor's ability to achieve various financial goals.

Web Sites for Mutual Funds

- Current mutual fund information and data at **www.personalwealth.com**
- Current information and financial performance on over 6,000 mutual funds and more than 7,800 stocks at **www.morningstar.net**
- Information and materials from the Mutual Fund Education Alliance and other sources may be accessed at **networth.galt.com**
- Investment information related to mutual funds may be obtained at **www.networth.quicken.com/investments, www.mfmag.com,** and **www.bloomberg.com**
- Information about no-load mutual funds at **www.no-load-funds.com/**
- Current articles on mutual funds from *Money* magazine at **www.money.com,** *Kiplinger's Personal Finance* magazine at **www.kiplinger.com,** *Business Week* at **www.businessweek.com,** *Worth* magazine at **www.worth.com,** and *Smart Money* at **www.smartmoney.com**

- Money market fund information at **www.moneyline.com/mlc**

(Note: Addresses and content of Web sites change, and new sites are created daily. Use the search engines discussed in Appendix B to update and locate Web sites for your current financial planning needs.)

PFP SHEET: 60

Short-Term Financial Planning Activities

1. Identify types of mutual funds that might be appropriate for your various financial goals and life situations.
2. Research the recent performance records and costs of various mutual funds that could be appropriate investments for you.

Long-Term Financial Planning Activities

1. Identify types of mutual funds that might be used for your long-term financial goals.
2. Develop a plan for selecting and monitoring your mutual fund portfolio.

CHAPTER 17

REAL ESTATE AND OTHER INVESTMENT ALTERNATIVES

OPENING CASE

REITS KEEP GROWING, BUT ARE THEY A GOOD INVESTMENT?

Some lucky people have the time and the inclination to search out individual real estate deals. But for most of us, the best way to buy real estate is through real estate investment trusts, or REITs (pronounced "reetz"). REIT was created by Congress in 1960, but it had never attracted much interest until recently. Today real estate has become a mainstream investment thanks to the rapid growth of REITs since the mid-1990s.

"Real estate is finally becoming more like every other American major industry—publicly traded and accessible to all investors. And REITs are the vehicle of change," says Mike Kirby, co-founder and principal of real estate research firm Green Street Advisors Inc.

REITs let investors enjoy some of the benefits of owning real estate "without buying dirt," says Mark Bass, a financial planner with Pennington, Bass & Associates in Lubbock, Texas. Bass says his clients typically invest 5 to 15 percent of their portfolios in real estate investment trusts.

Here are some of the advantages of REITs:

- *Consistent performance.* In 1997, REITs were up 29 percent over the last 12 months, compared with 25 percent for the S&P 500 stock index.
- *Regular income.* Because REITs are required by law to distribute 95 percent of their income to shareholders as dividends, they typically pay higher yields than stocks.
- *Diversification.* Owning REITs could cushion your portfolio if the stock market falls.
- *Liquidity.* As with other securities, you should be able to sell your shares. REITs offer the opportunity to invest in real estate the same way investors have invested in other publicly traded industries.

And here are some disadvantages:

- *Tax headaches.* If you hold your REITs in a taxable account, you need to know the amount of your distribution before you file your taxes. Unfortunately, REITs can't calculate the amount of their annual distribution until the end of the year, when they close their books.
- *Declining property values.* If property values decline, rents on apartments or office buildings will fall, and so will the value of your real estate investment trust.

With new REITs and REIT funds hitting the market every day, how do you find a good one? Look for one with experienced management and manageable debt, analysts say. Andrew Davis of Davis Real Estate Fund says he looks for managers who own a big stake in the company when he shops for REITs. Those managers are much less likely to make risky bets because their own money is at stake, he says. According to Davis, "Ultimately, REITs are the way real estate should be owned." Richard E. Rainwater, Chairman of Crescent Real Estate Equity, believes that 10 years from now the value of REITs will top $500 billion, and in 15 years it will hit $1 trillion. Fortunately, those REITs aren't' hard to find.

QUESTIONS

1. What are some of the advantages of REITs?
2. What are some of the disadvantages of REITs?
3. What are two characteristics of a good REIT?

SOURCES: Larry Light and Geoffrey Smith, "REITs Are Going Like a House of Fire," *Business Week,* June 2, 1997, pp. 121–24; Janice K. Glassman, "For Bargain Hunters, REITs Are Still Right," *Washington Post,* July 27, 1997, p. H01; Sandra Block, "Keen on Real Estate but Fear Risk? Look at REITs," *USA Today,* March 7, 1997, p. B6; Suzanne Woolley, Kathleen Morris, Richard A. Melcher, and Stephanie Anderson, "The New World of Real Estate," *Business Week,* September 22, 1997, pp. 78–87.

LEARNING
OBJECTIVES

After studying this chapter, you will be able to

L.O.1   Identify types of real estate investments.

L.O.2   Evaluate the advantages of real estate investments.

L.O.3   Assess the disadvantages of real estate investments.

L.O.4   Analyze the risks and rewards of investing in precious metals, gems, and collectibles.

INVESTING IN REAL ESTATE

L.O.1 Identify types of real estate investments.

Traditionally, Americans have invested in real estate. It is an asset that we can see, touch, and smell, and it is generally a good hedge against inflation. However, as you will see, the choices in real estate investment are bewildering for the new investor. Furthermore, the Tax Reform Act of 1986 has lessened the appeal of investing in real estate.

direct investment

Real estate investments are classified as direct or indirect. In **direct investment,** the investor holds legal title to the property. Direct real estate investments include single-family dwellings, duplexes, apartments, land, and nonresidential real estate.

indirect investment

With an **indirect investment,** investors appoint a trustee to hold legal title on behalf of all the investors in the group. Limited partnerships and syndicates, real estate investment trusts, mortgages, and mortgage pools are examples of indirect real estate investments.

Exhibit 17–1 on page 518 summarizes the advantages and disadvantages of the two types of investments.

Direct Real Estate Investments

Your Home as an Investment   Your home is, first, a place to live; second, it is an income shelter if you have a mortgage on it; finally, it is a possible hedge against inflation.

According to David Berson, chief economist at the Federal National Mortgage Association, Americans have about $8.7 trillion invested in single-family homes. Their equity, or the value of what they own outright after mortgage debt, amounts to about $5.6 trillion—some $500 billion more than people hold in stocks, bonds, and mutual funds combined. Generally, people feel driven to buy homes mainly for personal reasons, not as a result of financial analysis. Indeed, according to a study by the National Association of Realtors, the top two reasons most people give for buying are that they "preferred a larger home" or "wanted the tax advantages of home ownership."[1]

Home prices generally have climbed steadily over the years. During the past 150 years, owning a home produced a "real," or after-inflation, return of about 2.5 percent a year, roughly the same return yielded by a bond.[2]

EXHIBIT 17–1

Types, Advantages, and Disadvantages of Real Estate Investments

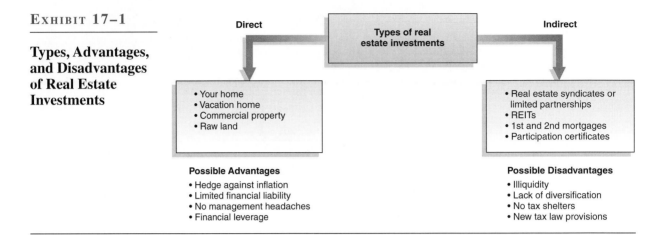

Your Vacation Home   If you have a vacation home, the after-tax cost of owning it has risen since 1987. Just how much it has risen depends largely on whether the Internal Revenue Service views the property as your second home or as a rental property. It is deemed a second home as long as you don't rent it for more than 14 days a year. In that case, you can write off your mortgage interest and property tax. If you rent the vacation home regularly, the size of your deductions is determined by whether you actively manage it and by the size of your income. According to one certified public accountant, "The primary reason you buy a vacation home is because you want to use it. Tax reasons…are way down on the list."[3]

commercial property

Commercial Property   The term **commercial property** refers to land and buildings that produce lease or rental income.[4] Such property includes duplexes, apartments, hotels, office buildings, stores, and many other types of commercial establishments. Aside from a home, the real property investment most widely favored by small investors is the duplex, fourplex, or small apartment building. Many investors have acquired sizable commercial properties by first investing in a duplex and then "trading up" to larger units as equity in the original property increases.

The investment potential of commercial property, unlike that of raw land or a personal residence, can be accurately measured. There are several methods for doing this, all of which compare the expected future income from a property with its cost. Exhibit 17–2 shows one method used to calculate the expected profitability of commercial properties. More sophisticated analytic methods are being used, but this method covers most of the areas investigated. Its greatest weaknesses are that it covers a maximum of three years and the expected market or sales price of the property plays no role in the analysis.

Exhibit 17–3 on page 520 contains information about a six-year-old, 10-unit apartment building, Outflow Apartments, that is assumed to be for sale. When such a property is placed on the market, the real estate broker listing it prepares information of the type contained in this exhibit. If the property is not listed, the seller prepares this information. Typically, only current-year information is supplied.

Financial Decision Trade-Off

Income and Expenses   *Gross scheduled income* (see Exhibit 17–2) is the total amount of income that would be obtained if the apartments were completely rented and all rents were paid. However, commercial properties are seldom fully rented, and rents sometimes cannot be collected. *Gross operating income* is what remains after these losses.

EXHIBIT 17–2

Current-Year Income Analysis for Outflow Apartments

Property name	Outflow Apartments			Type	Ten-Plex		
Location				List price	$200,000		
Assessed value:	$151,500	100%		Less loans	$140,000		
Land	30,000	20%		= List price equity $60,000			
Improvements	120,000	79%					
Personal property	1,500	1%					

	Year	%	Year 2	%	Year 3	%
Gross scheduled income	$ 30,000	100				
Less vacancy and credit losses	1,500	5				
= Gross operating income	28,500	95				
Less operating expenses:						
Taxes	5,700	19				
Utilities	1,200	4				
Insurance	300	1				
Management	2,400	8				
Services	200	1				
Supplies						
Maintenance	1,500	5				
Other	200	1				
Total operating expenses	11,500	39				
= Net operating income	17,000	56				
Less loan payments	16,022					
= Gross spendable income	978					
Plus principal repayment	2,868					
= Gross equity income	3,846					
Less depreciation	7,272					
= Taxable income	(3,426)					

SOURCE: Adapted with permission from Wilbur W. Widicus and Thomas E. Stitzel, *Personal Investing,* 5th ed. (Burr Ridge, IL: Richard D. Irwin, 1989), p. 334. © 1989 Richard D. Irwin.

Operating expenses are the nonfinancial expenses of operating the apartments. Traditionally, each expense category of this income statement is divided by gross scheduled income to provide a relative measure of each cost. Estimates of income and expenses must be made for new properties. Owners of existing properties typically provide the most recent year's income statement to prospective buyers. Taxes and utility expenses can usually be verified by examining receipts. It is much more difficult to check the accuracy of most other expense and income items.

Net operating income represents the income from the investment before financing payments and depreciation. A widely used measure of the gross profitability of such an investment is the ratio of net operating income (NOI) to the cost of the property. In this example, the ratio of operating income earned to the list price is

$$\frac{\text{NOI}}{\text{List price}} = \text{Rate of return}$$

$$\frac{\$17,000}{\$200,000} = 0.085, \text{ or } 8.5 \text{ percent}$$

A similar ratio of gross operating income to market price is also calculated. Appraisers and lenders often use both ratios.

Exhibit 17–3

Financing Schedule for Outflow Apartments

	Principal Amount	Term	Annual Payment	Interest Rate
Existing financing				
First loan	$100,000	25 years	$ 8,868	7½%
Proposed financing				
First loan	89,675	19	8,868	7½
Second loan	50,325	19	7,156	13

Repayment schedule, all loans

Year	Interest Paid	Principal Paid	Total Payment	Principal Remaining
1	$ 13,154	$2,868	$16,022	$137,132
2	12,892	3,130	16,022	134,002
3	12,604	3,418	16,022	130,584

SOURCE: Wilbur W. Widicus and Thomas E. Stitzel, *Personal Investing,* 5th ed. (Burr Ridge, IL: Richard D. Irwin, 1989), p. 337. © 1989 Richard D. Irwin.

Financing and Depreciation Charges   Financing and depreciation are so important that ever since the Tax Reform Act of 1986, they are handled separately from operating expenses. Beginning in 1987, depreciation stretches to 27½ years for residential buildings and 31½ years for other commercial property. The Tax Reform Act of 1986 dictates straight-line depreciation: An equal percentage of the cost must be deducted each year. In Exhibit 17–2, the allowed depreciation is $200,000 divided by 27½ years, or $7,272 per year.

Exhibit 17–3 shows a three-year loan schedule. This schedule assumes the purchaser can assume the balance of a 25-year, 7.5 percent loan ($89,675) and can obtain an additional loan at 13 percent, for total financing of $140,000. The original loan has 19 years remaining before it is paid off; the second loan will also have a 19-year maturity.

Returning to Exhibit 17–2, you can see how financing costs are deducted from net operating income to produce gross spendable income. Adding the yearly principal repayment on loans to gross spendable income produces gross equity income. Subtracting yearly depreciation costs from this figure gives a loss of $3,426 for the first year this investment is held. Gross spendable income and gross equity income are often divided by the amount of the investor's equity to compare returns with the equity investment.

Outflow Apartments' gross spendable income is only $978, but depreciation reduces the owner's taxable income by $3,426. If the owner were in the marginal 28 percent income tax bracket, his or her taxes would be lowered by

$$0.28 \times \$3,426 = \$959$$

This amount is often called a *tax saving.* Deducting this amount from the book loss shown on the income analysis form results in an after-tax cost of only $2,467:

$$\$3,426 - \$959 = \$2,467$$

The investment still produces a loss, but that loss is lowered by the investment's income tax effects.

Many real property investors are interested primarily in the yearly after-tax cash returns (or losses) from their investments. Traditionally, these returns are calculated by using the following format, in which amounts from Exhibit 17–3 have been rearranged to show the after-tax cash cost of holding Outflow Apartments:

Net operating income	$17,000
Less: Financing payments	16,022
= Gross spendable income	$ 978
Plus: Income tax benefit	959
Net spendable cash	$ 1,937

So far, Outflow Apartments appears to be an incredibly poor investment. However, we have not considered market price appreciation. Almost all real property prices in most parts of the United States have risen in recent years. Many people expect these price rises to continue and look to them for profits. They are quite willing to hold real property that breaks even on a cash basis or even runs a cash loss, hoping to take their profits in a lump sum when they sell the property.

The Outflow Apartments investment would be highly profitable if its value were to increase by 6 percent per year. The investment would then be worth $212,000 in one year, $224,720 in two, $238,203 in three, and $267,645 in five. Because the investor has never had more than $60,000 of equity in the apartments, large profits on invested equity would result if prices rose at this rate. Continued market price increases will cause real property to be sold at what seem to be unjustifiably high prices.

Under current tax laws, deductions such as mortgage interest, depreciation, property taxes, and other expenses of rental property are limited to the amount of rental income you receive. Any excess deductions are considered a passive loss and, with some exceptions, can be used only to offset income from a similar investment such as another rental property. A **passive activity** is a business or trade in which you do not materially participate, such as rental activity. **Passive loss** is the total amount of losses from a passive activity minus the total income from the passive activity.

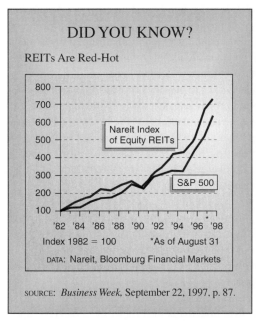

DID YOU KNOW?

REITs Are Red-Hot

Nareit Index of Equity REITs

S&P 500

'82 '84 '86 '88 '90 '92 '94 '96 '98

Index 1982 = 100   *As of August 31

DATA: Nareit, Bloomburg Financial Markets

SOURCE: *Business Week*, September 22, 1997, p. 87.

passive activity

passive loss

Financial Decision Trade-Off

Raw Land   Since the tax law changes of 1986, popular real estate investments, such as suburban garden apartments, no longer appeal to real estate investors. Instead, these investors have been favoring more exotic property, such as raw land ripe for development.

If land investments have promised tremendous gains, they have also posed enormous risks. With their money riding on a single parcel, investors could end up owning overpriced cropland in the event of a building slowdown or an economic downturn. Furthermore, land does not produce any cash flow.

Many investors buy land with the intention of subdividing it. Purchases of this kind are speculative because they involve many risks. You must be certain that water, sewers, and other utilities will be available. The most common and least expensive way to obtain water and sewer service is to hook onto existing facilities of an adjoining city or town.

Indirect Real Estate Investments

Indirect real estate investments include investing in real estate syndicates, real estate investment trusts, and participation certificates.

Bernice R. Hecker, a Seattle anesthesiologist, made her first real estate investment in 1985. She joined a partnership that bought an office building in Midland, Texas. "Why real estate? Probably superstition," she said. "I wanted a tangible asset. I felt I could evaluate a piece of property much more readily" than stocks, bonds, or a cattle ranch.[5]

Dr. Hecker used a real estate syndicate, one of the three basic indirect methods of investing in real estate: (1) real estate syndicates, which are partnerships that buy properties; (2) real estate investment trusts (REITs), which are stockholder-owned real estate companies; and (3) participation certificates sold by federal and state agencies. Indirect real estate investments are sold by most brokerage firms such as Merrill Lynch & Company.

syndicate

Real Estate Syndicates or Limited Partnerships   A **syndicate** is a temporary association of individuals or firms organized to perform a specific task that requires a large amount of capital.[6] The syndicate may be organized as a corporation, as a trust, or, most commonly, as a limited partnership.

The limited partnership works as follows. It is formed by a general partner, who has unlimited liability for its liabilities. The general partner then sells participation units to the limited partners, whose liability is generally limited to the extent of their initial investment, say, $5,000 or $10,000. Limited liability is particularly important in real estate syndicates because their mortgage debt obligations may exceed the net worth of the participants.

In addition to limited liability, a real estate syndicate provides professional management for its members. A syndicate that owns several properties may also provide diversification.

Traditionally, real estate syndicates have been tax shelters for the investors. However, the Tax Reform Act of 1986 has limited the creativity of real estate syndicators. It hits real estate syndicates particularly hard by preventing losses from "passive" investments in partnerships from offsetting income from other sources. It also limits deductions of interest and depreciation and increases the tax on capital gains.

real estate investment trust (REIT)

Real Estate Investment Trusts (REITs)   Another way to invest in real estate is the **real estate investment trust (REIT)**. A REIT is similar to a mutual fund or an investment company, and it trades on stock exchanges or over the counter. Like mutual funds, REITs pool investor funds. These funds, along with borrowed funds, are invested in real estate or used to make construction or mortgage loans.

There are three types of REITs: *equity REITs,* which invest in properties; *mortgage REITs,* which pool money to finance construction loans and mortgages on developed properties; and *hybrid REITs,* combinations of mortgage and equity REITs.

Federal law requires REITs to:

> **DID YOU KNOW?**
>
> You can contact NAREIT at 1–800–3NAREIT, or visit them at http://www.nareit.com.

- Distribute at least 95 percent of their net annual earnings to shareholders
- Refrain from engaging in speculative, short-term holding of real estate to sell for quick profits
- Hire independent real estate professionals to carry out certain management activities
- Have at least 100 shareholders; no more than half the shares may be owned by five or fewer people.

You may choose from among more than 300 REITs. Further information on REITs is available from the National Association of Real Estate Investments Trust, 1129 20th Street, NW, Washington, DC 20036. The accompanying Financial Planning in Action feature on page 523 summarizes REITs' remarkable revolution.

Investing in First and Second Mortgages   Mortgages and other debt contracts are commonly purchased by more well-to-do investors. Often the purchaser of a mortgage takes on some sort of risk that is unacceptable to the financial institutions from which mortgage financing is ordinarily obtained. Perhaps the mortgage is on a property for which there is no ready market. The title to the property may not be legally clear, or the title may not be

FINANCIAL PLANNING IN ACTION

REAL ESTATE'S REMARKABLE REVOLUTION

1960

Real estate investment trusts created by Congress to let individuals invest in real estate. REITs must distribute at least 95 percent of taxable income to shareholders but can avoid corporate taxes. REITs begin to flourish.

Mid-1970s

REIT market collapses because of high interest rates, excess leverage, and short-term financing. Many REITs go bust. REIT assets slump from $20 billion in 1974 to $7 billion in 1979.

1980s

New breed of REIT emerges, with lower leverage, stronger financing, and, after 1986, liberalized powers, thanks to tax changes. Rockefeller Center syndicated as a REIT.

1990

Commercial real estate market, hurt by thrift fiasco, collapses. Many empires, like the Reichmann's Olympia & York, go bankrupt. Rockefeller Center files for Chapter 11.

1991–92

Banks and other traditional sources cut off lending. Real estate execs seek alternate financing. "Opportunity" or "vulture" funds raise cash to buy distressed properties.

Taubman Centers, the holder of shopping centers and malls, pioneers "umbrella" REIT structure, called the UPREIT, which allows private owners to go public without having to pay capitals gains tax.

1993–95

Real estate market recovers. In 1993, a record 50 firms, including many old-line families, bring REITs public. REITs proliferate, move rapidly into malls and apartments. Billion of dollars of capital flow into industry.

1996

Consolidation phase begins. Simon Property Group and DeBartolo Realty merge, forming biggest REIT, with $3.1 billion market cap. Zell launches first hostile REIT bid. REIT stocks soar.

1997

REIT equity market hits $120 billion market cap. Commercial mortgage-backed market reaches $144 billion. Mortimer Zuckerman's Boston Properties launches a $900 million IPO, the biggest REIT ever. First prison REIT, CCA Prison Realty Trust, goes public. REITs start buying up many old-line private real estate companies.

SOURCE: *Business Week*, September 22, 1997, p. 86.

insurable. Nevertheless, many people purchase such mortgages. These investments may provide relatively high rates of return due to their special risk characteristics.

participation certificate (PC)

Participation Certificates   If you want risk proof real estate investment, participation certificates (PCs) are for you. A **participation certificate** is an equity investment in a pool of mortgages that have been purchased by one of several government agencies. Participation certificates are sold by federal agencies such as the Government National Mortgage Association (Ginnie Mae), the Federal Home Loan Mortgage Corporation (Freddie Mac), the Federal National Mortgage Association (Fannie Mae), and the Student Loan Marketing Association (Sallie Mae). A few states issue "little siblings," such as the State of New York Mortgage Agency (Sonny Mae) and the New England Education Loan Marketing Corporation (Nellie Mae).

Maes and Macs are guaranteed by agencies closely tied to the federal government, making them as secure as U.S. Treasury bonds and notes. At one time, you needed a minimum of $25,000 to invest in PCs. Thanks to Maes and Macs mutual funds, you now need as little as $1,000 to buy shares in a unit trust or a mutual fund whose portfolio consists entirely of these securities. Either way, you assume the role of a mortgage lender. Each

FINANCIAL PLANNING FOR LIFE'S SITUATIONS

UNCLE SAM AND HIS FAMILY

The government securities named Maes and Macs can offer safety and relatively high yields.

1. **Ginnie Mae—Government National Mortgage Association (GNMA).** Introduced the first mortgage-backed securities in 1970 and still dominates this market. The residential mortgage-backed securities are packaged in pools and then resold to investors as certificates ($25,000) or as shares by mutual funds. Regular payments to investors are guaranteed by the GNMA, an agency of the Department of Housing and Urban Development. Ginnie Maes are backed by the full faith and credit of the federal government. The average life of mortgages is 12 years.

2. **Freddie Mac—Federal Home Loan Mortgage Corporation (FHLMC).** Issues mortgage-backed securities similar to Ginnie Maes. The pools of fixed-rate home mortgages are made up of conventional home loans rather than mortgages insured by the FHA or the VA. The timely payment of interest and the *ultimate* payment of principal are guaranteed.

3. **Fannie Mae—Federal National Mortgage Association (FNMA).** Issues mortgage-backed securities similar to Ginnie Maes and Freddie Macs. The pools of fixed-rate home mortgages are similar to Freddie Macs but not to Ginnie Maes. Like Ginnie Maes, Fannie Maes guarantee a fair share of interest and principal *every month.* Like Ginnie Maes and Freddie Macs, newly issued Fannie Mae certificates require a

minimum investment of $25,000; the older certificates (whose principal has been partially paid off) require an investment of as little as $10,000.

4. **Sallie Mae—Student Loan Marketing Association.** Created by Congress in 1972 to provide a national secondary market for government-guaranteed student loans. Issues bonds, each backed by Sallie Mae as a whole rather than as specific pools of loans. Sallie Mae bonds are considered as safe as government Treasuries. Brokers sell bonds having minimum denominations of $10,000. You can also buy shares of Sallie Mae *stock;* the corporation is government chartered but publicly owned, and its shares are traded on the New York Stock Exchange.

5. **Sonny Mae—State of New York Mortgage Agency.** Issues bonds backed by fixed-rate, single-family home mortgages and uses proceeds to subsidize below-market-rate mortgages for first-time home buyers. As with ordinary bonds, interest on Sonny Maes is paid only until the bonds mature. Sonny Maes are exempt from federal income tax, and New York State residents do not pay state income tax on them.

6. **Nellie Mae—New England Education Loan Marketing Corporation.** A nonprofit corporation created by the Commonwealth of Massachusetts. Provides a secondary market for federally guaranteed student loans issued in Massachusetts and New Hampshire. The AAA-rated Nellie Mae bonds mature in three years and are sold in minimum denominations of $5,000.

month, as payments are made on the mortgages, you receive interest and principal by check, or, if you wish, the mutual fund will reinvest the amount for you.

The Financial Planning for Life's Situations feature above describes various types of participation certificates sold by federal and state agencies.

CONCEPT CHECK 17–1

1. What are four examples of direct investments in real estate?
2. What are four examples of indirect investments in real estate?
3. What is a syndicate? A REIT? A participation certificate (PC)?

ADVANTAGES OF REAL ESTATE INVESTMENTS

L.O.2 Evaluate the advantages of real estate investments.

For many types of real estate investments, blanket statements about their investment advantages and disadvantages are not possible. However, certain types of real estate investments may possess some of the advantages discussed in this section.

A Hedge against Inflation

Real property equity investments usually (but not always) provide protection against purchasing power risk. In some areas, the prices of homes have increased consistently. For example, prices are rising in the Midwest and in some Western areas, such as Colorado and Texas. "In Colorado Springs, multifamily housing is booming. All the inventory has dried up," says one financial planner.[7]

Easy Entry

You can gain entry to a shopping center or a large apartment building by investing $5,000 as a limited partner. (A limited partner's liability is restricted by the amount of his or her investment. A limited partner cannot take part in the management of the partnership.) The minimum capital requirements for the total venture may be as high as $1 million or more, which is beyond the limits of a typical real estate investor.

Limited Financial Liability

If you are a limited partner, you are not liable for losses beyond your initial investment. This can be important if the venture is speculative and rewards are not assured. General partners, however, must bear all financial risks.

No Management Concerns

If you have invested in limited partnerships, REITs, mortgages, or participation certificates, you need not worry about paperwork and accounting, maintenance chores, and other administrative duties.

Financial Leverage

Financial leverage is the use of borrowed funds for investment purposes. It enables you to acquire a more expensive property than you could on your own. This is an advantage when property values and incomes are rising. Assume you buy a $100,000 property with no loan and then sell it for $120,000. The $20,000 gain represents a 20 percent return on your $100,000 investment. Now assume you invest only $10,000 of your own money and borrow the other $90,000 (90 percent financing). Now you have made $20,000 on your $10,000 investment, or a 200 percent return.

For a brief overview of online real estate investments, see the Financial Planning for Life's Situations feature on page 526.

CONCEPT CHECK 17–2

1. What are the advantages of real estate investments?
2. How is financial leverage calculated?

DISADVANTAGES OF REAL ESTATE INVESTMENTS

L.O.3 Assess the disadvantages of real estate investments.

Real estate investments have several disadvantages. However, these disadvantages do not affect all kinds of real estate investments to the same extent.

FINANCIAL PLANNING FOR LIFE'S SITUATIONS

ONLINE REAL ESTATE INVESTMENTS: A PEARL IN EVERY OYSTER?

The explosion of online advertising on the Internet in one of the most talked-about topics in real estate investing today. But typing the words "real estate investments" when using a popular Internet search engine may yield a list of hundreds of sites, some much more useful than others. This makes it seem easier to find a pearl in an oyster than the investment that's right for you.

"The more information that becomes available on the Internet, the harder it becomes to find the information you're looking for," said Becky Swann, president and founder of Ired.com Inc., a Dallas-based company designed to serve as a "directory of directories" for real estate–related Internet sites.

Here is a brief overview of some of the more useful and creative destinations for sellers and buyers:

cyberhomes.com—This site claims to be the only online real estate search service with interactive street-level mapping. Once a property listed for sale has been identi- fied, a click on an icon will provide a Net surfer with a detailed map, complete with street names and area schools.

www.realtor.com—The National Association of Realtors in Washington, DC, claims to have the largest real estate site on the Internet, with over 839,000 active listings in the United States and Canada.

www.chicagotribune.com—Like most area newspapers, the *Chicago Tribune* maintains and permits free access to its classified real estate investment ads.

www.pacislands.com—This site is targeted at the investor looking for hot properties in the South Pacific. It features everything from thumbnail sketches of each area to an animated drawing of a Tahitian belly dancer!

One challenge in searching for an investment on the Internet is that the ease with which you can connect to a site is inversely proportional to its popularity. However, if you have Internet access, it can be easier to find your pearl!

SOURCES: Jay Romano, "http://buyandsellonline.com," *The New York Times,* July 27, 1997, p. 3; Liz Poppens, "Virtual Luau: Site Is a Paradise for Pacific Island Investors," *Chicago Tribune,* July 20, 1997, p. 3C.

Illiquidity

Perhaps the largest drawback of direct real estate investments is the absence of large, liquid, and relatively efficient markets for them. Whereas stocks or bonds generally can be sold in a few minutes at the market price, this is not the case for real estate. It may take months to sell commercial property or limited partnership shares.

Declining Property Values

As discussed earlier, real property investments usually provide a hedge against inflation. But during deflationary and recessionary periods, the value of such investments may decline. For example, thousands of developers, lenders, and investors have been victims of a deflation in commercial real estate that began sporadically in the early 1980s. Property values in Southern California, the Northeast, and some other regions are still declining.

Lack of Diversification

Diversification in direct real estate investments is difficult due to the large size of most real estate projects. REITs, Ginnie Maes, Freddie Macs, and other syndicates, however, do provide various levels of diversification.

Lack of a Tax Shelter

The Tax Reform Act of 1986 limits taxpayers' ability to use losses generated by real estate investments to offset income gained from other sources. Thus, investors cannot deduct their real estate losses from income generated by wages, salaries, dividends, and interest. In short, the tax shelter aspect of real estate syndicates no longer exists.

Long Depreciation Period

Before the Tax Reform Act of 1986 went into effect, commercial real estate could be depreciated within 18 years. Under the accelerated cost recovery system (ACRS), adopted in 1980, an investor was allowed to use accelerated depreciation methods to recover the costs. Now investors must use the straight-line depreciation method over 27½ years for residential real estate and over 31½ years for all other types of real estate.

Other provisions of the 1986 act affect real estate investments, and all reduce the value of the tax credits for such investments. Investors are not allowed to take losses in excess of the actual amounts they invest. Furthermore, the investment tax credit has been eliminated entirely for all types of real estate except low-income housing projects.

Management Problems

Financial Decision Trade-Off

Although investments in limited partnerships, REITs, mortgages, or participation certificates do not create management problems, buying and managing individual properties do. Along with the buildings come the responsibilities of management: finding reliable tenants, buying new carpeting, fixing the furnace when it breaks down in the middle of the night, and so on. Many people aren't willing to take on these responsibilities. "This is one reason I dislike small real estate investments," says one financial planner. "There should be a large enough amount of money that it is very important to you and you pay a lot of attention to it. Otherwise it won't work."[8]

If you believe investing in real estate is too risky or too complicated, you might want to consider other tangible investments such as gold and other precious metals, gems, and collectibles. But remember, these investments may entail both risk and reward.

CONCEPT   CHECK   17–3

---

1. What are the disadvantages of real estate investments?
2. What depreciation method is used for residential real estate?

INVESTING IN PRECIOUS METALS, GEMS, AND COLLECTIBLES

L.O.4 Analyze the risks and rewards of investing in precious metals, gems, and collectibles.

When the economy picks up, some investors predict higher inflation. Therefore, many think precious metals such as gold, platinum, and silver will regain some of their glitter. In this section, we discuss several methods for buying precious metals.

Gold

Gold prices tend to be driven up by factors such as fear of war, political instability, and inflation. On the other hand, easing of international tensions or disinflation causes a decline in gold prices. High interest rates also depress gold prices because they make it very expensive to carry gold as an investment.

EXHIBIT 17-4   **Fluctuations in the Price of Gold since 1976**

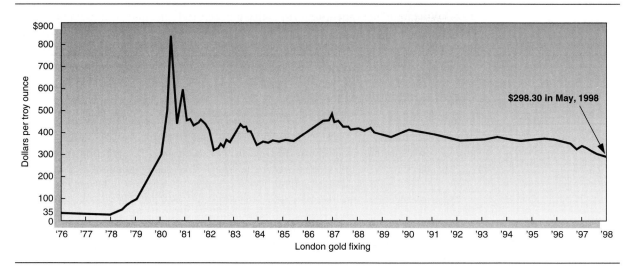

Many people have acquired gold directly. Many others have invested in gold through a number of other kinds of investments that serve a variety of purposes. Some of these investments promise quick profits at high risk, others preserve capital, and yet others provide income from dividends or interest. But all of them are subject to daily gold price fluctuations. Exhibit 17–4 shows gold price fluctuations between 1976 and May 1998.

Gold Bullion   Gold bullion includes gold bars and wafers. The basic unit of gold bullion is one kilogram (32.15 troy ounces of 0.995 fine gold). Coin dealers, precious metals dealers, and some banks sell gold bullion in amounts ranging from 5 grams (16/100 of a troy ounce) to 500 ounces or more. On small bars, dealers and banks add a 5 to 8 percent premium over the pure gold bullion value; on larger bars, the premium is usually 1 to 2 percent. Gold bullion poses storage problems, and unless the gold bar or wafer remains in the custody of the bank or dealer that sells it initially, it must be reassayed (retested for fineness) before being sold.

Gold Bullion Coins   You can avoid storage and assaying problems by investing in gold bullion coins. In the early 1980s, before South Africa's political problems intensified, South African krugerrands were the most popular gold bullion coins in the United States. Popular gold bullion coins today include Australia's kangaroo nugget, the Canadian gold maple leaf, the Mexican 50 peso, the Austrian 100 koronas, and the British sovereign. The new American eagle gold coin, the first gold bullion coin ever produced by the U.S. government, was issued in late 1986.

Most brokers require a minimum order of 10 coins and charge a commission of at least 2 percent.

Gold Stocks   In addition to investing in gold bullion and gold bullion coins, you may invest in gold by purchasing the common stocks of gold mining companies. Among the gold mining stocks listed on U.S. stock exchanges are those of Homestake Mining (based in the United States) and Campbell Red Lake and Dome Mines (based in Canada). Because such stocks often move in a direction opposite to that of the stock market as a whole, they may provide excellent portfolio diversification. You may also wish to examine closed-end investment companies with heavy positions in gold mining stocks, such as ARA, Ltd.

Silver, Platinum, and Palladium

Investments in silver, platinum, and palladium, like investments in gold, are used as a hedge against inflation and as a safe haven during political or economic upheavals. During the last 65 years, silver prices ranged from a historic low of 24.25 cents an ounce in 1932, to over $50 an ounce in early 1980, and then back to less than $4.37 an ounce in May 1998.

Two lesser-known precious metals, platinum and palladium, are also popular investments. Both have industrial uses as catalysts, particularly in automobile production. Some investors think increased car sales could mean higher prices for these metals. Platinum currently sells for about $400 an ounce and palladium for about $191.50 an ounce.

As discussed earlier, finding storage for your precious metals can be tricky. While $20,000 in gold, for example, occupies only as much space as a thick paperback book, $20,000 in silver weighs more than 200 pounds and could require a few safe deposit boxes. Such boxes, moreover, are not insured against fire and theft.

You should remember too that unlike stocks, bonds, and other interest-bearing investments, precious metals sit in vaults earning nothing. And whether you profit on an eventual sale depends entirely on how well you call the market.

Precious Stones

Precious stones include diamonds, sapphires, rubies, and emeralds. Precious stones appeal to investors because of their small size, ease of concealment, great durability, and potential as a hedge against inflation. Inflation and investor interest in tangible assets helped increase diamond prices 40-fold between 1970 and 1980. A few lucky investors made fortunes, and brokerage and diamond firms took up the investment diamond business.

Financial Decision
Trade-Off

Whether you are buying precious stones to store in a safe deposit box or to wear around your neck, there are a few risks to keep in mind. Diamonds and other precious stones are not easily turned into cash. It is difficult to determine whether you are getting a good stone. Diamond prices can be affected by the whims of De Beers Consolidated Mines of South Africa, Ltd., which controls 85 percent of the world's supply of rough diamonds, and by political instability in diamond-producing countries. Moreover, you should expect to buy at retail and sell at wholesale, a difference of at least 10 to 15 percent and perhaps as much as 50 percent.

> ### DID YOU KNOW?
>
> With all diamonds, the absence of color indicates a finer grade.

The best way to know exactly what you are getting, especially if you are planning to spend more than $1,000, is to insist that your stone be certified by an independent geological laboratory, one not connected with a diamond-selling organization. (The acknowledged industry leader in this area is the Gemological Institute of America.) The certificate should list the stone's characteristics, including its weight, color, clarity, and quality of cut. The grading of diamonds, however, is not an exact science, and recent experiments have shown that when the same diamond is submitted twice to the same institute, it can get two different ratings.

Sheet 60

Michael Roman, former chairman of the Jewelers of America, a trade group representing 12,000 retailers, stated that his group did not recommend diamonds as an investment and scoffed at the notion that local retail jewelers were realizing huge profits on diamond sales to misguided customers. He also did not believe in certification unless the stone in question is a high-grade diamond weighing at least one carat.

Despite the present rosy scenarios for precious metals and gems, the risks in trading them are sizable. Just ask investors who in 1980 bought gold at as much as $850 an ounce, platinum at $1,040 an ounce, silver at $48 an ounce, and a one-carat diamond at $62,000.

FINANCIAL PLANNING FOR LIFE'S SITUATIONS

21ST-CENTURY COLLECTIBLES

Don't touch that dial! You might be damaging a valuable antique. Connoisseurs are pegging vintage televisions and telephones, old-fashioned pinball machines, click-clacking stock tickers, and other relics of technology as the hot collectibles of the early 21st century. And don't forget those old personal computers. Today's baby boomers and busters are tomorrow's collectors, and the market has already begun to reflect their idiosyncratic tastes. The experts predict that homey items that evoke the Depression era—like Hummel figurines and tin canisters—will soon be gathering dust; mementos of the 20th century's revolutions in computers, photography, and technology will be valued as historical trophies.

Take note: The first Apple computer, introduced in 1976, now fetches several thousand dollars, a tasty boost from its original price of $666.66. The MITS Altair, a 1975 build-it-yourself personal computer kit, now brings more than $1,000. And the Kenbak I, considered the world's first personal computer by the Computer Museum in Boston, is on any serious computer collector's list. It was invented in 1971 by computer engineer John Blankenbaker; only 40 were made. Prices of computer manuals are also appreciating swiftly. Classic telephones, cameras, and televisions aren't in the same stratosphere, but it's more likely that people have them in their attics. The market for "vintage" televisions—those made from 1946 to the late 1950s—didn't even exist five years ago. Now a futuristic '50s Philco Predicta set brings about $175. Pink Princess phones with lighted dials are also hot.

In addition, Joe Camel and the Marlboro Man may soon be the hottest collectibles. Prices for some memorabilia are already climbing. Chris Cooper, a Texas collector, recently sold a cardboard Joe Camel figure for $150 to a man from Oklahoma. Cooper got it free from a grocery store. Old Joe Camel magazine ads that now sell for $5 to $10 will probably be worth a fortune in the future.

Some collectors are willing to pay thousands of dollars for exotic labels from firecrackers, such as a pre–World War II Golliwog label based on a then-popular English doll. Others are equally excited about schoolgirl stitchery these days. An old embroidered sampler decorated with the alphabet, numerals, houses, birds, or even a pious verse may be worth tens of thousands of dollars. At Sotheby's in New York recently, 135 samplers brought in $1.8 million, twice the presale estimate. An exquisite 1826 sampler by 14-year-old Anna Braddock of Burlington County, NJ, displaying a schoolhouse, children, and a barnyard, brought the top price of $145,000, three times the presale estimate.

To spot the art and collectibles markets that will surge in the early 21st century, look for one or more of the following: museum demand, corporate support, a rabid cult collector base, an oversold market, limited availability, or worldwide appeal. As with other types of investments, research and a careful purchasing plan can make collecting a financially rewarding venture.

SOURCES: Alexandra Peers, "Keep Everything," *The Wall Street Journal,* December 9, 1994, p. R8; Wendy Bounds, "Don't Throw Out That Old Ashtray Yet," *The Wall Street Journal,* June 26, 1997, p. B1; June Fletcher, "The People Don't Need a Match to Get a Bang Out of Firecrackers," *The Wall Street Journal,* July 1, 1997, p. B1; Sandra Dallas, "Schoolgirl Embroidery, Grown-Up Prices," *Business Week,* March 17, 1997, p. 122.

Collectibles

collectibles

Collectibles include rare coins, works of art, antiques, stamps, rare books, sports memorabilia, rugs, Chinese ceramics, paintings, and other items that appeal to collectors and investors. Each of these items offers the knowledgeable collector/investor both pleasure and the opportunity for profit. Many collectors have discovered only incidentally that items they bought for their own pleasure had gained greatly in value while they owned them.

Collecting can be a good investment and a satisfying hobby, but for many Americans it has recently become a financial disaster. For example, as the market for paintings by

Pablo Picasso and Andy Warhol has exploded, forgeries have become a significant problem. Art experts and law enforcement officials say that a new generation of collectors is being victimized by forgeries more sophisticated, more expensive, and more difficult to detect than ever before.

Nostalgia and limited availability will also fuel certain markets. With failed airlines and railroads becoming distant memories, count on Pan Am wing pins and Pullman porter badges to go up in value. Fanaticism, combined with a dwindling supply, will also push up prices of rock-and-roll record albums[9] (see the Financial Planning for Life's Situations feature on page 530 for more examples).

Rare-coin scams have increased, and many investors in rare coins have lost most of their investments as a result of fraudulent sales practices. If you are investing in coins, the Federal Trade Commission and the American Numismatic Association urge you to protect yourself by following these rules:

- Use common sense when evaluating any investment claims, and do not rush into buying.
- Make sure you know your dealer's reputation and reliability before you send money or authorize a credit card transaction.
- Do not be taken in by promises that the dealer will buy back your coins or that grading is guaranteed, unless you are confident that the dealer has the financial resources to stand behind these promises.
- Get a second opinion from another source about grade and value as soon as you receive your coins. So, before you buy, find out what remedies you will have if the second opinion differs.
- Be cautious about grading certificates, especially those furnished by coin dealers. Grading is not an exact science, and grading standards vary widely.
- Comparison shop. Visit several dealers before buying.[10]

Collecting for investment purposes is very different from collecting as a hobby. Like investing in real estate or the stock market, investing in collectibles should be approached with care.

Investment counselors caution that collectibles do not provide interest or dividends, that it may be difficult to sell them at the right price on short notice, and that if they become valuable enough, they must be insured against loss or theft.

Exhibit 17–5 on page 532 compares the annual rate of return on various tangible and intangible assets over the past 1, 5, 10, and 20 years.

DID YOU KNOW?

For a rare 1961 Chateau Petrusa, a subtly spicy Merlot, the average price was $2,696 a bottle.

SOURCE: *The Wall Street Journal*, May 2, 1997, p. B8.

CONCEPT CHECK 17–4

1. What are several methods for buying precious metals?
2. Why do precious stones appeal to investors?
3. What are collectibles?
4. How can you protect yourself from the fraud and fraudulent sales practices so prevalent in the collectibles market?

Exhibit 17–5   **In the Long Race, Stocks Win**

Assets	20 Years		10 Years		5 Years		1 Year	
	Rank	Return*	Rank	Return*	Rank	Return*	Rank	Return*
Stocks	1	13.1%	1	15.5%	2	10.4%	6	2.6%
Foreign exchange	2	11.9	3	13.0	1	10.6	5	3.3
Bonds	3	10.2	2	14.1	3	9.9	10	0.7
Stamps	4	9.1	10	−0.9	11	1.1	8	1.9
3-month Treasury bills	5	8.3	4	6.7	4	5.6	4	4.3
Diamonds	6	7.9	5	5.9	9	1.4	11	0.0
Housing	7	6.3	6	4.1	6	2.9	9	1.8
Consumer price index	8	5.7	7	3.6	5	3.5	7	2.1
Farmland	9	4.6	9	−0.7	7	2.4	2	6.4
Gold	10	4.5	8	−0.2	10	1.3	3	4.7
Oil	11	2.9	12	−5.2	12	−1.9	12	−9.8
Silver	12	1.0	11	−4.9	8	1.9	1	31.1
Sotheby's common		N/A		N/A	13	−3.3	13	−11.4

*Average annual return.

SOURCE: Sumner N. Levine, ed., *Business and Investment Almanac, 1995* (Burr Ridge, IL: Richard D. Irwin, 1995), p. 249. © Sumner N. Levine, 1995.

Summary

L.O.1 Identify types of real estate investments.

Real estate investments are classified as direct or indirect. Direct real estate investments, in which the investor holds legal title to the property, include a home, a vacation home, commercial property, and raw land. Indirect real estate investments include real estate syndicates, REITs, mortgages, and participation certificates.

L.O.2 Evaluate the advantages of real estate investments.

Real estate investments offer a hedge against inflation, easy entry, limited financial liability, no management headaches, and financial leverage.

L.O.3 Assess the disadvantages of real estate investments.

Real estate investments may have the disadvantages of illiquidity, declining values, lack of diversification, lack of a tax shelter, a long depreciation period, and management problems.

L.O.4 Analyze the risks and rewards of investing in precious metals, gems, and collectibles.

Some investors prefer to invest in precious metals such as gold, platinum, and silver; precious stones such as diamonds; or collectibles such as stamps, rare coins, works of art, antiques, rare books, and Chinese ceramics. Collectibles do not provide current income, and they may be difficult to sell quickly.

Glossary

collectibles Rare coins, works of art, antiques, stamps, rare books, and other items that appeal to collectors and investors. (p. 530)

commercial property Land and buildings that produce lease or rental income. (p. 518)

direct investment Investment in which the investor holds legal title to property. (p. 517)

indirect investment Investment in which a trustee holds legal title to property on behalf of the investors. (p. 517)

participation certificate An equity investment in a pool of mortgages that have been purchased by a government agency, such as Ginnie Mae. (p. 523)

passive activity A business or trade in which the investor does not materially participate. (p. 521)

passive loss The total amount of losses from a passive activity minus the total income from the passive activity. (p. 521)

real estate investment trust (REIT) A firm that pools investor funds and invests them in real estate or uses them to make construction or mortgage loans. (p. 522)

syndicate A temporary association of individuals or firms organized to perform a specific task that requires a large amount of capital. (p. 522)

REVIEW QUESTIONS

1. Compare and distinguish between direct and indirect real estate investments. Give an example of each. (L.O.1)
2. Distinguish among gross scheduled income, gross operating income, operating expenses, net operating income, and rate of return. (L.O.1)
3. Discuss major advantages of owning real estate directly and indirectly. (L.O.2)
4. What are several Internet sites related to real estate investments (L.O.2)

5. What are the disadvantages of real estate investments? (L.O.3)
6. What are the various ways of owning gold, silver, and platinum? (L.O.4)
7. Discuss some advantages and disadvantages of investing your money in collectibles such as stamps, rare coins, antiques, and sports memorabilia. (L.O.4)
8. What type of investment information can you obtain by using online computer services? (L.O.4)

FINANCIAL PLANNING PROBLEMS

1. *Calculating the Expected Profitability of Commercial Properties.* Exhibit 17–2 shows a current-year income analysis for Outflow Apartments. Perform second- and third-year income analyses for Outflow Apartments. Assume revenues and costs (except interest payments) will increase by 3 percent each year over the next two years. (L.O.1)
2. *Calculating Key Figures of Commercial Properties.* Based on the above analysis, answer the following questions. (L.O.1)
   a. What is the net operating income for year 2? For year 3?
   b. What is the gross spendable income for year 2? For year 3?
   c. What is the gross equity income for year 2? For year 3?
   d. What is the taxable income for year 2? For year 3?
3. *Calculating Taxable Income.* Why is taxable income declining in years 2 and 3? (L.O.1)

4. *Determining Income Tax Benefits.* What is the income tax benefit for year 2? For year 3? Why is this benefit decreasing? (L.O.1)
5. *Calculating Net Spendable Cash.* Calculate net spendable cash for years 2 and 3. Why is this figure increasing? (L.O.1)
6. *Calculating the Return on Investment.* Dave bought a rental property for $200,000 cash. One year later, he sold it for $240,000. What was the return on his $200,000 investment? (L.O.2)
7. *Calculating the Return on Investment Using Financial Leverage.* Suppose Dave invested only $20,000 of his own money and borrowed $180,000 (90 percent financing). What was his return on investment? (L.O.2)

PROJECTS AND APPLICATION ACTIVITIES

1. *Using the Internet to Obtain Information about Various Types of REITs.* Many REITs now maintain a Web page on the Internet. Visit a few Web sites of REIT companies 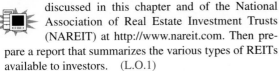 discussed in this chapter and of the National Association of Real Estate Investment Trusts (NAREIT) at http://www.nareit.com. Then prepare a report that summarizes the various types of REITs available to investors. (L.O.1)
2. *Assessing the Prices of Single-Family Dwellings.* Interview local real estate brokers and research current business magazines and the business section of the local newspaper to determine if the prices of single-family dwellings in your area have been increasing during the last 10 years. Prepare a written report indicating the reasons for the increase or decrease. (L.O.1)
3. *Assessing the Investment Potential of Commercial Real Estate.* Research current commercial real estate sections of local newspapers. How many listings do your find for duplexes? For fourplexes and small apartment buildings? Prepare an analysis of the investment potential of these properties. (L.O.1)

4. *Checking the Availability of Real Estate Limited Partnerships.* Call a few real estate and stock brokerage firms in your area to find out if any real estate limited partnerships are available for investors. (L.O.2)
5. *Comparing Mortgage Rates and Terms of a Loan.* Obtain duplex mortgage rates from your local commercial bank, a savings and loan association, and a credit union. Compare these rates and terms such as the down payment, loan costs (points), loan length, and maximum amount available to determine which of the three lenders offers the best financing. (L.O.3)
6. *Checking Current Prices of Precious Metals.* Listen to business news on radio or television. What are the current quotes for an ounce of gold and an ounce of silver? Are the prices of precious metals going up or down? How do the latest prices compare with the prices quoted in the chapter? What might be some reasons for fluctuations in the prices of precious metals? (L.O.4)

LIFE SITUATION CASE 17

INVESTING IN INDIUM, OSTRICH FARMING, AND GEMSTONES

Fraudulent telemarketing firms are selling indium, germanium, selenium, cadmium, and other "strategic metals" at greatly inflated prices. Recently Val Archer received a telephone call from Joe Johnson, an investment adviser. Joe began by assuring Val that "No," he didn't want her to invest a single cent. "Never invest with someone you don't know," he admonished. However, Joe wanted to demonstrate his firm's "research skill" by sharing with Val the forecast that indium was about to experience a significant price increase. Sure enough, the price soon went up.

A second telephone call from Joe didn't solicit an investment either. Joe simply wanted to share with Val a prediction that the price of indium was about to plummet. "Our forecasters will help you decide whether ours is the kind of firm you might someday want to invest with," he added. As predicted, the price of indium subsequently dropped.

By the time Val received a third call, she was a believer. She not only wanted to invest but insisted on it, and with a big enough investment to make up for the opportunities she had missed.

What Val did not know was that Joe had begun with a calling list of 400 names. On the first round of calls, he told 200 prospects that the price of indium would soon go up and the other 200 that it would go down. When the price went up, Joe made a second call to each of the 200 prospects whom he had given the "correct forecast." Of these, he told 100 that the next price of indium would move up and the other 100 that it would go down.

Once the predicted price decline occurred, Joe had a list of 100 people eager to invest. After all, how could you go wrong with such an infallible source of price forecasts?

Today scam artists like Joe Johnson are turning to the Internet to promote their schemes. They are using online computer services to promote familiar scams such as fraudulent stock offerings and exotic or high-tech investment opportunities such as ostrich farming, gold mining, gemstones, and wireless cable television.

Remember, *never* make an investment decision based solely on information obtained from a single source, whether electronic bulletin board, online chatroom, newspaper or direct-mail ad, telemarketer, or broadcast commercial. The National Fraud Information Center maintains a toll-free Consumer Assistance Service at 1–800–876–7060 to provide consumers with information about telemarketing and online scams. You may also access the Federal Trade Commission on the World Wide Web at http://www.ftc.gov.

QUESTIONS

1. What can you do to protect yourself from investment swindles like this one?
2. What can the federal and state governments do to stop such scams?
3. What other techniques do investment swindlers use?
4. What questions could you ask that might turn off investment swindlers?

USING THE INTERNET TO CREATE A PERSONAL FINANCIAL PLAN 17

COMPARING OTHER TYPES OF INVESTMENTS

Real estate and collectibles allow investors to achieve greater potential returns. However, these sometimes speculative ventures must be considered carefully in relation to your personal financial situation.

Web Sites for Real Estate and Other Investments

- Get real estate investment information at **www.financenter.com/** and "The Motley Fool" offers more at **www.fool.com/**
- As does **www.quicken.com** (**www.qfn.com**), the Cable News Network financial news service at **cnnfn.com/index.hmtl,** and the Center for Financial Well Being at **www.healthycash.com/center**

- Current real estate investments articles from *Money* magazine at **www.money.com,** from *Kiplinger's Personal Finance* magazine at **www.kiplinger.com,** *Business Week* at **www.businessweek.com,** *Worth* magazine at **www.worth.com,** and *Smart Money* at www.**smartmoney.com**
- Chicago Board of Trade at **www.cbot.com;** Chicago Mercantile Exchange at **www.cem.com**

(Note: Addresses and content of Web sites change, and new sites are created daily. Use the search engines discussed in Appendix B to update and locate Web sites for your current financial planning needs.)

PFP SHEET: 60

Short-Term Financial Planning Activities

1. Identify types of real estate and other investments that might serve your various financial goals and life situation.
2. Compare the cost of buying and operating various types of real estate investments.

Long-Term Financial Planning Activities

1. Identify real estate and other investments that might serve you in the future.
2. Develop a plan for selecting and monitoring real estate and other investments.

CONTINUOUS CASE FOR PART V

BUILDING AN INVESTMENT PROGRAM

Life Situation
Pam, 43; Josh, 45; children ages 16, 14, and 11

Financial Goals
- Build an investment portfolio that considers various risk factors

Financial Data

Monthly income	$ 4,900
Living expenses	4,450
Assets	262,700
Liabilities	84,600

With approximately 20 years to retirement, Pam and Josh Brock want to establish a more aggressive investment program to accumulate funds for their long-term financial needs. Josh does have a retirement program at work. This money, about $110,000, is invested in various conservative investments managed by professional money managers. In addition, the Brocks established their own investment program about four years ago, and today they have about $36,000 invested in conservative stocks and mutual funds.

In addition to their investment program, the Brocks have accumulated enough money to pay for the children's college educations. Also, they have $5,000 tucked away in a savings account that serves as the family's emergency fund. Finally, both will qualify for Social Security when they reach retirement age.

QUESTIONS

1. How would you rate the Brocks' financial condition at this stage in their lives?

2. Given the fact that Pam is 43 and Josh is 45, what investment goals would be most appropriate for this middle-aged couple?
3. According to Pam, "We both know we should have started our investment program sooner, but we always seemed to have 'emergencies' that took what extra money we had." Many investors feel the same way and, to compensate for a late start, often invest in highly speculative investments that promise large returns. Would you recommend such investments to a couple like the Brocks? Explain your answer.
4. Describe the investment portfolio you would recommend for the Brocks. Be sure to include *specific* types of investments (stocks, bonds, mutual funds, etc.), as well as information about the risk factor(s) associated with each investment alternative.

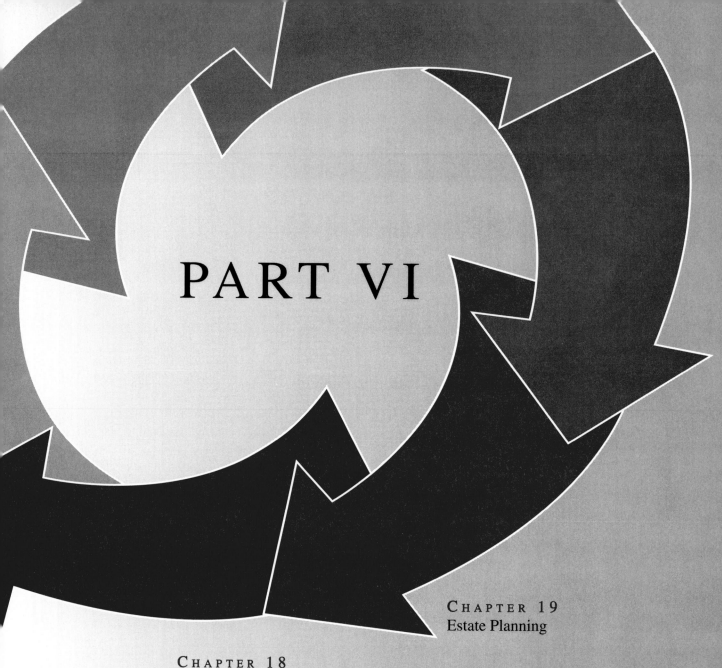

PART VI

CONTROLLING YOUR FINANCIAL FUTURE

For readers of this book, retirement may be 45 years, 30 years, or only a couple of years away. Whatever your life situation, planning for your later years requires an emphasis on good health maintenance, an ability to ask the right questions, and appropriate financial decisions.

Part VI of *Personal Finance* covers the final phase of personal financial planning activities. Retirement and estate plans should emphasize financial decisions for the benefit of you and your family now and in the future. In planning for the future, you must remember to continually reevaluate and revise your financial activities as your circumstances change.

The basic financial planning steps you should take now and in the future are simple. First, determine where you are now. Next, decide where you want to be in the future. Finally, select appropriate actions to keep you progressing toward your desired destination.

Chapter 18 emphasizes the need to start planning early for your retirement years and describes the important aspects of retirement planning. Chapter 19 explains the personal and legal aspects of estate planning. It discusses various types of trusts and estates and explains the effects of federal and state taxes on estate planning.

CHAPTER 18

RETIREMENT PLANNING

Opening Case

SANDWICH GENERATION: ONE FAMILY TRIES TO EASE THE BITE

The nest was empty, and Gail and John O'Neil were settling into a comfortable future. One daughter had been out of college for a couple of years and the other was halfway through. "I'd call John at work and say: 'Where should we go for dinner?'" recalls Gail, 48, a registered nurse who earns $30,000 a year. John, 57, a technical specialist at Abbott Laboratories, brings home $75,000.

Today, the O'Neils aren't splurging. As planned, 19-year-old Rebecca, a junior at Illinois State, returned to their four-bedroom house in Mundelein, Ill., for the summer. Then 24-year-old Texas Tech grad Jennifer unexpectedly moved back in April while searching for a job. A month later, John's mom, Evelyn, joined them from Florida, because she could no longer care for herself. Suddenly, the O'Neils epitomized the "sandwich generation," people squeezed financially by having to care for both older and younger family members—while also charting their own retirement course.

Drug Bills With three extra mouths to feed, it's been touch-and-go. Evelyn, 86, has periodic health problems—a frail heart that has undergone bypass surgery, failing eyesight, and Sundown dementia, a disorder that leaves her disoriented after dark. The couple paid for Evelyn's move back to Illinois. The former Raytheon supervisor gets $600 in Social Security checks per month and a $150 monthly pension. Much of that pays for her $300 monthly drug bills and for nearby Condell Day Center, a senior facility that she visits daily. (More than half of the $37-per-day bill is footed by the State of Illinois.)

Should Evelyn's health worsen, the O'Neils' long-term financial security would be jeopardized. They can borrow against the $10,000 cash value of their life insurance, or worse, tap into the $120,000 accumulated in retirement savings. John's pension, which he'll receive at 62, is worth $40,000. He hasn't decided whether to take that in a lump sum or as an annuity. The O'Neils, who are paying off $120,000 on their $210,000 home,

fret about when Grandma needs more tending than the day-care center can provide. Full-time nursing home care would cost up to $4,000 per month. Premiums on long-term care insurance are too expensive for Evelyn, but Gail is investigating a plan for the couple when they reach retirement age.

For now, the O'Neils are coping. They wisely set up mutual funds to pay for college costs. Rebecca's annual room, board, and tuition at Illinois State University is $10,000. They also took the advice of Jack Dunk, a senior financial adviser at American Express, who told them 10 years ago to combine their insurance policies into one to avoid duplicate fees. He also encouraged them to save through Abbott's stock purchase programs, which matches the first 2% put aside annually, pretax. John estimates the matching added about $2,500 a year to his savings.

However, with most of their retirement portfolio in Abbott stock, the O'Neils are placing a lot of faith in the continuing success of Abbott, whose stock price has climbed 322% in the past decade. Presently, there's little spare cash. Says Dunk: "For the sandwich generation, the dollars usually flow out and the future is on hold." And for Gail and John O'Neil, dining out is a pleasant memory.

QUESTIONS

1. What steps should John and Gail take to properly plan for their financial needs in retirement?
2. Is it possible for this couple to predict the exact amount of money they will need in retirement? Why or why not?
3. What types of expenses may increase or decrease during the retirement years?

SOURCE: Lisa Sanders, "Sandwich Generation: One Family Tries to Ease the Bite." *Business Week*, July 21, 1997, p. 84.

After studying this chapter, you will be able to

L.O.1   Recognize the importance of retirement planning.

L.O.2   Analyze your current assets and liabilities for retirement.

L.O.3   Estimate your retirement spending needs.

L.O.4   Identify your retirement housing needs.

L.O.5   Determine your planned retirement income.

L.O.6   Develop a balanced budget based on your retirement income.

WHY RETIREMENT PLANNING?

L.O.1 Recognize the importance of retirement planning.

Retirement can be a rewarding phase of your life. However, a successful, happy retirement doesn't just happen; it takes planning and continual evaluation. Thinking about retirement in advance can help you anticipate future changes and gain a sense of control over the future.

The ground rules for retirement planning are changing rapidly. Reexamine your retirement plans if you hold any of these misconceptions:

- My expenses will drop when I retire.
- My retirement will last only 15 years.
  - I can depend on Social Security and my company pension to pay for my basic living expenses.
  - My pension benefits will increase to keep pace with inflation.
  - My employer's health insurance plan and Medicare will cover my medical expenses.
  - There's plenty of time for me to start saving for retirement.
  - Saving just a little bit won't help.

It is vital to engage in basic retirement planning activities throughout your working years and to update your retirement plans periodically. While it is never too late to begin sound financial planning, you can avoid many unnecessary and serious difficulties by starting this planning early. Saving now for the future requires tackling the trade-offs between spending and saving.

DID YOU KNOW?

Retirement Planning

". . . up to 25 percent of current retirees consider their retirement to be . . . financially troubled. It is evident that most workers are not planning, and many have limited knowledge (about) retirement saving."

Employment Benefit Research Institute Issue Brief, January 1997

Tackling the Trade-Offs

Financial Decision Trade-Off

Although exceptions exist, the old adage "You can't have your cake and eat it too" is particularly true in planning for retirement. For example, if you buy state-of-the-art home stereo systems, drive expensive cars, and take extravagant vacations now, don't expect to retire with plenty of money.

EXHIBIT 18–1

**It's Never Too Late
to Start Planning
for Retirement**

Start young. A look at the performance of $2,000 of retirement plan investments over time at 4 percent shows the value of starting early. (in 1995 dollars)

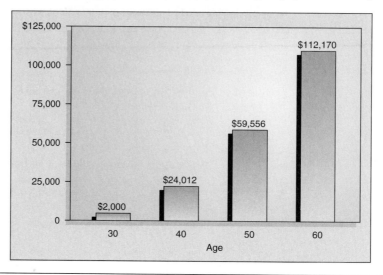

Even though baby boomers are more knowledgeable about saving and investing and can use various methods to manage their assets, the personal savings rate declined from more than 7 percent throughout the 1960s to just under 5 percent in 1996. But the savings crisis may be overstated. In a study conducted for Merrill Lynch & Company, Stanford University economist Douglas B. Bernheim found that, excluding the equity in their houses, baby boomers were saving only about one-third of what they will need in retirement. Yet when housing wealth is included, more than two-thirds of boomers likely will be able to maintain their current standard of living in retirement.[1]

Only saving now and curtailing current spending can ensure comfortable retirement later. Yet saving money doesn't come naturally to many young people. Ironically, although the time to begin saving is when you are young, the people who are in the best position to save are middle-aged.

Seventy-five percent of workers expect to live as well as, if not better than they do now when they retire, but only 25 percent of those surveyed have begun to save seriously for retirement.[2]

The Importance of Starting Early

Consider this: If from age 25 to 65 you invest $300 per month and earn an average of 9 percent interest a year, you'll have $1.4 million in your retirement fund. Waiting just 10 years until age 35 to begin your $300-a-month investing will yield $553,000, while waiting 20 years to begin this investment will produce only $201,000 at age 65. Exhibit 18–1 shows how even a $2,000 annual investment earning just 4 percent will grow.

For 40 years your life, and probably your family's life, revolve around your job. One day you retire, and practically every aspect of your life changes. There's less money, more time, and no daily structure.

You can expect to spend about 16 to 20 years in retirement—too many years to be bored, lonely, and broke. You want your retirement years to be rewarding, active, and rich in new experiences. But you have to plan, and plan early. It's never too early to begin planning for retirement; some experts even suggest starting while you are in school. Be certain you don't let your 45th birthday roll by without a comprehensive retirement plan. Remember, the longer you wait, the less you will be able to shape your life in retirement.

Retirement planning has both emotional and financial components. Emotional planning for retirement involves identifying your personal goals and setting out to meet them. Financial planning for retirement involves assessing your postretirement needs and income and plugging any gaps you find. Financial planning for retirement is critical for several reasons:

1. You can expect to live in retirement for up to 20 years. At age 65, the average life expectancy is 14 years for a man and 19 years for a woman.
2. Social Security and a private pension, if you have one, are most often insufficient to cover the cost of living.
3. Inflation may diminish the purchasing power of your retirement savings. Even a 3 percent rate of inflation will cause prices to double every 24 years.

You should anticipate your retirement years by analyzing your long-range goals. What does retirement mean to you? Does it mean an opportunity to stop work and relax, or does it mean time to travel, develop a hobby, or start a second career? Where and how do you want to live during your retirement? Once you have considered your retirement goals, you are ready to evaluate their cost and assess whether you can afford them.

> ## DID YOU KNOW?
>
> **Education Matters**
> Thirty-one percent of college grads have saved more than $50,000 toward retirement versus only 11 percent for their high school graduate counterparts.
>
> SOURCE: *Business Week*, July 21, 1997.

The Basics of Retirement Planning

Financial Decision
Trade-Off

Before you decide where you want to be financially, you have to find out where you are. Your first step, therefore, is to analyze your current assets and liabilities. Then estimate your spending needs and adjust them for inflation. Next, evaluate your planned retirement income. Finally, increase your income by working part time, if necessary. An attorney, for example, might choose to teach law. Recent articles and other retirement information may be accessed through online computer services. For further information, see Appendix B. Exhibit 18–2 on page 542 shows a few good sources for retirement planning using a personal computer.

CONCEPT   CHECK   18–1

1. Why is retirement planning important?
2. What are the four basic steps in retirement planning?

CONDUCTING A FINANCIAL ANALYSIS

L.O.2 Analyze your current assets and liabilities for retirement.

As you learned in Chapter 3, your assets include everything you own that has value: cash on hand and in checking and savings accounts; the current value of your stocks, bonds, and other investments; the current value of your house, car, jewelry, and furnishings; and the current value of your life insurance and pensions. Your liabilities are everything you owe: your mortgage, car payments, credit card balances, taxes due, and so forth. The difference between the two totals is your *net worth,* a figure you should increase each year as you move toward retirement. Use Exhibit 18–3 on page 543 to calculate your net worth now and at retirement.

EXHIBIT 18–2   **Using a Personal Computer for Retirement Planning**

Program	Cost	Format	Comments
Quicken Financial Planner Intuit (1–800–446–8848)	$40.00	Win 3.1/95 disk, Win 3.1/95 CD-ROM	Best buy for boomers. Lets you make year-by-year projections of income and expenses from now until age 125. Also lets you figure income and retirement benefits for you and your spouse separately.
Retireready Deluxe Individual Software (1–800–822–3522)	$49.95	Win 3.1/95 CD-ROM	So-so calculators. Real strengths: multimedia tutorials for retirement, topics A–Z. Also includes addresses and phone numbers for hundreds of private and government agencies.
Retire Secure Price Waterhouse (1–800–422–5579)	$45.00	Win 3.1/95 disk	What you'd expect from CPAs: jargony help screens and dull graphics, but calculators so robust that a pro would use them.
Retirement Planning Analyzer T. Rowe Price (1–800–541–5760)	$20.00	Win 3.1/Win95 disk	For $20, a good value: Not as thorough as the Quicken Financial Planner, but better at determining future tax rates and distinguishing tax-deferred from taxable accounts. Results: You may need less savings than you think.
Vanguard Retirement Manager Vanguard Group (1–800–999–1529)	$25.00	Win 3.1/95 disk, Win 3.1/95 CD-ROM Macintosh disk and CD-ROM	The pick for seniors. Handles with aplomb such prickly issues as minimum required distributions. Comes with 300-page book, *Investing During Retirement.*

Review Your Assets

Reviewing your assets to ensure they are sufficient for retirement is a sound idea. Make any necessary adjustments in your investments and holdings to fit your circumstances. In reviewing your assets, consider the following factors.

> ### DID YOU KNOW?
>
> **Home Sweet Home**
> According to a survey of 1,026 adults conducted in June 1997 for *Business Week* by Louis Harris & Associates Inc., 67% percent of people age 30 to 39 cite hefty housing expenses as an obstacle to their saving for retirement.

Housing   If you own your house, it is probably your biggest single asset. The amount tied up in your house, however, may be out of line with your retirement income. If it is, consider selling your house and buying a less expensive one. The selection of a smaller, more easily maintained house can also decrease your maintenance costs. The difference saved can be put into a savings account or certificates of deposit or into other income-producing investments. If your mortgage is largely or completely paid off, you may be able to get an annuity that provides you with extra income during retirement. In this arrangement, a lender uses your house as collateral to buy an annuity for you from a life insurance company. Each month, the lender pays you (the homeowner) from the annuity after deducting the mortgage interest payment. The mortgage principal, which was used to obtain the annuity, is repaid to the lender by probate after your death. This special annu-

reverse annuity mortgage

ity is known as a **reverse annuity mortgage (RAM)** or *equity conversion.*

Chicago-based Senior Income Reverse Mortgage Corporation (1–800–774–6266) offers a free consumers' information kit on reverse mortgages. The kit shows that the amount of money available depends on your age, the value of your home, and interest rates. For example, a 75-year-old couple with a $150,000 home in Chicago or the suburbs could receive a monthly check of about $900 for the next 10 years or $580 for as long as either partner lives in the home.[3]

EXHIBIT 18-3		Sample Figures	Your Figures
Review Your Assets, Liabilities, and Net Worth	**Assets: What We Own**		
	Cash:		
	Checking account	$ 800	_____
	Savings account	4,500	_____
	Investments:		
	U.S. savings bonds		
	(current cash-in value)	5,000	_____
	Stocks, mutual funds	4,500	_____
	Life insurance:		
	Cash value, accumulated dividends	10,000	_____
	Company pension rights:		
	Accrued pension benefit	20,000	_____
	Property:		
	House (resale value)	50,000	_____
	Furniture and appliances	8,000	_____
	Collections and jewelry	2,000	_____
	Automobile	3,000	_____
	Other:		
	Loan to brother	1,000	_____
	Gross assets	$108,800	_____
	Liabilities: What We Owe		
	Current unpaid bills	600	_____
	Home mortgage (remaining balance)	9,700	_____
	Auto loan	1,200	_____
	Property taxes	1,100	_____
	Home improvement loan	3,700	_____
	Total liabilities	$16,300	_____

Net worth: Assets of $108,800 minus liabilities of $16,300 equals $92,500.

Life Insurance   You may have set up your life insurance to provide support and education for your children. Now you may want to convert some of this asset into cash or income (an annuity). Another possibility is to reduce premium payments by decreasing the face value of your insurance. This will give you extra money to spend on living expenses or invest for additional income.

Other Investments   Evaluate any other investments you have. When you chose them, you may have been more interested in making your money grow than in getting an early return. Has the time come to take the income from your investments? You may now want to take dividends rather than reinvest them.

After thoroughly reviewing your assets, estimate your spending needs during your retirement years.

Your Assets after Divorce

Any divorce is difficult, particularly when it comes to a division of marital assets. Your pension benefits are considered marital property, which must be divided in a divorce. "Even if a person is not ready to retire, pension benefits are considered a marital asset subject to the division of property," says Howard Sharfstein, a partner in Schulte Roth & Zabel of New York.[4] Any retirement fund money, including a 401(k) plan or a profit-sharing

JONATHAN HOENIG SPEAKS
Retirement Redux: Planning for the Future

Retirement? Ah, yes: *retirement.* Better to save now and avoid the deprivation later. You know the spiel: Social Security, a joke; corporate pensions, all but eliminated; job security, gone; the Domino's 30-minute guarantee, abolished. With such an uncertain future, it is best one be prepared.

There are monetary returns, although I contend that the psychological feeling of safety that regular investing provides trumps all. While the boomers freak about not having saved enough for retirement, young people have time to spare. With a long-term horizon, investing is safe, easy, and relatively hassle free. Mutual funds have made retirement investing more convenient than sleeping through that 9AM class. Automatic investment plans can deduct as little as $25 a month from bank accounts or paychecks. Even pocket cash can get things rockin': Take that double tall latte ($2.39) and raisin cinnamon scone ($1.70) you snag at 'Bucks each morning and put it in an index fund. You'll have over $20,000 before your first midlife crisis. Keep it up until your second, and you'll have accumulated over $110,000—more than enough to pay for intensive therapy and a week in Boca. Systematic investing is

the fiscal equivalent of a tetanus shot: a regular bummer that doesn't hurt as bad as one initially believes.

If you are frightened of investing, worried that a crash or prolonged bear market will turn your retirement into an episode of Good Times, *you must chill!* Don't waste the Xanax worrying about the market, because the fact is that over a long period of time, stocks go up. Over a 20-year time horizon, the market's *worst* performance has been about 2.0 percent. While it might seem you can't afford to invest, the unfortunate reality is that you can't afford not to. With inflation humming along, common stock is the only asset class that will consistently keep you ahead.

IRAs, 401(k)s, pension plans—stock 'em full of quality mutual funds and chill. "Home runs" look great on the cover of *Money* magazine, but real wealth is born over time. Compound interest, or the titillating phenomenon of earning interest on interest, provides hefty gains to patient investors. This "get-rich-slowly" scheme won't get your picture in *Barron's* but is will provide for an adequate retirement. $100,000 will buy cases of Geritol once you get to Florida.

---

plan, set aside during a marriage and the dollar growth of a pension plan during a marriage are considered marital property.

Division of pension benefits generally depends on the length of the marriage. "In a five-year marriage the percentage of one person's assets given to the spouse is usually small," says Sharfstein. "In an eight-year marriage about 25 percent of the monetary assets earned by one partner may be given to the other partner. In a marriage that lasts more than 15 years there's generally a 50-50 split of the marital assets."[5]

Be warned: Many retirement-planning strategies accommodate the traditional husband-wife-kids family unit. But times have changed, and millions of nontraditional households have unique retirement needs. Nearly half of all American marriages end in divorce, creating difficulties for millions of adults thinking about their retirement years. Likewise, single parents, gays and lesbians, and individuals who choose to live together outside of marriage all have formidable retirement-planning challenges. See the accompanying Financial Planning for Life's Situations feature for suggestions.[6]

CONCEPT CHECK   18–2

1. How can you calculate your net worth today and at retirement?
2. What assets are considered marital assets?

FINANCIAL PLANNING FOR LIFE'S SITUATIONS

RETIREMENT PLANNING FOR VARIED LIFE SITUATIONS

- A divorcee should maximize contributions to retirement plan at work, and begin a separate savings account to protect retirement assets.

- A divorcee may consider taking out life insurance on an ex-spouse if he or she is responsible for child support; also buy disability insurance.

- Revise your estate plan after a divorce. In some states, a divorce doesn't automatically revoke your will or certain trusts if your ex-spouse is a beneficiary.

- An unmarried person should determine if an employer allows a joint-and-survivor benefit for a nonspouse. If so, inform your plan administrator while you're still employed, since the method of distribution can't be switched after you retire.

- An unmarried person should clearly indicate intentions in legally binding documents (be sure to have a will) since blood relatives will usually win in any disputes over assets that rise after death

- An unmarried person should consider techniques to minimize estate taxes, such as a charitable remainder trust.

- In family situations with strained relationships, a person should consider saving more than the usual 75 to 80 percent of gross preretirement income in anticipation that relatives may not provide future support.

SOURCE: Geoffrey Smith, "Nest-Egg Planning for the Not-So-Average Joe," *Business Week,* July 31, 1997, p. 80.

RETIREMENT LIVING EXPENSES

L.O.3 Estimate your retirement spending needs.

The exact amount of money you will need in retirement is impossible to predict. However, you can estimate the amount of money you will need by considering the changes you plan to make in your spending patterns and in where and how you live.

Your spending patterns will probably change. A study conducted by the Bureau of Labor Statistics on how families spend money shows that retired families use a greater share for food, housing, and medical care than nonretired families. Although no two families adjust their spending patterns to changes in the life cycle in the same manner, the tabulation in Exhibit 18–4 on page 546 can guide you in anticipating your own future spending patterns.

The following expenses may be lowered or eliminated:

- *Work expenses.* You will no longer have to make payments into your retirement fund. You will not be buying gas and oil for the drive back and forth to work or for train or bus fares. You may be buying fewer lunches away from home.

- *Clothing expenses.* You will probably need fewer clothes after you retire, and your dress may be more casual.

- *Housing expenses.* If you have paid off your house mortgage by the time you retire, your cost of housing may decrease (although increases in property taxes may offset this gain).

- *Federal income taxes.* Your federal income taxes will probably be lower. No federal tax has to be paid on some forms of income, such as railroad retirement benefits and certain veterans' benefits. A retirement credit is allowed for some sources of income, such as annuities. You will probably pay taxes at a lower rate because your taxable income will be lower.

EXHIBIT 18–4

How an "Average" Older (65+) Household Spends Its Money

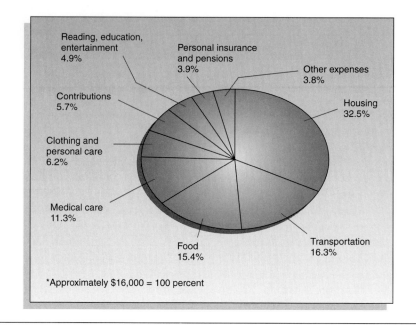

Reading, education, entertainment 4.9%

Personal insurance and pensions 3.9%

Other expenses 3.8%

Housing 32.5%

Contributions 5.7%

Clothing and personal care 6.2%

Medical care 11.3%

Food 15.4%

Transportation 16.3%

*Approximately $16,000 = 100 percent

SOURCE: U.S. Bureau of Labor Statistics.

Financial Decision Trade-Off

Under the U.S. Civil Service Retirement System, your retirement income is not taxed until you have received the amount you have invested in the retirement fund. After that, your retirement income is taxable.

You can also estimate which of the following expenses may increase:

- *Insurance.* The loss of your employer's contribution to health and life insurance will increase your own payments. Medicare, however, may offset part of this increased expense.
- *Medical expenses.* Although medical expenses vary from person to person, they tend to increase with age.
- *Expenses for leisure activities.* With more free time, many retirees spend more money on leisure activities. You may want to put aside extra money for a retirement trip or other large recreational expenses.
- *Gifts and contributions.* Many retirees who continue to spend the same amount of money on gifts and contributions find their spending in this area takes a larger share of their smaller income. Therefore, you may want to reevaluate such spending.

Using the worksheet in Exhibit 18–5 on page 547, list your present expenses and estimate what these expenses would be if you were retired. To make a realistic comparison, list your major spending categories, starting with fixed expenses such as rent or mortgage payments, utilities, insurance premiums, and taxes. Then list variable expenses—food, clothing, transportation, and so on, as well as miscellaneous expenditures such as medical expenses, entertainment, vacations, gifts, contributions, and unforeseen expenses.

Be sure you have an emergency fund for unforeseen expenses. Even when you are living a tranquil life, unexpected events can occur. Also, build a cushion to cope with inflation. Estimate high in calculating how much the prices of goods and services will rise.

EXHIBIT 18–5

Your Monthly Present Expenses and Your Estimated Monthly Retirement Expenses

	Monthly Expenses	
Item	Present	Retirement
Fixed expenses:		
Rent or mortgage payment	$_____	$_____
Taxes	_____	_____
Insurance	_____	_____
Savings	_____	_____
Debt payment	_____	_____
Other	_____	_____
Total fixed expenses	_____	_____
Variable expenses:		
Food and beverages	_____	_____
Household operation and maintenance	_____	_____
Furnishings and equipment	_____	_____
Clothing	_____	_____
Personal	_____	_____
Transportation	_____	_____
Medical care	_____	_____
Recreation and education	_____	_____
Gifts and contributions	_____	_____
Other	_____	_____
Total variable expenses	_____	_____
Total expenses	_____	_____

Adjust Your Expenses for Inflation

You now have a list of your likely monthly (and annual) expenses if you were to retire today. With inflation, however, those expenses will not be fixed. The potential loss of buying power due to inflation is what makes planning ahead so important. During the 1970s and the early 1980s, the cost of living increased an average of 6.1 percent a year, though the annual increase slowed to less than 4 percent between 1983 and 1998.

To help you plan for this likely increase in your expenses, use the inflation factor table in the Financial Planning Calculations feature on page 548.

CONCEPT CHECK 18–3

1. How can you estimate the amount of money you will need during retirement?
2. What expenses are likely to increase or decrease during retirement?
3. How might you adjust your expenses for inflation?

PLANNING YOUR RETIREMENT HOUSING

L.O.4 Identify your retirement housing needs.

Think about where you will want to live. If you think you will want to live in another city, it's a good idea to plan vacations in areas you might enjoy. When you find one that appeals to you, visit that area during various times of the year to experience the year-round climate.

FINANCIAL PLANNING CALCULATIONS

HOW MUCH INFLATION IS IN YOUR FUTURE?

Years to Retirement	**Estimated Annual Rate of Inflation between Now and Retirement**									
	4%	**5%**	**6%**	**7%**	**8%**	**9%**	**10%**	**11%**	**12%**	**13%**
5	1.2	1.3	1.3	1.4	1.5	1.5	1.6	1.7	1.8	1.8
8	1.4	1.5	1.6	1.7	1.8	2.0	2.1	2.3	2.5	2.7
10	1.5	1.6	1.8	2.0	2.2	2.4	2.6	2.8	3.1	3.4
12	1.6	1.8	2.0	2.3	2.5	2.8	3.1	3.5	3.9	4.3
15	1.8	2.1	2.4	2.8	3.2	3.6	4.2	4.8	5.5	6.3
18	2.0	2.4	2.8	3.4	4.0	4.7	5.6	6.5	7.7	9.0
20	2.2	2.7	3.2	3.9	4.7	5.6	6.7	8.1	9.6	11.5
25	2.7	3.4	4.3	5.4	6.8	8.6	10.8	13.6	17.0	21.1

1. Choose from the first column the approximate number of years until your retirement.

2. Choose an estimated annual rate of inflation. The rate of inflation cannot be predicted accurately and will vary from year to year. The 1997 inflation rate was less than 3 percent.

3. Find the inflation factor corresponding to the number of years until your retirement and the estimated annual inflation rate. (Example: 10 years to retirement combined with a 4 percent estimated annual inflation rate yields a 1.5 inflation factor.)

4. Multiply the inflation factor by your estimated retirement income and your estimated retirement expenses. (Example: $6,000 × 1.6 = $9,600.)

Total annual inflated retirement income: $ _____ .

Total annual inflated retirement expenses: $ _____ .

SOURCES: The above figures are from a compound interest table showing the effective yield of lump-sum investments after inflation that appeared in Charles D. Hodgman, ed., *Mathematical Tables from the Handbook of Chemistry and Physics* (Cleveland: Chemical Rubber Publishing, 1959); *Citicorp Consumer Views*, July 1985, pp. 2–3, © Citicorp, 1985; *Financial Planning Tables*, A. G. Edwards, August 1991.

Meet the people. Check into available activities, transportation, and taxes. Be realistic about what you will have to give up and what you will gain.

Where you live in retirement can influence your financial needs. You must make some important decisions about whether or not to stay in your present community and in your current home. Everyone has unique needs and preferences; only *you* can determine the location and housing that are best for you.

Financial Decision Trade-Off

Consider what moving involves. Moving is expensive, and if you are not satisfied with your new location, returning to your former home may be impossible. Consider the social aspects of moving. Will you want to be near your children, other relatives, and good friends? Are you prepared for new circumstances?

Type of Housing

Housing needs often change as people grow older. The ease and cost of maintenance and nearness to public transportation, shopping, temple, church/synagogue, and entertainment often become more important to people when they retire.

Many housing alternatives exist, several of which were discussed in Chapter 9. Here we will examine how each of the following alternatives would meet a retiree's housing needs.

Present Home   Staying in their present homes, whether a single-family dwelling, a condominium, or an apartment, is the alternative preferred by most people approaching retirement. That's what John and Virginia Wolf decided to do after John took early retirement at age 47 from his job as a service manager of a Van Nuys, California, Ford dealership in the late 1970s. Even though the couple had already paid off the mortgage on their small, three bedroom ranch house and could have leveraged into a bigger or fancier place, all John wanted to do was tinker in the garage and dabble in the stock market.[7] A recent survey of over 5,000 men and women revealed that 92 percent wanted to own their homes in retirement.[8]

Housesharing   You might consider sharing your home with others. Under this increasingly popular option, called *housesharing* or *shared* housing, two or more people, usually unrelated, live together in a house or a large apartment.

Accessory Apartment   An *accessory apartment* is a separate apartment built into a single-family house. Often a basement, garage, or other extra space is converted into such an apartment. This arrangement allows you to live independently without living alone.

ECHO Unit   An *elder cottage housing opportunity (ECHO)* unit is a small, freestanding home that is built on the same property as an existing residence. You might consider this alternative if you want to be near family and friends but retain the privacy of living in your own detached dwelling.

You may also want to look into some of the following alternatives. Remember to check with your local zoning board for any restrictions.

Boardinghouse/Rooming House   The accommodations in these facilities may include a bedroom, a sitting room, and a shared or private bathroom. The tenants usually eat together.

Single-Room Occupancy   Here a single room is rented at a specified price under a short-term, renewable lease. Widely varying facilities offer single-room occupancy. It is frequently found in converted hotels, schools, and factories.

Professional Companionship Arrangement   In this arrangement, you offer your services as a companion to a person who wants the help and company of another person in exchange for living accommodations.

Caretaker Arrangement   If you like caring for a home, gardening, or baby-sitting, you can reduce your costs for room and board by performing these tasks for a family whose home has an extra bedroom or apartment.

Commercial Rental   With commercial rentals, rooms are leased, usually for longer periods than the leases of single-room occupancies. Commercial rentals are found in apartment houses or auxiliary buildings of large, single-family homes.

One day you may conclude that living alone in your own housing unit is becoming too difficult. You should then examine the options in supportive housing. *Supportive housing* refers to a variety of housing arrangements from board and care homes to nursing homes. Among these arrangements are the following:

Board and Care Home   If you need help with food preparation and personal care but want to maintain as much independence as possible, a board and care home may be the answer.

Congregate Housing   If you are interested in living with a group that shares meals, congregate housing is an attractive option. Heavy housekeeping is provided, and staff is available to organize a variety of social and recreational activities.

Continuing Care Retirement Community   This option allows you to lead an independent lifestyle in a community that offers a full range of services and activities, including health care services. A contract, which you sign upon entering the community, specifies how much nursing care is provided, among other things.

Nursing Home   The nursing home option provides you with continuous medical care if you are frail and need nursing care services or have a disabling chronic condition.

Sheet 62

With so many choices, determining where to live in retirement is itself turning into a time-consuming job. But whether you want to race cars, go on a safari, or stay home to paint, the goal is to end up like Edna Cohen. "Don't feel bad if I die tomorrow," she says. "I've had a wonderful life." Who could ask for more?[9]

Whatever retirement housing alternative you choose, make sure you know what you are signing and understand what you are buying. The accompanying Financial Planning for Life's Situations feature on page 551 provides the vital statistics, advantages, and drawbacks of some of the most popular retirement communities.

Avoiding Retirement Housing Traps

All too many people make the move without doing enough research, and invariably it's a huge mistake. How can retirees avoid being surprised by hidden tax and financial traps when they move? Pros suggest that you call Right Choice, Inc., in South Hamilton, Massachusetts, (1–800–872–2294), or visit the company at www.rsmart.com. The company provides ReloSmart®, a new, easy-to-use software program that allows you to do unlimited relocation analyses. The cost is about $50.

Here are some tips from retirement specialists on how to uncover hidden taxes and other costs of a retirement area before moving there:

- Write or call the local chamber of commerce to get an economic profile and details on area property taxes.
- Contact the state's tax department to find out state income, sales, and inheritance taxes and special exemptions for retirees. If your pension will be taxed by the state you're leaving, check whether the new state will give you credit for those taxes.
- Subscribe to the Sunday edition of a local newspaper.
- Call a local CPA to find out which taxes are rising.
- Check with local utilities to estimate your energy costs. Visit the area in as many seasons as possible. Talk to retirees and other local residents about costs of health care, auto insurance, food, and clothing.
- Rent for a while instead of buying immediately.

CONCEPT   CHECK   18–4

1. What are the housing options for retirees?
2. What are the advantages and disadvantages of various housing options?

HOT RETIREMENT LOCALES: THE VITAL STATISTICS, ADVANTAGES, AND DRAWBACKS OF SOME OF THE MOST POPULAR COMMUNITIES

Place	Population by County	Per Capita Income	Leisure Activities	Crime Rate* per 100,000	Climate	Job Forecast† 1997–2005	Pros/Cons
Fairhope, AL	127,000	$21,000	Golf, boating, beaches	3,277 ▼	Subtropical	Above average ▲	+Near Mobile, AL.; good arts scene; low crime −Hurricane-prone; rising housing costs
Prescott, Prescott Valley, AZ	148,600	$18,800	Golf, hiking, sightseeing	3,662 ▼	Semi-arid mountain steppe	Above average ▲	+Victorian architecture; low crime; growing economy −Traffic congestion; few restaurants
Durango, CO	40,000	$22,700	Skiing, hiking, resident symphony	5,057 ■	Seasonal temperatures	Average ■	+Mountain college town; Victorian architecture −Cold, snowy winters; high housing costs, remote location
Port Charlotte, FL	140,000	$21,750	Golf, coastal boating, beaches	3,194 ▼	Subtropical	Above average ▲	+Low crime; growing economy; Gulf locale −Torrid summers; few cultural, artistic amenities
Camden, ME	38,500	$23,600	Coastal and inland water, parks	3,225 ▼	Seasonal temperatures	Average ■	+Coast location; low crime; good arts −Cold winters; costly housing; dim employment forecast
Petoskey, Harbor Springs, MI	28,300	$25,300	Great Lakes boating, beaches, fishing	4,641 ▼	Seasonal temperatures	Average ■	+Low crime; wonderful outdoor recreation −Severe winters; far from major cities, slow job growth
Oxford, MS	34,600	$17,300	University arts, hiking, parks	7,227 ▲	Almost subtropical	Average ■	+College town; good arts and culture; low taxes on retirement income −Humid summers; high property-crime rate; limited outdoor recreation
Branson, MO	35,300	$21,900	Lakes, hiking, national forests, country music	6,740 ▲	Hot, continental	Above average ▲	+Low cost of living; nearby water recreation; growing economy −High property crime rate; wet winters
Las Vegas, NV	1,060,000	$26,400	Gambling, golf, theater and symphony, parks	6,936 ▲	Arid, desert	Above average ▲	+Mild winters, expanding economy; big-city amenities like public transportation; lots of performing arts −High crime; congestion and sprawl; scorching summers
Tryon, NC	16,000	$26,300	Lake Lanier, national forest	1,975 ▼	Seasonal temperatures	Below average ▼	+Mild climate; low crime; horse country −Lack of big-city arts; poor employment outlook
San Juan Islands, WA	12,400	$32,500	Boating, beaches, parks	3,519 ▼	Marine climate	Average ■	+Unspoiled environment; low crime; no congestion −Isolation; accessible only by ferry; rising housing costs

▼ means the figure is below the national average by 10% or more; ▲ means it exceeds the average by at least 10%; ■ indicates it's within plus or minus 10%.

†Forecasts are for new jobs in finance, insurance, real estate, retail trade, and services—industries in which older adults find most opportunities. ■ means roughly the same growth rate as the U.S. average of 11.3%; ▲ is at least twice the average; ▼ is slower.

SOURCE: Eric Schine, "There's Never Any Reason for Us to Be Bored," *Business Week,* July 21, 1997, pp. 70–71.

PLANNING YOUR RETIREMENT INCOME

L.O.5 Determine your planned retirement income.

Once you have determined your approximate future expenses, you must evaluate the sources and amounts of your retirement income. Possible sources of income for many retirees are Social Security, other public pension plans, employer pension plans, personal retirement plans, and annuities.

Social Security

Social Security is the most widely used source of retirement income; it covers 97 percent of U.S. workers. Many Americans think of Social Security as benefiting only retired people. But it is actually a package of protection: retirement, survivors', and disability income. The package protects you and your family while you work and after you retire. Today more than 44 million people, almost one out of every six Americans, collect some kind of Social Security benefit.[10]

Social Security should not be the only source of your retirement income, however. It should be only a small part of your plan, or you won't live a very exciting retired life. Even the Social Security Administration cautions that Social Security was never intended to provide 100 percent of retirement income.

When and Where to Apply   Most people qualify for reduced Social Security retirement benefits at age 62; widows or widowers can begin collecting Social Security benefits earlier.

Three months before you retire, apply for Social Security benefits by telephoning the Social Security office at 1–800–772–1213. The payments will not start unless you apply for them. If you apply late, you risk losing benefits.

What Information Will You Need?   The Social Security office will tell you what proof you need to establish your particular case. Generally, you will be asked to provide the following:

- Proof of your age.
- Your Social Security card or Social Security number.
- Your W-2 withholding forms for the past two years.
- Your marriage license if you are applying for your spouse's benefits.
- The birth certificates of your children if you are applying for their benefits.

What if You Retire at 62 instead of 65?   Your Social Security benefits will be reduced if you retire before age 65. Currently there is a permanent reduction of five-ninths of 1 percent for each month you receive payments before age 65. Thus, if you retire at 62, your monthly payments will be permanently reduced by 20 percent of what they would be if you waited until 65 to retire. However, if you wait until 65 to collect Social Security, your benefits will not decrease. If you work after 65, your benefits will increase by one-fourth of 1 percent for each month past age 65 that you delay retirement, but only up to age 70.

Because of longer life expectancies, the full retirement age will be increased in gradual steps until it reaches 67. This change starts in 2003 and affects people born in 1938 and later. Look at Exhibit 18–6 on page 553 to determine your full retirement age.

Financial Decision Trade-Off

Estimating Your Retirement Benefits   The Social Security Administration will, upon request, provide a history of your earnings and an estimate of your future monthly benefits. To obtain this earnings and benefits statement, call 1–800–772–1213; or complete and

Exhibit 18–6

**Age to Receive Full
Social Security
Benefits**

Year of Birth	Full Retirement Age
1937 or earlier	65
1938	65 and 2 months
1939	65 and 4 months
1940	65 and 6 months
1941	65 and 8 months
1942	65 and 10 months
1943–54	66
1955	66 and 2 months
1956	66 and 4 months
1957	66 and 6 months
1958	66 and 8 months
1959	66 and 10 months
1960 and later	67

If your full retirement age is above 65 (that is, you were born after 1937), you still will be able to take your retirement benefits at age 62, but the reduction in your benefit amount will be greater than it is for people retiring now.

SOURCE: *Social Security: Retirement Benefits* (Washington, DC: Social Security Administration, February 1997), p. 5

mail Form SSA-7004, which you can obtain at any local Social Security office. You will receive the statement in about six weeks. The statement includes an estimate, in today's dollars, of how much you will get each month from Social Security when you retire—at age 62, 65, or 70—based on your earnings to date and your projected future earnings.

How to Become Eligible   To qualify for Social Security retirement benefits, you must have the required number of quarters of coverage. The number of quarters you need depends on your year of birth. People born after 1928 need 40 quarters to qualify for benefits.

DID YOU KNOW?

Frayed net
The average respondent who attended some college believes only 20 percent of his or her retirement income will come from Social Security.

SOURCE: *Business Week,* July 21, 1997, p. 60.

Minimum and Maximum Benefits   Social Security retirement benefits are based on earnings over the years. Exhibit 18–7 on page 554 shows approximate monthly Social Security benefits for workers at age 65.

Taxability of Social Security Benefits   Up to 85 percent of your Social Security benefits may be subject to federal income tax for any year in which your adjusted gross income plus your nontaxable interest income and one-half of your Social Security benefits exceed a base amount. For current information, telephone the Internal Revenue Service at 1–800–829–3676 for Publication 554, *Tax Benefits for Older Americans,* and Publication 915, *Tax Information on Social Security.*

If You Work after You Retire   Your Social Security benefits may be reduced if you earn above a certain amount a year, depending on your age and the amount you earn. You will receive all of your benefits for the year if your employment earnings do not exceed the annual exempted amount.

Benefits Increase Automatically   Social Security benefits increase automatically each January if the cost of living increased during the preceding year. Each year, the cost of living is compared with that of the year before. If it has increased, Social Security benefits increase by the same percentage.

EXHIBIT 18–7

Examples of Social Security Benefits

(approximate monthly benefits if you retire at full retirement age and had steady lifetime earnings)

	Your Age in 1997	Your Family	Your Earnings in 1996				
			$20,000	$30,000	$40,000	$50,000	$62,700 or More*
	45	You	$ 797	$1,063	$1,229	$1,354	$1,519
		You and your spouse†	1,195	1,594	1,843	2,031	2,278
	55	You	797	1,063	1,226	1,327	1,435
		You and your spouse†	1,195	1,594	1,839	1,990	2,152
	65	You	805	1,074	1,205	1,272	1,326
		You and your spouse†	1,207	1,611	1,807	1,908	1,989

*Use this column if you earned more than the maximum Social Security earnings base.

†Your spouse is assumed to be the same age you are. Your spouse may qualify for a higher retirement benefit based on his or her own work record.

NOTE: The accuracy of these estimates depends on the pattern of your actual past earnings and your earnings in the future. Your actual benefit will probably be higher because these estimates are shown in today's dollars.

SOURCE: *Social Security: Retirement Benefits* (Washington, DC: Social Security Administration, February 1997), p. 35

Spouse's Benefits   The full benefit for a spouse is one-half of the retired worker's full benefit. If your spouse takes benefits before age 65, the amount of the spouse's benefit is reduced to a low of 37.5 percent at age 62. However, a spouse who is taking care of a child who is under 16 or has a disability gets full (50 percent) benefits, regardless of age.

If you are eligible for both your own retirement benefits and for benefits as a spouse, Social Security pays your own benefit first. If your benefit as a spouse is higher than your retirement benefit, you'll get a combination of benefits equal to the higher spouse benefit.

DID YOU KNOW?

Social Security

Workers' confidence in their retirement income prospects dropped 12 percentage points over the past year. Only 7 percent are very confident Social Security and Medicare will pay benefits (at current levels).

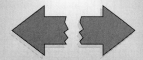

SOURCE: Employment Benefit Research Institute Issue Brief, January 1997.

The Future of Social Security   According to the Social Security Administration, the Social Security program is financially sound. The Social Security taxes received in recent years exceeded the Social Security benefits that were paid. Such surpluses are expected to continue until the year 2017, at which time a sizable reserve fund is expected to exist (see Exhibit 18–8).

However, some people are concerned about the future of Social Security. They contend that enormous changes since Social Security started nearly 63 years ago have led to promises that are impossible to keep. Longer life expectancies mean retirees collect benefits over a greater number of years. More workers are retiring early, thus entering the system sooner and staying longer. The flood of baby boomers who will begin retiring early in the next century will mean fewer workers to contribute to the system. In 1945, 45 workers supported every recipient. By 1995, that number had dropped to three. The Social Security Administration estimates the number will drop to two workers by 2050 (see Exhibit 18–9).

See the accompanying Financial Planning for Life's Situations feature on page 556 to learn about reform proposals to rescue our Social Security System.

Other Public Pension Plans

Besides Social Security, the federal government administers several other retirement plans (for federal government and railroad employees). Employees covered under these plans are not covered by Social Security. The Veterans Administration provides pensions

EXHIBIT 18–8

Social Security Income, Outgo, and Assets, 1985–2030*

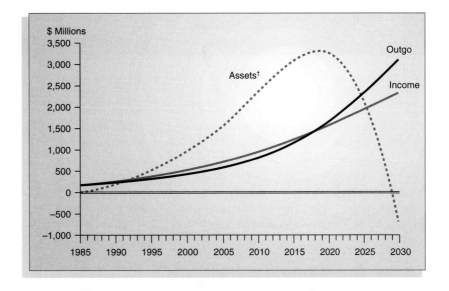

* Calendar-year data. Data for 1995 and beyond are projections.
†End-of-year data.
sources: Board of Trustees of the Social Security Administration, *Annual Report,* April 1995; *Economic Commentary,* Federal Reserve Bank of Cleveland, September 1997, p. 2.

EXHIBIT 18–9

The Number of Workers per Beneficiary Has Plummeted

Due to the increase in life expectancy, more people are receiving Social Security benefits for longer periods of time.

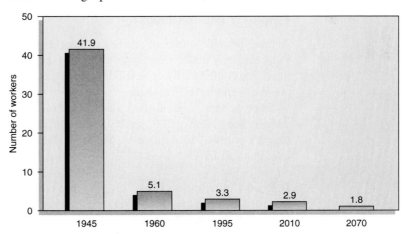

sources: Advisory Council on Social Security, 1994–95; *Southwest Economy* (Dallas: Federal Reserve Bank of Dallas, May–June 1997), p. 7.

for many survivors of men and women who died while in the armed forces and disability pensions for eligible veterans. The Railroad Retirement System is the only retirement system administered by the federal government that covers a single private industry. Many state, county, and city governments operate retirement plans for their employees.

FINANCIAL PLANNING FOR LIFE'S SITUATIONS

SUMMARY OF PROPOSALS FROM THE ADVISORY COUNCIL OF SOCIAL SECURITY

In January 1997, a federal advisory panel on Social Security put forth three comprehensive proposals for reforming the system. The 13-member council, formed in 1994, was asked to make recommendations to ensure the long-run solvency of Social Security. Members were drawn from academia, labor unions, and private industry.

The *maintain benefits* plan recommends several ways to increase Social Security revenues to allow the current program to continue. First, the proposal would increase the payroll tax rate from 12.4 to 14 percent over 50 years. The plan also recommends investing up to 40 percent of the Social Security trust fund in private equities. A politically appointed panel would oversee the selection of index funds; equity investments would remain under government ownership.

The *individual accounts* plan recommends increasing the payroll tax by 1.6 percentage points and allocating the additional revenues to individual accounts. Individual accounts would be converted to annuities when holders retire. Regular Social Security benefits also would be paid. The individual accounts would be maintained by the government, but individuals would choose among several investment options.

Under the *personal security accounts* proposal, the basis of Social Security would shift toward a system of individual accounts. Five percentage points of the current payroll tax would be allocated to individual accounts, which would be supplemented by a flat benefit equivalent to $410 in 1996. The individual accounts would be maintained by individuals, not the government, and subject to investment restrictions. The program would be phased in over time.

SOURCE: *Southwest Economy* (Dallas: Federal Reserve Bank of Dallas, May–June 1997), p. 10.

Employer Pension Plans

Another possible source of retirement income is the pension plan your company offers. With employer plans, your employer contributes to your retirement benefits, and sometimes you contribute too. Contributions and earnings on those contributions accumulate tax free until you receive them.

Since private pension plans vary, you should go to your firm's personnel office or union office to find out (1) when you become eligible for pension benefits and (2) what benefits you will be entitled to. Most employer plans are defined-benefit or defined-contribution plans.

defined-contribution plan

Defined-Contribution Plan   Over the last two decades, the defined-contribution plan has continued to grow rapidly while the number of defined-benefit plans has generally leveled off. A **defined-contribution plan** has an individual account for each employee; therefore, these plans are sometimes called *individual account plans*. The plan document describes the amount the employer will contribute, but it does not promise any particular benefit. When a plan participant retires or otherwise becomes eligible for benefits, the benefit is the total amount in the participant's account, including past investment earnings on amounts put into the account.

Defined-contribution plans include the following:

1. *Money-purchase pension plans.* Your employer promises to set aside a certain amount for you each year, generally a percentage of your earnings.

EXHIBIT 18–10

**An Early Start +
Tax-Deferred
Growth =
Greater Savings**

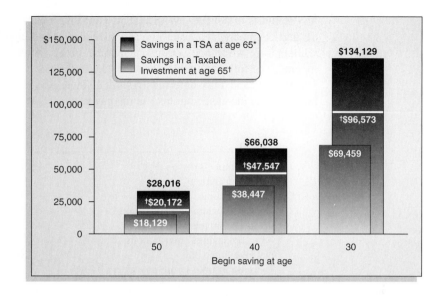

2. *Stock bonus plans.* Your employer's contribution is used to buy stock in your company for you. The stock is usually held in trust until you retire, at which time you can receive your shares or sell them at their fair market value.

3. *Profit-sharing plans.* Your employer's contribution depends on the company's profits.

401(k) (TSA) plans

4. *Salary reduction or 401(k) plans.* Under a **401(k) plan,** your employer makes nontaxable contributions to the plan for your benefit and reduces your salary by the same amounts. If your employer is a tax-exempt institution such as a hospital, university, or museum, the salary reduction plan is called a *Section 403(b) plan.* These plans are often referred to as *tax-sheltered annuity (TSA) plans.*

The Tax Reform Act of 1986 retains the $30,000 cap on annual contributions for money-purchase pension plans, stock bonus plans, and profit-sharing plans. Eventually, the annual limit on such plans will increase in response to inflation.

In 1994, the tax act reduced from $30,000 to $9,240 the maximum annual amount an employee can defer for a 401(k) plan. The maximum annual amount you may contribute to a 403(b) plan now ranges from $9,500 up to $12,500 if you have worked for the same employer for 15 years or more. The maximum can be higher in plans to which your employer contributes.

An Example: How Funds Accumulate   All earnings in a tax-sheltered annuity grow without current federal taxation. The fact that your dollars are saved on a pretax basis while your earnings grow tax deferred has a dynamic effect on the growth of your funds (see Exhibit 18–10).

Tax Benefits of a TSA   With a TSA, your investment earnings are tax deferred. Your savings compound at a faster rate and provide you with a greater sum than in an account without this advantage. Ordinary income taxes will be due when you receive the income. The following table illustrates the difference between saving in a conventional savings plan and a tax-deferred TSA for a single person earning $28,000 a year. Notice how you can increase your take-home pay with a TSA.

	Without TSA	With a TSA
Your income	$28,000	$28,000
TSA contribution	0	2,400
Taxable income	28,000	25,600
Estimated federal income taxes	5,319	4,647
Gross take-home pay	22,681	20,953
After-tax savings contributions	2,400	0
Net take-home pay	20,281	20,953
Increase in take-home pay with a TSA		**$ 672**

vesting

What happens to your benefits under an employer pension plan if you change jobs? One of the most important aspects of such plans is vesting. **Vesting** is your right to at least a portion of the benefits you have accrued under an employer pension plan (within certain limits), even if you leave the company before you retire.

defined-benefit plan

Defined-Benefit Plan   In a **defined-benefit plan,** the plan document specifies the benefits promised to the employee at the normal retirement age. The plan itself does not specify how much the employer must contribute annually. The plan's actuary determines the annual employer contribution required so that the plan fund will be sufficient to pay the promised benefits as each participant retires. If the fund is inadequate, the employer must make additional contributions. Because of their actuarial aspects, defined-benefit plans tend to be more complicated and more expensive to administer than defined-contribution plans.

Companies nationwide are switching their retirement plans to defined contributions from defined benefits. "Paternalistic employers are dying fast—if they're not already dead," says an actuary with an international consulting firm. The result is that "the shift to defined contributions has forced employees to take more responsibility for retirement. They have discretion as to how to invest the money and must make substantive decisions about their own financial futures."[11] It is estimated that by the year 2000, employees will be managing $1 trillion of their own retirement money in 401(k) retirement plans.

Plan Portability   Some pension plans allow portability. This feature enables you to carry earned benefits from one employer's pension plan to another's when you change jobs.

The Employee Retirement Income Security Act of 1974 (ERISA) sets minimum standards for pension plans in private industry and protects more than 50 million workers. Under this act, the federal government has insured part of the payments promised to retirees from private defined-benefit pensions. ERISA established the Pension Benefit Guaranty Corporation (PBGC), a quasi-governmental agency, to provide pension insurance. The PBGC's board of directors includes the secretaries of the U.S. Departments of Labor, the Treasury, and Commerce.

Use the checklist in Exhibit 18–11 on pages 559–60 to help you determine what your pension plan provides and requires.

EXHIBIT 18–11   Know Your Pension Plan Checklist

A. Plan Type Checklist

My plan is a:

Defined-benefit plan

☐ Integrated with Social Security.
☐ Nonintegrated.

Defined-contribution plan

☐ Integrated with Social Security.
☐ Nonintegrated.

My Social Security benefit:

☐ Will not be deducted from my plan benefit.
☐ Will be deducted from my plan benefit to the extent of _____ percent of the Social Security benefit I am due to receive at retirement.

B. Contributions Checklist

My pension plan is financed by:

☐ Employer contributions only.
☐ Employer and employee contributions.
☐ Union dues and assessments.

I contribute to my pension plan at the rate of $_____ per ☐ month ☐ week ☐ hour or _____ percent of my compensation.

C. Vesting Checklist

My plan provides:

☐ Full and immediate vesting.
☐ Cliff vesting.
☐ Rule of 45 vesting.
☐ Other (specify).

I need _____ more years of service to be fully vested.

D. Credited Service Checklist

I will have a year of service under my pension plan:

☐ If I work _____ hours in a 12-consecutive-month period.
☐ If I meet other requirements (specify).

The plan year (12-month period for which plan records are kept) ends on _____ of each year.
I will be credited for work performed:

☐ Before I became a participant in the plan.
☐ After the plan's normal retirement age.

As of now, _____ [date], I have earned _____ years of service toward my pension.

My plan's break-in-service rules are as follows: _____

_____

E. Retirement Benefit Checklist

I may begin to receive full normal retirement benefits at age _____.
Working beyond the normal retirement age ☐ will ☐ will not increase the pension paid to me when I retire.

I may retire at age _____ if I have completed _____ years of service. Apart from the age requirement,

I need _____ more years of service to be eligible for early retirement benefits.

(continued)

EXHIBIT 18-11   Know Your Pension Plan Checklist *(concluded)*

The amount of my normal retirement benefit is computed as follows: _____

The amount of my early retirement benefit is computed as follows: _____

My retirement benefit will be:
- ☐ Paid monthly for life.
- ☐ Paid to me in a lump sum.
- ☐ Adjusted to the cost of living.
- ☐ Paid to my survivor in the event of my death (see "Survivors' Benefit Checklist" below).

F. Disability Benefit Checklist

My plan ☐ does ☐ does not provide disability benefits.

My plan defines the term *disability* as follows: _____

To be eligible for disability retirement benefits, I must be _____ years old and must have _____ years of service.
A determination as to whether my condition meets my plan's definition of disability is made by:
- ☐ A doctor chosen by me.
- ☐ A doctor designated by the plan administrator.
- ☐ The Social Security Administration in deciding that I qualify for Social Security disability benefits.

I must send my application for disability retirement benefits to _____ within ____ months after I stop working.
If I qualify for disability benefits, I will continue to receive benefits:
- ☐ For life, if I remain disabled.
- ☐ Until I return to my former job.
- ☐ As long as I am eligible for Social Security disability benefits.

G. Survivors' Benefit Checklist

My pension plan ☐ provides ☐ does not provide a joint and survivor option or a similar provision for death benefits.
My spouse and I ☐ have ☐ have not rejected in writing the joint and survivor option.

Electing the joint and survivor option will reduce my pension benefit to _____.

My survivor will receive _____ per month for life if the following conditions are met (specify): _____
_____.

H. Plan Termination Checklist

My benefits ☐ are ☐ are not insured by the Pension Benefits Guaranty Corporation.

I. Benefit Application Checklist

My employer ☐ will ☐ will not automatically submit my pension application for me.

I must apply for my pension benefits ☐ on a special form that I get from _____ within _____ months
☐ before ☐ after I retire.
My application for pension benefits should be sent to _____.

I must furnish the following documents when applying for my pension benefits: _____.

If my application for pension benefits is denied, I may appeal in writing to _____

within _____ days.

J. Suspension of Benefits Checklist

- ☐ I am covered by a single-employer plan or by a plan involving more than one employer that does not meet ERISA's definition of a multiemployer plan.
- ☐ I am covered by a multiemployer plan as that term is defined in ERISA.

SOURCE: *Know Your Pension Plan* (Washington, DC: U.S. Department of Labor, 1992), pp. 5–10.

EXHIBIT 18–12		AGI—Single Returns	AGI—Joint Returns
Income Ranges and Deductibility Limits	1998	$30,000–$40,000	$50,000–$60,000
	1999	$31,000–$41,000	$51,000–$61,000
	2000	$32,000–$42,000	$52,000–$62,000
	2001	$33,000–$43,000	$53,000–$63,000
	2002	$34,000–$44,000	$54,000–$64,000
	2003	$40,000–$50,000	$60,000–$70,000
	2004	$45,000–$55,000	$65,000–$75,000
	2005	$50,000–$60,000	$70,000–$80,000
	2006	$50,000–$60,000	$75,000–$85,000
	2007+	$50,000–$60,000	$80,000–$100,000

For example, if you file a single return in 1998 and your AGI is $30,000 or less, your IRA contribution is fully deductible; if your AGI is $35,000, you will still be able to contribute the full $2,000, but only 50 percent will be deductible; and if your AGI is $40,000 or more, your contribution of up to $2,000 is nondeductible.

Personal Retirement Plans

In addition to the retirement plans offered by Social Security, other public pension plans, and employer pension plans, many individuals have set up personal retirement plans.

The two most popular personal retirement plans are individual retirement accounts (IRAs) and Keogh accounts.

individual retirement account (IRA)

Individual Retirement Accounts (IRAs)   The **individual retirement account (IRA),** which entails the establishment of a trust or a custodial account, is a retirement savings plan created for an individual. The Taxpayer Relief Act of 1997 includes several provisions designed to help you save for retirement. The act expanded rules on traditional IRAs and created a new type of IRA called the *Roth IRA* Plus.

The expansion of rules for existing IRAs allows more people to make deductible contributions and gain easier access to their funds. If you are under age 70½ and have earned income, you can contribute up to $2,000 to a traditional IRA. If you participate in an employer-sponsored retirement plan, see Exhibit 18–12 for the income ranges that determine what portion of your IRA contribution, if any, would be deductible under the new limits. If your adjusted gross income (AGI) is the lowest number on the range or less, your contribution will be fully deductible; if it is the highest number listed or more, it will be nondeductible. If your income falls somewhere in the middle, it will be partially deductible, depending on the exact amount. These ranges will go up every year until 2007. If your spouse is covered by a retirement plan at work but you aren't, you can still make a fully deductible IRA contribution until your AGI is $150,000 or more. New, penalty-free withdrawals are available for distributions made to cover qualified higher education expenses or up to $10,000 for first-time home buyer expenses.

Sheet 63

The Roth IRA Plus   Contributions are not tax deductible, but earnings accumulate tax free. You may contribute up to $2,000 per year (reduced by the amount contributed to a traditional IRA) if you are a single taxpayer with an AGI of less than $95,000 or less than $150,000 if you are filing jointly. You can make contributions even after age 70½. Five years after you establish your Roth IRA, you can take tax-free, penalty-free distributions if you are at least 59½ or will use the fund for first-time home buyer expenses.

Education IRA   The 1997 act also created a new IRA for education that allows individuals under certain income levels to contribute up to $500 per child under age 18. The contributions are not tax deductible, but they do provide tax-free distributions for education expenses.

You have an option to convert your traditional IRA to a Roth IRA Plus. Depending on your current age and your anticipated tax bracket in retirement, it may be a good idea to convert your traditional IRA into a Roth IRA Plus. If you are eligible for either a tax-deductible IRA or a Roth IRA Plus, which one is right for you? If you are saving for a first-time home purchase or retirement at age 59½, and these events are at least five years away, the Roth IRA Plus not only allows for penalty-free withdrawals but also tax-free distributions.

However, whether or not you are covered by a pension plan, you can still make nondeductible IRA contributions, and all of the income your IRA earns will compound tax deferred until you withdraw money from the IRA. Remember, the biggest benefit of an IRA lies in its tax-deferred earnings growth; the longer the money accumulates tax deferred, the bigger the benefit.

Exhibit 18–13 on page 563 shows the power of tax-deferred compounding of earnings, an important advantage offered by an IRA. Consider how compounded earnings transformed the lives of two savers, Abe and Ben. As the exhibit shows, Abe regularly invested $2,000 a year in an IRA for 10 years, from ages 25 to 35. Then Abe sat back and let compounding work its magic. Ben started making regular $2,000 annual contributions at age 35 and contributed for 30 years until age 65. As you can see, Abe retired with a much larger nest egg—over $192,000 more than Ben's. Moral? Get an early start on your plan for retirement.

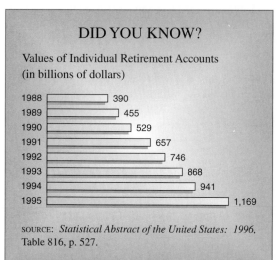

DID YOU KNOW?

Values of Individual Retirement Accounts
(in billions of dollars)

Year	Value
1988	390
1989	455
1990	529
1991	657
1992	746
1993	868
1994	941
1995	1,169

SOURCE: *Statistical Abstract of the United States: 1996,* Table 816, p. 527.

401(k)/403(b) Contributions versus IRA Contributions   How do 401(k) contributions compare with IRA contributions? As Exhibit 18–14 on page 564 shows, almost all of the advantages are with 401(k) contributions.

Simplified Employee Pension Plans–IRA (SEP–IRA)   A *SEP–IRA plan* is simply an individual retirement account funded by the employer. Each employee sets up an IRA account at a bank or a brokerage house. Then the employer makes an annual contribution of up to 15 percent of the employee's salary or $30,000, whichever is less.

The SEP–IRA is the simplest type of retirement plan if you are fully or partially self-employed. Your contributions, which can vary from year to year, are tax deductible, and earnings accumulate on a tax-deferred basis. A SEP–IRA has no IRS filing requirements, so paperwork is minimal.

Financial Decision
Trade-Off

Your investment opportunities for IRA funds are not limited to savings accounts and certificates of deposit. You can put your IRA funds in many kinds of investments—mutual funds, annuities, stocks, bonds, U.S.-minted gold and silver coins, real estate, and so forth. Only investments in life insurance, precious metals, collectibles, and securities bought on margin are prohibited.

IRA Withdrawals   When you retire, you will be able to withdraw your IRA in a lump sum, withdraw it in installments over your life expectancy, or place it in an annuity that guarantees payments over your lifetime. If you take the lump sum, the entire amount will be taxable as ordinary income and the only tax break you will have is standard five-year

EXHIBIT 18–13   **Tackling the Trade-Offs (saving now versus saving later)**

	Saver Abe				Saver Ben		
Age	Years	Contributions	Year-End Value	Age	Years	Contributions	Year-End Value
25	1	$2,000	$2,188	25	1	$ 0	$0
26	2	2,000	4,580	26	2	0	0
27	3	2,000	7,198	27	3	0	0
28	4	2,000	10,061	28	4	0	0
29	5	2,000	13,192	29	5	0	0
30	6	2,000	16,617	30	6	0	0
31	7	2,000	20,363	31	7	0	0
32	8	2,000	24,461	32	8	0	0
33	9	2,000	28,944	33	9	0	0
34	10	2,000	33,846	34	10	0	0
35	11	0	40,494	35	11	2,000	2,188
36	12	0	37,021	36	12	2,000	4,580
37	13	0	44,293	37	13	2,000	7,198
38	14	0	48,448	38	14	2,000	10,061
39	15	0	52,992	39	15	2,000	13,192
40	16	0	57,963	40	16	2,000	16,617
41	17	0	63,401	41	17	2,000	20,363
42	18	0	69,348	42	18	2,000	24,461
43	19	0	75,854	43	19	2,000	28,944
44	20	0	82,969	44	20	2,000	33,846
45	21	0	90,752	45	21	2,000	39,209
46	22	0	99,265	46	22	2,000	45,075
47	23	0	108,577	47	23	2,000	51,490
48	24	0	118,763	48	24	2,000	58,508
49	25	0	129,903	49	25	2,000	66,184
50	26	0	142,089	50	26	2,000	74,580
51	27	0	155,418	51	27	2,000	83,764
52	28	0	169,997	52	28	2,000	93,809
53	29	0	185,944	53	29	2,000	104,797
54	30	0	203,387	54	30	2,000	116,815
55	31	0	222,466	55	31	2,000	129,961
56	32	0	243,335	56	32	2,000	144,340
57	33	0	266,162	57	33	2,000	160,068
58	34	0	291,129	58	34	2,000	177,271
59	35	0	318,439	59	35	2,000	196,088
60	36	0	348,311	60	36	2,000	216,670
61	37	0	380,985	61	37	2,000	239,182
62	38	0	416,724	62	38	2,000	263,807
63	39	0	455,816	63	39	2,000	290,741
64	40	0	498,574	64	40	2,000	320,202
65	41	0	545,344	65	41	2,000	352,427
		$20,000				$62,000	

	Saver Abe		Saver Ben	
Value at retirement*		$545,344	Value at retirement*	$352,427
Less total contributions		$ 20,000	Less total contributions	$ 62,000
Net earnings		$525,344	Net earnings	$290,427

*The table assumes a 9 percent fixed rate of return, compounded monthly, and no fluctuation of the principal. Distributions from an IRA are subject to ordinary income taxes when withdrawn and may be subject to other limitations under IRA rules.

SOURCE: *The Franklin Investor* (San Mateo, CA: Franklin Distributors, Inc., January 1989)

EXHIBIT 18–14   **401(k)/403(b) versus Traditional IRA**

401(k)/403(b) Plans	Traditional IRA
Employers usually match employee contributions, so funds accumulate rapidly.	Contributions are not matched.
Salary deferrals reduce withholding and W-2 earnings immediately.	Contributions are taxed first and then qualify for a tax deduction.
Salary deferrals are made through affordable payroll deductions.	Contributions are usually made in single deposits at tax time, limiting affordability to available funds.
$10,000 limit.	$2,000 limit.
Available regardless of income level or participation income level or participation in other retirement programs.	May be unavailable if employee participates in other retirement programs or if income level exceeds a certain amount.
Permanent insurance protection can be provided.	Insurance not allowed.
May qualify for favorable tax treatment after age 59½.	Distributions taxed at ordinary income rates.
Withdrawals due to financial hardship allowed without penalty.	Withdrawals prior to age 59½ are subject to penalty tax.

income averaging. IRA withdrawals made before age 59½ are now subject to a 10 percent tax in addition to ordinary income tax, unless the participant dies or becomes disabled. You can avoid this tax if you roll over your IRA.

The Rollover IRA Strategy   If you change jobs or retire before age 59, one of your most attractive options for managing your retirement plan distribution will be the rollover IRA. This option enables you to avoid the early distribution penalty on pre–59½ distributions.

Keogh plan

Keogh Plans   A **Keogh plan,** also known an *H.R.10 plan* or a *self-employed retirement plan,* is a qualified pension plan developed for self-employed people and their employees. Generally, Keogh plans cannot discriminate in favor of a self-employed person or any employee. Both defined-contribution and defined-benefit Keogh plans have tax-deductible contribution limits, and other restrictions also apply to Keogh plans. Therefore, you should obtain professional tax advice before using this type of retirement plan. Whether you have an employer pension plan or a personal retirement plan, you must start withdrawing at age 70½ or the IRS will charge you a penalty.

Annuities

annuity

In Chapter 12, you learned what an annuity is and how annuities provide lifelong security. You can outlive the proceeds of your IRA, your Keogh plan, or your investments, but an **annuity** provides guaranteed income for life. Who should consider an annuity? One financial planner uses them for clients who have fully funded all other retirement plan options, including 401(k), 403(b), Keogh, and profit-sharing plans, but still want more money for retirement.[12]

You can buy an annuity as your individual retirement account with the proceeds of an IRA or a company pension, or as supplemental retirement income. You can buy an annuity with a single payment or with periodic payments. You can buy an annuity that will begin payouts immediately, or, as is more common, you can buy one that will begin payouts at a later date.

To the extent that annuity payments exceed your premiums, these payments are taxed as ordinary income as you receive them, but earned interest on annuities accumulates tax free until the payments begin. Annuities may be fixed, providing a specific income for life, or variable, with payouts above a guaranteed minimum level dependent on investment return. Either way, the rate of return on annuities is often pegged to market rates.

Types of Annuities   *Immediate annuities* are generally purchased by people of retirement age. Such annuities provide income payments at once. They are usually purchased with a lump-sum payment.

With *deferred annuities,* income payments start at some future date. Interest builds up on the money you deposit. Younger people often use such annuities to save money toward retirement.

A deferred annuity purchased with a lump sum is known as a *single-premium deferred annuity.* In recent years, such annuities have been popular because of the tax-free buildup during the accumulation period.

If you are buying a deferred annuity, you may wish to obtain a contract that permits flexible premiums. With such an annuity, your contributions may vary from year to year.

The cash value of your life insurance policy may be converted to an annuity. If you are over 65 and your children have completed their education and are financially self-sufficient, you may believe that you no longer need all of your life insurance coverage. An option in your life insurance policy lets you convert its cash value to a lifetime income.

Options in Annuities

You can decide on the terms under which your annuity pays off for you and your family. Exhibit 18–15 on page 566 summarizes the major options and their uses.

Which Annuity Option Is the Best?   The straight life annuity gives more income per dollar of outlay than any other type. But payments stop when you die, whether a month or many years after the payout begins.

Financial Decision Trade-Off

Should you get an annuity with a guaranteed return? Opinions differ. Some experts argue that it is a mistake to diminish your monthly income just to make sure your money is returned to your survivors. Some suggest that if you want to ensure that your spouse or someone else continues to receive annuity income after your death, you might choose the joint and survivor annuity. Such an annuity pays its installments until the death of the last designated survivor.

You have still another choice to make: how your annuity premiums are to be invested. With a fixed-dollar annuity, the money you pay is invested in bonds and mortgages that have a guaranteed return. Such an annuity guarantees you a fixed amount each payout period. With a variable annuity, the money you pay is generally invested in common stocks or other equities. The income you receive will depend on the investment results. Exhibit 18–16 on page 566 compares variable and fixed annuities.

An annuity guarantees lifetime income, but you have a choice regarding the form it will take. Discuss all of the possible options with your insurance agent. The costs, fees, and other features of annuities differ from policy to policy. Ask about sales and administrative charges, purchase and withdrawal fees, and interest rate guarantees. Also, as explained in Chapter 12, be sure to check the financial health of the insurance company.

Sheet 64

Will You Have Enough Money during Retirement?

Now that you have reviewed all the possible sources of your retirement income, estimate what your annual retirement income will be. Don't forget to inflate incomes or investments that increase with the cost of living (such as Social Security) to what they will be

Exhibit 18–15   **Income Annuity Options**

This exhibit gives you an approximate idea of how different income options compare. The amount of income you actually receive is based on factors such as how you invest, your age, your sex, and the income option you choose. Market conditions at any given time, especially interest rates, influence income amounts.

Income Option	Description	Common Uses	Typical Monthly Income*
Lifetime income. Also called *life income* or *life only*.	You receive income payments for the rest of your life. The income ceases upon your death.	Provides the most income per dollar invested of any lifetime option. Frequently used by single people with limited sources of additional income.	$923.71 per month for life.
Lifetime income with a minimum number of payments guaranteed. Also called *life with period certain*.	You receive income for the rest of your life. If you die before you receive a specific number of payments, your beneficiary will receive the balance of the number of income payments you choose.	Appropriate if you want a life income but dislike the risk of lost income in the event of premature death. People with heirs often consider this option.	$791.49 per month for life, 240-month minimum.
Lifetime income for two people. Also called *joint and survivor*.	Income payments are received for as long as either of the two people are alive. Upon the death of either person, income continues as a percentage of the original amount. Common percentages chosen for the survivor are 50, 66⅔, and 100%.	Often chosen by couples, who may choose the 100% option when there is little other income, or 50% or 66⅔% when there is other income. Lifetime income with period certain and installment refund† options are also available for joint-income plans.	$774.06 per month for as long as at least one of the people is alive, assuming the 100% option.

NOTE: The numbers above are hypothetical, and your actual income may differ. Only a portion of each payment would be taxable.

*Assumes a 65-year-old male with a 65-year-old spouse invests $100,000 and begins receiving income immediately.

†In an installment refund annuity, you receive an income for the rest of your life. However, if you die before receiving as much money as you paid in, your beneficiary receives regular income until the total payments equal that amount.

SOURCE: *Building Your Future with Annuities: A Consumer's Guide* (Fidelity Investments and U.S. Department of Agriculture, August 1991), p. 12.

Exhibit 18–16

A Comparison of Variable and Fixed Annuities

	Variable	Fixed
Tax-deferred earnings	Yes	Yes
Variety of income options	Yes	Yes
Annual investment ceiling	No	No
Investment flexibility	Yes	No
Potential for higher returns	Yes	No
Increased investment risk	Yes	No
Hedge against inflation	Yes	No
Security of principal and earnings	No	Yes
Guaranteed interest rate	No	Yes
Control over type of investment in the annuity	Yes	No

EXHIBIT 18–17

Sources of Income in Retirement

Social Security provides only 21 percent of the average retiree's annual income. On average, pension income accounts for about 19 percent, slightly less than that provided by Social Security.

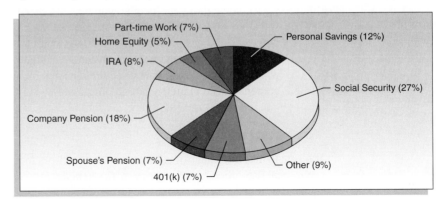

SOURCE: Social Security Administration, 1997.

when you retire. (Use the inflation factor table in the Financial Planning Calculations box on page 548.) Remember, one uncontrollable variable for retirees is inflation.

Now compare your total estimated retirement income with your total inflated retirement expenses, as figured earlier. If your estimated income exceeds your estimated expenses and a large portion of your planned income will automatically increase with the cost of living during your retirement, you are in good shape. (You should evaluate your plans every few years between now and retirement to be sure your planned income is still adequate to meet your planned expenses.)

If, however, your planned retirement income is less than your estimated retirement expenses, now is the time to take action to increase your retirement income. Also, if a large portion of your retirement income is fixed and will not increase with inflation, you should make plans for a much larger retirement income to meet your rising expenses during retirement.

Exhibit 18–17 summarizes the various sources of retirement income.

CONCEPT CHECK 18–5

1. What are possible sources of income for retirees?
2. What are examples of defined-contribution plans? How do they differ from defined-benefit plans?
3. What are the two most popular personal retirement plans?
4. What are annuities? What options are available in annuities? Which option is best?

LIVING ON YOUR RETIREMENT INCOME

L.O.6 Develop a balanced budget based on your retirement income.

As you planned your retirement, you estimated a budget or spending plan. Now you may find your actual expenses at retirement are higher than you anticipated.

The first step in stretching your retirement income is to make sure you are receiving all of the income to which you are entitled. Examine the possible sources of retirement income mentioned earlier to see whether you could qualify for more programs or additional benefits. What assets or valuables could you use as a cash or income source?

To stay within your income, you may also need to make some changes in your spending plans. For example, you can use your skills and time instead of your money. There are probably many things you can do yourself instead of paying someone else to do them. Take advantage of free and low-cost recreation such as walks, picnics, public parks, lectures, museums, libraries, art galleries, art fairs, gardening, and church and club programs.

Tax Advantages

Be sure to take advantage of all the tax savings retirees receive. For more information, ask your local IRS office for a free copy of *Tax Benefits for Older Americans*. If you have any questions about your taxes, get free help from someone at the IRS. You may need to file a quarterly estimated income tax return beginning with the first quarter of your first year of retirement.

Working during Retirement

You may want to work part time or start a new part-time career after you retire. Retirement work can provide you with a greater sense of usefulness, involvement, and self-worth and may be the ideal way to add to your retirement income. You may want to pursue a personal interest or hobby, or you can contact your state or local agency on aging for information about employment opportunities for retirees.

If you decide to work part time after you retire, you should be aware of how your earnings will affect your Social Security income. As long as you do not earn more than the annually exempt amount, your Social Security payments will not be affected. But if you earn more than the annual exempt amount, your Social Security payments will be reduced. Check with your local Social Security office for the latest information.

Investing for Retirement

The guaranteed income part of your retirement fund consists of money paid into lower-yield, very safe investments. This part of your fund may already be taken care of through Social Security or retirement plans, as discussed earlier. However, to offset inflation, your retirement assets must earn enough to keep up with, and even exceed, the rate of inflation. Here are some suggested investment strategies for 35-year-olds, 50-year-olds, and 65-year-olds.[13]

The 35-Year-Old's Strategy   Charles Cain, president of New York's Cain Asset Management Corporation, drew up a portfolio for 35-year-olds. According to Cain, since 35-year-olds have a relatively long time horizon, they "should be globally oriented, especially toward the emerging markets and along the Asian crescent." Cain says younger investors might want to put half their money into foreign stocks. He favors three funds: Warburg Pincus International Equity Fund, Lexington Worldwide Emerging Markets Fund, and T. Rowe Price New Asia Fund. Exhibit 18–18(*a*) on page 569 shows Cain's suggested investment portfolio for 35-year-olds.

EXHIBIT 18–18   **Suggested Investment Strategies for Life's Situations**

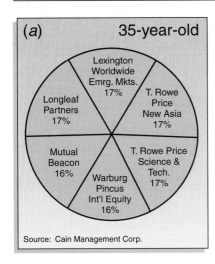

(a) 35-year-old

Lexington Worldwide Emrg. Mkts. 17%
T. Rowe Price New Asia 17%
Longleaf Partners 17%
Mutual Beacon 16%
Warburg Pincus Int'l Equity 16%
T. Rowe Price Science & Tech. 17%

Source: Cain Management Corp.

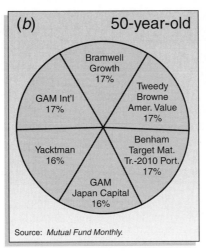

(b) 50-year-old

Bramwell Growth 17%
Tweedy Browne Amer. Value 17%
GAM Int'l 17%
Yacktman 16%
GAM Japan Capital 16%
Benham Target Mat. Tr.-2010 Port. 17%

Source: *Mutual Fund Monthly.*

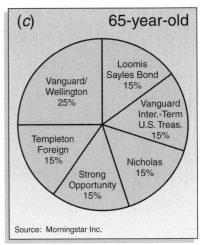

(c) 65-year-old

Loomis Sayles Bond 15%
Vanguard/ Wellington 25%
Vanguard Inter.-Term U.S. Treas. 15%
Templeton Foreign 15%
Nicholas 15%
Strong Opportunity 15%

Source: Morningstar Inc.

SOURCES: Cain Asset Management Corporation, *Mutual Fund Monthly;* Morningstar Inc.; Jonathan Clements, "Go Global, but Use Your Age as a Travel Guide," *The Wall Street Journal,* January 6, 1995, p. R5. Reprinted with permission.

The 50-Year-Old's Strategy   San Diego investment adviser Michael Stolper, who designed the portfolio for 50-year-olds (Exhibit 18–18(*b*)), is also betting heavily on foreign stocks. He has a third of his recommended portfolio in two overseas stock funds. "That reflects the fact that you have a global economic recovery, and the U.S. is 3½ years ahead of the rest of the world," says Stolper.

The 65-Year-Old's Strategy   As you approach retirement, you should bolster your bond position to 40 percent, advises Don Phillips, publisher of *Morningstar Mutual Funds,* a Chicago newsletter. Phillips put together the portfolio for 65-year-olds shown in Exhibit 18–18(*c*). He suggests that these investors put 30 percent of their money into two bond funds: Loomis Sayles Bond Fund and Vanguard Intermediate-Term U.S. Treasury Portfolio. In addition, Phillips recommends a 25 percent stake in Vanguard Wellington Fund, a balanced fund that typically owns a mix of 60 percent stocks and 40 percent bonds. If you combine the bonds in Vanguard Wellington with those held in the two pure bond funds, you end up with 40 percent of your overall portfolio in bonds and the rest in stocks.

Dipping into Your Nest Egg

Financial Decision Trade-Off

Should you draw on your savings? The answer depends on your financial circumstances, your age, and how much you want to leave to your heirs. Your savings may be large enough to allow you to live comfortably on the interest alone. Or you may need to make regular withdrawals to help finance your retirement. Dipping into savings isn't wrong, but you must do so with caution.

How long would your savings last if you drew on them for monthly income? If you have $10,000 in savings that earn 5.5 percent interest, compounded quarterly, you could take out $68 every month for 20 years before reducing this nest egg to zero. If you have $40,000, you could collect $224 every month for 30 years before exhausting your nest egg. For different possibilities, see Exhibit 18–19 on page 570.

EXHIBIT 18–19   **Dipping into Your Nest Egg**

Starting Amount of Nest Egg	You Can Reduce Your Nest Egg to Zero by Withdrawing This Much Each Month for the Stated Number of Years…					Or You Can Withdraw This Much Each Month and Leave Your Nest Egg Intact
	10 Years	15 Years	20 Years	25 Years	30 Years	
$ 10,000	$ 107	$ 81	$ 68	$ 61	$ 56	$ 46
15,000	161	121	102	91	84	69
20,000	215	162	136	121	112	92
25,000	269	202	170	152	140	115
30,000	322	243	204	182	168	138
40,000	430	323	272	243	224	184
50,000	537	404	340	304	281	230
60,000	645	485	408	364	337	276
80,000	859	647	544	486	449	368
100,000	1,074	808	680	607	561	460

NOTE: Based on an interest rate of 5.5 percent per year, compounded quarterly.

SOURCE: Select Committee on Aging, U.S. House of Representatives.

EXHIBIT 18–20   **Major Sources of Retirement Income: Advantages and Disadvantages**

Source	Advantages	Disadvantages
Social Security		
In planning	Forced savings	Increasing economic pressure on the system as U.S. population ages
	Portable from job to job	
	Cost shared with employer	
At retirement	Inflation-adjusted survivorship rights	Minimum retirement age specified
		Earned income partially offsets benefits
Employee Pension Plans		
In planning	Forced savings	May not be portable
	Cost shared or fully covered by employer	No control over how funds are managed
At retirement	Survivorship rights	Cost-of-living increases may not be provided on a regular basis
Individual Saving and Investing (Including Housing, IRA, and Keogh Plans)		
In planning	Current tax savings (e.g., IRAs)	Current needs compete with future needs
	Easily incorporated into family (i.e., housing)	Penalty for early withdrawal (IRAs and Keoghs)
	Portable	
	Control over management of funds	
At retirement	Inflation resistant	Some sources taxable
	Can usually use as much of the funds as you wish, when you wish	Mandatory minimum withdrawal restrictions (IRAs and Keoghs)
Postretirement Employment		
In planning	Special earning skills can be used as they are developed	Technology and skills needed to keep up may change rapidly
At retirement	Inflation resistant	Ill health can mean loss of this income source

FINANCIAL PLANNING IN ACTION

RETIREMENT CHECKLIST

As you approach retirement, assess your financial condition using the following checklist. Don't wait too long, or you will miss one or more opportunities to maximize your future financial independence.

	Yes	No
1. Do you talk regularly and frankly to family members about finances and agree on your goals and the lifestyle you will prefer as you get older?	☐	☐
2. Do you know what your sources of income will be after retirement, how much to expect from each source, and when?	☐	☐
3. Do you save according to your plan, shifting from growth-producing to safe, income-producing investments?	☐	☐
4. Do you know where your health insurance will come from after retirement and what it will cover?	☐	☐
5. Do you review your health insurance and consider options such as converting to cash or investments?	☐	☐
6. Do you have your own credit history?	☐	☐
7. Do you have a current will or a living trust?	☐	☐
8. Do you know where you plan to live in retirement?	☐	☐
9. Do you anticipate the tax consequences of your retirement plans and of passing assets on to your heirs?	☐	☐
10. Do your children or other responsible family members know where your important documents are and whom to contact if questions arise?	☐	☐
11. Do you have legal documents, such as a living will or a power of attorney, specifying your instructions in the event of your death or incapacitating illness?	☐	☐

SOURCE: Adapted from *Staying Independent,* American Express Consumer Affairs Office and IDS Financial Services Inc.

Exhibit 18–20 on page 570 summarizes major sources of retirement income and their advantages and disadvantages. Finally, use the accompanying Financial Planning in Action box to assess your financial condition as you approach retirement.

CONCEPT CHECK 18–6

1. What is the first step in stretching your retirement income?
2. How should you invest to obtain retirement income?

SUMMARY

L.O.1 Recognize the importance of retirement planning.

Retirement planning is important because you will probably spend many years in retirement; Social Security and a private pension may be insufficient to cover the cost of living; and inflation may erode the purchasing power of your retirement savings.

L.O.2 Analyze your current assets and liabilities for retirement.

Analyze your current assets (everything you own) and your current liabilities (everything you owe). The difference between your assets and your liabilities is your net worth. Review your assets to ensure they are sufficient for retirement.

L.O.3　Estimate your retirement spending needs.

Since the spending patterns of retirees change, it is impossible to predict the exact amount of money you will need in retirement. However, you can estimate your expenses. Some of those expenses will increase; others will decrease.

L.O.4　Identify your retirement housing needs.

Where you live in retirement can influence your financial needs. You are the only one who can determine the location and housing that are best for you. The types of housing available to retirees include their present homes, housesharing, accessory apartment, ECHO unit, boardinghouse, single-room occupancy, professional companionship agreement, caretaker arrangement, commercial rental, and supportive housing. Each of these living arrangements has advantages and disadvantages.

L.O.5　Determine your planned retirement income.

Estimate your retirement expenses and adjust those expenses for inflation using the appropriate inflation factor. Your possible sources of income during retirement include Social Security, other public pension plans, employer pension plans, personal retirement plans, and annuities.

L.O.6　Develop a balanced budget based on your retirement income.

Compare your total estimated retirement income with your total inflated retirement expenses. If your income approximates your expenses, you are in good shape; if not, determine additional income needs and sources.

GLOSSARY

annuity　A contract that provides an income for life. (p. 564)

defined-benefit plan　A plan that specifies the benefits the employee will receive at the normal retirement age.　(p. 558)

defined-contribution plan　A plan—profit sharing, money purchase, Keogh, or 401(k)—that provides an individual account for each participant; also called an *individual account plan.*　(p. 556)

401(k) (TSA) plan　A plan under which employees can defer current taxation on a portion of their salary.　(p. 557)

individual retirement account (IRA)　A special account in which the employee sets aside a portion of his or her income; taxes are not paid on the principal or interest until money is withdrawn from the account.　(p. 561)

Keogh plan　A plan in which tax-deductible contributions fund the retirement of self-employed people and their employees; also called an *H.R. 10 plan* or a *self-employed retirement plan.*　(p. 564)

reverse annuity mortgage　A mortgage in which the lender uses the borrower's house as collateral to buy an annuity for the borrower from a life insurance company; also called an equity conversion.　(p. 542)

vesting　An employee's right to at least a portion of the benefits accrued under an employer pension plan, even if the employee leaves the company before retiring.　(p. 558)

REVIEW QUESTIONS

1. If young professionals are worried about their retirement, what should they do about it? Where should they start? Where will you start? Outline your steps.　(L.O.1)
2. Why are many young professionals reluctant to plan for retirement?　(L.O.1)
3. What factors will you consider in reviewing your assets? What determines the suitability of those assets for retirement?　(L.O.2)
4. What expenses are likely to increase and decrease during retirement? Why?　(L.O.3)
5. Which type of housing will best meet your retirement housing needs?　(L.O.4)
6. What are possible sources of income during your retirement? How might annuities fit into your retirement plan?　(L.O.5)
7. What might be appropriate investment strategies for retirement income when your are 35? 50? 65? Explain your answers.　(L.O.6)

FINANCIAL PLANNING PROBLEMS

1. *Preparing a Net Worth Statement.* Prepare your net worth statement using the guidelines presented in Exhibit 18–3. (L.O.2)
2. *Comparing Spending Patterns during Retirement.* How will your spending patterns change during your retirement years? Compare your spending patterns with those shown in Exhibit 18–4.　(L.O.3)
3. *Evaluating Housing Options.* Which type of housing will best meet your housing needs in retirement? List the

advantages and disadvantages of your choice. Choose two locations and compare the costs.   (L.O.4)

4. *Calculating IRA Contributions.* Gene and Dixie Sladek both work. They have an adjusted gross income of $40,000, and they are filing a joint income tax return. What is the maximum IRA contribution they can make? How much of that contribution is tax deductible? (L.O.5)

5. *Calculating Net Pay and Spendable Income.* Assume your gross pay per pay period is $2,000 and you are in the 33 percent tax bracket. Calculate your net pay and spendable income in the following situations.   (L.O.5)

a. You save $200 per pay period after paying income tax on $2,000.

b. You save $200 per pay period in a tax-sheltered annuity.

6. *Calculating Monthly Withdrawals.* You have $50,000 in your retirement fund that is earning 5.5 percent per year, compounded quarterly. How many dollars in withdrawals per month would reduce this nest egg to zero in 20 years? How many dollars per month can you withdraw for as long as you live and still leave this nest egg intact? (L.O.6)

PROJECTS AND APPLICATION ACTIVITIES

1. *Conducting Interviews.* Survey friends, relatives, and other people to get their views on retirement planning. Prepare a written report of your findings.   (L.O.1)

2. *Obtaining Information about Reverse Mortgages.* Obtain a consumer information kit from Senior Income Reverse Mortgage Corporation in Chicago (1–800– 774–6266). Examine and evaluate the kit. How might a reverse mortgage help you or a family member?   (L.O.2)

3. *Using the Internet to Obtain Reverse Mortgage Information.*

   (*a*) Visit the Web site of the American Association of Retired Persons (AARP) at http://www.aarp.org. Locate the AARP Home Equity Information Center, which presents basic facts about reverse mortgages. 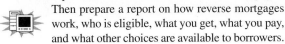 Then prepare a report on how reverse mortgages work, who is eligible, what you get, what you pay, and what other choices are available to borrowers.

   (*b*) Visit Fannie Mae's Web site at www.fanniemae. com/Homebuyer to find out about its reverse mortgage program.

4. *Determining Expenses during Retirement.* Read newspaper or magazine articles to determine what expenses are likely to increase and decrease during retirement. How

might this information affect your retirement-planning decisions?   (L.O.3)

5. *Evaluating Retirement Housing Options.* Which type of housing will best meet your retirement needs? Is such housing available in your community? Make a checklist of the advantages and disadvantages of your housing choice. (L.O.4)

6. *Writing Letters to Representatives in Congress.* Write a letter urging your representative in Congress to introduce or support legislation repealing the provisions of the present Social Security law that limit the earnings of Americans ages 65 to 69 who must work to provide for their needs.   (L.O.5)

7. *Requesting Personal Earnings and Benefits Statement.* Obtain Form SSA-7004 from your local Social Security office. Complete and mail the form to receive a personal earnings and benefits statement. Use the information in this statement to plan your retirement.   (L.O.5)

8. *Balancing a Retirement Budget.* Outline the steps you must take to live on your retirement income and balance your retirement budget.   (L.O.6)

LIFE SITUATION CASE 18

TO BE YOUNG, THRIFTY, AND IN THE BLACK: THE IMPORTANCE OF STARTING EARLY

Ann Farrell, a 28-year-old hydrogeologist, is one of the lucky ones. As a senior at Smith College in 1991, Farrell attended a seminar on investing early for retirement. "I remembered the figures if your started saving when you were young," she says. Indeed, the payoff is huge. Through compounding, 25-year-olds who invest $2,000 a year and stop at 34 will earn $142,000 more by the time they are 65 than someone who begins investing $2,000 at 35 and contributes $2,000 each year for the next 30 years, according to T. Rowe Price Associates.

Farrell already has $22,000 in her 401(k). That's a nice start compared to most of her peers. Public Agenda, a New

York-based market research firm, found that nearly 70% of polled adults aged 22 to 32 had saved less than $10,000 for retirement.

When Farrell was a new employee in 1991 at Roux Associates, an environmental consulting firm in Methuen, Mass., she was barred for a year from the company's Fidelity-managed 401(k) plan. Once eligible, she committed 8% of her paycheck in the two most aggressive stock funds offered (retirement growth and asset manager). The company matched 50% of her pretax contributions, up to 5% of her $28,000 salary.

Of course, it helped that her expenses were low. After graduation, Farrell—with only $500 to her name—moved back in with her parents, who charged her $200 a month for rent. She also traveled three out of every four weeks for work. "There is nowhere to spend money on the road," she claims. Still, she had to repay a $10,000 school loan and a $4,000 car loan. She also wanted to build an emergency slush fund. Once she began making headway on these goals, Farrell moved to her own place and gradually increased her pretax contribution to 10%. Last year, she upped it to 13% (the maximum) of her annual salary, which has hit $40,000. The government allows employees to make a pretax contribution of up to $9,500 a year. Farrell is currently chipping in about $5,000 a year.

Oddly, the lack of growth in environmental consulting has worked to Farrell's benefit. While most GenXers find themselves job-hopping every two years or so to get ahead, Farrell stayed put because there wasn't much movement in her industry. So she will become fully vested in her 401(k) this October, after five years in the plan.

But Farrell hasn't exhausted all her retirement savings possibilities. Even though IRA contributions are fully tax deductible only if a single person makes less than $35,000 a year ($50,000 for joint filers), Farrell can still benefit from the tax-deferred growth of the interest on her annual $2,000 contribution. For example, if she contributes $2,000 a year for 30 years, Farrell will earn $47,000 more in a nondeductible IRA than in a taxable account, assuming a 28% federal tax rate, according to T. Rowe Price Associates.

Farrell has done a lot right, but she has a long road ahead of her. When she makes her next move—she may leave her company and go to B-school—she needs to recognize the potholes that exist when protecting her retirement assets. For instance, if she decides to roll over her 401(k), she'll have to examine all of the investment options and rollover requirements. If she messes up, she could lose her head start on retirement savings.

QUESTIONS

1. What did Ann Farrell learn when she attended a seminar on retirement?
2. How much money did Ann originally commit to her 401(k) plan? In what funds did she invest her money?
3. What is the maximum contribution Ann can make to her 401(k) plan?
4. After how long and when did Ann become fully vested in her 401(k) plan?

SOURCE: Toddi Guttner, "To Be Young, Thrifty, and in the Black," *Business Week,* July 21, 1997, p. 76.

USING THE INTERNET TO CREATE A PERSONAL FINANCIAL PLAN 18

PLANNING FOR RETIREMENT

Long-term financial security is a common goal of most people. Retirement planning should consider both personal decisions (location, housing, activities) and financial factors (investments, pensions, living expenses).

Web Sites for Retirement Planning

- Retirement planning articles and assistance at **www.lifenet.com** and **www.savingsnet.com**
- Social Security Administration information and forms at **www.ssa.gov**
- Roth IRA information at **www.rothira.com** and **www.pensionplanners.com**
- Information about pension plans at **www.401k.com** and **www.wwebcom.com/retire**
- Useful investment and retirement planning assistance from American Express at **www.americanexpress.com/401k,** John Hancock at **www.jhancock.com,** Fidelity Investments at **www.personal.fidelity.com/retirement/toolkit.html,** and T. Rowe Price at **www.troweprice.com/retirement/retire.html.**
- Retirement and other information from the American Association of Retired Persons at **www.aarp.org**
- Current retirement articles from *Money* magazine at **www.money.com,** from *Kiplinger's Personal Finance*

magazine at **www.kiplinger.com,** *Business Week* at **www.businessweek.com,** *Worth* magazine at **www.worth.com,** and *Smart Money* at **www.smartmoney.com**

(Note: Addresses and content of Web sites change, and new sites are created daily. Use the search engines discussed in Appendix B to update and locate Web sites for your current financial planning needs.)

PFP SHEETS: 62–64

Short-Term Financial Planning Activities

1. Identify personal and financial retirement needs for various stages of your life.
2. Compare the benefits and cost of IRA, Roth IRA, and other pension plans (see PFP Sheet 63).

Long-Term Financial Planning Activities

1. Research costs and benefits of various housing alternatives (see PFP Sheet 62).
2. Estimate future retirement income needs and identify appropriate investments to meet those needs (see PFP Sheet 64).
3. Develop a plan for expanding personal interests and increasing contributions to retirement accounts.

CHAPTER 19

ESTATE PLANNING

OPENING CASE

RETIREMENT AND ESTATE PLANNING IN A MIDDLE-INCOME FAMILY

Bob, 42, is an account executive for a manufacturing company and makes $45,000 a year. His wife, Judy, also 42, is a teacher and makes $25,000 a year.

With a son and a daughter age 15 and 13, respectively, Bob and Judy want to make sure they have enough money for their children's educations. They also want to make sure they can retire with about 75 percent of their current monthly income when Bob is 64. Finally, Bob and Judy want to know how these goals and the overall status of their estate would be affected if either of them became disabled or died prematurely.

QUESTIONS

1. Assuming a modest rate of growth in their current capital plus monthly additions by each spouse, do you think Bob and Judy will be able to finance their children's educations? Would you recommend that they establish an education fund?

2. If Judy were to die prematurely, would the family face an income shortage? What if Bob died?

3. What suggestions do you have for Bob and Judy's estate planning? For example, what type of will do you recommend, and do you recommend a trust arrangement?

After studying this chapter, you will be able to

L.O.1 Analyze the personal aspects of estate planning.

L.O.2 Assess the legal aspects of estate planning.

L.O.3 Distinguish among various types and formats of wills.

L.O.4 Appraise various types of trusts and estates.

L.O.5 Evaluate the effects of federal and state taxes on estate planning.

WHY ESTATE PLANNING?

L.O.1 Analyze the personal aspects of estate planning.

estate

Your **estate** consists of everything you own. While you work, your objective is to accumulate funds for your future and for your dependents. However, your point of view will change. The emphasis in your financial planning will shift from accumulating assets to distributing them wisely. Your hard-earned wealth should go to those whom you wish to support and not to the various taxing agencies.

Contrary to widely held notions, estate planning, which includes wills and trusts, is not useful only to rich and elderly people. Trusts can be used for purposes other than tax advantages. Furthermore, most people can afford the expense of using them.

This chapter discusses a subject most people would rather avoid: death—your own or that of your spouse. Many people give little or no thought to setting their personal and financial affairs in order.

As you learned in the previous chapter, most people today live longer than those of previous generations and have ample time to think about and plan for the future. Yet a large percentage of people do little or nothing to provide for those who will survive them.

Planning for your family's financial security in the event of your death or the death of your spouse is not easy. Therefore, the objective of this chapter is to help you initiate discussions about questions you should ask before that happens. Does your spouse, for instance, know what all of the family's resources and debts are? Does your family have enough insurance protection?

The question of whether your family can cope financially without your own or your spouse's income and support is a difficult one. This chapter can't provide all of the answers, but it supplies a basis for sound estate planning for you and your family.

What Is Estate Planning?

estate planning

Estate planning is a definite plan for the administration and disposition of one's property during one's lifetime and at one's death. Thus, it involves both handling your property while you are alive and dealing with what happens to that property after your death.

Estate planning is an essential part of retirement planning and an integral part of financial planning. It has two components. The first consists of building your estate through savings, investments, and insurance. The second consists of transferring your estate, at your death, in the manner you have specified. As this chapter explains, an estate plan is usually implemented by a will and one or more trust agreements.

Nearly every adult engages in financial decision making and must keep important records. Whatever your status—single or married, male or female, taxi driver or corporate executive—you must make financial decisions that are important to you. Those decisions may be even more important to others in your family. Knowledge in certain areas and good recordkeeping can simplify those decisions.

At first, planning for financial security and estate planning may seem complicated. Although many money matters require legal and technical advice, if you and your spouse learn the necessary skills, you will find yourselves managing your money affairs more efficiently and wisely. Begin by answering the questionnaire in the accompanying Financial Planning in Action box on page 579 to see how much you and your family know about your own money affairs. You and your family should be able to answer some of these questions. The questions can be bewildering if the subjects are unfamiliar to you, but after reading this chapter, you'll be able to answer most of them.

If You Are Married

If you are married, your estate planning involves the interests of at least two people, and more if you have children. Legal requirements and responsibilities can create for married people problems that are entirely different than those of single people. Situations become more complex. Possessions accumulate. The need for orderliness and clarity increases.

Your death will mean a new lifestyle for your spouse. If you have no children or if the children have grown up and lead separate lives, your spouse will once again be single. The surviving spouse must confront problems of grief and adjustment. Daily life must continue. At the same time, the estate must be settled. If not, catastrophic financial consequences may result.

If children survive you, making sure that your estate can be readily analyzed and distributed may be all the more critical. If relatives or friends are beneficiaries, bequests have to be made known quickly and clearly.

Your desires and information about your estate have to be accessible, understandable, and legally proper. Otherwise, your beneficiaries may encounter problems and your intentions may not be carried out.

If You Never Married

Never having been married does not eliminate the need to organize your financial affairs. For people who live alone, as for married people, it is essential that important documents and personal information be consolidated and accessible.

Remember that in the event of your death, difficult questions and situations will confront some person at a time of severe emotional strain. That person may not be prepared to face them objectively. Probably the single most important thing you can do is take steps to see that your beneficiaries have the information and the knowledge they need to survive emotionally and financially if you die suddenly.

Everyone should take such steps. However, the need to take them is especially great if you are only 5 or 10 years away from retirement. By then, your possessions will probably be of considerable value. Your savings and checking account balances will probably be substantial. Your investment plans will have materialized. If you stop and take a look at where you are, you may be pleasantly surprised at the worth of your estate.

FINANCIAL PLANNING IN ACTION

ESTATE PLANNING CHECKLIST

Do you and your family members know the answers to the following questions?

	Yes	No
1. Can you locate your copies of last year's income tax returns?	☐	☐
2. Where is your safe deposit box located? Where is the key to it kept?	☐	☐
3. Do you know what kinds and amounts of life insurance protection you have?	☐	☐
4. Can you locate your insurance policies—life, health, property, casualty, and auto?	☐	☐
5. Do you know the names of the beneficiaries and contingent beneficiaries of your life insurance policies?	☐	☐
6. Do you know what type of health insurance protection you have and what the provisions of your health insurance policy are?	☐	☐
7. Do you and your spouse have current wills? Can you locate those wills, along with the name and address of the attorney who drafted them?	☐	☐
8. Do you have a separate record of the important papers you keep in your safe deposit box? Where is this record located?	☐	☐
9. Do you have a record of your spouse's Social Security number?	☐	☐
10. Can you locate your marriage certificate? The birth certificates of all the members of your family?	☐	☐
11. Do you know the name and address of your life insurance agent?	☐	☐
12. Do you have a clear understanding of what the principal financial resources and liabilities of your estate are?	☐	☐
13. Are you knowledgeable about simple, daily, and compound interest rates? About retirement funds and property ownership?	☐	☐
14. Have you given any thought to funerals and burial arrangements?	☐	☐
15. Do you know what papers and records will be important in the event of your death?	☐	☐
16. Can you explain the functions of a bank trust department, the meaning of joint ownership, and so forth?	☐	☐

SOURCE: *Planning with Your Beneficiaries* (Washington, DC: American Council of Life Insurance, Education, and Community Services, n.d.), p. 2.

New Lifestyles[1]

The times have changed, and millions of nontraditional households have unique estate planning problems. Nearly half of all American marriages end in divorce, creating headaches for millions of adults contemplating estate planning. Single parents and other single persons all have formidable estate planning challenges. Financial planners and estate attorneys universally offer such households the following self-serving, but smart advice: Plan early, and get expert help. The law provides plenty of protection for married couples, but it is rife with pitfalls for almost everyone else.

Single parents, divorced or not, should face the inevitable business of planning for their own death as part of retirement and estate planning. David Scott Sloan, chairman of trusts and estates at Sherburne, Powers & Needham, a law firm in Boston, says that simply leaving money to your kids can result in a huge estate tax bill, sharply decreasing the funds available if your estate is worth more than $625,000. Sloan recommends setting up a trust for the children's benefit.

Sheet 65

Unmarried couples face formidable retirement and estate planning challenges. A partner lacks any legal right to the companion's assets upon the companion's disability or death or upon the breakup of the partnership. Unmarried couples also lack the so-called marital deduction, which allows spouses to pass on everything they own to their surviving spouse tax free. Only the first $625,000 of an unmarried partner's assets is exempt from estate taxes. Estate planning is even more important for out-of-wedlock couples. For example, if no beneficiary is named on your pension plan, the plan sponsor is required to give the proceeds to your closest blood relative. So if you want your partner to receive the plan proceeds after you die, make sure he or she is named the beneficiary. Also, check to see if the plan allows unmarried partners to receive joint and survivor benefits.

People without children may face similar legal hurdles since they don't have massive child-rearing expenses. It is not uncommon for hostile blood relatives to launch—and win—nasty court battles over the ownership of assets after death.

The Opportunity Cost of Rationalizing

Financial Decision
Trade-Off

Daily living gets in the way of thinking about death. You mean to organize things that others need to know in case you die, but you haven't done this yet. One of your rationalizations may be that you are not sure about what information you need to provide.

Think about the outcome of your delay. Your beneficiary will meet people who offer specific types of assistance—morticians, clergy, lawyers, insurance agents, clerks of federal government agencies, and so on. These people will probably be strangers—sympathetic, courteous, and helpful, but disinterested. Also, your bereaved beneficiary may find it difficult to reveal confidences to them.

The moral is to plan your estate while you are in good health and think through the provisions carefully. Last-minute "death-bed" estate planning might fail to carry out your wishes.

CONCEPT   CHECK   19–1

1. Why is estate planning an important component of financial planning?
2. Why is estate planning important for single as well as married individuals? For "new" lifestyle individuals?

LEGAL ASPECTS OF ESTATE PLANNING

L.O.2 Assess the legal aspects of estate planning.

In the event of death, proof of claims must be produced or the claims will not be processed. If no thought was given to gathering the necessary documents beforehand (with a sufficient number of copies), a period of financial hardship may follow until proof is obtained. If needed documentation cannot be located, irretrievable loss of funds may occur. Your heirs may experience emotionally painful delays until their rights have been established.

Important papers include the following:

1. Birth certificates—yours, your spouse's, and your children's.
2. Marriage certificates—always important, but especially important if you or your spouse were married previously.

3. Legal name changes—judgment of court documents pertaining to any legal changes in the names that appear on birth certificates (especially important to protect the adopted children of a previous marriage or children who have been adopted through adoption agencies).
4. Military service records—the standard DD–214 (Armed Forces of the United States Report of Transfer or Discharge) or any other official statement of your military service details, if appropriate.

Here is a list of important documents for which proof is needed:

- Social Security documents.
- Veteran documents.
- Insurance policies.
- Transfer records of joint bank accounts.
- Safe deposit box records.
- Registration of automobiles.
- Title to stock and bond certificates.

You should have several copies of certain documents because when you submit a claim, the accompanying proof often becomes a permanent part of the claim file and is not returned. Remember too that in some circumstances, your children may be required to furnish proof of their parents' birth, marriage, or divorce.

Wills

will

One of the most vital records every adult should have is a written will. A **will** is the legal declaration of a person's mind as to the disposition of his or her property after death. Thus, a will is a way to transfer your property according to your wishes after you die.

Whether you prepare a will before you die or neglect to take that sensible step, you still have a will. If you fail to prepare your own will, the state in which you legally reside steps in and controls the distribution of your estate without regard for wishes you may have had but failed to define in legal form. Thus, if you die **intestate**—without a valid will—the state's law of descent and distribution becomes your will, as shown in Exhibit 19–1, on page 582.

intestate

Consider the opportunity cost of a husband and father who died without a will. By default, he has authorized his estate to be disposed of according to the provisions of the fictitious document in Exhibit 19–1. The wording in this exhibit represents a pattern of distribution that could occur unless you prepare a valid will specifying otherwise.

Financial Decision Trade-Off

This does not happen only to a husband. It could happen to anyone. To avoid such consequences, make a will! Consulting an attorney for this purpose can spare your heirs many difficulties, especially since the passage of the Economic Recovery Tax Act of 1981. This act created estate planning opportunities and problems for many people. It also created some difficult choices as to types of wills.

The Effect of Marriage or Divorce on Your Will   If you already have a will and are about to be married or divorced, review your will with an attorney for necessary changes. Upon divorce, only provisions favoring a former spouse are automatically revoked; provisions favoring family members of your ex-spouse, such as stepchildren, nieces, nephews, or in-laws, are not affected.

If you marry after you have made a will, the will is revoked automatically unless certain conditions are met. For example, marriage does not revoke a will if

EXHIBIT 19–1

My Last Will and Testament

The Opportunity Cost of Not Making a Will, or What Will the State Do to Your Property if You Die Intestate?

Being of sound mind and memory, I, _____, do hereby publish this as my last Will and Testament.

FIRST

I give my wife only one third of my possessions, and I give my children the remaining two thirds.

A. I appoint my wife as guardian of my children, but as a safeguard I require that she report to the Probate Court each year and render an accounting of how, why, and where she spent the money necessary for the proper care of my children.

B. As a further safeguard, I direct my wife to produce to the Probate Court a Performance Bond to guarantee that she exercise proper judgment in the handling, investing, and spending of the children's money.

C. As a final safeguard, my children shall have the right to demand and receive a complete accounting from their mother of all of her financial actions with their money as soon as they reach legal age.

D. When my children reach age 18, they shall have full rights to withdraw and spend their shares of my estate. No one shall have any right to question my children's actions on how they decide to spend their respective shares.

SECOND

Should my wife remarry, her second husband shall be entitled to one third of everything my wife possesses. Should my children need some of this share for their support, the second husband shall not be bound to spend any part of his share on my children's behalf.

A. The second husband shall have the sole right to decide who is to get his share, even to the exclusion of my children.

THIRD

Should my wife predecease me or die while any of my children are minors, I do not wish to exercise my right to nominate the guardian of my children.

A. Rather than nominating a guardian of my preference, I direct my relatives and friends to get together and select a guardian by mutual agreement.

B. In the event that they fail to agree on a guardian, I direct the Probate Court to make the selection. If the court wishes, it may appoint a stranger acceptable to it.

FOURTH

Under existing tax law, certain legitimate avenues are open to me to lower death rates. Since I prefer to have my money used for government purposes rather than for the benefit of my wife and children, I direct that no effort be made to lower taxes.

IN WITNESS WHEREOF, I have set my hand to this, my LAST WILL AND TESTAMENT, this _____ day of _____ 19 _____.

- The will indicates an intent that it not be revoked by a subsequent marriage.
- The will was drafted under circumstances indicating that it was in contemplation of marriage.

Because your existing will's legal status may be uncertain, you are better off drawing a new will to fit your new circumstances.

Cost of a Will   Legal fees for drafting a will vary with the complexities of your estate and family situation. A standard will costs between $200 and $350. The price varies from place to place, but generally the cost of writing a will is less than that for writing a living trust (to be discussed later in the chapter). Look for an attorney experienced in drafting wills and in estate planning.

1. What are the legal aspects of estate planning?
2. What is a will? Why is it an important estate planning tool?
3. How does marriage or divorce affect a will?

TYPES AND FORMATS OF WILLS

Types of Wills

L.O.3 Distinguish among various types and formats of wills.

A brief review of the types of wills will be helpful, since the tax effects of these wills differ. The four types of wills are the simple will, the traditional marital share will, the exemption trust will, and the stated dollar amount will.

simple will

Simple Will   A **simple will,** sometimes called an *I love you will,* leaves everything to the spouse. Such a will is sufficient for most smaller estates. However, if you have a large or complex estate, especially one involving business interests that you want to pass on to your children, a simple will may not meet your objectives. It may also create higher overall taxation, because everything would be taxed in your spouse's subsequent estate.

For example, in 1997, if your estate was $1.2 million and you left it all to your spouse, there would be no tax at your death. However, there would be a tax of $235,000 at your spouse's death, assuming the value of the estate remains constant. To avoid this, you could use a two-part marital will to split your estate into two halves, resulting in no tax at either death. If your spouse had separate property or if the value of your estate increased, the simple will would create higher taxation.

traditional marital share will

adjusted gross estate

Traditional Marital Share Will   The **traditional marital share will** leaves one-half of the **adjusted gross estate** (the gross estate minus debts and costs) to the spouse outright as a marital share. The other half of the adjusted gross estate might go to children or other heirs or be held in trust for the family. A trust can provide the spouse with a lifelong income and would not be taxed at the spouse's death.

Under this type of will, half of your estate is taxed at your death and half at your spouse's death. This results in the lowest overall amount of federal estate taxes on estates above a certain size (twice the exemption amount). However, there are other considerations. State inheritance taxes may be greater, especially at the first death, due to conflicting federal and state exemption and beneficiary classifications. Also, under this type of will, unlike a simple will or an exemption trust, federal estate taxes may have to be paid up front at the first death that will involve the loss of use of money. If your spouse has considerable assets in his or her own right, it might not be prudent to increase your spouse's estate by any amount. In such a situation, a will that equalizes estates might be better. Finally, the nine community-property states severely limit your options as to how to allocate your money.

exemption trust will

Exemption Trust Will   The **exemption trust will** has been gaining in popularity due to its increased exemption ($600,000 since 1987). Under this type of will, everything passes to your spouse with the exception of an amount equal to the exemption, which would pass into trust. The amount passed to your spouse can be by will, trust, or other means. The exemption trust can provide your spouse with a lifelong income.

There would be little or no tax at your death due to the combination of the exemption and the marital deduction. The exemption amount and any appreciation on it would not be taxed on your spouse's estate.

The main advantage of the exemption trust will is that it eliminates future taxation of the exemption amount and any growth in it. This may be an important factor if property values appreciate considerably.

stated dollar
amount will

Stated Dollar Amount Will   The **stated dollar amount will** allows you to pass on to your spouse any amount that satisfies your family objectives. These objectives may or may not include tax considerations. For example, you could pass the stated amount of $625,000 (in 1998). However, the stated amount might be related to anticipated income needs or to the value of personal items.

State law may dictate how much you must leave your spouse. Most states require that your spouse receive a certain amount, usually one-half or one-third. Some states require that such interests pass outright, and others permit life interests. The stated dollar amount will may satisfy such requirements and pass the balance to others. You may, for example, decide to pass most of your estate to your children, thereby avoiding subsequent taxation of your spouse's estate. It may also make sense to pass interests in a business to children who are involved in the business.

Such plans may increase taxes at your death, since not all of your property passes to your spouse. However, the taxes at your spouse's subsequent death would be lower. You can also leave your spouse an outright amount equal to the exemption with a life estate in the balance, or a life estate in trust.

The stated dollar amount has one major shortcoming. The will may leave specific dollar amounts to listed heirs and the balance to the surviving spouse. Although these amounts may be fine when the will is drafted, they can soon become obsolete. What if estate values suddenly decrease due to a business setback or a drop in the stock market? Consider an individual with an extensive equities portfolio who drafted a will in September 1987. After the October 17 market crash, the value of the portfolio may have shrunk by one-third. None of that decrease will be borne by those who were left specific dollar amounts. The entire decrease will be borne by the surviving spouse. Therefore, you should use percentages instead of designated amounts.[2]

Which Type of Will Is Best for You?   The four types of wills just discussed are your basic choices. Which one is best for you?

Prior to the Economic Recovery Tax Act of 1981, many experts advocated the traditional marital share will. Today many attorneys believe the exemption trust will is best. However, there is no one ideal will. Which will is best for you depends on factors such as the size of your estate, the future appreciation of your estate, inflation, the respective ages of you and your spouse, relative liquidity, and—most important—your objectives.

Formats of Wills

holographic will

Wills may be holographic or formal. A **holographic will** is a handwritten will that you prepare yourself. It should be written, dated, and signed entirely in your handwriting; no printed or typed information should be on its pages. It should not be witnessed. Some states, however, may not recognize a holographic will.

formal will

A **formal will** is usually prepared with an attorney's assistance. It may be either typed or on a preprinted form. You must sign the will and acknowledge it as your will in the pres-

beneficiary

ence of two witnesses, neither of whom is a **beneficiary** (a person you have named to receive property under the will). The witnesses must then sign the will in your presence.

The 10 Commandments of Making Your Will

1. Work closely with your spouse as you prepare your will. Seek professional help so that your family objectives can be met regardless of who dies first.
2. Write your will to conform with your current wishes. When your circumstances change (for example, when you retire or move to another state), review your will and, if appropriate, write a new one.
3. Do not choose a beneficiary as a witness. If such a person is called on to validate your will, he or she may not be able to collect an inheritance.
4. If you are remarrying, consider signing a prenuptial agreement to protect your children. If you sign such an agreement before the wedding, you and your intended spouse can legally agree that neither of you will make any claim on the other's estate. The agreement can be revoked later, if you both agree.

5. Consider using percentages rather than dollar amounts when you divide your estate. For example, if you leave $15,000 to a friend and the rest to your spouse, your spouse will suffer if your estate shrinks to $17,000.
6. Both you and your spouse should have a will, and those wills should be separate documents.
7. Be flexible. Don't insist that your heirs keep stock or run a cattle ranch. If you do so, they may suffer if economic conditions change.
8. Sign the original copy of your will and keep it in a safe place; keep an unsigned copy at home for reference.
9. Alter your will by preparing a new will or adding a codicil. Don't change beneficiaries by writing on the will itself; this may invalidate the will.
10. Select an executor or executrix who is both willing and able to carry out the complicated tasks associated with the job.

statutory will

A **statutory will** is one type of formal will. It is a preprinted form that may be obtained from lawyers and stationery stores. There are serious risks in using this or any other preprinted form. One risk is that such a form usually requires you to conform to rigid provisions, some of which may not be in the best interests of your beneficiaries. Also, if you change the preprinted wording, you may violate the law regarding wills, which may cause the changed sections or even the entire will to be declared invalid. There is also a risk that the form is out of date with respect to current law. It is always prudent to seek legal assistance in developing these documents.

Writing Your Will

The way to transfer your property according to your wishes is to write a will specifying those wishes. Joint ownership is no substitute for a will. Although jointly owned property passes directly to the joint owner and may be appropriate for some assets, such as your home, only a will allows you to distribute your property as a whole exactly as you wish. Select a person who will follow your instructions (your *executor* or *executrix*). By naming your own executor, you will eliminate the need for a court-appointed administrator, prevent unnecessary delay in the distribution of your property, and minimize estate taxes and settlement costs. See the accompanying Financial Planning for Life's Situations feature for guidance on important aspects of making a will.

Selecting an Executor   Select an executor or executrix who is both willing and able to carry out the complicated tasks associated with executing a will. These tasks are preparing an inventory of assets, collecting any money due, paying off any debts, preparing and filing all income and estate tax returns, liquidating and reinvesting other assets to pay off debts and provide income for your family while the estate is being administered,

EXHIBIT 19–2

Major Responsibilities of an Executor

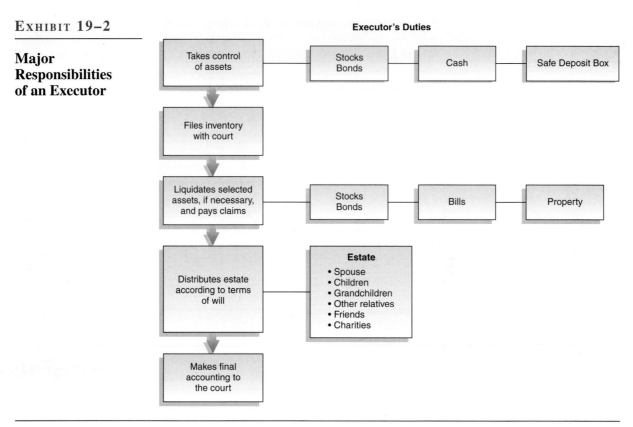

Executor's Duties

SOURCE: *Trust Services from Your Bank*, rev. ed. (Washington, DC: American Bankers Association, 1978), p. 9, © ABA 1978.

distributing the estate, and making a final accounting to your beneficiaries and to the probate court.

Your executor can be a family member, a friend, an attorney, an accountant, or the trust department of a bank. Fees for executors, whether professionals or friends, are set by state law. Exhibit 19–2 summarizes typical duties of an executor.

Selecting a Guardian   In addition to disposing of your estate, your will should name a guardian and/or trustee to care for minor children if both parents die at the same time, such as in an automobile accident or a plane crash. A **guardian** is a person who assumes the responsibilities of providing the children with personal care and of managing the estate for them. A **trustee,** on the other hand, is a person or an institution that holds or generally manages property for the benefit of someone else under a trust agreement.

You should take great care in selecting a guardian for your children. You want a guardian whose philosophy on raising children is similar to yours and who is willing to accept the responsibility.

Most states require a guardian to post a bond with the probate court. The bonding company promises to reimburse the minor's estate up to the amount of the bond if the guardian uses the property of the minor for his or her own gain. The bonding fee (usually several hundred dollars) is paid from the estate. However, you can waive the bonding requirement in your will.

Through your will, you may want to provide funds to raise your children. You could, for instance, leave a lump sum for an addition to the guardian's house and establish monthly payments to cover your children's living expenses.

guardian

trustee

The guardian of the minor's estate manages the property you leave behind for your children. This guardian can be a person or the trust department of a financial institution, such as a bank. Property that you place in trust for your children can be managed by the trustee rather than by the guardian of the minor's estate.

Altering or Rewriting Your Will

Sheet 66

Sometimes you will need to change provisions of your will. Consider one change involving the marital deduction. The old law limited the amount you could pass to your spouse tax free to one-half of your adjusted gross estate. But the Economic Recovery Tax Act of 1981 created an unlimited marital deduction. You can now pass any amount to your spouse tax free.

If you do have a will, you should review it. This is necessary even if you have already done some planning and your will refers to the old 50 percent marital deduction. Why? The new 100 percent marital deduction is not automatic. Congress would not alter or rewrite your will; this task was left to you. Therefore, unless you change your will or unless your state passes a law making the new definition applicable, you will have to rewrite your will to make the unlimited marital deduction apply. Because many choices are of a personal nature, few, if any, states will get involved. For example, some people may not want to leave the entire estate to their spouse, perhaps for valid tax reasons.

You should review your will if you move to a different state; if you have sold property mentioned in the will; if the size and composition of your estate have changed; if you have married, divorced, or remarried; or if new potential heirs have died or been born.

Don't make any changes on the face of your will. Additions, deletions, or erasures on a will that has been signed and witnessed can invalidate the will.

codicil

If only a few changes are needed in your will, adding a codicil may be the best choice. A **codicil** is a document that explains, adds, or deletes provisions in your existing will. It identifies the will being amended and confirms the unchanged sections of the will. To be valid, it must conform to the legal requirements for a holographic or formal will.

If you wish to make major changes in your will or if you have already added a codicil, preparing a new will is preferable to adding a new codicil. In the new will, however, include a clause revoking all earlier wills and codicils.

prenuptial agreement

If you are rewriting a will because of a remarriage, consider drafting a **prenuptial agreement.** This is a documentary agreement between spouses before marriage. In such agreements, one or both parties often waive a right to receive property under the other's will or under state law. Be sure to consult an attorney in drafting a prenuptial agreement.

Wills like some of those discussed in this section have existed for thousands of years; the oldest known will was written by the Egyptian pharaoh Uah in 2448 B.C. Recently a new type of will, called a *living will,* has emerged.

A Living Will

living will

A **living will** provides for your wishes to be followed if you become so physically or mentally disabled that you are unable to act on your own behalf. A living will is not a substitute for a traditional will. A person can prepare a living will in anticipation of death, and in that respect it resembles a traditional will. It enables an individual, while well, to express the intention that life be allowed to end if he or she becomes terminally ill. Many states recognize living wills, and you may consider writing one when you draw a conventional will. Exhibits 19–3 on page 588 and 19–4 on page 589 are examples of typical living wills.

To ensure the effectiveness of a living will, discuss your intention of preparing such a will with the people closest to you. You should also discuss this with your family doctor.

Exhibit 19–3

A Living Will: Example 1

To My Family, My Physician, My Lawyer, My Clergyman; To Any Medical Facility in Whose Care I Happen to Be; To Any Individual Who May Become Responsible for My Health, Welfare, or Affairs:

Death is as much a reality as birth, growth, maturity, and old age—it is the one certainty of life. If the time comes when I, _____, can no longer take part in decisions for my own future, let this statement stand as an expression of my wishes, while I am still of sound mind.

If the situation should arise in which there is no reasonable expectation of my recovery from physical or mental disability, I request that I be allowed to die and not be kept alive by artificial means or "heroic measures." I do not fear death itself as much as the indignities of deterioration, dependence, and hopeless pain. I, therefore, ask that medication be mercifully administered to me to alleviate suffering even though this may hasten the moment of death.

This request is made after careful consideration. I hope you who care for me will feel morally bound to follow its mandate. I recognize that this appears to place a heavy responsibility upon you, but it is with the intention of relieving you of such responsibility and of placing it upon myself in accordance with my strong convictions that this statement is made.

Signed _____

Date _____

Witness _____

Witness _____

Copies of this request have been given to _____

_____

_____

_____

source: *Don't Wait until Tomorrow* (Hartford, CT: Aetna Life and Casualty Company, n.d.), p. 10.

Sign and date your document before two witnesses. Witnessing shows that you signed of your own free will. Exhibit 19–5 on page 589 lists a few suggestions to ensure that a dying person's wishes are carried out.

Give copies of your living will to those closest to you, and have your family doctor place a copy in your medical file. Keep the original document readily accessible, and look it over periodically—preferably once a year—to be sure your wishes have remained unchanged. To verify your intent, redate and initial each subsequent endorsement.

A living will can become a problem. A once-healthy person may have a change of heart and prefer to remain alive even as death seems imminent. Living wills call for careful thought, but they do provide you with a choice as to the manner of your death.

Power of Attorney

power of attorney

Related to the concept of a living will is a power of attorney. A **power of attorney** is a legal document authorizing someone to act on your behalf. At some point in your life, you may become ill or incapacitated. You may then wish to have someone attend to your needs and your personal affairs. You can assign a power of attorney to anyone you choose.

The person you name can be given limited power or a great deal of power. The power given can be special—to carry out certain acts or transactions—or it can be general—to act completely for you. A conventional power of attorney is automatically revoked in a case of legal incapacity.

EXHIBIT 19–4

A Living Will: Example 2

Living Will Declaration

Declaration made this _____ day of _____ (month, year)

I, _____, being of sound mind, willfully and voluntarily make known my desire that my dying shall not be artificially prolonged under the circumstances set forth below, do hereby declare

If at any time I should have an incurable injury, disease, or illness regarded as a terminal condition by my physician and if my physician has determined that the application of life-sustaining procedures would serve only to artificially prolong the dying process and that my death will occur whether or not life-sustaining procedures are utilized, I direct that such procedures be withheld or withdrawn and that I be permitted to die with only the administration of medication or the performance of any medical procedure deemed necessary to provide me with comfort care.

In the absence of my ability to give directions regarding the use of such life-sustaining procedures, it is my intention that this declaration shall be honored by my family and physician as the final expression of my legal right to refuse medical or surgical treatment and accept the consequences from such refusal.

I understand the full import of this declaration, and I am emotionally and mentally competent to make this declaration.

Signed _____

City, County, and State of Residence _____

The declarant has been personally known to me, and I believe him or her to be of sound mind.

Witness _____

Witness _____

SOURCE: *Don't Wait until Tomorrow* (Hartford, CT: Aetna Life and Casualty Company, n.d.), p. 11.

EXHIBIT 19–5

A Checklist to Aid a Dying Person

Here are some steps estate planning specialists suggest to ensure that a dying person's wishes are carried out, to reduce taxes, and to make life easier for survivors.

Recommended Action	Benefits of This Action
Get a durable power of attorney	Appoints person to handle your financial affairs when you are unable to do so
Sign a living will or durable power of attorney for health care	Makes clear your wishes regarding your medical care
Update or make a will	Stipulates to whom you want to leave your assets
Set up a living trust	Avoids probate and allows trustee to manage your assets if you become incompetent
Make gifts up to $10,000 to children, other heirs.	Saves estate taxes
If you need cash, sell "loser" stocks or high-basis stocks	Low-basis stocks will get stepped-up basis for heirs.

SOURCE: Earl C. Gottschalk, Jr., "Taking Steps for the Terminally Ill," *The Wall Street Journal,* July 2, 1992, pp. C1, C10.

Letter of Last Instruction

In addition to your will, you should prepare a *letter of last instruction*. This document, though not legally enforced, can provide your heirs with important information. It should contain the details of your funeral arrangements. It should also contain the names of the people who are to be notified of your death and the locations of your bank accounts, safe deposit box, and other important items listed on page 581.

C O N C E P T   C H E C K   19–3

1. Distinguish among the four types of wills.
2. What are the two formats of wills?
3. What are the steps in writing your will?
4. What is a power of attorney?
5. What is a letter of last instruction?

TYPES OF TRUSTS AND ESTATES

L.O.4 Appraise various types of trusts and estates.

trustor

A trust is a property arrangement in which a trustee, such as a person or a bank trust department, holds title to, takes care of, and in most cases manages property for the benefit of someone else. The creator of the trust is called the **trustor** or *grantor*. A bank, as trustee, charges a modest fee for its services, generally based on the value of the trust assets. All trust assets added together are known as an *estate.*

trust

It is a good idea to discuss with your attorney the possibility of establishing a trust as a means of managing your estate. Basically, a **trust** is a legal arrangement through which a trustee holds your assets for your benefit or that of your beneficiaries. "Trusts today are used for everything from protecting assets from creditors to managing property for young children or disabled elders,"[3] according to one tax attorney.

revocable trust

Trusts are either revocable or irrevocable. If you establish a **revocable trust,** you retain the right to end the trust or change its terms during your lifetime. Revocable trusts avoid the often lengthy probate process, but they do not provide shelter from federal or state estate taxes. You might choose a revocable trust if you think you may need its assets for your own use at a later time or if you want to monitor the performance of the trust and the trustee before the arrangement is made irrevocable by your death. If you establish an

irrevocable trust

irrevocable trust, you cannot change its terms or end it. The trust becomes, for tax purposes, a separate entity, and the assets can't be removed, nor can changes be made by the grantor. Irrevocable trusts often are used by individuals with large estates to reduce estate taxes and avoid probate. Therefore, an irrevocable trust offers tax advantages not offered by a revocable trust.

Benefits of Establishing Trusts

Your individual circumstances dictate whether it makes sense to establish a trust. Here are some common reasons for setting up a trust. You can use a trust to

- Reduce or otherwise provide for payment of estate taxes.
- Avoid probate and transfer your assets immediately to your beneficiaries.
- Free yourself from management of your assets while you receive a regular income from the trust.

- Provide income for a surviving spouse or other beneficiaries.
- Ensure that your property serves a desired purpose after your death.

Trustee services are commonly provided by banks and, in some instances, by life insurance companies. An estate attorney can advise you about the right type of trust for you.

Types of Trusts

There are many types of trusts. Here we discuss 12 types: credit-shelter trusts, disclaimer trusts, marital-deduction trusts, living trusts, self-declaration trusts, testamentary trusts, life insurance trusts, charitable remainder trusts, qualified personal residence trusts, charitable lead trusts, generation-skipping trusts, and spendthrift trusts. Each of these types has particular advantages. Choose the type of trust that is most appropriate for your family situation.

credit-shelter trust

Credit-Shelter Trust   A **credit-shelter trust** is perhaps the most common estate planning trust. It is also known as a *bypass trust,* a *"residuary" trust,* an *A/B trust,* an *exemption equivalent trust,* or a *family trust.* It is designed to allow married couples, who can leave everything to each other tax free, to take full advantage of the exemption that allows $625,000 (in 1998) in every estate to pass free of federal estate taxes.

The Taxpayer Relief Act of 1997 increased the exemption amounts to $1 million by the year 2006 as follows:

1999	$ 650,000
2000	675,000
2001	675,000
2002	700,000
2003	700,000
2004	850,000
2005	950,000
2006	1,000,000

disclaimer trust

Disclaimer Trust   A **disclaimer trust** is appropriate for a couple who does not yet have enough assets to need a credit-shelter trust but may need one in the future. For example, a newly practicing physician who will soon finish paying off college loans might want to take this approach. With a disclaimer trust, the surviving spouse is left everything, but has the right to disclaim some portion of the estate. Anything disclaimed goes into a credit-shelter trust. This approach gives the surviving spouse the flexibility to shelter any wealth from estate taxes. However, if the estate fails to grow as expected, the survivor isn't locked into a trust structure.[4]

marital-deduction trust

Marital-Deduction Trust   With a **marital-deduction trust,** you can leave to your spouse any money that doesn't go into a credit-shelter trust. Whatever the amount, it is free of estate tax when you die, since it qualifies for the marital deduction. Perhaps the most popular form of marital trust is the *qualified terminable interest property trust,* or *Q-TIP.* Here the surviving spouse gets all trust income, which must be distributed at least once a year, and sometimes receives access to the principal as well. When the spouse dies, the assets go to whomever you specified in the trust documents. The trust assets are then taxed as part of the surviving spouse's estate.[5]

living trust

Living or Inter Vivos Trust   A **living trust,** or *inter vivos trust,* is a property management arrangement that you establish while you are alive. Well-structured estate plans often start with a living trust that becomes irrevocable at death, dividing itself into several other types of trusts, such as a credit-shelter trust. You simply transfer some property to a trustee, giving him or her instructions regarding its management and disposition while you are alive and after your death. A living trust has these advantages:

- It ensures privacy. A will is a public record; a trust is not.
- The property held in it avoids probate at your death. It eliminates probate costs and delays.
- It enables you to review your trustee's performance and to make changes if necessary.
- It can remove management responsibilities from your shoulders.
- It is less subject to dispute by disappointed heirs than a will is.
- It can guide your family and doctors if you become terminally ill or incompetent.

However, a living trust involves higher costs than creating a will, and funding a trust can be time consuming.

self-declaration trust

Self-Declaration Trust   A **self-declaration trust** is a variation of the living trust. Its unique feature is that the creator of the trust is also the trustee. The trust document usually includes a procedure for removing the creator of the trust as the trustee without going to court. Typically, one or more physicians or family members, or a combination of physicians and family members, have removal power. If the creator of the trust is removed, a named successor trustee takes over.

testamentary trust

Testamentary Trust   A **testamentary trust** is established by your will and becomes effective upon your death. Such a trust can be valuable if your beneficiaries are inexperienced in financial matters or if the potential estate tax is substantial. Like a living trust, a testamentary trust provides the benefits of asset management, financial bookkeeping, protection of the beneficiaries, and minimizing of estate taxes.

Newly acquired property can always be added to your trust. But what if you forget to change the title on some of your assets? A simple pourover will, written when the trust agreement is drafted is the answer. A *pourover* will is a simple document that states that anything you may have neglected to place in your trust during your lifetime should be placed in it at your death. While assets passing under a pourover will are generally probated, a small amount may be excluded from a probate.

life insurance trust

Life Insurance Trust   In many families, the proceeds of life insurance policies are the largest single asset of the estate. A **life insurance trust** is established while you are living. The trust receives your life insurance benefits upon your death and administers them in an agreed-on manner. Such a trust can be canceled if your family or financial circumstances change or if you wish to make new plans for the future.

Although common estate planning tools, life insurance trusts "aren't for the faint of heart," says one tax attorney. They require careful monitoring so that they don't run afoul of gift tax rules. Basically, the new gift tax rules allow a person to give away $10,000 a year to an unlimited number of people. The Taxpayer Relief Act of 1997 increased this amount in $1,000 increments, depending on the rate of inflation. For example, a 3 percent average annual inflation rate would mean no increase in the $1,000 amount until the end of the fourth year, when it would become $11,000. If you exceed this amount, you begin cutting into the lifetime credit that allows you to pass along $625,000 (in 1998) free of federal or gift taxes. Once you exceed this limit, you must pay gift tax.

charitable remainder trust

Charitable Remainder Trust   With a **charitable remainder trust,** you retain the right to the income but transfer that right to the charity upon death. If you have highly appreciated assets, it is a great way to improve your cash flow during your retirement and pursue a charitable interest at the same time. The biggest drawback is that you have to give away the asset irrevocably.

qualified personal residence trust (QPRT)

Qualified Personal Residence Trust   A **qualified personal residence trust (QPRT)** lets you get your home or vacation home out of your estate. You give your home to a trust but live in it for a term of, say, 10 years. At the end of that time, the home belongs to the continuing trust or to the trust beneficiaries, depending on how the trust is written.

charitable lead trust

Charitable Lead Trust   A **charitable lead trust** pays a specified charity income from a donated asset for a set number of years. When the term is up, the principal goes to the donor's beneficiaries with reduced estate or gift taxes. Such a trust has high setup and operating costs, however, which may make it impractical unless the assets involved are substantial. For this reason, it is a vehicle for very wealthy people, allowing them a way to keep an asset in the family but greatly reducing the cost of passing it on.[6]

generation-skipping trust

Generation-Skipping Trust   A **generation-skipping trust** allows you to directly leave a substantial amount of money to your grandchildren. That's because the federal government imposes a flat 55 percent tax on everything in excess of $1 million that you leave to your grandchildren's generation. In essence, it allows the government to make up for losing the opportunity to levy estate taxes on the middle generation. Like a credit-shelter trust, a generation-skipping trust can be used at the time of death to preserve the $1 million generation-skipping tax exemption for both spouses.[7]

spendthrift trust

Spendthrift Trust   If your beneficiary is too young or unable to handle money wisely, consider a **spendthrift trust.** Here the beneficiary receives small amounts of money at specified intervals. It prevents the beneficiary from squandering money or losing it in a bad investment.

There are still other types of specialized trusts. For example, a *pourover trust* is usually dormant during your lifetime, but it can be activated if you become disabled. It can be used to manage your insurance, qualified pension or profit-sharing plan proceeds, and your probate estate. A *Q-DOT (qualified domestic trust)* is for spouses who are not U.S. citizens. It provides the same marital deduction benefit that is available to citizen spouses. A *GRAT (grantor retained annuity trust)*, a *GRUT (grantor retained unitrust)*, and a *personal residence GRIT (grantor retained income trust)* permit grantors to use favorable rules for determining the amount of gift made to the trust.

Sheet 67

As you can see, trusts are complicated; therefore, you should seek a competent estate attorney in preparing this legal document. The purpose of all types of trusts is to preserve your estate for your heirs.

Estates

As mentioned earlier, your *estate* is everything you own (see Exhibit 19–6) on page 594. It includes all of your property—tangible and intangible, however acquired or owned, whether inside or outside the country. It may include jointly owned property, life insurance and employee benefits, and property you no longer own. Thus, an important step in estate planning is taking inventory of everything you own, such as

1. Cash, checking accounts, savings accounts, CDs, and money market funds.
2. Stocks, bonds (including municipals and U.S. savings bonds), mutual funds, commodity futures, and tax shelters.
3. Life insurance, employee benefits, and annuities.
4. Your home and any other real estate, land and buildings, furniture, and fixtures.

Exhibit 19–6

What Is Your Estate?

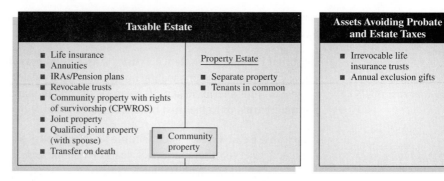

This exhibit shows which assets are included in your probate estate, the much larger number of assets included in your taxable estate, and the very few assets that can avoid both probate and estate taxes.

source: *Planning Your Estate* (A. G. Edwards & Sons, Inc., 1996), p. 6.

5. Farms, grain, livestock, machinery, and equipment.
6. Proprietorship, partnership, and close corporation interests.
7. Notes, accounts, and claims receivable.
8. Interests in trusts and powers of appointment.
9. Antiques, works of art, collections, cars, boats, planes, personal effects, and everything else.

community property

In the community-property states (Arizona, California, Idaho, Louisiana, Nevada, New Mexico, Texas, Wisconsin, and Washington), where each spouse owns 50 percent of the property, half of the community assets are included in each spouse's estate. **Community property** is "any property that has been acquired by either of the spouses during the marriage, but not by gift, devise, bequest or inheritance, or, often, by the income therefrom."[8] In the other, non–community-property states, property is included in the estate of the spouse who owns it. The way you own property can make a tax difference.

Joint Ownership   Joint ownership of property between spouses is very common. Joint ownership may also exist between parents and children, other relatives, or any two or more persons. While joint ownership may avoid *probate* (official proof of a will), creditor attachment, and inheritance taxes in some states, it does not avoid federal estate taxes. In fact, it may increase them.

There are three types of joint ownership, and each has different tax and estate planning consequences. First, if you and your spouse own property as *joint tenants with the right of survivorship (JT/WROS),* the property is considered owned 50–50 for estate tax purposes and will automatically pass to your spouse at your death, and vice versa. No gift tax is paid on creating such ownership, nor, due to the unlimited marital deduction, is any estate tax paid at the first death. However, this type of joint ownership may result in more taxes overall at the surviving spouse's later death than would be the case with a traditional marital share will, discussed earlier.

Second, if you and your spouse or anyone else own property as *tenants in common,* each individual is considered to own a proportionate share for tax purposes, and only your share is included in your estate. That share does not go to the other tenants in common at your death but is included in your probate estate and subject to your decision as to who gets it. While there are no gift or estate tax consequences between spouse joint owners, gifts of joint interests to children or others can create taxation.

Tenancy by the entirety, the third type of joint ownership, is limited to married couples. Under this type of joint ownership, both spouses own the property; when one spouse dies, the other gets it automatically. Neither spouse may sell the property without the consent of the other.

Joint ownership is a poor substitute for a will. It gives you less control over the disposition and taxation of your property. Your state laws govern the types and effects of joint ownership. Some states require that survivorship rights be spelled out in the deed, or at least abbreviated (for example, JT/WROS). Only your attorney can advise you on these matters.

Financial Decision
Trade-Off

Life Insurance and Employee Benefits   Life insurance proceeds are free of income tax, excluded from probate, and wholly or partially exempt from most state inheritance taxes. These proceeds are included in your estate for federal estate tax purposes if the policy contains any incidents of ownership such as the right to change beneficiaries, surrender the policy for cash, or make loans on the policy.

Assignment of ownership to your beneficiary or a trust can remove a life insurance policy from your estate. But if your spouse is the intended beneficiary, you do not need to assign ownership, since the proceeds will be free of estate tax due to the marital deduction.

Death benefits from qualified pension, profit-sharing, or Keogh plans are excluded from your estate unless they are payable to it or unless your beneficiary elects the special provision for averaging income tax in lump-sum distributions.

If there is "too much" money in your qualified retirement plan when you and your spouse die, your heirs could lose up to 80 percent in federal and state income taxes, estate tax, and the "excess accumulation" tax. Proper estate planning can minimize such confiscatory taxes.[9]

Lifetime Gifts and Trusts   Gifts or trusts with strings attached, such as retaining the income, use, or control of the property, are fully included at their date-of-death value, whether your rights are expressed or implied. For example, if you transfer title of your home to a child but continue to live in it, the home is taxed in your estate. Or if you put property in trust and retain a certain amount of control over the income or principal, the property is included in your estate even though you cannot obtain it yourself. Also, if you are the beneficiary of a trust established by someone else and you have general rights to the principal during life or the power to appoint it to anyone at death, that amount is included in your estate.

Settling Your Estate

If you have had a will drawn, you are *testate* in the eyes of the law, and an executor (named in your will) will carry out your wishes in due time. If you have not named an executor, the probate court (the court that supervises the distribution of estates) will appoint an administrator to carry out the instructions in your will.

If you don't have a will, you become *intestate* at your death. In that case, your estate is put under the control of a court-appointed administrator for distribution according to the laws of the state in which you reside.

CONCEPT CHECK 19–4

1. Differentiate among the 12 types of trusts.
2. What is included in an estate?
3. What are the three types of joint ownership?

Exhibit 19–7	Gross Estate	Settlement Costs	Net Estate	Percent Shrinkage
The Erosion of Probate and Estate Taxes				
Elvis Presley	$10,165,434	$ 7,374,635	$ 2,790,799	73%
John D. Rockefeller	26,905,182	17,124,988	9,780,194	64
Clark Gable	2,806,526	1,101,038	1,705,488	39
Walt Disney	23,004,851	6,811,943	16,192,908	30

SOURCE: Public court records, state probate courts.

FEDERAL AND STATE ESTATE TAXES

L.O.5 Evaluate the effects of federal and state taxes on estate planning.

The tax aspects of estate planning have changed considerably due to recent major changes in the federal tax structure. The maximum tax rate on estates and gifts, for example, is gradually declining. As Exhibit 19–7 shows, estate settlement costs can quickly deplete an estate.

You can reduce your taxable estate by giving away assets to anyone during your lifetime. (But don't give away assets just to reduce your estate tax liability if you may need those assets in your retirement.) No gift tax is due on gifts of up to $10,000 to any one person in any one year. (A married couple, acting together, may give up to $20,000 to one person in one year.)

For example, suppose that on January 2, 1998, Michael gave $10,000 worth of shares of a stock mutual fund to his son. On January 2, 2008, these shares are worth $50,000. As a result of this gift in 1998, Michael has removed from his estate the $10,000 gift plus $40,000 of appreciation, for a total of $50,000. All of this has been accomplished at no gift tax cost.

Types of Taxes

Federal and state governments levy various types of taxes that you must consider in planning your estate. The four major taxes of this kind are estate taxes, estate and trust income taxes, inheritance taxes, and gift taxes.

estate tax

Estate Taxes   An **estate tax** is a federal tax levied on the right of a deceased person to transmit his or her property and life insurance at death. Estate taxes have undergone extensive revision since the mid-1970s. The Economic Recovery Tax Act of 1981 made important tax concessions, particularly the unlimited marital deduction and the increased exemption equivalent shown in Exhibit 19–8 on page 597.

Under present law, with intelligent estate planning and properly drawn wills, you may leave all of your property to your surviving spouse free of federal estate taxes. The surviving spouse's estate in excess of $625,000 (in 1998) faces estate taxes of from 37 to 55 percent.

All limits have been removed from transfers between spouses during their lifetimes as well as at death. Whatever you give your spouse is exempt from gift and estate taxes. Gift tax returns need not be filed for interspousal gifts. There is still the possibility, however, that such gifts will be included in your estate if they were given within three years of your death.

DID YOU KNOW?

Just in the next five years, people will pay $100 billion of estate taxes.

SOURCE: American Society of CLU & ChFC, September 1997.

Estate and Trust Federal Income Taxes   In addition to the federal estate tax, estates and certain trusts must file federal income tax returns with the Internal Revenue Service. Generally, taxable income for estates and trusts is computed in much the same

EXHIBIT 19–8

Unified Estate and Gift Tax Schedule

As of 1997, each individual is entitled to a unified credit of $192,800, which is the amount of tax generated by a transfer of $600,000. In other words, no estate or gift taxes are assessed on the first $600,000 of a person's combined taxable gifts and transfers at death.

Taxable Estate

Over	Not Over	Pay	Percentage on Excess
$ 0	$ 10,000	$ 0	18
10,000	20,000	1,800	20
20,000	40,000	3,800	22
40,000	60,000	8,200	24
60,000	80,000	13,000	26
80,000	100,000	18,200	28
100,000	150,000	23,800	30
150,000	250,000	38,800	32
250,000	500,000	70,800	34
500,000	750,000	155,800	37
750,000	1,000,000	248,300	39
1,000,000	1,250,000	345,800	41
1,250,000	1,500,000	448,300	43
1,500,000	2,000,000	555,800	45
2,000,000	2,500,000	780,800	49
2,500,000	3,000,000	1,025,800	53
3,000,000 and over		1,290,800	55

Example:

Taxable estate	$1,000,000
Gross tax	345,800
Less credit	−192,800
Net tax due	$153,000

Unified Estate and Gift Tax Credit

Tax Credit	Equivalent Estate
$192,800	$600,000

manner as taxable income for individuals. Under the Tax Reform Act of 1986, trusts and estates must pay quarterly estimated taxes, and new trusts must use the calendar year as the tax year.

inheritance tax

Inheritance Taxes   An **inheritance tax** is levied on the right of an heir to receive all or part of the estate and life insurance proceeds of a deceased person. The tax payable depends on the net value of the property and insurance received. It also depends on the relationship of the heir to the deceased.

Inheritance taxes are imposed only by the state governments. Most states levy an inheritance tax, but the state laws differ widely as to exemptions, rates of taxation, and the treatment of property and life insurance. A reasonable average for state inheritance taxes would be 4 to 10 percent of your estate, with the higher percentages on larger amounts.

Over the past few years, many states have been phasing out their inheritance tax provisions, usually over a period of three or four years. This apparently reflects a desire to retain older and wealthy citizens as residents and to discourage them from leaving the states where they have lived most of their lives to seek tax havens in states such as Florida and Nevada. Increasingly, state legislatures have been questioning the equity of further taxes at death and are opting instead for sales and income taxes to provide state revenues.

gift tax

Gift Taxes   The federal and state governments levy a **gift tax** on the privilege of making gifts to others. A property owner can avoid estate and inheritance taxes by giving property during his or her lifetime. For this reason, the federal tax laws provide for taxes on gifts of property. The tax rates on gifts used to be only 75 percent of the tax rates on estates, but since 1976 the gift tax rates have been the same as the estate tax rates. Indeed, the tax rates are now called *unified transfer tax rates*.

Many states have gift tax laws. The state gift tax laws are similar to the federal gift tax laws, but the exemptions and dates for filing returns vary widely among the states.

As discussed earlier, the federal gift tax allows you to give up to $10,000 each year to any person without incurring gift tax liability or having to report the gift to the IRS. Note that the Taxpayer Relief Act of 1997 increased this amount in $1,000 increments, depending on rates of inflation in future years. Gifts from a husband or a wife to a third party are considered as having been made in equal amounts by each spouse. Consequently, a husband and wife may give as much as $20,000 per year to anyone without incurring tax liability.

Tax Avoidance and Tax Evasion

A poorly arranged estate may be subject to unduly large taxation. Therefore, you should study the tax laws and seek advice to avoid estate taxes larger than those the lawmakers intended you to pay. You should have a clear idea of the distinction between tax avoidance and tax evasion. *Tax avoidance* is the use of legal methods to reduce or escape taxes; *tax evasion* is the use of illegal methods to reduce or escape taxes.

Charitable Gifts and Bequests   Gifts made to certain recognized charitable or educational organizations are exempt from gift, estate, and inheritance taxes. Accordingly, such gifts or bequests (gifts through a will) represent one method of reducing or avoiding estate and inheritance taxes.

Calculation of Tax

The estate tax is applied not to your total gross estate but to your net taxable estate at death. *Net taxable estate* is your testamentary net worth after subtracting your debts, liabilities, probate costs, and administration costs. These items, all of which are taken off your estate before calculating your tax, are cash requirements to be paid by your estate. The Financial Planning Calculations feature on page 599 provides additional examples of figuring estate taxes.

Debts and Liabilities   In arriving at your taxable estate, the amount of your debts and other creditor obligations are subtracted. You are liable for the payment of these debts while living; your estate will be liable at your death. Your debts may include mortgages, collateralized loans, margin accounts, bank loans, notes payable, installment and charge accounts, and accrued income and property taxes. They may also include your last-illness and funeral expenses.

Probate and Administration Costs   Your estate administration costs will include fees for attorneys, accountants, appraisers, executors or administrators and trustees, court costs, bonding and surety costs, and miscellaneous expenses. These administration costs

FINANCIAL PLANNING CALCULATIONS

SAVING ON ESTATE AND GIFT TAXES THROUGH TRUSTS

Example 1 in the table below demonstrates how, upon the death of the surviving spouse, only one unified credit—that of the surviving spouse—will remain to offset the estate tax. The strategy in example 2 produces no estate tax on the first estate and reduces the surviving spouse's potential estate tax by the amount of property in this trust. This trust is known as a *credit-shelter* or *bypass trust*.

Example 1: $2,600,000 Estate

All to spouse (used full marital deduction in first estate)

First estate (deceased):	
Gross estate	$2,600,000
Marital deduction	(2,600,000)
Taxable estate	0
Tentative estate tax	0
Final tax	0
Second estate (surviving spouse):	
Gross estate	$2,600,000
Marital deduction	0
Taxable estate	2,600,000
Tentative estate tax	1,078,800
Estate tax credit	(192,800)
Final tax	886,000
Combined estate taxes	$ 886,000

Example 2: $2,000,000 Outright and in Trust to Spouse, $600,000 to Bypass Trust

Optimal marital deduction

First estate (deceased):	
Gross estate	$2,600,000
Marital deduction	(2,000,000)
Taxable estate	600,000
Tentative estate tax	$ 192,800
Estate tax credit	(192,800)
Final tax	0
Second estate:	
Gross estate	$2,000,000
Marital deduction	0
Taxable estate	$2,000,000
Tentative estate tax	780,800
Estate tax credit	(192,800)
Final tax	588,000
Combined estate taxes	588,000
Tax savings	$ 298,000

SOURCE: David Gerson and Charles Cangro, "Estate & Gift Tax: The Real Tax Problem," *Fundsfocus,* Neuberger Berman Management Inc., Fall 1994, p. 2.

---

may run 5 to 8 percent of your estate, depending on its size and complexity. While the percentage usually decreases as the size of the estate increases, it may be increased by additional complicating factors, such as handling a business interest.

Next, deductions are made for bequests to qualified charities and for property passing to your spouse (the marital deduction). That leaves your net taxable estate, to which the rates shown in Exhibit 19–8 on page 597 are applied to determine your gross estate tax.

Inheritance and estate taxes in your own state are additional costs, and these costs are not deductible in arriving at your taxable estate. In fact, you may have to pay inheritance taxes in two or more states, depending on the location of your property.

Paying the Tax

If, after having used various estate tax reduction techniques, you must still pay an estate tax, you should consider the best way to pay it. The federal estate tax is due and payable in cash nine months after your death. State taxes, probate costs, debts, and expenses also usually fall due within that time. These costs can, and often do, result in a real cash bind, because people rarely keep a lot of cash on hand. They derived their wealth from putting their money to work in businesses, real estate, or other investments. Estate liquidity—having enough cash to pay taxes and costs without forced sales of assets or heavy borrowing—is often a problem.

One way to handle the estate tax is to set aside or accumulate enough cash to pay it when it falls due. However, you may die before you have accumulated enough cash, and the cash you accumulate may be subject to income tax during your lifetime and to estate tax at your death.

Another way to handle the estate tax is for your family to sell assets to pay taxes. The first assets to be sold might be stocks, bonds, gold or silver coins, and similar liquid assets. However, these assets may be the source of your family's income after your death, and the market for them may be down. Assets such as real estate may also be sold, but prices on forced sales are usually only a fraction of the fair value.

Your family could consider borrowing; however, it is unusual to find a commercial lender that will lend money to pay back-taxes. If you do find one, it may require personal liability. In any event, borrowing does not solve the problem; it only prolongs it, adding interest costs in the process.

Borrowing from the IRS itself in the form of deferred payments or installments may be possible for reasonable cause. Tax extension and installment payment provisions are helpful, but they still leave a tax debt to be paid by your heirs at your death. Paying that debt, even over an extended period of time, could be a real burden and severely restrict their income and flexibility.

Life insurance may be a reasonable, feasible, and economical means of paying your estate tax. Instead of forcing your family to pay off the estate tax and other debts and costs by borrowing or selling, you can, through insurance, provide your family with tax-free cash at a fraction of the cost of borrowing.

Sheet 68

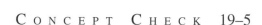

CONCEPT CHECK 19–5

1. What are the four types of taxes to consider in planning your estate?
2. How is estate tax calculated?
3. What are the various ways to handle the payment of estate tax?

SUMMARY

L.O.1 Analyze the personal aspects of estate planning.

Estate planning is an essential part of retirement planning and an integral part of financial planning. The first part of estate planning consists of building your estate; the second part consists of transferring your estate, at your death, in the manner you have specified. The personal aspects of estate planning depend on whether you are single or married. If you are married, your estate planning involves the interests of at least two people, and more if there are children. Never having been married does not eliminate the need to organize your financial affairs.

L.O.2 Assess the legal aspects of estate planning.

In the event of death, proof of claims must be produced or the claims will not be processed. Among the papers needed are birth certificates, marriage certificates, legal name changes, and military service records.

L.O.3 Distinguish among various types and formats of wills.

The four types of wills are the simple will, the traditional marital share will, the exemption trust will, and the stated dollar amount will. A will can be holographic or formal. Which type is best for you depends on your personal and financial circumstances.

L.O.4   Appraise various types of trusts and estates.

Establishing a trust can be an excellent way to manage your estate. Trusts are revocable or irrevocable. Popular forms of trusts include credit-shelter trusts, disclaimer trusts, marital-deduction trusts, living trusts, self-declaration trusts, testamentary trusts, life insurance trusts, charitable remainder trusts, qualified personal residence trusts, charitable lead trusts, generation-skipping trusts, and spendthrift trusts. An attorney's help is needed to establish a trust.

L.O.5   Evaluate the effects of federal and state taxes on estate planning.

The tax aspects of estate planning have changed considerably due to recent major changes in the federal tax structure. The four major federal and state taxes you must consider in planning your estate are estate taxes, estate and trust income taxes, inheritance taxes, and gift taxes.

GLOSSARY

adjusted gross estate   The gross estate minus debts and costs.   (p. 583)

beneficiary   A person who has been named to receive property under a will.   (p. 584)

charitable lead trust   A trust that pays a specified charity income from a donated asset for a set number of years. (p. 593)

charitable remainder trust   A trust in which the creator retains the right to the income but transfers that right to a charity upon his or her death.   (p. 592)

codicil   A document that modifies provisions in an existing will.   (p. 587)

community property   Any property that has been acquired by either spouse during the marriage.   (p. 594)

credit-shelter trust   A trust that allows married couples to leave everything to each other tax free.   (p. 591)

disclaimer trust   A trust designed for a couple who does not yet have enough assets to need a credit-shelter trust but may need one in the future.   (p. 591)

estate   Everything one owns.   (p. 577)

estate planning   A definite plan for the administration and disposition of one's property during one's lifetime and at one's death.   (p. 577)

estate tax   A federal tax on the right of a deceased person to transfer property and life insurance at death.   (p. 596)

exemption trust will   A will in which everything passes to the spouse except the exemption ($600,000 since 1987). (p. 583)

formal will   A will that is usually prepared with an attorney's assistance.   (p. 584)

generation-skipping trust   A trust that transfers a beneficial interest between two generations, where one generation is two or more generations subsequent to that of the creator.   (p. 593)

gift tax   A federal and state tax on the privilege of making gifts to others.   (p. 598)

guardian   A person who assumes responsibility for providing children with personal care and managing the deceased's estate for them.   (p. 586)

holographic will   A handwritten will.   (p. 584)

inheritance tax   A tax levied on the right of an heir to receive an estate.   (p. 597)

intestate   Without a valid will.   (p. 581)

irrevocable trust   A trust that cannot be altered or ended by its creator.   (p. 590)

life insurance trust   A trust whose assets are derived at least in part from the proceeds of life insurance.   (p. 592)

living trust   A trust that is created and provides benefits during the trustor's lifetime.   (p. 591)

living will   A document that enables an individual, while well, to express the intention that life be allowed to end if he or she becomes terminally ill.   (p. 587)

marital-deduction trust   A trust that leaves to the spouse any money that does not go into a credit-shelter trust.   (p. 591)

power of attorney   A legal document authorizing someone to act on one's behalf.   (p. 588)

prenuptial agreement   A documentary agreement between spouses before marriage.   (p. 587)

qualified personal residence trust (QPRT)   A trust that allows you to get your home or a vacation home out of your estate.   (p. 593)

revocable trust   A trust whose terms the trustor retains the right to change.   (p. 590)

self-declaration trust   A variation of the living trust in which the creator of the trust is also the trustee.   (p. 592)

simple will   A will that leaves everything to the spouse; also called an *I love you will*.   (p. 583)

spendthrift trust   A trust that permits the beneficiary to receive small amounts of money at specified intervals. (p. 593)

stated dollar amount will   A will that allows you to pass on to your spouse any amount that satisfies your family objectives.   (p. 584)

statutory will   A formal will on a preprinted form.   (p. 585)

testamentary trust   A trust established by the creator's will that becomes effective upon his or her death.   (p. 592)

traditional marital share will   A will in which the grantor leaves one-half of the adjusted gross estate to the spouse. (p. 583)

trust   A legal arrangement through which one's assets are held by a trustee.   (p. 590)

trustee   A person or an institution that holds or manages property for the benefit of someone else under a trust agreement.   (p. 586)

trustor   The creator of a trust; also called the *grantor*. (p. 590)

will   The legal declaration of a person's mind as to the disposition of his or her property after death.   (p. 581)

REVIEW QUESTIONS

1. Why should all individuals, married or single, engage in estate planning?   (L.O.1)
2. Why is a will an important estate planning tool?   (L.0.2)
3. Discuss the four types of wills, and list advantages and disadvantages of each type. Which type of will is best for you? Why?   (L.O.3)
4. What criteria might you use in selecting an executor? A guardian?   (L.O.3)
5. What is a living will? Who should have a living will? (L.O.3)
6. Distinguish between a revocable and an irrevocable trust. (L.O.4)

7. Discuss the 12 types of trusts. Which type of trust might be most appropriate for you and your family?   (L.O.4)
8. Discuss and distinguish among joint tenancy with the right of survivorship, tenancy in common, and tenancy by the entirety. Is one form of ownership more advantageous than the others? Explain.   (L.O.4)
9. Discuss the four types of taxes you should consider in planning your estate.   (L.O.5)
10. How is estate tax calculated, and when does it become due?   (L.O.5)

FINANCIAL PLANNING PROBLEMS

Refer to Exhibit 19–8 to solve the following problems. (L.O.5)
1. *Calculating Gross Tax, Amount of Credit, and Net Tax.* Bob and Kathy have a taxable estate of $1,500,000.
   a. What is the gross tax on this estate?
   b. What is the amount of credit?
   c. What is the net tax due?
2. *Calculating Gross Tax, Amount of Credit, and Net Tax.* Mike and Karen have a taxable estate of $3 million.
   a. What is the gross tax on this estate?
   b. What is the amount of credit?
   c. What is the net tax due?

3. *Calculating the Gift Tax.* In 1998, Joshua gave $10,000 worth of AT&T stock to his son. In 2008, the AT&T shares are worth $60,000.
   a. What was the gift tax in 1998?
   b. What is the total amount removed from Joshua's estate in 2008?
   c. What will be the gift tax in 2008?
4. *Calculating the Gift Tax.* In 1999, you gave a $10,000 gift to a friend. What is the gift tax?

PROJECTS AND APPLICATION ACTIVITIES

1. *Preparing a Written Record of Personal Information.* Prepare a written record of personal information that would be helpful to you and your heirs. Make sure to include the location of family records, your military service file, and other important papers; medical records; bank accounts; charge accounts; the location of your safe deposit box; U.S. savings bonds; stocks, bonds, and other securities; property owned; life insurance; annuities; and Social Security information.   (L.O.1)
2. *Developing Long-Term Estate Planning Goals.* Develop a list of specific long-term estate planning goals with your family. Discuss how those goals could be achieved even if you or your spouse died unexpectedly.   (L.O.1)

3. *Drafting a Simple Will.* Draft your simple will, using Exhibit 19–1 as a guideline. Whom will you appoint as a trustee or guardian for your minor children? Why? (L.O.2)
4. *Comparing Costs of Preparing a Will.* Contact several lawyers in your area to find out how much they would charge to prepare your simple will. Are their fees about the same?   (L.O.3)
5. *Using the Internet to Obtain Information about Wills.* Visit Metropolitan Life Insurance Company's Web page at http://www.lifeadvice.com. Using this information, prepare a report on the following: *(a)* Who needs a will? *(b)* elements of a will, naming a

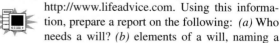

guardian, naming an executor, preparing a will, updating a will, estate taxes, where to keep your will, living will, etc.; *(c)* how is this report helpful in preparing your own will.

6. *Preparing the Letter of Last Instructions.* Prepare your own letter of last instructions.   (L.O.3)

7. *Determining Criteria in Choosing a Guardian.* Make a list of the criteria you will use in deciding who will be the guardian of your minor children if you and your spouse die at the same time.   (L.O.3)

8. *Using the Internet to Obtain Information about Estate Planning.* Visit the Prudential Insurance Company of America Web site at http://prudential.com/ estateplan. Gather information on various estate planning topics such as an estate planning worksheet; whether you need an estate plan; when to update your plan; estate taxes, wills, executors, trusts, etc. Then prepare a report to help you develop your estate plan.   (L.O.4)

9. *Establishing a Trust.* Discuss with your attorney the possibility of establishing a trust as a means of managing your estate.   (L.O.4)

10. *Obtaining Information from Your State Department of Revenue.* Ask your state department of revenue for brochures on state inheritance and gift taxes. What are the exemptions and rates of taxes? How are your property and life insurance treated for the purpose of inheritance tax? Of gift tax?   (L.O.5)

LIFE SITUATION CASE 19

ESTATE PLANNING FOR KURT AND CHRISTINE

Kurt and Christine Christoffer are concerned about what will happen to their estate when they are no longer around. Kurt is 75 and has been retired for the past 10 years. A successful pharmaceutical sales representative for a major company, Kurt worked hard, saved money, and invested wisely.

Kurt is worried about how Christine will manage after he dies. He is also concerned about his three married children and his grandchildren. Kurt's will, which he recently brought up to date, leaves everything to Christine. The three children are considered to be contingent beneficiaries. If anything happens to Christine, the estate will be shared equally among the three children.

Kurt has tried to establish the value of their estate. The residence is worth $500,000 according to an appraisal by a real estate agent a few months ago. They still have a $50,000 mortgage, however, so the actual net value of the home is $450,000. The Christoffers own a vacation home in Wisconsin worth approximately $150,000; this property has no mortgage. Kurt carries life insurance to provide liquid funds for his wife and family. He owns $200,000 in term and $150,000 in whole life insurance. The Christoffers have about $50,000 in savings accounts and certificates of deposit. According to Christine, their family assets, consisting of silver, china, crystal, antiques, and furniture, are worth about $200,000. In total, the Christoffers' taxable estate is $1,350,000.

QUESTIONS

1. What estate tax will the Christoffers' estate have to pay to the federal government?

2. On the basis of the estate tax that Kurt's estate may have to pay now and on the tax Christine's estate may have to pay later, would you advise Kurt to establish a trust that would reduce the amount of taxes that both estates will have to pay?

USING THE INTERNET TO CREATE A PERSONAL FINANCIAL PLAN 19

DEVELOPING AN ESTATE PLAN

Most people do not think they have enough assets to do estate planning. However, the planned transfer of resources with the use of a will, trusts, and other legal vehicles is a necessary phase of your total financial plan.

Web Sites for Estate Planning

■ Estate planning information at **www.webtrust.com**
■ Wills and estate planning information at **www.nolo.com** and at **www.mtpalermo.com**

■ Federal estate tax information at **www.irs.ustreas.gov**
■ Estate tax information at **www.lifenet.com/estate**
■ Current estate planning articles from *Money* magazine at **www.money.com,** from *Kiplinger's Personal Finance* magazine at **www.kiplinger.com,** *Business Week* at **www. businessweek.com,** *Worth* magazine at **www.worth.com,** and *Smart Money* at **www.smartmoney.com**

(Note: Addresses and content of Web sites change, and new sites are created daily. Use the search engines discussed in Appendix B to update and locate Web sites for your current financial planning needs.)

PFP SHEETS: 65–68

Short-Term Financial Planning Activities

1. Investigate the cost of a will. Decide on the type of will and provisions appropriate for your life situation (see PFP Sheet 66).
2. Using the IRS and other Web sites, identify recent estate tax law changes that may affect your financial planning decisions.

3. Compare the benefits and costs of different trusts that might be appropriate for your life situation (see PFP Sheet 67).

Long-Term Financial Planning Activities

1. Develop a plan for actions to be taken related to estate planning (see PFP Sheet 65).
2. Identify saving and investing decisions that would minimize future estate taxes (see PFP Sheet 68).

CONTINUOUS CASE FOR PART VI

PLANNING FOR TOMORROW

Life Situation
Pam, 48; Josh, 50; children ages 21, 19, and 16

Financial Goals
- Replenish savings used for college costs
- Plan for retirement in about 15 years
- Consider estate planning activities

Financial Data

Monthly income	$ 5,700
Living expenses	4,600
Assets	242,500
Liabilities	69,100

With two children in college, the Brocks once again find their life situation changing. Compared to five years ago, their total assets have decreased from $262,700 to $242,500 due to college expenses. The Brocks' oldest child will graduate next year, but the youngest will enter college in a couple of years. Therefore, the drain on the family's finances will continue.

The family's finances are adequate, but both Pam and Josh are beginning to worry about retirement. Over the years, Josh has taken advantage of different career opportunities. Today his annual salary, $68,400, is higher than it has ever been. But his employment changes have resulted in a smaller pension fund than would be available had he remained with the same organization. The current value of his pension plan is just over $115,000. The

investment program he and Pam started almost 10 years ago is growing and is now worth about $62,000. But they still worry whether they will have enough money to finance their retirement dreams when Josh retires in 15 years. According to Josh, "If I retired today, we couldn't maintain our current lifestyle. In fact, we couldn't even exist."

QUESTIONS
1. How would you rate the Brocks' financial condition at this stage in their lives?
2. Given that Pam is 48 and Josh is 50, what should be their major priorities as they continue planning for retirement?
3. What types of estate planning, if any, should the Brocks consider at this time?

APPENDIXES

A

APPENDIX A

USING A FINANCIAL PLANNER AND OTHER FINANCIAL PLANNING INFORMATION SOURCES

"ATM fees rise"

"Global currency fluctuations may affect consumer prices."

"Mortgage interest rates remain constant."

These are just a few of the possible influences on personal financial decisions that may occur each day. While this book offers the foundation you need for successful personal financial planning, changing social trends, economic conditions, and technology influence the decision-making environment. Your ability to continually supplement and update your knowledge is a skill that will serve you for a lifetime.

Various resources are available to assist you with personal financial decisions. These resources include printed materials, financial institutions, courses and seminars, the Internet and computer software, and financial planning specialists.

PRINTED MATERIALS

As Exhibit A–1 shows, a variety of personal finance periodicals are available to expand and update your knowledge. These periodicals, along with books on various personal finance topics, can be found in libraries.

In addition to these sources, a vast number of specialized publications are available. Financial planning newsletters key in on specific topics such as mutual funds, commodity investments, low-priced stocks, real estate investments, tax planning, and investments in gold and coins. You can find a newsletter on almost any financial area of interest to you.

As with any purchase, determine whether the amount you pay for a newsletter will provide an appropriate benefit. The financial newsletter industry is unregulated, and many publishers promise much more than they deliver. Not all investment services offer better information than other, less expensive resources. Request a sample copy of any newsletter before you subscribe.

E X H I B I T   A – 1   **Personal Financial Planning Periodicals**

The area of personal finance is constantly changing. You can keep up with changes by reading the following periodicals. You can subscribe to them, read them at your school or community library, or access them on the Internet.

Bottom Line/Personal
Box 1027
Milburn, NJ 07041
Web site: www.boardroom.com

Business Week
1221 Avenue of the Americas
New York, NY 10020
Web site: www.businessweek.com

Consumers Digest
5705 North Lincoln Ave.
Chicago, IL 60659
Web site:
    www.consumersdigest.com

Consumer Reports
Consumers Union
101 Truman Avenue
Yonkers, NY 10703-1057
Web site:
    www.consumerreports.org

Forbes
60 Fifth Avenue
New York, NY 10011
Web site: www.forbes.com

Fortune
Time & Life Building
Rockefeller Center
New York, NY 10020-1393
Web site: www.fortune.com

Kiplinger's Personal Finance
    Magazine
1729 H Street, NW
Washington, DC 20006
Web site: www.kiplinger.com

Money
Time & Life Building
Rockefeller Center
New York, NY 10020-1393
Web site: www.money.com

Smart Money
224 West 57th Street
New York, NY 10019
Web site: www.smartmoney.com

U.S. News & World Report
2400 N Street, NW
Washington, DC 20037-1196
Web site: www.usnews.com

The Wall Street Journal
200 Burnett Road
Chicopee, MA 01020
Web site: www.wsj.com

Worth
575 Lexington Avenue
New York, NY 10022
Web site: www.worth.com

FINANCIAL INSTITUTIONS

Some financial advisers, such as insurance agents and investment brokers, are affiliated with companies that sell financial services. Through national marketing efforts or local promotions, banks, savings and loan associations, credit unions, insurance companies, investment brokers, and real estate offices offer suggestions on budgeting, saving, investing, and other aspects of financial planning. These organizations may offer booklets, financial planning worksheets, Web sites, and other materials and information.

COURSES AND SEMINARS

Colleges and universities offer courses in investments, real estate, insurance, taxation, and estate planning that will enhance your knowledge of personal financial planning. The Cooperative Extension Service, funded through the U.S. Department of Agriculture, has offices located at universities in every state and in many counties (see your local telephone directory). Programs of these offices include community seminars and continuing education courses in the areas of family financial management, housing, consumer purchasing, health care, and food and nutrition. In addition, Cooperative Extension Service offices offer a variety of publications, videos, and software to assist consumers.

Civic clubs and community business organizations often schedule free or inexpensive programs featuring speakers and workshops on career planning, small-business management, budgeting, life insurance, tax return preparation, and investments. Financial institutions and financial service trade associations present seminars for current and prospective customers and members.

THE INTERNET AND SOFTWARE

The World Wide Web is becoming the most readily available information source in our society. When you sit down at your computer, you are able to get everything from money management tips and current interest rates to stock market quotes and sample wills.

Many personal financial planning software programs are on the market. Popular programs include *Managing Your Money, MS Money,* and *Quicken.* These programs help you analyze your current financial situation and project your future financial position. Specialized computer programs are also available for conducting investment analyses, preparing tax returns, and determining the costs of financing and owning a home. Remember, a personal computer cannot change your saving, spending, and borrowing habits; only *you* can do that. However, your computer can provide fast and current analyses of your financial situation and progress.

For further information on these topics, see Appendix B, "Technology for Personal Financial Planning: The Internet and Software."

FINANCIAL PLANNING SPECIALISTS

Various specialists can provide specific financial assistance and advice:

- *Accountants* specialize in tax matters and financial documents.
- *Bankers* assist with financial services and trusts.
- *Credit counselors* suggest ways to reduce spending and eliminate credit problems.
- *Certified financial planners* coordinate financial decisions into a single plan.
- *Insurance agents* sell insurance coverage to protect your wealth and property.
- *Investment brokers* provide information and handle transactions for stocks, bonds, and other investments.
- *Lawyers* help in preparing wills, estate planning, tax problems, and other legal matters.
- *Real estate agents* assist with buying and selling a home or other real estate.
- *Tax preparers* specialize in the completion of income tax returns and other tax matters.

In recent years, many of these specialists have expanded their services to include various aspects of financial planning. A financial planner's background or the company he or she represents is a good gauge of the financial planner's principal area of expertise. An accountant is likely to be most knowledgeable about tax laws, while an insurance company representative will probably emphasize how you can use insurance to achieve your financial goals.

Since many people devote much of their time to earning or using their income, many are unable to give their personal financial planning close attention. Financial planners can help you establish and accomplish financial goals by coordinating your financial decisions. These individuals operate under a variety of titles, such as *financial adviser, financial counselor,* and *money manager.*

Before employing the services of a financial planner, consider who the financial planners are, whether you need one, how to select one, and how financial planners are certified.

Who Are the Financial Planners?

Many financial planners represent major insurance companies or investment businesses. Financial planners may also be individuals whose primary profession is tax accounting, real estate, or law. Approximately 250,000 people call themselves financial planners. Financial planners are commonly categorized based on the four ways in which they are compensated:

1. **Fee-only planners** charge an hourly rate that may range from $75 to $200, or may charge a fixed fee of between less than $500 and several thousand dollars. Other fee-only planners may charge an annual fee ranging from .04 percent to 1 percent of the value of your assets.
2. **Fee-offset planners** start with an hourly fee or an annual fee. This charge is reduced by any commission earned from the sale of investments or insurance.
3. **Fee-and-commission planners** earn commissions from the investment and insurance products purchased and charge a fixed fee (ranging from $250 to $2,000) for a financial plan.
4. **Commission-only planners** receive their revenue from the commissions on sales of insurance, mutual funds, and other investments.

Consumers must be cautious about the fees charged and how these fees are communicated. A study by the Consumer Federation of America revealed that more than half of financial planners who told "mystery shoppers" that they offer "fee-only" services actually earned commissions or other financial rewards for implementing the recommendations made to their clients.

Do You Need a Financial Planner?

The two main factors that determine whether you need financial planning assistance are (1) your income and (2) your willingness to make independent decisions. If you earn less than $40,000 a year, you probably do not need a financial planner. Income of less than this amount does not allow for many major financial decisions once you have allocated for the spending, savings, insurance, and tax elements of your personal financial planning.

Taking an active role in your financial affairs can also reduce the need for a financial planner. Your willingness to keep up to date on developments related to investments, insurance, and taxes can reduce the amount of money you spend on financial advisers. This will require an ongoing investment of time and effort; however, it will enable you to control your own financial direction.

When deciding whether to use a financial planner, also consider the services he or she provides. First, the financial planner should assist you in assessing your current financial position with regard to spending, saving, insurance, taxes, and potential investments. Second, the financial planner should offer a clearly written plan with different courses of action. Third, the planner should take time to discuss the components of the plan and help you monitor your financial progress. Finally, the financial planner should guide you to other experts and sources of financial services as needed.

You may not always receive specific advice from a financial planner. Those who charge a flat fee may not give specific investment recommendations. Some consider this approach more objective than commission-based planners who promote products that increase their earnings.

How Should You Select a Financial Planner?

You can locate financial planners by using a telephone directory, contacting financial institutions, or obtaining references from friends, business associates, or professionals with whom you currently deal, such as insurance agents or real estate brokers.

When evaluating a financial planner, ask the following:

- Is financial planning your primary activity, or are other activities primary?
- Are you licensed as an investment broker or as a seller of life insurance?
- What is your educational background and formal training?
- What are your areas of expertise?
- Do you use experts in other areas, such as taxes, law, or insurance, to assist you with financial planning recommendations?
- What professional titles and certification do you possess?
- Am I allowed a free initial consultation?
- How is the fee determined? (Is this amount something you can afford?)
- Do you have an independent practice, or are you affiliated with a major financial services company?
- What are sample insurance, tax, and investment recommendations you make for clients?
- My major concern is _____. What would you suggest?
- May I see a sample of a written financial plan?
- May I see the contract you use with clients?
- Who are some of your clients whom I might contact?

Also, make sure you are comfortable with the planner and that the planner can clearly communicate. This type of investigation takes time and effort; however, remember that you are considering placing your entire financial future in the hands of one person.

How Are Financial Planners Certified?

While state and federal regulation of financial planners is expanding, the requirements for becoming a financial planner can vary from state to state. For example, Kansas requires that new financial advisers pass an exam that measures knowledge of stocks, bonds, and other investment products. Some states license individual investment advisers; in other states, firms are licensed but not individual advisers. A few states regulate neither individual advisers nor firms. Recent federal regulation requires that the largest financial advisers be monitored by the Securities and Exchange Commission.

Many financial planners use abbreviations for the titles they have earned. Some of these abbreviations are quite familiar, for example, CPA (certified public accountant), JD (doctor of law), and MBA (master of business administration); others include CFP (Certified Financial Planner), ChFC (Chartered Financial Consultant, in the life insurance industry), PFS (Personal Financial Specialist), AFC (Accredited Financial Counselor), CFA (Chartered Financial Analyst, handling stock and bond portfolios), AEP (Accredited Estate Planner), CRP (Certified Retirement Planner), RIA (Registered Investment Adviser, registered with SEC), EA (Enrolled Agent, tax specialist), and RFC (Registered Financial Consultant).

While these credentials provide some assurance of expertise, not all planners are licensed. The Better Business Bureau estimates that fraudulent planners take consumers for tens of millions of dollars in bad investments and advice each year. Financial planning activities such as insurance and investment security sales do come under regulatory control. Consumers should be wary of and investigate any financial planning action they are considering.

The following organizations and agencies may be contacted for further information about certification and regulation of financial planners:

- National Association of Personal Financial Advisors at 1–888–333–6659 (Web site: www.napfa.org).
- Certified Financial Planners Board of Standards at 1–888–273–6275 (Web site: www.cfpboard.org).
- International Association for Financial Planning at 1–800–945–4237 (Web site: www.iafp.org).
- Institute of Certified Financial Planners at 1–800–282–7526 (Web site: www.icfp.org).
- North American Securities Administrators Association at 1–888–-846–2722 (Web site: www.nassa.org).
- National Association of Insurance Commissioners at 816–842–3600 (Web site: www.naic.org).
- Securities and Exchange Commission at 1-800-732-0330 (Web site: www.sec.gov).
- American Institute of Certified Public Accountants at 1–800–862–4272 (Web site: www.aicpa.org).

HOW HELPFUL ARE COMPUTERIZED FINANCIAL PLANS?

Computerized financial plans can be an inexpensive alternative to using a financial planner. This low-priced advice can provide an appropriate financial direction. While the cost of a financial planner can range from a couple of hundred to several thousand dollars, computerized assistance ranges in price from nothing at all to a few hundred dollars.

Computerized financial advice may be available from many organizations. Investment brokers, insurance companies, and other financial institutions offer computerized financial evaluations and recommendations. For companies with a financial product to sell, computerized financial plans serve to attract new customers. Clients may have the option to meet with a company representative to interpret results. Again, beware of bias toward insurance or specific types of investments that may have been built into the computerized plan.

Despite drawbacks, computerized financial plans can have value. You are usually under no obligation to purchase products or services. The printed report assesses your current financial position and suggests actions you can take. You are not likely to get a lot of specific information, since this type of financial plan is designed to provide general advice for reaching financial goals.

WHAT CAREER OPPORTUNITIES ARE AVAILABLE IN PERSONAL FINANCE?

As you learn to handle your personal finances, you may wish to use your money management skills for a financial planning career. Employment in this field will require a basic knowledge of insurance, taxes, investments, and estate planning. Also important will be business subjects such as accounting, economics, and marketing, plus strong speaking, writing, and computer skills.

Your employment in financial planning may start with experience as a stockbroker, insurance agent, bank officer, or accountant. As your practical background increases, you can get involved as a personal financial planner through your employer, or you can start your own service. The field of financial services is creating a demand for people who desire to help others analyze and plan their finances. For further information about a career in financial planning, contact the organizations listed above.

APPENDIX B

TECHNOLOGY FOR PERSONAL FINANCIAL PLANNING: THE INTERNET AND SOFTWARE

"Let me e-mail you the latest mortgage rates that were on the Internet." A few years ago, this statement would have made no sense. Today, however, such statements are a routine part of our daily conversations.

Technology has evolved from room-size computers that process data in hours to notebook computers that allow instant retrieval of stock market prices from virtually any location. Personal computers can make personal financial decisions and recordkeeping more efficient. Improvements in technology have lowered prices of computers and made available software to help people budget, plan investments, and file their taxes by computer.

THE INTERNET

The foundation of computer network communications is the Internet. This "information highway" connects schools, government agencies, businesses, and homes through a global computer system. The main features of the Internet include:

- *E-mail,* which lets you send messages electronically from one computer to another.
- The *World Wide Web,* which allows you to browse through text, graphics, video clips, and sound bites from thousands of information sources.
- *Gophers,* computer sites with search programs run by companies and universities that give you easy access to library files and other databases.
- *FTP* (file transfer protocol), used to retrieve text files or download software from electronic libraries.
- *Discussion forums and message boards,* which allow people with similar interests to post questions and comments.

Most people access the Internet through their homes or another access site, such as a school or business location.

Several commercial online services are available to help you with personal financial planning activities. The cost of these services ranges from $12 to $20 per month. Most online services provide a wide variety of other services, including access to current news and sports, homework hot lines, reference materials, and discussion forums on a wide range of financial, economic, and political topics. Two of the most commonly used online services are

- *America Online* (www.aol.com), which offers a wide range of financial planning services such as investment information, stock quotes, online shopping, and access to recent articles from various personal finance and consumer information magazines. Users may download personal finance programs and obtain information about retirement planning, mutual funds, and portfolio management.
- *CompuServe* (www.compuserve.com) provides access to current stock prices, online shopping, and software for financial planning activities such as calculating net worth, determining loan payments, and researching potential investments. Users may also access various investment and financial planning information sources related to stocks, bonds, mutual funds, and other investments.

THE WORLD WIDE WEB AND PERSONAL FINANCIAL PLANNING

The World Wide Web makes it possible to access more information from your home or office than most libraries offer. You may use the Web for a variety of personal financial planning activities, including (1) researching current financial information; (2) obtaining programs to do financial planning calculations; (3) monitoring current stock and investment values; and (4) asking questions of experts and others through help lines, bulletin board services, and discussion forums. Some of the most useful Web sites providing current information on various personal finance topics include

- Standard and Poor's Personal Wealth at www.personalwealth.com.
- FinanCenter at www.financenter.com/.
- "The Motley Fool" at www.fool.com/.
- The Quicken Web site at www.quicken.com.
- The Cable News Network at cnnfn.com/index.hmtl.
- The Center for Financial Well-Being at www.healthycash.com/center.
- *Money* magazine at www.money.com; *Kiplinger's Personal Finance Magazine* at www.kiplinger.com; and *Business Week* at www.businessweek.com.
- The Federal Reserve System at www.bog.frb.fed.us.

Additional Web sites are offered at the end of each chapter in the "Using the Internet to Create a Personal Financial Plan" feature and on the inside front and back covers of this book.

USING SEARCH ENGINES

A search engine is a Web site that allows a user to locate information related to specfic topics. Some of the most commonly used search engines include

http://www.altavista.digital.com	http://www.excite.com
http://www.hotbot.com	http://www.infoseek.com
http://www.lycos.com	http://www.northernlight.com
http://www.search.com	http://www.webcrawler.com
http://www.yahoo.com	http://www.mamma.com

Various search engines operate in different manners and provide various features. Some search engines look for topic areas; others seek specific words. When conducting Web searches, be precise with your descriptive words. For example, use "mortgage rates" instead of "interest rates" to obtain information on the cost of borrowing to buy a home. Use "resumes" instead of "career planning" for assistance on developing a personal data sheet.

Searches may also be focused using the following descriptors:

- *consumer credit* will give you every document containing the words *consumer* or *credit.* (This resulted in 4,637,742 Web sites using an AltaVista search.)
- *consumer +credit* will provide documents containing both *consumer* and *credit.* (This resulted in 25,940 Web sites in an AltaVista search.)
- "consumer credit" will present only the documents in which the words *consumer credit* appear together. (This resulted in 28,769 Web sites.)
- "consumer credit laws" will provide a more precise search of documents about consumer credit laws. (This resulted in 218 Web sites.)

PERSONAL FINANCE SOFTWARE

Personal computer software is available to help you perform a variety of personal financial planning activities, from selecting a career to writing a will. Most specialized personal finance programs are available in a CD-ROM format as well as on disks. For information about the latest software, visit a computer store or read the articles and advertisements in magazines such as *PC Computing, PC Magazine, Computer Life, Windows, Family PC,* and *Home PC.*

Spreadsheets

A spreadsheet program such as Lotus 1-2-3, Excel, or Quattro can assist with various financial planning tasks. Spreadsheet software can store, manipulate, create projections, and report data for activities such as

- Creating budget categories and recording spending patterns.
- Maintaining tax records for different types of expenses, such as mileage, travel expenses, materials and supplies, and business-related costs.
- Calculating the growth potential of savings accounts and investments.
- Monitoring changes in the market value of investments.
- Keeping records of the value of items for a home inventory.
- Projecting needed amounts of life insurance and retirement income.

Money Management and Financial Planning Programs

Several integrated programs can help you maintain home financial records, create a budget, observe spending patterns, write checks, keep tax records, select and monitor investments, and project retirement needs. The most popular of these software packages include

Managing Your Money	*MS Money*	*Quicken*
MECA Software	Microsoft	Intuit
1–800–537–9993	1–800–426–9400	1-800-446-8848
(www.mymnet.com)	(www.microsoft.com)	(www.quicken.com)

Tax Software

Each year the software available to prepare federal and state tax returns becomes more helpful. Besides preparation and printing of the various forms and schedules, programs include tax-planning tips (with audio and video clips), audit warnings, and the ability to file your tax return electronically. Some of the most readily available tax software includes

TurboTax	*Kiplinger's TaxCut*
Quicken	Kiplinger
1–800–446–8848	1–800–235–4060
(www.turbotax.com)	(www.taxcut.com)

Investment Analysis Programs

Software designed for researching, trading, and monitoring an investment portfolio is also available. Most of these programs may be connected to online services to obtain current stock quotes and to buy and sell investments.

APPENDIX C

THE TIME VALUE OF MONEY
Future Value and Present Value Computations

"If I deposit $10,000 today, how much will I have for a down payment on a house in five years?"

"Will $2,000 saved a year give me enough money when I retire?"

"How much must I save today to have enough for my children's college education?"

As introduced in Chapter 1 and used to measure financial opportunity costs in other chapters, the *time value of money,* more commonly referred to as *interest,* is the cost of money that is borrowed or lent. Interest can be compared to rent, the cost of using an apartment or other item. The time value of money is based on the fact that a dollar received today is worth more than a dollar that will be received one year from today, because the dollar received today can be saved or invested and will be worth more than a dollar a year from today. Similarly, a dollar that will be received one year from today is currently worth less than a dollar today.

The time value of money has two major components: future value and present value. *Future value,* which is also referred to as *compounding,* is the amount to which a current sum will increase based on a certain interest rate and period of time. *Present value,* which is calculated through a process called *discounting,* is the current value of a future sum based on a certain interest rate and period of time.

In future value problems, you are given an amount to save or invest and you calculate the amount that will be available at some future date. With present value problems, you are given the amount that will be available at some future date and you calculate the current value of that amount. Both future value and present value computations are based on basic interest rate calculations.

INTEREST RATE BASICS

Simple interest is the dollar cost of borrowing or earnings from lending money. The interest is based on three elements:

- The dollar amount, called the *principal.*
- The *rate of interest.*
- The amount of *time.*

The formula for computing interest is

$$\text{Interest} = \text{Principal} \times \text{Rate of interest} \times \text{Time}$$

The interest rate is stated as a percentage for a year. For example, you must convert 12 percent to either 0.12 or $^{12}/_{100}$ before doing your calculations. The time element must also be converted to a decimal or fraction. For example, three months would be shown as either 0.25 or ¼ of a year. Interest for 2½ years would involve a time period of 2.5.

Example A   Suppose you borrow $1,000 at 5 percent and will repay it in one payment at the end of one year. Using the simple interest calculation, the interest is $50, computed as follows:

$$\$50 = \$1,000 \times 0.05 \times 1 \text{ (year)}$$

Example B   If you deposited $750 in a savings account paying 8 percent, how much interest would you earn in nine months? You would compute this amount as follows:

$$\begin{aligned} \text{Interest} &= \$750 \times 0.08 \times ¾ \text{ (or 0.75 of a year)} \\ &= \$45 \end{aligned}$$

Sample Problem 1   How much interest would you earn if you deposited $300 at 6 percent for 27 months? *(Answers to sample problems are on page 621.)*

Sample Problem 2   How much interest would you pay to borrow $670 for eight months at 12 percent?

FUTURE VALUE OF A SINGLE AMOUNT

The future value of an amount consists of the original amount plus compound interest. This calculation involves the following elements:

$$\begin{aligned} FV &= \text{Future value} \\ PV &= \text{Present value} \\ i &= \text{Interest rate} \\ n &= \text{Number of time periods} \end{aligned}$$

The formula for the future value of a single amount is

$$FV = PV(1 + i)^n$$

Example C   The future value of $1 at 10 percent after three years is $1.33. This amount is calculated as follows:

$$\$1.33 = \$1.00 (1 + 0.10)^3$$

Future value tables are available to help you determine compounded interest amounts (see Exhibit C–1 on page 622). Looking at Exhibit C–1 for 10 percent and three years, you can see that $1 would be worth $1.33 at that time. For other amounts, multiply the table factor by the original amount.

This may be viewed as follows:

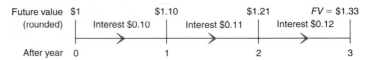

Example D   If your savings of $400 earn 12 percent, compounded *monthly,* over a year and a half, use the table factor for 1 percent for 18 time periods. The future value of this amount is $478.40, calculated as follows:

$$\$478.40 \; = \; \$400\,(1.196)$$

Sample Problem 3   What is the future value of $800 at 8 percent after six years?

Sample Problem 4   How much would you have in savings if you kept $200 on deposit for eight years at 8 percent, compounded *semiannually*?

FUTURE VALUE OF A SERIES OF EQUAL AMOUNTS (AN ANNUITY)

Future value may also be calculated for a situation in which regular additions are made to savings. The following formula is used:

$$FV \; = \; \frac{(1 \; + \; i)^n \; - \; 1}{i}$$

This formula assumes that (1) each deposit is for the same amount, (2) the interest rate is the same for each time period, and (3) the deposits are made at the end of each time period.

Example E   The future value of three $1 deposits made at the end of the next three years, earning 10 percent interest, is $3.31. This is calculated as follows:

$$\$3.31 \; = \; \$1 \; \frac{(1 \; + \; 0.10)^3 \; - \; 1}{0.10}$$

This may be viewed as follows:

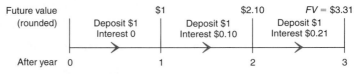

Using Exhibit C–2 on page 623, you can find this same amount for 10 percent for three time periods. To use the table for other amounts, multiply the table factors by the annual deposit.

Example F   If you plan to deposit $40 a year for 10 years, earning 8 percent compounded annually, use the table factor for 8 percent for 10 time periods. The future value of this amount is $579.48, calculated as follows:

$$\$579.48 \; = \; \$40(14.487)$$

Sample Problem 5   What is the future value of an annual deposit of $230 earning 6 percent for 15 years?

Sample Problem 6   What amount would you have in a retirement account if you made annual deposits of $375 for 25 years earning 12 percent, compounded annually?

PRESENT VALUE OF A SINGLE AMOUNT

If you want to know how much you need to deposit now to receive a certain amount in the future, use the following formula:

$$PV - \frac{1}{(1 + i)^n}$$

Example G   The present value of $1 to be received three years from now based on a 10 percent interest rate is $0.75. This amount is calculated as follows:

$$\$0.75 = \frac{\$1}{(1 + 0.10)^3}$$

This may be viewed as follows:

Present value (rounded)	$0.75	$0.83	$0.91	$1
		Discount (interest) $0.075	Discount (interest) $0.0825	Discount (interest) $0.0905
After year	0	1	2	3

Present value tables are available to assist you in this process (see Exhibit C–3 on page 624). Notice that $1 at 10 percent for three years has a present value of $0.75. For amounts other than $1, multiply the table factor by the amount involved.

Example H   If you want to have $300 seven years from now and your savings earn 10 percent, compounded *semiannually,* use the table factor for 5 percent for 14 time periods. In this situation, the present value is $151.50, calculated as follows:

$$\$151.50 = \$300(0.505)$$

Sample Problem 7   What is the present value of $2,200 earning 15 percent for eight years?

Sample Problem 8   To have $6,000 for a child's education in 10 years, what amount should a parent deposit in a savings account that earns 12 percent, compounded *quarterly?*

PRESENT VALUE OF A SERIES OF EQUAL AMOUNTS (AN ANNUITY)

The final time value of money situation allows you to receive an amount at the end of each time period for a certain number of periods. This amount is calculated as follows:

$$PV = \frac{1 - \frac{1}{(1 + i)^n}}{i}$$

Example I   The present value of a $1 withdrawal at the end of the next three years would be $2.49, calculated as follows:

$$\$2.49 = \$1 \left[\frac{1 - \dfrac{1}{(1 + 0.10)^n}}{0.10} \right]$$

This may be viewed as follows:

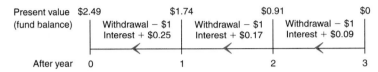

This same amount appears in Exhibit C–4 on page 625 for 10 percent and three time periods. To use the table for other situations, multiply the table factor by the amount to be withdrawn each year.

Example J   If you wish to withdraw $100 at the end of each year for 10 years from an account that earns 14 percent, compounded annually, what amount must you deposit now? Use the table factor for 14 percent for 10 time periods. In this situation, the present value is $521.60, calculated as follows:

$$\$521.60 = \$100(5.216)$$

Sample Problem 9   What is the present value of a withdrawal of $200 at the end of each year for 14 years with an interest rate of 7 percent?

Sample Problem 10   How much would you have to deposit now to be able to withdraw $650 at the end of each year for 20 years from an account that earns 11 percent?

USING PRESENT VALUE TO DETERMINE LOAN PAYMENTS

Present value tables can also be used to determine installment payments for a loan as follows:

$$\frac{\text{Amount borrowed}}{\text{Present value of a series table factor (Exhibit C–4)}} = \text{Loan payment}$$

Example K   If you borrow $1,000 with a 6 percent interest rate to be repaid in three equal payments at the end of the next three years, the payments will be $374.11. This is calculated as follows:

$$\frac{\$1,000}{2.673} = \$374.11$$

Sample Problem 11   What would be the annual payment amount for a $20,000, 10-year loan at 7 percent?

ANSWERS TO SAMPLE PROBLEMS

1. $300 × 0.06 × 2.25 years (27 months) = $40.50.
2. $670 × 0.12 × ⅔ (of a year) = $53.60.
3. $800(1.587) = $1,269.60. (Use Exhibit C–1, 8%, 6 periods.)
4. $200(1.873) = $374.60. (Use Exhibit C–1, 4%, 16 periods.)
5. $230(23.276) = $5,353.48. (Use Exhibit C–2, 6%, 15 periods.)
6. $375(133.33) = $49,998.75. (Use Exhibit C–2, 12%, 25 periods.)
7. $2,200(0.327) = $719.40. (Use Exhibit C–3, 15%, 8 periods.)
8. $6,000(0.307) = $1,842. (Use Exhibit C–3, 3%, 40 periods.)
9. $200(8.745) = $1,749. (Use Exhibit C–4, 7%, 14 periods.)
10. $650(7.963) = $5,175.95. (Use Exhibit C–4, 11%, 20 periods.)
11. $20,000/7.024 = $2,847.38. (Use Exhibit C–4, 7%, 10 periods.)

EXHIBIT C–1   **Future Value (Compounded Sum) of $1 after a Given Number of Time Periods**

Period	1%	2%	3%	4%	5%	6%	7%	8%	9%	10%	11%
1	1.010	1.020	1.030	1.040	1.050	1.060	1.070	1.080	1.090	1.100	1.110
2	1.020	1.040	1.061	1.082	1.103	1.124	1.145	1.166	1.188	1.210	1.232
3	1.030	1.061	1.093	1.125	1.158	1.191	1.225	1.260	1.295	1.331	1.368
4	1.041	1.082	1.126	1.170	1.216	1.262	1.311	1.360	1.412	1.464	1.518
5	1.051	1.104	1.159	1.217	1.276	1.338	1.403	1.469	1.539	1.611	1.685
6	1.062	1.126	1.194	1.265	1.340	1.419	1.501	1.587	1.677	1.772	1.870
7	1.072	1.149	1.230	1.316	1.407	1.504	1.606	1.714	1.828	1.949	2.076
8	1.083	1.172	1.267	1.369	1.477	1.594	1.718	1.851	1.993	2.144	2.305
9	1.094	1.195	1.305	1.423	1.551	1.689	1.838	1.999	2.172	2.358	2.558
10	1.105	1.219	1.344	1.480	1.629	1.791	1.967	2.159	2.367	2.594	2.839
11	1.116	1.243	1.384	1.539	1.710	1.898	2.105	2.332	2.580	2.853	3.152
12	1.127	1.268	1.426	1.601	1.796	2.012	2.252	2.518	2.813	3.138	3.498
13	1.138	1.294	1.469	1.665	1.886	2.133	2.410	2.720	3.066	3.452	3.883
14	1.149	1.319	1.513	1.732	1.980	2.261	2.579	2.937	3.342	3.797	4.310
15	1.161	1.346	1.558	1.801	2.079	2.397	2.759	3.172	3.642	4.177	4.785
16	1.173	1.373	1.605	1.873	2.183	2.540	2.952	3.426	3.970	4.595	5.311
17	1.184	1.400	1.653	1.948	2.292	2.693	3.159	3.700	4.328	5.054	5.895
18	1.196	1.428	1.702	2.026	2.407	2.854	3.380	3.996	4.717	5.560	6.544
19	1.208	1.457	1.754	2.107	2.527	3.026	3.617	4.316	5.142	6.116	7.263
20	1.220	1.486	1.806	2.191	2.653	3.207	3.870	4.661	5.604	6.727	8.062
25	1.282	1.641	2.094	2.666	3.386	4.292	5.427	6.848	8.623	10.835	13.585
30	1.348	1.811	2.427	3.243	4.322	5.743	7.612	10.063	13.268	17.449	22.892
40	1.489	2.208	3.262	4.801	7.040	10.286	14.974	21.725	31.409	45.259	65.001
50	1.645	2.692	4.384	7.107	11.467	18.420	29.457	46.902	74.358	117.390	184.570

EXHIBIT C–1   **(*Concluded*)**

Period	12%	13%	14%	15%	16%	17%	18%	19%	20%	25%	30%
1	1.120	1.130	1.140	1.150	1.160	1.170	1.180	1.190	1.200	1.250	1.300
2	1.254	1.277	1.300	1.323	1.346	1.369	1.392	1.416	1.440	1.563	1.690
3	1.405	1.443	1.482	1.521	1.561	1.602	1.643	1.685	1.728	1.953	2.197
4	1.574	1.630	1.689	1.749	1.811	1.874	1.939	2.005	2.074	2.441	2.856
5	1.762	1.842	1.925	2.011	2.100	2.192	2.288	2.386	2.488	3.052	3.713
6	1.974	2.082	2.195	2.313	2.436	2.565	2.700	2.840	2.986	3.815	4.827
7	2.211	2.353	2.502	2.660	2.826	3.001	3.185	3.379	3.583	4.768	6.276
8	2.476	2.658	2.853	3.059	3.278	3.511	3.759	4.021	4.300	5.960	8.157
9	2.773	3.004	3.252	3.518	3.803	4.108	4.435	4.785	5.160	7.451	10.604
10	3.106	3.395	3.707	4.046	4.411	4.807	5.234	5.696	6.192	9.313	13.786
11	3.479	3.836	4.226	4.652	5.117	5.624	6.176	6.777	7.430	11.642	17.922
12	3.896	4.335	4.818	5.350	5.936	6.580	7.288	8.064	8.916	14.552	23.298
13	4.363	4.898	5.492	6.153	6.886	7.699	8.599	9.596	10.699	18.190	30.288
14	4.887	5.535	6.261	7.076	7.988	9.007	10.147	11.420	12.839	22.737	39.374
15	5.474	6.254	7.138	8.137	9.266	10.539	11.974	13.590	15.407	28.422	51.186
16	6.130	7.067	8.137	9.358	10.748	12.330	14.129	16.172	18.488	35.527	66.542
17	6.866	7.986	9.276	10.761	12.468	14.426	16.672	19.244	22.186	44.409	86.504
18	7.690	9.024	10.575	12.375	14.463	16.879	19.673	22.091	26.623	55.511	112.460
19	8.613	10.197	12.056	14.232	16.777	19.748	23.214	27.252	31.948	69.389	146.190
20	9.646	11.523	13.743	16.367	19.461	23.106	27.393	32.429	38.338	86.736	190.050
25	17.000	21.231	26.462	32.919	40.874	50.658	62.669	77.388	95.396	264.700	705.640
30	29.960	39.116	50.950	66.212	85.850	111.070	143.370	184.680	237.380	807.790	2,620.000
40	93.051	132.780	188.880	267.860	378.720	533.870	750.380	1,051.700	1,469.800	7,523.200	36,119.000
50	289.000	450.740	700.230	1,083.700	1,670.700	2,566.200	3,927.400	5,988.900	9,100.400	70,065.000	497,929.000

EXHIBIT C–2   **Future Value (Compounded Sum) of $1 Paid in at the End of Each Period for a Given Number of Time Periods (an Annuity)**

Period	1%	2%	3%	4%	5%	6%	7%	8%	9%	10%	11%
1	1.000	1.000	1.000	1.000	1.000	1.000	1.000	1.000	1.000	1.000	1.000
2	2.010	2.020	2.030	2.040	2.050	2.060	2.070	2.080	2.090	2.100	2.110
3	3.030	3.060	3.091	3.122	3.153	3.184	3.215	3.246	3.278	3.310	3.342
4	4.060	4.122	4.184	4.246	4.310	4.375	4.440	4.506	4.573	4.641	4.710
5	5.101	5.204	5.309	5.416	5.526	5.637	5.751	5.867	5.985	6.105	6.228
6	6.152	6.308	6.468	6.633	6.802	6.975	7.153	7.336	7.523	7.716	7.913
7	7.214	7.434	7.662	7.898	8.142	8.394	8.654	8.923	9.200	9.487	9.783
8	8.286	8.583	8.892	9.214	9.549	9.897	10.260	10.637	11.028	11.436	11.859
9	9.369	9.755	10.159	10.583	11.027	11.491	11.978	12.488	13.021	13.579	14.164
10	10.462	10.950	11.464	12.006	12.578	13.181	13.816	14.487	15.193	15.937	16.722
11	11.567	12.169	12.808	13.486	14.207	14.972	15.784	16.645	17.560	18.531	19.561
12	12.683	13.412	14.192	15.026	15.917	16.870	17.888	18.977	20.141	21.384	22.713
13	13.809	14.680	15.618	16.627	17.713	18.882	20.141	21.495	22.953	24.523	26.212
14	14.947	15.974	17.086	18.292	19.599	21.015	22.550	24.215	26.019	27.975	30.095
15	16.097	17.293	18.599	20.024	21.579	23.276	25.129	27.152	29.361	31.772	34.405
16	17.258	18.639	20.157	21.825	23.657	25.673	27.888	30.324	33.003	35.950	39.190
17	18.430	20.012	21.762	23.698	25.840	20.213	30.840	33.750	36.974	40.545	44.501
18	19.615	21.412	23.414	25.645	28.132	30.906	33.999	37.450	41.301	45.599	50.396
19	20.811	22.841	25.117	27.671	30.539	33.760	37.379	41.446	46.018	51.159	56.939
20	22.019	24.297	26.870	29.778	33.066	36.786	40.995	45.762	51.160	57.275	64.203
25	28.243	32.030	36.459	41.646	47.727	54.865	63.249	73.106	84.701	98.347	114.410
30	34.785	40.588	47.575	56.085	66.439	79.058	94.461	113.280	136.310	164.490	199.020
40	48.886	60.402	75.401	95.026	120.800	154.760	199.640	259.060	337.890	442.590	581.830
50	64.463	84.579	112.800	152.670	209.350	290.340	406.530	573.770	815.080	1,163.900	1,668.800

EXHIBIT C–2   **(Concluded)**

Period	12%	13%	14%	15%	16%	17%	18%	19%	20%	25%	30%
1	1.000	1.000	1.000	1.000	1.000	1.000	1.000	1.000	1.000	1.000	1.000
2	2.120	2.130	2.140	2.150	2.160	2.170	2.180	2.190	2.200	2.250	2.300
3	3.374	3.407	3.440	3.473	3.506	3.539	3.572	3.606	3.640	3.813	3.990
4	4.779	4.850	4.921	4.993	5.066	5.141	5.215	5.291	5.368	5.766	6.187
5	6.353	6.480	6.610	6.742	6.877	7.014	7.154	7.297	7.442	8.207	9.043
6	8.115	8.323	8.536	8.754	8.977	9.207	9.442	9.683	9.930	11.259	12.756
7	10.089	10.405	10.730	11.067	11.414	11.772	12.142	12.523	12.916	15.073	17.583
8	12.300	12.757	13.233	13.727	14.240	14.773	15.327	15.902	16.499	19.842	23.858
9	14.776	15.416	16.085	16.786	17.519	18.285	19.086	19.923	20.799	25.802	32.015
10	17.549	18.420	19.337	20.304	21.321	22.393	23.521	24.701	25.959	33.253	42.619
11	20.655	21.814	23.045	24.349	25.733	27.200	28.755	30.404	32.150	42.566	56.405
12	24.133	25.650	27.271	29.002	30.850	32.824	34.931	37.180	39.581	54.208	74.327
13	28.029	29.985	32.089	34.352	36.786	39.404	42.219	45.244	48.497	68.760	97.625
14	32.393	34.883	37.581	40.505	43.672	47.103	50.818	54.841	59.196	86.949	127.910
15	37.280	40.417	43.842	47.580	51.660	56.110	60.965	66.261	72.035	109.690	167.290
16	42.753	46.672	50.980	55.717	60.925	66.649	72.939	79.850	87.442	138.110	218.470
17	48.884	53.739	59.118	65.075	71.673	78.979	87.068	96.022	105.930	173.640	285.010
18	55.750	61.725	68.394	75.836	84.141	93.406	103.740	115.270	128.120	218.050	371.520
19	63.440	70.749	78.969	88.212	98.603	110.290	123.410	138.170	154.740	273.560	483.970
20	72.052	80.947	91.025	102.440	115.380	130.030	146.630	165.420	186.690	342.950	630.170
25	133.330	155.620	181.870	212.790	249.210	292.110	342.600	402.040	471.980	1,054.800	2,348.800
30	241.330	293.200	356.790	434.750	530.310	647.440	790.950	966.700	1,181.900	3,227.200	8,730.000
40	767.090	1,013.700	1,342.000	1,779.100	2,360.800	3,134.500	4,163.210	5,529.800	7,343.900	30,089.000	120,393.000
50	2,400.000	3,459.500	4,994.500	7,217.700	10,436.000	15,090.000	21,813.000	31,515.000	45,497.000	80,256.000	165,976.000

EXHIBIT C–3   **Present Value of $1 to Be Received at the End of a Given Number of Time Periods**

Period	1%	2%	3%	4%	5%	6%	7%	8%	9%	10%	11%	12%
1	0.990	0.980	0.971	0.962	0.952	0.943	0.935	0.926	0.917	0.909	0.901	0.893
2	0.980	0.961	0.943	0.925	0.907	0.890	0.873	0.857	0.842	0.826	0.812	0.797
3	0.971	0.942	0.915	0.889	0.864	0.840	0.816	0.794	0.772	0.751	0.731	0.712
4	0.961	0.924	0.885	0.855	0.823	0.792	0.763	0.735	0.708	0.683	0.659	0.636
5	0.951	0.906	0.863	0.822	0.784	0.747	0.713	0.681	0.650	0.621	0.593	0.567
6	0.942	0.888	0.837	0.790	0.746	0.705	0.666	0.630	0.596	0.564	0.535	0.507
7	0.933	0.871	0.813	0.760	0.711	0.665	0.623	0.583	0.547	0.513	0.482	0.452
8	0.923	0.853	0.789	0.731	0.677	0.627	0.582	0.540	0.502	0.467	0.434	0.404
9	0.914	0.837	0.766	0.703	0.645	0.592	0.544	0.500	0.460	0.424	0.391	0.361
10	0.905	0.820	0.744	0.676	0.614	0.558	0.508	0.463	0.422	0.386	0.352	0.322
11	0.896	0.804	0.722	0.650	0.585	0.527	0.475	0.429	0.388	0.350	0.317	0.287
12	0.887	0.788	0.701	0.625	0.557	0.497	0.444	0.397	0.356	0.319	0.286	0.257
13	0.879	0.773	0.681	0.601	0.530	0.469	0.415	0.368	0.326	0.290	0.258	0.229
14	0.870	0.758	0.661	0.577	0.505	0.442	0.388	0.340	0.299	0.263	0.232	0.205
15	0.861	0.743	0.642	0.555	0.481	0.417	0.362	0.315	0.275	0.239	0.209	0.183
16	0.853	0.728	0.623	0.534	0.458	0.394	0.339	0.292	0.252	0.218	0.188	0.163
17	0.844	0.714	0.605	0.513	0.436	0.371	0.317	0.270	0.231	0.198	0.170	0.146
18	0.836	0.700	0.587	0.494	0.416	0.350	0.296	0.250	0.212	0.180	0.153	0.130
19	0.828	0.686	0.570	0.475	0.396	0.331	0.277	0.232	0.194	0.164	0.138	0.116
20	0.820	0.673	0.554	0.456	0.377	0.312	0.258	0.215	0.178	0.149	0.124	0.104
25	0.780	0.610	0.478	0.375	0.295	0.233	0.184	0.146	0.116	0.092	0.074	0.059
30	0.742	0.552	0.412	0.308	0.231	0.174	0.131	0.099	0.075	0.057	0.044	0.033
40	0.672	0.453	0.307	0.208	0.142	0.097	0.067	0.046	0.032	0.022	0.015	0.011
50	0.608	0.372	0.228	0.141	0.087	0.054	0.034	0.021	0.013	0.009	0.005	0.003

EXHIBIT C–3   **(*Concluded*)**

Period	13%	14%	15%	16%	17%	18%	19%	20%	25%	30%	35%	40%	50%
1	0.885	0.877	0.870	0.862	0.855	0.847	0.840	0.833	0.800	0.769	0.741	0.714	0.667
2	0.783	0.769	0.756	0.743	0.731	0.718	0.706	0.694	0.640	0.592	0.549	0.510	0.444
3	0.693	0.675	0.658	0.641	0.624	0.609	0.593	0.579	0.512	0.455	0.406	0.364	0.296
4	0.613	0.592	0.572	0.552	0.534	0.515	0.499	0.482	0.410	0.350	0.301	0.260	0.198
5	0.543	0.519	0.497	0.476	0.456	0.437	0.419	0.402	0.320	0.269	0.223	0.186	0.132
6	0.480	0.456	0.432	0.410	0.390	0.370	0.352	0.335	0.262	0.207	0.165	0.133	0.088
7	0.425	0.400	0.376	0.354	0.333	0.314	0.296	0.279	0.210	0.159	0.122	0.095	0.059
8	0.376	0.351	0.327	0.305	0.285	0.266	0.249	0.233	0.168	0.123	0.091	0.068	0.039
9	0.333	0.300	0.284	0.263	0.243	0.225	0.209	0.194	0.134	0.094	0.067	0.048	0.026
10	0.295	0.270	0.247	0.227	0.208	0.191	0.176	0.162	0.107	0.073	0.050	0.035	0.017
11	0.261	0.237	0.215	0.195	0.178	0.162	0.148	0.135	0.086	0.056	0.037	0.025	0.012
12	0.231	0.208	0.187	0.168	0.152	0.137	0.124	0.112	0.069	0.043	0.027	0.018	0.008
13	0.204	0.182	0.163	0.145	0.130	0.116	0.104	0.093	0.055	0.033	0.020	0.013	0.005
14	0.181	0.160	0.141	0.125	0.111	0.099	0.088	0.078	0.044	0.025	0.015	0.009	0.003
15	0.160	0.140	0.123	0.108	0.095	0.084	0.074	0.065	0.035	0.020	0.011	0.006	0.002
16	0.141	0.123	0.107	0.093	0.081	0.071	0.062	0.054	0.028	0.015	0.008	0.005	0.002
17	0.125	0.108	0.093	0.080	0.069	0.060	0.052	0.045	0.023	0.012	0.006	0.003	0.001
18	0.111	0.095	0.081	0.069	0.059	0.051	0.044	0.038	0.018	0.009	0.005	0.002	0.001
19	0.098	0.083	0.070	0.060	0.051	0.043	0.037	0.031	0.014	0.007	0.003	0.002	0
20	0.087	0.073	0.061	0.051	0.043	0.037	0.031	0.026	0.012	0.005	0.002	0.001	0
25	0.047	0.038	0.030	0.024	0.020	0.016	0.013	0.010	0.004	0.001	0.001	0	0
30	0.026	0.020	0.015	0.012	0.009	0.007	0.005	0.004	0.001	0	0	0	0
40	0.008	0.005	0.004	0.003	0.002	0.001	0.001	0.001	0	0	0	0	0
50	0.002	0.001	0.001	0.001	0	0	0	0	0	0	0	0	0

Exhibit C–4   **Present Value of $1 Received at the End of Each Period for a Given Number of Time Periods (an Annuity)**

Period	1%	2%	3%	4%	5%	6%	7%	8%	9%	10%	11%	12%
1	0.990	0.980	0.971	0.962	0.952	0.943	0.935	0.926	0.917	0.909	0.901	0.893
2	1.970	1.942	1.913	1.886	1.859	1.833	1.808	1.783	1.759	1.736	1.713	1.690
3	2.941	2.884	2.829	2.775	2.723	2.673	2.624	2.577	2.531	2.487	2.444	2.402
4	3.902	3.808	3.717	3.630	3.546	3.465	3.387	3.312	3.240	3.170	3.102	3.037
5	4.853	4.713	4.580	4.452	4.329	4.212	4.100	3.993	3.890	3.791	3.696	3.605
6	5.795	5.601	5.417	5.242	5.076	4.917	4.767	4.623	4.486	4.355	4.231	4.111
7	6.728	6.472	6.230	6.002	5.786	5.582	5.389	5.206	5.033	4.868	4.712	4.564
8	7.652	7.325	7.020	6.733	6.463	6.210	5.971	5.747	5.535	5.335	5.146	4.968
9	8.566	8.162	7.786	7.435	7.108	6.802	6.515	6.247	5.995	5.759	5.537	5.328
10	9.471	8.983	8.530	8.111	7.722	7.360	7.024	6.710	6.418	6.145	5.889	5.650
11	10.368	9.787	9.253	8.760	8.306	7.887	7.499	7.139	6.805	6.495	6.207	5.938
12	11.255	10.575	9.954	9.385	8.863	8.384	7.943	7.536	7.161	6.814	6.492	6.194
13	12.134	11.348	10.635	9.986	9.394	8.853	8.358	7.904	7.487	7.103	6.750	6.424
14	13.004	12.106	11.296	10.563	9.899	9.295	8.745	8.244	7.786	7.367	6.982	6.628
15	13.865	12.849	11.939	11.118	10.380	9.712	9.108	8.559	8.061	7.606	7.191	6.811
16	14.718	13.578	12.561	11.652	10.838	10.106	9.447	8.851	8.313	7.824	7.379	6.974
17	15.562	14.292	13.166	12.166	11.274	10.477	9.763	9.122	8.544	8.022	7.549	7.102
18	16.398	14.992	13.754	12.659	11.690	10.828	10.059	9.372	8.756	8.201	7.702	7.250
19	17.226	15.678	14.324	13.134	12.085	11.158	10.336	9.604	8.950	8.365	7.839	7.366
20	18.046	16.351	14.877	13.590	12.462	11.470	10.594	9.818	9.129	8.514	7.963	7.469
25	22.023	19.523	17.413	15.622	14.094	12.783	11.654	10.675	9.823	9.077	8.422	7.843
30	25.808	22.396	19.600	17.292	15.372	13.765	12.409	11.258	10.274	9.427	8.694	8.055
40	32.835	27.355	23.115	19.793	17.159	15.046	13.332	11.925	10.757	9.779	8.951	8.244
50	39.196	31.424	25.730	21.482	18.256	15.762	13.801	12.233	10.962	9.915	9.042	8.304

Exhibit C–4   (*Concluded*)

Period	13%	14%	15%	16%	17%	18%	19%	20%	25%	30%	35%	40%	50%
1	0.885	0.877	0.870	0.862	0.855	0.847	0.840	0.833	0.800	0.769	0.741	0.714	0.667
2	1.668	1.647	1.626	1.605	1.585	1.566	1.547	1.528	1.440	1.361	1.289	1.224	1.111
3	2.361	2.322	2.283	2.246	2.210	2.174	2.140	2.106	1.952	1.816	1.696	1.589	1.407
4	2.974	2.914	2.855	2.798	2.743	2.690	2.639	2.589	2.362	2.166	1.997	1.849	1.605
5	3.517	3.433	3.352	3.274	3.199	3.127	3.058	2.991	2.689	2.436	2.220	2.035	1.737
6	3.998	3.889	3.784	3.685	3.589	3.498	3.410	3.326	2.951	2.643	2.385	2.168	1.824
7	4.423	4.288	4.160	4.039	3.922	3.812	3.706	3.605	3.161	2.802	2.508	2.263	1.883
8	4.799	4.639	4.487	4.344	4.207	4.078	3.954	3.837	3.329	2.925	2.598	2.331	1.922
9	5.132	4.946	4.772	4.607	4.451	4.303	4.163	4.031	3.463	3.019	2.665	2.379	1.948
10	5.426	5.216	5.019	4.833	4.659	4.494	4.339	4.192	3.571	3.092	2.715	2.414	1.965
11	5.687	5.453	5.234	5.029	4.836	4.656	4.486	4.327	3.656	3.147	2.752	2.438	1.977
12	5.918	5.660	5.421	5.197	4.988	4.793	4.611	4.439	3.725	3.190	2.779	2.456	1.985
13	6.122	5.842	5.583	5.342	5.118	4.910	4.715	4.533	3.780	3.223	2.799	2.469	1.990
14	6.302	6.002	5.724	5.468	5.229	5.008	4.802	4.611	3.824	3.249	2.814	2.478	1.993
15	6.462	6.142	5.847	5.575	5.324	5.092	4.876	4.675	3.859	3.268	2.825	2.484	1.995
16	6.604	6.265	5.954	5.668	5.405	5.162	4.938	4.730	3.887	3.283	2.834	2.489	1.997
17	6.729	6.373	6.047	5.749	5.475	5.222	4.988	4.775	3.910	3.295	2.840	2.492	1.998
18	6.840	6.467	6.128	5.818	5.534	5.273	5.033	4.812	3.928	3.304	2.844	2.494	1.999
19	6.938	6.550	6.198	5.877	5.584	5.316	5.070	4.843	3.942	3.311	2.848	2.496	1.999
20	7.025	6.623	6.259	5.929	5.628	5.353	5.101	4.870	3.954	3.316	2.850	2.497	1.999
25	7.330	6.873	6.464	6.097	5.766	5.467	5.195	4.948	3.985	3.329	2.856	2.499	2.000
30	7.496	7.003	6.566	6.177	5.829	5.517	5.235	4.979	3.995	3.332	2.857	2.500	2.000
40	7.634	7.105	6.642	6.233	5.871	5.548	5.258	4.997	3.999	3.333	2.857	2.500	2.000
50	7.675	7.133	6.661	6.246	5.880	5.554	5.262	4.999	4.000	3.333	2.857	2.500	2.000

APPENDIX D

USING ELECTRONIC CALCULATORS FOR FINANCIAL DECISIONS

When doing calculations for personal finance decisions, three options are commonly available. First, the use of paper and pencil is appropriate for some estimates. However, more complex analyses may require the use of a personal computer with the software that accompanies this book or one of the programs discussed in Appendix B. Between these two extremes are situations in which you may want to use a calculator.

Today's financial calculators operate faster, possess more memory, and are programmed to do finance-related computations. Three of the most commonly used financial calculators are

- Hewlett-Packard HP–10B
- Sharp Electronics EL–733A
- Texas Instruments BA II Plus.

This reference presents key sequences needed to achieve a basic understanding of how to use these calculators to do computations related to time value of money, calculating consumer credit costs and home mortgage payments, computing investment returns, and projecting retirement income.

PREPARING YOUR CALCULATOR FOR FINANCIAL COMPUTATIONS

Several activities are required to get ready to use your financial calculator.

Clearing Entry and Memory Registers

To clear or "zero out" memory registers, use the following keystrokes:

Function	Hewlett-Packard HP-10B	Sharp Electronics EL-733A	Texas Instruments BA II Plus
Clear M(emory) registers	☐ CLEAR ALL	0 X→M	2nd MEM
			2nd CLR Work
Clear markup registers	☐ CLEAR ALL	2ndF CA	2nd CLR Work
Clear TVM registers	☐ CLEAR ALL	2ndF CA	2nd CLR TVM
Clear cash flow registers	☐ CLEAR ALL	2ndF CA	2nd CLR Work
Clear statistical registers	☐ {CLΣ}	2ndF CA	2nd CLR Work
Delete statistical data	☐ {Σ-}	CD	2nd DEL

NOTE: The ☐ key for HP-10B refers to the large orange square modifier key.

Setting Decimal Places

To set the display format to four decimal places, use the following key sequences:

- HP-10B: ☐ DISP 4
- EL-733A: 2ndF TAB 4
- BA II Plus: 2nd FORMAT 4 ENTER

For two decimal places, use 2 instead of 4 with the above sequence.
For a floating decimal point format, use the following:

- HP-10B: ☐ DISP .
- EL-733A: 2ndF TAB .
- BA II Plus: 2nd FORMAT 9 ENTER

Setting Compounding Frequency

The Sharp EL-733A is programmed for a compounding frequency of once per period. To change the compounding frequency on the HP-10B, enter 1 (or 12), then press ☐ P/Y .

The BA II Plus allows you to specify both the payment and the compounding frequency. This is done as follows: 2nd P/Y 1 ENTER then ☐ 1 ENTER . Press 2nd QUIT to return to calculator mode.

ACHIEVING FINANCIAL GOALS USING TIME VALUE OF MONEY CALCULATIONS

As discussed in Chapter 1 and Appendix C, future value and present value calculations, commonly referred to as the *time value of money,* are used to determine increases in an amount of money as a result of interest earned.

Future Value of a Single Amount

To calculate, for example, the future value of $7,000 at an annual rate of 10 percent (enter 1 for compounding frequency; see above) for 9 years, use the following key sequences:

INPUT	HP-10B	EL-733A	BA II Plus
Amount	− 7000 [PV]	− 7000 [PV]	− 7000 [PV]
Time periods	9 [N]	9 [n]	9 [N]
Interest rate	10 [I/YR]	10 [i]	10 [I/Y]
Result	[FV] 16,505.64	[COMP] [FV] 16,505.64	[CPT] [FV] 16,505.64

This deposit would grow to $16,505.64.

Future Value of a Series of Equal Amounts (Annuity)

If you want to know, for example, the future value of depositing $500 a year for 30 years in an account earning an annual rate of 6 percent, use the following key sequences:

INPUT	HP-10B	EL-733A	BA II Plus
Amount	− 500 [PMT]	− 500 [PMT]	− 500 [PMT]
Time periods	30 [N]	30 [n]	30 [N]
Interest rate	6 [I/YR]	6 [i]	6 [I/Y]
Result	[FV] − 39,529.09	[COMP] [FV] − 39,529.09	[CPT] [FV] 39,529.09

The result of this calculation would be $39,529.09.

Present Value of a Single Amount

Often a person wants to know how much to deposit today for that sum to grow to a desired amount in the future. For example, how much would you need to deposit today to have $10,000 in five years if your deposit is earning 8 percent? The key sequences to calculate the present value of a single amount are as follows:

INPUT	HP-10B	EL-733A	BA II Plus
Amount	10,000 [FV]	10,000 [FV]	10,000 [FV]
Time periods	5 [N]	5 [n]	5 [N]
Interest rate	8 [I/YR]	8 [i]	8 [I/Y]
Result	[PV] − 6,805.83	[COMP] [PV] − 6,805.83	[CPT] [PV] − 6,805.83

The amount you must deposit today is $6,805.83.

Present Value of a Series of Equal Amounts (Annuity)

You may want to determine the amount you must deposit now to allow you to withdraw a certain amount each year for a set number of years. For example, you may want to be able to withdraw $5,000 a year for the next four years from an account paying 6 percent annually. This present value of an annuity has the following key sequences:

INPUT	HP-10B	EL-733A	BA II Plus
Amount	5000 [PMT]	5000 [PMT]	5000 [PMT]
Time periods	4 [N]	4 [n]	4 [N]
Interest rate	6 [I/YR]	6 [i]	6 [I/Y]
Result	[PV] − 17,325.53	[COMP] [PV] − 17,325.53	[CPT] [PV] − 17,325.53

You must deposit $17,325.53 in this situation.

CONSUMER CREDIT AND HOME MORTGAGE CALCULATIONS

Buying on credit is very common for both consumer purchases and for financing a home. (Note: HP-10B and BA-II Plus users should change the compounding frequency to 12 times a year; see the "Setting Compounding Frequency" section above.)

Computing Credit Payments

You are offered a $10,000 auto loan for four years (48 months) with an annual percentage rate of 8.5 percent. The key sequence to determine the monthly payment is:

INPUT	HP-10B	EL-733A	BA II Plus
Loan amount	10,000 [PV]	10,000 [PV]	10,000 [PV]
Interest rate	8.5 [I/YR]	8.5 [÷] 12 [=] [i]	8.5 [I/Y]
Loan length: months	48 [N]	48 [n]	48 [N]
Result: payment	[PMT] −246.48	[COMP] [PMT] −246.48	[CPT] [PMT] −246.48

This results in a monthly payment of $246.48.

Determining APR

The annual percentage rate (APR) is the most commonly used figure for comparing different credit arrangements. Use the following key sequences to calculate APR for a $4,000, three-year (36-month) loan with monthly payments of $127.20:

INPUT	HP-10B	EL-733A	BA II Plus
Loan amount	4000 [PV]	4000 [PV]	4000 [PV]
Loan term: months	36 [N]	36 [n]	36 [N]
Monthly payment	127.20 [+/−] [PMT]	127.20 [+/−] [PMT]	127.20 [+/−] [PMT]
Result: interest rate	[I/YR] 9.0006	[COMP] [I] .75	[CPT] [I/Y] 9.006

The APR on this loan is about 9 percent. With the EL-733A, you must multiply the answer (.75) by 12 months to obtain the annual rate.

Fixed-Rate Mortgage Payments

Home buyers commonly pay for their housing purchases over periods of 15, 20, or 30 years. To calculate the monthly mortgage payment for a 15-year, $100,000 mortgage at 9.5 percent, use the following key sequence:

INPUT	HP-10B	EL-733A	BA II Plus
Mortgage amount	100,000 [PV]	100,000 [PV]	100,000 [PV]
Interest rate	9.5 [I/YR]	9.5 [÷] 12 [=] [i]	9.5 [I/Y]
Length of loan: months	180 [N]	180 [n]	180 [N]
Result: payment	[PMT] −1,044.22	[COMP] [PMT] −1,044.22	[CPT] [PMT] −1,044.22

The monthly payment for this 15-year mortgage is $1,044.22.

Loan Amortization Amount

Do not clear the data from the preceding example if you want to know (1) the remaining balance on the loan, (2) how much of a payment goes toward principal, and (3) how much goes for interest. For example, the 60th payment would use the following key sequences:

INPUT	HP-10B	EL-733A	BA II Plus
60th payment	60 [INPUT] [ ] [AMORT]	60	[2ND] [Amort] 60 [ENTER] [ ] 60 [ENTER]
Results:	Interest: [=] −642.05 Principal: [=] −402.17 Balance: [=] −80,698.95	Principal: [AMRT] −402.17 Interest: [AMRT] −642.05 Balance: [AMRT] −80,698.95	Balance: [ ] 80,698.95 Principal: [ ] −402.17 Interest: [ ] −642.05

The results of this calculation would be (1) $80,698.95 remaining balance, (2) $402.17 principal for this payment, and (3) $642.05 of the payment is for interest.

INVESTMENT AND RETIREMENT CALCULATIONS

Common investing and long-term financial security computations can also be determined using a financial calculator. (Note: HP-10B and BA II Plus users should set compounding frequency to 1 for these computations.)

Discounted Value of Securities

Certificates of deposit, zero-coupon bonds, and Treasury bills promise a single cash flow at some point in the future. To determine, for example, the current price of a zero-coupon bond (no annual interest) that has a maturity value of $1,000 in eight years and an annual expected return of 6 percent, use the following key sequence:

INPUT	HP-10B	EL-733A	BA II Plus
Maturity value	1,000 [FV]	1,000 [FV]	1,000 [FV]
Term: years	8 [N]	8 [n]	8 [N]
Interest rate	6 [I/YR]	6 [i]	6 [I/Y]
Result: Bond value	[PV] −627.41	[COMP] [PV] −627.41	[CPT] [PV] −627.41

The current price you should pay for this bond is $627.41.

Yield to Maturity for Bonds

The yield to maturity for a 10-year, $1,000 bond with a current market value of $880 and an annual interest payment of $80 (a stated rate of 8 percent) would be calculated using the following key sequence:

INPUT	HP-10B	EL-733A	BA II Plus
Current market price	880 [+/−] [PV]	880 [+/−] [PV]	880 [+/−] [PV]
Years to maturity	10 [N]	10 [n]	10 [N]
Interest payment	80 [PMT]	80 [PMT]	80 [PMT]
Maturity value	1000 [FV]	1000 [FV]	1000 [FV]
Result: yield to maturity	[I/YR] 9.9486	[COMP] [i] 9.9486	[CPT] [I/Y] 9.9486

The approximate yield to maturity would be 9.95 percent.

Projecting Needed Retirement Income

To estimate the need for a monthly income of $2,600 (based on today's dollars) when retiring in 20 years, with an annual inflation rate of 5 percent, use the following key sequence:

INPUT	HP-10B	EL-733A	BA II Plus
Current income	2600 PV	2600 PV	2600 PV
Years to retirement	20 N	20 n	20 N
Expected annual inflation	5 I/YR	5 i	5 I/Y
Result: projected future income	FV −6,898.57	COMP FV −6,898.57	CPT FV −6,898.57

You will need a monthly income of $6,898.57 in 20 years to buy what $2,600 buys today.

Determining Annual Contributions to a Retirement Fund

If you want a fund of $400,000 by retirement in 30 years and earn 7 percent a year over that time, use the following key sequence to determine the annual contribution:

INPUT	HP-10B	EL-733A	BA II Plus
Desired retirement account balance	400,000 FV	400,000 FV	400,000 FV
Years to retirement	30 N	30 n	30 N
Expected annual rate of return	7 I/YR	7 i	7 I/Y
Result: required annual deposit	PMT −4,234.56	COMP PMT −4,234.56	CPT PMT −4,234.56

This situation would require annual contributions of $4,234.56.

Portions of this reference have been adapted from Mark A. White, *Financial Analysis with an Electronic Calculator* (Burr Ridge, IL: Richard D. Irwin, 1993). For additional information about electronic calculators for analyzing financial decisions, refer to that text.

APPENDIX E

CONSUMER AGENCIES AND ORGANIZATIONS

The following government agencies and private organizations can offer information and assistance on various financial planning and consumer purchasing areas. These groups can serve your needs when you want to

- Research a financial or consumer topic area.
- Gather information for planning a purchase decision.
- Obtain assistance to resolve a consumer problem.

Section 1 provides an overview of federal, state, and local agencies and other organizations you may contact for information related to various financial planning and consumer topic areas. Section 2 lists state consumer protection offices that can assist you in local matters.

SECTION 1

Most federal agencies may be contacted through the Internet; several Web sites are noted. In addition, consumer information from several federal government agencies may be accessed at www.consumer.gov

Topic Area	Federal Agency	State, Local Agency; Other Organizations
Advertising False advertising Product labeling Deceptive sales practices Warranties	Federal Trade Commission Sixth and Pennsylvania Avenue, NW Washington, DC 20580 (202) 326–2222 (www.ftc.gov)	State Consumer Protection Office c/o State Attorney General or Governor's Office (see Section 2) Council of Better Business Bureaus 4200 Wilson Boulevard Arlington, VA 22203 (703) 276-0100 (www.bbb.org, *also:* www.fraud.org)
Air Travel Air safety Airport regulation Airline route	Federal Aviation Administration 800 Independence Avenue Washington, DC 20591 1–800–FAA–SURE (www.faa.gov)	International Airline Passengers Association Box 660074 Dallas, TX 75266 1–800–527–5888 (www.iapa.com)

SECTION 1   *(Continued)*

Topic Area	Federal Agency	State, Local Agency; Other Organizations
Appliances/Product Safety Potentially dangerous products Complaints against retailers, manufacturers	Consumer Product Safety Commission Washington, DC 20207 1–800–638–CPSC (www.cpsc.gov)	Major Appliance Consumer Action Panel (MACAP) 20 North Wacker Drive Chicago, IL 60606 1–800–621–0477
Automobiles New cars Used cars Automobile repairs Auto safety	Federal Trade Commission (see above) National Highway Traffic Safety Administration 400 Seventh Street, SW Washington, DC 20590 1–800–424–9393 (www.nhtsa.dot.gov)	AUTOCAP/National Automobile Dealers Association 8400 Westpark Drive McLean, VA 22102 (703) 821–7144 Center for Auto Safety 2001 S Street, NW Washington, DC 20009 (202) 328–7700
Banking, Financial Institutions Checking accounts Savings accounts Deposit insurance Financial services	Federal Deposit Insurance Corporation 550 17th Street, NW Washington, DC 20429 1–800–934–3342 (www.fdic.gov) Comptroller of the Currency 15th Street and Pennsylvania Avenue, NW Washington, DC 20219 (202) 447–1600 Federal Reserve Board Washington, DC 20551 (202) 452–3693 (www.bog.frb.fed.us) National Credit Union Administration 1775 Duke St. Alexandria, VA 22314 (703) 518–6300 (ncua.gov)	State Banking Authority (see Section 2) Credit Union National Association Box 431 Madison, WI 53701 (608) 231–4000 (www.cuna.org) American Bankers Association 1120 Connecticut Avenue, NW Washington, DC 20036 (202) 663–5000 (www.aba.com) U.S. Savings Bond rates 1–800–US–BONDS
Career Planning Job training Employment information	Coordinator of Consumer Affairs Department of Labor Washington, DC 20210 (202) 219–6060	State Department of Labor or State Employment Service
Consumer Credit Credit cards Deceptive credit advertising Truth-in-Lending Act Credit rights of women, minorities	Federal Trade Commission Sixth Street and Pennsylvania Avenue, NW Washington, DC 20580 (202) 326–2222 (www.ftc.gov)	Debt Counselors of America (www.dca.org) Consumer Credit Counseling Service 8701 Georgia Avenue, Suite 507 Silver Spring, MD 20910 1–800–388–2227 (www.nccs.org)
Environment Air, water pollution Toxic substances	Environmental Protection Agency Washington, DC 20460 1–800–438–4318 (indoor air quality) 1–800–426–4791 (drinking water safety) (www.epa.gov)	Clean Water Action Project 317 Pennsylvania Avenue, SE Washington, DC 20003 (202) 547–1196

Topic Area	Federal Agency	State, Local Agency; Other Organizations
Food Food grades Food additives Nutritional information	U.S. Department of Agriculture Washington, DC 20250 1–800–424–9121 (www.usda.gov) Food and Drug Administration 5600 Fishers Lane Rockville, MD 20857 (301) 443–3170 (www.fda.gov)	Center for Science in the Public Interest 1875 Connecticut Avenue, NW, Suite 300 Washington, DC 20009 (202) 332–9110 (www.cspinet.org)
Funerals Cost disclosure Deceptive business practices	Federal Trade Commission (see above)	Funeral Service Consumer Arbitration Program 11121 West Oklahoma Avenue Milwaukee, WI 53227 (414) 541–2500
Housing, Real Estate Fair housing practices Mortgages Community development	Department of Housing and Urban Development 451 Seventh Street, SW Washington, DC 20410 1–800–669–9777 (www.hud.gov)	National Association of Realtors 430 North Michigan Avenue Chicago, IL 60611 (312) 329–8200 National Association of Home Builders 15th and M Streets, NW Washington, DC 20005
Insurance Policy conditions Premiums Types of coverage Consumer complaints	Federal Trade Commission (see above) National Flood Insurance Program Box 459 Landam, MD 20706-0459 1–800–638–6620	State Insurance Regulator (see Section 2) American Council of Life Insurance 1001 Pennsylvania Avenue, NW Washington, DC 20004-2599 1–800–942-4242 Insurance Information Institute 110 William Street New York, NY 10038 (212) 669-9250 (www.iii.org)
Investments Stocks, bonds Mutual funds Commodities Investment brokers	Securities and Exchange Commission 450 Fifth Street, NW Washington, DC 20549 (202) 272–7440 (www.sec.gov) Commodity Futures Trading Commission 2033 K Street, NW Washington, DC 20581 (202) 254-8630	Investment Company Institute 1600 M Street, NW Washington, DC 20036 (202) 293–7700 (www.ici.org) National Association of Securities Dealers 1735 K Street, NW Washington, DC 20006 (202) 728–8000 National Futures Association 200 West Madison Street Chicago, IL 60606 1–800–621-3570 Securities Investor Protection Corp. 805 15th Street, NW, Suite 800 Washington, DC 20003 (202) 371–8300

SECTION 1   *(Concluded)*

Topic Area	Federal Agency	State, Local Agency; Other Organizations
Legal Matters Consumer complaints Arbitration	Department of Justice Office of Consumer Litigation Washington, DC 20530 (202) 514–2401	American Arbitration Association 140 West 51st Street New York, NY 10020 (212) 484–4000 American Bar Association 750 North Lake Shore Drive Chicago, IL 60611 (312) 988–5000 (abanet.org)
Mail Order Damaged products Deceptive business practices Illegal use of U.S. mail	U.S. Postal Service Washington, DC 20260-2100 (202) 268–4298 (www.usps.gov)	Direct Marketing Association 6 East 43rd Street New York, NY 10017 (212) 689–4977
Medical Concerns Prescription medications Over-the-counter medications Medical devices Health care	Food and Drug Administration (see above) Public Health Service 200 Independence Avenue, SW Washington, DC 20201 1–800–336–4797 (www.fda.gov)	American Medical Association 535 North Dearborn Chicago, IL 60610 (312) 645–5000 Public Citizen Health Research Group 2000 P Street Washington, DC 20036 (202) 872–0320
Retirement Old-age benefits Pension information Medicare	Social Security Administration 6401 Security Boulevard Baltimore, MD 21235 1–800–772–1213 (www.ssa.gov)	American Association of Retired Persons 601 E Street, NW Washington, DC 20049 (202) 434–2277 (www.aarp.org)
Taxes Tax information Audit procedures	Internal Revenue Service 1111 Constitution Avenue, NW Washington, DC 20204 1–800–829–1040 1–800–TAX–FORM (www.irs.ustreas.gov)	Department of Revenue (in your state capital city) The Tax Foundation One Thomas Circle Washington, DC 20005 (202) 822–9050 National Association of Enrolled Agents 6000 Executive Blvd. Rockville, MD 20852 1–800–424–4339
Telemarketing 900 numbers	Federal Communications Commission 1919 M Street, NW Washington, DC 20554 (202) 632–6999 (www.fcc.gov)	National Consumers League 815 Fifteenth Street, NW Washington, DC 20005 (202) 639–8140 (www.natlconsumersleague.org)
Utilities Cable television Utility rates	Federal Communications Commission 1919 M Street, NW Washington, DC 20554 (202) 632–6999 (www.fcc.gov)	State utility commission (in your state capital)

Information on additional government agencies and private organizations may be obtained from these publications:

Consumer's Resource Handbook
Consumer Information Center
Pueblo, CO 81009
www.pueblo.gsa.gov
(copies available at no charge)

Consumer Sourcebook
Gale Research, Inc.
Book Tower
Detroit, MI 48226
(available in many school and public libraries)

Section 2

This section provides contacts for state consumer protection, banking, and insurance agencies. Many state consumer protection offices may be accessed through the Web site of the National Association of Attorneys General at www.naag.org.

You may also find the Web site for your state consumer protection office by using a search engine with the following words: "(state)+consumer+protection+agency".

Some of the most informative state consumer protection Web sites that could be useful to all consumers include

- The Tennessee Divison of Consumer Affairs at www.state.tn.us/consumer.
- The Florida Department of Agriculture and Consumer Servcies at www/fl-ag.com.
- The New Jersey Consumer Affair Department at www.state.nj.us/lpa/ca/home.htm.
- The Minnesota attorney general at www.ag.state.mn.us/consumer.

Most state departments of insurance may be accessed on the Internet at www.fdn.net/state-doi.html.

The Web sites of state tax departments are available at www.taxadmin.org or www.best.com/~ftmexpat/html/taxsites.statelaw.html.

State Consumer Protection Offices	State Banking Authorities	State Insurance Regulators
Alabama Consumer Protection Division Office of Attorney General 11 South Union Street Montgomery, AL 36130 (334) 242–7334 1–800–392–5658 (toll-free in AL)	Superintendent of Banks 101 South Union Street Montgomery, AL 36130 (334) 242–3452	Insurance Commissioner 135 South Union Street, #200 Montgomery, AL 36130 (334) 269–3550
Alaska (contact Better Business Bureau in Anchorage)	Director of Banking, Securities and Corporations P.O. Box 110807 Juneau, AK 99811-0807 (907) 465-2521	Director of Insurance P.O. Box 110805 Juneau, AK 99811-0805 (907) 465–2515
Arizona Consumer Fraud Division Office of Attorney General 1275 West Washington Street Phoenix, AZ 85007 (602) 542–3702 1–800–352–8431 (toll-free in AZ)	Superintendent of Banks 2910 North 44th St. Phoenix, AZ 85018 (602) 255–4421 1–800–544–0708 (toll-free in AZ)	Department of Insurance 2910 North 44th Street, Suite 210 Phoenix, AZ 85018-7256 (602) 912–8444

SECTION 2   *(Continued)*

State Consumer Protection Offices	State Banking Authorities	State Insurance Regulators
Arkansas		
Consumer Protection Division Office of Attorney General 200 Catlett Prien 323 Center Street Little Rock, AR 72201 (501) 682–2341 1–800–482–8982 (toll-free in AR)	Bank Commissioner Tower Building 323 Center Street, Suite 500 Little Rock, AR 72201-2613 (501) 324–9019	Insurance Commissioner 1200 West 3rd St. Little Rock, AR 72201-1904 (501) 371–2600 1–800–852–5494
California		
California Department of Consumer Affairs 400 R Street, Suite 3000 Sacramento, CA 95814 (916) 445–4465 1–800–952–5200 (toll-free in CA)	Superintendent of Banks 111 Pine Street, Suite 1100 San Francisco, CA 94111-5613 (415) 263–8501 1–800–622–0620 (toll-free in CA)	Commissioner of Insurance 300 Capitol Mall, Suite 1500 Sacramento, CA 95814 (916) 445–5544 1–800–927–HELP (toll-free in CA)
Colorado		
Consumer Protection Unit Office of Attorney General 1525 Sherman St., 5th Floor Denver, CO 80203-1760 (303) 866–5189	State Bank Commissioner Division of Banking 1560 Broadway St., Suite 1175 Denver, CO 80202 (303) 894–7575	Commissioner of Insurance 1560 Broadway St., Suite 850 Denver, CO 80202 (303) 894–7499 (ext. 400)
Connecticut		
Department of Consumer Protection State Office Building 165 Capitol Avenue Hartford, CT 06106 (203) 566–2534 1–800–842–2649 (toll-free in CT)	Banking Commissioner 260 Constitution Plaza Hartford, CT 06103 (800) 240–8299	Insurance Commissioner P.O. Box 816 Hartford, CT 06142-0816 (203) 297–3800
Delaware		
Consumer Protection Unit Department of Justice 820 North French Street, 4th Floor Wilmington, DE 19801 (302) 577–3250	State Bank Commissioner 555 East Lockerman Street, Suite 210 Dover, DE 19901 (302) 739–4235 1–800–638–3376 (toll-free in DE)	Insurance Commissioner 841 Silver Lake Boulevard Dover, DE 19901 (302) 739–4251 1–800–282–8611 (toll-free in DE)
District of Columbia		

Department of Consumer and Regulatory
  Affairs
614 H Street, NW
Washington, DC 20001
(202) 727–7120
	Superintendent of Banking and Financial
	  Institutions
	714 14th St., NW (11th floor)
	Washington, DC 20005
	(202) 727–1563
		Superintendent of Insurance
		441 4th Street, NW
		One Judiciary Square, 8th Floor
		Washington, DC 20001
		(202) 727–8000 (ext. 3007)

Florida		
Department of Agriculture and Consumer Services Division of Consumer Services Mayo Building, 2nd Floor Tallahassee, FL 32399-0800 (904) 488–2221 1–800–435–7352 (toll-free in FL)	State Comptroller State Capitol Building Tallahassee, FL 32399-0350 (904) 488–6311 1–800–848–3792 (toll-free in FL)	Insurance Commissioner Plaza Level Eleven–The Capitol Tallahassee, FL 32399-0300 (904) 922–3100 1–800–342-2762 (toll-free in FL)
Georgia		
Governor's Office of Consumer Affairs Two M. L. King, Jr., Drive, SE Suite 356 Atlanta, GA 30334 (404) 656–3990 1–800–869–1123 (toll-free in GA)	Commissioner Banking and Finance 2990 Brandywine Road, Suite 200 Atlanta, GA 30341-5565 (404) 986–1633	Insurance Commissioner 2 Martin L. King, Jr., Drive Atlanta, GA 30334 (404) 656–2070
Hawaii		
Office of Consumer Protection Department of Commerce and Consumer Affairs Box 3767 Honolulu, HI 96813-3767 (808) 586–2636	Commissioner Financial Institutions P.O. Box 2054 Honolulu, HI 96805 (808) 586–2820	Insurance Commissioner P.O. Box 3614 Honolulu, HI 96811-3614 (808) 586–2790

SECTION 2   *(Continued)*

State Consumer Protection Offices	State Banking Authorities	State Insurance Regulators
Idaho		
Consumer Protection Unit Office of Attorney General 650 West State Street Boise, ID 83720-1000 (208) 334–2424 1–800–432–3545 (toll-free in ID)	Director Department of Finance 700 West State Street, 2nd Floor Boise, ID 83720-0031 (208) 334–3313	Director of Insurance 700 West State Street Boise, ID 83720 (208) 334–4320 1–800–721–3272 (toll-free in ID)
Illinois		
Consumer Protection Division Office of Attorney General 222 South College Springfield, IL 62706 (217) 782–0244 1–800–642–3112 (toll-free in IL)	Commissioner of Banks and Trust Companies 500 East Monroe Street Springfield, IL 62701 (217) 785–2837 1–800–634–5452 (toll-free in IL)	Director of Insurance 320 West Washington Street Springfield, IL 62767 (217) 782–4515
Indiana		
Consumer Protection Division Office of Attorney General 402 West Washington Street Indianapolis, IN 46204 (317) 232–6330 1–800–382–5516 (toll-free in IN)	Director Department of Financial Institutions 402 West Washington Street Indianapolis, IN 46204-2759 (317) 232–3955 1–800–382–4880 (toll-free in IN)	Commissioner of Insurance 311 West Washington Street, Suite 300 Indianapolis, IN 46204-2787 (317) 232–3250 1–800–622–4461 (toll-free in IN)
Iowa		
Consumer Protection Division Office of Attorney General 1300 East Walnut Street, 2nd Floor Des Moines, IA 50319 (515) 281–5926	Superintendent of Banking 200 East Grand, Suite 300 Des Moines, IA 50309 (515) 281–4014	Insurance Commissioner Lucas State Office Building, 6th Floor Des Moines, IA 50319 (515) 281–5705
Kansas		
Consumer Protection Division Office of Attorney General 301 West 10th Street Topeka, KS 66612-1597 (913) 296–3751 1–800–432–2310 (toll-free in KS)	State Bank Commissioner 700 Jackson Street, Suite 300 Topeka, KS 66603-3714 (913) 296–2266	Commissioner of Insurance 420 SW 9th Street Topeka, KS 66612 (913) 296–7829 1–800–432–2484 (toll-free in KS)
Kentucky		
Consumer Protection Division Office of Attorney General Box 2000 Frankfort, KY 40601-2000 (502) 562–2200 1–800–432–9257 (toll-free in KY)	Commissioner, Department of Financial Institutions 477 Versailles Road Frankfort, KY 40601 (502) 564–3390	Insurance Commissioner 215 West Main Street P.O. Box 517 Frankfort, KY 40601 (502) 564–6088
Louisiana		
Consumer Protection Section Office of Attorney General State Capitol Building Box 94095 Baton Rouge, LA 70804-9095 (504) 342–9638	Commissioner Financial Institutions P.O. Box 94095 Baton Rouge, LA 70804 (504) 925–4660	Commissioner of Insurance P.O. Box 94214 Baton Rouge, LA 70804-9214 (504) 342–1259
Maine		
Consumer and Antitrust Division Office of Attorney General State House Station Number 6 Augusta, ME 04333 (207) 624–8527 1–800–332–8529 (toll-free in ME)	Superintendent of Banking 36 State House Station Augusta, ME 04333-0036 (207) 624–8570	Superintendent of Insurance State House Station Number 34 Augusta, ME 04333-0034 (207) 624–8475 1–800–300–5000 (toll-free in ME)

SECTION 2   *(Continued)*

State Consumer Protection Offices	State Banking Authorities	State Insurance Regulators
Maryland		
Consumer Protection Division	Bank Commissioner	Insurance Commissioner
Office of Attorney General	501 St. Paul Place, 13th Floor	501 St. Paul Place, 7th Floor
200 St. Paul Place, 16th Floor	Baltimore, MD 21202	Baltimore, MD 21202
Baltimore, MD 21202-2021	(301) 333–6812	(410) 333–1782
(410) 528–8662		1–800–492–6116 (toll-free in MD)
Massachusetts		
Consumer Protection Division	Commissioner of Banks	Commissioner of Insurance
Department of Attorney General	100 Cambridge Street	470 Atlanta Avenue
1 Ashburton Place	Boston, MA 02202	Boston, MA 02110-2223
Boston, MA 02103	(617) 727–3145	(617) 521–7777
(617) 727–2200		
Michigan		
Consumer Protection Division	Commissioner	Commissioner of Insurance
Office of Attorney General	Financial Institutions Bureau	Insurance Bureau
Box 30213	P.O. Box 30224	611 West Ottawa Street
Lansing, MI 48909	Lansing, MI 48909	Lansing, MI 48933
(517) 373–1140	(517) 373–3460	(517) 373–0240
Minnesota		
Office of Consumer Services	Deputy Commissioner of Commerce	Commissioner of Commerce
Office of Attorney General	133 East 7th Street	133 East 7th Street
445 Minnesota St.	St. Paul, MN 55101	St. Paul, MN 55101
St. Paul, MN 55101	(612) 296–2135	(612) 296–2488
(612) 296–3353		
Mississippi		
Consumer Protection Division	Commissioner	Commissioner of Insurance
Office of Attorney General	Department of Banking and Consumer	1804 Walter Sillers Building
Box 22947	Finance	Jackson, MS 39201-1190
Jackson, MS 39225-2947	P.O. Box 23729	(601) 359–3569
(601) 359–4231	Jackson, MS 39225-3729	1–800–562–2957 (toll-free in MS)
1–800–281–4418 (toll-free in MS)	(601) 359–1031	
	1–800–844–2499 (toll-free in MS)	
Missouri		
Office of Attorney General	Commissioner of Finance	Director of Insurance
Box 899	P.O. Box 716	301 West High Street, Room 630
Jefferson City, MO 65102	Jefferson City, MO 65102	P.O. Box 690
(314) 751–3321	(314) 751–3242	Jefferson City, MO 65102
1–800–392–8222 (toll-free in MO)	1–800–722–3321 (toll-free in MO)	(573) 751–2640
		1–800–726–7390 (toll-free in MO)
Montana		
Consumer Affairs Unit	Commissioner	Commissioner of Insurance
Department of Commerce	Financial Institutions	126 North Sanders
1424 Ninth Avenue	Box 200546	Helena, MT 59601
Helena, MT 59620-0501	Helena, MT 59620-0546	(406) 444–2040
(406) 444–4312	(406) 444–2091	1–800–332–6148 (toll-free in MT)
Nebraska		
Consumer Protection Division	Director of Banking and Finance	Director of Insurance
Department of Justice	1200 N Street, Suite 311	941 "O" Street, Suite 400
2115 State Capitol, Box 98920	Lincoln, NE 68508	Lincoln, NE 68508
Lincoln, NE 68509	(402) 471–2171	(402) 471–2201
(402) 471–2682		
Nevada		
Commissioner of Consumer Affairs	Commissioner	Commissioner of Insurance
Department of Commerce	Financial Institutions	1665 Hot Springs Road
1850 East Sahara, Suite 101	406 East Second Street	Capitol Complex 152
Las Vegas, NV 89158	Carson City, NV 89710	Carson City, NV 89710
(702) 486–7355	(702) 687–4260	(702) 687–4270
1–800–362–5202 (toll-free in NV)		1–800–992-0900 (toll-free in NV)

SECTION 2   *(Continued)*

State Consumer Protection Offices	State Banking Authorities	State Insurance Regulators
New Hampshire Consumer Protection and Antitrust Division Office of Attorney General State House Annex Concord, NH 03301 (603) 271–3641	Bank Commissioner 169 Manchester Street Concord, NH 03301 (603) 271–3561	Insurance Commissioner 169 Manchester Street Concord, NH 03301-5151 (603) 271–2261 1–800–852–3416 (toll-free in NH)
New Jersey Division of Consumer Affairs P.O. Box 45027 Newark, NJ 07101 (201) 504–6534	Commissioner of Banking 20 West State Street, CN-325 Trenton, NJ 08625 (609) 292–3420	Commissioner Department of Insurance 20 West State Street, CN-329 Trenton, NJ 08625 (609) 984–2444
New Mexico Consumer and Economic Crime Division Office of Attorney General P.O. Drawer 1508 Santa Fe, NM 87504 (505) 827–6060 1–800–678–1508 (toll-free in NM)	Director Financial Institutions Division P.O. Box 25101 Santa Fe, NM 87504 (505) 827–7100	Superintendent of Insurance P.O. Drawer 1269 Santa Fe, NM 87504-1269 (505) 827–4698 1–800–947–4722 (toll-free in NM)
New York Bureau of Consumer Frauds and Protection Office of Attorney General State Capitol Albany, NY 12224 (518) 474–5481 1–800–771–7755 (toll-free in NY)	Superintendent of Banks Two Rector Street New York, NY 10006-1894 (212) 618–6653 1–800–522–3330 (toll-free in NY)	Superintendent of Insurance 160 West Broadway New York, NY 10013-3393 (212) 602–2488 1–800–342–3736 (toll-free in NY)
North Carolina Consumer Protection Section Office of Attorney General Department of Justice Building Box 629 Raleigh, NC 27602 (919) 733–7741	Commissioner of Banks P.O. Box 29512 Raleigh, NC 27626-0512 (919) 733–3016	Commissioner of Insurance Dobbs Building P.O. Box 26387 Raleigh, NC 27611 (919) 733–2004 1–800–662–7777 (toll-free in NC)
North Dakota Office of Attorney General 600 East Boulevard Bismarck, ND 58505 (701) 224–2210 1–800–472–2600 (toll-free in ND)	Commissioner of Banking and Financial Institutions 2900 N. 19th Street, #3 Bismarck, ND 58501-5305 (701) 328–9933	Commissioner of Insurance Capitol Building, 5th Floor 600 East Boulevard Avenue Bismarck, ND 58505-0320 (701) 224–2440 1–800–247–0560 (toll-free in ND)
Ohio Consumer Frauds and Crimes Section Office of Attorney General 30 East Broad Street State Office Tower, 25th Floor Columbus, OH 43266-0410 (614) 466–4986 1–800–282–0515 (toll-free in OH)	Superintendent of Banks 77 South High Street, 21st Floor Columbus, OH 43266-0549 (614) 466–2932	Director of Insurance 2100 Stella Court Columbus, OH 43215-1067 (614) 644–2658 1–800–686–1526 (toll-free in OH)
Oklahoma Assistant Attorney General for Consumer Affairs Office of Attorney General 4545 N. Lincoln Blvd., Suite 260 Oklahoma City, OK 73105 (405) 521–4274	Bank Commissioner 4545 North Lincoln Boulevard, Suite 164 Oklahoma City, OK 73105 (405) 521–2783	Insurance Commissioner 3814 Santa Fe Oklahoma City, OK 73118 (405) 521–2991 1–800–522–0071 (toll-free in OK)

SECTION 2   *(Continued)*

State Consumer Protection Offices	State Banking Authorities	State Insurance Regulators
Oregon		
Financial Fraud Section	Administrator	Insurance Commissioner
Department of Justice	Division of Finance and Corporate	350 Winter Street, NE
1162 Court Street, NE	Securities	Salem, OR 97310-0700
Salem, OR 97310	350 Winter Street, NE, Room 21	(503) 378–4636
(503) 378–4732	Salem, OR 97310	
	(503) 378–4140	
	1–800–PA–BANKS (toll-free in PA)	
Pennsylvania		
Bureau of Consumer Protection	Secretary of Banking	Insurance Commissioner
Office of Attorney General	333 Market Street, 16th Floor	1326 Strawberry Square, 13th Floor
Strawberry Square, 14th Floor	Harrisburg, PA 17101	Harrisburg, PA 17120
Harrisburg, PA 17120	(717) 787–6991	(717) 787–2317
(717) 787–9707	1–800–PABANKS (toll-free in PA)	
1–800–441–2555 (toll-free in PA)		
Puerto Rico		
Department of Consumer Affairs	Commissioner of Financial Institutions	Commissioner of Insurance
Minillas Station, Box 41059	1492 Ponce de Leon Ave. (No. 600)	Fernandez Juncos Station
Santurce, PR 00940-1059	San Juan, PR 00907-4192	P.O. Box 8330
(787) 721–0940	(707) 723–3131	Santurce, PR 00910
		(809) 722–8686
Rhode Island		
Consumer Protection Division	Associate Director and Superintendent of	Insurance Commissioner
Department of Attorney General	Banking and Securities	233 Richmond Street
72 Pine Street	233 Richmond Street, Suite 231	Providence, RI 02903-4233
Providence, RI 02903	Providence, RI 02903-4231	(401) 277–2223
(401) 274–4400	(401) 277–2405	
1–800–852–7776 (toll-free in RI)		
South Carolina		
Department of Consumer Affairs	Commissioner of Banking	Chief Insurance Commissioner
Box 5757	1015 Sumter Street, Room 309	P.O. Box 100105
Columbia, SC 29250–5757	Columbia, SC 29201	Columbia, SC 24201
(803) 734–9452	(803) 734–2001	(803) 737–6150
1–800–922–1594 (toll-free in SC)		1–800–768–3467 (toll-free in SC)
South Dakota		
Division of Consumer Affairs	Director of Banking	Director of Insurance
Office of Attorney General	State Capitol Building	Insurance Building
500 East Capitol Avenue	500 East Capitol Avenue	500 East Capitol
Pierre, SD 57501-5070	Pierre, SD 57501-5070	Pierre, SD 57501-3940
(605) 773-4400	(605) 773–3421	(605) 773–3563
1–800–300–1986 (toll-free in SD)		
Tennessee		
Antitrust and Consumer Protection Division	Commissioner	Commissioner of Insurance
Office of Attorney General	Financial Institutions	500 James Robertson Parkway
500 James Robertson Parkway	500 Charlotte Ave., 4th Floor	Nashville, TN 37243-0565
Nashville, TN 37243-0600	Nashville, TN 37243-0705	(615) 741–2218
(615) 741–4737	(615) 741–2236	1–800–342–4029 (toll-free in TN)
1–800–342–8385 (toll-free in TN)		
Texas		
Consumer Protection Division	Banking Commissioner	Consumer Services
Office of Attorney General	2601 North Lamar	Texas Department of Insurance
Capitol Station, Box 12548	Austin, TX 78705	P.O. Box 149104
Austin, TX 78711	(512) 479–1200	Austin, TX 78714-9104
(512) 463–2070		(512) 463–6464
		1–800–252–3439 (toll-free in TX)

SECTION 2   *(Concluded)*

State Consumer Protection Offices	State Banking Authorities	State Insurance Regulators
Utah		
Division of Consumer Protection Department of Commerce 160 East 300 South, Box 146704 Salt Lake City, UT 84114-6704 (801) 530–6601 1–800–721–7233 (toll-free in UT)	Commissioner Financial Institutions P.O. Box 89 Salt Lake City, UT 84110-0089 (801) 538–8830	Commissioner of Insurance 3110 State Office Building Salt Lake City, UT 84114 (801) 538–3805 1–800–439–3805 (toll-free in UT)
Vermont		

Assistant Attorney General
Public Protection Division
Office of Attorney General
109 State Street
Montpelier, VT 05609-1001
(802) 828–3171
	Commissioner of Banking, Insurance and
	  Securities
	89 Main St., 2nd Floor
	Montpelier, VT 05620-3101
	(802) 828–3307
		Commissioner of Banking, Insurance and
		  Securities
		89 Main St., Drawer 20
		Montpelier, VT 05620-3101
		(802) 828–4884

Virginia		
Antitrust and Consumer Litigation Section Office of Attorney General Supreme Court Building 900 East Main Street Richmond, VA 23219 (804) 786–2116 1–800–451–1525 (toll-free in VA)	Commissioner Financial Institutions P.O. Box 640 Richmond, VA 23218-0640 (804) 371–9657 1–800–552–7945 (toll-free in VA)	Commissioner of Insurance 1300 East Main Street Richmond, VA 23219 (804) 371–9694 1–800–552–7945 (toll-free in VA)
Washington		
Consumer Protection Division Office of Attorney General Box 40118 Olympia, WA 98504-0118 (360) 753–6210 1–800–551–4636 (toll-free in WA)	Supervisor of Banking P.O. Box 41023 Olympia, WA 98504-1203 (360) 753–6520 1–800–372–8303 (toll-free in WA)	Insurance Commissioner Insurance Building AQ21 Box 40255 Olympia, WA 98504-0255 (360) 753–3613 1–800–562–6900 (toll-free in WA)
West Virginia		
Consumer Protection Division Office of Attorney General 812 Quarrier Street, 6th Floor Charleston, WV 25301 (304) 348–8986 1–800–368–8808 (toll-free in WV)	Commissioner of Banking State Capitol Complex Building 3, Room 311 Charleston, WV 25305-0240 (304) 558–2294 1–800–642–9056 (toll-free in WV)	Insurance Commissioner 2019 Washington Street East Box 50540 Charleston, WV 25305-0540 (304) 558–3856 1–800–642–9004 (toll-free in WV)
Wisconsin		
Division of Trade and Consumer Protection Box 8911 Madison, WI 53708 (608) 224–4950 1–800–422–7128 (toll-free in WI)	Commissioner of Banking 101 East Wilson, 5th Floor Madison, WI 53707-7876 (608) 261–9555 1–800–452–3328 (toll-free in WI)	Commissioner of Insurance 121 East Wilson Madison, WI 53702 (608) 266–0103 1–800–236–8517 (toll-free in WI)
Wyoming		
Office of Attorney General 123 State Capitol Building Cheyenne, WY 82002 (307) 777–7874	Manager Division of Banking Herschler Building 3rd Floor East Cheyenne, WY 82002 (307) 777–7797	Commissioner of Insurance Herschler Building 122 West 25th Street Cheyenne, WY 82002-0440 (307) 777–7402 1–800–438–5768 (toll-free in WY)

ENDNOTES

CHAPTER 6

1. Peter Pae, "Credit Junkies," *The Wall Street Journal,* December 26, 1991, p. 1.
2. *Business Review* (Philadelphia: Federal Reserve Bank of Philadelphia, January–February 1992), p. 5.
3. *Nilson Report, Credit Card News,* and American Express Company, April 1994.
4. Amy Cortese, "The Ultimate Plastic," *Business Week,* May 19, 1997, pp. 119–22.
5. Experian Consumer Education Department, *Reports on Credit,* 1997.
6. *Cosigning a Loan: Facts for Consumers* (Washington, DC: Federal Trade Commission, Bureau of Consumer Protection, January 1988), p. 1.
7. Experian Consumer Education Department, *Reports on Credit.*
8. Vivian Marino, "In the Clear: Keep an Eye Out for Black Marks on Your Credit Report," *Chicago Tribune,* September 9, 1993, "Your Money" section, p. 1.
9. *Banking Legislation & Policy* (Philadelphia: Federal Reserve Bank of Philadelphia, April–June, 1997), pp. 3–4.

CHAPTER 7

1. *Lehman Brothers Global Economics,* based on data from the Federal Reserve Bank, U.S. Department of Commerce, and American Express Company, 1994.
2. *Debt Counseling,* rev. ed., AFL-CIO publication no. 140, March 1981.
3. *Business Week,* May 5, 1997, p. 54.
4. *At Home With Consumers* (Washington, DC.: Direct Selling Education Foundation, April 1997), p. 2.

CHAPTER 11

1. *U.S. Industrial Outlook* (Washington, DC: U.S. Government Printing Office,1994), p. 42-2; Health Care Financing Administration, press release, January 27, 1997; *Chicago Tribune,* January 13, 1998, p. 5.
2. *U.S. Industrial Outlook,* p. 42-5; *Chicago Tribune,* January 13 1998, p. 5.
3. *U.S. Industrial Outlook,* pp. 42-1, 42-2.

4. George Anders and Laurie McGinley, "Surgical Strike," *The Wall Street Journal,* May 6, 1997, p. A1.
5. "Federally Funded Health Services: Information on Seven Programs Serving Low Income Women and Children," *Reports and Testimony,* General Accounting Office/HRD-92-73 FS, May 28, 1992, p. 24.
6. *Insurance Handbook for Reporters,* 2nd ed. (Northbrook, IL: Allstate Insurance Group, 1985), p. 130.
7. *The Consumer's Guide to Disability Insurance* (Washington DC: Health Insurance Association of America, September 1991), p. 1.
8. *Source Book of Health Insurance Data* (Washington, DC: Health Insurance Association of America, 1991), pp. 95–96.
9. National Consumer League, *NCL Bulletin,* July–August 1994, p. 3.
10. The Agency for Health Care Policy and Research, *Examining Long-Term Care,* February 22, 1996, p. 6.
11. Eve Tahmincioglu, "The Catch-22 of Long-Term Care Insurance," *Kiplinger's Personal Finance,* May 1997, pp. 97–102.
12. Peter Weaver, "Long-Term Coverage Eligible for Tax Breaks," *Nation's Business,* February 1997, p. 62.
13. "Blue Cross and Blue Shield: Experiences of Weak Plans Underscore the Role of Effective State Oversight," *Report to the Chairman,* Permanent Subcommittee on Investigations, Committee of Governmental Affairs, U.S. Senate, General Accounting Office HEHS-94-71, April 1994, p. 1.
14. George J. Church, "Backlash Against HMOs," *Time,* April 14, 1997, pp. 32–36.
15. Jagadeesh Gokhale, "Medicare: Usual and Customary Remedies Will No Longer Work," *Economic Commentary,* Federal Reserve Bank of Cleveland, April 1997, p. 1.

CHAPTER 12

1. *1997 Life Insurance Fact Book* (Washington, DC.: American Council of Life Insurance, 1997), p. 11.
2. Lynn Asinof, "Group Life Insurance Often Costs More," *The Wall Street Journal,* September 3, 1991, p. C13.
3. *Chicago Tribune,* May 21, 1992, p. 3
4. *1996 Life Insurance Fact Book* (Washington, DC.: American Council of Life Insurance, 1996), p. 37.

CHAPTER 13

1. Nancy Dunnan, *Dun & Bradstreet Guide to $Your Investments: 1994* (New York: HarperCollins, 1994), p. 18.
2. Douglas Goldstein and Joyce Flory, *The Online Guide to Personal Finance and Investing* (Burr Ridge, IL: Irwin Professional Publishing, 1997), p. 2.
3. Ibid.

CHAPTER 14

1. "Holy Cow! That's Some Bull," *Newsweek,* July 28, 1997, p. 52.
2. Ibid.
3. John Downes and Jordan Elliot Goodman, eds., *Dictionary of Finance and Investment Terms* (Houppauge, NY: Barron's Educational Series, 1995), p. 406.
4. Ibid., p. 412.
5. Seth Godin, ed., *The 1997 Information Please Business Almanac* (Boston: Houghton Mifflin, 1996), p. 209.
6. Downes and Goodman, *Dictionary of Finance and Investment Terms,* p. 629.
7. Godin, *The 1997 Information Please Business Almanac,* p. 197.

CHAPTER 15

1. Leah Nathans Spiro and Kelley Holland, "The Trouble with Munis," *Business Week,* September 4, 1994, p. 45.
2. Ibid., p. 50.
3. Sumner N. Levine and Caroline Levine, *The Irwin Business and Investment Almanac 1996* (Burr Ridge, IL: Irwin Professional Publishing, 1996), p. 511.

CHAPTER 16

1. Information was obtained from the Internet on October 11, 1997. The Internet address is http://biz.yahoo.com/p/f/fqmx/h.html.
2. John Downes and Jordan Elliot Goodman, *Dictionary of Finance and Investment Terms* (Hauppauge NY: Barron's, 1995), p. 274.
3. *1997 Mutual Fund Fact Book* (Washington, DC: Investment Company Institute, 1997), pp. 19, 35.
4. Peter Lynch and John Rothchild, *Learn to Earn* (New York: Fireside Publishing, 1995), p. 124.
5. Prospectus for the American Mutual Fund, December 31, 1997, p. x.
6. *The Wall Street Journal,* October 10, 1997, p. C21.

CHAPTER 17

1. Barbara Donnelly Granito, "How to Manage the Real-Estate Balancing Act," *The Wall Street Journal,* August 12, 1994, p. C13.
2. Ibid.
3. Georgette Jasen, "Second Home Can Be Rewarding, but Not in the Investment Sense," *The Wall Street Journal,* August 23, 1994, p. C1.
4. This section is based on Wilbur W. Widicus and Thomas E. Stitzel, *Personal Investing,* 5th ed. (Burr Ridge, IL: Richard D. Irwin, 1989), pp. 321–23.
5. Joanne Lipman, "Land and Opportunity," *The Wall Street Journal,* December 2, 1995, p. D22.

6. William M. Pride, Robert J. Hughes, and Jack R. Kapoor, *Business,* 5th ed. (Boston: Houghton Mifflin, 1996), p. 128.
7. Lynn Asinof, "Real Estate Lures Investors Again after a Deep Slump," *The Wall Street Journal,* October 22, 1992, p. C1.
8. Ibid.
9. Alexandra Peers, "Keep Everything," *The Wall Street Journal,* December 9, 1994. p. R8.
10. *Consumer Alert: Investing in Rare Coins* (Washington, DC: Federal Trade Commission, n.d.).

CHAPTER 18

1. Kerry Capell, "How to Retire Successfully," *Business Week,* July 21, 1997, pp. 60–61.
2. "What's in Store for the Future?" *Financial Insights,* September 1992, p. 1.
3. "New Firm Specializes in Reverse Mortgages," *The Wheaton Leader,* March 30, 1994, business section, p. 2.
4. "Retirement Planning after Divorce," *Barron's,* August 31, 1992, p. 74.
5. Ibid.
6. Geoffrey Smith, "Nest-Egg Planning for the Not-So-Average Joe," *Business Week,* July 21, 1997, pp. 78–84.
7. Eric Schine, "There's Never Any Reason for Us to Be Bored," *Business Week,* July 21, 1997, pp. 70–76.
8. Jeanette A. Brandt, "Housing and Community Preferences: Will They Change in Retirement?" *Family Economics Review,* U.S. Department of Agriculture, May 1989, p. 7.
9. Schine, "There's Never Any Reason for Us to Be Bored," p. 76.
10. *Social Security: Understanding the Benefits* (Washington, DC: Social Security Administration, January 1997), p. 5.
11. Carol Kleinman, "Firms Shifting Retirement Planning, Risk to Workers," *Chicago Tribune,* January 19, 1992, sec. 8, p. 1.
12. Mary Rowland, "Pick Through the Annuity Tangle," *The New York Times,* February 16, 1992, p. 17.
13. Jonathan Clements, "Go Global, but Use Your Age as a Travel Guide," *The Wall Street Journal,* January 6, 1995, p. R5.

CHAPTER 19

1. This section is based on Geoffrey Smith, "Nest-Egg Planning for the Not-So-Average Joe," *Business Week,* July 21, 1997, pp. 78–84.
2. Murray Iseman, "Common Estate Planning Fiascoes," *Barron's,* January 2, 1989, p. 27.
3. Lynn Asinof, "Trust Funds Are Just for the Rich? Think Again," *The Wall Street Journal,* January 9, 1995, pp. C1, C10.
4. Ibid.
5. Ibid.
6. Lynn Asinof, "Estate Planning Techniques for the Rich," *The Wall Street Journal,* January 11, 1985, pp. C1, C18.
7. Ibid.
8. Chris J. Prestopino, *Introduction to Estate Planning* (Homewood, IL: Richard D. Irwin, 1989), p. 33.
9. *Looking Beyond Your Current Estate Plan,* American Society of CLU and ChFC, 1997.

INDEX

Blue-sky law, 450
Board and care home, 550
Boardinghouse, 549
Bodenheimer, Thomas, 350
Bodily injury liability, 317, 319, 325
Bond, 462, 463, 481
    annual interest, 469
    annual report, 477–478
    approximate market value, 469,
        483
    buying or selling, 476–478,
        480–481
    calculation of yield, 478,
        480–481
    comparing investments, 532
    convertible, 466, 484
    corporate: see Corporate bond
    coupon, 468
    general obligation, 474, 484
    government, 408, 472–476
    high-grade, 480
    information in newspaper, 476,
        477
    Internet, 488
    Jonathan Hoenig on, 474
    life situation, 487
    mechanics of transaction,
        471–472
    mortgage, 466, 484
    municipal, 474, 484
    in portfolio, 492
    registered, 468, 484
    repayment at maturity, 470
    researching, 468
    revenue, 474, 494
    times interest earned ratio, 482
    Treasury, 472, 473
    typical transaction, 470
    municipal, 474, 484
    serial, 467, 484
    yield to maturity for, 630
    zero-coupon, 469, 485, 630
Bond fund, 471, 497
Bond indenture, 464, 484
Bond ratings, 478, 480
Bond value, 469, 470
Book value, 440, 456, 457
Borden, Inc., 470
Borrow stock certificate, 454, 455
Borrowing, 24, 125
Boss, being your own, 52
Bottom Line/Personal, 607
Bounds, Wendy, 530
Braddock, Anna, 530
Brandname product, 235–236

Brandt, Jeanette A., 644
Brickman, Brian, 367
Bristol-Myers Squibb, 435
Broad form home insurance (HO-2),
    312, 313
Brobeck, Stephen, 154
Brock, Josh, 221, 391, 535, 604
Brock, Pam, 391, 535, 604
Brokerage services, 447, 450, 505
Budget, 62, 74, 84, 423–424; see also
    Financial statement
    annual summary, 81
    current situation, 74–75
    emergency fund and savings, 77
    evaluation, 80–82
    financial direction, 75–77
    fixed expenses, 77
    flexible, 13
    income, 77
    monthly, 78, 81
    recording system, 79–80
    spending patterns, 80
    variable expenses, 77
Budget allocation, 81
    after-tax, 76
    revisions, 80, 82
Budget variance, 80, 84
Bull market, 439, 457
Bump-up CD, 135
Bureau of Census, 67
Bureau of Labor Statistics, 16, 36, 76,
    87, 545
Burton, John, 132
Business contact, 39, 41
Business failure risk, 405
Business in home, 14
Business service, 37
Business Week, 29, 128, 424, 515
    bond funds and, 471
    collectibles and, 530
    education and, 540, 541
    estate planning and, 603
    financial planning and, 607, 613
    housing vs. retirement and, 542
    investments in, 501
    mutual fund ratings in, 502
    real estate in, 523
    REITs in, 521
    Social Security and, 553
    WWW site, 361, 488, 499, 515,
        534, 574
Buy-down, 288, 293
Buyer agent, 278, 280
Buyer protection insurance, 143
Buyer's market, 280

Buying
    leasing versus, 260
    residence, renting versus, 270
Buying long, 454
Buying service, 233
Bypass trust, 599

C

Cable News Network financial news,
    29, 613
Cafeteria-style employee benefit, 44,
    50
Cain, Charles, 568
Cain Asset Management Corporation,
    568, 569
Call feature, 466, 484
Call option, 455, 457
Callable CD, 135
Callable preferred stock, 432, 457
Cambridge Reports Inc., 327
Campus placement office, 39, 41
Campus project, 39
Campus recruiter, 41
Cangro, Charles, 599
Capacity (credit), 172, 175, 182
Capell, Kerry, 644
Capital (credit), 172, 175, 182
Capital appreciation fund, 497
Capital gain, 112, 113, 115, 416, 507
Capital gain distribution, 507, 511
Capital growth, 496
Capital loss, 113, 416
Capitalized cost, 258
Car buying service, 255, 260: see also
    Automobile
Career, 31, 50, 75
Career action plan, 35
Career development, 40, 47–48
    advancement, 34, 38
    changing careers, 48–50
    stages, 49
    training opportunities, 48
Career experience, sample action
    verbs, 55
Career fair, 41
Career information sources, 39–41
Career opportunities, 35
    economic conditions, 36
    industrial trends, 36–38
    influences, 36
    in personal finance, 611
    social influences, 35–36
Career path, 48–50

CONSUMER BUYING, TRANSPORTATION (Chapter 8; PFP Sheets 32–39)

What are the main sources of consumer information? (pages 228–229)

What techniques can be used to get the most for your money? (pages 234–239)

What actions can a person take to solve a consumer problem? (Exhibit 8-9, page 241)

How should a used car be evaluated? (Exhibit 8-A, page 252)

How can I best negotiate the price for a new vehicle? (pages 254–255)

When might leasing an motor vehicle be preferred to buying one? (pages 257–259)

WEB SITES FOR CONSUMER BUYING, TRANSPORTATION

Consumer Reports
www.consumerreports.org

Consumer topics
www.consumerworld.org

Brand, price, and feature comparisons
www.compare.net
www.pricescan.com

Government information sources
www.consumer.gov
www.pueblo.gsa.gov
www.ftc.gov

National Fraud Information Center
www.fraud.org

Better Business Bureau
www.bbb.org

Legal information for consumers
www.nolo.com
www.consumerlawpage.com

Motor vehicle purchasing tips
www.well.com/user/kr2/

Prices of new and used cars
www.edmunds.com
www.kbb.com

Leasing information
www.leasesource.com

Driving safety information
www.hwysafety.com

Crash test and insurance-related data
www.carsafety.org

HOUSING (Chapter 9; PFP Sheets 40–45)

What housing alternatives are available? (Exhibit 9-2, page 269)

Should I buy or rent my housing? (page 270)

What factors affect the price of a home? (pages 279–280)

How much of a mortgage can I qualify for? (Exhibit 9-8, page 282)

What are the main types of mortgages? (Exhibit 9-10, page 285)

What actions should be taken when selling a home? (pages 291–292)

WEB SITES FOR HOUSING

Renting vs. buying
www.financenter.com

Home buying guide
www.maxsol.com/homes/steps.htm

Home buying assistance
www.homefair.com/home
www.homeshark.com
www.ired.com

Mortgage information
www.bankrate.com
www.loan-page.com
www.hsh.com
www.microsurf.com

Adjustable rate mortgages
www.maxsol.com/homes/comparm.htm

FNMA (Fannie Mae)
www.homepath.com

Dept. of Housing & Urban Development
www.hud.gov

Mortgage pre-payment information
www.alfredo.wustl.edu/mort/

Reverse mortgages
www.hud.gov/rvrsmort.html

Mortgage cost calculator
www.centura.com/formulas/ca/c.html

INSURANCE (Chapters 10-12; PFP Sheets 46–54)

What types of risks are most commonly insured? (pages 302–304)

How much home insurance coverage do I need? (pages 315–316)

What factors affect the cost of automobile insurance? (pages 322–324)

How can I determine the amount of disability income insurance I need? (pages 338–341)

What are the main types of health insurance coverages? (pages 341–345)

How do I decide which health insurance coverage is best for me? (pages 347–369)

How much life insurance do I need? (pages 367–369)

What type of life insurance policy is best for my life situation? (pages 370–376)

How should I select an insurance agent? (pages 381–382)

What are the financial benefits of an annuity? (pages 385–387)

WEB SITES FOR INSURANCE

Insurance Research Council
www.ircweb.org

Basic insurance information
www.insure.com
www.iiaa.iix.com
www.iii.org

Rate information
www.insuremarket.com

Links to health-related sites
www.healthseek.com

Life & Health Info Foundation for Education
www.life-line.org

Health insurance options
www.northcoast.com/unlimited/
services_listing/greg_connors/gci.html

Long-term care issues
www.service.com/answers/health_insurance.html

Medicare (Social Security Administration)
www.ssa.gov

Medicare supplement information
www.naic.org

Determining life insurance needs
www.rightquote.com

Comparing coverages and costs
www.quotesmith.com
www.quickquote.com
www.accuquote.com

Life insurance information
www.insure.com

Planning assistance & rate information
www.insuremarket.com
www.lifenet.com

State insurance regulatory agencies
www.naic.org